PRESCHOOL PERIOD
(3 to 6 years)

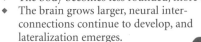

- Height and weight continue to increase rapidly.
- The body becomes less rounded, more muscular.
- The brain grows larger, neural inter-connections continue to develop, and lateralization emerges.
- Gross and fine motor skills advance quickly. Children can throw and catch balls, run, use forks and spoons, and tie shoelaces.
- Children begin to develop handedness.

- Children show egocentric thinking (viewing world from their own perspective) and "centration," a focus on only one aspect of a stimulus.
- Memory, attention span, and symbolic thinking improve, and intuitive thought begins.
- Language (sentence length, vocabulary, syntax, and grammar) improves rapidly.

- Children develop self-concepts, which may be exaggerated.
- A sense of gender and racial identity emerges.
- Children begin to see peers as individuals and form friendships based on trust and shared interests.
- Morality is rule-based and focused on rewards and punishments.
- Play becomes more constructive and cooperative, and social skills become important.

Preoperational stage	
Initiative-versus-guilt stage	
Phallic stage	
Preconventional morality level	

MIDDLE CHILDHOOD
(6 to 12 years)

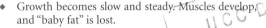

- Growth becomes slow and steady. Muscles develop, and "baby fat" is lost.
- Gross motor skills (biking, swimming, skating, ball handling) and fine motor skills (writing, typing, fastening buttons) continue to improve.

- Children apply logical operations to problems.
- Understanding of conservation (that changes in shape do not necessarily affect quantity) and transformation (that objects can go through many states without changing) emerge.
- Children can "decenter"–take multiple perspectives into account.
- Memory encoding, storage, and retrieval improve, and control strategies (meta-memory) develop.
- Language pragmatics (social conventions) and metalinguistic awareness (self-monitoring) improve.

- Children refer to psychological traits to define themselves. Sense of self becomes differentiated.
- Social comparison is used to understand one's standing and identity.
- Self-esteem grows differentiated, and a sense of self-efficacy (an appraisal of what one can and cannot do) develops.
- Children approach moral problems intent on maintaining social respect and accepting what society defines as right.
- Friendship patterns of boys and girls differ. Boys mostly interact with boys in groups, and girls tend to interact singly or in pairs with other girls.

Concrete operational stage
Industry-versus-inferiority stage
Latency period
Conventional morality level

Development ACROSS THE LifeSpan

ROBERT S. FELDMAN

University of Massachusetts at Amherst

Prentice Hall, Upper Saddle River, New Jersey 07458

Library of Congress Cataloging-in-Publication Data

Feldman, Robert S. (Robert Stephen),
    Development across the life span / Robert S. Feldman.
       p.   cm
    Includes bibliographical references and index.
    ISBN 0-13-199522-7
    1. Developmental psychology.   I. Title.
BF713.F45   1997   96-21207
155—dc20   CIP

Editor-in-Chief: Peter Janzow
Director of Production and Manufacturing: Barbara Kittle
Managing Editor: Bonnie Biller
Development Editor: Robert Weiss
Editorial/Production Supervision: Mary Rottino
Manufacturing Manager: Nick Sklitsis
Prepress and Manufacturing Buyer: Trisha Kenny
Creative Design Director: Leslie Osher
Interior and Cover Design: Joseph Rattan Design
Electronic Illustrations: Joseph Rattan Design
Photo Researcher: Eloise Marion
Editorial Assistant: Marilyn Coco

Acknowledgments for copyrighted material may
be found beginning on p. 727, which constitutes
an extension of this copyright page.

This book was set in Minion and Syntax Black by
Black Dot Graphics and was printed by Von Hoffman Company.
The cover was printed by Lehigh.

Printed in the United States of America
10 9 8 7 6 5 4 3 2 1

ISBN 0-13-199522-7

Prentice-Hall International (UK) Limited, *London*
Prentice-Hall of Australia Pty. Limited, *Sydney*
Prentice-Hall Canada, Inc. *Toronto*
Prentice-Hall Hispanoamericana, S.A., *Mexico*
Prentice-Hall of India Private Limited, *New Delhi*
Prentice-Hall of Japan, Inc. *Tokyo*
Simon & Schuster Asia Pte. Ltd., *Singapore*
Editoria Prentice-Hall do Brasil, Ltda., *Rio de Janeiro*

To Mom,
with love and affection

Brief Contents

Contents

PART 2
INFANCY: FORMING THE FOUNDATIONS OF LIFE

PART 3
THE PRESCHOOL YEARS

PART 4
THE MIDDLE CHILDHOOD YEARS

Chapter 10   Social and Personality Development in Middle Childhood 336

PART 5
ADOLESCENCE

Chapter 11   Physical and Cognitive Development in Adolescence   374

**PART 6
EARLY ADULTHOOD**

PART 7
MIDDLE ADULTHOOD

PART 8
LATE ADULTHOOD

PART 9
ENDINGS

Preface

This book tells a story: the story of our lives, and our parents' lives, and the lives of our children. It is the story of human beings, and how they get to be the way they are.

Unlike any other area of study, life-span development speaks to us in a very personal sense. It encompasses the range of human existence from its beginnings at conception to its inevitable ending at death. It is a discipline that deals with ideas and concepts and theories, but one that above all has at its heart people—our fathers and mothers, our friends and acquaintances, our very selves.

This text, *Development Across the Life Span*, seeks to capture the discipline in a way that sparks and nurtures and shapes students' interest. It is meant to excite readers about the field, to draw them into its way of looking at the world, and to mold their understanding of developmental issues. By exposing readers to both the current content and the promise inherent in life-span development, the text is designed to keep interest in the discipline alive long after students' formal study of the field has ended.

OVERVIEW

Development Across the Life Span provides a broad overview of the field of human development. It covers the entire range of human life, from the moment of conception through death. The text furnishes a comprehensive introduction to the field, covering basic theories and research findings and highlighting current applications outside the laboratory. It covers the life span chronologically, encompassing the prenatal period, infancy and toddlerhood, the preschool years, middle childhood, adolescence, early and middle adulthood, and later adulthood. Within these periods, it focuses on physical, cognitive, and social and personality development.

The book seeks to accomplish the following four major goals:

♦   First and foremost, the book is designed to provide a broad, balanced overview of the field of life-span development. It introduces readers to the theories, research, and applications that constitute the discipline, examining both the traditional areas of the field as well as more recent innovations. The text pays particular attention to the applications developed by life-span development specialists. Although not slighting theoretical material, the text emphasizes what we know about development across the life span demonstrating how this knowledge may be applied to real-world problems. In sum, the book highlights the interrelationships among theory, research, and application, accentuating the scope and diversity of the field. It also illustrates how life-span developmentalists use theory, research, and applications to help solve significant social problems.

♦   The second major goal of the text is to tie development to students' lives. Findings from the study of life-span development have a significant degree of relevance to students, and this text illustrates how these findings can be applied in a meaningful, practical sense. Applications are presented in a contemporaneous framework, including current news items, timely world events, and contemporary uses of life-span development that draw readers into the field. Numerous descriptive scenarios and vignettes reflect everyday situations in people's lives, explaining how they relate to the field. For example, each chapter begins with an opening prologue that provides a real-life situation relating to the chapter subject area. All chapters also have an "Informed Consumer of Development" section, which explicitly suggests ways to apply developmental findings to students' experience. These sections portray how these findings can be applied, in a practical, hands-on way. Each chapter also includes a feature called "Directions in Development" that discusses ways that developmental research is being used to answer the problems confronting society. For instance, policy issues such as the effects of day care on child development are considered. Finally, every chapter has an interview ("Speaking of Development") with a person working in a profession related to the chapter's topic. These interviews illustrate how a background in life-span development can be beneficial in a variety of vocations.

◆ The third goal of this book is to highlight both the commonalities and diversity of today's multicultural society. Consequently, every chapter has at least one "Developmental Diversity" section. These features explicitly consider how cultural factors relevant to development both unite and diversify our contemporary, global society. In addition, the book incorporates material relevant to diversity throughout every chapter.

◆ Finally, the fourth goal of the text is one that underlies the other three: making the field of life-span development engaging, accessible, and interesting to students. Life-span development is a joy both to study and teach, because so much of it has direct, immediate meaning to our lives. Because all of us are involved in our own developmental paths, we are tied in very personal ways to the content areas covered by the book. *Development Across the Life Span*, then, is meant to engage and nurture this interest, planting a seed that will develop and flourish throughout readers' lifetimes.

To accomplish this fourth goal, the book is user-friendly. Written in a direct, conversational voice, it replicates as much as possible a dialogue between author and student. The text is meant to be understood and mastered on its own, without the intervention of an instructor. To that end, it includes a variety of pedagogical features. Each chapter contains a "Looking Ahead" overview that sets the stage for the chapter, a running glossary, a numbered summary, and a list of key terms and concepts. In addition, each chapter has three "Review and Rethink" sections that provide an enumeration of the key concepts, as well as questions that promote and test critical thinking.

What this text is not. It is as important to delineate what this book is *not* meant to be as it is to say what it *is* intended to do. It is *not* an applied development book, focused solely on techniques for translating the knowledge base of development into answers to societal problems. Nor is it a theory-oriented volume, focusing primarily on the field's abstract theories. Instead, it blends and integrates theory, research, and applications.

Consequently, the text does not concentrate on a few isolated areas and present them in great depth. Rather, the focus is on the breadth of human development. The strategy of concentrating on the scope of the field permits the text to explore both the traditional core areas of the discipline and evolving, nontraditional areas of development.

The book does not attempt to provide a detailed historical record of the field. Instead, it looks at the here-and-now, drawing on the past where appropriate, but with a view toward delineating the discipline as it now stands and the directions toward which it is evolving. Similarly, although providing descriptions of classic studies, the emphasis is more on current research findings and trends.

Finally, the book seeks to provide a broad overview of the field of life-span development, integrating the theory, research, and applications of the discipline. It is meant to be a text that readers will want to keep in their own personal libraries, one that they will take off the shelf when considering problems related to that most intriguing of questions: How do people get to be the way they are?

SPECIFIC FEATURES

PROLOGUE: DOUBLING UP

Capt. Jim Tedesco, a volunteer firefighter from Paramus, N.J., looked across a crowded room at a firefighters' convention and was startled by what he saw. There was Mark Newman, another Paramus firefighter, and that was impossible. Newman, he knew, was back home in Paramus. But how many bald, 6-foot-6, 250-pound-plus New Jersey volunteer firemen are there who wear droopy mustaches, aviator-style eyeglasses, and a key ring on the right side of the belt?

At least two, it turned out. Striking up a conversation, Tedesco found that although the man he was speaking to looked, walked, talked, joked, and gestured just like Newman, his name was Gerald Levey. Then Tedesco learned that Levey had the same birth date as Newman—and that, like Newman, he, too, had been adopted in New York City.

Intrigued, Tedesco hatched a plan. After returning from the convention, he drove his friend Newman to Levey's firehouse in Tinton Falls, N.J., on the pretext of inspecting a new foam unit. When Newman walked in, Levey stared at him and muttered, "I've got to get a beer. That's my brother."

Newman, intent on the equipment he had come to see, walked right by Levey. "This is nothing but a pumper. So what's the big deal?" Newman complained. Tedesco grinned. "Mark, come over here and look at this firefighter," he said. "Doesn't he look familiar?" At last Newman looked at Levey. "You're right. He's big like me. He has a nose like me. He wears glasses like me. He's bald like me . . . I've got to get a beer." (Lang, 1987, p. 63)

Identical twins Mark Newman and Gerald Levey.

CHAPTER-OPENING PROLOGUES

Each chapter begins with a short vignette, describing an individual or situation that is relevant to the basic developmental issues being addressed in the chapter. For instance, the chapter on birth describes several actual births; one of the chapters on adolescence provides an account of Cedric Jennings' life as a student in an inner-city school; and a chapter on late adulthood discusses the lives of Eva and Joseph Solymosi, married for more than seven decades.

LOOKING AHEAD

For 31 years, twins Levey and Newman led separate, yet surprisingly parallel, lives. Although they were separated five days after birth and adopted by different families, their similarities go well beyond coincidence. Both are bachelors attracted to tall, slender women with long hair. Both love to fish and hunt. Both enjoy John Wayne movies and Chinese food. Both worked for a time in supermarkets. One got a degree in forestry; the other worked trimming trees. One installed fire alarms; the other installed sprinkler systems. Not only do they drink the same brand of beer but they hold the can the same way, pinkie curled underneath.

Mark Newman and Gerald Levey, and other twins like them, are more than mere curiosities. They also hold part of the key to one of the fundamental puzzles of human development: How do heredity and environment interact to make us the people we are?

In this chapter, we'll examine what life-span developmentalists and other scientists have learned about ways that heredity and the environment work in tandem to shape human behavior. We begin with the basics of heredity, examining how we receive our genetic endowment. We'll consider a burgeoning area of study, behavioral genetics, that specializes in the consequences of heredity on behavior. We'll also discuss what happens when genetic factors cause development to go awry, and how such problems are dealt with through genetic counseling.

Next, we'll discuss the interaction of heredity and environment. We'll consider the relative influence of genes and environment on a variety of characteristics, including physical traits, intelligence, and even personality.

Finally, we'll focus on the very first stage of development, tracing prenatal growth and change. We'll talk about the stages of the prenatal period, and how the prenatal environment offers both threats to—and the promise of—future growth.

LOOKING AHEAD SECTIONS

These opening sections orient readers to the topics to be covered, bridging the opening prologue with the remainder of the chapter and providing orienting questions.

DIRECTIONS IN DEVELOPMENT

Each chapter includes a section that describes current developmental research or research issues, applied to everyday problems. For instance, these sections include discussions of ways of dealing with violence, training parents, and reversing intellectual declines in the elderly.

Directions in Development

Genetic Counseling: *Predicting the Future from the Genes of the Present*

The last thing Joey Paulowsky needs is another bout with cancer. Only 7 years old, the Dallas native has already fought off leukemia, and now his family worries that Joey could be hit again. The Paulowsky family carries a genetic burden—a rare form of inherited cancer of the thyroid. Deborah, his mother, found a lump in her neck six years ago, and since then one family member has died of the cancer and 10 others have had to have their thyroids removed. "Do I have cancer?" Joey asks his mother. "Will it hurt?" The Paulowskys will know the answer next month, when the results of a genetic test will show whether their son carries the family's fateful mutation. (Brownlee, Cook, & Hardigg, 1994, p. 59)

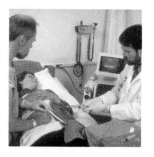

In amniocentesis, a sample of fetal cells is withdrawn from the amniotic sac and used to identify a number of genetic defects.

DEVELOPMENTAL DIVERSITY SECTION

Every chapter has at least one "Developmental Diversity" section incorporated into the text. These sections highlight issues relevant to today's multicultural society. Examples of these sections include discussions of cross-cultural differences in relationships, developing racial and ethnic awareness in childhood, adolescent race segregation, and racial differences in IQ and *The Bell Curve* controversy.<None>

Developmental Diversity:

Cultural Differences in Physical Arousal: Might a Culture's Philosophical Outlook Be Determined by Genetics?

The Buddhist philosophy, an inherent part of many Asian cultures, emphasizes harmony and peacefulness, and suggests that one should seek the eradication of human desire. In contrast, some of the traditional philosophies of Western civilization, such as those of Martin Luther and John Calvin, accentuate the importance of controlling the anxiety, fear, and guilt that are thought to be basic parts of the human condition.

INFORMED CONSUMER OF DEVELOPMENT

Every chapter includes information on specific uses that can be derived from research conducted by developmental investigators. For instance, the text provides concrete information on how to optimize the prenatal environment, how to assess language development, how to select a day-care provider, how to use discipline effectively, how to choose a career, and how to care for people with Alzheimer's disease.

The Informed Consumer of Development

Optimizing the Prenatal Environment

If you are contemplating ever having a child, by this point in the chapter you may be overwhelmed by the number of things that can go wrong. Don't be. Although the environment and genetics pose their share of risks, in the vast majority of cases, pregnancy and birth proceed without mishap. Moreover, there are several things that women can do to optimize the probability that pregnancy will progress smoothly—both before and during pregnancy. Among them:

◆ For women who are planning to become pregnant, several precautions are in order. First, women should have nonemergency X-rays only during the first two weeks after their menstrual periods. Second, women should be vaccinated against rubella (German measles) at least three, and preferably six, months before getting pregnant. Finally, women who are planning to become pregnant should avoid the use of birth control pills at least three months before trying to conceive, because of disruptions to hormonal production caused by the pills.

◆ Eat well, both before and during (and after, for that matter!) pregnancy. Pregnant mothers are, as the old saying goes, eating for two. This means that it is more essential than ever to eat regular, well-balanced meals.

SPEAKING OF DEVELOPMENT

Each chapter includes an interview with a person working in a field that uses the findings of life-span development. Among those interviewed are a toy designer, the chief of the marriage and family statistics branch of the U.S. Census Bureau, a former U.S. Secretary of Education, a child-care provider, a director of senior citizens programs, and others.

Speaking of Development

Lopa Malkan Wani

Born: 1965

Education: .... Cornell University, B.A. in biology, with a concentration in genetics; Sarah Lawrence College, M.S. in genetic counseling

Position: .... Genetic counselor for Genetrix, Inc.

Home: .... Sacramento, California

Not only has the field of genetics significantly advanced our understanding of the way we are put together but it has spawned a new occupation: genetic counselor. Genetic counselors help people deal with the potential consequences of the genes they carry.

Lopa Wani works in two major areas of the field. "The role of the genetic counselor is a dual one," she explains. "We are concerned with prenatal genetics and pediatric genetics, which deal with different issues.

"Prenatal genetics is concerned with both the period before conception, when we focus on planned pregnancies, and the period preceding birth, when we mostly offer counseling about the risks that might be present, tests for genetic conditions, and explain the options that are available.

Review and Rethink

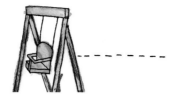

REVIEW

♦ Developmental specialists divide the prenatal period into three stages: germinal, embryonic, and fetal.

♦ The prenatal environment significantly influences the development of the baby. The diet, age, and illnesses of mothers can affect their babies' health and growth.

♦ Mothers who use drugs, alcohol, and tobacco can adversely affect the health and development of the unborn child. Fathers' and others' behaviors (e.g., smoking) can also affect the health of the unborn child.

♦ The vast majority of pregnancies and births proceed without mishap, and pregnant mothers can take positive steps to optimize their babies' chances for normal, healthy development.

RETHINK

♦ Based on your knowledge of prenatal development, do you think there is any truth in the opinion that pregnant women should avoid anger in order to spare their children from entering the world angry? Why or why not?

♦ Studies show that crack babies who are now entering school have significant difficulty dealing with multiple stimuli and forming close attachments. How might both genetic and environmental influences have combined to produce these results?

♦ In addition to avoiding smoking, do you think there are other steps fathers might take to help their unborn children develop normally in the womb? What are they and how might they affect the environment of the unborn child?

♦ Based on your knowledge of environmental influences on unborn children, what are some steps parents can take to give the fetus a healthy prenatal environment?

REVIEW AND RETHINK SECTIONS

Interspersed throughout each chapter are three short recaps of the chapters' main points, followed by questions designed to provoke critical thinking.

---

gametes   the sex cells from the mother and father that form a new cell at conception

fertilization   the process by which a sperm and an ovum—the male and female gametes, respectively—join to form a single new cell

zygote   the new cell formed by the process of fertilization

RUNNING GLOSSARY

Key terms are defined in the margins of the page on which the term is presented.

LOOKING BACK

What is our basic genetic endowment, and how do we receive it from our parents?

1. In humans, the adult female and male sex cells, or gametes, contain 23 chromosomes each. At fertilization, ovum and sperm unite to form a single new cell, called a zygote, in the female's uterus. The zygote receives a total of 46 chromosomes from its parents. Within the 46 chromosomes is the genetic blueprint—carried in some 100,000 genes—that will guide cell activity for the rest of the individual's life.

2. Gregor Mendel discovered an important genetic mechanism. In alleles, where two competing traits are present but only one can be expressed, the offspring may receive either similar or dissimilar genes from each parent. If the offspring receives dissimilar genes (one dominant and one recessive), the dominant gene will be expressed. If the offspring receives similar genes (two dominant or two recessive genes), that gene will be expressed. Traits such as hair and eye color and the presence of phenylketonuria (PKU) are alleles and follow this pattern, but relatively few inherited traits are governed by a single pair of genes in this way.

END-OF-CHAPTER MATERIAL

Each chapter ends with a numbered summary and a list of key terms and concepts. This material is designed to help students study and retain the information in the chapter.

KEY TERMS AND CONCEPTS

gametes (p. 42)   *chromosomes* (p. 43)
fertilization (p. 42)   *monozygotic twins* (p. 44)
zygote (p. 42)   *dizygotic twins* (p. 44)
genes (p. 43)   *genotype* (p. 47)

ANCILLARIES

Development Across the Life Span is accompanied by a superb set of ancillary teaching materials. They include the following:

Instructor Supplements

Instructor's Resource Manual, by Gayla Preisser and Susan Horton of Mesa Community College. The 3-hole-punched IRM contains a wealth of teaching tips and creative ideas for new and experienced instructors alike. Each chapter includes: Learning Objectives; Key Terms/Concepts; Chapter Outline; Lecture Suggestions; Cooperative Learning Activities; Critical Thinking Questions/Exercises; Assignment Ideas; Reflective Journal Exercise; PH Transparencies; Suggested Films and Videos; and Handouts that can be reproduced and distributed to students.

Teaching Transparencies for Human Development. A full set of color transparencies add visual impact to the study of child development. Designed in large format for use in lecture hall settings, many of these high-quality images are not found in the text.

Test Item File, by Lynne Blesz Vestal, contains over 1900 questions and a wide range of multiple-choice items of differing levels of difficulty. Also contains Short Answer/Essay and True/False questions.

Prentice Hall Custom Tests for Windows, Macintosh, and DOS. Prentice Hall's exclusive computerized testing software supports a full range of editing and graphics options, network test administration capabilities, and greater ease-of-use than ever before.

"800-Number" Telephone Test Preparation Service. A toll-free test preparation service is also available. Instructors may call an 800-number and select up to 200 questions from the Test Item File available with the text. Prentice Hall will format the test and provide an alternate version (if requested) and answer key(s), then mail it back within 48 hours, ready for duplication.

Videotape Support Materials

Speaking of Development Videos. This exclusive videotape program features interviews with eleven of the professionals highlighted within this text. Each segment visits the individual's workplace, and discusses their background in developmental issues and how it relates to their current job. The video may also provide students with some background information about future job opportunities.

ABC News/Prentice Hall Video Libraries
Lifespan Development, 1996
Child Development, 1995
Human Development, 1993
Three video libraries consisting of feature segments from award-winning programs such as *Nightline, 20/20, PrimeTime Live,* and *The Health Show* are available to qualified adopters of *Development Across the Life Span.*

Student Supplements

Study Guide, by Joyce Bishop, Golden West College. The entire Study Guide is written and designed with a unique, visual format to encourage active student involvement in the study process and to reinforce the text's pedagogical features. Each chapter includes the following: Class and Text Notes Study Outline; Learning Objectives; Critical Thinking and Workplace Application Questions; a wide range of practice multiple-choice questions with explanations for the correct answers; language-based activities to facilitate learning for non-native speakers; flash cards with key vocabulary terms and definitions; and labeling exercises based on graphics from the text.

***The New York Times* Supplement for Human Development.** When you adopt *Development Across the Life Span,* Prentice Hall and the New York Times will provide you with a complimentary student newspaper in quantities for your class. This collection of articles is designed to supplement classroom lectures and improve student access to current real-world issues and research.

ACKNOWLEDGMENTS

I am grateful to the following reviewers who provided a wealth of comments, criticism, and encouragement:

Martin W. Berkowitz, Marquette University; Peter J. Brady, Clark State Community College; Henri Sue Bynum, Indian River Community College; Craig Cowden, Northern Virginia Community College; Robin DesJardin, John Tyler Community College; Robert Frank, Oakton Community College; Robert Hensley, Kirkwood Community College; Russell Isabella, University of Utah; Robert D. Johnson, Arkansas State University; Elaine M. Justice, Old Dominion University; Albert A. Maisto, University of North Carolina at Charlotte; Cynthia Jones Neal, Wheaton College; Sherri Addis Palmer, Northeast Missouri State University; Robert F. Schultz, Fulton-Montgomery Community College; Ralph G. Soney, Western Piedmont Community College; Mary Helen C. Spear, Prince George's Community College; Linda Q. Thede, Kent State University; Frank Vitro, Texas Woman's University; Fred W. Vondracek, Penn State University.

Many others deserve a great deal of thanks. I am indebted to the many people who provided me with a superb education, first at Wesleyan University and later at the University of Wisconsin. Specifically, Karl Scheibe played a pivotal role in my undergraduate education, and the late Vernon Allen acted as mentor and guide through my graduate years. It was in graduate school that I learned about development, being exposed to such experts as Ross Parke, John Balling, Joel Levin, Herb Klausmeier, Frank Hooper, and many others.

My education continued when I became a professor. I am especially grateful to my colleagues at the University of Massachusetts, who make the university such as wonderful place in which to teach and do research.

Several people played central roles in the development of this book. Edward Murphy brought a keen intelligence and editorial eye to the process, and the book has been greatly strengthened by his considerable input. Lucy Rinehart and Erik Coats provided research assistance, and I am thankful for their help. Most of all, John Graiff was essential in juggling and coordinating the multiple aspects of writing a book, and I am very grateful for the substantial role he played.

I am also grateful to the superb Prentice Hall team that was instrumental in the inception and development of this text. Pete Janzow oversaw the project, always demonstrating his wisdom, canniness, and creativity. Phil Miller stood behind the project, and I am grateful for his continuing support. Barbara Muller, development editor, and Bob Weiss, head of development for psychology, provided expertise and uncommon guidance. On the production end of things, Mary Rottino, assistant managing editor, and Eloise Marion, photo researcher, helped in giving the book its distinctive look. Finally, thanks to Heidi Freund, who provided moral support with her infectious enthusiasm.

I also wish to acknowledge members of my family, who play such a pivotal role in my life. My brother, Michael, my sisters- and brothers-in-law, my nieces and nephews, all make up an important part of my life. In addition, I am always indebted to the older generation of my family, who led the way in a manner I can only hope to emulate. I will always be obligated to Ethel Radler, Harry Brochstein, and the late Mary Vorwerk. Most of all, the list is headed by my father, the late Saul Feldman, and my mother, Leah Brochstein.

In the end, it is my immediate family who deserve the greatest thanks. My three terrific kids, Jonathan, Joshua, and Sarah, not only are nice, smart, and good-looking, but also my pride and joy. And ultimately my wife, Katherine Vorwerk, provides the love and grounding that makes everything worthwhile. I thank them, with love.

Robert S. Feldman
University of Massachusetts at Amherst

About the Author

Robert S. Feldman is professor of psychology at the University of Massachusetts in Amherst, where he is Director of Undergraduate Studies. He was educated as an undergraduate at Wesleyan University, from where he graduated with High Honors, and received an M.S. and Ph.D. from the University of Wisconsin in Madison, specializing in social and developmental psychology.

His research on the development of nonverbal behavior in children has been published in more than 100 books, chapters, articles, and presentations. He has edited *Development of Nonverbal Behavior in Children* (Springer-Verlag), *Applications of Nonverbal Behavioral Theory and Research* (Erlbaum), and co-edited *Fundamentals of Nonverbal Behavior* (Cambridge University Press), and his research has been published in such journals as *Child Development, Journal of Early Intervention, Exceptional Children,* and the *Journal of Educational Psychology.* He is the recipient of grants from the National Institute of Mental Health and the National Institute of Disabilities and Rehabilitation Research. A past Fulbright lecturer and research scholar, he is a Fellow of the American Psychological Association and American Psychological Society.

During the course of nearly two decades as a college instructor, he has taught both undergraduate and graduate courses at Mount Holyoke College, Wesleyan University, and Virginia Commonwealth University, in addition to the University of Massachusetts.

Professor Feldman is an avid—if not particularly accomplished—pianist, and an excellent cook, despite his children's aversion to his experimentation with exotic cuisines. He lives with his three children and wife, a psychologist, in Amherst, Massachusetts, in a home overlooking the Holyoke mountain range.

Development Across the Lifespan

Beginnings

An Introduction to Life-span Development

CHAPTER OUTLINE

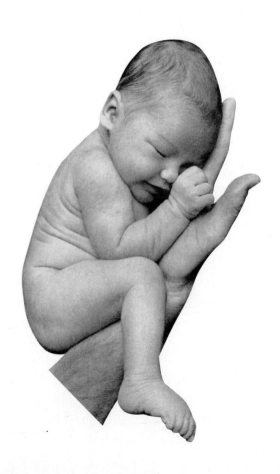

The Oklahoma City bombing illustrated the heroism of everyday people.

For the individuals who blew up the federal building in Oklahoma City, Oklahoma, killing 168 people—including 19 children younger than the age of six, the message was supposed to be one of terror and hatred for the U.S. government.

In some ways, though, just the opposite was communicated—a message about the heroism and bravery of everyday people who risked their own lives to pull victims from the wreckage, and about the people who came together as a community to help one another heal after the blast.

Consider, for instance, Rebecca Anderson. One of 20,000 volunteers who joined thousands of professional emergency workers, Rebecca rushed to the scene of the blast soon after seeing it on television. Without a helmet, she ran into the building three times, pulling several survivors out of the wreckage.

It was then that Rebecca, the mother of four children, was hit on the head by falling debris. She collapsed soon after. Rushed to the hospital, she developed a blood clot and slipped into a coma. Four days later, she was declared brain dead.

But even as she died, Rebecca continued to help. Because several months earlier she had indicated that she wished to be an organ donor, doctors transferred her heart and kidneys to patients requiring organ transplants. As a result, two more lives were saved.

LOOKING AHEAD

Although the Oklahoma City bombing can be looked at merely in terms of the terrorism—and heroism—involved, it also raises several significant issues related to development. For example, specialists in life-span development would look at the incident in the following ways.

- Life-span development experts who study the roots of violence might seek to examine the attitudes and values of the people who planted the bomb, seeking to explain the roots of such a violent outlook on life.

- Life-span developmentalists who investigate behavior at the level of biological functioning would seek to understand how living near the site of the blast influences future development by affecting the levels of certain bodily hormones.

- For life-span developmental specialists who examine the ways that thinking changes over the course of life, the explosion might be looked at in terms of how people calculate, and recalculate, the risks of future terrorist activity.

- Other life-span developmental experts, who focus on physical growth, might consider whether children who survived the blast had growth rates that differed from normal rates.

- Developmentalists who study the consequences of loss and death might seek to understand the experiences of people who lost family members and loved ones.

- Some developmental specialists might consider the decisions made by survivors to have children in the future, and whether any changes in fertility resulted from the blast.

- Because a day care center was destroyed in the blast, developmental experts might look for changes in the frequency with which people chose to use day care and made decisions regarding whether both spouses should work outside the home.

5

Although their interests might take many forms, all life-span developmental specialists share a common concern: understanding the growth and change that occur during the course of life. Taking many differing approaches, developmentalists study how both our biological inheritance from our parents and the environment in which we live jointly affect our behavior.

Some developmentalists focus on explaining how our genetic background can determine not only how we look but perhaps our very personality, and they explore ways to identify how much of our potential as human beings is provided—or limited—by heredity.

Other developmental specialists look to the environment, exploring ways in which our lives are shaped by the world that we encounter. They investigate the extent to which we are shaped by our early environments and how our current circumstances influence our behavior in both subtle and evident ways.

Whether they focus on heredity or environment, all life-span developmental experts acknowledge that neither heredity nor environment alone can account for the full range of human development and change. Instead, our understanding requires that we look at the joint effects of the interaction of heredity and environment, attempting to grasp how both, in the end, underlie human behavior.

In this chapter, we orient ourselves to the field of life-span development. We begin with a discussion of the scope of the field, illustrating the broad array of topics it covers and the full range of ages it examines, from the moment of conception to death. We also survey the key issues and controversies of the field.

Next, we continue with a consideration of the broad perspectives that life-span developmentalists take, from a focus on people's inner, unconscious lives and the interior operation of their minds, to people's outward, overt behavior.

Finally, we discuss the ways in which life-span developmental specialists use research to ask and answer questions. We discuss several research strategies, as well as ethical guidelines for conducting research. In sum, after reading this chapter, you'll be able to answer these questions:

- What is life-span development, and what areas of human life does it study?
- What are some primary influences on human development?
- What are the key issues in the field of life-span development?
- Which theoretical perspectives have guided thinking and research in life-span development?
- What role do theories and hypotheses play in the study of life-span development?
- How are research studies in life-span development conducted?

AN ORIENTATION TO LIFE-SPAN DEVELOPMENT

Have you ever marveled at the way an infant tightly grips your finger with tiny, perfectly formed hands? Or the way a preschooler methodically draws a picture? Or how an adolescent can make involved decisions about whom to invite to a party? Or the way a middle-aged politician can deliver a long, flawless speech from memory? Or how an 80-year-old grandfather is able to roughhouse with his grandchild?

If you have ever wondered about such things, you are asking the kinds of questions that scientists working in the field of life-span development pose. **Life-span development** is the discipline that studies patterns of growth, change, and stability in behavior that occur throughout the entire human life span.

Although the definition of the field seems straightforward, the simplicity is somewhat misleading. To understand what developmental psychology is actually about, we need to look underneath the various parts of the definition.

In its study of growth and change, life-span development takes a *scientific* approach. Like members of other scientific disciplines, developmental psychologists test their assumptions

life-span development *the discipline that studies patterns of growth, change, and stability in behavior that occur throughout the entire human life span*

about the nature and course of human development by applying scientific methods. As we'll see later in the chapter, they develop theories about development, and they use methodical, scientific techniques to validate the accuracy of their assumptions systematically.

Life-span development focuses on *human* development. Although there are developmental specialists who study the course of development in nonhuman species, the vast majority examine growth and change in people. Some seek to understand universal principles of development, whereas others focus on how cultural, racial, and ethnic differences affect the course of development. Still others aim to understand the unique aspects of individuals, looking at the traits and characteristics that differentiate one person from another. No matter what the approach, however, all life-span developmentalists view development as a lifelong, continuing process.

As developmental experts focus on the ways people change and grow during their lives, they also consider stability in people's lives. They ask in which areas, and in what periods, people show change and growth, and when and how their behavior reveals consistency and continuity with prior behavior.

Finally, life-span development focuses on growth, change, and stability throughout *every* part of people's lives, beginning with the moment of conception and continuing until death. Developmentalists assume that in some ways people continue to grow and change right up to the end of their lives, whereas in other respects their behavior remains stable. At the same time, developmental specialists believe that no particular, single periods of life govern all development. Instead, life-span developmentalists believe that every period of life contains the potential for both growth and declines in abilities, and that individuals have the capacity for substantial growth and change all the way through life.

CHARACTERIZING LIFE-SPAN DEVELOPMENT: THE SCOPE OF THE FIELD

Clearly, the definition of life-span development is broad and the scope of the field is extensive. Consequently, life-span development specialists cover several quite diverse areas, and a typical developmentalist specializes in two ways: topical area and age range.

For instance, some developmental specialists focus on **physical development,** examining the ways in which the body's makeup—the brain, nervous system, muscles, and senses, and the need for food, drink, and sleep—helps determine behavior. For example, one developmentalist specializing in physical development might examine the effects of malnutrition on the pace of growth in children, whereas another might look at how reaction time changes during adulthood.

Other developmental experts examine **cognitive development,** seeking to understand how growth and change in intellectual capabilities influence a person's behavior. Cognitive developmentalists examine learning, memory, problem solving, and intelligence. For example, specialists in cognitive development might want to see how intellectual abilities change over the course of life, or if cultural differences exist in the factors to which people attribute their academic successes and failures.

Finally, some developmental specialists focus on personality and social development. **Personality development** is the study of how the enduring characteristics that differentiate one person from another change over the lifespan, and **social development** is the way in which individuals' interactions with others and their social relationships grow, change, and remain stable over the course of life. A developmentalist interested in personality development might ask whether there are stable, enduring personality traits throughout the lifespan, whereas a specialist in social development might examine marriage and divorce during adulthood. (The major approaches are summarized in Table 1-1.)

Age Ranges and Individual Differences.   As they specialize in chosen topical areas, life-span development specialists typically look at particular age ranges. The life span is usually divided into broad age ranges: the prenatal period that occurs before birth; infancy and

physical development *development involving the body's physical makeup, including the brain, nervous system, muscles, and senses, and the need for food, drink, and sleep*

cognitive development *development involving the ways that growth and change in intellectual capabilities influence a person's behavior*

personality development *development involving the ways that the enduring characteristics that differentiate one person from another change over the life span*

social development *the way in which individuals' interactions with others and their social relationships grow, change, and remain stable over the course of life*

TABLE 1-1

APPROACHES TO LIFE-SPAN DEVELOPMENT

Orientation	Defining Characteristics	Examples of Questions Asked*
Physical development	Examines how brain, nervous system, muscles, sensory capabilities, needs for food, drink, and sleep affect behavior	What determines the sex of a child? (2) What are the long-term results of premature birth? (3) What are the benefits of breastfeeding? (4) What are the consequences of early or late sexual maturation? (11) What leads to obesity in adulthood? (13) How do adults cope with stress? (15) What are the outward and internal signs of aging? (17) How do we define death? (19)
Cognitive development	Examines intellectual abilities, including learning, memory, problem solving, and intelligence	What are the earliest memories that can be recalled from infancy? (5) What are the consequences of watching television? (7) Do spatial reasoning skills relate to music practice? (7) Are there benefits to bilingualism? (9) How does an adolescent's egocentrism affect his or her view of the world? (11) Are there ethnic and racial differences in intelligence? (9) How does creativity relate to intelligence? (13) Does intelligence decline in late adulthood? (17)
Personality and social development	Examines enduring characteristics that differentiate one person from another, and how interactions with others and social relationships grow and change over the lifetime	Do newborns respond differently to their mothers than to others? (3) What is the best procedure for disciplining children? (8) When does a sense of gender develop? (8) How can we promote cross-race friendships? (10) What are the causes of adolescent suicide? (12) How do we choose a romantic partner? (14) Do the effects of parental divorce last into old age? (18) Do people withdraw from others in late adulthood? (18) What are the stages of confronting death? (19)

*Numbers in parentheses indicate in which chapter the question is addressed.

toddlerhood (birth to age 3); the preschool period (ages 3 to 6); middle childhood (ages 6 to 12); adolescence (ages 12 to 20); young adulthood (ages 20 to 40); middle adulthood (ages 40 to 60); and late adulthood (age 60 to death).

Although most life-span developmentalists accept and employ these broad periods (and they are used to demarcate major parts of this book), the age ranges themselves are in many ways arbitrary. Although some have one clear-cut boundary (infancy begins with birth, the preschool period ends with entry into public school, and adolescence starts with sexual maturity), others do not.

For instance, consider the period of young adulthood, which is typically assumed to begin at age 20. That age, however, is notable only because it marks the end of the teen-age period. In fact, for many people, such as those enrolled in higher education, the age change from 19 to 20 has little special significance, coming as it does in the middle of the college years. Few sudden, substantial changes in physical, intellectual, personality, or social aspects of the individual are likely to occur at the midpoint of the college career.

In short, substantial individual differences exist in the timing of events in people's lives. In part, this is a biological fact of life: People mature at different rates and reach developmental milestones at different points. However, environmental factors also play a significant role in determining the age at which a particular event is likely to occur. For example, the typical age of marriage varies substantially from one culture to another, depending in part on the functions that marriage plays in a given culture.

It is important to keep in mind, then, that when developmental specialists discuss age ranges, they are talking about averages—the times when people, on average, reach particular milestones. Some people will reach the milestone earlier, some later, and many are likely to reach it just around the time of the average. It is only when people show substantial deviation from the average that such variation becomes noteworthy.

Furthermore, as people become older, it becomes more likely that they will deviate from the average and exhibit individual differences. In very young children a good part of developmental change is genetically determined and unfolds automatically, making development fairly similar across children. But as people age, environmental factors become more potent, leading to greater variability and individual differences as time passes.

The Links Between Topics and Ages.   Each of the broad topical areas of life-span development—physical, cognitive, and social and personality development—plays a role throughout the life span. Consequently, some developmentalists focus on physical development during the prenatal period, and others during adolescence. Some might specialize in social development during the preschool years, while others look at social relationships in old age. And still others might take a broader approach, looking at cognitive development through every period of life.

Developmentalists study people across the entire life span.

THE CONTEXT OF DEVELOPMENT: TAKING A BROAD PERSPECTIVE

Although considering the course of development in terms of physical, cognitive, and personality and social factors allows us to divide developmental influences into reasonably neat and compact packages, there is a real drawback to such a categorization: In the actual world, none of these broad influences occur in isolation from any other. Instead, there is a constant, ongoing interaction between the different types of influence. For instance, what occurs on a cognitive level has repercussions for personality, social, and physical development, whereas what is happening on a physical level has an impact on cognitive, personality, and social development.

The Ecological Approach to Development.   In acknowledging the problem with traditional approaches to life-span development, psychologist Urie Bronfenbrenner has proposed an alternative perspective, which he calls the **ecological approach** (Bronfenbrenner, 1979, 1989). This approach suggests that there are four levels of the environment that simultaneously influence individuals. Bronfenbrenner argues that we cannot fully understand development without considering how a person fits into each of these levels.

The *microsystem* is the everyday, immediate environment in which we lead our daily lives. Classrooms, workplaces, friends, families, teachers, and bosses all are examples of the influences that are part of the microsystem.

The *mesosystem* provides connections between the various aspects of the microsystem. Like links in a chain, the mesosystem binds students to teachers, employees to bosses, friends to one another. It also acknowledges indirect influences, such as those that affect a mother who has a bad day at the office and then is short-tempered with her daughter at home.

The *exosystem* represents broader influences, encompassing societal institutions such as local government, the community, schools, places of worship, and the local media. Each of these larger institutions of society can have an immediate, and major, impact on personal development, and each affects how the microsystem and mesosystem operate. For example, as we discuss in Chapter 7, the average child in the United States typically spends more time watching television than performing any other activity except sleeping for the first 18 years of life (Liebert & Sprafkin, 1988).

Finally, the *macrosystem* represents the larger cultural influences on an individual. Society in general, systems of governments, religious systems, political thought, and other broad, encompassing factors are parts of the macrosystem.

ecological approach   *the perspective suggesting that different levels of the environment simultaneously influence individuals*

Governmental bodies, such as this state assembly, illustrate the exosystem: societal institutions that influence personal development.

There are several advantages to taking an ecological approach to development. For one thing, the ecological approach emphasizes the interconnectedness of the influences on development. Because the various levels are related to one another, a change in one part of the system has an impact on other parts of the system. For instance, a parent's loss of a job (involving the mesosystem) has an impact upon a child's microsystem.

Conversely, changes on one environmental level may make little difference if other levels are not also changed. For instance, improving the school environment might have a negligible effect on academic performance if children receive little support for academic success in their home environments.

The ecological approach also illustrates that the influences among different family members are multidirectional. As we'll consider in Chapter 6, the relationship between parent and child reflects not just the parent's behavior but also what the child does to elicit responsiveness from the parent. For instance, infants who respond positively to parents trigger more positive behaviors on the part of the parents, which in turn spark more positive responses from the infants (Cohn & Tronick, 1989; Nwokah & Fogel, 1993).

Finally, the ecological approach stresses the importance of broad cultural factors that affect development. Developmental specialists increasingly look at how membership in cultural and subcultural groups influences behavior. For instance, it is clear that, in general, Western cultures tend to be *individualistic,* emphasizing personal identity, uniqueness, freedom, and the worth of the individual. In contrast, Asian cultures are largely *collectivistic,* promoting the idea that the group of society is more important than the individual. As explained in Chapter 12, such broad cultural values play an important role in shaping the ways that people view the world and behave (Kim et al., 1994).

Cohort and Normative Influences on Development: Developing with Others in a Social World.   Bob, born in 1947, is a baby boomer; he was born soon after the end of World War II, when an enormous bulge in the birth rate occurred as soldiers returned to the United States from overseas. His college years were passed at the height of protests against the Vietnam War and at a time when drug use was widespread throughout society. His mother, Leah, was born in 1921; she is part of the generation that passed its childhood and teenage years in the shadow of the Great Depression. Bob's son, Jon, was born in 1975. Now in college, he is a member of what has been called Generation X.

These people are in part products of the social times in which they live. Each belongs to a particular **cohort,** a group of people born at about the same time in the same place. Such major social events as wars, economic upturns and depressions, famines, and epidemics (like the one due to the AIDS virus) work similar influences on members of a particular cohort.

Cohort effects provide an example of **normative history-graded influences,** which are biological and environmental influences associated with a particular historical moment (Baltes, Reese, & Lipsitt, 1980; Baltes, 1987). For instance, people living in Oklahoma City, Oklahoma, in 1995 share both biological and environmental challenges due to the terrorist bombing of the federal building in that city.

Normative history-graded influences contrast with **normative age-graded influences,** which are biological and environmental influences similar for individuals in a particular age group, regardless of when or where they are raised. For instance, biological events such as puberty and menopause are universal events occurring at relatively the same time throughout all societies. Similarly, a sociocultural event such as entry into formal education can be considered a normative age-graded influence because it occurs in most cultures around age six.

Development is also affected by **normative sociocultural-graded influences,** which represent the impact of social and cultural factors present at a particular time for a particular individual, depending on such variables as race, ethnicity, social class, and subcultural membership. For example, sociocultural-graded influences are going to be considerably different for children who are white and affluent than for children who are members of a minority group and living in poverty.

Finally, **nonnormative life events** also influence development. These are specific, atypical events occurring in a particular person's life at a time when they do not happen to most people. For instance, experiencing at an early age the death of both parents, being involved in a serious auto accident, coming down with a deadly disease, or having a physical disability are all nonnormative life events.

KEY ISSUES AND QUESTIONS: DETERMINING THE NATURE— AND NURTURE—OF LIFE-SPAN DEVELOPMENT

As sciences go, life-span development is one of the new kids on the block. Although its roots can be traced back to the ancient Egyptians and Greeks, it did not become established as a separate field until the late nineteenth and early twentieth centuries.

From the time of its establishment, several key issues and questions have dominated the field. Among the major issues (summarized in Table 1-2) are the nature of developmental change, the importance of critical periods, life-span approaches versus more focused approaches, and the nature–nurture issue (Kagan, 1994; Parke, Ornstein, Rieser, & Zahn-Waxler, 1994).

Continuous Change Versus Discontinuous Change.   One of the primary issues challenging developmentalists is whether development proceeds in a continuous or discontinuous fashion. In **continuous change,** development is gradual, with achievements at one level building on those of previous levels. Continuous change is quantitative in nature; the basic underlying developmental processes that drive change remain the same over the course of the life span. Continuous change, then, produces changes that are a matter of degree, but not kind.

In contrast, **discontinuous change** occurs in distinct steps or stages. Each stage brings about behavior that is assumed to be qualitatively different from behavior at earlier stages.

As we'll see throughout future chapters, proponents of continuous change have offered alternatives to theories of development that assume that change is discontinuous, and the predominant view today is that most developmental growth is continuous. Still, both approaches have their merits, and developmentalists in both branches of the debate continue to press their cases. In fact, some have argued that taking an "either-or" position on the issue

cohort   *a group of people born at around the same time in the same place*

normative history-graded influences   *biological and environmental influences associated with a particular historical moment*

normative age-graded influences   *biological and environmental influences that are similar for individuals in a particular age group, regardless of when or where they are raised*

normative sociocultural-graded influences   *social and cultural factors present at a particular time for a particular individual, depending on such factors as race or ethnicity*

nonnormative life events   *specific, atypical events that occur in a particular person's life at a time when they do not happen to most people*

continuous change   *gradual development in which achievements at one level build on those of previous levels*

discontinuous change   *development that occurs in distinct steps or stages, with each stage bringing about behavior that is assumed to be qualitatively different from behavior at earlier stages*

TABLE 1-2

MAJOR ISSUES IN LIFE-SPAN DEVELOPMENT

Issue	Explanation
Continuous change vs. discontinuous change	In continuous change, development is gradual; the achievements at one level build on the previous ones. The underlying developmental processes driving the change remain the same over the course of the life span. In contrast, discontinuous change occurs in distinct steps or stages, with each stage bringing about behavior that is assumed to be qualitatively different from that seen at earlier stages.
Critical periods	A critical period is a particular time during development in which a particular event has its greatest consequences. Although early developmental psychologists placed great emphasis on the importance of critical periods, more recent thinking suggests that in many areas individuals may be more malleable than was first thought, particularly in the area of personality and social development.
Life-span approaches vs. focus on particular periods	Earlier developmental psychologists studying the life span focused attention primarily on the infancy and adolescence periods. Current thinking sees the entire life span as important for a number of reasons, including the discovery that developmental growth and change continue throughout every part of life.
Nature-nurture issue	Nature refers to traits, abilities, and capabilities that are inherited from one's parents. It encompasses any factor that is produced by the predetermined unfolding of genetic information. Nurture, on the other hand, involves the environmental influences that shape behavior. Some may be biological, whereas others are more social in nature. Some influences are a result of larger societal-level factors, such as the socio-economic opportunities available to members of minority groups.

is inappropriate. In their view, some types of developmental change may be continuous, whereas others are discontinuous. The debate, then, goes on (Rutter, 1987; Flavell, 1994).

Critical Periods: Gauging the Impact of Environmental Events.   If a woman comes down with a case of rubella (German measles) in the 11th week of pregnancy, the consequences for the child she is carrying are likely to be devastating: They include the potential for blindness, deafness, and heart defects. However, if she comes down with the exact same strain of rubella in the 30th week of pregnancy, damage to the child is unlikely.

The differing outcomes of the disease in the two periods demonstrate the concept of critical periods. A *critical period* is a specific time during development when a particular event has its greatest consequences.

Although early developmental psychologists placed great emphasis on the importance of critical periods, more recent thinking suggests that in many realms individuals may be more malleable than was first thought, particularly in the realm of personality and social development.

For instance, rather than permanent damage being caused by a lack of certain kinds of early social experiences, there is increasing evidence that later experiences can overcome earlier deficits. Consequently, instead of speaking of critical periods, more recent formulations identify *sensitive periods,* during which organisms are particularly susceptible to certain kinds of stimuli in their environments, but the absence of those stimuli does not always produce irreversible consequences (Bornstein, 1989).

Life-span Approaches Versus a Focus on Particular Periods.   On what part of the life span should life-span development focus its attention? For early developmentalists the answers tended to be "infancy" and "adolescence." Most attention was clearly concentrated on those two periods, largely to the exclusion of other parts of the life span.

Today, however, the story is different. The entire life span is now seen to be important, for several reasons. One is the discovery that developmental growth and change continue during every part of life—as we'll discuss throughout this book.

Furthermore, it is clear that to understand fully the social influences on people of a given age, we need to understand the people who are in large measure providing those influences. For instance, to understand development in infants, we need to unravel the effects of their parents' ages on their social environments. It is likely that a 15-year-old mother will present parental influences of a very different sort from those presented by a 37-year-old mother. Consequently, infant development is in part a consequence of adult development (Parke, 1988).

Nature Versus Nurture.   One of the enduring questions of life-span development involves how much of people's behavior is due to their genetically determined nature, and how much is due to nurture—to environmental factors. Having deep philosophical and historical roots, the issue has dominated much work in life-span development.

In this context, *nature* refers to traits, abilities, and capacities that are inherited from one's parents. It encompasses any factor that is produced by the predetermined unfolding of genetic information—a process known as **maturation.** These genetic, inherited influences are at work as we move from the one-cell organism that is created at the moment of conception to the billions of cells that make up a fully formed human. Nature influences whether our eyes are blue or brown, whether we have thick hair throughout life or go bald, and how good we are at athletics. Nature allows our brains to develop in such a way that we can read the words on this page.

In contrast, *nurture* refers to the environmental influences that shape behavior. Some of these influences may be biological, such as the impact of a pregnant mother's use of cocaine on her unborn child, or the amount and kind of food available to children. Other environmental influences are more social, such as the ways in which parents discipline their children and the effects of peer pressure on an adolescent. Finally, some influences are a result of larger, societal-level factors, such as the socioeconomic circumstances in which people find themselves.

If our traits and behavior were determined solely by either nature or nurture, there would probably be little debate regarding the issue. However, for most critical behaviors this is hardly the case. Take, for instance, one of the most controversial arenas: intelligence. As we'll consider in detail in Chapter 9, the question of whether intelligence is determined primarily by inherited, genetic factors—nature—or is shaped by environmental factors—nurture—has caused lively and often bitter arguments. Largely because of its social implications, the issue has spilled out of the scientific arena and into the realm of politics and social policy.

Consider the implications of the issue: If the extent of one's intelligence is primarily determined by heredity and consequently is largely fixed at birth, then efforts to improve intellectual performance later in life may be doomed to failure. In contrast, if intelligence is primarily a result of environmental factors, such as the amount and quality of schooling and stimulation to which one is exposed, then we would expect that an improvement in social conditions could bring about an increase in intelligence.

The issue becomes even more controversial when we try to determine the cause of racial differences in intelligence. For instance, the publication in 1994 of *The Bell Curve,* a book by psychologist Richard Herrnstein and sociologist Charles Murray, raised the issue of the source of differences in IQ scores between whites and African-Americans, as measured by traditional tests of intelligence. The controversy concerned whether such differences could be attributed more to nature—the argument of the authors—or nurture—the position taken by many other members of the psychological research community (Herrnstein & Murray, 1994; Nisbett, 1994; Jacoby & Glauberman, 1995; Kamin, 1995).

maturation   *the predetermined unfolding of sequences of behavior or traits produced by genetic causes*

The ferocity of the debate, and the importance of its resolution, illustrates the significance of issues that involve the nature–nurture question. As we address it in relation to several topical areas throughout this book, we should keep in mind that life-span developmentalists reject the notion that behavior is the result solely of either nature or nurture. Instead, the question is one of degree.

Furthermore, the interaction of genetic and environmental factors is a complex one, in part because certain genetically determined traits not only have a direct influence on children's behavior but also have an indirect influence in shaping children's *environments*. For example, a child who is consistently cranky and who cries a great deal—a trait that may be produced by genetic factors—may influence its environment by making its parents highly responsive to its insistent crying, in which they rush to comfort it whenever it cries. Their responsivity to the child's genetically determined behavior consequently becomes an environmental influence on the infant's subsequent development.

In sum, the question of how much of a given behavior is due to nature, and how much to nurture, is a challenging one. Ultimately, then, we should consider the two sides of the nature–nurture issue as opposite ends of a continuum, with particular behaviors falling somewhere between the two ends. Moreover, an analogous statement can be made regarding the other controversies that we have considered. For instance, continuous versus discontinuous development is not an either-or proposition; some forms of development fall toward the continuous end of the continuum, whereas others lie closer to the discontinuous end. In short, few statements about development involve either-or absolutes.

In the same way, a particular topical area can be approached on several different levels, and from several different angles, simultaneously. We discuss an example in the Directions in Development section.

Directions in Development

Violence: Dealing With a Modern-Day Plague Through Life-Span Development

When other children were hearing fairy tales, Garland Hampton heard bedtime stories about the day Uncle Robert killed two Milwaukee police officers, or the time Grandma, with both barrels, blew away the father of two of her children back in '62. By the time he was 9, he had seen his mother kill her boyfriend.

Now, at 15, locked up in the County Jail and awaiting trial on murder charges, Garland is still enough of a child that he is afraid he might cry when darkness falls.

But he is old enough to have had a nasty past of his own, too: at 10, there was trouble about stolen bicycles; at 12, he was picked up for shooting and wounding a gang rival; at 14, for carrying a .357 Magnum and a bag of cocaine, and now, gunning down a fellow gang member. Prosecutors say he is an adolescent menace to society, who must pay for his sins like a man.

Garland just says he is scared.

"I guess I been scared all my life," said Garland, a stocky boy with a hint of a 70's-style Afro, who cried as he talked about his life. "For me, living has been the same as running through hell with a gasoline suit on. I don't want people feeling sorry for me, but I really ain't had nothing good happen to me. The ax fell heavy on my head." (D. Terry, 1994, p. A1)

Garland Hampton

Garland's descent into violence is representative of the lives of many people in the United States today. Many observers have called the level of violence nothing less than an epidemic.

In fact, surveys find that violence and crime rank as the issue of greatest concern to most American citizens (*New York Times*/CBS News Poll). How can we explain the level of violence? How do people learn to be violent? How can we control, and remedy, aggression? And how can we discourage violence from occurring in the first place?

Developmentalists have sought to answer such questions from several different perspectives (APA Public Interest Directorate, 1993; Farley, 1993; Eron, Gentry, & Schlegel, 1994). Their work, illustrated by some representative approaches below, exemplifies some of the ways in which the field can provide concrete solutions to pressing problems.

- *Explaining the roots of violence.* Some developmentalists have looked at how early behavior problems may be associated with later difficulties in controlling aggression. For instance, Avashlom Caspi and colleagues are examining how a lack of control in early childhood is associated with later conduct disorders and antisocial behavior during adolescence (Caspi et al., 1995).

- *Dealing effectively with acts of aggression.* According to psychologist Arnold Goldstein of Syracuse University's Center for Research on Aggression, school teachers and administrators must be on the lookout for even mild forms of aggression, such as bullying and sexual harassment. Unless such forms of aggression are checked, they are likely to endure and to escalate into more blatant forms (Goldstein, 1994).

  Such "minor" forms of aggression are many. Name-calling, threats, thefts, extortion of lunch money, spreading of rumors, and racial and gender-based slurs all can have psychological and academic consequences. Additionally, major forms of aggression can have even more profound consequences—and they are becoming increasingly commonplace. For instance, gun violence is seen in almost two-thirds of all high schools and in one-fourth of junior high schools in the United States.

  To deal with such aggression, Goldstein has implemented a program that teaches students to "unlearn" aggression. Assuming that aggression is initially learned as a strategy—often successful—for dealing with conflict, the program teaches moral reasoning and new ways of controlling anger and handling conflict without aggression (Azar & McCarthy, 1994; Goldstein, 1994).

- *Seeking to prevent violence and other forms of juvenile delinquency.* Taking an ecological approach, some developmentalists have created violence prevention programs based on the assumption that families, peers, schools, and the community as a whole must be taken into account.

  For instance, the Yale Child Welfare Research Program provided a randomly chosen group of poor families with child care, medical care, and parent education regarding child development for the 17 months following the birth of their first children. The families also received home visits to help them obtain food and housing and to offer general advice. Ten years later, their children had better school attendance and were rated less aggressive by their teachers than were children in families who did not participate in the program. In addition, they were less likely than nonparticipants to stay out all night, steal, or be cruel to animals, according to their mothers. Developmental psychologist Edward Zigler says the program was also cost-effective: For each of the children in the program, the annual cost of remedial and support services was more than $1,000 lower than for those in the control group (Zigler, 1994).

As these examples illustrate, specialists in life-span development are making progress in dealing with the violence that is increasingly part of modern society. Furthermore, violence is just one example of the areas in which developmentalists are contributing their skills for the betterment of human society. As we'll see throughout this book, the field has much to offer.

Review and Rethink

REVIEW

- Life-span development, a scientific approach to understanding human growth and change thoughout life, encompasses physical, cognitive, and social and personality development.

- The ecological approach considers interrelationships among aspects of human development, and relationships between the individual and four levels of the environment.

- Membership in a cohort, based on age and place of birth, subjects people to influences based on historical events (normative history-graded influences). People are also subject to normative age-graded influences (experienced by all people at a given age), nonnormative life events (which are unique to an individual), and socio-cultural factors (normative sociocultural-graded influence).

- Four important issues in life-span development are continuity versus discontinuity in development, the importance of critical periods, whether to focus on certain periods or on the entire life span, and the nature–nurture controversy. Each issue is best seen not as an either-or choice, but as a continuum along which aspects of development can be placed.

RETHINK

- What sorts of questions would you expect a specialist studying cognitive development to ask? How about one studying personality or social development?

- What are some environmental factors that might influence the timing of human development?

- How might each of the four elements of the ecological approach influence a major developmental step, such as the decision to marry or not to marry?

- What are some events that might have a shared significance for members of your age cohort as normative history-graded influences? How might they produce different effects from events shared by members of different age cohorts?

- Can you think of one aspect of human development in each area (physical, cognitive, personality and social) that is affected by both nature and nurture?

THEORETICAL PERSPECTIVES

Until the seventeenth century in Europe, there was no concept of "childhood." Instead, children were simply thought of as miniature adults. They were assumed to be subject to the same needs and desires as adults, to have the same vices and virtues as adults, and to warrant no more privileges than adults. They were dressed the same as adults, and their work hours were the same as adults. Children also received the same punishments for misdeeds. If they stole, they were hanged; if they did well, they could achieve prosperity.

This view of childhood seems wrong-headed now, but at the time it is what passed for life-span development. From this perspective, there were no differences due to age; except for size, people were assumed to be virtually unchanging—at least on a psychological level—throughout most of the life span (Ariès, 1962).

Looking back over several centuries, it is easy to reject the medieval view of childhood; however, it is less clear how to formulate a contemporary substitute. Should our view of

Society's view of childhood, and what is appropriate to ask of children, has changed through the ages. These children worked full-time in mines in the early 1900s.

development focus on the biological aspects of change, growth, and stability over the life span? On the cognitive or social aspects? Or what?

In fact, developmentalists have produced a number of broad conceptual perspectives that represent approaches to development. Each broad perspective encompasses one or more **theories,** explanations and predictions concerning phenomena of interest. A theory provides a framework for understanding the relationships among an organized set of facts or principles.

We'll consider three major perspectives used by developmentalists: the psychodynamic, the behavioral, and the cognitive perspective. Each emphasizes somewhat different aspects of development and steers developmentalists in particular directions. Furthermore, each perspective continues to evolve and change, as befits a growing and dynamic discipline.

THE PSYCHODYNAMIC PERSPECTIVE: FOCUSING ON THE INNER PERSON

When Janet was six months old she was involved in a bloody automobile accident—or so her parents tell her, since she has no conscious recollection of it. Now, however, at age 24, she is having difficulty maintaining relationships, and her therapist is seeking to determine whether her current problems are a result of the earlier accident.

Looking for a such a link might seem a bit far-fetched, but to proponents of the **psychodynamic perspective,** it is not so improbable. Advocates of the psychodynamic perspective believe that behavior is motivated by inner forces, memories, and conflicts of which a person has little awareness or control. The inner forces, which may stem from one's childhood, continually influence behavior throughout the life span.

Freud's Psychoanalytic Theory. The psychodynamic perspective is most closely associated with a single person and theory: Sigmund Freud and his psychoanalytic theory. Freud, who lived from 1856 to 1939, was a Viennese physician whose revolutionary ideas about the unconscious determinants of behavior ultimately had a profound effect not only on psychology but on Western thought in general.

Freud's **psychoanalytic theory** suggests that unconscious forces act to determine personality and behavior. To Freud, the *unconscious* is a part of the personality about which a person is unaware. It contains infantile wishes, desires, demands, and needs that are hidden, because of their disturbing nature, from conscious awareness. Freud suggested that the unconscious is responsible for a good part of our everyday behavior.

theories *explanations and predictions concerning phenomena of interest, providing a framework for understanding the relationships among an organized set of facts or principles*

psychodynamic perspective *the approach that states behavior is motivated by inner forces, memories, and conflicts of which a person has little awareness or control*

psychoanalytic theory *the theory proposed by Freud that suggests that unconscious forces act to determine personality and behavior*

Sigmund Freud

id   *according to Freud, the raw, unorganized, inborn part of personality that is present at birth*

ego   *according to Freud, the part of personality that is rational and reasonable*

superego   *according to Freud, the aspect of personality that represents a person's conscience, incorporating distinctions between right and wrong*

psychosexual development   *according to Freud, a series of stages that children pass through in which pleasure, or gratification is focused on a particular biological function and body part*

fixation   *behavior reflecting an earlier stage of development*

psychosocial development   *the approach that encompasses changes both in the understanding individuals have of their interactions with others, others' behavior, and of themselves as members of society*

Erik Erikson

According to Freud, one's personality has three aspects: id, ego, and superego. The **id** is the raw, unorganized, inborn part of personality that is present at birth. It represents primitive drives related to hunger, sex, aggression, and irrational impulses. The id operates according to the *pleasure principle,* in which the goal is the immediate reduction of tension and the maximization of satisfaction.

The **ego** is the part of the personality that is rational and reasonable. Providing a reality check for the demands of the id, the ego acts as a buffer between the outside world and the primitive demands of the id. The ego operates on the *reality principle,* in which instinctual energy is restrained in order to maintain the safety of the individual and help integrate the person into society.

Finally, Freud proposed that the **superego** represents a person's conscience, incorporating distinctions between right and wrong. It develops around age five or six and is learned from an individual's parents, teachers, and other significant figures.

In addition to providing an account of the various parts of the personality, Freud also suggested the ways in which personality developed during childhood. He argued that **psychosexual development** occurred as children passed through a series of stages, in which pleasure, or gratification, was focused on a particular biological function and body part. As illustrated in Table 1-3, he suggested that pleasure shifted from the mouth (the *oral stage*) to the anus (the *anal stage*) and eventually to the genitals (the *phallic stage* and the *genital stage*).

If children are unable to gratify themselves sufficiently during a particular stage, or, conversely, if they receive too much gratification, fixation may occur. An adult with a **fixation** shows personality traits characteristic of an earlier stage of development because of an unresolved conflict from the earlier period. For instance, fixation at the oral stage might produce an adult unusually absorbed in oral activities—eating, talking, or chewing gum—or showing symbolic sorts of oral activities, such as "biting" sarcasm.

Erikson's Psychosocial Theory.   Psychoanalyst Erik Erikson (1902–1990) provided an alternative view of how society and culture both challenge and shape us. His theory of **psychosocial development** encompasses changes in our interactions with and understandings of one another, as well as in our knowledge and understanding of ourselves as members of society (Erikson, 1963).

Erikson's theory suggests that developmental change occurs throughout our lives in eight distinct stages (see Table 1-3). The stages emerge in a fixed pattern and are similar for all people.

Erikson argued that each stage presents a crisis or conflict that the individual must resolve. Although no crisis is ever fully resolved, making life increasingly complicated, the individual must at least address the crisis of each stage sufficiently to deal with demands made during the next stage of development.

Unlike Freud, who regarded development as relatively complete by adolescence, Erikson suggested that growth and change continue throughout the life span. For instance, as discussed further in Chapter 16, he argued that during middle adulthood people pass through the *generativity versus stagnation stage,* in which their contributions to family, community, and society can produce either positive feelings about the continuity of life—or a sense of stagnation and disappointment about what they are passing on to future generations.

Assessing the Psychodynamic Perspective.   It is hard for us to grasp the full significance of psychodynamic theories, represented by Freud's psychoanalytic theory and Erikson's theory of psychosocial development. Freud's introduction of the notion that unconscious influences affect behavior was a monumental accomplishment, and the fact that it seems at all reasonable to us shows how far the idea of the unconscious has pervaded thinking in

TABLE 1-3

FREUD'S AND ERIKSON'S THEORIES

Approximate Age	Freud's Stages of Psychosexual Development	Major Characteristics of Freud's Stages	Erikson's Stages of Psychosocial Development	Positive and Negative Outcomes of Erikson's Stages
Birth to 12-18 months	Oral	Interest in oral gratification from sucking, eating, mouthing, biting	Trust vs. mistrust	*Positive:* Feelings of trust from environmental support *Negative:* Fear and concern regarding others
12-18 months to 3 years	Anal	Gratification from expelling and withholding feces; coming to terms with society's controls relating to toilet training	Autonomy vs. shame and doubt	*Positive:* Self-sufficiency if exploration is encouraged *Negative:* Doubts about self, lack of independence
3 to 5-6 years	Phallic	Interest in the genitals; coming to terms with Oedipal conflict, leading to identification with same-sex parent	Initiative vs. guilt	*Positive:* Discovery of ways to initiate actions *Negative:* Guilt from actions and thoughts
5-6 years to adolescence	Latency	Sexual concerns largely unimportant	Industry vs. inferiority	*Positive:* Development of sense of competence *Negative:* Feelings of inferiority, no sense of mastery
Adolescence to adulthood (Freud) Adolescence (Erikson)	Genital	Reemergence of sexual interests and establishment of mature sexual relationships	Identity vs. role diffusion	*Positive:* Awareness of uniqueness of self, knowledge of role to be followed *Negative:* Inability to identify appropriate roles in life
Early adulthood (Erikson)			Intimacy vs. isolation	*Positive:* Development of loving, sexual relationships and close friendships *Negative:* Fear of relationships with others
Middle adulthood (Erikson)			Generativity vs. stagnation	*Positive:* Sense of contribution to continuity of life *Negative:* Trivialization of one's activities
Late adulthood (Erikson)			Ego-integrity vs. despair	*Positive:* Sense of unity in life's accomplishments *Negative:* Regret over lost opportunities of life

Western cultures. In fact, work by contemporary psychologists studying memory suggests that we carry with us memories—of which we are not consciously aware—that have a significant impact on our behavior (Kihlstrom, 1987; Westen, 1990; Jacoby & Kelley, 1992).

On the other hand, some of the most basic principles of Freud's psychoanalytic theory have been called into question because they have not been validated by subsequent research. In particular, the notion that people pass through stages in childhood that determine their adult personalities has little definitive research support. In addition, because much of

Freud's theory was based on a limited population of upper-middle-class Austrians living during a strict, puritanical era, it is questionable how applicable the theory is to broad, multicultural populations. Finally, because Freud's theory focuses primarily on male development, it has been criticized as sexist and may be interpreted as devaluing women. For such reasons, many developmental psychologists question Freud's theory (Guthrie & Lonner, 1986; Brislin, 1993; Crews, 1993).

Erikson's psychosocial theory has stood the test of time better than Freud's psychoanalytic theory. As we'll see in future chapters, Erikson's view that development continues throughout the life span is highly important—and has received considerable support. In fact, many of the specifics of Erikson's theory have been confirmed by later research (Whitbourne, Zuschlag, Elliot, & Waterman, 1992; Hetherington & Weinberger, 1993; Peterson & Stewart, 1993).

On the other hand, Erikson's theory also has its drawbacks. Like Freud's theory, it focuses more on men's than women's development. It is also vague in some respects, making it difficult for researchers to test rigorously. And, as is the case with psychodynamic theories in general, it is difficult to make definitive predictions about a given individual's behavior using the theory. In sum, then, the psychodynamic perspective provides good descriptions of past behavior, but imprecise predictions of future behavior.

THE BEHAVIORAL PERSPECTIVE: CONSIDERING THE OUTER PERSON

When Elissa Sheehan was three, a large brown dog bit her, and she needed dozens of stitches and several operations. From the time she was bitten, she broke into a sweat whenever she saw a dog, and in fact never enjoyed being around any pet.

To a developmental specialist using the behavioral perspective, the explanation for Elissa's behavior is straightforward: She has a learned fear of dogs. Rather than looking inside the organism at unconscious processes, the **behavioral perspective** suggests that the keys to understanding development are observable behavior and outside stimuli in the environment. If we know the stimuli, we can predict the behavior.

Behavioral theories reject the notion that people universally pass through a series of stages. Instead, people are assumed to be affected by the environmental stimuli to which they happen to be exposed. Developmental patterns, then, are personal, reflecting a particular set of environmental stimuli, and behavior is the result of continuing exposure to specific factors in the environment. Furthermore, developmental change is viewed in quantitative, rather than qualitative, terms. For instance, behavioral theories see advances in problem-solving capabilities as children age as a result of greater mental *capacities*, rather than changes in the *kind* of thinking that chidlren are able to bring to bear on a problem.

Classical Conditioning: Stimulus Substitution.   "Give me a dozen healthy infants, well-formed, and my own specified world to bring them up in and I'll guarantee to take any one at random and train him to become any type of specialist I might select—doctor, lawyer, artist, merchant-chief, and yes, even beggar-man and thief, regardless of his talents, penchants, tendencies, abilities, vocations and race of his ancestors" (Watson, 1925).

With these words, John B. Watson (1878–1958), one of the first American psychologists to advocate a behavioral approach, summed up the behavioral perspective. Watson believed strongly that we could gain a full understanding of development by carefully studying the stimuli that compose the environment. In fact, he argued that by effectively controlling a person's environment, it was possible to produce virtually any behavior.

As we'll consider further in Chapter 5, **classical conditioning** occurs when an organism learns to respond in a particular way to a neutral stimulus that normally does not evoke that type of response. For instance, if a dog is repeatedly exposed to the pairing of two stim-

behavioral perspective   the approach that suggests that the keys to understanding development are observable behavior and outside stimuli in the environment

classical conditioning   a type of learning in which an organism responds in a particular way to a neutral stimulus that normally does not bring about that type of response

uli, such as the sound of a bell and the presentation of meat, it may learn to react to the bell alone in the same way it reacts to the meat—by salivating and wagging its tail with excitement. Dogs do not typically respond to bells in this way; the behavior is a result of stimulus substitution.

The same process of classical conditioning explains how we learn emotional responses. In the case of dog-bite victim Elissa Sheehan, for instance, one stimulus has been substituted for another: Elissa's unpleasant experience with a particular dog (the initial stimulus) has been transferred to other dogs, and to pets in general.

Operant Conditioning.   In addition to classical conditioning, other types of learning derive from the behavioral perspective. In fact, the learning approach that probably has had the greatest influence is **operant conditioning,** a form of learning in which a voluntary response is strengthened or weakened by its association with positive or negative consequences.

In operant conditioning, formulated and championed largely by psychologist B.F. Skinner (1904–1990), individuals learn to act deliberately on their environments to bring about desired consequences. (Skinner, 1975). In a sense, then, people *operate* on their environments to bring about a desired state of affairs.

Whether or not people will seek to repeat a behavior depends on whether it is followed by reinforcement. *Reinforcement* is the process by which a stimulus is provided that increases the probability that a preceding behavior will be repeated. Hence, a student is apt to work harder in school if he or she receives good grades; workers are likely to labor harder at their jobs if their efforts are tied to pay increases; and people are more apt to buy lottery tickets if they are reinforced by winning at least occasionally.

Behavior that is reinforced, then, is more likely to be repeated in the future, whereas behavior that receives no reinforcement is likely to be discontinued, or, in the language of operant conditioning, *extinguished.* Principles of operant conditioning are used in **behavior modification,** a formal technique for promoting the frequency of desirable behaviors and decreasing the incidence of unwanted ones. Behavior modification has been used in a variety of situations, ranging from teaching severely retarded people the rudiments of language to helping people stick to diets (Bellack, Hersen, & Kazdin, 1990; Sulzer-Azaroff & Mayer, 1991; Malott, Whaley, & Malott, 1993).

operant conditioning   *a form of learning in which a voluntary response is strengthened or weakened, depending on its association with positive or negative consequences*

behavior modification   *a formal technique for promoting the frequency of desirable behaviors and decreasing the incidence of unwanted ones*

B.F. Skinner

social learning   learning by observing the behavior of another person, called a model

cognitive perspective   the approach that focuses on the processes that allow people to know, understand, and think about the world

Social Learning Theory: Learning Through Imitation.   Beavis and Butt-head, cartoon characters on MTV, discuss how enjoyable it is to set fires. On at least one occasion, one of them lights the other's hair on fire using matches and an aerosol spray can. Not long after seeing the show, five-year-old Austin Messner sets his bed on fire with a cigarette lighter, starting a blaze that killed his younger sister.

Cause and effect? We cannot know for sure, but it certainly seems possible, especially looking at the situation from the perspective of *social learning theory*. According to Albert Bandura and colleagues, a significant amount of learning is in the form of **social learning,** which is learning by observing the behavior of another person, called a *model* (Bandura, 1977).

Social learning theory holds that when we see the behavior of a model being rewarded, we are likely to imitate that behavior. For instance, in one classic experiment, children who were afraid of dogs were exposed to a model, nicknamed the "Fearless Peer," who was seen playing happily with a dog (Bandura, Grusec, & Menlove, 1967). After exposure, the children who previously had been afraid were more likely to approach a strange dog than were children who had not seen the model.

Bandura suggests that social learning proceeds in four steps (Bandura, 1986). First, an observer must pay attention and perceive the most critical features of a model's behavior. Second, the behavior must be successfully recalled. Third, the behavior must be reproduced accurately. Finally, the observer must be motivated to learn and carry out the behavior. Rather than learning being a matter of trial and error, as it is with operant conditioning, in social learning theory behavior is learned through observation.

Assessing the Behavioral Perspective.   Although they are part of the same general behavioral perspective, classical and operant conditioning on the one hand, and social learning theory on the other, disagree in some basic ways (Amsel, 1988). Both classical and operant conditioning consider learning in terms of external stimuli and responses, in which the only important factors are the observable features of the environment. In such an analysis, people and other organisms are "black boxes"; nothing that occurs inside the box is understood—nor much cared about, for that matter.

To social learning theorists, such an analysis is an oversimplification. They argue that what makes people different from rats and pigeons is mental activity in the form of thoughts and expectations. A full understanding of people's development, proponents maintain, cannot occur without moving beyond external stimuli and responses.

In many ways, social learning theory has come to predominate over classical and operant conditioning theories in recent decades. In fact, another perspective that focuses explicitly on internal mental activity has become enormously influential. This is the *cognitive approach,* which we consider next.

THE COGNITIVE PERSPECTIVE: EXAMINING THE ROOTS OF UNDERSTANDING

When three-year-old Jake is asked why it sometimes rains, he answers "so the flowers can grow." When his eleven-year-old sister Lila is asked the same question, she responds "because of evaporation from the surface of the Earth." And when their aunt Ajima, who is studying meteorology in graduate school, considers the same question, her extended answer includes a discussion of cumulonimbus clouds, the Coriolis effect, and synoptic charts.

To a developmentalist using the cognitive perspective, the difference in the sophistication of the answers is evidence of different degree of knowledge and understanding, or cognition. The **cognitive perspective** focuses on the processes that allow people to know, understand, and think about the world, and it emphasizes how people internally represent and contemplate the world. By using this perspective, developmentalists hope to understand how children and adults process information, and how their ways of thinking and understanding affect their behavior. They also seek to learn how cognitive abilities change as people develop, and the degree to which cognitive development represents quantitative and qualitative growth in intellectual abilities.

Piaget's Theory of Cognitive Development.   No single developmental psychologist has had a greater impact on the study of cognitive development than has Jean Piaget. A Swiss psychologist who lived from 1896 to 1980, Piaget proposed that all people passed in a fixed sequence through a series of universal stages of cognitive development. In each stage, he suggested, not only did the quantity of information increase, but the quality of knowledge and understanding changed as well. His focus was on the change in cognition that occurred as children moved from one stage to the next (Piaget, 1952, 1962, 1983).

Although we'll consider Piaget's theory in detail beginning in Chapter 5, we can get a broad sense of it by looking at some of its main features. Piaget suggested that human thinking is arranged into *schemes,* organized mental patterns that represent behaviors and actions. In infants, such schemes represent concrete behavior—a scheme for sucking, for reaching, and for each separate behavior. In older children, the schemes become more sophisticated and abstract. Schemes are like intellectual computer software that directs and determines how data from the world are looked at and dealt with (Achenbach, 1992).

Piaget suggested that the growth in children's understanding of the world can be explained by two basic principles. **Assimilation** is the process in which people understand an experience in terms of their current stage of cognitive development and way of thinking. In contrast, **accommodation** refers to changes in existing ways of thinking in response to encounters with new stimuli or events.

Assimilation occurs when current ways of thinking about and understanding the world are used to perceive and understand a new experience. For example, a young child who has not yet learned to count will look at a row of buttons that are closely spaced together and say there are fewer buttons in that row than in a row of the same number of buttons that are more spread out. The experience of counting buttons, then, is *assimilated* to already existing schemes that contain the principle "bigger is more."

Later, however, when the child is older and has had sufficient exposure to new experiences, the content of the scheme will undergo change. In understanding that the quantity of buttons is identical whether they are spread out or closely spaced, the child has *accommodated* to the experience. Assimilation and accommodation work in tandem to bring about cognitive development.

Assessing Piaget's Theory.   Piaget was without peer in influencing our understanding of cognitive development, and he is one of the towering figures in developmental psychology. He provided masterful descriptions of how intellectual growth proceeds during childhood—descriptions that have stood the test of literally thousands of investigations. By and large, then, Piaget's broad view of the sequence of cognitive development is accurate (Gratch & Schatz, 1987).

However, the specifics of the theory, particularly in terms of change in cognitive capabilities over time, have been called into question. For instance, some cognitive skills clearly emerge earlier than Piaget suggested. Furthermore, the universality of Piaget's stages has been disputed. A growing amount of evidence suggests that the emergence of particular cognitive skills occurs according to a different timetable in non-Western cultures. And in every culture, some people never seem to reach Piaget's highest level of cognitive sophistication: formal, logical thought.

Ultimately, the greatest criticism leveled at the Piagetian perspective is that cognitive development is not necessarily as discontinuous as Piaget's stage theory suggests. Remember that Piaget argued that growth proceeded in four distinct stages, in which the quality of cognition differed from one stage to the next.

However, many developmentalists argue that growth is considerably more continuous. These critics of the Piagetian approach suggest that an information-processing approach is

assimilation   *the process in which people understand an experience in terms of their current stage of cognitive development and way of thinking*

accommodation   *the process that changes existing ways of thinking in response to encounters with new stimuli or events*

more appropriate. *Information-processing* approaches to cognitive development, which seek to identify the ways individuals take in, use, and store information, assume that cognitive growth is typified more by quantitative than by qualitative change (Siegler, 1991). This viewpoint has garnered much support, and, as seen in later chapters, information-processing approaches have become an important alternative to Piagetian approaches.

WHICH APPROACH IS RIGHT? THE WRONG QUESTION

In our consideration of perspectives on development, we've looked at the three major ones: psychodynamic, behavioral, and cognitive. It would be natural to wonder which of the three—which are summarized in Table 1-4—provides that most accurate account of human development.

However, for several reasons, such a question is inappropriate. For one thing, each perspective emphasizes somewhat different aspects of development. For instance, the psychodynamic approach emphasizes emotions, motivational conflicts, and unconscious determinants of behavior. In contrast, behavioral perspectives emphasize overt behavior, paying far more attention to what people *do* than what goes on inside their heads, which is deemed largely irrelevant. Finally, the cognitive perspective takes quite the opposite tack, looking more at what people *think* than what they do.

Clearly, each perspective is based on its own premises and focuses on different aspects of development. Furthermore, the same developmental phenomenon can be looked at from a number of perspectives simultaneously.

In short, we can think of the different perspectives as analogous to a set of maps of the same general geographical area. One map may contain detailed depictions of roads; another map may show geographical features; another may show political subdivisions, such as cities, towns, and counties; and still another may highlight particular points of interest, such as scenic areas and historical landmarks. Each of the maps is accurate, but each provides a different point of view and way of thinking. No map alone is sufficient, but by considering them together we can come to a fuller understanding of the area in which we are interested.

In the same way, the various theoretical perspectives provide us with different ways of looking at development. Taking them together paints a full portrait of the myriad ways in which human beings change and grow over the course of their lives.

TABLE 1-4

MAJOR PERSPECTIVES ON LIFE-SPAN DEVELOPMENT

Perspective	Description
Psychodynamic	Advocates of the *psychodynamic perspective* believe that behavior is motivated by inner, unconscious forces, memories, and conflicts over which a person has little awareness and control. The inner forces, which may stem from childhood experiences, continually influence behavior throughout our entire lives. Major proponents: Sigmund Freud and Erik Erikson.
Behavioral	The *behavioral perspective* suggests that the focus of understanding development rests on observable behavior and outside stimuli in the environment. If we know what those stimuli are, we can predict how people will behave. Major proponents: John B. Watson, B.F. Skinner, and Albert Bandura.
Cognitive	The *cognitive perspective* focuses on the processes that allow people to know, understand, and think about the world, and it emphasizes how people internally represent and think about the world. It emphasizes how children and adults process information, and how their ways of thinking and understanding affect their behavior. Major proponent: Jean Piaget.

On the other hand, not all theories and claims derived from the various perspectives are accurate. How do we choose among competing explanations? The answer is *research*, which we consider in the final part of this chapter.

Developmental Diversity

How Culture, Ethnicity, and Race Influence Development

The culture in which people are raised plays a central role in their development.

> South American Mayan mothers are certain that almost constant contact between themselves and their infant children is necessary for good parenting, and they are physically upset if contact is not possible. They are shocked when they see a North American mother lay her infant down, and they attribute the baby's crying to the poor parenting of the North American. (Haviland, 1978; Morelli, Rogoff, Oppenheim, & Goldsmith, 1992)

Clearly, two views of good parenting are at odds in this passage. Is one correct and the other wrong?

Probably not, if we take into consideration the cultural context in which the mothers are operating. In fact, different cultures and subcultures have their own views of appropriate and inappropriate childrearing, just as they have different developmental goals toward which children are supposed to be aiming (Greenfield, 1995).

Consider, for instance, whether you agree that children should be taught that their classmates' assistance is indispensable to getting good grades in school, or that they should definitely plan to continue their fathers' businesses, or that children should follow their parents' advice in determining their career plans. If you have been raised in the dominant North American culture, it is likely that you would disagree with all three statements because they violate the premises of *individualism*, the dominant Western philosophy that emphasizes personal identity, uniqueness, freedom, and the worth of the individual.

On the other hand, if you were raised in a traditional Asian culture, your agreement with the three statements is considerably more likely. The reason? The statements are indicative of the value orientation known as *collectivism*, the notion that the well-being of the group is more important than that of the individual. People raised in collectivistic cultures tend to emphasize the welfare of the groups to which they belong, sometimes even at the expense of their own personal well-being.

The individualism–collectivism spectrum is one of several dimensions along which cultures differ, and it illustrates differences in the cultural contexts in which people operate. One of the challenges life-span developmentalists face is to take different cultural contexts into account.

Furthermore, they must consider not just broad cultural differences, such as those that separate North American and Asian cultures. They must take into account finer ethnic, racial, and socioeconomic differences if they are to achieve an understanding of how people change and grow throughout the life span. If developmentalists succeed in doing so, not only can they achieve a better understanding of human development but they may also be able to derive more precise applications for improving the human social condition.

Although life-span development is increasingly concerned with issues of human diversity, its forward movement has been slow, and in some ways it has actually moved backwards. For instance, between 1970 and 1989, only 4.6 percent of the articles published in *Developmental Psychology*, the premier journal of the discipline, focused on African-

American participants. Even worse, the number actually declined over that twenty-year period (Graham, 1992; MacPhee, Kreutzer, & Fritz, 1994).

On the other hand, as the proportion of minorities in American society continues to increase, it is probable that taking human diversity into account will become more commonplace. In fact, it is only by looking for differences among various ethnic and racial groups that specialists in life-span development can distinguish principles of development that are universal from ones that are culturally determined. It is likely, then, that life-span development will move from a discipline that focuses on North American and European development to one that embodies development across the globe.

Review and Rethink

REVIEW

- Three major theoretical perspectives have dominated the discipline of life-span development. The psychodynamic perspective looks primarily at the influence of internal, unconscious forces on development. Freud's psychoanalytic theory and Erikson's psychosocial theory are examples.

- A second perspective, the behavioral perspective, focuses on external, observable behaviors as the key to development. Classical conditioning, operant conditioning, and social learning theories are examples.

- The third major perspective is the cognitive perspective, which focuses on mental activity. Piaget's stage theory of development and information-processing approaches to development are examples.

- All three perspectives are valuable and none is complete, with each providing a part of the total picture.

- Culture, too, plays an important role in development, both broad culture and aspects of culture, such as race, ethnicity, and socioeconomic status.

RETHINK

- How might a person's unconscious affect his or her behavior? How were such behaviors explained before the concept of the unconscious was devised?

- Can you think of examples of conditioned responses and reinforcement in everyday life?

- How do the concepts of social learning and modeling relate to the mass media?

- In general, what does each theoretical perspective contribute to our understanding of human development?

- Can you think of examples of the ways culture (either broad culture or aspects of culture) affects human development?

RESEARCH METHODS

The Egyptians had long believed that they were the most ancient race on earth, and Psamtik [King of Egypt in the seventh century B.C.], driven by intellectual curiosity, wanted to prove that flattering belief. Like a good scientist, he began with a hypothesis: If children had no opportunity to learn a language from older people around them, they would spontaneously speak the primal, inborn language of humankind—the natural language of its most ancient people—which, he expected to show, was Egyptian.

To test his hypothesis, Psamtik commandeered two infants of a lower-class mother and turned them over to a herdsman to bring up in a remote area. They were to be kept in a sequestered cottage, properly fed and cared for, but were never to hear anyone speak so much as a word. The Greek historian Herodotus, who tracked the story down and learned what he calls "the real facts" from priests of Hephaestus in Memphis, says that Psamtik's goal "was to know, after the indistinct babblings of infancy were over, what word they would first articulate."

The experiment, he tells us, worked. One day, when the children were two years old, they ran up to the herdsman as he opened the door of their cottage and cried out "*Becos!*" Since this meant nothing to him, he paid no attention, but when it happened repeatedly, he sent word to Psamtik, who at once ordered the children brought to him. When he too heard them say it, Psamtik made inquiries and learned that *becos* was the Phrygian word for bread. He concluded that, disappointingly, the Phrygians were an older race than the Egyptians. (Hunt, 1993, pp. 1–2)

With the perspective of several thousand years, we can easily see the shortcomings—both scientific and ethical—in Psamtik's approach. Yet his procedure represents an improvement over mere speculation, and as such is sometimes looked upon as the first psychological experiment in recorded history (Hunt, 1993).

THEORIES AND HYPOTHESES: POSING DEVELOPMENTAL QUESTIONS

Questions such as those raised by Psamtik lie at the heart of life-span development. Is language innate? What are the effects of malnutrition on later intellectual performance? How do infants form relationships with their parents, and does participation in day care disrupt such relationships? Why are adolescents susceptible to peer pressure? Are there declines in intellectual abilities related to aging?

To resolve such questions, developmentalists rely on the **scientific method**, the process of posing and answering questions using careful, controlled techniques that include systematic, orderly observation and the collection of data.

The scientific method involves the formulation of theories, broad explanations, and predictions about phenomena of interest. All of us develop theories about development, based on our experience, folklore, and articles in magazines and newspapers. For instance, many people theorize that there is a crucial bonding period between parent and child immediately after birth, which is a necessary ingredient in forming a lasting parent–child relationship. Without such a bonding period, they assume, the parent–child relationship will be forever compromised.

Whenever we employ such explanations, we are developing our own theories. However, the theories of developmentalists are different. Whereas our own personal theories are built on unverified observations that are developed unsystematically, developmentalists' theories are more formal, based on a systematic integration of prior findings and theories. These theories allow developmentalists to summarize and organize prior observations, and they allow them to move beyond existing observations to draw deductions that may not be immediately apparent.

Theories are used to develop hypotheses. A **hypothesis** is a prediction stated in a way that permits it to be tested. For instance, someone who subscribes to the general theory that bonding is a crucial ingredient in the parent–child relationship might derive the more specific hypothesis that adopted children whose adoptive parents never had the chance to bond

scientific method   *the process of posing and answering questions using controlled, systematic techniques of data collection*

hypothesis   *a prediction stated in a way that permits it to be tested*

with them immediately after birth may ultimately have less secure relationships with their adoptive parents. Others might derive other hypotheses, such as that effective bonding occurs only if it lasts for a certain length of time, or that bonding affects the mother–child relationship, but not the father–child relationship. (In case you're wondering, these particular hypotheses have *not* been upheld; there are no long-term reactions to the separation of parent and child immediately following birth, even if the separation lasts several days.)

CHOOSING A RESEARCH STRATEGY: ANSWERING QUESTIONS

Once they have chosen a hypothesis to test, researchers must develop a strategy for testing its validity. There are two major categories of research: experimental research and correlational research. **Experimental research** is designed to discover *causal* relationships among various factors. In experimental research, researchers deliberately introduce a change in a situation to see the consequences of that change. For instance, a researcher conducting an experiment might vary the number of minutes that mothers and children interact immediately following birth, in an attempt to see whether the amount of bonding time affects the mother–child relationship.

In contrast, **correlational research** seeks to identify whether an association or relationship between two factors exists. Correlational research is unable to determine whether one factor causes changes in the other. For instance, correlational research could tell us if there is an association between the quality of a mother–child relationship when the child was two years old and the number of minutes that they were together just after birth. Such correlational research indicates if the two factors are *associated* or *related* to one another, but not if the initial contact caused the relationship to develop in a particular way.

Because experimental research is able to answer questions of causality, it represents the heart of developmental research. However, because some research questions cannot be answered through experiments, for either technical or ethical reasons, correlational research remains an important tool in the developmental researcher's toolbox.

Experiments: Determining Cause and Effect.   In an **experiment,** an investigator, called an *experimenter,* devises two different experiences for *subjects,* or *participants.* These two different experiences are called *treatments.* A **treatment** is a procedure applied by an investigator. One group of participants receives one of the treatments, while another group of participants receives either no treatment or an alternative treatment. The group receiving the treatment is known as the **treatment group;** the no-treatment or alternative-treatment group is called the **control group.**

Although the terminology may seem daunting at first, there is an underlying logic to it that helps to sort it out. Think in terms of a medical experiment in which the aim is to test the effectiveness of a new drug. In testing the drug, we wish to see if the drug successfully *treats* the disease. Consequently, the group that receives the drug would be called the *treatment* group. In comparison, another group of participants would not receive the drug treatment. Instead, they would be part of the no-treatment *control* group.

Similarly, suppose we wish to explore the consequences of exposure to movie violence on viewers' subsequent aggression. We might take a group of adolescents and show them films that contain a great deal of violent imagery. We would then measure their subsequent aggression. This group would constitute the treatment group. But we would also need another group—a control group. To fulfill this need, we might take a second group of adolescents, show them films that contain no aggressive imagery, and then measure their subsequent aggression. This would be the control group.

By comparing the amount of aggression displayed by members of the treatment and control groups, we would be able to determine if exposure to violent imagery produces aggression in viewers. And this is just what a group of researchers found: Running an experiment of this very sort, psychologist Jacques-Philippe Leyens and colleagues of the University of Louvain in Belgium found that the level of aggression rose significantly for the

experimental research   research designed to discover causal relationships between various factors

correlational research   research that seeks to identify whether an association or relationship between two factors exists

experiment   a process in which an investigator, called an experimenter, devises two different experiences for subjects or participants

treatment   a procedure applied by an investigator based on two different experiences devised for subjects and participants (See Experiment)

treatment group   the group receiving the treatment

control group   the group that receives either no treatment or alternative treatment

adolescents who had seen the movies containing violence (Leyens, Camino, Parke, & Berkowitz, 1975).

The central feature of this experiment—and all experiments—is the comparison of the consequences of different treatments. The use of both treatment and control groups allows researchers to rule out the possibility that something other than the experimental manipulation produced the results found in the experiment. For instance, if no control group was used, experimenters could not be certain that some other factor, such as the time of day the films were shown, the need to sit still during the movie, or even the mere passage of time, produced the changes observed. By employing a control group, then, experimenters can draw accurate conclusions about causes and effects.

Correlational Studies.   There are some situations that a researcher, no matter how ingenious, simply cannot control. For instance, no researcher would be able to assign different groups of infants to parents of high and low socioeconomic status in order to learn the effects of such status on subsequent development. Similarly, we cannot control what a group of children watch on television throughout their childhood years in order to learn if exposure to televised aggression later leads to aggressive behavior.

Because some experiments are logistically or ethically impossible, developmentalists employ an alternative procedure—correlational research. As mentioned earlier, correlational research examines the relationship between two variables to determine whether they are associated, or *correlated*.

For instance, researchers interested in the relationship between televised aggression and subsequent behavior have found that children who watch a good deal of aggression on television—murders, crime shows, shootings, and the like—tend to be more aggressive than those who watch only a little. In other words, as we'll discuss in greater detail in Chapter 8, both the viewing of aggression and the actual aggression are strongly associated, or correlated, with one another.

But does this mean that we can conclude that the viewing of televised aggression *causes* the more aggressive behavior of the viewers? Not at all. Consider some of the other possibilities: It might be that being aggressive in the first place makes children more likely to choose to watch violent programs. In such a case, then, it is the aggressive tendency that causes the viewing behavior, and not the other way around.

Researchers use a wide range of procedures to study human development.

case study   a research method involving extensive in-depth interviews with a particular individual or small group of individuals

survey research   sampling a group of people by assessing their behavior, thoughts, or attitudes, and then generalizing to a larger population

Or consider another possibility. Suppose that children who are raised in poverty are more likely to behave aggressively *and* to watch higher levels of aggressive television than those raised in more affluent settings. In this case, it is socioeconomic status that causes *both* the aggressive behavior and the television viewing. (The various possibilities are illustrated in Figure 1-1.)

In short, finding that two variables are correlated with one another proves nothing about causality. Although it is possible that the variables are linked causally, this is not necessarily the case.

On the other hand, correlational studies can provide us with important information. For instance, as we'll see in later chapters, we know from correlational studies that the closer the genetic link between two people, the more highly associated is their intelligence. We have learned that the more parents speak to their young children, the more extensive are the children's vocabularies. And we know that the better the nutrition that infants receive, the fewer the cognitive and social problems they experience later (Pollitt et al., 1993; Plomin, 1994b; Hart & Risley, 1995).

There are actually several types of correlational studies. For example, a **case study** involves extensive, in-depth interviews with a particular individual or small group of individuals. They often are used not just to learn about the individual being interviewed, but to derive broader principles or draw tentative conclusions that might apply to others.

Surveys represent another sort of correlational research. In **survey research**, people chosen to represent some larger population are asked questions about their attitudes, behavior, or thinking on a given topic. For instance, surveys have been conducted about parents' use of punishment on their children and on attitudes toward breast-feeding. From the responses, inferences are drawn regarding the larger population represented by the individuals being surveyed.

Choosing a Research Setting.   Deciding *where* to conduct an experiment may be as important as determining *what* to do. In the Belgian experiment described earlier on the

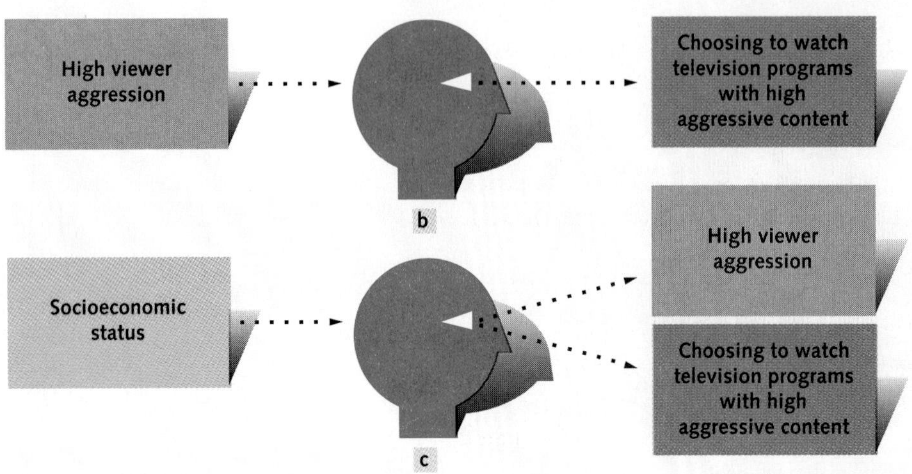

FIGURE 1-1

Finding a correlation between two factors does not imply that one factor *causes* the other factor to vary. For instance, suppose a study found that viewing television shows with high levels of aggression is correlated with actual aggression in children. The correlation may reflect at least three possibilities: (a) watching television programs containing high levels of aggression causes aggression in viewers; (b) children who behave aggressively choose to watch TV programs with high levels of aggression; or (c) some third factor, such as a child's socioeconomic status, leads both to high viewer aggression and to choosing to watch television programs with high viewer aggression.

influence of exposure to media aggression, the researchers used a real-world setting—a group home for boys who had been convicted of juvenile delinquency. They chose the location because it contained adolescents whose normal level of aggression was relatively high, and because they could incorporate showing the films into the everyday life of the home with minimal disruption.

In contrast, because it is typically more difficult to run an experiment in such real-world settings, most experiments in developmental psychology are conducted in laboratory settings. A **laboratory study** is a research investigation conducted in a controlled setting explicitly designed to hold events constant. The laboratory may be a room or building designed for research, as in a university's psychology department.

On the other hand, using a real-world setting like the one in the aggression experiment is the hallmark of a **field study**, a research investigation done in a naturally occurring setting. Field studies may be carried out in preschool classrooms, at community playgrounds, on school buses, or on street corners. (An example of the kind of information about children and families that can be obtained from field studies is provided in the Speaking of Development box on the next page.)

CONDUCTING DEVELOPMENTAL RESEARCH: CHOOSING A PROPER STRATEGY TO MEASURE CHANGE

For developmental experts, an interest in how people grow and change over the life span is central to their discipline. Consequently, one of the thorniest research issues they face concerns the measurement of change over age and time.

Longitudinal studies: Measuring individual change.   If you were interested in learning how a child's moral development changes between the ages of three and five, the most direct approach would be to take a group of three-year-olds and follow them until they were five, testing them periodically.

Such a strategy illustrates longitudinal research. In **longitudinal research**, the behavior of one or more individuals is measured as the subjects age. Longitudinal research measures change over time. By following many individuals over time, researchers can understand the general course of change across some period of life.

The granddaddy of longitudinal studies, which has become a classic, is a study of gifted children begun by Lewis Terman more than 75 years ago. In the study—which is still going on—a group of 1,500 children with high IQs were tested approximately every five years. Now in their 80s, the surviving participants—who call themselves "Termites"—have provided information on everything from intellectual accomplishment to personality and longevity, as we'll discuss in Chapter 18 (Terman & Oden, 1959; H.S. Friedman et al., 1995b).

Longitudinal studies can provide a wealth of information about change over time (Bullock, 1995). However, they have several drawbacks. For one thing, they require a tremendous investment of time, because developmentalists must wait for subjects to become older. Furthermore, there is a significant possibility of participant *attrition*, or loss, over the course of the research. Participants may drop out of a study, they may move away, or they may become ill or even die as the research proceeds.

Finally, participants who are observed or tested may become "test-wise" and perform better each time they are assessed as they become more familiar with the procedure. Consequently, despite the benefits of longitudinal research, particularly its ability to look at change within individuals, developmentalists often turn to other methods in conducting research. The alternative they choose most often: the cross-sectional study.

Cross-sectional Studies.   Let us return to the issue of moral development in children three to five years of age. Instead of using a longitudinal approach, and following the same children over several years, we might conduct the study by simultaneously looking at a group of 3-, 4-, and 5-year-olds.

laboratory study   a research investigation conducted in a controlled setting explicitly designed to hold events constant

field study   a research investigation carried out in a naturally occurring setting

longitudinal research   research in which the behavior of one or more individuals is measured as the subjects age

cross-sectional research   *research in which people of different ages are compared at the same point in time*

Such an approach typifies cross-sectional research. In **cross-sectional research**, people of different ages are compared at the same point in time. Cross-sectional studies provide information about differences in development between different age groups.

Cross-sectional research is considerably more economical in terms of time than is longitudinal research: Subjects are tested at just one point in time. For instance, Lewis Terman's study conceivably might have been completed 75 years ago if Terman had simply looked at a group of gifted 15-year-olds, 20-year-olds, 25-year-olds, and so forth, all the way through a group of 80-year-olds. Because the subjects would not be periodically tested, there would be no chance that they would become test-wise, and problems of subject attrition would not occur. Why, then, would anyone choose to use a procedure other than cross-sectional research?

The answer is that cross-sectional research brings its own set of difficulties. We can start with cohort effects. Recall that every person belongs to a particular *cohort*, the group of people born at about the same time in the same place. If we find that people of different ages vary along some dimension, it may be due to differences in cohort membership, not age per se.

Consider a concrete example: If we find in a correlational study that people who are 25 years old perform better on a test of intelligence than those who are 75 years old, there are

Speaking of Development

Donald J. Hernandez

Born: ·································· 1948

Education: ························· University of Illinois at Urbana, B.A. in sociology; University of California at Berkeley, M.A. and Ph.D. in sociology

Position: ·························· Chief of the Marriage and Family Statistics branch of the U.S. Bureau of the Census

Home: ····························· Silver Spring, Maryland

According to Donald J. Hernandez, when it comes to family life, there wasn't just one American Revolution; there have been five—and counting.

Hernandez, who conducts research on the evolution of the family, has uncovered statistics that put into clear perspective where the American family came from, and where it is today. Hernandez is the chief of the Marriage and Family Statistics branch of the U.S. Bureau of the Census, and he has published his research findings in a book entitled *America's Children: Resources from Family, Government and the Economy.*

Hernandez's findings indicate that over the past 150 years, the family in America has been completely transformed by a series of revolutions. "Three of these revolutions started in the 1800s," he explains. "The first was caused by the rise in nonfarm work by the father of the family. In the mid-1800s most families were farm families. Fathers, mothers, and children worked together on the farm, day in, day out, to support themselves. But by the mid-1900s most fathers worked outside the home much of the day, earning income to support the family, while the mother's role became that of homemaker.

"During the same period," Hernandez continues, "a second revolution occurred—this one in family size. While most families in the mid-1800s had eight or more children, the figure dropped to two or three children in the 1930s. There was enormous pressure at the time to move off farms and to have fewer children."

several explanations (which will be discussed in Chapter 17). Although the finding may be due to decreased intelligence in older people, it may also be attributable to cohort differences. The group of 75-year-olds may have had less education when they were younger than the 25-year-olds, because members of the older cohort were less likely to finish high school and attend college than members of the younger cohort. Or perhaps the older group performed less well because as infants they received less adequate nutrition than did members of the younger group. In short, we cannot fully rule out the possibility that differences we find between people of different age groups are due to cohort differences.

Cross-sectional studies have an additional disadvantage: They are unable to inform us about changes in individuals or groups. Although we can establish differences related to age, we cannot fully determine if such differences are related to change over time.

Cross-sequential Studies.   Because both longitudinal and cross-sectional studies have their drawbacks, researchers have turned to some compromise techniques. Among the most frequently employed are cross-sequential studies, which are essentially a combination of longitudinal and cross-sectional studies.

In **cross-sequential studies**, researchers examine a number of different age groups over several points in time. For instance, an investigator might annually examine the moral

cross-sequential studies   *the process by which researchers examine a number of different age groups over several points in time*

"In 1940, one in 10 children had a working mother. Today about 60 percent of children have mothers who work for pay"

"Not once in the last 50 years have the majority of children lived in Ozzie and Harriet families"

The third major change, according to Hernandez, was a marked increase in schooling for America's youngsters. "About half of children aged 5 to 19 were enrolled in school in 1870, but by the 1930s 95 percent of children 7 to 13, and 79 percent of children 14 to 17, were enrolled."

The next two revolutions uncovered by Hernandez involve women's entry into the workforce and the rise, since 1960, of the one-parent, mother-only family.

"In 1940, one in 10 children had a working mother. Today about 60 percent of children have mothers who work for pay," he explains. "Similarly, from 1940 to 1960 only six to eight percent of children lived in a mother-only family. As of 1993 the figure was close to 23 percent."

Various factors have contributed to the changes in the American family, says Hernandez, including the shift of the country's focus from agriculture to industry, new government policies, and the economy.

"There has been an increase of children born into poverty since the late 1970s. This is widely attributed to the rise in one-parent families, but the fact is that the economy and unemployment continue to be major contributors," he explains. "Parents face many obstacles. They don't have much money and they have to deal constantly with economic insecurity. This can lead to divorce. Economic factors have been very important influences on family changes, and on the poverty that results."

One statistic that amazed Hernandez clearly demonstrates that the so-called Ozzie and Harriet family is a myth. Hernandez defines such a family as one in which the father works full-time, the mother is not in the paid labor force, and all the children are born after the parents' only marriage.

"Not once in the last 50 years have the majority of children lived in Ozzie and Harriet families," he says. "In 1940, 41 percent of children under one year of age lived in such families. The figure jumped a bit—to 43 percent—in 1960. Estimates today indicate that less than one-fourth of children under one year of age live in families that meet the definition.

"To me this was a surprise," Hernandez admits. "When I calculated the statistics, I believed I would find a large majority of Ozzie and Harriet kids, at least in the recent past. I believed in the myth, too. But even when Ozzie and Harriet were on television in the 1950s, that's what it was—a myth."

behavior of a group of three-, four-, and five-year-olds over a period of three years. During that time, the three-year-olds would be tested at ages three, four, and five; the four-year-olds at ages four, five, and six; and the five-year-olds at ages five, six, and seven. Such an approach combines the advantages of longitudinal and cross-sectional research, and it permits developmental psychologists to tease out the consequences of age *change* versus age *differences*.

ETHICS AND RESEARCH: THE MORALITY OF RESEARCH

Return for a moment to the "study" conducted by Egyptian King Psamtik, in which two children were removed from their mother and held in isolation in an effort to learn about the roots of language. Clearly, such an experiment raises blatant ethical concerns, and nothing like it would ever be done today.

But sometimes ethical issues are more subtle. For instance, in seeking to understand the roots of aggressive behavior, U.S. government researchers proposed holding a conference in the mid-1990s to examine possible genetic roots of aggression. Based on work conducted by biopsychologists and geneticists, some researchers had begun to raise the possibility that genetic markers might be found that would allow the identification of children as being particularly violence prone. In such cases, it might be possible to track these violence-prone youngsters and provide interventions that might reduce the likelihood of later violence.

Critics objected strenuously, however. They argued that such identification might lead to a self-fulfilling prophecy. In such a case, children labeled as violence prone might be treated in a way that would actually *cause* them to be more aggressive than if they had not been so labeled. Ultimately, under intense political pressure, the conference was canceled (Horgan, 1993).

To help researchers deal with such ethical problems, the major organizations of developmentalists, including the Society for Research in Child Development and the American Psychological Association, have developed comprehensive ethical guidelines for researchers. Among the basic principles that must be adhered to are those involving freedom from harm, obtaining informed consent, avoiding the use of deception, and maintenance of subjects' privacy (American Psychological Association, 1992; Rosnow et al., 1993; Fisher & Fyrberg, 1994; Gurman, 1994).

Freedom from Harm.   Participants must be protected from physical and psychological harm. Their welfare, interests, and rights come before those of researchers. In research, subjects' rights always come first.

Informed Consent.   Consent must be obtained from subjects before their participation in a study. If they are above the age of seven, participants must voluntarily agree to be in a study. For those under 18, their parents or guardians must also provide consent.

The requirement for informed consent raises some difficult issues. Suppose, for instance, researchers wish to learn the psychological consequences of abortion on adolescents. Although they may be able to obtain the consent of an adolescent who has had an abortion to participate, the researchers may also need to get her parents' permission, because she is a minor. But suppose the parents have not been told by their daughter that she had had an abortion. In such a case, the mere request for permission from the parents would violate the privacy of the adolescent—leading to an ethical violation.

Use of Deception.   Although deception to disguise the true purpose of the experiment is permissible, any experiment that uses deception must undergo careful scrutiny by an independent panel before it is conducted. Suppose, for example, we want to know the reaction of subjects to success and failure. It is ethical to tell subjects that they will be playing a game when the true purpose is actually to observe how they respond to doing well or poorly on the task. However, such a procedure is only ethical if it causes no harm to participants, has been approved by a review panel, and ultimately includes a full debriefing for participants when the study is over.

Maintenance of Privacy. Subjects' privacy must be maintained. If they are videotaped during the course of a study, for example, they must give their permission for the videotapes to be viewed. Furthermore, access to the tapes must be carefully restricted.

The Informed Consumer of Development

Assessing Information on Development

If you immediately comfort crying babies, you'll spoil them.

If you let babies cry without comforting them, they'll be untrusting and clingy as adults.

***

Spanking is the best way to discipline your child.

Never hit your child.

***

If a marriage is unhappy, children are better off if their parents divorce than if they stay together.

No matter how difficult a marriage is, parents should avoid divorce for the sake of their children.

There is no lack of advice on the best way to raise a child or, more generally, to lead one's life. From best-sellers with unfathomable titles such as *Men Are from Mars, Women from Venus*, to magazine and newspaper columns that provide advice on every imaginable topic, each of us is exposed to tremendous amounts of information.

Yet not all advice is equally valid. The mere fact that something is in print or on TV does not automatically make it legitimate or accurate. Fortunately, there are ways of distinguishing when recommendations and suggestions are reasonable, and when they are not. Among the ways of determining if the advice should be accepted are the following.

♦ Consider the source of the advice. Recommendations from nationally respected organizations such as the American Medical Association, the American Psychological Association, and the American Academy of Pediatrics are likely to be the result of years of study, and their accuracy is probably high.

♦ Determine the credentials of the person providing advice. Information coming from established, acknowledged researchers and experts in a field is likely to be more accurate than that coming from someone whose credentials are obscure.

♦ Understand the difference between anecdotal evidence and scientific evidence. Anecdotal evidence is based on one or two instances of a phenomenon, haphazardly discovered or encountered. In contrast, scientific evidence is based on careful, systematic procedures. The evidence has been collected in a methodical, orderly manner.

♦ Keep cultural context in mind. Although a pronouncement may be valid in some contexts, it may not be true in all. For example, it is typically assumed that providing infants the freedom to move about and exercise their limbs facilitates their muscular development and mobility. Yet in some cultures, infants' movements are very restricted, and in a few they spend most of their time closely bound to their mothers (Super, 1976; Kaplan & Dove, 1987; Tronick, 1995). Although such infants may show delays in physical development, by late childhood they are indistinguishable from children raised in a less restrictive manner.

♦ Do not assume that because many people believe something, it is necessarily true. Scientific evaluation has often proven that some of the most basic presumptions about the effectiveness of various techniques are invalid. For instance, consider DARE, the Drug Abuse Resistance Education antidrug program that is used in about half the school systems in the United States. DARE is designed to prevent the spread of drugs through lectures and question-and-answer sessions run by specially trained police officers. One problem: Careful evaluation has found no evidence that the program works. Teachers, administrators, police officers, and taxpayers who support the program may like it—but it doesn't seem to reduce the use of drugs (Ennett, Tobler, Ringwalt, & Flewelling, 1994).

In short, the key to evaluating information relating to human development is to maintain a healthy dose of skepticism. No source of information is invariably, unfailingly accurate. By keeping a critical eye on the statements you encounter, you will be in a better position to determine the very real contributions made by developmentalists to understanding

Review and Rethink

REVIEW

♦ Theories in life-span development are systematically derived explanations of facts or phenomena. Theories suggest hypotheses, which are predictions that can be tested.

♦ Experimental research seeks to discover cause-and-effect relationships by the use of a treatment group and a control group. Correlational studies examine relationships between factors without demonstrating causality.

♦ Research studies may be conducted in laboratories, where conditions can be controlled effectively, or in field settings, where participants are subject to natural conditions.

♦ Researchers measure age-related change by longitudinal studies (same subjects at different ages), cross-sectional studies (different-age subjects at one time), and cross-sequential studies (different-age subjects at several times).

♦ Developmental researchers follow ethical guidelines relating to such issues as the prevention of harm to subjects, obtaining informed consent, avoiding the use of deception, and assuring privacy.

RETHINK

♦ Can you formulate a theory about one aspect of human development and a hypothesis that relates to it?

♦ What sort of research strategy would be appropriate for investigating each of the statements (about comforting babies, spanking, and divorce) at the beginning of the Informed Consumer box?

♦ Would a laboratory or a field setting be most appropriate for each research strategy you identified?

♦ Can you think of a correlation between two phenomena related to gender? What are some possible explanations for the correlation? How would you establish causality?

♦   What problems might affect a study of age-related changes in sexual attitudes and practices conducted at one time among a cross section of adults aged 18 to 50?

LOOKING BACK

What is life-span development, and what areas of human life does it study?

1. Life-span development is a scientific approach to questions about growth, change, and stability in human life. The scope of the field includes physical, cognitive, and social and personality development at all ages from conception to death.

2. The human life span is generally divided for convenience into broad periods, including the prenatal period, infancy and toddlerhood, the preschool period, middle childhood, adolescence, young adulthood, middle adulthood, and late adulthood. Individual and cultural differences affect the definition and application of these periods.

What are some primary influences on human development?

3. Because each area of development (physical, cognitive, social/personality) affects the others, some developmentalists take an ecological approach to development, which suggests that four levels of the environment simultaneously affect the individual: the microsystem, the mesosystem, the exosystem, and the macrosystem. The ecological approach stresses the interrelatedness of developmental areas and the importance of broad cultural factors in human development.

4. Each individual belongs to a cohort, a group of people born at around the same time and place and subject to similar influences. Membership in a cohort makes a person susceptible to normative history-graded influences, which contrast with normative age-graded influences (which occur at given ages to every cohort), nonnormative life events (which are individual), and normative sociocultural-graded influences.

What are the key issues in the field of life-span development?

5. Four key issues have been debated in the field of life-span development from its inception. One is whether developmental change in humans is continuous or discontinuous. Another is whether human development is largely governed by critical periods during which certain influences or experiences must occur for development to be normal. The third key issue is whether life-span development should focus on certain particularly important periods in human development (such as infancy or adolescence) or on the entire life span.

6. The fourth and most enduring and heated major issue in life-span development has probably been the nature-versus-nurture controversy: How much of human development is inherited (i.e., due to nature) and how much is learned through interactions with the environment (i.e., due to nurture)? This issue continues to be debated today.

7. Each of the four key issues is probably best regarded not as an either-or proposition, but as the ends of a continuum along which the various aspects of development are to be arrayed.

Which theoretical perspectives have guided thinking and research in life-span development?

8. Three major theoretical perspectives have dominated life-span development: the psychodynamic perspective (which focuses on inner, largely unconscious forces), the

behavioral perspective (which focuses on external, observable actions), and the cognitive perspective (which focuses on intellectual, mental processes).

9. The psychodynamic perspective is exemplified by the psychoanalytic theory of Sigmund Freud and the psychosocial theory of Erik Erikson. Freud focused attention on the unconscious, distinguishing three main elements: the impulsive id, the rational ego, and the moral superego. He also identified stages, associated with body parts and biological functions, through which children must pass successfully to avoid harmful fixations. Erikson extended the psychodynamic time focus to include the entire life span, identifying eight distinct stages of development, each characterized by a conflict, or crisis, to work out.

10. The behavioral perspective typically concerns stimulus-response learning, and is exemplified by classical conditioning (associating a neutral stimulus and a learned response), the operant conditioning of B.F. Skinner (in which voluntary responses are strengthened or weakened by reinforcement), and Bandura's social learning theory (in which people learn by observing the behavior of models).

11. Under the rubric of the cognitive perspective the most notable theorist is Jean Piaget, who identified developmental stages, involving qualitative changes in thinking, through which children pass. The two basic Piagetian principles are assimilation (fitting experiences into the current level of understanding) and accommodation (adjusting one's thinking to encompass new experiences). In contrast to the qualitative changes identified by Piaget, proponents of information-processing approaches explain cognitive growth as quantitative changes in mental processes and capacities.

12. Each theory and each perspective has value, and each is incomplete. The study of life-span development has benefited by the presence of alternative explanations, and it is best to regard the varying perspectives as partial views of the truth, which together can inform and enlighten one another and the field as a whole.

13. Culture is another important issue in developmental psychology. Many aspects of development are influenced not only by broad cultural differences but also by ethnic, racial, and socioeconomic differences within a particular culture.

What role do theories and hypotheses play in the study of life-span development?

14. Theories in a science such as life-span development are broad explanations of facts or phenomena of interest, based on a systematic integration of prior findings and theories. Hypotheses are theory-based predictions that can be tested.

15. Hypotheses are tested by two primary research strategies. Experimental research, involving the controlled manipulation of a situation, is designed to discover cause-and-effect relationships. Correlational research is designed to determine if two factors are associated with one another.

How are research studies in life-span development conducted?

16. Experiments in life-span development typically are conducted on subjects, or participants, who are divided into two groups, one of which—the treatment group—receives the experimental treatment and the other of which—the control group—does not. Following the treatment, differences between the treatment group and the control group can help the experimenter determine the effects of the treatment.

17. Correlational studies typically focus on groups of subjects with different characteristics, which are of interest because they are related to a researcher's hypothesis. If certain characteristics are found to be associated with other characteristics, a correlation is said to exist. Although correlational studies can provide a great deal of information, they lead to no direct conclusions about cause and effect.

18. Research may be conducted in a laboratory or in a real-world setting. Experiments are typically conducted in laboratory settings because of the difficulty of controlling variables in real-world settings. In field studies, data are gathered from participants in naturally occurring settings.

19. To measure change over time, researchers use three major strategies: longitudinal studies of the same participants over time, cross-sectional studies of different-age participants conducted at one time, and cross-sequential studies of different-age participants at several points in time. Longitudinal and cross-sectional studies have disadvantages that cross-sequential studies are designed to remedy.

20. Researchers must adhere to ethical guidelines pertaining, among other things, to protecting participants from harm, obtaining informed consent of participants, placing limits on the use of deception, and maintaining privacy.

KEY TERMS AND CONCEPTS

life-span development (p. 6)
physical development (p. 7)
cognitive development (p. 7)
personality development (p. 7)
social development (p. 7)
ecological approach (p. 9)
cohort (p. 11)
normative history-graded influences (p. 11)
normative age-graded influences (p. 11)
normative sociocultural-graded influences (p. 11)
nonnormative life events (p. 11)
continuous change (p. 11)
discontinuous change (p. 11)
maturation (p. 13)
theories (p. 17)
psychodynamic perspective (p. 17)
psychoanalytic theory (p. 17)
id (p. 18)
ego (p. 18)
superego (p. 18)
psychosexual development (p. 18)
fixation (p. 18)
psychosocial development (p. 18)

behavioral perspective (p. 20)
classical conditioning (p. 20)
operant conditioning (p. 21)
behavior modification (p. 21)
social learning (p. 21)
cognitive perspective (p. 22)
assimilation (p. 23)
accommodation (p. 23)
scientific method (p. 27)
hypothesis (p. 27)
experimental research (p. 28)
correlational research (p. 28)
experiment (p. 28)
treatment (p. 28)
treatment group (p. 28)
control group (p. 28)
case study (p. 30)
survey research (p. 30)
laboratory study (p. 31)
field study (p. 31)
longitudinal research (p. 31)
cross-sectional research (p. 32)
cross-sequential studies (p. 33)

CHAPTER 2

The Start of Life: Prenatal Development

CHAPTER OUTLINE

PROLOGUE: DOUBLING UP

Capt. Jim Tedesco, a volunteer firefighter from Paramus, N.J., looked across a crowded room at a firefighters' convention and was startled by what he saw. There was Mark Newman, another Paramus firefighter, and that was impossible. Newman, he knew, was back home in Paramus. But how many bald, 6-foot-6, 250-pound-plus New Jersey volunteer firemen are there who wear droopy mustaches, aviator-style eyeglasses, and a key ring on the right side of the belt?

At least two, it turned out. Striking up a conversation, Tedesco found that although the man he was speaking to looked, walked, talked, joked, and gestured just like Newman, his name was Gerald Levey. Then Tedesco learned that Levey had the same birth date as Newman—and that, like Newman, he, too, had been adopted in New York City.

Intrigued, Tedesco hatched a plan. After returning from the convention, he drove his friend Newman to Levey's firehouse in Tinton Falls, N.J., on the pretext of inspecting a new foam unit. When Newman walked in, Levey stared at him and muttered, "I've got to get a beer. That's my brother."

Newman, intent on the equipment he had come to see, walked right by Levey. "This is nothing but a pumper. So what's the big deal?" Newman complained. Tedesco grinned. "Mark, come over here and look at this firefighter," he said. "Doesn't he look familiar?" At last Newman looked at Levey. "You're right. He's big like me. He has a nose like me. He wears glasses like me. He's bald like me . . . I've got to get a beer." (Lang, 1987, p. 63)

LOOKING AHEAD

For 31 years, twins Levey and Newman led separate, yet surprisingly parallel, lives. Although they were separated five days after birth and adopted by different families, their similarities go well beyond coincidence. Both are bachelors attracted to tall, slender women with long hair. Both love to fish and hunt. Both enjoy John Wayne movies and Chinese food. Both worked for a time in supermarkets. One got a degree in forestry; the other worked trimming trees. One installed fire alarms; the other installed sprinkler systems. Not only do they drink the same brand of beer but they hold the can the same way, pinkie curled underneath.

Mark Newman and Gerald Levey, and other twins like them, are more than mere curiosities. They also hold part of the key to one of the fundamental puzzles of human development: How do heredity and environment interact to make us the people we are?

In this chapter, we'll examine what life-span developmentalists and other scientists have learned about ways that heredity and the environment work in tandem to shape human behavior. We begin with the basics of heredity, examining how we receive our genetic endowment. We'll consider a burgeoning area of study, behavioral genetics, that specializes in the consequences of heredity on behavior. We'll also discuss what happens when genetic factors cause development to go awry, and how such problems are dealt with through genetic counseling.

Next, we'll discuss the interaction of heredity and environment. We'll consider the relative influence of genes and environment on a variety of characteristics, including physical traits, intelligence, and even personality.

Finally, we'll focus on the very first stage of development, tracing prenatal growth and change. We'll talk about the stages of the prenatal period, and how the prenatal environment offers both threats to—and the promise of—future growth.

41

gametes   *the sex cells from the mother and father that form a new cell at conception*

fertilization   *the process by which a sperm and an ovum—the male and female gametes, respectively—join to form a single new cell*

zygote   *the new cell formed by the process of fertilization*

In sum, after reading this chapter, you will be able to answer these questions:

- What is our basic genetic endowment, and how do we receive it from our parents?
- How can human development go wrong, and what can be done to prevent or remedy genetic problems?
- How do the environment and genetics work together to determine human characteristics?
- Which human characteristics are significantly influenced by heredity?
- What happens during the prenatal stages of development?
- What threats are there to the fetal environment and what can be done about them?

HEREDITY

We humans begin the course of our lives simply.

Like individuals from tens of thousands of other species, we start as a single cell, a tiny speck probably weighing no more than one twenty-millionth of an ounce. But from this humble beginning, human development follows its own unique path, accomplishing a journey that leads to the flowering of humankind's vast potential.

What determines the process that transforms the single cell into something that we can more easily identify as a person? The answer is the human genetic code, transmitted at the moment of conception in the **gametes**, or sex cells, from the mother and father, and embedded in that single, first cell.

FERTILIZATION: THE MOMENT OF CONCEPTION

When most of us think about the facts of life, we tend to focus on the events that involve the moment when a male's *sperm* cells begin their journey toward a female's *ovum* (egg cell). Yet the act of sex that brings about the potential for conception is both the consequence and the start of a long string of events that precede and follow fertilization. **Fertilization**, or conception, is the process by which a sperm and an ovum—the male and female gametes, respectively—join to form a single new cell, called a **zygote**.

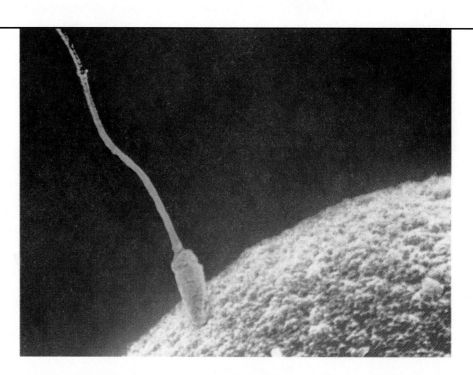

The moment of conception, when a sperm penetrates the egg at the point of fertilization.

Both the male's sperm and the female's ovum come with a history of their own. Females are born with about 400,000 ova located in the two ovaries (see Figure 2-1 for the basic anatomy of the male and female sex organs). However, the ova do not mature until the female reaches puberty. From that point until she reaches menopause, the female will ovulate about every 28 days. During ovulation, an egg is released from one of the ovaries and pushed by minute hair cells through the fallopian tube toward the uterus. If the ovum meets a sperm in the fallopian tube, fertilization takes place (Aitken, 1995).

Sperm, which look a little like microscopic tadpoles, have a shorter life span. They are created by the testicles at a rapid rate: An adult male typically produces several hundred million sperm a day. Consequently, the sperm ejaculated during sexual intercourse are of considerably more recent origin than the ovum to which they are heading.

When sperm enter the vagina, they begin a winding journey that takes them through the cervix, the opening into the uterus, and into the fallopian tube, where fertilization may take place. However, only a tiny fraction of the 300 million cells that are typically ejaculated during sexual intercourse ultimately survive the arduous journey. That's OK, though: It takes only one sperm to fertilize an ovum, and each sperm and ovum contain all the genetic data necessary to produce a new human.

genes   the basic unit of genetic information

chromosomes   rod-shaped portions of DNA that are organized in 23 pairs

GENES AND CHROMOSOMES: THE CODE OF LIFE

Genes are the basic unit of genetic information. Composed of sequences of *DNA (deoxyribonucleic acid)* molecules, genes determine the nature of every cell in the body and how it will function. Genes are the biological equivalent of "software" that programs the future development of all parts of the body's "hardware."

Humans have some 100,000 genes. The genes are arranged in specific locations and in a specific order along 46 **chromosomes**, rod-shaped portions of DNA that are organized in 23 pairs. Of the two chromosomes in each of the 23 pairs, one is provided by the mother and the other by the father at the time of fertilization. Through a cell replication process called *mitosis*, all the eventual cells of the body contain the same 46 chromosomes provided by the maternal and paternal gametes (sex cells). It is the uniting of the 23 maternal and 23 paternal chromosomes that provides the genetic blueprint that guides cell activity for the rest of the individual's life.

FIGURE 2-1

The basic anatomy of the sexual organs is illustrated in these cutaway side views.

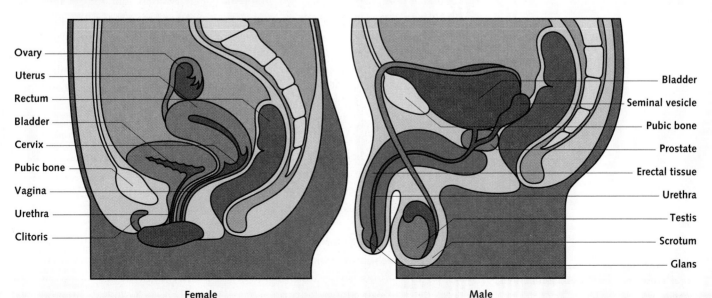

Female   Male

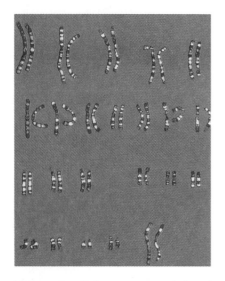

The 23 pairs of chromosomes, rod-shaped portions of DNA on which genes reside.

Specific genes in precise locations on the chain of chromosomes determine the nature and functioning of every cell in the body. For instance, genes determine which cells will ultimately become part of the heart and which will become part of the muscles of the leg. Genes also establish how different parts of the body will function: how rapidly the heart will beat, or how much strength a muscle will have.

If each parent provides just 23 chromosomes, where does the potential for the vast diversity of human beings come from? The answer resides primarily in the nature of the processes that underlie the cell division of the gametes. When gametes—sperm and ova—are formed in the adult human body in a process called *meiosis*, each gamete receives one of the (male or female) body's two pairs of 23 chromosomes. Because for each of the 23 pairs it is largely a matter of chance which member of the pair is contributed, there are 2^{23}, or some eight million, different combinations possible. Furthermore, other processes add to the variability of the genetic brew. The ultimate outcome: tens of *trillions* of possible genetic combinations.

With so many possible genetic mixtures provided by heredity, there is no likelihood that someday you'll bump into a genetic duplicate of yourself. There is one exception: an identical twin.

Multiple Births: Two—or More—for the Genetic Price of One.   Although it does not seem surprising when dogs and cats give birth to several offspring at one time, in humans multiple births are cause for comment. They should be: Less than two percent of all pregnancies produces twins. But why do multiple births occur at all?

Some multiple births occur when a cluster of cells in the ovum splits off within the first two weeks following fertilization. The result is two genetically identical zygotes, which, because they come from the same original zygote, are called monozygotic. **Monozygotic twins** are twins who are genetically identical. Any differences in their future development can be attributed only to environmental factors, for genetically they are exactly the same.

There is a second, and actually more common, mechanism that produces multiple births. In these cases, two separate ova are fertilized by two separate sperm at roughly the same time. Twins produced in this fashion are known as **dizygotic twins**. Because they are the result of two separate ovum-sperm combinations, they are no more genetically similar than two siblings born at different times.

Of course, not all multiple births produce only two babies. Triplets, quadruplets, and even more births are produced by either (or both) of the mechanisms that yield twins. Thus, triplets may be some combination of monozygotic, dizygotic, or trizygotic.

Although the chances of having a multiple birth are typically slim, the odds rise considerably with the use of fertility drugs meant to improve the chances that a couple will conceive a child. For example, one couple in ten using fertility drugs has dizygotic twins, compared to an overall figure of 1 in 86 for Caucasian couples in the United States. Older women, too, are more likely to have multiple births. Both the increased use of fertility drugs and the rising average age of mothers giving birth have contributed to the increase in multiple births over the last 25 years (see Figure 2-2).

Racial and ethnic differences also affect the rate of multiple births, probably due to inherited differences in the likelihood that more than one ovum will be released at a time (Vaughan, McKay, & Behrman, 1979). Of every 70 African-American couples, one has a dizygotic birth, compared with one out of 86 for Caucasian American couples. On the other hand, in some groups multiple births are unusually rare. For instance, in China just one in every 300 births produces dizygotic twins.

Boy or Girl? Establishing the Sex of the Child.   Recall that there are 23 matched pairs of chromosomes. Each chromosome is similar to the other member of its pair, with one exception—the 23rd chromosome, which is the one that determines the sex of the child. In females, the 23rd pair consists of two matching, relatively large X-shaped chromosomes,

monozygotic twins   *twins who are genetically identical*

dizygotic twins   *twins who are produced when two separate ova are fertilized by two separate sperm at roughly the same time*

Twins attending the annual twin convention in Twinsburg, Ohio, are monozygotic (identical) and dizygotic (non-identical).

appropriately identified as XX. In males, on the other hand, the members of the pair are dissimilar. One consists of an X-shaped chromosome, but the other is a smaller Y-shaped chromosome. This pair is identified as XY.

Because the production of gametes involves the receipt of just half of the chromosomal pairs in each parent, the ovum from the female will receive one of the two X chromosomes from the 23rd pair. However, because the male contributes either an X or a Y chromosome, the sperm will contain either an X or a Y from the 23rd pair.

The ultimate result of this process is that when an ovum and a sperm meet at fertilization, the ovum is sure to carry an X chromosome, but the sperm will carry either an X or a Y chromosome. If the sperm contributes an X chromosome, the child will have an XX pairing on the 23rd chromosome—and will be a female. On the other hand, if the sperm contributes a Y chromosome, the result will be an XY pairing—a male (see Figure 2-3).

It is clear from this process that it is the father's sperm that determines the sex of the child. Curiously, our understanding of how sex is determined is consistent with Aristotle's ancient notion that it is the man who determines his child's sex. However, Aristotle's explanation couldn't have been more wrong: He argued that the more sexually excited the man was, the more apt he was to produce a son.

FIGURE 2-2

MULTIPLE BIRTHS

Multiple births have increased significantly over the last 25 years.

(Adapted from *USA Weekend*, Nov. 25–27, 1995, p. 15)

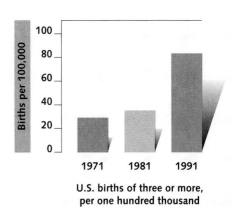

U.S. births of three or more, per one hundred thousand

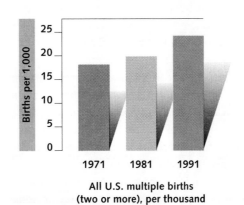

All U.S. multiple births (two or more), per thousand

FIGURE 2-3

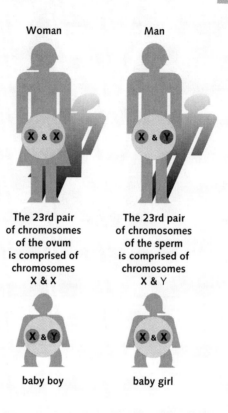

Woman

Man

The 23rd pair
of chromosomes
of the ovum
is comprised of
chromosomes
X & X

The 23rd pair
of chromosomes
of the sperm
is comprised of
chromosomes
X & Y

baby boy

baby girl

THE PAIRING OF
CHROMOSOMES X & Y

When an ovum and sperm meet at the
moment of fertilization, the ovum is certain
to provide an X chromosome, while the
sperm will provide either an X or a Y chromosome. If the sperm contributes its X chromosome, the child will have an XX pairing on
the 23rd chromosome and will be a girl. If the
sperm contributes a Y chromosome, the
result will be an XY pairing—a boy.

THE BASICS OF GENETICS: THE MIXING AND MATCHING OF HEREDITY

What determined the color of your hair? Why are you tall or short? What made you susceptible to hay fever? And why do you have so many freckles? To answer these questions, we
need to consider the basic mechanisms involved in the way that the genes we inherit from
our parents transmit information.

We can start by examining the discoveries of an Austrian monk, Gregor Mendel, in the
mid-1800s. In a series of simple yet convincing experiments, Mendel cross-pollinated pea
plants that always produced yellow seeds with pea plants that always produced green seeds.
The result was not, as one might guess, a plant with a combination of yellow and green
seeds. Instead, all of the resulting plants had yellow seeds. At first it appeared that the green-
seeded plants had had no influence.

However, additional research on Mendel's part proved that this was not true. When the
plants that had been produced by the combination of yellow- and green-seeded parent
plants were bred with one another, the consistent result was a ratio of three-quarters yellow
seeds to one-quarter green seeds.

Why did this 3-to-1 ratio of yellow to green seeds appear so consistently? It was
Mendel's genius to provide an answer. He argued that when two competing traits, such as a
green or yellow coloring of seeds, were both present, only one could be expressed. The one
that was expressed was called a *dominant trait,* whereas the one that was present in the
organism but not expressed was called a *recessive trait.* In the case of the pea plants, when
the two strains of purebred pea plants were bred, the offspring plants received genetic information from both parents. However, the yellow trait was dominant, and consequently the
recessive (green) trait did not assert itself.

Keep in mind, however, that genetic material relating to both parent plants is present in
the offspring, even though it cannot be seen. The genetic information is known as the

Gregor Mendel's pioneering experiments on pea plants provided the foundation for the study of genetics.

organism's **genotype**, the underlying combination of genetic material present (but outwardly invisible) in an organism. In contrast, a **phenotype** is the observable trait, the trait that actually is seen.

Although the offspring of the yellow-seeded and green-seeded pea plants all have yellow seeds (i.e., they have a yellow-seeded phenotype), the genotype consists of genetic information relating to both parents.

And what is the nature of the information in the genotype? To answer that question, let us turn from peas to people. In fact, the principles are the same not just for plants and humans, but for the majority of species.

Recall that parents transmit genetic information to their offspring via the chromosomes they contribute through the gamete they provide during fertilization. In cases of genes that govern *alleles*—genes for traits that may take alternate forms, such as hair or eye color—the offspring may receive similar or dissimilar genes from each parent. If the offspring receives similar genes, the organism is said to be *homozygous* for the trait. On the other hand, if the offspring receives different forms of the gene from its parents, it is said to be *heterozygous*. In the case of heterozygous alleles, the dominant characteristic is expressed. However, if the child happens to receive a recessive allele from each of its parents, and therefore lacks a dominant characteristic, it will display the recessive characteristic.

Transmission of Genetic Information in Humans.   We can see this process at work in humans by considering the transmission of *phenylketonuria (PKU)*, an inherited disorder in which a child is unable to make use of phenylalanine, an essential amino acid present in proteins found in milk and other foods. If left untreated, PKU allows phenylalanine to build up to toxic levels, causing brain damage and mental retardation.

Unlike most other characteristics, PKU is produced by a single pair of genes in the offspring, inherited from a particular pair of genes in the mother and the father. As shown in Figure 2-4, we can think of the pair in terms of *P*, a dominant gene that causes the normal production of phenylalanine, and *p*, a recessive gene that produces PKU. In cases in which neither parent is a PKU carrier, both the mother's and the father's pairs of genes are the dominant form, symbolized as *PP*. Consequently, no matter which member of the pair is contributed by the mother and father, the resulting pair of genes in the child will be *PP*, and the child will not have PKU.

genotype   *the underlying combination of genetic material present (but not outwardly visible) in an organism*

phenotype   *the observable trait, the trait that actually is seen*

However, consider what happens if one of the parents has a recessive *p* gene. In this case, which we can symbolize as *Pp*, the parent will not have PKU, since the normal *P* gene is dominant. But the recessive gene can be passed down to the child. This is not so bad: If the child has only one recessive gene, it will not suffer from PKU. But what if both parents

FIGURE 2-4

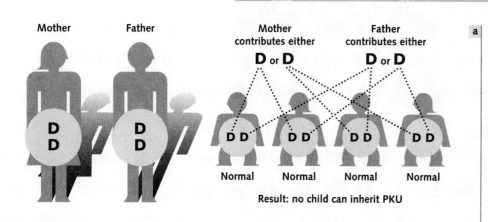

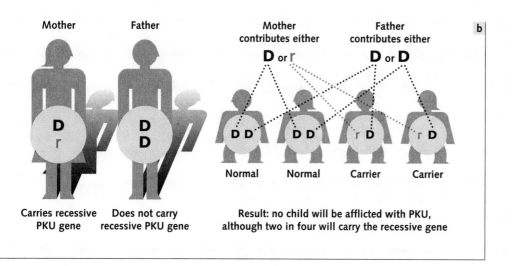

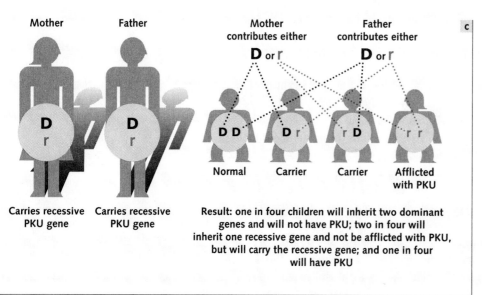

PKU, a disease that causes brain damage and mental retardation, is produced by a single pair of genes inherited from one's mother and father. If neither parent carries a gene for the disease (a), a child cannot develop PKU. Even if one parent carries the recessive gene, but the other doesn't (b), the child cannot inherit the disease. However, if both parents carry the recessive gene (c), there is a one in four chance that the child will have PKU.

carry a recessive *p* gene? In this case, although neither parent has the disorder, it is possible for the child to receive a recessive gene from both parents. The child's genotype for PKU then will be *pp*, and he or she will have the disorder.

Remember, though, that even children whose parents both have the recessive gene for PKU have only a 25 percent chance of inheriting the disorder. Owing to the laws of probability, 25 percent of children with *Pp* parents will receive the dominant gene from each parent (*PP*), and 50 percent will receive the dominant gene from one parent and the recessive gene from the other (*Pp* or *pP*). Only the unlucky 25 percent who receive the recessive gene from each parent and end up with the genotype *pp* will suffer from PKU.

The basic principles that explain the transmission of PKU underlie the transmission of all genetic information from parent to child. However, in some respects, the case of PKU is simpler than most cases of genetic transmission. Relatively few traits are governed by a single pair of genes. Instead, most traits are the result of **polygenic inheritance**, a combination of multiple gene pairs responsible for the production of a particular trait.

Furthermore, some genes come in several alternate forms, and still others act to modify the way that particular genetic traits (produced by other alleles) are displayed. And some traits, such as blood type, are produced by genes in which neither pair of genes can be classified as purely dominant or recessive. Instead, the trait is expressed in terms of a combination of the two genes—such as type AB blood.

A number of recessive genes, called *X-linked*, are located only on the X chromosome. Recall that in females, the 23rd pair of chromosomes is an XX pair, whereas in males it is an XY pair. One result is that males have a higher risk for a variety of X-linked disorders, because males lack a second X chromosome that can counteract the genetic information that produces the disorder. For example, males are significantly more apt to have red-green color blindness, a disorder produced by a set of genes on the X chromosome.

Similarly, hemophilia, a blood disorder, is produced by X-linked genes. Hemophilia has been a recurrent problem in the royal families of Europe, as illustrated in Figure 2-5, which shows the inheritance of hemophilia in many of the descendants of Britain's Queen Victoria.

Behavioral Genetics: Extending Mendel's Discoveries. Mendel's achievements in recognizing the basics of genetic transmission of traits were trailblazing. However, they mark only the beginning of our understanding of the ways that particular sorts of characteristics are

polygenic inheritance *inheritance in which a combination of multiple gene pairs is responsible for the production of a particular trait*

FIGURE 2-5

Hemophilia, a blood-clotting disorder, has been an inherited problem throughout the royal families of Europe, as illustrated by the descendants of Queen Victoria of Britain.

(Adapted from Kimball, 1983.)

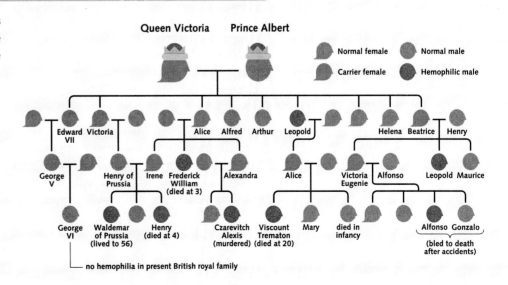

behavioral genetics   *the study of the effects of heredity on behavior*

Down syndrome   *a disorder produced by the presence of an extra chromosome on the 21st chromosome pair, once referred to as mongolism*

sickle-cell anemia   *a blood disorder that gets its name from the shape of the red blood cells in those who have it*

passed on from one generation to the next. The most recent approach to deciphering the effect of heredity is through a rapidly burgeoning field known as behavioral genetics. As the name implies, **behavioral genetics** studies the effects of heredity on behavior. Rather than simply examining stable, unchanging characteristics such as hair or eye color, behavioral genetics takes a broader approach, considering how our personality and behavioral habits are affected by genetic factors. Behavioral genetics represents the melding of interests of psychologists, who focus on the causes of behavior, and geneticists, who focus on the processes that permit the transmission of characteristics through heredity (Kimble, 1993; Rowe, 1993; McClearn, 1993; Bouchard, 1994; Lander & Schork, 1994).

The promise of behavioral genetics is substantial. For one thing, researchers working within the field have gained a better understanding of the specifics of the genetic code that underlies human behavior and development. Such advances have provided knowledge of the workings of genetics at both a molecular and chemical level. Furthermore, scientists are learning how various behavioral difficulties, including psychological disorders such as schizophrenia, may have a genetic basis (Plomin, 1990, 1994c). Even more important, researchers are seeking to identify how genetic defects may be remedied. To understand how that possibility might come about, we need to consider the ways in which genetic factors, which normally cause development to proceed so smoothly, may falter.

INHERITED AND GENETIC DISORDERS: WHEN DEVELOPMENT GOES AWRY

Phenylketonuria is just one of several disorders that may be inherited. Like a bomb that is harmless until its fuse is lit, a recessive gene responsible for a disorder may be passed on unknowingly from one generation to the next, revealing itself only when, by chance, it is paired with another recessive gene. It is only when two recessive genes come together like a match and a fuse that the gene will express itself and a child will inherit the genetic disorder.

But there is another way that genes are a source of concern: In some cases, genes become physically damaged. For instance, genes may break down because of wear-and-tear or chance events occurring during the cell division processes of meiosis and mitosis. Sometimes genes, for no known reason, spontaneously change their form, a process called *spontaneous mutation.* Alternatively, certain environmental factors, such as exposure to X-rays, may produce a malformation of genetic material. When such damaged genes are passed on to a child, the results can be disastrous.

In addition to PKU, which occurs once in every 10,000 to 20,000 births, other inherited and genetic disorders include:

◆ *Down syndrome.* As we noted earlier, people have 46 chromosomes, arranged in 23 pairs. One exception is individuals with **Down syndrome**, a disorder produced by the presence of an extra chromosome on the 21st chromosome pair. Once referred to as mongolism, Down syndrome is the most frequent cause of mental retardation. It occurs in about one out of 500 births, although the risk is much greater in mothers who are unusually young or old (Cicchetti & Beeghly, 1990).

◆ *Sickle-cell anemia.* Approximately 10 percent of the African-American population carries genes that produce sickle-cell anemia, and one African-American in 400 actually has the disease. **Sickle-cell anemia** is a blood disorder that gets its name from the shape of the red blood cells in those who have it. Symptoms include poor appetite, stunted growth, swollen stomach, and yellowish eyes. People afflicted with the most severe form of the disease rarely live beyond childhood. However, for those with less severe cases, medical advances have produced significant increases in life expectancy.

- *Tay-Sachs disease.* Occurring mainly in Jews of Eastern European ancestry, **Tay-Sachs disease** usually causes death before its victims reach school age. There is no treatment for the disorder, which produces blindness and muscle degeneration prior to death.

- *Klinefelter's syndrome.* One male out of every 400 is born with **Klinefelter's syndrome**, the presence of an extra X chromosome. The resulting XXY complement produces underdeveloped genitals, extreme height, and enlarged breasts. Klinefelter's syndrome is one of several genetic abnormalities that result from receiving the improper number of sex chromosomes. For instance, there are disorders produced by an extra Y chromosome (XYY), a missing second chromosome (X0), and three X chromosomes (XXX). Such disorders are typically characterized by problems relating to sexual characteristics and by intellectual deficits (Sorenson, 1992).

Although we have been focusing on inherited factors that can go awry, it is important to note that in the vast majority of cases, the genetic mechanisms with which we are endowed work quite well. Overall, just under 95 percent of children born in the United States are healthy and normal. For the some 250,000 who are born with some sort of physical or mental disorder, appropriate intervention often can help treat—and in some cases cure—the problem.

Moreover, because of advances in behavioral genetics, genetic difficulties increasingly can be forecast, anticipated, and planned for before a child's birth. In fact, as scientists' knowledge regarding the specific location of particular genes expands, predictions of what the genetic future may hold are becoming increasingly exact, as we discuss in the Directions in Development section on the next page (Cook-Deegan, 1994).

ROLE OF THE ENVIRONMENT IN DETERMINING THE EXPRESSION OF GENES: FROM GENOTYPES TO PHENOTYPES

It is important to keep in mind that the expression of particular traits is affected by factors other than genetics alone. The environment also plays a crucial role in determining the degree to which an individual's genotypic potential reaches fruition.

For instance, consider **temperament**, patterns of arousal and emotionality that represent consistent and enduring characteristics in an individual. Suppose we found—as increasing evidence suggests is the case—that a small percentage of children are born with temperaments that produce an unusual degree of physiological reactivity. Having a tendency to shrink from anything unusual, such infants react to novel stimuli with a rapid increase in heartbeat and unusual excitability of the limbic system of the brain (Kagan & Snidman, 1991). Such heightened reactivity to stimuli at the start of life, which seems linked to inherited factors, is also likely to cause children, by the time they are four or five, to be considered shy by their parents and teachers. But not always: Some of them behave indistinguishably from their peers at the same age (Rothbart, Ahadi, & Hershey, 1994).

What makes the difference? The answer seems to be the environment in which the children are raised. Youngsters whose parents encourage them to be outgoing by arranging supportive opportunities for them to engage in new activities may overcome their shyness. In contrast, children raised in a stressful environment marked by marital discord or a prolonged illness may be more likely to retain their shyness later in life (Kagan, Arcus, & Snidman, 1993; Pedlow, Sanson, Prior, & Oberklaid, 1993).

Such findings illustrate that many traits represent **multifactorial transmission**, meaning that they are determined by a combination of both genetic and environmental factors. In multifactorial transmission, a genotype provides a particular range within which a phenotype may achieve expression. For instance, people with a genotype that permits them to gain weight easily may never be slim, no matter how much they diet. They may be *relatively* slim, given their genetic heritage, but they may never be able to get beyond a certain

Tay-Sachs disease   *an untreatable disorder that produces blindness and muscle degeneration prior to death*

Klinefelter's syndrome   *a disorder resulting from the presence of an extra X chromosome that produces underdeveloped genitals, extreme height, and enlarged breasts*

temperament   *patterns of arousal and emotionality that are consisitent and enduring characterisitics of an individual.*

multifactorial transmission   *traits that are determined by a combination of both genetic and environmental factors in which a genotype provides a range within which a phenotype may be expressed*

degree of thinness. In many cases, then, it is the environment that determines the way in which a particular genotype will be expressed as a phenotype (Wachs, 1992, 1993; Plomin, 1994c).

Conversely, certain genotypes are relatively unaffected by environmental factors. In such cases, development follows a preordained pattern, relatively independent of the specific environment in which a person is raised. For instance, research on pregnant women who were severely malnourished during famines caused by World War II found that their children were, on average, unaffected physically or intellectually as adults (Stein, Susser, Saenger, & Marolla, 1975). Similarly, no matter how much people eat health food they are not going to grow beyond certain genetically imposed limitations in height.

Ultimately, of course, it is the unique interaction of inherited and environmental factors that determines people's patterns of development. As Jerome Kagan observed:

> No human quality, psychological or physiological, is free of the contribution of events both within and outside the organism. . . . [E]very psychological quality is like a pale gray fabric woven from thin black threads, which represent biology, and thin white ones, which represent experience. But it is not possible to detect any quite black or white threads in the gray cloth. (Kagan, Arcus, & Snidman, 1993, p. 209)

Directions in Development

Genetic Counseling: Predicting the Future from the Genes of the Present

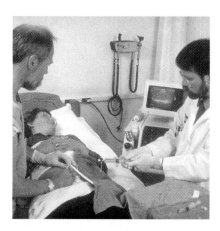

In amniocentesis, a sample of fetal cells is withdrawn from the amniotic sac and used to identify a number of genetic defects.

> The last thing Joey Paulowsky needs is another bout with cancer. Only 7 years old, the Dallas native has already fought off leukemia, and now his family worries that Joey could be hit again. The Paulowsky family carries a genetic burden—a rare form of inherited cancer of the thyroid. Deborah, his mother, found a lump in her neck six years ago, and since then one family member has died of the cancer and 10 others have had to have their thyroids removed. "Do I have cancer?" Joey asks his mother. "Will it hurt?" The Paulowskys will know the answer next month, when the results of a genetic test will show whether their son carries the family's fateful mutation. (Brownlee, Cook, & Hardigg, 1994, p. 59)

The answer will be delivered by a member of a field that, just a few decades ago, was nonexistent: genetic counseling. **Genetic counseling** focuses on helping people deal with issues relating to inherited disorders.

Genetic counselors use a variety of data in their work (Lindhout, Frets, & Niermeijer, 1991). For instance, couples contemplating having a child may seek to determine the risks involved in a future pregnancy. In such a case, a counselor will take a thorough family history, seeking any familial incidence of birth defects that might indicate a pattern of recessive or X-linked genes. In addition, the counselor will take into account factors such as the age of the mother and father and any previous abnormalities in other children they may have already had.

Typically, genetic counselors suggest a thorough physical examination. Such an exam may identify physical abnormalities which potential parents may have and not be aware of.

genetic counseling   *the discipline that focuses on helping people deal with issues relating to inherited disorders*

In addition, samples of blood, skin, and urine may be used to isolate and examine specific chromosomes. Possible genetic defects, such as the presence of an extra sex chromosome, can be identified by assembling a *karyotype*, a chart containing enlarged photos of each of the chromosomes.

If the woman is already pregnant, testing of the unborn child itself is possible. In **amniocentesis**, a small sample of fetal cells is drawn by a tiny needle inserted into the amniotic fluid surrounding the unborn fetus. By analyzing the fetal cells, technicians can identify a variety of genetic defects. In addition, they can determine the sex of the child. Although there is always a danger to the fetus in such an invasive procedure, amniocentesis is generally safe when carried out between the 12th and 16th weeks of pregnancy.

An additional test, **chorionic villus sampling (CVS)**, can be employed even earlier. The test involves taking small samples of hairlike material that surrounds the embryo. The CVS test can be done between the 8th and 11th week of pregnancy. However, because it is riskier than amniocentesis and can identify fewer genetic problems, its use is relatively infrequent.

Other tests that are less invasive and therefore less risky are also possible. For instance, the unborn child may be examined through **ultrasound sonography**, in which high-frequency sound waves are used to bombard the mother's womb. These waves produce a

amniocentesis the process of identifying genetic defects by examining a small sample of fetal cells drawn by a needle inserted into the amniotic fluid surrounding the unborn fetus

chorionic villus sampling (CVS) a test used to find genetic defects that involves taking samples of hairlike material that surrounds the embryo

ultrasound sonography a process in which high-frequency sound waves scan the mother's womb to produce an image of the unborn baby whose size and shape can then be assessed

TABLE 2-1

GENETIC TESTS

DNA TESTS AVAILABLE NOW

Disease	Description	Incidence	Cost
Adult polycystic kidney disease	Multiple kidney growths	1 in 1,000	$350
Alpha-1-antitrypsin deficiency	Can cause hepatitis, cirrhosis of the liver, emphysema	1 in 2,000 to 1 in 4,000	$200
Charcot-Marie-Tooth disease	Progressive degeneration of muscles	1 in 2,500	$250–$350
Familial adenomatous polyposos	Colon polyps by age 35, often leading to cancer	1 in 5,000	$1,000
Cystic fibrosis	Lungs clog with mucus; usually fatal by age 40	1 in 2,500 Caucasians	$125–$150
Duchenne/Becker muscular dystrophy	Progressive degeneration of muscles	1 in 3,000 males	$300–$900
Hemophilia	Blood fails to clot properly	1 in 10,000	$250–$350
Fragile X syndrome	Most common cause of inherited mental retardation	1 in 1,250 males; 1 in 2,500 females	$250
Gaucher's disease	Mild to deadly enzyme deficiency	1 in 400 Ashkenazi Jews	$100–$150
Huntington's disease	Lethal neurological deterioration	1 in 10,000 Caucasians	$250–$300
"Lou Gehrig's disease" (ALS)	Fatal degeneration of the nervous system	1 in 50,000, 10% familial	$150–$450
Myotonic dystrophy	Progressive degeneration of muscles	1 in 8,000	$250
Multiple endocrine neoplastia	Endocrine gland tumors	1 in 50,000	$900
Neurofibromatosis	*Café au lait* spots to large tumors	1 in 3,000	$900
Retinoblastoma	Blindness; potentially fatal eye tumors	1 in 20,000	$1,500
Spinal muscular atrophy	Progressive degeneration of muscles	7 in 100,000	$100–$900
Tay-Sachs disease	Lethal childhood neurological disorder	1 in 3,600 Ashkenazi Jews	$150
Thalassemia	Mild to fatal anemia	1 in 100,000	$300

Tests of the Future

Alzheimer's	Most likely multiple genes involved	4 million cases	Not available
Breast cancer	Five to 10% of all cases are thought to be hereditary	2.6 million cases	Not available
Diabetes	Most likely multiple genes involved	13–14 million cases	Not available
Nonpolyposis colon cancer	Several genes cause up to 20% of all cases	150,000 cases per year	Not available
Manic-depression	Most likely multiple genes involved	2 million cases	Not available

rather indistinct, but useful, image of the unborn baby, whose size and shape can then be assessed. By using ultrasound sonography repeatedly, developmental patterns can be determined. After the various tests are complete and all possible information is available, the couple will meet with the genetic counselor again. Typically, counselors avoid giving specific recommendations. Instead, they lay out the facts and present various options, ranging from doing nothing to taking more drastic steps, such as terminating the pregnancy through abortion. Ultimately, it is the parents who must decide what course of action to follow.

The newest role of genetic counselors involves testing to identify whether an individual is susceptible to future disorders because of genetic abnormalities. For instance, *Huntington's disease*, a devastating, always fatal disorder marked by tremors and intellectual deterioration, typically does not appear until people reach their 40s. However, genetic testing can identify much earlier whether a person carries the flawed gene that produces Huntington's disease. Presumably, people's knowledge that they carry the gene can help them prepare themselves for the future.

In addition to Huntington's disease, there is an ever-increasing number of other disorders that can be predicted on the basis of genetic testing (see Table 2-1). Although such testing may bring welcome relief from future worries—if the results are negative—positive results may produce just the opposite effect. In fact, genetic testing raises difficult practical and ethical questions.

Suppose, for instance, a person who thought she was susceptible to Huntington's disease was tested in her 20s and found that she did not carry the defective gene. Obviously, she would experience tremendous relief. But suppose she found that she did carry the gene and was therefore going to get the disease. She might well experience depression and remorse. In fact, some studies show that 10 percent of people who find they have the flawed gene that leads to Huntington's disease never recover fully on an emotional level (Nowak, 1994a).

Furthermore, genetic testing is a complicated issue. It rarely provides a simple yes or no answer. Typically, it presents a range of probabilities, which many people find difficult to comprehend. For instance, many patients interpret "a risk of about 50 percent" as meaning that their chances are either zero or 100 percent. In addition, people are increasingly demanding the latest genetic test, even if evidence is scanty that they are at appreciable medical risk of having a particular disease (Brownlee et al., 1994).

ALTERNATE ROUTES TO PREGNANCY: GIVING NATURE A BOOST

For some couples, conception presents a major challenge. In fact, some 15 percent of couples suffer from **infertility**, the inability to conceive after 12 to 18 months of trying to become pregnant.

Infertility is produced by several causes. In some cases, it is the age of the parents (the older the parents, the more likely infertility will occur), previous use of birth control pills, illicit drugs or cigarettes, or previous bouts of sexually transmitted diseases. In other cases, men have an abnormally low sperm count, which decreases the chances that a sperm will successfully fertilize an ovum. And still other cases of infertility are a result of the woman's *mother* taking certain drugs during pregnancy.

Whatever the cause of infertility, several approaches provide alternate paths to conception. Some difficulties can be corrected through the use of drugs or surgery. Another option may be **artificial insemination**, in which a man's sperm is placed directly into a woman's

infertility   the inability to conceive after 12 to 18 months of trying to become pregnant

artificial insemination   a process of fertilization in which a man's sperm is placed directly into a woman's vagina by a physician

vagina by a physician. In some situations, the woman's husband provides the sperm; in others it is an anonymous donor from a sperm bank.

In some cases, in vitro fertilization is employed. **In vitro fertilization (IVF)** is a procedure in which a woman's ova are removed from her ovaries, and a man's sperm are used to fertilize the ova in a laboratory. The fertilized egg is then implanted in either the woman who provided the donor eggs or in a *surrogate mother*, a woman who agrees to carry the child to term. Surrogate mothers may also be used in cases in which the mother is unable to conceive; the surrogate mother, who is artificially inseminated by a father, agrees to give up the infant after its birth.

The use of a surrogate mother presents a variety of ethical and legal issues, as well as many emotional concerns. In some cases, surrogate mothers have decided to refuse to give up the child after its birth; in others the surrogate mother has sought to have a role in the child's life. In such cases, the rights of the mother, father, surrogate mother, and ultimately the baby are in conflict.

How do children conceived using emerging reproductive technologies such as in vitro fertilization fare? Recent evidence shows that they do quite well. In fact, one study suggests that the quality of parenting in families who have used such techniques may even be superior to that of naturally conceived children. Furthermore, the later psychological adjustment of children conceived using in vitro fertilization and artificial insemination is no different from that of children conceived using natural techniques (Golombok, Cook, Bish, & Murray, 1995).

in vitro fertilization (IVF)   *a procedure in which a woman's ova are removed from her ovaries, and a man's sperm are used to fertilize the ova in a laboratory*

Review and Rethink

REVIEW

♦ In humans, the male sex cell (the sperm) and the female sex cell (the ovum) provide the developing baby with 23 chromosomes each, through which the baby inherits characteristics from both mother and father.

♦ A genotype is the underlying combination of genetic material present in an organism, but invisible; a phenotype is the visible trait, the expression of the genotype. Within a range predetermined by the genotype, environmental factors play a significant role in determining the way in which that genotype will be expressed as a phenotype.

♦ The field of behavioral genetics, a combination of psychology and genetics, studies the effects of genetics on behavior.

♦ Several inherited and genetic disorders are due to damaged or mutated genes, including phenylketonuria (PKU), Down syndrome, sickle-cell anemia, Tay-Sachs disease, and Klinefelter's syndrome.

♦ Genetic counselors use a variety of data and techniques to advise future parents of possible genetic risks to their unborn children.

♦ Among the alternate routes to conception are artificial insemination and in vitro fertilization (IVF).

RETHINK

♦ How can the study of identical twins like Mark Newman and Gerald Levey, who were separated at birth, help researchers determine the effects of genetic and environmental factors on human development? How might you design such a study?

- How can you inherit some traits from your mother and some from your father? How can you have some traits that are unlike either parent's? How might inherited characteristics "skip a generation," as they are often said to do?

- How might adopted children develop traits similar to those of their adoptive parents? What sorts of traits do you think might be shared or be different in adoptive families?

- What are some ethical and philosophical questions that surround the issue of genetic counseling? Might it sometimes be unwise to know ahead of time about possible genetically linked disorders that could afflict your child or yourself?

- What are some examples of how the genotype might limit the expression of the phenotype? How might environment affect the ways in which the genotype is realized as the phenotype?

THE INTERACTION OF HEREDITY AND ENVIRONMENT

Nature versus nurture. Heredity versus environment. Genetic influences versus situational influences.

However we choose to state it, each of the previous statements reflects an enduring question that has intrigued and puzzled life-span developmentalists about the root causes

Speaking of Development

Lopa Malkan Wani

Born: ························ 1965

Education: ······················· Cornell University, B.A. in biology, with a concentration in genetics; Sarah Lawrence College, M.S. in genetic counseling

Position: ······················· Genetic counselor for Genetrix, Inc.

Home: ····························· Sacramento, California

Not only has the field of genetics significantly advanced our understanding of the way we are put together but it has spawned a new occupation: genetic counselor. Genetic counselors help people deal with the potential consequences of the genes they carry.

Lopa Wani works in two major areas of the field. "The role of the genetic counselor is a dual one," she explains. "We are concerned with prenatal genetics and pediatric genetics, which deal with different issues.

"Prenatal genetics is concerned with both the period before conception, when we focus on planned pregnancies, and the period preceding birth, when we mostly offer counseling about the risks that might be present, tests for genetic conditions, and explain the options that are available.

of human behavior. Is behavior produced by inherited, genetic influences, or is it triggered by factors in the environment?

The answer is: There is no answer. As developmental research accumulates, it is becoming increasingly clear that to view behavior as due to *either* genetic or environmental factors is inappropriate. A given behavior is not caused just by genetic factors; nor is it caused solely by environmental forces. Instead, as we first discussed in Chapter 1, the behavior is the product of some combination of the two. The more appropriate question, then, is *how much* of the behavior is caused by genetic factors, and *how much* by environmental factors. (See, for example, the range of possibilities for the determinants of intelligence, illustrated in Figure 2-6.)

ANSWERING THE NATURE–NURTURE RIDDLE

Developmental specialists have used several strategies to try to answer the question of the degree to which traits, characteristics, and behavior are produced by genetic and environmental factors, respectively. In seeking an answer, they have turned to studies involving both nonhuman species and humans (Plomin & McClearn, 1993; Kimble, 1993; Plomin, 1994a).

Nonhuman Studies: Controlling both Genetics and Environment.   One approach to understanding the relative contribution of heredity and environment makes use of non-

"To some people a four percent risk factor is a large risk, while to others it isn't"

"If the person feels that the risk is great enough, we proceed to explore the types of testing that are available"

"In pediatric genetics, on the other hand, we work with a child who already has the problem or who may have a problem that needs to be identified."

The disorders that Wani and her colleagues deal with are sometimes carried from one generation to the next by recessive genes. "When both parents carry the same non-working gene, we refer to that as an autosomal recessive condition," explains Wani. "There is a 25 percent chance that the child of that sort of union will be affected by the disorder." Diseases carried by recessive genes include Tay-Sachs disease, cystic fibrosis, and sickle-cell anemia, according to Wani.

"The first thing we assess is the parents' view of the condition—what their feelings are. Some people may not view the condition as serious. They might not want to go ahead with the tests for the condition," she explains. "We also have to be sure they understand the disorder, that they have an accurate perception of it."

According to Wani, risk assessment is very important—but equally important is the carrier's perception of the risk. "To some people a four percent risk factor is a large risk, while to others it isn't," she says. "If the person feels that the risk is great enough, we proceed to explore the types of testing that are available."

Staying in touch with parents and reading their signals carefully is a significant part of the counselor's work. "When a pregnancy is diagnosed as abnormal, people don't necessarily hear what you tell them the first time. They also have strong feelings of guilt and shame when they find out they are carrying a recessive gene," Wani concludes. "But there's nothing to be ashamed of. All of us carry about five to seven recessive genes that simply don't work right. Every one of us."

human animals. It is relatively simple to develop breeds of animals that are genetically similar to one another in terms of specific traits. The people who raise Butterball turkeys at Thanksgiving do it all the time, producing turkeys that grow especially rapidly so that they can be brought to market inexpensively. Similarly, strains of laboratory animals can be bred to share similar genetic backgrounds.

By observing animals with similar genetic backgrounds in different environments, scientists can determine, with reasonable precision, the effects of specific kinds of environmental stimulation. Conversely, researchers can examine groups of animals that have been bred to have significantly *different* genetic backgrounds on particular traits. Then, by exposing such animals to identical environments, they can determine the role that genetic background plays.

Of course, the drawback to using nonhumans as research subjects is that we cannot be sure how well the findings we obtain can be generalized to people. Still, the opportunities that animal research offers are substantial.

Human Studies: Exploiting Genetic Similarities and Dissimilarities.   Obviously, researchers cannot control either the genetic backgrounds or the environments of humans in the way they can with nonhumans. However, nature conveniently has provided the potential to carry out various kinds of "natural experiments"—in the form of twins.

Recall that identical, monozygotic twins such as Mark Newman and Gerald Levey, whose story we read at the beginning of the chapter, share an identical genetic code. Because their inherited backgrounds are precisely the same, any variations in their behavior must be due entirely to environmental factors. In a world devoid of ethics, it would be rather simple for researchers to make use of identical twins to draw unequivocal conclusions about the role of nature and nurture. For instance, by separating identical twins at birth and placing them in totally different environments, researchers could assess the impact of environment unambiguously. Obviously, ethical considerations make this impossible. However, a fair number of cases exist in which identical twins are put up for adoption at birth and are raised in substantially different environments. Such instances allow us to draw fairly confident

FIGURE 2-6

Intelligence is produced by a range of possible causes, spanning the nature–nurture continuum.

Nature				Nurture
Intelligence is provided entirely by genetic factors; environment plays no role. Even a highly enriched environment and excellent education make no difference.	Although largely inherited, intelligence is affected by extremely enriched or deprived environment.	Intelligence is affected both by a person's genetic endowment and environment. A person genetically predisposed to low intelligence may perform better if raised in an enriched environment or worse in a deprived environment. Similarly, a person genetically predisposed to higher intelligence may perform worse in a deprived environment, or better in an enriched environment.	Although intelligence is largely a result of environment, genetic abnormalities may produce mental retardation.	Intelligence depends entirely on the environment. Genetics plays no role in determining intellectual success.

Possible Causes

conclusions about the relative contributions of genetics and environment (Lykken, McGue, Tellegen, & Bouchard, 1993b; LaBuda, Gottesman, & Pauls, 1993).

Still, the data from monozygotic twins raised in different environments are not always without bias. Adoption agencies typically take the characteristics (and wishes) of birth mothers into account when they place babies in adoptive homes. For instance, children tend to be placed with families of the same race and religion. Consequently, even when monozygotic twins are placed in different adoptive homes, there are often similarities in the two home environments. The consequence is that researchers cannot always unambiguously attribute differences in behavior to genetics or environment.

Dizygotic twins, too, present opportunities to learn about the relative contributions of heredity and situational factors. Recall that dizygotic twins are genetically no more similar than siblings in a family born at different times. It is possible to compare behavior within pairs of dizygotic twins with that of pairs of monozygotic twins (who are genetically identical). If monozygotic twins are more similar on a particular trait, on average, than dizygotic twins, we can assume that genetics plays an important role in determining the expression of that trait (e.g., Schulman, Keith, & Seligman, 1993).

Still another approach is to study people who are totally unrelated to one another and who therefore have dissimilar genetic backgrounds, but who share an environmental background. For instance, a family that adopts, at the same time, two very young and unrelated children probably will provide them with quite similar environments throughout their childhood. In this case, similarities in the children's characteristics and behavior can be attributed with some confidence to environmental influences (Segal, 1993).

Finally, developmental researchers have examined groups of people in light of their degree of genetic similarity. For instance, if we find a high association on a particular trait between biological parents and their children, but a weaker association between adoptive parents and their children, we have evidence for the importance of genetics in determining the expression of that trait. Conversely, if there is a stronger association on a trait between adoptive parents and their children than between biological parents and their children, we have evidence for the importance of the environment in determining that trait. In general, when a particular trait tends to occur at similar levels among genetically similar individuals, but tends to vary more among genetically more distant individuals, we can assume that genetics plays an important role in the development of that trait.

Developmental researchers have used all these approaches, and more, to study the relative impact of genetic and environmental factors. What have they found? Before turning to their specific findings, it is important to state the general conclusion resulting from decades of research: Virtually all traits, characteristics, and behaviors are the joint result of the combination and interaction of nature and nurture. Like love and marriage and horses and carriages, genetic and environmental factors work in tandem to create the unique individual that each of us is and will become.

PHYSICAL TRAITS: FAMILY RESEMBLANCES

When patients entered the examining room of Dr. Cyril Marcus, they didn't realize that sometimes they were actually being treated by his identical twin brother, Dr. Stewart Marcus. So similar in appearance and manner were the twins that even long-time patients were fooled by this admittedly unethical behavior, which occurred in a bizarre case made famous in the film *Dead Ringers*.

Monozygotic twins are merely the most extreme example of the fact that the more genetically similar two people are, the more likely they are to share physical characteristics. Tall parents tend to have tall children, and short ones tend to have short children. Obesity, which is defined as being more than 20 percent above the average weight for a given height, also has a strong genetic component. For example, in one study, pairs of identical twins were put on diets that contained an extra 1,000 calories a day—and ordered not to exercise. Over a three-month period, the twins gained almost identical amounts of weight. More-

Some traits—like curly hair—have a clear genetic component.

over, different pairs of twins varied substantially in how much weight they gained, with some pairs gaining almost three times as much weight as other pairs (Bouchard et al., 1990a). Other, less obvious physical characteristics also show strong genetic influences. For instance, blood pressure, respiration rates, and even the age at which life ends are more similar in closely related individuals than in those who are less genetically similar (Jost & Sontag, 1944; Sorensen, Nielsen, Andersen, & Teasdale, 1988; Price & Gottesman, 1991).

INTELLIGENCE

No other issue involving the relative influence of heredity and environment has generated more research than the topic of intelligence. Why? The main reason is that intelligence, generally measured in terms of an IQ score, is a core human characteristic; IQ is strongly related to success in scholastic endeavors and, somewhat less strongly, to other types of achievement.

Let us first consider the degree to which intelligence is related to genetic factors. The answer is unambiguous: Genetics plays a significant role in intelligence. Both overall intelligence and specific subcomponents of intelligence (such as spatial skills, verbal skills, and memory) show strong effects for heredity (Cardon, Fulker, DeFries, & Plomin, 1992; Pedersen, Plomin, Nesselroade, & McClearn, 1992; McGue, Bouchard, Iacono, & Lykken, 1993; Cardon & Fulker, 1993). As can be seen in Figure 2-7, the closer the genetic link between two individuals, the greater the correspondence of their overall IQ scores.

Not only is genetics an important influence on intelligence, but the impact increases with age. For instance, as fraternal (i.e., dizygotic) twins move from infancy to adolescence, their IQ scores become less similar. In contrast, the IQ scores of identical (monozygotic) twins become increasingly similar over the course of time. These opposite patterns suggest the intensifying influence of inherited factors with increasing age (Wilson, 1983; McGue et al., 1993; Brody, 1993).

Although it is clear that heredity plays an important role in intelligence, investigators are much more divided on the question of how to quantify that role. Perhaps the most

FIGURE 2-7

MEDIAN CORRELATION

The closer the genetic link between two individuals, the greater the correspondence between their IQ scores.

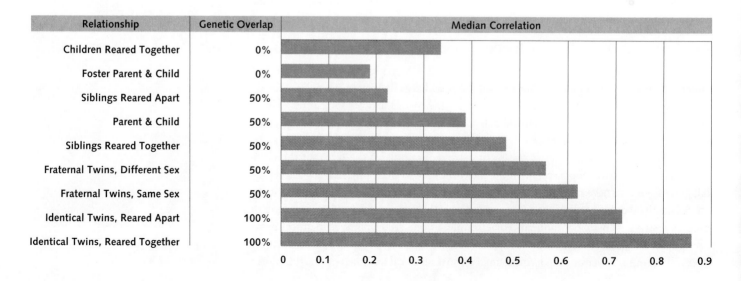

Relationship	Genetic Overlap	Median Correlation
Children Reared Together	0%	
Foster Parent & Child	0%	
Siblings Reared Apart	50%	
Parent & Child	50%	
Siblings Reared Together	50%	
Fraternal Twins, Different Sex	50%	
Fraternal Twins, Same Sex	50%	
Identical Twins, Reared Apart	100%	
Identical Twins, Reared Together	100%	

0   0.1   0.2   0.3   0.4   0.5   0.6   0.7   0.8   0.9

extreme view is held by psychologist Arthur Jensen, who argues that as much as 80 percent of intelligence is a result of the influence of heredity (Jensen, 1969). Others have suggested more modest figures, ranging from 50 percent to 70 percent (e.g., Weinberg, 1989; Bouchard, et al. 1990b; Plomin, DeFries, & McClearn, 1990b).

It is important to keep in mind that although heredity clearly plays an important role in intelligence, it is hardly the only factor. Even the most extreme estimates of the role of genetics still allow for environmental factors to play a significant part (Storfer, 1990). In fact, in terms of public policy for maximizing people's intellectual success, the issue is not whether primarily hereditary or environmental factors underlie intelligence. Instead, as developmental psychologist Sandra Scarr suggests, we should be asking what can be done to maximize the intellectual development of each individual (Scarr & Carter-Saltzman, 1982).

GENETIC AND ENVIRONMENTAL INFLUENCES ON PERSONALITY: BORN TO BE OUTGOING?

Although it seems reasonable to most people that such characteristics as race and eye color are inherited, the notion that personality characteristics are affected by genetic factors seems less credible. However, increasing evidence supports the conclusion that at least some personality traits have at least some genetic components (Rowe, 1993; D. Smith, 1993; Bouchard, 1994).

For example, neuroticism and extroversion are among the personality factors that have been linked most directly to genetic factors. The term *neuroticism*, when considered in the context of personality, refers to the degree of moodiness, touchiness, or sensitivity an individual characteristically displays. In other words, neuroticism reflects emotional reactivity. *Extroversion* is the degree to which a person seeks to be with others, to behave in an outgoing manner, and generally to be sociable (Loehlin, 1992; Bergeman et al., 1993; Plomin, 1994c).

How do we know which personality traits reflect genetics? Again, the evidence comes largely from studies of twins. For instance, in one large-scale study, personality psychologist Auke Tellegen and colleagues studied the personality traits of hundreds of pairs of twins. Because a good number of the twins were genetically identical but had been raised apart, it was possible to determine with some confidence the influence of genetic factors (Tellegen et al., 1988).

Tellegen found that certain traits reflected the contribution of genetics considerably more than others. As you can see in Figure 2-8, social potency (the tendency to be a masterful, forceful leader who enjoys being the center of attention) and traditionalism (strict endorsement of rules and authority) are strongly associated with genetic factors.

Other research has revealed genetic influences on other, less central personality traits. For example, a person's political attitudes, religious interests and values, and even attitudes toward human sexuality seem to have genetic components. Even the amount of television that people watch appears to have a genetic component (Eysenck, 1976; Plomin et al., 1990a; Waller et al., 1990; Loehlin, 1992; Coccaro, Bergeman & McClearn, 1993; Lykken et al., 1993b; Schulman et al., 1993).

It may seem far-fetched that factors such as TV viewing levels are affected by genetics. Admittedly, it is hardly likely that evolution has provided humans with a gene that controls TV watching. How, then, could genetics play a role in a behavior that is so purely a part of contemporary life?

The answer comes from considering what is involved in watching television: It is a passive, solitary activity, one that largely precludes involvement in more social activities. Consequently, the influence of genetics may be indirect. For instance, we know that genetics plays an important role in determining a person's general level of extroversion. It may be that people who are relatively extroverted are less likely to watch television, an activity that hinders social involvement with others. On the other hand, a more introverted person may

FIGURE 2-8

Social Potency	61%
A person high in this trait is masterful, a forceful leader who likes to be the center of attention.	
Traditionalism	60%
Follows rules and authority, endorses high moral standards and strict discipline.	
Stress Reaction	55%
Feels vulnerable and sensitive and is given to worries and is easily upset.	
Absorption	55%
Has a vivid imagination readily captured by rich experience; relinquishes sense of reality.	
Alienation	55%
Feels mistreated and used, that "the world is out to get me."	
Well Being	54%
Has a cheerful disposition, feels confident and optimistic.	
Harm Avoidance	50%
Shuns the excitement of risk and danger, prefers the safe route even if it is tedious.	
Aggression	48%
Is physically aggressive and vindictive, has taste for violence and is "out to get the world."	
Achievement	46%
Works hard, strives for mastery, and puts work and accomplishment ahead of other things.	
Control	43%
Is cautious and plodding, rational and sensible, likes carefully planned events.	
Social Closeness	33%
Prefers emotional intimacy and close ties, turns to others for comfort and help.	

These traits are among the personality factors that are related most closely to genetic factors. The higher the percentage, the greater the degree to which the trait reflects the influence of heredity.

(Adopted from Tellegen et al., 1988).

be more apt to watch television largely because it involves only minimal social interaction.

Such reasoning helps illustrate the importance of inherited factors in determining personality. However, it also points out once again the critical interplay between nature and nurture. In homes that have a TV set, an individual's personality tendencies that are shaped by genetic factors may be exhibited in a particular way. But in homes that lack a TV set, these tendencies may be expressed in quite different behaviors. There is a constant interplay, then, between heredity and environment. In fact, the way in which nature and nurture interact may be reflected not just in the behavior of individuals but also in the very foundations of a culture, as we will see next.

Developmental Diversity:

Cultural Differences in Physical Arousal: Might a Culture's Philosophical Outlook Be Determined by Genetics?

The Buddhist philosophy, an inherent part of many Asian cultures, emphasizes harmony and peacefulness, and suggests that one should seek the eradication of human desire. In contrast, some of the traditional philosophies of Western civilization, such as those of

Martin Luther and John Calvin, accentuate the importance of controlling the anxiety, fear, and guilt that are thought to be basic parts of the human condition.

Could such philosophical approaches reflect, in part, genetic factors? That is the controversial suggestion made by developmental psychologist Jerome Kagan and his colleagues, who speculate that the underlying temperament of a given society, determined genetically, may predispose people in that society toward a particular philosophy (Kagan et al., 1993).

Kagan bases his admittedly speculative suggestion on well-confirmed findings that show clear differences in temperament between Caucasian and Asian children. For instance, one study that compared four-month-old infants in China, Ireland, and the United States found several relevant differences. In comparison to the Caucasian-American babies and the Irish babies, the Chinese babies had significantly lower motor activity, irritability, and vocalization (see Table 2-2).

Kagan suggests that the Chinese, who enter the world temperamentally calmer, may find Buddhist philosophical notions of serenity more in tune with their natural inclinations. In contrast, Westerners, who are emotionally more volatile and tense, and who report higher levels of guilt, are more likely to be attracted to philosophies that articulate the necessity of controlling the unpleasant feelings that they are more apt to encounter in their everyday experience (Kagan et al., 1994).

It is important to note that this does not mean that one philosophical approach is necessarily better, or worse, than the other. Nor does it mean that either of the temperaments from which the philosophies are thought to spring is superior or inferior to the other. Similarly, we must keep in mind that any single individual within a culture can be more or less temperamentally volatile, and that the range of temperaments found even within a particular culture is vast. Finally, as we noted in our initial discussion of temperament, environmental conditions can have a significant effect on the portion of a person's temperament that is not genetically determined.

Still, the notion that the very basis of culture—its philosophical traditions—may be affected by genetic factors is intriguing. More research is necessary to determine just how the unique interaction of heredity and environment within a given culture may produce a framework for viewing and understanding the world.

TABLE 2-2

MEAN BEHAVIORAL SCORES FOR MOTOR ACTIVITY, CRYING, FRETTING, VOCALIZING, AND SMILING FOR CAUCASIAN-AMERICAN , IRISH, AND CHINESE 4-MONTH-OLD INFANTS

Behavior	American	Irish	Chinese
Motor activity	48.6	36.7	11.2
Crying (in seconds)	7.0	2.9	1.1
Fretting (% trials)	10.0	6.0	1.9
Vocalizing (% trials)	31.4	31.1	8.1
Smiling (% trials)	4.1	2.6	3.6

(*Source*: Kagan, Arcus, & Snidman, 1993)

PSYCHOLOGICAL DISORDERS: THE ROLE OF GENETICS AND ENVIRONMENT

Lori Schiller began to hear voices when she was a teenager in summer camp. Without warning, the voices screamed, "You must die! Die! Die!" She ran from her bunk into the darkness, where she thought she could get away. Camp counselors found her screaming as she jumped wildly on a trampoline. "I thought I was possessed," she said later (Bennett, 1992).

In a sense, Lori was possessed: possessed with schizophrenia, one of the most severe types of psychological disorder. Normal and happy through childhood, Lori's world took a tumble during adolescence as she increasingly lost her hold on reality. For the next two decades, she would be in and out of institutions, struggling to ward off the ravages of the disorder.

What was the cause of Schiller's mental disorder? Increasing evidence suggests that schizophrenia is brought about by genetic factors. The disorder runs in families, with some families showing an unusually high incidence. Moreover, the closer the genetic links between someone with schizophrenia and another family member, the more likely it is that the other person will also develop schizophrenia. For instance, a monozygotic twin has close to a 50 percent risk of developing schizophrenia when the other twin develops the disorder (see Figure 2-9). On the other hand, a niece or nephew of a person with schizophrenia has less than a 5 percent chance of developing the disorder (Gottesman, 1991, 1993; Prescott & Gottesman, 1993).

However, these data also illustrate that genetics alone is not responsible for the disorder. If genetics were the sole cause, the risk for an identical twin would be 100 percent. Consequently, other factors account for the disorder, ranging from structural abnormalities

FIGURE 2-9

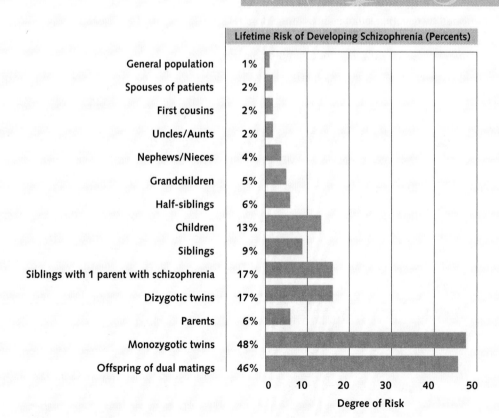

Lifetime Risk of Developing Schizophrenia (Percents)

General population	1%
Spouses of patients	2%
First cousins	2%
Uncles/Aunts	2%
Nephews/Nieces	4%
Grandchildren	5%
Half-siblings	6%
Children	13%
Siblings	9%
Siblings with 1 parent with schizophrenia	17%
Dizygotic twins	17%
Parents	6%
Monozygotic twins	48%
Offspring of dual matings	46%

Degree of Risk

The psychological disorder of schizophrenia has clear genetic components. The closer the genetic links between someone with schizophrenia and another family member, the more likely it is that the other person will also develop schizophrenia.

(*Source:* Gottesman, I.I., 1991.)

in the brain to a biochemical imbalance (Iacono & Grove, 1993; Wang, Black, Andreasen, & Crowe, 1993).

It also seems that even if individuals harbor a genetic predisposition toward schizophrenia, they are not destined to develop the disorder. Instead, they may inherit an unusual sensitivity to stress in the environment. If stress is low, schizophrenia will not occur. But if stress is sufficiently strong, it will lead to schizophrenia. Conversely, for someone with a strong genetic predisposition toward the disorder, even relatively weak environmental stressors may lead to schizophrenia (Gottesman, 1991; Fowles, 1992).

Several other psychological disorders have been shown to be related, at least in part, to genetic factors. For instance, major depression, alcoholism, autism, and attention-deficit hyperactivity disorder have significant inherited components (McGuffin & Katz, 1993; McGue, 1993; Eaves et al., 1993; Shields, 1973).

The example of schizophrenia and other genetically related psychological disorders also illustrates a fundamental principle regarding the relationship between heredity and environment, one that underlies much of our previous discussion. Specifically, the role of genetics is often to produce preparedness for a future course of development. When and whether a certain behavioral characteristic will actually be displayed depends on the nature of the environment. Thus, although a predisposition for schizophrenia may be present at birth, people typically do not show the disorder until adolescence—if at all.

Similarly, certain other kinds of traits are more likely to be displayed as the influence of parents and other socializing factors declines. For example, adopted children may, early in their lives, display traits that are relatively similar to their adoptive parents', given the overwhelming influence of the environment on young children. In contrast, as they get older and their parents' influence declines, genetically influenced traits may begin to manifest themselves as unseen genetic factors begin to play a greater role (Loehlin, 1992; Caspi & Moffitt, 1991, 1993).

According to developmentalist Sandra Scarr (1992, 1993), the genetic endowment provided to children by their parents not only determines their genetic characteristics but also actively influences their environment. Because of **active genotype-environment effects**, children focus on those aspects of their environment that are most congruent with their genetically determined abilities. At the same time, they pay less attention to those aspects of the environment that are less compatible with their genetic endowment. For instance, a particularly well-coordinated child may be more apt to try out for Little League baseball, while her less-coordinated—but more musically endowed—friend might be more apt to try out for an after-school chorus. In each case, the children are actively producing an environment in which their genetically determined abilities can flourish.

But the relationship between genetics and environment can be more subtle. In some cases, there are **passive genotype-environment effects**, in which *parents'* genes are associated with the environment in which children are raised. For example, a particularly sports-oriented parent, who has genes that promote good physical coordination, may provide many opportunities for a child to play sports. Similarly, there are **evocative genotype-environment effects**, in which a child's genes elicit a particular type of environment. For instance, an infant's demanding behavior may cause parents to be more attentive to the infant's needs than they would were the infant less demanding.

In sum, determining whether behavior is primarily attributable to nature or nurture is a bit like shooting at a moving target. Not only are behaviors and traits a joint outcome of genetic and environmental factors, but the relative influence of genes and environment for specific characteristics shifts over the course of people's lives. Although the pool of genes we inherit at birth sets the stage for our future development, the constantly shifting scenery and the other characters in our lives determine just how our development eventually plays out.

Developmental psychologist Sandra Scarr.

active genotype-environment effects
effects on behavior produced when a child focuses on aspects of his or her environment that are congruent with his or her genetic endowment

passive genotype-environment effects
effects on behavior produced when parents' genes lead to a particular kind of environment

evocative genotype-environment effects
effects on behavior produced when a child's genes elicit a particular kind of environment

Review and Rethink

REVIEW

- Human characteristics and behavior are a joint outcome of genetic and environmental factors. The extent to which a given trait is caused by genetic factors or environmental factors varies from trait to trait and over time.

- Scientists use both nonhuman and human studies to analyze the different contributions of genetics and environment. Individuals with identical genetic backgrounds and different environmental influences and, conversely, individuals with different genetic backgrounds and highly similar environmental influences are studied to tease out the varying influences of nature and nurture.

- Genetic influences have been identified in physical characteristics, intelligence, personality traits and behaviors, and psychological disorders.

- There is some speculation that entire cultures may be predisposed genetically toward certain types of philosophical viewpoints and attitudes.

RETHINK

- How might a different environment from the one you experienced have affected the development of personality characteristics that you believe you inherited from one or both of your parents?

- Do you think dizygotic (i.e., fraternal) twins are likely to be more similar to one another than two siblings born of the same parents at different times? Why? What genetic or environmental factors help determine your answer?

- What sort of study might you design to examine whether "handedness" (the tendency to be either right-handed or left-handed) is determined more by genetics or environment?

- The prologue of this chapter said that identical twins Mark Newman and Gerald Levey both enjoy John Wayne movies and Chinese food. How might these personal preferences be influenced by genetic factors?

- Some people have used the proven genetic basis of intelligence to argue against strenuous educational efforts on behalf of individuals with below-average IQs. Does this viewpoint make sense based on what you have learned about heredity and environment? Why or why not?

- A friend with a schizophrenic sister has just learned that her grandfather also had this disorder. Using your knowledge of the role of genetics and environment, what would you tell your friend about her chances of developing schizophrenia?

PRENATAL GROWTH AND CHANGE

From the moment of conception, development proceeds relentlessly, guided by the complex set of genetic guidelines inherited from the parents, and influenced from the start by environmental factors. Starting as a single cell produced by the alliance of ovum and sperm at the instant of conception, prenatal growth proceeds in an orderly, yet surprisingly rapid, pace.

THE STAGES OF THE PRENATAL PERIOD: THE ONSET OF DEVELOPMENT

Developmentalists divide the prenatal period into three phases: the germinal, embryonic, and fetal stages. They are summarized in Table 2-3.

The Germinal Stage: Fertilization to 2 Weeks.   The **germinal stage**, the first—and shortest—stage of the prenatal period, takes place during the first two weeks following conception. It is characterized by methodical cell division and the attachment of the organism to the wall of the uterus. Cell division gets off to a quick start: Three days after fertilization, the zygote consists of some 32 cells, and by the next day the number doubles. Within a week, the zygote is made up of 100 to 150 cells, and the number rises with increasing rapidity.

In addition to increasing in number, the cells of the zygote become increasingly specialized. For instance, some cells form a protective layer around the zygote, while others begin to establish the rudiments of a placenta and umbilical cord. When fully developed, the *placenta* serves as a conduit between the mother and fetus, providing nourishment and oxygen via the *umbilical* cord. In addition, waste materials from the developing child are removed through the umbilical cord.

The Embryonic Stage: 2 to 8 Weeks.   By the end of the germinal period—just two weeks after conception—the zygote is firmly secured to the wall of the mother's uterus. At this point, the child is called an *embryo.*

The **embryonic stage** is the period from two to eight weeks following fertilization. During this time, significant growth occurs in the major organs and body systems. At the beginning of the embryonic stage, the developing child has three distinct layers, each of which will ultimately form a different set of structures as development proceeds.

The outer layer of the embryo, the *ectoderm*, will form skin, hair, teeth, sense organs, and the brain and spinal cord. The *endoderm*, the inner layer, produces the digestive system, liver, pancreas, and respiratory system. Sandwiched between the ectoderm and endoderm is the *mesoderm*, from which the muscles, bones, blood, and circulatory system are forged. Every part of the body is formed from these three layers.

An observer looking at an embryo at the end of the embryonic stage would be hard-pressed to identify it as human. Only an inch long, an 8-week-old embryo has what appear

germinal stage   the first—and shortest—stage of the prenatal period which takes place during the first 2 weeks following conception

embryonic stage   the period from 2 to 8 weeks following fertilization during which significant growth occurs in the major organs and body systems

TABLE 2-3

STAGES OF THE PRENATAL PERIOD

GERMINAL	EMBRYONIC	FETAL
Fertilization to 2 Weeks	**2 Weeks to 8 Weeks**	**8 Weeks to Birth**
The germinal stage is the first and shortest, characterized by methodical cell division and the attachment of the organism to the wall of the uterus. Three days after fertilization the zygote consists of 32 cells, a number that doubles by the next day. Within a week the zygote multiplies to 100–150 cells. The cells become specialized, with some forming a protective layer around the zygote.	The zygote is now designated an embryo. The embryo develops three layers, which ultimately form a different set of structures as development proceeds. The layers are: Ectoderm: Skin, sense organs, brain, spinal cord. Endoderm: Digestive system, liver, respiratory system. Mesoderm: Muscles, blood, circulatory system. The embryo is one inch long.	The fetal stage formally starts when the differentiation of the major organs has occurred. Now called a fetus, the individual grows rapidly as length increases 20 times. At four months the fetus weighs an average of four ounces; at seven months, three pounds; and at the time of birth the average child weighs just over seven pounds.

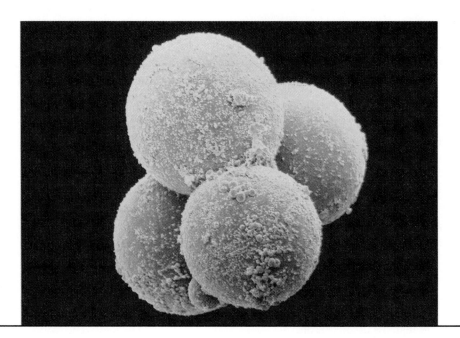

On the second day following fertilization, in the germinal stage, the organism consists of four cells.

fetal stage   *the stage that begins at about 8 weeks after conception and continues until birth*

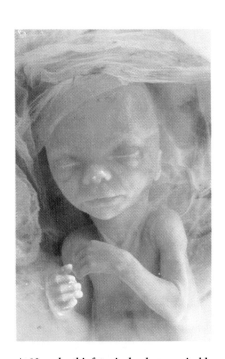

At 12 weeks, this fetus is clearly recognizable as a human.

to be gills and a taillike structure. On the other hand, a closer look reveals several familiar features. Rudimentary eyes, nose, lips, and even teeth can be recognized, and the embryo has stubby bulges that will form arms and legs.

The Fetal Stage: 8 Weeks to Birth.   It is not until the final period of prenatal development, the fetal stage, that the developing child becomes instantly recognizable. The **fetal stage** starts at about 8 weeks after conception and continues until birth. The fetal stage formally starts when the differentiation of the major organs has occurred.

Now called a *fetus*, the developing child undergoes astoundingly rapid change during the fetal stage. For instance, it increases in length some twenty times, and its proportions change dramatically. At 2 months, about half the fetus is what will ultimately be its head; by 5 months, the head accounts for just over a quarter of its total size (see Figure 2-10).

The fetus also increases in weight substantially. At four months, the fetus weighs an average of about four ounces; at seven months, it weighs about three pounds; and at the time of birth the average child weighs just over seven pounds.

At the same time, the complexity of the organism increases rapidly. Organs become more differentiated and operational. By 3 months, the fetus swallows and urinates. In addition, the interconnections between the different parts of the body become more complex and integrated. Arms develop hands; hands develop fingers; fingers develop nails.

As this is happening, the fetus makes itself known to the outside world. Although mothers may at first be unaware in the earliest stages of pregnancy that they are, in fact, pregnant, the fetus now becomes increasingly active. By 4 months, a mother can feel the movement of her child, and several months later others can feel the baby's kicks through the mother's skin.

During the fetal stage, the fetus develops a wide repertoire of different types of activities. In addition to the kicks that alert its mother to its presence, the fetus can turn, do somersaults, cry, hiccup, clench its fist, open and close its eyes, and suck its thumb. It also is capable of hearing and can even respond to sounds that it hears repeatedly (Lecanuet, Granier-Deferre, & Busnel, 1995b). For instance, researchers Anthony DeCasper and Melanie Spence (1986) asked a group of pregnant mothers to read aloud a Dr. Seuss story, the poem *The Cat in the Hat*, two times a day during the latter months of pregnancy. Three days after the babies were born, they appeared to recognize the story they had heard, responding more to it than to another story that had a different rhythm.

FIGURE 2-10

PROPORTIONS OF GROWTH

During the fetal period, the proportions of the body change dramatically. At 2 months, the head represents about half the fetus, but by the time of birth, it is one-quarter of its total size.

(*Source*: Robbins, 1929.)

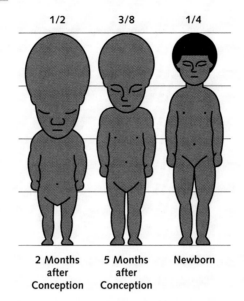

2 Months after Conception   5 Months after Conception   Newborn

Just as no two adults are alike, no two fetuses are the same. Although development during the prenatal period follows the broad patterns outlined here, there are significant differences in the specific nature of individual fetuses' behavior. Some fetuses are exceedingly active, whereas others are more sedentary. Some spend most of their time sucking their thumbs; others never do this at all. Some have relatively quick heart rates; others have slower rates, with the typical range varying between 120 to 160 beats per minute (Lecanuet, Fifer, Krasnegor, & Smotherman, 1995a).

Such differences in fetal behavior are due in part to genetic characteristics inherited at the moment of fertilization. Other kinds of differences, though, are brought about by the nature of the environment in which the child spends its first 9 months of life. As we will see, there are numerous ways in which the prenatal environment of infants affects their development—in good ways and bad.

THE PRENATAL ENVIRONMENT: THREATS TO DEVELOPMENT

According to the Siriono people of South America, if a pregnant woman eats the meat of certain kinds of animals, she runs the risk of having a child who may act and look like those animals. According to opinions offered on daytime television talk programs such as the Oprah Winfrey show, a pregnant mother should avoid getting angry in order to spare her child from entering the world with anger (Cole, 1990).

Such views are largely the stuff of folklore. However, it is true that certain aspects of mothers' and fathers' behavior, both before and after conception, can produce lifelong consequences for the child. Some consequences show up immediately, whereas others, more insidious, may not appear until years after birth. In fact, half are not apparent before birth (Jacobson et al., 1985).

Some of the most profound consequences are brought about by teratogenic agents. A **teratogen** is a factor that produces a birth defect. Although it is the job of the placenta to keep teratogens from reaching the fetus, the placenta is not entirely successful at this, and probably every fetus is exposed to some teratogens. Furthermore, the timing of exposure to a teratogen is crucial. At some phases of prenatal development, a teratogen may have only a minimal impact. At other periods, however, the consequences may be profound (see Figure 2-11).

teratogen   *a factor that produces a birth defect*

FIGURE 2-11

Depending on their state of development, various parts of the body vary in their sensitivity to teratogens.

(From Moore, 1974.)

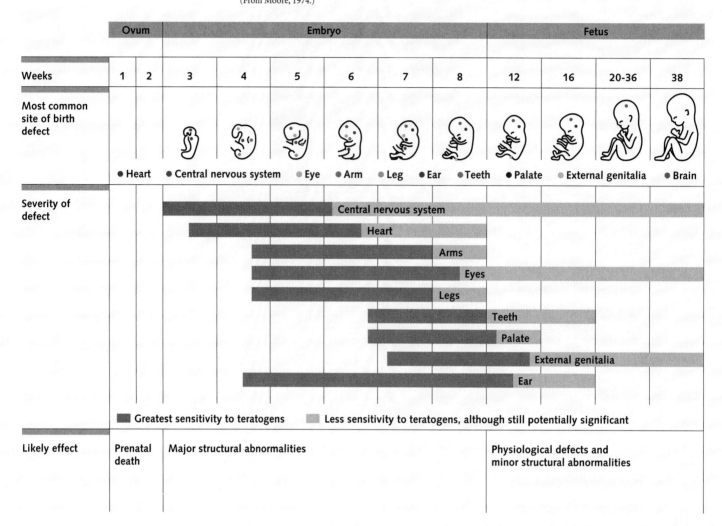

Mothers' Diet.   Most of our knowledge of the environmental factors affecting the developing fetus comes from the study of the mother. For instance, a mother's diet clearly plays an important role in bolstering the development of the fetus. A mother who eats a varied diet high in nutrients is apt to have fewer complications during pregnancy, an easier labor, and a generally healthier baby than a mother whose diet is restricted in nutrients (J.L. Brown, 1987; Morgane et al., 1993).

The problem of diet is of immense global concern. In 1992 the World Food Council estimated that there were 550 million hungry people in the world. Even worse, the number of people vulnerable to hunger was thought to be close to a *billion*. Clearly, restrictions in diet that bring about hunger on such a massive scale affect millions of children born to women living in those conditions (United Nations, 1994).

Fortunately, there are ways to counteract the types of maternal malnourishment that affect prenatal development. Dietary supplements given to mothers can reverse some of the problems produced by a poor diet (Crosby, 1991; Prentice, 1991). Furthermore, research shows that babies who were malnourished as fetuses, but who are subsequently raised in enriched environments, can overcome some of the effects of their early malnourishment (Grantham-McGregor et al., 1994). However, the reality is that few of the world's children whose mothers were malnourished *before* their birth are apt to find themselves in enriched environments after birth (Garber, 1981; Zeskind & Ramey, 1981; Ricciuti, 1993).

Mothers' Age.   With a great deal of medical help from her physicians, Rosanna Della Corta, a 62-year-old woman in Italy, gave birth in 1994. At the time, she was the oldest woman ever known to have become a mother. Most of the media attention, which was substantial, focused on the potential psychological difficulties for a child whose mother would be so atypically old.

However, the mother's advanced age probably had an impact on physical aspects of her pregnancy and birth, as well as potentially on her child's future development. Specifically, research shows that mothers who give birth when over the age of 30 are at greater risk for a variety of pregnancy and birth complications than are younger ones. For instance, they are more apt to give birth prematurely, and their children are more likely to have low birth weights (Berkowitz, Skovron, Lapinski, & Berkowitz, 1990; Cnattingius, Berendes, & Forman, 1993; Vercellini et al., 1993).

Furthermore, older mothers are considerably more likely to give birth to children with Down syndrome, a form of mental retardation. For mothers over 40, the incidence of Down syndrome is one percent; for mothers over 50, the incidence increases to 25 percent (Gaulden, 1992).

The risks involved in pregnancy are greater not only for unusually old mothers but also for atypically young women. Women who become pregnant during adolescence—and such pregnancies actually encompass 20 percent of all pregnancies—are more likely to have premature deliveries. Furthermore, the mortality rate of infants born to adolescent mothers is double that for mothers in their 20s. Keep in mind, though, that the higher mortality rate for younger pregnancies may reflect more than just physiological problems related to the mothers' young age. The heightened mortality rate is also a consequence of adverse social and economic factors, which may have set the stage for the adolescent to become pregnant in the first place.

Mothers' Illness.   Depending on when it strikes, an illness in a pregnant woman can have devastating consequences. For instance, the onset of *rubella* (German measles) in the mother prior to the 11th week of pregnancy is likely to cause serious consequences in the baby, including blindness, deafness, heart defects, or brain damage. In later stages of a pregnancy, however, adverse consequences of rubella become increasingly less likely.

Several other diseases may affect a developing fetus, again depending on when the illness is contracted. For instance, *chicken pox* may produce birth defects, whereas *mumps* may increase the risk of miscarriage.

Some sexually transmitted diseases such as *syphilis* can be transmitted directly to the fetus, who will be born suffering from the disease. In some cases, sexually transmitted diseases such as *gonorrhea* are communicated to the child as it passes through the birth canal to be born.

The newest, and probably the deadliest, of the diseases to affect a newborn is *AIDS (acquired immune deficiency syndrome)*. Mothers who have the disease or who merely are carriers of the virus may pass it on to their fetuses through the blood that reaches the placenta. If the fetuses contract the disease—and some 30 percent of infants born to mothers with AIDS are born with the virus—they face a devastating path. Many have birth abnormalities, including small, misshapen faces, protruding lips, and brain deterioration. Ninety percent experience neurological symptoms exemplified by intellectual delays and deficits, and loss of motor coordination, facial expressions, and speech. Because AIDS causes a breakdown of the immune system, these babies are extremely susceptible to infection. The long-term prognosis for infants born with AIDS is grim: Although drugs such as AZT may stave off the symptoms of the disease, survival beyond infancy is unusual (Brouwers et al., 1990; Nyhan, 1990; Chin, 1994; Frenkel & Gaur, 1994; HMHL, 1994).

Mother's Drug Use.   A mother's use of many kinds of drugs—both legal and illegal—poses serious risks to the unborn child. Even over-the-counter remedies for common ailments can have surprisingly injurious consequences. For instance, aspirin taken for a headache can lead to bleeding in the fetus. Moreover, impairments in the physical development of four-year-olds have been linked to the frequent use of aspirin during pregnancy (Barr, Streissguth, Darby, & Sampson, 1990).

Even drugs prescribed by medical professionals have sometimes proven to have disastrous consequences. In the 1950s, many women who were told to take *thalidomide* for morning sickness during their pregnancies gave birth to children with stumps instead of arms and legs. Although unknown to the physicians who prescribed the drug, thalidomide inhibited the growth of limbs that normally would have occurred during the first three months of pregnancy.

Some drugs taken by mothers cause difficulties in their children literally decades after they were taken. As recently as the 1970s, the artificial hormone *DES (diethylstilbestrol)* was frequently prescribed to prevent miscarriage. Only later was it found that the daughters of mothers who took DES stood a much higher than normal chance of developing a rare form of vaginal or cervical cancer, and they had more difficulties during their pregnancies (Herbst, 1981). Sons of mothers who had taken DES had their own problems, including a higher than average rate of reproductive difficulties (Herbst, 1981).

Illicit drugs may pose equally great, and sometimes even greater, risks for the environments of prenatal children. For one thing, the purity of drugs purchased illegally varies significantly, so drug users can never be quite sure what specifically they are ingesting. Furthermore, the effects of some commonly used illicit drugs can be particularly devastating.

Consider, for instance, the use of *marijuana*. Certainly one of the most commonly used illegal drugs—millions of people in the United States have admitted trying it—marijuana used during pregnancy can restrict the oxygen that reaches the fetus. Its use can lead to infants who are irritable, nervous, and easily disturbed (Feng, 1993).

During the early 1990s, *cocaine* use by pregnant women led to an epidemic of thousands of so-called crack babies. Some estimates put the incidence of children born to mothers who have used cocaine during pregnancy at one in fifty (Julien, 1992; Sturner, et al., 1991).

Cocaine produces an intense restriction of the arteries leading to the fetus, causing a significant reduction in the flow of blood and oxygen. This process increases the risks of fetal death. At birth, children whose mothers were addicted to cocaine may themselves be addicted to the drug and may have to suffer through the agonies of withdrawal. Even if not addicted, they may be born with significant problems. They are often shorter and weigh less than average, and they may have serious respiratory problems, visible birth defects, or seizures. They behave quite differently from other infants: Their reactions to stimulation are muted, but once they start to cry, it may be nearly impossible to soothe them (Chasnoff, Hunt, & Kaplan, 1989; Julien, 1992; Alessandri, Sullivan, Imaizumi, & Lewis, 1993; Gottwald & Thurman, 1994; Lewis & Bendersky, 1995).

It is difficult to focus on the long-term effects of mothers' cocaine use in isolation, because such drug use is often accompanied by poor nurturing following birth (Richardson & Day, 1994; Myers et al., 1992). However, results of studies of crack babies who are just now entering school are discouraging. These children seem to have difficulty dealing with multiple stimuli and forming close attachments to others (Rist, 1990; Azuma & Chasnoff, 1993; Lewis & Bendersky, 1995).

Alcohol and Tobacco Use by Mothers.   A pregnant woman who reasons that having a drink every once in a while or smoking an occasional cigarette has no appreciable effect on her unborn child is, in all likelihood, kidding herself: Increasing evidence suggests that even small amounts of alcohol and nicotine can disrupt the development of the fetus.

Mothers' use of alcohol can have profound consequences for the unborn child. For instance, studies have found that maternal consumption of an average of just two alcoholic drinks a day during pregnancy is associated with lower intelligence in their offspring at age seven. Other research concurs, suggesting that relatively small quantities of alcohol taken during pregnancy can have future adverse effects on children's behavior and psychological functioning (Streissguth, Barr, & Sampson, 1990; Barr, Konner, Bakeman, & Adamson, 1991; Shriver & Piersel, 1994).

The children of alcoholics, whose mothers consume substantial quantities of alcohol during pregnancy, are at an even greater risk. Approximately one out of every 750 infants is born with **fetal alcohol syndrome (FAS)**, a disorder that may include below-average intelligence and sometimes mental retardation, delayed growth, and facial deformities. Today, FAS is the primary cause of mental retardation with a known cause (Able & Sokol, 1987; Streissguth et al., 1990; Feng, 1993).

Because of the risks associated with alcohol, physicians today counsel pregnant women (and even those who are trying to become pregnant) to avoid drinking any alcoholic beverages. In addition, they caution against another practice proven to have an adverse effect on an unborn child: smoking.

Smoking produces several consequences, none good. For starters, smoking reduces the oxygen content and increases the carbon monoxide of the mother's blood, which quickly reduces the oxygen available to the fetus. In addition, the nicotine and other toxins in cigarettes slow the respiration rate of the fetus and speed up its heart.

The ultimate result is an increased possibility of miscarriage and a higher likelihood of death during infancy. In fact, recent estimates suggest that smoking by pregnant women leads to the 115,000 miscarriages and the deaths of 5,600 babies in the United States alone each year (Feng, 1993; DiFranza & Lew, 1995).

Smokers are two times as likely as nonsmokers to have babies with an abnormally low birth weight, and babies born to smokers tend to be shorter, on average, than those of nonsmokers. Some studies have even found that both language and intellectual development are delayed in children of mothers who smoked during pregnancy (Lefkowitz, 1981; Fried & Watkinson, 1990).

Do Fathers Affect the Prenatal Environment?   It would be easy to reason that once the father has done his part in the sequence of events leading to fertilization, he would have no role in the *prenatal* environment of the fetus. In fact, developmentalists have in the past generally shared this view, and there is little research investigating fathers' influence on the prenatal environment.

However, it is becoming increasingly clear that fathers also play a role in affecting the prenatal environment. For instance, the second-hand smoke from the cigarettes of fathers can affect both the mother and the unborn child. One study found that the greater the level of the father's smoking, the less the child weighed at birth (Lester & Van Theil, 1977; Rubin et al., 1986). Similarly, there are some associations between the development of certain kinds of tumors in a child and the nature of a father's occupation, although the explanation for the relationship is far from clear. Still, it does appear that fathers, and probably other family members as well, have an impact on the prenatal environment (Campbell, Poland, Waller & Ager, 1992).

fetal alcohol syndrome (FAS)   *a disorder caused by the pregnant mother consuming substantial quantities of alcohol during pregnancy, potentially resulting in mental retardation and delayed growth in the child*

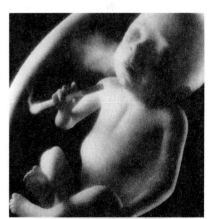

As this advertisement points out, smoking during pregnancy presents several significant risks to the unborn child.

The Informed Consumer of Development

Optimizing the Prenatal Environment

If you are contemplating ever having a child, by this point in the chapter you may be over-whelmed by the number of things that can go wrong. Don't be. Although the environment and genetics pose their share of risks, in the vast majority of cases, pregnancy and birth pro-ceed without mishap. Moreover, there are several things that women can do to optimize the probability that pregnancy will progress smoothly—both before and during pregnancy. Among them:

- For women who are planning to become pregnant, several precautions are in order. First, women should have nonemergency X-rays only during the first two weeks after their menstrual periods. Second, women should be vaccinated against rubella (German measles) at least three, and preferably six, months before getting pregnant. Finally, women who are planning to become pregnant should avoid the use of birth control pills at least three months before trying to conceive, because of disruptions to hor-monal production caused by the pills.

- Eat well, both before and during (and after, for that matter!) pregnancy. Pregnant mothers are, as the old saying goes, eating for two. This means that it is more essential than ever to eat regular, well-balanced meals.

- Do not use alcohol and other drugs. The evidence is clear that many drugs pass directly to the fetus and may cause birth defects. It is also clear that the more one drinks, the greater the risk to the fetus. The best advice: Do not use *any* drug unless directed by a physician.

- Monitor caffeine intake. Although it is still unclear whether caffeine produces birth defects, it is known that the caffeine found in coffee, tea, and chocolate can pass to the fetus, acting as a stimulant. Because of this, you probably should not drink more than a few cups of coffee a day.

- Whether pregnant or not, don't smoke. This holds true for mothers, fathers, and any-one else in the vicinity of the pregnant mother; research suggests that smoke in the fetal environment can affect birth weight.

- Exercise regularly. In most cases, women can maintain their customary exercise level. According to a 1994 advisory from the American College of Obstetricians and Gynecologists, "There are no data in humans to indicate that pregnant women should limit exercise intensity and lower target heart rates because of potential adverse effects" (ACOG, 1994). On the other hand, extreme exercise should be avoided, especially on very hot or very cold days. "No pain, no gain" isn't applicable during pregnancy (Warrick, 1991; Brody, 1994a).

Review and Rethink

REVIEW

◆ Developmental specialists divide the prenatal period into three stages: germinal, embryonic, and fetal.

◆ The prenatal environment significantly influences the development of the baby. The diet, age, and illnesses of mothers can affect their babies' health and growth.

◆ Mothers who use drugs, alcohol, and tobacco can adversely affect the health and development of the unborn child. Fathers' and others' behaviors (e.g., smoking) can also affect the health of the unborn child.

◆ The vast majority of pregnancies and births proceed without mishap, and pregnant mothers can take positive steps to optimize their babies' chances for normal, healthy development.

RETHINK

◆ Based on your knowledge of prenatal development, do you think there is any truth in the opinion that pregnant women should avoid anger in order to spare their children from entering the world angry? Why or why not?

◆ Studies show that crack babies who are now entering school have significant difficulty dealing with multiple stimuli and forming close attachments. How might both genetic and environmental influences have combined to produce these results?

◆ In addition to avoiding smoking, do you think there are other steps fathers might take to help their unborn children develop normally in the womb? What are they and how might they affect the environment of the unborn child?

◆ Based on your knowledge of environmental influences on unborn children, what are some steps parents can take to give the fetus a healthy prenatal environment?

LOOKING BACK

What is our basic genetic endowment, and how do we receive it from our parents?

1. In humans, the adult female and male sex cells, or gametes, contain 23 chromosomes each. At fertilization, ovum and sperm unite to form a single new cell, called a zygote, in the female's uterus. The zygote receives a total of 46 chromosomes from its parents. Within the 46 chromosomes is the genetic blueprint—carried in some 100,000 genes— that will guide cell activity for the rest of the individual's life.

2. Gregor Mendel discovered an important genetic mechanism. In alleles, where two competing traits are present but only one can be expressed, the offspring may receive either similar or dissimilar genes from each parent. If the offspring receives dissimilar genes (one dominant and one recessive), the dominant gene will be expressed. If the offspring receives similar genes (two dominant or two recessive genes), that gene will be

expressed. Traits such as hair and eye color and the presence of phenylketonuria (PKU) are alleles and follow this pattern, but relatively few inherited traits are governed by a single pair of genes in this way.

How can human development go wrong, and what can be done to prevent or remedy genetic problems?

3. Genes may become physically damaged due to wear-and-tear, environmental factors such as exposure to X-rays, or chance events during cell division. Sometimes genes spontaneously mutate, for no known reason. If damaged genes are passed on to the child, the result can be a genetic disorder such as Down syndrome, sickle-cell anemia, Tay-Sachs disease, and Klinefelter's syndrome.

4. Behavioral genetics studies the genetic basis of human behavior. It focuses on personality characteristics and behaviors, as well as certain psychological disorders such as schizophrenia.

5. The study of genetic factors in behavior is leading to important discoveries relating to the minute workings of genetics at the molecular and chemical levels. The future promise is that researchers will learn how to remedy certain genetic defects.

6. Genetic counselors use data from many sources to identify potential genetic abnormalities in women and men who plan to have children. Tests can also be performed on already developing fetuses, including amniocentesis, chorionic villus sampling (CVS), and ultrasound sonography.

7. Recently, genetic counselors have begun testing individuals for genetically based disorders that may eventually appear in the individuals themselves, rather than in their children. Ethical and practical issues relating to this sort of genetic counseling are complex and are still being worked out.

8. Infertility, the inability to conceive after 12 to 18 months of trying to become pregnant occurs in some 15 percent of couples. Among the treatments are the use of drugs, surgery, artificial insemination, in vitro fertilization, and the use of surrogate mothers.

How do the environment and genetics work together to determine human characteristics?

9. Behavioral characteristics are often determined by a combination of genetics and environment. Genetically based traits represent a potential, called the genotype, which may be affected by the environment in different ways for different individuals. The actuality that is ultimately expressed is called the phenotype.

10. A disorder such as schizophrenia provides insight into the ways heredity and environment work together. Genetic factors alone do not produce schizophrenia, but they may produce a sensitivity toward environmental factors, such as stress, that can lead to schizophrenia. Other disorders, including alcoholism and autism, work similarly.

11. To work out the different influences of heredity and environment, researchers use nonhuman studies and human studies, particularly of twins. Identical twins adopted at birth and reared in different environments are especially helpful in such research. Other human studies compare the characteristics of dizygotic and monozygotic twins; the characteristics of unrelated children adopted together into the same environment; and the characteristics shared by adoptive parents and their children versus those shared by biological parents and their children.

Which human characteristics are significantly influenced by heredity?

12. The most important research finding is that virtually all human traits, characteristics, and behaviors are the result of the combination and interaction of nature and nurture.

13. Many physical characteristics, including height, obesity, blood pressure, respiration rate, and life span, show strong genetic influences.

14. Intelligence contains a strong genetic component, but it can be significantly influenced by environmental factors.

15. Some personality traits, including neuroticism and extroversion, have been linked to genetic factors. Other aspects of personality, such as attitudes, values, and interests, also seem to have a genetic component. Some personal behaviors, such as preferences for leisure activities, may be genetically influenced through the mediation of inherited personality traits.

16. There has been some speculation that entire cultures may show a genetic predisposition toward one set of beliefs and values—one philosophy—over a different one.

What happens during the prenatal stages of development?

17. The germinal stage (fertilization to two weeks) is marked by rapid cell division and specialization, and the attachment of the zygote to the wall of the uterus. During the embryonic stage (two to eight weeks), three layers begin to grow and specialize. The ectoderm forms skin, hair, teeth, sense organs, and the brain and spinal cord. The mesoderm forms muscles, blood, and the circulatory system. The endoderm produces the digestive system, liver, pancreas, and respiratory system.

18. The fetal stage (eight weeks to birth) is characterized by a rapid increase in complexity and differentiation of the organs. The fetus becomes active and most of its systems operational. Even at the fetal stage, genetic differences produce differences in behavior.

What threats are there to the fetal environment and what can be done about them?

19. Characteristics and behaviors of the mother have the most direct influence on prenatal development. Factors in the mother that may affect the unborn child include diet, age, illnesses, and drug, alcohol, and tobacco use. The behaviors of fathers and others in the environment may also affect the health and development of the unborn child.

20. Pregnant women can give their unborn children the best chance of a healthy development by eating well; avoiding alcohol, unprescribed drugs, and smoking; limiting caffeine intake; and exercising regularly.

KEY TERMS AND CONCEPTS

gametes (p. 42)
fertilization (p. 42)
zygote (p. 42)
genes (p. 43)
chromosomes (p. 43)
monozygotic twins (p. 44)
dizygotic twins (p. 44)
genotype (p. 47)
phenotype (p. 47)
polygenic inheritance (p. 49)
behavioral genetics (p. 50)
Down syndrome (p. 50)
sickle-cell anemia (p. 50)
Tay-Sachs disease (p. 51)
Klinefelter's syndrome (p. 51)
temperament (p. 51)

multifactorial transmission (p. 51)
genetic counseling (p. 52)
amniocentesis (p. 53)
chorionic villus sampling (CVS) (p. 53)
ultrasound sonography (p. 53)
infertility (p. 54)
artificial insemination (p. 54)
in vitro fertilization (IVF) (p. 55)
active genotype-environment effects (p. 65)
passive genotype-environment effects (p. 65)
evocative genotype-environment effects (p. 65)
germinal stage (p. 67)
embryonic stage (p. 67)
fetal stage (p. 68)
teratogen (p. 69)
fetal alcohol syndrome (FAS) (p. 73)

Birth
and the Newborn Infant

CHAPTER OUTLINE

PROLOGUE: LABOR OF LOVE

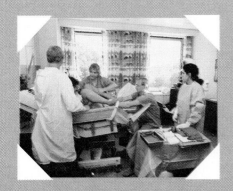

After carefully researching different techniques for childbirth, Anitra Ellis and her husband, Corelyou, picked a local family birthing center for the delivery of their twins. When Anitra went into labor, the Ellises drove the 15 miles to the Gentle Birth Center Medical Group, where four midwives were available to assist.

Labor was an active process for Anitra. Standing the entire time, she walked around and talked with her husband. She was encouraged to eat and drink whenever she wanted, and she was given a massage when her back started to feel sore.

Labor lasted some 18 hours, and the delivery was smooth. Corelyou Hayes Ellis IV was born first, followed by his sister, Erynn Emon Ellis. Just five hours after the birth, the whole family was at home, and Anitra and Corelyou were resting comfortably. As her parents watched, Erynn, the smaller of the two babies, used her arm to push herself over.

The experience of giving birth was likely very different for Anitra Ellis's mother. For her, the process probably began when she was wheeled into a hospital room crowded with women in various stages of labor. No husbands or other family members could be present, and standard operating procedure was to administer a strong dose of general anesthetic. Because of the drug, the mother was completely unaware of being taken to the delivery room and giving birth. The first time she saw her newborn, it was already several hours old and still groggy from the drugs administered to its mother. (Knight, 1994)

LOOKING AHEAD

Despite variations in the processes of labor and delivery for Anitra and her mother, the birth undoubtedly brought equal joy to the parents. The entry into this world of a newborn, who so readily triggers the hopes, aspirations, and unconditional love of its parents, is a remarkable event.

Yet the excitement and wonder of the moment of birth is far overshadowed by the extraordinary nature of the newborn itself. It enters the world with a surprising array of capabilities, ready from the first moments of life outside the womb to respond to the world and the people in it.

This chapter will both examine the events leading to the delivery and birth of a child and take an initial look at the newborn. We first consider labor and delivery, exploring how the process proceeds as well as several alternative approaches.

We next examine some of the possible complications of birth. Although most births progress without a hitch, we investigate the problems that sometimes occur, ranging from premature births to infant mortality.

Finally, we investigate the extraordinary range of capabilities of newborns. We'll look not only at their physical and perceptual abilities but also at the way they enter the world with skills that help form the foundations of their future relationships with others.

In sum, after reading this chapter, you will be able to answer these questions:

♦ What is the normal process of labor?

♦ What happens immediately after the baby is born?

♦ What choices do parents have regarding the birthing process?

♦ What complications can occur at birth and what are their causes, effects, and treatments?

♦ What capabilities does the newborn have?

BIRTH

neonate   *the term used for newborns*

Her head was cone-shaped at the top. Although I knew this was due to the normal movement of the head bones as she came through the birth canal and that this would change in a few days, I was still startled. She also had some blood on the top of her head and was damp, a result of the amniotic fluid in which she had spent the last nine months. There was some white, cheesy substance over her body, which the nurse wiped off just before she placed her in my arms. I could see a bit of downy hair on her ears, but I knew this, too, would disappear before long. Her nose looked a little as if she had been on the losing end of a fistfight: It was squashed into her face, flattened by its trip through the birth canal. But as she seemed to fix her eyes on me and grasped my finger, it was clear that she was nothing short of perfect. (Adapted from Brazelton, 1969)

For those of us accustomed to thinking of newborns in the images of baby food commercials, this portrait of a typical newborn may be surprising. Yet most **neonates**—the term used for newborns—are born resembling this one. Make no mistake, however: Despite their temporary blemishes, babies are a welcome sight to their parents from the moment of their birth.

The neonate's outward appearance is caused by a variety of factors in its journey from the mother's uterus, down the birth canal, and out into the world. We can trace its passage, beginning with the release of the chemicals that initiate the process of labor.

LABOR: THE PROCESS OF BIRTH BEGINS

For the average mother, about 266 days after conception, an as-yet-unidentified factor triggers the process that leads to birth. At that point, the hormone *oxytocin* is released by the mother's pituitary gland. When the concentration of oxytocin becomes high enough, the uterus begins periodic contractions.

During the prenatal period, the uterus, which is composed of muscle tissue, slowly expands as the fetus grows. Although for most of the pregnancy it is inactive, after the fourth

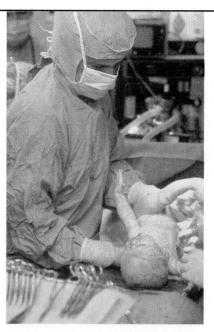

The image of newborns portrayed in commercials differs dramatically from reality.

month it occasionally contracts in order to ready itself for the eventual delivery. These contractions, called *Braxton-Hicks contractions*, are sometimes termed "false labor" owing to the fact that they do not necessarily signify that the baby will be born soon.

When birth is actually imminent, the uterus begins to contract intermittently. Its increasingly intense contractions act as if it were a vise, opening and closing to force the head of the fetus against the *cervix*, the neck of the uterus that separates it from the vagina. Eventually, the force of the contractions becomes strong enough to propel the fetus slowly down the birth canal until it enters the world as a newborn (Mittendorf, Williams, Berkey, & Cotter, 1990).

Labor proceeds in three stages (see Figure 3-1). In the *first stage of labor*, the uterine contractions initially occur about every 8 to 10 minutes and last about 30 seconds. As labor proceeds, the contractions occur more frequently and last longer. Toward the end of labor, the contractions may occur every 2 minutes and last almost 2 minutes. As the contractions increase in intensity, the mother's cervix becomes wider, eventually expanding enough to allow the baby's head (the widest part of the body) to pass through.

This first stage of labor is the longest. Its duration varies significantly, depending on the mother's age, race, ethnicity, and number of prior pregnancies, and a variety of other factors involving both the fetus and the mother. Typically, labor takes sixteen to 24 hours for firstborn children, but there are wide variations. Births of subsequent children usually involve shorter periods of labor.

During the *second stage of labor*, the baby's head starts to move through the cervix and birth canal. During this stage, which typically lasts about 90 minutes, the baby's head emerges more with each contraction, increasing the size of the vaginal opening. Because the area between the vagina and rectum must stretch a good deal, an incision called an *episiotomy* is sometimes made to increase the size of the opening of the vagina. However, this practice has been increasingly criticized in recent years as potentially causing more harm than good, and in developed areas of the world other than the United States episiotomies are uncommon (Klein et al., 1994).

FIGURE 3-1

THE THREE STAGES OF LABOR

Stage 1

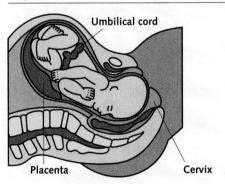

Uterine contractions initially occur every 8 to 10 minutes and last 30 seconds. Toward the end of labor, contractions may occur every 2 minutes and last as long as 2 minutes. As the contractions increase, the cervix, which separates the uterus from the vagina, becomes wider, eventually expanding to allow the baby's head to pass through.

Stage 2

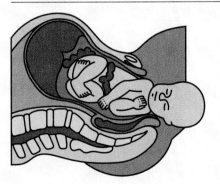

The baby's head starts to move through the cervix and birth canal. Typically lasting around 90 minutes, the second stage ends when the baby has completely left the mother's body.

Stage3

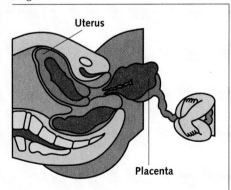

The child's umbilical cord (still attached to the neonate) and the placenta are expelled from the mother. This stage is the quickest and easiest, taking just a few minutes.

The second stage of labor ends when the baby has completely left the mother's body. Finally, the *third stage of labor* occurs when the child's umbilical cord (still attached to the neonate) and the placenta are expelled from the mother. This stage is the quickest and easiest, taking just a few minutes.

The nature of a woman's reactions to labor reflect, in part, cultural factors. Although there is no evidence that the physiological aspects of labor differ among women of different cultures, expectations about labor and interpretations of its pain do vary significantly from one culture to another.

For instance, there is a kernel of truth to popular stories of pregnant women in certain societies putting down the tools with which they are tilling their fields, stepping aside and giving birth, and immediately returning to work with their neonates wrapped and bundled on their backs. Accounts of the !Kung people in Africa describe the woman in labor sitting calmly beside a tree and without much ado—or assistance—successfully giving birth to a child and quickly recovering. On the other hand, many societies regard childbirth as dangerous, and some even view it in terms befitting an illness. Such cultural perspectives color the way that people in a given society view the experience of childbirth (Shostak, 1981; Chalmers, Enkin, & Keirse, 1989; Cole, 1992).

BIRTH: FROM FETUS TO NEONATE

The exact moment of birth occurs when the fetus, having left the uterus through the cervix, passes through the vagina to emerge fully from its mother's body. In most cases, babies automatically make the transition from taking in oxygen via the placenta to using their lungs to breathe air. Consequently, as soon as they are outside the mother's body, most newborns spontaneously cry. This helps them to clear their lungs and to breathe on their own.

What happens next varies from situation to situation and from culture to culture. In Western cultures, health care workers are almost always on hand to assist with the birth. In the United States, 99 percent of births are attended by professional health care workers, but worldwide only about 50 percent of births have professionals in attendance (United Nations, 1990).

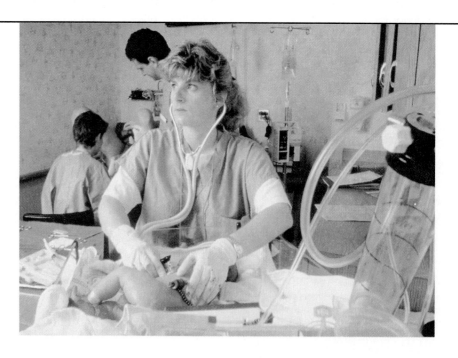

The Apgar scale is used at birth to measure several indications of good health.

The Apgar Scale. In most cases, the newborn infant first undergoes a quick visual inspection. Parents may be counting fingers and toes, but trained health care workers look for something more. Typically, they employ the **Apgar scale**, a standard measurement system that looks for a variety of indications of good health (see Table 3-1). Developed by physician Virginia Apgar in 1953, the scale directs attention to five basic qualities, recalled most easily by using Apgar's name as a guide: *a*ppearance (color), *p*ulse (heart rate), *g*rimace (reflex irritability), *a*ctivity (muscle tone), and *r*espiration (respiratory effort).

Using the scale, health care workers assign the neonate a score ranging from 0 to 2 on each of the five qualities, producing an overall score that can range from 0 to 10. The vast majority of children score 7 or above. The ten percent of neonates who score under 7 require help to start breathing. Newborns who score under 4 need immediate, life-saving intervention. Scores that remain between 0 and 3 after 20 minutes indicate that severe problems are likely to be present. On the other hand, most of the components of the Apgar score are based on subjective factors, and parents sometimes place too much emphasis on the specific score (Jepson, Talashek, & Tichy, 1991).

Although low Apgar scores may indicate problems or birth defects that were already present in the fetus, the process of birth itself may sometimes cause difficulties. Among the most profound are those relating to a temporary deprivation of oxygen.

At various junctures during labor, the fetus may not get sufficient oxygen for any of a number of reasons. For instance, the umbilical cord may become pinched during a prolonged contraction, thereby cutting off the supply of oxygen to the fetus. The cord may also get wrapped around the neck of the fetus or another part of its body, or an unusual positioning of the fetus within the birth canal may cause the cord to be restricted. It is even possible that the stresses of traveling through the birth canal may cause the baby to grasp the umbilical cord and squeeze it (Bornstein & Lamb, 1992).

Lack of oxygen for a few seconds is not particularly harmful to the fetus, but deprivation for any longer time may cause serious harm. A restriction of oxygen, or *anoxia*, lasting a few minutes can produce brain damage as unoxygenated brain cells, which never can regenerate, die. Furthermore, anoxia can lead to such an increase in blood pressure that bleeding occurs in the brain.

Physical Appearance and Initial Encounters. After assessing the newborn's health, health care workers next deal with the remnants of the child's passage through the birth canal. Recall the description of the thick, greasy substance that covers the newborn. This material, called *vernix*, smoothes the passage through the birth canal; it is no longer needed once the child is born and is quickly cleaned away. Newborns' bodies are also covered with a fine, dark fuzz

Apgar scale a standard measurement system that looks for a variety of indications of good health in newborns

TABLE 3-1

APGAR SCALE

Sign*	0	1	2
Appearance (color)	Blue, pale	Body pink, extremities blue	Entirely pink
Pulse (heart rate)	Absent	Slow (below 100)	Rapid (over 100)
Grimace (reflex irritability)	No response	Grimace	Coughing, sneezing, crying
Activity (muscle tone)	Limp	Weak, inactive	Strong, active
Respiration (breathing)	Absent	Irregular, slow	Good, crying

*Each sign is rated in terms of absence or presence from 0 to 2; highest overall score is 10.
(*Source*: Adapted from Apgar, 1953.)

bonding *close physical and emotional contact between parent and child during the period immediately following birth, argued by some to affect later relationship strength*

known as *lanugo*; this soon disappears. The newborn's eyelids may be puffy owing to an accumulation of fluids during labor, and it may have other blood or fluids on parts of its body.

After cleansing, the newborn is usually returned to the mother and to the father, if he is present. The everyday and universal occurrence of childbirth makes it no less miraculous to parents, and most cherish this time to make their first acquaintance with their child.

However, the importance of the initial encounter between parent and child has become a matter of considerable controversy. Some psychologists and physicians argued in the 1970s and early 1980s that **bonding**, the close physical and emotional contact between parent and child during the period immediately following birth, was a crucial ingredient for forming a lasting relationship between parent and child. Their arguments were based in part on research conducted on nonhuman species such as ducklings. This work showed that there was a critical period just after birth when organisms exhibited a particular readiness to learn, or *imprint*, from other members of their species who happened to be present (Lorenz, 1957).

According to the concept of bonding applied to humans, a critical period begins just after birth and lasts only a few hours. During this period actual skin-to-skin contact between mother and child supposedly leads to deep, emotional bonding (Klaus & Kennell, 1976; deChateau, 1980). The corollary to this assumption is that if circumstances prevent such contact, the bond between mother and child will forever be lacking in some way. Because medical practices prevalent at the time often left little opportunity for sustained mother and child physical contact immediately after birth, the suggestion was received with alarm. The idea was taken seriously and generated a substantial amount of public attention (Eyer, 1992).

There was just one problem: Scientific evidence for the notion was lacking. When developmentalists carefully reviewed the research literature, they found little support for the idea. Although it does appear that mothers who have early physical contact with their babies are more responsive to them than those who do not have such contact, the difference lasts only a few days. Furthermore, there are no lingering reactions to separations immediately following birth, even separations of several days. Such news is reassuring to parents whose children must receive immediate, intensive medical attention just after birth, as well as to parents who adopt children and are not present at all at their births (M. Lamb, 1982a; Goldberg, 1983; Myers, 1987; Eyer, 1994).

APPROACHES TO CHILDBIRTH: WHERE MEDICINE AND ATTITUDES MEET

> Ester Iverem knew herself well enough to know that she didn't like the interaction she had with medical doctors. So she opted for a nurse-midwife at Manhattan's Maternity Center where she was free to use a birthing stool and to have her husband, Nick Chiles, by her side. When contractions began, Iverem and Chiles went for a walk, stopping periodically to rock—a motion, she says, "similar to the way children dance when they first learn how, shifting from foot to foot." That helped her work through the really powerful contractions.
>
> "I sat on the birthing chair [a Western version of the traditional African stool, which lies low to the ground and has an opening in the middle for the baby to come through] and Nick was sitting right behind me. When the midwife said 'Push!' the baby's head just went 'pop!,' and out he came." Their son, Mazi (which means "Sir" in Ibo) Iverem Chiles, was placed on Ester's breast while the midwives went to prepare for his routine examination. (Knight, 1994, p. 122)

For something as natural as giving birth, which occurs throughout the nonhuman animal world apparently without much thought, parents in the Western world have developed a variety of strategies—and some very strong opinions. Should the birth take place in a hospital or in the home? Should a physician, a nurse, or a midwife assist? Is the father's presence desirable? Should siblings and other family members be on hand to participate in the birth?

Most of these questions cannot be answered definitively, primarily because the choice of childbirth techniques often comes down to a matter of values and opinions. No single procedure will be effective for all mothers and fathers, and no conclusive research evidence has proven that one procedure is significantly more effective than another.

The abundance of choices is largely due to a reaction to traditional medical practices that had been prevalent in the United States until the early 1970s. Before that time, the typical procedure went something like this: A woman in labor was placed in a room with many other women, all of whom were in various stages of childbirth, and some of whom were screaming in pain. Fathers and other family members were not allowed to be present. The mother's pubic hair was shaved, and she was given an enema. Just before delivery, she was rolled into a delivery room, where the birth took place. Often the woman was so drugged that she was not aware of the birth at all.

Physicians argued that such procedures were necessary to ensure the health of the newborn and the mother. However, critics charged that alternatives were available that not only would maximize the medical well-being of the participants in the birth but would also represent an emotional and psychological improvement (Pascoe, 1993).

Pain and Childbirth.   Any woman who has delivered a baby will agree that childbirth is painful. But how painful, exactly, is it?

Such a question is largely unanswerable. One reason is that pain is a subjective, psychological phenomenon, one that cannot be easily measured. No one is able to answer the question of whether their pain is "greater" or "worse" than someone else's pain, although some studies have tried to quantify it. For instance, in one survey women were asked to rate the pain they experienced during labor on a 1-to-5 scale, with 5 being the most painful (Yarrow, 1992). Nearly half (44 percent) said "5," and an additional one-quarter said "4."

Furthermore, because pain is usually a sign that something is wrong in one's body, we have learned to react to pain with fear and concern. Yet during childbirth, pain is actually a signal that the body is working appropriately—that the contractions that are meant to propel the baby through the birth canal are doing their job. Consequently, the experience of pain during labor is difficult for women in labor to interpret, thereby potentially increasing their anxiety and making the contractions seem even more painful.

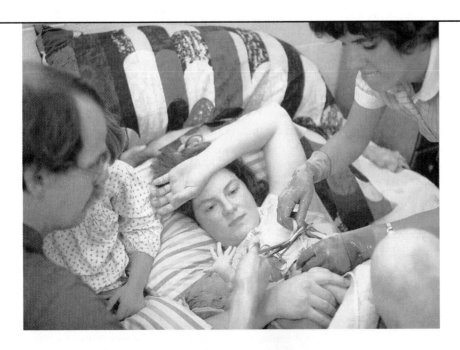

A midwife helps in this home delivery.

Ultimately, the nature of every woman's delivery depends on a complex series of factors. They encompass such variables as how much preparation and support she has before and during delivery, her culture's view of pregnancy and delivery, and the specific nature of the delivery itself (Seibel & McCarthy, 1993; Davis-Floyd, 1994).

Use of Anesthesia and Pain-reducing Drugs.   Among the greatest advances of modern medicine is the ongoing discovery of drugs that reduce pain. However, the use of medication during childbirth is a practice that has both benefits and pitfalls.

It is clear that drugs hold the promise of greatly reducing, and even eliminating, pain associated with labor, which can be extreme. However, pain reduction comes at a cost: The stronger the drug, the greater its effects on the fetus and neonate. The reason is pharmacologically simple: Drugs administered during labor reach not just the mother but the fetus as well. Because of the small size of the fetus relative to the mother, drug doses that might have only a minimal effect on the mother can have a magnified effect on the fetus.

Many studies have demonstrated the results of the use of anesthesia during delivery. Some consequences are immediate: Anesthetics may temporarily depress the flow of oxygen to the fetus and slow labor (Brackbill, 1979; Hollenbeck, Gewirtz, Sebris, & Scanlon, 1984; Thorpe et al., 1993). In addition, neonates whose mothers have been anesthetized are less physiologically responsive and show poorer motor control during the first days of life after birth. And the effects may be lasting: Research shows that during the course of the first year, progress in sitting up, standing, and other physical activities is somewhat slower for children whose mothers received drugs during labor (Brackbill & Broman, 1979; Murray, Dolby, Nation, & Thomas, 1981; Garbaciak, 1990; Douglas, 1991).

The effects of drugs show up in other, less obvious ways. For example, anesthetic use can produce differences in the nature of the interactions between mother and child (Scanlon & Hollenbeck, 1983; Hollenbeck et al., 1984). Even after the physical effects of the drugs have worn off and the infants are behaving in the same way as infants whose mothers did not receive drugs, mothers report feeling differently about their babies. Several reasons account for this difference. It may be that mothers who choose to avoid medication during delivery hold more positive attitudes toward giving birth and toward their babies in the first place. More probably, the presence or absence of drugs in the infants' systems causes behavioral differences in the infants themselves, which in turn elicit differing reactions from their mothers.

On the other hand, not all studies find that the use of drugs during labor invariably affects the neonate negatively. In fact, some researchers argue that drugs, as they are currently employed during labor, produce only minimal risks to the fetus and neonate. For instance, one study found no differences in strength, touch sensitivity, activity level, irritability, and sleep between children whose mothers had been given drugs during labor and those whose mothers had received no drugs (Kraemer et al., 1985).

The wisdom of using drugs to control pain during labor is a difficult issue, pitting legitimate concerns regarding pain control against potential—and in many cases, uncertain—concerns for the neonate. Joint guidelines issued by the American Academy of Pediatrics and the American College of Obstetricians and Gynecologists (AAP/ACOG, 1992) suggest that the proper use of minimal amounts of drugs for pain relief is reasonable and has no significant effect on a child's later well-being. Ultimately, the decision to use or not to use anesthetic drugs must be made by the mother, in conjunction with the father and medical care providers.

Alternative Birthing Procedures.   Possible hazards due to the use of anesthetics during labor, as well as concerns about other traditional birth practices, have led to the development of several alternative strategies designed to minimize the need for anesthetics (M. Smith, 1990; Mathews & Zadak, 1991). Among the major ones:

◆ *Lamaze birthing techniques.* The Lamaze method has achieved widespread popularity in the United States. Based on the writings of Dr. Fernand Lamaze, the method makes use of basic psychological techniques involving relaxation training (Lamaze, 1970). Typically, mothers-to-be undergo a series of weekly training sessions in which they learn exercises that help them relax various parts of the body on command. A "coach," most typically the father, is trained along with the future mother. The training allows women to cope with painful contractions with a relaxation response, rather than by tensing up, which may make the pain more acute. In addition, the women learn to focus on a relaxing stimulus, such as a tranquil scene in a picture. The goal is to learn how to deal positively with pain and to relax at the onset of a contraction.

Does the procedure work? Most mothers, as well as fathers, report that a Lamaze birth is a very positive experience. They enjoy the sense of mastery that they gain over the process of labor, a feeling of control over what can be a formidable experience (Bing, 1983; Wideman & Singer, 1984; Mackey, 1990). On the other hand, we cannot be sure that parents who choose the Lamaze method aren't already more highly motivated about the experience of childbirth than parents who do not choose the technique. It is therefore possible that the accolades they express after Lamaze births are due to their initial enthusiasm, and not to the Lamaze procedures themselves.

Although it is not possible to pinpoint definitively the specific consequences of Lamaze preparation for childbirth, one thing is certain: Participation in Lamaze procedures, as well as other *natural childbirth techniques* in which the emphasis is on educating the parents about the process of birth and minimizing the use of drugs, is relatively rare among members of lower income groups, including many members of ethnic minorities. Parents in these groups may not have transportation, time, or the financial resources to attend childbirth preparation classes. The result is that women in lower income groups tend to be less prepared for the events of labor and consequently may suffer more pain and anguish during childbirth (Ball, 1987).

◆ *The Leboyer method.* Consider the abrupt transition faced by a neonate. Accustomed to floating in a pool of warm water (the amniotic fluid) for nine months, hearing only muffled sounds and seeing light only dimly, the newborn is violently thrust into a very different world outside the mother. How might this transition be facilitated?

According to French physician Frederick Leboyer (pronounced "Leh-boy-AY"), the optimal approach is to maintain the environment of the womb as long as possible

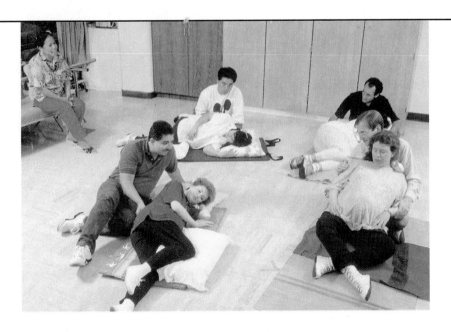

In Lamaze classes, parents are taught relaxation techniques to prepare for childbirth and to reduce the need for anesthetics.

after birth (Leboyer, 1975). Under Leboyer's method, delivery rooms are kept softly lighted and a hushed atmosphere prevails. As soon as the baby is born, it is placed on the mother's stomach and then floated in a pool of warm water. The umbilical cord is not cut immediately after birth, as is traditionally done to compel the baby to breathe on its own. Instead, the cord is left intact, allowing the neonate to acclimate gradually to an air-breathing world.

Although the Leboyer technique gained some popularity in the early 1980s, today only one remnant is seen frequently: Newborns are often placed on the warmth of the mother's stomach just after birth.

♦ *Family birthing centers.* When Jill Rakovich became pregnant for the third time, she and her husband, Milos, decided they wanted to find a less forbidding locale than the traditional delivery room. They had both found this setting uncomfortable and grim when their two older children were born.

After researching the possibilities, Jill discovered a family birthing center located close to a nearby hospital. The center consisted of rooms decorated like homey bedrooms. Unlike the typical forbidding hospital room, these looked warm and inviting, although they also were equipped with several pieces of medical equipment. When labor began, Jill and Milos went to the birthing center and settled into one of the rooms. Labor proceeded smoothly, and, as her husband watched, Jill gave birth to her third child.

Speaking of Development

Kathy McKain

Born: ···························· 1958

Education: ····················· University of Pittsburgh, B.S. in nursing; University of Pennsylvania, M.N.S. (Master of Nursing and Science)

Position: ······················ Coordinator of midwifery for Birthplace–Midwifery Services of Western Pennsylvania Hospital

Home: ························· Pittsburgh, Pennsylvania

One of the most ancient of professions, midwifery, still fills a crucial niche in today's high-tech society, providing an alternative to a traditional in-hospital birth.

For the past six years, Kathy McKain has helped scores of women give birth, as a midwife and as coordinator of midwifery services at a modern urban hospital.

"Our basic idea as we approach the care of a woman and her family is a respect for the fact that this is her body, her pregnancy, and her experience," she explains. "We try hard to make the environment conducive to the family's developmental concerns. For instance, many women who are giving birth already have children, and so we provide a comfortable

The decision to use a birthing center is becoming increasingly common. In the majority of cases labor and delivery are uneventful, permitting births to occur in the relatively relaxed, homelike setting the birthing center provides. Furthermore, in the event of complications, equipment is at hand. Supporters of birthing centers suggest that they provide a more comfortable, less stressful environment than a hospital room, offering a setting that may facilitate labor and delivery (Eakins, 1986).

Because of the popularity of the philosophy behind birthing centers, many hospitals have opened birthing rooms of their own. The increasing prevalence of birthing centers reflects the view that childbirth is a natural part of life that should not be rigidly isolated from its other aspects. Rather than medical events that involve a passive patient and a dictatorial physician, labor and delivery are now typically viewed as participatory experiences involving the mother, the father, other family members, and care providers acting jointly.

This philosophy also has implications for the choice of care provider. In place of a traditional *obstetrician*, a physician who specializes in delivering babies, some parents are turning to a *midwife*, a childbirth attendant who stays with the mother throughout labor and delivery. Midwives—often nurses specializing in childbirth—are used primarily for pregnancies in which no complications are expected. Although the use of midwives is increasing in the United States, they are employed in only a minority of

"Our basic idea as we approach the care of a woman and her family is a respect for the fact that this is her body, her pregnancy, and her experience."

"Our goal is to keep the mother and baby together the entire time. While there could be an exception where the baby needs some separation, we generally see mother and child as a unit."

waiting room and playroom, and we welcome the other children in to participate in their mother's visits. Incorporating family members into the process seems to work well.

"We discuss with the mother the fact that the pregnancy can be a life crisis or a major developmental milestone, rather than just a medical event," says McKain. "Along the way we talk about a lot of things in addition to the physical aspects of birth. We talk about the relationship between the woman and her partner, the planned or unplanned nature of the pregnancy, and the life changes that the pregnancy and the baby will cause. In many birthing processes, the mental side is neglected, but we consider it our responsibility to cover that side, too.

"Our goal is to keep the mother and baby together the entire time. While there could be an exception where the baby needs some separation, we generally see mother and child as a unit. We teach our midwives to deliver the baby right to the mother. They do their cleaning up and assessing of the baby right there, in the mother's arms.

"A great majority of women we see are planning to nurse their babies. We believe the baby is prepared at birth with the sucking and swallowing reflexes, and we capitalize on that fact."

In a typical year Birthplace sees more then 200 births and 450 annual checkups, according to McKain. Stays are generally no longer than four to twelve hours. Birthplace staff make a follow-up home visit with the newborn and mother.

Summing up her practice, McKain says, "There are so many issues that need to be addressed. We feel it is important to deal with the meaning of the birth to the mother."

births (DeClercq, 1992). In contrast, midwives help deliver some 80 percent of babies in other parts of the world. Moreover, in countries at all levels of economic development many births successfully take place at home. For instance, more than a third of all births in the Netherlands occur at home (Treffers, Eskes, Kleiverda, & van Alten, 1990).

What kind of setting and care provider are optimal? In the majority of cases, it does not make a great deal of difference. Naturally, arrangements for care should be made thoughtfully and in advance, and backup medical help should be on call. If a birth is to occur outside a traditional hospital, such a hospital should be no more than five or ten minutes away. Furthermore, for pregnancies that stand a high risk of complications—such as those of women whose previous deliveries have been difficult—a hospital setting is preferable (Rusting, 1990).

The Informed Consumer of Development

Dealing with Labor

Every woman who is soon to give birth has some fear of labor. Most have heard gripping tales of extended 48-hour labors or vivid descriptions of the pain that accompanies labor. Still, few mothers would dispute the notion that the rewards of giving birth are worth the effort. Indeed, polls show that almost two-thirds of women report feeling "very positive" about the births of their children (Yarrow, 1992).

There is no single right or wrong way to deal with labor. However, experts suggest several strategies that can help make the process as positive as possible (Salmon, 1993):

◆ Be flexible. Although you may have carefully worked out beforehand a scenario about what to do during labor, don't feel an obligation to follow through exactly. If a strategy is ineffective, turn to another one.

◆ Communicate with your health care providers. Let them know what you are experiencing. They may be able to suggest ways to deal with what you are encountering. By examining you, they will also be able to explain just what stage of labor you are in.

◆ Remember that labor is . . . laborious. Labor is aptly named: It takes hard work and can be exhausting. Expect that you may become fatigued, but realize that as the final stages of labor occur, you may well get a second wind.

◆ Accept your partner's support. If a spouse or other partner is present, allow that person to make you comfortable and provide support. A partner's encouragement may be critical.

◆ Be realistic and honest about your reactions to pain. Even if you had planned an unmedicated delivery, realize that you may find the pain difficult to tolerate. At that point, consider the use of drugs. Above all, don't feel that asking for pain medication is a sign of failure. It isn't.

◆ Focus on the big picture. Keep in mind that labor is part of a process that ultimately leads to an event unmatched in the joy that it can bring.

Review and Rethink

REVIEW

◆ In the first stage of labor, contractions increase in frequency, duration, and intensity until the baby's head is able to pass through the cervix. In the second stage, the baby moves through the cervix and birth canal and leaves the mother's body. In the third stage, the umbilical cord and placenta emerge.

◆ Immediately after birth, birthing attendants usually examine the neonate using a measurement system such as the Apgar scale.

◆ Many birthing options are available to parents today. They may weigh the advantages and disadvantages of anesthetic drugs during birth, and they may choose alternatives to traditional hospital birthing, including the Lamaze method, the Leboyer method, the use of a birthing center, and the use of a midwife.

RETHINK

◆ Why might cultural differences exist in expectations and interpretations of labor? Do you think such cultural differences are due primarily to physical or psychological factors?

◆ Although 99 percent of U.S. births are attended by professional medical workers or birthing attendants, this is the case in only about 50 percent of births worldwide. What do you think are some causal factors and implications of this statistic?

◆ What arguments have been advanced by those who consider the bonding process— close physical contact between parent and child immediately after birth—an essential ingredient in forming a normal parent–child relationship? Why might some parents have found this position alarming?

◆ What are some arguments for and against the use of pain-reducing drugs during birth? What advice would you give a mother-to-be about anesthetics, and why?

◆ Which elements of various birthing techniques, including more traditional and less traditional ones, do you think are most likely to contribute to the well-being of the newborn and its family? Why?

BIRTH COMPLICATIONS

> In addition to the usual complimentary baby supplies that most hospitals bestow on new mothers, the maternity nurses at Greater Southeast Hospital have become practiced in handing out "grief baskets."
>
> Inside are items memorializing one of [Washington, D.C.'s] grimmest statistics—an infant mortality rate that's more than twice the national average. The baskets contain a photograph of the dead newborn, a snip of its hair, the tiny cap it wore, and a yellow rose. (Thomas, 1994, p. A14)

The infant mortality rate in Washington, D.C., capital of the richest country in the world, is 16.7 deaths per 1,000 births, exceeding the rate of countries such as Sri Lanka, Panama, Chile, and Jamaica. Overall, the United States ranks 22nd in the world in infant mortality, with 7.9 deaths for every 1,000 live births (National Center for Health Statistics, 1993a; Eberstadt, 1994; Singh & Yu, 1995).

Why is infant survival less likely in the United States than in other, less developed countries? To answer this question, we need to consider the nature of the problems that can occur during labor and delivery.

preterm infants infants who are born prior to 38 weeks after conception. (Also known as premature infants)

low-birthweight infants infants that weight less than 2,500 grams (about 5 1/2 pounds) at birth

small-for-gestational-age infants infants who, because of delayed fetal growth, weigh 90 percent or less than the average weight of infants of the same gestational age

PRETERM INFANTS: TOO SOON, TOO SMALL

On the morning of January 7, as Jewel McNeill's labor pains grew stronger and stronger, a nurse came into the delivery room. Did the McNeills have any plans for burying their baby? she asked grimly. Would they want an autopsy? Jewel recalls her using the phrase "disposing of the fetus." Her husband, Michael, noticed a receptacle that looked like a trash can at the bottom of the table. This, he thought, would be his baby's only cradle. According to the hospital's calculations, Jewel was no more than 22 weeks pregnant—18 weeks short of full term. The baby would weigh barely a pound and its lungs would be too undeveloped to sustain life. The doctor told Jewel to start pushing. Better to end the agony. A few minutes later, at exactly 10:08 a.m., Briana Adia-Jewel McNeill was born.

Alive.

Her eyes were open, her arms and legs were wiggling and she began to cry. To Jewel, it sounded like a cry for help. (Katrowitz, 1988, p. 62)

If Briana had been born only a decade or so earlier, her cry might have been ignored. Yet today, like the other six to seven percent of infants in the United States who are born early, Briana has a significantly higher chance of survival.

Preterm infants, or premature infants, are born prior to 38 weeks after conception. Because they have not had time to develop fully as fetuses, preterm infants are at high risk for illness and death (Holmes, Reich, & Y. Gyurke, 1989).

The degree of risk faced by preterm babies varies a great deal (Bornstein & Lamb, 1992). The main factor in determining the extent of danger is the child's weight at birth, which has great significance as an indicator of the extent of the baby's development. Although the average newborn weighs around 3,400 grams (about 7-$\frac{1}{2}$ pounds), **low-birthweight infants** weigh less than 2,500 grams (around 5-$\frac{1}{2}$ pounds). Although only seven percent of all newborns in the United States fall into the low-birthweight category, they account for the majority of newborn deaths. Although most low-birthweight infants are preterm, some are small-for-gestational-date babies. **Small-for-gestational-age infants** are babies who, because of delayed fetal growth, weigh 90 percent or less than the average weight of infants of the same gestational age (Meisels & Plunkett, 1988; Shiono & Behrman, 1995).

If the degree of prematurity is not too great and weight at birth is not extremely low, the threat to the child's well-being is relatively minor. In such cases, the main treatment may

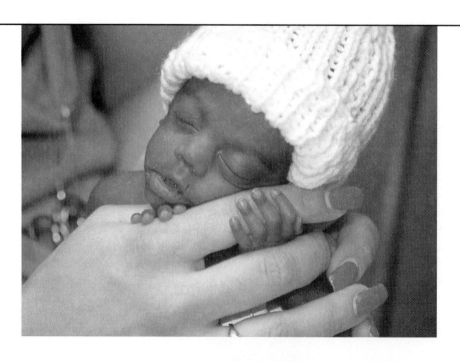

Preterm infants stand a much greater chance of survival today than they did even a decade ago.

be to keep the baby in the hospital to gain weight. Additional weight is critical because fat layers help prevent chilling in neonates, who are not terribly efficient at regulating body temperature.

Newborns who are born more prematurely and who have significantly below-average birthweights face a tougher road. For them, simply staying alive is a major task. For instance, low-birthweight infants are highly vulnerable to infection. Furthermore, because their lungs have not had sufficient time to develop completely, premature babies have problems taking in sufficient oxygen. As a consequence, they may experience *respiratory distress syndrome (RDS)*, with potentially fatal consequences.

To deal with respiratory distress syndrome, low-birthweight infants are often placed in *incubators*, enclosures in which temperature and oxygen content are controlled. The exact amount of oxygen is carefully monitored. Too low a concentration of oxygen will not provide relief, and too high a concentration can damage the delicate retinas of the eyes, leading to permanent blindness.

The immature development of preterm neonates makes them unusually sensitive to stimuli in their environment. They can easily be overwhelmed by the sights, sounds, and sensations they experience, and their breathing may be interrupted or their heart rates may slow. Furthermore, they are often unable to move smoothly; their arm and leg movements are uncoordinated, causing them to jerk about and appear startled. Such behavior is quite disconcerting to parents (T.M. Field, 1990).

Despite the difficulties they experience at birth, the majority of preterm infants eventually develop normally in the long run. However, the tempo of development often proceeds more slowly for preterm children, compared to youngsters born at full term, and more subtle problems sometimes emerge later. For example, by the end of one year, only 10 percent of prematurely born infants display significant problems, and only 5 percent are seriously disabled. By the age of 6, however, approximately 38 percent have mild problems that call for special educational interventions. For instance, some preterm children show learning disabilities, behavior disorders, or lower-than-average IQ scores. Others have difficulties with physical coordination. Still, some 60 percent of preterm infants are free of even minor problems (Bregman & Kimberlin, 1993; Herrgard et al., 1993; Lee & Barratt, 1993; Liaw & Brooks-Gunn, 1993; Bradley et al., 1994; Mandich et al., 1994; Hack, Klein, & Taylor, 1995).

Very-low-birthweight Infants: The Smallest of the Small.   The story is less positive for the most extreme cases of prematurity—very-low-birthweight infants. **Very-low-birthweight infants** weigh under 1,250 grams (about 2¼ pounds) or, regardless of weight, have been in the womb fewer than thirty weeks.

Very-low-birthweight infants are not only tiny (some fitting easily in the palm of the hand) but they hardly seem even to belong to the same species as full-term newborns. Their eyes may be fused shut and their earlobes may look like flaps of skin on the sides of their heads. Their skin is a darkened red color, whatever their race.

Very-low-birthweight babies are in grave danger from the moment they are born because of the immaturity of their organ systems. Before the last two decades, these babies would not have survived outside the mother. However, medical advances have led to a much higher chance of survival, pushing the **age of viability**, the point at which an infant can survive prematurely, to about 24 weeks—some 4 months earlier than the term of a normal delivery. At the same time, such advances have not been without their costs, both developmental and financial.

The physical and cognitive problems experienced by low-birthweight and preterm babies are even more pronounced in very-low-birthweight infants, with astonishing financial consequences. For instance, the costs of keeping very-low-birthweight infants alive are enormous. A three-month stay in an incubator in an intensive care unit can run hundreds of thousands of dollars, and not infrequently—some 50 percent of the time—the infant ultimately dies, despite massive medical intervention.

very-low-birthweight infants infants who weigh less than 1250 grams (around 2 1/4 pounds) or, regardless of weight, have been in the womb less than thirty weeks

age of viability the point at which an infant can survive a premature birth

Even if a very-low-birthweight preterm infant survives, the medical costs can continue to mount. For instance, one estimate suggests that the average monthly cost of medical care for such infants during the first 3 years of life may be between three and fifty times higher than the medical costs for a full-term child. Such astronomical costs have raised significant ethical debate about the advisability of expending substantial financial and human resources in cases in which a positive outcome may be very unlikely (Shankaran, Cohen, Linver, & Zonia, 1988; Beckwirth & Rodning, 1991; McCormick, 1992; Sung, Vohr, & Oh, 1993; Lewit, Baker, Corman, & Shiono, 1995).

The difficult issues surrounding very-low-birthweight infants are not likely to diminish in the years ahead. In fact, as medical capabilities progress, the age of viability is likely to be pushed even further back. On the other hand, developmental researchers are formulating new strategies for dealing with preterm infants in the hope of improving their lives. We consider some of these programs in the Directions in Development section.

Causes of Preterm and Low-birthweight Deliveries.   Although half of preterm and low-birthweight births are unexplained, several known causes account for the remainder (See Table 3-2; Goldberg & DiVitto, 1983; Friedman & Sigman, 1992; Radetsky, 1994; Paneth, 1995). In some cases, difficulties relating to the mother's reproductive system cause such births. For instance, mothers carrying twins have unusual stress placed on them, leading to premature labor. In fact, most multiple births are preterm to some degree.

In other cases, preterm and low birthweight babies are a result of the immaturity of the mother's reproductive system. Young mothers—under the age of 15—are more prone to

TABLE 3-2

FACTORS ASSOCIATED WITH INCREASED RISK OF LOW BIRTHWEIGHT

I. Demographic Risks
  A. Age (less than 17; over 34)
  B. Race (minority)
  C. Low socioeconomic status
  D. Unmarried
  E. Low level of education

II. Medical Risks Predating Pregnancy
  A. Parity (0 or more than 4)
  B. Low weight for height
  C. Genitourinary anomalies/surgery
  D. Selected diseases such as diabetes, chronic hypertension
  E. Nonimmune status for selected infections such as rubella
  F. Poor obstetric history, including previous low-birthweight infant, multiple spontaneous abortions
  G. Maternal genetic factors (such as low maternal weight at own birth)

III. Medical Risks in Current Pregnancy
  A. Multiple pregnancy
  B. Poor weight gain
  C. Short interpregnancy interval
  D. Hypotension
  E. Hypertension/preeclampsia/toxemia
  F. Selected infections such as asymptomatic bacteriuria, rubella, and cytomegalovirus
  G. First or second trimester bleeding
  H. Placental problems such as placenta previa, abruptio placentae

  I. Hyperemesis
  J. Ologohydramnios/polyhydramnios
  K. Anemia/abnormal hemoglobin
  L. Isoimmunization
  M. Fetal anomalies
  N. Incompetent cervix
  O. Spontaneous premature rupture of membrane

IV. Behavioral and Environmental Risks
  A. Smoking
  B. Poor nutritional status
  C. Alcohol and other substance abuse
  D. DES exposure and other toxic exposure, including occupational hazards
  E. High altitude

V. Health Care Risks
  A. Absent or inadequate prenatal care
  B. Iatrogenic prematurity

VI. Evolving Concepts of Risks
  A. Stress, physical and psychosocial
  B. Uterine irritability
  C. Events triggering uterine contractions
  D. Cervical changes detected before onset of labor
  E. Selected infections such as mycoplasma and chlamydia trachomatis
  F. Inadequate plasma volume expansion
  G. Progesterone deficiency

Adapted from Committee to Study the Prevention of Low Birthweight (1985).

deliver prematurely than are older ones. In addition, a woman who has not had much time between pregnancies is more likely to deliver a preterm or low-birthweight infant than is a woman who has given her reproductive system a chance to recover from a prior delivery.

Finally, factors that affect the general health of the mother, such as nutrition, level of medical care, amount of stress in the environment, and economic support, all are related to prematurity and low birthweight. Racial factors are also implicated, not because of race per se, but because members of racial minorities have disproportionately lower incomes. For instance, the percentage of low-birthweight infants born to African-American mothers is double that for Caucasian American mothers. (Goldberg & DiVitto, 1983; Kleinman, 1992; National Center for Health Statistics, 1993b; Radetsky, 1994; Cohen, 1995.)

Directions in Development

Treating Preterm Infants: Effective Interventions

To most parents, stroking and soothingly caressing their babies seem to come naturally. What they probably don't know, though, is that touch does more than calm their babies: It triggers a complex chemical reaction that assists infants in their efforts to survive.

According to research conducted by developmentalist Tiffany Field, preterm infants who were massaged for 15 minutes three times a day gained weight some 50 percent faster than did preterm infants of the same age who were not stroked (see Figure 3-2). The massaged infants also were more active and responsive to stimuli. Ultimately, the preterm infants who were massaged were discharged earlier from the hospital, and their medical costs were significantly lower than for infants in the unmassaged group (T.M. Field, 1988, 1995).

The benefits of massage seem to stem from the physiological stimulation it provides. Preterm neonates housed in incubators often face a world consisting of the continuous sound of oxygen being pumped in and steady, bright lights overhead. The act of massage may provide environmental variation, and it also may stimulate the production of chemicals in the brain that instigate growth (Schanberg & Field, 1987; Schanberg, Field, Kuhn, & Bartolome, 1993; T.M. Field, 1990, 1991, 1995; Tronick, 1995).

Not every type of stimulation is successful in producing gains in preterm newborns, however. Stimulation that is too strong or rough can be harmful; stimulation that is too light can be irritating. Finally, in the case of very-low-birthweight infants, too much stimulation can overwhelm the infants' efforts to stabilize their internal physiological environments (Lester & Tronick, 1990; Als, 1992; Wheeden, Scafidi, Field, & Ironson, 1993).

Other approaches to improving the outcomes for low-weight and preterm newborns are geared to both parents and their children. For instance, in one successful program, approximately one thousand preterm newborns, each weighing under 5.5 pounds, were divided into two groups (Infant Health and Development Program, 1990; Gross, Brooks-Gunn, & Spiker, 1992). Parents of the children in one group received special instruction in their homes from health care experts. During the visit, the parents were given information on health and development and were provided with a program of games and activities meant to improve the cognitive, social, and language skills of their children. In addition, when the children reached one year of age, they were placed in a special educational day care program, with one teacher for every three children. At age 2, the ratio changed to one teacher for every four children.

FIGURE 3-2

The weight gain of premature infants who were systematically massaged was greater than those who did not receive the massage.

(*Source*: Adapted from Field, 1990.)

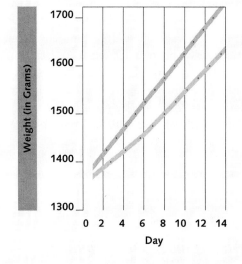

Infants with massage

Infants without massage

In comparison to youngsters in the second group—who received no special training—the children in the treatment group achieved impressive results. Treated children had significantly higher IQ scores than did those who received no special treatment. Average IQ scores of the lightest babies, who had weighed under 4.4 pounds at birth, were more than 13 points higher. Average IQ gains for the heavier babies, who weighed between 4.4 and 5.5 pounds at birth, were not as great—some 7 points higher—but still significant.

Results such as these have important implications for public policy. They suggest that intervention programs to help preterm and low-weight babies should begin with the very start of life. By intervening early, developmentalists might well diminish—and possibly prevent—future problems.

POSTMATURE BABIES: TOO LATE, TOO LARGE

One might imagine that a baby who spends extra time in the womb might have some advantages, given the opportunity to continue growth undisturbed by the outside world. Yet the reality is different. **Postmature infants**—those still unborn 2 weeks after the mother's due date—face several risks.

For example, the blood supply from the placenta may become insufficient to nourish the fetus adequately. Consequently, the blood supply to the brain may be decreased, leading to the potential of brain damage. Similarly, labor becomes riskier (for both the child and the mother) as a fetus who may be equivalent in size to a 1-month-old infant has to make its way through the birth canal (Boylan, 1990).

In some ways, difficulties involving postmature infants are more easily prevented than those involving preterm babies: Medical practitioners can induce labor artificially if the pregnancy continues too long. Not only can certain drugs bring on labor, but physicians also have the option of performing Cesarean deliveries, a form of delivery we consider next.

CESAREAN DELIVERY: INTERVENING IN THE PROCESS OF BIRTH

As Elena entered her 18th hour of labor, the obstetrician who was monitoring her progress began to look concerned. She told Elena and her husband, Pablo, that the fetal monitor revealed that the fetus's heart rate had begun to repeatedly fall after

postmature infants   *infants still unborn two weeks after the mother's due date*

each contraction. After trying some simple remedies, such as repositioning Elena on her side, the obstetrician came to the conclusion that the fetus was in distress. She told them that the baby should be delivered immediately, and to accomplish that, she would have to carry out a Cesarean delivery.

Elena became one of the almost one million mothers in the United States who have a Cesarean delivery each year. In a **Cesarean delivery**, the baby is surgically removed from the uterus, rather than traveling through the birth canal.

Several types of difficulties during the birthing process can lead to Cesarean deliveries. Fetal distress is the most frequent cause. For instance, if the fetus appears to be in some danger, as indicated by a sudden rise in its heart rate or if blood is seen coming from the mother's vagina during labor, a Cesarean may be performed. Cesarean deliveries are also used in some cases of *breech position*, in which the baby is positioned feet first in the birth canal, or *transverse position*, in which the baby lies crosswise in the uterus, or when the baby's head is so large it has trouble moving through the birth canal.

The use of routine fetal heartbeat monitoring has contributed to a soaring rate of Cesarean deliveries. For instance, almost 25 percent of all children in the United States are born in this way, up some 500 percent from the early 1970s (National Center for Health Statistics, 1993a). What benefits have resulted from this increase?

According to critics, very few. Other countries have substantially lower rates of Cesarean deliveries (see Figure 3-3), and there is no association between successful birth consequences and the rate of Cesarean deliveries (Notzon, 1990). In addition, Cesarean deliveries carry dangers. A Cesarean is major surgery, and recovery can be relatively lengthy, particularly when compared to a normal delivery. In addition, the risk of maternal infection is higher with Cesarean deliveries (Mutryn, 1993; Shearer, 1993).

Finally, a Cesarean delivery presents some risks for the baby. Although Cesarean babies are spared the stresses of passing though the birth canal, their relatively easy passage into the world may deter the normal release of certain stress-related hormones, such as catecholamines, into the newborn's bloodstream. Because these hormones help prepare the neonate to deal with the stress of the world outside the womb, their absence may be detrimental to the newborn child. In fact, research indicates that babies who have not experienced labor due to a Cesarean delivery are more prone to initial breathing problems upon birth than those who experience at least some labor prior to being born via a Cesarean delivery (Lagercrantz & Slotkin, 1986; Hales, Morgan, & Thurnau, 1993).

Owing in part to the increase in Cesarean deliveries that results from their use, fetal monitoring devices that measure the baby's heartbeat during labor are no longer employed routinely, in accordance with current recommendations from medical authorities. These experts cite research evidence that the outcomes are no better for newborns who have been monitored than for those who have not been monitored, and that monitors give false alarms regarding the presence of fetal distress with disquieting regularity (Levano et al., 1986; Albers & Krulewitch, 1993). On the other hand, monitors can play a critical role in high-risk pregnancies and in cases of preterm and postmature babies.

INFANT MORTALITY AND STILLBIRTH

The joy that accompanies the birth of a child is completely reversed when a newborn dies. The relative rarity of their occurrence makes infant deaths even harder for parents to bear.

Infant mortality is defined as death within the first year of life. The overall rate in the United States is 8.5 deaths per 1,000 live births (Wegman, 1993). Infant mortality has been declining since the 1960s, and U.S. government officials expect to meet their goal of lowering the overall rate to 7 deaths per 1,000 live births.

Sometimes a child does not even live beyond its passage through the birth canal. **Stillbirth**, the delivery of a child who is not alive, occurs in less than one delivery out of 100. Sometimes the death is detected before labor begins. In this case, labor is typically induced, or physicians

Cesarean delivery a birth in which the baby is surgically removed from the uterus, rather than traveling through the birth canal

infant mortality death within the first year of life

stillbirth the delivery of a child who is not alive, occuring in less than one delivery in 100

FIGURE 3-3

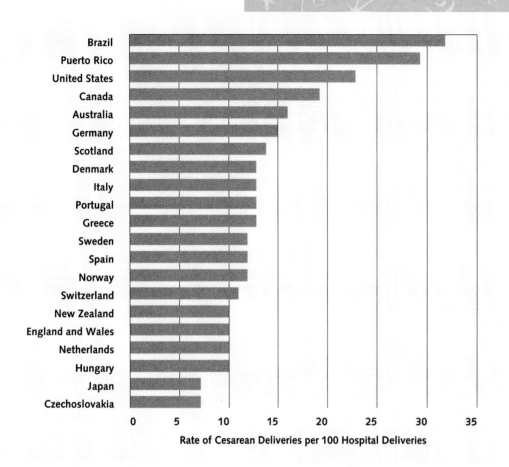

The rate at which Cesarean deliveries are performed varies substantially from one country to another.

(*Source*: Adapted from Notzon, 1990.)

may carry out a Cesarean delivery in order to remove the body from the mother as soon as possible. In other cases of stillbirth, the baby dies during its travels through the birth canal.

Whether the death is a stillbirth or occurs after the child is born, the loss of a baby is a tragic occurrence. The impact on parents is significant: They move through the same stages of grief and mourning as they experience when an older loved one dies. In fact, the cruel juxtaposition of the first dawning of life and an unnaturally early death may make the loss particularly difficult to accept and deal with. Depression is a common aftermath (DeFrain, Martens, Stork, & Stork, 1991; Brockington, 1992).

Developmental Diversity

Overcoming Racial and Cultural Differences in Infant Mortality

The general decline in the U.S. infant mortality rate over the past several decades masks some significant, and startling, racial differences. In particular, African-American babies are more than twice as likely to die before age one than white babies (see Figure 3-4). In fact, if current trends continue, by the turn of the century, the mortality rate for African-American infants will be three times that for Caucasian infants (National Center for Health Statistics, 1993b; Singh & Yu, 1995).

FIGURE 3-4

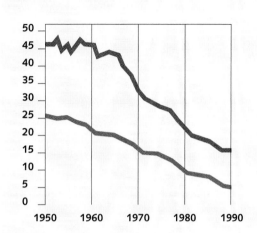

African-American

White

Although infant mortality is dropping for both African-American and Caucasian children, the death rate is still twice as high for African-American youngsters. These figures show the number of deaths in the first year of life for every 1,000 live births.

(*Source*: National Center for Health Statistics, 1995.)

Furthermore, the overall U. S. rate of infant mortality is higher than the rate in many other countries (see Figure 3-5). The United States ranks behind 22 other industrialized nations. Its mortality rate is more than double that of Japan, which has the lowest mortality rate of any country in the world.

What makes the United States fare so poorly in terms of newborn survival? One answer is that America has a higher rate of low-birthweight and preterm deliveries than many other countries. In fact, when U.S. infants are compared to infants of the same weight who are born in countries with lower mortality, the differences in mortality rates disappear (Paneth, 1995; Wilcox, Skjaerven, Buekens, & Kiely, 1995).

Another reason for the higher U.S. mortality rate relates to economic diversity. The United States has a higher proportion of people living in poverty than do many other countries. Because people in lower economic categories are less likely to have adequate medical care and be less healthy, the relatively high proportion of economically deprived individuals in the United States has an impact on the overall mortality rate (Aved, Irwin, Cummings, & Findeisen, 1993).

Furthermore, many countries do a significantly better job providing prenatal care to mothers-to-be than does the United States. For instance, low-cost—even free—care, both before and after delivery, is often available in other countries. Paid maternity leave is frequently provided to pregnant women, lasting in some cases as long as 51 weeks (see Table 3-3). In certain European countries, women receive a comprehensive package of services involving general practitioner, obstetrician, and midwife. Pregnant women receive many privileges, such as transportation benefits for visits to health care providers. In Norway, pregnant women may be given living expenses for up to ten days so they can be close to a hospital when it is time to give birth. And when their babies are born, new mothers receive, for just a small payment, the assistance of trained home helpers (C. A. Miller, 1987).

In the United States, the story is very different. The lack of national health care insurance or a national health policy means that prenatal care is often haphazardly provided to the poor. About one out of every six pregnant women has insufficient prenatal care. Some 20 percent of Caucasian women and close to 40 percent of African-American women who are pregnant receive no prenatal care early in their pregnancies. Five percent of white mothers and 11 percent of black mothers do not see a health-care provider until the last three months of pregnancy; some never see a health care provider at all. In fact, the percentage of pregnant women in the United States who receive virtually no prenatal care has actually increased in the 1990s from previous years (National Center for Health Statistics, 1993c; Thomas, 1994; Johnson, Primas, & Coe, 1994).

FIGURE 3-5

The rate of infant mortality is higher in the United States than for other industrialized countries.

(*Source: The World Factbook*, 1994.)

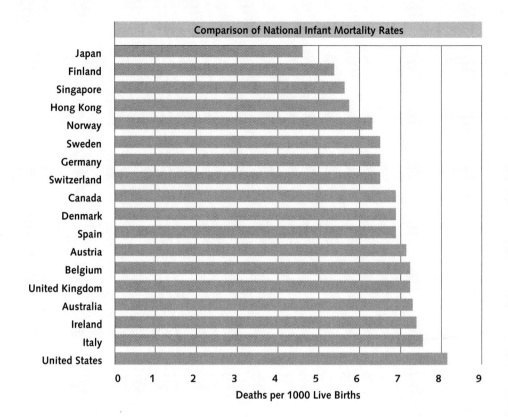

The ultimate outcome of the deficiency in prenatal services to women with low incomes is the higher likelihood of death for their infants. Yet this unfortunate state of affairs can be changed if greater support is provided. A start would be to ensure that all economically disadvantaged pregnant women have access to free or inexpensive high-quality medical care from the very beginning of pregnancy. Furthermore, barriers that prevent poor women from reaching such care should be reduced. For instance, programs can be devel-

TABLE 3-3

MATERNITY-LEAVE POLICIES IN OTHER COUNTRIES: GUARANTEED BY LAW

	Maximum Weeks Allowed	Percent of Salary Replaced
Sweden*	51	90
France	16–38	84
Italy	20	80
Britain	18	90
Canada	15	60
Germany	14	100
Japan	14	60
Netherlands	7	100

*For both parents combined.
(*Source: Caminiti, 1992.)

oped that help pay for transportation to a health facility or for the care of older children while the mother is making a health care visit (Aved et al., 1993).

Finally, programs that provide basic education for all mothers-to-be are of paramount importance. Increasing the level of understanding of the potential risks involved in child-bearing could prevent many problems before they actually occur (Carnegie Task Force on Meeting the Needs of Young Children, 1994; Fangman et al., 1994).

Review and Rethink

REVIEW

♦ Largely because of low birthweight, preterm infants may have substantial difficulties after birth and later in life, although most preterm babies ultimately develop normally.

♦ Very-low-birthweight infants are in special danger because of the immaturity of their organ systems. With massive intervention and at high cost, infants who have spent as little as 24 weeks in their mothers' bodies can now be helped to survive.

♦ Preterm and low-birthweight deliveries can be caused by health, age, and pregnancy-related factors in the mother. Income (and, because of its relationship with income, race) is also an important factor, with lower income leading to a higher incidence of low-birthweight babies.

♦ Cesarean deliveries, which occur with unusual frequency in the United States, are performed with postmature babies or when the fetus is in distress, in the wrong position, or unable to progress through the birth canal.

♦ Infant mortality rates can be affected by the availability of inexpensive health care and good education programs for mothers-to-be. The infant mortality rate in the United States is higher than the rate in many other countries and is higher for low-income families than for higher-income families.

RETHINK

♦ What are some ethical considerations relating to the provision of intensive medical care to very-low-birthweight babies? Do you think such interventions should be routine practice? Why or why not?

♦ Effective educational programs have been devised for treating preterm infants. What are some public policy implications of this fact? What arguments, pro and con, can be made regarding such efforts?

♦ Why do you think the number of Cesarean deliveries has increased dramatically in the United States in recent years? What sort of policy for families and physicians would you design to govern the use of Cesarean procedures?

♦ Why do you think the United States lacks educational and health care policies that could reduce infant mortality rates overall and among poorer people? What arguments would you make to change this situation?

THE COMPETENT NEWBORN

In one sense, we are all born too soon.

The size of the brain of the average newborn is just one-quarter what it will be at adulthood. In comparison, the brain of the macaque monkey, who is born after just 24 weeks of gestation, is 65 percent of its adult size. Because of the relative puniness of the infant human brain, some observers have suggested that we are propelled out of the womb some six to twelve months sooner than we ought to be.

In reality, evolution probably knew what it was doing: If we stayed inside our mothers' bodies an additional half-year to a year, our heads would be so large that we would never manage to get through the birth canal (Schultz, 1969; Gould, 1977; Kotre & Hall, 1990).

The relatively underdeveloped brain of the human newborn helps explain the infant's apparent helplessness. Neonates arrive in the world quite incapable of successfully caring for themselves. Because of this, the earliest views of newborns focused on the things that they could not do, comparing them rather unfavorably to older members of the human species.

Today, however, such beliefs have taken a backseat to more favorable views of the neonate. As developmentalists have begun to understand more about the nature of newborns, they have come to the realization that infants enter this world with an astounding array of capabilities.

PHYSICAL COMPETENCE: MEETING THE DEMANDS OF A NEW ENVIRONMENT

The world faced by a neonate is remarkably different from the one it experienced in the womb. Consider, for instance, the significant changes in functioning that the newly born Jamilla Castro, who weighed a robust 8 pounds 2 ounces at birth, encounters as she begins the first moments of life in her new environment (summarized in Table 3-4).

Jamilla's most immediate task is to bring sufficient air into her body. Inside her mother, air was delivered through the umbilical cord, which also provided a means for the removal of carbon dioxide. The realities of the outside world are different: Once the umbilical cord is cut, Jamilla's respiratory system must begin its lifetime's work.

For Jamilla, the task is automatic. As we noted earlier, most neonates begin to breathe on their own as soon as they are exposed to air. The ability to breathe immediately is a good indication that the respiratory system of the normal neonate is reasonably well developed, despite its lack of rehearsal in the womb.

Neonates emerge from the uterus more practiced in other types of physical activities. For example, newborns such as Jamilla show several **reflexes**—unlearned, organized involuntary responses that occur automatically in the presence of certain stimuli. Some of these reflexes are well rehearsed, having been present for several months before birth. The *sucking reflex* and the *swallowing reflex* permit the neonate to begin right away to ingest food. The *rooting reflex*, which involves turning in the direction of a source of stimulation (such as a light touch) near the mouth, is also related to eating. It guides the infant toward potential sources of food that are near its mouth, such as a mother's nipple.

Not all of the reflexes that are present at birth lead the newborn to seek out desired stimuli such as food. For instance, Jamilla can cough, sneeze, and blink—reflexes that help her to avoid stimuli that are potentially bothersome or hazardous.

Jamilla's sucking and swallowing reflexes, which help her to consume her mother's milk, are coupled with the new-found ability to digest nutriments. The neonate's digestive system initially produces *meconium*, a greenish-black material that is a remnant of the neonate's days as a fetus. The digestive tract immediately begins to process newly ingested nourishment.

Because their livers, a critical component of the digestive system, do not always work effectively at first, almost half of all newborns develop a distinctly yellowish tinge to their

reflexes *unlearned, organized involuntary responses that occur automatically in the presence of certain stimuli*

TABLE 3-4

JAMILLA CASTRO'S FIRST ENCOUNTERS UPON BIRTH

1. As soon as she is through the birth canal, Jamilla automatically begins to breathe on her own despite no longer being attached to the umbilical cord that provided precious air in the womb.
2. Reflexes–unlearned, organized involuntary responses that occur in the presence of stimuli–begin to take over. Sucking and swallowing reflexes permit Jamilla immediately to ingest food.
3. The rooting reflex, which involves turning in the direction of a source of stimulation, guides Jamilla toward potential sources of food that are near her mouth, such as her mother's nipple.
4. Jamilla begins to cough, sneeze, and blink–reflexes that help her avoid stimuli that are potentially bothersome or hazardous.
5. Her senses of smell and taste are highly developed. Physical activities and sucking increase when she smells peppermint. Her lips pucker when a sour taste is placed on her lips.
6. Objects with colors of blue and green seem to catch Jamilla's attention more than other colors, and she reacts sharply to loud, sudden noises. She will also continue to cry if she hears others newborns cry, but will stop if she hears a recording of her own voice crying.

bodies and eyes. This change in color is a symptom of *neonatal jaundice*. It is most likely to occur in preterm and low-weight neonates, and it is typically not dangerous. Treatment most often consists of placing the baby under fluorescent lights or administering drugs.

THE NEWBORN'S SENSORY CAPABILITIES: EXPERIENCING THE WORLD

Just after Jamilla was born, her father was certain that she looked directly at him. Did she, in fact, see him?

This is a hard question to answer for several reasons. For one thing, when psychologists talk of "seeing," they mean both a sensory reaction due to the stimulation of the visual sensory organs and an interpretation of that stimulation (the distinction, as you might recall from an introductory psychology class, between sensation and perception). Furthermore, as we'll discuss further when we consider sensory capabilities during infancy in Chapter 4, it is tricky, to say the least, to pinpoint the specific sensory skills of newborns who lack the ability to explain what they are experiencing.

Still, we do have some answers to the question of what newborns are capable of seeing and, for that matter, questions about their other sensory capabilities. For example, it is clear that neonates such as Jamilla can see to some extent. Although their visual acuity is not fully developed, newborns actively pay attention to certain types of information in their environment (Haith, 1980, 1991).

For instance, neonates pay closest attention to portions of scenes in their field of vision that are highest in information, such as objects that sharply contrast with the rest of their environment. Furthermore, infants can discriminate different levels of brightness. There is even evidence suggesting that newborns have a sense of size constancy, seemingly aware that objects stay the same size even though the size of the image on the retina varies with distance (Slater, Mattock, & Brown, 1990).

And not only can neonates distinguish different colors, but they seem to prefer particular ones. For example, they are able to distinguish among red, green, yellow, and blue, and they take more time staring at blue and green objects—suggesting a partiality for those colors (Adams, Mauer, & Davis, 1986).

Newborns are also clearly capable of hearing. They react to certain kinds of sounds, showing startle reactions to loud, sudden noises, for instance. The also exhibit familiarity with certain sounds. For example, newborns continue to cry when they hear other newborns crying. On the other hand, a crying newborn who hears a recording of its own crying is more likely to stop crying, as if it recognizes the familiar sound (Martin & Clark, 1982).

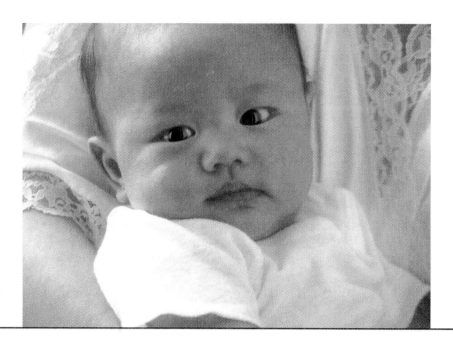

Newborns actively pay attention to their environments.

As with vision, the degree of auditory acuity is not as great as it will be later. The auditory system is not completely developed. Moreover, amniotic fluid, which is initially trapped in the middle ear, must drain out before the newborn can fully hear (Reinis & Goldman, 1980).

In addition to sight and hearing, the other senses also function quite adequately in the newborn. It is obvious that newborns are sensitive to touch. For instance, they respond to stimuli such as the hairs of a brush, and they are aware of puffs of air so weak that adults cannot notice them. The senses of smell and taste are also well developed. Newborns suck and increase other physical activity when the odor of peppermint is placed near the nose. They also pucker their lips when a sour taste is placed on them, and respond with suitable facial expressions to other tastes as well. Such findings clearly indicate that the senses of touch, smell, and taste are not only present at birth but are reasonably sophisticated (Sarnat, 1978; Jacklin, Snow, & Maccoby, 1981; Rosenstein & Oster, 1988; Mistretta, 1990).

In one sense, the sophistication of the sensory systems of newborns such as Jamilla is not surprising. After all, the typical neonate has had nine months to prepare for his or her encounter with the outside world. As we discussed in Chapter 2, human sensory systems begin their development well before birth. Furthermore, some researchers suggest that the passage through the birth canal places babies in a state of heightened sensory awareness, preparing them for the world that they are about to encounter for the first time (Bornstein & Lamb, 1992).

FOUNDATIONS OF SOCIAL COMPETENCE: RESPONDING TO OTHERS

Soon after Jamilla was born, her older brother looked down at her in her crib and opened his mouth wide, pretending to be surprised. Jamilla's mother, looking on, was amazed when it appeared that Jamilla imitated his expression, opening her mouth as if she were surprised.

Researchers registered surprise of their own when they first found that newborns did indeed have the capability to imitate others' behavior. Although infants were known to have all the muscles in place to produce facial expressions related to basic emotions, the actual appearance of such expressions was assumed to be largely random.

However, research beginning in the late 1970s suggested a different conclusion. For instance, developmental researchers demonstrated that, when exposed to an adult modeling a behavior that the infant already performed spontaneously, such as opening the mouth or sticking out the tongue, the newborn was apt to imitate the behavior (Meltzoff & Moore, 1977).

Developmental psychologist Tiffany Field.

Even more exciting were findings from studies conducted by developmental specialist Tiffany Field and her colleagues (Field, 1982; Field & Walden, 1982; Field, Cohen, Garcia, & Greenberg, 1984b). They initially showed that infants could discriminate among such basic facial expressions as happiness, sadness, and surprise. They then exposed newborns to an adult model with a happy, sad, or surprised facial expression. The results were clear: The newborns produced a reasonably accurate imitation of the adult's expression (see Figure 3-6).

Subsequent research, conducted just minutes after birth and in a variety of cultures, has shown that imitative capabilities appear to be a universal characteristic of newborns (Kaitz, Meschulach-Sarfaty, Auerbach, & Eidelman, 1988; Reissland, 1988). Imitative skills are more than a mere curiosity. Effective social interaction with others relies in part on the ability to react to other people in an appropriate manner and to understand the meaning of others' emotional states. Consequently, the imitative capability of newborns provides an important foundation for social interaction later in life (Phillips, Wagner, Fells, & Lynch, 1990).

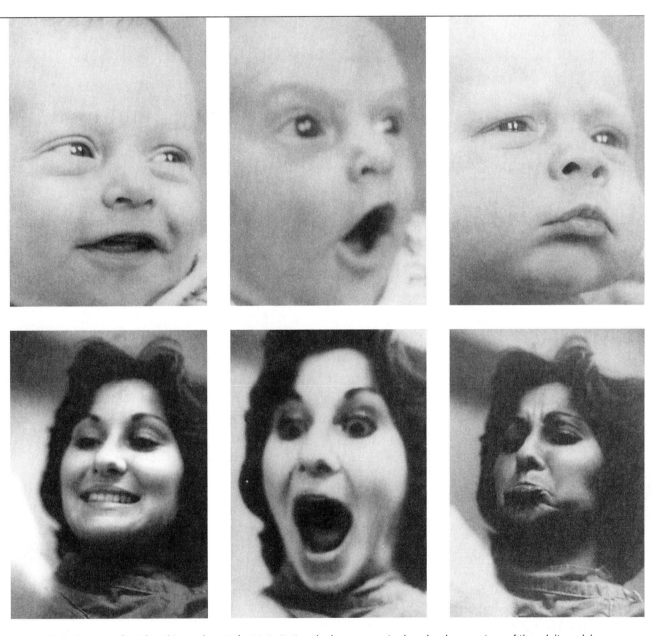

FIGURE 3-6   It is clear that this newborn infant is imitating the happy, surprised, and sad expressions of the adult model.

(Courtesy of Dr. Tiffany Field.)

TABLE 3-5

FACTORS THAT ENCOURAGE SOCIAL INTERACTION BETWEEN FULL-TERM NEWBORNS AND THEIR PARENTS

Full-Term Newborn	Parent
Has organized states	Helps regulate infant's states
Attends selectively to certain stimuli	Provides these stimuli
Behaves in ways interpretable as specific communicative intent	Searches for communicative intent
Responds systematically to parent's acts	Wants to influence newborn, feel effective
Acts in temporally predictable ways	Adjusts actions to newborn's temporal rhythms
Learns from, adapts to parent's behavior	Acts repetitively and predictably

(*Source*: Eckerman and Ochler, 1992.)

In addition to their imitative abilities, several other aspects of newborns' behavior act as forerunners for more formal types of social interaction that will develop more fully in the future. As shown in Table 3-5, certain characteristics of neonates mesh with parental behavior to help produce a social relationship between child and parent, as well as social relationships with others (Eckerman & Oehler, 1992).

For example, newborns cycle through various states of arousal, ranging from deep sleep to great agitation. Although immediately after birth these cycles are disrupted, they quickly become more regularized. Caregivers become involved when they seek to aid the infant in transitions from one state to another. For instance, a father who rhythmically rocks his crying daughter in an effort to calm her is engaged in a joint activity that is a prelude to future social interactions of different sorts. Similarly, newborns tend to pay particular attention to their mothers' voices (Hepper, Scott, & Shahidullah, 1993). In turn, parents and others modify their speech when talking to infants, using a different pitch and tempo than they use with older children and adults (DeCasper & Fifer, 1980; Fernald, 1984).

The ultimate outcome of the social interactive capabilities of the newborn infant, and the responses such behavior brings about from parents, is to pave the way for future social interactions. Just as the neonate shows remarkable skills on a physical and perceptual level, then, its social capabilities are no less sophisticated.

The Informed Consumer of Development

First Encounters: Interacting with a Newborn

If you are the relative or friend of a woman who has just given birth, you may be anticipating your initial encounter with the new baby with some degree of trepidation. In fact, people tend to interact with newborns in very different ways. Some approach newborns gingerly, acting as though they are confronting a representative of an alien society; others show no hesitation in touching and stroking them and hoisting them vigorously into the air.

Is there an optimal way of interacting with newborns? Although there are no hard-and-fast rules, several principles can guide your first encounters with a newborn:

- ◆ Prepare yourself: Newborns may look slightly "unfinished." As we discussed earlier, delivery is not an easy experience for a baby: Its head may be misshapen and its nose and ears squashed down. Hairlike material may cover its shoulder blades and spine, its skin may be wrinkled, and its color may be bluish or yellowish. Most of this will change in a few days.

- ◆ Hold the baby securely. Keep in mind that newborns have been in the close confines of the womb for nine months; thus, they need to become accustomed to the newfound freedom of movement that the world provides. Consequently, they should not be dangled in the air or otherwise treated roughly. In fact, in some cultures, newborns are routinely wrapped up firmly in blankets—a procedure called *swaddling*.

- ◆ Speak gently. Because the sense organs of babies are operative even before birth, they can readily hear voices and other sounds in their surroundings. In fact, because the stimulation from their passage through the birth canal may make them particularly sensitive to stimuli, one should take care not to speak too loudly. But do speak to the newborn: As we'll see in the next few chapters, linguistic stimulation is crucial to the development of language skills.

- ◆ Keep to yourself any suspicions that something may be wrong with the child. Unless you are a pediatrician or an expert in infant development, you do not have the knowledge to make such a pronouncement. Furthermore, what you are seeing may not be a true sample of the baby's behavior, particularly if the mother has received medication during labor. Remember that every baby is different, and that a baby's appearance and behavior on its first day of life will change substantially in just a few days.

Review and Rethink

REVIEW

- ◆ Neonates, born with brains that are only a fraction of their ultimate size, are in many ways helpless. Nevertheless, studies of what newborns *can* do, rather than what they *cannot* do, have revealed some surprising capabilities.

- ◆ Newborns' respiratory and digestive systems begin to function at birth. They come equipped with an array of reflexes to help them eat, swallow, find food, and avoid unpleasant stimuli.

- ◆ Newborns' sensory competence includes the ability to distinguish objects in the visual field and to see color differences; the ability to hear and to discern familiar sounds; and sensitivity to touch, odors, and tastes.

- ◆ Newborns develop the foundations of social competence early. Sophisticated imitative capabilities help them react appropriately to other people's emotional states and to manage the beginnings of social interaction.

RETHINK

- ◆ Developmental researchers no longer view the neonate as a helpless, incompetent creature, but rather as a remarkably competent, developing human being. What do you think are some implications of this change in viewpoint for methods of childrearing and child care?

♦ How do newborns' reflexes help them in their new environment? How might the fetus have developed such organized responses to stimuli?

♦ How does the newborn's imitative capability help the child to develop social competence later in life? In what ways might this process be different or similar for a baby born without sight?

♦ How should a person who is meeting a newborn for the first time act toward the baby and its parents? Why?

LOOKING BACK

What is the normal process of labor?

1. Labor proceeds in three stages. The first stage begins with 30-second contractions occurring about every 8 to 10 minutes. The frequency, duration, and intensity of the contractions increase until the mother's cervix expands enough to permit the baby's head to pass through.

2. In the second stage of labor, which lasts about 90 minutes, the baby begins to move through the cervix and birth canal and ultimately leaves the mother's body.

3. In the third stage of labor, which lasts only a few minutes, the umbilical cord and placenta are expelled from the mother.

What happens immediately after the baby is born?

4. After it emerges, the newborn, or neonate, is usually inspected by health care workers using a standard measurement system such as the Apgar scale.

5. Health care workers inspect the newborn for signs of irregularities. One of the most serious problems that can be caused by the birth process itself is a temporary deprivation of oxygen, which can bring serious harm if it lasts longer than a few seconds.

6. After it is cleaned, the newborn is returned to its mother and father for its first encounter with those who will love and care for it.

What choices do parents have regarding the birthing process?

7. Parents today have a variety of options concerning the process of giving birth, including the use or nonuse of pain-suppressing drugs, and a range of alternative birthing techniques, including the Lamaze method, the Leboyer method, the use of birthing centers versus hospitals, and the use of midwives versus obstetricians.

8. Helpful strategies for women facing the pains of labor include maintaining a flexible mind about birthing methods, communicating frankly and frequently with health care workers, having realistic expectations about fatigue and pain, accepting the support of a partner, and focusing on the joyful event in which labor ends.

What complications can occur at birth and what are their causes, effects, and treatments?

9. Preterm, or premature, infants are born under 38 weeks following conception. Preterm infants generally have low birthweight, which can cause chilling, vulnerability to infection, respiratory distress syndrome, and hypersensitivity to environmental stimuli.

10. Some children who were born prematurely may also show adverse effects later in life, including slowed development, learning disabilities, behavior disorders, below-average IQ scores, and problems with physical coordination.

11. Very-low-birthweight infants are in special danger because of the immaturity of their organ systems. However, medical advances have pushed the age of viability of the infant back to about 24 weeks following conception.

12. The costs of treating very-low-birthweight infants, at birth and later in life, are very high, a fact that raises serious ethical questions about the wisdom of such massive medical intervention.

13. Several treatment strategies for preterm infants appear to be effective, including regular massage and educational programs designed to improve cognitive, social, and language skills.

14. Causal factors in preterm and low-birthweight deliveries include multiple births, the young age of the mother, a short time between pregnancies, and general health factors in the mother.

15. Another factor in low birthweight is income. Women with lower incomes have a higher incidence of low-birthweight babies than do those with higher incomes. The question of income also entails race, as members of racial minorities have disproportionately lower incomes.

16. Postmature babies, who spend extra time in their mothers' wombs, are also at risk. However, physicians can artificially induce labor or perform a Cesarean delivery to address this situation.

17. Cesarean deliveries are performed when the fetus is in distress, in the wrong position, or unable to progress through the birth canal. The United States has an unusually high incidence of Cesarean deliveries, which many critics consider unjustified because of dangers to mother and child from this procedure.

18. The infant mortality rate in the United States is higher than the rate in many other countries, and higher for low-income families than for higher-income families. Improvements in the availability of high-quality but inexpensive medical care and in pregnancy-related education could change this situation.

What capabilities does the newborn have?

19. Although apparently helpless, human newborns have remarkable capabilities. They quickly master the breathing of air through the lungs, and they are equipped with reflexes to help them eat, swallow, find food, and avoid unpleasant stimuli.

20. Newborns' sensory capabilities are also sophisticated. Although their sensory systems will increase in acuity as they age, even as newborns they have some visual discrimination, can hear quite well, are sensitive to touch, and can smell and taste.

21. Newborns are able to imitate the behavior of others, a capability that helps them form social relationships and facilitates the development of social competence.

KEY TERMS AND CONCEPTS

neonate (p. 80)

Apgar scale (p. 83)

bonding (p. 84)

preterm infants (p. 92)

low-birthweight infants (p. 92)

small-for-gestational-age infants (p. 92)

very-low-birthweight infants (p. 93)

age of viability (p. 93)

postmature infants (p. 96)

Cesarean delivery (p. 97)

infant mortality (p. 97)

stillbirth (p. 97)

reflexes (p. 102)

Infancy:
Forming the Foundations of Life

Physical Development

CHAPTER OUTLINE

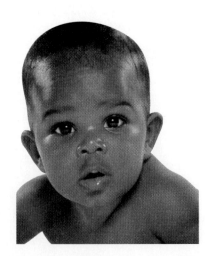

PROLOGUE: FIRST STEPS

I was in the kitchen, on the phone, when my son Ben appeared in the doorway, his finger-tips on the doorjamb for balance. Gradually he let go to toddle toward me, stringing one impossible step after another. He held his arms up in the air and moved his feet mechanically, stiffly stepping forward with slow deliberation at first and then awkwardly picking up speed, propelled by a force he couldn't quite control. His every step defied a law of motion, and he seemed poised to tumble, at any moment, in any direction. "He's walking!" I screamed to the long-distance operator on the other end of the line as Ben lunged for my knees in a moment of pure triumph. (Israeloff, 1991, p. 54)

LOOKING AHEAD

Ben Israeloff's first steps at the age of nine months capped a succession of milestones that brought him closer to full mobility and caused his parents sheer joy. His accomplishment, however remarkable, was only one of many that characterize the dramatic physical attainments during infancy.

In this chapter we consider the nature of physical development during the period of infancy, which starts at birth and continues until the second birthday. We begin by considering the pace of growth during infancy: obvious changes in height and weight, but also less apparent changes in the nervous system. We also consider how infants quickly develop stable patterns in which their basic activities, such as sleeping, eating, and attending to the world, take on some degree of order.

Our discussion then turns to motor development, the development of skills that eventually will allow an infant to roll over, take the first step, and pick up a pin from the floor—skills that ultimately form the basis for later and even more complex behaviors. We start with basic, genetically determined reflexes and consider how even these may be modified on the basis of experience. We also discuss the nature and timing of the development of particular physical skills, examining whether their emergence can be speeded up. We also consider the importance of early nutrition to their development.

Finally, we explore the development of the senses during infancy. We'll investigate how several individual sensory systems operate, and we'll look at how data from the sense organs are sorted out and transformed into meaningful information.

In sum, after reading this chapter, you'll be able to answer these questions:

◆ How do the human body and nervous system develop?

◆ Does the environment affect the pattern of development?

◆   What are reflexes and how are they useful?

◆   How universal are the schedule and sequence of motor development?

◆   What is the role of nutrition in physical development, and what food is best for infants?

◆   How do the senses develop, and what sensory capabilities do infants possess?

GROWTH AND STABILITY

The average newborn weighs in at just over seven pounds, which is probably less than the weight of the turkey most of us ate last Thanksgiving. Its length is a mere 20 inches, shorter than a loaf of French bread. It is helpless; if left to fend for itself, it could not survive.

Yet after just a few years, the story is very different. Babies are much larger, they are mobile, and they become increasingly independent. How does this growth happen? We can answer this question first by describing the changes in weight and height that occur over the first two years of life, and then by examining some of the principles that underlie and direct that growth.

PHYSICAL GROWTH: THE RAPID ADVANCES OF INFANCY

Over the first 2 years of a human's life, growth occurs at a rapid pace (see Figure 4-1). By the age of five months, the average infant's birthweight has doubled to about 15 pounds. By the first birthday, the infant's weight has tripled to approximately 22 pounds. Although the pace of weight gain slows during the second year, it is still continuous. By the end of its second year, the average child weighs four times its birthweight.

The weight gains of infancy are matched by increased length. By the end of the first year, the typical baby stands a proud 30 inches tall, an average increase from birth of almost a foot. By its second birthday, it usually attains a height of three feet.

Not all parts of an infant's body grow at the same rate. For instance, as we saw first in Chapter 2, at birth the head accounts for one-quarter of the newborn's entire body size. During the first 2 years of life, the rest of the body begins to catch up. By the age of two the baby's head is only one-fifth of body length, and by adulthood it is only one-eighth (see Figure 4-2). Furthermore, a growing body of evidence suggests that growth is not regular and continuous, as originally thought. Instead, recent research suggests that it occurs in short spurts, separated by periods of days in which there is little or no growth (Lampl, Cameron, Veldhuis, & Johnson, 1995).

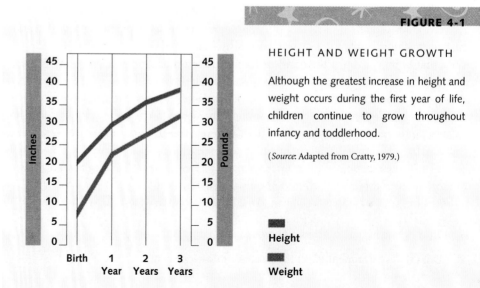

FIGURE 4-1

HEIGHT AND WEIGHT GROWTH

Although the greatest increase in height and weight occurs during the first year of life, children continue to grow throughout infancy and toddlerhood.

(*Source*: Adapted from Cratty, 1979.)

■ Height

■ Weight

FIGURE 4-2

DECREASING PROPORTIONS

At birth, the head represents one-quarter of the neonate's body size. By adulthood, the head is only one-eighth the size of the body.

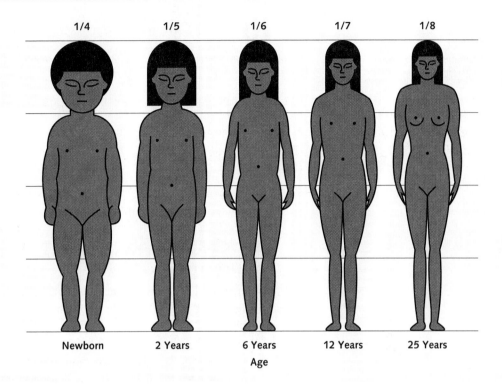

The disproportionately large size of infants' heads at birth is an example of one of the major principles that govern growth: the cephalocaudal principle, which relates to the direction of growth. The **cephalocaudal principle** states that growth follows a pattern that begins with head and upper body parts and then proceeds to the rest of the body. Reflecting Greek and Latin roots meaning "head-to-tail," the cephalocaudal growth principle means that we develop visual abilities (located in the head) well before we master the ability to walk (closer to the end of the body). The cephalocaudal principle operates both prenatally and after birth.

Several other principles (summarized in Table 4-1) help explain the patterns by which growth occurs. The **proximodistal principle** states that development proceeds from the center of the body outward. Based on the Latin words for "near" and "far," the proximodistal principle means that the trunk of the body grows before the extremities of the arms and legs. Similarly, it is only after growth has occurred in the arms and legs that the fingers and toes can grow. Furthermore, the development of the ability to use various parts of the body also follows the proximodistal principle. For instance, the effective use of the arms precedes the ability to use the hands.

Another major principle of growth concerns the way complex skills build upon simpler ones. The **principle of hierarchical integration** states that simple skills typically develop separately and independently. Later, however, these simple skills are integrated into more complex ones. Thus, the relatively complex skill of grasping something in the hand cannot be mastered until the developing infant learns how to control—and integrate—the movements of the individual fingers.

Finally, the last major principle of growth is the **principle of the independence of systems**, which suggests that different body systems grow at different rates. This principle means that growth in one system does not necessarily imply that growth is occurring in others. For instance, Figure 4-3 illustrates the patterns of growth for three very different systems: body size, which we have already discussed, the nervous system, and sexual characteristics. As you can see, both the rate and the timing of these different aspects of growth are independent (Bornstein & Lamb, 1992).

cephalocaudal principle   *the principle that growth follows a pattern that begins with head and upper body parts*

proximodistal principle   *the principle that development proceeds from the center of the body outward*

principle of hierarchical integration   *the principle stating that simple skills typically develop separately and independently but are later integrated into more complex skills*

principle of the independence of systems   *the principle of growth that suggests that different body systems grow at different rates*

TABLE 4-1

THE MAJOR PRINCIPLES GOVERNING GROWTH

Cephalocaudal Principle	Proximodistal Principle	Principle of Hierarchical Integration	Principle of the Independence of Systems
Growth follows a pattern that begins with the head and upper body parts and then proceeds to the rest of the body. Based on Greek and Latin roots meaning "head-to-tail."	Development proceeds from the center of the body outward. Based on the Latin words for "near" and "far."	Simple skills typically develop separately and independently. Later they are integrated into more complex skills.	Different body systems grow at different rates.

THE NERVOUS SYSTEM AND BRAIN: THE FOUNDATIONS OF DEVELOPMENT

Whatever feelings, movements, and thoughts an infant may experience are brought about by the same complex network: the infant's nervous system. The *nervous system* comprises the brain and the nerves that extend throughout the body.

Although estimates vary, infants are born with between 100 *billion* and 200 *billion neurons*, the basic nerve cells of the nervous system. To reach this number, neurons multiply at an amazing rate prior to birth. In fact, at some points in prenatal development, cell division creates some 250,000 additional neurons every minute. This pace is necessary, though: Because virtually no new neurons are created after birth, the number created in the womb is a lifetime's worth.

We can liken the changes that the brain undergoes in its development after birth to the actions of a farmer who, in order to strengthen the vitality of a fruit tree, prunes away unnecessary branches. In the same way, the ultimate capabilities of the brain are brought about in part by a "pruning down" of unnecessary neurons. As the infant's experience of the world increases, neurons that do not become interconnected become unnecessary. They

FIGURE 4-3

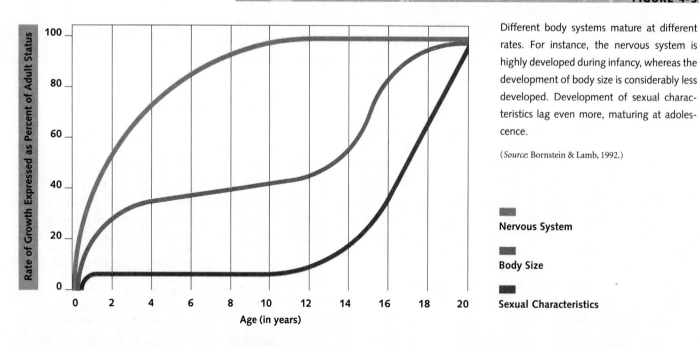

Different body systems mature at different rates. For instance, the nervous system is highly developed during infancy, whereas the development of body size is considerably less developed. Development of sexual characteristics lag even more, maturing at adolescence.

(*Source*: Bornstein & Lamb, 1992.)

Nervous System

Body Size

Sexual Characteristics

eventually die out, increasing the efficiency of the nervous system. Unlike most other aspects of growth, then, the development of the nervous system proceeds most effectively through the loss of cells (Black & Greenough, 1986; Lipsitt, 1986b; Kolb, 1989).

Although the creation of neurons stops just after birth, neurons continue to increase in size. In fact, the brain triples its weight in the first 2 years of life, and it reaches more than three-quarters of its adult weight and size by the age of 2. The intricacy of neural connections continues to increase throughout life.

Brain development, much of which unfolds automatically owing to genetically predetermined patterns, is also susceptible to environmental influences. **Plasticity**, the degree to which a developing structure or behavior is susceptible to experience, is relatively great for the brain. For instance, the nature of an infant's sensory experience affects both the size of individual neurons and the structure of their interconnections. Consequently, compared with those brought up in more enriched environments, infants raised in severely restricted settings are likely to show differences in brain structure and weight (Rosenzweig & Bennett, 1976; Gottlieb, 1991).

Work with nonhumans has been particularly illuminating in revealing the nature of the brain's plasticity. For instance, some studies have compared rats raised in an unusually visually stimulating environment to those raised in more typical, and less interesting, cages. Results of such research show that areas of the brain associated with vision are both thicker and heavier for the rats reared in enriched settings (Black & Greenough, 1986).

Conversely, environments that are unusually barren or in some way restricted may impede the brain's development. Again, work with nonhumans provides some intriguing data. In one study kittens were fitted with goggles that restricted their vision so that they could view only vertical lines. When the cats grew up and had their goggles removed, they were unable to see horizontal lines, although they saw vertical lines perfectly well. Analogously, kittens whose goggles restricted their vision of vertical lines early in life were effectively blind to vertical lines during their adulthood—although their vision of horizontal lines was accurate (Hirsch & Spinelli, 1970).

On the other hand, when goggles are placed on older cats who have lived relatively normal kittenhoods, such results are not seen after the goggles are removed. The conclusion is that there is a critical period for the development of vision. A **critical period** is a specific, but limited, time span, usually early in an organism's life, during which the organism is particularly susceptible to environmental influences relating to some particular facet of development. A critical period may be associated with a behavior—such as the development of full vision— or with the development of a structure of the body, such as the configuration of the brain.

The existence of critical periods raises several important issues. For one thing, it suggests that unless an infant receives a certain level of early environmental stimulation during a critical period, it may suffer damage or fail to develop capabilities that can never be fully remedied. If this is true, providing successful later intervention for such children may prove to be particularly challenging.

The opposite question also arises: Does an unusually high level of stimulation during critical periods produce developmental gains beyond what a more commonplace level of stimulation would provide?

Such questions have no simple answers. Determining how unusually impoverished or enriched environments affect later development is one of the central questions addressed by developmental researchers seeking to maximize opportunities for developing children (Fisher & Lerner, 1994; Lamb, 1994).

INTEGRATING THE BODILY SYSTEMS: THE LIFE CYCLES OF INFANCY

In the first days of life, the infant shows a jumble of different behavioral patterns. The most basic activities—sleeping, eating, crying, attending to the world—are controlled by a variety of bodily systems. Although each of these individual behavioral patterns may be func-

plasticity   the degree to which a developing structure or behavior is susceptible to experience

critical period   a specific, but limited, time span, usually early in an organism's life, during which the organism is particularly susceptible to environmental influences relating to some particular facet of development

rhythms *repetitive, cyclical patterns of behavior*

state *the degree of awareness displayed to both internal and external stimulation*

tioning effectively, it takes some time and effort for infants to learn to integrate the separate systems. In fact, one of the neonate's major missions is to integrate its individual behaviors (Thoman & Whitney, 1990; Thoman, 1990).

Rhythms and States.   One of the most important ways that behavior becomes integrated is through the development of various body **rhythms**, repetitive—cyclical patterns of behavior. Some rhythms are immediately obvious, such as the change from wakefulness to sleep. Others are more subtle, but still easily noticeable, such as breathing and sucking patterns. Still other rhythms may require careful observation to be noticed. For instance, newborns may go through periods in which they jerk their legs in a regular pattern every minute or so. Although some of these rhythms are apparent just after birth, others emerge slowly over the first year as the nervous system becomes more integrated (Thelen, 1979; Robertson, 1982).

One of the major rhythms relates to an infant's **state**—the degree of awareness it displays to both internal and external stimulation. As can be seen in Table 4-2, such states include various levels of wakeful behaviors, such as alertness, fussing, and crying, and different levels of sleep as well. Each change in state brings about an alteration in the amount of stimulation required to get the infant's attention (Brazelton, 1973; Thoman & Whitney, 1990; Karmel, Gardner, & Magnano, 1991).

Some of the different states that infants experience produce changes in electrical activity in the brain. These changes are reflected in different patterns of electrical *brain waves*, which can be measured by a device called an *electroencephalogram*, or *EEG*. Starting at three months before birth, the nature of these brain-wave patterns changes significantly until the infant reaches the age of three months, when a more mature pattern emerges and the brain waves stabilize (Parmalee & Sigman, 1983).

Sleep: Perchance to Dream?   At the beginning of infancy, the major state that occupies a baby's time is sleep—much to the relief of exhausted parents, who often regard sleep as a welcome respite from caregiving responsibilities. On average, newborns sleep some 16 to 17 hours daily. However, wide variations exist. Some sleep more than 20 hours; others sleep as little as 10 hours a day (Parmalee, Wenner, & Schulz, 1964).

Even though infants sleep a lot, you probably shouldn't ever wish to "sleep like a baby," despite popular wisdom. For one thing, the sleep of infants comes in fits and starts. Rather

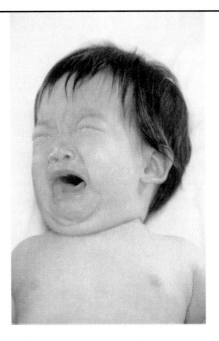 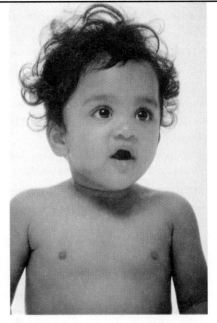

Infants cycle through various states, including crying and alertness. These states are integrated through bodily rhythms.

TABLE 4-2

PRIMARY BEHAVIORAL STATES

STATES	CHARACTERISTICS	PERCENTAGE OF TIME WHEN ALONE IN STATE
Awake States		
Alert	Attentive or scanning, the infant's eyes are open, bright, and shining.	6.7
Nonalert waking	Eyes are usually open, but dull and unfocused. Varied, but typically high motor activity.	2.8
Fuss	Fussing is continuous or intermittent, at low levels.	1.8
Cry	Intense vocalizations occurring singly or in succession.	1.7
Transition States Between Sleep and Waking		
Drowse	Infant's eyes are heavy-lidded, but opening and closing slowly. Low level of motor activity.	4.4
Daze	Open, but glassy and immobile eyes. State occurs between episodes of Alert and Drowse. Low level of activity.	1.0
Sleep-wake transition	Behaviors of both wakefulness and sleep are evident. Generalized motor activity; eyes may be closed, or they open and close rapidly. State occurs when baby is awakening.	1.3
Sleep States		
Active sleep	Eyes close; uneven respiration; intermittent rapid eye movements. Other behaviors: smiles, frowns, grimaces, mouthing, sucking, sighs, and sigh-sobs.	50.3
Quiet sleep	Eyes are closed and respiration is slow and regular. Motor activity limited to occasional startles, sigh-sobs, or rhythmic mouthing.	28.1
Transitional Sleep State		
Active-quiet transition sleep	During this state, which occurs between periods of Active Sleep and Quiet Sleep, the eyes are closed and there is little motor activity. Infant shows mixed behavioral signs of Active Sleep and Quiet Sleep.	1.9

(*Source*: Adapted from Thoman, & Whitney, 1990.)

than covering one long stretch, sleep initially comes in spurts of about two hours, followed by periods of wakefulness. Because of this, infants are "out of sync" with the rest of the world, for whom sleep comes at night and wakefulness during the day.

Luckily for their parents, infants eventually settle into a more adultlike pattern. After a week, babies sleep a bit more at night and are awake for slightly longer periods during the day. Typically, by the age of 16 weeks infants begin to sleep as much as six continuous hours at night, and daytime sleep falls into regular naplike patterns. Most infants sleep through the night by the end of the first year, and the total amount of sleep they need each day is down to about 15 hours (Thoman & Whitney, 1989).

Hidden beneath the supposedly tranquil sleep of infants is another cyclic pattern. During periods of sleep, infants' heart rates increase and become irregular, their blood pressure rises, and they begin to breathe more rapidly (Schechtman & Harper, 1991; Ferrari, Kelsall, Rennie, & Evans, 1994). Sometimes, although not always, their closed eyes begin to move in a back-and-forth pattern, as if they were viewing an action-packed scene. This period of active sleep is similar, although not identical, to the **rapid eye movement (REM) sleep** found in older children and adults and is associated with dreaming.

rapid eye movement (REM) sleep   the *period of sleep that is found in older children and adults and is associated with dreaming*

Infants sleep in spurts, often making them out of sync with the rest of the world.

At first, this active, REM-like sleep takes up roughly one-half of an infant's sleep, compared with just 20 percent of an adult's sleep (see Figure 4-4). However, the quantity of active sleep quickly declines, and by the age of 6 months it amounts to just one-third of total sleep time (Coons & Guilleminault, 1982).

The appearance of active sleep periods that are similar to REM sleep in adults raises the intriguing question of whether infants dream during those periods. No one knows the answer, although it seems unlikely. First of all, young infants do not have much to dream about, given their relatively limited experiences. Furthermore, the brain waves of sleeping infants appear to be qualitatively different from those of adults who are dreaming. It is not until the baby reaches three or four months of age that the wave patterns become similar to those of dreaming adults, suggesting that young infants aren't dreaming during active sleep—or at least aren't doing so in the same way as adults do (McCall, 1979; Parmalee & Sigman, 1983).

Although the patterns that infants show in their wakefulness-sleep cycles seem largely preprogrammed by genetic factors, environmental influences also play a part. For instance, both long- and short-term stressors in infants' environments can affect their sleep patterns. When environmental circumstances keep babies awake, sleep, when at last it comes, is apt to be less active (and quieter) than usual.

Furthermore, cultural practices affect the sleep patterns of infants. For example, among the Kipsigis of Africa, infants sleep with their mothers at night and are allowed to nurse whenever they wake. In daytime, they accompany their mothers during daily chores, often napping while strapped to their mothers' backs. The result of this practice is that infants among the Kipsigis do not sleep through the night until much later than do babies in Western societies. In fact, for the first 8 months of life, Kipsigis infants do not sleep much longer than three hours at a stretch. In comparison, 8-month-old infants in the United States may sleep as long as eight hours at a time (Boismier, 1977; Super & Harkness, 1982; Cole, 1992; Anders & Taylor, 1994).

SIDS: The Unanticipated Killer.   For a tiny percentage of infants, the rhythm of sleep is interrupted by a deadly affliction: sudden infant death syndrome, or SIDS. **Sudden infant death syndrome (SIDS)** is a disorder in which seemingly healthy infants die in their sleep. Put to bed for a nap or for the night, an infant simply never wakes up.

No known cause has been found to explain SIDS, which afflicts some two of every thousand infants, or some 7,000 children in the United States annually. Although it seems to

sudden infant death syndrome (SIDS)
a disorder in which seemingly healthy infants die in their sleep

FIGURE 4-4

REM SLEEP THROUGH THE LIFE SPAN

As we age, the proportion of REM sleep decreases; the amount of total sleep time declines.

(*Source*: Adapted from Roffwarg, Muzio, & Dement, 1966.)

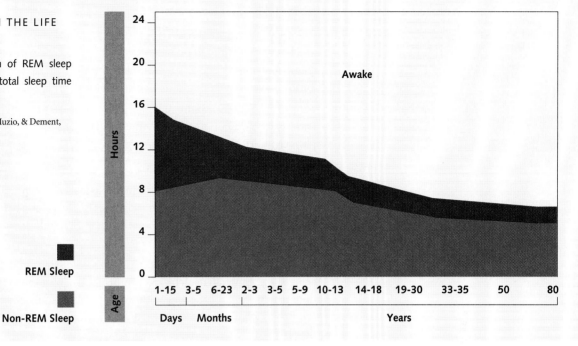

occur when the normal patterns of breathing during sleep are interrupted, scientists have been unable to discover why that might happen. It is clear that infants do not smother or choke; they die a peaceful death, simply ceasing to breathe. No means for preventing the syndrome have been found, which occurs most often for children under the age of six months. It is the leading cause of death in children under the age of 1 year (Burns & Lipsitt, 1991).

Certain factors increase the risk of SIDS. For instance, boys and African-Americans are at greater risk. In addition, low birthweight and low Apgar scores found at birth are associated with SIDS, as are having a mother who smokes during pregnancy. Still, no clear-cut factor predicts with any certainty which infant is most likely to be susceptible to the problem; SIDS is found in children of every race and socioeconomic class and in children who have had no apparent health problems (Burns & Lipsitt, 1991; DiFranza & Lew, 1995).

Because parents have no preparation for the death of an infant from SIDS, the event is particularly devastating. Parents often feel guilt, fearing that they were neglectful or have somehow contributed to their child's death. Yet such guilt is unwarranted: Nothing has been identified that can prevent the death.

Review and Rethink

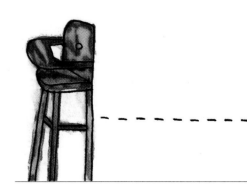

REVIEW

- The major principles of growth are the cephalocaudal principle (growth proceeds from top to bottom), the proximodistal principle (growth proceeds outward), the principle of hierarchical integration (complex skills build on simple skills), and the principle of the independence of systems (different body systems grow at different rates).

- Development of the nervous system entails first the development of billions of neurons, which mostly occurs before birth, and then the formation through the infant's experience of useful interconnections among the neurons.

◆   Brain development depends on both genetic and environmental factors. Plasticity, the susceptibility of a developing organism to environmental influences, is relatively high for the brain.

◆   Researchers have identified critical periods during the development of body systems and behaviors—limited periods when the organism is particularly susceptible to environmental influences. If environmental influences are disturbed during a critical period, development may also be disturbed.

◆   Babies integrate their individual behaviors by developing rhythms—repetitive, cyclical patterns of behavior. A major rhythm relates to the infant's state—the awareness it displays to internal and external stimulation.

RETHINK

◆   The cephalocaudal principle seems to imply that babies should learn how to talk before they learn how to walk, and yet most babies can walk long before they can form understandable utterances. How does another major growth principle explain this apparent contradiction?

◆   Research indicates that there is a critical period during childhood for normal language acquisition. Individuals deprived of normal language stimulation as babies and children may never use language with the same skill as others who were not so deprived. For babies who are born deaf, what are the implications of this research finding, particularly with regard to signed languages?

◆   This chapter describes critical periods during which infants may be either helped or harmed in their development by their exposure to environmental influences. What are the implications of such critical periods for public policy relating to infant care?

◆   What are some cultural influences on infants' daily patterns of behavior that operate in the culture of which you are a part? How do they differ from the influences of other cultures (either within or outside the United States) of which you are aware?

MOTOR DEVELOPMENT

Suppose you were hired by a genetic engineering firm to redesign newborns and were charged with replacing the current version with a new, more mobile one. The first change you would probably consider in carrying out this (luckily fictitious) job would be in the conformation and composition of the baby's body.

The shape and proportions of newborn babies are simply not conducive to easy mobility. Their heads are so large and heavy that young infants lack the strength to raise them. Because their limbs are short in relation to the rest of the body, their movements are further impeded. Furthermore, their bodies are mainly fat, with a limited amount of muscle; the result is that they lack strength (Illingworth, 1973).

Fortunately, it doesn't take too long before infants begin to develop a remarkable amount of mobility. In fact, even at birth they have an extensive repertoire of behavioral possibilities brought about by innate reflexes, and their range of motor skills grows rapidly during the first 2 years of life.

REFLEXES: OUR INBORN PHYSICAL SKILLS

When her father pressed 3-day-old Christina's palm with his finger, she responded by tightly winding her small fist around his finger and grasping it. When he moved his finger upward, she held on so tightly that it seemed he might be able to lift her completely off her crib floor.

The Basic Reflexes.   In fact, her father was right: Christina probably could have been lifted in this way. The reason for her resolute grip was activation of one of the dozens of reflexes

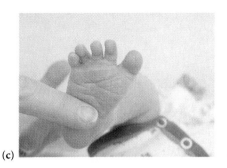

(a)   (b)   (c)

Infants showing (a) the rooting and grasping reflex, (b) the startle reflex, and the (c) the Babinski reflex.

with which infants are born. **Reflexes** are unlearned, organized, involuntary responses that occur automatically in the presence of certain stimuli. As we first noted in Chapter 2, when we discussed reflexes relating to the intake of food, newborns enter the world with an expansive repertoire of behavioral patterns that, when activated, help them adapt to their new surroundings and serve to protect them.

As we can see from the list of reflexes in Table 4-3, many reflexes clearly represent behavior that has survival value, helping to ensure the well-being of the infant. For instance, the *swimming reflex* makes a baby who is lying face down in a body of water paddle and kick in a sort of swimming motion. The obvious consequence of such behavior is to help the baby move from danger and survive until a caregiver can come to its rescue. Similarly, the *eye blink reflex* seems designed to protect the eye from too much direct light, which might damage the retina.

reflexes   *unlearned, organized, involuntary responses that occur automatically in the presence of certain stimuli*

TABLE 4-3

SOME BASIC REFLEXES IN INFANTS

Reflex	Approximate Age of Disappearance	Description	Possible Function
Rooting Reflex	3 weeks	Neonate's tendency to turn its head toward things that touch its cheek.	Food intake
Stepping Reflex	2 months	Movement of legs when held upright with feet touching the floor.	Prepares infants for independent locomotion
Swimming Reflex	4–6 months	Infant's tendency to paddle and kick in a sort of swimming motion when lying face down in a body of water.	Avoidance of danger
Moro Reflex	6 months	Activated when support for the neck and head is suddenly removed. The arms of the infant are thrust outward and then appear to grasp onto something.	Similar to primates' protection from falling
Babinski Reflex	8–12 months	An infant fans out its toes in response to a stroke on the outside of its foot.	Unknown
Startle Reflex	Remains in different form	An infant, in response to a sudden noise, flings out its arms, arches its back, and spreads its fingers.	Protection
Eye Blink Reflex	Remains	Rapid shutting and opening of eye on exposure to direct light.	Protection of eye from direct light
Sucking Reflex	Remains	Infant's tendency to suck at things that touch its lips.	Food intake
Gag Reflex	Remains	An infant's reflex to clear its throat.	Prevents choking

Given the protective value of many reflexes, it might seem beneficial for them to remain with us for our entire lives. In fact, some do: The eye blink reflex remains functional throughout the full lifespan. On the other hand, quite a few reflexes, such as the swimming reflex, disappear after a few months. Why should this be the case?

Most researchers attribute the gradual disappearance of reflexes to the increase in voluntary control over behavior that occurs as infants become more able to control their muscles. In addition, it may be that reflexes form the foundation for future, more complex behaviors. As these more intricate behaviors become well learned, they subsume the earlier reflexes (Minkowski, 1967; Touwen, 1984; Myklebust & Gottlieb, 1993).

It may even be that the use of reflexes stimulates parts of the brain responsible for more complex behaviors. For example, some researchers argue that exercise of the stepping reflex helps the brain's cortex to develop later the ability to walk. As evidence, developmental psychologist Philip R. Zelazo and his colleagues conducted a study in which they provided two-week-old infants practice in walking for four sessions of three minutes each over a six-week period. The results showed that the children who had the walking practice actually began to walk unaided several months earlier than those who had had no such practice. Zelazo suggests that the training produced stimulation of the stepping reflex, which in turn led to stimulation of the brain's cortex, readying the infant earlier for independent locomotion (Zelazo, Zelazo, & Kolb, 1972; Zelazo, 1983; Zelazo, Zelazo, Cohen, & Zelazo, 1993).

Do these findings suggest that parents should make out-of-the-ordinary efforts to stimulate their infant's reflexes? Probably not. Although the evidence shows that intensive practice may produce an earlier appearance of certain motor activities, there is no evidence that the activities are performed qualitatively any better in practiced infants than in unpracticed infants. Furthermore, even when early gains are found, they do not seem to produce ultimately an adult who is more proficient in motor skills.

In fact, structured exercise may do more harm than good: According to the American Academy of Pediatricians, structured exercise for infants may lead to muscle strain, fractured bones, and dislocated limbs, consequences that far outweigh the unproven benefits that may come from the practice (American Academy of Pediatricians, 1988).

The Universality of Reflexes.   Although reflexes are, by definition, genetically determined and universal throughout all infants, there are actually some cultural variations in the ways they are displayed. For instance, consider the *Moro reflex*, which is activated when support for the neck and head is suddenly removed. The Moro reflex consists of the infant's arms thrusting outward and then appearing to seek to grasp onto something. Most scientists feel that the Moro reflex represents a left-over response that we humans have inherited from our nonhuman ancestors. The Moro reflex is an extremely useful behavior for monkey babies, who travel about by clinging to their mothers' backs. If they lose their grip, they fall down unless they are able to grasp quickly onto their mother's fur—in a Moro-like reflex (Prechtl, 1982).

Although the Moro reflex is found in all humans, it appears with significantly different vigor in different children. Some differences reflect cultural and ethnic variations. For instance, Caucasian infants show a pronounced response to situations that produce the Moro reflex. Not only do they fling out their arms, but they also cry and respond in a generally agitated manner. In contrast, Navajo babies react to the same situation much more calmly. Their arms do not flail out as much, and they cry only rarely (Freedman, 1979).

In some cases, reflexes can serve as helpful diagnostic tools for pediatricians. Because reflexes emerge and disappear on a regular timetable, their absence—or presence—at a given point of infancy can provide a clue that something may be amiss in an infant's development. (Even for adults, physicians include reflexes in their diagnostic bag of tricks, as anyone knows who has had his or her knee tapped with a rubber mallet to see if the lower leg jerks forward.)

Although some reflexes may be remnants from our prehuman past and seemingly have little usefulness in terms of survival today, they still may serve a very contemporary function. According to some developmental researchers, some reflexes may promote caregiving and nurturance on the part of adults in the vicinity. For instance, Christina's father, who found his daughter gripping his finger tightly when he pressed her palm, probably cares little that she is simply responding with an innate reflex. Instead, he will more likely view his daughter's action as responsiveness to him, a signal perhaps of increasing interest and affection on her part. As we will see in Chapter 6, when we discuss the social and personality development of infants, such apparent responsiveness can help cement the growing social relationship between an infant and its caregivers (Bell & Ainsworth, 1972; Belsky, Rovine, & Taylor, 1984).

MOTOR DEVELOPMENT IN INFANCY: LANDMARKS OF PHYSICAL ACHIEVEMENT

Probably no physical changes are more obvious—and more eagerly anticipated—than the increasing array of motor skills that babies acquire during infancy. Most parents can remember their child's first steps with a sense of pride and awe at how quickly she or he changed from a helpless infant, unable even to roll over, into a person who could navigate quite effectively in the world (Thelen, 1995).

Gross Motor Skills.   Even though the motor skills of newborns are not terribly sophisticated, at least compared with attainments that will soon appear, infants still are able to accomplish some kinds of movement. For instance, when placed on their stomachs they wiggle their arms and legs and may try to lift their heavy heads. As their strength increases, they are able to push hard enough against the surface on which they are resting to propel their bodies in different directions. They often end up moving backwards rather than forwards, but by the age of 6 months they become rather accomplished at moving themselves in particular directions. These initial efforts are the forerunners of crawling, in which they coordinate the motions of their arms and legs and propel themselves forward. Crawling appears typically between 8 and 10 months. (Figure 4-5 provides a summary of some of the milestones of normal motor development.)

Walking comes later. At about the age of 9 months, most infants are able to walk by supporting themselves on furniture, and by the end of the first year of life, most can walk well on their own.

At the same time that infants are learning to move around, they are perfecting the ability to remain in a stationary sitting position. At first, babies cannot remain seated upright without support. But they quickly master this ability, and most are able to sit without support by the age of 6 months.

Fine Motor Skills.   As infants are perfecting their gross motor skills, such as sitting upright and walking, they are also making advances in their fine motor skills (see Table 4-4). For instance, by the age of 3 months, infants show some ability to coordinate the movements of their limbs (Thelen, 1994).

Furthermore, although infants are born with a rudimentary ability to reach toward an object, this ability is neither very sophisticated nor very accurate, and it disappears about the age of 4 weeks. A different and more precise form of reaching reappears at 4 months. It takes some time for infants to coordinate successful grasping after they reach out, but in fairly short order they are able to reach out and hold onto an object of interest (Mathew & Cook, 1990; Rochat & Goubet, 1995).

The sophistication of fine motor skills continues to grow. By the age of 11 months, infants are able to pick objects as small as marbles off the ground—presenting care providers with issues of safety, since the place such objects often go next is the mouth. And by the time they are 2, children can carefully hold a cup, bring it to their lips, and take a drink without spilling a drop.

FIGURE 4-5

0 month: fetal posture	**1 month:** chin up	**2 months:** chest up	**3 months:** reach and miss
4 months: sit with support	**5 months:** sit on lap, grasp object	**6 months:** sit on high chair, grasp dangling object	**7 months:** sit alone
8 months: stand with help	**9 months:** stand holding furniture	**10 months:** creep	**11 months:** walk when led
12 months: pull to stand by furniture	**13 months:** climb stair steps	**14 months:** stand alone	**15 months:** walk alone

MILESTONES OF MOTOR DEVELOPMENT

(Adapted from Shirley, 1993.)

Developmental Norms: Comparing the Individual to the Group.   It is important to keep in mind that the timing of the milestones that we have been discussing is based on **norms**, which represent the average performance of a large sample of children of a given age. They permit comparisons between a particular child's performance on a particular behavior and the average performance of the children in the norm sample.

For instance, one of the most widely used techniques to determine infants' normative standing is the **Brazelton Neonatal Behavioral Assessment Scale (NBAS)**, a measure designed to determine infants' neurological and behavioral responses to their environment. The NBAS provides a supplement to the traditional Apgar test (discussed in Chapter 3) that is given immediately following birth. Taking about 30 minutes to administer, the NBAS includes 27 separate categories of responses that comprise four general aspects of infants'

norms   *the average performance of a large sample of individuals of a given age*

Brazelton Neonatal Behavioral Assessment Scale (NBAS)   *a measure designed to determine infants' neurological and behavioral responses to their environment*

TABLE 4-4

MILESTONES OF FINE MOTOR DEVELOPMENT

Age (months)	Skill
3	Opens hand prominently
3.5	Grasps rattle
8.5	Grasps with thumb and finger
11	Holds crayon adaptively
14	Builds tower of two cubes
16	Places pegs in board
24	Imitates strokes on paper
33	Copies circle

Source: Adapted from Frankenburg et al., 1992, and Bayley, 1969.)

behavior: interactions with others (such as alertness and cuddliness); motor behavior; physiological control (such as the ability to be soothed after being upset); and responses to stress (Brazelton, Nugent, & Lester, 1987; Brazelton, 1973, 1990).

Although the norms provided by scales such as the NBAS are useful in making broad generalizations about the timing of various behaviors and skills, they must be interpreted with caution. Because norms are averages, they mask substantial individual differences in the times when children attain various achievements. They also may hide the fact that the sequence in which various behaviors are achieved may differ somewhat from one child to another.

Furthermore, norms are useful only to the extent that they are based on data from a large, heterogeneous, culturally diverse sample of children. Unfortunately, many of the norms on which developmentalists have traditionally relied have been based on groups of infants who are predominantly Caucasian and from the middle and upper socioeconomic strata (e.g., Gesell, 1946). This limitation would not be critical if no differences existed in the timing of development in children from different cultural, racial, and social groups. But they do. For example, as a group, African-American babies show more rapid motor development than do Caucasian babies throughout infancy. Moreover, significant variations are related to cultural factors, as we discuss next (Werner, 1972; Rosser & Randolph, 1989; Brazelton, 1991).

Developmental Diversity

The Cultural Dimensions of Motor Development

Among the Ache people, who live in the rain forest of South America, infants face an early life of physical restriction. Because the Ache lead a nomadic existence, living in a series of tiny camps in the rain forest, open space is at a premium. Consequently, for the first few years of life, infants spend nearly all their time in direct physical contact with their mothers. Even when they are not physically touching their mothers, they are permitted to venture no more than a few feet away.

Infants among the Kipsigis people, who live in a more open environment in rural Kenya, Africa, lead quite a different existence. Their lives are filled with activity and exercise. Parents seek to teach their children to sit up, stand, and walk from the earliest days of infancy. For example, very young infants are placed in shallow holes in the ground designed to keep them in an upright position. Parents begin to teach their children to walk starting at the eighth week of life. The infants are held with their feet touching the ground, and they are pushed forward.

Clearly, the infants in these two societies lead very different lives (Super, 1976; Kaplan & Dove, 1987). But do the relative lack of early motoric stimulation for Ache infants and the efforts of the Kipsigis to encourage motoric development really matter?

The answer is both yes and no. Yes, in that Ache infants tend to show delayed motor development, relative both to Kipsigis infants and to children raised in Western societies. Although their social abilities are no different, Ache children tend to begin walking at about 23 months, about a year later than the typical child in the United States. In contrast, Kipsigis children, who are encouraged in their motor development, learn to sit up and walk several weeks earlier, on average, than U.S. children.

In the long run, however, the differences among Ache, Kipsigis, and Western children disappear. By late childhood, there is no evidence of differences in general, overall motor skills among Ache, Kipsigis, and Western youngsters.

Variations in the timing of motor skills seem to depend in part on parental expectations of what is the "appropriate" schedule for the emergence of specific skills. For instance, one study examined the motor skills of infants who lived in a single city in England, but whose mothers varied in ethnic origin. In the research, English, Jamaican, and Indian mothers' expectations were first assessed regarding several markers of their infants' motor skills. The Jamaican mothers expected their infants to sit and walk significantly earlier than did the English and Indian mothers, and the actual emergence of these activities was in line with their expectations. The source of the Jamaican infants' earlier mastery seemed to lie in the treatment of the children by their parents. For instance, Jamaican mothers gave their children practice in stepping quite early in infancy (Hopkins & Westra, 1989, 1990).

In sum, the time at which specific motor skills appear is in part determined by cultural factors. Activities that are an intrinsic part of a culture are more apt to be purposely taught to infants in that culture, leading to the potential of their earlier emergence (Nugent, Lester, & Brazelton, 1989).

It is not all that surprising that children in a given culture who are expected by their parents to master a particular skill, and who are taught components of that skill from an early age, are more likely to be proficient in that skill earlier than children from other cultures with no such expectations and no such training. The larger question, however, is whether the earlier emergence of a basic motor behavior in a given culture has lasting consequences for specific motor skills and for achievements in other domains. On this issue, the jury is still out (Bloch, 1989).

What is clear, however, is that there are certain genetically determined constraints on how early a skill can emerge. It is physically impossible for one-month-old infants to stand and walk, regardless of the encouragement and practice they may get within their culture. Parents who are eager to accelerate their infants' motoric development, then, should be cautioned not to hold overly ambitious goals. In fact, they might well ask themselves whether it matters if an infant acquires a motor skill a few weeks earlier than his or her peers. The most reasonable answer is no. Although some parents may take pride in a child who walks earlier than other babies (just as some parents may be concerned over a delay of a few weeks), in the long run the timing of this activity will probably make no difference.

NUTRITION IN INFANCY: FUELING MOTOR DEVELOPMENT

The rapid physical growth that occurs during infancy is fueled by the nutrients that infants receive. Without proper nutrition, infants not only cannot reach their physical potential, but they suffer cognitive and social consequences as well (Pollitt et al., 1993; Pollitt, 1994).

marasmus *a disease characterized by the cessation of growth*

Malnutrition.   The condition of having an improper amount and balance of nutrients, *malnutrition,* produces several results, none good. For instance, children living in many developing countries, where they are more susceptible to malnourishment and at greater risk for disease than are children in more industrialized, affluent countries, begin to show a slower growth rate by the age of 6 months. By the time they reach the age of 2, their height and weight are only 95 percent the height and weight of children in more industrialized countries. Furthermore, children who have been chronically malnourished during infancy later score lower on tests of IQ and tend to do less well in school. These effects may linger even if the children's diet has improved substantially (Barrett & Frank, 1987; Sigman, Neumann, Jansen, & Bwibo, 1989; Gorman & Pollitt, 1992; Grantham-McGregor et al., 1994).

The problem of malnutrition is greatest in underdeveloped countries, where almost ten percent of infants are severely malnourished. In the Dominican Republic, for instance, 13 percent of youngsters under age 3 are underweight, and 21 percent have stunted growth. In other areas, the problem is even worse. In South Asia, for example, almost 60 percent of all children are underweight (World Food Council, 1992; see Figure 4-6).

Problems of malnourishment are not restricted to third-world countries, however. In the United States, the richest nation in the world, some 14 million children live in poverty, which puts them at risk for malnutrition. In fact, although overall poverty rates are no worse than they were 20 years ago, the poverty rate for children under the age of 3 has increased. Some one-quarter of families who have children 2 years old and younger live in poverty. And, as we can see in Figure 4-7, the rates are even higher for African-American and Hispanic families, as well as for single-parent families (Einbinder, 1992; Carnegie Task Force on Meeting the Needs of Young Children, 1994).

Although these children rarely become severely malnourished, owing to adequate social safety nets, they remain susceptible to *undernutrition,* in which there is some deficiency in diet. In fact, some surveys find that as many as a quarter of 1- to 5-year-old youngsters in the United States have diets that fall below the minimum caloric intake recommended by nutritional experts (Barrett & Frank, 1987; U.S. Bureau of the Census, 1992).

Severe malnutrition during infancy can lead to several disorders. Malnutrition during the first year can produce **marasmus**, a disease characterized by the cessation of growth.

FIGURE 4-6

The number of underweight children under the age of 5 years in developing countries is substantial.

(*Source*: World Food Council, 1992.)

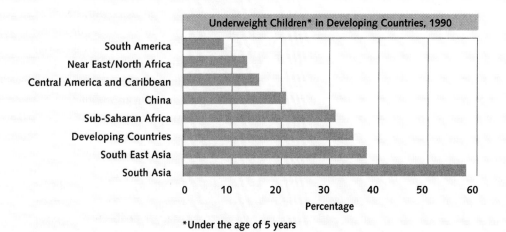

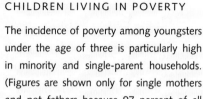

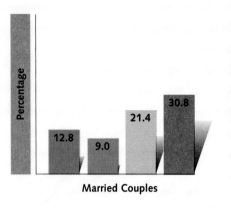

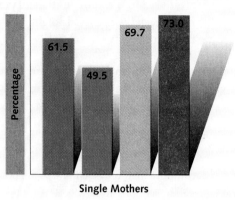

CHILDREN LIVING IN POVERTY

The incidence of poverty among youngsters under the age of three is particularly high in minority and single-parent households. (Figures are shown only for single mothers and not fathers because 97 percent of all children under three who live with a single parent live with their mothers; only 3 percent live with their fathers.)

(*Source*: Einbinder, 1992.)

Race and Ethnic Background: ■ All ■ White ■ African-American ■ Hispanic

Marasmus, attributable to a severe deficiency in proteins and calories, causes the body to waste away and ultimately results in death. Older children are susceptible to **kwashiorkor,** a disease in which a child's stomach, limbs, and face swell with water. To a casual observer, it appears that a child with kwashiorkor is actually chubby. However, this is an illusion: The child's body is in fact struggling to make use of the few nutrients that are available.

Although the consequences are not as severe as those of malnutrition, undernutrition also has its long-term costs. For instance, there is increasing evidence that children's later cognitive development is affected by even mild to moderate undernutrition (Sigman, 1995).

Obesity.   Although it is clear that malnourishment during infancy has potentially disastrous consequences for an infant, the effects of *obesity*, defined as weight greater than 20 percent above the average for a given height, are less clear. For one thing, there appears to be no correlation between obesity during infancy and obesity at the age of 16 years. (There is an association between obesity after the age of six and adult weight, however.)

Furthermore, although some research suggests that overfeeding during infancy may lead to the creation of unnecessary fat cells, which remain in the body throughout life, it is not clear that an abundance of fat cells necessarily leads to adult obesity (Wright, 1987). In fact, genetic factors are an important determinant of obesity (Knittle, 1975; Bouchard et al., 1990a; Fabsitz, Carmelli, & Hewitt, 1992).

In sum, obesity during infancy is not a major concern. On the other hand, the societal view that "a fat baby is a healthy baby" is not necessarily correct, either. Rather than focusing on their infant's weight, parents should concentrate on providing appropriate nutrition. At least during the period of infancy, concerns about weight need not be central, as long as infants are provided with an appropriate diet.

Although everyone agrees on the importance of receiving proper nutrition during infancy, just how to reach that goal is a source of controversy. Because infants are not born with the ability to eat or digest solid food, at first they exist solely on a liquid diet. But just what should that liquid be—a mother's breast milk or a formula of commercially processed cow's milk with vitamin additives? The answer has been a major source of contention.

kwashiorkor   *a disease in which a child's stomach, limbs, and face swell with water*

Breast or Bottle: Which is Better?   Some forty years ago, if a mother asked her pediatrician whether breast-feeding or bottle-feeding was better, she would have received a simple and clear-cut answer: Bottle-feeding was the preferred method. During the 1940s, the general belief among child care experts was that breast-feeding was an obsolete method that put children unnecessarily at risk.

With bottle-feeding, the argument went, parents could keep track of the amount of milk their baby was receiving and could thereby ensure that the child was taking in sufficient nutrients. In contrast, mothers who breast-fed their babies could never be certain just how much milk their infants were getting. Furthermore, use of the bottle was said to help mothers keep their feedings to a rigid, one-bottle-every-4-hours schedule—at that time the recommended procedure.

Today, however, a mother would get a very different answer to the same question. Child care authorities agree: For the first four to six months of life, there is no better food for an infant than breast milk (American Academy of Pediatrics, 1982). Breast milk not only contains all the nutrients necessary for growth, but it also seems to offer some degree of immunity to a variety of childhood diseases, such as respiratory infections and diarrhea. Breast milk is more easily digested than is cow's milk or formula, and it is sterile, warm, and convenient for the mother to dispense (Eiger, 1987; Howie et al., 1990). And, as we discuss later in the Directions in Development section, it may even hold health-related advantages for mothers.

Breast-feeding also holds significant emotional advantages for both mother and child. Most mothers report that the experience of breast-feeding brings about feelings of intimacy and closeness that are incomparable to any other experiences with their infants (K. Epstein, 1993). At the same time, infants, whose rooting and sucking reflexes are genetically well designed to find nourishment and satisfaction from breast-feeding, seem to be calmed and soothed by the experience (Eiger & Olds, 1987).

Despite the advantages of breast-feeding, only about half of all new mothers in the United States employ it. This is actually a decline from the peak that was reached in 1982, when almost two-thirds of all new mothers breast-fed their babies (see Figure 4-8).

Breast or bottle? Although infants receive adequate nourishment from breast- or bottle-feeding, most authorities agree "breast is best."

FIGURE 4-8

BREAST-FEEDING TRENDS
1970–1992

Beginning in the early 1970s and extending for the next 10 years, the percentage of mothers who were breast-feeding increased steadily. However, the rate has declined since that point, except for a slight rise at the beginning of the 1990s. In addition, the rate of mothers who breast-feed has been more than twice as high for white women as for African-American women.

(*Source:* Ross Laboratories, 1993.)

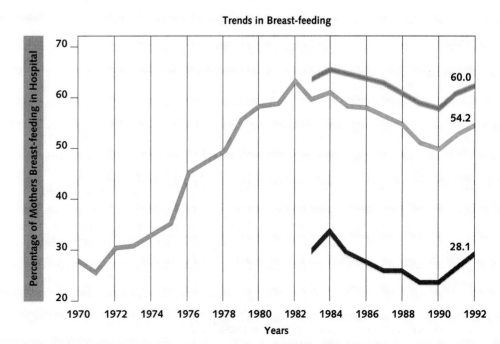

Trends in Breast-feeding

White   African   Total
American

Although recent figures suggest that breast-feeding may once again be on the rise, the decline that occurred in the 1980s is surprising (Ross Laboratories, 1993).

Issues of age, social status, and race influence the decision whether to breast-feed. Rates of breast-feeding are highest among women who are older, have better educations, and are of higher socioeconomic status (Richardson & Champion, 1992). Moreover, there are ethnic and racial group differences. For instance, breast-feeding among white mothers in the United States occurs at a rate almost double that for African-American mothers (Child Health USA '93, 1993).

If authorities are in agreement about the benefits of breast-feeding, why in so many cases do women not breast-feed? In some cases, they cannot. Some women have difficulties producing milk, whereas others are taking some type of medicine or have an infectious disease such as AIDS that could be passed on to their infants through breast milk. Sometimes, infants are too ill to nurse successfully. And in many cases of adoption, where the birth mother is unavailable after giving birth, the adoptive mother has no choice but to bottle-feed.

Speaking of Development

J. Kenneth Whitt

Born: ·································· 1946

Education: ····················· B.A., Psychology, University of Virginia; Ph.D., Clinical Psychology, University of Texas

Position: ························· Child Development Researcher

Home: ····························· Chapel Hill, North Carolina

Although malnutrition in infants is often thought of as a condition more prevalent in underdeveloped countries, it can also be found in the richest of nations such as the United States.

But the causes of malnutrition, in many cases, are not what they may appear to be on the surface, and a further diagnosis can reveal the root problem and provide treatment that will restore the infant's development.

According to Dr. Kenneth Whitt, professor of psychiatry and pediatrics at the University of North Carolina School of Medicine, when children show abnormally slow growth and development in their first three years, it is known as failure to thrive.

"Traditionally, failure to thrive was considered to have either an organic or nonorganic basis," Whitt explained. Although organic failure to thrive is produced by a physical cause such as the inability to digest food properly, "nonorganic failure to thrive was considered to be produced by caregiver neglect or psychopathology of the caregiver."

Determining the cause of failure to thrive has proved challenging. For instance, looking at the point where a child's growth begins to show a change may be a starting point in finding the ultimate reason for the malnutrition, according to Whitt.

"If we notice that a child begins to fall off his or her growth curve, but does not fit failure to thrive criteria until much later, we have to trace back to where the failure to thrive began," he said. "We ask whether there was something that happened in that time developmentally that can give us a clue as to what was going on."

In other cases, the decision not to breast-feed is based on practical considerations. Women who hold jobs outside the home may not have sufficiently flexible schedules to breast-feed their infants. This problem is particularly true with less affluent women who may have less control over their schedules. Such problems also may account for the lower rate of breast-feeding among mothers of lower socioeconomic status.

Education is also an issue: Some women simply do not receive adequate information and advice regarding the advantages of breast-feeding, and they choose to use formula because it seems an appropriate choice. Indeed, some hospitals may inadvertently encourage the use of formula by including it in the gift packets new mothers receive as they leave the hospital.

In developing countries, the use of formula is particularly problematic. Because formula often comes in powdered form that is to be mixed with water, local pollution of the water supply can make formula particularly dangerous. Yet until the early 1980s, manufacturers aggressively sold formula in such countries, touting it as the "modern" choice. It took a massive, worldwide boycott of products manufactured by Nestlé, a major

"While at first it appeared to be a simple eating disorder, something didn't seem to fit. Why would a child develop this pattern of behavior? There was nothing in the infant's social history that would indicate a reason for it."

"One of the ways we use our understanding of child development is to provide a link to families so as not to struggle with feeding."

Whitt noted that there have been numerous cases in which the caregiver was initially considered to have been the source of failure to thrive, but after closer scrutiny a different cause emerged. "For instance, infants were admitted who had nonorganic failure to thrive, but it was found that a number of the cases didn't fit with the history from a social/emotional perspective."

For example, one case of failure to thrive occurred in an 11-month-old where it seemed as though the child was simply refusing to eat. As Whitt explained, "His refusing to eat appeared to be a behavior problem. However, after talking with the child's caregivers, it was discovered that this problem had been occurring since the infant was 5 or 6 months of age.

"While at first it appeared to be a simple eating disorder, something didn't seem to fit. Why would a child develop this pattern of behavior at a time when attachment is the norm? There was nothing in the infant's social history that would indicate a reason for deviation from normal developmental expectations."

"More importantly, the pattern of refusal is a more typical response during a later period when the child strives to organize autonomous behavior and struggles to separate and individuate emotionally from the primary caregiver. This absence of 'goodness-of-fit' between expected developmental challenges and observed patterns of behavior gave cause to question the 'non-organic' assumptions of etiology in this case."

Ultimately, though, Whitt's research team identified the true cause. "It was found that the child had lactose intolerance and was unable to digest milk properly. Within a few days after changing the formula, he began to recover," Whitt said.

Understanding how feeding emerges in normal development is an important part of understanding failure to thrive and malnutrition, according to Whitt. "Kids of all ages are trying to be competent," Whitt explained. "One of the ways we use our understanding of child development is to provide a rationale to families so as to decrease struggles over feeding.

"Have them look at finger feeding, allowing the child to feed him- or herself and not worry about the mess. It's a beginning to help families to plug into the normal developmental process, and a way to help them and physicians in treating eating disorders."

manufacturer of formula, to end the company's promotion of bottle-feeding (J. L. Fox, 1984). Formula containers now include labels that advertise the benefits of breast-feeding and the dangers associated with bottle-feeding, and free samples are no longer supplied to mothers.

Educational, social, and cultural support for breast-feeding is particularly important. For instance, physicians need to educate their patients about the importance of the practice and to provide specific information on just how to breast-feed. (Although breast-feeding is

Directions in Development

Understanding the Benefits of Breast-feeding

"Breast is best." This slogan has been widely publicized by groups seeking to increase the practice of breast-feeding. The notion that breast-feeding is superior to bottle-feeding recently has taken on new credibility, as research by developmental researchers has found new benefits—not only for infants but also for mothers.

For instance, recent research suggests that women who breast-feed may have lower rates of ovarian cancer and breast cancer prior to menopause. Furthermore, the hormones produced during breast-feeding help shrink the uteruses of women following birth, enabling their bodies to return more quickly to a pre-pregnancy state. These hormones also may inhibit ovulation, thereby preventing pregnancy and helping to space the birth of additional children (Herbst, 1994; Ross & Yu, 1994).

Although it is clear that mothers may derive some benefit from breast-feeding, it is their infants who are helped the most, in ways that are only now becoming apparent. Although it has been known for some time that breast-feeding helps provide some protection from respiratory and stomach illnesses, new evidence suggests that breast milk has other, more subtle virtues.

For instance, several recent studies have found that breast-fed infants have higher levels of docosahexaenoic acid (DHA) in their brains and retinas than do infants who have been bottle-fed (Neuringer, 1993). Because research with nonhumans suggests that a deficit of DHA leads to irreversible changes, it is possible—although highly speculative—that higher levels of the chemical may enhance the brain functioning of children who have been breast-fed (Rogan & Gladen, 1993).

Much current work is focused on understanding how other components of breast milk may enhance growth. For instance, some researchers are examining how an epidermal growth factor present in breast milk may advance the development of the digestive and respiratory systems in infants. Furthermore, there is evidence that preterm infants ultimately may do better cognitively as a result of being fed breast milk during infancy (Lucas et al., 1992; Brody, 1994b).

Obviously, breast-feeding is not the solution to every problem faced by infants, and the millions of individuals who have been raised on formula should not be concerned that they have suffered irreparable harm. But it does continue to be clear that the slogan "breast is best" is right on target.

a natural act, mothers require a bit of practice to learn how to hold the baby properly, position the nipple correctly, and deal with such potential problems as sore nipples.)

Introducing Solid Foods: When and What?   Although pediatricians agree that breast milk is the ideal initial food, at some point infants require more nutriments than breast milk alone can provide. The American Academy of Pediatrics suggests that babies benefit from solids starting at about 4 to 6 months of age (American Academy of Pediatrics, 1992).

Solid foods are introduced into an infant's diet gradually, one at a time. Most often cereal comes first, followed by strained fruits. Vegetables typically are introduced next, and ultimately other kinds of food, such as eggs, fish, and meat, are added.

The exact amount of solid foods is hard to specify. In part, it depends on the activity level of the particular infant. Highly active youngsters require more calories than do those who are relatively sedentary.

The timing of *weaning*, the cessation of breast-feeding, varies greatly. In developed countries such as the United States, weaning typically occurs as early as three or four months. On the other hand, in certain subcultures within the United States, breast-feeding may continue for two or three years. Recommendations from the American Academy of Pediatrics suggest that infants be fed breast milk for the first 6 to 12 months (American Academy of Pediatrics, 1992).

Infants generally start solid foods at around 4 to 6 months, gradually working their way up to a variety of different foods.

Review and Rethink

REVIEW

♦ Reflexes, which are universal and genetically acquired physical behaviors, have many uses. Some reflexes help the infant survive and remain safe in its new environment, others serve as the basis of later-learned behaviors such as walking, and still others seem to help infants and caregivers form intimate social relationships.

♦ During infancy children achieve a series of landmarks in their physical development. The schedule and order of these landmarks are generally consistent across children. However, significant individual and cultural variations exist, and any norms used to describe the timing of developmental milestones should be regarded with caution.

♦ Training and cultural expectations can affect the timing of the development of motor skills. Whether such manipulation of the developmental schedule produces lasting effects remains an open question.

♦ Nutrition strongly affects physical development. Malnutrition, which is especially a problem in developing countries, can slow growth, affect intellectual performance, and cause diseases such as marasmus and kwashiorkor. Negative effects are also suffered by the victims of undernutrition, which exists even in developed countries.

♦ The advantages of breast-feeding are numerous, including nutritional, immunological, emotional, and physical benefits for the infant, and physical and emotional benefits for the mother as well. Factors of age, education, socioeconomic status, health, and practicality influence mothers' willingness and ability to breast-feed.

RETHINK

♦ What are some examples of reflexive behaviors not mentioned in this chapter that are part of your physical repertoire? How are they useful? Are the behaviors you named really innate, automatic reflexes, or are they learned responses?

♦ In what ways does the practice of training infants to accelerate their motor-skill development recall the relationship between genotype and phenotype? What sorts of constraints might there be on the results of such training?

♦ What advice might you give a friend who is concerned about the fact that her infant is still not walking at 14 months, when every other baby she knows started walking by the first birthday?

♦ How would you design an experiment to determine whether early development of physical skills produces lasting effects? Why do you think a definitive answer to this question has not yet been found? How would you eliminate factors other than early development from your study?

♦ Given that malnourishment negatively affects physical growth, how can it also adversely affect IQ scores and school performance, as reported in this chapter?

DEVELOPMENT OF THE SENSES

According to William James, one of the founders of the field of psychology, the world of the infant was a "blooming, buzzing confusion" (James, 1890/1950). Was he right?

In this case, James's wisdom failed him. For although the world that the infant senses lacks the clarity and stability that we can distinguish as adults, from the earliest days of infancy the world grows increasingly comprehensible as an infant's ability both to sense and to perceive the environment develops.

The processes that underlie infants' understanding of the world around them are sensation and perception. **Sensation** is the stimulation of the sense organs, and **perception** is the sorting out, interpretation, analysis, and integration of stimuli involving the sense organs and brain. Sensation is the responsiveness of the sense organs to stimulation, whereas perception is the interpretation of that stimulation. Sorting out infants' capabilities in the realm of sensation and perception presents a challenge to the ingenuity of investigators.

VISUAL PERCEPTION: SEEING THE WORLD

From the time of his birth, everyone who met little Lee Eng felt that he gazed at them intently. His eyes seemed to meet those of visitors. They seemed to bore deeply, and knowingly, into the faces of people who were looking at him.

How good in fact was Lee's vision, and what, precisely, could he make out of his environment? Quite a bit. According to some estimates, a newborn's distance vision ranges from 20/200 to 20/600, which means that the infant cannot discern visual material beyond 20 feet that an adult with normal vision is able to see from a distance of between 200 and 600 feet (M.M. Haith, 1991).

These figures indicate that infants' distance vision is some 10 to 30 times poorer than the average adult's, perhaps suggesting that the vision of infants is inadequate. However, looking at the figures from a different perspective suggests a revised interpretation: The vision of newborns provides the same degree of distance acuity as the uncorrected vision of many adults who wear eyeglasses or contact lenses. (If you wear glasses or contact lenses, remove them to get a sense of what an infant can see of the world.) Furthermore, infants' distance vision grows increasingly acute. By 6 months of age, the average infant's vision is already 20/20—in other words, identical to that of adults (Aslin, 1987).

sensation   the stimulation of the sense organs

perception   the sorting out, interpretation, analysis, and integration of stimuli involving the sense organs and brain

Other visual abilities grow rapidly. For instance, *binocular vision*, the ability to combine the images coming to each eye to see depth and motion, is achieved at around 14 weeks. Depth perception is a particularly useful ability, as a classic study on the topic indicates. In this study, carried out by developmental psychologists Eleanor Gibson and Richard Walk (1960), infants were placed on a sheet of heavy glass. A checkered pattern appeared under half of the glass sheet, making it seem that the infant was on a stable floor. However, in the middle of the glass sheet, the pattern dropped down several feet, forming an apparent "visual cliff." The question Gibson and Walk asked was whether infants would willingly crawl across the cliff when called by their mothers (see Figure 4-9).

The results were unambiguous. Most of the infants in the study, who ranged in age from 6 to 14 months, could not be coaxed over the apparent cliff. Clearly the ability to perceive depth had already developed in most of them by that age. On the other hand, the experiment did not pinpoint when depth perception emerged, since only infants who had already learned to crawl could be tested. But other experiments, in which infants of 2 and 3 months were placed on their stomachs above the apparent floor and above the visual cliff, revealed differences in heart rate between the two positions (Campos, Langer, & Krowitz, 1970). Still, such findings do not permit us to know whether infants are responding to depth itself, or merely to the *change* in visual stimuli that occurs when they are moved from a lack of depth to depth.

Infants also show clear visual preferences that are present from birth. For example, when given a choice, infants reliably prefer to look at stimuli that include patterns than to look at simpler stimuli (see Figure 4-10). How do we know? Developmental psychologist Robert Fantz (1963) created a classic test. He built a chamber in which babies could lie on their backs and see pairs of visual stimuli above them. Fantz could determine which of the stimuli the infants were looking at by observing the reflections of the stimuli in their eyes.

FIGURE 4-9 The "visual cliff" examines the depth perception of infants. Most infants in the age range of 6 to 14 months cannot be coaxed to cross the cliff, apparently responding to the fact that the patterned area drops several feet.

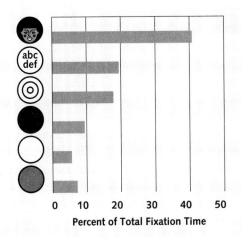

FIGURE 4-10

In a classic experiment, researcher Robert Fantz found that 2- and 3-month-old infants preferred to look at more complex stimuli than simple ones.

(Adapted from Fantz, 1961.)

Fantz's work was the impetus for a great deal of research on the preferences of infants, most of which points to a critical conclusion: Infants are genetically pre-programmed to prefer certain kinds of stimuli. Just minutes after birth, infants show a preference for real faces over scrambled ones. They also show preferences for certain colors, shapes, and configurations of various stimuli. Such capabilities may be a reflection of the existence of highly specialized cells in the brain that react to stimuli of a particular pattern, orientation, shape, and direction of movement (Hubel & Wiesel, 1979; Haith, 1991; Gallant, Braun & VanEssen, 1993).

However, genetics is not the sole determinant of infant visual preferences. Just a few hours after birth, infants have already learned to prefer their own mother's face to other faces. Such findings provide another clear piece of evidence of how heredity and environmental experiences are woven together to determine an infant's capabilities (Goren, Sarty, & Wu, 1975; Field et al., 1984a).

AUDITORY PERCEPTION: THE WORLD OF SOUND

What is it about a mother's lullaby that helps soothe a crying, fussy baby? Some clues emerge when we look at the capabilities of infants in the realm of auditory sensation and perception.

It is clear that infants hear from the time of birth—and even before. As we noted in Chapter 3, the ability to hear begins prenatally. Even in the womb, the fetus responds to sounds outside of its mother.

Because they have had some practice in hearing before birth, it is not surprising that infants have reasonably good auditory perception after birth. In fact, for certain very high and very low frequencies, infants actually are more sensitive to sound than are adults—a sensitivity that seems to increase during the first two years of life. On the other hand, infants are initially less sensitive than are adults to middle-range frequencies. Eventually, however, their capabilities within the middle range improve (Fenwick & Morrongiello, 1991).

It is not fully clear what leads to the improvement during infancy in sensitivity to sounds, although it may be related to the maturation of the nervous system. More puzzling is why after infancy, children's ability to hear very high and low frequencies gradually declines. One explanation may be that exposure to high levels of noise may diminish capacities at the extreme ranges (Schneider, Trehub, & Bull, 1980; Kryter, 1983; Trehub, Schneider, Morrongiello, & Thorpe, 1988, 1989).

In addition to the ability to detect sound, infants need several other abilities in order to hear effectively. For instance, *sound localization* permits infants to discern the direction from which a sound is emanating. Compared to adults, infants have a slight handicap in this task because effective sound localization requires the use of the slight difference in the times at which a sound reaches our two ears. Because infants' heads are smaller than those of adults, the difference in timing of the arrival of sound at the two ears is less than it is in adults.

However, despite the potential limitation brought about by their smaller heads, infants' sound localization abilities are actually fairly good even at birth, and they reach adult levels of success by the age of one year (Clifton, 1992).

Interestingly, their improvement is not steady: Although we don't know why, the accuracy of sound localization actually declines between birth and two months of age, but then begins to increase (Aslin, 1987; Schneider, Bull, & Trehub, 1988; Trehub et al., 1989).

Infant discrimination of groups of different sounds, in terms of their patterns and other acoustical characteristics, is also quite good. For instance, the change of a single note in a six-tone melody can be detected by infants as young as 6 months old. They also react to changes in musical key (Trehub, Thorpe, & Morrongiello, 1985). In sum, they listen with a keen ear to the melodies of lullabies sung to them by their parents!

Even more important to their ultimate success in the world, young infants are capable of making the fine discriminations that their future understanding of language will require (Bijeljac-Babic, Bertoncini, & Mehler, 1993). For instance, in one classic study, a group of 1- to 4-month-old infants sucked on nipples that activated a recording of a person saying "ba" every time they sucked (Eimas, Sigueland, Jusczyk, & Vigorito, 1971). At first, their interest in the sound made them suck vigorously. Soon, though, they became acclimated to the sound (through a process called *habituation*, discussed in Chapter 5) and sucked with less energy. On the other hand, when the experimenters changed the sound to "pa," the infants immediately showed new interest and sucked with greater vigor once again. The clear conclusion: Infants as young as a month old could make the distinction between the two similar sounds.

Even more intriguingly, young infants are able to discriminate certain characteristics that differentiate one language from another. For instance, in one study a short English-language passage was recited to a group of 5-month-old infants. Later, the infants were able to distinguish a different English-language passage from a passage that was presented in Spanish. The sound discrimination occurred despite the fact that the English and Spanish passages were similar in meter, number of syllables, and speed of recitation (Bahrick & Pickens, 1988; Moon, Cooper, & Fifer, 1993).

Given their ability to discriminate a difference in speech as slight as the difference between two consonants, it is not surprising that infants can distinguish different people on the basis of voice. In fact, from an early age they show clear preferences for some voices over others. For instance, in one experiment newborns were allowed to suck a nipple that turned on a recording of a human voice reading a story. The infants sucked significantly longer when the voice was that of their mother than when the voice was that of a stranger (DeCasper & Fifer, 1980; Fifer, 1987).

How do such preferences arise? One hypothesis is that prenatal exposure to the mother's voice is the key. As support for this conjecture, researchers point to the fact that newborns do not show a preference for their fathers' voices over other male voices. Furthermore, newborns prefer listening to melodies sung by their mothers before they were born to melodies that were not sung before birth. It seems, then, that the prenatal exposure to their mothers' voices—although muffled by the liquid environment of the womb—helps shape infants' listening preferences (DeCasper & Prescott, 1984; Panneton, 1985).

SMELL AND TASTE

What do infants do when they smell a rotten egg? Pretty much what adults do—crinkle their noses and generally look unhappy. On the other hand, the scent of bananas and butter produces a pleasant reaction on the part of infants (Steiner, 1979).

Infants react to unpleasant tastes from birth.

The sense of smell is so well developed, even among very young infants, that at least some 12- to 18-day-old babies can distinguish their mothers on the basis of smell alone. For instance, in one experiment infants were exposed to the smell of gauze pads worn under the arms of adults the previous evening. Infants who were being breast-fed were able to distinguish their mothers' scent from those of other adults. However, not all infants could do this: Those who were being bottle-fed were unable to make the distinction. Moreover, both breast-fed and bottle-fed infants were unable to distinguish their fathers on the basis of odor (Cernoch & Porter, 1985; Porter, Bologh, & Makin, 1988).

Taste, like smell, shows surprising sophistication during infancy—in part because the two capabilities are related. Some taste preferences are well developed at birth, such as disgust over bitter tastes. At the same time, infants seem to have an innate sweet tooth—even before they have teeth: Very young infants smile when a sweet-tasting liquid is placed on their tongues. They also suck harder at a bottle if it is sweetened (Crook, 1978, 1987; Steiner, 1979; Rosenstein & Oster, 1988; Forges & Lipsitt, 1993).

SENSITIVITY TO PAIN AND TOUCH

When Eli Rosenblatt was 8 days old, he participated in the ancient Jewish ritual of circumcision. As he lay nestled in his father's arms, the foreskin of his penis was removed. Although Eli shrieked in what seemed to his anxious parents as pain, he soon settled down and went back to sleep. Others who had watched the ceremony assured his parents, with great authority, that at Eli's age babies do not really experience pain, at least not in the same way that adults do.

Were Eli's relatives accurate in saying that young infants do not feel pain? In the past, many medical practitioners would have agreed. In fact, because they assumed that infants did not experience pain in truly bothersome ways, many physicians routinely carried out medical procedures, and even some forms of surgery, without the use of painkillers or anesthesia. Their argument was that the risks from the use of anesthesia outweighed the potential pain that the young infants experienced.

Contemporary Views on Infant Pain.   Today, however, it is widely acknowledged that infants are born with the capacity to feel pain. Obviously, no one can be sure if the experience of pain in children is identical to that in adults, any more than we can tell if an adult friend who complains of a headache is experiencing pain that is more or less severe than our own pain when we have a headache.

What we do know is that pain produces signs of distress in infants, such as a rise in heartbeat, sweating, facial expressions indicative of discomfort, and changes in the intensity and tone of crying (Johnston, 1989). Such evidence indicates that infants do, in fact, experience pain. There also seems to be a developmental progression in reactions to pain. For example, a newborn who has her heel pricked for a blood test responds with signs of distress, but it takes her several seconds to show the response. In contrast, only a few months later, the same procedure brings a much more immediate reaction. It is possible that the delayed response in infants is produced by the relatively slower transmission of information within the newborn's nervous system (Porter, Porges, & Marshall, 1988; Anand & Hickey, 1987, 1992; Bornstein & Lamb, 1992).

In response to increasing support for the notion that infants experience pain, medical experts now endorse the use of anesthesia and painkillers during surgery for even the youngest infants. According to the American Academy of Pediatrics, painkilling drugs are appropriate in most types of surgery, although minor surgical procedures—such as circumcision—still may be done without their use.

Responding to Touch.   It clearly does not take the sting of pain to get an infant's attention. Even the youngest infants respond to gentle touches, such as a soothing caress, which can calm a crying, fussy baby (Stack & Muir, 1992).

In fact, touch is one of the most highly developed sensory systems in a newborn. It is also one of the first to develop; there is evidence that by 32 weeks after conception, the entire body is sensitive to touch. Furthermore, several of the basic reflexes present at birth, such as the rooting reflex, require touch sensitivity to operate: An infant must sense a touch near the mouth in order automatically to seek a nipple to suck (M.M. Haith, 1986).

Infants' abilities in the realm of touch are particularly helpful in their efforts to explore the world. Several theorists have suggested that one of the ways children gain information about the world is through touching. For instance, at the age of 6 months, infants are apt to place almost any object in their mouths, apparently taking in data about its configuration from their sensory responses to the feel of it in their mouths (Ruff, 1989).

MULTIMODAL PERCEPTION: COMBINING INDIVIDUAL SENSORY INPUTS

When Eric Pettigrew was 7 months old, his grandparents presented him with a squeaky rubber doll. As soon as he saw it, he reached out for it, grasped it in his hand, and listened as it squeaked. He seemed delighted with the gift.

One way of considering Eric's sensory reaction to the doll is to focus on each of the senses individually: what the doll looked like to Eric, how it felt in his hand, and what it sounded like. In fact, this approach has dominated the study of sensation and perception in infancy.

However, we might take another approach: We might examine how the various sensory responses are integrated with one another. Instead of looking at each individual sensory response, we could consider how the responses work together and are combined to produce Eric's ultimate reaction. The **multimodal approach to perception** considers how information that is collected by various individual sensory systems is integrated and coordinated.

Although the multimodal approach is a relatively recent innovation in the study of how infants understand their sensory world, it raises some fundamental issues about the development of sensation and perception. For instance, some researchers argue that sensations are initially integrated with one another in the infant, whereas others maintain that the infant's sensory systems are initially separate and that development leads to increasing integration (Rose & Ruff, 1987; Bahrick, 1989; Legerstee, 1990).

We do not yet know which view is correct. However, it does appear that by an early age infants are able to relate what they have learned about an object through one sensory chan-

multimodal approach to perception   the approach that considers how information collected by various individual sensory systems is integrated and coordinated

The senses of sight and touch are integrated by infants through multimodal perception.

nel to what they have learned about it through another. For instance, even one-month-old infants are able to recognize by sight objects that they have previously held in their mouths but never seen (Meltzoff, 1981; Steri & Spelke, 1988). Clearly, some cross-talk between various sensory channels is already possible a month after birth.

The success of infants at multimodel perception is another example of the sophisticated perceptual abilities of infants, which continue to grow throughout the period of infancy. These increasing capabilities are mirrored by the growth of cognitive abilities, as discussed in the next chapter.

The Informed Consumer of Development

Exercising Your Infant's Body and Senses

We have seen how the kind of experiences that infants encounter as they grow is reflected in their motor and sensory development. For instance, recall how cultural expectations and environments affect the age at which various physical milestones, such as the timing of the first step, occur. Does this suggest that parents are well advised to try to accelerate their infants' timetables?

Although experts disagree, most feel that such acceleration yields little advantage. No data suggest that a child who walks at ten months ultimately has any advantage over one who walks at 15 months.

On the other hand, it does seem reasonable for parents to ensure that their infants receive some level of physical and sensory stimulation. The goal, according to Jane Clark, an expert in kinesiology (the science of human anatomy and movement), is not to get children to achieve motoric milestones early, but "to raise active, confident children who will become healthy, active adults who feel good about their bodies and who value physical activity for its intrinsic benefits and rewards" (Israeloff, 1991). There are several specific ways to accomplish this goal:

- Carry a baby in different positions—in a backpack, in a frontpack, or in a football hold with the infant's head in the palm of your hand and its feet lying on your arm.

- Let infants explore their environment. Do not contain them too long in a barren environment. Let them crawl or wander around an environment—after first making it childproof by removing dangerous objects.

- Engage in "rough-and-tumble" play. Wrestling, dancing, and rolling around on the floor—if not violent—are activities that are fun and that stimulate older infants' motoric and sensory systems.

- Let babies touch their food and even play with it. Infancy is too early to start teaching infants very much about the etiquette of table manners.

- Provide toys that stimulate the senses. For instance, brightly colored, textured toys with movable parts are enjoyable and help hone infants' senses.

- Above all, do not focus so much on the goal of stimulating an infant's motoric and sensory abilities that you miss out on the joy and wonder of his or her continuing development.

Review and Rethink

REVIEW

♦ Sensation refers to the activation of the sense organs by external stimuli. Perception is the analysis, interpretation, and integration of sensations.

♦ Infants' abilities in the sensory realm are surprisingly well developed at or shortly after birth. Their perceptions through sight, hearing, smell, taste, and touch help them explore and begin to make sense of the world.

♦ Very early, infants can see depth and motion, distinguish colors and patterns, localize and discriminate sounds, recognize the sound of their mothers' voices, and discern their mothers by smell alone. Moreover, infants can relate some perceptions received through one sensory channel to those received through another.

♦ Infants are sensitive to pain and to touch. Most medical authorities now subscribe to procedures, including anesthesia, that minimize infants' pain.

♦ Parents and caregivers should help infants engage in physical activities that will help them grow into healthy adults who feel confident about their bodies.

RETHINK

♦ Given what was said earlier in this chapter about the way the brain and nervous system develop, what sort of sensory environment would probably be most conducive to healthy neural development in the infant? Why?

♦ Are the processes of sensation and perception always linked? Is it possible to sense without perceiving? To perceive without sensing? How?

♦ In this chapter it was said that the nervous system develops by "pruning down" unnecessary neurons that do not form links with other neurons. Do you think an infant's early preference for the sounds of its home language gives evidence that such a process operates in the area of language development? How?

♦ The "ba"–"pa" experiment described in this chapter—in which sucking intensity decreased once babies became used to the "ba" sound, and then increased again when "ba" was changed to "pa"—was used to show that infants can discriminate highly similar sounds. Another conclusion might be that infants prefer novelty. How might a preference for novelty facilitate infant development?

♦ Individuals born without the use of one sense often develop unusual abilities in one or more other senses. Do you think this phenomenon might relate to the argument about whether integration of the senses precedes differentiation, or vice versa? How?

LOOKING
BACK

How do the human body and nervous system develop?

1. Human babies grow rapidly, especially during the first two years of life. By the end of that time, the average baby in the United States has grown from 20 to 36 inches in height and from 7 to about 22 pounds.

2. The nervous system, which includes the brain and the nerves of the body, contains a

huge number of neurons, virtually all of which grow before birth. For neurons to survive and become useful, they must form interconnections with other neurons based on the infant's experience of the world.

3. Major principles that govern human growth include the cephalocaudal principle (growth proceeds from upper body to lower), the proximodistal principle (growth proceeds from the center of the body outward), the principle of hierarchical integration (simple skills are grasped first and then integrated into more complex ones), and the principle of the independence of systems (different body systems grow at different rates).

Does the environment affect the pattern of development?

4. Brain development, largely predetermined genetically, also contains a strong element of plasticity—a susceptibility to environmental influences.

5. Studies have shown that many aspects of development, including both behaviors and body structures, occur during critical periods when the organism is particularly susceptible to environmental influences. If interactions between baby and environment are affected during the critical period, development may be affected as well.

6. One of the primary tasks of the infant is the development of rhythms—cyclical patterns that integrate individual behaviors. An important rhythm pertains to the infant's state—the degree of awareness it displays to stimulation. The infant experiences various states during both sleep and wakefulness. Normal rhythms can be disturbed, as evidenced by sudden infant death syndrome, or SIDS.

What are reflexes and how are they useful?

7. Reflexes are unlearned, automatic responses to stimuli that help newborns survive and protect themselves. Some reflexes also have value as the foundation for future, more conscious behaviors.

8. Reflexes, although genetically determined and universal, are susceptible to some cultural variations. Reflexes also have utility as diagnostic devices for doctors and even as facilitators to promote caregiving and nurturing emotions in adults.

How universal are the schedule and sequence of motor development?

9. The development of gross and fine motor skills proceeds along a generally consistent timetable in normal children. However, caution should be applied to the interpretation of norms used to describe "average" behavior. Not only do individual variations exist, but cultural factors influence development and may not be reflected in norms that are not carefully determined to include cultural variations.

10. The development of motor skills reflects cultural differences. Within limits that are set genetically, the onset of certain motor skills can be speeded up or slowed down, depending on cultural expectations and practices. In the long term, it is unclear whether such differences in timing have lasting effects on the ultimate level of motor skill achieved by the individual.

What is the role of nutrition in physical development, and what food is best for infants?

11. Adequate nutrition is essential for physical development. Malnutrition and undernutrition affect physical aspects of growth and may also affect IQ and school performance.

12. Breast-feeding has distinct advantages over bottle-feeding, including the nutritional completeness of breast milk, its provision of a degree of immunity to certain childhood diseases, and its easy digestibility. In addition, breast-feeding offers significant physical and emotional benefits to both child and mother.

13. The decision whether to breast-feed or bottle-feed depends on a number of factors, including mother's age, socioeconomic status, health issues, practical constraints, and level of knowledge of the benefits of breast-feeding.

How do the senses develop, and what sensory capabilities do infants possess?

14. Sensation, the stimulation of the sense organs, differs from perception, the interpretation and integration of sensed stimuli.

15. Infants' visual perception is quite good. Although infants' vision is less acute than is adults' at first, within six months infants achieve adult levels of distance acuity. Moreover, the early achievement of binocular vision permits sophisticated perception of depth and motion by infants.

16. Auditory perception, which begins in the womb, is well developed in infants. They can localize sound, discriminate sound patterns and tones, and make fine sound discriminations that will be essential in the later development of language.

17. The senses of smell and taste are surprisingly sophisticated in infants. Infants react as adults do to pleasant and unpleasant odors and tastes, and even very young infants can recognize their mothers' scents.

18. The nature of infants' experiences of pain is not entirely understood, but it is clear that infants react negatively to painful stimuli. Infants use their highly developed sense of touch to explore and experience the world.

19. Whether all sensations are initially integrated in infants and later become differentiated, or initially separate senses later become increasingly integrated, is an unresolved issue. However, infants are clearly able to relate perceptions from one sensory source to those from a different sensory source.

20. Although attempts to accelerate infants' achievement of motoric milestones are probably unwise and fruitless, parents should encourage and participate with their babies in physical activity and provide room for them to explore. Such activity can help them become healthy, active, and confident adults.

KEY TERMS AND CONCEPTS

cephalocaudal principle (p. 115)
proximodistal principle (p. 115)
principle of hierarchical integration (p. 115)
principle of the independence of systems (p. 115)
plasticity (p. 117)
critical period (p. 117)
rhythms (p. 118)
state (p. 118)
rapid eye movement (REM) sleep (p. 119)
sudden infant death syndrome (SIDS) (p. 120)

reflexes (p. 123)
norms (p. 126)
Brazelton Neonatal Behavioral Assessment Scale (NBAS) (p. 126)
marasmus (p. 129)
kwashiorkor (p. 130)
sensation (p. 136)
perception (p. 136)
multimodal approach to perception (p. 141)

Cognitive Development

CHAPTER OUTLINE

As I waited with my six-year-old son in stalled traffic on the West Side Highway, at the end of a long day, we were both feeling haggard and hungry. My son was yearning for a chocolate Easter egg. "The one you gave me when we were at Caroline's with white inside, and then yellow inside that. I wish I had one now."

I was amazed that Nicholas could remember that Easter at Caroline's; he had been less than two. And why couldn't I remember buying that egg? . . .

"I wish I had some of the gumbo we tried last year in New Orleans," I replied as we inched along in traffic.

"What's New Orleans?" Nicholas asked.

"What's New Orleans!" I cried in shock. I told him it was incredible to me that he could forget the outlandish costumes, the bands playing Dixieland music in the streets, the steamboat on the Mississippi River. Nicholas's face looked blank. He could recall perfectly a chocolate he had eaten when he was 19 months old, but he had completely missed 3 days of unforgettable pageantry just last year. (Ellsberg, 1994, p. 31)

How well will these flowers be recalled several years later?

LOOKING AHEAD

As this account suggests, in certain cases memories of infancy can remain for years. But just how accurate are such recollections, and when—and how—are our earliest memories formed?

We address these and related questions in this chapter as we consider cognitive development during the first years of life. To do this, we consider the work of developmental researchers who seek to understand how infants develop their knowledge and understanding of the world. We first discuss the work of Swiss psychologist Jean Piaget, whose theory of developmental stages served as a highly influential impetus for a considerable amount of work on cognitive development. We'll look at both the limitations and the contributions of this important developmentalist.

We then turn to the basic processes by which cognitive growth occurs. After considering how learning takes place, we turn to memory in infants and the ways in which infants process, store, and retrieve information. We discuss the controversial issue of the recollection of events that occurred during infancy. We also address individual differences in intelligence.

Finally, we consider language, the medium by which infants develop communication with others. We look at the roots of language in prelinguistic speech and trace the milestones indicating the development of language skills in the progression from first words to first phrases and sentences. We also look at the characteristics of communication addressed to infants and examine some surprising universals in the nature of such communication across different cultures.

In sum, after reading this chapter, you'll be able to answer these questions:

♦ What can we learn about children's views of the world from Piaget's theories of cognitive development?

♦ How do infants process information and learn about the world?

♦ What sorts of memories do infants have?

♦ How can we measure infant intelligence, and how does it relate to adult intelligence?

♦ By what processes do children learn to use language?

♦ How do children influence the language that adults use to address them?

PIAGET'S APPROACH TO COGNITIVE DEVELOPMENT

Action = Knowledge.

In certain ways, this equation sums up Swiss psychologist Jean Piaget's view of how infants attain an understanding of the world. He argues that infants do not acquire knowledge from facts communicated by others, nor through sensation and perception. Instead, Piaget suggests that knowledge is the product of direct motor behavior. Although many of his basic explanations and propositions have been challenged by subsequent research, as we'll discuss later, the view that in significant ways infants learn by doing remains unquestioned (Piaget, 1952, 1962, 1983).

As we first noted in Chapter 1, Piaget's theory is based on a stage approach to development. He assumes that all children pass through a series of universal stages in a fixed order. He also believes that not only does the quantity of information acquired in each stage increase, but—even more importantly—the quality of knowledge and understanding also grows. Some approaches to cognition focus on the content of an individual's knowledge about the world, such as might be assessed in a traditional intelligence test. In contrast, Piaget's theory suggests that the focus should be on the change in understanding that occurs as the child moves from one stage to another.

For instance, several kinds of changes in knowledge about what can and cannot occur in the world develop during infancy. Consider an infant who, during an experiment, is exposed to an impossible event, such as seeing her mother simultaneously in three identical versions (due to some clever trickery with mirrors). A 3-month-old infant shows no disturbance over the multiple apparitions and in fact will interact happily with each. However, by 5 months of age, the child becomes quite agitated at the sight of multiple mothers. Apparently by this time the child has figured out that she has but one mother, and viewing three at a time is thoroughly alarming (Bower, 1977). To Piaget, such reactions indicate growth in an underlying mastery of principles regarding the way the world operates.

Swiss psychologist Jean Piaget.

According to Piaget, such cognitive development occurs in an orderly fashion. Children pass through four major stages as they move from birth through adolescence: sensorimotor, preoperational, concrete operational, and formal operational. Piaget suggests that movement from one stage to the next occurs when a child reaches an appropriate level of physical maturation and is exposed to relevant types of experience. Without such experience, children are assumed to be incapable of reaching their cognitive potential.

Piaget contends that two principles underlie the growth in children's understanding of the world: assimilation and accommodation. **Assimilation** is the process in which people understand an experience in terms of their current stage of cognitive development and way of thinking. Assimilation occurs, then, when a stimulus or event is perceived and understood in accordance with existing patterns of thought.

In contrast, **accommodation** refers to changes in existing ways of thinking that occur in response to encounters with new stimuli or events. When existing ways of thinking and understanding become altered to fit or match novel experiences, accommodation takes place.

Piaget gives a name to the shifting patterns of understanding that characterize infancy: schemes. A **scheme** is an organized pattern of sensorimotor functioning, a representation in the nervous system of action upon the world. Schemes are like computer programs: They direct and determine how data from the world are considered and dealt with (Achenbach, 1992).

assimilation   *the process in which people understand an experience in terms of their current stage of cognitive development and way of thinking*

accommodation   *changes in existing ways of thinking that occur in response to encounters with new stimuli or events*

scheme   *an organized pattern of sensorimotor functioning*

Schemes are illustrated by the way in which an infant reacts when given a new cloth book. The infant will touch it, mouth it, perhaps try to tear it or bang it on the floor. To Piaget, each of these actions may be representative of a scheme, and they are the infant's way of gaining knowledge and understanding of the book. Adults, on the other hand, would use a different scheme upon encountering the book. Far from picking it up and putting it in their mouths or banging it on the floor, they would probably be drawn to the letters on the page, seeking to understand the book through the meaning of the printed words—a very different approach.

In newborns, schemes are primarily limited to reflexes, such as sucking and rooting. Quickly, however, schemes become more sophisticated as infants become more advanced in their motor capabilities—to Piaget, a signal of the potential for more advanced cognitive development.

Because the sensorimotor stage of development begins at birth and continues until the child is about 2 years old, we'll consider it here in detail. (Future chapters will discuss development during the other stages.) In discussing the specific substages of the sensorimotor period, it may at first appear that they unfold with great regularity, as infants reach a particular age and smoothly proceed into the next substage. However, the reality of cognitive development, Piaget admits, is somewhat different. First, the ages at which infants actually reach a particular stage vary a good deal among different children. The exact timing of a stage reflects an interaction between the infant's level of physical maturation and the nature of the social environment in which the child is being raised. Consequently, although Piaget contends that the order of the substages does not change from one child to the next, the timing can and does vary to some degree.

Furthermore, Piaget argues that development is a more gradual process than the demarcation of different stages might seem to imply. Specifically, infants do not go to sleep one night in one substage and wake up the next morning in the next one. Instead, there is a rather steady shift in behavior as a child moves toward the next stage of cognitive development. Infants also pass through periods of transition, in which some aspects of their behavior reflect the next higher stage, while other aspects are indicative of their current stage (see Figure 5-1).

THE SENSORIMOTOR PERIOD: CHARTING THE COURSE OF EARLY COGNITIVE GROWTH

Piaget suggests that the **sensorimotor stage**, the initial major stage of cognitive development, can be broken down into six substages (summarized in Table 5-1), and described in turn.

sensorimotor stage   *according to Piaget the initial stage of cognitive development, spanning birth to about 2 years of age, during which knowledge develops from physically acting on objects*

FIGURE 5-1

TRANSITIONS

Infants do not suddenly shift from one stage of cognitive development to the next. Instead, Jean Piaget argues that there is a period of transition, in which some behavior reflects one stage, while other behavior reflects the more advanced stage.

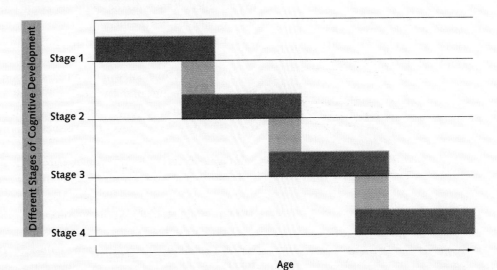

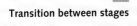
Transition between stages

TABLE 5-1

PIAGET'S SIX SUBSTAGES OF THE SENSORIMOTOR STAGE

Substage	Age	Description	Example
SUBSTAGE 1: Simple reflexes	First month of life	During this period, the various reflexes that determine the nature of the infant's interactions with the world are at the center of its cognitive life.	The sucking reflex causes the infant to suck at anything placed in its lips.
SUBSTAGE 2: First habits and primary circular reactions	From 1 to 4 months	At this age infants begin to coordinate what were separate actions into single, integrated activities.	An infant might combine grasping an object with sucking on it, or staring at something with touching it.
SUBSTAGE 3: Secondary circular reactions	From 4 to 8 months	During this period, infants take major strides in shifting their cognitive horizons beyond themselves and begin to act upon the outside world.	A child who repeatedly picks up a rattle in her crib and shakes it in different ways to see how the sound changes is demonstrating her ability to modify her cognitive scheme about shaking rattles.
SUBSTAGE 4: Coordination of secondary circular reactions	From 8 to 12 months	In this stage infants begin to use more calculated approaches to producing events, coordinating several schemes to generate a single act. They achieve object permanence during this stage.	An infant will push one toy out of the way to reach another toy that is lying, partially exposed, under it.
SUBSTAGE 5: Tertiary circular reactions	From 12 to 18 months	At this age infants develop what Piaget regards as the deliberate variation of actions that bring desirable consequences. Rather than just repeating enjoyable activities as in Substage 4, infants appear to carry out miniature experiments to observe the consequences.	A child will drop a toy repeatedly, varying the position from which he dropped it, carefully observing each time to see where it fell.
SUBSTAGE 6: Beginnings of thought	From 18 months to 2 years	The major achievement of Substage 6 is the capacity for mental representation or symbolic thought. Piaget argued that only at this stage can infants imagine where objects that they cannot see might be.	Children can even plot in their heads unseen trajectories of objects, so that if a ball rolls under a piece of furniture, they can figure out where it is likely to emerge on the other side.

Substage 1: Simple Reflexes.   This first substage of the sensorimotor period encompasses the first month of life. During this time, the various reflexes that determine the nature of the infant's interactions with the world are at the center of its cognitive life. For example, the sucking reflex causes the infant to suck at anything placed in its lips. This sucking behavior, according to Piaget, provides the newborn with information about objects—information that paves the way to the next substage of the sensorimotor period.

At the same time, some of the reflexes become modified as a result of the infant's experience with the nature of the world. For instance, an infant who is being breast-fed, but who also receives supplemental bottles, may begin to make modifications in how it sucks depending on whether the nipple it is sucking is on a breast or a bottle.

Substage 2: First Habits and Primary Circular Reactions.   The second substage of the sensorimotor period occurs from 1 to 4 months of age. In this period, infants begin to coordinate what were separate actions into single, integrated activities. For instance, an infant might combine grasping an object with sucking on it, or staring at something with touching it.

If an activity engages children's interests, they may repeat it over and over, simply for the sake of continuing to experience it. *Primary circular reactions* are schemes reflecting an infant's repetition of interesting or enjoyable actions, just for the enjoyment of doing them.

Thus, when an infant first puts his thumb in his mouth and begins to suck, it is a mere chance event. However, when he repeatedly sucks his thumb in the future, it represents a primary circular reaction that he is repeating because the sensation of sucking is pleasurable.

Substage 3: Secondary Circular Reactions.   This substage occurs between 4 and 8 months of age. During this period, infants take major strides in shifting their cognitive horizons beyond themselves and begin to act upon the outside world. For instance, when infants, through chance activities, produce an enjoyable event in their environment, they now seek to repeat that event. A child who repeatedly picks up a rattle in her crib and shakes it in different ways to see how the sound changes is demonstrating her ability to modify her cognitive scheme about shaking rattles. She is engaging in what Piaget calls *secondary circular reactions*: schemes regarding repeated actions meant to bring about a desirable consequence. The major difference between primary circular reactions and secondary circular reactions is whether the infant's activity is focused on the infant and his or her own body (primary circular reactions), or involves actions relating to the world outside (secondary circular reactions).

During the third substage, the degree of vocalization increases substantially as infants come to notice that if they make noises, other people around them will respond with noises of their own. Similarly, infants begin to imitate the sounds made by others. Vocalization becomes a secondary circular reaction that ultimately helps lead to the development of language and the formation of social relationships.

Substage 4: Coordination of Secondary Circular Reactions.   One of the major leaps forward in terms of cognitive development comes as infants move through the substage termed *coordination of secondary circular reactions*, which lasts from about 8 to 12 months of age. Before this stage, behavior involved direct action on objects. When something caught an infant's interest, she attempted to repeat the event using a single scheme. However, in Substage 4, infants begin to use more calculated approaches to producing events, coordinating several schemes to generate a single act. For instance, they will push one toy out of the way to reach another toy that is lying, partially exposed, under it. They also begin to anticipate upcoming events. Piaget tells of his son Laurent who at 8 months "recognizes by a certain noise caused by air that he is nearing the end of his feeding and, instead of insisting on drinking to the last drop, he rejects his bottle." (Piaget, 1952, pp. 248–249).

Infants' new-found purposefulness, their ability to use means to attain particular ends, and their skill in anticipating future circumstances all owe their appearance in part to the developmental achievement of object permanence that emerges in Substage 4. **Object permanence** is the realization that people and objects exist even when they cannot be seen. It is a simple principle, but its mastery has profound consequences.

Consider, for instance, how a 7-month-old infant named Chu, who has yet to learn the idea of object permanence, reacts when his father, who has been shaking a rattle in front of him, takes the rattle and places it under a blanket. To Chu, who has not mastered the concept of object permanence, the rattle no longer exists, and he will make no effort to look for it.

Several months later, when Chu is in Substage 4, the story is quite different (see Figure 5-2). This time, as soon as his father places the rattle under the blanket, Chu tries to toss the cover aside, eagerly searching for the rattle. Chu clearly has learned that the object continues to exist even when it cannot be seen. For the infant who achieves an understanding of object permanence, then, out of sight is decidedly not out of mind.

The attainment of object permanence extends not only to inanimate objects but also to people. It gives Chu the security that his father and mother still exist even when they have left the room. This awareness is likely a key element in the development of social attachments, examined in Chapter 6. The recognition of object permanence also feeds infants' growing assertiveness: As they realize that an object taken away from them doesn't just cease

object permanence *the realization that people and objects exist even when they cannot be seen*

FIGURE 5-2

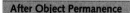

Before Object Permanence

After Object Permanence

OBJECT PERMANENCE

Before infants have understood the idea of object permanence, they will not search for an object that has been hidden right before their eyes. But several months later, they will search for it, illustrating that they have attained object permanence.

to exist, but is merely somewhere else, their only-too-human reaction may be to want it back—and want it back quickly.

Although the understanding of object permanence emerges in Substage 4, it is only a rudimentary understanding. It takes several months for the concept to be fully comprehended, and infants continue during this time to make certain kinds of errors relating to object permanence. For instance, they often are fooled when they watch as a toy is first hidden under one blanket and then under a second blanket. In seeking out the toy, Substage-4 infants most often turn to the first hiding place, ignoring the blanket under which the toy is currently located—even though the hiding was done in plain view.

Substage 5: Tertiary Circular Reactions.   This substage is reached at about the age of 12 months and extends to 18 months. As the name of the stage indicates, during this period infants develop what Piaget labeled *tertiary circular reactions*, schemes regarding the deliberate variation of actions that bring desirable consequences. Rather than just repeating enjoyable activities, as they do with secondary circular reactions, infants appear to carry out miniature experiments to observe the consequences.

For example, Piaget observed his son Laurent dropping a toy swan repeatedly, varying the position from which he dropped it, carefully observing each time to see where it fell. Instead of just repeating the action each time (as in a secondary circular reaction), Laurent made modifications in the situation to learn about their consequences. As you may recall from our discussion of research methods in Chapter 1, this behavior represents the essence of the scientific method: An experimenter varies a situation in a laboratory to learn the effects of the variation. To infants in Substage 5, the world is their laboratory, and they spend their days leisurely carrying out one miniature experiment after another.

What is most striking about infants' behavior during Substage 5 is their interest in the unexpected. Unanticipated events are not only treated as interesting but as something to be explained and understood. Infants' discoveries can lead to new-found skills, some of which may cause a certain amount of chaos. For instance, an infant may pull at a tablecloth in order to reach a plate of cookies or throw a water toy into the tub with increasing vigor to see how high the water splashes.

Substage 6: Beginnings of Thought.   This final stage of the sensorimotor period lasts from about 18 months to 2 years. The major achievement of Substage 6 is the capacity for mental representation or symbolic thought. Piaget argued that only at this stage can infants imagine where objects that they cannot see might be. They can even plot in their heads unseen trajectories of objects, so that if a ball rolls under a piece of furniture, they can figure out where it is likely to emerge on the other side.

Because of children's new abilities to create internal representations of objects, their understanding of causality also becomes more sophisticated. For instance, consider Piaget's description of his son Laurent's efforts to open a garden gate:

> Laurent tries to open a garden gate but cannot push it forward because it is held back by a piece of furniture. He cannot account either visually or by any sound for the cause that prevents the gate from opening, but after having tried to force it he suddenly seems to understand; he goes around the wall, arrives at the other side of the gate, moves the armchair which holds it firm, and opens it with a triumphant expression. (Piaget, 1954, p. 296)

The attainment of mental representation also permits another important development: the ability to pretend. Using the skill of what Piaget refers to as **deferred imitation**, in which a person who is no longer present is imitated later, children are able to pretend that they are driving a car, feeding a doll, or cooking dinner long after they have witnessed such scenes played out in reality.

deferred imitation   an act in which a person who is no longer present is imitated later

APPRAISING PIAGET: SUPPORT AND CHALLENGES

Most developmentalists would probably agree that in many significant ways, Piaget's descriptions of how cognitive development proceeds during infancy are quite accurate (Harris, 1983, 1987). However, when many of the specifics of Piagetian theory are considered, there is substantial disagreement over the validity of the theory and its predictions.

Let us start with what is clearly correct about the Piagetian approach. Piaget was a masterful reporter of children's behavior, and his descriptions of their growth during infancy remain a monument to his powers of observation. Furthermore, literally thousands of studies have supported Piaget's view that children learn much about the world by acting on objects in their environment. Finally, the broad outlines sketched out by Piaget of the sequence of cognitive development and the increasing cognitive accomplishments that occur during infancy are generally accurate (Gratch & Schatz, 1987).

On the other hand, specific aspects of the theory have come under increasing scrutiny—and criticism—in the decades since Piaget conducted his pioneering work. For example, some developmentalists question the stage conception that forms the basis of Piaget's theory. To critics, development proceeds in a much more continuous fashion than Piaget's stage theory suggests. Rather than showing major leaps of competence at the end of one stage and the beginning of the next, improvement comes in more gradual increments, growing step-by-step in a skill-by-skill manner.

Moreover, Piaget's notion that cognitive development is grounded in motor activities has been disputed. Some developmentalists charge that such a view ignores the importance of the sophisticated sensory and perceptual systems present from a very early age in infancy—systems about which Piaget knew little, since so much of the research illustrating their sophistication was done relatively recently (Butterworth, 1994). (See, for instance, the accompanying Directions in Development section on infants' mathematical skills.) Critics also point to research showing that children born without arms and legs owing to their mothers' use of once-legal drugs during pregnancy (such as Thalidomide) develop quite normally on a cognitive level, despite their lack of practice with motor activities (Decarrie, 1969).

To bolster their views, Piaget's critics also point to recent studies that cast doubt on Piaget's view that infants are incapable of mastering the concept of object permanence until

With the attainment of the cognitive skill of deferred imitation, children are able to imitate people and scenes they have witnessed in the past.

they are close to a year old. For instance, some work suggests that younger infants may not appear to understand object permanence because the techniques used to test their abilities are too insensitive (Baillargeon & DeVos, 1991).

It may be that a 4-month-old doesn't search for a rattle hidden under a blanket because she has not learned the motor skills necessary to do the searching—not because she doesn't understand that the rattle still exists. Similarly, the apparent inability of young infants to comprehend object permanence may reflect more about their memory deficits than their lack of understanding of the concept: The memories of young infants may be poor enough that they simply do not recall the earlier concealment of the toy (Diamond, 1991). In fact, when more age-appropriate tasks were employed, some researchers found indications of object permanence in children as young as 3-½ months (Baillargeon, 1987; Mandler, 1990; Spelke, 1991).

Other types of behavior likewise seem to emerge earlier than Piaget suggested. For instance, recall the ability of neonates to imitate basic facial expressions of adults just hours after birth, as we discussed in Chapter Three. The presence of such skill at such an early age contradicts Piaget's view that, initially, infants are able to imitate only behavior that they see in others, using parts of their own body that they can plainly view—such as the hands and feet. In fact, facial imitation suggests that humans are born with a basic, innate capability for imitating others' actions, a capability that depends on certain kinds of environmental experiences (Meltzoff & Moore, 1989), but one that Piaget believed develops later in infancy.

Some of the most powerful evidence against Piaget's views emerges from work with children in non-Western cultures. For instance, some evidence suggests that the timing of the emergence of various cognitive skills among children in non-Western societies differs from the timing observed in children living in Europe and the United States. Infants raised in the Ivory Coast of Africa, for example, reach the various substages of the sensorimotor period at an earlier age than do infants reared in France (Dasen, Inhelder, LaVallee, & Retschitzki, 1978). This is not altogether surprising, for parents in the Ivory Coast of Africa tend to emphasize motor skills more heavily than do parents in Western societies, thereby providing greater opportunity for practice of those skills.

Despite the problems we have addressed regarding Piaget's view of the sensorimotor period, even his most passionate critics concede that he has provided us with a masterful description of the broad outlines of sensorimotor development during infancy. His failings seem to be in underestimating the capabilities of younger infants and in his claims that sensorimotor skills develop in a consistent, fixed pattern. Still, his influence has been enormous, and although the focus of many contemporary developmentalists has shifted to newer information-processing approaches that we discuss next, Piaget remains a towering and pioneering figure (Beilin & Pufall, 1992; Demetriou, Shayer, & Efklides, 1993; Siegler, 1994.).

Directions in Development

Mathematical Skills: The Pluses and Minuses of Infancy

Can 5-month-old infants add and subtract?

Surprisingly, yes, according to recent research—yielding an answer that contradicts Piaget's view of infants' cognitive capabilities. Based on data collected by developmental psychologist Karen Wynn, infants as young as 5 months can calculate the outcome of simple addition and subtraction problems (Wynn, 1992).

To arrive at this conclusion, Wynn developed an ingenious procedure. As illustrated in the photo in Figure 5-3, infants first were shown an object—a four-inch-high Mickey Mouse statuette. A screen then came up, hiding the statuette. Next, the experimenter showed the infants a second, identical Mickey Mouse, and then placed it behind the same screen.

Finally, depending on the experimental condition, one of two outcomes occurred. In the "correct addition" condition, the screen dropped, revealing the two statuettes (analogous to 1 + 1 = 2). But in the "incorrect addition" condition, the screen dropped to reveal just one statuette (analogous to the incorrect 1 + 1 = 1).

Because infants look longer at unexpected occurrences than at expected ones, the researchers examined the pattern of infants' gaze in the different conditions. In support of the notion that infants can distinguish between correct and incorrect addition, the infants in the experiment gazed longer at the incorrect result than at the correct one. In a similar procedure, infants looked longer at incorrect subtraction problems than at correct ones. The conclusion: Infants have rudimentary mathematical skills.

These results suggest that infants may have an innate ability to comprehend certain basic mathematical functions. This inborn proficiency may form the basis of future understanding of more complex mathematics. Furthermore, the presence of such early mathematical skills lends weight to the notion that other basic skills may have innate components, and it calls into question some of Piaget's fundamental views of the infant's capabilities.

FIGURE 5-3   Mickey Mouse math. Research by Dr. Karen Wynn found that 5-month-olds like Michelle Follet, pictured here, reacted differently according to whether the number of Mickey Mouse statuettes they saw represented correct or incorrect addition.

Review and Rethink

REVIEW

- ◆ Jean Piaget's theory of human cognitive development involves a succession of stages through which children progress from birth to adolescence.

- ◆ As humans move from one stage to another, the way they understand the world changes as a function of their maturation and their experiences.

- The sensorimotor stage, from birth to about 2 years, involves a gradual progression through simple reflexes, single coordinated activities, interest in the outside world, purposeful combinations of activities, manipulation of actions to produce desired outcomes, and symbolic thought.

- Piaget, whose influence has been substantial, is respected as a careful observer of children's behavior and a generally accurate interpreter of the way human cognitive development proceeds.

- Critics of Piaget fault him for underestimating infants' capabilities and for regarding as universal some aspects of human development that appear to be subject to cultural and individual variations.

RETHINK

- In this chapter, an individual's approach to a book is used as an example of a difference in scheme between children and adults. Can you think of other examples of different ways that adults and children understand and interpret objects or events in their worlds?

- Can you think of examples of the principles of assimilation and accommodation at work in child development? Do these principles function in adult human learning?

- In what ways do you think the concept of object permanence might foster the infant's social and emotional development?

- Why is the emergence of a capacity for mental representation essential for the development of thought? In what ways do you think the mental representations of a blind infant differ from those of a sighted infant? In what ways might they be the same?

- In general, what are some implications for childrearing practices of Piaget's observations about the ways children gain an understanding of the world?

INFORMATION-PROCESSING APPROACHES TO COGNITIVE DEVELOPMENT

At the age of 3 months, Carrie Nordstrom breaks into a smile as her brother Nate stands over her crib, picks up a doll, and makes a whistling noise through his teeth. In fact, Carrie never seems to tire of Nate's efforts at making her smile, and soon whenever Nate appears and simply picks up the doll, her lips begin to curl into a smile.

Clearly, Carrie remembers Nate and his humorous ways. But how did she learn this? What is it that makes Nate distinctive to her? How does she come to associate Nate's presence with previous entertaining encounters?

To answer questions such as these, we need to diverge from the road that Piaget laid out for us. Rather than seeking to identify the universal milestones in cognitive development through which all infants pass, as Piaget tried to do, we must consider the processes by which individuals acquire and use the information to which they are exposed. We need, then, to focus less on the qualitative changes in infants' mental lives and consider more closely their quantitative capabilities.

Information-processing approaches to cognitive development seek to identify the way that individuals take in, use, and store information (Siegler, 1991). According to this approach, the quantitative changes in infants' abilities to organize and manipulate information represent the hallmarks of cognitive development.

Taking this perspective, cognitive growth is characterized by increasing sophistication in information processing, similar to the way a computer program becomes more sophisticated and useful as the programmer modifies it and as the size of the computer's memory and its computational sophistication increase. Information-processing approaches, then, focus on the types of "mental programs" that people use when they seek to solve problems (Mehler & DuPoux, 1994).

information-processing approaches the model that seeks to identify the way that individuals take in, use, and store information

THE BASICS OF LEARNING: STARTING SIMPLY

Six-month-old Michael Samedi was on a car ride with his family when a thunder-storm suddenly began. The storm rapidly became violent, and flashes of lightning were quickly followed by loud thunderclaps. Michael was clearly disturbed and began to sob. With each new thunderclap, the pitch and fervor of his crying increased. Unfortunately, before very long it wasn't just the sound of the thunder that would raise Michael's anxiety; the sight of the lightning alone was enough to make him bawl in fear. In fact, even as an adult, Michael feels his chest tighten and his stomach churn at the mere sight of lightning.

Classical Conditioning.   The source of Michael's fear is **classical conditioning**, a basic type of learning first identified by Ivan Pavlov. In classical conditioning an organism learns to respond in a particular way to a neutral stimulus that normally does not trigger that type of response.

You have probably heard of the initial demonstration of classical conditioning, which involved Pavlov's research with dogs. Pavlov discovered that by repeatedly pairing two stim-uli, such as the sound of a bell and the arrival of meat, he could make hungry dogs learn to respond (in this case by salivating) not only when the meat was presented but even when the bell was sounded without the presence of meat (Pavlov, 1927).

The key feature of classical conditioning is stimulus substitution, in which a stimulus that does not naturally bring about a particular response is paired with a stimulus that does evoke that response. Repeatedly presenting the two stimuli together results in the second stimulus taking on the properties of the first. In effect, the second stimulus is substituted for the first.

Classical conditioning underlies the learning of both pleasurable and undesired responses. For example, our earlier example of Carrie Nordstrom, who smiles when her brother Nate picks up her doll, may be viewed as an example of classical conditioning: The mere presence of Nate brings the same reaction to the now-conditioned Carrie as would Nate's earlier playing with her doll. On the other hand, Michael Samedi's fear of lightning is also brought about by classical conditioning: The lightning has become a substitute stim-ulus for thunder, and each stimulus now evokes the response of fear.

One of the earliest examples of the power of classical conditioning in shaping human emotions was demonstrated in the case of an 11-month-old infant called Little Albert in the research report (Watson & Rayner, 1920). Although he initially adored furry animals and showed no fear of rats, Albert learned to fear them when, during a laboratory demonstra-tion, a loud noise was sounded every time he played with a cute and harmless white rat. In fact, the fear generalized to other furry objects, including rabbits and even a Santa Claus

classical conditioning   a type of learning in which an organism responds in a particular way to a neutral stimulus that normally does not trigger that type of response

Ivan Pavlov's research with dogs laid the groundwork for our understanding of clas-sical conditioning.

operant conditioning a form of learning
in which a voluntary response is strengthened
or weakened, depending on its association
with positive or negative consequences

habituation the decrease in the response to
a stimulus that occurs after repeated presentations of the same stimulus

mask. (By the way, such a demonstration would be considered unethical today, and it would never be conducted.)

Infants are capable of learning very early through classical conditioning. For instance, 1- and 2-day-old newborns who are stroked on the head just before being given a drop of a sweet-tasting liquid soon learn to suck and to turn their heads at the head-stroking alone (Blass, Ganchrow, & Steiner, 1984). Clearly, classical conditioning is in operation from the time of birth.

Operant Conditioning. But classical conditioning is not the only mechanism through which infants learn; they also respond to **operant conditioning**, a form of learning in which a voluntary response is strengthened or weakened, depending on its association with positive or negative consequences. As we first discussed in Chapter 1, in operant conditioning, infants learn to act deliberately on their environments to bring about some desired consequence. An infant who learns that crying in a certain way is apt to bring her parents' immediate attention is displaying operant conditioning.

Like classical conditioning, operant conditioning functions from the earliest days of life. For instance, researchers have found that even newborns readily learn through operant conditioning to keep sucking on a nipple when it permits them to continue hearing their mothers read a story or to listen to music (Butterfield & Siperstein, 1972; DeCasper & Fifer, 1980; Lipsitt, 1986b).

Habituation. Probably the most primitive form of learning is **habituation**, or the decrease in the response to a stimulus that occurs after repeated presentations of the same stimulus.

Habituation in infants relies on the fact that the presentation of a novel stimulus typically produces an orienting response, in which the infant quiets, becomes attentive, and experiences a slowed heart rate. But when the novelty wears off owing to repeated exposure to the stimulus, the infant no longer reacts with an orienting response. However, when a new and different stimulus is presented, the infant once again reacts with an orienting response. When this happens, we can say that the infant has learned to recognize the original stimulus and to distinguish it from others.

Habituation occurs in every sensory system of infants, and researchers have studied the phenomenon in several ways. One is to examine changes in sucking, which stops temporarily when a new stimulus is presented. This reaction is not unlike that of an adult who temporarily puts down his knife and fork when a dinner companion makes an interesting statement to which he wishes to pay particular attention. Other study techniques include measuring heart rate, respiration rate, and the length of time an infant looks at a particular stimulus.

The ability to learn through habituation is clearly present at birth, and it becomes more pronounced over the first 12 weeks of infancy. As a consequence, habituation is linked to physical and cognitive maturation, and difficulties involving habituation represent a signal of developmental problems (Rovee-Collier, 1987; Braddick, 1993; Tamis-Lemonda & Bornstein, 1993).

Are There Limits on Learning? Although the three basic processes of learning that we have considered—classical conditioning, operant conditioning, and habituation (summarized in Table 5-2)—are all present at birth, they face considerable constraints. According to researchers Marc Bornstein and Michael Lamb (1992), three factors limit the success of learning during infancy. One is the *behavioral state* of the infant. For learning to occur, infants must be in a sufficiently attentive state to sense, perceive, and recognize the relationship between various stimuli and responses. Without at least a minimal level of attentiveness, learning will not be possible (Papousek & Bernstein, 1969).

Natural constraints on learning represents a second limiting factor. Not all behaviors are physically possible for an infant, and infants' perceptual systems, which are not fully developed at birth, may not be sufficiently refined to respond to, or even notice, a particular stim-

TABLE 5-2

THREE BASIC PROCESSES OF LEARNING

Type	Description	Example
Classical conditioning	A situation in which an organism learns to respond in a particular way to a neutral stimulus that normally does not bring about that type of response.	One-and two-day-old newborns are stroked on the head just before being given a drop of a sweet-tasting liquid. They soon learn to suck and turn their heads at the head-stroking alone.
Operant conditioning	A form of learning in which a voluntary response is strengthened or weakened, depending on its positive or negative consequences.	An infant who learns that crying in a certain way is apt to bring her parents' immediate attention is displaying operant conditioning.
Habituation	The decrease in the response to a stimulus that occurs after repeated presentations of the same stimulus.	The most primitive form of learning, habituation occurs in every sensory system of infants. It relies on the fact that the presentation of a novel stimulus typically produces an orienting response, in which the infant quiets, becomes attentive, and experiences a slowed heart rate.

ulus. Consequently, certain types of classical and operant conditioning that are possible with older individuals are ineffective with infants.

Finally, *motivational constraints* may limit learning. For learning to occur, the response involved must not be so taxing on infants that they simply are unmotivated to respond. If the response is too demanding, learning may fail to appear not because the infants haven't learned an association between a stimulus and a response, but because they just don't have the energy or skills to proceed (Rovee-Collier, 1987).

Despite these limitations, infants show great capacities to learn. But just how far do the capabilities of infants extend beyond the basic learning processes? Research on memory in infants illustrates just how competent infants are in other regards.

MEMORY DURING INFANCY: THEY MUST REMEMBER THIS . . .

Think back to the beginning of the chapter. Nicholas was a 6-year-old who remembered quite clearly an Easter egg he was given when he was less than 2—yet had difficulty recalling more current events. How likely is it that Nicholas's memories are accurate? To answer this question, we need to consider the qualities of memory that exist during infancy.

Memory Capabilities in Infancy.   Certainly, infants have **memory** capabilities, defined as the process by which information is initially recorded, stored, and retrieved. As we've seen, the ability of infants to distinguish new stimuli from old, as illustrated by habituation, implies that some memory of the old must be present. Unless infants had some memory of an original stimulus, it would be impossible for them to recognize that a new stimulus differed from the earlier one.

However, infants' capability to habituate and show other basic forms of learning tells us little about how age brings about changes in the capacities of memory and in its fundamental nature. Consider the question of capacity: Do infants' memory capabilities increase as they get older? The answer is clearly affirmative. In one study, infants were taught that

memory   the process by which information is initially recorded, stored, and retrieved

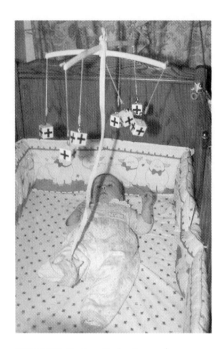

FIGURE 5-4   Early signs of memory. Infants who had learned the association between a moving mobile and kicking showed surprising recall ability if they were exposed to a reminder.

they could move a mobile hanging over the crib by kicking (see Figure 5-4). It took only a few days for 2-month-olds to forget their training, but 6-month-old infants still remembered for as long as 3 weeks (Rovee-Collier, 1984, 1993).

Furthermore, infants who were later prompted to recall the association between kicking and moving the mobile showed evidence that the memory continued to exist even longer. Infants who had received just two training sessions lasting 9 minutes each still recalled about a week later, as illustrated by the fact that they began to kick when placed in the crib with the mobile. Two weeks later, however, they made no effort to kick, suggesting that they had forgotten entirely.

But they hadn't: When a reminder was given—a look at a moving mobile—the memory was apparently reactivated. In fact, the infants could remember the association, following prompting, for as long as an additional month (Sullivan, Rovee-Collier, & Tynes, 1979). Other evidence confirms these results, suggesting that hints can reactivate memories that at first seem lost, and that the older the infant, the more effective such prompting is (Enright, Rovee-Collier, Fagen, & Caniglia, 1983; Rovee-Collier, 1987; Rovee-Collier & Hayne, 1987; Hayne & Rovee-Collier, 1995).

Is the nature of memory in infants different from that in older children and adults? Some researchers suggest that memory during infancy is dependent on particular neurological systems in the brain—specifically, the hippocampus—and that memory in later life involves additional structures of the brain (C.A. Nelson, 1995).

On the other hand, although the nature of information and the parts of the brain involved in memory may differ during infancy, other researchers suggest that information is processed similarly throughout the life span. According to memory expert Carolyn Rovee-Collier, people, regardless of their age, gradually lose memories, although they may regain them if reminders are provided. Moreover, the more times a memory is retrieved, the more enduring the memory becomes (Rovee-Collier, 1993).

The Duration of Memories.   Although the processes that underlie memory retention and recall seem similar throughout the life span, the quantity of information stored and recalled does differ markedly as infants develop. Older infants can remember information longer, and they can retrieve it more rapidly.

Researchers disagree on the age from which memories can be retrieved. Some research supports the notion of **infantile amnesia**, the lack of memory for experiences that occurred prior to 3 years of age. For instance, consider whether you can recall the birth of a younger brother or sister. For most college students, if the birth happened before they reached the age of 3, they can remember virtually nothing about the event (Sheingold & Tenney, 1982).

However, other research shows surprising retention in infants. For example, Nancy Myers and her colleagues exposed a group of 6-month-old youngsters to an unusual series of events in a laboratory, such as intermittent periods of light and dark and unusual sounds. When the children were later tested at the age of 18 months or 30 months, they demonstrated clear evidence that they had some memory of their participation in the earlier experience. Not only did particular behaviors, such as reaching, reflect their earlier participation but they also seemed more familiar with the testing situation itself, showing more willingness to remain in the situation than did a control group of same-age children (Myers, Clifton, & Clarkson, 1987; Perris, Myers, & Clifton, 1990).

Such findings are consistent with evidence that the physical record of a memory in the brain appears to be relatively permanent, suggesting that memories, even from infancy, may be enduring (Newcombe & Fox, 1994). Conversely, the fact that memories may be stored somewhere in the recesses of the brain does not mean that they can be easily, or accurately, retrieved. Memories are susceptible to interference from other, newer information, which may displace or block out the older information, thereby preventing its recall (Potter, 1990). Furthermore, recall of memories is sensitive to the environmental context in which the memories were initially formed. If changes have occurred in the context relating to the ini-

infantile amnesia   *the lack of memory for experiences that occurred prior to 3 years of age*

tial memories, then recall may be difficult, if not impossible (Ceci & Hembrooke, 1993; Rovee-Collier, 1993).

Ultimately, the issue of whether memories formed during infancy are retained into adulthood remains an open—and controversial—issue. Although infants' memories may be highly detailed and can be enduring if the infants experience repeated reminders, it is still not clear how accurate those memories remain over the course of the life span. In fact, research shows that early memories are susceptible to misrecollection if people are exposed to related, and contradictory, information following the initial formation of the memory. Not only does such new information potentially impair recall of the original material, but the new material may be inadvertently incorporated into the original memory, thereby corrupting its accuracy (Rovee-Collier, Borza, Adler, & Boller, 1993; Fivush, 1995).

In sum, the data suggest that, at least theoretically, it is possible for memories to remain intact from a very young age—if subsequent information does not interfere with them. This is a big "if," because most memories are likely to involve experiences that are somehow related to subsequent experiences and therefore susceptible to interference. Ultimately, it may be that the validity of recollections of memories from infancy needs to be evaluated on a case-by-case basis.

INDIVIDUAL DIFFERENCES IN INTELLIGENCE: IS ONE INFANT SMARTER THAN ANOTHER?

> Maddy Rodriguez is a bundle of curiosity and energy. At 6 months of age, she cries heartily if she cannot reach a toy, and when she sees a reflection of herself in a mirror, she gurgles and seems, in general, to find the situation quite amusing.
>
> ***
>
> Jared Lynch, at 6 months, is a good deal more inhibited than Maddy. He doesn't seem to care much when a ball rolls out of his reach, losing interest in it rapidly. And, unlike Maddy, when he sees himself in a mirror, he pretty much ignores the reflection.

As anyone who has spent any time at all observing more than one baby can tell you, not all infants are alike. Some are full of energy and life, apparently displaying a natural-born curiosity, whereas others seem, by comparison, somewhat less interested in the world around them. Does this mean that such infants differ in intelligence?

Answering questions about how and to what degree infants vary in their underlying intelligence is not easy. Although it is clear that different infants show significant variations in their behavior, the issue of just what types of behavior may be related to cognitive ability is complicated. Interestingly, the examination of individual differences between infants was the initial approach taken by developmental psychologists to understand cognitive development, and such issues still represent an important focus within the field.

What is Infant Intelligence? Before we can address whether and how infants may differ in intelligence, we need to consider what is meant by the term "intelligence." Psychologists have yet to agree upon a general definition of intelligent behavior, even among adults. Is it the ability to do well in scholastic endeavors? Competence in navigating across treacherous seas, such as that shown by peoples of the South Pacific, who have no knowledge of Western navigational techniques? Proficiency in business negotiations?

The problem of defining intelligence in infants is even more problematic than with adults. Is it the speed with which a new task is learned through classical or operant conditioning? Is it the rapidity of habituation, or is it the age at which an infant learns to crawl or walk? Furthermore, even if we are able to identify particular behaviors that seem validly to differentiate one infant from another in terms of intelligence during infancy, we need to address a further, and probably more important, issue: How well do measures of infant intelligence relate to eventual adult intelligence?

Determining what is meant by intelligence in infants represents a major challenge for developmentalists.

TABLE 5-3

APPROACHES USED TO DETECT DIFFERENCES IN INTELLIGENCE DURING INFANCY

Developmental Quotient	Formulated by Arnold Gesell, the developmental quotient is an overall developmental score that relates to performance in four domains: motor skills (balance and sitting), language use, adaptive behavior (alertness and exploration), and personal-social (feeding and dressing).
Bayley Scales of Infant Development	Developed by Nancy Bayley, the Bayley Scales of Infant Development evaluate an infant's development from 2 to 30 months. The Bayley Scales focus on two areas: mental (senses, perception, memory, learning, problem solving, and language), and motor abilities (fine and gross motor skills).
Visual-recognition memory measurement	Measures of visual-recognition memory, the memory of and recognition of a stimulus that has been previously seen, also relate to intelligence. The more quickly an infant can retrieve a representation of a stimulus from memory, the more efficient, presumably, is that infant's information processing.

Clearly such questions are not simple, and no simple answers have been found. However, developmental researchers have devised several approaches (summarized in Table 5-3) to illuminate the nature of individual differences in intelligence during infancy.

Developmental Scales.   Developmental psychologist Arnold Gesell formulated the earliest measure of infant development, which was designed to screen out normally developing babies from those with atypical development (Gesell, 1946). Gesell based his scale on examinations of hundreds of babies. He compared their performance at different ages to learn what behaviors were most common at a particular age. If an infant varied significantly from the norms of a given age, he or she was considered to be either developmentally delayed or advanced.

Gesell's primary motivation in developing his norms was to screen out abnormally developing infants for purposes of adoption. Following the lead of researchers who sought to quantify intelligence through a specific score (known as an *intelligence quotient*, or IQ, score), Gesell developed a **developmental quotient** (DQ), which is an overall developmental score that relates to performance in four domains: motor skills (for example, balance and sitting), language use, adaptive behavior (such as alertness and exploration), and personal-social (for example, feeding and dressing).

Later researchers were motivated by different goals. For instance, Nancy Bayley developed one of the most widely used measures for infants. **The Bayley Scales of Infant Development** evaluate an infant's development from 2 to 30 months (Bayley, 1969). The Bayley Scales focus on two areas: mental and motor abilities. The mental scale focuses on the senses, perception, memory, learning, problem solving, and language; the motor scale evaluates fine and gross motor skills (see Table 5-4). Like Gesell's approach, the Bayley Scale yields a developmental quotient (DQ). A child who scores at an average level—meaning average performance for other children at the same age—receives a score of 100.

The virtue of approaches such as those taken by Gesell and Bayley is that they provide a good snapshot of an infant's current developmental level. Using them, we can tell in an objective manner if a particular infant falls behind or is ahead of his or her same-age peers.

developmental quotient   *an overall developmental score that relates to performance in four domains: motor skills, language use, adaptive behavior, and personal-social*

Bayley Scales of Infant Development   *a measure that evaluates an infant's development from 2 to 30 months*

They are particularly useful in identifying infants who are substantially behind their peers, and who therefore need immediate special attention (Culbertson & Gyurke, 1990).

On the other hand, except in extreme cases, such scales are not very good at all in predicting a child's future course of development. A child whose development lags behind her peers at the age of 1 year, as identified by these measures, does not necessarily display slow development at age 5, or 12, or 25. The association between most measures of behavior during infancy and adult intelligence, then, is minimal (Bornstein & Sigman, 1986; L.S. Siegel, 1989; DiLalla et al., 1990).

Because it is difficult with these global measures to obtain measures of infant intelligence that are related to later intelligence, investigators have turned in the last decade to other techniques that may help assess intelligence in a meaningful way. Some have proven to be quite useful.

Information-processing Approaches to Individual Differences in Intelligence. When we speak of intelligence in everyday parlance, we often differentiate between "quick" individuals and those who are "slow." Actually, according to research on the speed of information processing, such terms hold some truth. Contemporary approaches to infant intelligence suggest that the speed with which infants process information may correlate most strongly with later intelligence, as measured by IQ tests administered during adulthood.

For instance, infants who process information efficiently ought to be able to learn about stimuli more quickly, and thus we would expect that they would turn their attention away from a given stimulus more rapidly than would those who are less efficient at information processing. Similarly, measures of **visual-recognition memory**, the memory of and recognition of a stimulus that has been previously seen, also relate to IQ. The more quickly an infant can retrieve a representation of a stimulus from memory, the more efficient, presumably, is that infant's information processing (Tamis-LeMonda & Bornstein, 1993).

Research using an information-processing framework is clear in suggesting a relationship between information processing and cognitive abilities: Measures of how quickly infants lose interest in stimuli that they have previously seen, as well as their responsiveness

visual-recognition memory *memory and recognition of a stimulus that has been previously seen*

TABLE 5-4

SAMPLE ITEMS FROM THE BAYLEY SCALES OF INFANT DEVELOPMENT

MENTAL SCALE		MOTOR SCALE	
Age (in Months)	Item	Age (in Months)	Item
0.1	Responds to sound of rattle	0.1	Lifts head when held at shoulder
1.5	Social smile	1.8	Turns: side to back
2.0	Visually recognizes mother	2.3	Sits with support
3.8	Turns head to sound of cube	3.2	Turns: back to side
4.1	Reaches for cube	5.3	Pulls to sitting
4.8	Discriminates stranger	6.4	Rolls: back to stomach
6.0	Looks for fallen spoon	6.6	Sits alone steadily
7.0	Vocalizes 4 different syllables	8.1	Pulls to standing
9.1	Responds to verbal request	9.6	Walks with help
13.4	Removes pellet from bottle	11.7	Walks alone
14.2	Says two words	14.6	Walks backward
18.8	Uses words to make wants known	16.1	Walks upstairs with help
19.3	Names one picture (e.g., dog)	23.4	Jumps off floor

Source: Adapted from N. Bayley (1969).

to new stimuli, correlate moderately well with later measures of intelligence. Infants who are more efficient information processors during the 6 months following birth tend to have higher intelligence scores between 2 and 12 years of age, as well as higher scores on other measures of cognitive competence (Thompson, Fagen, & Fulker, 1991; Rose, Feldman, & Wallace, 1992; Perleth, Lehwald, & Browder, 1993; Rolfe, 1994; Rose & Feldman, 1995; Slater, 1995; Sigman et al., in press).

Other research suggests that abilities related to the *multimodal approach to perception*, which we considered in Chapter 4, may offer clues about later intelligence. For instance, the information-processing skill of cross-modal transference is associated with intelligence. **Cross-modal transference** is the ability to identify a stimulus that has previously only been experienced through one sense by using another sense. For instance, a baby who is able to recognize by sight a screwdriver that she has only previously touched, but not seen, is displaying cross-modal transference. Research has found that cross-modal transference, which requires a high level of abstract thinking, at age 1 is associated with intelligence scores several years later (Rose & Ruff, 1987; Spelke, 1987; Rose, Feldman, Wallace, & McCarton, 1991).

Although information-processing efficiency and cross-modal transference abilities

Speaking of Development

Ellen Sackoff

Born: ································· 1949

Education: ······················ Hood College, B.A. in art
City University of New York, M.A. in developmental psychology

Position: ························· Managing partner for the Discovery Group

Home: ···························· New York City

How would you like to blend your educational background and personal interests and end up in a job developing, evaluating, and marketing new products for children, including toys? That's just what Ellen Sackoff did.

Armed with an art degree, Sackoff started her work life as a textile designer. But she wanted something more. She was determined to combine her art background with her interest in human behavior. So she started a company that designs and develops toys for infants.

As a managing partner of the Discovery Group, Sackoff uses her background in development to alert parents about the best toys of the year and tests toys for the Children's Television Wokshop.

"One might wonder why the field of child development would be involved in making toys for infants," she observes. "The reason is that play has long been a major area of research in psychology. Psychologists look at the play of animals and humans, and they think about what constitutes play and what its role is in development.

during infancy relate moderately well to later IQ scores, we need to keep in mind two qualifications. First, even though an association exists between early information-processing capabilities and later measures of IQ, the correlation is only moderate in strength. Other factors, such as the degree of environmental stimulation, also play a crucial role in helping to determine adult intelligence. Consequently, we should not assume that intelligence is somehow permanently fixed in infancy.

Second, and perhaps even more important, intelligence measured by traditional IQ tests relates to a particular type of intelligence, one that emphasizes abilities that lead to academic, and certainly not artistic or professional, success. Consequently, predicting that a child may do well on IQ tests later in life is not the same as predicting that the child will be successful later in life.

Still, the relatively recent finding that an association exists between efficiency of information processing and later IQ scores has changed how we view the consistency of cognitive development across the lifespan. Whereas the earlier reliance on scales such as the Bayley led to the misconception that little continuity existed, the more recent information-processing approaches suggest that cognitive development unfolds in a more orderly and continuous manner from infancy to the later stages of life.

"People now are focusing more and more on making toys that tune into children's developmental stages."

"If toys are truly tools for play, then let's give babies tools that work well, tools that keep their attention."

"For infants, play serves an important function in their exploration of the world. It is all they do. Through their explorations, infants learn about their world."

Involving child-development experts in the design of toys for infants is a relatively new phenomenon, but already there appears to be considerable demand for it.

"Play contributes to all aspects of development," Sackoff explains. "People now are focusing more and more on making toys that tune into children's developmental stages. We make use of the fact that the development of a child follows a fairly universal course.

"In the first few months, we know that infants rely on their eyes and ears, but particularly their eyes. Babies focus more on objects that have sharp contrasts, and that is why there has been a proliferation of black-and-white toys. A lot of bold primary colors are used as well, but pastels are not used much because infants do not see their lack of contrast well."

Another development fact used by toy developers in the creation of new products is that babies like to look at faces, largely because faces are in constant movement.

"Things that move are fascinating to infants. The constant movement and changing of a face are what keep a baby's attention," Sackoff notes. "Many toys incorporate images of faces even though the image is static."

A toy with high play value, according to Sackoff, is one that will sustain infants' interest over time. Children tend to get bored playing with the same toy all the time.

"We test toys largely through observation of kids. We try to see which features are used, and which are not," she adds. "This is the basis for removing weak features and emphasizing strong ones.

"Play is important, and good toys are therefore important," she says. "If toys are truly tools for play, then let's give babies tools that work well, tools that keep their attention."

Even if they don't understand the meaning of the words, infants still benefit from being read to.

The Informed Consumer of Development

What Can You Do to Promote Infants' Cognitive Development?

All parents want their children to reach their full cognitive potential, but sometimes efforts to reach this goal take a bizarre path. For instance, some parents pay hundreds of dollars to enroll in workshops with names such as "How to Multiply Your Baby's Intelligence," and they buy books with titles such as *How to Teach Your Baby to Read* (Sharpe, 1994).

Do such efforts ever succeed? Although some parents swear they do, there is no scientific support for the efficacy of such programs. For example, despite the many cognitive skills of infants, it should be clear that no infant skill will permit a child actually to read. Furthermore, "multiplying" a baby's intelligence is impossible, and such organizations as the American Academy of Pediatrics and the American Academy of Neurology have denounced programs that claim to do so.

On the other hand, there are things that can be done to promote cognitive development in infants. The following suggestions, based upon findings of developmental psychologists, offer a starting point (Meyerhoff & White, 1986; Schwebel, Maher, & Fagley, 1990; Schulman, 1991):

- Provide infants the opportunity to explore the world. As Piaget suggests, children learn by doing, and they need the opportunity to explore and probe their environment. Make sure that environment contains a variety of toys, books, and other sources of stimulation. (Also see the Speaking of Development box.)

- Be responsive to infants, on both a verbal and a nonverbal level. Try to *speak* to babies, as opposed to *at* them. Ask questions, listen to their responses, and provide further communication.

- Read to your infants. Although they may not understand the meaning of your words, they will respond to your tone of voice and the intimacy provided by the activity. Reading together also begins to create a lifelong reading habit.

- Keep in mind that you do not have to be with an infant 24 hours a day. Just as infants need time to explore their world on their own, parents and other caregivers need time off from childcare activities.

- Don't push infants nor expect too much too soon. Your goal should not be to create a genius; it should be to provide a warm, nurturing environment that will allow an infant to reach his or her potential.

Review and Rethink

REVIEW

- Information-processing approaches to the study of cognitive development complement qualitative approaches such as Piaget's by considering quantitative changes in children's abilities to organize and use information.

- Even young infants are capable of learning through such simple means as classical conditioning, operant conditioning, and habituation.

- Infants clearly have memory capabilities from a very early age, although both the duration and the accuracy of such memories over the long term are unresolved questions.

- Traditional measures of infant intelligence focus on behavioral attainments, which can help identify developmental delays or advances. However, these measures are not strongly related to measures of adult intelligence.

- Information-processing approaches to assessing intelligence rely on variations in the speed with which infants process information. Infants' speed of information processing correlates moderately with adult measures of IQ.

RETHINK

- According to this chapter, classical conditioning relies on stimulus substitution. Can you think of examples of the use of classical conditioning on adults in everyday life, in such areas as entertainment, advertising, or politics?

- What information from this chapter could you use to refute the claims of books or educational programs that promise to help parents multiply their babies' intelligence or instill advanced intellectual skills in infants?

- This chapter refers to the issue of the duration and accuracy of early childhood memories as "controversial." What sorts of controversies arise out of this issue? Can such controversies be resolved? How?

- In what way is the use of such developmental scales as Gesell's or Bayley's helpful? In what way is it dangerous? How would you maximize the helpfulness and minimize the danger?

- Information-processing speed in infants correlates moderately well with one sort of adult intelligence. Might there be other indicators in infants that correlate with other adult skills or intelligences? Of what use would such indicators be? What would be their limitations?

THE ROOTS OF LANGUAGE

Mama. No. Cookie. Dad. Jo.

When an infant utters his or her first word, no matter what it is, it marks the start of a transformation from an entity with talents seemingly not so different from those possessed by animals of many other species to an entity with skills that are, arguably, unique to human beings.

But those initial words are just the first and most obvious manifestations of language. Many months earlier, infants were using language to comprehend the world around them. How does this linguistic ability develop? What is the pattern and sequence of language development? And how does the use of language mark a transformation in the cognitive world of infants and their parents? We'll consider these questions, and others, as we address the development of language during the first years of life.

THE FUNDAMENTALS OF LANGUAGE: FROM SOUNDS TO SYMBOLS

Language, the systematic, meaningful arrangement of symbols, provides the basis for communication. But it does more than this: It is closely tied to the way infants think and how they understand the world. It enables them to reflect on people and objects and to convey their thoughts to others.

language   *the systematic, meaningful arrangement of symbols that provides the basis for communication*

In considering the development of language, we need to distinguish between linguistic *comprehension*, the understanding of speech, and linguistic *production*, the use of language to communicate. One principle underlies the relationship between the two: Comprehension precedes production. An 18-month-old may be able to understand a complex series of directions ("pick up your coat from the floor and put it on the chair by the fireplace") but may not yet have strung more than two words together. Comprehension, then, begins earlier than production, and throughout infancy comprehension increases at a faster rate than production. For instance, during infancy comprehension of words expands at a rate of 22 new words a month, whereas production of words increases at a rate of about nine new words a month (Benedict, 1979). Other forms of language ability show the same pattern, with comprehension consistently preceding production (see Figure 5-5).

Prelinguistic Communication.   Consider the following "dialogue" between a mother and her 3-month-old child (C.E. Snow, 1977b):

FIGURE 5-5

Throughout infancy, the comprehension of speech precedes the production of speech.

(*Source*: Adapted from Bornstein & Lamb, 1992.)

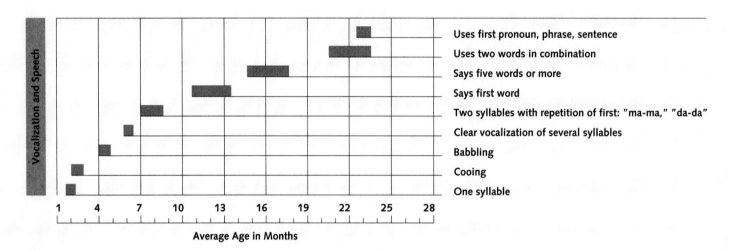

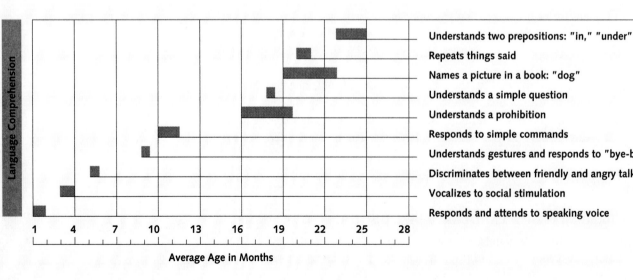

Mother	Infant
	[Smiles]
Oh, what a nice little smile!	
Yes, isn't that pretty?	
There now.	
There's a nice little smile.	
	[Burps]
What a nice wind as well!	
Yes, that's better, isn't it?	
Yes.	
Yes.	
	[Vocalizes]
Yes!	
There's a nice noise.	

prelinguistic communication *communication through sounds, facial expressions, gestures, imitation, and other nonlinguistic means*

babbling *making speechlike but meaningless sounds*

Although we tend to think of language in terms of the production first of words and then of groups of words, infants actually begin to communicate linguistically well before they say their first word. Spend 24 hours with even a very young infant and you will hear a variety of sounds: cooing, crying, gurgling, murmuring, and various types of other noises. These sounds, although not meaningful in themselves, play an important role in linguistic development, paving the way for true language (Bloom, 1993).

Prelinguistic communication is communication through sounds, facial expressions, gestures, imitation, and other nonlinguistic means. When a father responds to his daughter's "ah" with an "ah" of his own, and then the daughter repeats the sound, and the father responds once again, they are engaged in prelinguistic communication. Clearly, the "ah" sound has no particular meaning. However, its repetition, which mimics what will later be the give-and-take of conversation, teaches the infant something about turn-taking (Dromi, 1993).

The most obvious manifestation of prelinguistic communication is **babbling**, making speechlike but meaningless sounds that start at the age of 2 or 3 months and continues until about the age of 1 year. When they babble, infants repeat the same vowel sound over and

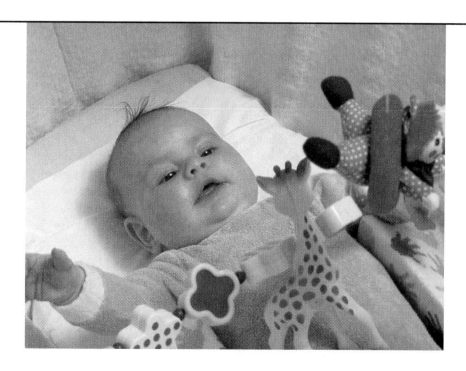

Infants spontaneously babble, making speech-like but meaningless sounds, even when no other person is present.

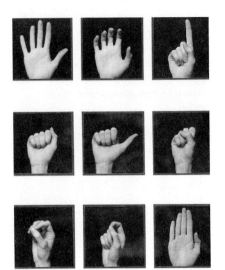

Deaf infants who are exposed to sign language do their own type of babbling, related to the use of signs.

over, changing the pitch from high to low (as in "ee-ee-ee," repeated at different pitches). After the age of 5 months, the sounds of babbling begin to expand, reflecting the addition of consonants (such as "bee-bee-bee-bee").

Babbling is a universal phenomenon, accomplished in the same way throughout all cultures. While they are babbling, infants spontaneously produce all of the sounds found in every language, not just the language they hear people around them speaking. In fact, even deaf children display their own form of babbling: Infants who cannot hear and who are exposed to sign language show their own form of babbling, but they use their hands instead of their voices (Jakobson, 1971; Petitto & Marentette, 1991).

The form of babbling follows a progression from sounds that are the simplest to make to more complex sounds. Babies start with sounds that involve the lips ("p" or "b"), and then proceed to sounds that involve the tongue ("d" or "n"). Later babbling involves nasal or dental sounds ("m" or "t") (Menyuk, 1995).

Although exposure to a particular language does not seem to influence babbling at first, experience eventually does make a difference. By the age of 6 months, babbling differs according to the language to which infants are exposed (Blake & de Boysson-Bardies, 1992). The difference is so noticeable that even untrained listeners can distinguish between babbling infants who have been raised in cultures in which French, Arabic, or Cantonese languages are spoken (Locke, 1983; de Boysson-Bardies, Sagart, & Durand, 1984; Boysson-Bardies & Vihman, 1991; Vihman, 1991).

Babbling may be the most obviously languagelike achievement of early infancy, but there are other indications of prelinguistic speech. For instance, consider 5-month-old Marta, who spies her red ball just beyond her reach. After reaching for it and finding that she is unable to get to it, she makes a cry of anger that alerts her parents that something is amiss, and her mother hands it to her. Communication, albeit prelinguistic, has occurred.

Four months later, when Marta faces the same situation, she no longer bothers to reach for the ball and doesn't respond in anger. Instead, she holds out her arm in the direction of the ball, but now, with great purpose, seeks to catch her mother's eye. When her mother sees the behavior, she knows just what Marta wants. Clearly, Marta's communicative skills—although still prelinguistic—have taken a leap forward.

Even these prelinguistic skills are supplanted in just a few months, when the gesture gives way to a new communicative skill: producing an actual word. Marta's parents clearly hear her say "ball."

First Words.   When a mother and father first hear their child say "Mama" or "Dada," which may occur as early as 9 months, it is hard to be anything but delighted. But their initial enthusiasm may be dampened a bit when they find that the same sound is used to ask for a cookie, a doll, and a ratty old blanket.

First words generally are spoken somewhere near the age of 10 to 14 months. Linguists differ on just how to recognize that a first word has actually been uttered. Some say it is when an infant clearly understands words and can produce a sound that is close to a word spoken by adults, such as a child who uses "mama" for any request she may have. Other linguists use a stricter criterion for the first word; they restrict "first word" to cases in which children give a clear, consistent name to a person, event, or object. In this view, "mama" counts as a first word only if it is consistently applied to the same person, seen in a variety of situations and doing a variety of things, and is not used to label other people (Kamhi, 1986; Bornstein & Tamis-LeMonda, 1989).

Although disagreement exists over when we can say a first word has been uttered, there is no disputing the fact that once an infant starts to produce words, the rate of increase in vocabulary is rapid. By the age of 15 months, the average child has a vocabulary of 10 words. The child's vocabulary methodically expands until the one-word stage of language development ends at about 18 months when a sudden spurt in vocabulary occurs. In just a short period—a few weeks somewhere between 16 and 24 months of age—a child's vocabulary typically increases from 50 to 400 words (Bates, Bretherton, & Snyder, 1988).

As you can see from the list in Table 5-5, the first words in children's early vocabularies typically regard objects and things, both animate and inanimate. Most often they refer to people or objects who constantly appear and disappear ("Mama"), to animals ("kitty"), or to temporary states ("wet"). These first words are often **holophrases**, one-word utterances that depend on the particular context in which they are used to determine meaning. For example, a youngster may use the phrase "ma" to refer to his mother's coming in and out or to ask for something to eat (K. Nelson, 1981; Clark, 1983; Dromi, 1987).

First Sentences. When Aaron was 19 months old, he heard his mother coming up the back steps, as she did every day just before dinner. Aaron turned to his father and distinctly said, "Ma come." In stringing those two words together, Aaron took a giant step in his language development.

The increase in vocabulary that comes at about 18 months is accompanied by another accomplishment: the linking together of individual words into sentences that convey a single thought. Although a good deal of variability exists in the time at which children first create two-word phrases, it is generally about 8 to 12 months after they say their first word.

The linguistic advance represented by two-word combinations is important because the linkage not only provides labels for things in the world but also indicates the relations between them. For instance, the combination may declare something about possession ("Mama key") or recurrent events ("Dog bark"). Interestingly, most early sentences do not represent demands or even necessarily require a response. Instead, they are often merely comments and observations about events occurring in the child's world (Slobin, 1970; Halliday, 1975).

holophrases one-word utterances that depend on the particular context in which they are used to determine meaning

TABLE 5-5

COMPREHENSION AND PRODUCTION OF WORDS

	Comprehension Percentage	Production Percentage
1. *Nominals (Words referring to "things")*	56	61
Specific (people, animals, objects)	17	11
General (words referring to all members of a category)	39	50
Animate (objects)	9	13
Inanimate (objects)	30	37
Pronouns (e.g., this, that, they)	1	2
2. *Action words*	36	19
Social action games (e.g., peek-a-boo)	15	11
Events (e.g., "eat")	1	NA
Locatives (locating or putting something in specific location)	5	1
General action and inhibitors (e.g., "don't touch")	15	6
3. *Modifiers*	3	10
Status (e.g., "all gone")	2	4
Attributes (e.g., "big")	1	3
Locatives (e.g., "outside")	0	2
Possessives (e.g., "mine")	1	1
4. *Personal-social*	5	10
Assertions (e.g., "yes")	2	9
Social expressive (e.g., "bye-bye")	4	1

Note: Percentage refers to percentage of children who include this type of word among their first 50 words.
Adapted from Benedict (1979).

telegraphic speech   *speech in which words not critical to the message are left out*

underextension   *the act of using words too restrictively, common among children just mastering spoken language*

overextension   *words used too broadly, overgeneralizing their meaning*

Two-year-olds using two-word combinations tend to employ particular sequences that are similar to the ways in which adult sentences are constructed. For instance, sentences in English typically follow a pattern in which the subject of the sentence comes first, followed by the verb, and then the object ("Josh threw the ball"). Children's speech most often uses a similar order, although not all the words are initially included. Consequently, a child might say "Josh threw" or "Josh ball" to indicate the same thought. What is significant is that the order is typically not "threw Josh" or "ball Josh," but rather the usual order of English, which makes the utterance much easier for an English speaker to comprehend (R. Brown, 1973; Maratsos, 1983).

Although the creation of two-word sentences represents an advance, the language used by children still is by no means adultlike. For instance, 2-year-olds produce **telegraphic speech**: Words not critical to the message are left out, similar to the way we might write a telegram for which we were paying by the word. Rather than saying, "I showed you the book," a child using telegraphic speech might say, "I show book." "I am drawing a dog" might become "Drawing dog" (see Table 5-6).

Early language has other characteristics that differentiate it from the language used by adults. For instance, consider Sarah, who refers to the blanket she sleeps with as "Blankey." When her Aunt Ethel gives her a new blanket, Sarah refuses to call the new one a "blankey," restricting the word to her original blanket.

Sarah's inability to generalize the label of "blankey" to blankets in general is an example of **underextension**, using words too restrictively, which is common among children just mastering spoken language. Underextension occurs when language novices think that a word refers to a specific concept, instead of to all examples of the concept (Caplan & Barr, 1989).

As infants grow more adept with language, the opposite phenomenon sometimes occurs. In **overextension**, words are used too broadly, overgeneralizing their meaning. For example, when Sarah referred to buses, trucks, and tractors as "cars," she was guilty of overextension, making the assumption that any object with wheels must be a car. Although overextension reflects speech errors, it also shows that advances are occurring in the child's thought processes: The child is beginning to develop general mental categories and concepts (Behrend, 1988).

SPEAKING TO CHILDREN: THE LANGUAGE OF MOTHERESE

Say the following sentence aloud: Do you like the apple dumpling?

Now pretend that you are going to ask the same question of an infant, and speak it as you would for the child's ears.

TABLE 5-6

CHILDREN'S IMITATION OF SENTENCES SHOWING DECLINE OF TELEGRAPHIC SPEECH

	Eve, 25.5 Months	Adam, 28.5 Months	Helen, 30 Months	Ian, 31.5 Months	Jimmy, 32 Months	June, 35.5 Months
I showed you the book.	I show book.	(I show) book.	C	I show you the book.	C	Show you the book.
I am very tall.	(My) tall.	I (very) tall.	I very tall.	I'm very tall.	Very tall.	I very tall.
It goes in a big box.	Big box.	Big box.	In big box.	It goes in the box.	C	C
I am drawing a dog.	Drawing dog.	I draw dog.	I drawing dog.	Dog.	C	C
I will read the book.	Read book.	I will read book.	I read the book.	I read the book.	C	C
I can see a cow.	See cow.	I want see cow.	C	Cow.	C	C
I will not do that again.	Do–again.	I will that again.	I do that.	I again.	C	C

C = correct imitation.

Source: Adapted from R. Brown & C. Fraser (1963).

Chances are several things happened when you translated the phrase for the infant. First of all, the wording probably changed, and you may have said something like, "Does baby like the apple dumpling?" At the same time, the pitch of your voice probably rose, your general intonation most likely had a singsong quality, and you probably separated your words carefully.

motherese   *a style of speech directed toward infants that is characterized by short, simple sentences*

Motherese, or Infant-directed Speech.   The shift in your language was due to an attempt to use what has been called **motherese,** a style of speech directed toward infants. Motherese is characterized by short, simple sentences, and it typically refers to concrete objects in the baby's environment. Pitch becomes higher, the range of frequencies increases, and intonation is more varied. There is also repetition of words, and topics are restricted to items that are assumed to be comprehensible by infants. Sometimes motherese includes amusing sounds that are not even words, imitating the prelinguistic speech of infants. In other cases, it has little formal structure, but is similar to the kind of telegraphic speech that infants use as they develop their own language skills (Swanson, Leonard, & Grandour, 1992).

Motherese changes as children become older. Near the end of the first year, motherese takes on more adultlike qualities. Sentences become longer and more complex, although individual words are still spoken slowly and deliberately. Pitch is also used to focus attention on particularly important words.

Because it is inexactly named—fathers and other adults use the same kind of speech with infants, not just mothers—motherese has come to be called *infant-directed speech.* Whatever name is used, however, the way in which adults speak to children plays an important role in infants' acquisition of language. Newborns show more positive responses to such speech than to regular language, a fact that suggests that they may be particularly receptive to it (Fernald, 1991; Hepper, Scott, & Shahidullah, 1993). Furthermore, some research suggests that unusually extensive exposure to motherese early in life is related to the comparatively early appearance of first words and earlier linguistic competence in other areas (Bornstein & Ruddy, 1984; Hoff-Ginsberg, 1986; Cooper & Aslin, 1990, 1994; Hampson & Nelson, 1993).

Gender Differences.   To a girl, a bird is a birdie, a blanket a blankie, and a dog a doggy. To a boy, a bird is a bird, a blanket a blanket, and a dog a dog.

At least that is what parents of boys and girls appear to think, as illustrated by the language they use toward their sons and daughters. Virtually from the time of birth, the language parents employ with their children differs depending on the child's sex, according to research conducted by developmental psychologist Jean Berko Gleason (Gleason, 1987; Gleason, Perlmann, Ely, & Evans, 1994).

Gleason found that, by the age of 32 months, girls hear twice as many diminutives (words such as "kitty" or "dolly" instead of "cat" or "doll") as boys hear. Although the use of diminutives declines with increasing age, their use consistently remains higher in speech directed at girls than in speech directed at boys (see Figure 5-6).

Parents also are more apt to respond differently to children's requests depending on the child's gender. For instance, when turning down a child's request, mothers are likely to respond with a firm "no" to a male child, but to soften the blow to a female child by providing a diversionary response ("Why don't you do this instead?") or by somehow making the refusal less direct. Consequently, boys tend to hear firmer, clearer language, while girls are exposed to warmer phrases, often referring to inner emotional states (Perlmann & Gleason, 1990).

Do such differences in language directed at boys and girls during infancy affect their behavior as adults? Although no direct evidence supports such an association, it is clear that men and women use different sorts of language as adults. For instance, as adults, women tend to use more tentative, less assertive language than do men. We don't know whether these differences are a reflection of early linguistic experiences, but such findings are certainly intriguing (Matlin, 1987; Tannen, 1991).

Motherese, or, more precisely, infant-directed speech, includes the use of short, simple sentences and is said in a pitch that is higher than that used with older children and adults.

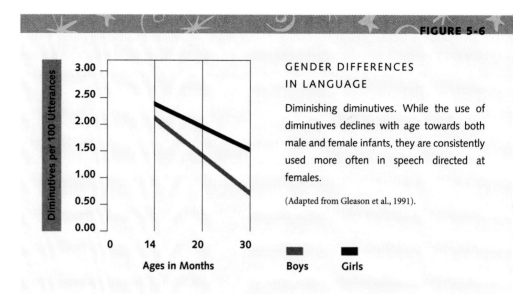

FIGURE 5-6

GENDER DIFFERENCES IN LANGUAGE

Diminishing diminutives. While the use of diminutives declines with age towards both male and female infants, they are consistently used more often in speech directed at females.

(Adapted from Gleason et al., 1991).

Developmental Diversity

Is Infant-Directed Speech Similar Across All Cultures?

Do mothers in the United States, Japan, and Italy speak the same way to their infants?

In some respects, they clearly do. Although the words themselves differ across languages, the way the words are spoken is quite similar. According to a growing body of research, basic similarities exist across cultures in the nature of infant-directed speech (Grieser & Kuhl, 1988; Papousek & Papousek, 1991).

Consider, for instance, the comparison in Table 5-7 of the major characteristics of speech directed at infants used by native speakers of English and Spanish. Of the ten most

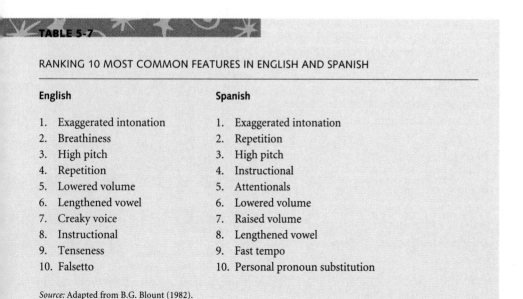

TABLE 5-7

RANKING 10 MOST COMMON FEATURES IN ENGLISH AND SPANISH

English	Spanish
1. Exaggerated intonation	1. Exaggerated intonation
2. Breathiness	2. Repetition
3. High pitch	3. High pitch
4. Repetition	4. Instructional
5. Lowered volume	5. Attentionals
6. Lengthened vowel	6. Lowered volume
7. Creaky voice	7. Raised volume
8. Instructional	8. Lengthened vowel
9. Tenseness	9. Fast tempo
10. Falsetto	10. Personal pronoun substitution

Source: Adapted from B.G. Blount (1982).

FIGURE 5-7

INFANT-DIRECTED SPEECH.

Across a variety of cultures, both mothers and fathers use speech pitch of a higher frequency when speaking to infants than to other adults.

(Source: Fernald et al, 1989).

Adult-Directed Speech

Infant-Directed Speech

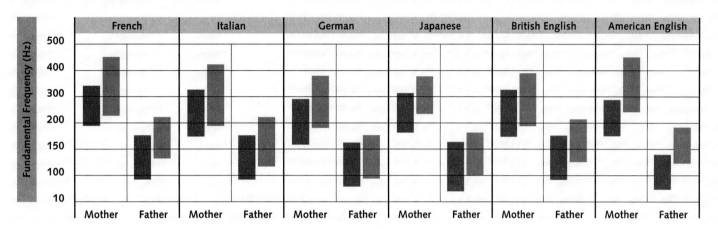

frequent features, six are common to both: exaggerated intonation, high pitch, lengthened vowels, repetition, lower volume, and instructional emphasis (that is, heavy stress on certain key words, such as emphasizing the word "ball" in the sentence, "No, that's a *ball*") (Blount, 1982).

More precise comparisons, across a broader range of languages, reveal other similarities. For instance, Figure 5-7 shows the remarkable similarities in speech pitch among speakers of different languages when they are directing speech to infants, as opposed to adults (Fernald et al., 1989). It is particularly interesting that in every case mothers raise their pitch more than do fathers when speaking to infants. Furthermore, speakers of American English show the greatest differences between speech to an infant and speech to an adult.

The cross-cultural similarities in infant-directed speech are so great, in fact, that they appear in some facets of language specific to particular types of interactions. For instance, evidence comparing American English, German, and Mandarin Chinese speakers shows that in each of the languages, pitch rises when a mother is attempting to get an infant's attention or produce a response, whereas pitch falls when she is trying to calm an infant (Papousek & Papousek, 1991).

Why do we find such similarities across very different languages? One hypothesis is that the characteristics of infant-directed speech activate innate responses in infants. For instance, infants seem to prefer infant-directed speech over adult-directed speech, suggesting that their perceptual systems may be more responsive to such characteristics. Another explanation is that infant-directed speech facilitates language development, providing cues as to the meaning of speech before infants have developed the capacity to understand the meaning of words (Fernald & Kuhl, 1987; Fernald, 1989).

The Informed Consumer of Development

Assessing Language Development

Given the critical role that language plays in cognitive development, parents often are concerned that their infant's language development proceeds on schedule. Although no hard-and-fast rules obtain, given the wide variability in the timing of children's first words and the ways their vocabularies develop (Shore, 1994), several guidelines indicate whether language development is normal. An infant who does the following is probably developing normally, according to psycholinguist Anne Dunlea (Fowler, 1990; Yarrow, 1990):

◆   *Understanding at least some things that are heard.* This means that, at the minimum, the child has some receptive language and is capable of hearing. For instance, most children can discriminate between friendly and angry speech by the age of 6 months.

◆   *Producing sounds, such as a raspberry noise, at about 6 or 7 months of age.* Children who are deaf may end prelinguistic speech at this point, even if they produced it earlier, because they cannot hear themselves.

◆   *Using gestures to communicate.* Pointing and reaching are often forerunners of language. By the age of 9 months, most children look toward an object pointed to by an adult, and most use pointing themselves before the end of their first year.

◆   *Pretending to use language.* Even if the words make no sense, children may pretend to use language before they actually begin to speak, indicating that they at least know how language functions.

What if the applicaton of these guidelines suggests that an infant has a hearing problem? It would be reasonable to have a pediatrician evaluate your child. Keep in mind, however, the wide range of variations in language development among different children, and the fact that the vast number of children develop quite normally.

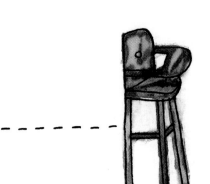

Review and Rethink

REVIEW

◆   Before they speak their first word, infants understand many adult utterances and engage in several forms of prelinguistic communication, including the use of facial expressions, gestures, and babbling.

◆   Children typically produce their first words between 10 and 14 months, and they rapidly increase their vocabularies from that point on, especially during a spurt at about 18 months.

◆   Children's language development proceeds through a pattern of holophrases, two-word combinations, and telegraphic speech. Their linguistic development reflects their growing sense of the relations between objects in the world, and their acquisition of general mental categories and concepts.

◆ When speaking to infants, adults of all cultures tend to use infant-directed speech, or motherese. This type of speech seems to appeal to infants and to facilitate their linguistic development.

◆ According to some research, adults tend to speak more indirectly to girls and more directly to boys, which may contribute to behavioral differences later in life.

RETHINK

◆ Many linguists believe that humans have an innate linguistic ability that permits children to develop the language of their environment naturally. What evidence for this viewpoint do you find in this chapter?

◆ What are some ways in which children's linguistic development reflects their acquisition of new ways of interpreting and dealing with their world?

◆ Infants prefer motherese to regular language. Given what you have learned about research involving infants, how do you think researchers might have established this fact?

◆ Do you think the stages of linguistic development for a signed language mirror those for a spoken language? What similarities and differences might there be?

◆ What are some implications of differences in the ways adults speak to boys and girls? How might such speech differences contribute to later differences not only in speech, but in attitudes?

LOOKING BACK

What can we learn about children's views of the world from Piaget's theories of cognitive development?

1. Jean Piaget, a Swiss psychologist, was a highly influential theorist and researcher most noted for his pioneering work in child development. His basic premise is that infants achieve their understanding of the world through direct motor behavior, rather than from other people or through sensation and perception.

2. Piaget's stage theory asserts that children pass through stages of cognitive development in a fixed order. The stages represent changes not only in the quantity of knowledge infants gain but also in the quality of that knowledge. Their schemes, or organized patterns of understanding aspects of the world, shift as they progress from stage to stage.

3. According to Piaget, all children pass gradually through the four major stages of cognitive development (sensorimotor, preoperational, concrete operational, and formal operational) and their various substages when the children are at an appropriate level of maturation and are exposed to relevant types of experiences.

4. In the Piagetian view, children's understanding grows through assimilation of their experiences into their current way of thinking or through accommodation of their current way of thinking to their experiences.

5. During the sensorimotor period, which stretches from birth to about 2 years old, and which Piaget divides into six substages, infants progress from the use of simple reflexes, through the development of repeated and integrated actions that gradually increase in complexity, to the ability to generate purposeful effects from their actions. By the end

of the sixth substage of the sensorimotor period, infants are beginning to engage in symbolic thought.

6. An important concept in the Piagetian view is object permanence, the realization that people and objects continue to exist even when they are not seen. This concept is regarded as developing during the fourth substage of the sensorimotor period.

7. Piaget's theories have had great influence on the study of development. Modern psychologists agree that he was an unparalleled observer of child behavior, that his insights into the ways children learn are correct, and that the broad outlines of his stages of development are accurate. However, they criticize his underestimation of infants' abilities and his assumption that the pattern of cognitive development is universal, instead of potentially influenced by cultural and other factors.

How do infants process information and learn about the world?

8. Information-processing approaches to the study of cognitive development seek to learn how individuals receive, organize, store, and retrieve information. Such approaches differ from and supplement qualitative approaches such as Piaget's by considering quantitative changes in children's abilities to process information.

9. From birth, infants learn through such simple means as habituation (a decreased response due to familiarity), classical conditioning (a response displaced from one stimulus to another), and operant conditioning (an increased response due to association with desirable consequences).

10. For all their abilities, infants' learning is clearly limited by their behavioral state, by natural constraints, and by motivational factors influenced by the demands of the learning task.

What sorts of memories do infants have?

11. Infants have memory capabilities from their earliest days, as evidenced by their ability to habituate and to learn in other basic ways. With prompting, they can retrieve memories after considerable intervals.

12. The accuracy of infant memories is a matter of debate. Evidence shows that some information taken in by the infant at a very early age can be successfully stored and retrieved. However, evidence also shows that infant memories are susceptible to interference from later experiences and memories.

How can we measure infant intelligence and how does it relate to adult intelligence?

13. Traditional measures of infant intelligence, such as Gesell's developmental quotient and the Bayley Scales of Infant Development, focus on average behavior observed at particular ages in large numbers of children. Such measures can help identify developmental delays or advances at given points in time. However, they do not effectively predict adult intelligence.

14. Information-processing approaches to assessing intelligence rely on variations in the speed with which infants process information. Infants' speed of information processing appears to correlate moderately well with adult measures of IQ. However, this finding has limited application because intelligence is not a fixed quantity during the lifespan, is influenced by environmental factors, and includes aspects and components not measured by IQ tests.

By what processes do children learn to use language?

15. Prelinguistic communication involves the use of sounds, gestures, facial expressions, imitation, and other nonlinguistic means to express thoughts and states. Babbling is a

form of prelinguistic communication, which proceeds through regular stages and, with other forms of prelinguistic communication, prepares the infant for speech.

16. Infants typically produce their first words between the ages of 10 and 14 months. Thereafter, vocabulary increases rapidly, especially during a spurt at about 18 months. At approximately the same time, children typically begin to link words together into primitive sentences that express single thoughts.

17. Beginning speech is characterized by the use of holophrases, in which a single word conveys more complex meaning based on its context; telegraphic speech, in which only essential sentence components are used; underextension, in which an overly restrictive meaning is assigned to a word; and overextension, in which an overly generalized meaning is assigned to a word.

18. Features of the child's home language begin to emerge as early as the babbling stage, when sounds other than those of the home language gradually disappear. In addition, the grammar of the home language begins to be reflected even in telegraphic speech, when word order mirrors that used by mature speakers of the home language.

How do children influence the language that adults use to address them?

19. Adult language is influenced by the children to whom it is addressed. Infant-directed speech (also called motherese) takes on characteristics, surprisingly invariant across cultures, that make it appealing to infants and that probably facilitate language development.

20. Adult language also exhibits differences based on the gender of the child to whom it is directed. For example, some research indicates that adult speech addressed to boys is more direct than speech addressed to girls. It is possible that gender differences in the language heard during infancy may have effects that emerge later in life.

KEY TERMS AND CONCEPTS

assimilation (p. 148)

accommodation (p. 148)

scheme (p. 148)

sensorimotor stage (of cognitive development) (p. 149)

object permanence (p. 151)

deferred imitation (p. 153)

information-processing approaches (p. 156)

classical conditioning (p. 157)

operant conditioning (p. 158)

habituation (p. 158)

memory (p. 159)

infantile amnesia (p. 160)

developmental quotient (p. 162)

Bayley Scales of Infant Development (p. 162)

visual-recognition memory (p. 163)

cross-modal transference (p. 163)

language (p. 167)

prelinguistic communication (p. 169)

babbling (p. 169)

holophrases (p. 171)

telegraphic speech (p. 172)

underextension (p. 172)

overextension (p. 172)

motherese (p. 173)

CHAPTER 6

INFANCY

Social and Personality Development

CHAPTER OUTLINE

PROLOGUE: THE VELCRO CHRONICLES

It was during the windy days of March that the problem in the day care center first arose. Its source: 10-month-old Russell Ruud. Otherwise a model of decorum, Russell had somehow learned how to unzip the Velcro chin strap to his winter hat. He would remove the hat whenever he got the urge, seemingly oblivious to the potential health problems that might follow.

But that was just the start of the real difficulty. To the chagrin of the teachers in the day care center, not to speak of the children's parents, soon other children were following his lead, removing their own caps at will.

Russell's mother, made aware of the anarchy at the day care center—and the other parents' distress over Russell's behavior—pleaded innocent. "I never showed Russell how to unzip the Velcro," claimed his mother, Judith Ruud, an economist with the Congressional Budget Office in Washington, D.C. "He learned by trial and error, and the other kids saw him do it one day when they were getting dressed for an outing." (Goleman, 1993, p. C10)

By then, though, it was too late for excuses: Russell, it seems, was an excellent teacher. Keeping the children's hats on their heads proved to be no easy task. Even more ominous was the thought that if the infants could master the Velcro straps on their hats, would they soon be removing the Velcro fasteners on their shoes and removing *them?*

LOOKING AHEAD

Russell's behavior embodies what recent research suggests is a heretofore unsuspected outcome of infants' participation in day care: the acquisition of new skills and abilities from more "expert" peers. Infants, as we will see, have an amazing capacity to learn from other children, and their interactions with others can play a central role in their developing social and emotional worlds.

This chapter considers social and personality development in infancy. We begin by examining the emotional lives of infants, considering which emotions they feel and how well they can decode others' emotions. We also consider how infants use others to determine how to react, and their views of their own and others' mental lives.

We then turn to a consideration of social relationships, looking at how bonds of attachment are forged and the ways in which infants interact with family members and peers.

Finally, the chapter considers the characteristics that differentiate one infant from another. We'll discuss differences in the way children are treated depending on their gender. We'll consider the nature of family life at the close of the twentieth century and how it differs from earlier eras. The chapter closes with a look at the benefits and costs of infant day care outside the home, a child-care option increasingly employed.

In sum, after reading this chapter, you'll be able to answer these questions:

- Do infants have emotions?

- How do infants interpret the emotions of others?

- What are some characteristics of infants' mental life?

- What is attachment in infancy, and how does it relate to the future social competence of individuals?

- What roles do mothers, fathers, and infants play in social development?

- What sorts of interactions do infants engage in with caregivers and other children?

- What are some of the ways that infants differ from one another?

◆   How are societal changes reflected in family life and child-care practices?

◆   Is day care beneficial or harmful for infants?

FORMING THE ROOTS OF SOCIABILITY

Germaine smiles when he catches a glimpse of his mother. Tawanda looks angry when her mother takes away the spoon that she is playing with. Sydney scowls when a loud plane flies by overhead.

A smile. A look of anger. A scowl. The emotions of infancy are written all over a baby's face. Yet do infants experience emotions in the same way that adults do? When do they become capable of understanding what others are experiencing emotionally? And how do they use others' emotional states to make sense of their environment? We consider some of these questions as we seek to understand how infants develop emotionally and socially.

EMOTIONS IN INFANCY: DO INFANTS EXPERIENCE EMOTIONAL HIGHS AND LOWS?

Anyone who spends any time at all around infants knows they display facial expressions that seem indicative of their emotional states. In situations where we expect them to be happy, they seem to smile; when we might assume they are frustrated, they show anger; and when we might expect them to be unhappy, they look sad (see Figure 6-1).

In fact, these basic facial expressions are remarkably similar across the most diverse cultures. Whether we look at babies in India, the United States, or the jungles of New Guinea, the expression of basic emotions is the same. Furthermore, the nonverbal expression of emotion, called *nonverbal encoding*, is fairly consistent throughout the life span. These consistencies have led researchers to conclude that the capacity to display basic emo-

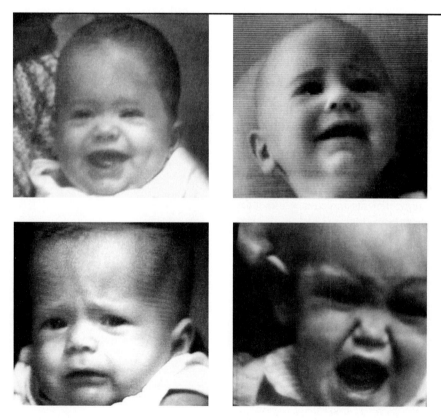

FIGURE 6-1   Infants appear to display a wide range of emotional expressions.

tions is innate (Feldman, 1982; Camras, Malatesta, & Izard, 1991; Ekman & O'Sullivan, 1991).

Infants appear to display a fairly wide range of emotional expressions. According to research on what mothers see in their children's nonverbal behavior, almost all think that by the age of 1 month, their babies have expressed interest and joy. In addition, 84 percent of mothers believe their infants have expressed anger, 75 percent surprise, 58 percent fear, and 34 percent sadness (Johnson et al., 1982).

Experiencing Emotions.   Does the capability of infants to encode emotions nonverbally in a consistent, reliable manner mean that they actually *experience* emotions, and—if they do—is the experience similar to that of adults? These questions are not easy to answer.

The fact that children display nonverbal expressions in a manner similar to that of adults does not necessarily mean that the actual experience is identical. In fact, if the nature of such displays is innate, it is possible that facial expressions can occur spontaneously, without any emotional experience accompanying them. Nonverbal expressions, then, might be emotionless in young infants, in much the same way that our knee reflexively jerks forward, without the involvement of emotions, when a physician taps it.

However, most developmental specialists believe otherwise: They argue that the nonverbal expressions of infants represent emotional experiences. In fact, developmental psychologist Carroll Izard suggests in his **differential emotions theory** that emotional expressions not only reflect emotional experiences but also help in the regulation of emotion itself. Izard argues that infants are born with an innate repertoire of emotional expressions, reflecting basic emotional states. These basic expressions are expanded and modified as infants and children grow older and become more adept at controlling their nonverbal behavioral expressions and more sophisticated in their ability to experience a wider array of emotions (Izard, 1977; Izard & Malatesta, 1987; Camras et al., 1991).

In sum, infants do appear to experience emotions, although the range of emotions at birth is fairly restricted. However, as they get older, infants both display and experience a wider range of increasingly complex emotions (N.F. Fox, 1994).

Smiling.   As Luz lay sleeping in her crib, her mother and father caught a glimpse of the most beautiful smile crossing her face. Her parents were sure that Luz was having a pleasant dream. Were they right?

Probably not. The earliest smiles expressed during sleep probably have little meaning, although no one can be absolutely sure. However, by 6 to 9 weeks it is clear that babies begin to smile reliably at the sight of stimuli that please them, including toys, mobiles, and—to the delight of parents—people. Smiling in response to other individuals is considered a **social smile**, in comparison to smiling at nonhuman stimuli.

Actually, the first smiles tend to be relatively indiscriminate, as infants first begin to smile at the sight of almost anything they find amusing. However, as they get older, they become more selective in their smiles, and their social smiles become directed toward particular individuals, not just anyone (Wolff, 1963).

Furthermore, by the age of 18 months, social smiling, directed more toward mothers and other caregivers, becomes more frequent than smiling directed toward nonhuman objects. Moreover, if an adult is unresponsive to a child, the amount of smiling decreases. In sum, by the end of the second year children are quite purposefully using smiling to communicate their positive emotions, and they are sensitive to the emotional expressions of others (Jones & Raag, 1989; Jones, Collins, & Hong, 1991; Toda & Fogel, 1993).

Decoding Others' Facial and Vocal Expressions.   You may recall from Chapter Three that neonates are able to imitate adults' facial expressions, a capability that is apparent even minutes after birth (Kaitz, Meschulach-Sarfaty, Auerbach, & Eidelman, 1988; Reissland, 1988). Although newborns' imitative abilities certainly do not mean that they can understand the

differential emotions theory   *the theory that emotional expressions not only reflect emotional experiences but also help in the regulation of emotion itself*

social smile   *smiling in reference to other individuals*

True social smiles emerge by the age of 6 to 9 weeks.

meaning of others' facial expressions, such imitation does pave the way for future *nonverbal decoding* abilities, which begin to emerge fairly soon. Using these abilities, infants can interpret others' facial and vocal expressions that carry emotional meaning.

Although relatively little attention has been given to infants' perception of vocal expressions, it does appear that they are able to discriminate happy and sad vocal expressions at the age of 5 months. Infants also seem to be able to discriminate vocal expressions of emotion at a slightly earlier age than they discriminate facial expressions (Walker-Andrews & Grolnick, 1983; Walker-Andrews & Lennon, 1991).

Developmental specialists know more about the *sequence* in which nonverbal facial decoding ability progresses. In the first 6 to 8 weeks, infants' visual precision is sufficiently limited that they cannot pay much attention to others' facial expressions. But they soon begin to discriminate among different facial expressions of emotion and even seem to be able to respond to differences in emotional intensity conveyed by facial expressions. They also respond to unusual facial expressions. For instance, they show distress when their mothers pose bland, unresponsive, neutral facial expressions (Klinnert et al., 1983; Kuchuk, Vibbert, & Bornstein, 1986; Lamb, Morrison, & Malkin, 1987; Nelson, 1987).

By the time they reach the age of 4 months, infants may already have begun to understand the emotions that lie behind the facial and vocal expressions of others. How do we know this? One important clue comes from a study in which 7-month-old infants were shown a pair of facial expressions relating to joy and sadness and, simultaneously, heard a vocalization representing either joy (a rising tone of voice) or sadness (a falling tone of voice). The infants paid more attention to the face that matched the tone, suggesting that they had at least a rudimentary understanding of the emotional meaning of facial expressions and voice tones (Phillips et al., 1990).

In sum, infants learn early both to encode and to decode emotions. Such abilities play an important role not only in helping them experience their own emotions but—as we see next—in using others' emotions to understand the meaning of ambiguous social situations.

SOCIAL REFERENCING: FEELING WHAT OTHERS FEEL

When 23-month-old Brooke watches as her mother and father loudly argue with one another, she glances at her older brother. He appears unperturbed by the scene, having witnessed it all too often in the past, and he wears a small smile of embarrassment on his face. On seeing this, Brooke smiles slightly, too, mimicking her brother's facial expression.

Like Brooke, most of us have been in situations in which we feel uncertain. In such cases, we sometimes turn to others to see how they are reacting. This reliance on others, known as social referencing, helps us decide what an appropriate response ought to be.

Social referencing is the intentional search for information to help explain the meaning of uncertain circumstances and events. Social referencing is used to clarify the meaning of a situation by reducing our uncertainty about what is occurring (Campos & Stenberg, 1981; Klinnert, 1984).

Social referencing first tends to occur about the age of 8 or 9 months (Walden & Ogan, 1988). It is a fairly sophisticated social ability: Infants need it not only to understand the significance of others' behavior, such as their facial expressions, but also to realize that others' behavior has meaning with reference to specific circumstances (Rosen, Adamson, & Bakeman, 1992).

Infants make particular use of facial expressions in their social referencing. For instance, in one study infants were given an unusual toy to play with. The amount of time they played with it depended on their mothers' facial expressions. When their mothers displayed disgust, they played with the toy significantly less than when their mothers appeared pleased. Furthermore, when given the opportunity to play with the same toy later, the infants revealed lasting consequences of their mothers' earlier behavior, despite the mothers' now neutral-appearing facial reactions (Hornik, Risenhoover, & Gunner, 1987; Hornik, & Gunnar 1988).

Although it is clear that social referencing begins fairly early in life, developmental researchers are still not certain *how* it operates. Consider, for instance, one possibility: It may be that observing someone else's facial expression brings about the emotion the expression represents. That is, an infant who views someone looking sad may come to feel sad herself, and her behavior may be affected. On the other hand, it may be the case that viewing another's facial expression simply provides information. In this case, the infant does not experience the particular emotion represented by another's facial expression; she simply uses the display as data to guide her own behavior.

Both explanations for social referencing have received support, and so we still do not know which is correct. What we do know is that social referencing is most likely to occur

social referencing   the intentional search for information to help explain the meaning of uncertain circumstances and events

Social referencing is used by children to help explain the meaning of circumstances and events that they find puzzling.

when a situation breeds uncertainty and ambiguity. Furthermore, infants who reach the age when they are able to use social referencing become quite upset if they receive conflicting nonverbal messages from their mothers and fathers. Mixed messages, then, are a real source of stress for an infant (Walden & Baxter, 1989; Hirshberg, 1990; Hirshberg & Svejda, 1990; Camras & Sachs, 1991).

THE DEVELOPMENT OF SELF: DO INFANTS KNOW WHO THEY ARE?

> Elysa, 8 months old, crawls past the full-length mirror that hangs on a door in her parents' bedroom. She barely pays any attention to her reflection as she moves by. On the other hand, her cousin Brianna, who is almost 2 years old, stares at herself in the mirror as she passes and laughs as she touches her forehead with her fingers.

Perhaps you have had the experience of catching a glimpse of yourself in a mirror and noticing a hair out of place. You probably reacted by attempting to push the unruly hair back into place. Your reaction shows more than that you care about how you look. It implies that you have a sense of yourself, the awareness and knowledge that you are an independent social entity to which others react, and which you attempt to present to the world in ways that reflect favorably upon you.

We are not, however, born with the knowledge that we exist independently from others and the larger world. Although it is difficult to demonstrate, the youngest infants—like all animals other than some apes—do not seem to have a sense of themselves as individuals. They do not recognize likenesses of themselves, whether in photos or in mirrors, and they show no evidence of being able to distinguish themselves from other people (Gallup, 1977).

The roots of self-awareness begin to grow at about the age of 12 months. We know this from a simple but ingenious experimental technique known as the *mirror and rouge task*. In it, an infant's nose is secretly colored with a dab of red rouge, and the infant is seated in front of a mirror. If infants touch their noses or attempt to wipe off the rouge, we have evidence that they have at least some knowledge of their physical characteristics. For them, this awareness is one step in developing an understanding of themselves as independent objects.

Although some infants as young as 12 months seem startled on seeing the rouge spot, for most a reaction does not occur until between 17 and 24 months of age. It is also about this age that children begin to show awareness of their own capabilities. For instance, infants between the ages of 23 and 25 months sometimes begin to cry when asked in experiments to imitate a complicated sequence of behaviors involving toys, although they readily accomplish simpler ones. According to developmental psychologist Jerome Kagan, their reaction

Research suggests that this 18-month-old is exhibiting a clearly-developed sense of self.

suggests that they are conscious that they lack the capability to carry out difficult tasks, and are unhappy about it—a reaction that provides a clear indication of self-awareness (M. Lewis & Brooks-Gunn, 1979; Kagan, 1981; Lipka & Brinthaupt, 1992; Asendorpf & Baudonniere, 1993).

In sum, by the time they reach the age of 18 to 24 months, infants have developed at least the rudiments of awareness of their own physical characteristics, and they understand that their appearance is stable over time. Although it is not clear how far this awareness extends, it is becoming increasingly evident that, as we discuss next, infants have not only a basic understanding of themselves but also the beginnings of an understanding of how the mind operates—what has come to be called a "theory of mind" (Damon & Hart, 1992).

THEORY OF MIND: INFANTS' PERSPECTIVES ON THE MENTAL LIVES OF OTHERS—AND THEMSELVES

What are infants' thoughts about thinking? According to developmental psychologist John Flavell, infants begin to understand certain things about the mental processes of themselves and others at quite an early age. Flavell has investigated children's **theory of mind**, their knowledge and beliefs about the mental world. Theories of mind represent the explanations that children use to explain how others think.

For instance, cognitive advances during infancy permit older infants to come to see people in ways that are very different from other objects. They learn to see others as *compliant agents*, beings similar to themselves who behave under their own power and who have the capacity to respond to infants' requests (Flavell, 1993; C. Lewis & Mitchell, 1994; Flavell, Green, & Flavell, 1995).

In addition, children's capacity to understand intentionality and causality grows during infancy. They begin to grasp that others' behaviors have some meaning and that the behaviors they see people enacting are designed to accomplish particular goals, in contrast to the "behaviors" of inanimate objects (Parritz, Mangelsdorf, & Gunnar, 1992; Gelman & Kalish, 1993; Golinkoff, 1993).

By the age of 2, infants begin to demonstrate the rudiments of **empathy**, an emotional response that corresponds to the feelings of another person. At 24 months of age, infants sometimes comfort others or show concern for them (Zahn-Waxler, Robinson, & Emde, 1992). To do this, they need to be aware of others' emotional states. Further, during their second year infants begin to use deception, both in games of "pretend" and in outright attempts to fool others. A child who plays "pretend" and who uses falsehoods must be aware that others hold beliefs about the world—beliefs that can be manipulated (Leslie, 1987; J. Dunn, 1991).

In sum, by the end of infancy children have developed the rudiments of a theory of mind. This theory represents a kind of folk psychology. It helps children to understand the actions of others and it affects their own behavior (Wellman, 1990; Moses & Chandler, 1992).

By the age of 2, children demonstrate the foundations of empathy, an emotional response that corresponds to the feelings of another person.

theory of mind   *children's knowledge and beliefs about the mental world*

empathy   *an emotional response that corresponds to the feelings of another person*

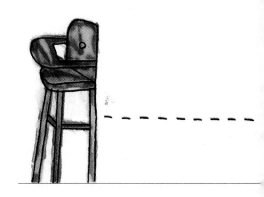

Review and Rethink

REVIEW

- Infants appear both to express and to experience emotions, at first displaying a limited range, and then a wider range reflecting increasingly complex emotional states.

- Infants from different cultures use similar facial expressions to convey basic emotional states. As the infant matures, the meaning of an expression such as the smile grows increasingly specific, with a more limited range of applicability.

◆   The ability to decode the nonverbal facial and vocal expressions of others develops early in infants. By 8 or 9 months, infants begin to use such nonverbal decoding to clarify situations of uncertainty and determine appropriate responses, an ability termed *social referencing*.

◆   Infants are not at first aware that they exist separately from the rest of the world. They develop self-awareness gradually, starting after 12 months of age.

◆   By the age of 2, children have developed the rudiments of a theory of mind, including a realization that people are essentially different from inanimate objects, a growing sense of intentionality and causality, fundamental feelings of empathy, and the ability to pretend and to deceive.

RETHINK

◆   If the facial expressions that convey basic emotions are similar across cultures, how do such expressions arise? Can you think of facial expressions that are culture-specific? How do they arise?

◆   Why might the ability to discriminate vocal expressions emerge earlier than the ability to discriminate facial expressions?

◆   In what situations do adults rely on social referencing to work out appropriate responses? How might social referencing be used to manipulate individuals' responses?

◆   How might a child's developing sense of empathy be fostered by parents and other caregivers?

◆   How do Flavell's ideas about a growing sense of causality, pretense, and deception in children compare to Piaget's notions of experimentation and deferred imitation by children?

FORGING RELATIONSHIPS

Louis became the center of attention on the way home [from the hospital]. His father brought Martha, aged 5, and Tom, aged 3, to the hospital with him when Mrs. Moore was discharged. Martha rushed to see "her" new baby and ignored her mother. Tom clung to his mother's knees in the reception hall of the hospital.

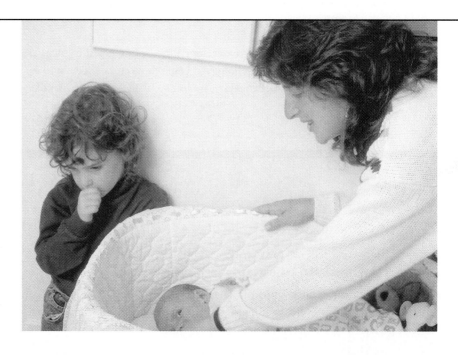

The lack of enthusiasm displayed by this older sibling illustrates the challenges posed by the arrival of a new member of the family.

A hospital nurse carried Louis to the car, placing him in Mrs. Moore's arms for the ride home. The two older children immediately climbed over the seat and swamped mother and baby with their attention. Both children stuck their faces into his, smacked at him, and talked to him. They soon began to fight over him with loud voices. The loud argument and the jostling of his mother upset Louis and he started to cry. He let out a wail that came like a shotgun blast into the noisy car. The children quieted immediately and looked with awe at this new infant. His insistent wails drowned out their bickering. He had already asserted himself in their eyes. Martha's lip quivered as she watched her mother attempt to comfort Louis, and she added her own soft cooing in imitation of her mother. Tom squeezed even closer to his mother, put his thumb in his mouth, and closed his eyes to shut out the commotion. (Brazelton, 1983, p. 48)

The arrival of a newborn brings a dramatic change to a family's dynamics. No matter how welcome a baby's birth, it causes a fundamental shift in the roles that people play within the family. The mother and father must start to build a relationship with their infant, and older children must adjust to the presence of a new member of the family and build their own alliance with their infant brother or sister.

Although the process of social development during infancy is neither simple nor automatic, it is crucial: The bonds that grow between infants and their parents, family, and others provide the foundation for a lifetime's worth of social relationships.

ATTACHMENT: FORMING SOCIAL BONDS

The most important form of social development that occurs during infancy is **attachment**, the positive emotional bond that develops between a child and a particular individual. The nature of our attachment during infancy has repercussions for how we relate to others throughout the rest of our lives (Greeberg, Cicchetti, & Cummings, 1990; Kochanska, 1995).

To understand attachment, the earliest researchers turned to the bonds that form between parents and children in the nonhuman animal kingdom. For instance, ethologist Konrad Lorenz (1965) studied the poultry equivalent of attachment by observing newborn goslings, who have an innate tendency to follow their mother, the first moving object to which they typically are exposed after birth. Lorenz found that goslings whose eggs were raised in an incubator and who viewed *him* after hatching would follow *his* every movement, as if he were their mother. He labeled this process *imprinting*: rapid, innate learning that takes place during a critical period and that involves attachment to the first moving object observed.

Lorenz's findings suggested that attachment was based on biologically determined factors, and other theorists agreed. For instance, Freud suggested that attachment grew out of a mother's ability to satisfy a child's oral needs.

On the other hand, the ability to provide food and other physiological needs is not as crucial as Freud and other theorists first thought. In a classic study, psychologist Harry Harlow gave infant monkeys the choice of cuddling a wire "monkey" that provided food or a soft, terry cloth "monkey" that was warm but did not provide food (see Figure 6-2). Their preference was clear: They would spend most of their time clinging to the cloth "monkey," although they made occasional expeditions to the wire monkey to nurse (Harlow & Zimmerman, 1959). This research clearly illustrates that food alone is insufficient to bring about attachment. Furthermore, these findings are congruent with the research we discussed in Chapter 3 showing no evidence for the existence of a critical bonding period between human mothers and infants immediately after birth.

The earliest work on human attachment, which is still highly influential, was carried out by John Bowlby (1951). Bowlby's theorizing about attachment had a biological basis, although it was supplemented by observations of emotionally disturbed children with whom he worked in a London clinic.

attachment   the positive emotional bond that develops between a child and a particular individual

FIGURE 6-2   Harlow's monkeys.

Mary Ainsworth, who devised the "strange situation" to measure infant attachment.

Ainsworth strange situation   *a sequence of staged episodes that illustrate the strength of attachment between a child and (typically) his or her mother*

In Bowlby's view, attachment is based primarily on infants' needs for safety and security—their genetically determined motivation to avoid predators. As they develop, infants come to learn that their safety is best provided by a particular individual, a realization that ultimately leads to the development of a special relationship, typically with the mother. Bowlby suggests that this single relationship is qualitatively different from the bonds formed with others, including the father—a suggestion that, as we'll see later, has been a source of some subsequent dispute.

Bowlby also suggests, somewhat ironically, that attachment—which has its roots in the desire to seek the protective security of the mother—is critical in allowing an infant to explore the world. According to his view, having strong, firm attachment provides a kind of home base away from which growing children can progressively roam as they become more independent.

Using Bowlby's theorizing as a base, developmental psychologist Mary Ainsworth developed a widely used experimental technique to measure attachment (Ainsworth, Blehar, Waters, & Wall, 1978). The **Ainsworth strange situation** consists of a sequence of staged episodes that illustrate the strength of attachment between a child and (typically) his or her mother. The "strange situation" follows this general eight-step pattern: (1) The mother and baby enter an unfamiliar room; (2) the mother sits down, leaving the baby free to explore; (3) an adult stranger enters the room and converses first with the mother and then with the baby; (4) the mother exits the room, leaving the baby alone with the stranger; (5) the mother returns, greeting and comforting the baby, and the stranger leaves; (6) the mother departs again, leaving the baby alone; (7) the stranger returns; and (8) the mother returns and the stranger leaves (Ainsworth et al., 1978).

Infants' reactions to the various aspects of the strange situation vary considerably, depending on the nature of their attachment to their mothers. One-year-olds show three major patterns: securely attached, avoidant, and ambivalent (summarized in Table 6-1). *Securely attached* children use the mother as a kind of home base, at ease in the strange situation as long as she is present. They explore independently, returning to her occasionally. When she leaves, though, they act upset, and they go to her as soon as she returns. Most children—about two-thirds—fall into the securely attached category.

In contrast, children labeled *avoidant* do not seek proximity to the mother, and after the mother has left, they seem to avoid her when she returns. It is as if they are angered by her behavior. Some 20 percent of children are found to be in the avoidant category at 1 year of age.

Finally, the last group of children are labeled *ambivalent*, displaying a combination of positive and negative reactions to their mothers. Ambivalent children are in such close contact with the mother that they may not explore their environment much. They may be anx-

TABLE 6-1

CLASSIFICATIONS OF INFANT ATTACHMENT

	CLASSSIFICATION CRITERIA				
Label	Proximity Seeking	Contact Maintaining	Proximity Avoiding	Contact Resisting	Crying
Avoidant	Low	Low	High	Low	Low (pre-separation), high or low (separation), low (reunion)
Secure	High	High (if distressed)	Low	Low	Low (pre-separation), high or low (separation), low (reunion)
Ambivalent	High	High (often pre-separation)	Low	High	Occasionally (pre-separation), high (separation), moderate to high (reunion)

(*Source:* Waters, 1978.)

In this illustration of the strange situation, the infant first explores the playroom on his own, as long as his mother is present. But when she leaves, he begins to cry. On her return, however, he is immediately comforted and stops crying. The conclusion: he is securely attached.

ious even before the mother leaves, and when she does they show great distress. But upon her return, they show ambivalent reactions, simultaneously seeking close contact but also hitting and kicking her. About 12 percent of 1-year-olds fall into the ambivalent classification (Cassidy & Berlin, 1994).

Although Ainsworth identified only three categories, a more recent expansion of her work suggests that there is a fourth category—*disorganized-disoriented*; these children show inconsistent, often contradictory behavior, such as approaching the mother when she returns but not looking at her. Their confusion suggests that they may be the least securely attached children of all (Egeland & Farber, 1984; O'Connor, Sigman, & Brill, 1987).

The explicit classification of a child into an attachment style would be of only minor consequence were it not for the fact that the nature of attachment between infants and their mothers seems to have significant consequences for relationships at later stages of life. For example, research has found that boys who were securely attached at the age of 1 year showed fewer psychological difficulties at older ages than did avoidant or ambivalent children. Similarly, children who were securely attached as infants tended to be more socially and emotionally competent later than were those with the other attachment styles, and others viewed them more positively. Ultimately, some research suggests that the nature of romantic relationships in adult life is associated with the kind of attachment style developed during infancy (Lewis, Feiring, McGuffog, & Jaskir, 1984; Shaver, Hazan, & Bradshaw, 1988; Ainsworth, 1989; Ainsworth & Bowlby, 1991; Holmes, 1994).

On the other hand, we cannot say that having something other than a secure attachment style as a child invariably leads to difficulties later in life, nor that having a secure attachment at age 1 always leads to good adjustment later on (Lamb et al., 1984). In fact, some evidence suggests that children with avoidant and ambivalent attachment—as measured by the strange situation—do quite well, particularly when we look at experimental findings from different cultures.

Developmental Diversity

Are There Cross-cultural Differences in Attachment?

Recall that the work on attachment was initially inspired by John Bowlby's observations of the biologically motivated efforts of the young of other species to seek safety and security. From these observations, Bowlby suggested that seeking attachment was a biological universal, one that we should find not only in other species but also among humans. Such reasoning suggests that we should see attachment strivings in all humans, regardless of their culture.

However, research has brought this contention into question. For example, one study of German infants showed that most fell into the avoidant category (Grossmann, Grossman, Huber, & Wartner, 1982). Other studies, conducted in Israel and Japan, have found a smaller proportion of infants who were securely attached than in the United States (Sagi et al., 1985; Takahashi, 1986; Sagi, 1990).

More recent analyses confirm not only that there are differences in the distribution of infants into the various types of attachment, but that subcultural differences also exist even within particular societies (van Ijzendoorn & Kroonenberg, 1988; Sagi, van Ijzendoorn, & Koren-Karic, 1991; Sagi et al., 1994). Do such findings suggest that we should abandon the notion that attachment is a universal biological tendency?

Not necessarily. Most of the data on attachment have been obtained by using the Ainsworth strange situation, which may not be the most appropriate measure in non-Western cultures. For example, Japanese parents seek to avoid separation and stress during infancy, and they do not strive to foster independence to the same degree as do parents in many Western societies. Because of their relative lack of prior experience in separation, then, infants placed in the strange situation may experience unusual stress—producing the appearance of less secure attachment in Japanese children. If a different measure of attachment were to be used, one that might be administered later in infancy, more Japanese infants could well be classified as secure (Takahashi, 1990; Nakagawa, Lamb, & Miyaki, 1992).

In sum, it may be that cross-cultural and within-cultural differences in attachment reflect the nature of the measure employed. On the other hand, it is still possible that Bowlby's claim that the desire for attachment is universal was too strongly stated. In fact, more recent approaches view attachment as not entirely biologically determined, but rather as susceptible to cultural norms and expectations.

Specifically, some developmental theorists suggest that attachment should be viewed as a general tendency, but one that is modifiable according to how actively caregivers in a society seek to instill independence in their children. Consequently, secure attachment may be seen earliest in cultures that promote independence, but may be delayed in societies in which independence is a less important cultural value (van Ijzendoorn & Tavecchio, 1987).

PRODUCING ATTACHMENT: ROLES OF THE MOTHER, FATHER, AND INFANT

> As 5-month-old Annie cries passionately, her mother comes into the room and gently lifts her from her crib. After just a few moments, as her mother rocks Annie and speaks softly, Annie's cries cease, and she cuddles in her mother's arms. But the moment her mother places her back in the crib, Annie begins to wail again, leading her mother to pick her up once more.

The pattern is familiar to most parents. The infant cries, the parent reacts, and the child responds in turn. Yet such seemingly insignificant sequences as these, repeatedly occurring in the lives of infants and parents, help pave the way for the development of relationships among children, their parents, and the rest of the social world. We consider next how each of the major caregivers and the infant play a role in the development of attachment.

Mothers and Attachment.   Sensitivity to their infants' needs and desires is the hallmark of mothers of securely attached infants. Such a mother tends to be aware of her child's moods, and she takes into account her youngster's feelings as she interacts with him or her. She is also responsive during face-to-face interactions, provides feeding "on demand," and is warm and affectionate to her infant (T.M. Field, 1987b; Pederson et al., 1990; Ainsworth, 1993; Isabella, 1993).

It is not only a matter of responding in *any* fashion to their infants' signals that separates mothers of securely attached and insecurely attached children. Mothers of secure infants tend to provide the appropriate level of response. For example, research shows that overly responsive mothers are just as likely to have insecurely attached children as underresponsive mothers (Belsky et al., 1984).

The research showing the correspondence between mothers' sensitivity to their infants and the security of the infants' attachment is consistent with Ainsworth's arguments that attachment depends on how mothers react to their infants' social overtures. Ainsworth suggests that mothers of securely attached infants respond rapidly and positively to them. In contrast, the way for mothers to produce insecurely attached infants, according to Ainsworth, is to ignore their behavioral cues, to behave inconsistently with them, and to ignore or reject their social efforts.

But how do mothers know how to respond to their infants' cues? One answer is that they learn from their own mothers. For instance, mothers tend to have attachment styles that are similar to those developed by their infants. In fact, some research finds substantial stability in attachment patterns from one generation to the next (Benoit & Parker, 1994).

On the other hand, it is important to keep in mind that mothers' (and others') behavior toward infants is, in part, a reaction to the children's ability to provide effective cues. A mother may not be able to respond effectively to a child whose own behavior is unrevealing, misleading, or ambiguous. As we will see, the kind of cues a child gives off may in part determine how successful the mother will be in responding to the infant.

Infants' Behavior and Attachment. As we first noted in Chapter 2, and as discussed in greater detail later in this chapter, infants are born with particular temperaments—patterns of arousal and emotionality that represent consistent and enduring characteristics. Do such temperamental differences, as well as other individual differences, affect attachment?

The evidence is mixed. Some researchers find associations between attachment and temperament; others do not. Most evidence seems to suggest that there is some relationship, although it is not particularly strong. For instance, one study examined infants' temperaments at 2 days of age, as determined by their behavior when a dummy was withdrawn from them. The results showed an association between their early reactions and whether they later were securely or insecurely attached. It may be that temperament relates to the manner in which infants demonstrate their security or insecurity, but that temperament has only minor effects on actual attachment (Belsky & Rovine, 1987; Vaughn, Lefever, Seifer, & Barglow, 1989; Calkins & Fox, 1992; Vaughn et al., 1992; Goldsmith & Harman, 1994).

Other individual differences between infants are likely related to attachment. For example, infants vary considerably in how much emotion they display nonverbally. Some are "poker-faced," showing little expressivity, whereas others' reactions tend to be much more easily decoded (Field et al., 1982; Feldman & Rimé, 1991). It seems reasonable to assume that more expressive infants provide more easily discernible cues to others, thereby easing the way for caregivers to be more successful in responding to their needs.

Fathers and Attachment. Up to now we have barely touched upon one of the key players involved in the upbringing of a child: the father. In fact, if you looked at the early theorizing and research on attachment, you would find little mention of the father and his potential contributions to the life of the infant (Russell & Radojevic, 1992).

There are at least two reasons for this. First, John Bowlby, who provided the initial theory of attachment, suggested that there was something unique about the mother—child relationship. He saw the mother as uniquely equipped, biologically, to provide sustenance

Attachment styles are stable from one generation to the next.

for the child, and he concluded that this capability led to the development of a special relationship between mothers and their children. Second, the early work on attachment was influenced by the traditional social views of the time, which considered it "natural" for the mother to be the primary caregiver, while the father's role was to work outside the home to provide a living for his family.

Several factors led to the demise of this view. One was that societal norms changed, and fathers began to take a more active role in childrearing activities. More important, it became increasingly clear from research findings that—despite societal norms that relegated fathers to secondary childrearing roles—some infants formed their primary initial relationship with their fathers. Moreover, many infants had strong attachment relationships with more than one individual (M.E. Lamb, 1982b; Goossens & van Ijzendoorn, 1990; Volling & Belsky, 1992).

For example, one study found that although most infants formed their first primary relationship with one person, approximately one-third had multiple relationships, and it was difficult to determine which attachment was primary (Schaffer & Emerson, 1964). Furthermore, by the time the infants were 18 months old, most had formed multiple relationships. In sum, infants may develop attachments not only to their mothers but also to a variety of other individuals (Parke & Tinsley, 1987; Fox, Kimmerly, & Schafer, 1991).

Still, the nature of attachment between infants and mothers, on the one hand, and infants and fathers, on the other, is not identical (Cox, Owen, Henderson, & Margand, 1992; Pipp, Easterbrooks, & Brown, 1993). For example, when they are in unusually stressful circumstances, infants prefer to be soothed by their mothers rather than by their fathers (M.E. Lamb, 1977).

One reason for qualitative differences in attachment involves the differences in what fathers and mothers do with their children. Mothers spend a greater proportion of their time feeding and directly nurturing their children. In contrast, fathers spend more time, proportionally, playing with infants. Nevertheless, almost all fathers do contribute to child care: Surveys show that 95 percent say they do some child-care chores every day. But they still, on average, do less than mothers. For instance, 30 percent of fathers with wives who work do three or more hours of daily child care, in comparison with 74 percent of employed married mothers who spend that amount of time in child-care activities (see Figure 6-3; Parke, 1981; NSFH, 1988; Jacobsen & Edmondson, 1993).

Furthermore, the nature of fathers' play with their infants is often quite different from that of mothers. Fathers engage in more physical, rough-and-tumble activities with their

Some children form their primary initial relationship with their fathers, and some have more than one strong attachment relationship.

FIGURE 6-3

Who's caring for the children? It's mostly not fathers: Even in families in which the mother works outside the home, only 30 percent of fathers put in more than three hours daily caring for their preschooler.

(Source: National Survey of Families and Households, 1988.)

· · · · ·
Average for all married fathers with a preschooler

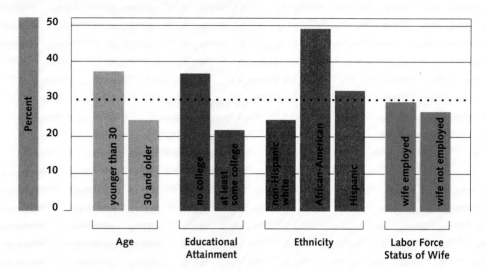

Fathers Who Spend 3 or More Hours a Day Caring for a Preschooler

children. In contrast, mothers play traditional games such as peek-a-boo and games with more verbal elements (Power & Parke, 1982; Lamb, 1986; Parke, 1990).

These differences in the ways that fathers and mothers play with their children occur even in the minority of families in the United States in which the father is the primary caregiver. Moreover, the differences occur in very diverse cultures: Fathers in Australia, Israel, India, and Japan all engage more in play than in caregiving, as do fathers of the Aka Pygmy tribe in central Africa (Lamb, 1987; Roopnarine, 1992).

INFANT INTERACTIONS: DEVELOPING A WORKING RELATIONSHIP

It is clear that infants may develop multiple attachment relationships, and that over the course of time the specific individuals with whom the infant is primarily attached may change. These variations in attachment highlight the fact that the development of relationships is an ongoing process, not only during infancy but throughout the lifespan.

What processes underlie the development of relationships during infancy? One answer comes from studies that examine how parents interact with their children. For instance, across almost all cultures, mothers behave in typical ways with their infants. They tend to exaggerate their facial and vocal expressions—the nonverbal equivalent of the "motherese" that they use when they speak to infants (as we discussed in Chapter Five). Similarly, they often imitate their infants' behavior, responding to distinctive sounds and movements by repeating them. There are even types of games, such as peek-a-boo, itsy-bitsy spider, and pat-a-cake, that are nearly universal (T.M. Field, 1979, 1990).

According to the **mutual regulation model**, infants and parents learn to communicate emotional states to one another and to respond appropriately. For instance, both infant and parent act jointly to regulate turn-taking behavior, with one individual waiting until the other completes a behavioral act before starting another. Consequently, at the age of 3 months, infants and their mothers have about the same influence on each other's behavior. Interestingly, by the age of 6 months, infants have more control over turn-taking, although both partners once again become roughly equivalent in terms of mutual influence by the time the infant is 9 months (Tronick & Gianino, 1986; Cohn & Tronick, 1983, 1989; Nwokah & Fogel, 1993).

mutual regulation model *an approach where infants and parents learn to communicate emotional states to one another and to respond appropriately*

Games like peek-a-boo, which are close to universal across cultures, illustrate the development of relationships.

reciprocal socialization   *a process in which infants' behaviors invite further responses from parents and other caregivers*

One of the ways in which infants and parents signal each other when they interact is through facial expressions. Even quite young infants are able to read, or decode, the facial expressions of their caregivers, and they react to those expressions (Lelwica & Haviland, 1983; Camras et al., 1991).

For example, an infant whose mother, during an experiment, displays a stony, immobile facial expression reacts by making a variety of sounds, gestures, and facial expressions of her own in response to such a puzzling situation—and possibly to elicit some new response from her mother. Infants also show more happiness themselves when their mothers appear happy, and they look at their mothers longer. On the other hand, infants are apt to respond with sad looks and to turn away when their mothers display unhappy expressions (Termine & Izard, 1988).

In sum, the development of attachment in infants does not merely represent a reaction to the behavior of the people around them. Rather, there is a process of **reciprocal socialization**, in which infants' behaviors invite further responses from parents and other caregivers. In turn, the caregivers' behaviors bring about a reaction from the child, continuing the cycle (Egeland, Pianta, & O'Brien, 1993). Ultimately, these actions and reactions lead to an increase in attachment, forging and strengthening bonds between infants and caregivers. Figure 6-4 summarizes the sequence of infant–caregiver interaction, known as the *Attachment Behavioral System* (Bell & Ainsworth, 1972; Ainsworth & Bowlby, 1991).

INFANTS' SOCIABILITY WITH THEIR PEERS: INFANT–INFANT INTERACTION

How sociable are infants with other children? Although it is clear that they do not form "friendships" in the traditional sense, they do react positively to the presence of peers from early in life, and they engage in rudimentary forms of social interaction (T.M. Field, 1990).

FIGURE 6-4

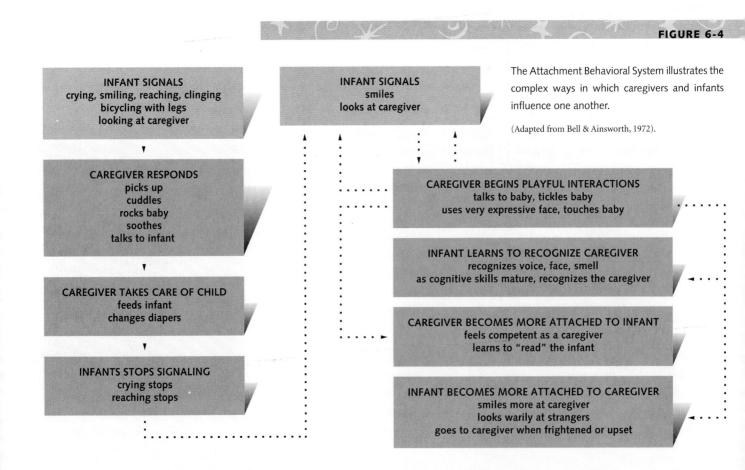

The Attachment Behavioral System illustrates the complex ways in which caregivers and infants influence one another.

(Adapted from Bell & Ainsworth, 1972).

INFANT SIGNALS
crying, smiling, reaching, clinging
bicycling with legs
looking at caregiver

CAREGIVER RESPONDS
picks up
cuddles
rocks baby
soothes
talks to infant

CAREGIVER TAKES CARE OF CHILD
feeds infant
changes diapers

INFANTS STOPS SIGNALING
crying stops
reaching stops

INFANT SIGNALS
smiles
looks at caregiver

CAREGIVER BEGINS PLAYFUL INTERACTIONS
talks to baby, tickles baby
uses very expressive face, touches baby

INFANT LEARNS TO RECOGNIZE CAREGIVER
recognizes voice, face, smell
as cognitive skills mature, recognizes the caregiver

CAREGIVER BECOMES MORE ATTACHED TO INFANT
feels competent as a caregiver
learns to "read" the infant

INFANT BECOMES MORE ATTACHED TO CAREGIVER
smiles more at caregiver
looks warily at strangers
goes to caregiver when frightened or upset

Infants' sociability is expressed in several ways. From the earliest months of life they smile, laugh, and vocalize while looking at their peers. They show more interest in peers than in inanimate objects, and they pay greater attention to other infants than they do to a mirror image of themselves (Fogel, 1980; Field, 1981; Field & Roopnarine, 1982).

Conversely, infants are not consistently sociable. For one thing, by the end of the first year they start to show more interest in inanimate toys as they become better able to manipulate objects and to move around in the world. Furthermore, they begin to show preferences for people with whom they are familiar compared with those they do not know. For example, studies of identical twins show that twins exhibit a higher level of social behavior toward each other than toward an unfamiliar infant (Field & Roopnarine, 1982; Field, 1990).

Still, an infant's level of sociability generally rises as it gets older. Nine- to 12-month-olds mutually present and accept toys, particularly if they know each other. They also play social games, such as peek-a-boo or crawl-and-chase (Vincze, 1971; Endo, 1992). Such behavior is important, for it serves as a foundation for future social exchanges involving the elicitation of responses from others and the offering of reactions to those responses (Brownell, 1986; Howes, 1987).

Finally, as infants age, they begin to imitate each other (Russon & Waite, 1991). For instance, 14-month-olds who are familiar with one another sometimes reproduce each other's behavior (Mueller & Vandell, 1979). Not only does such imitation serve a social function but it can also be a powerful teaching tool, as we discuss in the accompanying Directions in Development section.

Directions in Development

Infants Teaching Infants: When Babies Become Experts

"Expert" infants can teach their peers how to play with complicated toys, according to researcher Andrew Meltzoff and colleagues.

Think back to the story of 10-month-old Russell Ruud at the start of the chapter. He showed the other children in his day care center how he could remove his hat by unfastening the Velcro straps, and soon others were following his lead.

According to Andrew Meltzoff, a developmental psychologist at the University of Washington, Russell's ability to impart this information is only one example of how so-called expert babies are able to teach skills and information to other infants. And, according to the research of Meltzoff and his colleagues, the abilities learned from the "experts" are retained and later utilized to a remarkable degree (Hanna & Meltzoff, 1993; Meltzoff & Moore, 1994).

In an innovative series of studies, Meltzoff and his colleagues devised a procedure to illustrate the sophistication of the teaching process. In one study, for instance, they created five toys, each attractive to a 1-year-old. Although simple to play with, each toy had to be worked in a particular manner for it to function correctly. For example, one toy was a plastic cup that would contract only if pushed in a particular way.

The experimenters then demonstrated to a group of infants, all about 17 months old, how to play with one of the five toys. The infants were allowed to play with it on their own until they had mastered it.

The next phase of the study was conducted in a day care center. The infants—now expert in the use of the toy—were allowed to play with it while other one-year-olds watched. However, the observers were not immediately given the opportunity to use the toy; they could only observe the "expert" play with it.

Two days later, however, when they were by themselves in their own homes, the observer infants got their opportunity to play with the toy. The result was that nearly three-quarters of the observer babies were able to play correctly with the toy. In comparison, only one-quarter of a control group of infants who had not seen an expert's demonstration were able to play appropriately with it (Hanna & Meltzoff, 1993).

The results are clear in suggesting the importance of exposure to other children's activities in promoting learning. Moreover, learning by exposure is a powerful phenomenon, one that starts early in life. For example, recent evidence shows that even 6-week-old infants perform delayed imitation of a novel stimulus to which they have earlier been exposed, such as an adult sticking the tongue out the side of the mouth (Meltzoff & Moore, 1994).

Finding that infants learn new behaviors, skills, and abilities from exposure to other children has several implications. For one thing, it suggests that interactions between infants provide more than social benefits; they may also have an impact on children's future cognitive development. Even more important, these findings illustrate a possible benefit that infants derive from participation in day care (which we consider later in this chapter). Although we don't know for sure, the opportunity to learn from their peers may prove to be a lasting advantage for infants in group day care settings.

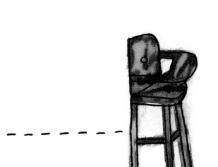

Review and Rethink

REVIEW

- Attachment, the positive emotional bond between an infant and a significant individual, may be genetically based, and different patterns of attachment seem to relate to a person's later social competence as an adult.

- Mothers and their babies generally form the primary social attachment in infancy, and the quality of the attachment is related to the warmth and effectiveness of the mother's responses to her baby's social overtures. Traditionally, the father's role has been seen as less central, and the nature of fathers' and mothers' attachments to their babies is qualitatively different.

- By the amount of emotion they display nonverbally, infants to some extent may affect the nature and quality of their caregivers' responses to them, and consequently the quality of the attachment between themselves and their caregivers.

- Infants and those with whom they interact engage in reciprocal socialization as they mutually adjust to one another's interactions.

- Infants react differently to other children than to inanimate objects, and they gradually engage in increasing amounts of peer social interaction, even participating in reciprocal teaching and learning.

RETHINK

- In what sort of society might the attachment style labeled "avoidant" be encouraged by cultural attitudes toward childrearing? In such a society, would characterizing the infant's consistent avoidance of its mother as anger be an accurate interpretation?

◆ In what ways might overly responsive and underresponsive caregivers equally contribute to insecure attachment in their infants?

◆ Does the importance of infants' early attachment to primary caregivers have social policy implications relating to working parents? Do current policies reveal societal assumptions pertaining to the different roles of mothers and fathers?

◆ Can you discern a relationship between reciprocal socialization and operant conditioning?

◆ Why do you think that learning from their peers is so effective for young children? Does this finding have implications for educational practices?

DIFFERENCES AMONG INFANTS

"It's a boy." "It's a girl."

One of these two statements, or some variant, is probably the first announcement made in the delivery room after the birth of a child. Why does this differentiation occur, and what are the implications of dividing children so rigorously according to gender?

We turn now to such questions as we consider some of the differences we find among infants and the lives they lead—differences not only in gender but also in their overall personality, temperament, the nature of infants' families, and in the ways in which infants are cared for.

PERSONALITY DEVELOPMENT: THE CHARACTERISTICS THAT MAKE INFANTS UNIQUE

The origins of **personality**, the sum total of the enduring characteristics that differentiate one individual from another, begin during infancy. From birth onward, infants begin to show unique, stable traits and behaviors that ultimately lead to their development as distinct, special individuals (Halverson, Kohnstamm, & Martin, 1994).

According to psychologist Erik Erikson, whose approach to personality development we first discussed in Chapter 1, infants' early experiences are responsible for shaping one of the key aspects of their personalities: whether they will be basically trusting or mistrustful.

Erikson's theory of psychosocial development considers how individuals come to understand themselves and the meaning of others'—and their own—behavior (Erikson, 1963). The theory suggests that developmental change occurs throughout a person's life in eight distinct stages, the first of which occurs in infancy.

According to Erikson, infancy marks the time of the **trust-versus-mistrust stage**, encompassing birth to 18 months. During this period, infants develop a sense of trust or mistrust, largely depending on how well their needs are met by their caretakers. Erikson suggests that if infants are able to develop trust, they experience a sense of hope, which permits them to feel they can fulfill their needs successfully. On the other hand, feelings of mistrust lead infants to see the world as harsh and unfriendly, and they may have later difficulties in forming close bonds with others.

Erikson argues that personality is primarily shaped by infants' experiences. However, as we discuss next, other developmental psychologists concentrate on consistencies of behavior that are present at birth. These consistencies are viewed as largely genetically determined and as providing the raw material of personality.

TEMPERAMENT: STABILITIES IN INFANT BEHAVIOR

Sarah's parents thought there must be something wrong. Unlike her older brother, Josh, who had been so active as an infant that he seemed to never be still, Sarah was much more

personality   the sum total of the enduring characteristics that differentiate one individual from another, beginning during infancy

Erikson's theory of psychosocial development   the theory that considers how individuals come to understand themselves and the meaning of others'—and their own—behavior

trust-versus-mistrust stage   the period where infants develop a sense of trust or mistrust, largely depending on how well their needs are met by their caretakers

temperament *patterns of arousal and emotionality that are consistent and enduring characteristics of an individual*

placid. She took long naps, and was easily soothed on those relatively rare occasions when she became agitated. What could be producing her extreme calmness?

The most likely answer: The difference between Sarah and Josh reflected differences in temperament. As we first discussed in Chapter 2, **temperament** encompasses patterns of arousal and emotionality that are consistent and enduring characteristics of an individual.

Temperament refers to *how* children behave, as opposed to *what* they do or *why* they do it (Thomas & Chess, 1984). As we noted in Chapter 2, infants show temperamental differences in general disposition from the time of birth. These differences appear to be largely determined by genetic factors, although there is also evidence that the prenatal environment and the nature of a child's birth may also have some influence. Regardless of cause, temperament is quite consistent, with longitudinal studies showing stability from infancy well into adolescence (Riese, 1990; Pedlow et al., 1993; Guerin & Gottfried, 1994; Sanson et al., 1994; Caspi et al., 1995).

Several dimensions of behavior reflect temperament. One central dimension is *activity level*, which reflects the degree of overall movement. Some babies (like Sarah) are relatively placid, and their movements are slow and almost leisurely. In contrast, the activity level of other infants (like Josh) is quite high, with strong, restless movements of the arms and legs.

Another important dimension of temperament is *irritability*. Some infants are easily disturbed and cry easily; others are relatively easygoing. Irritable infants fuss a great deal, and they are easily upset. They are also difficult to soothe when they do begin to cry. Such irritability is relatively stable: Researchers find that infants who are irritable at birth remain irritable at the age of 1, and even at age 2 they are still more easily upset than are infants who were not irritable just after birth (Riese, 1987; Worobey & Bajda, 1989). (Other aspects of temperament are listed in Table 6-2.)

Categorizing Temperament: Easy, Difficult, and Slow-to-warm Babies. Because temperament can be viewed along so many dimensions, some development psychologists have asked whether there are broader categories that can be used to describe children's overall behavior. According to Alexander Thomas and Stella Chess (1984), who carried out a large-scale longitudinal study of a group of infants in New York, babies can be described according to one of several profiles:

- ◆ *Easy babies.* Easy babies have a positive disposition. Their body functions operate regularly, and they are adaptable. They are generally positive, showing curiosity about new situations and their emotions are moderate or low in intensity. This category applies to about 40 percent (the majority) of infants.

- ◆ *Difficult babies.* These infants have more negative moods, and they are slow to adapt to new situations. When confronted with a new situation, they tend to withdraw. About 10 percent of infants belong in this category.

- ◆ *Slow-to-warm babies.* These children are inactive, showing relatively calm reactions to their environment. Their moods are generally negative, and they withdraw from new situations, adapting slowly. Approximately 15 percent of infants are slow-to-warm.

As for the remaining 35 percent, they cannot be consistently categorized. These children show a variety of combinations of characteristics. For instance, one infant may have relatively sunny moods, but react negatively to new situations, or another may show little stability of any sort in terms of general temperament.

The Consequences of Temperament: Does Temperament Matter? The obvious question to emerge from the findings of the relative stability of temperament is whether a particular kind of temperament is beneficial. The answer seems to be that no single type of temperament is invariably good or bad. Instead, children's long-term adjustment depends on the

TABLE 6-2

DIMENSIONS OF TEMPERAMENT

Dimension	Temperament
Activity level	Proportion of active time periods to inactive time periods
Approach-withdrawal	The response to a new person or object, based on whether the child accepts the new situation or withdraws from it
Adaptability	How easily the child is able to adapt to changes in his or her environment
Quality of mood	The contrast of the amount of friendly, joyful, and pleasant behavior with unpleasant, unfriendly behavior
Attention span and persistence	The amount of time the child devotes to an activity and the effect of distraction on that activity
Distractibility	The degree to which stimuli in the environment alter behavior
Rhythmicity (regularity)	The regularity of basic functions such as hunger, excretion, sleep, and wakefulness
Intensity of reaction	The energy level or reaction of the child's response
Threshold of responsiveness	The intensity of stimulation needed to elicit a response

goodness of fit of their particular temperament and the nature and demands of the environment in which they find themselves. For instance, children with a low activity level and low irritability may do particularly well in an environment in which they are left to explore on their own and generally allowed to direct their own behavior. In contrast, high activity level, highly irritable children may do best with greater direction, which permits them to channel their energy in particular directions (Thomas & Chess, 1977, 1980; Mangelsdorf et al., 1990; Bornstein & Lamb, 1992).

Some research does suggest that certain temperaments are, in general, more adaptive than others. For instance, Thomas and Chess found that difficult children, in general, were more likely to show behavior problems by school age than those who were classified as easy children in infancy (Thomas, Chess, & Birch, 1968). But not all difficult children experience problems. The key determinant seems to be the way in which parents react to their infants' difficult behavior. If they react by showing anger and inconsistency—which their child's difficult, demanding behavior readily evokes—then the child is ultimately more likely to experience behavior problems. Conversely, parents who display more warmth and consistency in their responses are more likely to have children who avoid later problems (Crockenberg, 1986; Belsky, Fish, & Isabella, 1991).

Cultural differences also have a major influence on the consequences of a particular temperament. For instance, children who would be described as "difficult" in Western cultures actually seem to have an advantage in the East African Masai culture. The reason? Because mothers offer their breast to their infants only when they fuss and cry, irritable, more difficult infants are apt to receive more nourishment than more placid "easy" infants. Particularly when environmental conditions are bad, such as during a drought, difficult babies are apt to have an advantage (deVries, 1984).

Recent approaches to temperament grow out of the framework of behavioral genetics that we discussed in Chapter 2. For instance, David Buss and Robert Plomin (1984) argue that temperamental characteristics represent inherited traits that are fairly stable across the life span. These traits are seen as making up the core of personality and playing a substantial role in future development.

GENDER: WHY DO BOYS WEAR BLUE AND GIRLS WEAR PINK?

From the moment of birth, girls and boys are treated differently. Their parents send out different kinds of birth announcements. They are given different clothes to wear and different-colored blankets. The toys that are chosen for them differ (Bridges, 1993).

gender   *the sense of being male or female*

Parents play with them differently: From birth on, fathers tend to interact more with sons than with daughters, whereas mothers interact more with daughters (Parke & Sawin, 1980). Because, as we noted earlier in the chapter, mothers and fathers play in different ways (with fathers typically engaging in more physical, rough-and-tumble activities and mothers in traditional games such as peek-a-boo), male and female infants are clearly exposed to different styles of activity and interaction from their parents (Power & Parke, 1982; M.E. Lamb, 1986; Parke, 1990; Grant, 1994).

The behavior exhibited by girls and boys is interpreted in very different ways by adults. For instance, in one experiment researchers showed adults a video of an infant whose name was given as either "John" or "Mary" (Condry & Condry, 1976). Although it was the same baby performing a single set of behaviors, adults perceived "John" as adventurous and inquisitive, while "Mary" was fearful and anxious. Clearly, adults view the behavior of children through the lens of **gender**, the sense of being male or female. ("Gender" and "sex" are not the same: Sex typically refers to sexual anatomy and sexual behavior, whereas gender refers to the perception of maleness or femaleness related to membership in a particular society; Stern & Karraker, 1989; Pomerleau, Bolduc, Malcuit, & Cossette, 1990; Burnham & Harris, 1992.)

Although it is obvious that boys and girls live, to some extent, in different worlds owing to their respective gender, there is a considerable amount of argument over both the extent and causes of such gender differences. Some gender differences are fairly clear from the time of birth. For example, male infants tend to be more active and fussier than female infants. Boys grimace more, although no gender difference exists in the overall amount of crying, and boys' sleep tends to be more disturbed than that of girls. There is also some evidence that male newborns are more irritable than female newborns, although the findings are inconsistent (Moss, 1974; Phillips, King, & DuBois, 1978; Eaton & Enns, 1986).

However, the overall differences between male and female infants are generally minor. In fact, in most ways infants seem so similar that usually adults cannot discern whether a baby is a boy or girl. Furthermore, it is important to keep in mind that the differences among individual boys, and the differences among individual girls, are much more extensive than the average differences found when boys and girls are compared (Langlois, Ritter, Roggman, & Vaughn, 1991; Unger & Crawford, 1992; Beal, 1994).

Gender differences emerge more clearly as children age—and become increasingly influenced by the gender roles that society sets out for them. For instance, by the age of a year, infants are able to make distinctions between males and females. Furthermore, girls prefer to play with dolls or stuffed animals, whereas boys seek out blocks and trucks. Often, of course, these are the only options available to them because of the choices their parents and other adults have made in the toys they provide (Poulin-Dubois, Serbin, Kenyon, & Derbyshire, 1994).

Children's preferences for certain kinds of toys are reinforced by their parents, although parents of boys are more apt to be concerned about their child's choices than are parents of girls. For example, 1-year-old boys receive more positive reactions for playing with transportation and construction-type toys than do girls. Moreover, the amount of reinforcement boys receive for playing with toys that society deems appropriate increases with age, and boys receive increasing discouragement for playing with toys that society views as more acceptable for girls. On the other hand, girls who play with toys seen by society as "masculine" are less discouraged for their behavior than are boys who play with toys seen as "feminine" (Eisenberg, Wolchik, Hernandez, & Pasternack, 1985; Fagot & Hagan, 1991).

By the time they reach the age of 2, boys behave more independently and less compliantly than do girls. Much of this behavior can be traced to parental reactions to earlier behavior. For instance, when a child takes his or her first steps, parents tend to react differently, depending on the child's gender: Boys are encouraged more to go off and explore the

Parents of girls who play with toys related to activities associated with boys are apt to be less concerned than parents of boys who play with toys typically associated with girls.

world, whereas girls are hugged and kept close. In general, exploratory behavior tends to be encouraged more in boys than in girls. It is hardly surprising, then, that by 2 years, girls tend to show less independence and greater compliance (Fagot, 1978; Brooks-Gunn & Matthews, 1979; Kuczynski & Kochanska, 1990).

In sum, differences in behavior between boys and girls begin in infancy, and—as we will see in future chapters—continue to be seen throughout the life span. Although gender differences have complex causes, representing some combination of innate, biologically related factors and environmental factors, they play a profound role in the social and emotional development of infants. Boys and girls are treated differently on the basis of gender from birth onward, and this differential treatment produces dissimilar worlds for members of the two sexes, even during infancy.

FAMILY LIFE IN THE 1990S: OZZIE AND HARRIET GO THE WAY OF THE DINOSAURS

A look back at television shows of the 1950s (such as *Ozzie and Harriet* and *Leave It to Beaver*) finds a world of families portrayed in a way that today seems oddly old-fashioned and quaint: mothers and fathers, married for years, and their good-looking children making their way in a world that seems to have few, if any, serious problems.

As we discussed in Chapter 1, even in the 1950s such a view of family life was overly romantic and unrealistic. Today, however, it is broadly inaccurate, representing only a minority of families in the United States. A quick review of statistics collected by the U.S. Census Bureau tells the story (Bird & Melville, 1994; Carnegie Task Force, 1994; Gelles, 1994):

♦ The number of single-parent families has increased dramatically in the last two decades, as the number of two-parent households has declined. Approximately 56 percent of white children live with both parents, whereas just one-quarter of African-American children and one-third of Hispanic children live with both parents. If current trends continue, 60 percent of all children will live at some time during their lives with a single parent (Demo & Acock, 1991; U.S. Bureau of the Census, 1991a).

The view of the family, as reflected in media depictions ranging from Ozzie and Harriet to Roseanne, has changed radically from the 1950s to the present.

- The average size of families is shrinking. Today, 2.6 people occupy the average household, compared to 2.8 in 1980. The number of people living in nonfamily households (without any relatives) is nearly 30 million.

- In 1960, 5 percent of all births in the United States were to unmarried mothers. By the 1990s, more than 25 percent of births were to unmarried mothers.

- Every minute, an adolescent in the United States gives birth.

- More than five million children under the age of 3 are cared for by other adults while their parents work, and more than half of mothers of infants work outside the home.

- In 1990, one-quarter of families with children under 3 years of age lived in poverty in the United States. The rates are even higher for African-American and Hispanic families, and for single-parent families of young children. More children under 3 live in poverty than do older children, adults, or the elderly (Einbinder, 1992).

Such statistics are disheartening. At the very least, they suggest that infants are being raised in environments in which substantial stressors are present, factors that make raising children, never easy even under the best circumstances, an unusually difficult task.

On the other hand, society is adapting to the new realities of family life in the 1990s. Several kinds of social support exist for the parents of infants, and society is evolving new institutions to help in their care. One example is the growing array of child-care provisions available to help working parents.

INFANT DAY CARE

Should infants be placed in day care? For many parents, there is little choice: Economic realities, or the desire to maintain a career, require that their children be left in the care of others for a portion of the day, typically in infant day care settings. In fact, recent figures indicate that almost 25 percent of preschool children whose mothers work outside the home spend their days in day care centers (see Figure 6-5). Do such arrangements have any discernible effects on infant development?

High-quality infant day care seems to produce only minor differences from home care in most respects, and some aspects of development may even be enhanced.

The answer, while not definitive, is reassuring: High-quality day care seems to produce only minor differences from home care in most respects, and it may even enhance certain aspects of development. For example, most research finds little or no difference in the strength of parental attachment bonds of infants who have been in day care compared with infants raised solely by their parents. Furthermore, various studies have found clear benefits from participation in day care. For instance, compared with children not in day care, children who participated in day care during their first year showed higher levels of play, laughing, and touching; they kicked and pushed less; and they were found to be more sociable and cooperative (Haskins, 1985; Phillips et al., 1987; Field et al., 1988; Howes, Phillips, & Whitebook, 1992; Fein, Gariboldi, & Boni, 1993).

In addition, infant day care may have lasting beneficial effects. Research examining children from low-income families who had participated in day care from infancy through 3 years of age found advantages in terms of cognitive and academic achievement at the age of 12 (Campbell & Ramey, 1994).

FIGURE 6-5

Where are children cared for? Although most youngsters spend their days at home, almost one quarter of children younger than 5 years of age whose mothers work outside the home spend their days in day care centers.

(Source: U.S. Bureau of the Census, 1991b; Child Health USA, 1993.)

Child's home
Day care or preschool
Nonrelative's home
Relative's home
Other

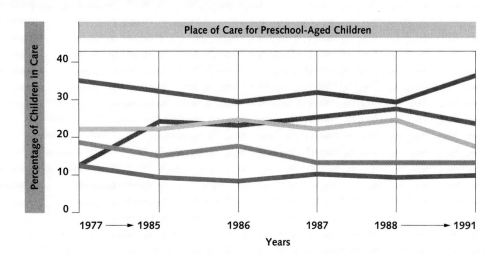

On the other hand, some research has yielded mixed, and some negative, results regarding the outcomes of infant day care (Matlock & Green, 1990). For example, one study found that high-risk, poor children who had secure attachment to their mothers showed negative, avoidant, and more aggressive behavior several years after participating in infant day care. Conversely, the results were not uniformly negative: For insecurely attached infants, participation in infant day care was associated with more positive outcomes. Apparently, involvement in day care acted as a protective factor for the children who had come from insecurely attached backgrounds (Egeland & Hiester, 1995).

Other research finds that participation in infant day care may actually produce less secure attachment. One study found that infants involved in care outside the home for more than twenty hours a week during their first year show less secure attachment to their mothers than those who have not been in day care. Moreover, boys in day care for 35 or more hours a week show some evidence of less secure attachment to their fathers (Chase-Lansdale & Owen, 1987; Belsky & Rovine, 1988).

Other research points to further potential drawbacks of day care—at least in extensive quantities—during infancy. For instance, infants who spend their first year in full-time day care have sometimes been found to exhibit more aggression, less obedience, and more neg-

Speaking of Development

Melinda Rauch

Born: ·································· 1966

Education: ····················· University of Colorado at Denver, B.A. in psychology

Position: ························· Infant/toddler teacher for HeartsHome Early Learning Center in Houston, Texas

Home: ···························· Spring, Texas

Upon graduation from college, Melinda Rauch answered an ad for a preschool teacher, expecting that it would be just a temporary job. As it turned out, her love of children guided her to her current vocation.

For the past four-and-a-half years, Rauch has worked with infants and toddlers at HeartsHome, providing far more than basic day care services.

"We meet our children's basic needs by making sure they're happy, clean, dry, and fed, but we also meet their developmental needs by teaching them to take turns, get along with others, and accept that they don't always get their own way," Rauch says.

ative reactions to frustration than infants who were cared for at home. Furthermore, some research suggests that children who spend more time in day care may adjust less successfully when they get to kindergarten (Rubenstein, Howes, & Boyule, 1981; Haskins, 1985; Bates et al., 1994).

Although such findings are troubling, their implications may be less far-reaching than we might at first assume. For instance, not all of the children in the studies were enrolled in high-quality day care settings; many were in less-than-optimal situations. Furthermore, some of the findings may not be entirely that negative: The greater aggression and lower compliance found in some studies may simply reflect increased assertiveness among children who have more experience in the company of groups of other youngsters (Howes et al., 1992; Aviezer, van Ijzendoorn, Sagi, & Schuengel, 1994).

Finally, there is no assurance that the personalities and socioeconomic status of children who are in day care are similar to those of children who are raised in the home by parents. Although the use of day care is prevalent throughout all segments of society, it is likely that certain groups are overrepresented in day care centers. Consequently, until more research is done on just who makes use of day care and how it is used by members of different segments of society, we won't be able to understand fully the consequences of participation. Furthermore, research must take into account the quality of day care centers and

"We also meet their developmental needs by teaching them to take turns, get along with others"

Activities that include teaching are an integral part of an infant's day at HeartsHome, according to Rauch. "We work with infants from 6 weeks to 3 years old, and we vary the activities by age group. We do a lot of sensory play with different substances, such as rice, cornmeal, and water. When we do artwork, we don't focus on the products that the child creates so much as on the process the child uses in creating.

"Everything is a hands-on experience," she explains. "Basically, I take a crayon and model what to do with it. Then I put the crayon in their hands and help them make the same motions. Often they'll stick it in their mouths, and so we'll have a learning experience that crayons aren't food. We can go through several learning experiences just using crayons."

Getting along with others is an important socialization task, and Rauch says she works with children as young as 18 months on the concept of sharing.

"We don't expect them to learn the concept completely at 18 months, but we will use a popular toy like mini-basketballs to teach sharing. There may be more than one of a particular item, but it's still a problem when all the children want to do the same thing at the same time. I try to explain turn-taking, and then I might take the child who doesn't have the item and guide him or her to read a book or play with another toy. It's important to give them a sense that there are alternatives."

"When we do artwork, we don't focus on the products that the child creates so much as on the process the child uses in creating."

the specific activities they engage in to optimize the potential benefits and minimize the negative consequences of care outside the home (Clarke-Stewart, Gruber, & Fitzgerald, 1994; Appelbaum, 1995).

The Informed Consumer of Development

Choosing the Right Infant Care Provider

If there is one finding that emerges with crystal clarity from research conducted on the consequences of infant day care, it is that benefits occur only when day care is of high quality (Zigler & Styfco, 1994). But what distinguishes high-quality day care from low-caliber programs?

The American Psychological Association suggests considering these questions in choosing a program (Committee on Children, Youth and Families, 1994):

- Are there enough providers? A desirable ratio is one adult for every three to four infants.

- Are group sizes manageable? Even with several providers, a group of infants should not be larger than eight.

- Do the individuals providing the care seem to like what they are doing? You should find out what their motivation is.

- Is day care just a temporary job, or is it a career? Are the care providers experienced? Do they seem happy in the job, or is offering day care just a way to earn money?

- What do the caregivers do during the day? They should spend their time playing with, listening and talking to, and paying attention to the children. They should seem genuinely interested in the children, rather than merely going through the motions of caring for them.

- Are the children safe and clean? The environment should be one in which infants can move around and not be endangered. The equipment and furniture should be in good repair. Moreover, the providers should adhere to the highest levels of cleanliness. After changing a baby's diaper, providers should wash their hands.

- What training do the providers have in caring for children? They should know the basics of infant development, have an understanding of how normal children develop, and be alert to signs that development may depart from normal patterns.

- Finally, is the environment happy and cheerful? Day care is not just a babysitting service: For the time an infant is there, it is the child's whole world. You should feel fully comfortable and confident that the day care center is a place where your infant will be treated as an individual.

In addition to following these guidelines, you can contact the National Association for the Education of Young Children, from which you may be able to get the name of a resource and referral agency in your area. Write to NAEYC Information Service, 1834 Connecticut Ave. NW, Washington, DC 20009; or call (800) 424-2460.

Review and Rethink

REVIEW

◆ Personality is the sum total of the enduring characteristics that differentiate one individual from an other. According to Erik Erikson, the first stage of psychosocial development is the trust-versus-mistrust stage.

◆ Temperament encompasses enduring levels of arousal and emotionality that are characteristic of an individual.

◆ Gender differences become more pronounced as infants age, owing mostly to environmental influences, especially the different expectations, attitudes, and actions displayed by parents and other adults toward boys and girls.

◆ Substantial changes in the nature of the family have brought about corresponding adjustments in the ways children are nurtured and reared.

◆ Day care can have neutral, positive, or negative effects on the social development of children, depending largely on its quality.

◆ Research on the effects of day care must take into account the varying quality of different day care settings and the social characteristics of the parents who tend to use day care.

RETHINK

◆ Does the concept of social referencing, studied in this chapter, help explain the development of gender-based behavioral differences in young children? How?

◆ The "John" and "Mary" video experiment described in this chapter demonstrates how identical actions of boys and girls can be interpreted differently. Can you think of examples of the same phenomenon occurring in adulthood?

◆ What are some social implications of the changes in family life described in this chapter? What sorts of family policies might be instituted to address these changes?

◆ Can you relate the issue of day care to the phenomenon of attachment studied earlier in this chapter? What factors complicate the relationship between day care and attachment?

◆ How might social attitudes toward such issues as women's careers and alternative lifestyles influence studies of the effects of day care and the interpretation of their findings?

LOOKING
BACK

Do infants have emotions?

1. Infants display a variety of facial expressions that appear to reflect their basic emotional states. This is called nonverbal encoding. The basic facial expressions that infants display are similar across cultures.

2. Infants experience emotions that correspond to their facial displays. A basic repertoire of expressions and emotional states appears to be innate and to grow in sophistication and complexity as the child ages and gradually experiences a wider array of emotions.

How do infants interpret the emotions of others?

3. Infants also develop early the capability of nonverbal decoding: determining the emotional states of others based on their facial and vocal expressions.

4. Through a process called social referencing, infants from the age of 8 or 9 months use the expressions of others to clarify ambiguous situations and learn appropriate reactions to them.

What sort of mental life do infants have?

5. Although at first infants are not aware that they exist independently from others and the larger world, they begin to develop self-awareness from about the age of 12 months.

6. Infants are also developing a theory of mind at this time: knowledge and beliefs about how they and others think. Their theory of mind gradually helps them understand that humans differ from other entities, that humans act with a sense of purpose, that effects have causes and causes have effects, that the emotions of others can be shared through empathy, and that beliefs can be manipulated through pretense and deception.

What is attachment in infancy, and how does it relate to the future social competence of individuals?

7. Attachment, a strong, positive emotional bond that forms between an infant and one or more significant persons, is a crucial factor in enabling individuals to develop social relationships. Bowlby's theory that attachment is based primarily on infants' genetic motivation to seek safety from predators, and Lorenz's theory that infants are biologically driven to "imprint" on a caregiving individual—typically the mother—during a critical period soon after birth, suggest that attachment is a genetically determined trait, although some would contend that it has significant cultural aspects.

8. Ainsworth's "strange situation" measure classifies infants into one of three major attachment patterns: securely attached, avoidant, and ambivalent. A fourth pattern, disorganized-disoriented, was added later. Research suggests an association between an infant's attachment pattern and his or her adult social and emotional competence. Cultural factors probably affect interpretation of this measure.

What roles do mothers, fathers, and infants play in social development?

9. Mothers' interactions with their babies have been found to be particularly important for social development. Mothers who respond effectively to their babies' social overtures appear to contribute to the babies' ability to become securely attached.

10. Infants' temperamental differences have at most a slight association with their attachment patterns, but infants who tend to display their emotions nonverbally provide cues that facilitate caregiver responses conducive to secure attachment.

11. Infants may form primary attachments with their fathers, but this is less usual than with their mothers. Furthermore, attachment to fathers differ qualitatively from attachment to mothers, at least partly because fathers and mothers interact differently with their babies.

What sorts of interactions do infants engage in with caregivers and other children?

12. Through a process of reciprocal socialization, infants and caregivers interact and affect one another's behavior, which strengthens their mutual relationship.

13. From an early age, infants engage in rudimentary forms of social interaction with other children, and their level of sociability rises as they age, eventually encompassing the ability to learn effectively from one another. Social interactions with other children serve as a foundation for future social exchanges and relationships.

What are some of the ways that infants differ from one another?

14. The origins of personality, the sum total of the enduring characteristics that differentiates one individual from another, are found during infancy. According to Erikson's theory of psychosocial development, infants are initially in the trust-versus-mistrust stage, encompassing birth to 18 months. During this period, infants develop a sense of trust or mistrust, largely depending on how well their needs are met by their caretakers.

15. Temperament encompasses enduring levels of arousal and emotionality that are characteristic of an individual. Several dimensions, such as activity level and irritability, reflect temperament. Temperamental differences are reflected in the broad classification of infants into easy, difficult, and slow-to-warm categories.

16. Although biologically based behavioral differences between boy and girl infants exist, they are minor compared to their behavioral similarities. However, as infants age, gender differences become more pronounced, mostly due to the influence of environmental factors.

17. Differences between boys and girls are accentuated by parental expectations and behavior. Mothers and fathers display different interaction patterns with their children, the toy and play preferences of boys and girls differ and are differently encouraged by parents, and boys' and girls' actions are interpreted differently by parents and other adults.

How are societal changes reflected in family life and child-care practices?

18. Family life in the United States is rapidly changing. The size of the average family has decreased, and there are now more single-parent families, unmarried and very young mothers, working parents, and children born into poverty than ever before.

Is day care beneficial or harmful for infants?

19. Day care, a social response to the changing nature of the family, can be beneficial to the social development of children, fostering social interaction and cooperation, if it is of high quality.

20. On the other hand, some research has found negative outcomes from day care, including increased levels of aggression and disobedience in day care children and a decreased ability among young infants to form secure attachments to their parents. These findings pertain to children involved in large amounts of day care each week.

21. Studies of the effects of day care should increasingly take into account factors related to the quality of the day care provided and to the characteristics of the parents who tend to use day care as a childrearing strategy.

22. Overall, high-quality day care appears to have few or no negative effects on children, and it may even have positive effects in terms of social development. High-quality day care can be recognized by the ratio of providers to children, the quality of the facilities, the nature of the activities provided, and the attitudes and expertise of the providers.

KEY TERMS AND CONCEPTS

differential emotions theory (p. 183)

social smile (p. 183)

social referencing (p. 185)

theory of mind (p. 187)

empathy (p. 187)

attachment (p. 189)

Ainsworth strange situation (p. 190)

mutual regulation model (p. 195)

reciprocal socialization (p. 196)

personality (p. 199)

Erikson's theory of psycholosocial development (p. 199)

trust-versus-mistrust stage (p. 199)

temperament (p. 208)

gender (p. 200)

The Preschool Years

Physical and Cognitive Development

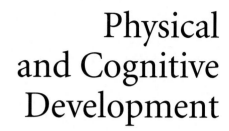

CHAPTER OUTLINE

PROLOGUE: GETTING READY

The night before my younger child, Will, started kindergarten, neither he nor I could sleep. Mingled with his excitement was, I imagined, concern over some of the worries that he had expressed to my husband and me: Would he be smart enough? Would he be able to read? Would there be enough time at school to play? Similar doubts haunted my own dreams like the Wild Things; I wondered whether I should have left Will in preschool for another year (with an August birthday, he would be one of the youngest in his class), whether his skills would be as advanced as the other children's, whether his teacher would appreciate his charms, tolerate his mishaps, and love him no matter what, as we do—and how I would survive without a little one at my heels.

The next morning, I helped Will get dressed in the new outfit that we had bought weeks earlier and carefully laid out the night before. To avoid last-minute panic, I'd packed his favorite lunch and his backpack the night before. After a photo session, we set off together. Although he clutched my hand on the walk to the classroom, Will lined up with his classmates as if he had been doing it for years, and trotted into the class with nary a backward glance. (Fishel, 1993, p. 165)

LOOKING AHEAD

In one sense, the preschool years mark a time of preparation: a period spent anticipating and getting ready for the start of a child's formal education, where society begins to pass on its intellectual tools to a new generation.

But it is a mistake to take the label "preschool" too literally. The years between 3 and 6 are hardly a mere way-station in life, an interval spent waiting for the next, more important period to start. Instead, the preschool years are a time of tremendous change and growth, where physical, intellectual, and social development proceeds at a rapid pace.

This chapter focuses on the physical, cognitive, and linguistic growth that occurs during the preschool years. We begin by considering the nature of physical change during those years. We discuss weight and height, nutrition, and health and wellness. We consider changes in the brain and its neural byways, and we touch on some intriguing findings relating to gender differences in the way that the brain functions. We also look at how both gross and fine motor skills change over the preschool years.

Intellectual development is the focus of much of the remainder of the chapter. We examine the major approaches to cognitive development, including Piaget's theory, information-processing approaches, and a view of cognitive development that takes culture into account.

Finally, the chapter considers the important advances in language development that occur during the preschool years. We end with a discussion of several factors that influence cognitive development, including exposure to television and participation in child care and preschool programs.

After reading this chapter you'll be able to answer the following questions:

◆ How do children's bodies and nutritional requirements change during the preschool years?

◆ What health problems potentially affect preschool children?

215

- How do preschool children's brains and physical skills develop?
- How does Piaget interpret cognitive development during the preschool years?
- How do other views of cognitive development differ from Piaget's?
- How do children's linguistic abilities develop in the preschool years?
- What effects does television have on preschoolers?
- What kinds of preschool educational programs are available in the United States, and what effects do they have?

PHYSICAL GROWTH

It is an unseasonably warm spring day at the Cushman Hill preschool, one of the first after a long winter. The children in Mary Scott's class have happily left their winter coats in the classroom for the first time this spring, and they are excitedly playing outside. Jessie plays a game of catch with Germaine, while Sarah and Molly climb on the jungle gym. Craig and Marta chase one another, while Jesse and Bernstein try, with gales of giggles, to play leap-frog. Virginia and Ollie sit across from each other on the teeter-totter, successively bumping it so hard into the ground that they both are in danger of being knocked off. Erik, Jim, Scott, and Paul race around the perimeter of the playground, running for the sheer joy of it.

These same children, now so active and mobile, were unable even to crawl or walk just a few years earlier. The advances in their physical abilities that have occurred in such a short time are nothing short of astounding. Just how far they have developed is apparent when we look at the specific changes they have undergone in their size, shape, and physical abilities.

THE GROWING BODY

Two years after birth, the average child in the United States weighs in at about 25 to 30 pounds and is close to 34 inches tall—roughly half the height of the average adult. Children grow steadily during the preschool period, and by the time they are 6 years old they weigh, on average, about 46 pounds and stand 46 inches tall (see Figure 7-1).

Individual Differences in Height and Weight.   These averages mask great individual differences in height and weight. For instance, ten percent of 6-year-olds weigh 55 pounds or more, and ten percent weigh 36 pounds or less. Furthermore, average differences in height and weight between boys and girls increase during the preschool years. Although at age 2 the differences are relatively small, by the age of 6 boys begin to be taller and heavier, on average, than girls.

Furthermore, profound differences in height and weight exist between children in economically developed countries and those in developing countries. The better nutrition and health care received by children in developed countries translates into significant differences in growth. For instance, the average Swedish 4-year-old is as tall as the average 6-year-old in Bangladesh (United Nations, 1990).

Differences in height and weight also reflect economic factors within the United States. For instance, more than ten percent of children in the United States whose family incomes are below the poverty level are among the shortest five percent of all preschool-age children (Barrett & Frank, 1987; Egan, 1994; Sherry, Springer, Connell, & Garrett, 1992).

Changes in Body Shape and Structure.   If we compare the bodies of a 2-year-old and a 6-year-old, we find that the bodies vary not only in height and weight but also in shape. During the preschool years, boys and girls become less chubby and roundish and more slender. They begin to burn off some of the fat they have carried from their infancy,

FIGURE 7-1

Gaining height and weight. The preschool years are marked by steady increases in height and weight. The figures show the median point for boys and girls at each age, in which 50 percent of children in each category are above this height or weight level and 50 percent are below.

(Adapted from Lowrey, 1986).

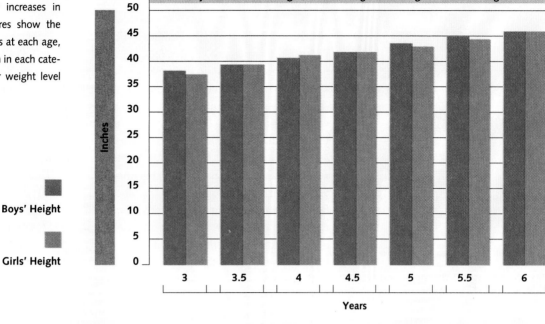

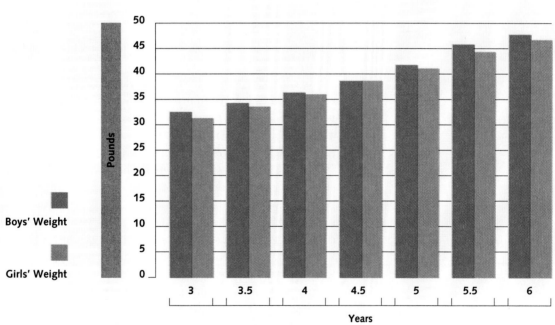

and they no longer have a pot-bellied appearance. Moreover, their arms and legs lengthen, and the size relationship between the head and the rest of the body becomes more adultlike. In fact, by the time children reach age 6, their proportions are quite similar to those of adults.

The changes in size, weight, and appearance we see during the preschool years are only the tip of the iceberg. Internally, other physical changes are occurring. Children grow stronger as their muscle size increases and their bones become sturdier. The sense organs

Providing preschoolers with a variety of foods helps ensure good nutrition.

continue their development. For instance, the *eustachian tube* in the ear, which carries sounds from the external part of the ear to the internal part, moves from a position that is almost parallel to the ground at birth to a more angular position. This change sometimes leads to an increase in frequency of earaches during the preschool years.

Nutrition: Eating the Right Foods.   Nutritional needs change during the preschool years. Because the rate of growth during this period is slower than during infancy, preschoolers need less food to maintain their growth. The change in food consumption may be so noticeable that parents sometimes worry that their preschooler is not eating enough. However, children tend to be quite adept at maintaining an appropriate intake of food, if provided with nutritious meals. In fact, anxiously encouraging children to eat more than they seem to want naturally may lead them to increase their food intake beyond an appropriate level.

Ultimately, some children's food consumption can become so high as to lead to **obesity**, which is defined as a body weight more than 20 percent higher than the average weight for a person of a given age and height. Obesity is brought about by both biological and social factors. There is a clear genetic component of obesity, illustrated by the fact that adopted children tend to have weights that are more similar to those of their birth parents than those of their adoptive parents. In addition, children who are obese during the preschool years tend to have responded more to sweet tastes at birth and to have been more responsive at birth to environmental stimuli (Biron, Mongeau, & Bertrand, 1977; Rodin & Hall, 1987; Unger, Kreeger, & Christoffel, 1990; Schlicker, Borra, & Regan, 1994).

The degree of encouragement—or discouragement—parents provide on the subject of eating also plays a role in obesity. For instance, some parents may strongly encourage their preschoolers to eat in the mistaken belief that their youngsters are not eating enough. Conversely, other parents may place strong restraints on children's food intake to prevent obesity.

In either case, such behavior may prevent children from developing their own internal controls over eating. Without such controls, children may become less aware of their internal hunger cues—and may ultimately become obese. For instance, a recent study of a group of children aged 3 to 5 found that those with the highest proportion of body fat had mothers who exerted the greatest level of control over the amount of food their children ate (Johnson & Birch, 1994). Furthermore, the more control the mothers in the study reported exerting, the less self-regulation of food intake their youngsters exhibited. In sum, strong parental involvement in what children eat may suppress the children's natural ability to monitor and control their food intake, and this may lead to obesity and even to more severe eating problems in the future (Rodin & Hall, 1987; Brownell & Rodin, 1994).

How do parents ensure that their children have good nutrition without turning mealtimes into a tense, adversarial situation? In most cases, the best strategy is to make sure that a variety of foods, low in fat and high in nutritional content, is available. Foods that have a relatively high iron content are particularly important: Iron deficiency anemia, which causes chronic fatigue, is one of the prevalent nutritional problems in developed countries such as the United States. High-iron foods include dark green vegetables (such as broccoli), whole grains, and some types of meat (Ranade, 1993).

On the other hand, like adults, preschool children are not going to find all foods equally appealing, and children should be given the opportunity to develop their own natural preferences. As long as their overall diet is adequate, no single food is indispensable.

Health and Illness.   For the average child in the United States, a runny nose due to the common cold is the most frequent—and happily, the most severe—kind of health problem during the preschool years. In fact, the majority of children in the United States are reasonably healthy during this period.

---

obesity   *body weight more than 20 percent higher than the average weight for a person of a given age and height*

This was not always the case. Before the discovery of vaccines and the routine immunization of children, the preschool period was a dangerous time. Even today, this period is risky in certain lower socioeconomic segments of the U.S. population, as well as in many parts of the world. In fact, probably because of the lack of a national health care policy in the United States and the complacency on the part of government officials, the proportion of children immunized in the United States has fallen during some portions of the last two decades—at the same time it has been rising in many third-world countries (Williams, 1990).

Directions in Development

The Search for a Supervaccine

Vaccine researchers liken their quest to the search for the Holy Grail: developing a "supervaccine" that will protect every child in the world from all the major preventable childhood diseases.

To accomplish this daunting task, the Children's Vaccine Initiative (CVI) was begun in the early 1990s with the backing of leaders of many countries around the globe and a confederation of international organizations, such as the United Nations Children's Fund and the World Health Organization. The CVI was designed to attack a problem that has prevented millions of children from being vaccinated against the diseases of childhood.

The problem has been that today's vaccines, while effective, must be administered in six separate doses—something that is simply impossible to accomplish in most developing countries. In addition, many vaccines require refrigeration and must be administered by injection. In this context, a supervaccine that simultaneously prevented all major childhood diseases, that could last some period without refrigeration, and that could be administered orally in a single dose would clearly be an important accomplishment. With such a vaccine it would become at least theoretically feasible to provide protection for all the world's children (Gibbins, 1994).

The need certainly exists for such a supervaccine. More than two million youngsters needlessly die each year from measles, influenza, polio, tetanus, diphtheria, tuberculosis, and other diseases that can be prevented.

For the moment, a supervaccine remains more a goal than a reality. Several preliminary problems must be overcome. For instance, it is unclear how many antibodies a child is capable of accepting at a single time. Moreover, vaccines differ in stability, which means that, for purposes of preservation, different vaccines require different preparations. To produce a supervaccine, some means must be discovered to preserve simultaneously several different types of vaccine.

On the other hand, the goal does not seem to be unreachable. Several combined vaccines are already on the market. For example, one vaccine now being sold in Europe combines diphtheria, tetanus, pertussis (whooping cough), and polio protection. In light of such developments, the goal of creating a supervaccine for the next century seems achievable.

THE GROWING BRAIN

The brain grows at a faster rate than any other part of the body. Two-year-olds have brains that are about three-quarters the size and weight of an adult brain. By age 5, children's brains weigh 90 percent of average adult brain weight. In comparison, the average 5-year-old's total body weight is just 30 percent of average adult body weight (Lowrey, 1986; Schuster & Ashburn, 1986; Nihart, 1993).

Why does the brain grow so rapidly? One reason is an increase in the number of interconnections among cells. These interconnections allow for more complex communication between neurons—and permit the rapid growth of cognitive skills that we'll discuss later in the chapter. In addition, the amount of myelin—protective insulation that surrounds parts of neurons—increases, which speeds the transmission of electrical impulses along brain cells but also adds to brain weight.

The two halves of the brain also begin to become increasingly differentiated and specialized (see Figure 7-2). For instance, **lateralization**, the process in which certain functions are located more in one hemisphere of the brain than the other, becomes more pronounced during the preschool years.

For almost all right-handed individuals, and a majority of left-handed people, the left hemisphere concentrates on tasks that necessitate verbal competence, such as speaking, reading, thinking, and reasoning. The right hemisphere develops its own strengths, especially in nonverbal areas such as comprehension of spatial relationships, recognition of patterns and drawings, music, and emotional expression (Kitterle, 1991; Hellige, 1994; Zaidel, 1994).

Each of the two hemispheres begins to process information in a slightly different manner. Whereas the left hemisphere considers information sequentially, one piece of data at a time, the right hemisphere processes information in a more global manner, reflecting on it as a whole (Gazzaniga, 1983; Springer & Deutsch, 1989).

Despite the specialization of the hemispheres, we need to keep in mind that in most respects the two hemispheres of the brain act in tandem. They are interdependent, and the differences between the two are minor. Furthermore, many individual differences exist in the nature of lateralization. For example, many of the 10 percent of people who are left-handed or ambidextrous (able to use both hands interchangeably) have language centered in their right hemispheres or have no specific language center.

Even more intriguing are differences in lateralization related to gender and culture. For instance, starting during the first year of life and continuing in the preschool years, boys and girls show some hemispheric differences associated with lower body reflexes and the processing of auditory information (Shucard, Shucard, Cummins, & Campso, 1981; Grattan, DeVos, Levy, & McClintock, 1992). Furthermore, males clearly tend to show greater lateralization of language in the left hemisphere; among females, however, language is more evenly divided between the two hemispheres (Gur et al., 1982). Such differences may help explain why—as examined later in the chapter—a female's language development proceeds at a more rapid pace during the preschool years than does a male's language development.

We still do not know the source of the difference in lateralization between females and males. One explanation is genetic: that female and male brains are predisposed to function in slightly different ways. Such a view is supported by data suggesting that minor structural differences exist between males' and females' brains. For instance, a section of the *corpus callosum*, a bundle of fibers connecting the hemispheres of the brain, is proportionally larger in women than in men. Furthermore, studies conducted among other species, such as primates, rats, and hamsters, have found size and structural differences in the brains of males and females (Hammer, 1984; Allen, Hines, Shryne, & Gorski, 1989).

---

lateralization   *the process in which certain functions are located more in one hemisphere of the brain than the other*

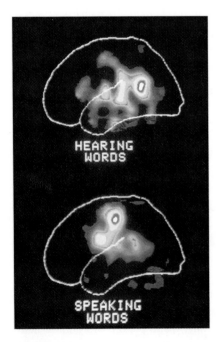

FIGURE 7-2   These scans show how different parts of the brain are activated during particular tasks, illustrating the increasing specialization of the brain.

Before we accept a genetic explanation for the differences between female and male brains, we need to consider an equally plausible alternative: It may be that verbal abilities emerge earlier in girls because girls receive greater encouragement for verbal skills than boys do. For instance, there is evidence suggesting that, even as infants, girls are spoken to more than boys. Such higher levels of verbal stimulation may produce growth in particular areas of the brain that does not occur in boys (Beale, 1994). Consequently, environmental factors rather than genetic ones may lead to the gender differences we find in brain lateralization. Once again, we find that teasing out the relative impact of heredity and environment is a challenging task.

MOTOR DEVELOPMENT

As their parents watched from the edge of the summer school playground, 3-year-old Jorge tore after Henry, with Cary in hot pursuit. Eleanor and Heidi threw a ball to each other. Mick and Satra sat at a bench, painstakingly cutting out paper flowers with a scissors for a party that afternoon. It was hard for their parents to recall that just a few years earlier, these same children were not even able to lift up their heads or roll over, let alone walk.

In their motor development, preschool children have come a long way since birth. Both their gross and fine motor skills have become increasingly fine-tuned.

Gross Motor Skills.   By the time they are 3, children have mastered a variety of skills: jumping, hopping on one foot, skipping, and running. By 4 and 5, their skills have become more refined, as they gain increasing control over their muscles. For instance, at age 4 they can throw a ball with enough accuracy that a friend can catch it, and by age 5 they can toss a ring and have it land on a peg 5 feet away. Five-year-olds can learn to ride bikes, climb ladders, and ski downhill—activities that all require a good bit of coordination (Clark & Humphrey, 1985). (Table 7-1 summarizes major gross motor skills that emerge during the preschool years.)

One reason that motor skills develop at such a rapid clip during the preschool years is that children spend a great deal of time practicing them. During this period, the general level of activity is extraordinarily high: Preschoolers seem to be perpetually in motion. In

TABLE 7-1

MAJOR GROSS MOTOR SKILLS IN EARLY CHILDHOOD

3-Year-Olds	4-Year-Olds	5-Year-Olds
Cannot turn or stop suddenly or quickly	Have more effective control of stopping, starting, and turning	Start, turn, and stop effectively in games
Jump a distance of 15 to 24 inches	Jump a distance of 24 to 33 inches	Can make a running jump of 28 to 36 inches
Ascend a stairway unaided, alternating the feet	Descend a long stairway alternating the feet, if supported	Descend a long stairway alternating the feet, if supported
Can hop, using largely an irregular series of jumps with some variations added	Hop 4 to 6 steps on one foot	Easily hop a distance of 16 feet

(*Source:* C. Corbin 1973.)

fact, the activity level is higher at age 3 than at any other point in the entire life span (Eaton & Yu, 1989; Poest, Williams, Witt, & Atwood, 1990).

Girls and boys differ in certain aspects of gross motor coordination, in part because of differences in muscle strength, which is somewhat greater in boys than in girls. For instance, boys can typically throw a ball better and jump higher. Furthermore, a boy's overall activity level tends to be greater than a girl's (Eaton & Yu, 1989). On the other hand, girls generally surpass boys in tasks that involve the coordination of limbs. For instance, at the age of 5, girls are better than boys at jumping jacks and balancing on one foot (Cratty, 1979).

Fine Motor Skills.   At the same time gross motor skills are developing, children are progressing in their ability to use fine motor skills, which involve more delicate, smaller body movements. These skills encompass such varied activities as using a fork and spoon, cutting with scissors, tying one's shoelaces, and playing the piano.

The skills involved in fine motor movements require a good deal of practice, as anyone knows who has watched a 4-year-old struggling painstakingly to copy letters of the alphabet. Yet fine motor skills show clear developmental patterns. At the age of 3, children are already able to draw a circle and square with a crayon, and they can undo their clothes when they go to the bathroom. They can put a simple jigsaw puzzle together, and they can fit blocks of different shapes into matching holes. On the other hand, they do not show much polish in accomplishing such tasks: For instance, they may try to force puzzle pieces into place.

By age 4, preschoolers' fine motor skills are considerably better. They can draw a person that looks like a person, and they can fold paper into triangular designs. And by the time they are 5, they are able to hold and manipulate a thin pencil properly. Furthermore, almost all show a clear preference at this time for the use of one hand over another—the development of **handedness.**

Actually, some signals of future handedness are seen early in infancy, when infants may show a preference for one side of their bodies over another. By the age of 7 months, some infants seem to favor one hand by grabbing more with it than the other (Ramsay, 1980; Michel, 1981). Conversely, many children show no preference until the end of the preschool years.

By age 5, though, most children display a clear-cut tendency to use one hand over the other, with 90 percent being right-handed and ten percent left-handed. Furthermore, more boys than girls are left-handed.

Much speculation has been devoted to the meaning of handedness, fueled in part by long-standing myths about the sinister nature of left-handedness. (In fact, the word "sinister" itself is derived from the Latin word meaning "on the left.") In Islamic cultures, for instance, the left hand is generally used in going to the toilet, and it is considered unciv-

handedness   *the preference of using one hand over another*

During the preschool years, children grow in both gross and fine motor skills.

ilized to serve food with that hand. Many artistic portrayals of the devil show him as left-handed.

However, there is no scientific basis for myths that suggest there is something wrong with being left-handed. In fact, some evidence exists that left-handedness may be associated with certain advantages. For example, a study of 100,000 students who took the Scholastic Assessment Test (SAT) showed that 20 percent in the highest-scoring category were left-handed, double the proportion of left-handed people in the general population. Moreover, such individuals as Michelangelo, Leonardo da Vinci, Benjamin Franklin, and Pablo Picasso were left-handed (Bower, 1985).

Although some educators of the past tried to force left-handed children to use the right hand, particularly when learning to write, thinking has changed. Most teachers now encourage children to use whichever hand they prefer. Still, most left-handed people will agree that the design of desks, scissors, and most other everyday objects favors those who are right-handed. In fact, the world is so "right-biased" that it may prove to be a dangerous place for those who are left-handed: Left-handed people have more accidents and are at greater risk of dying younger than are right-handed people (Coren, 1989; Coren & Halpern, 1991).

The Informed Consumer of Development

Keeping Preschoolers Healthy

There's no way around it: Even the healthiest preschooler occasionally gets sick. Social interaction with others ensures that illnesses are going to be passed from one child to another. However, some diseases are preventable, and others can be minimized if simple precautions are taken:

- Preschoolers should eat a well-balanced diet containing the proper nutrients, particularly foods with sufficient protein. (The recommended daily energy intake for children age 24 months is about 1,300 calories, and for those age 4 to 6 it is about 1,700 calories.) Because preschoolers' stomachs are small, they may need to eat as often as five to seven times a day.

- Children should get as much sleep as they wish. Being run-down, from lack of either nutrition or sleep, makes children more susceptible to illness.

- Children should avoid contact with others who are ill. Parents should ensure that children wash their hands after playing with other youngsters who are obviously sick. Cold germs are often carried from one person to another via the hands.

- Ensure that children follow an appropriate schedule of immunizations. As illustrated in Table 7-2 (next page), current recommendations state that a child should have received nine different vaccines and other preventive medicines in five to seven separate visits to the doctor.

- Finally, if a child does get ill, remember this: Minor illnesses during childhood sometimes provide immunity to more serious illnesses later on.

TABLE 7-2

RECOMMENDED CHILD VACCINATION SCHEDULE OF THE PUBLIC HEALTH SERVICE'S IMMUNIZATION PRACTICES ADVISORY COMMITTEE

Age	DTP[3]	Poliomyelitis[4]	MMR[5]	HIB[1] Option 1	HIB[1] Option 2	HBV[2] Option 1	HBV[2] Option 2
Birth	-	-	-	-	-	x	-
1–2 months	-	-	-	-	-	x	x
2 months	x	x	-	x	x	-	-
4 months	x	x	-	x	x	-	x
6 months	x	-	-	x	-	-	-
6–8 months	-	-	-	-	-	x	x
12 months	-	-	-	-	x	-	-
15 months	x[6]	x[6]	x[7]	x	-	-	-
4–6 years[8]	x	x	x[9]	-	-	-	-

[1]HIB = Haemophilus b conjugate vaccine. HIB vaccine is given in either a 4-dose schedule (option 1) or a 3-dose schedule (option 2), depending on the type of vaccine used.

[2]HBV = Hepatitis B vaccine. HBV can be given simultaneously with DTP, poliomyelitis, MMR, and Haemophilus b conjugate vaccine at the same visit.

[3]DTP = Diphtheria, tetanus, and pertussis vaccine, combined.

[4]Poliomyelitis vaccine may be live oral polio vaccine in drops (OPV) or killed (inactivated) polio vaccine by injection (IPV).

[5]MMR = Measles, mumps, and rubella vaccine, combined.

[6]Many experts recommend this vaccine at 18 months of age.

[7]In some areas, this dose of MMR vaccine may be given at 12 months.

[8]Before school entry.

[9]Many experts recommend this dose of MMR vaccine be given at entry to middle or junior high school.

Source: Child Health USA '93.

Review and Rethink

REVIEW

♦ The preschool period is marked by steady physical growth. Children's bodies increase in height and weight, and they change in shape and structure.

♦ Nutrition significantly affects physical growth. Preschoolers tend to eat less than they did as babies, but they generally regulate their food intake appropriately, given nutritious options and the freedom to develop their own choices and controls.

♦ Most diseases to which preschoolers are susceptible have been controlled in the developed countries by immunization. However, in developing countries and among economically disadvantaged sectors of developed countries, immunization programs have been less successful.

♦ Brain growth is rapid during the preschool years. In addition, the brain develops lateralization, a tendency of the two hemispheres to adopt specialized tasks within the context of a unified brain.

◆ Gross and fine motor development also advances rapidly during the preschool years. During this period, boys' and girls' gross motor skills begin to diverge, and children develop handedness.

RETHINK

◆ How might biology and environment combine to affect the physical growth of a child adopted as an infant from a developing country and taken to a more industrialized country to live?

◆ Aside from obesity, to what other sorts of eating problems might overly controlling parents contribute? How?

◆ If the left hemisphere of the brain tends to process information more sequentially, and the right hemisphere more globally, how might the union of the two hemispheres be beneficial for processing different kinds of inputs from sight, hearing, touch, taste, and smell?

◆ How do genetics and culture interact to enable boys, in general, to play baseball more proficiently than girls? Can a girl overcome these factors to become a proficient baseball player? Why or why not?

◆ Assuming it can be shown that left-handers perform disproportionately well on tests of scholastic aptitude, should parents train their children to become left-handed? Why or why not?

INTELLECTUAL DEVELOPMENT

Three-year-old Sam was talking to himself. As his parents listened with amusement from another room, they could hear him using two very different voices. "Find your shoes," he said in a low voice. "Not today. I'm not going. I hate the shoes," he said in a higher-pitched voice. The lower voice answered, "You are a bad boy. Find the shoes, bad boy." The higher-voiced response was "No, no, no."

Sam's parents realized that he was playing a game with his imaginary friend, Gill. Gill was a bad boy who often disobeyed his mother, at least in Sam's imagination. In fact, according to Sam's musings, Gill often was guilty of misdeeds for which his parents blamed Sam.

In some ways, the intellectual sophistication of 3-year-olds is astounding. Their creativity and imagination leap to new heights, their language is increasingly sophisticated, and they reason and think about the world in ways that would have been impossible even a few months earlier. But what underlies the dramatic advances in intellectual development that start in the preschool years and continue throughout that period? We can consider several approaches, starting with a look at Piaget's findings on the cognitive changes that occur during the preschool years.

PIAGET'S STAGE OF PREOPERATIONAL THINKING

The Swiss psychologist Jean Piaget, whose stage approach to cognitive development we discussed in Chapter 5, saw the preschool years as a time of both stability and great change. He suggested that the preschool years fit entirely into a single stage of cognitive development—the preoperational stage—which lasts from the age of 2 years until about 7 years.

During the **preoperational stage**, children's use of symbolic thinking grows, mental reasoning emerges, and the use of concepts increases. Children become better at representing events internally, and they grow less dependent on the use of direct sensorimotor activity to understand the world around them. Yet they are still not capable of **operations**: organized, formal, logical mental processes. It is only at the end of the preoperational stage that the ability to carry out operations comes into play.

preoperational stage   according to Jean Piaget, the stage where children's use of symbolic thinking grows, mental reasoning emerges, and the use of concepts increases

operations   organized, formal, and logical mental processes

According to Piaget, a key aspect of preoperational thought is *symbolic function*, the ability to use a mental symbol, a word, or an object to stand for or represent something that is not physically present. For example, during this stage, preschoolers can use a mental symbol for a car (the word "car"), and they likewise understand that a small toy car is representative of the real thing. Because of their ability to use symbolic function, children have no need to get behind the wheel of an actual car to understand its basic purpose and use.

Symbolic function is at the heart of one of the major advances that occurs in the preoperational period: the increasingly sophisticated use of language. As we'll discuss later in this chapter, children make substantial progress in language skills during the preschool period.

It is important to consider Piaget's approach to cognitive development within the appropriate historical context and in light of more recent research findings. Recall, as we discussed in Chapter 5, that his theory is based on extensive observations of relatively few children. Despite his insightful and ground-breaking observations, recent experimental investigations suggest that, in certain regards, Piaget underestimated children's capabilities. Nevertheless, the broad outlines of his approach, which we'll consider here, provide a useful means of thinking about the advances in cognitive ability that occur during the preschool years.

The Relation Between Language and Thought.   Piaget suggests that language and thinking are inextricably intertwined, and that the advances in language that occur during the preschool years offer several improvements over the type of thinking possible during the earlier sensorimotor period. For instance, thinking embedded in sensorimotor activities is relatively slow, for it depends on actual movements of the body that are bound by human physical limitations. In contrast, the use of symbolic thought allows preschoolers to represent actions symbolically, permitting much greater speed.

Even more important, the use of language allows children to think beyond the present to the future. Consequently, rather than being grounded in the immediate here-and-now, preschoolers can imagine future possibilities through language. A third advantage is that preschoolers in the preoperational period can use language to consider several possibilities at the same time (Piaget & Inhelder, 1969; Wadsworth, 1971). In contrast, sensorimotor thought progresses in a linear, step-by-step way—the same way that children in the sensorimotor stage move from one sequential activity to the next.

Do the increased language abilities of preschoolers lead to increased thinking proficiency, or do the improvements in thinking during the preoperational period lead to enhancements in language ability? This question—whether thought determines language, or language determines thought—is one of the enduring and most controversial questions within the field of psychology. Piaget's answer is that language grows out of cognitive advances, rather than the other way around. He argues that improvements during the earlier sensorimotor period are necessary for language development, and that continuing growth in cognitive ability during the preoperational period provides the foundation for language ability. Consequently, Piaget argues that language development is based on the development of more sophisticated modes of thinking—and not the other way around.

Centration: What You See is What You Think.   Place a dog mask on a cat and what do you get? According to 3- and 4-year-old preschoolers, a dog. To them, a cat with a dog mask ought to bark like a dog, wag its tail like a dog, and eat dog food. In every respect, the cat has been transformed into a dog (DeVries, 1969).

Piaget suggests that the root of this belief is **centration**, a key element, and limitation, of the thinking of children in the preoperational period. It is the process of concentrating on one limited aspect of a stimulus and ignoring other aspects.

Preschoolers are unable to consider all available information about a stimulus. Instead, they focus on superficial, obvious elements that are within their sight. These external elements come to dominate preschoolers' thinking, leading to inaccuracy in thought.

centration   *the process of concentrating on one limited aspect of a stimulus and ignoring other aspects*

FIGURE 7-3

Which row contains more buttons? When preschoolers are shown these two rows and asked the question of which row has more buttons, they usually respond that the lower row contains more, because it looks longer. They answer in this way even though they know quite well that ten is greater than eight.

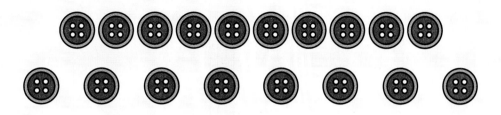

For example, consider what preschoolers say when they are shown two rows of buttons, one with ten buttons that are closely spaced together, and the other with eight buttons spread out to form a longer row (see Figure 7-3). If asked which of the rows contains more buttons, children who are 4 or 5 usually choose the row that looks longer, rather than the one that actually contains more buttons. This occurs despite the fact that children this age know quite well that ten is more than eight.

The cause of the children's mistake is that the visual image dominates their thinking. Rather than taking into account their understanding of quantity, they focus on appearance. To a preschooler, appearance is everything.

Egocentrism: The Inability to Take Others' Perspectives. One hallmark of the preoperational period is egocentric thinking. **Egocentric thought** is thinking that does not take into account the viewpoints of others. Preschoolers do not understand that others have different perspectives from their own. Egocentric thought takes two forms: the lack of awareness that others see things from a different physical perspective, and the failure to realize that others may hold thoughts, feelings, and points-of-view different from theirs. (Note what egocentric thought does *not* imply: that preoperational children intentionally think in a selfish or inconsiderate manner.)

Egocentric thinking underlies children's lack of concern over their nonverbal behavior and the impact it has on others. For instance, a 4-year-old who is given an unwanted gift of socks when he was expecting something more desirable may frown and scowl as he opens the package, unaware that his face can be seen by others and may reveal his true feelings about the gift (Feldman, 1992).

Egocentrism lies at the heart of several types of behavior during the preoperational period. For instance, preschoolers may talk to themselves, even in the presence of others, and at times they simply ignore what others are telling them. Rather than being a sign of eccentricity, such behavior illustrates the egocentric nature of preoperational children's thinking: the lack of awareness that their behavior acts as a trigger to others' reactions and responses. Consequently, a considerable amount of verbal behavior on the part of preschoolers has no social motivation behind it but is meant for the preschoolers' own consumption.

Similarly, egocentrism can be seen in hiding games with children during the preoperational stage. In a game of hide-and-seek, 3-year-olds may attempt to hide by covering their faces with a pillow—even though they remain in plain view. Their reasoning: If they cannot see others, others cannot see them. They assume that others share their view.

Incomplete Understanding of Transformation. Children in the preoperational period are unable to understand the notion of **transformation**, the process in which one state is changed into another. For instance, adults know that if a pencil that is held upright is allowed to fall down, it passes through a series of successive stages until it reaches its final,

---

egocentric thought *thinking that does not take into account the viewpoints of others*

transformation *the process in which one state is changed into another*

FIGURE 7-4

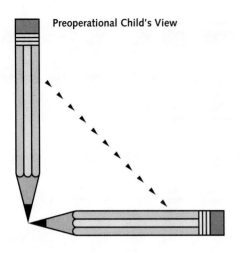 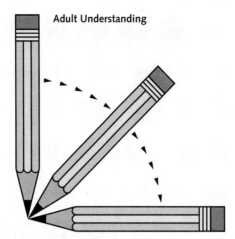

THE FALLING PENCIL.

Children in Piaget's preoperational stage do not understand that as a pencil falls from the upright to the horizontal position it moves through a series of intermediary steps. Instead, they think that there are no intermediate steps in the change from the upright to horizontal position.

horizontal resting spot (see Figure 7-4). In contrast, children in the preoperational period are unable to envision or recall the successive transformations that the pencil followed in moving from the upright to the horizontal position. If asked to reproduce the sequence in a drawing, they draw the pencil upright and lying down, with nothing in between. Basically, they ignore the intermediate steps.

Similarly, a preoperational child who sees several slugs during a walk in the woods may believe that they are all the same slug. The reason: She views each sighting in isolation and is unable to reconstruct the transformation from one sighting to the next.

Emergence of Intuitive Thought.   Because Piaget labeled the preschool years as the "*pre-operational period*," it is easy to assume that this is a period of marking time, waiting for the more formal emergence of operations. As if to support this view, many of the characteristics of the preoperational period highlight cognitive skills that the preschooler has yet to master. However, the preoperational period is far from idle. Cognitive development proceeds steadily, and in fact several new types of ability emerge. A case in point: the development of intuitive thought.

Intuitive thought reflects preschoolers' use of primitive reasoning and their avid acquisition of knowledge about the world. From about age 4 through 7, children's curiosity blossoms. They constantly seek out the answers to a wide variety of questions.

At the same time, children may act as if they are authorities on particular topics, feeling certain that they have the correct—and final—word on an issue. If pressed, they are unable to back up their reasoning, and they are inattentive to how they know what they know. In other words, their intuitive thought leads them to believe that they know answers to all kinds of questions, but there is little or no logical basis for this confidence in their understanding of the way the world operates.

On the other hand, the intuitive thinking that children display in the late stages of the preoperational period has certain qualities that prepare them for more sophisticated forms of reasoning. For example, by the end of the preoperational stage, preschoolers begin to understand the notion of *functionality*, which refers to the concept that actions, events, and outcomes are related to one another in fixed patterns. For instance, preschoolers come to understand that pushing harder on the pedals makes a bicycle move faster, or that pressing a button on a remote control makes the TV change channels.

Furthermore, children begin to show an awareness of the concept of identity in the later

intuitive thought   *thinking that reflects preschoolers' use of primitive reasoning and their avid acquisition of knowledge about the world*

stages of the preoperational period. *Identity* is the understanding that certain things stay the same, regardless of changes in shape, size, and appearance. For instance, knowledge of identity allows one to understand that a lump of clay contains the same amount of clay regardless of whether it is clumped into a ball or stretched out like a snake. Comprehension of identity is necessary for children to develop a cognitive skill that, according to Piaget, marks the transition from the preoperational period to the next one: an understanding of conservation.

Conservation: Learning That Appearances Are Deceiving.   Consider the following scenario:

> Four-year-old Jaime is shown two drinking glasses of different shapes. One is short and broad, the other tall and thin. A teacher half-fills the short, broad glass with apple juice. The teacher then pours the juice into the tall, thin glass. The juice fills the tall glass almost to the brim. The teacher asks Jaime a question: Is there more juice in the second glass than there was in the first?

If you view this as an easy task, so do children like Jaime. They have no trouble answering the question. However, they almost always get the answer wrong.

Most 4-year-olds respond that there is more apple juice in the tall, thin glass than there was in the short, broad one. In fact, if the juice is poured back into the shorter glass, they are quick to say that there is now less juice than there was in the taller glass (see Figure 7-5).

The reason for the error in judgment is that children of this age do not understand the principle of conservation. **Conservation** is the knowledge that quantity is unrelated to the arrangement and physical appearance of objects. During the preoperational period, preschoolers are unable to understand that changes in one dimension (such as appearance) do not necessarily mean that other dimensions (such as quantity) are changed.

Children who do not yet understand the principle of conservation feel quite comfortable in asserting that the amount of liquid changes as it is poured between glasses of different sizes. They simply are unable to realize that the transformation in appearance does not imply a transformation in quantity.

The inability to conserve manifests itself in several ways during the preoperational period. For example, if 5-year-olds are shown a row of checkers and asked to build a row that is "the same," the row they typically build will be identical in length—but it may vary in the number of checkers. Similarly, if shown two rows of checkers, each with the same number of checkers, but one with the checkers more spread out, children in the preoperational stage will reason that the two rows are not equal.

The lack of conservation also manifests itself in children's understanding of area, as illustrated by Piaget's cow-in-the field problem (Piaget, Inhelder, & Szeminska, 1960). In the problem, two sheets of green paper, equal in size, are shown to a child, and a toy cow is placed in each field. Next, a toy barn is placed in each field, and children are asked which cow has more to eat. The typical—and, so far, correct—response is that the cows have the same amount.

conservation *the knowledge that quantity is unrelated to the arrangement and physical appearance of objects*

FIGURE 7-5   Which container contains more? Even after seeing that the amount of liquid in the two cups is identical (left), and watching while the liquid in one cup is poured into the glass, most 4-year-olds believe that the glass contains more liquid than the cup (right).

In the next step, a second toy barn is placed in each field. But in one field, the barns are placed adjacent to one another, while in the second field, they are separated from one another. Children who have not mastered conservation usually say that the cow in the field with the adjacent barns has more grass to eat than the cow in the field with the separated barns. In contrast, children who can conserve answer, correctly, that the amount available is identical. (Some other conservation tasks are shown in Figure 7-6.)

Why do children in the preoperational stage make errors on tasks that require conservation? Piaget suggests that the main reason is that their tendency toward centration prevents them from focusing on the relevant features of the situation. Furthermore, they cannot follow the sequence of transformations that accompanies changes in the appearance of a situation.

Evaluating Piaget's Approach to Cognitive Development.   Piaget, a masterful observer of children's behavior, provides a detailed portrait of preschoolers' cognitive abilities. His rich description of how children view the world is simply unmatched by most other accounts of cognitive development.

However, Piaget's portrait is both incomplete and, in certain respects, flawed. Several aspects of his theory seriously underestimate children's capabilities. Take, for instance, Piaget's views of how children in the preoperational period understand number. He contends that preschoolers' thinking is seriously handicapped, as evidenced by their performance on tasks involving reversibility and conservation. Yet recent experimental work suggests otherwise.

For example, developmental psychologist Rochel Gelman has found in her research that children as young as age 3 can readily discern the difference between rows of two and three toy animals, regardless of the animals' spacing. Furthermore, older children are able to note differences in number, performing tasks such as identifying which of two numbers is larger. In fact, as we noted in Chapter 5, some developmental researchers find evidence that even infants can calculate simple addition and subtraction problems (Gelman, 1972; Wynn, 1992).

Based on such evidence, Gelman concludes that children have an innate ability to count, one akin to the ability to use language that some theorists see as universal and genetically determined. Such a conclusion is clearly at odds with Piagetian notions, which suggest that children's numerical abilities do not blossom until after the preoperational period.

Some developmental researchers also believe that cognitive skills develop in a more continuous manner than Piaget's state theory implies. Rather than thought changing in quality, as Piaget argues, critics of Piaget suggest that developmental changes are more quantitative in nature. The underlying processes that produce cognitive skill are regarded by such critics as undergoing only minor changes with age (Gelman & Baillargeon, 1983; Case, 1991).

There are further difficulties with Piaget's view of cognitive development. His contention that conservation does not emerge until the end of the preoperational period and, in some cases, even later, has not stood up to careful experimental scrutiny. For instance, performance on conservation tasks can be improved by providing preoperational children with certain kinds of training and experiences. The mere possibility of enhancing performance argues against the Piagetian view that children in the preoperational period have not reached a level of cognitive maturity that would permit them to understand conservation (D. Field, 1987a).

Clearly, children are more capable at an earlier age than Piaget's account would lead us to believe. Why did Piaget underestimate children's cognitive abilities? One answer is that he tended to concentrate on preschoolers' *deficiencies* in thinking, focusing his observations on children's lack of logical thought. In contrast, more recent theorists have focused more on children's competence. By shifting the question, they have found increasing evidence for a surprising degree of competence in preschoolers.

FIGURE 7-6

COMMON TESTS OF CHILDREN'S UNDERSTANDING OF THE PRINCIPLE
OF CONSERVATION.

Type of Conservation	Modality	Change in Physical Appearance	Average Age Concept is Grasped
Number	Number of elements in a collection 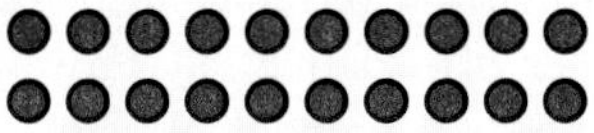	Rearranging or dislocating elements 	6–7 years
Substance (mass)	Amount of a malleable substance (e.g., clay or liquid) 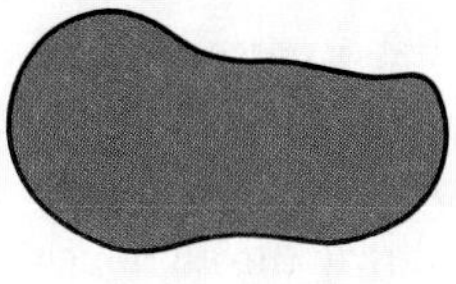	Altering shape 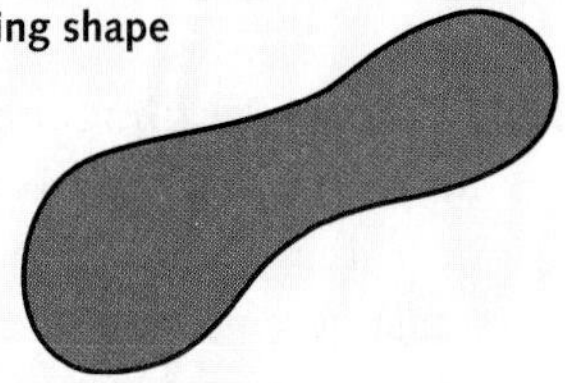	7–8 years
Length	Length of a line or object 	Altering shape or configuration 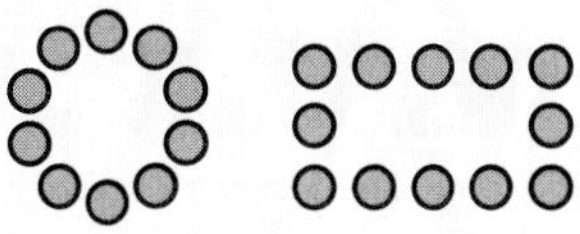	7–8 years
Area	Amount of surface covered by a set of plane figures 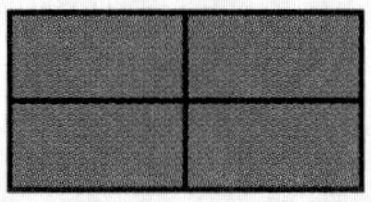	Rearranging the figures 	8–9 years
Weight	Weight of an object	Altering shape 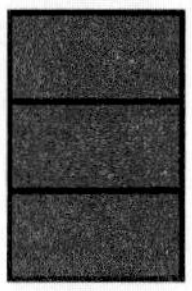	9–10 years
Volume	Volume of an object (in terms of water displacement) 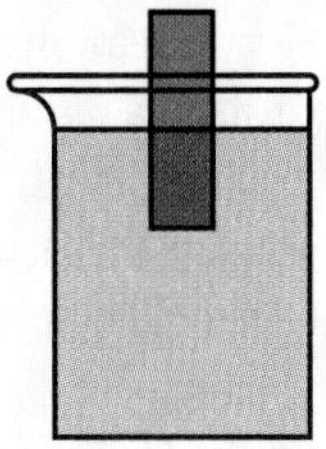	Altering shape 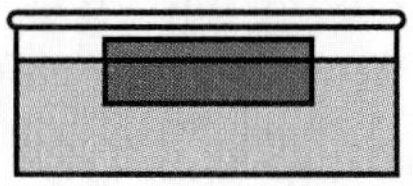	14–15 years

How specific and accurate will this preschooler's memory of this event be in the future?

INFORMATION-PROCESSING APPROACHES TO COGNITIVE DEVELOPMENT

Even as an adult, Paco has clear recollections of his first trip to a farm, which he took when he was 3 years old. He was visiting his godfather, who lived in Puerto Rico, and the two of them went to a nearby farm. Paco recounts seeing what seemed like hundreds of chickens, and he clearly recalls his fear of the pigs, who seemed huge, smelly, and frightening. Most of all he recalls the thrill of riding on a horse with his godfather.

That Paco has a clear memory of his farm trip is not surprising: Most people have unambiguous, and seemingly accurate, memories dating as far back as the age of 3. But are the processes used to form memories during the preschool years similar to those that operate later in life? More broadly, what general changes in the processing of information occur during the preschool years?

Memory: Recalling the Past.   Think back to your own earliest memory. If you are like most people, it probably is of an event that occurred after the age of 3.

According to Katherine Nelson (1989), **autobiographical memory**, memory of particular events from one's own life, does not achieve much accuracy until after age 3. Accuracy then increases gradually and slowly throughout the preschool years (K. Nelson, 1989, 1992).

Preschoolers recollections of events that happened to them are sometimes, but not always, accurate. For instance, 3-years-olds can remember fairly well central features of routine occurrences, such as the sequence of events involved in eating at a restaurant. In addition, preschoolers are typically accurate in their responses to open-ended questions (Goodman & Reed, 1986; K. Nelson, 1986; Price & Goodman, 1990).

One important determinant of the accuracy of preschoolers' autobiographical memories is how soon they are assessed. Unless an event is particularly vivid or meaningful, it is not likely to be remembered at all. Moreover, not all autobiographical memories last into later life. For instance, the first day of preschool may be remembered by a 3-year-old 6 months later, but the event may not be recalled at all later in life.

Furthermore, preschoolers' autobiographical memories not only fade, but the ones that are remembered may not be wholly accurate. For instance, preschoolers have difficulty describing certain kinds of information, such as complex causal relationships, and may oversimplify recollections. Their memories are also susceptible to the suggestions of others. For example, if preschoolers are repeatedly asked questions about an event they do not at first remember, the question itself may send them the message that they "ought" to remember it. Consequently, they may feel obliged to report recalling the event, even if they really don't (Ceci & DeSimone, 1992; Ceci & Bruck, 1993; Marche & Howe, 1995). (A discussion of another type of information-processing skill in preschoolers is found in the Directions in Development section.)

Information Processing and the Continuities of Cognitive Development.   According to information-processing approaches, cognitive development consists of gradual improvements in the ways people perceive, understand, and remember information. With age and practice, preschoolers process information more efficiently and with greater sophistication, and they are able to handle increasingly complex problems. In the eyes of proponents of information-processing approaches, it is these quantitative advances in information processing—and not the qualitative changes suggested by Piaget—that constitute cognitive development (Case, 1991).

autobiographical memory   *memory of particular events from one's own life*

Directions in Development

Spatial Reasoning Skills: Music to a Preschooler's Ear?

Some research suggests that preschoolers' spatial reasoning abilities improve as a result of musical training.

Learning the notes on a piano may do more than produce the ability to make music: It may also lead to an increase in spatial abilities.

At least that is the conclusion of researchers who studied the effects of teaching preschoolers to play the piano, as well as involving them in organized singing activities. In the research, Frances Rauscher and colleagues reasoned that musical activity is associated with particular neural firing patterns in the brain related to spatial reasoning skills (Rauscher et al., 1994).

To test the hypothesis, researchers taught a group of 3- and 4-year-olds to play the piano over an 8-month period, instructing them in the fundamentals of the keyboard and rudimentary music theory. In addition, the children participated in daily 30-minute group singing sessions.

In comparison to a control group of preschoolers who did not receive musical training, the musically sophisticated children performed better on measures of spatial reasoning that involved assembling objects into a whole. In contrast, there was no difference between the two groups on tasks that did not involve spatial reasoning.

Although more work is needed to validate these findings and to determine if the effects of musical training are lasting, the results are intriguing. Not only do they suggest that certain kinds of training in one domain, such as music, can have consequences for skills in other areas, such as spatial skills, but they also have applied implications. For instance, they argue that so-called educational "frills," which are the activities that are often the first to be jettisoned by school systems facing financial crises, might well promote significant basic skills.

For instance, dramatic changes in the nature of attention occur as preschoolers become older: They have longer attention spans, can pay attention to more than one dimension of an object simultaneously, and can monitor and plan what they are attending to more effectively (Flavell, 1977; Siegler, 1989; Kail, 1991). Such increasing attentional abilities place some of Piaget's findings in a different light. For example, increased attention allows older children to attend to both the height *and* the width of tall and short glasses into which liquid is poured. This permits them to understand that the amount of liquid in the glasses stays the same when it is poured back and forth. Preschoolers, in contrast, are unable to attend to both dimensions simultaneously, and thus are less able to conserve.

In sum, information-processing approaches view the changes that occur in children's cognitive abilities during the preschool years as analogous to the way a computer program becomes more sophisticated as a programmer modifies it on the basis of experience. These approaches focus on changes in the kinds of "mental programs" that children invoke when approaching problems. By focusing on the improvements in cognitive performance that these changes bring about, we can come closer to understanding the hallmarks of developmental change during the preschool years (Mehler & Dupoux, 1994; Siegler, 1994).

Developmental Diversity

Vygotsky's View of Cognitive Development: Taking Culture into Account

> As her daughter watches, a member of the Chilcotin Indian tribe prepares a salmon for dinner. When the daughter asks a question about a small detail of the process, the mother takes out another salmon and repeats the entire process. According to the tribal view of learning, understanding and comprehension can come only from grasping the total procedure, and not from learning about the individual subcomponents of the task. (Tharp, 1989)

The Chilcotin view of how children learn about the world stands in contrast to the prevalent view of Western society, in which the general assumption is that only by mastering the separate parts of a problem can one fully comprehend it. Do differences in the ways different cultures and societies approach problems have an influence on cognitive development? According to Russian developmental psychologist Lev Vygotsky, the answer is a clear yes.

In an increasingly influential view, Vygotsky argues that the focus of cognitive development should be on a child's social and cultural world. Instead of concentrating on individual performance, as do both Piagetian and information-processing approaches, Vygotsky focuses on the social aspects of development and learning. He holds that cognitive development proceeds as a result of social interactions in which partners jointly work to solve problems. Because of the assistance that such adult and peer partners provide, children gradually grow intellectually and begin to function on their own (Vygotsky, 1978; Wertsch & Tulviste, 1992; Davydov, 1995).

Vygotsky argues that the nature of the partnership that adults and peers provide is determined largely by cultural and societal factors. For instance, culture and society establish the institutions, such as preschools and play groups, that promote development by providing opportunities for cognitive growth. Furthermore, by emphasizing particular tasks, culture and society shape the nature of specific cognitive advances. Unless we look at what is important and meaningful to members of a given society, we may seriously underestimate the nature and level of cognitive abilities that ultimately will be attained (Belmont, 1994).

Vygotsky proposes that a child's cognitive abilities increase through exposure to information that resides within the child's **zone of proximal development (ZPD)**, which is the level at which a child can *almost*, but not fully, comprehend or perform a task on his or her own. When appropriate instruction occurs within the ZPD, students are able to increase their understanding or master new tasks. For cognitive development to occur, then, new information must be presented—by parents, teachers, or more skilled peers—within the ZPD (Rogoff, 1990; Steward, 1995).

In sum, Vygotsky's view is that the specific nature of cognitive development cannot be understood without taking the cultural and social context of a society into account. The focus of preschoolers' comprehension of the world, the specific sequence in which their cognitive development proceeds, and the nature of their understanding are all outcomes of their interactions with their parents, peers, and other members of society.

Lev Vygotsky's approach to cognitive development argues that the tasks, ranging from cooking to weaving, that a culture emphasizes influence children's cognitive abilities.

zone of proximal development (ZPD)
according to Lev Vygotsky, the level at which a child can almost, but not fully, comprehend or perform a task on his or her own

Review and Rethink

REVIEW

♦   According to Jean Piaget, children in the preoperational stage develop symbolic function, a qualitative change in their thinking that is the foundation of further cognitive advances, including the development of language and intuitive thought.

♦   Preoperational children use intuitive thought to explore and draw conclusions about the world, and their thinking begins to encompass the important notions of functionality and identity.

♦   Recent developmental researchers, although acknowledging Piaget's gifts and contributions, take issue with his emphasis on children's limitations and his underestimation of their capabilities.

♦   Proponents of information-processing approaches argue that quantitative changes in children's processing skills, such as memory and attention, largely account for their cognitive development.

♦   Lev Vygotsky believes that children develop cognitively within a context of culture and society that influences the path and sequence of their development.

RETHINK

♦   Do you agree with Piaget that symbolic thought does not emerge until children leave the sensorimotor period? How might you design a study to investigate the presence or absence of symbolic thought in very young children?

♦   In your view, how do thought and language interact in preschoolers' development? Is it possible to think without language? How do prelingually deaf children think?

♦   How does the Piagetian concept of identity relate to the concept of conservation?

♦   Are there cultural aspects to intuitive thought? Do you believe children in all cultures develop logical thinking identically, or are there cultural differences? Why?

♦   How might learning in one skill, such as music, work to improve performance in a skill such as spatial understanding? Might there be other such links between seemingly different cognitive areas?

THE GROWTH OF LANGUAGE AND LEARNING

I tried it out and it was very great!
This is a picture of when I was running through the water with Mommy.
Where you are going when I go to the fireworks with Mommy and Daddy?
I didn't know creatures went on floats in pools.
We can always pretend we have another one.
And the teacher put it up on the counter so no one could reach it.
I really want to keep it while we're at the park.
You need to get your own ball if you want to play "hit the tree."
When I grow up and I'm a baseball player, I'll have my baseball hat, and I'll put
    it on, and I'll play baseball. (Schatz, 1994, p. 179)

Listen to Ricky, at the age of 3. In addition to recognizing most letters of the alphabet, printing the first letter of his name, and writing the word "Hi," he is readily capable of producing the complex sentences quoted above.

During the preschool years, children's language skills reach new heights of sophistication. They begin the period with reasonable linguistic capabilities, although with significant gaps in both comprehension and production. In fact, no one would mistake the language used by a 3-year-old for that of an adult. However, by the end of the preschool years, they can hold their own with adults, both comprehending and producing language that has many of the qualities of adults' language. How does this transformation occur?

LANGUAGE DEVELOPMENT

The two-word utterances of the 2-year-old soon increase in both number of words and scope. Indeed, language blooms so rapidly between the late 2s and the mid-3s that researchers have yet to understand the exact pattern. What is clear is that sentence length increases at a steady pace, and the ways in which children at this age combine words and phrases to form sentences—known as **syntax**—doubles each month. By the time a preschooler is 3, the various combinations reach into the thousands (see Table 7-3 for an example of one child's growth in the use of language; Pinker, 1994).

In addition to the increasing complexity of sentences, enormous leaps occur in the number of words children use. By age 6 the average child has a vocabulary of approximately 14,000 words. To reach this number, preschoolers acquire vocabulary at a rate of nearly one new word every 2½ hours, 24 hours a day (Clark, 1983).

By the age of 3, preschoolers routinely use plurals and possessive forms of nouns (such as "boys" and "boy's"), employ the past tense (adding "-ed" at the end of words), and use articles ("the" and "a"). They can ask, and answer, complex questions ("Where did you say my book is?" and "Those are trucks, aren't they?").

Preschoolers' skills extend to the appropriate formation of words that they have never before encountered. For example, in one classic experiment, preschool children were shown cards with drawings of a cartoonlike bird, such as those shown in Figure 7-7 (on page 238) (Berko, 1958). The experimenter told the children that the figure was a "wug," and then showed them a card with two of the cartoon figures. "Now there are two of them," the children were told, and they were then asked to supply the missing word in the sentence, "There are two _____" (the answer to which, as *you* no doubt know, is "wugs").

Not only did children show that they knew rules about the plural forms of nouns but they also understood possessive forms of nouns and the third-person singular and past-tense forms of verbs—all for words that they never had previously encountered, since they were nonsense words with no real meaning.

Preschoolers also learn what *cannot* be said as they acquire the principles of grammar. **Grammar** is the system of rules that determine how our thoughts can be expressed. For instance, preschoolers come to learn that "I am sitting" is correct, whereas the similarly structured "I am knowing [that]" is incorrect. Although they still make frequent mistakes of one sort or another, 3-year-olds follow the principles of grammar most of the time. Some errors are very noticeable—such as the use of "mans" and "wents"—but these errors are actually quite rare, occurring between one-tenth of a percent and 8 percent of the time. Put another way, more than 90 percent of the time young preschoolers are correct in their grammatical constructions (de Villiers & de Villiers, 1992; Pinker, 1994).

syntax   the way in which words and phrases are combined to form sentences

grammar   the rules that determine how our thoughts can be expressed verbally

TABLE 7-3

GROWING SPEECH CAPABILITIES

Over the course of just a year, the sophistication of the language of a boy named Adam increases amazingly, as these speech samples show:

2 years, 3 months:	Play checkers. Big drum. I got horn. A bunny-rabbit walk.
2 years, 4 months:	See marching bear go? Screw part machine. That busy bulldozer truck.
2 years, 5 months:	Now put boots on. Where wrench go? Mommy talking bout lady. What that paper clip doing?
2 years, 6 months:	Write a piece of paper. What that egg doing? I lost a shoe. No, I don't want to sit seat.
2 years, 7 months:	Where piece a paper go? Ursula has a boot on. Going to see kitten. Put the cigarette down. Dropped a rubber band. Shadow has hat just like that. Rintintin don't fly, Mommy.
2 years, 8 months:	Let me get down with the boots on. Don't be afraid a horses. How tiger be so healthy and fly like kite? Joshua throw like a penguin.
2 years, 9 months:	Where Mommy keep her pocket book? Show you something funny. Just like turtle make mud pie.
2 years, 10 months:	Look at that train Ursula brought. I simply don't want put in chair. You don't have paper. Do you want little bit, Cromer? I can't wear it tomorrow.
2 years, 11 months:	That birdie hopping by Missouri in bag. Do want some pie on your face? Why you mixing baby chocolate? I finish drinking all up down my throat. I said why not you coming in? Look at that piece a paper and tell it. Do you want me tie that round? We going turn light on so you can't see.
3 years, 0 months:	I going come in fourteen minutes. I going wear that to wedding. I see what happens. I have to save them now. Those are not strong mens. They are going sleep in wintertime. You dress me up like a baby elephant.
3 years, 1 month:	I like to play with something else. You know how to put it back together. I gon' make it like a rocket to blast off with. I put another one on the floor. You went to Boston University? You want to give me some carrots and some beans? Press the button and catch it, sir. I want some other peanuts. Why you put the pacifier in his mouth? Doggies like to climb up.
3 years, 2 months:	So it can't be cleaned? I broke my racing car. Do you know the light wents off? What happened to the bridge? When it's got a flat tire it's need a go to the station. I dream sometimes. I'm going to mail this so the letter can't come off. I want to have some espresso. The sun is not too bright. Can I have some sugar? Can I put my head in the mailbox so the mailman can know where I are and put me in the mailbox? Can I keep the screwdriver just like a carpenter keep the screwdriver?

Source: Pinker (1994).

Private Speech and Social Speech.   Over the course of the preschool years, children's use of **private speech**, spoken language that is not intended for others, is common. As much as 20 percent to 60 percent of what children say is private speech, and such speech is a normal practice during even later stages of childhood. In fact, some research suggests that its use grows over the preschool years, peaking between the ages of 4 and 7. On the other hand, private speech becomes more secretive as children grow older and realize that talking to one-self is discouraged. Consequently, older children tend to whisper private speech, or they silently move their lips rather than speak out loud (Berk, 1992; Quay & Blaney, 1992; Berk & Landau, 1993).

Some developmental researchers suggest that private speech performs an important function. For instance, Lev Vygotsky suggests that it facilitates children's thinking and that youngsters use it to help them control their behavior. In his view, private speech ultimately serves an important social function, allowing children to solve problems and reflect upon

private speech   *spoken language that is not intended for others*

FIGURE 7-7

This is a wug.

Now there is another one.
There are two of them.
There are two _____ .

Even though no preschooler—like the rest of us—is likely to have ever before encountered a wug, they are able to produce the appropriate word to fill in the blank (which, for the record, is *wugs*).

(Adapted from Berko, 1958).

difficulties they encounter. He suggests further that private speech is a forerunner to the internal dialogues that we use when we reason with ourselves during thinking. Clearly, Vygotsky's views are at odds with those of Piaget, who suggests that private speech is egocentric and a sign of immature thought and ultimately a failure to communicate effectively (Vygotsky, 1962, 1986).

The preschool years also mark the growth of **social speech**, speech directed toward another person and meant to be understood by that person. Before the age of 3, children may seem to be speaking only for their own entertainment, apparently uncaring whether anyone else can understand. However, during the preschool years, children begin to direct their speech to others, wanting others to listen and becoming frustrated when they cannot make themselves understood. As a result, they begin to adapt their speech to others. Recall that Piaget contended that most speech during the preoperational period was egocentric: Preschoolers were seen as taking little account of the effect their speech was having on others. However, more recent experimental evidence suggests that children are somewhat more adept in taking others into account than Piaget initially suggested.

The Origins of Language Development. The immense strides in language development during the preschool years raise a fundamental question: How does proficiency in language come about? Linguists are deeply divided on how to answer this question.

One response comes from the basic principles of learning. According to the **learning theory approach**, language acquisition follows the basic laws of reinforcement and conditioning discussed in Chapter 5. For instance, a child who articulates the word "da" may be hugged and praised by her father, who jumps to the conclusion that she is referring to him. This reaction reinforces the child, who is more likely to repeat the word. In sum, the learning theory perspective on language acquisition suggests that children learn to speak by being rewarded for making sounds that approximate speech. Through the process of *shaping*, language becomes more and more similar to adult speech (Skinner, 1957).

social speech   speech directed toward another person and meant to be understood by that person

learning theory approach   the theory that language acquisition follows the basic laws of reinforcement and conditioning

There is a problem, though, with the learning theory approach. It doesn't seem to explain adequately how readily children acquire the rules of language. For instance, novice users of language are reinforced not only when they use grammatically impeccable language but also when they make errors. Parents are apt to be just as responsive if their child says, "Why the dog won't eat?" as they are if the child phrases the question more correctly ("Why won't the dog eat?"). Both forms of the question are understood correctly, and both elicit the same response; reinforcement is provided for both correct and incorrect language usage. Under such circumstances, learning theory is hard-put to explain how children learn to speak properly.

Still other problems exist with learning theory explanations. For instance, research shows that children are able to move beyond specific utterances they have heard and to produce novel phrases, sentences, and constructions. Furthermore, children can apply rules to nonsense words. In one study, 4-year-olds heard the nonsense verb "to pilk" in the sentence "the bear is pilking the horse." Later, when asked what was happening to the horse, they responded by placing the nonsense verb in the correct tense and voice: "He's getting pilked by the bear."

Such conceptual difficulties with the learning theory approach have led to the development of an alternative approach, championed by the linguist Noam Chomsky (1968, 1978, 1991), who argues that a genetically determined, innate mechanism directs the development of language. He suggests that people are born with an innate capacity to use language that emerges, more or less automatically, owing to maturation.

Chomsky's analysis of different languages suggests that all the world's languages share a similar underlying structure, which he calls **universal grammar**. In this view, the human brain is wired with a neural system called the **language-acquisition device (LAD)** that both permits the understanding of language structure and provides a set of strategies and techniques for learning the particular characteristics of the language to which a child is exposed. In this view, language is uniquely human, made possible by a genetic predisposition to both comprehend and produce words and sentences (Lust, Hermon, & Kornfilt, 1994; Lust, Suner, & Whitman, 1995).

Like the learning theory approach, the view that language represents an innate ability unique to humans has its critics. For instance, some researchers argue that certain primates are able to learn at least the basics of language, an ability that calls into question the uniqueness of the human linguistic capacity. Other critics suggest that we must identify mechanisms other than either a language-acquisition device or learning theory principles if we are to understand fully the processes that underlie language development (MacWhinney, 1991; Savage-Rumbaugh et al., 1993).

In sum, the origins of language remain a hotly contested question. What is obvious is that language development proceeds at an extraordinarily rapid clip during the preschool years. Of course, not all children's development proceeds at the same rate, as the results of recent research on the relationship between poverty and language use—which we consider next—makes perfectly clear.

Poverty and Language Development.   The language that preschoolers hear at home has profound consequences for future cognitive success, according to results found by psychologists Betty Hart and Todd Risley (1995) in a landmark study. The researchers studied the language used by a group of parents of varying levels of affluence as they interacted with their children over a 2-year period. Coding some 1,300 hours of everyday interactions between parents and children produced several major findings:

♦ The rate at which language was addressed to children varied significantly according to the economic level of the family. As can be seen in Figure 7-8, the greater the affluence of the parents, the more they spoke to their children.

universal grammar Noam Chomsky's theory that all the world's languages share a similar underlying structure

language-acquisition device (LAD) a neural system that both permits the understanding of language structure and provides a set of strategies and techniques for learning the particular characteristics of the language to which a child is exposed

FIGURE 7-8

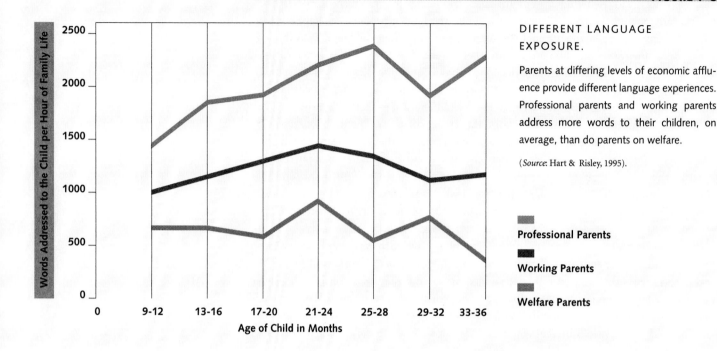

DIFFERENT LANGUAGE
EXPOSURE.

Parents at differing levels of economic affluence provide different language experiences.
Professional parents and working parents
address more words to their children, on
average, than do parents on welfare.

(*Source:* Hart & Risley, 1995).

■ Professional Parents

■ Working Parents

■ Welfare Parents

♦ In a typical hour, parents classified as professionals spent almost twice as much time
interacting with their children as did welfare parents.

♦ By the age of 4, children in welfare families were likely to have been exposed to some 13
million fewer words than youngsters in families classified as professionals.

♦ The kind of language used in the home differed between the various types of families.
Children in welfare families were apt to hear prohibitions ("no" or "stop," for example)
twice as frequently as do youngsters in professional families.

Ultimately, the study found that the type of language to which children were exposed
was associated with performance on tests of intelligence. The greater the number and diversity of words a child heard, for instance, the better the performance of the children at age 3
on a variety of measures of intellectual achievement.

Clearly, such findings argue for the importance of early exposure to language, both in
terms of quantity and variety. It also suggests that intervention programs that teach parents
to use more varied and higher quantities of language may be useful in alleviating some of
the damaging consequences of poverty.

The research is also consistent with an increasing body of evidence demonstrating
that family income and poverty have powerful consequences on general cognitive
development and children's behavior. Children raised in poorer homes tend to have
lower IQ scores and do worse on other measures of cognitive development by the
age of 5. Furthermore, the longer children live in poverty, the more severe are the
consequences. Poverty not only reduces the educational resources available to children; it also has such negative effects on *parents* that it limits the psychological support
that they can give to their children. In short, the consequences of poverty are severe, and
they linger (Duncan, Brooks-Gunn, & Klebanov, 1994; Bolger, Patterson, Thompson,
& Kupersmidt, 1995).

TELEVISION: LEARNING FROM THE MEDIA

> It's a Thursday afternoon at Unitel Studio on Ninth Avenue, where *Sesame Street* is taping its nineteenth season. Hanging back in the wings is a newcomer on the set, a compact young woman with short blonde hair named Judy Sladky. Today is her screen test. Other performers come to New York aspiring to be actresses, dancers, singers, comedians. But Sladky's burning ambition is to be Alice, a shaggy mini-mastodon who will make her debut later this season as the devoted baby sister of Aloysius Snuffle-upagus, the biggest creature on the show. (Helman, 1987, p. 50)

Ask almost any preschooler, and she or he will be able to identify Snuffle-upagus, as well Big Bird, Bert, Ernie, and a host of other characters: They are members of the cast of *Sesame Street*, the most successful television show in history targeted at preschoolers; its audience is in the millions.

But *Sesame Street* is not all that preschoolers are watching, for TV plays a central role in many U.S. households. In fact, it is one of the most potent and widespread stimuli to which children are exposed, with the average preschooler watching some 20 to 30 hours of TV a week (Rosemond, 1988).

Television: Ubiquitous Presence, Uncertain Consequences.   Almost every home in the United States has a television set, and more than half of all households own more than one. Statistics show there are more TVs than toilets in this country. These televisions do not sit idle: It has been estimated that the average American child spends more time watching television than talking to adults, playing with siblings, or attending school (Singer & Singer, 1983; Liebert & Sprafkin, 1988; Van Evra, 1990).

Despite television's ubiquitous presence, the consequences of watching so much television are not fully clear. For instance, research suggests that children do not fully understand the plots of the stories they are viewing, particularly in longer programs. They are unable to recall significant story details after viewing a program, and the inferences they make about the motivations of characters are limited and often erroneous. Moreover, preschool children may have difficulty separating fantasy from reality in TV programming (Parke & Slaby, 1983; Rule & Ferguson, 1986; Wright, Huston, Reitz, & Piemyat, 1994).

On the other hand, some kinds of information are likely to be understood relatively well by children. For instance, preschoolers are able to decode the facial expressions they see on television. However, the emotional displays that they view differ from what they find in the everyday, nontelevised world.

For example, one examination of the nonverbal behavior on the TV shows viewed most frequently by children found that nonverbal displays of emotion occurred at the surprisingly high rate of some 200 emotional expressions per hour. Furthermore, although a wide range of emotions was observed, depictions of certain emotions (such as happiness and sadness) were displayed considerably more frequently than were others (for instance, fear and disgust). Consequently, televised displays of emotion occur at high frequencies and diverge from what happens in the real world (Houle & Feldman, 1991; Coats & Feldman, 1995).

In sum, preschool children's understanding of what they see on television is typically incomplete and not fully accurate. This problem is compounded by the fact that much of what they view on TV is not representative of what actually happens in the real world. On the other hand, as they get older and their information-processing capabilities improve, preschoolers' understanding of the material they see on television also improves (Wright et al., 1994). They remember things more accurately, and they become better able to focus on the central message of a show. This suggests that the powers of the medium of television may be harnessed to bring about cognitive gains—exactly what the producers of *Sesame Street* set out to do (Van Evra, 1990).

***Sesame Street:* A Teacher in Every Home?**   *Sesame Street* is, without a doubt, the most popular educational program for children in the United States. Almost half of all preschoolers in the United States watch the show, and it is broadcast in almost 100 different countries and in 13 foreign languages. Characters like Big Bird and Kermit the Frog have become familiar throughout the world, to both adults and preschoolers (Liebert & Sprafkin, 1988).

Sesame Street was devised with the express purpose of providing an educational experience for preschoolers. Its specific goals include teaching letters and numbers, increasing vocabulary, and teaching preliteracy skills. Has *Sesame Street* achieved its goals? Most evidence suggests that it has.

For example, a 2-year longitudinal study compared three groups of 3- and 5-year-olds: those who watched cartoons or other programs, those who watched the same amount of *Sesame Street,* and those who watched little or no TV. Children who watched *Sesame Street* had significantly larger vocabularies than did those who watched other programs or those who watched little television. These findings held regardless of the children's gender, family size, and parent education and attitudes. Such findings are consistent with earlier evaluations of the program, which concluded that viewers showed dramatic improvements in skills that were directly taught, such as alphabet recitation, and improvements in other areas that were not directly taught, such as reading words (Bogatz & Ball, 1972; Rice, Huston, Truglio, & Wright, 1990).

The most recent evaluation of the show finds that not only are preschoolers in lower income households who watch the show better prepared for school, but that they also perform significantly higher on several measures of verbal and mathematics ability at ages 6 and 7 than do those who do not watch it (see Figure 7-9). Furthermore, viewers of *Sesame Street* spend more time reading than do nonviewers. And by the time they are 6 and 7, viewers of *Sesame Street* and other educational programs tend to be better readers and judged more positively by their teachers (Huston & Wright, 1995).

On the other hand, *Sesame Street* has not been without its critics. For instance, some educators claim the frenetic pace at which different scenes are shown makes viewers less receptive to the traditional forms of teaching that they will experience when they begin school. Traditional teaching moves at a slower pace, and the lessons are typically less visually appealing than those presented on *Sesame Street.* However, careful evaluations of the program find no evidence that viewing *Sesame Street* leads to declines in enjoyment of traditional schooling (Van Evra, 1990).

In sum, results of research on the consequences of watching *Sesame Street* are largely positive. Still, it is important to keep in mind the difficulties of carrying out evaluations of the effects of viewing. For instance, parents who encourage their children to watch a show reputed to improve academic performance may also encourage their children's academic performance in other spheres. Consequently, it may be the parents' high level of encouragement, and not the program itself, that leads to children's improved cognitive performance. Without the use of true experiments—which are difficult, if not impossible, to carry out because it is hard to maintain experimental control of what children watch in their homes—conclusions about the consequences of TV viewing remain uncertain. (We'll discuss this issue more in Chapter Eight, when we consider the consequences of viewing violence in the media.)

EARLY CHILDHOOD EDUCATION: TAKING THE "PRE" OUT OF THE PRESCHOOL PERIOD

The term "preschool period" is something of a misnomer: Almost three-quarters of children in the United States are enrolled in some form of care outside the home, much of which is designed either explicitly or implicitly to teach skills that will enhance both intellectual and social abilities. Several reasons account for this increase, but one major factor is the rise in the number of families in which both parents work outside the home. For instance, a high proportion of fathers work outside the home, and close to 60 percent of women with children under age 6 are employed, most of them full-time (Gilbert, 1994).

However, there is another reason, one less tied to the practical considerations of child care: Developmental researchers have found increasing evidence that children can benefit substantially from involvement in some form of educational activity before they enroll in formal schooling, which typically takes place at age 5 or 6 in the United States. When compared to children who stay at home and have no formal educational involvement, those youngsters enrolled in *good* preschools experience clear cognitive and social benefits (McCartney, 1984; Haskins, 1989; Clarke-Stewart, 1993).

The Varieties of Early Education.   The variety of early education alternatives is vast. Some outside-the-home care for children is little more than babysitting, while other options are designed to promote intellectual and social advances. Among the major choices of the latter type are the following:

♦   **Day care centers** typically provide care for children all day while their parents are at work. Although many day care centers were first established as safe, warm environments where children could be cared for and could interact with other youngsters, today their purpose tends to be broader, aimed at providing some form of intellectual stimulation. Still, their primary purpose tends to be more social and emotional than cognitive.

Some day care is provided in family day care centers, small operations run in private homes. Because such centers are often unlicensed, the quality of care can be uneven, and parents should investigate carefully before enrolling their children. In contrast, providers of center-based care, which is offered in institutions such as school classrooms, community centers, and churches and synagogues, are licensed and regulated by governmental authorities. Because teachers in such programs are more

day care centers   *places that typically provide care for children all day, while their parents are at work*

FIGURE 7-9

THE BENEFITS OF *SESAME STREET*.

Children who watched more of *Sesame Street* and other informative TV shows during the preschool years later scored better at age 7 than did those who watched mostly cartoons.

(Adapted from Wright & Huston, 1995.)

Test Score Advantage

Test Score Disadvantage

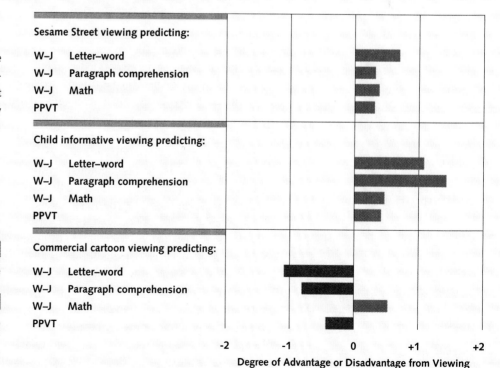

In many industrialized countries other than the United States, preschool education receives significantly more national support.

often trained professionals than those who provide family day care, the quality of care is often higher and more stable.

- **Preschools** (or **nursery schools**) are more explicitly designed to provide intellectual and social experiences for children. Because they tend to be more limited in their schedules, typically providing care for only 3 to 5 hours per day, preschools mainly serve children from middle and higher socioeconomic levels.

    Like day care centers, preschools vary enormously in the activities they provide. Some emphasize social skills; others focus on intellectual development. Some do both. For instance, Montessori preschools, which use a method developed by Italian educator Maria Montessori, employ a carefully designed set of materials to create an environment that fosters sensory, motor, and language development.

- **School day care** is provided by some local school systems in the United States. Almost half the states in the United States fund prekindergarten programs for 4-year-olds, often targeted at disadvantaged children. Because they typically are staffed by more well-trained teachers than less-regulated day care centers, school day care programs are often of higher quality than other early education alternatives.

How effective are such programs? According to developmental psychologist Alison Clarke-Stewart, who has studied the issue extensively, preschoolers enrolled in day care centers show intellectual development that at least matches that of children at home, and often is better. For instance, some studies find that day-care preschoolers are more verbally fluent, show memory and comprehension advantages, and even achieve higher IQ scores than do at-home children (Clarke-Stewart, 1993). Other studies find that early participation in day care is particularly helpful for children from impoverished home environments or otherwise at risk (Caughy, DiPietro, & Strobino, 1994; Reynolds, 1994).

Analogous advantages are found in social development. Children in high-quality programs tend to be more self-confident, independent, and knowledgeable about the social world in which they live than do those who do not participate. Conversely, not all the outcomes of outside-the-home care are positive: Children in day care have been found to be less polite, less compliant, less respectful of adults, and sometimes more competitive and aggressive than their peers (Belsky, Steinberg, & Walker, 1982; Thornburg, Pearl, Crompton, & Ispa, 1990; Bates et al., 1991).

preschools (or nursery schools)   *a child care facility designed to provide intellectual and social experiences for youngsters*

school day care   *child care facility provided by some local school systems in the United States*

It is important to keep in mind that not all early childhood care programs are equally effective. As we observed of infant day care in Chapter Six, one key factor is program *quality*: High-quality care provides intellectual and social benefits; low-quality care not only is unlikely to furnish benefits, but poor programs actually may harm children (Phillips et al., 1994).

How can we define "high quality"? Several characteristics are important; they are analogous to those that pertain to infant day care (see Chapter Six). For example, high-quality facilities have well-trained care providers. Furthermore, both the overall size of the group and the ratio of care providers to children are critical. Single groups should not have many more than 14 to 20 children, and there should be no more than five to ten 3-year-olds per caregiver, or seven to ten 4- or 5-year-olds per caregiver. Finally, the curriculum of a child care facility should not be left to chance, but should be carefully planned out and coordinated among the teachers (National Research Council, 1991; Cromwell, 1994).

No one knows how many programs in the United States can be considered "high quality," but there are many fewer than desirable. In fact, the United States lags behind almost every other industrialized country in the quality of its day care, as well as in its quantity and affordability.

Preschools Around the World: Why Does the United States Lag Behind?   In France and Belgium, accessibility to preschool is a legal right. In Sweden and Finland, preschoolers whose parents work have day care provided, if it is wanted. Russia has an extensive system of state-run *yasli-sads*, nursery schools and kindergartens, attended by 75 percent of urban children aged 3 to 7.

In contrast, the United States has no coordinated national policy on preschool education—or on the care of children in general. There are several reasons for this. For one, decisions about education have traditionally been left to the states and local school districts. For another, the United States has no tradition of teaching preschoolers, unlike other countries

FIGURE 7-10

THE PURPOSE BEHIND PRESCHOOL.

To parents in China, Japan, and the United States, the main purpose of preschools is very different. Whereas parents in China see preschools mainly as a way of giving children a good start academically, parents in Japan see them primarily as a means of giving children the experience of being a member of a group. In contrast, parents in the U.S. view preschools as a way of making children more independent, although obtaining a good academic start and group experience are also important.

China ▮

United States ▮

Japan ▮

(Based on Tobin, Wu, & Davidson, 1989.)

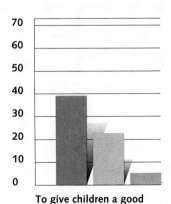

To give children a good start academically

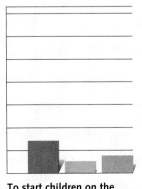

To start children on the road to being good citizens

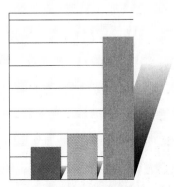

To give children experience being a member of a group

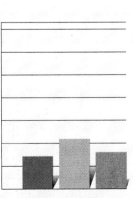

To make young children more independent and self-reliant

in which preschool-age children have been enrolled in formal programs for decades. Finally, the status of preschools in the United States has been traditionally low. Consider, for instance, that preschool and nursery school teachers are the lowest paid of all teachers. (Salaries increase as students' ages rise. Thus, college and high school teachers are paid most, whereas preschool and elementary school teachers are paid least.)

Finally, the quantity and nature of preschools may differ from one country to another according to the views that different societies hold of the purpose of early childhood education (Lamb, Ketterlinus, & Fracasso, 1992). For instance, in a cross-country comparison of preschools in China, Japan, and the United States, researchers found that parents in the three countries view the purpose of preschools very differently. Whereas parents in China tend to see preschools primarily as a way of giving youngsters a good start academically, Japanese parents view them primarily as a way of giving children the opportunity to be members of a group. In the United States, in comparison, parents regard the primary purpose of preschools as making children more independent and self-reliant, although obtaining a good academic start and having group experience are also important (Tobin, Wu, & Davidson, 1989).

Preparing Preschoolers for Academic Pursuits: Does Head Start Truly Provide a Head Start?   Although many programs designed for preschoolers focus primarily on social and

Speaking of Development

Yolanda Garcia

Born: 1952

Education: .... B.A., Combined Social Sciences, History, Sociology, and Political Science, University of California at Santa Barbara; M.A., Administration, Child Welfare, and Public Policy, University of Chicago School of Social Services; M.A., Education Administration, San Jose State University, California

Position: .... Head Start Director

Home: .... San Jose, California

As an undergraduate student, Yolanda Garcia had to work to put herself through school, and as a result she found a job working with preschoolers. That, coupled with a desire to work in the field of social services, prepared her for her life's vocation as part of one of the federal government's most well-known programs: Head Start.

emotional factors, some programs are geared primarily toward promoting cognitive gains and preparing preschoolers for the more formal instruction that they will experience when they start kindergarten. In the United States, the best-known program designed to promote future academic success is Head Start. Born in the 1960s when the United States declared a War on Poverty, the program has served over 13 million children and their families. Although it was designed to serve the "whole child," including children's physical health, self-confidence, social responsibility, and social and emotional development, the program has been scrutinized most closely in relation to the goal of improving cognitive processes (U.S. Department of Education, 1992; Zigler, Styfco, & Gilman, 1993; Zigler & Styfco, 1994).

Whether Head Start is seen as successful or not depends on the lens through which one is looking. If, for instance, the program is expected to provide long-term increases in IQ scores, it is a disappointment. Although graduates of Head Start programs tend to show immediate IQ gains, these increases do not last. On the other hand, it is clear that preschoolers who participate in Head Start are more ready for future schooling than those who do not. Furthermore, graduates of Head Start programs have better future school adjustment than do their peers, and they are less likely to be in special education classes or to be retained in grade. Finally, some research suggests that ultimately Head Start graduates show higher academic performance at the end of high school, although the gains are modest (Hebbeler, 1985; McKey et al., 1985; Lee, Brooks-Gunn, Schnur, & Liaw, 1990).

"The children learn by doing, with the teacher helping the children develop cognitive skills and reinforcing their interest areas."

"Teachers will guide the child through the processes that build on their level of cognitive development."

As the Director of the Children Services Department, a branch of the Santa Clara County Office of Education, Garcia is responsible for the Head Start program that serves 1,799 youngsters at 56 facilities in two counties.

"In Head Start classes, the children learn by doing," she explained, "with the teacher helping the children develop cognitive skills and reinforcing their interest areas. The teacher guides the children based on their interest and sets up an environment that is conducive to the child's interest."

Much of the teaching and planning is done through a variety of learning activities, according to Garcia. The children themselves play an active role in their education.

"We utilize an open framework of learning where teachers plan with the children. The teacher becomes the observer, recorder, and the guide from one step in the learning process to the next," she explained. "Teachers will guide the child through the processes that build on their level of cognitive development."

The goal of each Head Start program, according to Garcia, is to have a ratio of one teacher to seven students. This ratio, she says, allows for quality interaction.

"It also allows the teacher to individualize the teaching, permitting group activities to be based on what the teacher knows about the individuals making up the specific group of children."

In addition, results from other types of preschool readiness programs indicate that those who participate and graduate are less likely to repeat grades, and they complete school more frequently than do those who are not in the program. Moreover, according to a cost-benefit analysis of one preschool readiness program, for every dollar spent on the program, taxpayers saved seven dollars by the time the graduates reached the age of 27 (Schweinhart, Barnes, & Weikart, 1993).

Should We Seek to Improve Cognitive Skills During the Preschool Years?   Not everyone agrees that programs that seek to enhance academic skills during the preschool years are a good thing. In fact, according to developmental psychologist David Elkind, U.S. society tends to push children so rapidly that they begin to feel stress and pressure at a young age (Elkind, 1984, 1988).

Elkind argues that academic success is largely dependent upon factors out of parents' control, such as inherited abilities and a child's rate of maturation. Consequently, children of a particular age cannot be expected to master educational material without taking their current level of cognitive development into account.

Rather than arbitrarily expecting children to master material at a particular age, Elkind suggests that a better strategy is to provide an environment in which learning is encouraged, but not pushed. By creating an atmosphere in which learning is facilitated—for instance, by reading to preschoolers or taking them on visits to museums—parents will allow children to proceed at their own pace, rather than one that pushes them beyond their limits.

Although Elkind's suggestions are appealing—it is certainly hard to argue that increases in children's anxiety levels and stress should be avoided—they are not without their detractors. For instance, some educators have argued that pushing children is largely a phenomenon of the middle and higher socioeconomic levels, possible only if parents are relatively affluent. For poorer youngsters, whose parents may not have substantial resources available to push their children nor the easy ability to create an environment that promotes learning, the benefits of formal programs that promote learning are likely to outweigh their drawbacks.

The Informed Consumer of Development

Promoting Cognitive Development in Preschoolers: From Theory to the Classroom

We've considered the notion that one focus of the preschool period should be on promoting future academic success, and we have also discussed the alternative view that pushing children too hard academically may be hazardous to their well-being.

There is, however, a middle ground. Drawing on research that examines cognitive development during the preschool years, we can make several suggestions for parents and preschool teachers who wish to improve the academic readiness of children without creating undue stress. Among them are the following:

- Both parents and teachers should be aware of the stage of cognitive development, with its capabilities and limitations, that each individual child has reached. Unless they are aware of a child's current level of development, it will be impossible to provide appropriate materials and experiences.

- Instruction should be at a level that reflects—but is just slightly higher than—each student's current level of cognitive development. Piaget, for instance, suggests that cognitive growth is more likely to occur when both information and material are of moderate novelty. With too little novelty, children will be bored; with too much, they will be confused.

- Instruction should be individualized as much as possible. Because children of the same age may hover around different levels of cognitive development, curriculum materials that are prepared individually stand a better chance of success.

- Students should be kept actively engaged in learning, and they should be allowed to pace themselves as they move through new material.

- Opportunities for social interaction—both with other students and with adults—should be provided. By receiving feedback from others and observing how others react in given situations, preschoolers learn new approaches and ways of thinking about the world.

- Students should be allowed to make mistakes. Cognitive growth often flows from confronting errors.

- Because cognitive development can occur only when children have achieved the appropriate level of maturation, preschoolers should not be pushed too far ahead of their current state of cognitive development. For instance, although it may be possible through intensive training to get preoperational children to recite, in a rote manner, the correct response to a conservation problem, this does not mean that they will have true comprehension of what they are verbalizing.

Ultimately, keep in mind that children require *developmentally appropriate educational practice*, which is education based on both typical development and the unique characteristics of a given child (Bredekamp, 1989; Cromwell, 1994).

Review and Rethink

REVIEW

- In the preschool years, children rapidly increase in linguistic ability, developing an improved sense of grammar and shifting gradually from private to social speech.

- Learning theorists believe that basic learning processes adequately account for language development, whereas Noam Chomsky and his followers argue that humans have an innate language capacity that naturally facilitates language development.

- The effects of television on preschoolers are unclear. Some people are concerned about the emotional messages children are receiving; others are hopeful about the use of television as an educational tool.

- Preschool educational programs are beneficial if they are of high quality, with trained staff, good curriculum, proper group sizes, and small staff–student ratios. With the exception of Head Start, the U.S. government pays comparatively little attention to early childhood education.

- Although some contend that attempting to improve preschoolers' cognitive skills causes undue stress, most researchers would agree that preschool children benefit from a developmentally appropriate, individualized, and supportive environment for learning.

RETHINK

- Is private speech egocentric or useful? Do adults ever use private speech? What function does it serve?

- American Sign Language (ASL) is generally regarded as a true language. What characteristics must ASL have to fit Noam Chomsky's conception of a language? Do you think humans are genetically predisposed to acquire a language such as ASL?

- If Chomsky is correct about the language acquisition device, why do children raised in isolation not develop language naturally? Why do adults have such difficulty learning a second language?

- Why is it difficult to set up an experiment on the effects of children's TV viewing? Why are results from TV viewing experiments so inconclusive?

- In this chapter, various negative outcomes of child care outside the home were mentioned, such as a lack of politeness and compliance. Do you think such outcomes are related to cultural views of the purpose of preschool programs?

LOOKING BACK

How do children's bodies and nutritional requirements change during the preschool years?

1. Children's physical growth during the preschool period proceeds steadily. Differences in growth rate reflect individual differences, gender, and economic status. In addition to gaining height and weight, the body of the preschooler undergoes changes in shape and structure. Children grow more slender, and their bones and muscles strengthen.

2. Preschoolers need less food than they did in the early years. Primarily, they require balanced nutrition. If parents and caregivers provide a good variety of healthful foods, children will, in general, naturally achieve an appropriate intake of nutrients.

What health problems potentially affect preschool children?

3. Obesity is caused by both genetic and environmental factors. One strong environmental influence appears to be parents and caregivers, who may substitute their own interpretations of their children's food needs for the children's internal tendencies and controls.

4. Children in the preschool years are susceptible to a range of dangerous diseases. In the economically developed world, immunization programs have largely controlled most life-threatening diseases during those years. However, in economically disadvantaged sectors of the world—and in some areas of the United States—immunization is not completely effective.

How do preschool children's brains and physical skills develop?

5. Brain growth is particularly rapid during the preschool years, with the number of interconnections among cells and the amount of myelin around neurons increasing greatly.

Through the process of lateralization, the two halves of the brain begin to specialize in somewhat different tasks—a process partially influenced by gender and culture. However, despite lateralization, the two hemispheres function as a unit and in fact differ only slightly.

6. Both gross and fine motor skills advance rapidly during the preschool years, a time when children are extraordinarily active. During this time, gender differences in gross motor skill levels begin to emerge clearly, fine motor skills are honed by practice, and handedness begins to assert itself, with the great majority of children turning out right-handed.

How does Jean Piaget interpret cognitive development during the preschool years?

7. The intellectual development of preschoolers, which is rapid and dramatic, has been observed and interpreted by numerous theoreticians. Among the most influential is Jean Piaget, whose preoperational stage of cognitive development coincides with these years.

8. During Piaget's preoperational stage, children are as yet unable to perform mental operations: organized, formal, logical thinking. However, their cognitive abilities involve symbolic function, which permits quicker and more effective thinking than in the previous stage. This is because the ability to manipulate mental representations provides freedom from the limitations of sensorimotor learning. According to Piaget, improved cognitive abilities in the preoperational period enable significant improvements in language.

9. Piaget focuses on certain limitations of children's thinking during the preoperational stage, including centration (concentration on limited aspects of stimuli), egocentric thought (thinking that fails to take into account others' viewpoints), and an imperfect understanding of transformation (the interim processes involved in changes of state).

10. According to Piaget, children in the preoperational stage do engage in intuitive thought for the first time, actively applying rudimentary reasoning skills to the acquisition of world knowledge. Their intuitive thinking leads to other advances—such as an understanding of the concepts of functionality and identity—that position them for the major cognitive changes that attend the next stage of development. Their main deficit is in failing to grasp conservation, the notion that the quantity of objects is unaffected by changes in their appearance.

How do other views of cognitive development differ from Piaget's?

11. More recent work by developmental researchers suggests that Piaget's views of children's development, though based on gifted intuitions and intensive observations, focused excessively on children's limitations rather than on their capabilities. These researchers have found evidence of significantly greater cognitive capabilities in preschoolers than Piaget proposed.

12. A different approach to cognitive development is taken by proponents of information-processing theories. One focus of these researchers is on ways preschoolers store and recall information in the form or memories. They find that preschool children's autobiographical memories, inaccessible or unreliable at first, begin to achieve some degree of accuracy after age 3. Another important focus is on the effects on cognitive development of quantitative changes in information-processing abilities (such as attention). They conclude that changes in preschoolers' cognitive abilities are more gradual and more purely quantitative than Piaget theorized.

13. Lev Vygotsky's view of children's learning is becoming increasingly influential. He pro-

poses that the nature and progress of children's cognitive development are dependent on the children's social and cultural context. According to Vygotsky, children's cognitive abilities are developed in socially supported ways as children and others work together to solve problems that reside in the children's zone of proximal development—the level of cognitive skill at which the children can almost, but not quite, perform a task.

How do children's linguistic abilities develop in the preschool years?

14. The burst in language ability that occurs during the preschool years is dramatic. Children rapidly progress from two-word utterances to longer, more sophisticated expressions that reflect their growing vocabularies and emerging grasp of grammar. They also proceed along a continuum from private speech to more social speech.

15. One theory of how humans develop language is the learning theory approach, which assumes that adults and children use basic behavioral processes—such as conditioning, reinforcement, and shaping—in language learning. A radically different approach is proposed by Noam Chomsky, who holds that humans are genetically endowed with a language-acquisition device, which permits them to detect and use the principles of universal grammar that underlie all languages.

What effects does television have on preschoolers?

16. Television has become a ubiquitous presence in children's lives in the United States and other developed countries. The effects of television on preschool children are unclear. Although preschoolers' comprehension of TV storylines is imperfect, they can decode facial expressions accurately. Preschoolers' sustained exposure to emotions and situations that are not representative of the real world have raised concerns about children's TV viewing. On the other hand, the fact that preschoolers can derive meaning from television programs has led to such targeted programs as *Sesame Street*, designed to bring about cognitive gains in viewers.

What kinds of preschool educational programs are available in the United States, and what effects do they have?

17. Early childhood educational programs, offered as center-based or school-based day care or as preschool, can lead to cognitive and social advances. The quality of such programs largely determines their effectiveness, with staff expertise, curriculum, group size, and caregiver–child ratios being factors most directly influencing quality.

18. The United States lacks a coordinated national policy on preschool education, an unusual characteristic among developed nations. Federal neglect in this area reflects systemic factors relating to the federal–state division of responsibility, tradition, and the low status of preschools in the United States.

19. The major federal initiative in U.S. preschool education has been the Head Start program. Head Start, aimed at less advantaged children, has yielded mixed results: no permanent gains in IQ scores, but an increased likelihood of good school adjustment and somewhat higher academic performance, and a decreased likelihood of retention in grade and assignment to special education classes.

20. Although it may not be either advisable or effective to push preschool children aggressively toward higher academic achievement, providing an individually tailored educational program that is developmentally appropriate and set in a good social context creates a supportive atmosphere in which children can pursue their own learning and increase their academic readiness.

KEY TERMS AND CONCEPTS

obesity (p. 218)

lateralization (p. 220)

handedness (p. 222)

preoperational stage (p. 225)

operations (p. 225)

centration (p. 226)

egocentric thought (p. 227)

transformation (p. 227)

intuitive thought (p. 228)

conservation (p. 229)

autobiographical memory (p. 232)

zone of proximal development (ZPD) (p. 234)

syntax (p. 236)

grammar (p. 236)

private speech (p. 237)

social speech (p. 238)

learning theory approach (p. 238)

universal grammar (p. 239)

language-acquisition device (LAD) (p. 239)

day care centers (p. 243)

preschools (or nursery schools) (p. 244)

school day care (p. 244)

CHAPTER 8

THE PRESCHOOL YEARS

Social and Personality Development

CHAPTER OUTLINE

PROLOGUE: CAUTION—MORPHING MAY BE HAZARDOUS TO A TEACHER

LOOKING AHEAD

FORMING A SENSE OF SELF

Self-concept: Thinking about the self

Psychosocial development

Developmental Diversity

Developing Racial and Ethnic Awareness

Gender identity: Developing femaleness and maleness

Review and Rethink

PRESCHOOLERS' SOCIAL WORLDS

Preschool social life: The development of friendships

Playing by the rules: The work of play

Discipline: Teaching desired behavior

Directions in Development

Successful Parenting: Teaching Parents to Parent

Child abuse and psychological maltreatment: The grim side of family life

Speaking of Development

David S. Kurtz

Resilience: Overcoming the odds

The Informed Consumer of Development

Disciplining Children

Review and Rethink

MORAL DEVELOPMENT AND AGGRESSION

Developing morality: Following society's rights and wrongs

Aggression and violence in preschoolers

The Informed Consumer of Development

Increasing Moral Behavior and Reducing Aggression in Preschoolers

Review and Rethink

LOOKING BACK

KEY TERMS AND CONCEPTS

PROLOGUE: CAUTION—MORPHING MAY BE HAZARDOUS TO A TEACHER

It's 8:30 A.M. and 30 preschoolers are kicking and karate-chopping their way into Fannie Elliott's classroom.

Ms. Elliott, a teacher at Kedren Headstart Preschool in Los Angeles, is aghast. "Why," she asks the four-year-olds, "do you do what you do?" Still breathless from their romp, they shout almost in unison: "We are the Power Rangers."

Like many grown-ups these days, Ms. Elliott lives in a strange world in which, at any moment, small children may suddenly turn into frenzied, brawling boxers. Emulating the teenage heroes of the hit television show "The Mighty Morphin Power Rangers," legions of tots are fighting in classrooms. . . .

"One simply has to say 'Trini' [a ranger's name] and abracadabra, the little curmudgeons transform before my very eyes into an entire martial-arts army," Ms. Elliott says. First come grunts and groans, then cries of "Hi-Yah!" as the children's eyes take on a bewitched glint. Soon the classroom erupts into a Bruce Lee festival, she says, as the children "tumble and run around so the enemy won't attack them." (Pereira, 1994, p. A1)

LOOKING AHEAD

Ms. Elliott's experience is not unique: A poll of preschool teachers found that 96 percent had witnessed a Morphin-inspired act of aggression (Carlsson-Paige & Levin, 1994).

Why is the aggression displayed by characters in such television shows as the *Mighty Morphin Power Rangers* so appealing to preschool-age viewers, and does observing fictional violence lead to actual aggression? More broadly, what are the factors that determine how preschoolers interact with one another, and how does personality and social development proceed during this period?

These and many other questions are addressed in this chapter. We begin by examining how preschool-age children continue to form a sense of self, focusing on how they develop their self-concepts. We especially examine issues of self relating to gender, a central aspect of children's views of themselves and others.

Preschoolers' social lives are the focus of the next part of the chapter. We look at how children play with one another, examining the various types of play. We consider how parents and other authority figures use discipline to shape children's behavior. We also look at a grimmer side of family interaction: child abuse and psychological maltreatment.

Finally, we examine two sides of the coin of preschoolers' social behavior: moral development and aggression. We consider how children develop a notion of right and wrong, and how that development can lead them to be helpful to others. We also look at the other side of the coin—aggression—and we examine the factors that lead preschoolers to behave in a way that hurts others. We end on an optimistic note: considering how we may help preschoolers to be more moral, and less aggressive, individuals.

In sum, after reading this chapter, you'll be able to answer these questions:

♦ How do preschool children develop a concept of themselves?

♦ How do children develop a sense of racial identity and gender?

♦ In what sorts of social relationships do preschoolers engage?

◆   How do the nature and function of play change over time?

◆   What sorts of disciplinary styles do parents employ, and what effects do they have?

◆   What factors contribute to child abuse and neglect?

◆   How do children develop a moral sense?

◆   Is aggression normal in preschoolers, and how does it develop?

FORMING A SENSE OF SELF

Although the question "Who am I?" is not explicitly posed by most preschoolers, it underlies a considerable amount of development during the preschool years. During this period, children wonder about the nature of the self, and the way they answer the "Who am I?" question may affect them for the rest of their lives.

SELF-CONCEPT: THINKING ABOUT THE SELF

If you ask preschoolers to specify what makes them different from other children, they readily respond with answers like, "I'm a good runner" or "I like to color" or "I'm a big girl." Such answers relate to **self-concept**—their identity, or their set of beliefs about what they are like as individuals (Eder, 1990; Breakwell, 1992; Hattie, 1992).

The statements that compose children's self-concepts are not necessarily accurate. In fact, preschool youngsters typically overestimate their skills and knowledge across all domains of expertise. Consequently, their view of the future is quite rosy: They expect to win the next game they play, to beat all opponents in an upcoming race, and even to write great stories when they grow up. Even when they have just experienced failure at a task, they are likely to expect to do well in the future (Stipek & Hoffman, 1980; Ruble, 1983; Damon & Hart, 1988).

Preschoolers also begin to develop a view of self that reflects the way their particular culture considers the self. Such views pervade a culture, sometimes in subtle ways. For instance, one well-known saying in Western societies states that "the squeaky wheel gets the grease." On the other hand, children in Asian cultures are exposed to a different perspective; they are told that "the nail that stands out gets pounded down." Such adages represent two very different views of the world. In the view that predominates in Western cultures, one should seek to get the attention of others by standing out and making one's needs known. In contrast, the predominant Asian perspective suggests that individuals should attempt to blend in and refrain from making themselves distinctive (Markus & Kitayama, 1991; Triandis, 1995).

Such varying philosophies may lead to differences in how children begin to view the self during the preschool years. Asian societies tend to have a **collectivistic orientation**, promoting the notion of interdependence. People in such cultures tend to regard themselves as parts of a larger social network in which they are interconnected with others.

In contrast, children in Western cultures are more likely to develop an independent view of the self, reflecting an **individualistic orientation** that emphasizes personal identity and uniqueness of the individual. They are more apt to see themselves as self-contained and autonomous, in competition with others for scarce resources. Consequently, children in Western cultures are more likely to focus on their uniqueness and what sets them apart from others—what makes them special.

In sum, preschoolers' self-concepts are a result not only of how their parents treat them. Additional influences are the views of their society and their exposure to the dominant philosophy of their culture (Marjoribanks, 1994).

PSYCHOSOCIAL DEVELOPMENT

According to psychoanalyst Erik Erikson (1963), by the time children reach the preschool years, they have already passed through several stages of psychosocial development. As we

---

self-concept   *peoples' identity, or their set of beliefs about what they are like as individuals*

collectivistic orientation   *the orientation promoting the notion of interdependence in which people tend to regard themselves as parts of a larger social network*

individualistic orientation   *the orientation that emphasizes personal identity and uniqueness of the individual*

discussed in Chapter 6, **psychosocial development** encompasses changes both in the understandings individuals have of themselves as members of society, and in their comprehension of the meaning of others' behavior.

Erikson suggests that, throughout life, society and culture present particular challenges, which shift as people age. As we noted in Chapter 6, Erikson suggests that people pass through eight distinct stages, each of which necessitates resolution of a crisis or conflict.

In the early part of the preschool period, children enter the **autonomy-versus-shame-and-doubt stage** (18 months to 3 years). During this period, children develop independence and autonomy if parents encourage exploration and freedom. On the other hand, if they are restricted and protected, children feel shame, self-doubt, and unhappiness.

The preschool years also encompass the **initiative-versus-guilt stage**, which lasts from about age 3 to age 6. It is during this period that children's views of themselves undergo major change as preschoolers face conflicts between, on the one hand, the desire to act independently of their parents and, on the other hand, the guilt that comes from the unintended consequences of their actions. In essence, preschoolers come to realize that they are people in their own right, and they begin to make decisions and to shape the kind of individuals they will become.

psychosocial development   the approach that encompasses changes both in the understanding individuals have of themselves as members of society, and in their comprehension of the meaning of others' behavior

autonomy-versus-shame-and-doubt stage   the period during which children develop independence and autonomy if parents encourage exploration and freedom

initiative-versus-guilt stage   the period when preschoolers come to realize that they are people in their own right, and they begin to make decisions and to shape the kind of people that they will become

Developmental Diversity

Developing Racial and Ethnic Awareness

The preschool years mark an important turning point for children. Their answer to the question of who they are begins to take into account their racial and ethnic identity.

For most preschoolers, racial awareness comes relatively early. Certainly, even infants are able to distinguish different skin colors; their perceptual abilities allow for such color distinctions quite early in life. However, it is only later that children begin to attribute meaning to different racial characteristics. By the time they are 3 or 4 years of age, preschoolers distinguish between blacks and whites and begin to understand the significance that society places on racial membership.

Furthermore, some preschoolers begin to have preferential feelings for members of their own racial group over others (Katz, 1976). On the other hand, many minority children feel ambivalence over the meaning of their racial identity. Some preschoolers experience **race dissonance**, the phenomenon in which minority youngsters indicate preferences for white values or people. Thus, some studies find that as many as 90 percent of African-American children, when asked about their reactions to drawings of black and white children, react more negatively to the drawings of black children than to those of white children. However, these negative reactions did not translate into lower self-esteem for the African-American subjects. Instead, their preferences appear to be a result of the powerful influence of the dominant white culture, rather than a disparagement of their own racial characteristics (N. Holland, 1994).

Ethnic identity emerges somewhat later. For instance, in one study of Mexican-American ethnic awareness, preschoolers displayed only a limited knowledge of their ethnic identity. However, as they became older, their understanding of their racial background grew in both magnitude and complexity. In addition, those preschoolers who were bilingual, speaking both Spanish and English, were most apt to be aware of their racial identity (Bernal, 1994).

By the time they are 3 or 4 years of age, preschoolers distinguish between members of different races and begin to understand the significance of race in society.

race dissonance   the phenomenon in which minority children indicate preferences for majority values or people

If parents react positively to this transformation toward independence, they help their children resolve the inherent pull—between taking initiative and experiencing guilt—that is characteristic of this period. Conversely, parents who discourage their children's efforts to seek independence may contribute to a sense of guilt that persists throughout their lives.

GENDER IDENTITY: DEVELOPING FEMALENESS AND MALENESS

Boys' awards: Very Best Thinker, Most Eager Learner, Most Imaginative, Most Enthusiastic, Most Scientific, Best Friend, Mr. Personality, Hardest Worker, Best Sense of Humor.

Girls' awards: All-Around Sweetheart, Sweetest Personality, Cutest Personality, Best Sharer, Best Artist, Biggest Heart, Best Manners, Best Helper, Most Creative.

What's wrong with this picture? To one parent, whose daughter received one of the girls' awards during a kindergarten graduation ceremony, quite a bit. While the girls were getting pats on the back for their pleasing personalities, the boys were receiving awards for their intellectual and analytical skills (Deveny, 1994).

Such a situation is not rare: Girls and boys often live in very different worlds. Differences in the ways in which males and females are treated begin at birth (as we noted in Chapter Six), continue during the preschool years, and—as we'll see later—extend throughout the life span.

Gender, the sense of being male or female, is well established by the time children reach the preschool years. (As we first noted in Chapter 6, "gender" and "sex" do not mean the same thing. *Sex* typically refers to sexual anatomy and sexual behavior, whereas *gender* refers to the perception of maleness or femaleness related to membership in a given society.) By the age of 2, children consistently label themselves and those around them as male or female (Fagot & Leinbach, 1993; Signorella, Bigler, & Liben, 1993; Poulin-Dubois et al., 1994).

One way in which gender is manifested is in play. During the preschool years, boys increasingly play with boys and girls with girls, a trend that increases during middle childhood. Actually, girls begin the process of preferring same-sex playmates a little earlier than

During the preschool period, differences in play, relating to gender, become more pronounced. In addition, boys tend to play with boys, and girls with girls.

do boys. Girls first have a clear preference for interacting with other girls at age 2, while boys do not show much preference for same-sex partners until age 3 (Fagot, 1991; Lloyd & Duveen, 1991; Serbin, Moller, Powlishta, & Gulko, 1991; Benenson, 1994; Ramsey, 1995).

Such same-sex preferences appear in many cultures. For instance, studies of kindergartners in mainland China show no examples of mixed-gender play. Similarly, gender outweighs ethnic variables when it comes to play: A Hispanic boy would rather play with a Caucasian boy than with a Hispanic girl (Whiting & Edwards, 1988; Shepard, 1991; Fishbein & Imai, 1993; Martin, 1993; Turner, Gervai, & Hinde, 1993).

Preschoolers also begin to hold expectations about appropriate behavior for girls and boys. In fact, their expectations about gender-appropriate behavior are even more rigid and gender-stereotyped than are those of adults, and they may be less flexible during the preschool years than at any other point in the life span. For instance, beliefs in gender stereotypes become more pronounced up to age 5, and they have already started to become somewhat less rigid by age 7. On the other hand, gender expectations do not disappear, and the content of gender stereotypes held by preschoolers is similar to that held traditionally by adults in society (Urberg, 1982; Golombok & Fivush, 1994).

And what is the nature of preschoolers' gender expectations? Like adults, preschoolers expect that males are more apt to have traits involving competence, independence, forcefulness, and competitiveness. In contrast, females are viewed as more likely to have traits such as warmth, expressiveness, nurturance, and submissiveness. Although these are *expectations* and say nothing about the way that men and women actually behave, such expectations both provide the lens through which preschoolers view the world and affect their own behavior and the way they interact with their peers and with adults (Signorella et al., 1993).

The prevalence and strength of preschoolers' gender expectations, and differences in behavior between boys and girls, have proven puzzling. Why should gender play such a powerful role during the preschool years (as well as during the rest of the life span)? Developmental researchers have proposed several explanations.

Biological Perspectives on Gender.   Recall that gender relates to the sense of being male or female, whereas sex refers to the physical characteristics that differentiate males and females. It would hardly be surprising to find that the physical characteristics associated with sex might themselves lead to gender differences, and this in fact has been shown to be true.

For example, some research has focused on girls whose mothers had, prior to being aware that they were pregnant, inadvertently taken drugs that contained high levels of *androgens* (male hormones). These androgen-exposed girls are more likely to display behaviors associated with male stereotypes than are their sisters who were not exposed to androgens (Money & Ehrhardt, 1972). Androgen-exposed girls prefer boys as playmates and spend more time than other girls playing with toys associated with the male role, such as cars and trucks. Similarly, girls prenatally exposed to unusually high levels of female hormones are apt to display more behaviors that are stereotypically female than is typical (Berenbaum & Hines, 1992; Hines & Kaufman, 1994).

Moreover, as we first noted in Chapter 7, some research suggests that biological differences exist in the structure of female and male brains. For instance, part of the *corpus callosum*, the bundle of nerves connecting the hemispheres of the brain, is proportionally larger in women than in men (Whitelson, 1989). To some theoreticians, evidence such as this suggests that gender differences may be produced by biological factors.

Before accepting such contentions, however, it is important to note that alternative explanations abound. For example, it may be that the corpus callosum is proportionally larger in women as a result of certain kinds of experiences that influence brain growth in particular ways. If this is true, environmental experience produces biological change—and not the other way around.

identification   *the process in which children attempt to be similar to their same-sex parent, incorporating the parent's attitudes and values*

In sum, as in many other domains involving the interaction of inherited, biological characteristics and environmental influences, it is difficult to attribute behavioral characteristics unambiguously to biological factors. Because of this difficulty, we must consider other explanations for gender differences.

Psychoanalytic Perspectives.   You may recall from Chapter 1 that Freud's psychoanalytic theory suggests that we move through a series of stages related to biological urges. To Freud, the preschool years encompass the *phallic stage*, in which the focus of a child's pleasure relates to genital sexuality. Freud suggests that the anatomical differences between males and females become particularly evident to preschoolers, and that at about the age of 5, boys begin to develop sexual interests in their mothers, viewing their fathers as rivals. As a consequence, boys conceive a desire to kill their fathers—just as Oedipus did in the ancient Greek tragedy. However, because they view their fathers as all-powerful, boys develop a fear of retaliation, which takes the form of *castration anxiety*. To overcome this fear, boys repress their desires for their mothers and instead begin to identify with their fathers, attempting to be as similar to them as possible. **Identification** is the process in which children attempt to be similar to their same-sex parent, incorporating the parent's attitudes and values.

Girls, according to Freud, go through a different process. They begin to feel sexual attraction toward their fathers and experience *penis envy*—a view that not unexpectedly has led to accusations that Freud viewed women as inferior to men. To resolve their penis envy, girls ultimately identify with their mothers, attempting to be as similar to them as possible.

In the cases of both boys and girls, the ultimate result of identifying with the same-sex parent is that the children adopt their parents' gender attitudes and values. In this way, says Freud, society's expectations about the ways females and males "ought" to behave are perpetuated into new generations.

If you are like many people, you may find it difficult to accept Freud's elaborate explanation of gender differences. So do most developmental specialists, who believe that gender development is best explained by other mechanisms. In part, they base their criticisms of Freud on the lack of scientific support for his theories. For example, children learn gender stereotypes much earlier than the age of 5. Furthermore, this learning occurs even in single-parent households. Conversely, some aspects of psychoanalytic theory have

According to social learning approaches, children observe the behavior of same-sex adults and come to imitate it.

been supported, such as findings indicating that preschoolers whose same-sex parents support sex-stereotyped behavior tend to demonstrate that behavior also. Still, far simpler processes can account for this phenomenon, and many developmental researchers have searched for explanations of gender differences other than Freud's (Mussen, 1969; Maccoby, 1980).

Social-learning Approaches. According to social-learning approaches, children learn gender-related behavior and expectations from their observation of others. In this view, children watch the behavior of their parents, teachers, and even peers. Their observation of the rewards that these others attain for acting in a gender-appropriate manner leads them to conform to such behavior themselves.

The media, and in particular television, also play a role in perpetuating traditional views of gender-related behavior from which preschoolers may learn. For instance, TV shows typically define female characters in terms of their relationships with males. Furthermore, females are more apt to appear with males, whereas female-female relationships are relatively uncommon. Also, females appear as victims far more often than do males (Mackey & Hess, 1982; Signorelli, 1987; Condry, 1989).

Television also presents men and women in traditional gender roles. Although such shows as *ER* and *Murphy Brown* portray women in atypical, counter-stereotypical roles, these shows generally go unwatched by preschoolers. Instead, preschoolers are exposed to repeats of older programs such as *Leave It to Beaver* and *The Brady Bunch*, which portray women and men in highly traditional roles. Such models, according to social-learning theory, are apt to have a powerful influence on preschoolers' definitions of appropriate behavior (Signorelli, 1990).

In some cases, learning of social roles does not involve models, but occurs more directly. For example, most of us have heard preschoolers being told by their parents to act like a "little girl" or "little man." What this generally means is that girls should behave politely and courteously, or that boys should be tough and stoic—traits associated with society's traditional stereotypes of men and women. Such direct training sends a clear message about the behavior expected of a preschooler.

Cognitive Approaches. In the view of some theorists, the desire to form a clear sense of identity leads children to establish a *gender identity*, a sense of themselves as male or female. To do this, they develop a **gender schema**, a cognitive framework that organizes information relevant to gender (Bem, 1987; Stangor, Lynch, Changming, & Glass, 1992).

Gender schemas are developed early in life, forming a lens through which preschoolers view the world. For instance, preschoolers use their increasing cognitive abilities to develop "rules" about what is right, and what is inappropriate, for males and females. Thus, some girls decide that wearing pants is inappropriate for a female, and they apply the rule so rigidly that they refuse to wear anything but dresses. Or a preschool boy may reason that since makeup is typically worn by females, it is inappropriate for him to wear makeup even when he is in a preschool play and all the other boys and girls are wearing it.

Can we reduce the objectionable consequences of viewing the world in terms of gender schemas? According to Sandra Bem, one way is to encourage children to be **androgynous**, a state in which gender roles encompass characteristics thought typical of both sexes. For instance, androgynous males may be encouraged to be assertive (typically viewed as a male-appropriate trait) but at the same time to be warm and tender (usually viewed as female-appropriate traits). Similarly, girls might be encouraged to be both empathetic and tender (typically seen as female-appropriate traits), and competitive, aggressive, and independent (typical male-appropriate traits).

Like the other approaches to gender development (summarized in Table 8-1), the cognitive perspective does not imply that differences between the two sexes are in any way

gender schema *a cognitive framework that organizes information relevant to gender*

androgynous *a state in which gender roles encompass characteristics thought typical of both sexes*

TABLE 8-1

FOUR APPROACHES TO GENDER DEVELOPMENT

Perspective	Key Concepts
Biological	Inborn, genetic factors produce gender differences.
Psychoanalytic	Gender development is the result of moving through a series of stages related to biological urges.
Social learning	Children learn gender-related behavior and expectations from their observation of others' behavior.
Cognitive	Through the use of gender schemas, developed early in life, preschoolers form a lens through which they view the world. They use their increasing cognitive abilities to develop "rules" about what is appropriate for males and females.

improper or inappropriate. Instead, it suggests that preschoolers should be taught to treat others as individuals. Furthermore, preschoolers need to learn the importance of fulfilling their own talents, acting as individuals and not as representatives of a particular gender.

Review and Rethink

REVIEW

◆ During the preschool years, children develop their self-concepts, beliefs about themselves that they derive from their own perceptions, their parents' behaviors, and society.

◆ According to Erik Erikson's psychosocial development theory, preschool children are mainly dealing with their desire to achieve a certain amount of autonomy and independence from their parents, as well as feeling guilty about this desire.

◆ Racial and ethnic awareness begins to form in the preschool years. Members of minority groups may experience race dissonance before establishing a sense of identity with their race and ethnicity.

◆ Gender awareness also develops in the preschool years. Explanations of this phenomenon, which emphasizes the action of universal factors within the individual, include purely biological explanations and psychoanalytical explanations such as Freud's.

◆ While the social-learning approach to explaining gender expectations focuses on the influence of society, the cognitive approach focuses on the individual's formation of a cognitively based gender schema.

RETHINK

◆ Is an individual's self-concept fully formed by the time he or she reaches adulthood? What processes might influence an adult's self-concept?

◆ How would you relate Erikson's stages of trust-versus-mistrust, autonomy-versus-shame-and-doubt, and initiative-versus-guilt to the issue of secure attachment discussed in an earlier chapter?

◆ How might the black power and black pride movements of the 1960s and 1970s have addressed issues of self-concept for African-Americans? In what ways might these movements have affected white Americans' self-concepts?

◆   What are the distinctions among gender differences, gender expectations, and gender stereotypes? How are they related?

◆   Why do cognitive approaches to gender differences appear to offer the most hope of causing changes in gender expectations? What is a gender schema, what are its contents, and how might a schema change over time?

PRESCHOOLERS' SOCIAL WORLDS

To Nicole and Diana Schoo, the movie *Home Alone* probably didn't seem too funny. For them, the tale of a child mistakenly left behind by his vacationing parents was all too similar to their own experience. In their case, though, their abandonment was no comic error: Their parents intentionally left them behind.

Diana, age 4, and her older sister Nicole, age 9, were found at home—alone— while their parents were on a 9-day vacation in Acapulco, Mexico. It was not the first time the girls had been left unattended; their parents had left them unaccompanied while they went off on a 4-day visit to Massachusetts the previous summer.

Local authorities who learned of the girls' plight arrested the Schoo parents on their return from Acapulco. The Schoos faced charges on two felony counts of child abandonment and cruelty to children, and a misdemeanor charge of child endangerment.

For an increasing number of preschoolers, life does not mirror what we see in reruns of *The Cosby Show* or *Leave It to Beaver*. Many face the realities of an increasingly complicated world. For instance, as we'll discuss in more detail in Chapter 10, children are increasingly likely to live with only one parent. In 1960, less than 10 percent of all children under the age of 18 lived with one parent; by 1989, almost a quarter lived in a single-parent household. In fact, in 1993, almost 50 percent of all children experienced their parents' divorce and lived with one parent for an average of 5 years (Carnegie Task Force, 1994).

Still, for most children the preschool years are not a time of upheaval and turmoil. Instead, the period encompasses a growing interaction with the world at large. For instance, preschoolers begin to develop genuine friendships with other youngsters, in which close ties emerge.

PRESCHOOL SOCIAL LIFE: THE DEVELOPMENT OF FRIENDSHIPS

When Juan was 3, he had his first best friend, Emilio. Juan and Emilio, who lived in the same apartment building in San Jose, were inseparable. They played incessantly with toy cars, racing them up and down the apartment hallways until some of the neighbors began to complain about the noise. They pretended to read to one another, and sometimes they slept over at each other's apartment—a big step for a three-year-old. Neither boy seemed more joyful than when he was with his "best friend"—the term each used for the other.

At about the age of 3, children develop real friendships. Although they play together earlier, much of their activity involves simply being in the same place at the same time, without real social interaction.

Something changes around age 3. Peers come to be seen not as miniature, less powerful adults, but as individuals who hold some special qualities and rewards. Although preschoolers' relations with adults reflect children's needs for care, protection, and direction, their relations with peers are based more on the desire for companionship, play, and entertainment.

Furthermore, as they get older, preschoolers' conception of friendship gradually evolves. With age, they come to view friendship as a continuing state, a stable relationship that has meaning beyond the immediate moment, one that bears implications for future activity (Furman & Bierman, 1983).

The quality of interactions that children have with friends changes during the preschool period. The focus of friendship in 3-year-olds is the enjoyment of carrying out shared activities—doing things together and playing jointly. Older preschoolers, however, pay more attention to abstract concepts such as trust, support, and shared interests (Park, Lay, & Ramsay, 1993).

Even at the age of 3, preschoolers are interested in maintaining smooth social relations with their friends. They try to create a sense of agreement with one another and attempt to avoid disagreement. In fact, they are more concerned with avoiding disagreement than are older preschoolers, who more readily accept dissension as the occasional outcome of a social relationship (Gottman & Parkhurst, 1980).

Why Are Some Children More Popular than Others?   Not all preschoolers form close friendships with others in the way that Juan and Emilio did. In fact, some children have relatively few friends, experiencing difficulty in interacting with others and forming stable relationships.

Several qualities are associated with popularity during the preschool years, some of which persist throughout much of the life span. For instance, one unfortunate by-product of society's emphasis on physical attractiveness is the "beautiful is good" stereotype, which suggests that physical attractiveness is linked to other positive qualities. Not only are physically attractive preschoolers judged more likable, by both peers and adults, than less attractive preschoolers, but their behavior is interpreted in light of their attractiveness (Dion, 1972). As a result, physically attractive children who misbehave are judged more leniently than those who are less attractive. In sum, those who are physically attractive are liked more than those who are unattractive, beginning in the preschool years and continuing into old age (Dion, 1972; Berscheid & Walster, 1974; Hatfield & Sprecher, 1986).

But it is not only physical attractiveness that determines popularity. Preschoolers' social skills and behavior play an even more important role. For instance, disliked children are more likely to display aggressive behavior, to be disruptive, and to impose themselves on their peers. They are less cooperative, and they do not take turns (Newcomb, Bukowski, & Pattee, 1993; Mendelson, Aboud, & Lanthier, 1994).

In contrast, children who are more popular are more outgoing and sociable. They speak more, and nonverbally they are more positive, smiling more often than those who are less popular. In general, they have a greater understanding of others' emotions and are more sensitive to the meaning of others' nonverbal behavior (Roopnarine & Honig, 1985; Philippot, Feldman, & McGee, 1990; Garner, Jones, & Miner, 1994).

Improving Children's Social Skills.   Are unpopular preschoolers destined for a life with few friends? Not necessarily. The social skills that make some children more popular than others can be promoted and actually taught by parents and preschool teachers.

For instance, children can be taught to be more cooperative, to share with others, and to play with others in appropriate ways. At the same time, they can be encouraged to decrease the incidence of aggressive behaviors that put others off, and to avoid taking things from others (Roopnarine & Honig, 1985; Bierman, Miller, & Stabb, 1987; Ogilvy, 1994).

In addition, parents can promote positive peer relations by providing a warm, supportive home environment. A good deal of research evidence shows that children with parents who were rejecting or authoritarian tend to be less socially skilled than those with more parental support. The evidence suggests that strong, positive relationships between parents and children facilitate children's relationships with others (Hartup, 1989; Hinde, Tamplin, & Barrett, 1993; Sroufe, 1994).

PLAYING BY THE RULES: THE WORK OF PLAY

In Minka Arafat's class of 3-year-olds, Minnie bounces her doll's feet on the table as she sings softly to herself. Ben pushes his toy car across the floor, making motor noises. Sarah chases Abdul around and around the perimeter of the room.

Categorizing Play. These 3-year-olds are engaged in **functional play**—simple, repetitive activities typical of 3-year-olds. Functional play may involve objects, such as dolls or cars, or repetitive muscular movements like skipping, jumping, or rolling and unrolling a piece of clay. Functional play, then, involves doing something for the sake of being active, rather than with the aim of creating some end product (K.H. Rubin, Fein, & Vandenberg, 1983).

As children get older, functional play declines. By the time they are 4, children become involved in a more sophisticated form of play. In **constructive play** children manipulate objects to produce or build something. A child who builds a house out of Legos or puts a puzzle together is involved in constructive play: He or she has an ultimate goal—the production of something. Such play is not necessarily aimed at creating something novel, for children may repeatedly build a house of blocks, let it fall into disarray, and then rebuild it.

Constructive play permits youngsters to test their developing physical and cognitive skills and to practice their fine muscle movements. They gain experience in solving problems about the ways and the sequences in which things fit together (Tegano, Lookabaugh, May, & Burdette, 1991). They also learn to cooperate with others—a development we observe as the social nature of play shifts during the preschool period.

The Social Aspects of Play. If two preschoolers are sitting at a table side by side, each putting a different puzzle together, are they engaged jointly in play?

According to pioneering work done by Mildred Parten (1932), the answer is yes. She suggests that these preschoolers are engaged in **parallel play**, in which children play with similar toys, in a similar manner, but do not interact with each other. Parallel play is typical for children during the early preschool years. Preschoolers also engage in another form of play, a highly passive one, called **onlooker play**. Here children simply watch others at play, but do not actually participate themselves. They may look on silently, or they may make comments of encouragement or advice.

As they get older, however, preschoolers engage in more sophisticated forms of social play involving a greater degree of interaction. In **associative play** two or more children actu-

functional play   simple, repetitive activities typical of 3-year-olds that may involve objects or repetitive muscular movements

constructive play   play in which children manipulate objects to produce or build something

parallel play   activity in which children play with similar toys, in a similar manner, but do not interact with each other

onlooker play   a passive form of play in which children simply watch others at play but do not actually participate themselves

associative play   activity where two or more children actually interact with one another by sharing or borrowing toys or materials, although they do not do the same thing

In parallel play, children play with similar toys, in a similar manner, but don't necessarily interact with one another.

TABLE 8-2

Type of Play	Definition of Type of Play
Functional play	Functional play involves simple, repetitive activities typical of 3-year-olds. It may involve objects, such as dolls or cars, or repetitive muscular movements like skipping, jumping, or rolling and unrolling a piece of clay.
Constructive play	By the time they are 4, children become involved in more sophisticated play in which they manipulate objects to produce or build something. A child who builds a house out of Legos or puts together a puzzle is involved in constructive play. This type of play permits children to test their developing physical and cognitive skills as well as practice their fine muscle movements.
Parallel play	Children who engage in parallel play use similar toys, in a similar manner, but do not interact with each other. This form of play is typical of children during the early preschool years.
Onlooker play	In onlooker play, children simply watch others at play, but do not actually participate themselves. They may look on silently, or they may make comments of encouragement or advice. This type of play is common among preschoolers.
Associative play	As they get older, preschoolers are involved in the greater degree of interaction of associative play. Here, two or more children actually interact with one another by sharing or borrowing toys or materials, although they do not do the same thing.
Cooperative play	In cooperative play, children genuinely play with one another, taking turns, playing games, or devising contests.

ally interact with one another by sharing or borrowing toys or materials, although they do not do the same thing. In **cooperative play**, children genuinely play with one another, taking turns, playing games, or devising contests. (The various types of play are summarized in Table 8-2.)

Although associative and cooperative play do not typically become prevalent until children reach the end of the preschool years, both the amount and the kind of social experience children have had significantly influence the nature of play. For instance, children who have had substantial preschool experience are apt to engage in more social forms of behavior, such as associative and cooperative play, fairly early in the preschool years than those with less experience (Roopnarine, Johnson, & Hooper, 1994).

Furthermore, solitary and onlooker play continue in the later stages of the preschool period. There are simply times when children prefer to play by themselves. And when newcomers join a group, one strategy for becoming part of the group—often successful—is to engage in onlooker play, waiting for an opportunity to join the play more actively (P.K. Smith, 1978; Howes, Unger, & Seidner, 1989).

Children's cultural background also results in different styles of play. For example, comparisons of Korean-Americans and Anglo-Americans find that Korean-American children engage in a higher proportion of parallel play than do their Anglo-American counterparts, whereas Anglo-American preschoolers are involved in more pretend play (Farver, Kim, & Lee, 1995; see Figure 8-1).

DISCIPLINE: TEACHING DESIRED BEHAVIOR

While no one is looking—she thinks—Kerry goes into her brother Jesse's bedroom, where he has been saving the last of his Halloween candy. Just as Kerry takes Jesse's last Reese's Peanut Butter Cup, the children's mother walks into the room and immediately takes in the situation.

If you were Kerry's mother, which of the following reactions seems most reasonable?

1. Tell Kerry that she must go to her room and stay there for the rest of the day, and that

cooperative play   *play in which children genuinely play with one another, taking turns, playing games, or devising contests*

FIGURE 8-1

COMPARING PLAY COMPLEXITY

An examination of Korean-American and Anglo-American preschoolers' play complexity finds clear differences in patterns of play.

(*Source:* Adapted from Farver, Kim, & Lee, 1995).

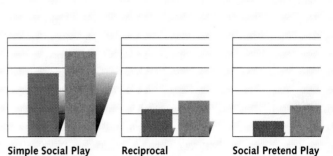

Korean-American

Anglo-American

she is going to lose access to her favorite blanket, the one she sleeps with every night and during naps.

2. Mildly tell Kerry that what she did was not such a good idea, and she shouldn't do it in the future.

3. Explain why her brother Jesse was going to be upset, and tell her that she must go to her room for an hour as punishment.

Each of these three alternative responses represents one of the three major parenting styles that, according to classic research by Diana Baumrind (1971, 1980), characterize most parents' patterns of discipline. **Authoritarian parents** are controlling, punitive, rigid, cold. Their word is law, and they value strict, unquestioning obedience from their children. They also do not tolerate expressions of disagreement.

Permissive parents, in contrast, provide lax and inconsistent feedback. They require

authoritarian parents parents who are controlling, punitive, rigid, cold

permissive parents parents who provide lax and inconsistent feedback

The way in which children are disciplined has important consequences for children's development in a variety of areas.

authoritative parents   *parents who are firm, setting clear and consistent limits*

little of their children, and they do not see themselves as holding much responsibility for how their children turn out.

There are actually two types of permissive parents. *Permissive-indifferent* parents are unusually uninvolved in their children's lives; they show little interest or concern with their children's well-being. In contrast, *permissive-indulgent* parents are more involved with their children, but they place little or no limits or control on their behavior.

Finally, **authoritative parents** are firm, setting clear and consistent limits. Although they tend to be relatively strict, like authoritarian parents, they are more receptive to disagreement from their children. They also try to reason with their children, giving explanations for why they should behave in a particular way and communicating the rationale for any punishment they may impose. The children of authoritative parents are encouraged to be independent. (These different parenting styles are summarized in Table 8-3.)

Does the particular style of parental discipline result in differences in children's behavior? The answer, according to Diana Baumrind, is very much yes—although, as you might expect, there are many exceptions.

Children of authoritarian parents tend to be withdrawn, showing relatively little sociability. They are not very friendly, often behaving uneasily around their peers. Girls who are raised by authoritarian parents are especially dependent on their parents, whereas boys are unusually hostile.

Permissive parents have children who, in many ways, share the undesirable characteristics of children of authoritarian parents. Children with permissive-indifferent parents tend to be dependent and moody, low in social skills, and to have low self-control. Permissive-indulgent parenting results in children with lower self-control and who feel that they are especially privileged. Such children also have lower social skills.

Children of authoritative parents fare best. They generally are independent, friendly with their peers, self-assertive, and cooperative. They have strong motivation to achieve, and they are typically successful and likable.

Clearly, authoritative parents appear to be the most likely to produce successful children. But not always. For instance, in a significant number of cases the children of authoritarian and permissive parents develop quite successfully. Moreover, parents are not entirely consistent: Although the authoritarian, permissive, and authoritative patterns describe general styles, sometimes parents switch from their dominant mode to one of the others. For instance, when a child darts into the street, even the most laid-back and permissive parent is likely to react in an authoritarian manner, laying down strict demands about safety. In

TABLE 8-3

PARENTAL DISCIPLINE STYLES

Type	Characteristics	Relationship with Children
Authoritarian	controlling, punitive, rigid, cold	Their word is law, and they value, strict, unquestioning obedience from their children. They also do not tolerate expressions of disagreement.
Permissive-indifferent	lax and inconsistent feedback	They are usually uninvolved in their children's lives; they show little interest or concern with their children's well-being.
Permissive-indulgent	lax and inconsistent feedback	They are more involved with their children, but they place little or no limits or control on their behavior.
Authoritative	firm, setting clear and consistent limits	Although they tend to be relatively strict, like authoritarian parents, they are more receptive to disagreement from their children and encourage them to be independent. They also try to reason with their children, giving explanations for why they should behave in a particular way and communicating the rationale for any punishment they may impose.

Drawing by R. Chast; ©1995 The New Yorker Magazine, Inc.

such cases, authoritarian styles might be most effective (Kuczynski, 1984; Bayer & Cegala, 1992; Darling & Steinberg, 1993; Steinberg et al., 1994).

Furthermore, the findings regarding childrearing styles are chiefly applicable to Western society. As we discuss in the Directions in Development section, the style of parenting that is most successful may depend quite heavily on the norms of a particular culture—and what parents in a particular culture are taught regarding appropriate childrearing practices (Papps et al., 1995).

Directions in Development

Successful Parenting: Teaching Parents to Parent

Chiao shun. Guan.

When parents in China seek advice on the best childrearing practices, they are likely to encounter these two terms and unlikely to hear about the virtues of authoritative parenting with which parents in Western societies are apt to be regaled. The reason relates not only to differences in parenting advice but also to a wide cultural gulf between Eastern and Western conceptions of childrearing practices.

According to developmental psychologist Ruth Chao, the concept of *chiao shun* suggests that parents should be strict, rigid, and controlling—much like authoritarian parents in the United States. But the rationale behind *chiao shun* is different. *Chiao shun* implies that parents have a duty to train their children to adhere to socially and culturally desirable standards of behavior, particularly those manifested in good school performance (Chao, 1994).

The notion of rigid control of children grows out of the concept of *guan*, which literally means "to govern." But the concept is broader than the literal meaning; it encompasses notions of caring for and loving children. Thus, to provide strict control is a measure of parents' involvement in and concern for the welfare of their children. More broadly, such a notion derives from the teachings of Confucius, who emphasized the importance of maintaining harmonious relations with others.

Chiao shun and *guan* result in views of the most appropriate childrearing practices that are very different from their Western counterparts. Parents in China are encouraged to be highly directive with their children, pushing them to excel and controlling their behavior to a considerably higher degree than parents typically do in Western countries. And it works: Children of Asian parents tend to be quite successful, particularly academically (Steinberg, Dornbusch, & Brown, 1992).

In contrast, the childrearing advice given to parents in the United States conveys a very different message. Parents are generally advised to use authoritative methods, and explicitly to avoid authoritarian measures. Interestingly, though, it wasn't always this way. Until World War II, the point of view that dominated the advice literature was authoritarian, apparently founded on Puritan religious influences that suggested that children had Original Sin or that they needed to have their wills broken (Smuts & Hagen, 1985).

In sum, the childrearing practices that parents are urged to follow reflect cultural perspectives about the nature of children, as well as about the appropriate role of parents. No single parenting pattern or style, then, is likely to be universally appropriate nor invariably to produce successful children. Instead, cultural context must be taken into account.

CHILD ABUSE AND PSYCHOLOGICAL MALTREATMENT: THE GRIM SIDE OF FAMILY LIFE

The figures are gloomy and disheartening: At least five children are killed by their parents or caretakers every day, and 140,000 others are physically injured every year. Overall, more than 3 million children are abused or neglected in the United States annually (Ards & Harrell, 1993; Mones, 1995; U.S. Advisory Board on Child Abuse and Neglect, 1995). The abuse takes several forms, ranging from actual physical abuse to psychological mistreatment (see Figure 8-2).

Physical Abuse.　Although child abuse can occur in any household, regardless of economic well-being or the social status of the parents, it is most frequent in families living in stressful environments. Conditions of poverty, single-parent households, and families with higher-than-average levels of marital conflict create such environments. Child abuse is also related to the presence of violence between spouses (Dodge, Bates, & Pettit, 1990; Margolin, 1995; Milner, 1995).

Children with certain characteristics are more prone to be the victims of child abuse. Abused children are more likely to be fussy, resistant to control, and not readily adaptable to new situations. They have more headaches and stomachaches, experience more bedwetting, are generally more anxious, and may show developmental delays. Moreover, victims are most vulnerable to abuse at certain ages: Both 3- and 4-year-olds, as well as 15- to 17-year-olds, are the most likely to be abused by their parents (Gil, 1970; Steinmetz, 1987; Gelles & Cornell, 1990; Straus & Gelles, 1990; Putnam, 1995).

It is critical to keep in mind that labeling children as being at higher risk for receiving abuse does not make them responsible for their abuse; the family members who carry out

FIGURE 8-2

CHILD ABUSE IN THE UNITED STATES

(*Source*: American Humane Association, 1991.)

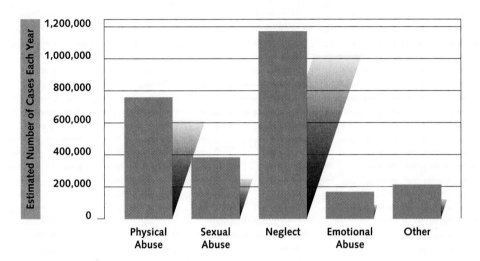

the abuse are at fault. Statistical findings simply suggest that children with such character-istics are more at risk of being the recipients of family violence.

Why does physical abuse occur? Most parents certainly don't intend to abuse their children. In fact, most parents who abuse their children later express bewilderment and dismay at their own behavior.

One reason for child abuse is the vague demarcation between permissible and impermissible forms of physical violence. Societal folklore says that spanking is not merely acceptable, but often necessary and desirable. For example, one survey found that almost half of mothers with children under 4 years of age had spanked their child in the previous week, and almost 20 percent of mothers believe it is appropriate to spank a child less than 1 year of age (Socolar & Stein, 1995).

In a case that shocked the nation, 6-year-old Elisa Izquierdo was the victim of prolonged child abuse throughout her short life. The abuse culminated with her death after her mother—who was convinced that her daughter harbored "evil spirits"—threw her against a concrete wall. When she was found by authorities, there was no part of her body that was not cut or bruised from repeated beatings.

cycle-of-violence hypothesis   *the theory that abuse and neglect suffered by children predispose them as adults to abuse and neglect their own children*

Unfortunately, the line between "spanking" and "beating" is not clear, and spankings begun in anger can escalate easily into abuse. Furthermore, despite common wisdom, the use of physical punishment of any sort is *not* recommended by child-care experts (Committee for Rights and Legal Matters, 1989; Greven, 1990; Welker, 1991). (For a guide to when punishment crosses the line into abuse, see Table 8-4.)

Many other societies do not make the distinctions between acceptable violence and abuse that we find in the United States. For instance, Sweden outlaws *any* form of physical punishment directed toward a child. In many other countries, such as China, social norms work against the use of physical punishment, and its use is rare (Kessen, 1979). In contrast, the values of personal freedom and responsibility prevalent in the United States foster a social climate in which high levels of child abuse occur.

Another factor that leads to high rates of abuse is the privacy with which child care is conducted in Western societies. Unlike other cultures, in which childrearing is seen as the joint responsibility of several people and even society as a whole, in most Western cultures—and particularly the United States—children are raised in private, isolated households. Because child care is seen as the sole responsibility of the parent, other people are typically not available when a parent's patience is tested.

One additional source of abuse is insensitivity to age norms on the part of parents. Abusive caregivers may have unrealistically high expectations regarding children's abilities to be quiet and compliant at a particular age. Their children's failure to meet these unrealistic expectations may provoke abuse (L. Peterson, 1994).

Finally, abuse inflicted on youngsters is often associated with violence that the abusers themselves have suffered as children. According to the **cycle-of-violence hypothesis**, the abuse and neglect that children suffer predispose them as adults to abuse and neglect their own children (Widom, 1989; Dodge et al., 1990).

The cycle-of-violence hypothesis suggests that victims of abuse have learned from their childhood experiences that violence is an appropriate and acceptable form of discipline. Violence is consequently perpetuated from one generation to another, as each generation learns to behave abusively through its participation in an abusive, violent family (Feshbach, 1980; Straus & Gelles, 1990; Ney, Fung, & Wickett, 1993).

Conversely, although many cases exist in which abusive parents have themselves suffered abuse as children, being abused as a child does not inevitably lead to abuse of one's own children. In fact, statistics show that only about one-third of people who were abused

TABLE 8-4

WHAT ARE THE WARNING SIGNS OF CHILD ABUSE?

Because child abuse is typically a secret crime, identifying the victims of abuse is particularly difficult. Still, there are several signs in a child that indicate that he or she is the victim of violence (Robbins, 1990):

- visible, serious injuries that have no reasonable explanation
- bite or choke marks
- burns from cigarettes or immersion in hot water
- feelings of pain for no apparent reason
- fear of adult or care providers
- inappropriate attire in warm weather (long sleeves, long pants, high-necked garments)–possibly to conceal injuries to the neck, arms, and legs
- extreme behavior–highly aggressive, extremely passive, extremely withdrawn
- fear of physical contact

If you suspect a child is a victim of aggression, it is your responsibility to act. Call your local police or the department of social services in your city or state, or call the National Center on Child Abuse and Neglect (Washington, DC) at (202)245-2856. Talk to a teacher or a member of the clergy. Remember, by acting decisively you can literally save someone's life.

or neglected as children abuse their own children; the remaining two-thirds of people abused as children do not turn out to be child abusers. Clearly, suffering abuse as a child is not the full explanation for child abuse in adults.

Psychological Maltreatment.   Child abuse does not necessarily take the form of direct physical injury. In fact, sometimes neglect—such as that inflicted on the children in the Schoo family, described earlier—can be as devastating.

Unlike physical abuse, in which children suffer actual bodily injury and punishment, **psychological maltreatment** occurs when parents or other caregivers harm children's behavioral, cognitive, emotional, or physical functioning (Hart & Brassard, 1987). Psychological maltreatment can occur through either overt behavior or neglect.

For example, abusive parents may frighten, belittle, or humiliate their children, thereby intimidating and harassing them. Children may be made to feel like disappointments or failures, or they may be constantly reminded that they are a burden to their parents. Parents may tell their children that they wish they had never had children and specifically that they wish that their children had never been born. Children may be threatened with abandonment or even death. In other instances, older children may be exploited. They may be forced to seek employment and then to give their earnings to their parents.

In other cases of psychological maltreatment, the abuse takes the form of neglect. Parents may ignore their children or act emotionally unresponsive to them. In such cases, children may be given unrealistic responsibilities or may be left to fend for themselves, as in the case of the Schoo youngsters.

No one knows how much psychological maltreatment occurs each year; figures separating psychological maltreatment from other types of abuse are not routinely gathered. The lack of trustworthy statistics stems from obstacles standing in the way of unambiguously identifying cases of psychological maltreatment. Most such maltreatment occurs in the privacy of people's homes. Furthermore, psychological maltreatment typically causes no physical damage, such as bruises or broken bones, to alert physicians, teachers, and other authorities. Consequently, many cases of psychological maltreatment probably are not identified.

What are the consequences of psychological maltreatment? Although some children are sufficiently resilient to survive the abuse and grow into psychologically healthy adults, in many cases lasting damage results. For example, psychological maltreatment has been associated with low self-esteem, lying, misbehavior, and underachievement in school. In extreme cases, it can produce criminal behavior, aggression, and murder. In other instances, children who have been psychologically maltreated become depressed and even commit suicide (Hart & Brassard, 1987; Vondra, Barnett, & Cicchetti, 1990; Malinosky-Rummell & Hansen, 1993; Leiter & Johnsen, 1994; Perez & Widom, 1994).

RESILIENCE: OVERCOMING THE ODDS

Not all children succumb to the mistreatment and abuse that life thrusts on them. In fact, some do surprisingly well, considering the type of problems they have encountered. What enables some youngsters to overcome stress and trauma that in most cases scars others for life?

Resilience refers to the ability to overcome circumstances that place a child at high risk for psychological or physical damage. Several factors seem to reduce and, in certain cases, eliminate some children's reactions to difficult environments that in others produce profoundly negative consequences, such as extremes of poverty, prenatal stress, or homes that are racked with violence or other forms of social disorder.

According to developmental psychologist Emmy Werner (1995), resilient children have temperaments that evoke positive responses from a wide variety of caregivers. They tend to be affectionate, easygoing, and good-natured. They are easily soothed as infants, and they

psychological maltreatment   abuse that occurs when parents or other caregivers harm children's behavioral, cognitive, emotional, or physical functioning

resilience   the ability to overcome circumstances that place a child at high risk for psychological or physical damage

are able to elicit care from the most nurturant people in whatever environment in which they find themselves. In short, because of their pleasant temperaments, they are able to evoke whatever support is present in a given setting. In a sense, then, resilient children are successful in making their own environments by drawing out behavior in others that is necessary for the child's own development.

Similar traits are associated with resilience in older youngsters. The most resilient school-age children are those who are socially pleasant, outgoing, and have good communication skills. They tend to be relatively intelligent, and they are independent, feeling that they can shape their own fate and are not dependent on others or on luck (Werner & Smith, 1992; Werner, 1993, 1995).

The characteristics of resilient children suggest ways of increasing the chances of children who are at risk from a variety of developmental threats. For instance, in addition to decreasing their exposure to factors that put them at risk in the first place, we need to increase their competence and teach them ways of dealing with their situation. In fact, programs that have been successful in helping especially vulnerable children have a common thread: They provide competent and caring adult models who can teach problem-solving skills and help them to communicate their needs to those who are in a position to aid them (Schorr, 1988; Haggerty, Garmezy, Rutter, & Sherrod, 1994; Hetherington & Blechman, 1996).

Speaking of Development

David S. Kurtz

Born: ···························· 1960

Education: ···················· University of California at Irvine, B.S. in biology and B.A. in psychology; California State University, Fullerton, M.A. in experimental psychology; California School of Professional Psychology, Los Angeles, M.A. and Ph.D. in clinical psychology

Position: ····················· Associate director of the Childhelp Los Angeles Center

Home: ························· Glendale, California

What is it like to pick up the phone and hear the voice of an abused child reaching out for help? Dr. David Kurtz knows.

For most of his 8 years with the Childhelp Los Angeles Center, Dr. Kurtz worked in crisis intervention. He was one of the many counselors working the phones at the National Child Abuse Hotline located at Childhelp.

Currently the associate director of the center, Dr. Kurtz still finds occasion to provide help and support via the phone lines.

"Those who call us with a child-abuse issue may be the parents of an abused child, a neighbor who has witnessed child abuse, or an adult who was a victim of abuse 20 or 30 years ago," says Dr. Kurtz. "But children who call in, or those who represent them, are given priority. They are put at the front of the line.

"For younger children the caller is usually a sibling or an adult who is representing the abused child," he says, adding that there are also occasions when a parent may call about his or her own frustrations with a very young child.

"We often explore developmental issues when parents call us," he notes. "Often we find

The Informed Consumer of Development

Disciplining Children

The question of how best to discipline children has been raised for generations. Answers coming from developmental researchers today include the following (Lamb et al., 1992; Grusec & Goodnow, 1994; Wierson & Forehand, 1994; O'Leary, 1995):

♦ For most children in Western cultures, authoritative parenting is best. Parents should be firm and consistent, providing clear direction for desirable behavior. Reprimands for misbehavior should be immediate and brief. Authoritative disciplinarians provide rules, but they explain why those rules make sense in language that children can understand.

♦ Spanking is never an appropriate discipline technique, according to the American Academy of Pediatrics. Not only is spanking less effective than other techniques in curbing undesireable behavior, but it also leads to additional, unwanted outcomes. For

"Often we find that a significant part of parents' frustration is attributable to their unrealistic expectations of what children are capable of doing at a given age.

"A child is going to be very, very scared and will be dealing with confused feelings of shame, guilt, and fear that the abuser—who is usually a close family member—is going to get into trouble."

that a significant part of parents' frustration is attributable to their unrealistic expectations of what children are capable of doing at a given age.

"An example of this is a highly frustrated woman who called us after returning from a grocery shopping trip with her child. She had a very strong impulse to slap the child, and she was afraid she would lose control. The child kept pulling items off the shelves at the store, and she was convinced the child was doing it purposefully to upset her.

"When we asked how old the child was, she said 10 months. We explained that her child was much too young to be acting purposefully in that way, and that the child was not trying to get at her. Clearly, this parent was not alone. Many parents who have to deal with some sort of disciplinary issue would benefit from a better understanding of child development."

Dr. Kurtz emphasizes the importance of establishing as trusting a relationship as possible with the stressed people who are looking for help on this issue. "When people call, it's essential to build a rapport with them. The general policy at the Hotline is that the counselors do not give their names, but with children we make an exception," he says. "A child is going to be very, very scared and will be dealing with confused feelings of shame, guilt, and fear that the abuser—who is usually a close family member—is going to get into trouble."

instance, children who are spanked are significantly more aggressive toward their peers than are those who have not been spanked (Strassberg, Dodge, Pettit, & Bates, 1994).

♦ Tailor parental discipline to the characteristics of the child and the situation. Keep in mind that—as we first discussed in Chapter 2—children have different temperaments that may predispose them to be more or less accepting of discipline. Try to keep the child's particular personality qualities in mind, and adapt discipline to it.

♦ A related suggestion is more controversial. Lawrence Steinberg and his colleagues (Steinberg et al., 1994) cite evidence that the consequences of authoritarian parenting styles do not appear to be as negative among minority youth as they are among majority youth. These researchers suggest that some children from economically disadvantaged families may benefit from more authoritarian styles of parenting. They believe that authoritarianism may be beneficial for children in unusually difficult living situations. It also may be the case that ethnic and cultural factors lead to differences in the perception of parental authoritarianism. However, this view remains controversial.

♦ Defuse difficult situations with humor and playfulness, and provide alternative activities. Some parents and children engage in repetitive battles, in which each participant vies to be the winner and to make the other party the loser. For instance, bedtime can be the source of a nightly struggle between a resistant child and an insistent parent. Parental strategies for gaining compliance that involve making the situation enjoyable—such as reading a bedtime story or engaging in a nightly "wrestling" match with the child—can defuse potential battles and turn bedtime into an opportunity for fun.

Review and Rethink

REVIEW

♦ In the preschool years, children develop their first true friendships on the basis of personal characteristics, trust, and shared interests. Popularity becomes an issue, influenced by both physical and social characteristics.

♦ The character of preschoolers' play changes over time, growing more sophisticated, interactive, and cooperative, and relying increasingly on social skills.

♦ Disciplinary styles vary individually and from culture to culture. In the United States, parents may be classified as authoritarian, permissive, or authoritative, with the authoritative style being in most cases the most effective.

♦ Owing largely to cultural factors, child abuse is comparatively prevalent in the United States. Abuse can be physical or psychological, and it is associated with both social and personal factors.

♦ According to the cycle-of-violence hypothesis, child abuse may be perpetuated across generations because individuals who were abused as children show a tendency to be abusers as adults.

RETHINK

♦ Do you believe the association between physical attractiveness and popularity is caused by biological or environmental factors? Why?

◆ Are the styles and strategies of children's play that we explored in this chapter, such as parallel play and onlooker play, mirrored in adult life in realms of interaction other than play?

◆ Why might the children of authoritative and of permissive parents equally tend to have sociability problems as adults?

◆ Some people believe that researching and identifying personality traits of abused children, such as fussiness or failure to adapt to new situations, contributes to a tendency to blame the victim. What do you think? Why are such studies conducted?

◆ We have seen that one factor contributing to the prevalence of child abuse in the United States is the strong value placed on individual privacy in this culture. What sorts of policies regarding privacy and child abuse do you think are appropriate? Why?

MORAL DEVELOPMENT AND AGGRESSION

During snack time at preschool playmates Jan and Meg inspected the goodies in their lunch boxes. Jan found two appetizing cream-filled cookies. Meg's snack offered less tempting carrot and celery sticks. As Jan began to munch on one of her cookies Meg looked at the cut-up vegetables and burst into tears. Jan responded to Meg's distress by offering her companion one of her cookies, which Meg gladly accepted. Jan was able to put herself in Meg's place, understand Meg's thoughts and feelings, and act compassionately. (Katz, 1989, p. 213)

In this short scenario we see many of the key elements of morality, as it is played out among preschoolers. Changes in children's views of morality and in their moral conduct are an important element of growth during the preschool years.

Yet, at the same time these changes are occurring, both the degree and the nature of aggressive behavior displayed by preschoolers are also changing. We can consider the development of morality and aggression as two sides of the coin of human conduct.

DEVELOPING MORALITY: FOLLOWING SOCIETY'S RIGHTS AND WRONGS

Moral development refers to changes in people's sense of justice and of what is right and wrong, and in their behavior related to moral issues. Developmental specialists have considered moral development in terms of children's reasoning about morality, their attitudes toward moral transgressions, and their behavior when faced with moral issues. In the process of studying moral development, several approaches have evolved (Langford, 1995).

Piaget's View of Moral Development.   Consider the following exchange:

Q. *How did you get to know the rules [of the game of marbles]?*
A. When I was quite little my Daddy showed me.
Q. *And how did your daddy know?*
A. My Daddy just knew. No one told him . . .
Q. *Who invented the game of marbles?*
A. My Daddy did. . . . (Piaget, 1932, p. 55)

When a preschooler feels, as does this 5-year-old, that a game was invented by no less an authority figure than his father, it is no wonder that he would adhere rigidly to its rules.

According to Jean Piaget, who was one of the first to study questions of moral development, the view expressed by the child quoted above is representative of a broad form of moral thinking known as heteronomous morality (Piaget, 1932).

moral development the changes in people's sense of justice and of what is right and wrong, and in their behavior related to moral issues

heteronomous morality according to Piaget, the initial stage of moral development, in which rules are seen as invariant, unchangeable, and beyond people's influence and control

immanent justice the notion that rules that are broken earn immediate punishment

Heteronomous morality is the initial stage of moral development in which rules are seen as invariant, unchangeable, and beyond people's influence and control. Children in the heteronomous morality stage, which lasts from about age 4 through age 7, may play a game while following their own idiosyncratic version of its rules or not fully grasping the actual rules. Nevertheless, they enjoy playing with others, even though every participant may be playing according to his or her own set of personal rules. Piaget suggests that every child may "win" such a game, because winning is equated with having a good time, as opposed to truly competing with others.

Heteronomous morality ultimately is replaced by two later stages of morality: incipient cooperation and autonomous morality. In the *incipient cooperation stage*, which lasts from approximately age 7 to age 10, children's games become more clearly social as children actually learn the rules and play according to a shared conception of them. However, it is not until the *autonomous cooperation stage*, which begins at about age 10, that children become fully aware that game rules can be modified if the people who play them agree. The later transition into more sophisticated forms of moral development—which we will consider in Chapter 10—also is reflected in school-age children's understanding that rules of law are created by people, and they are subject to change according to the will of people.

Until these later stages are reached, however, children's reasoning about rules and issues of justice is bounded in the concrete. For instance, consider the following two stories:

> A little boy who is called John is in his room. He is called to dinner. He goes into the dining room. But behind the door there was a chair, and on the chair there was a tray with fifteen cups on it. John couldn't have known there was all this behind the door. He goes in, the door knocks against the tray, bang go the fifteen cups, and they all get broken!
>
> Once there was a little boy whose name was Henry. One day when his mother was out he tried to get some jam out of the cupboard. He climbed up on to a chair and stretched out his arm. But the jam was too high up and he couldn't reach it and have any. But while he was trying to get it he knocked over a cup. The cup fell down and broke. (Piaget, 1932, p. 122)

Piaget found that a preschool child, in the heteronomous morality stage, judges the child who broke the 15 cups worse than the one who broke just one. In contrast, children who have moved beyond the heteronomous morality stage consider the child who broke the one cup naughtier. The reason: Children in the heteronomous morality stage do not take *intention* into account.

Children in the heteronomous stage of moral development also believe in **immanent justice**, which is the notion that rules that are broken earn immediate punishment. Preschool children believe that if they do something wrong, they will be punished instantly—even if no one sees them carrying out their misdeeds. In contrast, older children understand that punishments for misdeeds are determined and meted out by people. Others are seen as making judgments about the severity of a transgression, and as taking intentionality into account in determining the nature of the penalty to be imposed.

Evaluating Piaget's Approach to Moral Development. Recent research suggests that although Piaget was on the right track in his description of how moral development proceeds, his approach suffers from the same problem we encountered in his theory of cognitive development. Specifically, Piaget underestimated the age at which children's moral skills are honed.

It is now clear that preschool children understand the notion of intentionality by about age 3, and this allows them to make judgments based on intent at an earlier age than Piaget supposed. Specifically, when provided with moral questions that emphasize intent, preschoolers judge someone who is intentionally bad as more "naughty" than someone who is unintentionally bad, but who creates more objective damage. Moreover, by the age of 4, they judge intentional lying as wrong (Yuill & Perner, 1988; Bussey, 1992).

Social-learning Approaches to Morality.   Social-learning approaches to moral development stand in stark contrast to Piaget's approach. While Piaget emphasizes how limitations in preschoolers' cognitive development lead to particular forms of moral *reasoning*, social-learning approaches focus more on how the environment in which preschoolers operate produces moral *behavior*.

According to social-learning approaches, the best predictor of children's moral conduct is whether they have received positive reinforcement for acting in a morally appropriate way. For instance, when Claire's mother tells her she has been a "good girl" for sharing a box of candy with her brother Dan, Claire's behavior has been reinforced. As a consequence, she is more likely to engage in sharing behavior in the future.

Not all moral behavior has to be directly performed, and subsequently reinforced, for learning to occur. According to social-learning approaches, children also learn moral behavior by observing the behavior of others, called *models* (Bandura, 1977). Models who are seen to receive reinforcement for their behavior are imitated, and ultimately observers learn to perform the behavior themselves. For example, when Claire's friend Jake watches Claire share her candy with her brother, Jake is more likely to engage in sharing behavior himself at some later point.

Quite a few studies illustrate the power of models, and of social learning more generally, in producing moral behavior in preschoolers. For instance, experiments have shown that children who view someone behaving generously or unselfishly are apt to follow the model's example, subsequently behaving in a generous or unselfish manner themselves when put in a similar situation (Midlarsky & Bryan, 1972; Kim & Stevens, 1987). Furthermore, the reverse holds true: If a model behaves selfishly, children who observe such behavior tend to behave more selfishly themselves (Staub, 1971; Grusec, 1982, 1991).

Not all models are equally effective in producing moral, helpful responses. For instance, preschoolers are more apt to model the behavior of warm, responsive adults than of adults who appear colder. Furthermore, models viewed as highly competent or high in prestige are more effective than others (Yarrow, Scott, & Waxler, 1973; Bandura, 1977).

Children do more than unthinkingly mimic behavior that they see rewarded in others. By observing moral conduct, they are reminded of society's norms about the importance of moral behavior, as conveyed by parents, teachers, and other powerful authority figures. The observation of others demonstrating moral conduct illustrates the connection between particular situations and certain kinds of behavior. This increases the likelihood that similar situations will elicit similar behavior in the observer.

Consequently, modeling paves the way for the development of more general rules and principles in a process called **abstract modeling**. Rather than always modeling the particular behavior of others, older preschoolers begin to develop generalized principles that underlie the behavior they observe. After observing repeated instances in which a model is rewarded for acting in a morally desirable way, children begin the process of inferring and learning the general principles of moral conduct (Bandura, 1991).

Empathy and Moral Behavior.   According to some developmentalists, **empathy**—the understanding of what another individual feels—lies at the heart of some kinds of moral behavior. Consider, for example, a scene in a city playground. Four-year-old Ezra sees his playmate Ned trip, fall, and begin to cry. Ezra goes to Ned, telling him not to feel bad, and offers to push him on a swing. For Ezra to understand that Ned needed comforting, it was necessary for Ezra to feel empathy with Ned's unhappiness—to realize that he was hurt and warranted sympathy.

The roots of empathy grow early. One-year-old infants cry when they hear other infants crying. By 2 and 3, toddlers will offer gifts and spontaneously share toys with other children

abstract modeling the process through which modeling paves the way for the development of more general rules and prinicples

empathy the understanding of what another individual feels

and adults, even if they are strangers (Stanjek, 1978; Radke-Yarrow, Zahn-Waxler, & Chapman, 1983; Zahn-Wexler & Radke-Yarrow, 1990).

During the preschool years, empathy continues to grow. Some theorists believe that increasing empathy—as well as other positive emotions such as sympathy and admiration—leads children to behave in a more moral fashion. In addition, some negative emotions—such as anger at an unfair situation or shame over previous transgressions—also may promote moral behavior (Damon, 1988; Farver & Branstetter, 1994).

The concept that negative emotions may promote moral development is one that Freud first suggested in his theory of psychoanalytic personality development. You'll recall from Chapter 1 that Freud argued that a child's *superego*, the part of the personality that represents societal do's and don'ts, is developed through resolution of the Oedipal conflict. Children come to identify with their same-sex parent, incorporating that parent's standards of morality to avoid unconscious guilt raised by the Oedipal conflict.

Whether or not we accept Freud's account of the Oedipal conflict and the guilt it produces—and most developmental specialists do not, as we saw in Chapter 1—it is consistent with more recent findings. These suggest that preschoolers' attempts to avoid experiencing negative emotions sometimes lead them to act in more moral, helpful ways. For instance, one reason that children help others is to avoid the feelings of personal distress that they experience when they are confronted with another person's unhappiness or misfortune (Eisenberg & Fabes, 1991).

AGGRESSION AND VIOLENCE IN PRESCHOOLERS

Four-year-old Eshu couldn't hold his anger and frustration in any more. Although he usually was mild-mannered, when Billy began to tease him about the split in his pants and kept it up for several minutes, Eshu finally snapped. Rushing over to Billy, Eshu pushed him to the ground and began to hit him with his small, closed fists. Because he was so distraught, Eshu's punches were not terribly effective, but they were severe enough to hurt Billy and bring him to tears before the preschool teachers could intervene.

Although violence of this sort is relatively rare among preschoolers, aggression is not uncommon. The potential for verbal hostility, shoving matches, kicking, and other forms of aggression is present throughout the preschool period, although the degree to which aggression is acted out changes as children become older.

Aggression, both physical and verbal, is present throughout the preschool period.

Social learning explanations of aggression suggest that children's observation of aggression on television can result in actual aggression.

Aggression is intentional injury or harm to another person (L. Berkowitz, 1993). Infants do not act aggressively; it is hard to contend that their behavior is *intended* to hurt others, even if they inadvertently manage to do so. On the other hand, by the time they reach preschool age, children demonstrate true aggression.

During the early preschool years, some of the aggression is addressed at attaining a desired goal, such as getting a toy away from another person or using a particular space occupied by someone else. Consequently, in some ways the aggression is inadvertent, and minor scuffles may in fact be a typical part of early preschool life.

Conversely, extreme and sustained aggression is a cause of concern. In most children, the amount of aggression declines as they move through the preschool years. Most learn to use language to express their wishes, and they become increasingly able to negotiate with others. Typically, both the frequency and the average length of episodes of aggressive behavior decline in the preschool years (Cummings, Iannotti, & Zahn-Waxler, 1989).

Although declines in aggression are typical, some children remain aggressive throughout the preschool period. Furthermore, aggression is a relatively stable characteristic: The most aggressive preschoolers tend to be the most aggressive children during the school-age years, and the least aggressive preschoolers tend to be the least aggressive school-age children (Olweus, 1982; Parke & Slaby, 1983; Minde, 1992). Still, it is the rare child who does not demonstrate at least an occasional act of aggression.

The Roots of Aggression.   How can we explain the aggression of preschoolers? Some theoreticians suggest that to behave aggressively is an instinct, part and parcel of the human condition. For instance, Freud's psychoanalytic theory suggests that we all have a death drive, which leads us to act aggressively toward others as we turn our inward hostility outward (Freud, 1920). According to ethologist Konrad Lorenz, an expert in animal behavior, animals—including humans—share a fighting instinct that stems from primitive urges to preserve territory, maintain a steady supply of food, and weed out weaker animals (Lorenz, 1966, 1974).

Similar arguments are made by **sociobiologists,** scientists who consider the biological roots of social behavior. They argue that aggression facilitates the goal of strengthening the species and its gene pool as a whole. As a result, aggressive instincts promote the survival of one's genes to pass on to future generations (McKenna, 1983; Reiss, 1984).

Although instinctual explanations of aggression are logical, most developmental researchers believe they are not the whole story (Bandura, 1978). Not only do instinctual

aggression   *intentional injury or harm to another person*

sociobiologists   *scientists who consider the biological roots of social behavior*

explanations fail to take into account the increasingly sophisticated cognitive abilities that humans develop as they get older, but they also have relatively little experimental support. Moreover, they provide little guidance in determining when and how children, as well as adults, will behave aggressively, other than noting that aggression is an inevitable part of the human condition. Consequently, developmentalists have turned to other approaches to explain aggression and violence.

Social-learning Approaches to Aggression.   The day after Eshu lashed out at Billy, Lynn, who had watched the entire scene, got into an argument with Ilya. They verbally bickered for a while, and suddenly Lynn balled her hand into a fist and tried to punch Ilya. The preschool teachers were stunned: It was rare for Lynn to get upset, and she had never displayed aggression before.

Is there a connection between the two events? Most of us would answer yes, particularly if we subscribed to the view, suggested by social-learning approaches, that aggression is largely a learned behavior. *Social-learning approaches to aggression* contend that aggression is based on prior learning. To understand the causes of aggressive behavior, then, we should look at the system of rewards and punishments existing in a child's environment.

Social-learning approaches to aggression emphasize how social and environmental conditions teach individuals to be aggressive. For instance, preschoolers may learn that they can continue to play with the most desirable toys by declining aggressively their classmates' requests for sharing. In the parlance of social-learning theory, they have been reinforced for acting aggressively, and they are more likely to behave aggressively in the future.

Reinforcement also comes in less direct ways. A good deal of research suggests that exposure to aggressive models leads to increased aggression, particularly if the observers are themselves angered, insulted, or frustrated. For example, Albert Bandura and colleagues illustrated the power of models in a classic study of preschoolers (Bandura, Ross, & Ross, 1963) (see Figure 8-3). One group of children watched a film of an adult playing aggres-

FIGURE 8-3   This series of photos is from Albert Bandura's classic Bobo doll experiment, designed to illustrate social learning of aggression. The photos clearly show how the adult model's aggressive behavior (in the first row) is imitated by children who had viewed the aggressive behavior (second and third rows).

sively and violently with a Bobo doll (a large, inflated plastic dummy that always returns to an upright position after being pushed down). In comparison, children in another condition watched a film of an adult playing sedately with a set of Tinkertoys. Later, the preschoolers were allowed to play with a number of toys, which included both the Bobo doll and the Tinkertoys. But first, the youngsters were led to feel frustration by being refused the opportunity to play with a favorite toy.

Consistent with social-learning approaches, the preschoolers modeled the behavior of the adult who they had viewed. Those who had seen the aggressive model playing with the Bobo doll were considerably more aggressive than those who had watched the calm, unaggressive model playing with the Tinkertoys.

Later research has supported this early study, and it is clear that exposure to aggressive models increases the likelihood that aggression on the part of observers will follow. These findings have profound consequences, particularly when we consider the high levels of television viewing of preschoolers. The average preschooler watches 3 hours of TV *each day*, and even children whose parents don't own television sets watch from 1 to 2 hours a day— at friends' homes (Condry, 1989).

Although television has clear cognitive impacts, as we discussed in Chapter 7, it has other, and perhaps even more important, consequences for frequent viewers. In particular, because it contains so much violent content (see Figure 8-4), the medium can have a powerful influence on the subsequent aggressive behavior of viewers (Liebert & Sprafkin, 1988; Wood, Wong, & Chachere, 1991; Sanson & diMuccio, 1993).

As we noted in the prologue to this chapter, TV programs such as the *Mighty Morphin Power Rangers* are watched by millions of preschoolers, who later imitate the Rangers' violent behavior during play. This is no surprise, given social-learning theory. But does the playful enactment of aggression later turn into the real thing, producing children (and later adults) who demonstrate more actual—and ultimately deadly—aggression?

FIGURE 8-4

ACTS OF VIOLENCE

An analysis of the violence shown on the major TV networks and several cable channels in Washington, DC, on just one particular weekday found acts of violence during every time period.

(*Source:* Center for Media and Public Affairs, 1995).

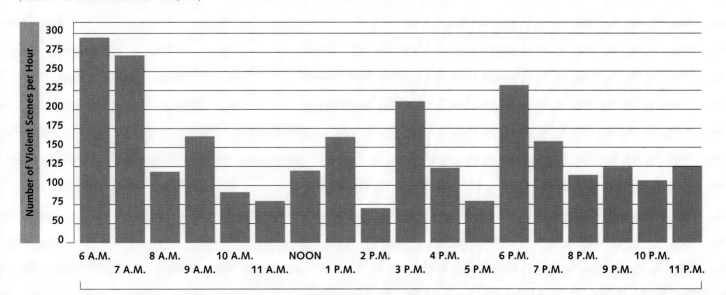

It is hard to answer the question definitively, primarily because no true experiments outside laboratory settings have been conducted. Although it is clear that observation of laboratory aggression on television leads to higher levels of aggression, evidence showing that real-world viewing of aggression is associated with subsequent aggressive behavior is correlational. (Think, for a moment, of how we might conduct a true experiment involving children's viewing habits. It would require that we control children's viewing of TV in their homes for extended periods, exposing some to a steady diet of violent shows and others to nonviolent ones—something that most parents would not agree to.)

Despite the fact that the results are primarily correlational and therefore inconclusive, the weight of research evidence is clear in suggesting that observation of televised aggression does lead to subsequent aggression. For example, in one longitudinal study, children's preferences for violent TV shows at age 8 were related to the seriousness of criminal convictions by age 30 (Huesmann, 1986). Other evidence supports the notion that observation of media violence can lead to a greater readiness to act aggressively and to an insensitivity to the suffering of victims of violence (Linz, Donnerstein, & Penrod, 1988; Bushman & Geen, 1990; Comstock & Strasburger, 1990).

Fortunately, the same principles of social-learning theory that lead preschoolers to learn aggression from television suggest ways of reducing the negative influence of the medium. For instance, children can be explicitly taught critical-viewing skills that influence their interpretation of televised models. In such training, they are taught that violence is not representative of the real world, that the viewing of violence is objectionable, and that they should refrain from imitating the behavior they have seen on television (Huesmann et al., 1983; Eron & Huesmann, 1985; Zillman, 1993).

Furthermore, just as exposure to aggressive models leads to aggression, observation of *non*aggressive models can *reduce* aggression. Preschoolers do not learn from others only how to be aggressive; they can also learn how to avoid confrontation and to control their aggression, as we'll discuss later.

Cognitive Approaches to Aggression: The Thoughts Behind Violence.   Two children, waiting for their turn in a game of kickball, inadvertently knock into one another. One child's reaction is to apologize; the other's is to shove, saying angrily, "Cut it out!"

Despite the fact that each child bears the same responsibility for the minor event, very different reactions result. The first child interprets the event as an accident; the second sees it as a provocation and reacts with aggression.

The cognitive approach to aggression suggests that the key to understanding moral development is to examine preschoolers' interpretations of others' behavior and of the environmental context in which a behavior occurs. According to developmental psychologist Kenneth Dodge and his colleagues, some children are more prone than others to assume that actions are aggressively motivated. They are unable to pay attention to the appropriate cues in a situation, and they fail to interpret the behaviors in a given situation accurately. Instead, they assume—often erroneously—that what is happening is related to others' hostility. Subsequently, in deciding how to respond, they base their behavior on their inaccurate interpretation of others' behavior. In sum, they may behave aggressively in response to a situation that never in fact existed (Dodge & Coie, 1987; Dodge & Crick, 1990).

Although the cognitive approach to aggression provides a description of the process that leads some children to behave aggressively, it is less successful in explaining how certain children come to be inaccurate perceivers of situations in the first place. Furthermore, it doesn't tell why such inaccurate perceivers so readily respond with aggression, and why they assume that aggression is an appropriate and even desirable response.

Conversely, cognitive approaches to aggression are useful in pointing out a means to reduce aggression: By teaching preschoolers to be more accurate interpreters of a situation, we can induce them to be less prone to view others' behavior as motivated by hostility, and consequently less likely to respond with aggression themselves.

The Informed Consumer of Development

Increasing Moral Behavior and Reducing Aggression in Preschoolers

Based on our discussions of moral development and the roots of aggression, we can identify several methods for encouraging preschoolers' moral conduct and reducing the incidence of aggression. Among the most practical and readily accomplished are the following (Bullock, 1988):

- ◆ Provide opportunities for preschoolers to observe others acting in a cooperative, helpful, prosocial manner. Furthermore, encourage them to interact with peers in joint activities in which they share a common goal. Such cooperative activities can teach the importance and desirability of working with—and helping—others.

- ◆ Don't ignore aggressive behavior. Parents and teachers should intervene when they see aggression in preschoolers, and they should send a clear message that aggression is an unacceptable means to resolve conflicts.

- ◆ Help preschoolers devise alternative explanations for others' behavior. This is particularly important for children who are prone to aggression and who may be apt to view others' conduct as more hostile than it actually is. Parents and teachers should help such children see that the behavior of their peers has several possible interpretations.

- ◆ Monitor preschoolers' TV viewing, particularly the violence that is shown. Evidence shows that observation of televised aggression results in subsequent increases in children's levels of aggression. At the same time, encourage preschoolers to watch particular shows that are designed, in part, to increase the level of moral conduct, such as *Sesame Street, Mr. Rogers' Neighborhood*, and *Barney*.

- ◆ Help preschoolers understand their feelings. When children become angry—and there are times when almost all children do—they need to learn how to deal with their feelings in a constructive manner. Tell them *specific* things they can do to improve the situation ("I see you're really angry with Jake for not giving you a turn. Don't hit him, but tell him you want a chance to play with the game.")

- ◆ Explicitly teach reasoning and self-control. Preschoolers can understand the rudiments of moral reasoning, and they should be reminded why certain behaviors are desirable. For instance, explicitly saying "If you take all the cookies, others will have no dessert" is preferable to saying, "Good children don't eat all the cookies."

Review and Rethink

REVIEW

- ◆ Jean Piaget believed that preschoolers are in the heteronomous morality stage of moral development, which includes the sense that rules of conduct are unchangeable and beyond human control, and that actions, not intentions, determine morality.

- Social-learning approaches to moral development emphasize the importance of reinforcement for moral actions and the observation of models of moral conduct.

- Although some developmental researchers place the development of empathy at the heart of a child's moral development, negative emotions such as anger at unfairness and shame over previous misdeeds may also be important.

- Aggression, which in mild forms is normal in preschoolers and in extreme forms unusual and disturbing, typically declines in frequency and duration as children become more able to use language to negotiate disputes.

- Ethologists and sociobiologists regard aggression as an innate human characteristic, whereas proponents of social-learning and cognitive approaches focus on learned aspects of aggression and on ways to teach nonaggressive behavior.

RETHINK

- If high-prestige models of behavior are particularly effective in influencing moral attitudes and actions, are there implications for individuals in such industries as sports, advertising, and entertainment?

- How does the process of abstract modeling operate in the development of moral principles?

- Do empathy, anger at unfairness, and shame continue to operate in the moral development of adults? How?

- Why are biological explanations of aggression insufficient? What more is needed?

- If television and aggression are ever conclusively linked, what will be the social-policy implications? Why do children enjoy watching acts of aggression and violence on television?

LOOKING BACK

How do preschool children develop a concept of themselves?

1. An important issue during the preschool years is the development of self-concept. Preschoolers' self-concepts are formed partly from their own perceptions and estimations of their characteristics, partly from their parents' behavior toward them, and partly from cultural influences.

2. According to Erik Erikson, individuals pass through eight stages of psychosocial development. During the preschool years, they first pass through the autonomy-versus-shame-and-doubt stage (18 months to 3 years), in which children develop independence and autonomy, or feel shame, self-doubt, and unhappiness. Later, in the initiative-versus-guilt stage (ages 3 to 6), preschoolers face conflicts between the desire to act independently of their parents and the guilt that comes from the unintended consequences of their actions.

How do children develop a sense of racial identity and gender?

3. Two human traits of which preschoolers become aware are race/ethnicity and gender. Each presents complex issues to resolve. Racial attitudes are formed largely in response to the children's environment, including parents and other influences. Children of minority backgrounds may experience race dissonance, in which their own race appears to them to be less desirable than the majority race; only later will they develop racial and ethnic identity.

4. Gender differences emerge early in the preschool years as children form expectations about what is appropriate and inappropriate for each sex. Their expectations generally conform to widely held societal stereotypes.

5. The reason for the strong gender expectations held by preschoolers is unclear. Some researchers point to genetic factors, such as hormones and brain structures, as evidence for a biological explanation of gender expectations. Freud's psychoanalytic theories used the concepts of Oedipal urges, castration anxiety, identification, and penis envy to explain gender expectations, a framework that many later researchers have found cumbersome and inaccurate.

6. Social-learning theorists believe that environmental influences, including parents, teachers, peers, and the media, cause preschoolers to develop their stereotyped understandings of gender. Another approach is more cognitive: that children form gender schemas, cognitive frameworks that organize information that the children gather about gender.

In what sorts of social relationships do preschoolers engage?

7. Preschool social relationships begin to encompass genuine friendship, which develops from children's emerging appreciation of other children as particularly enjoyable individuals, and which takes on a dimension of stability and trust.

8. Popularity among preschoolers is linked to physical characteristics, such as attractiveness, and behavioral characteristics, such as social skills and sensitivity to others. Some of the characteristics that tend to make children popular can be taught; others may relate to the type of home environment the child experiences.

How do the nature and function of play change over time?

9. The nature of play changes during these years. Children progress from repetitive, functional play to more creative and constructive play. In addition, the social nature of play changes, moving through solitary play, parallel play, onlooker play, associative play, and cooperative play, with increasing demands for organization and social skill.

What sorts of disciplinary styles do parents employ, and what effects do they have?

10. Disciplinary styles differ both individually and culturally. In the United States and other Western societies, parents' styles tend to be mostly authoritarian, permissive, or authoritative, with the last being regarded as the most effective. In some Asian countries, an emphasis on social harmony provides support for a more authoritarian style, which can be quite effective in its home setting.

11. Children of authoritarian and permissive parents may suffer consequences in terms of sociability. Dependency, hostility, and low self-control are often effects of these parenting styles. Children of authoritative parents tend to be more independent, friendly, self-assertive, and cooperative.

What factors contribute to child abuse and neglect?

12. Child abuse occurs with alarming frequency in the United States and other countries, especially in stressful home environments. Firmly held notions regarding family privacy and a folklore that supports the use of "the rod" in childrearing contribute to the high rate of abuse in the United States. Moreover, the cycle-of-violence hypothesis points to the likelihood that individuals abused as children may turn into abusers as adults.

13. Child abuse can take highly physical forms, but it can also be more subtle. Psychological maltreatment may involve neglect of parental responsibilities, emotional negligence, intimidation or humiliation, unrealistic demands and expectations, or exploitation of

children. Psychological maltreatment may have lasting behavioral and psychological effects.

How do children develop a moral sense?

14. The process of moral development during the preschool years has been studied by several researchers. Piaget believed that children at this age are in the heteronomous morality stage of moral development, characterized by a belief in external, unchangeable rules of conduct. These rules do not take intention into account, merely acts. The belief in immanent justice—sure, immediate punishment for all misdeeds—is also a characteristic of this stage.

15. In contrast, social-learning approaches to morality emphasize interactions between environment and behavior in moral development. According to these approaches, models of behavior play an important role in development, providing not only specific examples of appropriate actions, but also the basis for establishing abstract principles of moral behavior.

16. Some developmental researchers believe that a child's development of empathy, which begins early in life, underlies many kinds of moral behavior. Other emotions, including the negative emotions of anger and shame that were emphasized in Freud's psychoanalytic theories of personality development, may also promote moral behavior.

Is aggression normal in preschoolers, and how does it develop?

17. Aggression, which involves intentional harm to another person, begins to emerge in the preschool years. Mild forms of aggression appear to be virtually universal, but extreme aggression, which occurs infrequently, is cause for concern. As children age and improve their language skills, acts of aggression typically decline in frequency and duration, although aggressive or nonaggressive tendencies in the individual are relatively stable throughout the school years.

18. Whether aggression is innate or learned is a topic of theory and research. Some ethologists, such as Konrad Lorenz, believe that aggression is simply a biological fact of human—and all animal—life, a belief also held by many sociobiologists, who focus on the individual's instinctual desire to pass genes on to the next generation, a desire that leads to aggressive intraspecies competition.

19. On the other hand, social-learning theorists, disturbed by the lack of experimental support for the view that aggression is innate—and by its failure to account for cognition and to explain in detail how aggression operates—focus on learned aspects of aggressive behavior. In their view the environment—including models of behavior and social reinforcement—is of primary importance. The hypothesis that television can induce aggressive behavior has been studied and has found experimental support.

20. The cognitive approach to aggression emphasizes the role of interpretations of the behaviors of others in determining aggressive or nonaggressive responses. By teaching children to consider multiple interpretations of others' acts, proponents of the cognitive approach hope to reduce aggressive responses.

KEY TERMS AND CONCEPTS

self-concept (p. 256)
collectivistic orientation (p. 256)
individualistic orientation (p. 256)
psychosocial development (p. 257)
autonomy-versus-shame-and-doubt stage (p. 257)

initiative-versus-guilt stage (p. 257)
race dissonance (p. 257)
identification (p. 260)
gender schema (p. 261)
androgynous (p. 261)
functional play (p. 265)

constructive play (p. 265)
parallel play (p. 265)
onlooker play (p. 265)
associative play (p. 265)
cooperative play (p. 266)
authoritarian parents (p. 267)
permissive parents (p. 267)
authoritative parents (p. 268)
cycle-of-violence hypothesis (p. 272)

psychological maltreatment (p. 273)
resilience (p. 273)
moral development (p. 277)
heteronomous morality (p. 278)
immanent justice (p. 278)
abstract modeling (p. 279)
empathy (p. 279)
aggression (p. 281)
sociobiologists (p. 281)

The Middle Childhood Years

CHAPTER 9

THE MIDDLE
CHILDHOOD YEARS
Physical and Cognitive Development

CHAPTER OUTLINE

PROLOGUE: THE WORLD AT 10

Alex Ruck is a 10-year-old with a sly smile and the energy of liquid lightning, as a family friend once put it. . . . On any given afternoon, Alex and his friends, David, Wan-Tei and Chubs, go skateboarding or snowboarding or play pickup games of football, basketball, hockey, or one of their own invention called Werewolf Hide-and-Seek. In this variation of the classic game, kids who hide but get caught must pretend they are being mauled by were-wolves . . .

Like many 10-year-olds, Alex plays Little League baseball every spring, usually as a shortstop or pitcher. He's just an "OK" player, he says. When he reads—usually before going to bed at 9 P.M.—he favors books like *Fangs of Evil* or *Zombie Camp*. He dresses in baggy T-shirts, sweats, and flannel shirts, along with a well-worn pair of Converse high tops. . . .

School is getting tough for Alex—he usually finishes his six-hour school day with an hour or two of homework ahead. Sports are becoming more competitive, too. He's on a community-center swim team and practices three times a week, all year round; his coaches say he swims better than most kids in his age group.

Alex's daily school-bus ride takes him from his stable, mostly white neighborhood to a public magnet school, East Hills International Studies Academy, in the middle of a housing project. It is a few miles and half a world from his house. East Hills is about 60% black, and has students from Russia, Africa, China, and the Middle East. Both privileged and poor families send their kids to East Hills; about 70% of its student body is bused in. Alex mixes with a wide variety of kids in classes and at lunch. The school has an aggressive mediation program that defuses fights before they get out of control; serious arguments break out very rarely. The children find common ground in TV shows, new computer games, or hated teachers.

There are harsher truths, too. Two bodies have been found within several hundred yards of the school in the past 2 years. Last year, when a tree branch fell on Alex's school bus, the children hit the floor screaming: They thought it was a gunshot. Alex won't wear a red, black, and white Starter jacket he got last year to school because, he says, those are gang col-ors. "I don't want to get shot," he explains matter-of-factly. . . .

He is generally attentive and quiet in class, sometimes placing his head on the desk as he listens. One recent day starts in science and takes him through two math classes, where Alex struggles through a test on fractions and works some negative numbers on calculators.

In reading class, the kids are excited to learn they will hear a narrative version of *Hamlet*, read by their teacher, Carol Beavers, who has been telling them the stories of Shakespeare this year. "All right, Hamlet!" one student yells. But the narrative is very literal, summarizing the stage actions as well as the story. Some children listen closely, but others seem to lose track of the story. Ms. Beavers admits some of her pupils probably forget what they heard the minute they walk out the door. "But my objective is to foster an interest, to try to get them to understand the plot," she says. "I just want to lay a groundwork."

In science, Alex studies birds on a computer program, and late in the day he appalls some girls by balancing his bubble gum on his nose.

"That's disgusting," one of them snipes.

Alex smiles. . . . (Murray, 1995, pp. B1–B2)

LOOKING
AHEAD

To Alex Ruck, life at age 10 is both simple and complex. Although able to indulge his passion for sports and computer games, at the same time he must confront the pressures of school and the larger world, which can include substantial violence and danger. Still a child, yet lacking much of the innocence we expect of children, Alex confronts a challenging world.

This chapter, which considers some of the central facets of Alex's life, focuses on the physical and cognitive aspects of middle childhood. Beginning at age 6 and continuing to the start of adolescence at about age 12, these years are often referred to as the "school years" because for most children, they mark the beginning of formal education. These are also years of significant physical and cognitive growth.

We begin our consideration of middle childhood by examining physical development. We discuss how children's bodies change, and the twin problems of malnutrition and—the other side of the coin—childhood obesity. We also consider both typical development and some of the special needs that affect exceptional children's sensory and physical abilities.

Next, we turn to cognitive development in middle childhood. We examine several approaches, including Piagetian and information-processing theories. We look at language development and the critical questions revolving around bilingualism—an increasingly pressing social issue in the United States owing to the growing diversity of the school-age population.

Finally, we consider several issues involving schooling. After discussing the scope of education throughout the world, we examine multicultural education. The chapter ends with a discussion of intelligence, a characteristic closely tied to school success. We look at the nature of IQ tests and at the education of children who are below and above the intellectual norm.

In sum, after reading this chapter, you will be able to answer these questions:

♦   In what ways do children grow during the school years, and what factors influence their growth?

♦   What are the nutritional needs of school-age children, and what are some causes and effects of improper nutrition?

♦   What sorts of special needs manifest themselves in the middle childhood years, and how can they be met?

♦   In what ways do children develop cognitively during these years, according to major theoretical approaches?

♦   How does language develop during the middle childhood period, and what special circumstances pertain to children for whom English is not the first language?

♦   What are some trends in schooling worldwide and in the United States?

♦   How can intelligence be measured, and how are children who fall outside the normal range of intelligence to be educated?

PHYSICAL DEVELOPMENT

Dusty Nash, an angelic-looking blond child of seven, awoke at five one recent morning in his Chicago home and proceeded to throw a fit. He wailed. He kicked. Every muscle in his 50-pound body flew in furious motion. Finally, after about 30 minutes, Dusty pulled himself together sufficiently to head downstairs for break-

fast. While his mother bustled about the kitchen, the hyperkinetic child pulled a box
of Kix cereal from the cupboard and sat on a chair.

But sitting still was not in the cards this morning. After grabbing some cereal
with his hands, he began kicking the box, scattering little round corn puffs across
the room. Next he turned his attention to the TV set, or rather, the table supporting
it. The table was covered with checkerboard Con-Tact paper, and Dusty began peel-
ing it off. Then he became intrigued with the spilled cereal and started stomping it
to bits. At this point his mother interceded. In a firm but calm voice she told her son
to get the stand-up dust pan and broom and clean up the mess. Dusty got out the
dust pan but forgot the rest of the order. Within seconds he was dismantling the
plastic dust pan, piece by piece. His next project: grabbing three rolls of toilet paper
from the bathroom and unraveling them around the house. (Wallis, 1994, p. 43)

It was only 7:30 A.M.

Dusty Nash suffers from a disorder that just a few decades ago no one had heard of—
attention-deficit hyperactivity disorder. Although not common, occurring in only three to
five percent of the school-age population, the disorder represents one of several challenges
that children might face as they pass through middle childhood. Yet even in children without identifiable difficulties, the range of skills and abilities encompassed by typical development is enormous. We'll first consider typical physical growth during middle childhood,
and then return to look at exceptional children, such as Dusty, whose development does not
conform to typical patterns.

THE GROWING BODY

Slow but steady.

If three words could characterize the nature of growth during middle childhood, it
would be these. Especially when compared to the swift growth during the first 5 years of life
and the remarkable growth spurt characteristic of adolescence, middle childhood is relatively tranquil.

On the other hand, the body has not shifted into neutral. Physical growth continues,
although at a more stately pace. For instance, while they are in elementary school, children
in the United States grow, on average, 2 to 3 inches a year. By the age of 11, the average girl
is 4 feet 10 inches tall and the average boy is slightly shorter at 4 feet 9-½ inches tall. This is
the only time during the life span when girls are, on average, taller than boys. This height

Seven-year-old Dusty Nash's high energy
and low attention span is due to attention-
deficit hyperactivity disorder, which occurs
in three to five percent of the school-age
population.

difference reflects the slightly more rapid physical development of girls, who start their adolescent growth spurt about the age of 10.

Weight gain follows a similar pattern. During middle childhood, both boys and girls gain from 5 to 7 pounds a year. Weight also becomes redistributed. As the rounded look of "baby fat" disappears, children's bodies become more muscular and their strength increases.

Average height and weight increases disguise significant individual differences, as anyone who has seen a line of fourth graders walking down a school corridor has doubtless noticed. Variations of a half-foot between children of the same age are not unusual, and well within normal ranges.

Cultural Patterns of Growth.   Because most children in North America receive sufficient nutrients to reach their full potential, most height and weight differences among North American youngsters are due to genetically determined variability. In other parts of the world, inadequate nutrition and disease take their toll, producing children who are shorter and who weigh less than they would had they sufficient nutrients. The discrepancies can be dramatic: Children in poorer areas of cities such as Calcutta, Hong Kong, and Rio de Janeiro are smaller than their counterparts in affluent areas of the same cities.

Other variations in height and weight are the result of genetic factors relating to racial and ethnic background. For instance, children from Asian and Oceanic Pacific backgrounds tend to be shorter, on average, than those with northern and central European heritages. However, even within particular racial and ethnic groups there is significant variation. Furthermore, we cannot attribute racial and ethnic differences solely to inherited factors, because dietary customs, as well as possible variations in levels of affluence, also may contribute to the differences.

Promoting Growth with Hormones: Should Short Children Be Made to Grow?   The makers of Protropin, an artificial human growth hormone that can make short children taller, had a problem: They needed to find short children in order to promote the use of their drug. One of the ways they solved their problem was by paying for surveys to identify short children in schools.

Although such practices are legal, they are on the fringe of ethical conduct, at least according to some developmental specialists. The problem is not so much whether the drug is effective in increasing the growth of unusually short children—it is—but whether drug manufacturers are being overly aggressive in their quest to market the drug to potential patients (Kolata, 1994).

The problem is a new one: Artificial hormones to promote growth have become available only in the last decade. Today some 20,000 children who have insufficient natural growth hormone are taking such drugs. But some observers question whether shortness is a serious enough problem to warrant the use of the drug, which is costly and has potential side effects. Furthermore, in some cases, the drug may lead to the premature onset of puberty, which may—ironically—restrict later growth.

On the other hand, there is no denying that artificial growth hormones are effective in increasing children's height. In fact, for those children whose height is projected to be well below normal, the effect of such drugs can be dramatic. In some cases Protropin has added well over a foot in height to extremely short children, placing them within normal height ranges.

Severe malnutrition, like that experienced by this child in Somalia, not only has profound physical consequences, but ultimately can slow cognitive development substantially.

Nutrition.   The level of nutrition that children experience during their lives significantly affects many aspects of their behavior. For instance, longitudinal studies over many years in Guatemalan villages show that children's nutritional backgrounds are related to several dimensions of social and emotional functioning at school age. Children who had received more nutrients were more involved with their peers, showed more positive emotion, had less anxiety, and had more moderate activity levels than did their peers who had received less adequate nutrition. Furthermore, the children with a better nutritional history were more eager to explore new environments, showed more persistence in frustrating situations, were more alert on some types of activities, and generally displayed higher energy levels and more self-confidence (Barrett & Frank, 1987; see Figure 9-1).

Nutrition is also linked to cognitive performance. For instance, in one study, children in Kenya who were well nourished performed better on a test of verbal abilities and on other cognitive measures than those who had mild to moderate undernutrition. Other research suggests that malnutrition may influence cognitive development by dampening children's curiosity, responsiveness, and motivation to learn (Sigman et al., 1989; Ricciuti, 1993).

Although undernutrition and malnutrition clearly lead to physical, social, and cognitive difficulties, in some cases overnutrition—the intake by a child of too many calories—presents problems of its own, particularly when it leads to childhood obesity.

Childhood Obesity.   When Ruthellen's mother asks if she would like a piece of bread with her meal, Ruthellen replies that she better not—she thinks that she may be getting fat. Ruthellen, who is of normal weight and height, is six years old.

Although height can be of concern to both children and parents during middle childhood, maintaining the appropriate weight is an even greater worry for many. In fact, concern about weight can border on an obsession, particularly among girls. For instance, many six-year-old girls worry about becoming "fat," and they try to avoid foods that they think are likely to make them put on weight. Why? Their concern is probably due to the U.S. preoccupation with being slim, which permeates every sector of society (Feldman, Feldman, & Goodman, 1988).

What is ironic about the widely held view that thinness is a virtue is that increasing numbers of children are becoming obese. *Obesity* is defined as body weight that is more than 20 percent above the average for a person of a given age and height. By this definition, some ten percent of all children are obese—a proportion that is growing. In fact, since the 1960s, obesity among children aged 6 to 11 has risen by 54 percent (D.R. Lamb, 1984; Gortmaker, Dietz, Sobol, & Welher, 1987; Ungrady, 1992; Troiano, Flegal, Kuczmarski, & Campbell, 1995).

Several factors account for childhood obesity. As we first noted in Chapter 7, obesity is caused by a combination of genetic and social characteristics. For instance, increasing

FIGURE 9-1

NUTRITION AND BEHAVIOR.

Children who received higher levels of nutrients had more energy and felt more self-confident than did those whose nutritional intake was lower.

(Adapted from Barrett & Radke-Yarrow, 1985).

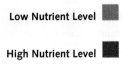

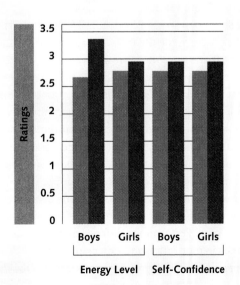

evidence suggests that particular inherited genes are related to obesity and predispose certain children to be overweight (Zhang et al., 1994).

At the same time, obesity cannot be attributable solely to inherited factors, for it is hard to link the rise in obesity over the past several decades to changes in the gene pool. Clearly, various social factors must also enter into children's weight problems.

In addition to society's preoccupation with slimness as a sign of beauty, an additional social ingredient in obesity is parental worry about their children's weight. Parents who are particularly involved in their youngsters' eating habits, and who exhibit controlling behavior regarding them, may produce children who lack internal controls to regulate their own food intake (Johnson & Birch, 1994; Brownell & Rodin, 1994).

Another important social factor that determines obesity is exercise—or rather, the lack of exercise (Epstein, 1992). School-age children, by and large, tend to engage in relatively little exercise and are not particularly fit (Wolf, Gortmaker, Cheung, & Gray, 1993). For instance, approximately 40 percent of boys 6 to 12 are unable to do more than one pull-up, and one-fourth cannot do any. Furthermore, school fitness surveys reveal that American children have shown little or no improvement in the amount of exercise they get, despite national efforts to increase the level of fitness of school-age youngsters. In one survey, for example, two-thirds of children tested failed to meet minimum standards set by the U.S. President's Council on Physical Fitness and Sports (Ungrady, 1992).

Why, when our visions of childhood include children running happily on school playgrounds, playing sports, and chasing one another in games of tag, is the actual level of exercise relatively low? One answer is that many youngsters are closeted in their homes, watching television.

The correlation between TV viewing and obesity is strong: The more television children watch, the more likely they are to be overweight (Dietz, 1987). Several reasons account for this pattern. For one thing, TV viewing is a sedentary activity; few people engage in vigorous exercise while watching TV. Another factor is that children tend to snack while watching television, thereby increasing their caloric intake beyond nutritional need. It is even possible that frequent exposure to commercials for food products entices habitual TV viewers to be overly interested in food and eating.

MOTOR DEVELOPMENT

The fact that the level of fitness of school-age children is not as high as we would desire doesn't mean that such children are physically incapable. In fact, even without regular exercise, children's gross and fine motor skills develop substantially over the course of the school years.

Gross Motor Skills.   One important improvement in gross motor skills is in the realm of muscle coordination. Watching a softball player pitch a ball past a batter to her catcher, or a runner reach the finish line in a race, we are struck by the huge strides that these children have made since the more awkward days of preschool.

During middle childhood, children master many types of skills that earlier they could not perform well. For instance, riding a bike, ice skating, swimming, and skipping rope are readily mastered by most school-age youngsters (Cratty, 1986; see Figure 9-2).

Do boys and girls differ in their motor skills? Traditionally, developmental researchers had concluded that gender differences in gross motor skills become increasingly pronounced during these years, with boys outperforming girls (Espenschade, 1960). However, more recent research casts some doubt on this conclusion. When comparisons are made between boys and girls who regularly take part in similar activities—such as softball—gender variations in gross motor skills are minimized (Hall & Lee, 1984).

Why? Performance differences were probably found in the first place because of differences in motivation and expectations. Society told girls that they would do worse than boys in sports, and the girls' performance reflected that message.

FIGURE 9-2

GROSS MOTOR SKILLS DEVELOPED BY CHILDREN BETWEEN THE AGES OF 6 AND 12 YEARS.

(Adapted from Cratty, 1979).

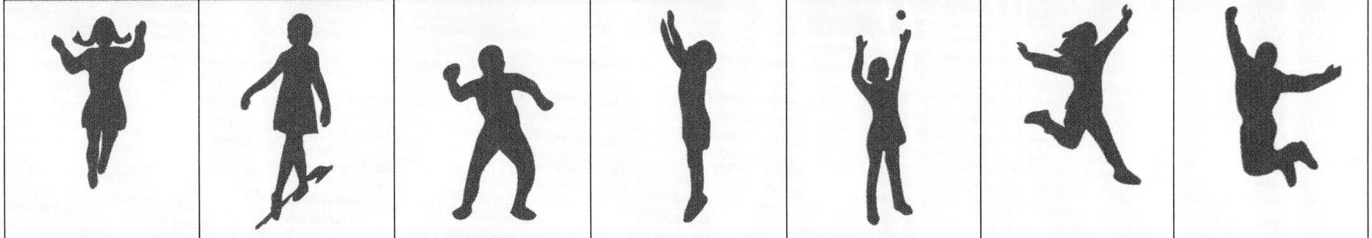

6 Years	7 Years	8 Years	9 Years	10 Years	11 Years	12 Years
Girls superior in accuracy of movement; boys superior in more forceful, less complex acts. Can throw with the proper weight shift and step. Acquire the ability to skip.	Can balance on one foot with eyes closed. Can walk on a 2-inch-wide balance beam without falling off. Can hop and jump accurately into small squares (hopscotch). Can correctly execute a jumping-jack exercise.	Can grip objects with 12 pounds of pressure. Can engage in alternate rhythmical hopping in a 2-2, 2-3, or 3-3 pattern. Girls can throw a small ball 33 feet; boys can throw a small ball 59 feet. The number of games participated in by both sexes is the greatest at this age.	Girls can vertical jump 8.5 inches over their standing height, plus reach; boys can vertical jump 10 inches over their standing height plus reach. Boys can run 16.6 feet per second and throw a small ball 41 feet; girls can run 16 feet per second and throw a small ball 41 feet.	Can judge and intercept directions of small balls thrown from a distance. Both girls and boys can run 17 feet per second .	Boys can achieve standing broad jump of 5 feet; girls can achieve standing broad jump of 4.5 feet.	Can achieve high jump of 3 feet.

Today, however, society's message has changed, at least officially. For instance, the American Academy of Pediatrics suggests that boys and girls should engage in the same sports and games, and that they can do so together in mixed-sex groups. There is no reason to separate the sexes in physical exercise and sports until puberty, when the smaller size of females begins to make them more susceptible to injury in contact sports (American Academy of Pediatrics, 1989a).

Fine Motor Skills.   Typing at a computer keyboard; writing in cursive with pen and pencil; drawing detailed pictures: These are just some of the accomplishments that depend on improvements in fine motor coordination that occur during early and middle childhood. Both 6- and seven-year-olds are able to tie their shoes and fasten buttons; by age 8, they can use each hand independently; and by 11 and 12, they can manipulate objects with almost as much capability as they will show in adulthood.

One of the reasons for advances in fine motor skills is that the amount of myelin in the brain increases significantly between the ages of 6 and 8 (Lecours, 1982). You may recall from Chapter 7 that *myelin* provides protective insulation that surrounds parts of nerve cells. Because increased levels of myelin raise the speed at which electrical impulses travel between neurons, messages can reach muscles more rapidly and control them better.

CHILDREN WITH SPECIAL NEEDS

What would it be like if every letter that is underlined in this sentence appeared to you to be reversed? To children with one form of learning disability, called *dyslexia*, this is in fact the case every time they try to read or write.

visual impairment   *difficulties in seeing that may include blindness or partial sightedness*

auditory impairment   *a special need that involves the loss of hearing or some aspect of hearing*

Dyslexia is just one of several special needs of school-age children. These special needs embody some of the major challenges to both caretakers and teachers. We turn now to the most prevalent exceptionalities that affect children of normal intelligence, considering sensory difficulties, learning disabilities, and attention-deficit disorders. (We'll consider the special needs of children who are significantly below and above average in intelligence later in the chapter.)

Sensory Difficulties: Visual, Auditory, and Speech Problems.   Anyone who has temporarily lost his or her eyeglasses or a contact lens has had a glimpse of how difficult even rudimentary, everyday tasks must be for those with sensory impairments. To function with less than typical vision, hearing, or speech can be a tremendous challenge.

Visual impairment can be considered in both a legal and an educational sense. The definition of legal impairment is quite straightforward: *Blindness* is visual acuity of less than 20/200 after correction (meaning the inability to see even at 20 feet what a typical person can see at 200 feet), while *partial sightedness* is visual acuity of less than 20/70 after correction.

Even when the legal limits of impairment are not reached, however, visual impairment in an educational sense can be present. For one thing, the legal criterion pertains solely to distance vision, whereas most educational tasks require close-up vision. In addition, the legal definition does not consider abilities in the perception of color, depth, and light—all of which might influence a student's educational success. About one student in a thousand requires special education services relating to a visual impairment.

Although most severe visual problems are identified fairly early, it sometimes happens that an impairment goes undetected. Furthermore, visual problems can emerge gradually as children develop physiologically and changes occur in the visual apparatus of the eye. Parents must be aware of the signals of visual problems in their children. Frequent eye irritation (redness, sties, or infection), continual blinking and facial contortions when reading, holding reading material unusually close to the face, difficulty in writing, and frequent headaches, dizziness, or burning eyes are some of the signs of visual problems.

Another relatively frequent special need relates to **auditory impairment**. Not only do auditory impairments cause academic problems but they can also produce social difficulties, for considerable peer interaction takes place through informal conversation. Hearing loss, which affects some 1 to 2 percent of the school-age population, is not simply a matter of not hearing enough. Rather, auditory problems can vary along a number of dimensions (U.S. Department of Education, 1987).

In some cases of hearing loss, only a limited range of frequencies, or pitches, is affected. For example, the loss may be great at pitches in the normal speech range yet quite minor in other frequencies, such as those of very high or low sounds. In addition, a child may require different levels of amplification at different frequencies. For this reason, a hearing aid that indiscriminately amplifies all frequencies equally may be ineffective.

The age of onset of a hearing loss is critical in determining the degree to which a child can adapt to the impairment. If the loss of hearing occurs in infancy, the effects will probably be much more severe than if it occurs after the age of 3. The reason relates to the critical role that hearing plays in the development of language. Children who have had little or no exposure to the sound of language are unable to understand or produce oral language themselves. On the other hand, loss of hearing after a child has learned language will not have serious consequences on subsequent linguistic development.

Severe and early loss of hearing is also associated with difficulties in abstract thinking. Because hearing-impaired children may have limited exposure to language, abstract concepts that can be understood fully only through the use of language may be less well understood than concrete concepts that can be illustrated visually (Hewett & Forness, 1974).

Auditory difficulties are sometimes accompanied by speech impairments. A speech impairment is one of the most public types of exceptionality: Every time the child speaks aloud, the impairment is obvious to listeners. In fact, the definition of **speech impairment** suggests that speech is impaired when it deviates so much from the speech of others that it calls attention to itself, interferes with communication, or produces maladjustment in the speaker (Van Riper, 1972). In other words, if a child's speech sounds impaired, it probably is. Speech impairments are present in 3 to 5 percent of the school-age population (U.S. Department of Education, 1987).

Stuttering, which entails substantial disruption in the rhythm and fluency of speech, is the most common speech impairment. Despite a great deal of research on the topic, no single cause has been identified. Although the disfluencies of stuttering are relatively normal in young children—and occasionally occur in normal adults—chronic stuttering can be a severe problem. Not only does stuttering hinder communication but it can also produce embarrassment and stress in children, who may become inhibited from conversing with others and speaking aloud in class.

Parents and teachers can adopt several strategies for dealing with stuttering. For starters, attention should not be drawn to the stuttering, and children should be given sufficient time to finish what they begin to say, no matter how protracted the statement becomes. It does not help stutterers for others to finish their sentences for them or otherwise correct their speech (Onslow, 1992).

Learning Disabilities.   Some 2.3 million school-age children in the United States are officially labeled as having **learning disabilities**, characterized by difficulties in the acquisition and use of listening, speaking, reading, writing, reasoning, or mathematical abilities (National Joint Committee on Learning Disabilities, 1989; Roush, 1995).

Such a broad definition encompasses a wide and heterogeneous variety of difficulties. For instance, some children suffer from dyslexia, a reading disability that can result in the reversal of letters during reading and writing, confusion between left and right, and difficulties in spelling. Although the causes of dyslexia are unknown, increasing evidence suggests that visual information may reach the brain in an improper sequence, producing the kind of difficulties such as the letter reversals described earlier (Livingston, Adam, & Bracha, 1993).

The causes of learning disabilities are not well understood. Although they are generally attributed to some form of brain dysfunction, probably due to genetic factors, some experts suggest that they are produced by such environmental causes as poor early nutrition or allergies (Mercer, 1992).

Attention-deficit hyperactivity disorder (ADHD) is marked by inattention, impulsiveness, a low tolerance for frustration, and generally a great deal of inappropriate activity. Although all children show such traits some of the time, for those diagnosed with ADHD such behavior is common and interferes with their home and school functioning (Barkley, 1995).

Although it is hard to know how many children have the disorder, most estimates put the number at from 3 to 5 percent of the school-age population, or some 3.5 million Americans under the age of 18. What is clear is that a child who has ADHD is likely to have difficulty staying on task and working toward goals, have limited self-control, be easily distracted, and—above all—be physically active. An ADHD child can be a whirlwind of activity, exhausting the energy and patience of parents, teachers, and even peers (Baker, 1994).

The treatment of children with ADHD has been a source of considerable controversy. Because it has been found that doses of Ritalin or Dexadrine (which, paradoxically, are stimulants) reduce activity levels in hyperactive children, many physicians routinely prescribe drug treatment (Wallace, 1994).

Although in many cases such drugs are effective in increasing attention span and compliance, in some cases the side effects are considerable, and the long-term health consequences of this treatment are unclear. Furthermore, although drugs often help scholastic performance in the short run (Weber, Frankenberger, & Heilman, 1992), the long-term evi-

speech impairment   *speech that is impaired when it deviates so much from the speech of others that it calls attention to itself, interferes with communication, or produces maladjustment in the speaker*

stuttering   *substantial disruption in the rhythm and fluency of speech; the most common speech impairment*

learning disabilities   *difficulties in the acquisition and use of listening, speaking, reading, writing, reasoning, or mathematical abilities*

attention-deficit hyperactivity disorder (ADHD)   *a learning disability marked by inattention, impulsiveness, a low tolerance for frustration, and generally a great deal of inappropriate activity*

dence for continuing improvement is mixed. In fact, some studies suggest that after a few years, children treated with drugs do not perform any better academically than do untreated children (McDaniel, 1986).

What are the most common signs of ADHD? Although it is often difficult to distinguish between children who simply have a high level of activity and those with ADHD, some of the most common symptoms include persistent difficulty in finishing tasks, following instructions, and organizing work; inability to watch an entire TV program; frequent interruption of others; and a tendency to jump into a task before hearing all the instructions. If a child is suspected of having ADHD, he or she should be evaluated by a specialist. (Parents can receive support from the Center for Hyperactive Child Information, P.O. Box 66272, Washington, DC 20035.)

The Informed Consumer of Development

Keeping Children Fit

> Here is a brief portrait of a contemporary American: Sam works all week at a desk and gets no regular physical exercise. On weekends he spends many hours sitting in front of the TV, often snacking on sodas and sweets. Both at home and at restaurants, his meals feature high-calorie, fat-saturated foods. (Segal & Segal, 1992, p. 235)

Although this sketch could apply to many adult men and women, Sam is actually a 6-year-old. He is one of many school-age children in the United States who get little or no regular exercise, and who consequently are physically unfit and at risk for obesity and other health problems.

However, several approaches can be taken to encourage children to become more physically active (Squires, 1991; O'Neill, 1994):

- ◆ *Make exercise fun.* For children to build the habit of exercising, they need to find it enjoyable. Activities that keep youngsters on the sidelines or that are overly competitive may give children with inferior skills a lifelong distaste for exercise.

- ◆ *Gear activities to the child's physical level and motor skills.* For instance, use child-size equipment that can make participants feel successful.

- ◆ *Encourage the child to find a partner.* It could be a friend, a sibling, or a parent. Exercising can involve a variety of activities, such as roller skating or hiking, but almost all activities are carried out more readily if someone else is also doing them.

- ◆ *Start slowly.* Sedentary children—those who haven't habitually engaged in physical activity—should start off gradually. For instance, they could begin with 5 minutes of exercise a day, 7 days a week. Over ten weeks, they could move toward a goal of 30 minutes of exercise 3 to 5 days a week.

- ◆ *Urge, but do not push too hard, participation in organized sports activities.* Not every child is athletically inclined, and pushing too hard for involvement in organized sports may backfire. Make participation and enjoyment the goals of such activities, not winning.

- ◆ *Do not make physical activity, such as jumping jacks or push-ups, a punishment for unwanted behavior.*

◆ *Schools and parents should encourage children to participate in an organized physical fitness program.* For instance, the Cooper Institute for Aerobics Research has designed a program called the "Fitnessgram," which is used by 2 million children in 3,000 schools around the United States. (For more information, write Cooper Institute for Aerobics Research, 12330 Preston Road, Dallas, Texas 75230.)

Review and Rethink

REVIEW

◆ During the middle childhood years, the body grows at a slow but steady pace that is influenced by both genetic and social factors.

◆ Adequate nutrition is important for physical, social, and cognitive development in the middle childhood years, but overnutrition, in the form of obesity, should be avoided.

◆ Children substantially improve their gross and fine motor skills during the school years, with muscular coordination and manipulative skills advancing to near-adult levels.

◆ Many school-age children have special needs, particularly in the areas of vision, hearing, and speech, which should be addressed early by parents and teachers to avoid unduly hindering the development of cognitive, linguistic, and social skills. Some youngsters also have learning disabilities.

◆ Attention-deficit hyperactivity disorder (ADHD), marked by attention, organization, and activity problems, affects between 3 and 5 percent of the school-age population. Treatment through the use of drugs is highly controversial.

RETHINK

◆ Under what circumstances would you recommend the use of a growth hormone such as Protropin? Is shortness primarily a physical or a cultural problem?

◆ Do proven links among affluence, nutrition, and the development of cognitive and social skills provide insight into the notion of "the cycle of poverty"? How might the cycle be broken?

◆ Do you believe early hearing loss affects the ability to learn to read? How?

◆ In general, are social attitudes toward people with speech impairments supportive? How would you advise children to treat a youngster with a noticeable speech impairment?

◆ Before accepting the treatment of ADHD with drugs, what questions would you want answered about the child and the drugs?

INTELLECTUAL DEVELOPMENT

Jared's parents were delighted when he came home from kindergarten one day and explained that he had learned why the sky was blue. He talked about Earth's atmosphere—although he didn't pronounce the word correctly—and how tiny bits of moisture in the air reflected the sunlight. Although his explanation had rough edges

concrete operational stage   *the period of cognitive development between 7 and 12 years of age, which is characterized by the active, and appropriate, use of logic*

decentering   *the ability to take multiple aspects of a situation into account*

(he couldn't quite grasp what the "atmosphere" was), he still had the general idea, and that, his parents felt, was quite an achievement for their 5-year-old.

* * *

Fast-forward 6 years. Jared, now 11, had already spent an hour laboring over his evening's homework. After completing a two-page worksheet on multiplying and dividing fractions, he had begun work on his U.S. Constitution project. He was taking notes for his report, which would explain what political factions had been involved in the writing of the document and how the Constitution had been amended since its creation.

Jared, of course, is not alone in having made vast intellectual advances during his middle childhood. In this period, cognitive abilities broaden, and children become increasingly able to understand and master complex skills. At the same time, though, their thinking is still not fully adultlike.

What are the advances, and the limitations, in thinking during childhood? Several perspectives provide us with an understanding of what goes on cognitively during middle childhood.

PIAGETIAN APPROACHES TO COGNITIVE DEVELOPMENT

Let us return for a moment to Jean Piaget's view of the preschooler, which we considered in Chapter 7. From Piaget's perspective, the preschooler thinks *preoperationally*. This type of thinking is largely egocentric, and preoperational children lack the ability to use *operations*—organized, formal, logical mental processes.

The Rise of Concrete Operational Thought.   All this changes, according to Piaget, during the **concrete operational stage**, which coincides with the school years and which occurs between 7 and 12 years of age. This stage is characterized by the active, and appropriate, use of logic. Concrete operational thought involves applying *logical* operations to concrete problems. For instance, when children in the concrete operational stage are confronted with a conservation problem (such as determining whether the amount of liquid poured from one container to another container of a different shape stays the same), they use cognitive and logical processes to answer, no longer being influenced solely by appearance. Consequently, they easily—and correctly—solve conservation problems. Because they are less egocentric, they can take multiple aspects of a situation into account, an ability known as **decentering**.

Cognitive development makes substantial advances during middle childhood.

The shift from preoperational thought to concrete operational thought does not happen overnight, of course. During the 2 years before children move firmly into the concrete operational period, they shift back and forth between preoperational and concrete operational thinking. For instance, they typically pass through a period when they can answer conservation problems correctly but cannot articulate why they did so. When asked to explain the reasoning behind their answers, they may respond with an unenlightening, "Because."

However, once concrete operational thinking is fully engaged, children show several cognitive advances. For instance, they attain the concept of *reversibility*, which is the notion that processes that transform a stimulus can be reversed, returning it to its original form. Grasping reversibility permits children to understand that a ball of clay that has been squeezed into a long, snakelike rope can be returned to its original state. More abstractly, it allows school-age children to understand that if 3 + 5 equals 8, then 5 + 3 also equals 8—and, later during the period, that 8 − 3 equals 5.

Concrete operational thinking also permits children to understand such concepts as the relationship between time and speed. For instance, consider the problem shown in Figure 9-3, in which two cars start and finish at the same points in the same amount of time, but travel different routes. Children who are just entering the concrete operational period reason that the cars are traveling at the same speed. However, between the ages of 8 and 10, children begin to draw the right conclusion: that the car traveling the longer route must be moving faster if it arrives at the finish point at the same time as does the car traveling the shorter route.

Still, despite the advances that occur during the concrete operational stage, children still experience one critical limitation in their thinking. They remain tied to concrete, physical reality. Furthermore, they are unable to understand truly abstract or hypothetical questions, or ones that involve formal logic.

Piaget in Perspective: Piaget Was Right, Piaget Was Wrong.   As we have seen in our prior consideration of Piaget's views in Chapters 5 and 7, researchers following in Piaget's footsteps have found much to cheer about—as well as much to criticize.

Piaget was a virtuoso observer of children, and his many books contain pages of brilliant, careful observations of children at work and play. Furthermore, his theories have powerful educational implications, and many schools employ principles derived from his views to guide the nature and presentation of instructional materials (Flavell, 1985; Ravitch, 1985).

FIGURE 9-3

TRAVEL TIME

After being told that the two cars traveling the Routes 1 and 2 start and end their journeys in the same amount of time, children who are just entering the concrete operational period still reason that the cars are traveling at the same speed. Later, however, they reach the correct conclusion: that the car traveling the longer route must be moving at a higher speed if it starts and ends its journey at the same time as the car traveling the shorter route.

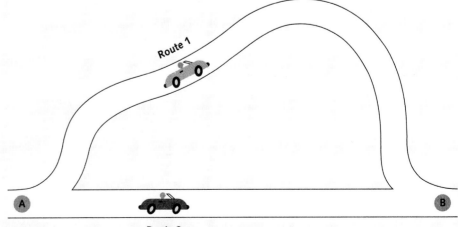

Route 1

A

Route 2

B

In some ways, then, Piaget's approach was quite successful in describing cognitive development. At the same time, though, critics have raised compelling, and seemingly legitimate, grievances about his approach. As we have noted before, many researchers argue that Piaget underestimated children's capabilities, in part because of the limited nature of the mini-experiments he conducted. When a broader array of experimental tasks is used, children show less consistency within stages than Piaget would predict (Siegler, 1994).

Furthermore, Piaget seems to have misjudged the age at which children's cognitive abilities emerge. As might be expected from our earlier discussions of Piaget's stages, increasing evidence suggests that children's capabilities emerge sooner than Piaget envisioned. Some children show evidence of a form of concrete operational thinking before the age of 7, the time at which Piaget suggested these abilities first appear.

The opposite phenomenon also seems to occur: Cross-cultural research implies that some children never leave the preoperational stage, failing to master conservation and to develop concrete operations. For example, pioneering work by Patricia Greenfield (1966) found that among the Wolof children in Senegal, a West African country, only half of children aged 10 to 13 understood conservation of liquid. Studies in such other non-Western areas as the jungles of New Guinea and Brazil and remote villages in Australia confirmed her findings: Not everyone reached the concrete operational stage (Dasen, 1977). It appeared that Piaget's claims that his stages provided a universal description of cognitive development were exaggerated.

On the other hand, we should not entirely dismiss the Piagetian approach. For one thing, subsequent research has found that with proper training in conservation, children in non-Western cultures who do not conserve can readily learn to do so. For instance, in one study urban Australian children—who develop concrete operations on the same timetable as Piaget suggested—were compared to rural Aborigine children, who typically do not demonstrate an understanding of conservation at the age of 14 (Dasen, Ngini, & Lavallee, 1979). When the rural Aborigine children were given training, they began to conserve as adequately as their urban counterparts, although with a time lag of about three years (see Figure 9-4).

Such research suggests that in some ways Piaget may have been more right than wrong: Although school-age children in some cultures may differ from Westerners in the demonstration of certain cognitive skills, it is unlikely that they lack the ability to perform concrete operations. Instead, the most probable explanation of the difference is that the non-Western

Research conducted in such places as remote areas of Australia shows that, contrary to Piaget's assertion, not everyone reaches the concrete operational stage.

FIGURE 9-4

CROSS-CULTURAL CONSERVATION

Rural Australian Aborigine children trail their urban counterparts in the development of their understanding of conservation; with training they later catch up. Without training, about half of 14-year-old Aborigines do not have an understanding of conservation.

(Adapted from Dasen, Ngini, & Lavallee, 1979).

Urban Australians

Rural Australian Aborigines

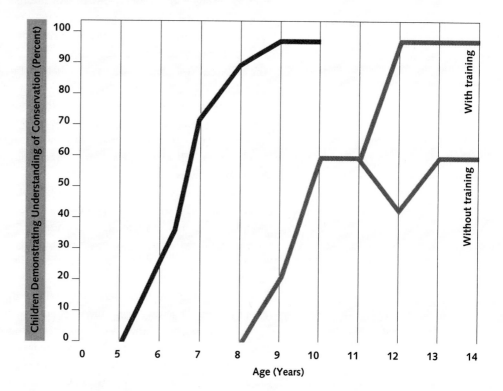

children have had different sorts of experiences from those that permit children in Western societies to perform well on Piagetian measures of conservation and concrete operations. The progress of cognitive development, then, cannot be understood without looking at the nature of a child's culture (Jahoda & Lewis, 1988; Beilin & Pufall, 1992).

INFORMATION PROCESSING IN MIDDLE CHILDHOOD

It is a real feat for first graders to learn basic math tasks, such as addition and subtraction of single-digit numbers, as well as the spelling of simple words such as "dog" and "run." But by the time they reach the sixth grade, children are able to work with fractions and decimals, and "exhibit" and "residence" are typical spelling words.

According to *information-processing approaches*, children become increasingly sophisticated in their handling of information. Like computers, they can process more data as the size of their memories increases and the "programs" they use to process information become increasingly sophisticated.

Memory. What is needed for a child to remember a piece of information? Three processes must all function properly: encoding, storage, and retrieval. *Encoding* is the process by which information is initially recorded in a form usable to memory. Children who were never taught that 5 + 6 = 11, or who didn't pay attention when they were exposed to this fact, will never be able to recall it. They never encoded the information in the first place. But mere exposure to a fact is not enough; the information also has to be *stored*. In our example, the information that 5 + 6 = 11 must be placed and maintained in the memory system. Finally, proper functioning of memory requires that material that is stored in memory must be *retrieved*. Through retrieval, material in memory storage is located, brought into awareness, and used.

memory   *the process by which information is initially encoded, stored, and retrieved*

meta-memory   *an understanding about the processes that underlie memory, which emerges and improves during middle childhood*

In sum, **memory** is the ability to encode, store, and retrieve information. The process can be thought of as analogous to the combined operation of a computer's keyboard (encoding), hard drive (storage), and screen (retrieval). Only when all three components are operating are children able to recall information successfully.

During middle childhood, short-term memory capacity improves significantly. For instance, children are increasingly able to hear a string of digits (1-5-6-3-4) and then repeat the string in reverse order (4-3-6-5-1). At the start of the preschool period, they can remember and reverse only about two digits; by the beginning of adolescence they can perform the task with as many as six digits. In addition, they use more sophisticated strategies for recalling information, which can be improved with training (Roodenrys, Hulme, & Brown, 1993; Ardila & Rosselli, 1994; Bjorklund, Schneier, Cassel, & Ashley, 1994; Halford, Mayberry, O'Hare, & Grant, 1994).

Memory capacity may shed light on another issue in cognitive development. Some developmental researchers suggest that the difficulty children experience in solving conservation problems just before the preschool period might stem from memory limitations (Siegler & Richards, 1982). They argue that young children simply may not be able to recall all the necessary pieces of information that enter into the correct solution of conservation problems.

Meta-memory, an understanding about the processes that underlie memory, also emerges and improves during middle childhood. By the time they enter first grade, children have a general notion of what memory is, and that some people have "good" memories and others "bad" memories (Schneider & Pressley, 1989; Lewis & Mitchell, 1994).

School-age children's understanding of memory becomes more sophisticated as they grow older and increasingly engage in *control strategies*—conscious, intentionally used tactics to improve cognitive processing. For instance, school-age youngsters are aware that rehearsal, the repetition of information, is a useful strategy for improving memory, and they increasingly employ it over the course of middle childhood. Similarly, they progressively make more effort to organize material into coherent patterns, a strategy that permits them to recall it better. For instance, when faced with remembering a list including cups, knives, forks, and plates, older school-age children are more likely to group the items into coherent patterns—cups and plates, forks and knives—than children just entering the school-age years (Howe & O'Sullivan, 1990; Weed, Ryan, & Day, 1990; Pressley & Van Meter, 1993).

Improving Memory.   Can children be trained to be more effective in the use of control strategies? The answer is decidedly yes. School-age children can be taught to apply particular strategies, although such teaching is not a simple matter. For instance, children need to know not only how to use a memory strategy, but also when and where to use it most effectively. But if such information is conveyed by teachers and parents, it can be a genuine boon to children (O'Sullivan, 1993).

Take, for example, an innovative technique called the keyword strategy, which can help students learn the vocabulary of a foreign language, the capitals of the states, or other information in which two sets of words or labels are paired. In the *keyword strategy*, one word is paired with another that sounds like it. For instance, in learning foreign-language vocabulary, a foreign word is paired with a common English word that has a similar sound. The English word is the keyword. Thus, to learn the Spanish word for duck (*pato*, pronounced *pot-o*), the keyword might be "pot"; for the Spanish word for horse (*caballo*, pronounced *cob-eye-yo*), the keyword might be "eye." Once the keyword is chosen, children then form a mental image of the two words interacting with one another. For instance, a student might use an image of a duck taking a bath in a pot to remember the word *pato*, or a horse with bulging eyes to remember the word *caballo* (Pressley & Levin, 1983; Pressley, 1987).

LANGUAGE DEVELOPMENT: WHAT WORDS MEAN

If you listen to what school-age children say to one another, their speech, at least at first hearing, sounds not too different from that of adults. However, the apparent similarity is deceiving. The linguistic sophistication of children—particularly at the start of the school-age period—still requires refinement to reach adult levels of expertise.

Mastering the Mechanics of Language.   For instance, vocabulary continues to increase during the school years. Although children know thousands of words, they continue to add new words to their vocabularies, and at a fairly rapid clip. For instance, the average 6-year-old has a vocabulary of from 8,000 to 14,000 words, whereas the vocabulary grows by another 5,000 words between the ages of 9 and 11.

Furthermore, school-age children's mastery of grammar improves. For instance, the use of the passive voice is rare during the early school-age years (as in "The dog was walked by Jon," compared with the active voice "Jon walked the dog"). Six- and 7-year-olds only infrequently use conditional sentences, such as "If Sarah will set the table, I will wash the dishes." However, over the course of middle childhood, the use of both passive voice and conditional sentences increases. In addition, children's understanding of *syntax*, the rules that indicate how words and phrases can be combined to form sentences, grows during middle childhood.

By the time they reach first grade, most children pronounce words quite accurately. However, certain *phonemes*, units of sound, remain troublesome. For instance, the ability to pronounce *j, v, th,* and *zh* sounds develops later than does the ability to pronounce other phonemes.

School-age children also may have difficulty decoding sentences when the meaning depends on *intonation*, or tone of voice. For example, consider the sentence, "George gave a book to David and he gave one to Bill." If the word "he" is emphasized, the meaning is "George gave a book to David and David gave a different book to Bill." But if the intonation emphasizes the word "and," then the meaning changes to "George gave a book to David and George also gave a book to Bill." Such subtleties are not easily sorted out by school-age children (Moshman, Glover, & Bruning, 1987; Woolfolk, 1993).

Children also become more competent during the school years in their use of *pragmatics*, the rules governing the use of language to communicate in a social context. Pragmatics concern children's ability to use appropriate and effective language in a given social setting.

For example, although children are aware of the rules of conversational turn-taking at the start of the early childhood period, their use of these rules is sometimes primitive. Consider the following conversation between 6-year-olds Yonnie and Max:

YONNIE: My dad drives a Fedex truck.

MAX: My sister's name is Molly.

YONNIE: He gets up really early in the morning.

MAX: She wet her bed last night.

Later, however, conversations show more give-and-take, with the second child actually responding to the comments of the first. For instance, this conversation between 11-year-olds Mia and Josh reflects a more sophisticated mastery of pragmatics:

MIA: I don't know what to get Claire for her birthday.

JOSH: I'm getting her earrings.

MIA: She already has a lot of jewelry.

JOSH: I don't think she has that much.

metalinguistic awareness   an understanding of one's own use of language

bilingualism   the use of more than one language

How Language Promotes Self-control.   The growing sophistication of their language helps school-age youngsters control their behavior. For instance, in one experiment, children were told that they could have one marshmallow treat if they chose to eat one immediately, but two treats if they waited. Most of the children, who ranged in age from 4 to 8, chose to wait, but the strategies they used while waiting differed significantly.

The 4-year-olds often chose to look at the marshmallows while waiting, a strategy that was not terribly effective. In contrast, 6- and 8-year-olds used language to help them overcome temptation, although in different ways. The 6-year-olds spoke and sang to themselves, reminding themselves that if they waited they would get more treats in the end. The 8-year-olds focused on aspects of the marshmallows that were not related to taste, such as their appearance, which helped them to wait.

Metalinguistic Awareness.   One of the most significant developments in middle childhood is the increasing **metalinguistic awareness** of children, which is an understanding of one's own use of language. By the time they are 5 or 6, children understand that language is governed by a set of rules. Whereas in the early years these rules are learned and comprehended implicitly, during middle childhood youngsters come to understand them more explicitly (Kemper & Vernooy, 1993).

Metalinguistic awareness helps children achieve comprehension when information is fuzzy or incomplete. For instance, when preschoolers are given ambiguous or unclear information, they rarely ask for clarification, and they tend to blame themselves if they do not understand. By the time they reach the age of 7 or 8, children realize that miscommunication may be due to factors attributable not only to themselves but also to the person communicating with them. Consequently, school-age children are more likely to ask for clarifications of information that is unclear to them (Beal & Belgrad, 1990; Kemper & Vernooy, 1993).

BILINGUALISM: SPEAKING IN MANY TONGUES

> For picture day at New York's P.S. 217, a neighborhood elementary school in Brooklyn, the notice to parents was translated into five languages. That was a nice gesture, but insufficient: More than 40 percent of the children are immigrants whose families speak any one of 26 languages, ranging from Armenian to Urdu (Leslie, 1991, p. 56).

From the smallest towns to the biggest cities, the voices with which children speak are changing. In seven states, including Texas, New York, and Colorado, more than a quarter of the students are not native English speakers. In fact, English is the second language for more than 32 million Americans (U.S. Bureau of the Census, 1993; see Figure 9-5).

Although **bilingualism** (use of more than one language) presents a challenge to the teachers of children who speak English either haltingly or, initially, not at all, increasing evidence suggests that knowing more than one language may present distinct cognitive advantages.

For instance, speakers of two languages show greater cognitive flexibility. Because they have a wider range of linguistic possibilities to choose from as they assess a situation, they can solve problems with greater creativity and versatility (Romaine, 1994).

Bilingual students often have greater metalinguistic awareness, understanding the rules of language more explicitly. They might even score higher on tests of intelligence, according to some research. For example, one survey of French- and English-speaking school-age children in Canada found that bilingual students scored significantly higher on both verbal and nonverbal tests of intelligence than did those who spoke only one language (Lambert & Peal, 1972; Hakuta & Garcia, 1989; Ricciardelli, 1992; Genesee, 1994).

Finally, because many linguists contend that universal processes underlie language acquisition, as we noted in Chapter 7, instruction in a native language may enhance instruc-

The increasing diversity of the United States is illustrated by this girl scout troop, sponsored by a Buddhist church.

FIGURE 9-5

THE VOICES OF AMERICA

The number of U.S. residents over the age of 5 who speak a language other than English at home.

(*Source*: U.S. Bureau of the Census, 1991).

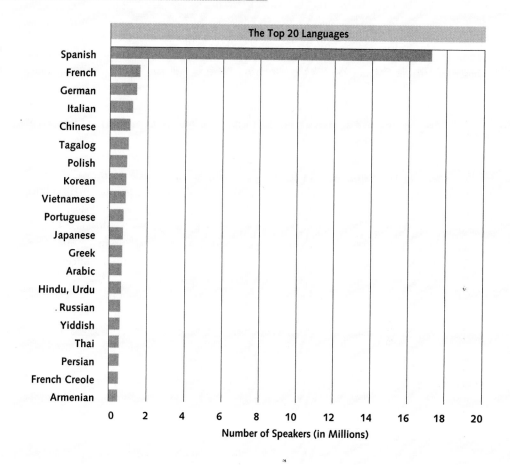

The Top 20 Languages

Spanish
French
German
Italian
Chinese
Tagalog
Polish
Korean
Vietnamese
Portuguese
Japanese
Greek
Arabic
Hindu, Urdu
Russian
Yiddish
Thai
Persian
French Creole
Armenian

0 2 4 6 8 10 12 14 16 18 20

Number of Speakers (in Millions)

tion in a second language. Consequently, students who enter school speaking no English may be successfully taught in their native languages, while at the same time learning English. There is no evidence that children will be overwhelmed cognitively by simultaneous instruction in their native languages and in English. In fact, as we discuss next, many educators believe that second-language learning should be a regular part of elementary schooling (Lindholm, 1991; Perozzi & Sanchez, 1992; Yelland, Pollard, & Mercuri, 1993).

Developmental Diversity

The Benefits of Bilingualism: Children Do Swimmingly in Language-Immersion Programs

One by one, the first graders recite the characters the teacher has drawn on the board. Only it's not the ABCs that these six- and seven-year-olds are rattling off but the hiragana characters of the Japanese language.

The students in this inner-city public-school classroom have no Japanese heritage. In fact, almost all of them are African-American. But all day long, they hear only Japanese from their teachers. They recite their math problems in Japanese. Their language readers open from left to right as in Japan. When the teacher asks in Japanese, "Do you understand?" the children chirp, "Hai." (Reitman, 1994, p. B1)

These students, enrolled in Detroit's Foreign Language Immersion and Cultural Studies School, are participating in a program designed to capitalize on younger children's ability to learn second languages with relative ease. The school represents a sharp departure from traditional language instruction. In what is called a *language immersion program*, the school teaches all of its subjects in a foreign language.

Children in language immersion programs make rapid advances with the foreign language in which they are being taught, for several reasons. One is that, unlike older youngsters, they have not learned to be frightened by the task of learning a language. Furthermore, they feel relatively little embarrassment if they mispronounce words or make grammatical errors.

For those enrolled in language immersion programs, learning a second language provides several benefits beyond command of the language. It can also raise self-esteem due to the sense of mastery that comes from achieving proficiency in a difficult subject. Moreover, it can make students more sensitive to other cultures. Furthermore, although parents sometimes worry that their children's progress in English will be limited by their concentration on a foreign language, such concerns seem misplaced. Research suggests that children in

Speaking of Development

Lauro Cavazos

Born: ································· 1927

Education: ······················ Texas Tech University, B.A.; M.A. Texas Tech University, 1951; Ph.D. Iowa State University, 1954; numerous honorary degrees

Position: ·························· United States Secretary of Education, 1988–1990

Home: ····························· Concord, Massachusetts

By the year 2000 many facets of society in America will change, and much of that change will be the result of education, according to Lauro F. Cavazos, former Secretary of Education (1988–90) in the administration of President George Bush.

In his cabinet position Cavazos worked toward three main goals: raising the expectations of students, teachers, and parents; providing access to quality education for all students, especially those most at risk of failing; and promoting the notion that quality education is the responsibility of every member of society. This was a tremendous task, considering the growing diversity of the student population.

"First of all, we're finally starting to recognize that there is cultural diversity and acknowledge it in a serious fashion," says the sixth-generation Texan. "Already some 30 percent of the students in elementary and secondary public education are Hispanic or African-

immersion programs perform as well as their peers, and sometimes even better, in English grammar, reading comprehension, and tests of English vocabulary (Larsen-Freeman & Long, 1991).

On the other hand, not all language immersion programs are successful. The most positive results have come from programs in which majority group children are learning languages that are not spoken by the dominant culture. In contrast, when minority group children who enter school knowing only a language other than English are immersed in English-only programs, the results are less positive. In fact, children from minority language backgrounds enrolled in English-only programs sometimes perform worse in both English *and* their native languages than do same-age peers (Genesee, 1994).

Clearly, the effectiveness of language immersion programs varies widely. Furthermore, such programs are difficult to operate administratively. Finding an adequate number of bilingual teachers can be difficult, and teacher and student attrition can be a problem. Still, the results of participation in immersion programs can be impressive, particularly as knowledge of multiple languages becomes less of a luxury and more of a necessity in today's multicultural world.

"We're finally starting to recognize that there is cultural diversity and acknowledge it in a serious fashion."

American, and these numbers are going to continue to grow as we approach the turn of the century."

Noting the increase in bilingual students, Cavazos points out that the trend will have an impact on the areas of literature, history, geography, and economics, among others—all contributing to the changing of American society.

"We need to recognize that diversity is a bonus in America," he notes. "I'm a strong supporter of bilingual education, but certain conditions need to be met in order for it to work. First, I think non-English-speaking students need to learn English as quickly as possible, hopefully within a year, but at most three years. Second, they should retain their original language, whatever that language is—Cambodian, Spanish, or whatever. And third, each group should be expected to add to the culture of America, because America is an amalgamation of many different cultures. We need to recognize that America is already a pluralistic society."

Maintaining that one of America's biggest problems is an education deficit, Cavazos stresses the importance of the educational development of children.

"We need to recognize that diversity is a bonus in America."

"Some 27 million Americans are illiterate, and 40 million to 50 million Americans read at the fourth-grade level," he says. "We have 600,000 to 700,000 youngsters who drop out of school each year, and we haven't had a significant increase in SAT scores in years. I call that the education deficit.

"Our first major goal is to help those students who are in need—the minorities, handicapped, students in special education, and so forth. Our second central goal is to support good research. I've had tremendous resistance to some of the things I've said, and some people really take offense," Cavazos states. "But if we don't change things, in one or two generations this nation is going to be in serious trouble."

Review and Rethink

REVIEW

- According to Jean Piaget, school-age children are in the concrete operational stage of cognitive development, which is characterized by the application of logical processes to concrete problems.

- Information-processing approaches attribute cognitive development during the school years to quantitative improvements in memory and in the sophistication of the mental programs that the school-age child can handle.

- The three processes of memory—encoding, storage, and retrieval—come under increasing control during the school years, and the development of meta-memory permits the use of control strategies to improve cognitive processing and memorization.

- Language development in middle childhood is characterized by improvements in vocabulary, syntax, and pragmatics; by the use of language as a self-control device; and by the growth of metalinguistic awareness.

- Bilingualism, the ability to speak more than one language, can produce improvements in cognitive flexibility, metalinguistic awareness, and even IQ test performance, but simple immersion in the language of the dominant culture can be problematic for children of other cultures.

RETHINK

- Do you think a non-Western Piaget working in a different culture might have developed a theory of stages involving cognitive tasks that Western children would have difficulty performing without explicit instruction? Why?

- Why do control strategies such as grouping into patterns and using keywords work? What do they tell us about memory?

- This chapter suggested that two rules of pragmatics, which govern the social uses of language, are (1) that speakers should take turns, and (2) that speakers should address the same topic. Can you think of other rules of pragmatics?

- Do adults use language as a self-control device? How?

- Why might instruction in one's first language enhance instruction in another language, such as English? Do the notions of metalinguistic awareness and universal grammar relate to this phenomenon?

SCHOOLING: THE THREE R'S (AND MORE) OF MIDDLE CHILDHOOD

As the eyes of the six other children in his reading group turned to him, Glenn shifted uneasily in his chair. Reading had never come easily to him, and he always felt anxious when it was his turn to read aloud. But as his teacher nodded in encouragement, he plunged in, hesitantly at first, then gaining momentum as he read the story about a mother's first day on a new job. He found that he could read the passage quite nicely, and he felt a surge of happiness and pride at his accomplishment. When he was done, he broke into a broad smile as his teacher said simply, "Well done, Glenn."

It is small moments such as these, repeated over and over, that make—or break—a child's educational experience. Schooling marks a time when society formally attempts to transfer its accumulated body of knowledge, beliefs, values, and wisdom to new generations. The success with which this transfer is managed determines, in a very real sense, the future fortunes of the world.

SCHOOLING AROUND THE WORLD: WHO GETS EDUCATED?

In the United States, as in most developed countries, a primary school education is both a universal right and a legal requirement. Virtually all children are provided with a free education through the 12th grade.

Children in other parts of the world are not so fortunate. In 1990, more than 100 million children, 60 percent of them female, did not have access to even a primary school education. An additional 100 million youngsters did not complete a basic education, and overall more than 960 million individuals (two-thirds of them women) were illiterate throughout their lives (see Figure 9-6). Projections suggest that by the year 2000 more than 160 million of the world's children will not have access to even a primary school education (World Conference on Education for All, 1990).

In almost all developing countries, fewer females receive formal education than do males, a discrepancy found at every level of schooling. Even in developed nations, women lag behind men in their exposure to science and technological topics. These differences reflect widespread and deeply held cultural and parental biases that favor males over females.

WHAT MAKES CHILDREN READY FOR SCHOOL?

Do children who are younger than most of the other children in their grade suffer as a result? According to traditional wisdom, the answer is yes. Because younger children are assumed to be slightly less advanced developmentally than their peers, it has been assumed that such youngsters would be at a competitive disadvantage.

However, recent research has begun to dispel this view. According to a massive study conducted by developmental psychologist Frederick Morrison, children who are among the

FIGURE 9-6

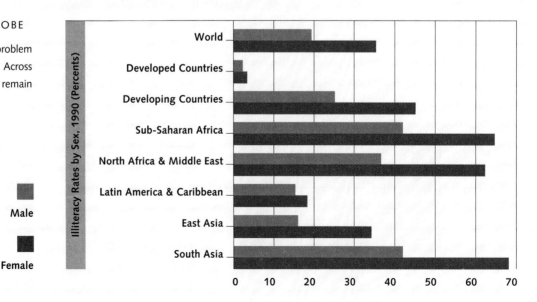

ILLITERACY ACROSS THE GLOBE

Illiteracy remains a significant problem worldwide, particularly for women. Across the world, close to a billion people remain illiterate throughout their lives.

(*Source*: UNESCO, 1990.)

Male

Female

youngest in first grade progress at the same rate as the oldest. Although they were slightly behind older first graders in reading, the difference was negligible. It was also clear that parents who chose to hold their children back in kindergarten, thereby ensuring that they would be among the oldest in first grade and after, were not doing their children a favor. These older children did no better than their younger classmates (DeAngelis, 1994; Bisanz, Morrison, & Dunn, 1995).

Clearly, then, age relative to same-grade peers is not, by itself, a particularly important factor in determining school success. If age does not matter, what did have an impact on school success? It turned out that several factors relating to parental influence played a large role. For example, the parents' attitude toward reading was important, as were parents' intelligence and educational background.

In sum, evidence suggests that age, per se, is not a critical indicator of when children should start school. Instead, the start of formal schooling is more reasonably tied to overall developmental readiness, the product of a complex combination of several factors.

EDUCATIONAL TRENDS: BEYOND THE THREE R'S

Schooling in the 1990s is very different from what it was as recently as a decade ago; U.S. schools are experiencing a definite return to the educational fundamentals embodied in the traditional three R's (reading, writing, and arithmetic). As can be seen in the model curriculum promoted by the U.S. Department of Education (Table 9-1), the emphasis on educational basics is strong. This trend marks a departure from the 1970s and 1980s, when the emphasis was on socio-emotional issues and on allowing students to choose study topics on the basis of their interests, instead of in accordance with a set curriculum.

The elementary classrooms of the 1990s also stress issues of individual accountability. Teachers are more likely to be held responsible for their students' learning, and both students and teachers are more likely to be required to take tests, developed at the state or national level, to assess their competence (Woolfolk, 1993).

Furthermore, increased attention is being paid to issues involving student diversity and multiculturalism. And with good reason: The demographic makeup of students in the United States is undergoing an extraordinary shift. For instance, the proportion of Hispanics will in all likelihood more than double in the next 50 years. Moreover, by the year 2050, Caucasians will make up just over half of the total population of the United States (U.S. Bureau of the Census, 1993; see Figure 9-7). Consequently, educators have been taking multicultural concerns more and more seriously.

FIGURE 9-7

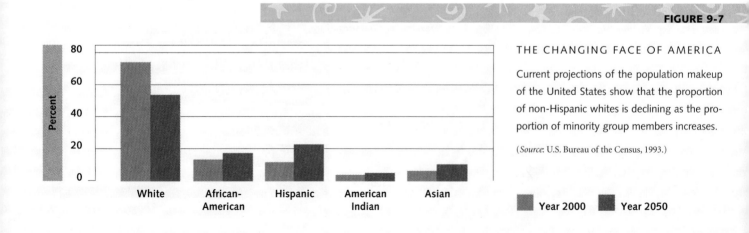

THE CHANGING FACE OF AMERICA

Current projections of the population makeup of the United States show that the proportion of non-Hispanic whites is declining as the proportion of minority group members increases.

(*Source*: U.S. Bureau of the Census, 1993.)

Year 2000   Year 2050

TABLE 9-1

JAMES MADISON ELEMENTARY SCHOOL: A MODEL CURRICULUM FOR KINDERGARTEN THROUGH GRADE 6

Subject	Kindergarten Through Grade 3	Grades 4 Through 6
ENGLISH	*INTRODUCTION TO READING AND WRITING* (phonics, silent and oral reading, basic rules of grammar and spelling, vocabulary, writing and penmanship, elementary composition, and library skills)	*INTRODUCTION TO CRITICAL READING* (children's literature, independent reading and book reports, more advanced grammar, spelling and vocabulary, and composition skills)
SOCIAL STUDIES	*INTRODUCTION TO HISTORY, GEOGRAPHY AND CIVICS* (significant Americans, explorers, Native Americans, American holidays, customs, and symbols, citizenship, and landscape, climate, and mapwork)	Grade 4: *U.S. HISTORY TO CIVIL WAR* Grade 5: *U.S. HISTORY SINCE 1865* Grade 6: *WORLD HISTORY TO THE MIDDLE AGES*
MATHEMATICS	*INTRODUCTION TO MATHEMATICS* (numbers, basic operations, fractions and decimals, rounding, geometric shapes, measurement of length, area, and volume, bar graphs, and estimation and elementary statistics)	*INTERMEDIATE ARITHMATIC AND GEOMETRY* (number theory, negative numbers, percentages, and exponents, line graphs, the Pythagorean theorem, and basic probability)
SCIENCE	*INTRODUCTION TO SCIENCE* (plants and animals, the food chain, the solar system, rocks and minerals, weather, magnets, energy and motion, properties of matter, and simple experiments)	Grade 4: *EARTH SCIENCE AND OTHER TOPICS* Grade 5: *LIFE SCIENCE AND OTHER TOPICS* Grade 6: *PHYSICAL SCIENCE AND OTHER TOPICS*
FOREIGN LANGUAGE	*(OPTIONAL)*	*INTRODUCTION TO FOREIGN LANGUAGE* (basic vocabulary, grammar, reading, writing, conversation, and cultural material)
FINE ARTS	*MUSIC AND VISUAL ART* (songs, recordings, musical sounds and instruments, painting, craftmaking, and visual effects)	*MUSIC AND VISUAL ART* (great composers, musical styles and forms, elementary music theory, great painters, interpretation of art, and creative projects)
PHYSICAL EDUCATION AND HEALTH	*PHYSICAL EDUCATION AND HEALTH* (body control, fitness, sports, games, and exercises, sportsmanship, safety, hygiene, nutrition, and drug prevention education)	*PHYSICAL EDUCATION AND HEALTH* (team and individual sports, first aid, drug prevention education, and appropriate sex education)

Source: U.S. Department of Education (1988).

Developmental Diversity

Multicultural Education

Ever since the earliest period of formal education in the United States, classrooms have been populated by individuals from a broad range of backgrounds and experiences. Yet it is only relatively recently that variations in student backgrounds have been viewed as one of the major challenges—and opportunities—that educators face.

In fact, both the diversity of background and the experience in the classroom relates to a fundamental objective of education: to provide a formal mechanism to transmit the information a society holds important. As the famous anthropologist Margaret Mead observed, "In its broadest sense, education is the cultural process, the way in which each newborn human infant, born with a potentiality for learning greater than that of any other mammal, is transformed into a full member of a specific human society, sharing with the other members of a specific human culture" (Mead, 1942, p. 633).

Culture, then, can be thought of as a set of behaviors, beliefs, values, and expectations shared by members of a particular society. But although culture is often thought of in a relatively broad context (as in "Western culture" or "Asian culture"), it is also possible to focus on particular *subcultural* groups within a larger, more encompassing culture. For example, we can consider particular racial, ethnic, religious, socioeconomic, or even gender groups within the United States as manifesting characteristics of a subculture.

Membership in a cultural or subcultural group might be of only passing interest to educators were it not for the fact that students' cultural backgrounds have a substantial impact on the way that they—and their peers—are educated. In fact, in recent years a considerable amount of thought has gone into establishing **multicultural education**, a form of education in which the goal is to help minority students develop competence in the culture of the majority group while maintaining positive group identities that build on their original cultures (La Fromboise, Coleman, & Gerton, 1993).

Cultural Assimilation or Pluralistic Society?   Multicultural education developed in part as a reaction to a **cultural assimilation model**, which fostered the view of American society as the proverbial melting pot. According to this view, the goal of education was to assimilate individual cultural identities into a unique, unified American culture. In practical terms this meant that students were discouraged from speaking their native tongues and were totally immersed in English.

In the early 1970s, however, educators and members of minority groups began to suggest that the cultural assimilation model ought to be replaced by a **pluralistic society model**. According to this conception, American society is made up of diverse, coequal cultural groups that should preserve their individual cultural features.

The pluralistic society model grew in part from the belief that teachers, by discouraging children's use of their native tongues, denigrated their cultural heritages and lowered their self-esteem. Furthermore, because instructional materials inevitably feature culture-specific events and understandings, children who were denied access to their own cultural materials might never be exposed to important aspects of their backgrounds. For example, English-language texts rarely present some of the great themes that appear throughout Spanish literature and history (such as the search for the Fountain of Youth and the Don Juan legend). Hispanic students immersed in such texts might never come to understand important components of their own heritage.

multicultural education   a form of education in which the goal is to help minority students develop competence in the culture of the majority group while maintaining positive group identities that build on their original cultures

cultural assimilation model   the model that fostered the view of American society as the proverbial melting pot

pluralistic society model   the concept that American society is made up of diverse, coequal cultural groups that should preserve their individual cultural features

Ultimately, educators began to argue that the presence of students representing diverse cultures enriched and broadened the educational experience of all students. Pupils and teachers exposed to people from different backgrounds could better understand the world and gain greater sensitivity to the values and needs of others.

Fostering a Bicultural Identity.   Today, most educators agree that the pluralistic society model is the most valid one for schooling, and that minority children should be encouraged to develop a **bicultural identity**. They recommend that children be supported in maintaining their original cultural identities while they integrate themselves into the dominant culture. This view suggests that an individual can live as a member of two cultures, with two cultural identities, without having to choose one over the other (LaFromboise, Coleman, & Gerton, 1993).

However, the means of achieving the goal of biculturalism are far from clear. Consider, for example, children who enter a school speaking only Spanish. The traditional "melting-pot" technique would be to immerse the children in classes taught in English while providing a crash course in English-language instruction (and little else) until the children demonstrate a suitable level of proficiency. Unfortunately, the traditional approach has a considerable drawback: Until the students master English, they fall further and further behind their peers who entered school already knowing English.

More contemporary approaches emphasize a bicultural strategy, in which children are encouraged to maintain simultaneous membership in more than one culture. Instruction begins in the child's native language and shifts as rapidly as possible to include English.

Even after the children have mastered English, some instruction in the native language continues. At the same time, the school conducts a program of multicultural education for all students, in which teachers present material on the cultural backgrounds and traditions of speakers of all the languages spoken in the school. Such instruction is designed to enhance the self-image of speakers from both majority and minority cultures.

Successful bicultural programs also attempt to bring multiple languages into the context of everyday social interactions. Children are encouraged to use a variety of languages in their social relationships, and to become equally adept at several languages.

Although most educational experts favor bicultural approaches, the general public does not always agree. For instance, a national "English only" movement has as one of its goals the prohibition of school instruction in any language other than English. Whether such a perspective will prevail remains to be seen.

INTELLIGENCE: DETERMINING INDIVIDUAL STRENGTHS

"Why should you tell the truth?" "How far is Los Angeles from New York?" "A table is made of wood; a window of _____."

As ten-year-old Hyacinth sat hunched over her desk, trying to answer a long series of questions like these, she tried to guess the point of the test she was taking in her fifth-grade classroom. Clearly, the test didn't cover material that her teacher, Ms. White-Johnston, had talked about in class.

"What number comes next in this series: 1, 3, 7, 15, 31, _____?"

As Hyacinth continued to work her way through the questions, she gave up trying to guess the rationale for the test. She'd leave that to her teacher, she sighed to herself. Rather than attempting to figure out what it all meant, she simply tried to do her best on the individual test items.

bicultural identity   *the maintaining of one's original cultural identity while integrating into the dominant culture*

The French educator Alfred Binet originated the intelligence test

Hyacinth might be surprised to learn that she was not alone in questioning the meaning and import of the items on the test she was taking. For although the test items were painstakingly developed, many developmental specialists would admit to harboring their own doubts as to whether questions such as these are appropriate to the task of assessing what they are designed to measure: intelligence.

Understanding just what is meant by the concept of intelligence has proven to be a major challenge for researchers interested in delineating what separates intelligent from unintelligent behavior. Although nonexperts have their own conceptions of intelligence (one survey found, for instance, that lay persons feel that intelligence consists of three components: problem-solving ability, verbal ability, and social competence), it has been more difficult for experts to concur (Sternberg, Conway, Ketron, and Bernstein, 1981; Weinberg, 1989; J.E. Davidson, 1990). Still, a general definition of intelligence is possible: **Intelligence** is the capacity to understand the world, think rationally, and use resources effectively when faced with challenges (Wechsler, 1975).

Part of the difficulty in defining intelligence stems from the many—and sometimes unsatisfactory—paths that have been followed over the years in the quest to distinguish more intelligent people from less intelligent ones. To understand how researchers have approached the task of devising batteries of assessments, called *intelligence tests*, we need to consider some of the historical milestones in the area of intelligence.

Intelligence Benchmarks: Differentiating the Intelligent from the Unintelligent.   The Paris school system was faced with a problem at the turn of the century: A significant number of French children were not benefiting from regular instruction. Unfortunately, these children—many of whom we would now call mentally retarded—were generally not identified early enough to shift them to special classes. The French minister of instruction approached psychologist Alfred Binet with the problem of devising a technique for the early identification of students who might benefit from instruction outside the regular classroom.

Binet tackled his task in a thoroughly practical manner. His years of observing school-aged children suggested to him that previous efforts to distinguish intelligent from unintelligent students—some of which were based on reaction time or keenness of sight—were off the mark. Instead, he launched a trial-and-error process in which items and tasks were administered to students who had been previously identified by teachers as being either "bright" or "dull." Tasks that the bright students completed correctly and the dull students failed to complete correctly were retained for the test. Tasks that did not discriminate between the two groups were discarded. The end result of this process was a test that reliably distinguished students who had previously been identified as fast or slow learners.

Binet's pioneering efforts in intelligence testing left three important legacies. The first was his pragmatic approach to the construction of intelligence tests. Binet did not have theoretical preconceptions about what intelligence was. Instead, he used a trial-and-error approach to psychological measurement that continues to serve as the predominant approach to test construction today. His definition of intelligence as *that which his test measured* has been adopted by many modern psychologists, and it is particularly popular among test developers who respect the widespread utility of intelligence tests but wish to avoid arguments about the underlying nature of intelligence.

Our second inheritance from Binet stems from his focus on linking intelligence and school success. Binet's procedure for constructing an intelligence test ensured that intelligence—defined as performance on the test—and school success would be virtually one and the same. Binet's intelligence test and its current successors, then, have become reasonable indicators of the degree to which students possess attributes that contribute to successful school performance. Unfortunately, they do not provide particularly useful information regarding a vast number of other attributes that are largely unrelated to academic proficiency.

Finally, Binet developed a procedure of assigning each intelligence test score to a **mental age**, the age of the children taking the test who, on average, achieved that score. For

intelligence   *the capacity to understand the world, think with rationality, and use resources effectively when faced with challenges*

mental age   *the typical intelligence level found for people at a given chronological age*

example, if a 6-year-old girl received a score of 30 on the test, and this was the average score received by 10-year-olds, her mental age would be considered 10 years. Similarly, a 15-year-old boy who scored a 90 on the test—thereby matching the mean score for 15-year-olds—would be assigned a mental age of 15 years.

Although assigning a mental age to students provides an indication of whether or not they are performing at the same level as their peers, it does not permit adequate comparisons between students of a different **chronological**, or physical, **age**. By using mental age alone, for instance, it would be assumed that a 15-year-old responding with a mental age of 17 years would be as bright as a 6-year-old responding with a mental age of 8 years, when actually the 6-year-old would be showing a much greater *relative* degree of brightness.

A solution to this problem comes in the form of the **intelligence quotient**, or **IQ score**, a measure of intelligence that takes into account a student's mental *and* chronological age. The traditional method of calculating an IQ score uses the following formula, in which MA stands for mental age and CA for chronological age:

$$IQ\ SCORE = \frac{MA}{CA} \times 100.$$

As a bit of trial-and-error with this formula demonstrates, people whose mental age (MA) is equal to their chronological age (CA) will always have an IQ of 100. Furthermore, if the chronological age exceeds the mental age—implying below-average intelligence—the score will be below 100; and if the chronological age is lower than the mental age—suggesting above-average intelligence—the score will be above 100.

Using this formula, we can return to our earlier example of a 15-year-old who scores at a 17-year-old mental age. This student's IQ is $^{17}/_{15} \times 100$, or 113. In comparison, the IQ of a 6-year-old scoring at a mental age of 8 is $^8/_6 \times 100$, or 133—a higher IQ score than the 15-year-old's.

Although the basic principles behind the calculation of an IQ score still hold, scores today are calculated in a more mathematically sophisticated manner and are known as *deviation IQ scores*. The average deviation IQ score remains set at 100, but tests are now devised so that the degree of deviation from this score permits the calculation of the proportion of people who have similar scores. For instance, approximately two-thirds of all people fall within 15 points of the average score of 100, achieving scores between 85 and 115. As scores rise or fall beyond this range, the percentage of people in the same score category falls significantly.

Measuring IQ: Present-day Approaches to Intelligence.   Although tests of intelligence have become increasingly sophisticated since the time of Binet in terms of the accuracy with which they measure IQ, most of them can still trace their roots to his original work in one way or another. For example, one of the most widely used tests—the **Stanford-Binet Intelligence Scale**—began as an American revision of Binet's original test. The test consists of a series of items that vary according to the age of the person being tested. For instance, young children are asked to answer questions about everyday activities or to copy complex figures. Older people are asked to explain proverbs, solve analogies, and describe similarities between groups of words. The test is administered orally, and test-takers are given progressively more difficult problems until they are unable to proceed.

The **Wechsler Intelligence Scale for Children–Revised (WISC–R)** and its adult version, the **Wechsler Adult Intelligence Scale–Revised (WAIS-R)**, are two other widely used intelligence tests that provide separate measures of verbal and performance (or nonverbal) skills, as well as a total score. As you can see from the sample items in Figure 9-8, the verbal tasks are traditional word problems testing skills such as understanding a passage, while typical nonverbal tasks are copying a complex design, arranging pictures in a logical order, and assembling objects. The separate portions of the test allow for easier identification of any specific problems a test-taker may have. For example, significantly higher scores on the performance part of the test than on the verbal part may indicate difficulties in linguistic development.

chronological (or physical) age   the actual age of the child taking the intelligence test

intelligence quotient (IQ score)   a measure of intelligence that takes into account a student's mental and chronological age

Stanford-Binet Intelligence Scale   a test that consists of a series of items that vary according to the age of the person being tested

Wechsler Intelligence Scale for Children–Revised (WISC–R)   a test for children that provides separate measures of verbal and performance (or nonverbal) skills, as well as a total score

Wechsler Adult Intelligence Scale–Revised (WAIS-R)   a test for adults that provides separate measures of verbal and performance (or nonverbal) skills, as well as a total score

FIGURE 9-8

SAMPLE ITEMS FOUND ON THE WECHSLER INTELLIGENCE SCALES FOR CHILDREN (WISC–III).

Name	Goal of Item	Example
VERBAL SCALE		
Information	Assess general information	Where does honey come from?
Comprehension	Assess understanding and evaluation of social norms and past experience	Why do we use an umbrella when it rains?
Arithmetic	Assess math reasoning through verbal problems	Alice found three baseballs in a field. She gives two to her friend Jocelyn. How many baseballs does Alice have left?
Similarities	Test understanding of how objects or concepts are alike, tapping abstract reasoning	In what way are birds and airplanes alike?
PERFORMANCE SCALE		
Digit symbol	Assess speed of learning	Match symbols to numbers using key. 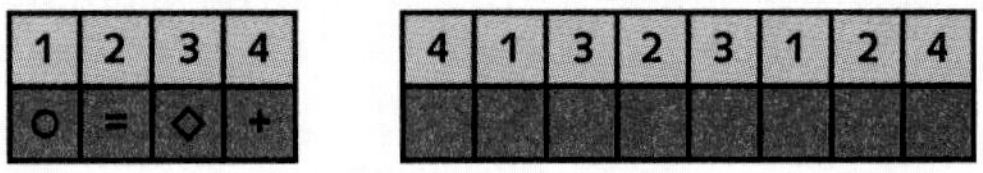
Picture completion	Visual memory and attention	Identify what is missing. 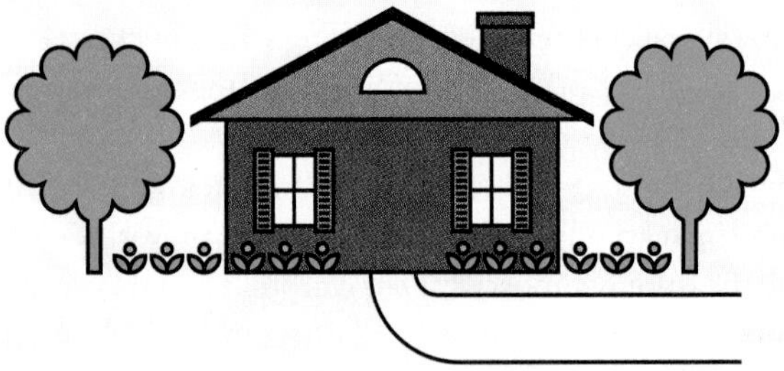
Object assembly	Test understanding of relationship of parts to wholes	Put pieces together to form a whole. 

What IQ Tests Don't Tell: Alternative Conceptions of Intelligence. The intelligence tests used most frequently in school settings today share an underlying premise: Intelligence is composed of a single, unitary mental ability factor, commonly called *g* (Spearman, 1927). The *g* factor is assumed to underlie performance on every aspect of intelligence, and it is the *g* factor that intelligence tests presumably measure.

However, many theorists dispute the notion that intelligence is unidimensional (Weinberg, 1989). For example, some psychologists suggest that in fact two kinds of intelligence exist: fluid intelligence and crystallized intelligence (Cattell, 1967, 1987). **Fluid intelligence** is the ability to deal with new problems and situations. For example, a student asked to group a series of letters according to some criterion or to remember a set of numbers would be using fluid intelligence. In contrast, **crystallized intelligence** is the store of information, skills, and strategies that people have acquired through their use of fluid intelligence. A student would likely be relying on crystallized intelligence to solve a puzzle or deduce the solution to a mystery, in which it was necessary to draw on past experience.

Other theorists divide intelligence into an even greater number of parts. For example, psychologist Howard Gardner suggests that we have seven distinct intelligences, each relatively independent (see Table 9-2). Gardner suggests that these separate intelligences operate not in isolation, but together, depending on the type of activity in which we are engaged (Gardner & Hatch, 1989; Kornhaber, Krechevsky, & Gardner, 1991).

Taking another tack, psychologist Robert Sternberg suggests that intelligence is best thought of in terms of information processing. In this view, the way in which people store material in memory and later use it to solve intellectual tasks provides the most precise conception of intelligence. Rather than focusing on the structure of intelligence in the form of its various subcomponents, then, information-processing approaches examine the processes that underlie intelligent behavior (Sternberg, 1987, 1990).

Researchers who have broken tasks and problems into their component parts have noted critical differences in the nature and speed of problem-solving processes between those who score high and those who score low on traditional IQ tests (Sternberg, 1982). For instance, when verbal problems such as analogies are broken into their component parts, it becomes clear that people with higher intelligence levels differ from others not only in the number of problems they ultimately are able to solve but also in their method of solving the problems. People with high IQ scores spend more time on the initial stages of problem solving, retrieving relevant information from memory. In contrast, those who score lower on traditional IQ tests tend to spend less time on the initial stages, instead skipping ahead and making less informed guesses. The processes used in solving problems, then, may reflect important differences in intelligence.

Sternberg's work on information-processing approaches to intelligence has led him to develop the **triarchic theory of intelligence**. According to this model, intelligence consists of three aspects of information processing: the componential element, the experiential element, and the contextual element. The componential aspect of intelligence reflects how efficiently people can process and analyze information. Efficiency in these areas allows people to infer relationships among different parts of a problem, solve the problem, and then evaluate their solution. Individuals who are strong on the componential element score highest on traditional tests of intelligence.

The experiential element is the insightful component of intelligence. People who have a strong experiential element can easily compare new material with what they already know, and they can combine and relate facts that they already know in novel and creative ways. Finally, the contextual element of intelligence concerns practical intelligence, or ways of dealing with the demands of the everyday environment.

In Sternberg's view, people vary in the degree to which each of these three elements is present, and a person's success on a given task reflects the match between the task and the person's specific pattern of strength on the three components of intelligence (Sternberg, 1985, 1991).

fluid intelligence   *the ability to deal with new problems and situations*

crystallized intelligence   *the store of information, skills, and strategies that people have acquired through education and prior experiences, and through their previous use of fluid intelligence*

triarchic theory of intelligence   *the model that states intelligence consists of three aspects of information processing: the componential element, the experiential element, and the contextual element*

TABLE 9-2

GARDNER'S SEVEN INTELLIGENCES

1. *Musical intelligence* (skills in tasks involving music). Case example:
   When he was 3, Yehudi Menuhin was smuggled into the San Francisco Orchestra concerts by his parents. The sound of Louis Persinger's violin so entranced the youngster that he insisted on a violin for his birthday and Louis Persinger as his teacher. He got both. By the time he was 10 years old, Menuhin was an international performer.

2. *Bodily kinesthetic intelligence* (skills in using the whole body or various portions of it in the solution of problems or in the construction of products or displays, exemplified by dancers, athletes, actors, and surgeons). Case example:
   Fifteen-year-old Babe Ruth played third base. During one game, his team's pitcher was doing poorly and Babe loudly criticized him from third base. Brother Mathias, the coach, called out, "Ruth, if you know so much about it, *you* pitch!" Babe was surprised and embarrassed because he had never pitched before, but Brother Mathias insisted. Ruth said later that at the very moment he took the pitcher's mound, he *knew* he was supposed to be a pitcher.

3. *Logical mathematical intelligence* (skills in problem solving and scientific thinking). Case example:
   Barbara McClintock won the Nobel Prize in medicine for her work in microbiology. She describes one of her breakthroughs, which came after thinking about a problem for half an hour...: "Suddenly I jumped and ran back to the {corn} field. At the top of the field (the others were still at the bottom) I shouted, "Eureka, I have it!'"

4. *Linguistic intelligence* (skills involved in the production and use of language). Case example:
   At the age of 10, T.S. Elliot created a magazine called *Fireside*, to which he was the sole contributor. In a three-day period during his winter vacation, he created eight complete issues.

5. *Spatial intelligence* (skills involving spatial configurations, such as those used by artists and architects). Case example:
   Navigation around the Caroline Islands...is accomplished without instruments.... During the actual trip, the navigator must envision mentally a reference island as it passes under a particular star and from that he computes the number of segments completed, the proportion of the trip remaining, and any corrections in heading.

6. *Interpersonal intelligence* (skills in interacting with others, such as sensitivity to the moods, temperaments, motivations, and intentions of others). Case example:
   When Anne Sullivan began instructing the deaf and blind Helen Keller, her task was one that had eluded others for years. Yet, just two weeks after beginning her work with Keller, Sullivan achieved a great success. In her words, "My heart is singing with joy this morning. A miracle has happened! The wild little creature of two weeks ago has been transformed into a gentle child."

7. *Intrapersonal intelligence* (knowledge of the internal aspects of oneself; access to one's own feelings and emotions). Case example:
   In her essay "A Sketch of the Past," Virginia Woolf displays deep insight into her own inner life through these lines, decribing her reaction to several specific memories from her childhood that still, in adulthood, shock her: "Though I still have the peculiarity that I receive these sudden shocks, they are now always welcome; after the first surprise, I always feel instantly that they are particularly valuable. And so I go on to suppose that the shock-receiving capacity is what makes me a writer."

   Source: Adapted from Walters & Gardner (1986).

Directions in Development

Racial Differences in IQ and *The Bell Curve* Controversy

A "jontry" is an example of a

(a) rulpow	(c) spudge
(b) flink	(d) bakwoe

If you were to find an item such as this on an intelligence test that you were taking, your immediate—and quite legitimate—reaction would likely be to complain. How could a test that purports to measure intelligence include test items that incorporate meaningless terminology?

But suppose, instead, that you found the following item, which at first may appear to be equally inappropriate:

A "handkerchief head" is

(a) a cool cat   (c) an "Uncle Tom"

(b) a porter   (d) a hoddi

Although this example may seem equally improper to you, you might feel otherwise if you were familiar with the language used in predominately African-American areas of certain cities and rural sections of the United States. For unlike the first example, which was made up of nonsense syllables, the second example uses meaningful words that a small but significant minority of English speakers would have little trouble understanding. In fact, one might argue that an intelligence test using the language of the second example would be more appropriate to administer to people who spoke that language than a traditional intelligence test using standard English.

The second item (the correct answer to which is "c," by the way) is drawn from a series of questions devised by sociologist Adrian Dove, as part of a pseudo-intelligence test designed to make a point (Dove, 1968). Dove contended that cultural experience played a crucial role in determining intelligence test scores, and he suggested that traditional measures of intelligence were biased in favor of white, upper- and middle-class students and against groups with different cultural experiences.

Dove created his "test" in reaction to a long-standing debate regarding the finding that members of certain racial groups consistently score lower on IQ tests than do members of other groups. For example, the mean score of African-Americans tends to be about 15 IQ points lower than the mean score of whites—although the measured difference varies a great deal depending on the particular IQ test employed (e.g., Humphreys, 1992).

The question that emerges from such differences, of course, is whether they reflect actual differences in intelligence, or, instead, are caused by bias in the intelligence tests themselves in favor of majority groups and against minorities. For example, if whites perform better than African-Americans because of their greater familiarity with the language used in the test items, the test hardly can be said to provide a fair measure of the intelligence of African-Americans. Similarly an intelligence test that used language such as that used in Dove's test could not be considered an impartial measure of intelligence for whites.

The question of how to interpret differences between intelligence scores of different cultural groups lies at the heart of one of the major controversies for life span developmentalists: To what degree is an individual's intelligence determined by heredity and how much by environment? The issue is crucial because of its social implications. For instance, if intelligence is primarily determined by heredity and is therefore largely fixed at birth, attempts to alter intelligence later in life will meet with limited success. On the other hand, if intelligence is largely environmentally determined, modifying social conditions is a more promising strategy for bringing about increases in intelligence.

***The Bell Curve* Controversy.** Although investigations into the relative contributions of heredity and environment to intelligence have been conducted for decades, the smoldering debate became a raging fire with the publication in 1994 of a book by Richard J. Herrnstein and Charles Murray, titled *The Bell Curve*. In the book, Herrnstein and Murray argue that the average 15-point IQ difference between whites and African-Americans is due primarily to heredity rather than environment. Furthermore, they argue that this IQ difference accounts for the higher rates of poverty, lower employment, and higher use of welfare among minority groups, as compared with majority groups (Herrnstein & Murray, 1994).

Herrnstein and Murray contend that whites score higher than African-Americans on traditional IQ tests even when socioeconomic status (SES) is taken into account. Specifically, middle- and upper-SES African-Americans tend to score lower than do middle- and upper-SES whites, just as lower-SES African-Americans score lower on average than lower-SES whites. Herrnstein and Murray use this evidence to argue that the IQ score difference between whites and African-Americans is primarily due to genetic factors.

The conclusions reached by Herrnstein and Murray raised a storm of protest, and many researchers who examined the data reported in the book came to conclusions that were quite different. Most developmental researchers responded by arguing that the differences between races in measured IQ can be explained by environmental differences between the races. Furthermore, critics maintain that there is little evidence to suggest that IQ is related to poverty and other social ills. Indeed, some researchers go further, suggesting that IQ scores are unrelated in meaningful ways to later success in life (e.g., McClelland, 1993; Sternberg & Wagner, 1993; Nisbett, 1994; Jacoby & Glauberman, 1995).

These experts base their conclusions on several arguments. For one thing, even when socioeconomic conditions are supposedly held constant, wide variations remain among different households. Furthermore, living conditions of African-Americans and whites are hardly identical, even when their socioeconomic status is similar. We cannot rule out the possibility, then, that environmental differences exist between Caucasian and African-American families that are identical in socioeconomic status. Furthermore, there is little evidence that high IQ scores produce either financial or social success.

Finally, members of cultural and social minority groups may score lower than members of the majority group due to the nature of the intelligence tests themselves. As we discussed earlier, traditional intelligence tests might discriminate against minority groups who have not had exposure to the same environment as have majority group members (Miller-Jones, 1989).

In sum, most members of the developmental community believe that Herrnstein and Murray came to a conclusion about the source of racial IQ differences that is not supported by evidence. Still, the view set forth in *The Bell Curve* remains noteworthy, and it is likely to continue to influence both political and developmental agendas.

"I don't know anything about the bell curve, but I say heredity is everything."

Drawing by C. Bansotti; ©1994 The New Yorker Magazine, Inc.

BELOW AND ABOVE INTELLIGENCE NORMS: MENTAL RETARDATION AND THE INTELLECTUALLY GIFTED

Although Connie kept pace with her classmates in kindergarten, by the time she reached first grade she was academically the slowest in almost every subject. It was not that she didn't try, but rather that it took her longer than other students to catch on to new material, and she regularly required special attention to keep up with the rest of the class.

On the other hand, in some areas she excelled: When asked to draw or produce something with her hands, she not only matched her classmates' performance but exceeded it, producing beautiful work that was much admired by her classmates. Although the other students in the class felt that there was something different about Connie, they were hard-pressed to identify the source of the difference, and in fact they didn't spend much time pondering the issue.

least restrictive environment *the setting that is most similar to that of children without special needs*

mainstreaming *an educational approach in which exceptional children are integrated to the extent possible into the traditional educational system and are provided with a broad range of educational alternatives*

Connie's parents and teacher, though, knew what made her special. Extensive testing in kindergarten had shown that Connie's intelligence was well below normal, and she was officially classified as a special-needs student.

If Connie had been attending school before 1975, she would most likely have been removed from her regular class as soon as her low IQ was identified and placed in a class taught by a special-needs teacher. Often consisting of students with a hodgepodge of afflictions, including emotional difficulties, severe reading problems, and physical disabilities such as multiple sclerosis, such classes were traditionally kept separate and apart from the regular educational process.

However, all that changed in 1975, when Congress passed Public Law 94-142, the Education for All Handicapped Children Act. The intent of the law—an intent that has been largely realized—was to ensure that children with special needs received a full education in the **least restrictive environment**, the setting that is most similar to that of children without special needs.

In practice, the law has meant that children with special needs must be integrated into regular classrooms and regular activities to the greatest extent possible, as long as doing so is educationally beneficial. Children are to be isolated from the regular classroom only for those subjects that are specifically affected by their exceptionality; for all other subjects they are to be taught with nonexceptional children in regular classrooms. Of course, some children with severe handicaps still need a mostly or entirely separate education, depending on the extent of their condition. But the goal of the law is to integrate exceptional children and typical children to the fullest extent possible.

This educational approach to special education, designed to end the segregation of exceptional students as much as possible, has come to be called **mainstreaming**: Exceptional children are integrated to the extent possible into the traditional educational system and are provided with a broad range of educational alternatives.

Ending Segregation by Intelligence Levels: The Benefits of Mainstreaming. In many respects, the introduction of mainstreaming—while clearly increasing the complexity of classroom teaching—was a reaction to failures of traditional special education. For one thing, there was little research support for the advisability of special education for exceptional students. Research that examined such factors as academic achievement, self-concept, social adjustment, and personality development generally failed to discern any advantages for special-needs children placed in special, as opposed to regular, education classes (Dunn, 1968; Wang, Peverly, & Catalano, 1987). Furthermore, separate systems designed to educate minorities separately from majorities historically tend to be inferior—as an examination of schools that were once segregated on the basis of race clearly demonstrates.

An additional important argument in favor of mainstreaming concerns the issue of labeling students—as "mentally deficient," or "emotionally disturbed," or whatever category

mental retardation *a significantly subaverage level of intellectual functioning that occurs with related limitations in two or more skill areas*

was used in determining that they should be relegated to special education classes. Labeling students—which is frequently done with little precision—often produces negative expectations regarding their capabilities, which in turn can lead to behavior in themselves and others that actually causes the expectations to be fulfilled. Furthermore, being labeled negatively can lead to a decrease in peer acceptance and self-concept. For example, research has found that a behavior is viewed more negatively when it is carried out by a student labeled "mentally retarded" than when the same behavior is performed by a presumably "normal" student (Archibald, 1974; Cook & Wollersheim, 1976).

Ultimately, though, the most compelling argument in favor of mainstreaming is philosophical: Because special-needs students must ultimately function in a normal environment, greater experience with their peers ought to enhance their integration into society and to affect their learning positively. Mainstreaming, then, provides a mechanism to equalize the opportunities available to all children. The ultimate objective of mainstreaming is to ensure that all individuals, regardless of handicaps, will have—to the greatest extent possible—opportunities to choose their goals on the basis of a full education, enabling them to obtain a fair share of life's rewards (Reynolds & Birch, 1977; Fuchs & Fuchs, 1994).

Does the reality of mainstreaming live up to its promise? To some extent the benefits extolled by proponents have been realized, at least where mainstreaming is done with care and classroom teachers receive substantial support. Furthermore, mainstreaming provides important benefits not only for exceptional children but also for typical children. For instance, typical children in mainstreamed classes come to understand the nature of others' disabilities better and, at least potentially, come to hold more positive attitudes toward those with disabilities. In sum, everyone—typical and exceptional children alike—can potentially benefit from mainstreaming (Kauffman, 1993; Daly & Feldman, 1994; Scruggs & Mastropieri, 1994).

Below the Norm: Mental Retardation. Approximately 1 to 3 percent of the school-age population is considered to be mentally retarded. The wide variation in these incidence estimates stems from the breadth of the most widely accepted definition of mental retardation, which leaves ample room for interpretation. According to the American Association on Mental Retardation (AAMR), **mental retardation** refers to "substantial limitations in present functioning" characterized by "significantly subaverage intellectual functioning,

This boy, who has been identified as mentally retarded, is mainstreamed into this fifth grade class.

existing concurrently with related limitations in two or more of the following applicable adaptive skill areas: communication, self-care, home living, social skills, community use, self-direction, health and safety, functional academics, leisure and work. Mental retardation manifests before age 18" (AAMR, 1992).

Although "subaverage intellectual functioning" can be measured in a relatively straightforward manner—using standard IQ tests—it is more difficult to determine how to gauge limitations in "applicable adaptive skills." Ultimately, this imprecision leads to a lack of uniformity in the ways experts apply the label of "mental retardation." Furthermore, it has resulted in significant variation in the abilities of people who are categorized as mentally retarded. Accordingly, mentally retarded individuals range from those who can be taught to work and function with little special attention to those who are virtually untrainable and who never develop speech or such basic motor skills as crawling or walking (Matson & Mulick, 1991).

In addition, even when objective measures such as IQ tests are used to identify mentally retarded individuals, discrimination may occur against children from ethnically diverse backgrounds. Most traditional intelligence tests are standardized using white, English-speaking, middle-class populations. As a result, children from different cultural backgrounds may perform poorly on the tests—not because they are retarded, but because the tests use questions that are culturally biased in favor of majority group members. In fact, one classic study found that in one California school district, Mexican-American students were ten times more likely to be placed in special education classes than were whites (Mercer, 1973).

The vast majority of the mentally retarded—some 90 percent—have relatively low levels of deficits. Classified with **mild retardation**, they score in the range of 50 or 55 to 70 on IQ tests. Typically, their retardation is not even identified before they reach school, although their early development often is slower than average. Once they enter elementary school, their retardation and their need for special attention usually become apparent. With appropriate training, these students can reach a third- to sixth-grade educational level, and although they cannot carry out complex intellectual tasks, they are able to hold jobs and function quite independently and successfully.

Intellectual and adaptive limitations become more apparent, however, at higher levels of mental retardation. People whose IQ scores range from about 35 or 40 to 50 or 55 are classified with **moderate retardation**. Composing between 5 and 10 percent of those classified as mentally retarded, the moderately retarded display distinctive behavior early in their lives. They are slow to develop language skills, and their motor development is also affected. Regular schooling is usually not effective in training the moderately retarded to acquire academic skills, because generally they are unable to progress beyond the second-grade level. Still, they are capable of learning occupational and social skills, and they can learn to travel independently to familiar places. Typically, they require moderate levels of supervision.

At the most significant levels of retardation—those who are classified with **severe retardation** (IQs ranging from about 20 or 25 to 35 or 40) and **profound retardation** (IQs below 20 or 25)—the ability to function is severely limited. Usually, such people have little or no speech, poor motor control is the norm, and they may need 24-hour nursing care. At the same time, though, some individuals with severe retardation are capable of learning basic self-care skills, such as dressing and eating, and they may even develop the potential to become partially independent as adults. Still, the need for relatively high levels of care continues throughout the life span, and most severely and profoundly retarded people are institutionalized for the majority of their lives.

Above the Norm: The Gifted and Talented.   Consider this situation:

I was standing at the front of the room explaining how the earth revolves and how, because of its huge size, it is difficult for us to realize that it is actually round. All of

mild retardation *retardation in which IQ is in the range of 50 or 55 to 70*

moderate retardation *retardation in which IQ is from 35 or 40 to 50 or 55*

severe retardation *retardation in which IQ ranges from about 20 or 25 to 35 or 40*

profound retardation *retardation in which the IQ score is below 20 or 25*

a sudden, Spencer blurted out, "The earth isn't round." I curtly replied, "Ha, do you think it's flat?" He matter-of-factly said, "No, it's a truncated sphere." I quickly changed the subject. Spencer said the darndest things. (Payne, Kauffman, Brown, & DeMott, 1974, p. 94)

It sometimes strikes people as curious that the gifted and talented are considered to have a form of exceptionality. Yet—as the above quote suggests—the three to five percent of school-age children who are gifted and talented present special challenges of their own.

What students are considered to be **gifted and talented**? Because of the breadth of the term, little agreement exists among researchers on a single definition. However, the federal government considers the term "gifted" to include "children who give evidence of high performance capability in areas such as intellectual, creative, artistic, leadership capacity, or specific academic fields, and who require services or activities not ordinarily provided by the school in order to fully develop such capabilities" (Sec 582, P.L. 97-35). Intellectual capabilities, then, represent only one type of exceptionality; unusual potential in areas outside the academic realm are also included in the concept. Gifted and talented children have so much potential that they, no less than students with low IQs, warrant special concern (Azar, 1995).

Although the stereotypic description of the gifted—particularly those with exceptionally high intelligence—would probably include adjectives such as "unsociable," "poorly adjusted," and "neurotic," such a view is far off the mark. In fact, most research suggests that highly intelligent people also tend to be outgoing, well adjusted, and popular (Stanley, 1980).

For instance, one landmark, long-term study of 1,500 gifted students, which began in the 1920s, found that the gifted did better in virtually every dimension studied. Not only were they smarter than average but they were also healthier, better coordinated, and psychologically better adjusted than their less intelligent classmates. Furthermore, their lives played out in ways that most people would envy. The subjects received more awards and distinctions, earned more money, and made many more contributions in art and literature than did the average person. For example, by the time they had reached the age of 40, they had collectively produced more than 90 books, 375 plays and short stories, and 2,000 articles, and they had registered more than 200 patents. Perhaps not surprisingly, they reported greater satisfaction with their lives than did the nongifted (Terman & Oden, 1947; Sears, 1977; Shurkin, 1992).

Yet being gifted and talented is no guarantee of success in school, as we can see if we consider the particular components of the category. For example, the verbal abilities that allow the eloquent expression of ideas and feelings can equally permit the expression of glib and persuasive statements that happen to be inaccurate. Furthermore, teachers may sometimes misinterpret the humor, novelty, and creativity of unusually gifted children, considering their intellectual fervor to be disruptive or inappropriate. And peers are not always sympathetic: Some very bright children try to hide their intelligence in an effort to fit in better with other students (Feldman, 1982).

Two main approaches to educating the gifted and talented have been devised: acceleration and enrichment (Feldhusen, 1989). **Acceleration** allows gifted students to move ahead at their own pace, even if this means skipping to higher grade levels. The materials that students receive under acceleration programs are not necessarily different from what other students receive; they simply are provided at a faster pace than for the average student.

An alternative approach is **enrichment**, through which students are kept at grade level but are enrolled in special programs and given individual activities to allow greater depth of study on a given topic. In enrichment, the material provided to gifted students differs not only in the timing of its presentation but also in its sophistication. Thus, enrichment materials are designed to provide an intellectual challenge to the gifted student, encouraging higher-order thinking.

gifted and talented   *children who show evidence of high performance capability in areas such as intellectual, creative, artistic, leadership capacity, or specific academic fields*

acceleration   *special programs that allow gifted students to move ahead at their own pace, even if this means skipping to higher grade levels*

enrichment   *an approach through which students are kept at grade level but are enrolled in special programs and given individual activities to allow greater depth of study on a given topic*

Acceleration programs can be remarkably effective. Most studies have shown that gifted students who begin school even considerably earlier than their age-mates do as well as or better than those who begin at the traditional age (Rimm & Lovance, 1992). One of the best illustrations of the benefits of acceleration is the "Study of Mathematically Precocious Youth," an ongoing program at Johns Hopkins University in Baltimore. In this program, seventh and eighth graders who have unusual abilities in mathematics participate in a variety of special classes and workshops. Results have been nothing short of sensational, with students successfully completing college courses and sometimes even enrolling in college early. Some students have even graduated from college before the age of 18(Stanley & Benbow, 1983; Brody & Benbow, 1987).

The Informed Consumer of Development

Creating an Atmosphere that Promotes School Success

What makes children succeed in school? Although there are many factors, some of which we'll be discussing in the next chapter, there are several practical steps that can be taken to maximize children's chances of success. Among them:

◆ *Promote a "literacy environment."* Parents should read to their children and familiarize them with books and reading. Adults should provide reading models: Children should see that reading is an important activity in the lives of the adults with whom they interact.

◆ *Talk to children.* Discuss events in the news, talk about their friends, and share hobbies. Getting children to think about and discuss the world around them is one of the best preparations for school.

◆ *Provide a place for children to work.* This can be a desk, a corner of a table, or an area of a room. What's important is that it be a separate, designated area.

◆ *Encourage children's problem-solving skills.* To solve a problem, youngsters should learn to identify their goal, what they know, and what they don't know; to design and carry out a strategy; and, finally, to evaluate their result.

Review and Rethink

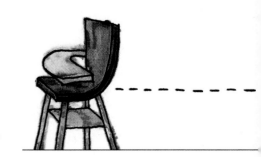

REVIEW

◆ Schooling in the United States, which is nearly universally available, has recently focused on the basic academic skills, student and teacher accountability, and multiculturalism.

♦ Multicultural education is in transition from a melting pot model of cultural assimilation to a pluralistic society model, in which coexisting cultures make unique contributions to the whole.

♦ The measurement of intelligence has traditionally been a matter of testing skills that promote academic success and calculating the ratio of mental age (measured in relation to average test performance by age group) to chronological age.

♦ Recent theories of intelligence suggest that the concept of academic intelligence may be insufficient, and that there may be several distinct intelligences or several components of intelligence that reflect different ways of processing information.

♦ U.S. educators are attempting to deal with substantial numbers of exceptional individuals whose intellectual and other skills are significantly lower or higher than normal.

RETHINK

♦ Is an educational focus on the basic academic skills appropriate? How does the theory that there are multiple intelligences related to this issue?

♦ Should instruction be provided to children in the United States in their home languages or only in English? Why?

♦ How do fluid intelligence and crystallized intelligence interact? Which of the two is likely to be more influenced by genetic factors, and which by environmental factors? Why?

♦ What are the advantages of mainstreaming? What challenges does it present? Are there situations in which you would not support mainstreaming?

♦ Some people argue that expending additional resources on gifted and talented children is wasteful, for these children will succeed anyway. What is your opinion of this suggestion, and why?

LOOKING BACK

In what ways do children grow during the school years, and what factors influence their growth?

1. The middle childhood years are characterized by slow and steady growth, with children gaining, on average, about 5 to 7 pounds per year and 2 to 3 inches. Weight is redistributed as baby fat disappears.

2. In part, growth is genetically determined, but societal factors such as affluence, dietary habits, nutrition, and disease also contribute significantly. Growth can be artificially induced by hormones, but the use of drugs for this purpose raises ethical questions.

3. During the middle childhood years, great improvements occur in gross motor skills in both boys and girls. Cultural expectations, rather than actual genetic differences, probably underlie most gross motor skill differences between boys and girls. Fine motor skills also develop rapidly, largely because of increases in the level of myelin in the brain.

What are the nutritional needs of school-age children, and what are some causes and effects of improper nutrition?

4. Adequate nutrition is important because of its many effects on children in the school

years. In addition to purely physical effects, well-nourished children generally show superior social and emotional functioning and better cognitive performance.

5. Obesity can be a problem in middle childhood. Although partially influenced by genetic factors, obesity also is associated with excessive parental interference with children's development of internal controls regarding eating, overindulgence in sedentary activities such as TV viewing, and lack of physical exercise.

What sorts of special needs manifest themselves in the middle childhood years, and how can they be met?

6. Special needs of many sorts show their clearest effects during the school years. Visual, auditory, and speech impairments, as well as other learning disabilities, can lead to academic and social problems and must be handled with sensitivity and appropriate assistance.

7. Children with attention-deficit hyperactivity disorder (ADHD) exhibit another form of special need. ADHD is characterized by inattention, impulsiveness, failure to complete tasks, lack of organization, and excessive amounts of uncontrollable activity. Treatment of ADHD by drugs is highly controversial because of unwanted side effects and doubts about long-term consequences.

In what ways do children develop cognitively during these years, according to major theoretical approaches?

8. Intellectually, children in the school years grow substantially. According to Jean Piaget, they enter the concrete operational period and for the first time become capable of applying logical thought processes to concrete problems. They grasp the notion of reversibility and come to understand concepts such as the relationship between speed and time.

9. Piaget's view has limitations, namely his tendency to underestimate the capabilities of children and to overestimate the universality of his stages (which appear to have a significant cultural dimension). Nevertheless, the notion of concrete operational thinking has clear applications in Western cultures and has influenced educational principles and practices positively.

10. According to information-processing approaches, children's intellectual development in the school years is more quantitative than qualitative, with substantial increases in memory capacity, and in the sophistication of the "programs" children can handle, accounting for their rapid cognitive development.

11. Children's memory, including the ability to encode, store, and retrieve information, increases dramatically during the school years, and their increased understanding of the processes that underlie memory (meta-memory) enables them to use control strategies to improve cognitive processing and memorization.

How does language develop during the middle childhood period, and what special circumstances pertain to children for whom English is not the first language?

12. The language development of children in the school years is also substantial, with improvements in vocabulary, syntax, and pragmatics. Despite these advances, school-age children's language is still not as proficient as it will become in adulthood, and some pronunciation and comprehension difficulties are normal.

13. Improvements in language help children control their behavior through linguistic strategies. Moreover, their growing metalinguistic awareness permits them to realize that language use is rule-governed and is subject to breakdowns for which they are not solely responsible, and which can be remedied by seeking clarification.

14. Bilingualism is an increasingly prevalent phenomenon in the school years. There is evidence that many children who are taught all subjects in the first language, with simultaneous instruction in English, experience few deficits and several linguistic and cognitive advantages. However, immersion programs, which work well when majority children are immersed during the school day in a minority language, do not work as well the other way around: when minority children are immersed in the language of the majority.

What are some trends in schooling worldwide and in the United States?

15. Schooling, which is available to nearly all youngsters in most developed countries, is not as accessible to children, especially girls, in many less developed nations. The time at which schooling begins should be determined by the child's overall developmental readiness, rather than by age alone.

16. Schooling in the United States appears to be moving from a socio-emotional focus on the student to a stronger emphasis on academic basics and student and teacher accountability.

17. Multiculturalism and diversity are significant issues in U.S. schools, where the melting pot society, in which minority cultures were assimilated to the majority culture, is being replaced by the pluralistic society, in which individual cultures maintain their own identities while participating in the definition of a larger culture. For minority children especially, this means the development of a bicultural identity, and the presence of other cultures in schools can enhance the education of all students.

How can intelligence be measured, and how are children who fall outside the normal range of intelligence educated?

18. Intelligence testing has traditionally focused on factors that differentiate successful academic performers from unsuccessful ones. The intelligence quotient, or IQ, reflects the ratio of a person's mental age to his or her chronological age, based on average test performance for individuals of a given chronological age. More recently, other conceptualizations of intelligence have emerged, focusing on different types of intelligence or on different aspects of the information-processing task. The related issues of cultural bias in IQ testing and the relationship among race, socioeconomic status, and IQ are highly controversial and hotly debated.

19. The education of people who fall significantly below the intellectual norm has long been problematic. Today's thinking focuses on placing children with exceptionalities—including intellectual deficits—in the least restrictive environment, typically the regular classroom. If done properly, this strategy can benefit all students and permit the exceptional student to focus on strengths rather than weaknesses. Many mentally retarded youngsters can learn basic life and academic skills, but the classification of children into the retarded category is highly controversial and may reflect cultural biases.

20. Gifted and talented children, whatever their advantages, appear to need special educational programs and materials to permit their gifts to flourish. These have been made available mainly through acceleration and enrichment programs.

KEY TERMS AND CONCEPTS

visual impairment (p. 300)
auditory impairment (p. 300)
speech impairment (p. 301)
stuttering (p. 301)

learning disabilities (p. 301)
attention-deficit hyperactivity disorder (ADHD) (p. 301)
concrete operational stage (p. 304)

decentering (p. 304)

memory (p. 308)

meta-memory (p. 308)

metalinguistic awareness (p. 310)

bilingualism (p. 310)

multicultural education (p. 318)

cultural assimilation model (p. 318)

pluralistic society model (p. 318)

bicultural identity (p. 319)

intelligence (p. 320)

mental age (p. 321)

chronological (or physical) age (p. 321)

intelligence quotient (IQ score) (p. 321)

Stanford-Binet Intelligence Scale (p. 321)

Wechsler Intelligence Scale for
  Children–Revised (WISC-R) (p. 321)

Wechsler Adult Intelligence Scale–Revised
  (WAIS-R) (p. 321)

fluid intelligence (p. 323)

crystallized intelligence (p. 323)

triarchic theory of intelligence (p. 323)

least restrictive environment (p. 327)

mainstreaming (p. 327)

mental retardation (p. 328)

mild retardation (p. 329)

moderate retardation (p. 329)

severe retardation (p. 329)

profound retardation (p. 329)

gifted and talented (p. 330)

acceleration (p. 330)

enrichment (p. 330)

CHAPTER 10

THE MIDDLE
CHILDHOOD YEARS
Social and Personality
Development

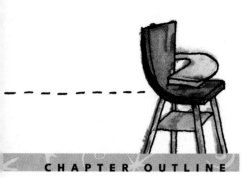

CHAPTER OUTLINE

PROLOGUE: KEVIN

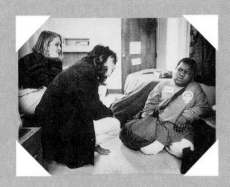

It is a cold, bleak Friday afternoon in Kansas City, and inside this second-floor dorm room at the Gillis Center, the atmosphere seems no less gloomy. Emily McLane, 24, one of the center's 42 child-care specialists, is getting Kevin ready for the weekend. "Okay, time to pack up," she tells him cheerfully. "You're going home." Suddenly the first-grader explodes in anger, scowling and clenching his fists. Although these weekend trips home to his grandmother's are routine, they still mean leaving the orderly world of Gillis for the chaos of home, where his mother's drug problems have shattered the family's stability. "Kevin," McLane asks as the boy's anger gradually subsides, "do you need a *hug?*" Kevin's face softens. "Yes," he says, melting into the young woman's arms. (Arias, 1995, pp. 35–36)

LOOKING AHEAD

Like many residential treatment centers, the Gillis Center serves a variety of children. Some have severe emotional and behavioral problems, while others are orphans—children without parents whose problems keep them from being adopted. Others have families lost to crime, drugs, or violence, and unable to care adequately for children.

Of course, youngsters like Kevin are the exception. For most children in the United States, home is with their biological fathers and mothers, and a more typical range of peer relationships, school, and family affects development.

But regardless of their circumstances and fortune, children face a range of challenges during middle childhood in terms of their social and personality development, which we consider in this chapter. We start by examining the changes that occur in the ways children see themselves, including their views of their personal characteristics and their self-esteem. We also discuss several approaches to moral development.

Next, the chapter turns to relationships during middle childhood. We discuss the stages of friendship and the ways gender and race affect how and with whom children interact. We also look at how to improve children's social competence.

The last part of the chapter examines two major societal institutions in children's lives: family and school. We consider the consequences of divorce, latchkey children, and the phenomenon of group care. Finally, we look at schooling, considering such topics as how children explain their academic performance and how teachers' expectations can affect student performance.

In sum, after reading this chapter, you will be able to answer the following questions:

- In what ways do children's views of themselves change during the middle childhood years?

- How do children in these years develop a sense of self-esteem?

- Through what stages does moral development proceed as children age?

- What sorts of relationships and friendships do children have in the middle school years?

- What are the causes and effects of popularity and unpopularity?

- How do gender and race affect friendships?

- How do today's diverse family arrangements affect children?

- How do subjective interpretations of successes and failures, by oneself and by others, contribute to school outcomes?

THE DEVELOPING SELF

Nine-year-old Karl Haglund is perched in his eagle's nest, a treehouse built high in the willow that grows in his backyard. Sometimes he sits there alone among the tree's spreading branches, his face turned toward the sky, a boy clearly enjoying his solitude. Sometimes he's with his friend, engrossed in the kind of talk that boys find fascinating.

This morning Karl is busy sawing and hammering. "It's fun to build," he says. "I started the house when I was 4 years old. Then when I was about 7, my dad built me this platform. 'Cause all my places were falling apart and they were crawling with carpenter ants. So we destroyed them and then built me a deck. And I built on top of it. It's stronger now. You can have privacy here, but it's a bad place to go when it's windy 'cause you almost get blown off." (Kotre & Hall, 1990, p. 116)

Karl's growing sense of competence is reflected in the passage above, as he describes how he and his father built his treehouse. Conveying what psychologist Erik Erikson calls "industriousness," Karl's quiet pride in his accomplishment illustrates one of the ways in which children's views of themselves evolve.

UNDERSTANDING ONE'S SELF: A NEW RESPONSE TO "WHO AM I?"

During middle childhood, children continue their efforts to answer the question "Who am I" as they seek to understand the nature of the self. Although the question does not yet have the urgency it will assume in adolescence, elementary-school-age youngsters still seek to pin down their place in the world.

The Shift in Self-understanding from the Physical to the Psychological.   Several changes in children's views of themselves during middle childhood illustrate the quest for self-understanding. For one thing, they begin to view themselves less in terms of external, physical attributes and more in terms of psychological traits (Aboud & Skerry, 1983).

For instance, 6-year-old Carey describes herself as "a fast runner and good at drawing"—both characteristics dependent on skill in external, motoric activities. In contrast, 11-year-old Trisha characterizes herself as "pretty smart, friendly, and helpful to my friends." Trisha's portrayal is based on psychological characteristics, inner traits that are more abstract than the younger child's descriptions. The use of inner traits to determine self-concept results from the child's increasing cognitive skills, a development that we discussed in Chapter 9.

In addition to shifting focus from external characteristics to internal, psychological traits, children's views of self become more differentiated. As they get older, children discover that they may be good at some things, and not so good at others. Ten-year-old Ginny, for instance, comes to understand that she is good at arithmetic but not very good at spelling; 11-year-old Malcolm determines that he is good at softball but doesn't have the stamina to play soccer very well.

Furthermore, children's self-concepts become divided into personal and academic spheres. In fact, research on students' self-concepts in English, mathematics, and nonacademic realms has found that the separate self-concepts are not always correlated, although there is overlap among them.

Furthermore, as can be seen in Figure 10-1, self-concept in each of the three domains can be further broken down. For instance, the nonacademic self-concept includes the components of physical appearance, peer relations, and physical ability. In sum, self-concept becomes increasingly differentiated as children mature (Marsh, 1990; Marsh & Holmes, 1990).

Social Comparison.   If someone asks you how good you are at math, how would you respond? Most of us would compare our performance to others who are roughly of the

FIGURE 10-1

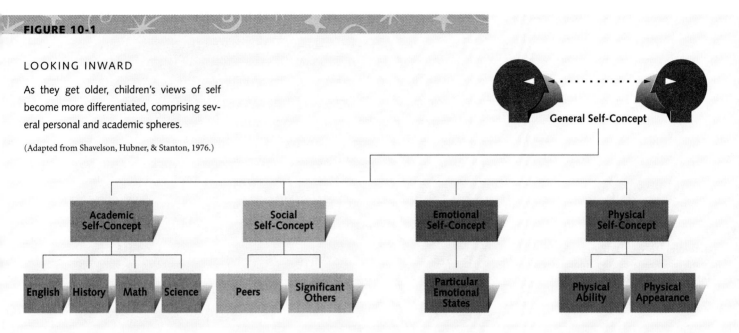

LOOKING INWARD

As they get older, children's views of self become more differentiated, comprising several personal and academic spheres.

(Adapted from Shavelson, Hubner, & Stanton, 1976.)

General Self-Concept

Academic Self-Concept

Social Self-Concept

Emotional Self-Concept

Physical Self-Concept

English   History   Math   Science

Peers   Significant Others

Particular Emotional States

Physical Ability   Physical Appearance

same age and educational level. It is unlikely that we would answer the question by comparing ourselves either to Albert Einstein or to a kindergartner just learning about numbers.

Elementary-school-age children begin to follow the same sort of reasoning when they seek to understand how able they are. Whereas earlier they tended to consider their abilities in terms of absolutes, now they begin to use social-comparison processes to determine their levels of accomplishment during middle childhood.

Social comparison is the desire to evaluate one's own behavior, abilities, expertise, and opinions by comparing them to those of others. According to a theory first suggested by psychologist Leon Festinger (1954), when concrete, objective measures of ability are lacking, people turn to *social reality* to evaluate themselves. Social reality refers to understanding that is derived from how others act, think, feel, and view the world.

But who provides the most adequate comparison? Generally, children compare themselves to individuals who are similar along relevant dimensions. Consequently, when they cannot objectively evaluate their ability, children during middle childhood increasingly look to others who are similar to themselves (Ruble, Boggiano, Feldman, & Loebl, 1989; Wood, 1989; Suls & Wills, 1991).

Although children typically compare themselves to similar others, in some cases—particularly when their self-esteem is at stake—students choose to make *downward social comparisons* with others who are obviously less competent or successful (Pyszczynski, Greenberg, & LaPrelle, 1985).

Downward social comparison protects self-image. By comparing themselves to those who are less able, children ensure that they will come out on top and thereby preserve an image of themselves as successful.

Downward social comparison helps explain why some students in elementary schools with low achievement levels are found to have stronger academic self-esteem than very capable students in schools with high achievement levels. The reason seems to be that students in the low-achievement schools observe others who are not doing terribly well academically, and they feel relatively good by comparison. In contrast, students in the high-achievement schools may find themselves competing with a more academically proficient group of students, and their perception of their performance may suffer in comparison. In some ways, then, it is better to be a big fish in a small pond than a small fish in a big one (Marsh & Parker, 1984).

social comparison   the desire to evaluate one's own behavior, abilities, expertise, and opinions by comparing them to those of others

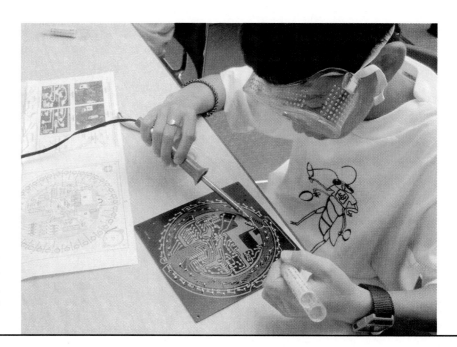

According to Erik Erikson, middle childhood encompasses the industry-versus-inferiority stage, characterized by a focus on meeting the challenges presented by the world.

PSYCHOSOCIAL DEVELOPMENT: INDUSTRY VERSUS INFERIORITY

According to Erik Erikson, whose approach to psychosocial development we last discussed in Chapter 8, middle childhood encompasses the **industry-versus-inferiority stage**. Lasting from roughly age 6 to age 12, the industry-versus-inferiority stage is characterized by a focus on efforts to attain competence in meeting the challenges presented by parents, peers, school, and the other complexities of the modern world.

Success in this stage brings with it feelings of mastery and proficiency and a growing sense of competence. Conversely, difficulties in this stage lead to feelings of failure and inadequacy. As a result, children may withdraw both from academic pursuits, showing less interest and motivation to excel, and from interactions with peers.

Attaining a sense of industry during the middle childhood years has lasting consequences. For example, one study examined how childhood industriousness and hard work were related to adult behavior by following a group of 450 males over a 35-year period, starting in early childhood. Males who were most industrious and hard-working during childhood were most successful as adults, both in occupational attainment and in their personal lives. In fact, childhood industriousness was more closely associated with adult success than was intelligence or family background (Vaillant & Vaillant, 1981).

SELF-ESTEEM: EVALUATING THE SELF

Children do not dispassionately view themselves just in terms of an itemization of physical and psychological characteristics. Instead, they think of themselves as being good, or bad, in particular ways. **Self-esteem** is an individual's overall and specific positive and negative self-evaluation. Whereas self-concept reflects beliefs and cognitions about the self, self-esteem is more emotionally oriented (Baumeister, 1993).

Self-esteem develops in important ways during middle childhood. Children increasingly compare themselves to others, and as they do, they assess how well they measure up to society's standards. In addition, they increasingly develop their own internal standards of success, and they can see how well they compare to those.

One of the advances that occurs during middle childhood is an increasing differentiation of self-esteem. At the age of 7, most youngsters have self-esteem that reflects a global, undifferentiated view of themselves. If their overall self-esteem is positive, they assume that they are relatively good at all things. Conversely, if their overall self-esteem is negative, they

industry-versus-inferiority stage the period from age 6 to 12 characterized by a focus on efforts to attain competence in meeting the challenges presented by parents, peers, school, and the other complexities of the modern world

self-esteem an individual's overall and specific positive and negative self-evaluation

assume that they are inadequate at most things (Marsh & Shavelson, 1985; Harter, 1990a). As children progress into the middle childhood years, however, their self-esteem becomes differentiated: higher for some areas that they evaluate, and lower for others.

Change and Stability in Self-esteem.   Generally, the self-esteem of most children tends to increase during middle childhood, with a brief decline around the age of twelve. Although there are probably several reasons for the decline, the main one appears to be the school transition that typically occurs about this age: Students leaving elementary school and entering either middle school or junior high school show a decline in self-esteem, which then gradually rises again (Eccles et al., 1989).

Children with chronically low self-esteem face a tough road, in part because their self-esteem becomes enmeshed in a cycle of failure that grows increasingly difficult to break. Assume, for instance, that Harry, a student with chronically low self-esteem, is facing an important test. Because of his low self-esteem, he expects to do poorly. As a consequence, he is quite anxious—so anxious that he is unable to concentrate well and study effectively. Furthermore, he may decide not to study much, because he feels that if he is going to do badly anyway, why bother studying?

Ultimately, of course, Harry's high anxiety and lack of effort bring about the result he expected: He does poorly on the test. This failure, which confirms Harry's expectation, reinforces his low self-esteem, and the cycle of failure continues (see Figure 10-2).

Race and Self-esteem.   If you were part of a minority group whose members routinely experienced prejudice and discrimination, how might your self-esteem be affected?

For many decades, developmental researchers hypothesized—and found supportive evidence for the notion—that members of minority groups would feel lower self-esteem than would members of majority groups. In particular, the evidence seemed clear that African-Americans had lower self-esteem than Caucasians (Deutsch, 1968).

Some of the first evidence was found in a set of pioneering studies a generation ago, in which African-American children were shown a black doll and a white doll (K.B. Clark & Clark, 1947). In the study, the children received a series of requests, including "Give me the doll that looks bad" and "Give me the doll that is a nice color." In every case, the African-American children preferred white dolls over black ones. The interpretation that was drawn from the study: The self-esteem of the African-American children was low.

Subsequent research in the 1950s and 1960s supported the notion that children showed lower self-esteem as a consequence of being members of minority groups that were dis-

FIGURE 10-2

A CYCLE OF LOW SELF-ESTEEM

Because children with low self-esteem may expect to do poorly on a test, they may experience high anxiety and not work as hard as those with higher self-esteem. As a result, they actually do perform badly on the test, which in turn confirms their negative view of themselves.

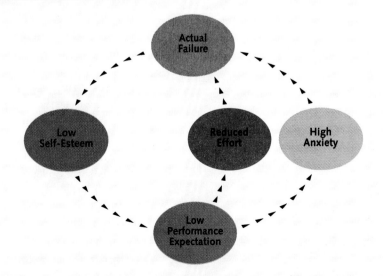

In pioneering research conducted several decades ago, African-American girls' preference for white dolls was viewed as an indication of low self-esteem. More recent evidence, however, suggests that whites and African-American children show little difference in self-esteem.

criminated against. In fact, some research even suggested that members of minority groups preferred members of majority groups to members of their own groups, and that they rejected membership in their own groups, showing a form of self-hatred due to minority-group status (Milner, 1983).

More recent theorizing, however, sheds a different light on the issue of self-esteem and racial group membership. According to French psychologist Henri Tajfel (1982), members of a minority group are likely to accept the negative views held by a majority group only if they perceive that there is little realistic possibility of changing the power and status differences between the groups.

On the other hand, if the existing differences between majority and minority group members are viewed as illegitimate, unstable, and potentially changeable, then minority group members will place the blame for the prejudice and discrimination they experience on societal forces and prejudice, and not on themselves. In this case, self-esteem between African-Americans and whites should not differ.

In fact, societal attitudes favoring group pride and ethnic awareness for minority group members, as well as increased sensitivity to the importance of multiculturalism in general, have become considerably more widespread in the last several decades. Such attitudes have resulted in a narrowing of measured differences in self-esteem between members of different ethnic groups (Garbarino, 1985; Harter, 1990b; Duckitt, 1994).

SELF-EFFICACY: BUILDING EXPECTATIONS OF THE SELF

"Will I do well in arithmetic?" "How will I be able to complete this project?" "Can I make the after-school basketball team?"

These questions are typical of those that children ask themselves during the elementary school years. How each is answered depends in large measure on a child's **self-efficacy**, which refers to learned expectations that one is capable of carrying out a behavior or producing a desired outcome in a particular situation (Bandura, 1986, 1993; Schunk, 1991).

Self-efficacy is critical to children's success because it motivates greater effort and persistence in the face of a challenging task. As a result, children with high self-efficacy are more likely to be successful, whether the realm is academics or athletics (Bandura & Schunk, 1981; Taylor, Locke, Lee, & Gist, 1984; Scheier & Carver, 1992).

Self-efficacy develops over the course of middle childhood. By observing their own prior successes and failures on particular tasks, children begin to develop a sense of how well they can expect to do within a particular domain. For instance, a child who has even moderate success roller-blading for the first time is on the road to developing self-efficacy in that

self-efficacy *learned expectations that one is capable of carrying out a behavior or producing a desired outcome in a particular situation* domain, and is more likely to try it in the future. In contrast, a child who has little initial success is less likely to try it in the future.

There are other sources of children's self-efficacy. For instance, observation of others' success (or failure) in an activity can affect a child's sense of self-efficacy. Direct reinforcement from others, in the form of praise or encouragement, is also an important determinant (Bandura, 1988).

MORAL DEVELOPMENT

> Your wife is near death from an unusual kind of cancer. One drug exists that the physicians think might save her—a form of radium that a scientist in a nearby city has recently developed. The drug, though, is expensive to manufacture, and the scientist is charging ten times what the drug costs him to make. He pays $1,000 for the radium and charges $10,000 for a small dose. You have gone to everyone you know to borrow money, but you can get together only $2,500—one-quarter of what you need. You've told the scientist that your wife is dying and asked him to sell it more cheaply or let you pay later. But the scientist has said, "No, I discovered the drug and I'm going to make money from it." In desperation, you consider breaking into the scientist's laboratory to steal the drug for your wife. Should you do it?

According to developmental psychologist Lawrence Kohlberg and his colleagues, the answer that children give to this question reveals central aspects of their sense of morality and justice. He suggests that people's responses to moral dilemmas such as this one reveal the stage of moral development they have attained—as well as yielding information about their general level of cognitive development (Kohlberg, 1984; Colby & Kohlberg, 1987).

Kohlberg contends that people pass through a series of stages in the evolution of their sense of justice and in the kind of reasoning they use to make moral judgments. Primarily due to cognitive characteristics that we discussed earlier, school-age children tend to think either in terms of concrete, unvarying rules ("It is always wrong to steal" or "I'll be punished if I steal") or in terms of the rules of society ("Good people don't steal" or "What if everyone stole?").

By the time they reach adolescence, however, individuals are able to reason on a higher plane, typically having attained Piaget's stage of formal operations. They are capable of comprehending abstract, formal principles of morality, and they consider cases such as the one presented above in terms of broader issues of morality and of right and wrong ("Stealing may be justifiable if you are following your own standards of conscience").

Kohlberg suggests that moral development can best be understood within the context of a three-level sequence, which is further subdivided into six stages (see Table 10-1). At the lowest level, *preconventional morality* (Stages 1 and 2), people follow unvarying rules based on rewards and punishments. For example, a student at the preconventional level might evaluate the moral dilemma posed in the story above by saying that it was not worth stealing the drug because if you were caught, you would go to jail.

In the next level, that of *conventional morality* (Stages 3 and 4), people approach moral problems in terms of their own position as good, responsible members of society. Thus, students who decide *against* stealing the drug because they think they would feel guilty or dishonest, and students who decide *in favor of* stealing the drug because if they did nothing in this situation they would be unable to face others, would be reasoning at the conventional level of morality.

Finally, individuals using *postconventional morality* (Level 3; Stages 5 and 6) invoke universal moral principles that are considered broader than the rules of the particular society in which they live. Students who feel that they would condemn themselves if they did not steal the drug because they would not be living up to their own moral principles would be reasoning at the postconventional level.

TABLE 10-1

KOHLBERG'S SEQUENCE OF MORAL REASONING

		MOTOR SCALE	
Level	Stage	In Favor of Stealing	Against Stealing
LEVEL 1 Preconventional morality: At this level, the concrete interests of the individual are considerd in terms of rewards and punishments.	**STAGE 1** Obedience and punishment orientation: At this stage, people stick to rules in order to avoid punishment, and obedience occurs for its own sake.	"If you let your wife die, you will get in trouble. You'll be blamed for not spending the money to save her, and there'll be an investigation of you and the druggist for your wife's death."	"You shouldn't steal the drug because you'll get caught and sent to jail if you do. If you do get away, your conscience will bother you thinking how the police will catch up with you at any minute."
	STAGE 2 Reward orientation: At this stage, rules are followed only for a person's own benefit. Obedience occurs because of rewards that are received.	"If you do happen to get caught, you could give the drug back and you wouldn't get much of a sentence. It wouldn't bother you much to serve a little jail term, if you have your wife when you get out."	"You may not get much of a jail term if you steal the drug, but your wife will probably die before you get out, so it won't do much good. If your wife dies, you shouldn't blame yourself; it isn't your fault she has cancer."
LEVEL 2 Conventional morality: At this level, people approach moral problems as members of society. They are interested in pleasing others by acting as good members of society.	**STAGE 3** "Good boy" morality: Individuals at this stage show an interest in maintaining the respect of others and doing what is expected of them.	"No one will think you're bad if you steal the drug, but your family will think you're an inhuman husband if you don't. If you let your wife die, you'll never be able to look anybody in the face again."	"It isn't just the druggist who will think you're a criminal; everyone else will, too. After you steal the drug, you'll feel bad thinking how you've brought dishonor on your family and yourself; you won't be able to face anyone again."
	STAGE 4 Authority and social-order-maintaining morality: People at this stage conform to society's rules and consider that "right" is what society defines as right.	"If you have any sense of honor, you won't let your wife die just because you're afraid to do the only thing that will save her. You'll always feel guilty that you caused her death if you don't do your duty to her."	"You're desperate and you may not know you're doing wrong when you steal the drug. But you'll know you did wrong after you're sent to jail. You'll always feel guilty for your dishonesty and law-breaking."
LEVEL 3 Postconventional morality: At this level, people use moral principles which are seen as broader than those of any particular society.	**STAGE 5** Morality of contract, individual rights and democratically accepted law: People at this stage do what is right because of a sense of obligation to laws which are agreed upon within society. They perceive that laws can be modified as part of changes in an implicit social contract.	"You'll lose other people's respect, not gain it, if you don't steal. If you let your wife die, it will be out of fear, not out of reasoning. So you'll just lose self-respect and probably the respect of others, too."	"You'll lose your standing and respect in the community and violate the law. You'll lose respect for yourself if you're carried away by emotion and forget the long-range point of view."
	STAGE 6 Morality of individual principles and conscience: At this final stage, a person follows laws because they are based on universal ethical principles. Laws that violate the principles are disobeyed.	"If you don't steal the drug, and if you let your wife die, you'll always condemn yourself for it afterward. You won't be blamed and you'll have lived up to the outside rule of the law but you won't have lived up to your own standards of conscience."	"If you steal the drug, you won't be blamed by other people, but you'll condemn yourself because you won't have lived up to your own conscience and standards of honesty."

Source: Adapted from Kohlberg (1969).

Kohlberg's theory proposes that people move through the periods of moral development in a fixed order and that they are unable to reach the highest stage until about the age of 13, due to deficits in cognitive development that are not overcome until then (Kurtines & Gewirtz, 1987). However, not everyone is presumed to reach the highest stages: Kohlberg has found that only about 25 percent of all adults rise above the fourth stage of his model, into the level of postconventional morality.

Unfortunately, although Kohlberg's theory provides a good account of the development of moral *judgments*, it is less adequate in predicting moral *behavior* (Malinowski & Smith, 1985; Snarey, 1985). For example, one experiment found that 15 percent of students who reasoned at the postconventional level of morality—the highest category— cheated on a task, although they were not as prone to cheating as those at lower levels; some 55 percent of those at the conventional level and 70 percent of those at the preconventional level also cheated (Kohlberg, 1975; Kupfersmid & Wonderly, 1980). Clearly, though, knowing what is morally right does not always mean acting that way (Killen & Hart, 1995).

Still, a good deal of research suggests that aspects of moral conduct are clearly related to Kohlberg's levels of moral reasoning, although the results are often complex and not easy to interpret. For instance, children who reason at Stage 1 and Stage 3 tend to be the best behaved in school, whereas those who reason at Stage 2 are more apt to exhibit poor social behavior in school settings. Such findings suggest that we have not heard the last word on Kohlberg's stages (Richards, Bear, Stewart, & Norman, 1992; Bear & Rys, 1994; Langford, 1995).

Moral Development in Girls.   An aspect of Kohlberg's theory that has proved particularly problematic is the difficulty it has explaining *girls'* moral judgments. Because the theory initially was based largely on data from males, some researchers have argued that it does a better job describing boys' moral development than girls'.

In fact, psychologist Carol Gilligan (1982, 1987) has suggested an alternative account of the development of moral behavior in girls. She suggests that differences in the ways boys and girls are raised in our society lead to basic distinctions in how men and women view moral behavior. According to her, boys view morality primarily in terms of broad principles such as justice or fairness, whereas girls see it in terms of responsibility toward individuals and willingness to sacrifice themselves to help specific individuals within the context of particular relationships. Compassion for individuals, then, is a more prominent factor in moral behavior for women than it is for men (Gilligan, Ward, & Taylor, 1988; Gilligan, Lyons, & Hanmer, 1990).

Because Kohlberg's theory considers moral behavior largely in terms of principles of justice, it is inadequate in describing the moral development of females. This accounts for the surprising finding that women typically score at a lower level than do males on tests of moral judgments using Kohlberg's stage sequence. In Gilligan's view, a female's morality is centered more on individual well-being than on moral abstractions, and the highest levels of morality are represented by compassionate concern for the welfare of others.

Gilligan views morality as developing among females in a three-stage process. In the first stage, termed "Orientation toward individual survival," females first concentrate on what is practical and best for them, gradually making a transition from selfishness to responsibility, in which they think about what would be best for others. In the second stage, termed "Goodness as self-sacrifice," females begin to think that they must sacrifice their own wishes to what other people want, ultimately making the transition from "goodness" to "truth," in which they take into account their own needs plus those of others. Finally, in the third stage, "Morality of nonviolence," women come to see that hurting anyone is immoral—including hurting themselves. This realization establishes a moral equivalence between themselves and others and represents, according to Gilligan, the most sophisticated level of moral reasoning. (The stages are summarized in Table 10-2.)

It is obvious that Gilligan's sequence of stages is quite different from that of Kohlberg, and some researchers have suggested that her rejection of Kohlberg's work is too sweeping

TABLE 10-2

GILLIGAN'S THREE STAGES OF MORAL DEVELOPMENT FOR WOMEN

STAGE 1 Orientation toward individual survival	In this first stage a female initially concentrates on what is practical and best for her, gradually making a transition from selfishness to responsibility, in which she thinks about what would be best for others.
STAGE 2 Goodness as self-sacrifice	In the second stage she begins to think that she must sacrifice her own wishes to what other people want, ultimately making the transition from "goodness" to "truth" in which she takes into account her own needs and those of others.
STAGE 3 Morality of nonviolence	In the final stage, she comes to see that hurting anyone–including herself–is immoral. This realization establishes a moral equivalence between herself and others and, according to Gilligan, represents the most sophisticated level of moral reasoning.

Source: Gilligan (1982).

and that gender differences are not as pronounced as first thought (Colby & Damon, 1987). For instance, some research has found that both males and females use similar "justice" and "care" orientations in making moral judgments. Clearly, the question of how boys and girls differ in their moral orientations is far from settled (McGraw & Bloomfield, 1987; Jadack, Hyde, Moore, & Keller, 1995).

Review and Rethink

REVIEW

♦ In the middle childhood years, children begin to use social comparison to develop self-concepts involving psychological rather than physical characteristics and differentiation into distinct domains.

♦ According to Erik Erikson, children at this time are in the industry-versus-inferiority stage, focusing on efforts to achieve competence and to meet increasingly complex challenges.

♦ During the middle childhood years, self-esteem develops significantly through comparisons with others and the formation of internal standards of success; if self-esteem is low, the result can be a cycle of failure.

♦ Self-efficacy—a sense of one's own capabilities—develops over the course of middle childhood through reflections on one's own performance, observations of others, and feedback.

♦ According to Lawrence Kohlberg, moral development proceeds from a concern with rewards and punishments, through a focus on social conventions and rules, toward a sense of universal moral principles—a theoretical construct that appears to apply more accurately to males than to females.

RETHINK

♦ Does the fact that students in low-achievement schools often have higher academic self-esteem than students in high-achievement schools argue against high-achievement schools? Why or why not?

◆ If industriousness is a more accurate predictor of future success than IQ, how might industriousness be measured? How might an individual's industriousness be improved? Should this be a focus of schooling?

◆ What is an example of the relationship between low self-esteem and the cycle of failure in an area other than academics? How might the cycle of failure be broken?

◆ Kohlberg and Gilligan each postulate the existence of three major levels of moral development. Are any of their levels comparable? In which level of either theory do you think that the largest discrepancy between males and females would be observed?

◆ Might cultural differences in the stages of moral development cast doubt on the universality of either Kohlberg's or Gilligan's theories?

RELATIONSHIPS: BUILDING FRIENDSHIP

In Lunch Room Number Two, Jamillah and her new classmates chew slowly on sandwiches and sip quietly on straws from cartons of milk. They huddle into their seats, staring blankly ahead, in awe of what's happening. The school principal moves among them with a microphone. "We eat quietly and we eat in our seats. No one gets up." On this day, no one seems inclined to test him. Boys and girls look timidly at the strange faces across the table from them, looking for someone who might play with them in the schoolyard, someone who might become a friend.

For these children, what happens in the schoolyard will be just as important as what happens in the school. And when they're out on the playground, there will be no one to protect them. No child will hold back to keep from beating them at a game, humiliating them in a test of skill, or harming them in a fight. No one will run interference or guarantee membership in a group. Out on the playground, it's sink or swim. No one automatically becomes your friend. (Kotre & Hall, 1990, pp. 112–113)

As Jamillah and her classmates demonstrate, friendship comes to play an increasingly important role during middle childhood. Children grow progressively more sensitive to the importance of friends, and building and maintaining friendships becomes a large part of children's social lives.

The formation of friendships influences children's development in several ways. For instance, friendships provide children with information about the world and other people, as well as about themselves. Friends provide emotional support that allows youngsters to respond more effectively to stress. Friends can teach children how to manage and control their emotions, and help them to interpret their own emotional experiences.

Friendships also provide a training ground for communicating and interacting with others, and they can foster intellectual growth. Finally, friendships allow children to practice their skills in forming close relationships with others—skills that will become increasingly important in their future lives (Asher & Parker, 1991; Hartup, 1992).

STATUS AMONG SCHOOL-AGE CHILDREN: ESTABLISHING ONE'S POSITION

Who's on top? Although school-age children are not likely to articulate such a question, the reality of children's friendships is that they exhibit clear hierarchies in terms of status. **Status** is the evaluation of a role or person by other relevant members of a group. Children who have higher status have greater access to available resources, such as games, toys, books, and information. In contrast, lower-status children are more likely to follow the lead of children of higher status.

Status is an important determinant of children's friendships. High-status children tend to form friendships with higher-status individuals, whereas lower-status children are more

status   *the evaluation of a role or person by other relevant members of a group* likely to have friends of lower status. The number of friends a child has is also related to status: Higher-status youngsters are more apt to have a greater number of friends than those of lower status.

But it is not only the quantity of social interactions that separates high-status children from lower-status children; the nature of their interactions is different. Higher-status children are more likely to be viewed as friends by other children. They are more likely to form *cliques*, groups that are viewed as exclusive and desirable, and they tend to interact with a greater number of other children. In contrast, children of lower status are more likely to play with younger or less popular children (Ladd, 1983).

Popularity, then, is a reflection of children's status. School-age youngsters who are mid to high in status are more likely to initiate and coordinate joint social behavior, making their general level of social activity higher than that of children low in social status (Erwin, 1993).

STAGES OF FRIENDSHIP

During middle childhood, a child's conception of the nature of friendship undergoes some profound changes. According to developmental psychologist William Damon, a child's view of friendship passes through three distinct stages (Damon, 1977; Damon & Hart, 1988).

In the first stage, which ranges from about 4 to 7 years of age, children see friends as others who like them and with whom they share toys and other activities. They view the children with whom they spend the most time as their friends. For instance, a kindergartner who was asked "How do you know that someone is your best friend?" responded in this way:

> I sleep over at his house sometimes. When he's playing ball with his friends he'll let me play. When I slept over, he let me get in front of him in 4-squares. He likes me. (Damon, 1983, p. 140)

What children in this first stage don't do much of, however, is to take others' personal qualities into consideration. For instance, they do not see their friendships as being based upon their peers' unique positive personal traits. Instead, they use a very concrete approach to deciding who is a friend, primarily dependent upon others' behavior. They like those who share and with whom they can share, whereas they don't like those who don't share, who hit, or who don't play with them. In sum, in the first stage, friends are viewed largely in terms of presenting opportunities for pleasant interactions.

In the next stage, however, children's view of friendship becomes more complicated. Lasting from about age 8 to age 10, this stage covers a period in which children take others' personal qualities and traits into consideration. In addition, friends are viewed in terms of the kinds of rewards they provide. For instance, consider how an 8-year-old girl explains why another girl is her "best friend":

> She never disagrees, she never eats in front of me, she never walks away when I'm crying, and she helps me on my homework. (Damon, 1988, pp. 80–81)

Clearly, this girl's view of friendship is based on the responsivity of her "best friend" to her needs, not just on how often they engage in shared activities. In fact, the centerpiece of friendship in this second stage is mutual trust. Friends are seen as those who can be counted on to help out when they are needed. This means that violations of trust are taken very seriously, and friends cannot make amends for such violations just by engaging in positive play, as they might at earlier ages. Instead, the expectation is that formal explanations and formal apologies must be provided before a friendship can be reestablished.

The third stage of friendship begins toward the end of middle childhood, from 11 to 15 years of age. During this period, children begin to develop the view of friendship that they hold during adolescence. Although we'll discuss this perspective in detail in Chapter 12, the main criteria for friendship now shift toward intimacy and loyalty. Friendship is characterized by psychological closeness, mutual disclosure, and exclusivity. By the time they reach the end of middle childhood, children seek out friends who will be loyal (Newcomb & Bagwell, 1995).

Consider, for instance, the following sixth grader's response to the question "How do you know that someone is your best friend?":

> If you can tell each other things that you don't like about each other. If you get in a fight with someone else, they'd stick up for you. If you can tell them your phone number and they don't give you crank calls. If they don't act mean to you when other kids are around. (Damon, 1983, p. 140)

The twin themes of intimacy and loyal support are clearly sounded in this child's response. By the end of middle childhood, then, children come to view friendship not so much in terms of shared activities as in terms of the psychological benefits that friendship brings.

Children also develop clear ideas about which behaviors they seek in their friends—and which they dislike. As can be seen in Table 10-3, fifth and sixth graders most enjoy others who invite them to participate in activities and who are helpful, both physically and psychologically. In contrast, displays of physical or verbal aggression, among other behaviors, are disliked.

INDIVIDUAL DIFFERENCES IN FRIENDSHIP: WHAT MAKES A CHILD POPULAR?

Why is it that some children are the schoolyard equivalent of the life of the party, while others are social isolates, whose overtures to others are dismissed or disdained?

Developmental researchers have attempted to answer this question by examining individual differences in popularity, seeking to identify the reasons why some youngsters climb the ladder of popularity while others remain firmly on the ground.

What Personal Characteristics Lead to Popularity?   Popular children share several personality characteristics. They are usually helpful, cooperating with others on joint projects. They are also funny, tending to have good senses of humor and to appreciate others'

TABLE 10-3

THE MOST-LIKED AND LEAST-LIKED BEHAVIORS THAT CHILDREN NOTE IN THEIR FRIENDS, IN ORDER OF IMPORTANCE

Most-Liked Behaviors	Least-Liked Behaviors
Having a sense of humor	Verbal aggression
Being nice or friendly	Expressions of anger
Being helpful	Dishonesty
Being complimentary	Being critical or criticizing
Inviting one to participate in games, etc.	Being greedy or bossy
Sharing	Physical aggression
Avoiding unpleasant behavior	Being annoying or bothersome
Giving one permission or control	Teasing
Providing instructions	Interfering with achievements
Loyalty	Unfaithfulness
Performing admirably	Violating of rules
Facilitating achievements	Ignoring others

Adapted from Zarbatany, Hartmann, & Rankin (1990).

social competence *the collection of individual social skills that permit individuals to perform successfully in social settings*

neglected children *children who receive relatively little attention from their peers in the form of either positive or negative interactions*

rejected children *children who are actively disliked, and whose peers may react to them in an obviously negative manner*

social problem solving *the use of strategies for solving social conflicts in ways that are satisfactory both to oneself and to others*

attempts at humor. Compared with children who are less popular, they are better able to understand others' emotional experiences by more accurately reading their nonverbal behavior. In sum, popular children are high in **social competence**, the various social skills that permit individuals to perform successfully in social settings (Feldman, Philippot, & Custrini, 1991; Erwin, 1993; Hubbard & Coie, 1994).

Popular children are not totally self-sufficient. They show interest in others, and they are not afraid to ask for others' help when necessary. At the same time, though, they are not overly reliant on others. Consequently, popular children maintain a balance between independence and dependence (Hartup, 1970; Rubin, Daniels-Beirness, & Hayvren, 1982).

When they enter a new social situation, popular children have a sense of what is occurring and learn to adapt their behavior to the situation. They are aware that it takes time to build relationships and that they may only gradually become a full member of a new group (Putallaz, 1983; Asher, 1983).

Children who are unpopular, in contrast, can be sad figures, for school-age peers can be particularly unwelcoming to social outcasts. Unpopular children may be the last chosen to participate in activities with other children, or they may be actively discriminated against in classroom activities.

On the other hand, unpopular children are not always unhappy children, and they often have at least some friends. For example, one study showed that only a moderate association existed between unpopularity in school and children's reports of how lonely they were. One explanation may be that the children who are unpopular in school compensate by playing with neighborhood friends or siblings (Asher, Hymel, & Renshaw, 1984; Vandell & Hembree, 1994).

What makes some children unpopular? Some are unliked because they are immature, acting silly or in ways that are more appropriate to younger children. Others are overly aggressive, showing hostility to their peers or acting in an overbearing manner; still others are so withdrawn that they permit little interaction. Some children are unpopular because they are far from society's stereotypes of physical attractiveness. Consequently, children who are unusually obese or thin, who "look funny," or who are extremely slow academically may find themselves in the unenviable role of class outcast (Dodge & Crick, 1990).

Lack of popularity may take one of two forms (Asher & Parker, 1991). **Neglected children** are those who receive relatively little attention from their peers. They are not necessarily disliked; they just do not receive much attention in the form of either positive or negative interactions. It turns out, however, that neglected children do not fare all that badly. Although they see themselves as less socially competent than other children, they often don't feel less happy or accepted than their more popular peers (Erwin, 1993).

On the other hand, a second form of unpopularity—active rejection—is more harmful. **Rejected children** are actively disliked, and their peers may react to them in an obviously negative manner. Rejected children are disruptive, aggressive, uncooperative, short-tempered, and unfriendly. In general, they lack social competence. Moreover, their behavior is often seen as a problem not only by other children but also by adults (Volling, Mackinnon, Rabiner, & Baradaran, 1993; DeRosier, Kupersmidt, & Patterson, 1994; Boivin, Dodge, & Coie, 1995).

The long-term outcomes for rejected children can be quite negative. Rejected children are more likely to be poorly adjusted and to show delinquency in their later lives than popular or neglected children. Of course, it is not clear whether these difficulties are caused by their rejection by their peers, or by behavior problems that may have led them to become rejected in the first place.

Social Problem-solving Abilities.   Another factor that relates to children's popularity is their skill at **social problem solving**. This refers to the use of strategies for solving social conflicts in ways that are satisfactory both to oneself and to others. Because social conflicts among school-age youngsters are a not infrequent occurrence—even among the best of friends—successful strategies for dealing with them are an important element of social success (Hay, 1984).

According to developmental psychologist Kenneth Dodge, successful social problem solving proceeds through a series of steps that correspond to children's information-processing strategies (see Figure 10-3). Dodge argues that the manner in which children solve social problems is a consequence of the decisions that they make at each point in the sequence (Dodge, 1985; Dodge, Pettit, McClasky, & Brown, 1986; Dodge & Crick, 1990; Dodge & Price, 1994).

By carefully delineating each of the stages, Dodge provides a means by which interventions can be targeted toward a specific child's deficits. For instance, some children routinely misinterpret the meaning of other children's behavior (Step 2), and then respond according to their misinterpretation.

Consider, for example, Frank, a fourth grader, who is playing a game with Bill. While playing the game, Bill begins to get angry because he is losing. If Frank mistakenly assumes that Bill is angry not because he is losing but because of something that Frank has done, Frank's misunderstanding may lead *him* to react with anger, making the situation more volatile. If Frank had interpreted the source of Bill's anger more accurately, Frank might have been able to behave in a more effective manner, thereby defusing the situation.

Generally, children who are popular are better at interpreting the meaning of others' behavior. Furthermore, they possess a wider inventory of techniques for dealing with social problems. In contrast, less popular children tend to be less effective at understanding the causes of others' behavior, and their strategies for dealing with social problems are more limited (Vitaro & Pelletier, 1991).

FIGURE 10-3

PROBLEM-SOLVING STEPS

Children's problem solving proceeds through several steps involving different information-processing strategies.

(*Source*: Based on Dodge, 1985.)

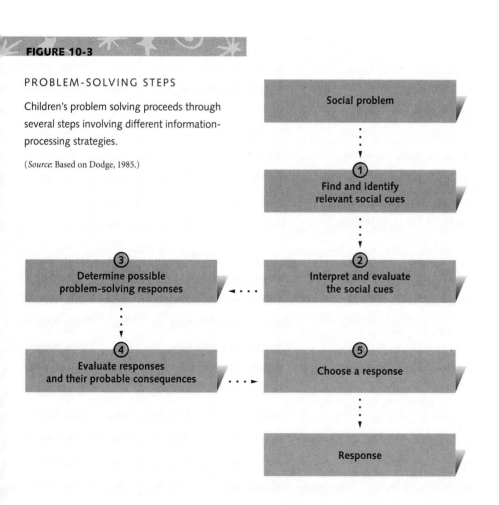

A variety of factors lead some children to be unpopular and socially isolated from their peers.

Teaching Social Competence.   Can anything be done to help unpopular children learn social competence? Happily, the answer appears to be yes. Several programs have been developed to teach youngsters those social skills that seem to underlie general social competence. For example, in one experimental program, a group of unpopular fifth and sixth graders were taught the skills that underlie such abilities as holding a conversation with friends. They were taught ways to disclose material about themselves, to learn about others by asking questions, and to offer help and suggestions to others in a nonthreatening way. Compared with a group of children who did not receive such training, the children who were trained interacted more with their peers, held more conversations, developed higher self-esteem, and—most critically—were more accepted by their peers than before training (Bierman & Furman, 1984).

Similarly, children in another program were taught to be more adept at decoding the meaning of facial expressions, thereby becoming more sensitive to others' emotions and moods. As a result of their training, some youngsters in the program became noticeably better at making friends and getting along with their teachers (Nowicki & Duke, 1994).

GENDER AND FRIENDSHIPS: THE SEX SEGREGATION OF MIDDLE CHILDHOOD

Boys are idiots. Girls have cooties. At least those are the typical views offered by boys and girls regarding members of the opposite sex during the elementary school years. Avoidance of the opposite sex becomes quite pronounced during this time, to the degree that the social networks of most boys and girls consist almost entirely of same-sex groupings (Gottman, 1986; Adler, Kless, & Adler, 1992).

When boys and girls make occasional forays into the other gender's territory, the action often has romantic overtones. For instance, girls may threaten to kiss a boy, or boys might try to lure girls into chasing them. Such behavior, termed "border work," helps to emphasize the clear boundaries that exist between the two sexes. In addition, it may pave the way for future interactions that do involve romantic or sexual interests when school-age children reach adolescence and cross-sex interactions become more socially endorsed (Thorne, 1986; Beal, 1994).

The lack of cross-gender interaction in the middle childhood years means that boys' and girls' friendships are restricted to members of their own gender. However, the nature of friendships within the two genders is quite different.

Boys typically have larger networks of friends than do girls, and they tend to play in groups, rather than pairing off. The status hierarchy is usually fairly blatant, with an acknowledged leader and members falling into particular levels of status. Because of this fairly rigid **dominance hierarchy**, rankings that represent the relative social power of those in the group, members of higher status can safely question and oppose children lower in the hierarchy (Beal, 1994).

Boys tend to be concerned with their place in the status hierarchy, and they attempt to maintain their status and improve upon it. This makes for a style of play known as *restrictive play*, in which interactions are interrupted when a child feels that his status is challenged. Thus, a boy who believes that he is unjustly challenged by a peer of lower status may attempt to end the interaction by scuffling over a toy or otherwise behaving assertively. Consequently, boys' play tends to come in bursts, rather than in more extended, tranquil episodes (Boulton & Smith, 1990; Benenson & Apostoleris, 1993).

The language of friendship used among boys reflects their concern over status and challenge. For instance, consider this conversation between two African-American boys who were good friends:

Child 1:   Why don't you get out of my yard.
Child 2:   Why don't you *make* me get out the yard.
Child 1:   I *know* you don't want that.
Child 2:   You're not gonna make me get out the yard cuz you can't.
Child 1:   Don't force me.
Child 2:   You can't. Don't force me to hurt you *(snickers)*. (Goodwin, 1990, p. 37)

Friendship patterns among girls are quite different. Rather than having a wide network of friends, school-age girls focus on one or two "best friends" who are of relatively equal status. In contrast to boys, who seek out status differences, girls profess to avoid differences in status, preferring to maintain friendships at equal-status levels.

Conflicts among school-age girls are solved through compromise, by ignoring the situation, or by giving in, rather than by seeking to make one's own point of view prevail. In sum, the goal is to smooth over disagreements, making social interaction easy and nonconfrontational (Goodwin, 1990).

According to developmental psychologist Carole Beal, the motivation of girls to solve social conflict indirectly does not stem from a lack of self-confidence or from apprehension over the use of more direct approaches. In fact, when school-age girls interact with other girls who are not considered friends or with boys, they can be quite confrontational. However, among friends their goal is to maintain equal-status relationships—ones lacking a dominance hierarchy (Beal, 1994).

The language used by girls tends to reflect their view of relationships. Rather than blatant demands ("Give me the pencil"), girls are more apt to use language that is less confrontational and directive. Girls tend to use indirect forms of verbs, such as "Let's go to the movies" or "Would you want to trade books with me?" rather than "I want to go to the movies" or "Let me have these books" (Goodwin, 1980, 1990).

Interestingly, the segregation of friendships according to gender occurs in almost all societies. Why should this be? In nonindustrialized societies, same-gender segregation may be the result of the types of activities that children engage in. For instance, in many cultures, boys are assigned one type of chore and girls another. Segregation in activities leads to the development of same-gender friendships (Harkness & Super, 1985; Whiting & Edwards, 1988).

dominance hierarchy   *rankings that represent the relative social power of those in a group hierarchy*

Developmental Diversity

Promoting Cross-race Friendships: Integration In and Out of the Classroom

Are friendships color-blind? For the most part, the answer is no. Children's closest friendships tend largely to be with others of the same race. In fact, as children age there is a decline in the number and depth of friendships outside their own racial group. By the time they are 11 or 12, it appears that African-American children become particularly aware of and sensitive to the prejudice and discrimination directed toward members of their race, and they are more apt to make ingroup-outgroup distinctions (Singleton & Asher, 1979; Hartup, 1983).

For instance, when third graders from one long-time integrated school were asked to name a best friend, approximately one-quarter of Caucasian children and two-thirds of African-American children chose a child of the other race. In contrast, by the time they reached 10th grade, no more than 10 percent of whites and 5 percent of African-Americans named a different-race best friend (Singleton & Asher, 1979; Asher, Singleton, & Taylor, 1982).

Although closest friendships tend to be with others of the same race, members of different racial and ethnic groups can show a high degree of mutual acceptance, particularly in schools with ongoing integration efforts.

On the other hand, although they may not choose each other as best friends, Caucasians and African-Americans—as well as members of other minority groups—can show a high degree of mutual acceptance. This pattern is particularly true in schools with ongoing integration efforts. This makes sense: A good deal of research supports the notion that contact between majority and minority group members can reduce prejudice and discrimination.

Contact between different racial groups is effective for several reasons. For one thing, people may find that they have more in common with members of other racial groups than they had expected. This realization leads to greater attraction. In addition, as people learn more about members of other racial groups, their previously held but inaccurate biases may be reduced (Stephan, 1985; Gaertner et al., 1990).

Contact among members of different races can open access to information about a broader range of educational and occupational opportunities, as well as cultural and leisure choices. It can also reduce anxieties and fears that members of both minority and majority groups hold about people outside their group. Finally, contact offers the opportunity to view members of other racial groups as individuals rather than as representatives of some vague, distant, and homogeneous group (Desforges et al., 1991; Wells & Crain, 1994).

On the other hand, contact between members of majority and minority groups does not invariably increase cross-racial acceptance. Contact is effective only if several important conditions are met (S.W. Cook, 1984). First, the contact must occur in equal-status settings. It hardly seems realistic to expect, for instance, that hiring an African-American custodian in a school will reduce the prejudice of white students; placing white and African-American same-status students together in the same classes would be of greater benefit.

A second important factor concerns the intimacy of the interaction between group members. Majority and minority group members must be cooperatively involved in activities that are important to them. They need to know each other on an informal basis and as individuals.

Finally, the situation must support interracial interaction and favor equality. It must allow the disconfirmation of negative stereotypes and permit individuals to interact under a variety of circumstances (Stephan, 1985, 1986; Gerard, 1988; N. Miller & Brewer, 1990).

In sum, contact can be an effective means of promoting acceptance and friendship among school-age children as long as the conditions outlined above are met. Fortunately, in most elementary school settings, this can be the case. Students in the same class can be made to feel that they are of relatively equal status; they can be guided, through various teaching techniques, to interact closely and cooperatively; and teachers can communicate the importance of interracial interaction and equality.

In addition, majority and minority group interaction can spill over outside of school once it occurs in the classroom. For example, students attending schools with a substantial minority population report relatively frequent interracial contacts after school. However, there remains a higher likelihood that a minority group member will have a majority group friend than that a majority group member will have a minority group friend. This tendency is not surprising, particularly in schools in which the minority group population is proportionately small relative to the majority group. In such cases, on a statistical basis alone we would expect fewer opportunities for majority group members to interact with minority group members (DuBois & Hirsch, 1990; Howes & Wu, 1990).

The Informed Consumer of Development

Increasing Children's Social Competence

It is clear that building and maintaining friendships is critical in children's lives. Is there anything that parents and teachers can do to foster children's social competence?

The answer is a clear yes. Among the strategies that can work are the following:

- Encourage social interaction. Teachers can devise ways in which children are led to take part in group activities, and parents can encourage membership in such groups as Brownies and Cub Scouts or participation in team sports.

- Teach listening skills to children. Show them how to listen carefully and respond to both the underlying meaning of a communication and its overt content.

- Make children aware that people display emotions and moods nonverbally; consequently, they should pay attention to others' nonverbal behavior, not only to what others are saying on a verbal level.

- Teach conversational skills, including the importance of asking questions and self-disclosure. Encourage students to use "I" statements in which they clarify their own feelings or opinions, and avoid making generalizations about others.

- Don't ask children to choose teams or groups publicly. Instead, assign children randomly: It works just as well in ensuring a distribution of abilities across groups and avoids the public embarrassment of a situation in which some children are chosen last.

Review and Rethink

REVIEW

♦ Children pass through three stages in their understanding of the nature of friendship, from the sharing of enjoyable activities, through the consideration of personal traits that can meet their needs, to a focus on intimacy and loyalty.

♦ Friendships in childhood display status hierarchies, with popular, high-status children manifesting social competence and engaging in more relationships; low-status children becoming followers; and unpopular children being either neglected or rejected by their peers.

♦ Because social competence affects popularity, improvements in such abilities as social problem solving and social information processing can lead to better interpersonal skills and greater popularity.

♦ Boys and girls engage increasingly in same-sex friendships, with boys' friendships involving group relationships, dominance hierarchies, and restrictive play, and girls' friendships characterized by equal-status pairings, cooperation, compromise, and the avoidance of confrontation.

♦ Interracial friendships decrease in frequency as children age, but equal-status contacts among members of different races can promote mutual acceptance and appreciation.

RETHINK

♦ Do you think the stages of friendship are a childhood phenomenon, or do adults' friendships display similar stages?

♦ Is there a "cycle of success" in the relationship between social competence and popularity? A cycle of failure in their opposites?

♦ How does the increasing sophistication of cognitive skills contribute to social competence? Does social competence relate to one of Howard Gardner's seven intelligences?

♦ Do you think boys' and girls' different approaches to friendship are primarily genetic or environmental? In what ways might they be influenced by cultural factors?

♦ Is it possible to decrease the segregation of friendships along racial lines? What factors would have to change in individuals or in society?

FAMILY AND SCHOOL: SHAPING CHILDREN'S BEHAVIOR IN MIDDLE CHILDHOOD

The routine is similar every day. Five days a week, after school gets out, 10-year-old Marlene O'Connor gets off the school bus and trudges up the hill to her home. She takes the house key, which she keeps on a string around her neck to avoid losing it, and opens the front door to her empty home. Locking the door behind her, she turns on the television and calls her mother, who is at work as a service representative for an Ohio electric utility. After chatting briefly with her mother, assuring her that she is well, Marlene turns her attention to the television as she eats a snack she has found in the kitchen. She watches TV until her mother and father return home a few hours later.

Is Marlene paying a price because both her parents work outside the home? This question is one of several that we need to address as we consider how children's schooling and home life profoundly affect their lives during middle childhood.

THE FAMILY: THE CHANGING HOME ENVIRONMENT

> The original plot goes like this: first comes love. Then comes marriage. Then comes Mary with a baby carriage. But now there's a sequel: John and Mary break up. John moves in with Sally and her two boys. Mary takes the baby Paul. A year later Mary meets Jack, who is divorced with three children. They get married. Paul, barely 2 years old, now has a mother, a father, a stepmother, a stepfather, and five stepbrothers and stepsisters—as well as four sets of grandparents (biological and step) and countless aunts and uncles. And guess what? Mary's pregnant again. (Katrowitz & Wingert, 1990, p. 24)

We've already noted in earlier chapters the changes that have occurred in the structure of the family over the last few decades. With a soaring divorce rate, an increase in the number of parents who both work outside of the home, and a rise in single-parent families, the environment faced by children passing through middle childhood in the 1990s is very different from the one that prior generations faced.

The Consequences of Divorce. Having divorced parents is no longer very distinctive. Compared with three-quarters 30 years ago, only about half of children in the United States will pass through childhood living with both of their parents, each of whom has been married only one time (Jacobson, 1987). The rest will live in single-parent homes; or with stepparents, grandparents, or other nonparental relatives; and some will end up in foster care. Minority groups have been hit particularly hard by these trends: More than half of all black children and almost one-third of all Hispanic children live in homes with only one parent.

How do children react to divorce? The answer depends on how soon you ask the question following a divorce, as well as how old the children are at the time. Immediately after a divorce, the results can be quite devastating. Both children and parents may show several types of psychological maladjustment for a period that may last from 6 months to 2 years. For instance, children may be anxious, experience depression, or show sleep disturbances and phobias. Even though children most often live with their mothers following a divorce, the quality of the mother–child relationship declines in the majority of cases (Gottman, 1993; Guttman, 1993).

During the early stage of middle childhood, youngsters whose parents are divorcing often tend to blame themselves for the breakup. By the age of 10, children feel pressure to choose sides, taking the position of either the mother or the father. They thereby experience some degree of divided loyalty (Wallerstein & Blakeslee, 1989).

On the other hand, the consequences of divorce become less devastating from 18 months to 2 years later. After reaching a low point approximately a year following the divorce, most children begin to return to their predivorce state of psychological adjustment. Still, twice as many children of divorced parents require psychological counseling as do children from intact families (Zill, 1983; Hetherington, Stanley-Hogan, & Anderson, 1989).

Several factors relate to how youngsters react to divorce. One is the economic standing of the family the child is living with. In many cases, divorce brings a decline in both parents' standards of living. When this occurs, children may be thrown into poverty, which can have a negative effect on many aspects of their upbringing.

In other cases, the negative consequences of divorce are less severe than they might otherwise be because the divorce reduces the hostility and anger in the home. Because the predivorce household was overflowing with parental strife, in some cases the relative lack of conflict of a postdivorce household may be beneficial to children. This is particularly true for children who maintain a close, positive relationship with the parent with whom they do not live. Consequently, for some children, living with parents who have an intact but unhappy marriage, high in conflict, has more and stronger negative consequences than experiencing a parental divorce (Booth & Edwards, 1989; Cherlin, 1993; Gelles, 1994; Gottfried & Gottfried, 1994; Davies & Cummings, 1994).

Living in Blended Families.   For many children, the aftermath of divorce includes the subsequent remarriage of one or both parents. In fact, more than 10 million households in the United States contain at least one spouse who has remarried. More than 5 million remarried couples have at least one stepchild living with them in what has come to be called **blended families**. Experts predict that by the year 2000, over 50 percent of children born in the last decade will be stepdaughters and stepsons (Glick, 1989; U.S. Bureau of the Census, 1991b).

Living in a blended family is challenging for the children involved. There often is a fair amount of *role ambiguity*, in which roles and expectations are unclear. Children may be uncertain about their responsibilities, how to behave to stepparents and stepsiblings, and how to make a host of decisions that have wide-ranging implications for their role in the family. For instance, a child in a blended family may have to choose which parent to spend each vacation and holiday with, or to decide between the conflicting suggestions they have received from biological parent and stepparent (Cherlin, 1993; Dainton, 1993).

How do school-age youngsters in blended families fare? In many cases, surprisingly well. In comparison to adolescents, who have more difficulties, school-age children often adjust relatively smoothly to blended arrangements, for several reasons. For one thing, the family's financial situation is often improved after a parent remarries. In addition, in a blended family more people are available to share the burden of household chores. Finally, the fact that the family contains more individuals can increase the opportunities for social interaction (Hetherington & Clingempeel, 1992; Hetherington et al., 1989).

On the other hand, not all children adjust well. Some find the disruption of routine and of established networks of family relationships difficult. For instance, a child who is used to having her mother's complete attention may find it difficult to observe her mother showing interest and affection to a stepchild. The blending of families does not always proceed smoothly.

When Both Parents Work: How Do Children Fare?   In most cases, children whose parents both work full-time outside of the home fare quite well. Most research suggests that children whose parents are loving, are sensitive to their children's needs, and provide appropriate substitute care develop no differently from children in families in which one of the parents does not work (Kamerman & Hayes, 1982; L.W. Hoffman, 1989).

One reason that children whose mothers and fathers both work develop no differently relates to the psychological adjustment of the parents. In general, women who are satisfied with their lives tend to be more nurturing with their children. When work provides a high level of satisfaction, then, mothers who work outside the home may be more psychologically supportive of their children. Thus, it is not so much a question of whether a mother chooses to work full-time, to stay at home, or to arrange some combination of the two. What matters is how satisfied she is with the choices she has made (Scarr, Phillips, & McCartney, 1989; Barnett & Rivers, 1992; Gilbert, 1994).

Although we might expect that children whose parents both work would spend comparatively less time with their parents than children with one parent at home full-time, research suggests otherwise. Children with mothers and fathers who work full-time spend essentially the same amount of time with family, in class, with friends, and alone as do children in families where one parent stays at home (Galambos & Dixon, 1984; Richards & Duckett, 1991, 1994).

Furthermore, as much time is spent on family meals and evening activities for children in families in which mothers are employed as in families in which mothers are not employed. In fact, some evidence suggests that working parents try to compensate for time

---

blended families *a remarried couple that has at least one stepchild living with them*

that they are away from home, spending even more time in the evenings with their children than do parents who do not both work.

On the other hand, the parent with whom children spend their time may be different. For instance, one survey of 10- to 13-year-olds found that children whose mothers were employed full-time spent more time alone with their fathers than did children whose mothers were not so employed (Richards & Duckett, 1994).

Latchkey Children.   Although children in families in which both parents work typically fare well, their success is due in part to the availability of adequate substitute care. For many children, however, no care is available, and they return after school to empty houses. These are so-called **latchkey children**, youngsters who let themselves into their homes after school and wait alone until their parents return from work.

Concern about latchkey children has centered on their lack of supervision and the emotional costs of being alone. However, research has not identified many differences between latchkey children and children who return to homes with parents. Although many children report negative experiences while at home by themselves (such as loneliness), they seem emotionally undamaged by the experience. In addition, if they stay at home by themselves rather than "hanging out" unsupervised with friends, they may avoid involvement in activities that can lead to difficulties (Long & Long, 1983; Steinberg, 1986).

In sum, the consequences of being a latchkey child are not necessarily harmful. In fact, children may develop an enhanced sense of independence and competence. Furthermore, the time spent alone provides an opportunity to work uninterrupted on homework or school projects. Some findings even suggest that children with employed parents can have higher self-esteem because they feel they are contributing to the household in significant ways (L.W. Hoffman, 1989).

Single-parent Families.   Almost one-quarter of all children under the age of 18 in the United States live with only one parent. If present trends continue, almost three-quarters of American children will spend some portion of their lives in a single-parent family before they are 18 years old. For minority children, the numbers are even higher: Some 60 percent of African-American children and 35 percent of Hispanic children under the age of 18 live in single-parent homes (Demo & Acock, 1991; U.S. Bureau of the Census, 1990b, 1994).

Single-parent households reflect several situations (see Figure 10-4). The most prevalent are cases in which there never was a spouse (that is, the parent never married), the

The consequences of being a so-called latchkey child are not necessarily harmful, and may even lead to a greater sense of independence and competence.

latchkey children   *children who let themselves into their homes after school and wait alone until their caretakers return from work*

FIGURE 10-4

The composition of single-parent families. For both African-Americans and Caucasians, the single parent who is present is the mother.

(*Source*: Suro, 1992.)

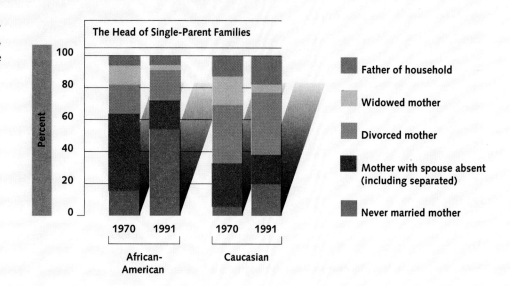

The Head of Single-Parent Families

- Father of household
- Widowed mother
- Divorced mother
- Mother with spouse absent (including separated)
- Never married mother

1970   1991
African-American

1970   1991
Caucasian

spouses have divorced, or the spouse is absent. In the vast majority of cases, the single parent who is present is the mother.

What consequences are there for children living in homes with just one parent? This is a difficult question to answer. Much depends on whether a second parent was present earlier and, if so, whether the two parents got along with each other or were constantly fighting. In cases of high parental strife, the decrease in overall tension and anxiety in a household reduced to a single parent may actually enhance a child's adjustment (Gongla & Thompson, 1987; Gottman & Katz, 1989).

Furthermore, the economic status of the single-parent family plays a role in determining the consequences on children. Living in relative poverty—and single-parent families are often less well-off financially than two-parent families—has a negative impact on children.

In sum, the impact of living in a single-parent family is not, by itself, invariably negative or positive. Given the large number of single-parent households, the stigma that once existed toward such families has largely declined. The ultimate consequences for children depend on a variety of factors that accompany single parenthood, such as the economic status of the family, the amount of time that the parent is able to spend with the child, and the degree of stress in the household.

The Consequences of Group Care: Orphanages in the 1990s.   The term "orphanage" evokes images of pitiful youngsters clothed in rags, eating porridge out of tin cups and housed in huge, prisonlike institutions.

The reality today is different. Even the term "orphanage" is rarely used, having been replaced by *group home* or *residential treatment center*. Typically housing a relatively small number of children, group homes are used for youngsters—like Kevin, described at the beginning of the chapter—whose parents are no longer able to care for them adequately.

Group care has grown significantly in the last decade. In fact, in just the 4-year period from 1987 to 1991, the number of children in group or foster care increased by more than 50 percent. Today, close to a half million youngsters in the United States live in such situations (Carnegie Task Force on Meeting the Needs of Young Children, 1994).

About three-quarters of children in group care are victims of neglect and abuse. Most of them can be returned to their homes, following intervention with their families by social service agencies. But the remaining one-quarter are so psychologically damaged due to abuse or other causes that, once they are placed in group care, they are likely to remain there

(a)

(b)

Although the orphanages of the early 1900s were crowded and institutional (a), today the equivalent, called group homes or residential treatment centers (b), are much more pleasant.

throughout childhood. With severe problems, such as high levels of aggression or anger, they are largely unadoptable. No family wants to house them even temporarily in a foster home (Fanshel, Finch, & Grundy, 1990; Sugden, 1995).

Although some politicians have suggested that an increase in group care is a solution to complex social problems associated with unwed mothers who become dependent on welfare, experts in providing social services and psychological treatment are not so sure. For one thing, group homes cannot always consistently provide the support and love potentially available in a family setting. Moreover, group care is hardly cheap: It can cost some $40,000 annually to support a child in group care—about ten times the cost of maintaining a child in foster care or on welfare (Cox & Cox, 1985; Fanshel, Finch, & Grundy, 1990, 1992).

Other experts argue that group care is neither inherently good nor bad. Instead, the consequences of living away from one's family may be quite positive, depending on the particular characteristics of the staff of the group home and whether child and youth care workers are able to develop an effective, stable, and strong emotional bond with a specific child. (Table 10-4 shows the personal characteristics of the best—and worst—child and youth care workers.) On the other hand, if a worker is unable to form a meaningful relationship with a child in a group home, the results may well be unfavorable (Shealy, 1995).

THE SCHOOL: THE ACADEMIC ENVIRONMENT

Where do children spend most of their time? During the school year, at least, more of the day is spent in the classroom than anywhere else. It is not surprising, then, that schools have a profound impact on children's lives, shaping and molding not only their way of thinking but also the way they view the world. We turn now to a number of critical aspects of schooling in middle childhood.

TABLE 10-4

PERSONAL CHARACTERISTICS OF THE BEST AND WORST CHILD AND YOUTH CARE WORKERS

The best workers:	The worst workers:
Flexible	Exhibits pathology
Mature	Selfish
Integrity	Defensive
Good judgment	Dishonest
Common sense	Abusive
Appropriate values	Abuses drugs/alcohol
Responsible	Uncooperative
Good self-image	Poor self-esteem
Self-control	Rigid
Responsive to authority	Irresponsible
Interpersonally adept	Critical
Stable	Passive-aggressive
Unpretentious	Inappropriate boundaries
Predictable/consistent	Unethical
Nondefensive	Authoritarian/coercive
Nurturant/firm	Inconsistent/unpredictable
Self-aware	Avoidant
Empowering	Doesn't learn from experience
Cooperative	Poor role model
Good role model	Angry/explosive

Adapted from Shealy (1995).

attributions *people's understanding of the reasons behind their behavior*

How Children Explain Academic Success and Failure.   Most of us, at one time or another, have done poorly on a test. Think back to how you felt when you received a bad grade. Did you feel shame? Anger at the teacher? Fear of the consequences? According to psychologist Bernard Weiner (1985, 1994), your response in such situations is determined largely by the particular causes to which you attribute your failure. And the kinds of attributions you make ultimately determine how hard you strive to do well on future tests.

Weiner has proposed a theory of motivation based on people's **attributions**, i.e., their understanding of the reasons behind their behavior. He suggests that people attempt to determine the causes of their academic success or failure by considering three basic dimensions: (1) whether the cause is internal (dispositional) or external (situational); (2) whether the cause is stable or unstable; and (3) whether the cause is controllable or uncontrollable.

Consider, for instance, a student named Henry who gets a 98, the highest score in the class, on an exam. To what can he attribute his success? He might think it is a result of his ability, his effort in studying for the test, or the fact that he was rested and relaxed when he took the exam. Because each of these factors is related to what Henry is or has done, they are internal attributions. But note how they differ on the other dimensions: Ability is a sta-

Speaking of Development

Sam Schmidt

Born: ·························· 1966

Education: ····················· University of Nebraska at Lincoln, B.A. in business administration

Position: ·························· Family teacher at Boys Town

Home: ··························· Boys Town, Nebraska

Following graduation from college 4½ years ago, Sam and Kristin Schmidt became house parents, or as they are called at Boys Town, Family Teachers, in one of the 76 individual homes at Boys Town.

"Many of the kids who come to Boys Town have been physically or sexually abused, and almost all of them have been emotionally abused," Sam Schmidt says. "They have a distorted perception of how to treat other children and adults. We try to teach them appropriate boundaries and to gradually build relationships with others to the point of where they are comfortable and confident with other people.

"A major problem in our children is their behavior patterns, which they have learned in a dysfunctional family setting or in and around their neighborhood. Boys Town combines a family style environment with skill-based training to help remediate these learned behaviors," says Schmidt. "We teach them a lot of different skills, such as how to follow instructions, accept criticism, and agree and disagree appropriately with adults."

Boys Town has its own middle school and high school, and the same techniques are applied there as are used in the home, according to Schmidt. One of the basic approaches is called SODAS, or *S*ituation, *O*ptions, *D*isadvantages, *A*dvantages, and *S*olution.

"We start by asking the children to write down what the situation is—say, taking out the trash," Sam Schmidt explains. "They then think of two or three options, such as 'I will

ble, enduring factor, whereas study effort and degree of relaxation are both unstable and can fluctuate from one test to another. Finally, study effort and degree of relaxation differ from each other in terms of controllability: Although amount of effort is controllable, degree of relaxation may not be.

The attributions people make have important implications for their perceptions of their performance. For example, the internal-external dimension is related to esteem-related emotions. When a success is attributed to internal factors, students tend to feel pride; but failure attributed to internal factors causes shame. On the other hand, the stability dimension determines future expectations about success and failure. Specifically, when students attribute success or failure to factors that are relatively stable and invariant, they are apt to expect similar performance in the future. In contrast, when they attribute performance to unstable factors such as effort or luck, their expectations about future performance are relatively unaffected.

Finally, the controllability dimension affects emotions that are directed toward others. If children feel that failure was due to factors within their control—e.g., lack of effort—they are apt to experience anger; but if the failure was uncontrollable, they are likely to feel sadness or pity.

"A major problem in our children is their behavior patterns, which they have learned in a dysfunctional family setting or in and around their neighborhood."

do it' and 'I won't do it.' Then they write down the advantages and disadvantages of each option and think about them. This process usually helps them arrive at a solution."

Another motivational tool used at Boys Town is a point system. Positive points are awarded for good behavior and point fines for negative behavior.

"Once a day the point cards are totaled, and if the kids have enough points they get privileges like watching television, going to the gym, or using the telephone," Schmidt says. "If they don't make the point total, they are assigned academic work or other work, or they may have to write on a problem-solving situation. They can earn back half of the negative point fine by acknowledging the fine itself.

"When they come here they learn the basic skills, and usually they respond to them very well," he adds. "Many of them do it over time, until, gradually, appropriate behavior becomes internalized and they do it without thinking about it."

"Gradually, appropriate behavior becomes internalized and they do it without thinking about it."

Cultural Comparisons: Individual Differences in Attribution.   Not everyone comes to the same conclusions about the sources of success and failure. In fact, among the strongest influences on people's attributions are their race, ethnicity, and socioeconomic status. Because different experiences give us different perceptions about the ways things in the world fit together, it is not surprising that there are subcultural differences in how achievement-related behaviors are understood and explained.

One important difference is related to racial factors: African-Americans are less likely than Caucasians to attribute success to internal rather than external causes. Specifically, African-American children sometimes feel that task difficulty and luck (external causes) are the major determinants of their performance outcomes, and even if they put in maximum effort, prejudice and discrimination will prevent them from succeeding (Ogbu, 1988; Graham, 1994).

An attributional pattern that overemphasizes the importance of external causes is maladaptive. Attributions to external factors reduce a student's sense of personal responsibility for success or failure. But when attributions are based on internal factors, they suggest that a change in behavior—such as increased effort—can bring about a change in success (Graham, 1992, 1994).

African-Americans are not the only group susceptible to maladaptive attributional patterns. Women, for example, often attribute their unsuccessful performance to low ability, an uncontrollable factor. Ironically, though, they do not attribute successful performance to high ability, but to factors outside their control. A belief in this pattern suggests the conclusion that even with future effort, success will be unattainable. Females who hold these views may be less inclined to expend the effort necessary to improve their rate of success (Dweck & Bush, 1976; D.A. Phillips & Zimmerman, 1990; Dweck, 1991).

Furthermore, members of different cultures show clear-cut differences in attributional patterns, as we discuss in the Directions in Development section.

Directions in Development

Cultural Differences in Attributions for Academic Performance: Explaining Asian Academic Success

Consider two students, Ben and Hannah, each performing poorly in school. Suppose you thought that Ben's poor performance was due to unalterable, stable causes, such as a lack of intelligence, whereas Hannah's was produced by temporary causes, such as a lack of hard work. Who would you think would ultimately do better in school?

If you are like most people, you'd probably predict that the outlook was better for Hannah. After all, Hannah could always work harder, but it is hard for someone like Ben to develop higher intelligence.

According to psychologist Harold Stevenson, this reasoning lies at the heart of the superior school performance of Asian students, compared with students in the United States. Stevenson's research suggests that teachers, parents, and students in the United States are likely to attribute school performance to stable, internal causes, while people in Japan, China, and other East Asian countries are more likely to see temporary, situational factors as the cause of their performance. The Asian view, which stems in part from ancient Confucian writings, tends to accentuate the necessity of hard work and perseverance.

Students, teachers, and parents in Asian countries are more likely to attribute school performance to situational factors such as how hard they work, while people in western cultures are more likely to attribute performance to stable, internal causes, such as underlying intelligence.

This cultural difference in attributional styles is displayed in several ways. For instance, surveys show that mothers, teachers, and students in Japan and Taiwan all believe strongly that students in a typical class tend to have the same amount of ability. In contrast, mothers, teachers, and students in the United States are apt to disagree, arguing that there are significant differences in ability among the various students (see Figure 10-5).

It is easy to imagine how such different attributional styles can influence teaching approaches. If, as in the United States, students and teachers seem to believe that ability is fixed and locked in, poor academic performance will be greeted with a sense of failure and reduced motivation to work harder to overcome it. In contrast, Japanese teachers and students are apt to see failure as a temporary setback owing to their lack of hard work. After making such an attribution, they are more apt to expend increased effort on future academic activities.

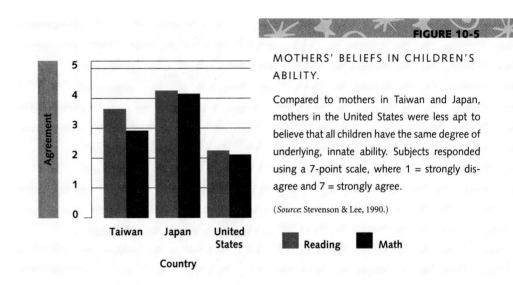

FIGURE 10-5

MOTHERS' BELIEFS IN CHILDREN'S ABILITY.

Compared to mothers in Taiwan and Japan, mothers in the United States were less apt to believe that all children have the same degree of underlying, innate ability. Subjects responded using a 7-point scale, where 1 = strongly disagree and 7 = strongly agree.

(*Source*: Stevenson & Lee, 1990.)

Reading   Math

Some psychologists have suggested that these different attributional orientations may explain the fact that Asian students frequently outperform American students in international comparisons of students achievement (Geary, Fan, & Bow-Thomas, 1992). Because Asian students tend to assume that academic success results from hard work, they may put greater effort into their schoolwork than do American students, who believe that their inherent ability determines their performance. These arguments suggest that the attributional style of students and teachers in the United States might well be maladaptive (Stevenson, 1992; Stevenson & Stigler, 1992; Stevenson, Chen, & Lee, 1993; Chen & Stevenson, 1995).

Expectation Effects: How Others' Expectancies Influence Children's Behavior.   Suppose you were told at the beginning of a new school year that the students in your class had taken a test described in this way:

All children show hills, plateaus, and valleys in their scholastic progress. A study being conducted at Harvard with the support of the National Science Foundation is interested in those children who show an unusual forward spurt of academic progress. These spurts can and do occur at any level of academic and intellectual functioning. When these spurts occur in children who have not been functioning too well academically, the result is familiarly referred to as "late blooming."

As part of our study we are further validating a test which predicts the likelihood that a child will show an inflection point or "spurt" within the near future. This test which will be administered in your school will allow us to predict which youngsters are most likely to show an academic spurt. . . . The development of the test for predicting inflections or "spurts" is not yet such that *every* one of the top 20 percent will show the spurt or "blooming" effect. But the top 20 percent of the children *will* show a more significant inflection or spurt within the next year or less than will the remaining 80 percent of the children. (R. Rosenthal & Jacobson, 1968, p. 66)

Consider your reaction to the children on the list of "bloomers" identified by the test. Would you treat them differently from the children who were not so designated?

If the results of a classic, but controversial, study are any guide, your answer should be affirmative: Teachers do, in fact, seem to treat youngsters for whom they have expectations of improvement differently from those for whom they have no such expectations (R. Rosenthal & Jacobson, 1968). In the experiment, elementary school teachers were told at the beginning of a new school year that five children in their classes would be likely to "bloom" in the upcoming year, based on the test described above. In reality, however, the information was bogus: The names of the children had simply been picked at random, although the teachers didn't know that. The teachers received no further details from the experimenters for the rest of the year.

At the end of the year, the children completed an intelligence test that was identical to one taken a year earlier. According to the experimenters, the results showed that clear differences existed in the intellectual growth of the so-called bloomers, compared with that of the other members of their classes. Those randomly designated as likely to make significant gains did, in fact, improve more than the other children. However, the results were not uniform: The greatest differences were found for children in first and second grades, with smaller differences for children in grades three through six.

When the findings of the experiment, reported in a book dubbed *Pygmalion in the Classroom* (Rosenthal & Jacobson, 1968), were published, they caused an immediate stir among educators—and among the public at large. The reason for this furor was the implication of the results: If merely holding high expectations is sufficient to bring about gains in achievement, wouldn't holding low expectations lead to slowed achievement? And because teachers sometimes may hold low expectations about children from lower socioeconomic and minority backgrounds, did this mean that children from such backgrounds were destined to show low achievement throughout their educational careers?

Although the original experiment has been criticized on methodological and statistical grounds (R. Snow, 1969; Wineburg, 1987), enough new evidence has been amassed to make it clear that the expectations of teachers are communicated to their students and can in fact bring about the expected performance. The phenomenon has come to be called the **teacher expectancy effect**—the cycle of behavior in which a teacher transmits an expectation about a child and actually brings about the expected behavior (Babad, 1992).

The teacher expectancy effect can be viewed as a special case of a broader concept known as the *self-fulfilling prophecy*, in which a person's expectation is capable of bringing about an outcome (Snyder, 1987). For instance, physicians have long known that providing patients with placebos (fake, inactive drugs) can sometimes "cure" them, simply because the patients expect the medicine to work.

In the case of teacher expectancy effects, the basic explanation seems to be that teachers, after forming an initial expectation about a child's ability, transmit it to the child

teacher expectancy effect *the cycle of behavior in which a teacher transmits an expectation about a child and thereby actually brings about the expected behavior* through a complex series of verbal and nonverbal cues. These communicated expectations in turn indicate to the child what behavior is appropriate, and the child behaves accordingly (Harris & Rosenthal, 1986; Rosenthal, 1987, 1994).

Once teachers have developed expectations about a child, by what method do they transmit them? Generally, four major factors relate to the transmission of expectations (Harris & Rosenthal, 1986; Rosenthal, 1994):

◆ *Classroom social-emotional climate.* Teachers create a warmer, more accepting environment for children for whom they hold high expectations than for those from whom they expect less. They convey more positive attitudes by smiling and nodding more often, and they look at high-expectation children more frequently.

◆ *Feedback.* When teachers hold high expectations for a child, they provide more positive evaluations of the child's work and they are more accepting of the child's ideas. In contrast, low-expectation children receive more criticism and little or no feedback in some situations. Even when low-expectation children do well, the kind of feedback teachers offer is less positive than when a high-expectation child does well.

◆ *Input to children.* Children who are expected to do well receive greater quantities of material from their teachers, and they are asked to complete more difficult material. Consequently, they are given more opportunities to perform well.

◆ *Output from teachers.* Teachers initiate more contacts with high-expectation children, and the overall number of contacts between teachers and high-expectation children is higher than with low-expectation children. As a result, high-expectation children have more opportunities to respond in class.

The final link in the chain of events that encompasses the teacher expectation effect is the child. And given the range of teacher behaviors brought about by teacher expectations, it is hardly surprising that children's performance would be significantly affected. Clearly, children who encounter a warm socio-emotional climate, who are the recipients of more feedback from their teachers, who are given more material to complete, and who have more contact with teachers are going to develop more positive self-concepts, be more motivated, and work harder than those who receive negative treatment or neglect. Ultimately, the high-expectation children are likely to perform better in class.

The cycle, then, is complete: A teacher who expects a child to do better treats that child more positively. The child responds to such treatment and eventually performs in accord with the teacher's expectations. But note that the cycle does not stop there: Once children behave congruently with the teacher's expectations, the expectations are reinforced. As a consequence, a child's behavior ultimately may cement the expectation initially held by the teacher (see Figure 10-6).

We should also note that expectations are an omnipresent phenomenon in classrooms and are not the province of teachers alone. For instance, children develop their own expectations about their teacher's competence, based on rumors and other bits of information, and they communicate their expectations to those teachers. In the end, a teacher's behavior may be brought about in significant measure by children's expectations (Feldman & Prohaska, 1979; Feldman & Theiss, 1982; Jamieson, Lydon, Stewart, & Zanna, 1987).

It is also important to keep in mind that the classroom is not the only place in which expectations operate. *Any* setting in which one person holds an expectation about a child, and vice versa, may produce analogous expectation effects. Clearly, children's views of themselves and of their behavior are in part a consequence of what others expect of them (Eden, 1990; Harris et al., 1992).

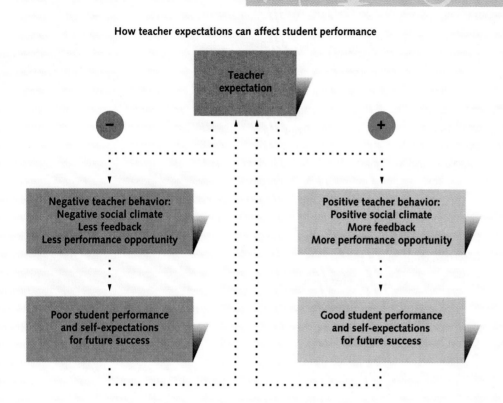

How teacher expectations can affect student performance

Teacher expectation

− (Negative)

Negative teacher behavior:
Negative social climate
Less feedback
Less performance opportunity

Poor student performance
and self-expectations
for future success

+ (Positive)

Positive teacher behavior:
Positive social climate
More feedback
More performance opportunity

Good student performance
and self-expectations
for future success

FIGURE 10-6

How teacher expectations can affect student performance. Teachers who hold a positive or negative expectation about a student can actually bring about the expected behavior.

Review and Rethink

REVIEW

◆ Divorce can cause psychological difficulties in children during the middle school years, but the consequences depend on such factors as financial circumstances and the comparative levels of tension in the family before and after the divorce.

◆ Children whose parents work outside the home usually receive about the same amount of parental attention and care as do children with an at-home parent, and latchkey children may develop independence and enhanced self-esteem from their experience.

◆ Having a single parent can have either positive or negative effects, depending on financial circumstances, the amount of parent–child interaction, and the level of tension in the family.

◆ People attribute successes and failures to factors according to their attributional patterns, which seem to differ along individual, cultural, and gender dimensions.

◆ Expectancies can affect the behavior of both the person holding and the person receiving them, eventually producing outcomes that reflect and confirm the expectancies.

RETHINK

◆ How might the development of self-esteem in middle childhood be affected by a divorce? By a family situation characterized by constant hostility and tension between parents?

◆ Politicians often speak of "family values." How does this term relate to the diverse family situations covered in this chapter, including divorced parents, single parents, blended families, working parents, latchkey children, abusive families, and group care?

◆ Can you think of ways in which the attributions people apply to others may work to confirm stereotypes along racial or gender lines?

◆ How might the negative expectancies of a teacher work to produce results that confirm those expectancies? Are expectancies related to attributions?

◆ Do expectancies operate outside the classroom, among adults? How?

LOOKING BACK

In what ways do children's views of themselves change during the middle childhood years?

1. Children in the middle school years begin to view themselves in terms of psychological characteristics rather than physical ones. In addition, they begin to differentiate their self-concepts into different areas.

2. Children use social comparison as an important means of arriving at an evaluation of their behavior, abilities, expertise, and opinions. Generally, they measure themselves against relevant others in their environment.

3. According to Erik Erikson, children in the middle childhood years are in the industry-versus-inferiority stage, during which they focus on achieving competence and responding to a wide range of personal challenges. Their success or failure at meeting these challenges affects their sense of competence and can have lifelong consequences.

How do children in these years develop a sense of self-esteem?

4. In addition to working on their self-concepts, children in the middle childhood years are also developing self-esteem, an evaluation of their overall worth as individuals. In general, although self-esteem grows steadily during these years, a temporary dip appears at around age 12, most likely attributable primarily to the transition from elementary school to the next higher school level.

5. Children with chronically low self-esteem can become trapped in a cycle of failure in which low self-esteem feeds on itself by producing low expectations and poor performance. Members of minority groups that are the objects of discriminatory practices can experience low self-esteem unless they are convinced that the discriminatory practices they undergo are illegitimate and can be changed.

6. Children also develop a sense of self-efficacy during these years, using reflections on their own behavior, observations of the behavior of others, and feedback from others to form expectations about what they are capable of doing and achieving.

Through what stages does moral development proceed as children age?

7. Children develop both morally and in other ways. According to Lawrence Kohlberg, people pass through three major levels and six stages of moral development, from pre-conventional morality (motivated by rewards and punishments), through conventional morality (motivated by social reference), to postconventional morality (motivated by a sense of universal moral principles)—a level that many individuals do not attain. Carol Gilligan has sketched out an alternative progression for girls, from an orientation toward individual survival, through goodness as self-sacrifice, to the morality of nonviolence.

What sorts of relationships and friendships do children have in the middle school years?

8. Children's friendships, which are important aspects of their intellectual and emotional lives, display clear status hierarchies, with high status leading to a greater number of friendships and interactions, access to more desirable resources, and membership in preferred social groupings.

9. Children's understanding of friendship passes through stages, from a focus on mutual liking and time spent together, through the consideration of personal traits and the rewards that friendship provides, to an appreciation of intimacy and loyalty.

What are the causes and effects of popularity and unpopularity?

10. Popularity in children is related to traits that underlie social competence, including cooperation, humor, understanding, adaptability, and skill at social problem solving. Unpopularity can result from socially unacceptable behavior, physical unattractiveness, or "differentness."

11. Popular children engage in activities that promote social development and skill. Unpopular children may be simply neglected by their peers, in which case they may not suffer serious consequences, or they may be rejected by their peers, in which case their ultimate social adjustment is endangered.

12. Because of the importance of social interactions and friendships, developmental specialists have engaged in efforts to improve children's social skills. One focus has been on improving social problem-solving skills or, following the information-processing approach of Kenneth Dodge, on deficits in children's processing of social information that affect their exercise of social skills.

How do gender and race affect friendships?

13. Gender is a significant factor in friendship. Not only do boys and girls increasingly prefer same-gender friendships, but friendships among males have different characteristics than do friendships among females. Male friendships are characterized by groups larger than pairs, status hierarchies, and restrictive play to address status challenges. Female friendships tend to involve one or two close relationships, equal status among friends, and a reliance on cooperation, compromise, and the avoidance of confrontation.

14. Race also influences the formation of friendships, with cross-race friendships diminishing in frequency as children age. Nevertheless, equal-status interactions among members of different racial groups can lead to improved understanding, mutual respect and acceptance, and a decreased tendency to stereotype.

How do today's diverse family arrangements affect children?

15. Immediately after a divorce, the effects on middle-school-age children can be serious, but they tend to diminish after about 18 to 24 months. Major factors in the seriousness of the consequences are the financial condition of the family and the hostility level

between spouses before the divorce. The blended families that often result from divorce and remarriage present challenges to the child, but can also offer opportunities for increased social interaction.

16. Children in families in which both parents work outside the home generally fare well, because their parents' sense of career fulfillment often translates into satisfaction in the home, and because most working parents try hard to spend time with their children. When both parents work, their children often must fend for themselves in an empty home after school (as "latchkey children"), a requirement that can lead to independence and a sense of competence and contribution.

17. Living in a single-parent family does not in itself lead to negative consequences. Factors affecting children in single-parent families are the same as those affecting children of divorce: the financial condition of the family and, if there had been two parents, the level of hostility that existed between them.

18. Children in group care, whose numbers are increasing, tend to have been victims of neglect and abuse before their group-care placement. Many can be helped and placed with their own or other families, but about 25 percent of them are so psychologically damaged that they will never be adopted or taken into a foster home and will spend their childhood years in group care.

How do subjective interpretations of successes and failures, by oneself and by others, contribute to school outcomes?

19. People attach attributions to their academic successes and failures, which may be (1) internal or external, (2) stable or unstable, and (3) controllable or uncontrollable. Differences in attributional patterns are not only individual but also appear to be influenced by culture and gender. Some attributional patterns that overemphasize an uncontrollable factor (such as luck), a stable, internal factor (such as low ability), or an external factor (such as task difficulty) to explain failure may be maladaptive.

20. The expectancies of others, particularly teachers, can produce outcomes that conform to those expectancies. Expectancies can cause differences in the ways teachers deal with students, which may lead to modified behavior on the part of students, which in turn may confirm the teachers' initial expectancies.

KEY TERMS AND CONCEPTS

social comparison (p. 339)

industry-versus-inferiority stage (p. 340)

self-esteem (p. 340)

self-efficacy (p. 342)

status (p. 347)

social competence (p. 350)

neglected children (p. 350)

rejected children (p. 350)

social problem solving (p. 350)

dominance hierarchy (p. 353)

blended families (p. 358)

latchkey children (p. 359)

attributions (p. 362)

teacher expectancy effect (p. 366)

Adolescence

CHAPTER 11

Physical and Cognitive Development

CHAPTER OUTLINE

Recently, a student was shot dead by a classmate during lunch period outside Frank W. Ballou Senior High. It didn't come as much of a surprise to anyone at the school, in this city's most crime-infested ward. Just during the current school year, one boy was hacked by a student with an ax, a girl was badly wounded in a knife fight with another female student, five fires were set by arsonists, and an unidentified body was dumped next to the parking lot.

But all is quiet in the echoing hallways at 7:15 A.M., long before classes start on a spring morning. The only sound comes from the computer lab, where 16-year-old Cedric Jennings is already at work on an extra-credit project, a program to bill patients at a hospital. Later, he will work on his science-fair project, a chemical analysis of acid rain.

He arrives every day this early and often doesn't leave until dark. The high-school junior with the perfect grades has big dreams: He wants to go to Massachusetts Institute of Technology. (Suskind, 1994, p. 1)

LOOKING AHEAD

Cedric is one of a tiny group of students who have an average of B or better at their huge inner-city high school in Washington, DC. This cadre of achievers is a lonely group, the frequent target of threats and actual violence. Yet Cedric perseveres, intent on getting a college education and succeeding academically and, ultimately, in life.

Why do students such as Cedric overcome the extremes of poverty and violence that they face, while others are less successful? More broadly, what are the challenges that all adolescents face, and how do they confront those challenges?

In this chapter and the next, we consider the basic issues and questions that underlie adolescence. **Adolescence** is the developmental stage that lies between childhood and adulthood. It begins and ends imprecisely, starting just before the teenage years and ending just after them. This imprecision reflects the nature of society's treatment of the period: Adolescents are considered to be no longer children, but not yet adults. Clearly, though, adolescence is a time of considerable physical and psychological growth and change.

This chapter focuses on physical and cognitive growth during adolescence. We begin by considering the extraordinary physical maturation that occurs during adolescence, triggered by the onset of puberty. We discuss the consequences of early and late maturation, as well as nutrition and eating disorders.

Next we turn to a consideration of cognitive development during adolescence. After reviewing several approaches to understanding changes in cognitive capabilities, we examine school performance, focusing on the ways that socioeconomic status, ethnicity, and race affect scholastic achievement.

The chapter concludes with a discussion of several of the major threats to adolescents' well-being. We'll focus on drug, alcohol, and tobacco use, as well as sexually transmitted diseases.

adolescence the developmental stage that *lies between childhood and adulthood*

After reading this chapter you'll be able to answer the following questions:

♦ What physical changes do adolescents experience?

♦ What are the consequences of early and late maturation?

♦ What nutritional needs and concerns do adolescents have?

♦ How does cognitive development proceed during adolescence?

♦ What factors affect adolescent school performance?

♦ Why do adolescents use dangerous substances, and what are the warning signs of substance abuse?

♦ What dangers do adolescent sexual practices present, and how can these dangers be avoided?

PHYSICAL MATURATION

For the male members of the Awa tribe, the beginning of adolescence is marked by an elaborate and—to Western eyes—gruesome ceremony marking the transition from childhood to adulthood. First the boys are whipped for 2 or 3 days with sticks and prickly branches. Through the whipping, the boys atone for their previous infractions and honor tribesmen who were killed in warfare.

But that's just for starters. In the next phase of the ritual, sharpened sticks are punched into the boys' nostrils, producing a considerable amount of blood. Then, adults force a 5-foot length of vine into the boys' throats, causing them to choke and vomit. Finally, deep cuts are made in the boys' genitals. Jeering onlookers poke at the cuts to make them bleed even more.

Most of us probably feel gratitude that we did not have to endure such physical trials when we entered adolescence. But members of Western cultures do have their own rites of passage into adolescence, admittedly less fearsome, such as bar mitzvahs and bat mitzvahs at age 13 for Jewish boys and girls, and confirmation ceremonies in many Christian denominations (Myerhoff, 1982; Dunham et al., 1986).

Regardless of the nature of the ceremonies celebrated by various cultures, their underlying purpose tends to be similar from one culture to the next: symbolically celebrating the onset of the physical changes that take a child to the doorstep of adulthood.

GROWTH DURING ADOLESCENCE: THE RAPID PACE OF PHYSICAL AND SEXUAL MATURATION

The growth in height and weight during adolescence can be breathtaking. In only a few months, an adolescent can grow several inches and require a virtually new wardrobe. In fact, over just a 4-year period, boys and girls undergo a transformation, at least in physical appearance, from children to young adults.

The dramatic changes during adolescence constitute the adolescent growth spurt, a period of very rapid growth in height and weight. During the adolescent growth spurt, height and weight increase as quickly as they did during infancy. On average, boys grow 4.1 inches a year and girls 3.5 inches a year. Some adolescents grow as much as 5 inches in a single year (Tanner, 1972).

Boys' and girls' adolescent growth spurts begin at different times. On average, girls start their spurts 2 years earlier than do boys, and they complete them earlier as well. As you can see in Figure 11-1, girls begin their spurts about age 10, whereas boys don't start until about age 12. For the 2-year period starting at age 11, girls tend to be a bit taller than boys. This doesn't last, however: By the age of 14, boys, on average, are taller than girls—a state of affairs that persists for the remainder of the life span.

FIGURE 11-1

Patterns of growth are depicted in two ways. The figure on the left shows height at a given age, whereas the figure on the right shows the height *increase* that occurs from birth through the end of adolescence. These figures illustrate how girls begin their growth spurt about age 10, while boys don't start until about age 12. However, by the age of 14, boys tend to be taller than girls.

(Adapted from Marshall, 1978.)

Boy
Girl

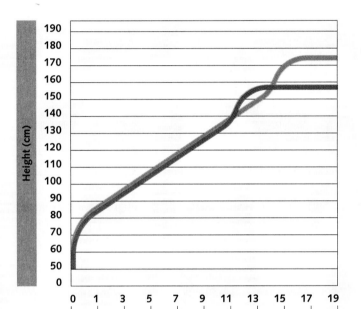
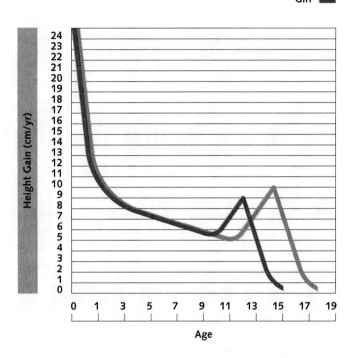

PUBERTY: THE START OF SEXUAL MATURATION

Like the growth spurt, **puberty**, the period during which the sexual organs mature, begins earlier for girls than for boys. Girls start puberty at about age 11 or 12, and boys begin at about age 13 or 14. However, wide variations occur among individuals. For example, some girls begin puberty as early as 8 or 9 or as late as 16 years of age.

Puberty begins when children's bodies begin to produce androgens (male hormones) or estrogens (female hormones) at adult levels. This surge in the production of hormones leads to the growth spurt and puberty.

What triggers the start of puberty? Although we know what happens when it begins, no one has yet identified the reason that it begins at a particular time. However, it is clear that environmental and cultural factors play a role. For example, **menarche**, the onset of menstruation, and probably the most conspicuous signal of puberty in girls, varies greatly in different parts of the world. In poorer, developing nations, menstruation begins later than in more economically advantaged countries. Even within wealthier countries, girls in more affluent groups begin to menstruate earlier than less affluent girls (see Figure 11-2). Consequently, it appears that girls who are better nourished and healthier are more apt to start menstruation at an earlier age than are those who suffer from malnutrition or chronic disease.

Other factors can affect the timing of menarche. For instance, environmental stress can bring about an earlier onset. To illustrate, one recent study found that girls from divorced families or families high in interparental conflict tended to begin menstruation earlier than

puberty   the period during which the sexual organs mature, beginning earlier for girls than for boys

menarche   the onset of menstruation

FIGURE 11-2

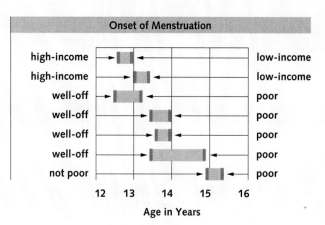

Onset of Menstruation

USA (African descent)	high-income		low-income
USA (European descent)	high-income		low-income
Hong Kong	well-off		poor
Tunis	well-off		poor
Baghdad	well-off		poor
South Africa (Bantu, urban)	well-off		poor
Transkei reserve (Bantu, rural)	not poor		poor

12   13   14   15   16
Age in Years

The onset of menstruation occurs earlier in more economically advantaged countries than those that are poorer. But even in wealthier countries, girls living in more affluent circumstances begin to menstruate earlier than girls living in less affluent situations.

(Adapted from Eveleth & Tanner, 1976.)

primary sex characteristics   *characteristics associated with the development of the organs and structures of the body that directly relate to reproduction*

secondary sex characteristics   *the visible signs of sexual maturity that do not involve the sex organs directly*

Both males and females undergo significant bodily changes during adolescence, and they show increased interest in their physical appearance.

did girls from families with lower levels of stress (Wierson, Long, & Forehand, 1993; Graber, Brooks-Gunn, & Warren, 1995).

Within the United States, historical patterns of menarche are congruent with what we find in other cultures. Near the end of the nineteenth century, menstruation began, on average, about age 14 or 15, compared with today's 11 or 12. The earlier onset today is likely the result of reduced disease and improved nutrition.

Does this mean that the age at which puberty starts will continue to decline? Probably not. It is likely that there is a genetically determined limit on how early menstruation can occur. In fact, we may have reached it already: For the last few decades, despite generally rising health and affluence, there has been no further decline in the age at which puberty begins (Malina, 1979; Bullough, 1981; Dreyer, 1982).

Menstruation is just one of several changes in puberty that are related to the development of **primary sex characteristics**, which are associated with the development of the organs and structures of the body directly related to reproduction. In contrast, **secondary sex characteristics** are the visible signs of sexual maturity that do not involve the sex organs directly.

For instance, girls experience development of primary sex characteristics through changes in the vagina and uterus as a result of maturation. Secondary sex characteristics include the development of breasts and pubic hair. Breasts begin to grow at about the age of 10, and pubic hair begins to appear at about age 11. Underarm hair is seen about two years later.

Boys' sexual maturation follows a somewhat different course. In terms of primary sex characteristics, the penis and scrotum begin to grow at an accelerated rate about the age of 12, and they reach adult size about 3 or 4 years later. By the age of 14, the average boy is able to have his first ejaculation, although his body has already been producing sperm for a few years. At the same time, there is development in secondary sex characteristics. Pubic hair begins to grow about the age of 12, followed by the growth of underarm and facial hair. Finally, boys' voices deepen as the vocal cords become longer and the larynx larger. (Figure 11-3 summarizes the changes that occur in sexual maturation during early adolescence.)

BODY IMAGE: REACTIONS TO PHYSICAL CHANGES IN ADOLESCENCE

Unlike infants, who also undergo extraordinarily rapid growth, adolescents are well aware of what is happening to their bodies, and they may react with horror or joy. Few, though, are neutral about the changes they are witnessing.

FIGURE 11-3

The changes in sexual maturation that occur for males and females during early adolescence.

(Adapted from Tanner, 1978.)

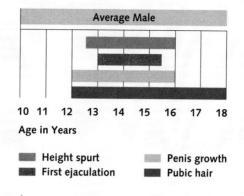

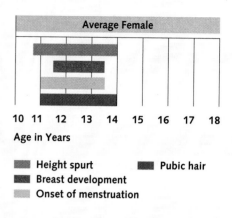

For instance, menarche produces several psychological consequences. Western society has in the past emphasized the more negative aspects of menstruation, such as the potential of cramps and messiness, and girls tended to react to menarche with anxiety (Ruble & Brooks-Gunn, 1982). Today, however, society's view of menstruation tends to be more positive, in part because menstruation has been demystified and discussed more openly. (For instance, TV commercials for tampons are commonplace.) As a consequence, menarche is typically accompanied by an increase in self-esteem, a rise in status, and greater self-awareness (Brooks-Gunn & Reiter, 1990).

In some ways, a boy's first ejaculation is roughly equivalent to menarche in a girl. However, while girls generally tell their mothers about the onset of menstruation, boys rarely mention their first ejaculation to either their parents or their friends (Stein & Reiser, 1994). Moreover, there is little evidence that the first ejaculation causes boys much anxiety or worry (Gaddis & Brooks-Gunn, 1985). There are several possible explanations for this: It may be that the event is actually of little concern or interest to boys, and therefore not worthy of mention. However, it seems more likely that boys see the first ejaculation as part of their sexuality, an area about which they are quite uncertain and which they are therefore reluctant to discuss with others.

How children react to the onset of puberty depends, in part, on when it happens. Girls and boys who mature either earlier or later than most of their peers are especially affected by the timing of puberty.

THE TIMING OF PUBERTY: THE CONSEQUENCES OF EARLY AND LATE MATURATION

What are the social consequences of early or late maturation? One of the most persistent questions addressed by psychologists who specialize in adolescence is whether early and late maturation bring with them any particular advantages or disadvantages. The answer, it turns out, differs for boys and girls.

For boys, early maturation is largely a plus. Early maturing boys tend to be more successful at athletics, presumably because of their larger size. Furthermore, they tend to be more popular and to have a more positive self-concept.

On the other hand, early maturation in boys does have a down side. Boys who mature early are more apt to have difficulties in school, and they are more likely to become involved in delinquency and substance abuse. The reason: Their larger size makes it more likely that they will seek out the company of older boys who may involve them in activities that are inappropriate for their age.

Overall, though, early maturation appears to be generally beneficial for boys. Ultimately, early maturers end up being more responsible and cooperative in later life (Livson & Peskin, 1980; Duncan et al., 1985; Andersson & Magnusson, 1990).

The story is a bit different for early maturing girls. In their case, the obvious changes in their bodies—such as the development of breasts—may lead them to feel uncomfortable and different from their peers. Moreover, because girls, in general, mature earlier than do boys, early maturation tends to come at a very young age in the girl's life. Early maturing girls may have to endure ridicule from their less mature classmates.

On the other hand, early maturation is not a completely negative experience for girls. Girls who mature earlier tend to be sought after more as potential dates, and their popularity may enhance their self-concept. Still, they may not be socially ready to participate in the kind of dating situations that most girls only have to deal with later, and such situations can be psychologically challenging for early maturing girls. Moreover, the conspicuousness of their deviance from their later-maturing classmates may have a negative effect on them (Simmons & Blyth, 1987).

Whether girls face difficulties with early maturation depends in part on cultural norms and standards. For instance, in the United States, the notion of female sexuality is looked upon with a degree of ambivalence. Consequently, the outcome of early maturation might be negative. On the other hand, in countries in which attitudes about sexuality are more liberal, results of early maturation could be more positive. For example, in Germany, which has a more open view of sex, early maturing girls have higher self-esteem than do such girls in the United States. Furthermore, the consequences of early maturation vary even within the United States, depending on the views of girls' peer groups and on prevailing community standards regarding sex (Silbereisen, Peterson, Albrecht, & Kracke, 1989; Richards, Kinney, Benet, & Merzel, 1990; Petersen, in press).

As with early maturation, the situation with late maturation is mixed, although in this case boys fare worse than girls. For instance, boys who are smaller and lighter than their more mature peers tend to be viewed as less attractive. Because of their smaller size, they are at a disadvantage when it comes to sports activities. Furthermore, because of the social convention that boys should be taller than their dates, the social lives of late-maturing boys may suffer. Ultimately, these difficulties may lead to a decline in self-concept. In fact, the disadvantages of late maturation for boys may extend well into adulthood (Mussen & Jones, 1957; Livson & Peskin, 1980).

The picture for late-maturing girls, on the other hand, is a bit more complicated. Girls who mature later may be overlooked in dating and other mixed-sex activities during junior high school and middle school, and they may have relatively low social status (Apter, Golatzer, Beth-Halachmi, & Laron, 1981; Clarke-Stewart & Friedman, 1987). However, by the time they are in 10th grade and have begun to mature visibly, late-maturing-girls' satisfaction with themselves and their bodies may be greater than that of early maturers. In fact, late-maturing girls may end up with fewer emotional problems. The reason? Late-maturing girls are more apt to fit the societal ideal of a slender, "leggy" body type than early maturers, who tend to look heavier in comparison (Simmons & Blythe, 1987; Petersen, 1988).

In sum, the reactions to early and late maturation present a complex picture. Some developmental psychologists suggest that the concern over early and later maturation, and over the effects of puberty in general, may have been overemphasized in the past (Petersen & Crockett, 1985; Paikoff & Brooks-Gunn, 1990). Rather than focusing on the growth spurt and sexual maturation that occur during adolescence, they suggest that other factors, such as changes in peer groups, family dynamics, and, particularly, schools and other societal institutions, may be more pertinent in determining an adolescent's behavior. As we have seen repeatedly, we need to take into consideration the complete constellation of factors affecting individuals in order to understand their development.

NUTRITION, FOOD, AND EATING DISORDERS: FUELING THE GROWTH OF ADOLESCENCE

A rice cake in the afternoon, an apple for dinner. That was Heather Rhodes's typical diet her freshman year at St. Joseph's College in Rensselaer, Indiana, when she began to nurture a fear (exacerbated, she says, by the sudden death of a friend) that she was gaining weight. But when Rhodes, now 20, returned home to Joliet, Illinois, for summer vacation a year and a half ago, her family thought she was melting away. "I could see the outline of her pelvis in her clothes . . .," says Heather's mother, so she and the rest of the family confronted Heather one evening, placing a bathroom scale in the middle of the family room. "I told them they were attacking me and to go to hell," recalls Heather, who nevertheless reluctantly weighed herself. Her 5'7" frame held a mere 85 pounds—down 22 pounds from her senior year in high school. "I told them they rigged the scale," she says. It simply didn't compute with her self-image. "When I looked in the mirror," she says, "I thought my stomach was still huge and my face was fat." (Sandler, 1994, p. 56)

Heather Rhodes suffered from anorexia nervosa, a severe eating disorder in which people refuse to eat, while denying that their behavior and appearance are out of the ordinary.

Heather's problem: a severe eating disorder, anorexia nervosa.

The rapid physical growth of adolescence is fueled by an increase in food consumption. Particularly during the growth spurt, adolescents eat substantial quantities of food, increasing their intake of calories rather dramatically. During the teenage years, the average girl requires some 2,200 calories a day, and the average boy 2,800.

Of course, not just any calories help nourish adolescents' growth. Several key nutrients are essential, including in particular calcium and iron. The calcium provided by milk helps bone growth, which may prevent the later development of osteoporosis—the thinning of bones—that affects 25 percent of women later in their lives. Similarly, iron is necessary to prevent iron-deficiency anemia, an ailment that is not uncommon among teenagers.

For most adolescents, the major nutritional issue is ensuring the consumption of a sufficient balance of appropriate foods. But for a substantial minority, nutrition can be a major concern and can create a real threat to health. Among the most prevalent problems: obesity and more severe eating disorders like the one afflicting Heather Rhodes.

Obesity.   The most common nutritional concern during adolescence is obesity. As we discussed in earlier chapters (see Chapters 4, 7, and 9), *obesity* is defined as body weight that is more than 20 percent above the average for a given age and height. Under this definition, some 5 percent of adolescents are formally classified as obese, and an additional 15 percent are overweight to some degree (Gans, 1990).

Although adolescents are obese for the same reasons as are younger children, the psychological consequences may be particularly severe during a time of life when body image is of special concern. Furthermore, the potential health consequences of obesity during adolescence are also problematic. For instance, obesity taxes the circulatory system, increasing the likelihood of high blood pressure and diabetes. Finally, obese adolescents stand an 80 percent chance of becoming obese adults.

Anorexia Nervosa and Bulimia.   The desire to avoid obesity sometimes becomes so strong that it turns into a problem itself. For instance, Heather Rhodes suffered from **anorexia nervosa**, a severe eating disorder in which individuals refuse to eat, while denying that their behavior and appearance, which may become skeleton-like, are out of the ordinary.

Anorexia is a severe psychological disorder; some 15 to 20 percent of its victims literally starve themselves to death. It primarily afflicts women between the ages of 12 and 40; those most susceptible are intelligent, successful, and attractive white adolescent girls from affluent homes (Hsu, 1990; Button, 1993).

In the early stages, anorexics' lives become centered on food. Even though they eat little, they may go shopping often, collect cookbooks, talk about food, or cook huge meals for others. Although they may be incredibly thin, their body images are so distorted that

anorexia nervosa   a severe eating disorder in which individuals refuse to eat, while denying that their behavior and appearance, which may become skeleton-like, are out of the ordinary

bulimia *an eating disorder characterized by binges on large quantities of food, followed by purges of the food through vomiting or the use of laxatives*

they see their reflections in mirrors as disgustingly fat, and they try to lose more and more weight. Even when they look like skeletons, they are unable to see what they have become.

Bulimia, another eating disorder, is characterized by binges on large quantities of food, followed by purges of the food through vomiting or the use of laxatives. Bulimics might eat an entire gallon of ice cream or a whole package of tortilla chips. But after such a binge, sufferers experience powerful feelings of guilt and depression, and they intentionally purge themselves of the food.

Although the weight of a person with bulimia remains fairly normal, the disorder is quite hazardous. The constant vomiting and diarrhea of the binge-and-purge cycles can produce a chemical imbalance that can lead to heart failure.

The exact reasons for the occurrence of eating disorders are not clear, although several factors appear to be implicated. For one thing, girls who mature earlier than their peers and who have a higher level of body fat are more susceptible to eating disorders during later adolescence. In addition, several psychological problems are also associated with subsequent eating disorders. Girls who show clinical levels of depression are more likely to develop eating disorders later (Nagel & Jones, 1992; Graber, Brooks-Gunn, Paikoff, & Warren, 1994).

Some theorists suggest that a biological cause lies at the root of both anorexia nervosa and bulimia. In fact, there appear to be genetic components to the disorders, and in some cases doctors have found hormonal imbalances in sufferers (Gold et al., 1986; Holland, Sicotter, & Treasure, 1988; Condit, 1990; Irwin, 1993; Treasure & Tiller, 1993).

Other attempts at explaining the eating disorders emphasize psychological and social factors. For instance, some experts suggest that the disorders are a result of overdemanding parents or by-products of other family difficulties (Miller, McCluskey-Fawcett, & Irving, 1993). In addition, the societal preference for slender bodies and disapproval of obesity may contribute to the disorder (Crandall & Biernat, 1990; Rothblum, 1990; Logue, 1991; Sohlberg & Strober, 1994).

There are also clear cultural causes. Anorexia nervosa, for instance, is found only in cultures that idealize slender female bodies. Because in most places such a standard does not hold, anorexia is not prevalent outside the United States. For instance, there is no anorexia in all of Asia, with two interesting exceptions: the upper classes of Japan and of Hong Kong, where Western influence is greatest. Furthermore, anorexia nervosa is a fairly recent disorder. It was not seen in the seventeenth and eighteenth centuries, when the ideal of the female body was a plump corpulence (Kleinman, 1991; Carson, Butcher, & Coleman, 1992).

Because anorexia nervosa and bulimia are products of both biological and environmental causes, treatment typically involves multiple approaches. For instance, both psychological therapy and dietary modifications are likely to be needed for successful treatment (Fairburn et al., 1993; Lask & Bryant-Waugh, 1993; Schmidt & Treasure, 1993).

Review and Rethink

REVIEW

- Adolescence is a period of rapid physical growth, including the hormonal and bodily changes associated with puberty. Girls typically begin their growth spurts and puberty about two years earlier than do boys.

- Puberty, whose timing is due to a combination of biological, cultural, and environmental factors, can cause reactions in adolescents ranging from confusion to increased self-esteem.

- Early or late maturation can bring advantages and disadvantages. The disadvantages are largely due to dissonance between physical maturity and emotional and psychological maturity.

- Adequate nutrition is essential in adolescence because of the need to fuel physical growth. Changing physical needs and environmental pressures can induce obesity or an obsession with avoiding obesity that can manifest itself as an eating disorder.

- The two most common eating disorders among adolescents are anorexia nervosa and bulimia. Both are serious and involve multiple causes, and both must be treated with a combination of physical and psychological therapies.

RETHINK

- Why do you think the passage to adolescence is regarded in many cultures as such a significant transition that it calls for unique ceremonies?

- What are some of the educational implications of the variations in maturation rate that adolescents experience? How can a teacher help students deal with the wide variety of changes they are witnessing and participating in?

- In what ways might the popularity of early developing boys and girls offer both benefits and threats?

- How can societal and environmental influences contribute to the emergence of an eating disorder?

- Why must the treatment of eating disorders typically involve multiple therapies, rather than simply a change in diet?

COGNITIVE DEVELOPMENT AND SCHOOLING

The bedtime stories Aleksandr Khazanov's father told him were multiplication tables and long division.

When Aleksandr was 14—a little over a year after his family immigrated to Brooklyn as refugees from Russia—his math teacher at Stuyvesant High School watched him whiz through differential equations and felt the boy was so advanced that he could learn more studying on his own.

Last summer, at 15, long before he was old enough to get his driver's license, Aleksandr took qualifying exams for Pennsylvania State University's doctoral program in math. He passed all three tests on the first try.

So when Aleksandr submitted a paper to the Westinghouse Science Talent Search competition, the most prestigious science contest for high school students, the Stuyvesant coordinator for contest entries, Stan Teitel, took an extraordinary step.

"I had the audacity to call up Westinghouse and question them as to whether they had someone advanced enough to understand his paper," Mr. Teitel said. "I'm telling you, this kid is way above the rest of us." (Belluck, 1995, p. A1)

The people at Westinghouse must have agreed: Aleksandr Khazanov was named a finalist in the contest.

Although most adolescents do not reach the heights of mathematical sophistication that Aleksandr attained—nor do most adults, for that matter—their intellectual abilities do make significant gains during adolescence. In fact, by the end of the period, adolescents' cognitive proficiencies match those of adults in major respects.

Aleksandr Khazanov

What is it that sets adolescents' thinking apart from that of younger children? One of the major changes is the ability to think beyond the concrete, current situation to what *might* or *could* be. Adolescents are able to keep in their heads a variety of abstract possibilities, and they can see issues in relative, as opposed to absolute, terms. Instead of viewing problems as having black-and-white solutions, they are capable of perceiving shades of gray (Keating, 1980, 1990).

As was the case with other stages of life, we can use several approaches to explain adolescents' cognitive development. We'll begin by returning to Jean Piaget's theory, which has had a significant influence on how developmentalists think about thinking during adolescence.

PIAGETIAN APPROACHES TO COGNITIVE DEVELOPMENT

Fourteen-year-old Siena is asked to solve a problem that anyone who has seen a grandfather's clock may have pondered: What determines the speed at which a pendulum moves back and forth? In the version of the problem that she is asked to solve, Siena is given a weight hanging from a string. She is told that she can vary several things: the length of the string, the weight of the object at the end of the string, the amount of force used to push the string, and the height to which the weight is raised in an arc before it is released.

Siena doesn't remember, but she was asked to solve the same problem when she was 8 years old. At that time, she was in the concrete operational period, and her efforts to solve the problem were not very successful. For instance, she approached the problem haphazardly, with no systematic plan of action. She simultaneously tried to push the pendulum harder *and* shorten the length of the string *and* increase the weight on the string. Because she was varying so many factors at once, when the speed of the pendulum changed she had no way of knowing which factor or factors made a difference.

Now, however, Siena is much more systematic. Rather than immediately beginning to push and pull at the pendulum, she stops a moment and thinks. Then, just like a scientist conducting an experiment, she varies only one factor at a time. By examining each variable separately and systematically, she is able to come to the correct solution: The length of the string determines the speed of the pendulum.

Using Formal Operations to Solve Problems.   Siena's approach to the pendulum question, a problem devised by Jean Piaget, illustrates that she has moved into the formal operations period (Piaget & Inhelder, 1958). The **formal operations period** is the stage at which people develop the ability to think abstractly. Most people reach it at the start of adolescence, about the age of 12.

By bringing formal principles of logic to bear on problems they encounter, adolescents in the formal operations period are able to consider problems in abstract rather than in concrete terms. They are able to test their understanding by systematically carrying out rudimentary experiments on problems and situations and observing what their experimental "interventions" bring about.

Although Piaget proposed that children enter the formal operational stage at the beginning of adolescence, you may recall that he also hypothesized that—as with all the stages of cognitive development—full capabilities do not emerge suddenly, at one stroke. Instead, they gradually unfold through a combination of physical maturation and environmental experiences. According to Piaget, it is not until adolescents are about 15 years old that they are fully settled in the formal operations stage.

In fact, some evidence suggests that a sizable proportion of people hone their formal operational skills at a later age, and in some cases, never fully employ formal operational thinking at all. For instance, most studies show that only 40 to 60 percent of college students and adults fully achieve formal operational thinking, and some estimates run as low as 25 percent (Keating & Clark, 1980; Sugarman, 1988).

Adolescents also differ for cultural reasons in their use of formal operations. For instance, individuals in isolated, scientifically unsophisticated societies and who have little

formal operations period   *the stage at which people develop the ability to think abstractly* formal education are less likely to perform at the formal operations level than are formally educated individuals in more technologically sophisticated societies (Jahoda, 1980; Segall, Dasen, Berry, & Poortinga, 1990).

Does this mean that adolescents (and adults) from cultures in which formal operations tend not to emerge are incapable of attaining them? Not at all. A more probable conclusion is that the scientific reasoning that characterizes formal operations is not equally valued in all societies. If everyday life does not require or promote a certain type of reasoning, it is irrational to expect people to employ that type of reasoning when confronted with a problem (Greenfield, 1976; Shea, 1985).

Evaluating Piaget's Approach.   Each time we've considered Piaget's theory in previous chapters, several concerns have cropped up. Let's summarize some of the issues here:

♦ Piaget suggests that cognitive development proceeds in universal, steplike advances that occur at particular stages. Yet we find significant differences in cognitive abilities from one person to the next, especially when we compare individuals from different cultures. Furthermore, we find inconsistencies in the performance of tasks even within the same individual—tasks that, if Piaget was correct, the person ought to perform uniformly well once she or he reaches a given stage (Siegler, 1994).

♦ The notion of stages proposed by Piaget suggests that cognitive abilities do not grow gradually or smoothly. Instead, the stage point-of-view implies that cognitive growth is typified by relatively rapid shifts from one stage to the next. In contrast, many developmentalists argue that cognitive development proceeds in a more continuous fashion, increasing not so much in qualitative leaps forward as in quantitative accumulations (Gelman & Baillargeon, 1983; Case, 1991).

♦ Because of the nature of the tasks Piaget employed to measure cognitive abilities, critics suggest that he miscalculated the age at which certain capabilities emerge. It is now widely accepted that infants and children are more sophisticated at an earlier age than Piaget asserted (Bornstein & Sigman, 1986).

♦ Piaget had a relatively narrow view of what is meant by *thinking* and *knowing*. To Piaget knowledge consists primarily of the kind of understanding displayed in the pendulum problem. However, as we discussed in Chapter 9, psychologists such as Howard Gardner suggest that we have many kinds of intelligence, separate from and independent of one another (Gardner & Hatch, 1989; Kornhaber, Krechevsky, & Gardner, 1991).

These criticisms of Piaget's approach to cognitive development have considerable merit. On the other hand, Piaget made momentous contributions to our understanding of cognitive development, and his work remains highly influential. He was a brilliant observer of children's and adolescents' behavior, although his focus on particular aspects of their cognitive lives may have been too narrow. His theory was the impetus for an enormous number of studies on the development of thinking capacities and processes, and it also spurred a good deal of classroom reform. Finally, his bold statements about the nature of cognitive development provided a springboard from which many opposing positions on cognitive development bloomed, such as the information-processing perspective, to which we turn next (Demetrious, Shayer, & Efklides, 1993).

INFORMATION-PROCESSING PERSPECTIVES

To proponents of information-processing approaches to cognitive development, growth in mental abilities proceeds gradually and continuously. Unlike Piaget's view that the increasing cognitive sophistication of the adolescent is a reflection of stagelike spurts, the **information-processing perspective** sees changes in cognitive abilities as gradual transformations in the capacity to take in, use, and store information.

In this view, increases in information-processing capabilities lie at the heart of the advances in mental ability seen during adolescence. Developmental advances are brought

information-processing perspective   *the model that seeks to identify the way that individuals take in, use, and store information*

metacognition   *the knowledge that people have about their own thinking processes, and their ability to monitor their cognition*

about by progressive changes in the ways people organize their thinking about the world, develop strategies for dealing with new situations, sort facts, and achieve advances in memory capacity and perceptual abilities (Keating & Clark, 1980; Gagne, 1985; Burbules & Lin, 1988; Wellman & Gelman, 1992).

And the cognitive strides made during adolescence are considerable. Although general intelligence—as measured by traditional IQ tests—remains stable, dramatic improvements evolve in the specific mental abilities that underlie intelligence. Verbal, mathematical, and spatial abilities increase. Memory capacity grows, and adolescents become more adept at effectively dividing their attention between more than one stimulus at a time—such as simultaneously studying for a biology test and listening to a *Hootie and the Blowfish* CD.

Furthermore, adolescents grow increasingly sophisticated in their understanding of problems, their ability to grasp abstract concepts and to think hypothetically, and their comprehension of the possibilities inherent in situations. They also know more about the world; their store of knowledge increases as the amount of material to which they are exposed grows and their memory capacity enlarges (Pressley, Cariglia-Bull, Deane, & Schneider, 1987). Taken as a whole, the mental abilities that underlie intelligence show a marked improvement during adolescence, peaking at about age 20 (see Figure 11-4).

The Growth of Metacognition.   According to information-processing explanations of cognitive development during adolescence, one of the most important reasons for advances in mental abilities is the growth of **metacognition**, or the knowledge that people have about their own thinking processes, and their ability to monitor their cognition.

For example, as adolescents improve their understanding of their memory capacity, they get better at gauging how long they need to study a particular kind of material to memorize it for a test. Furthermore, they can judge when they have fully memorized the material considerably more accurately than when they were younger. These improvements in metacognitive abilities permit adolescents to comprehend and master school material more effectively (Flavell, 1979; R. Garner & Alexander, 1989; T.O. Nelson, 1990, 1994).

Conversely, advances in metacognition do not always produce positive results. For instance, metacognition may make adolescents particularly introspective and self-conscious—two hallmarks of the period that, as we see next, may produce a high degree of egocentrism.

Egocentrism in Adolescents' Thinking.   Carlos is furious at his parents. He sees them as totally unfair because, when he borrows their car, they insist that he call home and let them know where he is. Eleanor is angry at Molly because Molly inadvertently bought earrings just like hers, and Molly insists on sometimes wearing them to school. Josh is upset with his

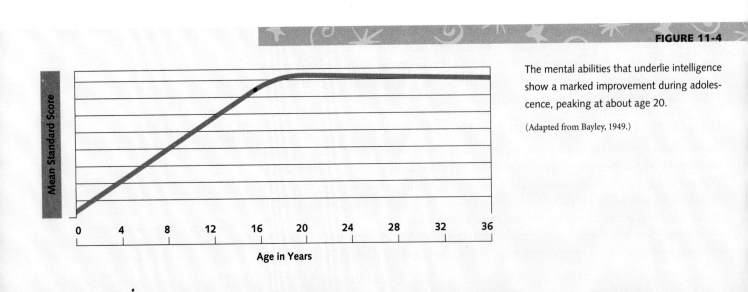

FIGURE 11-4

The mental abilities that underlie intelligence show a marked improvement during adolescence, peaking at about age 20.

(Adapted from Bayley, 1949.)

biology teacher, Ms. Sebastian, for giving a long, difficult midterm exam on which he didn't do well.

Each of these adolescents is furious, angry, or upset over what may seem like not-so-unreasonable behavior on the part of others. Why? It is quite possible that the cause lies in the egocentrism that may sometimes dominate adolescents' thinking.

According to developmental psychologist David Elkind, this period of life fosters **adolescent egocentrism**, a state of self-absorption in which the world is viewed from one's own point-of-view (Elkind, 1967, 1985). Egocentrism makes adolescents highly critical of authority figures such as parents and teachers, unwilling to accept criticism, and quick to find fault with others' behavior.

The kind of egocentrism we see in adolescence helps explain why adolescents sometimes perceive that they are the focus of everyone else's attention. In fact, adolescents may develop what has been called an **imaginary audience**, fictitious observers who pay as much attention to the adolescents' behavior as they do themselves.

Because of adolescents' newly sophisticated metacognitive abilities, they readily imagine that others are thinking about them, and they may construct elaborate scenarios about others' thoughts. Unfortunately, these scenarios may suffer from the same kind of egocentrism as the rest of their thinking. The imaginary audience is usually perceived as focusing on the one thing that adolescents think most about: themselves. For instance, a student sitting in a class may be sure a teacher is focusing on her, and a teenager at a basketball game may just know that everyone around is focusing on the pimple on his chin.

Egocentrism leads to a second distortion in thinking: the notion that one's experiences are unique. Adolescents develop **personal fables**, the view that what happens to them is unique, exceptional, and shared by no one else. For instance, teenagers whose romantic relationships have ended may feel that no one has ever experienced the hurt they feel, that no one has ever been treated so badly, that no one can understand what they are going through.

Personal fables also may make adolescents feel invulnerable to the risks that threaten others. They may think that there is no need to use condoms during sex, as the personal fables they construct make them immune to pregnancy and to sexually transmitted diseases such as AIDS. They may drive after drinking, because their personal fables paint them as careful drivers, always in control. Much of adolescents' risk-taking may well be traced to the personal fables they construct for themselves (Dolcini et al., 1989; Arnett, 1995).

SCHOOL PERFORMANCE

Do the advances that occur in cognitive abilities in adolescence translate into improvements in school performance? Curiously, the answer is no, at least if we use students' grades as the measure of school performance. On average, students' grades *decline* during the course of schooling (Schulenberg, Asp, & Petersen, 1984; Simmons & Blyth, 1987).

The reason for this decline is not entirely clear. Obviously, the nature of the material to which students are exposed becomes increasingly complex and sophisticated over the course of adolescence. But the growing cognitive abilities of adolescents might be expected to compensate for the increased sophistication of the material. Thus, we need to look to other explanations to account for the grade decline.

A better explanation seems to relate not to student performance but to teachers' grading practices. It turns out that teachers grade older adolescents more stringently than younger ones. Even though the level of sophistication of student performance, in an absolute sense, may be improving, their grades don't necessarily reflect the improvement (Simmons & Blyth, 1987).

Socioeconomic Status and School Performance: Individual Differences in Achievement.
Despite the ideal that all students are entitled to the same opportunity in the classroom, it is very clear that certain groups have more educational advantages than do others. One of

adolescent egocentrism a state of self-absorption in which the world is viewed from one's own point-of-view

imaginary audience fictitious observers who pay as much attention to the adolescents' behavior as they do themselves

personal fables the view held by some adolescents that what happens to them is unique, exceptional, and shared by no one else

the most telling indicators of this reality is the relationship between educational achievement and socioeconomic status (SES).

Middle- and high-SES students earn higher grades, score higher on standardized tests of achievement, and complete more years of schooling than do students from lower-SES homes. This disparity does not, of course, start in adolescence; the same findings hold for children in lower grades. However, by the time students are in high school, the effects of socioeconomic status become even more pronounced (Garbarino & Asp, 1981).

Why do students from middle- and high-SES homes show, in general, greater academic success? Several explanations abound, most involving environmental factors. For one thing, children living in poverty lack many of the advantages enjoyed by other youngsters. Their nutrition and health might be less adequate. Often living in crowded conditions, they may have few places to do homework. Their homes may lack the books and computers found in more economically advantaged households.

Furthermore, parents living in poverty are less likely to be involved in their children's schooling—a factor related to school success. Poorer adolescents, who may live in impoverished areas of cities with high levels of violence, may also attend older and generally inadequate schools with run-down facilities and a higher incidence of violence. Taken together, these factors clearly result in a less-than-optimal learning environment (Garbarino, Dubrow, Kostelny, & Pardo, 1992; Grolnick & Slowiaczek, 1994).

Although most developmentalists reject the approach, some researchers point to genetic factors as a source of SES differences in educational attainment. According to the controversial argument advanced by the authors of *The Bell Curve* (discussed in Chapter Nine), lower school performance of children living in poverty might be due to inherited differences in intelligence levels. According to this argument, the parents' lower IQ scores lead them into poorer-paying professions and a life of poverty. The children, inheriting their parents' low IQ and subject to the harsh conditions of poverty, are unlikely to do well in school. So goes the argument (Herrnstein & Murray, 1994).

There are several reasons to reject this reasoning. For one thing, there is substantial variation in school performance *within* a particular SES level—often, in fact, more than the variation *between* students of different SES. Put another way, there are many low-SES students who perform far better than the average performance of higher-SES students. Likewise, many higher-SES students perform well below the average performance of lower-SES students.

More important, the consequences of environment are particularly potent. Students from impoverished backgrounds may be at a disadvantage from the day they begin their schooling. Consequently, they may perform less well initially than their more affluent peers. As they grow older, their school performance may continue to lag, and in fact their disadvantage may snowball. Because later school success builds heavily on basic skills presumably learned early in school, children who experience problems early may find themselves falling increasingly behind the academic eight-ball as adolescents (Huston, 1991; Phillips et al., 1994).

Ethnic and Racial Differences in School Achievement.   Do various ethnic groups and races perform differently in school? Although the answer is fairly simple—it is "yes, they do"—reasons for the differences are as hard to come by as they were when we examined socioeconomic differences in school performance (Dornbusch, Ritter, & Steinberg, 1992).

Achievement differences between ethnic and racial groups are significant, and they paint a troubling picture of American education. For instance, data on school achievement indicate that, on average, African-American and Hispanic students tend to perform at lower levels, receive lower grades, and score lower on standardized tests of achievement than do Caucasian students (see Table 11-1). In contrast, Asian-American students tend to receive higher grades than Caucasian students.

Moreover, as shown in Figure 11-5, even continuing enrollment in school differs according to race. For instance, by the time they reach high school age, the proportion of

TABLE 11-1

PERFORMANCE ON TESTS OF ACHIEVEMENT

Reading, 1987–88	9-Year-Olds	13-Year-Olds	17-Year-Olds
National average	211.8	257.5	290.1
White	217.7	261.3	294.7
Black	188.5	242.9	274.4
Hispanic	193.7	240.1	270.8
Writing, 1988	**4th Graders**	**9th Graders**	**11th Graders**
National average	173.3	208.2	220.7
White	180.0	213.1	225.3
Black	150.7	190.1	206.9
Hispanic	162.2	197.2	202.0
Mathematics, 1985–86	**9-Year-Olds**	**13-Year-Olds**	**17-Year-Olds**
National average	222.0	269.0	302.0
White	227.0	274.0	308.0
Black	202.0	249.0	279.0
Hispanic	205.0	254.0	283.0

National Assessment of Educational Progress scales in reading, writing, and mathematics range from 0 to 500.
Source: National Center for Education Statistics, *Digest of education statistics* (1990).

minority students still enrolled in school is lower than the proportion of Caucasian students (U.S. Bureau of the Census, 1994).

What is the source of such ethnic and racial differences in academic achievement? Clearly, much of the difference is due to socioeconomic factors: Because more African-American and Hispanic families live in poverty, their economic disadvantage may be reflected in their school performance. In fact, when we take socioeconomic levels into account by comparing different ethnic and racial groups at the same socioeconomic level, achievement differences diminish (Woolfolk, 1993; Steinberg et al., 1992; Luster & McAdoo, 1994).

But socioeconomic factors are not the full story. For instance, anthropologist John Ogbu (1974, 1992) argues that members of certain minority groups may perceive school success as relatively unimportant. They may believe that societal prejudice in the workplace will dictate tha]t they will not succeed, no matter how much effort they expend. The conclusion is that hard work in school will have no eventual payoff.

FIGURE 11-5

The proportion of individuals enrolled in high school differs according to racial and ethnic background.

(*Source*: U.S. Bureau of the Census, 1990b.)

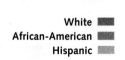

White �
African-American ▇
Hispanic ▒

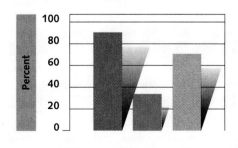

There are significant differences in school achievement between members of different racial and ethnic groups.

Furthermore, Ogbu suggests that members of minority groups who enter a new culture voluntarily are more likely to be successful in school than those who are brought into a new culture against their will. For instance, he notes that Korean children who are the sons and daughters of voluntary immigrants to the United States tend to be, on average, quite successful in school. On the other hand, Korean children in Japan, whose parents were forced to immigrate during World War II and work as forced laborers, tend to do relatively poorly in school. The reason for the disparity? Ogbu argues that the children of parents who were forced to immigrate are less likely to succeed than those whose parents immigrated voluntarily (Ogbu, 1992: Gallagher, 1994).

Another factor in the differential success of various ethnic and racial group members has to do with attributions for academic success. As we discussed in Chapter 10, students from many Asian cultures tend to view achievement as the consequence of temporary situational factors, such as how hard they work. In contrast, African-American students are more apt to view success as the result of external causes over which they have no control, such as luck. Students who subscribe to the belief that effort will lead to success, and then expend that effort, are more likely to do better in school than students who believe that effort makes less of a difference (Stevenson, 1992; Stevenson & Stigler, 1992; Stevenson, Chen, & Lee, 1992; Graham, 1986, 1990).

Another explanation for ethnic differences in adolescent performance comes from psychologist Laurence Steinberg. He and his colleagues suggest that differences in adolescents' beliefs about the consequences of not doing well in school may account for ethnic and racial differences in school performance.

Specifically, Steinberg argues that African-American and Hispanic students tend to believe that they can succeed *despite* poor school performance. This belief may cause them to put less effort into their studies. In contrast, Asian-American students tend to believe that if they do not do well in school, they are unlikely to get good jobs and be successful. Asian-Americans, then, are motivated to work hard in school by a fear of the consequences of poor academic performance (Steinberg et al., 1992).

Research on ethnic and racial differences in achievement suggests a strategy for improving the performance of groups that do less well in school. If, in fact, the root of the problem is the belief that poor academic performance brings few negative consequences, society needs to provide a clearer message about the value of education and to make the point that school failure clearly has negative consequences. More broadly, adolescent minority group members need to believe that their future success depends, in part, on their academic performance, and that—despite the societal hurdles faced by minority group members—they can overcome such barriers and succeed.

Directions in Development

Are There Psychological Costs to Academic Achievement? It Depends on Your Culture

> On a brisk Saturday morning, while most of their friends were relaxing at home, 16-year-old Jerry Lee and eight other Asian teenagers huddled over their notebooks and calculators for a full day of math and English lessons.
>
> During the week, they all attend public schools in the city. But every Saturday, they go to a Korean hag-won, or cram school, in Flushing to spend up to seven hours immersed in the finer points of linear algebra or Raymond Chandler.
>
> "I complain, but my mom says I have to go," said Jerry, a Stuyvesant High School student from Sunnyside, Queens, who has already scored a 1520 on the Scholastic Assessment Test for college, but is shooting for a perfect 1600. "It's like a habit now." (A. Dunn, 1995, p. 1)

Long a tradition in Korea, Japan, and China, cram schools have begun to spring up in the United States as Asian parents, committed to the success of their children, demand them in increasing numbers.

Cram schools are a fixture in Asian society, where competition for success begins as young as age 4 or 5. By the time children reach adolescence, competition to attend prestigious schools has reached fever pitch. Some high-school-age students spend hours every day after school and on weekends in instruction that goes beyond what is covered in public schooling.

Being pushed to attend cram school is one type of intense pressure under which Asian children are often placed. In fact, although the scholastic performance of children in Asia typically exceeds that of children in the United States, critics suggest that such success comes at the price of increased stress, psychological burdens, and depression (e.g., Holman, 1991; Watanabe, 1992).

Not so—at least according to recent research that casts doubt on the critics' contentions. Developmental Psychologist David Crystal and his colleagues examined psychological adjustment in a group of 11th-grade students in the United States, China, and Japan. Compared with the U.S. students, the Asian students reported that their parents held higher expectations for their academic achievement and were less satisfied with their academic success (Crystal et al., 1994).

Despite the higher parental pressure, both Japanese and Chinese students experienced lower levels of stress than did their U.S. counterparts. As can be seen in Figure 11-6, over 75 percent of U.S. students said they felt stress once a week or almost every day. In comparison, 50 percent or fewer of Japanese and Chinese students reported such frequent stress.

Furthermore, Japanese students were less depressed and in general had lower academic anxiety than their U.S. counterparts. Chinese students also reported lower levels of anxiety

FIGURE 11-6

THE EXPERIENCE OF STRESS

Although more than 75 percent of U.S. students say they feel stress once a week or almost every day, only 50 percent or fewer of Japanese and Chinese students report such frequent stress.

(*Source*: Crystal et al., 1994.)

USA ▩   Taiwan ▩   Japan ▩

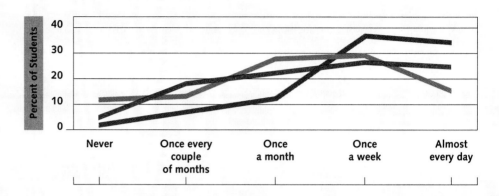

regarding academic performance than did U.S. students, although they did suffer somewhat more often from depression and health-related problems than U.S. and Japanese students.

Why should U.S. students experience greater stress and anxiety than Asian students, who are subject to significantly greater demands from their parents? One explanation may be that students in the United States view academics as only one of many spheres in which they need to achieve. As we'll discuss more in Chapter 12, social relationships play a major role in U.S. adolescents' lives. In addition, many adolescents experience pressures about dating or part-time jobs. Consequently, pressures and competition between academic and social pursuits may contribute to U.S. students' high levels of stress.

In contrast, Asian students perceive that the major task they face during adolescence is achieving high levels of academic success. Other demands are clearly secondary. As a consequence, they may be more focused on the pursuit of academic excellence and feel less conflict from competing demands.

Although the full explanation for these findings remains to be seen, one lesson is clear: High academic achievement of the sort attained by students in Japan and China does not necessarily come at the expense of psychological adjustment.

Review and Rethink

REVIEW

◆ Adolescence, with its substantial cognitive advances, corresponds to Piaget's formal operations period, a stage characterized by abstract reasoning and an experimental approach to problems.

◆ According to the information-processing perspective, the cognitive advances of adolescence are quantitative and gradual, involving improvements in many aspects of thinking and memory.

- Improved metacognition is one of the cognitive advances of adolescence, enabling the monitoring of thought processes and of mental capacities.

- Adolescents are susceptible to adolescent egocentrism, which can cause social problems, and to the perception that their behavior is constantly observed by an imaginary audience. They also construct personal fables that stress their uniqueness and immunity to harm.

- Declines in school performance during adolescence have been attributed to teachers' grading practices. Academic performance is also linked in complex ways to socioeconomic status and to race and ethnicity.

RETHINK

- When faced with complex problems, do you think most adults spontaneously apply formal operations like those used to solve the pendulum problem? Why or why not?

- If a gifted observer had focused on one or more of Howard Gardner's *other* intelligences (i.e., not academic intelligence), do you think he or she would have observed stages of development like Piaget's cognitive stages?

- In what ways does adolescent egocentrism complicate adolescents' social and family relationships? Do adults entirely outgrow egocentrism and personal fables?

- Is socioeconomic status (SES) destiny? How would you examine and critique *The Bell Curve* contention that low IQ ultimately leads to low SES, rather than the other way around?

- We have seen that members of some groups tend to deny the link between school success and success in life. What sorts of environmental factors or role models might support this denial? If the link were in fact proved to be nonexistent, would the necessary conclusion be that academic effort and achievement have no value?

THREATS TO ADOLESCENTS' WELL-BEING

Like most parents, I had thought of drug use as something you worried about when your kids got to high school. Now I know that, on the average, kids begin using drugs at 11 or 12, but at the time that never crossed our minds. Ryan had just begun attending mixed parties. He was playing Little League. In the eighth grade, Ryan started getting into a little trouble—one time he and another fellow stole a fire extinguisher, but we thought it was just a prank. Then his grades began to deteriorate. He began sneaking out at night. He would become belligerent at the drop of a hat, then sunny and nice again. By then he was pretty heavy into drugs, but we were denying what we saw. You build up this trust with your child, and the last thing you want to do is break it. But looking back, there were signs everywhere. His room was filled with bottles of eye drops, to cover the redness from smoking marijuana. Money was missing from around the house, and he began burning incense in his room.

It wasn't until Ryan fell apart at 14 that we started thinking about drugs. He had just begun McLean High School, and to him, it was like going to drug camp every day. Back then, everything was so available. He began cutting classes, a common tip-off, but we didn't hear from the school until he was flunking everything. It turned out that he was going to school for the first period, getting checked in, then leaving and smoking marijuana all day. (Shafer, 1990, p. 82)

Ryan's parents learned all too soon that marijuana was not the only drug Ryan was using. As his friends later admitted, Ryan was what they called a "garbage head." He'd try anything, including cocaine, PCP, alcohol, and LSD. Despite efforts to curb his use of drugs, Ryan never succeeded in stopping. He died at the age of 16, hit by a passing car after wandering into the street during an episode of drug use.

addictive drugs   *drugs that produce a biological or psychological dependence in users, leading to increasingly powerful cravings for them*

Although most cases of adolescent drug use produce far less extreme results, the use of drugs, as well as other kinds of substance use and abuse, represents the primary threat to health during adolescence, which is usually one of the healthiest periods of life. Let us consider some of these preventable problems, such as drug, alcohol, and tobacco use, as well as sexually transmitted diseases.

ILLEGAL DRUGS

How prevalent is illegal drug use during the adolescent period? Very prevalent, and rising. For instance, the most recent annual survey of nearly 50,000 U.S. high school students showed that one in four high school sophomores and one in three seniors said they had smoked marijuana at least once within the last year. Even eighth graders are using the drug: Some 13 percent said they had smoked the drug during the past year, and 8 percent said they had smoked it within the last 30 days (see Figure 11-7). Almost half of high school seniors have used an illegal drug at least once in their lives (O'Malley, Johnston, Bachman, 1995).

The use of marijuana and other illegal drugs is rising. Although drug use declined in the 1980s—the "just say no" campaigns seem to have been effective—it began to rise again in the 1990s. For instance, current figures on marijuana usage are almost double what they were in 1991. Furthermore, the number of high school seniors who disapprove of the occasional use of marijuana dropped from 79 percent to 69 percent.

The use of other illegal drugs has also grown recently. In contrast to the early 1990s, more high school students report having used cocaine, crack, hallucinogenic drugs, heroin, and stimulants at least once during the previous year. On the other hand, the use of drugs by adolescents is less prevalent than it was in the late 1970s and early 1980s. During that period, surveys found that more than 50 percent of high school seniors had used marijuana.

Why do adolescents use drugs? There are multiple reasons. Some relate to the perceived pleasurable experience drugs may provide, and others to the escape from the pressures of everyday life that drugs temporarily permit. Some adolescents try drugs simply for the thrill of doing something illegal. Especially in adolescence, the alleged drug use of well-known role models, such as movie star River Phoenix or Mayor Marion Barry of Washington, DC (who served time in prison for the use of cocaine), may also contribute. Finally, peer pressure plays a role: Adolescents, as we'll discuss in greater detail in Chapter 12, are particularly susceptible to the perceived standards of their peer groups (Dinges & Oetting, 1993; McDonald & Towberman, 1993; Epstein et al., 1995; Julien, 1995; Petraitis, Flay, & Miller, 1995).

The use of illegal drugs is dangerous in several respects. For instance, some drugs are addictive. **Addictive drugs** are substances that produce a biological or psychological dependence in users, leading to increasingly powerful cravings for them. When drugs produce a biological addiction, their presence in the body becomes so common that the body is unable

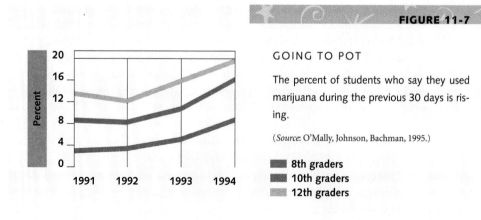

FIGURE 11-7

GOING TO POT

The percent of students who say they used marijuana during the previous 30 days is rising.

(*Source*: O'Mally, Johnson, Bachman, 1995.)

■ 8th graders
■ 10th graders
■ 12th graders

The use of marijuana among high school students has increased significantly since the early 1990s.

to function in their absence. Drugs can also produce a psychological addiction. In such cases, people grow to depend on drugs to cope with the everyday stress of life.

In addition, if drugs are used as an escape, they may prevent adolescents from confronting—and potentially solving—the problems that led them to drug use in the first place. Finally, drugs may be dangerous because even casual users of less hazardous substances can "graduate" to more dangerous forms of substance abuse. For instance, those who smoke marijuana are 85 times more likely to use cocaine than those who do not (Toch, 1995). (For more on efforts to deal with adolescent drug use, see the Speaking of Development feature.)

ALCOHOL: USE AND ABUSE

More than 75 percent of college students have something in common: They've consumed at least one alcoholic drink during the previous thirty days. More than 40 percent say they have had five or more drinks within the past 2 weeks, and some 16 percent consume 16 or more drinks each week. High school students are also drinkers: Some 76 percent of high school seniors report having had an alcoholic beverage in the last year (Carmody, 1990; NIAAA, 1990; Center on Addiction and Substance Abuse, 1994).

One of the most troubling patterns is the frequency of binge drinking among college students. Binge drinking is defined for men as drinking five or more drinks in one sitting; for women, who tend to weigh less and whose bodies absorb alcohol less efficiently, binge drinking is defined as four drinks in one sitting.

Recent surveys find that some 50 percent of male college students and 39 percent of female college students say they participated in binge drinking during the previous 2 weeks (see Figure 11-8). Even for lighter drinkers and nondrinkers, this high level of drinking among their peers affects their college experience. For instance, two-thirds of lighter drinkers reported that they had had their studying or their sleep disturbed by drunk students. Approximately one-third had been insulted or humiliated by a drunk student, and 25 percent of women said they had been the target of an unwanted sexual advance by a drunk classmate (Wechsler, Isaac, Grodstein, & Sellers, 1994).

Why do adolescents start to drink? Some believe it is the "adult" thing to do. Others drink for the same reason that they use drugs: It releases inhibitions and tension and reduces stress (Fromme & Rivet, 1994). Of course, the same chemical reaction that produces

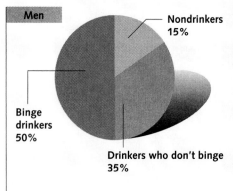

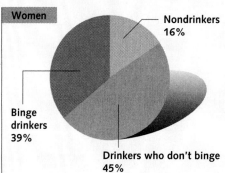

Men

Nondrinkers
15%

Binge
drinkers
50%

Drinkers who don't binge
35%

Women

Nondrinkers
16%

Binge
drinkers
39%

Drinkers who don't binge
45%

BINGE DRINKING AMONG
COLLEGE STUDENTS

For men, binge drinking was defined as consuming five or more drinks in one sitting; for
women, the total was four or more.

(*Source*: Wechsler, Isaac, Grodstein, & Sellers, 1994.)

Speaking of Development

Doreen Gail Branch

Born: ································· 1958

Education: ···················· Howard University, Washington, DC, BS and MA in Psychology

Position: ······················· Research Associate for the National Public Service Research
Institute

Home: ···························· Greenbelt, Maryland

Substance abuse of alcohol, tobacco, and drugs cuts across all segments of the population,
but one group that is particularly vulnerable to their allure is adolescents. In an effort to create effective preventative programs, Doreen Branch is working as part of a community services coalition project in Maryland's Prince George's County. The coalition serves adolescents between the ages of 12 and 18.

"We are currently looking at the community and how the different parts can band
together to battle alcohol, tobacco, and other drug abuse problems, as well as those associated with their use," said Branch.

Initially starting college as a pre-medical student, Branch decided to try her hand at
psychology. She was immediately attracted to the discipline, finding that it required more
thought and creativity than merely memorizing a text. Her new interest ultimately led her
to seek a masters degree in psychology, and shortly after graduating she joined the National
Public Service Research Institute.

One major goal of her work is to provide youth with alternatives to using drugs and to
introduce them to other activities. "Many people are familiar with midnight basketball programs," she said, "but our efforts go beyond them. For instance, one of the things we are
developing is a tennis program that not only teaches tennis, but also provides mentoring to

these results can also make adolescents feel depressed, cloud their judgment, impair memory, and reduce motoric skills necessary for driving. These consequences are the greatest danger of alcohol use.

For some adolescents—perhaps as many as a third—alcohol use becomes a habit that cannot be controlled. *Alcoholics*, those with alcohol problems, learn to depend on alcohol and are unable to control their drinking. They also become increasingly immune to the consequences of drinking, and therefore need to drink ever-larger amounts of liquor to bring about the positive effects they crave. Some drink throughout the day, while others go on binges in which they consume huge quantities of alcohol (NIAAA, 1990; Morse & Flavin, 1992).

The reasons why some adolescents become alcoholic is not fully known. Genetics plays a role: Alcoholism runs in families. On the other hand, not all alcoholics have others in their family who drink too much. In cases such as these, alcoholism may be triggered by efforts to deal with environmental stress (Bushman, 1993; Boyd, Howard, & Zucker, 1995).

TOBACCO

Even though most adolescents are well aware of its dangers, many still indulge in smoking. While recent figures show that, overall, a smaller proportion of adolescents smoke than in

"We have to educate students on drugs, and we need to inform them of the dangers of even a little drug use."

"Many adolescents that we deal with do not believe that marijuana, and sometimes even cocaine, are harmful."

at-risk adolescents." She notes that such a program emphasizes that there are other things to do with one's time than use drugs.

"We have to educate students on drugs, and we need to inform them of the dangers of even a little drug use. Many adolescents that we deal with do not believe that marijuana, and sometimes even cocaine, are harmful," Branch added.

Branch is also studying how tobacco and alcohol manufacturers use advertising to influence teenagers. "One of the things that we are trying to do is to change local policies in terms of billboards that cater to the advertising of cigarettes and alcohol. While many of these advertisements are in the poorest sections of town, all teenagers can be influenced by them," she said.

One tactic she has used to deter adolescents' drug use has been to ask them to write, produce, and act in their own commercials on the dangers of drug and alcohol abuse. Another was to provide funding for a large meeting, the "Kiamsha Youth Empowerment Conference." With the help of adult mentors, Maryland adolescents organized the meeting largely by themselves.

"The issues discussed at the conference included drugs, sex, violence, and spirituality," said Branch. "The whole conference was planned and conducted by teenagers. They hit on a lot of issues that kids have to deal with, and—in part because it was planned by the adolescents themselves—it was a great success."

The portrayal of Joe Camel as a hip and smooth character has helped to maintain the image of smoking as a "cool" activity.

Drawing by R. Chast; © 1995 The New Yorker Magazine, Inc.

prior decades, the numbers remain substantial. Furthermore, within certain groups the numbers are increasing. For instance, smoking is more prevalent among girls, and in several countries, including Austria, Norway, and Sweden, the proportion of girls who smoke is higher than the proportion of boys (Chollat-Traquet, 1992; Bartecchi, MacKenzie, & Schrier, 1995).

Adolescents smoke despite growing social sanctions against the habit. As the dangers of second-hand smoke become more apparent, many people look down on smokers. More environments, including schools and places of business, have become "smoke-free," a trend that makes it increasingly difficult to find a place to smoke. Furthermore, the health dangers of smoking are hardly in dispute: Every package of cigarettes carries a warning that smoking is linked to a higher mortality rate, and even adolescents who smoke admit that they know the dangers.

Why, then, do adolescents begin to smoke and then maintain the habit? One reason is that smoking is still considered sexy and hip. Advertisements for cigarettes depict attractive individuals smoking, and clever ads, such as the highly successful "Joe Camel" series, make an effective pitch to young males. In fact, children as young as 6 identify Joe Camel as readily as Mickey Mouse (Lipman, 1992; Bartecchi et al., 1995; Ono, 1995).

There are also other reasons. Nicotine, the active chemical ingredient of cigarettes, can produce biological and psychological dependency; it also produces a pleasant emotional state that smokers seek to maintain (Pomerleau & Pomerleau, 1989; Nowak, 1994a). Furthermore, exposure to parents and peers who smoke increases the chances that an adolescent will take up the habit (Botvin, Epstein, Schinke, & Diaz, 1994; Webster, Hunter, & Keats, 1994). Finally, smoking is sometimes seen as an adolescent rite of passage: Trying cigarettes is looked upon as a sign of growing up. Although one or two cigarettes do not usually produce a lifetime smoker, it doesn't take much more. In fact, people who smoke as few as ten cigarettes early in their lives stand an 80 percent chance of becoming habitual smokers (Salber, Freeman, & Abelin, 1968; Bowen, Kahl, Mann, & Peterson, 1991; Stacy et al., 1992).

Developmental Diversity

Selling Death: Pushing Smoking to the Less Advantaged

In Dresden, Germany, three women in miniskirts offer passers-by a pack of Lucky Strikes and a leaflet that reads: "You just got hold of a nice piece of America." Says a local doctor, "Adolescents time and again receive cigarettes at such promotions."

A Jeep decorated with the Camel logo pulls up to a high school in Buenos Aires. A woman begins handing out free cigarettes to 15- and 16-year-olds during their lunch recess.

At a video arcade in Taipei, free American cigarettes are strewn atop each game. At a disco filled with high school students, free packs of Salems are on each table. (Ecenbarger, 1993, p. 50)

If you are a cigarette manufacturer and you find that the number of people using your product is declining, what do you do? U.S. companies have sought to carve out new markets by turning to the least advantaged groups of people, both at home and abroad. For instance, in the early 1990s the R.J. Reynolds tobacco company designed a new brand of cigarettes it named "Uptown." The advertising used to herald its arrival made clear who the target was: African-Americans living in urban areas (M. Quinn, 1990). Because of subsequent protests, the tobacco company withdrew Uptown from the market.

In addition to seeking new converts in the United States, tobacco companies aggressively recruit adolescent smokers abroad. In many developing countries the number of smokers is still low. Tobacco companies are seeking to increase this number through marketing strategies designed to hook adolescents on the habit by means of free samples. In addition, in countries where American culture and products are held in high esteem, advertising suggests that the use of cigarettes is an American—and consequently prestigious—habit (Sesser, 1993).

The strategy is effective. For instance, in some Latin American cities as many as 50 percent of teenagers smoke. According to the World Health Organization, smoking will prematurely kill some 200 million of the world's children and adolescents; overall, 10 percent of the world's population will die because of smoking (Ecenbarger, 1993).

SEXUALLY TRANSMITTED DISEASES: ONE COST OF SEX

In the fall of 1990, Krista Blake was 18 and looking forward to her first year at Youngstown State University in Ohio. She and her boyfriend were talking about getting married. Her life was, she says, "basic, white-bread America." Then she went to the doctor, complaining about a backache, and found out she had the AIDS virus.

Blake had been infected with HIV, the virus that causes AIDS, 2 years earlier by an older boy, a hemophiliac. "He knew that he was infected, and he didn't tell me," she says. "And he didn't do anything to keep me from getting infected, either." (Becahy, 1992, p. 49)

AIDS.   Krista Blake is not alone: **Acquired immunodeficiency syndrome**, or **AIDS**, is now the leading cause of death among young people. AIDS has no cure and ultimately brings death to those who are infected with the HIV virus that produces the disease.

acquired immunodeficiency syndrome (AIDS) a sexually transmitted disease, produced by the HIV virus, that has no cure and ultimately causes death

Although most adolescents are well aware of the importance of safer sex practices, their feelings of invulnerability sometimes lead them to believe that their chances of contracting a sexually-transmitted disease are minimal—especially when they are well-acquainted with their partner.

Because AIDS is spread primarily through sexual contact, it is classified as a **sexually transmitted disease (STD)**. Although it began as a problem that primarily afflicted homosexuals, it has spread to other populations, including heterosexuals and intravenous drug users. Minorities have been particularly hard-hit: African-Americans and Hispanics account for some 40 percent of AIDS cases, although they make up only 18 percent of the population.

In the United States, experts estimate that by the beginning of 1995, some two million people will have been infected with the virus. Worldwide, the figures are mind-boggling: By the year 2000, it is estimated that some 30 million people will be carrying the AIDS virus (HMHL, 1994).

AIDS and Adolescent Behavior.   Although it is no secret how AIDS is transmitted— through the exchange of bodily fluids, including semen and blood—it has proven difficult to motivate teenagers to employ safer sex practices that can prevent its spread. On the one hand, the use of condoms during sexual intercourse has increased, and people are less likely to engage in casual sex with new acquaintances (Kolata, 1991; Catania et al., 1992; Kelly, 1995).

However, the use of safer sex practices is far from universal. Adolescents, who—as we discussed earlier in the chapter—are prone to engage in risky behavior due to feelings of invulnerability, are likely to believe that their chances of contracting AIDS are minimal. This is particularly true when adolescents perceive that their partner is "safe"—someone they know well and with whom they are involved in a relatively long-term relationship (Moore & Rosenthal, 1991; Fisher & Fisher, 1992; Kelly et al., 1993; Pryor & Reeder, 1993; D.A. Rosenthal & Shepherd, 1993).

Unfortunately, unless an individual knows the complete sexual history and HIV status of a partner, unprotected sex remains risky business. And learning a partner's complete sexual history is difficult. It is often inaccurately communicated out of embarrassment, a sense of privacy, or simply forgetfulness.

Short of celibacy, a solution regarded as improbable for many adolescents involved in relationships, there is no certain way to avoid AIDS. However, health experts suggest several strategies for making sex safer; these are listed in Table 11-2.

Other Sexually Transmitted Diseases.   Although AIDS is the deadliest of sexually transmitted diseases, others are far more common (see Figure 11-9). In fact, one in four adoles-

sexually transmitted disease (STD) a disease that is spread through sexual contact

TABLE 11-2

SAFER SEX: PREVENTING THE TRANSMISSION OF AIDS

Health psychologists and educators have devised several guidelines to help prevent the spread of AIDS. Among them are the following:

- **Use condoms.** The use of condoms greatly reduces the risk of transmission of the virus that produces AIDS, which occurs through exposure to bodily fluids such as semen or blood.
- **Avoid high-risk behaviors.** Such practices as unprotected anal intercourse or the exchange of needles used in drug use greatly increase the risk of AIDS.
- **Know your partner's sexual history.** Knowing your sexual partner and his or her sexual history can help you to evaluate the risks of sexual contact.
- **Consider abstinence.** Although not always a practical alternative, the only certain way of avoiding AIDS is to refrain from sexual activity altogether.

cents contracts an STD before graduating from high school. Overall, some 2.5 million teenagers contract an STD each year (Gans, 1990; Alan Guttmacher Institute, 1993a); Barringer, 1993).

Chlamydia, a disease caused by a parasite, is the most common STD. Initially it has few symptoms, but later it causes burning urination and a discharge from the penis or vagina. It can lead to pelvic inflammation and even to sterility.

Another common STD is **genital herpes**, a virus not unlike the cold sores that sometimes appear around the mouth. The first symptoms of herpes are often small blisters or sores around the genitals, which may break open and become quite painful. Although the sores may heal after a few weeks, the disease often recurs after an interval, and the cycle repeats itself. When the sores reappear, the disease, for which there is no cure, is contagious.

Several other STDs are frequent among adolescents. *Trichomoniasis*, an infection in the vagina or penis, is caused by a parasite. Initially without symptoms, it can eventually cause a painful discharge. *Gonorrhea* and *syphilis* are the STDs that have been recognized for the longest time; cases were recorded by ancient historians. Until the advent of antibiotics, both diseases were deadly; today both can be treated quite effectively.

chlamydia   *the most common sexually transmitted disease, caused by a parasite*

genital herpes   *a common sexually transmitted disease that is a virus and not unlike cold sores that sometimes appear around the mouth*

FIGURE 11-9

Best estimates for sexually transmitted diseases (STDs) among adolescents.

(*Source*: Sexually Transmitted Diseases (STDs) in the United States, 1993c.)

3 million teenagers, about 1 person in 8 aged 13–19 and about 1 in 4 of those who have had sexual intercourse, acquire an STD every year. Among the most common:

Chlamydia: Chlamydia is more common among teenagers than among older men and women; in some studies, 10 to 29 percent of sexually active adolescent girls and 10 percent of teenage boys have been found to be infected with chlamydia.

Gonorrhea: Adolescents aged 15–19 have higher rates of gonorrhea than do sexually active men and women in any 5-year age group between 20–44.

Pelvic Inflammatory Disease: In 1987–1988 women aged 15–19 had the highest rate of hospitalization for acute pelvic inflammatory disease (PID).

Human Papillomavirus: Up to 15 percent of sexually active women aged 13–19 have been found in some studies to be infected with human papillomavirus (HPV).

Syphilis: Infectious syphilis rates more than doubled between 1986 and 1990 among women aged 15–19.

The Informed Consumer of Development

Hooked on Drugs or Alcohol?

Although it is not always easy to determine if an adolescent has a drug or alcohol abuse problem, there are some signals. Among them:

Identification with the drug culture

- Drug-related magazines or slogans on clothing
- Conversation and jokes that are preoccupied with drugs
- Hostility discussing drugs
- Collection of beer cans

Signs of physical deterioration

- Memory lapses, short attention span, difficulty concentrating
- Poor physical coordination, slurred or incoherent speech
- Unhealthy appearance, indifference to hygiene and grooming
- Bloodshot eyes, dilated pupils

Dramatic changes in school performance

- Marked downturn in grades—not just from C's to F's, but from A's to B's and C's; assignments not completed
- Increased absenteeism or tardiness

Changes in behavior

- Chronic dishonesty (lying, stealing, cheating); trouble with the police
- Changes in friends; evasiveness in talking about new ones
- Possession of large amounts of money
- Increasing and inappropriate anger, hostility, irritability, secretiveness
- Reduced motivation, energy, self-discipline, self-esteem
- Diminished interest in extracurricular activities and hobbies (Adapted from Franck & Brownstone, 1991, pp. 593–594.)

If an adolescent—or anyone else, for that matter—fits any of the above descriptors, help is probably needed. It is possible to get advice from a national hotline. For alcohol difficulties, the National Council on Alcoholism can be reached at (800) 622-2255; for drug problems, the National Institute on Drug Abuse is available at (800) 662-4357. In addition, those who need advice can find a local listing for Alcoholics Anonymous or Narcotics Anonymous in the telephone book. Finally, the National Council on Alcoholism and Drug Dependence can be reached at 12 West 21 St., New York, NY 10010, for help with alcohol and drug problems.

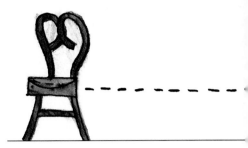

Review and Rethink

REVIEW

◆ Illegal drug use is prevalent among adolescents, who may regard drugs as a way to find pleasure, avoid pressure, or gain the approval of peers. Drug use is dangerous because it can escalate, become addictive, and prevent the confrontation of problems.

◆ The use of alcohol is also popular among adolescents, often out of a desire to appear adult or to lessen inhibitions. Impaired judgment and motor control are the main dangers of alcohol use.

◆ A third substance that constitutes a serious health hazard to adolescents is tobacco. Despite the well-known dangers of smoking, adolescents often engage in the practice to enhance their images or emulate adults.

◆ AIDS is the most serious of the sexually transmitted diseases, ultimately causing its victims death. Safe-sex practices or sexual abstinence can prevent AIDS, although these strategies are often ignored by adolescents.

◆ Other sexually transmitted diseases affect adolescents, such as chlamydia, genital herpes, trichomoniasis, gonorrhea, and syphilis.

RETHINK

◆ In what ways do characteristics of adolescent development that have been studied in this chapter contribute to adolescents' tendencies to abuse drugs?

◆ How might you address an adolescent's claim that his use of marijuana is harmless and totally under his control?

◆ How do adolescents' concerns about self-image and perception that they are the center of attention contribute to smoking and alcohol use?

◆ What adolescent tendencies contribute to the spread of sexually transmitted diseases? Are these tendencies exclusively adolescent?

◆ Why do adolescents' increased cognitive abilities, including the ability to reason and to think experimentally, fail to deter them from irrational behavior such as drug and alcohol abuse, tobacco use, and unsafe sex practices?

LOOKING BACK

What physical changes do adolescents experience?

1. The adolescent years are marked by a physical growth spurt that mirrors the rapid growth rate of infancy. Girls' growth spurts begin about age 10, about 2 years earlier than boys' growth spurt.

2. The most significant event during adolescence is the onset of puberty, which begins for most girls about age 11 and for most boys at about age 13. The timing of puberty is linked both to cultural and environmental factors and to biological ones. As puberty commences, the body begins to produce male or female hormones at adult levels, the sex organs develop and change, menstruation and ejaculation begin, and other body changes occur.

3. The physical changes that accompany puberty, which adolescents usually experience with keen interest, often have psychological effects, which may involve an increase in self-esteem and self-awareness, as well as some confusion and uncertainty about sexuality.

What are the consequences of early and late maturation?

4. Those who mature either early or late experience mixed consequences. For boys, early maturation can lead to increased athleticism, greater popularity, and a more positive self-concept. For girls, although early maturation can lead to increased popularity and an enhanced social life, they may also experience embarrassment over the changes in their bodies that differentiate them from their peers. Furthermore, early physical maturation can lead both boys and girls into activities and situations for which they are not adequately prepared.

5. Late maturation, because it results in smaller size, can put boys at a distinct physical and social disadvantage, which can affect self-concept and have lasting negative consequences. Girls who mature late may suffer neglect by their peers of both sexes, but ultimately they appear to suffer no lasting ill effects and may even benefit from late maturation.

What nutritional needs and concerns do adolescents have?

6. While most adolescents have no greater nutritional worries than fueling their growth with appropriate foods, some are obese or overweight, and they may suffer psychological and physical consequences. Furthermore, a substantial number are excessively concerned about obesity, to the point of contracting an eating disorder.

7. Two major eating disorders that affect adolescents are anorexia nervosa, a refusal to eat because of a perception of being overweight, and bulimia, a cycle of binge eating followed by purges of food. Both biological and environmental factors appear to contribute to these disorders, and treatment typically involves psychological therapy and dietary changes.

How does cognitive development proceed during adolescence?

8. Cognitive growth during adolescence is rapid and substantial, with notable gains in the ability to think abstractly, to reason accurately, and to view possibilities in relative rather than absolute terms.

9. Adolescence coincides with Piaget's formal operations period of development, the stage at which people begin to engage in abstract thought and experimental reasoning. In this area as in others, Piaget is now regarded as having ignored individual and cultural differences, underestimated children's capabilities, overemphasized the qualitative nature of cognitive advances, and too narrowly defined cognition.

10. According to information-processing approaches, cognitive growth during adolescence is gradual and quantitative, involving improvements in mental organization and strategies; memory capacity; perceptual abilities; verbal, mathematical, and spatial abilities; attention; problem solving; and knowledge.

11. Another major area of cognitive development, according to the information-processing view, is the growth of metacognition, which permits adolescents to monitor their thought processes and accurately assess their cognitive capabilities.

12. Hand-in-hand with the development of metacognition is the growth of adolescent egocentrism, a self-absorption that makes it hard for adolescents to accept criticism and tolerate authority figures. Adolescents may play to an imaginary audience of critical observers, and they may develop personal fables, which emphasize the uniqueness of their experiences and plight, and their supposed invulnerability to risks.

What factors affect adolescent school performance?

13. School performance during the adolescent years declines, probably because of increased demands placed on students and more stringent grading practices than before.

Socioeconomic status is directly related to school achievement levels, largely because environmental factors relating to health, nutrition, living conditions, parental availability, and deteriorating schools negatively affect students of low socioeconomic status.

14. Race and ethnicity are also related to school achievement. Differences are linked to socioeconomic factors, the circumstances under which a minority group enters the majority culture, attributional patterns regarding success factors, and belief systems regarding the link between school success and success in life.

Why do adolescents use dangerous substances, and what are the warning signs of substance abuse?

15. The use of illicit drugs is alarmingly prevalent among adolescents, who are motivated by pleasure-seeking, pressure-avoidance, the desire to flout authority, or the imitation of role models. Not only can drug use escalate and lead to addiction but adolescents' avoidance of underlying problems can also have serious effects.

16. Alcohol use is also prevalent among adolescents, who may view drinking as a way to lower inhibitions or to manifest adult behavior. The impairment of judgment and motor skills is one of the main dangers of alcohol consumption, although secondary dangers to others—including personal and sexual aggression—are also serious.

17. Even though the dangers of smoking are well known and accepted by adolescents, tobacco use continues. Despite a reduction in smoking among adolescents in general, smoking within some groups has actually increased. Adolescents who smoke appear to be motivated by a desire to appear adult and "cool."

18. Among the warning signs that an adolescent may have a problem with drugs or alcohol are identification with the drug culture, evidence of physical deterioration, dramatic declines in school performance, and significant changes in behavior.

What dangers do adolescent sexual practices present, and how can these dangers be avoided?

19. AIDS is now the leading cause of death among young people, affecting minority populations with particular severity. Adolescent behavior patterns and attitudes, such as shyness, self-absorption, and a belief in personal invulnerability, militate against the use of safe-sex practices that can prevent the disease.

20. Other sexually transmitted diseases, including chlamydia, genital herpes, trichomoniasis, gonorrhea, and syphilis, occur frequently among the adolescent population and can be prevented by safe-sex practices or abstinence.

KEY TERMS AND CONCEPTS

adolescence (p. 375)

puberty (p. 377)

menarche (p. 377)

primary sex characteristics (p. 378)

secondary sex characteristics (p. 378)

anorexia nervosa (p. 381)

bulimia (p. 382)

formal operations period (p. 384)

information-processing perspective (p. 385)

metacognition (p. 386)

adolescent egocentrism (p. 387)

imaginary audience (p. 387)

personal fables (p. 387)

addictive drugs (p. 394)

acquired immunodeficiency syndrome (AIDS) (p. 399)

sexually transmitted disease (STD) (p. 400)

chlamydia (p. 401)

genital herpes (p. 401)

CHAPTER 12

ADOLESCENCE

Social and Personality Development

CHAPTER OUTLINE

PROLOGUE: NUKET CURRAN

The first thing you notice about 17-year-old Nuket Curran is her hair. Her light brown locks are trimmed close on the back and sides—like those of a typical male in the 1950s. The entire top is roached, standing straight up for about an inch and a half. From the right side, just above and behind her ear, hangs a long, very thin braid.

"I started out looking like everyone else," she says. "In ninth grade I was more, like preppy. Had the bob, it was down to here—just standard-looking. And then I got an under-cut; it was called a wedge. Then I cut one side off and then I shaved it off and then I just had long, long bangs and black in my hair. It was, like, striped black and my natural color. Then it was red—cherry cola red—and black. Then it was orange and black. I looked like Halloween. Then it was blond and black. I just felt like doing it, you know, and I can't do that when I'm 35. I can't get a job looking like that. So why not just do it now?

"People said, 'Well, she's dyeing her hair to be different.' In a way that's true. I mean, it's just a different way of expressing myself. I don't like to call it punk or new wave or any other terminology. It's a way of showing that I'm just another human being that's different from every other human being. I'm so bored with how everyone dresses the same. They have plain hair and plain everything. It's just monotonous. They're afraid to, like, stand out, to be themselves. And I just felt like I was being myself." (Kotre & Hall, 1990, pp. 178–179)

LOOKING AHEAD

No one would mistake Nuket—named by her parents for the Turkish word meaning "mountain flower"—for plain and monotonous. A nonconformist by nature, she epitomizes the rebelliousness that traditionally has been thought to typify the adolescent period.

Yet Nuket is less of a rebel than her appearance would suggest—a characterization that recent evidence suggests applies to most adolescents. Research increasingly shows that most people pass through adolescence without much turmoil in their lives. Although they may "try on" different roles and flirt with activities that their parents find objectionable, the majority of adolescents pass through the period in relative tranquillity (Peterson, 1988; Steinberg, 1993).

This is not to say that the transitions adolescents pass through are less than highly challenging (Eccles et al., 1993; Laursen & Collins, 1994; Compas, Hinden, & Gerhardt, 1995; Crockett & Crouter, 1995). As we'll see in this chapter, in which we examine the personality and social development of the period, adolescence brings about major changes in the ways in which individuals must deal with the world.

We begin by considering how adolescents form their views of themselves. We look at self-concept and self-esteem, and at identity development. We also examine two major psychological difficulties: depression and suicide.

Next, we discuss relationships during adolescence. We consider how adolescents reposition themselves within the family, and how the influence of family members declines in some spheres as peers take on new importance. We also examine the ways in which adolescents interact with their friends, and the determinants of popularity and rejection.

Finally, the chapter considers dating and sexual behavior. We look at the role of dating in adolescents' lives, and we consider sexual behavior and the standards that govern adolescents' sex lives. Finally, we look at teenage pregnancy, and at programs that seek to prevent unwanted pregnancy.

In sum, after reading this chapter, you'll be able to answer these questions:

♦ How does the development of self-concept, self-esteem, and identity proceed during adolescence?

♦ What dangers do adolescents face as they deal with the stresses of adolescence?

♦ How does the quality of relationships with family and peers change during adolescence?

♦ What are gender and race relations like in adolescence?

♦ What does it mean to be popular and unpopular in adolescence, and how do adolescents respond to peer pressure?

♦ What are the functions and characteristics of dating during adolescence?

♦ How does sexuality develop in the adolescent years?

♦ Why is teenage pregnancy a particular problem in the United States, and what can be done about it?

IDENTITY: ASKING "WHO AM I?"

Turning 13 was an important period of my life. It was the time when I started to mature physically. It also was the time when more girls started to notice me. My personality changed a lot from a boring nerd to an energetic, funny and athletic kid.

As my year went on as a 13-year-old, as if things couldn't get better, they surprisingly did! My life as a child had ended. I was now a teenager. This just goes to show you that turning 13 meant turning into a new person.

Patrick Backer (1993, p. 2)

As you go to school, things get harder. You sort of realize that you're getting older. Adults treat you like an adult and don't give you the breaks you got when you're a child.

To be 13 you have journeyed only half way to the *real* world. Then you notice that you're going to high school and think of the next 4 years and then college. Next you vote, a house, job and kids. It seems your life passes right before your eyes.

Mieko Ozeki (1993, p. 2)

When I turned 13 it was like starting a new life. It was the year I was finally going to be allowed to do more things. For one thing I was able to hang out later. I wasn't a child anymore. I knew it and my parents knew it, too.

During adolescence, questions of identity become increasingly crucial.

I really can't think of a more important birthday besides your first one.

Dmitri Ponomarev (1993, p. 2)

These voices of adolescents resonate with a common theme: a keen awareness and self-consciousness regarding their newly forming place in society and life. During adolescence, questions like "Who am I?" and "Where do I belong in the world?" begin to take a front seat.

Why should issues of identity become so important during adolescence? One reason is that adolescents' intellectual capacities become more adultlike. They can now understand—and appreciate—such abstract issues as the importance of establishing their position in society and the need to form a sense of themselves as individuals. Another reason is that the dramatic physical changes during puberty make adolescents acutely aware of their own bodies—and of the fact that others are reacting to them in ways to which they are unaccustomed.

Whatever the cause, adolescence often brings substantial changes in teenagers' self-concepts and self-esteem—in sum, their notions of their own identity.

SELF-CONCEPT: CHARACTERIZING THE CHARACTERISTICS OF ADOLESCENCE

Ask Louella to describe herself and she says, "Others look at me as laid-back, relaxed, and not worrying too much. But really, I'm often nervous and emotional."

The fact that Louella distinguishes others' views of her from her own perceptions represents a developmental advance of adolescence. In childhood, Louella would have characterized herself according to a list of traits that would not differentiate her view of herself and others' perspectives. However, adolescents are able to make the distinction, and when they try to describe who they are, they take both their own and others' views into account (Harter, 1990b).

This broadening view of themselves is one aspect of adolescents' increasing discernment and perception in their understanding of who they are. The view of the self becomes more organized and coherent, and they can see various aspects of the self simultaneously. Furthermore, they look at the self from a psychological perspective, viewing traits not as concrete entities but as abstractions.

In some ways, however, the increasing differentiation of self-concept is a mixed blessing, especially during the earlier years of adolescence. At that time, adolescents may be troubled by the multiple aspects of their personalities. During the beginning of adolescence, for instance, teenagers may want to view themselves in a certain way ("I'm a sociable person and love to be with people"), and they may become concerned when their behavior is inconsistent with that view ("Even though I want to be sociable, sometimes I can't stand being around my friends and just want to be alone"). By the end of adolescence, however, teenagers accept the fact that different situations elicit different behaviors and feelings (Harter, 1990a; Pyryt & Mendaglio, 1994).

SELF-ESTEEM: EVALUATING WHO YOU ARE

Knowing who you are and *liking* who you are represent two different things. Although adolescents become increasingly accurate in understanding who they are (their self-concept), this knowledge does not guarantee that they like themselves (their self-esteem) any better. In fact, their increasing accuracy in understanding themselves permits them to see themselves fully—warts and all.

The same cognitive sophistication that allows adolescents to differentiate various aspects of the self also leads them to evaluate those aspects in different ways. For instance, an adolescent may have high self-esteem in terms of academic performance, but lower self-esteem in terms of relationships with others. Or it may be just the opposite, as articulated by this adolescent:

How much do I *like* the kind of person I am? Well, I like some things about me, but I don't like others. I'm glad that I'm popular since it's really important to me to have friends. But in school I don't do as well as the really smart kids. That's OK, because if you're too smart you'll lose your friends. So being smart is just not that important. Except to my parents. I feel like I'm letting them down when I don't do as well as they want. (Harter, 1990a, p. 364)

What determines an adolescent's self-esteem? Several factors make a difference. One is gender: Particularly during early adolescence, girls' self-esteem tends to be lower and more vulnerable than boys' (Simmons & Rosenberg, 1975; Simmons, Brown, Bush, & Blyth, 1978; Cairns, McWhirter, Duffy, & Barry, 1990). One reason is that, compared to boys, girls are more highly concerned about physical appearance and social success—in addition to academic achievement. Although boys are also concerned about these things, their attitudes are often more casual. Moreover, traditional societal messages may be interpreted as suggesting that female academic achievement is a roadblock to social success. Girls hearing such messages, then, are in a difficult bind: If they do well academically, they jeopardize their social success. No wonder that the self-esteem of adolescent girls is more fragile than that of boys (Unger & Crawford, 1992).

Socioeconomic status (SES) and race also influence self-esteem. Adolescents of higher SES generally have higher self-esteem than those of lower SES, particularly during middle and later adolescence. It may be that the social status factors that especially enhance one's standing and self-esteem—such as having more expensive clothes or a car—become more conspicuous in the later periods of adolescence (Savin-Williams & Demo, 1983; Van Tassel-Baska, Olszewski-Kubilius, & Kulieke, 1994).

Race also plays a role in self-esteem, although the findings are not entirely consistent. Early studies argued that minority status would lead to lower self-esteem. This finding led to the hypothesis—initially supported—that African-Americans and Hispanics would have lower self-esteem than Caucasians. Researchers' explanations for this finding were straightforward: Societal prejudice would be incorporated into the self-concepts of the targets of the prejudice, making them feel disliked and rejected.

However, more recent research paints a different picture. Most findings now suggest that African-Americans differ little from whites in their levels of self-esteem (Harter, 1990b). Why should this be? One explanation is that social movements within the African-American community that bolster racial pride help support African-American adolescents. In fact, research finds that a stronger sense of racial identity is related to a higher level of self-esteem in African-Americans and Hispanics (Phinney, Lochner, & Murphy, 1990).

Another reason for overall similarity in self-esteem levels between minority and majority adolescents is that teenagers in general focus their preferences and priorities on those aspects of their lives at which they are best. Consequently, African-American youths may concentrate on the things that they find most satisfying and gain self-esteem from being successful at them (Hunt & Hunt, 1975; Phinney & Alipuria, 1990).

Finally, self-esteem may be influenced not by race alone, but by a complex combination of factors. For instance, some developmental specialists have considered race and gender simultaneously, coining the term *ethgender* to refer to the joint influence of race and gender. One study that simultaneously took both race and gender into account found that African-American and Hispanic males had the highest levels of self-esteem, whereas Asian and Native American females had the lowest levels (Martinez, & Dukes, 1991; Dukes & Martinez, 1994).

IDENTITY FORMATION IN ADOLESCENCE: CHANGE OR CRISIS?

According to Erik Erikson, whose theory we last discussed in Chapter 10, the search for identity inevitably leads some adolescents into substantial psychological difficulties as they encounter the adolescent identity crisis (Erikson, 1963). Erikson's theory regarding this stage, which is summarized with his other stages in Table 12-1, suggests that adolescence is the time of the **identity-versus-role-diffusion stage**.

During the identity-versus-role-diffusion stage, teenagers seek to determine what is unique and distinctive about themselves. They strive to discover their particular strengths and weaknesses and the roles they can best play in their future lives. In short, they seek to understand their identity.

In Erikson's view, adolescents who stumble in their efforts to find a suitable identity may follow several dysfunctional courses. They may adopt socially unacceptable roles, such as that of deviant, or they may have difficulty forming and maintaining long-lasting close personal relationships later on in life. In general, their sense of self becomes "diffuse," failing to organize around a central, unified core identity.

On the other hand, those who are successful in forging an appropriate identity set a course that provides a foundation for future psychosocial development. They learn their unique capabilities, and they develop an accurate sense of who they are. They are prepared to set out on a path that takes full advantage of what their unique strengths permit them to do (Kahn, 1985; Zimmerman, Csikszentmihalyi, & Getzels, 1985; Blustein & Palladino, 1991; Archer & Waterman, 1994).

As any student knows who has been repeatedly asked by parents and friends "What's your major?" and "What are you going to do when you graduate?," societal pressures are high during the identity-versus-role-diffusion stage. Adolescents feel pressure to make choices about what their life's work will be, or—at the very least—to decide whether their post-high-school plans include work or college. These are new choices, because up to this point, at least in the United States, society has laid out a universal educational track for all students. However, the track ends at high school; consequently, adolescents face difficult choices about which of several possible future paths they will follow.

During the identity-versus-role-diffusion period, adolescents increasingly rely on their friends and peers as sources of information. At the same time, their dependence on adults

identity-versus-role-diffusion stage *the period during which teenagers seek to determine what is unique and distinctive about themselves*

TABLE 12-1

A SUMMARY OF ERIKSON'S STAGES

Stage	Approximate Age	Positive Outcomes	Negative Outcomes
1. Trust vs. mistrust	Birth–1.5 years	Feelings of trust from environmental support	Fear and concern regarding others
2. Autonomy vs. shame and doubt	1.5–3 years	Self-sufficiency if exploration is encouraged	Doubts about self, lack of independence
3. Initiative vs. guilt	3–6 years	Discovery of ways to initiate actions	Guilt from actions and thoughts
4. Industry vs. inferiority	6–12 years	Development of sense of competence	Feelings of inferiority, no sense of mastery
5. Identity vs. role diffusion	Adolescence	Awareness of uniqueness of self, knowledge of role to be followed	Inability to identify appropriate roles in life
6. Intimacy vs. isolation	Early adulthood	Development of loving, sexual relationships and close friendships	Fear of relationships with others
7. Generativity vs. stagnation	Middle adulthood	Sense of contribution to continuity of life	Trivialization of one's activities
8. Ego-integrity vs. despair	Late adulthood	Sense of unity in life's accomplishments	Regret over lost opportunities of life

Source: Erikson (1963).

declines. As we'll discuss later in the chapter, this increasing dependence on the peer group enables adolescents to forge close relationships. It also helps them to clarify their own identities as they compare themselves to others.

Because of the pressures of the identity-versus-role-diffusion period, Erikson suggests that many adolescents pursue a *psychological moratorium*, a period during which adolescents take time off from the upcoming responsibilities of adulthood and explore various roles and possibilities.

On the other hand, many adolescents cannot, for practical reasons, pursue a psychological moratorium involving a relatively leisurely exploration of various identities. For instance, some adolescents, for economic reasons, must work part-time after school and then take jobs immediately after graduation from high school. As a result, they have little time to experiment with identities and engage in a psychological moratorium. Does this mean such adolescents will be psychologically damaged in some way? Probably not. In fact, the satisfaction that can come from successfully holding a part-time job while attending school may be a sufficient psychological reward to outweigh the inability to try out various roles.

MARCIA'S APPROACH TO IDENTITY DEVELOPMENT: UPDATING ERIKSON

Using Erikson's theory as a springboard, psychologist James Marcia suggests that identity can be seen in terms of four categories, called *statuses*. The identity statuses depend on whether each of two characteristics—crisis and commitment—is present or absent. *Crisis* is a period of identity development in which an adolescent consciously chooses among various alternatives and makes decisions. *Commitment* is psychological investment in a course of action or an ideology (Marcia, 1966, 1980).

By conducting lengthy interviews with adolescents, Marcia proposed four categories of adolescent identity (see Table 12-2).

1. **Identity achievement**. Following a period of crisis during which they consider various alternatives, adolescents commit to a particular identity. Teenagers of this identity status have successfully thought through who they are and what they want to do. They tend to be the most psychologically healthy, higher in achievement motivation and moral reasoning than adolescents of any other status.

2. **Identity foreclosure**. These are adolescents who have committed to an identity, but who did not do it by passing through a period of crisis in which they explored alternatives. Instead, they accepted others' decisions about what was best for them. Typical adolescents in this category are a son who enters the family business because it is

identity achievement   *the particular identity to which teenagers commit following a period of crisis during which they consider various alternatives*

identity foreclosure   *the state of adolescents who prematurely commit to an identity without adequately exploring alternatives*

TABLE 12-2

MARCIA'S FOUR CATEGORIES OF ADOLESCENT DEVELOPMENT

		COMMITMENT	
		PRESENT	ABSENT
EXPLORATION	PRESENT	Identity achievement	Moratorium
	ABSENT	Identity foreclosure	Identity diffusion

Source: Marcia (1980).

expected of him, and a daughter who decides to become a physician simply because her mother is one. Although foreclosers are not necessarily unhappy, they tend to have what can be called "rigid strength": Happy and self-satisfied, they also have a high need for social approval and tend to be authoritarian.

3. **Identity diffusion**. Some adolescents in this category consider various alternatives, but never commit to one. Others in this group never even get that far, not even considering their options in any conscious way. They tend to be flighty, shifting from one thing to the next. While they may seem carefree, their lack of commitment impairs their ability to form close relationships. In fact, they are often socially withdrawn.

4. **Moratorium**. Although adolescents in the moratorium category have explored various alternatives to some degree, they have not yet committed themselves. As a consequence, they show relatively high anxiety and experience psychological conflict. On the other hand, they are often lively and appealing, seeking intimacy with others. Adolescents of this status typically settle on an identity, but only after something of a struggle.

It is important to note that adolescents are not necessarily stuck in one of the four categories. For instance, even though a forecloser may have settled upon a career path during early adolescence with little active decision making, he or she may reassess the choice later and move into another category. For some individuals, then, identity formation may take place beyond the period of adolescence (Marcia, 1980; Flum, 1994).

On the other hand, most research suggests that identity gels by the age of 18. In fact, the freshman year of college is, for many individuals, a time of considerable movement toward establishing an identity (Waterman & Waterman, 1981; Waterman, 1982).

DEPRESSION AND SUICIDE: PSYCHOLOGICAL DIFFICULTIES IN ADOLESCENCE

Although by far the majority of teenagers weather the search for identity—as well as the other challenges presented by the period—without major psychological difficulties, some find adolescence particularly stressful. Some, in fact, develop severe psychological problems. Two of the most vexing are adolescent depression and suicide.

Adolescent Depression. No one is immune from periods of sadness and bad moods, and adolescents are no exception. The end of a relationship, failure at an important task, the

identity diffusion the category in which adolescents consider various identity alternatives, but never commit to one, or never even consider identity options in any conscious way

moratorium the category in which adolescents may have explored various identity alternatives to some degree, but have not yet committed themselves

Between 25 and 40 percent of girls, and 20 to 35 percent of boys, experience occasional episodes of depression during adolescence, although the incidence of major depression is far lower.

death of a loved one—all may produce profound feelings of sadness, loss, and grief. In situations such as these, depression is a fairly typical reaction.

How common are feelings of depression in adolescence? Although figures are hard to come by, some estimates suggest that 20 to 35 percent of boys and 25 to 40 percent of girls report having experienced depressed moods in the previous 6 months. Reports of feeling "sad and hopeless" are even higher: Almost two-thirds of teenagers say they have experienced such feelings at one time or another (see Figure 12-1). Conversely, only a small minority of adolescents—some 3 percent—experience *major depression*, a full-blown psychological disorder in which depression is severe and lingers for long periods (Gans, Blyth, Elsby, & Gaveras, 1990; Petersen, Compas, & Brooks-Gunn, 1991; Petersen et al., 1993).

Gender, ethnic, and racial differences also are found in depression rates. As is the case among adults, adolescent girls, on average, experience depression more often than do boys. Furthermore, some studies have found that African-American adolescents have higher rates of depression than do Caucasian youths, although not all research supports this conclusion. Native Americans, too, appear to have higher rates of depression (Fleming & Offord, 1990; Nettles & Pleck, 1990).

Depression has several causes. In cases of severe, long-term depression, biological factors are often involved. Some adolescents, for instance, seem to be genetically predisposed to experience depression (Ehlers, Frank, & Kupfer, 1988; Brooks-Gunn, Petersen, & Compas, 1994).

However, environmental and social factors relating to the extraordinary changes in the social lives of adolescents are also an important cause (Aseltine, Gore, & Colten, 1994). Thus, an adolescent who experiences the death of a loved one or grows up with a depressed parent is at a higher risk of depression (Hammen, 1991). In addition, being unpopular, having few close friends, and experiencing rejection are associated with adolescent depression (Vernberg, 1990).

One of the most puzzling questions about depression is why its incidence is higher among girls than boys. Some psychologists speculate that stress is more pronounced for girls than for boys in adolescence, owing to the many, sometimes contradictory, aspects of the traditional female gender role. For instance, consider the plight of an adolescent girl who, accepting traditional gender roles, is worried both about doing well in school and

FIGURE 12-1

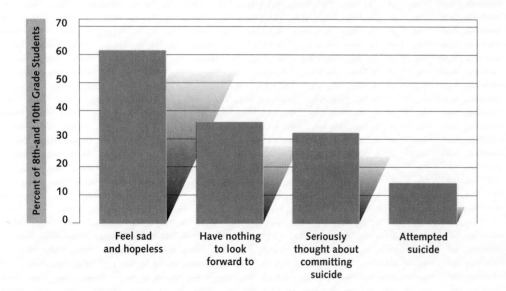

FEELINGS OF DEPRESSION
AMONG ADOLESCENTS

Almost two-thirds of adolescents have experienced some symptoms of depression at some point, according to surveys.

(Adapted from National Adolescent Student Health Survey, cited in J. Gans, 1990.)

about being popular. If she feels that academic success undermines her popularity, she is placed in a difficult bind.

There may also be other causes of girls' generally higher levels of depression during adolescence. They may be more apt than boys to react to stress by turning inward, thereby experiencing a sense of helplessness and hopelessness. In contrast, boys more often react by externalizing the stress and acting more impulsively or aggressively, or by turning to drugs and alcohol. One factor that doesn't seem to cause the higher incidence of female depression is female hormones: Little evidence links hormonal production in adolescent girls to depression (Rutter & Garmezy, 1983; Gjerde, Block, & Block, 1988; Petersen, Sarigiani, & Kennedy, 1991; Nolen-Hoeksema & Girgus, 1994; Lewinsohn, Roberts, Seeley, & Rohde, 1994).

Adolescent Suicide.   Elyssa Drazin was 16. Although her grades had gone down in the previous 6 months, she was still a pretty good student. Her social life had picked up over the last 2 years, and she had been involved with Jake Segool. In the past month, however, the relationship had cooled considerably, and Jake had told her he wanted to date other girls. Elyssa was devastated, and—as she wrote in a note that was found on her desk—she could not bear the thought of seeing Jake holding hands with another girl. She took a large quantity of sleeping pills and became one of the thousands of adolescents who take their own lives each year.

The rate of adolescent suicide in the United States has tripled in the last 30 years. In fact, one teenage suicide occurs every 90 minutes, for an annual rate of 12.2 suicides per 100,000 adolescents. Moreover, the reported rate may actually understate the true number of suicides; parents and medical personnel are often reluctant to report a death as suicide, preferring to label it an accident. Even with underreporting, suicide is the third most common cause of death in the 15-to-24-year-old age group, after accidents and homicide (Henry, Stephenson, Hanson, & Hargett, 1993).

The rate of suicide is higher for boys than for girls, although girls *attempt* suicide more frequently. Males are more successful because of the methods they use: Boys tend to employ more violent means, such as guns, whereas girls are more apt to choose the more peaceful strategy of drug overdose. Some estimates suggest that there are as many as 200 attempted suicides for every successful one (Hawton, 1986; Berman & Jobes, 1991; Gelman, 1994).

The rate of adolescent suicide has tripled in the last 30 years. These girls console one another following the suicide of a classmate in their New Jersey high school.

cluster suicide   *a situation in which one suicide leads to attempts by others to kill themselves*

The reasons behind the increase in adolescent suicide over past decades are unclear. The most obvious explanation is that the stress experienced by teenagers has increased, leading those who are most troubled to be more likely to commit suicide (Elkind, 1984). But why should stress have increased just for adolescents? The suicide rate for other segments of the population has remained fairly stable over the same time period.

Although an explanation for the increase in adolescent suicide has not been found, it is clear that certain factors heighten the risk of suicide. One factor is depression. Depressed teenagers who are experiencing a profound sense of hopelessness are at greater risk of committing suicide. In addition, social inhibition, perfectionism, and a high level of anxiety are related to a greater risk of suicide (Cimbolic & Jobes, 1990; Petersen et al., 1993; Lewinsohn, Rohde, & Seeley, 1994).

Some cases of suicide are associated with family conflicts and adjustment difficulties. Others follow a history of abuse and neglect. The rate of suicide among drug and alcohol abusers is also relatively high. As can be seen in Figure 12-2, those contemplating suicide cite several other factors as well (Garland & Zigler, 1993; Brent, Perper, Moritz, & Liotus, 1994).

Some suicides appear to be caused by exposure to the suicide of others. In **cluster suicide**, one suicide leads to attempts by others to kill themselves. For instance, some high schools have experienced a series of suicides following a well-publicized case. As a result, many schools have established crisis intervention teams to counsel students when one student commits suicide (Hazell, 1993).

There are several warning signs that should sound an alarm regarding the possibility of suicide. Among them:

- direct or indirect talk about suicide, such as "I wish I were dead" or "You won't have me to worry about any longer"

- school difficulties, such as missed classes or a decline in grades

- making arrangements as if preparing for a long trip, such as giving away prized possessions or arranging for the care of a pet

- writing a will

FIGURE 12-2

These problems were the ones most frequently cited by callers to a suicide-prevention hotline who were contemplating suicide.

(*Source:* Samaritans, 1991.)

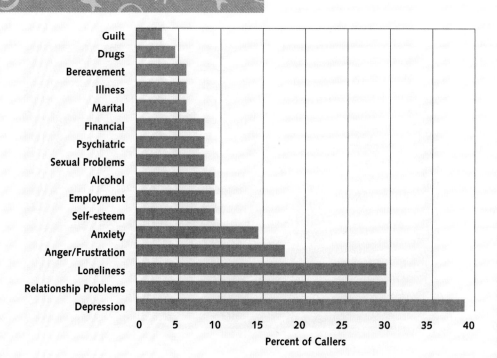

- loss of appetite or excessive eating

- general depression, including a change in sleeping patterns, slowness and lethargy, and uncommunicativeness

- dramatic changes in behavior, such as a shy person suddenly acting outgoing

- preoccupation with death in music, art, or literature.

The Informed Consumer of Development

Deterring Adolescent Suicide

If you suspect that an adolescent, or anyone else for that matter, is contemplating suicide, don't stand idly by. Act! The U.S. Public Health Service makes several suggestions for what to do:

- Listen without judging, giving the person an understanding forum in which to try to talk things through.

- Talk specifically about suicidal thoughts, such as: Does the person have a plan? Has he or she bought a gun? Where is it? Has he or she stockpiled pills? Where are they? The Public Health Service notes that, "contrary to popular belief, such candor will not give a person dangerous ideas or encourage a suicidal act."

- Evaluate the situation, distinguishing between general upset and more serious danger, as when suicide plans *have* been made. If the crisis is acute, *do not leave the person alone.*

- Be supportive; let the person know you care and try to break down his or her feelings of isolation.

- Take charge of finding help, without concern about invading the person's privacy. Do not try to handle the problem alone; get professional help immediately.

- Make the environment safe, removing from the premises (not just hiding) weapons such as guns, razors, scissors, medication, and other potentially dangerous household items.

- Do not keep suicide talk or threats secret; these are calls for help and warrant immediate action.

- Do not challenge, dare, or use verbal shock treatment. They can have tragic effects.

- Make a contract with the person, getting a promise or commitment, preferably in writing, not to make any suicidal attempt until you have talked further.

- Beware of elevated moods and seemingly quick recoveries; sometimes they are illusory, reflecting the relief of finally deciding to commit suicide or the temporary release of talking to someone, though the underlying problems have not been resolved (based on Franck & Brownstone, 1991, pp. 445–446).

For immediate help with a suicide-related problem, call (800) 448-3000, a national hot line staffed with trained counselors.

Review and Rethink

REVIEW

◆ Self-concept during adolescence grows more differentiated as the view of the self becomes more organized, broader, and more abstract, and takes account of the views of others.

◆ Self-esteem, too, grows increasingly differentiated as the adolescent develops the ability to place different values on different aspects of the self. Factors of gender, race, and socioeconomic status appear to influence self-esteem.

◆ Both Erik Erikson's identity-versus-role-diffusion stage and James Marcia's four identity statuses focus on the adolescent's struggle to determine an identity and a role in society. Adolescents tend to rely on friends and peers in the face of societal pressures; they may react in dysfunctional ways and may seek a psychological moratorium to explore role possibilities.

◆ One of the dangers that adolescents face is depression, a psychological disorder with biological, environmental, and social causes that affects girls more than boys.

◆ Suicide is now the third most common cause of death among 18-to-24-year-olds. Those who deal with adolescents should familiarize themselves with the warning signs of suicide and with ways to prevent it.

RETHINK

◆ How does the adolescent's changing self-concept relate to changes in his or her cognitive development?

◆ What are some consequences of the shift from reliance on adults to reliance on peers? Are there advantages? Dangers?

◆ Do you believe that all four of Marcia's identity statuses can lead to reassessment and different choices later in life? Do you think some statuses are more likely than others to produce this type of rethinking? Why?

◆ Why are females more likely to experience depression than males? How would you design a study to explore the possible effects of biological versus environmental factors?

◆ What obligations do you have to a friend who confides in you the intention to commit suicide and asks you to respect confidentiality?

RELATIONSHIPS: FAMILY AND FRIENDS

Slim and dark, with a passing resemblance to actress Demi Moore, Leah is dressed up and ready to go to the first real formal dance of her life. True, the smashing effect of her short beaded black dress is marred slightly by the man's shirt she insists on wearing to cover her bare shoulders. And she is in a sulk. Her boyfriend, Sean Moffitt, is 4 minutes late, and her mother, Linda, refuses to let her stay out all night at a coed sleep-over party after the dance.

When Sean arrives with his mother, Pam, Leah reluctantly sheds the work shirt. She greets Sean shyly, not sure he'll approve of that afternoon's makeover by hairdresser and manicurist. Sean, an easygoing youth with dimples and rosy cheeks, squirms in his tuxedo. Leah recombs his hair and makes him remove his earring. "None of the guys are wearing them to the dance," she declares. (She's wrong. A few moments later, their friends Melissa and Erik arrive, and Erik is wearing his earring.)

Leah's father, George, suggests a 2 A.M. curfew: Leah hoots incredulously. Sean pitches the all-nighter, stressing that the party will be chaperoned. Leah's mother has already talked to the host's mother, mortifying Leah with her off-hand comment that a coed sleepover seemed "weird." Rolling her eyes, Leah persists: "It's not like anybody's really going to sleep!" Sean asks his mother for another $20. "Why did the amount suddenly jump?" she asks, digging into her purse. (Graham, 1995, p. B1)

autonomy   *having independence and a sense of control over one's life*

This snapshot of the life of 16-year-old Leah Brookner of Norwalk, Connecticut, provides a glimpse of some of the complex, interdependent relationships in which adolescents are involved. As Leah juggles parents, friends, and romantic partners, her life—and those of other adolescents—seems, at times, like an intricate jigsaw puzzle in which not all the pieces fit together perfectly.

The social world of adolescents is considerably wider than that of younger children. As adolescents' relationships with people outside the home grow increasingly important, their interactions with their families evolve and take on a new, and sometimes difficult, character (Montemayor, Adams, & Gulotta, 1994).

FAMILY TIES: REASSESSING RELATIONS WITH RELATIONS

When Pepe Lizzagara entered junior high school, his relationship with his parents changed drastically. Although relations were quite good previously, by the middle of seventh grade, tensions grew. In Pepe's view, his parents always seemed to be "on his case." Instead of giving him more freedom, which he felt he deserved at age 13, they actually seemed to be getting more restrictive.

Pepe's parents would probably suggest that they were not the source of the tension in the household—Pepe was. From their point of view, Pepe, with whom they had established what seemed to be a stable relationship throughout much of his childhood, suddenly seemed transformed. Like Nuket Curran (described in the chapter prologue), whose hair color shifted almost as frequently as her moods, Pepe presented novel, and often bewildering, behavior.

The Quest for Autonomy.   Parents are sometimes angered, and even more frequently puzzled, by adolescents' conduct. Children who have previously accepted their parents' judgments, declarations, and guidelines begin to question—and sometimes rebel against—their parents' views of the world.

One reason for these clashes is the shift in the roles that both children and parents must deal with during adolescence. Adolescents increasingly seek **autonomy**, independence and a sense of control over their lives. Most parents intellectually realize that this shift is a normal part of adolescence, representing one of the primary developmental tasks of the period, and in many ways they welcome it as a sign of their children's growth. However, in many cases the day-to-day realities of adolescents' increasing autonomy may prove difficult for them to deal with (Smetana, 1995).

In most families, teenagers' autonomy grows gradually over the course of adolescence. For instance, one study of changes in adolescents' views of their parents found that increasing autonomy led them to perceive parents less in idealized terms and more as individuals in their own right. At the same time, adolescents came to depend more on themselves, and to feel more like separate individuals (see Figure 12-3).

The increase in adolescent autonomy is reflected in the relationship between parents and teenagers. At the start of adolescence, the relationship tends to be asymmetrical: Parents hold most of the power and influence over the relationship. By the end of adolescence, however, power and influence have become more balanced, and parents and children end up in a more symmetrical, or egalitarian, relationship. Power and influence are shared, although parents typically retain the upper hand.

generation gap *a divide between parents and children in attitudes, values, aspirations, and worldviews*

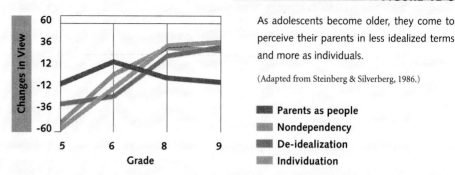

FIGURE 12-3

As adolescents become older, they come to perceive their parents in less idealized terms and more as individuals.

(Adapted from Steinberg & Silverberg, 1986.)

■ Parents as people
■ Nondependency
■ De-idealization
■ Individuation

The degree of autonomy that is eventually achieved varies from one family to the next. Furthermore, cultural factors play an important role. In Western societies, which tend to value individualism, adolescents seek autonomy at a relatively early stage of adolescence. In contrast, Asian societies are *collectivistic*; they promote the idea that the well-being of the group is more important than that of the individual. In such societies, adolescents' aspirations to achieve autonomy are less pronounced (Feldman & Rosenthal, 1990; Kim et al., 1994).

The Myth of the Generation Gap.   It might be thought that one factor motivating adolescents' efforts to attain autonomy is the discrepancy between parents' and teenagers' views of the world. According to this argument, there is a **generation gap**, a deep divide between parents and children in attitudes, values, aspirations, and worldviews.

The reality, however, is quite different. The generation gap, when it exists, is really quite narrow. Adolescents and their parents tend to see eye-to-eye in a variety of domains. Republican parents have Republican children; members of the Christian Right have children who espouse similar views; parents who advocate for abortion rights have children who are pro-abortion. On social, political, and religious issues, parents and adolescents tend to be in agreement, and children's worries mirror those of their parents. They also have similar career aspirations and attitudes about work. In fact, on most issues of attitudes and values, the differences between one adolescent and another are far greater than the differences between parents and their adolescent children (Conger, 1977; Feather, 1980; Youniss, 1989; Chira, 1994).

Similarly, there is typically no generation gap in the value that parents and adolescents place on the relationship they have with one another. Despite their quest for autonomy and independence, most adolescents have deep love, affection, and respect for their parents—reciprocating the feelings that their parents have for them. Although there are notable exceptions, with some parent–adolescent relationships marked by significant strife, the majority of relationships are more positive than negative. In fact, there is no evidence suggesting that family problems are worse during adolescence than at any other stage of development (Steinberg, 1990, 1993).

On the other hand, parents' and adolescents' relationships are not always sweetness and light. For instance, parents and adolescents often hold different views on matters of personal taste such as music preferences and styles of dress. Significant strife may occur between parents and adolescents, particularly during early adolescence, when conflicts between children's efforts to achieve autonomy and parental reactions are more pronounced than at any other time.

Why should strife be greater during early adolescence than at later stages of the period? According to developmentalist Judith Smetana, the reason involves differing definitions of,

More conflict between parents and their children occurs during the early stages of adolescence than at later stages of the period.

and rationales for, appropriate and inappropriate conduct. Parents may feel, for instance, that getting one's ear pierced in three places is inappropriate because society traditionally deems it inappropriate. On the other hand, adolescents may view the issue in terms of personal choice (Smetana, 1988, 1989; Smetana, Yau, & Hanson, 1991).

Furthermore, the newly sophisticated reasoning of adolescents (discussed in the previous chapter) leads teenagers to think about parental rules in more complex ways. Consequently, arguments that were convincing to a school-age child ("Do it because I tell you to do it") are less compelling to an adolescent.

Although at first the argumentativeness and assertiveness of early adolescence may lead to an increase in conflict, in many ways they play an important role in the evolution of parent–child relationships. Although parents may at first react defensively to the challenges that their children present, and may grow inflexible and rigid, in most cases they eventually come to realize that their children *are* growing up.

Parents also come to see that their adolescent children's arguments are often compelling and not so unreasonable, and that their daughters and sons can, in fact, be trusted with more freedom. Consequently, they become more yielding, allowing and eventually perhaps even encouraging independence. As this process occurs during the middle stages of adolescence, the combativeness of early adolescence declines.

Of course, this pattern does not hold for all adolescents. Although the majority of teenagers maintain stable relations with their parents throughout adolescence, as many as 20 percent pass through a fairly rough time (Dryfoos, 1990). We'll consider some of the factors that place adolescents at risk later in the chapter.

RELATIONSHIPS WITH PEERS: THE IMPORTANCE OF BELONGING

In the eyes of numerous parents, the most fitting symbol of adolescence is the telephone. For many of their children, it appears to be an indispensable lifeline, sustaining ties to friends with whom they may have already spent many hours earlier in the day.

The seemingly compulsive need to communicate with friends is symbolic of the role that peers play in adolescence. Continuing the trend that began in middle childhood, adolescents spend increasing amounts of time with their peers, and the importance of peer relationships grows as well. In fact, there is probably no period of life in which peer relationships are as important as they are in adolescence (Youniss & Haynie, 1992).

reference group   *groups of people with whom one compares oneself*

cliques   *groups of from two to twelve people whose members have frequent social interactions with one another*

crowds   *a larger group than a clique, comprised of individuals who share particular characteristics but who may not interact with one another*

sex cleavage   *sex segregation in which boys interact primarily with boys, and girls primarily with girls*

Several reasons account for the prominence of peers during adolescence (Coleman, 1980). For one thing, peers provide the opportunity to compare and evaluate opinions, abilities, and even physical changes—a process called *social comparison*. Because physical and cognitive changes are so pronounced, especially during the early stages of puberty, adolescents turn increasingly to others who share, and consequently can shed light on, their own experiences.

Parents are unable to provide social comparison. Not only are they well beyond the changes that adolescents undergo, but adolescents' questioning of adult authority and their motivation to become more autonomous make parents, other family members, and adults in general inadequate and invalid sources of knowledge. Who is left to provide such information? Peers.

Finally, adolescence is a time of experimentation, of trying out new roles and conduct. Peers provide information about what roles and behavior are most acceptable by serving as a **reference group**, groups of people with whom one compares oneself.

Reference groups present a set of *norms*, or standards, against which adolescents can judge their social success. An adolescent need not even belong to a group for it to serve as a reference group. For instance, unpopular adolescents may find themselves belittled and rejected by members of a popular group, yet use that more popular group as a reference group.

Cliques and Crowds: Belonging to a Group.   Even if they do not belong to the group they use for reference purposes, adolescents typically are part of some identifiable group. In fact, one of the consequences of the increasing cognitive sophistication of adolescents is the ability to group others in more discriminating ways. Rather than defining people in concrete terms relating to what they do ("football players" or "musicians"), adolescents use more abstract terms packed with greater subtleties ("jocks" or "the artsy-craftsy crowd") (B. Brown, 1990; Montemayor et al., 1994).

What are the typical groups to which adolescence belong? There are actually two types: cliques and crowds. **Cliques** are groups of from two to twelve people whose members have frequent social interactions with one another. In contrast, **crowds** are larger, comprising individuals who share particular characteristics but who may not interact with one another. For instance, "toughs," "jocks," and "brains" are separate crowds currently found in the typical high school.

There is a surprisingly high level of agreement among adolescents regarding the characteristics of members of particular groups. For instance, one study found that "jocks" and "normals" were seen as dressing casually, whereas "populars" were viewed as more stylish dressers. "Normals" and "jocks" were perceived as friendly; "populars" and "jocks" were cliquish. "Populars" and "jocks" tried hard in school; "druggies" and "toughs" hate school (Brown, Lohr, & Trujillo, 1983; see Figure 12-4).

Of course, these descriptions are merely stereotypes, and they do not necessarily represent the actual characteristics of individual group members. Still, the stereotypes are powerful and widespread, and the expectation that people in a particular crowd behave in a certain way may constrain members' behavior. In fact, the stereotype may actually bring about the expected behavior—another example of a self-fulfilling prophecy.

Gender Relations.   At the very start of adolescence, groups tend to mirror the makeup of middle childhood groups in that they are composed almost universally of same-sex individuals. Boys hang out with boys; girls hang out with girls. Technically, this sex segregation is called the **sex cleavage**.

However, the situation changes in short order as members of both sexes enter puberty. Both the hormonal surge that marks puberty and causes the maturation of the sex organs, and societal pressures suggesting that the time is appropriate for romantic involvement, lead to a change in the ways the opposite sex is viewed. Rather than seeing every member of the

FIGURE 12-4

Various high school groups are seen as having very different characteristics.

(Adapted from Brown, Lohr, & Trujillo, 1983.)

Legend:
- Casual, athletic dress
- Stylish dress and grooming
- Friendly
- Cliquish
- Enjoy, try hard at academics
- Hate school

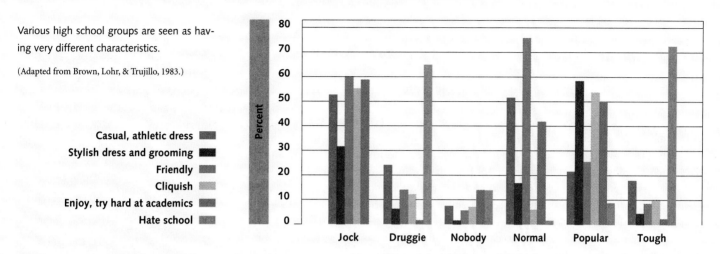

opposite sex as "annoying" and "a pain," boys and girls begin to regard each other with greater interest, in terms of both personality and sexuality.

When this change occurs, boys' and girls' cliques, which previously had moved along parallel but separate tracks, begin to converge. Adolescents begin to attend boy–girl dances or parties, although most of the time the boys still spend their time with boys, and the girls with girls (Csikszentmihalyi & Larson, 1984). (Think back to your own early adolescence, and perhaps you'll recall dances with boys lined up on one side of the room and girls on the other.)

A little later, however, adolescents increasingly spend time with members of the opposite sex (Dunphy, 1963). New cliques emerge, composed of both males and females. Not everyone participates initially: Early on, the teenagers who are leaders of the same-sex cliques and who have the highest status pilot the way. Eventually, however, most adolescents find themselves in cliques that include boys and girls.

The sex segregation of childhood continues during the early stages of adolescence. However, by the time of middle adolescence, this segregation decreases, and boys' and girls' cliques begin to converge.

Developmental Diversity

Race segregation: The great divide of adolescence

When Philip McAdoo, a [student] at the University of North Carolina, stopped one day to see a friend who worked on his college campus, a receptionist asked if he would autograph a basketball for her son. Because he was African-American and tall, "she just assumed that I was on the basketball team," recounted McAdoo.

Jasme Kelly, an African-American sophomore at the same college, had a similar story to tell. When she went to see a friend at a fraternity house, the student who answered the door asked if she was there to apply for the job of cook.

White students, too, find racial relations difficult and in some ways forbidding. For instance, Jenny Johnson, a white 20-year-old junior, finds even the most basic conversation with African-American classmates difficult. She describes a conversation in which African-American friends "jump at my throat because I used the word 'black' instead of African-American. There is just such a huge barrier that it's really hard . . . to have a normal discussion." (Sanoff & Minerbrook, 1993, p. 58)

Even in schools that are racially integrated, members of different races interact relatively little.

The pattern of race segregation found at the University of North Carolina is repeated over and over in schools and colleges throughout the United States: Even at desegregated schools with a high proportion of minority students, members of different races interact very little. Moreover, even if they have a friend of a different race within the confines of a school, most adolescents do not interact with that friend outside of school (DuBois & Hirsch, 1990).

It doesn't start out this way. During elementary school and even during early adolescence, there is a fair amount of integration among the races. However, by middle and late adolescence, the amount of race segregation is striking (Shrum, Cheek, & Hunter, 1988; Spencer & Dornbusch, 1990; Spencer, 1991).

Why should race segregation be the rule, even in schools that have been desegregated for some time? One reason is that minority students may actively seek support from others who share their minority status. Furthermore, by associating primarily with other members of their own minority group, they are able to affirm their own identity.

Other explanations for campus segregation are less positive. For instance, socioeconomic status (SES) differences between the races may keep integration between the races at low levels. Racial differences tend to mirror SES differences: People from minority groups are overrepresented in lower SES groups (Coleman, 1961), just as people from the majority group are overrepresented in higher SES groups. Because cliques tend to comprise members who are of similar SES, they also display very little racial integration. It is possible, then, that apparent racial differences in interaction patterns are really due to SES characteristics, and not to race per se.

Another explanations for the lack of interaction between members of different racial groups relates to differences in academic performance. Because minority group members tend to experience less school success than do members of the majority group, as we discussed in Chapter 10, it may be that the segregation between the races is based not on race itself but on academic achievement.

Specifically, some students attend schools in which classes are assigned on the basis of students' prior levels of academic success. If minority group members experience less success, they may find themselves in classes with proportionally fewer majority group members. Similarly, majority students may be in classes with few minority students. Such class assignment practices, then, might inadvertently maintain and promote race segregation. This pattern would be particularly prevalent in schools where rigid academic tracking is practiced, with students assigned to "low," "medium," and "high" tracks depending on their prior achievement (Hallinan & Williams, 1989).

Finally, the lack of racial interaction in school might reflect negative attitudes held by both majority and minority students. Minority students may feel that the white majority is prejudiced, discriminatory, and hostile, and they may prefer to stick to same-race groups. Conversely, majority students may assume that minority group members are antagonistic and unfriendly. Such mutually destructive attitudes reduce the likelihood that meaningful interaction can take place (Miller & Brewer, 1984).

Is the voluntary racial segregation found during adolescence inevitable? No. For instance, adolescents who have had extensive interactions with members of different races earlier in their lives are more likely to have friends of different races. Furthermore, schools that actively promote contact between members of different racial groups in mixed-ability classes may create an environment in which cross-race friendships can flourish (Schofield & Francis, 1982).

Still, the task is daunting. Many societal pressures act to keep members of different races from interacting with one another. Furthermore, cliques may actively promote norms that discourage group members from crossing racial lines to form new friendships.

Cliques and crowds undergo yet another transformation at the end of adolescence: They become less powerful and may, in fact, succumb to the increased pairing-off that occurs between males and females. Rather than the clique being the center of adolescents' social lives, then, boy–girl interaction becomes the focus.

POPULARITY AND REJECTION

Most adolescents have well-tuned antennae when it comes to determining who is popular and who is not. In fact, for some teenagers, concerns over popularity—or lack of it—may be a central focus of their lives.

Actually, the social world of adolescents is divided not only into popular and unpopular individuals; the differentiations are more complex (see Table 12-3). For instance, some adolescents are controversial; in contrast to *popular* adolescents, who are mostly liked, *controversial* adolescents are liked by some and disliked by others. Furthermore, there are *rejected* adolescents, who are uniformly disliked, and *neglected* adolescents, who are neither liked nor disliked. In most cases, however, popular and controversial adolescents tend to be similar in that their overall status is higher, whereas rejected and neglected adolescents share a generally lower status.

For instance, popular and controversial adolescents have more close friends, engage more frequently in activities with their peers, and disclose more about themselves to others than do less popular students. They are also more involved in extracurricular school activities. In addition, they are well aware of their popularity, and they are less lonely than are their less popular classmates (Franzoi, Davis, & Vasquez-Suson, 1994).

In contrast, the social world of rejected and neglected adolescents is considerably more negative. They have fewer friends, engage in social activities less frequently, and have less contact with the opposite sex. They see themselves—accurately, it turns out—as less popular, and they are more likely to feel lonely.

Unpopular adolescents fall into several categories. Controversial adolescents are liked by some and disliked by others; rejected adolescents are uniformly disliked; and neglected adolescents are neither liked nor disliked.

CONFORMITY: PEER PRESSURE IN ADOLESCENCE

Whenever Aldos Henry said he wanted to buy a particular brand of sneakers or a certain style of shirt, his parents complained that he was just giving in to peer pressure and told him to make up his own mind about things.

In arguing with Aldos, his parents were subscribing to a view of adolescence that is quite prevalent in U.S. society: that teenagers are highly susceptible to **peer pressure**, the influence of one's peers to conform to their behavior and attitudes. Were his parents correct?

Research suggests that it all depends. In some cases, adolescents *are* highly susceptible to the influence of their peers. For instance, when considering what to wear, whom to date, and what movies to see, adolescents are apt to follow the lead of their peers. On the other hand, when it comes to many nonsocial matters, such as choosing a career path or trying to solve a problem, they are more likely to turn to an experienced adult (Phelan, Yu, & Davidson, 1994).

peer pressure   *the influence of one's peers to conform to their behavior and attitudes*

TABLE 12-3

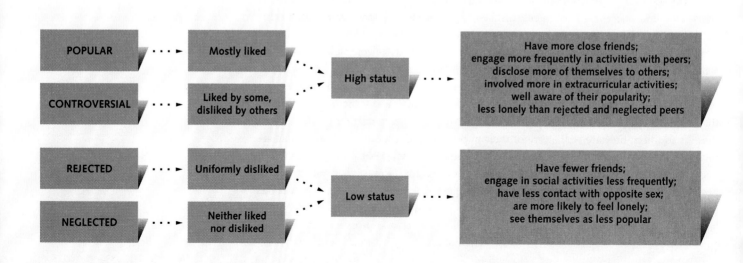

In short, particularly in middle and late adolescence, teenagers turn to those they see as experts on a given dimension (Young & Ferguson, 1979). If they have social concerns, they turn to the people most likely to be experts—their peers. On the other hand, if the problem is one about which parents or other adults are most likely to have expertise, teenagers tend to turn to them for advice and are most susceptible to their opinions.

Overall, then, it does not appear that susceptibility to peer pressure suddenly soars during adolescence. Instead, adolescence brings about a change in the people to whom an individual conforms. Whereas children conform fairly consistently to their parents during childhood, in adolescence conformity shifts to include the peer group, in part because pressures to conform increase.

Ultimately, however, adolescents conform less to both peers *and* adults as they develop increasing autonomy over their lives. As they grow in confidence and in the ability to make their own decisions, adolescents are more apt to remain independent and to reject pressures from others, no matter who those others are (Steinberg & Silverberg, 1986; Steinberg, 1993; Crockett & Crouter, 1995.)

JUVENILE DELINQUENCY: THE CRIMES OF ADOLESCENCE

Although the vast majority of them are law-abiding citizens, adolescents, along with young adults, are more likely to commit a crime than any other age group. This state of affairs has partly to do with the definition of certain behaviors (such as drinking), which are illegal for adolescents but not for older individuals. But even when such crimes are disregarded, adolescents are disproportionately involved in violent crimes, such as murder, assaults, and rape, and property crimes, involving theft, robbery, and arson.

For example, almost 20 percent of serious violent crimes are committed by adolescents, either alone or in groups. Another 8 percent are committed by adolescents in conjunction with older offenders. Overall, a quarter of all serious violent crime involves an adolescent. Furthermore, the numbers are growing. Over the past decade, the arrest rate for violent crimes rose almost 60 percent among adolescents. Experts predict that if the present trends continue, by the year 2010, the number of arrests of juveniles for a violent crime will more than double (Juvenile Justice Clearinghouse, 1995).

Why do adolescents become involved in criminal activity? Some offenders are known as **undersocialized delinquents**, adolescents who are raised with little discipline, or with harsh, uncaring parental supervision. These children have never been appropriately socialized, and they simply have not learned standards of conduct to regulate their own behavior. Undersocialized delinquents typically begin criminal activities at an early age, well before the onset of adolescence.

Undersocialized delinquents share several characteristics. They tend to be relatively aggressive and violent fairly early in life, behaviors that lead them to be rejected by their peers and to fail academically. They also are more likely to have been diagnosed with attention deficit disorder as children and tend to be less intelligent than average (Patterson, DeBaryshe, & Ramsey, 1989).

Undersocialized delinquents often suffer from psychological difficulties, and as adults they fit a psychological category called the *antisocial personality disorder*. They are relatively unlikely to be successfully rehabilitated, and many undersocialized delinquents live on the margins of society throughout their lives (Farrington, 1991; D.O. Lewis et al., 1994; Ronka & Pulkkinen, 1995; Tate, Reppucci, & Mulvey, 1995).

On the other hand, most adolescent offenders are **socialized delinquents**, who know and subscribe to the norms of society and who are fairly normal psychologically. For them, transgressions committed during adolescence do not lead to a life of crime. Instead, most socialized delinquents pass through a period during adolescence where they engage in some petty crimes, but they do not continue law-breaking into adulthood.

Socialized delinquents are typically highly influenced by their peers, and their delinquency often occurs in groups. In addition, some research suggests that parents of social-

undersocialized delinquents adolescents who are raised with little discipline, or with harsh, uncaring parental supervision

socialized delinquents adolescents who know and subscribe to the norms of society; they are fairly normal psychologically

ized delinquents supervise their children's behavior less closely (W. Miller, 1958; Dornbusch et al., 1985; Windle, 1994; Fletcher, Darling, Steinberg, & Dornbusch, 1995).

Review and Rethink

REVIEW

♦ The search for autonomy causes a sometimes painful readjustment in relations between teenagers and their parents, due partly to different definitions of appropriate and inappropriate behavior. However, the generation gap is actually less wide than is generally thought.

♦ Belonging becomes a significant issue in adolescence, with cliques and groups serving as reference groups and offering a ready means of social comparison. Sex cleavage gradually diminishes, until boys and girls begin to pair off.

♦ Racial separation increases during adolescence, bolstered by socioeconomic status differences, different academic experiences, and mutually distrustful attitudes.

♦ Degrees of popularity in adolescence include popular, controversial, neglected, and rejected adolescents. More popular adolescents engage in more friendships, activities, and intergender relationships than do less popular adolescents.

♦ Adolescents tend to conform to their peers, and to be susceptible to peer pressure, in areas in which they regard their peers as experts, and to conform to adults in areas of perceived adult expertise. In general, conformity to others decreases during adolescence.

♦ Adolescents are disproportionately involved in criminal activities, although most do not commit crimes. Juvenile delinquents can be categorized as either undersocialized or socialized delinquents.

RETHINK

♦ In what ways do you think parents with different styles—authoritarian, authoritative, and permissive—tend to react to attempts to establish autonomy during adolescence?

♦ Why does there appear to be no real generation gap in most attitudes, despite adolescents' need to question authority?

♦ In what ways does membership in cliques or crowds constrain behavior? Do such groupings disappear in adulthood?

♦ What school policies do you think would be most effective in decreasing racial segregation?

♦ How do the findings about conformity and peer pressure reported in this chapter relate to adolescents' developing cognitive abilities?

DATING, SEXUAL BEHAVIOR, AND TEENAGE PREGNANCY

Night has eased into day, but it is all the same for Tori Michel, 17. Her 5-day-old baby, Caitlin, has been fussing for hours, though she seems finally to have settled into the pink-and-purple car seat on the living-room sofa. "She wore herself out," explains Tori, who lives in a two-bedroom duplex in this St. Louis suburb with her mother, Susan, an aide to handicapped adults. "I think she just had gas."

Motherhood was not in Tori's plans for her senior year at Fort Zumwalt South High School—not until she had a "one-night thing" with James, a 21-year-old she met through friends. She had been taking birth-control pills but says she stopped after breaking up with a long-term boyfriend. "Wrong answer," she now says ruefully.

When she learned she was pregnant last January, Tori decided against having an abortion. "It just doesn't seem right," she says. Her mother, who divorced her husband Robert 2 years ago, supported her daughter's decision. James is no longer in the picture. . . . Tori cannot help but admit she's a bit shell-shocked. Finishing school, she insists, is her priority. "Ever since I've had Caitlin, I haven't felt like a teenager. I've felt like a mom," she says. "I think it happened too fast." (Gleick, Reed, & Schindehette, 1994, p. 40)

Three A.M. feedings, diaper changes, and visits to the pediatrician are not part of most people's vision of adolescence. Yet millions of teenagers become mothers, a problematic trend in the United States, with ramifications for every segment of society.

In the remainder of the chapter we'll consider several aspects of adolescents' relationships with one another. Just as one thing sometimes leads to another in the real world, we'll first consider dating, then sexual behavior, and then adolescent pregnancy.

DATING: BOY MEETS GIRL IN THE 1990s

It took him almost a month, but Sylvester Chiu finally got up the courage to ask Jackie Durbin to go to the movies. It was hardly a surprise to Jackie, though: Sylvester had first told his friend Erik about his resolve to ask Jackie out, and Erik had told Jackie's friend Cynthia about Sylvester's plans. Cynthia, in turn, had told Jackie, who was primed to say yes when Sylvester finally did call.

Welcome to the complex world of dating, an important ritual of adolescence. By the time most girls are 12 or 13, and boys 13 or 14, they begin to engage in dating. By the age of 16, more than 90 percent of teenagers have had at least one date, and by the end of high school, some three-quarters of adolescents have been steadily involved with someone (Dickenson, 1975; McCabe, 1984).

The Functions of Dating.   Although on the surface dating may seem to be simply part of a pattern of courtship that can potentially lead to marriage, it actually serves other functions as well. For instance, dating is a means of learning how to establish intimacy with other individuals. Furthermore, it can provide entertainment and, depending on the status of the person one is dating, prestige. It even can be used in developing a sense of one's own identity (Skipper & Nass, 1966; Savin-Williams & Berndt, 1990; Sanderson & Cantor, 1995).

Just how well dating serves such functions, particularly the development of psychological intimacy, is an open question. What specialists in adolescence do know, however, is surprising: Dating in early and middle adolescence is not terribly successful at facilitating intimacy. On the contrary, dating is often a superficial activity in which the participants so rarely let down their guards that they never become truly close and never expose themselves emotionally to each other. Psychological intimacy may be lacking even when sexual activity is part of the relationship (Douvan & Adelson, 1966; Savin-Williams & Berndt, 1990).

True intimacy becomes more common during later adolescence. At that point, the dating relationship may be taken more seriously by both participants, and it may be seen as a means of selecting a mate and as a potential prelude to marriage (an institution we'll consider in Chapter 14).

Dating in Minority Groups.   Cultural influences affect dating patterns among minority adolescents, particularly those whose parents have come to the United States from other countries. Minority parents may try to control their children's dating behavior in an effort to preserve the minority group's traditional values (Spencer & Dornbusch, 1990).

For example, Asian parents may be especially conservative in their attitudes and values, in part because they themselves may have had no experience of dating. (In many cases, the parents' marriage was arranged by others, and the entire concept of dating is unfamiliar.) They may insist that dating be conducted with chaperones, or not at all. As a consequence, they may find themselves involved in substantial conflict with their children (Sung, 1985).

SEXUAL RELATIONSHIPS: PERMISSIVENESS WITH AFFECTION

The maturation of the sexual organs during the start of adolescence opens a new range of possibilities in relations with others: sexuality. In fact, sexual behavior and thoughts are among the central concerns of adolescents. Almost all adolescents think about sex, and many think about it a good deal of the time (Coles & Stokes, 1985).

Masturbation.   For most adolescents, their initiation into sexuality comes from **masturbation**, sexual self-stimulation. Almost half of all adolescent boys and a quarter of adolescent girls report that they have engaged in masturbation. The frequency of masturbation shows a sex difference: Male masturbation is most frequent in the early teens and then begins to decline; females begin more slowly and reach a maximum later (Oliver & Hyde, 1993).

Although masturbation is widespread, it still may produce feelings of shame and guilt. Several reasons account for this. One is that adolescents may believe that masturbation signifies the inability to find a sexual partner—an erroneous assumption; statistics show that three-quarters of married men and 68 percent of married women report masturbating between 10 and 24 times a year (Hunt, 1974). Another reason is the legacy of shame remaining from misguided past views. For instance, nineteenth-century physicians and laypersons warned of horrible effects of masturbation, including "dyspepsia, spinal disease, headache, epilepsy, various kinds of fits . . ., impaired eyesight, palpitation of the heart, pain in the side and bleeding at the lungs, spasm of the heart, and sometimes sudden death" (Gregory, 1856). Suggested remedies included bandaging the genitals, covering them with a cage, tying the hands, male circumcision without anesthesia (so that it might better be remembered), and for girls, the administration of carbolic acid to the clitoris. One physician, J.W. Kellogg, believed that certain grains would be less likely to provoke sexual excitation—leading to his invention of corn flakes (Michael, Gagnon, Laumann, & Kolata, 1994).

The reality is different. Today, experts on sexual behavior view masturbation as a normal, healthy, and harmless activity (Leitenberg, Detzer, & Srebnik, 1993). In fact, some suggest that it provides a useful means of learning about one's own sexuality.

Sexual Intercourse.   Although it may be preceded by many different types of sexual intimacy, including deep kissing, massaging, petting, and oral sex, sexual intercourse remains a major milestone in the perceptions of most adolescents. Consequently, the focus of researchers investigating sexual behavior has been on the act of intercourse.

The age at which adolescents first have sexual intercourse has been steadily declining over the last 50 years. Overall, about half of adolescents begin having intercourse between the ages of 15 and 18, and at least 80 percent have had sex before the age of 20 (Seidman & Reider, 1994).

There are racial and gender differences in the timing of first intercourse (Leigh, Morrison, Trocki, & Temple, 1994). For instance, half of all African-American males have intercourse by the time they are 15, and half of all Hispanic males by the time they are about 16-½. In comparison, it is not until age 17 that half of white males have had sexual intercourse. The pattern is a little different for females: Half of all black females have had intercourse by the time they are about 17, while half of all white females and half of all Hispanic females have intercourse by the time they are 18 (Michael et al., 1994; see Figure 12-5).

Clearly, sexual activities are taking place earlier during adolescence than they did in prior eras. This is in part a result of a change in societal norms governing sexual conduct. The prevailing norm several decades ago was the *double standard*, in which premarital sex

---

masturbation   *sexual self-stimulation*

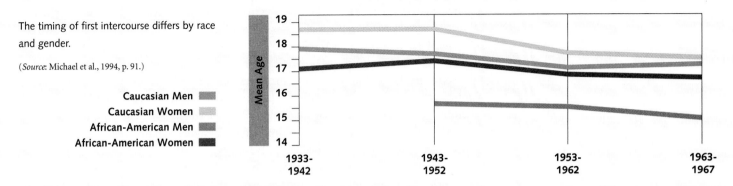

FIGURE 12-5

The timing of first intercourse differs by race and gender.

(*Source*: Michael et al., 1994, p. 91.)

Caucasian Men
Caucasian Women
African-American Men
African-American Women

was considered permissible for males but not for females. Women were told by society that "nice girls don't," while men heard that premarital sex was permissible—although they should be sure to marry virgins.

Today, however, the double standard has largely been supplanted by a new norm, called *permissiveness with affection*. According to this standard, premarital intercourse is viewed as permissible for both men and women if it occurs in the context of a long-term, committed, or loving relationship (Reiss, 1960; Hyde, 1994).

On the other hand, the demise of the double standard has not been complete. Attitudes toward sexual conduct are typically more lenient for males than for females. The nature of this difference extends across very different cultures. For instance, in Mexico, where there are strict standards against premarital sex, males are considerably more likely than females to have premarital sex (Liskin, 1985; Spira, Bajos, Bejin, & Beltzer, 1992; Johnson, Wadsworth, Wellings, & Bradshaw, 1992).

SEXUAL ORIENTATION: HETEROSEXUALITY AND HOMOSEXUALITY

When we consider adolescents' sexual development, the most frequent pattern is *heterosexuality*, sexual attraction and behavior directed to the opposite sex. Yet some teenagers do not follow this path. Instead, they experience *homosexual* feelings, sexual attraction to members of their own sex.

At one time or another, about 20 to 25 percent of adolescent boys, and 10 percent of adolescent girls, have at least one same-sex sexual encounter. However, many fewer adolescents become exclusively homosexual. Although accurate figures are difficult to obtain, estimates range from a low of 1.1 percent to a high of 10 percent. Most experts believe that between 4 and 10 percent of both men and women are exclusively homosexual during extended periods of their lives (Kinsey, Pomeroy, & Martin, 1948; McWhirter, Sanders, & Reinisch, 1990; Alan Guttmacher Institute, 1993b; Michael et al., 1994).

The difficulty in determining the proportion of people who are homosexual is due, in part, to the fact that homosexuality and heterosexuality are not completely distinct sexual orientations. Alfred Kinsey, a pioneer sex researcher, argued that sexual orientation should be viewed as a continuum, in which "exclusively homosexual" was at one end and "exclusively heterosexual" at the other (Kinsey et al., 1948). In-between are people who show both homosexual and heterosexual behavior.

The factors that induce people to develop as heterosexual or homosexual are not well understood. Increasing evidence suggests that genetic and biological factors may play an important role. For instance, evidence from studies of twins shows a higher joint incidence of homosexuality in identical twins than in nontwins. Other research finds that various structures of the brain are different in homosexuals and heterosexuals, and hormone production also seems to be linked to sexual orientation (LeVay, 1993; Gladue, 1994; Berenbaum & Snyder, 1995; Meyer-Bahlburg et al., 1995).

On the other hand, evidence of a biological cause is not yet conclusive, given that most findings are based on small samples (Byne & Parsons, 1994). Consequently, some researchers have suggested that family or peer environmental factors play a role. For example, Freud argued that homosexuality was the result of inappropriate identification with the opposite-sex parent (Freud, 1922/1959).

The difficulty with Freud's theoretical perspective and other, similar perspectives that followed is that there simply is no evidence to suggest that any particular family dynamic or childrearing practice is consistently related to sexual orientation. Similarly, explanations based on learning theory, which suggest that homosexuality arises because of rewarding, pleasant homosexual experiences and unsatisfying heterosexual ones, do not appear to be the complete answer (A. Bell & Weinberg, 1978; Isay, 1990).

In short, there is no accepted explanation of why some adolescents develop a heterosexual orientation and others a homosexual orientation. Most experts believe that sexual orientation develops out of a complex interplay of genetic, physiological, and environmental factors (Gladue, 1994).

What is clear is that adolescents who find themselves attracted to members of the same sex face a difficult time (Anderson, 1994). Society still harbors great ignorance and prejudice regarding homosexuality, persisting in the belief that people have a choice in the matter—which they do not. The result is that adolescents who find themselves to be homosexual are at greater risk for depression, and suicide rates are significantly higher for homosexual adolescents than for heterosexual adolescents.

Ultimately, though, most adolescents come to grips with their sexual orientation. Once they are past adolescence, homosexuals have the same overall degree of mental and physical health as do heterosexuals. Homosexuality is not considered a psychological disorder by any of the major psychological or medical associations, and all of them endorse efforts to reduce discrimination against homosexuals (Bersoff & Ogden, 1991; Herek, 1993; Patterson, 1994).

THE EPIDEMIC OF TEENAGE PREGNANCY

Every minute of the day, an adolescent in the United States gives birth. Every year, over a million women under the age of 20—one in every 10 teenage girls—become pregnant, and the pregnancy rate among teenage women aged 15–19 has increased 23 percent in the last two decades. Approximately half of all adolescent mothers are unmarried, and in some

The stresses of adolescence are magnified for homosexuals, who often face societal prejudice. Eventually, however, most adolescents come to grips with their sexual orientation, as these students at a symposium exemplify.

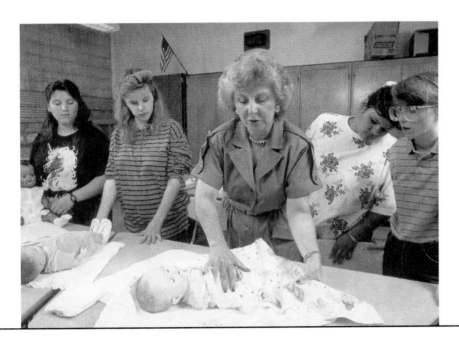

One of the difficulties faced by teenage mothers is their lack of knowledge about proper child-care techniques. These adolescents are enrolled in a class designed to teach them about infant care.

inner cities, 80 percent of teenagers who have babies are not married. Frequently, a mother must care for her child without the help of the father (Stevens-Simon & White, 1991; Alan Guttmacher Institute, 1994).

The results of an unintended pregnancy can be devastating to both mother and child. Without financial or emotional support, a mother may have to abandon her own education; consequently, she may be relegated to unskilled, poorly paying jobs for the rest of her life. In other cases, she may develop long-term dependency on welfare. Her physical and mental health may suffer (B.C. Miller, 1992; Baldwin, 1993; Prodromidis et al., 1994; Ambuel, 1995). (See Speaking of Development)

The children of teenage mothers also do not fare well when compared to children of older mothers. They are more likely to suffer from poor health and to show poorer school performance. Later, they are more likely to become teenage parents themselves, creating a cycle of pregnancy and poverty from which it is very difficult to extricate themselves (Furstenberg, Brooks-Gunn, & Morgan, 1987; Carnegie Task Force, 1994).

The severity of the problem of teenage pregnancies is peculiarly American. If we look at other industrialized countries, we find much lower rates of teenage pregnancy (Alan Guttmacher Institute, 1988; see Figure 12-6). Although it might be suspected that the higher rates of pregnancy in the United States are due to more frequent or earlier sexual activity, that is not the case. For instance, there is little difference among industrialized countries in the age at which adolescents first have sexual intercourse.

What does differ is the use of birth control. Teenage girls in the United States are much less likely to use contraception than teenagers in other countries. And even when they do use birth control, teenagers in the United States are less likely to use effective methods (Musick, 1993).

However, ineffective birth control is only part of the cause. An additional factor is that, despite increasing rates of premarital sexual behavior, people in the United States remain basically intolerant of premarital sex, and they are unwilling to provide the type of sex education that might reduce the rate of teenage pregnancies.

Although adolescent pregnancy and parenthood are difficult problems, some teenagers successfully break the poverty-and-pregnancy cycle. Two key factors for teenage mothers are completing high school and postponing future births. Social programs that help young mothers complete their education and that support them in other basic ways are critically important (Furstenberg et al., 1987; Buchholz & Korn-Bursztyn, 1993; Rauch-Elnekaone, 1994).

Directions in Development

Preventing Adolescent Pregnancies: Sex Education Programs That Work

According to surveys, almost 90 percent of Americans agree that all children should have sex education. Just what that sex education should consist of, however, is a question that elicits far less agreement.

Some proponents of sex education hold that the only appropriate message is 100 percent abstinence. However, there is little scientific evidence that such a message is effective: When carefully evaluated, the efficacy of programs that teach only abstinence is not conclusively supported (APA Public Policy Office, 1995). Particularly for adolescents who are already sexually active, abstinence is not a compelling message.

However, several types of sex education programs are effective. According to recent analyses, delays of two or more years in first sexual intercourse have been brought about in junior and senior high school students involved in such programs, compared with students

Speaking of Development

Patricia Canessa

Born: ························· 1948

Education: ······················ University of Chile, B.S. in biology; University of Colombia, M.A. in psychology; Northwestern University, Evanston, Illinois, M.A. in psychology; University of Rome, Italy, Ph.D. in family therapy

Position: ····················· Department director, the Arts of Living Institute

Home: ························ Chicago, Illinois

When a young teenage girl faces pregnancy, it can be a tough world, but for the past 24 years the Arts of Living Institute has helped hundreds of pregnant teenagers, aged 14 to 19, find new lives, raise healthy children, and make the transition from teenager to mother a bit more easily.

Department director Patricia Canessa, who has been with the institute for the past 10 years, notes that its success rate is attributable to a comprehensive program designed not only for the health of the pregnant teenager and her baby, but also for the new mother's social development.

Eighty-five to 90 percent of the pregnant teenagers who reach the institute come from the poorest areas of Chicago and are living below the poverty line, according to Canessa.

not in the programs. Furthermore, such programs reduced unprotected sexual intercourse by 40 percent among adolescents who were already sexually active (Ubell, 1995).

Effective programs make use of the basic concepts of learning theory, including reinforcement and modeling. They teach specific social skills that permit adolescents to say no effectively and to anticipate the pressures that they may confront in sexual situations. For instance, students are taught:

◆ that they will benefit—socially, physically, economically—from avoiding disease and averting unwanted pregnancy.

◆ how to delay first intercourse. Students learn—and practice, through role-playing with classmates—how to anticipate and avert sexual advances deftly and even pleasantly.

◆ how to get and use protection—usually condoms—if they are already sexually active.

◆ how to develop, through practice, confidence that the skills being learned will actually work in real-life situations (Ubell, 1995, p. 19–20).

Effective programs use exercises and games that promote student involvement. For instance, they employ role-playing and involve homework in which teenagers discuss sex with their parents. They also address the realities of caring for a baby. Teenagers

"We need . . . to be aware of potential conditions that might affect the pregnancy, such as a sexually transmitted disease or a urinary tract infection—two major contributors to low birth weight."

"The target of the program is comprehensive: to change a pattern of dysfunctional behaviors that cross generations, to break a cycle of behavior."

"Once the girl comes in with a parent, guardian, or relative who lives in the household, we gather the basic information, and a social worker then performs an extensive psychosocial assessment," Canessa explains.

"During the psychosocial assessment we explain the importance of developing the ability to do three things: establish social interactions, develop cognitively through academic accomplishments, and succeed behaviorally in a structured situation such as the school, the family, or the community."

The psychosocial assessment also covers the current living situation, a history of the family, and the precipitating factors that led to the current pregnancy, as perceived by the teenager. A health assessment follows the psychosocial assessment.

"We need know what the girl has been doing for prenatal care and to be aware of potential conditions that might affect the pregnancy, such as a sexually transmitted disease or a urinary tract infection—two major contributors to low birth weight," Canessa adds.

The teenager's reproductive history and a family health history are also taken. "We follow this with a brief parenting evaluation in which we stress the importance of the father and assess the role he will play in prenatal care, delivery, and parenting. The father can be interviewed either alone or with the girl," Canessa says. "We look at his educational level and his plans in terms of vocation, social development, and engagement in co-parenting activities."

Efforts are also made to reintegrate the girl into school. "The target of the program is comprehensive: to change a pattern of dysfunctional behaviors that cross generations, to break a cycle of behavior," says Canessa. "In working with the families we try to change the mother–daughter relationship so that the daughter–baby relationship is changed as well."

often have a romanticized view of what childrearing is all about. Exercises designed to make adolescents truly understand single parenthood drive home the difficulties involved.

No sex education program can be 100 percent effective. Still, researchers are making advances in producing programs that are increasingly effective. However, such programs are highly sensitive to political demands and pressures, and their implementation depends in part on the nation's political and social climate.

Review and Rethink

REVIEW

- ◆ The functions of dating in adolescence include intimacy, entertainment, and prestige. The ability to achieve intimacy develops gradually during the period.

- ◆ Masturbation, once viewed very negatively, is now generally regarded as a normal and harmless practice that continues into adulthood.

- ◆ Sexual intercourse is a major milestone that most people reach during adolescence. The age of first intercourse reflects cultural differences, and has been declining over the last 50 years.

- ◆ Sexual orientation, which is most accurately viewed as a continuum rather than as discrete categories, develops as the result of a complex combination of factors.

- ◆ Teenage pregnancy is a major problem in the United States, with negative consequences for adolescent mothers and their children. Effective sex education can reduce the incidence of teenage pregnancy.

RETHINK

- ◆ What factors in early and middle adolescence work against the achievement of true intimacy in dating?

- ◆ Do you think old social attitudes toward masturbation decreased its incidence? Are modern attitudes toward the practice likely to cause an increase? Why or why not?

- ◆ Why is the age of first intercourse declining? What factors contribute to a double standard toward sex for males and females?

- ◆ How might the interplay of genetic, physiological, and environmental factors influence sexual orientation? Can people decide to be or not to be homosexual or heterosexual?

- ◆ Are social programs that help pregnant teenagers complete high school and postpone future pregnancies giveaways? Do they benefit only pregnant teenagers, or are the benefits broader?

LOOKING BACK

How does the development of self-concept, self-esteem, and identity proceed during adolescence?

1. During adolescence, self-concept differentiates to encompass others' views as well as one's own. Adolescents become more perceptive as their views of themselves grow more organized and coherent, include multiple aspects simultaneously, and regard personal traits more abstractly than before. Sometimes this differentiation can cause confusion as different situations elicit behaviors that reflect a complex, rather than a simple, definition of the self.

2. The differentiation of self-concept permits a similar differentiation in self-esteem. Adolescents are able to evaluate particular aspects of themselves differently. Self-esteem can be affected not only by personal factors but also by gender, socioeconomic status, and race.

3. According to Erik Erikson, adolescents are in the identity-versus-role-diffusion stage, seeking to discover their individuality and identity. Faced with societal pressures to make important life decisions, adolescents may experience confusion and may sometimes exhibit dysfunctional reactions. They come to rely for help and information more on friends and peers than on adults, and some adolescents may undertake a psychological moratorium to explore various roles and possibilities.

4. In an expansion of Erikson's work, James Marcia finds four identity statuses that are determined by the presence or absence of crisis and commitment. The four stages are identity achievement, identity foreclosure, identity diffusion, and moratorium. People may fall into one category during adolescence, and later in life may reassess their choices and move into a different category.

What dangers do adolescents face as they deal with the stresses of adolescence?

5. Many adolescents have feelings of sadness and hopelessness, and some experience major depression, a psychological disorder with enduring effects. Biological, environmental, and social factors contribute to depression, and there are gender, ethnic, and racial differences in the likelihood of its occurrence. The fact that the incidence of depression is higher among girls than among boys may be due to confusing societal expectations for girls and differences in the ways boys and girls react to stress.

6. The rate of adolescent suicide is rising, with suicide now the third most common cause of death in the 15-to-24-year-old bracket. The reasons for this increase are not fully understood, but adolescent stresses and family situations are being examined closely for causal links.

7. Individuals who come into contact with adolescents should be aware of the warning signs of suicide, including talk about suicide, school problems, making a will, or communicating long-term plans for possessions or pets, depression, eating problems, and dramatic changes in behavior. When suicide is suspected, the proper steps include listening and being actively supportive, finding help, removing hazards, and maintaining close contact.

How does the quality of relationships with family and peers change during adolescence?

8. Adolescents' quest for autonomy often brings confusion and tension to their relationships with their parents, as parents and children work out their changing roles and strike a new balance of power. In part, the tension can be attributed to differences in

parents' and children's definitions of appropriate and inappropriate behavior, but the actual "generation gap" between parents' and teenagers' attitudes is usually small.

9. Peers are important during adolescence because they provide a means of social comparison and offer reference groups against which to judge social success. Relationships among adolescents are characterized by the need to belong, whether to a clique or a crowd. Group membership brings peer acceptance, but can limit behavior by imposing stereotypical expectations.

What are gender and race relations like in adolescence?

10. The strict sex cleavage characterizing gender relations in middle childhood and early adolescence diminishes at puberty. Boys and girls begin to spend time together in groups and, toward the end of adolescence, to pair off.

11. In general, segregation between the races increases in middle and late adolescence, even in schools with a diverse student body. Racial separation may be due not only to race per se but also to socioeconomic status, different academic achievement and class assignments, and mutually distrustful attitudes. A very high degree of consistent interaction between adolescents of different races can help alleviate segregation.

What does it mean to be popular and unpopular in adolescence, and how do adolescents respond to peer pressure?

12. Degrees of popularity during adolescence include popular and controversial adolescents (on the high end of popularity) and neglected and rejected adolescents (on the low end). Popular adolescents enjoy a greater number of friendships, activities, and relationships with the opposite sex than do their less popular peers.

13. The phenomenon of peer pressure during adolescence is not as simple as often thought. In actuality, adolescents rely on and conform to their peers in areas where they regard their peers as experts, and they rely on and conform to adults in areas of adult expertise. As adolescents grow in confidence, their conformity to both peers and adults declines.

14. Although most do not commit crimes, adolescents are disproportionately involved in criminal activities. Juvenile delinquents can be categorized as either undersocialized or socialized delinquents. Undersocialized delinquents are raised with harsh or uncaring parental supervision and begin criminal activity prior to adolescence. In contrast, socialized delinquents know and subscribe to the norms of society and are fairly normal psychologically. They are less likely to be involved in crime past adolescence.

What are the functions and characteristics of dating during adolescence?

15. During adolescence, dating has several functions, serving as a way for adolescents to establish intimacy, as a form of entertainment, and even as a means of achieving social prestige.

16. Development of psychological intimacy is difficult at first, due to early adolescents' unwillingness to expose themselves psychologically. True intimacy comes later, as adolescents mature, gain confidence, and take relationships more seriously.

How does sexuality develop in the adolescent years?

17. For most adolescents, masturbation serves as their initiation into sexuality. Past views of masturbation have changed, and today this widespread practice is generally regarded as normal and harmless.

18. Sexual intercourse, which generally begins in the teens, is regarded as a major milestone. The age of first intercourse has declined over the past 50 years, as the double standard that restricted premarital sex exclusively to men and "bad girls" has faded and

as the norm of permissiveness with affection has gained ground.

19. Most people's sexual orientation is largely or entirely heterosexual, with between 4 and 10 percent being mostly or exclusively homosexual. Sexual orientation, which should probably be viewed as a continuum rather than as independent categories, apparently develops out of a complex interplay of genetic, physiological, and environmental factors. Because they face societal disapproval, homosexual adolescents are at greater risk for depression and suicide than are heterosexual adolescents.

Why is teenage pregnancy a particular problem in the United States, and what can be done about it?

20. Pregnancy among teenagers is reaching epidemic proportions in the United States, with about 10 percent of girls under 20 becoming pregnant each year. Adolescent childbirth can have highly negative effects for mother and child. The incidence of both contraception and sex education is comparatively low in the United States, which contributes to the high rate of adolescent pregnancy.

21. Effective sex education holds out the promise of decreasing the incidence of teenage pregnancy. Effective sex education involves more than simple advocacy of abstinence; it also teaches the benefits of avoiding unwanted pregnancies, practical methods of delaying first intercourse and averting sexual advances, and ways to get and use protection.

KEY TERMS AND CONCEPTS

identity-versus-role-diffusion stage (p. 411)
identity achievement (p. 412)
identity foreclosure (p. 412)
identity diffusion (p. 413)
moratorium (p. 413)
cluster suicide (p. 416)
autonomy (p. 419)
generation gap (p. 420)

reference group (p. 422)
cliques (p. 422)
crowds (p. 422)
sex cleavage (p. 422)
peer pressure (p. 426)
undersocialized delinquents (p. 427)
socialized delinquents (p. 427)
masturbation (p. 430)

PART 6

Early Adulthood

Physical and Cognitive Development

CHAPTER OUTLINE

Spotting him as he emerges from beneath a shady tree, the coach goes over and places one arm across the runner's sweaty back. Even though Tony Gorczyca has just claimed an Olympic victory in the 5,000 meters, his coach is not about to let it go to his head.

"It sure got boring watching you run around in circles," the coach, Dave Landau, says as he squints against the blazing sun. "You looked like a gerbil out there."

Gorczyca pauses momentarily, letting Landau's words sink in, then shoots back his reply: "Anytime you want to race, let me know."

It is a warm retort, made of friendship. After a spring of training together, these two Montgomery County [Maryland] residents have established a bond of respect that extends far beyond the white lanes of the track. And while he himself is a marathoner, Landau knows Gorczyca could pose a challenge were they to race—even though Gorczyca is mentally retarded and suffers from a disease that has left him with an under-developed right leg and arm, blind in one eye and prone to violent seizures. (Wisnia, 1994, p. D5)

LOOKING AHEAD

Most young adults do not face the physical challenges—let alone the mental hurdles—that Tony Gorczyca faces. In fact, for most people, early adulthood is a time when the body acts as if on automatic pilot: People are at the peak of their physical health and fitness. Intellectually, too, early adults are enjoying the height of their cognitive abilities.

At the same time, considerable development continues during this period, which starts at the end of adolescence (about age 20) and continues until roughly the start of middle age (about age 40). As we'll see throughout this and the following chapter, significant changes occur as new opportunities arise and people choose to take on (or to forgo) a new set of roles as spouse, parent, and worker.

This chapter focuses on physical and cognitive development. It begins with a look at the physical changes that extend into early adulthood. We'll see that growth not only continues, but also various motor skills change. We look at diet and weight, examining the prevalence of obesity. We also consider stress and coping during the early years of adulthood.

The chapter then turns to cognitive development. Although traditional approaches to cognitive development regarded adulthood as an inconsequential plateau, we'll examine some new theories that suggest that significant cognitive growth occurs during adulthood. We'll also consider the nature of adult intelligence and how life events are reflected in cognitive development.

Finally, the last part of the chapter considers college, the institution that shapes intellectual growth for those who attend. After considering who goes to college, we'll consider how gender and race are related to achievement. We end by looking at some reasons why students drop out of college, and we examine some of the adjustment problems that college students face.

In short, after reading this chapter, you'll be able to answer these questions:

◆ How does the body develop during early adulthood, and to what risks are young adults exposed?

443

♦ What are the effects of stress, and what can be done about it?

♦ Does cognitive development continue in young adulthood?

♦ How is intelligence defined today, and what causes cognitive growth in young adults?

♦ Who attends college today, and how is the college population changing?

♦ What do students learn in college, and what difficulties do they face?

PHYSICAL DEVELOPMENT AND STRESS

It's 5:00 P.M. Rosa Convoy, a 25-year-old single mother, has just finished her work as a receptionist at a dentist's office and is on her way home. She has exactly two hours to pick up her daughter, Zoe, from day care, get home, make and eat dinner, pick up and return with a babysitter from down the street, say goodbye to Zoe, and get to her 7 o'clock programming class at a local community college. It's a marathon she runs every Tuesday and Thursday night, and she knows she doesn't have a second to spare if she wants to reach the class on time.

It doesn't take an expert to know what Rosa Convoy is experiencing: stress. Like those of other young adults, Rosa's days pass in a blur of activity, sometimes, it seems, taxing her body—and mind—to the breaking point.

How well Rosa can cope with the multiple demands she faces depends on a complex interplay between physical and psychological factors (Hetherington & Blechman, 1995). As we'll see, although most people reach the height of their physical capacities in young adulthood, the stress produced by the challenges of life may sometimes be overwhelming.

PHYSICAL DEVELOPMENT AND THE SENSES

In most respects, physical development and maturation are complete at early adulthood. Most people are at the peak of their physical capabilities. They have attained their full height, and their limbs are proportional to their size, rendering the gangliness of adolescence a memory. People in their early 20s tend to be healthy, vigorous, and energetic.

On the other hand, not all growth is complete. Some people, particularly late maturers, continue to gain height in their early 20s. Furthermore, certain parts of the body do not fully mature until early adulthood. For instance, the brain continues to grow in both size and weight, reaching its maximum during early adulthood. Brain-wave patterns may also reveal change during early adulthood, although many people in their early 20s show mature patterns (Haug, 1991; Scheibel, 1992; Friedman, Berman, & Hamberger, 1993).

The senses are as sharp as they will ever be. Although there are changes in the elasticity of the eye—a continuation of an aging process that may begin as early as 10—they are so minor that they produce no deterioration in vision. It is not until the 40s, as we'll see in Chapter 15, that eyesight changes sufficiently to be noticeable.

Hearing, too, is at its peak. However, a gender difference emerges: Women can detect higher tones more readily than can men (McGuinness, 1972). In general, though, the hearing of both men and women is quite good. Under quiet conditions the average young adult can hear the ticking of a watch 20 feet away.

The other senses, including taste, smell, and sensitivity to touch and pain, are excellent, and they remain that way throughout early adulthood. These senses do not begin to deteriorate until people are in their 40s or 50s.

MOTOR FUNCTIONING, FITNESS, AND HEALTH: STAYING WELL

If you are a professional athlete, most people probably consider you to be over the hill by the time you leave your 20s. Although there are notable exceptions (think of baseball star Nolan Ryan, who was still playing in his 40s, for instance), even athletes who train constantly tend to lose their physical edge once they reach their 30s. In some sports, the peak passes even earlier. In swimming, for instance, women reach their peak at age 18, and men at age 20 (Schultz & Curnow, 1988).

Most professional athletes—as well as the rest of us—are at the peak of their psychomotor abilities during early adulthood. Reaction time is quicker, muscle strength is greater, and eye-hand coordination is better than at any other period (Salthouse, 1993; Sliwinski, Buschke, Kuslansky, & Senior, 1994).

Physical Fitness.   The physical prowess that typically characterizes early adulthood doesn't come naturally, however; nor does it come to everyone. For people to reach their physical potential, they must exercise and maintain a proper diet.

The benefits of exercise are hardly secret: In the United States, jazzercize and aerobics classes, Nordic Traks and Nautilus workouts, and jogging and swimming are common and seemingly ubiquitous activities. Yet the conspicuousness of exercise activities is misleading. No more than 10 percent of Americans are involved in sufficient regular exercise to keep them in good physical shape, and less than a quarter engage in even moderate regular exercise (MMWR, 1989; Kaplan, Sallis, & Patterson, 1993). Furthermore, the opportunity to exercise is largely an upper- and middle-class phenomenon; people of lower socioeconomic status (SES) often have neither the time nor the money to engage in regular exercise (Atkins, Senn, Rupp, & Kaplan, 1990).

However, the advantages to those who do become involved in regular exercise programs are many. Exercise increases cardiovascular fitness, meaning that the heart and circulatory system operate more efficiently. Furthermore, lung capacity increases, raising endurance. Muscles become stronger, and the body is more flexible and manueverable. The range of movement is greater, and the muscles, tendons, and ligaments are more elastic. Moreover, exercise during this period helps reduce *osteoporosis*, the thinning of the bones, in later life.

Exercise also may optimize the immune response of the body, helping it fight off disease. Exercise may even decrease stress and anxiety and reduce depression. It can provide people with a sense of control over their bodies, as well as impart a feeling of accomplishment (Brown, 1991; P.A. Gross, 1991).

Regular exercise provides another, ultimately more important reward: It increases longevity. In brief, the higher the level of fitness, the lower the death rate (see Figure 13-1; Blair et al., 1989).

Health.   Although a lack of exercise may produce poor health (and worse), health risks, in general, are relatively slight in early adulthood. During this period, people are less susceptible to colds and other minor illnesses than they were as children, and when they do come down with illnesses, they usually get over them quickly.

Adults in their 20s and 30s stand a higher risk of dying from accidents, primarily those involving automobiles, than from most other causes. But there are other killers: Among the leading sources of death for people 25 to 34 are AIDS, cancer, heart disease, and suicide. Amid the grim statistics of mortality, age 35 represents a significant milestone. It is at that point that illness and disease overtake accidents as the leading cause of death—the first time this is true since infancy.

Not all people fare equally well during early adulthood. For instance, men are more apt to die than are women, primarily due to men's higher involvement in automobile accidents. Furthermore, African-Americans have twice the death rate of Caucasians, and minorities in general have a higher likelihood of dying than the Caucasian majority.

Professional athletes, like tennis player Jana Novotna, are at the peak of their psychomotor abilities during early adulthood.

FIGURE 13-1

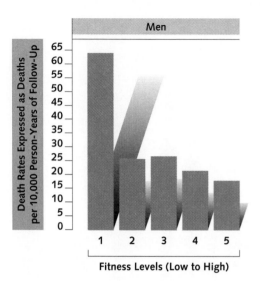

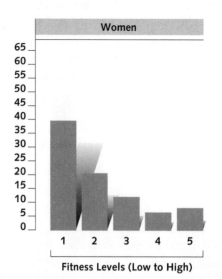

THE RESULT OF FITNESS: LONGEVITY.

The greater the fitness level, the lower the death rate tends to be for both men and women.

(*Source*: Blair et al., 1989.)

Another major cause of death for men is violence, particularly in the United States, where the murder rate is significantly higher than in any other developed country (see Figure 13-2). Compare, for instance, the U.S. murder rate of 21.9 per 100,000 men to Japan's 0.5 murders per 100,000 men—a difference in magnitude of more than 4,000 percent. Statistics like this one have led some observers to conclude that violence is "as American as apple pie" (Fingerhut & Kleinman, 1990; Berkowitz, 1993).

Murder rates also depend significantly on racial factors. Although murder is the fifth most frequent cause of death for young adult white Americans, it is *the* most likely cause of death for African-Americans, and it is a significant factor for Hispanic-Americans. In some areas of the country, a young black male has a higher probability of being murdered than a

The murder rate in the United States is significantly higher than in any other developed country.

FIGURE 13-2

The murder rate (per 100,000 men) is far higher in the United States than in any other developed country.

(*Source*: Fingerhut & Kleinman, 1990.)

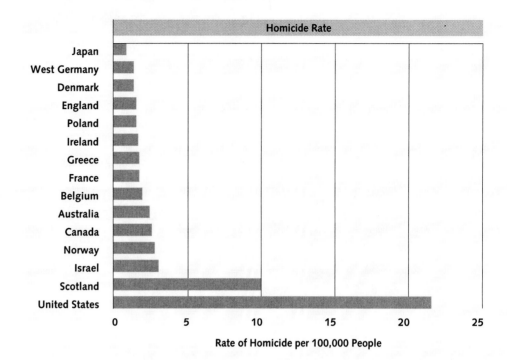

soldier in the Vietnam War had of being killed. Overall, an African-American male has a 1 in 21 chance of being murdered during his lifetime. In contrast, a white male has a 1 in 131 chance of being murdered (CDC, 1991; Berkowitz, 1993; Triandis, 1994).

EATING, NUTRITION, AND OBESITY: A WEIGHTY CONCERN

Most young adults know what foods are nutritionally sound and how to maintain a balanced diet; they just don't bother to follow the rules. And the rules are not all that difficult to follow.

Good Nutrition. According to guidelines provided by the U.S. Department of Agriculture, people can achieve good nutrition by eating foods that are low in fat, such as vegetables, fruits, whole grain foods, fish, poultry, lean meats, and low-fat dairy products. In addition, increased consumption of whole-grain foods and cereal products, vegetables (including dried beans and peas), and fruit helps people raise the amount of complex carbohydrates and fiber they ingest. Milk and other sources of calcium also need to be included to prevent osteoporosis. Finally, everyone should reduce salt intake (U.S.D.A., 1992; see Figure 13-3).

During adolescence, a poor diet doesn't always present a significant problem. For instance, teenagers do not suffer too much from a diet high in junk foods and fat because they are undergoing such tremendous growth. The story changes when they reach young adulthood, however. With growth tapering off, young adults must reduce the caloric intake they were used to during adolescence.

Many do not. Although most people enter young adulthood with average bodies in terms of height and weight, they gradually put on weight if their poor dietary habits remain unchanged (Insel & Roth, 1991).

Obesity. The population of the United States is growing—in more ways than one. Obesity, defined as body weight that is 20 percent or more above the average weight for a

FIGURE 13-3

THE CURRENT U.S. GOVERNMENT NUTRITIONAL GUIDELINES.

Foods at the base of the pyramid are those that are needed most often; the ones at the top should be eaten infrequently.

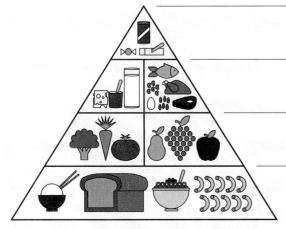

The small tip of the pyramid shows fats, oils, and sweets. These are foods such as salad dressings and oils, cream, butter, margarine, sugars, soft drinks, candies, and sweet desserts. These foods provide calories and little else nutritionally. Most people should use them sparingly.

On this level of the Food Guide Pyramid are two groups of foods that come mostly from animals: milk, yogurt, and cheese; and meat, poultry, fish, dry beans, eggs, and nuts. These foods are important for protein, calcium, iron, and zinc.

This level includes foods that come from plants–vegetables and fruits. Most people need to eat more of these foods for the vitamins, minerals, and fiber they supply.

At the base of the Food Guide Pyramid are breads, cereals, rice, and pasta–all foods from grains. You need the most servings of these foods each day.

(Adapted from U.S. Department of Agriculture, 1995.)

person of a given height, is on the rise in the United States: The proportion of the population classified as obese increased by 31 percent from 1980 to 1991 (National Center for Health Statistics, 1994).

Some 7 percent of men and 10 percent of women between the ages of 20 and 25 are classified as obese. The numbers edge up throughout adulthood: At each age increment, a larger percentage of people is classified as obese.

Furthermore, it is not only weight that increases with age; so does the amount of fat in the body. By the age of 18, men's bodies contain approximately 15 to 18 percent body fat, and women's bodies are 20 to 25 percent body fat. However, by the age of 50, body fat in men usually doubles, and body fat in women typically increases by 50 percent (Bray, 1983, 1990).

The exact processes that lead people to become obese remain a mystery. Some evidence suggests that genetic factors may be at the core of the problem. For instance, researchers have identified specific genes that produce inherited obesity in mice, as well as a gene in humans that appears almost identical. The gene regulates the size of the body's fat stores, apparently by controlling the release of particular types of hormones. It seems plausible, then, that inherited factors play a role in obesity (Y. Zhang et al., 1994b).

On the other hand, environmental and social factors may also be at work in producing obesity. Obese people might be oversensitive to external eating cues based on social standards, such as eating meals at a certain time regardless of whether or not they are hungry. At the same time, they may be less sensitive to the internal cues that, in nonobese people, regulate hunger. For example, when bowls of crackers are placed near people in experiments who have just consumed sandwiches, obese people eat more crackers than do nonobese people—ignoring internal physiological cues that tell them they are already full (Schachter, Goldman, & Gordon, 1968).

Other research suggests that obese individuals may have higher weight set points than do people of normal weight. The **weight set point** is the particular level of weight that the body strives to maintain (Nisbett, 1972; Kupfermann, 1991; Stallone & Stunkard, 1991). The weight set point acts as a type of internal weight thermostat, calling for either more or less food intake, depending on the amount of nutrients required by the body.

weight set point *the particular level of weight that the body strives to maintain*

According to the weight-set-point explanation, obese individuals have weight set points that are unusually high, making them particularly vulnerable to external, social cues about foods. Consequently, they are more likely to eat and perpetuate their obesity. Furthermore, as they become obese, their fat cells increase in number and size, which leads to a further rise in weight set point. This cycle obviously makes it very difficult to lower the weight set point—and lose weight permanently (Logue, 1991).

In fact, weight control is a difficult, and often losing, battle for many young adults. Most people who diet ultimately regain the weight they have lost, and they become involved in a see-saw cycle of weight gain and loss (Heatherton, Polivy, & Herman, 1991; Lowe, 1993). In fact, some obesity experts now argue that the rate of dieting failure is so great that people may want to avoid dieting altogether. Instead, if people eat the foods they really want in moderation, they may be able to avoid the binge eating that often occurs when diets fail. Even though obese people may never reach their desired weight, they may, according to this reasoning, ultimately control their weight more effectively (Polivy & Herman, 1985, 1991).

Developmental Diversity

Physical Disabilities: Coping With Physical Challenges

The physically-challenged face a variety of obstacles, despite the passage of the Americans with Disabilities Act in 1990, which mandates full access to public establishments.

Some 43 million Americans are physically challenged, according to the official definition of *disability*—a condition that substantially limits a major life activity such as walking or vision. Like Tony Gorczyca, whose story began this chapter, people with disabilities face a difficult, challenging path.

Statistics paint a grim picture of a minority group that is undereducated and underemployed. Fewer than 10 percent of people with major handicaps have finished high school, and fewer than 25 percent of disabled men and 15 percent of disabled women work fulltime. Overall, between 50 and 75 percent of all adults with handicaps are unemployed (U.S. Commission on Civil Rights, 1983).

Furthermore, even if people with disabilities do find work, the positions are often routine and low-paying. For example, 46 percent of workers with disabilities earn less than $15,000 per year, compared with 22 percent of nondisabled workers (Schaefer & Lamm, 1992).

Individuals with disabilities face several kinds of barriers to leading full lives that are completely integrated into the broader society. Some barriers are physical. Despite passage of the landmark Americans with Disabilities Act (ADA) in 1990, which mandates full access to public establishments such as stores, office buildings, hotels, and theaters, people in wheelchairs still cannot gain access to many older buildings.

Another barrier—sometimes harder to overcome than a physical one—is prejudice and discrimination. People with disabilities sometimes face pity or avoidance from nondisabled people. Some nondisabled people focus so much on the disability that they overlook other characteristics, reacting to a person with a disability only as a problem category and not as an individual. Others treat people with disabilities as though they were children (Heward & Orlansky, 1988). Ultimately, such treatment can take its toll on the way people with disabilities think about themselves.

STRESS AND COPING: DEALING WITH LIFE'S CHALLENGES

Few of us need much of an introduction to **stress**, the response to events that threaten or challenge us. Stress is a part of nearly everyone's existence, and our lives are crowded with events and circumstances, known as *stressors*, that produce threats to our well-being. Stressors need not be unpleasant events: Even the happiest events, such as starting a long-sought-after job or planning a wedding, can produce stress (Sarason, Johnson, & Siegel, 1978; Brown & McGill, 1989).

Stress triggers several outcomes. The most immediate is typically a biological reaction, as certain hormones, secreted by the adrenal glands, cause a rise in heart rate, blood pressure, respiration rate, and sweating. In some situations, these immediate effects may be beneficial because they produce an "emergency reaction" in the sympathetic nervous system by which people are better able to defend themselves from a sudden, threatening situation.

On the other hand, long-term, continuous exposure to stressors may result in a reduction of the body's ability to deal with stress. As stress-related hormones are constantly secreted, the heart, blood vessels, and other body tissues may deteriorate. As a consequence, people become more susceptible to diseases as their ability to fight off germs declines (Kiecolt-Glaser & Glaser, 1986; Schneiderman, 1983; Cohen, Tyrrell, & Smith, 1991).

The Origins of Stress   Not every situation produces stress. What makes some situations stressful? According to psychologists Richard Lazarus and Susan Folkman, people move through a series of stages, depicted in Figure 13-4, that determine whether they will experience stress (Lazarus & Folkman, 1984; Lazarus, 1968, 1991).

Primary appraisal is the first step—the assessment of an event to determine whether its implications are positive, negative, or neutral. If the event is seen as primarily negative, it is appraised in terms of the harm that it has caused in the past, how threatening it is likely to be, and how likely it is that the challenge can be resisted successfully.

Secondary appraisal follows. This is the assessment of whether one's coping abilities and resources are adequate to overcome the harm, threat, or challenge posed by the potential stressor. At this point in the process, people try to determine whether they will be able to confront the dangers in the situation. If resources are lacking, and the potential threat is great, they will experience stress.

stress   *the response to events that threaten or challenge people*

primary appraisal   *the assessment of an event to determine whether its implications are positive, negative, or neutral*

secondary appraisal   *the assessment of whether one's coping abilities and resources are adequate to overcome the harm, threat, or challenge posed by the potential stressor*

Although we commonly think of negative events, such as auto mishaps, leading to stress, even welcome events can be stressful.

FIGURE 13-4

STEPS LEADING TO THE PERCEPTION OF STRESS.

The way in which a potential stressor is appraised determines whether stress will be experienced.

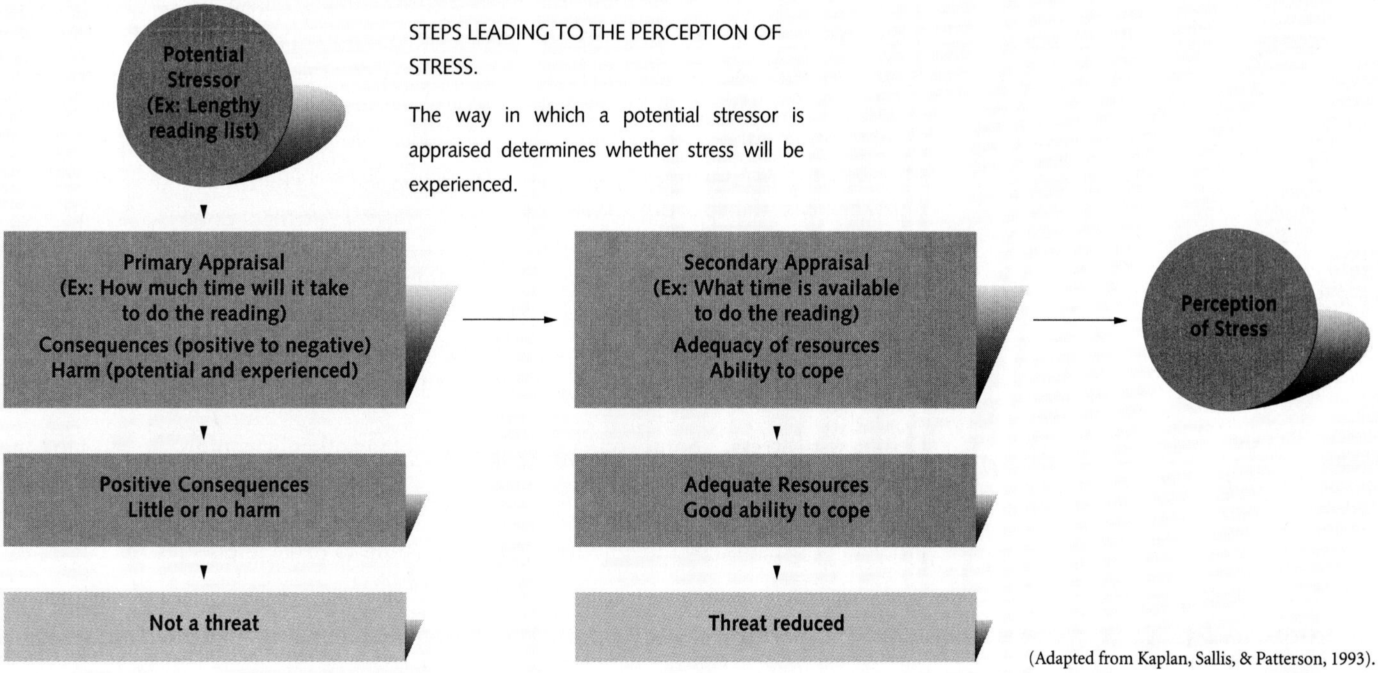

Potential Stressor
(Ex: Lengthy reading list)

▼

Primary Appraisal
(Ex: How much time will it take to do the reading)
Consequences (positive to negative)
Harm (potential and experienced)

Secondary Appraisal
(Ex: What time is available to do the reading)
Adequacy of resources
Ability to cope

Perception of Stress

▼

Positive Consequences
Little or no harm

Adequate Resources
Good ability to cope

▼

Not a threat

Threat reduced

(Adapted from Kaplan, Sallis, & Patterson, 1993).

Clearly, stress is a very personal response. Some people in early adulthood find hang gliding and rock climbing diverting and entertaining; for the rest of us, such activities would bring about a good deal of stress.

Still, some general principles help predict when an event will be appraised as stressful. Psychologist Shelley Taylor (1991) suggests the following:

♦ Events and circumstances that produce negative emotions are more likely to lead to stress than are events that are positive. For example, planning for the adoption of a new baby produces less stress than dealing with the illness of a loved one.

♦ Situations that are uncontrollable or unpredictable are more likely to produce stress than are those that can be controlled and predicted. Professors who give surprise quizzes in their classes produce more stress than do those whose quizzes are scheduled in advance.

♦ Events and circumstances that are ambiguous and confusing produce more stress than those that are unambiguous and clear. If they cannot easily understand a situation, people must struggle simply to comprehend it, rather than to deal with it directly.

♦ People who must accomplish simultaneously many tasks that strain their capabilities are more likely to experience stress than those who have fewer things to do.

The Consequences of Stress.   If enough stress is experienced in a short time span, it can have formidable costs. Over the long run, the constant wear-and-tear caused by the physiological arousal that occurs as the body tries to fight off stress produces negative effects. For instance, headaches, backaches, skin rashes, indigestion, chronic fatigue, and even the common cold are stress-related illnesses (Kiecolt-Glaser & Kiecolt-Glaser, 1991; Cohen, Tyrrell, & Smith, 1993).

Stress may also lead to **psychosomatic disorders**, medical problems caused by the interaction of psychological, emotional, and physical difficulties. For instance, ulcers,

psychosomatic disorders   *medical problems caused by the interaction of psychological, emotional, and physical difficulties* asthma, arthritis, and high blood pressure may—although not invariably—be produced by stress (Lepore, Palsane, & Evans, 1991).

Stress can even cause more serious, life-threatening, illnesses. According to some research, the greater the number of stressful events a person experiences over the course of a year, the more likely he or she is to have a major illness (see Table 13-1; Holmes & Rahe, 1967).

Before you start computing whether you are overdue for a major illness, however, keep in mind some important limitations to the research. Not everyone who experiences high stress becomes ill, and the weights given to particular stressors probably vary from one person to the next. Furthermore, there is a kind of circularity to such enumerations of stressors: Because the research is correlational, it is possible that someone who has a major illness to begin with is more likely to experience some of the stressors on the list. For example, a person may have lost a job *because* of the effects of an illness, rather than developing an illness because he or she lost a job. Still, the list of stressors does at least provide a way to consider how most people react to various potentially stressful events in their lives.

Coping with Stress.   Some young adults are better than others at **coping**, the effort to control, reduce, or tolerate the threats that lead to stress. What is the key to successful coping?

Some people use *problem-focused coping*, by which they attempt to manage a stressful problem or situation by directly changing the situation to make it less stressful. For exam-

coping   *the effort to control, reduce, or learn to tolerate the threats that lead to stress*

Speaking of Development

Patricia Norris

Born: ································· 1932

Education: ······················· University of California at Santa Barbara, B.A. in psychology; Union Institute, Cincinnati, Ohio, Ph.D. in psychology.

Position: ························· Director of psychoneuroimmunology at the Life Sciences Institute of Mind-Body Health

Home: ···························· Topeka, Kansas

After 14 years as director of the Biofeedback and Psychophysiology Center at the Menninger Clinic in Topeka, Kansas, Patricia Norris went into private practice in 1994.

Today, as director of psychoneuroimmunology—the study of the relationship between the body's immune system and psychological factors—at the Life Sciences Institute of Mind-Body Health, Norris works with people who face stress and pain in their everyday lives.

"Just about everyone would agree that any patient who goes to a doctor is experiencing stress on several levels, whether the stress is psychological or physical," she says. "Our main work here focuses on teaching self-regulation, helping people to discover how their own bodies respond—in helpful or unhelpful ways—and to learn to respond consciously and healthfully to all types of things, including panic, anxiety, pain, and life's events. Self-regulation is the bottom line.

"Biofeedback is a technique that people can observe and use. They can watch their hearts actually beat slower," she notes, "and then they can learn to use their knowledge as a tool for self-regulation."

Through biofeedback, Norris teaches patients how to control their muscles and blood flow, a strategy that she has found works well in helping relieve both pain and stress.

ple, a man who is having on-the-job difficulties might speak to his boss and ask that his responsibilities be modified.

Other people employ *emotion-focused coping*, which involves the conscious regulation of emotion. For instance, a mother who is having trouble finding appropriate care for her child while she is at work might tell herself that she should look at the bright side: At least she has a job in a difficult economy (Folkman & Lazarus, 1980, 1988).

Coping is also aided by the presence of *social support*, assistance and comfort supplied by others. Turning to others in the face of stress can provide both emotional support (in the form of a shoulder to cry on) and practical, tangible support (such as a temporary loan) (Sarason, Sarason, & Pierce, 1990; Lepore, Evans, & Schneider, 1991; Croyle & Hunt, 1991; Lepore et al., 1991; Spiegel, 1993).

Finally, even if people do not consciously cope with stress, some psychologists suggest that they may use unconscious defensive coping mechanisms about which they are not aware and which aid in stress reduction. *Defensive coping* involves unconscious strategies that distort or deny the true nature of a situation. For instance, people may deny the seriousness of a threat, trivializing a life-threatening illness, or they may say to themselves that academic failure on a series of tests is unimportant. The problem with such defensive coping is that it does not deal with the reality of the situation; it merely avoids or ignores the problem.

"Our main work here focuses on teaching self-regulation, helping people to discover how their own bodies respond."

"If we think of stress as what is going on in our lives, there isn't much that we can do about it. But if we think of stress as a response, there's a lot we can do. We can actually learn to change the response on a physiological and psychological level," she explains.

"We start with learning to change reactions. It's not your life that is killing you; it's your reactions to it," Norris says. "People aren't capable of dealing with stress until they learn internal strategies for changing their reactions. Once they are able to change their reactions, they can decide to make bigger and more central changes.

"For instance, people with high blood pressure know they should exercise and cut out salt, but because of their tension they don't do it. Once they're able to manage their stress, they can begin to make the changes they need in their lives to treat the high blood pressure itself.

"Many times people's stress patterns come out of their early developmental history. As they start to change some of their stress reactions, they often get in touch with very early life events, beliefs, or 'scripts' they wrote for themselves. Probably all of our stress patterns are developmental in nature."

"If we think of stress as what is going on in our lives, there isn't much that we can do about it. But if we think of stress as a response, there's a lot we can do."

TABLE 13-1

WILL STRESS IN YOUR LIFE PRODUCE ILLNESS?

Using the following scale, you can assess the degree of stress in your life (Rahe & Arthur, 1978). To do this, take the stressor value given beside each event you have experienced and multiply it by the number of occurrences over the past year (up to a maximum of four), then add up the scores.

87	Experienced the death of a spouse	50	Changed to a different line of work
77	Getting married	49	Had a major change in amount of independence and responsibility
77	Experienced the death of a close family member	47	Had a major change in responsibilities at work
76	Getting divorced	46	Experienced a major change in use of alcohol
74	Experienced a marital separation from mate	45	Revised personal habits
68	Experienced the death of a close friend	44	Had trouble with school administration
68	Experienced pregnancy or fathered a pregnancy	43	Held a job while attending school
65	Had a major personal injury or illness	43	Had a major change in social activities
62	Were fired from work	42	Had trouble with in-laws
60	Ended a marital engagement or a steady relationship	42	Had a major change in working hours or conditions
58	Had sexual difficulties	42	Changed residence or living conditions
58	Experienced a marital reconciliation with your mate	41	Had your spouse begin or cease work outside the home
57	Had a major change in self-concept or self-awareness	41	Changed your choice of major field of study
56	Experienced a major change in the health or behavior of a family member	41	Changed dating habits
54	Became engaged to be married	40	Had an outstanding personal achievement
53	Had a major change in financial status	38	Had trouble with your boss
52	Took on a mortgage or loan of less than $10,000	38	Had a major change in amount of participation in school activities
52	Had a major change in use of drugs	37	Had a major change in type and/or amount of recreation
50	Had a major conflict or change in values	36	Had a major change in church activites
50	Had a major change in the number of arguments with your spouse	34	Had a major change in sleeping habits
50	Gained a new family member	33	Took a trip or vacation
50	Entered college	30	Had a major change in eating habits
50	Changed to a new school	26	Had a major change in the number of family get-togethers
		22	Were found guilty of minor violations of the law

A total score of 1,435 or higher places you in a high-stress category. According to Marx, Garrity, & Bowers (1975), a high score increases the chances of experiencing a future stress-related illness, although it certainly does not guarantee it.

The Informed Consumer of Development

Coping with Stress

Although no single formula can cover all cases of stress, some general guidelines can help all of us cope with the stress that is part of our lives. Among them are the following (Holahan & Moos, 1987, 1990; Greenglass & Burke, 1991; Kaplan et al., 1993; Sacks, 1993).

◆ Seek control over the situation producing the stress. Putting yourself in charge of a situation that is producing stress can take you a long way toward coping with it.

TABLE 13-2

HOW TO ELICIT THE RELAXATION RESPONSE

Some general advice on regular practice of the relaxation response:

- Try to find 10 to 20 minutes in your daily routine; before breakfast is a good time.
- Sit comfortably.
- For the period you will practice, try to arrange your life so you won't have distractions. Put the phone on the answering machine, and ask someone else to watch the kids.
- Time yourself by glancing periodically at a clock or watch (but don't set an alarm). Commit yourself to a specific length of practice, and try to stick to it.

There are several approaches to eliciting the relaxation response. Here is one standard set of instructions:

Step 1. Pick a focus word or short phrase that's firmly rooted in your personal belief system. For example, a nonreligious individual might choose a neutral word like *one* or *peace* or *love*. A Christian person desiring to use a prayer could pick the opening words of Psalm 23, *The Lord is my shepherd;* a Jewish person could choose *Shalom.*

Step 2. Sit quietly in a comfortable position.

Step 3. Close your eyes.

Step 4. Relax your muscles.

Step 5. Breathe slowly and naturally, repeating your focus word or phrase silently as you exhale.

Step 6. Throughout, assume a passive attitude. Don't worry about how well you're doing. When other thoughts come to mind, simply say to yourself, "Oh, well," and gently return to the repetition.

Step 7. Continue for 10 to 20 minutes. You may open your eyes to check the time, but do not use an alarm. When you finish, sit quietly for a minute or so, at first with your eyes closed and later with your eyes open. Then do not stand for one or two minutes.

Step 8. Practice the technique once or twice a day.

Source: Benson (1993).

- Redefine "threat" as "challenge." Changing the definition of a situation can make it seem less threatening. "Look for the silver lining" isn't bad advice.

- Get social support. Almost any difficulty can be faced more easily with the help of others. Friends, family members, and even telephone hot lines staffed by trained counselors can provide significant support. (For help in identifying appropriate hot lines, the U.S. Public Health Service maintains a "master" toll-free number that can provide phone numbers and addresses of many national groups. Call 800-336-4794.)

- Use relaxation techniques. Procedures that reduce the physiological arousal brought about by stress can be particularly effective. Techniques that produce relaxation, such as transcendental meditation, Zen and yoga, progressive muscle relaxation, and even hypnosis, have been shown to be effective in reducing stress. One that works particularly well was devised by physician Herbert Benson, and is illustrated in Table 13-2 (Benson, 1993).

- If all else fails, keep in mind that a life without any stress at all would be a dull one. Stress is a natural part of life, and successfully coping with it can be a gratifying experience.

Review and Rethink

REVIEW

♦ By young adulthood, the body and the senses are generally at their peak, but growth, particularly in the brain, is proceeding.

♦ Young adults are generally as fit and healthy as they will ever be, and accidents present the greatest risk of death. In the United States, violence is also a significant risk, particularly for nonwhite males.

♦ Health must be maintained by proper diet and exercise. Obesity, which is caused by a combination of biological and environmental factors, is increasingly a problem for young adults.

♦ People with physical disabilities face not only physical barriers in today's society but also psychological barriers caused by prejudice and stereotyping.

♦ Stress, which is a healthy reaction in small doses, can be harmful to body and mind if it is frequent or of long duration.

RETHINK

♦ If the advantages of exercise and proper nutrition are evident, why are obesity and poor physical fitness so widespread in the United States? Are these inevitable consequences of a high standard of living?

♦ Why is violence so prevalent in the United States, as compared with other societies?

♦ What sorts of interpersonal barriers do people with disabilities face? How can those barriers be removed?

♦ Why are there individual differences in people's reactions to stress? Do you think there are also cultural differences?

♦ The evidence that stress causes disease is called "correlational." What does this mean? Is it possible to design an experiment that would conclusively establish a casual link?

COGNITIVE DEVELOPMENT

> John is known to be a heavy drinker, especially when he goes to parties. Mary, John's wife, warns him that if he comes home drunk one more time, she will leave him and take the children. Tonight John is out late at an office party. He comes home drunk. Does Mary leave John?

An adolescent who hears this situation (drawn from research by Labouvie-Vief, 1986) may find the case to be open-and-shut: Mary leaves John. But in early adulthood, the answer becomes a bit less clear. We'll see that as people enter adulthood, they become less concerned with the sheer logic of situations and instead take into account real-life concerns that may influence and temper behavior in particular situations.

INTELLECTUAL GROWTH IN EARLY ADULTHOOD

If cognitive development were to follow the same pattern as physical development, we would expect to find little new intellectual growth in early adulthood. In fact, Jean Piaget, whose theory of cognitive development played such a prominent role in our earlier discussions of intellectual change, argued that by the time people left adolescence, their thinking, at least qualitatively, had largely become what it would be for their rest of their lives.

Was Piaget's view correct? Increasing evidence suggests that arguments like his might well be flawed.

Postformal Thought.   Developmentist Giesela Labouvie-Vief (1980, 1986) suggests that the nature of thinking changes qualitatively during early adulthood. She asserts that thinking based solely on formal operations (Piaget's final stage, reached during adolescence) is insufficient to meet the demands placed on young adults. The complexity of society, which requires specialization, and the increasing challenge of finding one's way through all that complexity require thought that is not necessarily based on pure logic.

Instead, thinking that employs metaphors, confronts society's paradoxes, and involves a more subjective understanding may be especially adaptive, according to Labouvie-Vief. Such thinking is more flexible; it allows for interpretive processes and reflects the fact that reasons behind events in the real world are subtle, painted in shades of gray rather than in black-and-white (Labouvie-Vief, 1990).

To demonstrate how this sort of thinking develops, Labouvie-Vief presented experimental subjects, ranging in age from 10 to 40, with scenarios similar to the John and Mary scenario at the beginning of this section. Each story had a clear, logical conclusion. However, the story could be interpreted differently if real-world demands and pressures were taken into account.

In responding to the scenarios, adolescents relied heavily on the logic inherent in formal operations. For instance, they would predict that Mary would immediately pack up her bags and leave with the children when John came home drunk. After all, that's what she said she would do.

On the other hand, young adults were less prone to use strict logic in determining a character's likely course of action. Instead, they would consider various possibilities that might come into the picture in a real-life situation: Would John be apologetic and beg Mary not to leave? Did Mary really mean it when she said she'd leave? Does Mary have some alternative place to go?

In short, young adults exhibited what Labouvie-Vief calls **postformal thought**, thinking that goes beyond Piaget's formal operations. Rather than being based on purely logical processes, with absolutely right and wrong answers to problems, postformal thought acknowledges that adult predicaments must sometimes be solved in relativistic terms.

In short, postformal thought acknowledges a world that sometimes lacks clearly right and wrong solutions to problems, a world in which logic may fail to resolve complex human questions. Instead, finding the best resolution to difficulties may involve drawing upon and integrating prior experiences.

Schaie's Stages of Development.   Developmentalist K. Warner Schaie (1977/1978) offers another perspective on postformal thought (Schaie, Willis, Jay, & Chipuer, 1989; Schaie & Willis, 1993). Taking up where Piaget left off, Schaie suggests that adults' thinking follows a set pattern of stages (illustrated in Figure 13-5). But Schaie focuses on the ways in which information is *used* during adulthood, rather than on changes in the acquisition and understanding of new information, as in Piaget's approach.

Consequently, Schaie labels the first stage of cognitive development the **acquisitive stage**, which encompasses all of childhood and adolescence. He suggests that before adulthood, the main cognitive developmental task is acquisition of information. But this information is largely squirreled away for future use. In fact, much of the rationale for education during childhood and adolescence is to prepare people for future activities.

The situation changes considerably in early adulthood, however. Instead of targeting the future use of knowledge, the focus shifts to the here-and-now. Schaie suggests that young adults enter the **achieving stage**, in which intelligence is applied to specific situations involving the attainment of long-term goals regarding careers, family, and societal contributions. During the achieving stage, young adults must confront and resolve several major

According to Giesela Labouvie-Vief, the nature of thought changes qualitatively during early adulthood.

postformal thought   *thinking that acknowledges that adult predicaments must sometimes be solved in relativistic terms*

acquisitive stage   *according to Schaie, the first stage of cognitive development encompassing all of childhood and adolescence, in which the main developmental task is to acquire information*

achieving stage   *the point reached by young adults in which intelligence is applied to specific situations involving the attainment of long-term goals regarding careers, family, and societal contributions*

FIGURE 13-5

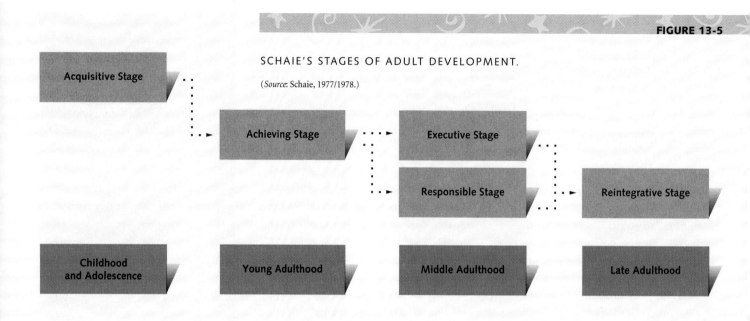

SCHAIE'S STAGES OF ADULT DEVELOPMENT.

(*Source*: Schaie, 1977/1978.)

issues, and the decisions they make—such as what job to take and whom to marry—have implications for the rest of their lives.

During the late stages of early adulthood and in middle adulthood, people move into the responsible and executive stages. In the **responsible stage**, the major concerns of middle-aged adults relate to their personal situations: protecting and nourishing their spouses, families, and careers.

Sometime later during middle adulthood, many people (but not all) enter the **executive stage**. Here people take a broader perspective that includes concerns about the world. Rather than focusing only on their own lives, people in the executive stage also put energy into nourishing and sustaining societal institutions. They may become involved in town government, religious congregations, service clubs, charitable groups, factory unions—organizations that have a larger purpose in society. People in the executive stage, then, look beyond their individual situations.

Old age marks entry into the final period, the **reintegrative stage**, the period of late adulthood during which the focus is on tasks that have personal meaning. In this stage, people no longer focus on acquiring knowledge as a means of solving potential problems they may encounter. Instead, their information acquisition is directed toward particular issues that specifically interest them. Furthermore, they have less interest in—and patience for—things that they do not see as having some immediate application to their lives. Thus, the abstract issue of whether the federal budget should be balanced may be of less concern to an elderly individual than whether the government should provide universal health care.

INTELLIGENCE: WHAT MATTERS IN EARLY ADULTHOOD?

Your year on the job has been generally favorable. Performance ratings for your department are at least as good as they were before you took over, and perhaps even a little better. You have two assistants. One is quite capable. The other just seems to go through the motions and is of little real help. Even though you are well liked, you believe that there is little that would distinguish you in the eyes of your superiors from the nine other managers at a comparable level in the company. Your goal is rapid promotion to an executive position. (Based on Wagner & Sternberg, 1985, p. 447)

responsible stage   the stage where the major concerns of middle-aged adults relate to their personal situations, including protecting and nourishing their spouses, families, and careers

executive stage   the period in middle adulthood when people take a broader perspective than earlier, including concerns about the world

reintegrative stage   the period of late adulthood during which the focus is on tasks that have personal meaning

How do you meet your goal?

The way in which adults answer this question has a great deal to do with their future success, according to psychologist Robert Sternberg. The question is one of a series designed to assess a particular type of intelligence that may have more of an impact on future success than the type of intelligence measured by traditional IQ tests (of the sort we discussed in Chapter 9).

In his **triarchic theory of intelligence**, Sternberg suggests that intelligence is made up of three major components: componential, experiential, and contextual (see Figure 13-6). The *componential* aspect relates to the mental components involved in analyzing data used in solving problems, especially problems involving rational behavior. It relates to people's ability to select and use formulas, to choose appropriate problem-solving strategies, and in general to make use of what they have been taught. The *experiential* component refers to the relationship between intelligence, people's prior experience, and their ability to cope with new situations. This is the insightful aspect of intelligence, which allows people to relate what they already know to a new situation and an array of facts never before encountered. Finally, the *contextual* component of intelligence involves the degree of success people demonstrate in facing the demands of their everyday, real-world environments. For instance, the contextual component is involved in adapting to on-the-job professional demands (Sternberg, 1985a, 1991).

Traditional intelligence tests, which yield an IQ score, tend to focus on the componential aspect of intelligence. Yet increasing evidence suggests that a more useful measure, particularly when one is looking for ways to compare and predict adult success, is the contextual component—the aspect of intelligence that has come to be called *practical intelligence*.

Practical Intelligence: Using Common Sense.   According to Robert Sternberg, the IQ score that most traditional tests produce relates quite well to academic success. However, IQ seems to be unrelated to other types of achievement, such as career success. For example, although it is clear that success in business settings requires some minimal level of the sort of intelligence measured by IQ tests, the rate of career advancement and the ultimate success of business executives is only marginally related to IQ scores (Wagner & Sternberg, 1991; Sternberg & Wagner, 1986, 1993; McClelland, 1993).

Sternberg contends that success in a career necessitates a type of intelligence—called **practical intelligence**—that is substantially different from that involved in traditional academic pursuits. Whereas academic success is based on knowledge of particular types of information, obtained largely from reading and listening, practical intelligence is learned primarily by observing others and modeling their behavior. People who are high in practi-

triarchic theory of intelligence   *Sternberg's theory that intelligence is made up of three major components: componential, experiential, and contextual*

practical intelligence   *intelligence that is learned primarily by observing others and modeling their behavior*

FIGURE 13-6

STERNBERG'S TRIARCHIC
THEORY OF INTELLIGENCE.

(Based on Sternberg, 1985.)

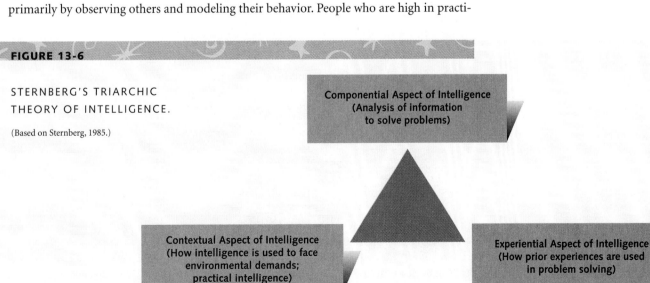

Componential Aspect of Intelligence
(Analysis of information
to solve problems)

Contextual Aspect of Intelligence
(How intelligence is used to face
environmental demands;
practical intelligence)

Experiential Aspect of Intelligence
(How prior experiences are used
in problem solving)

cal intelligence can extract and deduce broad principles and norms about appropriate behavior, and can apply them in particular situations (see Figure 13-8).

Of course, business is not the only sphere in which practical intelligence is important. Psychologist Seymour Epstein argues that *constructive thinking*, a form of practical intelligence, underlies success in such areas as social relationships and physical and emotional health. Constructive thinkers are able to control their emotions effectively and deal with challenges in ways that lead to success. Rather than just complaining about an objectionable situation, for instance, constructive thinkers take action (Epstein & Meier, 1989; Atwater, 1992; Epstein, 1994).

Creativity: Novel Thought. The hundreds of musical compositions of Wolfgang Amadeus Mozart, who died at the age of 35, were largely written during early adulthood. The same is true of many other creative individuals: Their major works were produced during early adulthood (Dennis, 1966; see Figure 13-7).

One reason for the higher productivity of early adulthood may be what psychologist Sarnoff Mednick (1963) proposed: "Familiarity breeds rigidity." By this he meant that the more people know about a subject, the less likely they are to be creative in that area. According to such reasoning, people in early adulthood may be at the peak of their creativity because many of the problems they encounter on a professional level are novel. As they get older, however, and become more familiar with the problems, their creativity may be stymied.

Conversely, many people do not reach their pinnacle of creativity until much later in life. For instance, Buckminster Fuller did not devise his major contribution, the geodesic

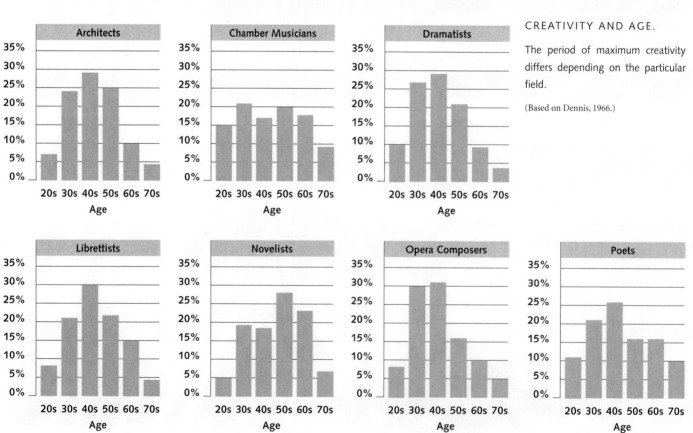

FIGURE 13-7

CREATIVITY AND AGE.

The period of maximum creativity differs depending on the particular field.

(Based on Dennis, 1966.)

FIGURE 13-8

MEASURING PRACTICAL INTELLIGENCE IN FOUR DOMAINS.

(*Source*: Sternberg & Wagner, 1993).

Management

You are responsible for selecting a contractor to renovate several large buildings. You have narrowed the choice to two contractors on the basis of their bids and after further investigation, you are considering awarding the contract to the Wilson & Sons Company. Rate the importance of the following pieces of information in making your decision to award the contract to Wilson & Sons.

_____ The company has provided letters from satisfied former customers.

_____ The Better Business Bureau reports no major complaints about the company.

_____ Wilson & Sons has done good work for your company in the past.

_____ Wilson & Sons' bid was $2000 less than the other contractor's (approximate total cost of the renovation is $325,000).

_____ Former customers whom you have contacted strongly recommended Wilson & Sons for the job.

Sales

You sell a line of photocopy machines. One of your machines has relatively few features and is inexpensive, at $700, although it is not the least expensive model you carry. The $700 photocopy machine is not selling well and it is overstocked. There is a shortage of the more elaborate photocopy machines in your line, so you have been asked to do what you can to improve sales of the $700 machine. Rate the following strategies for maximizing your sales of the slow-moving photocopy machine.

_____ Stress with potential customers that although this model lacks some desirable features, the low price more than makes up for it.

_____ Stress that there are relatively few models left at this price.

_____ Arrange as many demonstrations as possible of the machine.

_____ Stress simplicity of use, since the machine lacks confusing controls that other machines may have.

Academic Psychology

It is your second year as an assistant professor in a prestigious psychology department. This past year you published two unrelated empirical articles in established journals. You don't, however, believe there is yet a research area that can be identified as your own. You believe yourself to be about as productive as others. The feedback about your first year of teaching has been generally good. You have yet to serve on a university committee. There is one graduate student who has chosen to work with you. You have no external source of funding, nor have you applied for any.

Your goals are to become one of the top people in your field and to get tenure in your department. The following is a list of things you are considering doing in the next two months. You obviously cannot do them all. Rate the importance of each by its priority as a means of reaching your goals.

_____ Improve the quality of your teaching.

_____ Write a grant proposal.

_____ Begin a long-term research project that may lead to a major theoretical article.

_____ Concentrate on recruiting more students.

_____ Begin several related short-term research projects, each of which may lead to an empirical article.

_____ Participate in a series of panel discussions to be shown on the local public television station.

College Student Life

You are enrolled in a large introductory lecture course. Requirements consist of 3 exams and a final. Please indicate how characteristic it would be of your behavior to spend time doing each of the following if your goal were to receive an A in the course.

_____ Attend class regularly.

_____ Attend optional weekly review sections with the teaching fellow.

_____ Read assigned text chapters thoroughly.

_____ Take comprehensive class notes.

_____ Speak with the professor after class and during office hours.

Poet Maya Angelou, who spoke at the 1993 presidential inauguration, has maintained a steady pattern of creative productivity throughout adulthood.

dome, until he was in his 50s. Frank Lloyd Wright designed the Guggenheim Museum in New York at age 70. Charles Darwin and Jean Piaget were still writing influential works well into their 70s, and Picasso was painting in his 90s. Furthermore, when we look at overall productivity, as opposed to the period of a person's most important output, we find that productivity remains fairly steady throughout adulthood, particularly in the humanities (Simonton, 1989).

Overall, the study of creativity reveals few consistent developmental patterns. One reason for this is the difficulty of determining just what constitutes an instance of **creativity**, which is defined as combining responses or ideas in novel ways. Because definitions of what is "novel" may vary from one person to the next, it is hard to identify a particular behavior unambiguously as creative (Glover, Ronning, & Reynolds, 1989; Isaksen & Murdock, 1993; Sasser-Coen, 1993).

That ambiguity has not stopped psychologists from trying. For instance, one important component of creativity is a person's willingness to take risks that may result in potentially high payoffs (Sternberg & Lubart, 1992). Creative people are analogous to successful stock market investors who try to follow the "buy low, sell high" rule. Creative people develop and endorse ideas that are unfashionable or regarded as wrong ("buying low"). They assume that the ideas will eventually come to be viewed more positively, and at that time others will see the value of the ideas and embrace them ("selling high").

LIFE EVENTS AND COGNITIVE DEVELOPMENT

Marriage. The death of a parent. Starting a first job. The birth of a child. Buying a house.

The course of life comprises many events such as these—important milestones on the path through the life span. Such occurrences, whether they are welcome or unwanted, clearly may bring about stress, as we saw earlier in this chapter. But do they also cause cognitive growth?

Although the research is still spotty, and largely based on case studies, some evidence suggests that major life events may lead to cognitive growth. For instance, the birth of a child—a profound event—might trigger fresh insights into the nature of one's relationships with relatives and ancestors, one's broader place in the world, and the role one has in per-

creativity   combining responses or ideas in creative ways

petuating humanity. Similarly, the death of a loved one may cause people to reevaluate what is important to them, and to look anew at the manner in which they lead their lives (Feldman, Biringen, & Nash, 1981; Haan, 1985).

In sum, the ups and downs of life events may lead young adults to think about the world in novel, more complex, sophisticated, and often less rigid ways. Rather than applying formal logic to situations—a strategy of which they are fully capable—they instead apply the broader perspective of postformal thought. Such thinking allows them to deal more effectively with the complex social worlds (discussed in Chapter 14) of which they are a part.

Review and Rethink

REVIEW

- Piaget's view that cognitive development peaks at the end of adolescence is now being reconsidered, as evidence mounts for postformal thought, a type of thinking that goes beyond logic to encompass interpretive and subjective thinking.

- According to Warner Schaie, people pass through five stages in the way they use information: acquisitive, achieving, responsible, executive, and reintegrative.

- New views of intelligence are emerging, including the triarchic theory and a focus on practical intelligence, which is based on experience and observation of others.

- Creativity is widely regarded as reaching its height during early adulthood, which may be because young adults view even long-standing problems as novel situations.

- Major life events seem to contribute to cognitive growth by providing opportunities and incentives to rethink one's self and one's world.

RETHINK

- Can you think of situations that you would deal with differently as an adult than as an adolescent? Do the differences reflect postformal thinking?

- What might be some consequences of Schaie's stages of thought in mixed-age settings, such as the workplace?

- If practical intelligence depends on the environment and on observations of others, how might the nature of practical intelligence differ across cultural and socioeconomic environments?

- How is practical intelligence related to social competence?

- What does "familiarity breeds rigidity" mean? Can you think of examples of this phenomenon from your own experience?

COLLEGE: PURSUING HIGHER EDUCATION

For Enrico Vasquez, there was never any doubt: He was headed for college. Enrico, the son of a wealthy Cuban immigrant who had made a fortune in the medical supply business after fleeing Cuba 5 years before Enrico's birth, had had the importance of education constantly drummed into him by his family. In fact, the question was never *whether* he would go to college, but what college he would be able to get into.

As a consequence, Enrico found high school to be a pressure cooker: Every grade and extracurricular activity was seen as helping—or hindering—his chances of admission to a "good" college.

Armando Williams's letter of acceptance to Dallas County Community College is framed on the wall of his mother's apartment. To her, the letter represents nothing short of a miracle, an answer to her prayers. Growing up in a neighborhood saturated with drugs and drive-by shootings, Armando had always been a hard worker and a "good boy," in his mother's view. But when he was growing up she never even entertained the possibility of his making it to college. To see him reach this stage in his education fills her with joy.

Whether a student's enrollment seems almost inevitable or signifies a triumph over the odds, attending college is a significant accomplishment. Although students already enrolled may feel that college attendance is nearly universal, this is not the case at all: Nationwide, a minority of high school graduates enter college.

THE DEMOGRAPHICS OF HIGHER EDUCATION

What types of students enter college? Like the population as a whole, college students are primarily white and middle class. Although nearly 40 percent of white high school graduates enter college, just 29 percent of African-American and 31 percent of Hispanic graduates enter college (see Figure 13-9). Even more striking, although the absolute number of minority students enrolled in college has increased, the *proportion* of the minority population that does enter college has *decreased* over the last decade—a decline that most education experts attribute to changes in the availability of financial aid.

Furthermore, the proportion of students who enter college but ultimately never graduate is substantial. Only about 40 percent of those who start college finish 4 years later with a degree. Although about half of those who don't receive a degree in 4 years eventually do finish, the other half never get a college degree. For minorities, the picture is even worse: The national drop-out rate for African-American college students stands at 70 percent (Minorities in Higher Education, 1990).

On the other hand, the sheer number of minority students attending college is rising dramatically, and minority students make up an increasingly larger proportion of the college population. These trends reflect changes in the racial and ethnic composition of the United States, and they are important because higher education remains an important way for families to improve their economic well-being (Kates, 1995).

For instance, by the year 2000, the U.S. Department of Education projects an increase

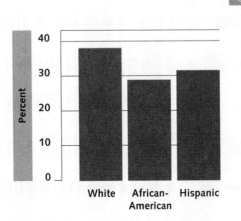

FIGURE 13-9

COLLEGE PARTICIPATION BY HIGH SCHOOL GRADUATES.

The proportion of African-Americans and Hispanics who enter college after graduating from high school is lower than the proportion of whites.

(*Source*: U.S. Bureau of the Census, 1990a.)

of 13 percent in African-American college attendance and 22 percent in Hispanic college attendance over levels ten years earlier. Over the same period, enrollment of whites is projected to rise only 6 percent (U.S. Department of Education, 1992). Already at some colleges, such as the University of California at Berkeley, whites have shifted from the majority to the minority as what is traditionally called "minority" representation has increased significantly.

WHAT DO COLLEGE STUDENTS LEARN?

The response to this question is not only "math" or "hotel management" or even "life-span development," although that is part of the answer. Clearly, students gain a body of knowledge that may help them function more effectively in the world. However, college is more than that: It is a period of developmental growth that encompasses mastery not just of particular bodies of knowledge, but of ways of understanding the world.

For example, psychologist William Perry (1970) examined the ways in which students grew intellectually and morally during college. In comprehensive interviews with a group of students at Harvard University, he found that students entering college tended to use *dualistic thinking* in their views of the world. For instance, they reasoned that something was right, or it was wrong; people were good, or they were bad; and others were either for them, or against them.

However, as they encountered new ideas and points of view from other students and their professors, their dualistic thinking declined. Students increasingly realized that issues can have more than one plausible side, and that it is possible to hold multiple perspectives on an issue. This *multiple thinking* was characterized by a shift in the way the students viewed authorities: Instead of presupposing that experts had all the answers, they began to assume that their own thinking on an issue had validity if their position was well argued and rational.

In fact, they had entered a stage in which knowledge and values were regarded as *relativistic*. Rather than seeing the world as having absolute standards and values, they argued that different societies, cultures, and individuals could have different standards and values, all of them equally valid.

GENDER AND COLLEGE PERFORMANCE

> I registered for a calculus course my first year at DePauw. Even twenty years ago I was not timid, so on the very first day I raised my hand and asked a question. I still have a vivid memory of the professor rolling his eyes, hitting his head with his hand in frustration, and announcing to everyone, "Why do they expect me to teach calculus to girls?" I never asked another question. Several weeks later I went to a football game, but I had forgotten to bring my ID. My calculus professor was at the gate checking IDs, so I went up to him and said, "I forgot my ID but you know me, I'm in your class." He looked right at me and said, "I don't remember you in my class." I couldn't believe that someone who changed my life and whom I remember to this day didn't even recognize me. (Sadker & Sadker, 1994, p. 162)

Although such incidents of blatant sexism are less likely to occur today, prejudice and discrimination directed at women are still a fact of college life. For instance, the next time you are in class, consider the gender of your classmates—and the subject matter of the class. Although men and women attend college in roughly equal proportions, there is significant variation in the classes they take. Classes in education and the social sciences, for instance, typically have a larger proportion of women than men; and classes in engineering, the physical sciences, and mathematics tend to have more men than women.

Even women who start out in mathematics, engineering, and the physical sciences are more likely than men to drop out. For instance, the attrition rate for women in such fields during the college years is two-and-a-half times greater than the rate for men. Ultimately, although white women make up 43 percent of the U.S. population, they earn just 22 percent of the bachelor of science degrees and 13 percent of the doctorates, and they hold only 10 percent of the jobs in physical science, math, and engineering.

Differences in gender distribution and attrition rates across subject areas are no accident. They reflect the powerful influence of gender stereotypes that operate throughout the world of education—and beyond. For instance, when women in their first year of college are asked to name a likely career choice, they are much less apt to choose careers that have traditionally been dominated by men, such as engineering or computer programming, and more likely to choose professions that have traditionally been populated by women, such as nursing and social work (Glick, Zion, & Nelson, 1988; CIRE, 1990).

These initial expectations about the fields that are of interest to them are reflected in students' anticipation of their entering and peak salaries once they leave college. Women expect to earn less than men, both when they start their careers and when they are at their peaks (Major & Konar, 1984; Martin, 1989; Jackson, Gardner, & Sullivan, 1992). These expectations jibe with reality: On average, women earn 70 cents for every dollar that men earn. Moreover, women who are members of minority groups do even worse: African-American women earn 62 cents for every dollar men make, whereas for Hispanic women the figure is 54 cents (U.S. Bureau of Labor Statistics, 1993).

Male and female college students also have different expectations regarding their areas of competence. For instance, one survey asked first-year college students whether they were above or below average on a variety of traits and abilities. As can be seen in Figure 13-10, men were more likely than women to think of themselves as above average in overall academic and mathematical ability, competitiveness, and emotional health.

Both male and female college instructors treat men and women differently in their classes, even though the different treatment is largely unintentional and the instructors are unaware of their actions. For instance, teachers call on men in class more frequently than they call on women, and they make more eye contact with men than they do with women. Furthermore, male students are more likely to receive extra help from their instructors than are women. Finally, the quality of the responses received by male and female students differs, with male students receiving more positive reinforcement for their comments than do

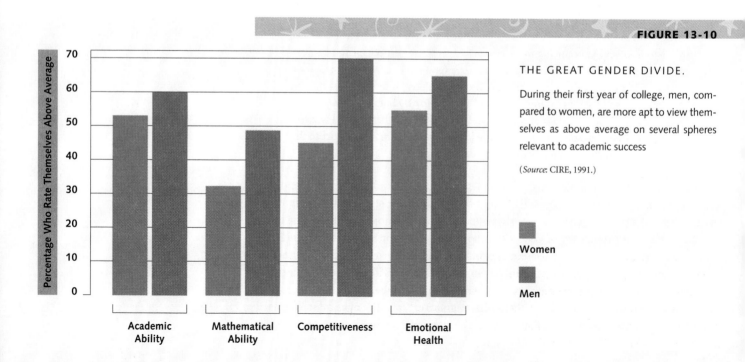

FIGURE 13-10

THE GREAT GENDER DIVIDE.

During their first year of college, men, compared to women, are more apt to view themselves as above average on several spheres relevant to academic success

(*Source*: CIRE, 1991.)

■ Women

■ Men

TABLE 13-3

GENDER BIAS IN THE CLASSROOM

The course on the U.S. Constitution is required for graduation, and more than fifty students, approximately half male and half female, file in. The professor begins by asking if there are questions on next week's midterm. Several hands go up.

BERNIE: Do we have to memorize names and dates in the book? Or will the test be more general?
PROFESSOR: You do have to know those critical dates and people. Not every one but the important ones. If I were you, Bernie, I would spend time learning them. Ellen?
ELLEN: What kind of short-answer questions will there be?
PROFESSOR: All multiple choice.
ELLEN: Will we have the whole class time?
PROFESSOR: Yes, we'll have the whole class time. Anyone else?
BEN (calling out): Will there be an extra-credit question?
PROFESSOR: I hadn't planned on it. What do you think?
BEN: I really like them. They take some of the pressure off. You can also see who is doing extra work.
PROFESSOR: I'll take it under advisement. Charles?
CHARLES: How much of our final grade is this?
PROFESSOR: The midterm is 25 percent. But remember, class participation counts as well. Why don't we begin?

The professor lectures on the Constitution for twenty minutes before he asks a question about the electoral college. The electoral college is not as hot a topic as the midterm, so only four hands are raised. The professor calls on Ben.

BEN: The electoral college was created because there was a lack of faith in the people. Rather than have them vote for the president, they voted for the electors.
PROFESSOR: I like the way you think. (He smiles at Ben, and Ben smiles back.) Who could vote? (Five hands go up, five out of fifty.) Angie?
ANGIE: I don't know if this is right, but I thought only men could vote.
BEN (calling out): That was a great idea. We began going downhill when we let women vote. (Angie looks surprised but says nothing. Some of the students laugh, and so does the professor. He calls on Barbara.)
BARBARA: I think you had to be pretty wealthy, own property–
JOSH (not waiting for Barbara to finish, calls out): That't right. There was a distrust of the poor, who could upset the democracy. But if you had property, if you had something at stake, you could be trusted not to do something wild. Only property owners could be trusted.
PROFESSOR: Nice job, Josh. But why do we still have electors today? Mike?
MIKE: Tradition, I guess.
PROFESSOR: Do you think it's tradition? If you walked down the street and asked people their views of the electoral college, what would they say?
MIKE: Probably they'd be clueless. maybe they would think that it elects the Pope. People don't know how it works.
PROFESSOR: Good, Mike. Judy, do you want to say something? (Judy's hand is at "half-mast," raised but just barely. When the professor calls her name, she looks a bit startled.)
JUDY (speaking very softly): Maybe we would need a whole new constitutional convention to change it. And once they get together to change that, they could change anything. That frightens people, doesn't it? (As Judy speaks, a number of students fidget, pass notes, and leaf through their books; a few even begin to whisper.)

(*Source:* Sadker & Sadker, 1994.)

female students—exemplified by the startling illustration in Table 13-3 (Epperson, 1988; AAUW, 1992; Sadker & Sadker, 1994).

The different treatment of men and women in the college classroom has led some educators to argue in favor of single-sex schools for women. They point to evidence that the rate of participation and ultimately the success of women in the sciences is greater for graduates of women's colleges than for graduates of coeducational institutions. Furthermore, some research suggests that women who attend same-sex colleges may show higher self-esteem than those attending coeducational colleges, although the evidence is not entirely consistent on this count (M. Smith, 1990; Miller-Bernal, 1993).

According to some research, women who attend same-sex colleges have a higher rate of participation in classes and have higher self-esteem than women who attend coeducational institutions of higher learning.

Why might women do better in single-sex colleges? One reason is that they receive more attention than they would in coeducational settings, where instructors are affected, however inadvertently, by societal biases. In addition, women's colleges tend to have more female instructors than coeducational institutions, and they thereby provide more role models for women. Finally, women attending women's colleges may receive more encouragement for participation in nontraditional subjects such as mathematics and science than those in coeducational colleges. In fact, such an explanation lies at the heart of an innovative program designed to increase women's success in nontraditional areas, as discussed in the accompanying Directions in Development section.

Directions in Development

Overcoming Racial and Gender Barriers to Achievement

When women take college classes in math, science, and engineering, they are more likely to do poorly than men who enter college with the same level of preparation and identical SAT scores. Strangely, though, this phenomenon does not hold true for other areas of the curriculum, where men and women perform at similar levels (Steele, 1992).

According to psychologist Claude Steele, the reason has to do with women's acceptance of society's stereotypes about achievement in particular domains. Steele suggests that women are no strangers to society's dominant view that some subjects are more appropriate areas of study for women than others are. In fact, the pervasiveness of the stereotype makes women who attempt to achieve in traditionally "inappropriate" fields highly vulnerable (Steele, & Aronson, 1995).

Specifically, because of the strength and pervasiveness of such stereotypes, the performance of women seeking to achieve in nontraditional fields may be hindered as they are distracted by worries about the failure that society predicts for them. In some cases, a woman may decide that failure in a male-dominated field, because it would confirm societal stereotypes, presents such great risks that, paradoxically, the struggle to succeed is not worth the effort. In that instance, the woman may not even try very hard.

On the other hand, there is a bright side to Steele's analysis: If women can be convinced that societal stereotypes regarding achievement are invalid, then their performance might well improve. And in fact, this is just what Steele found in a series of experiments he conducted at the University of Michigan and Stanford University.

In one study male and female college students were told they would be taking two math tests: one in which there were gender differences—men supposedly performed better than women—and a second in which there were no gender differences. In reality, the tests were entirely similar, drawn from the same pool of difficult items. The reasoning behind the experimental manipulation was that women would be vulnerable to societal stereotypes on a test that they thought supported those stereotypes, but would not be vulnerable on a test supposedly lacking gender differences.

The results fully supported Steele's reasoning. When the women were told there were gender differences in the test, they greatly underperformed the men. But when they were told there were no gender differences, they performed virtually the same as the men.

In short, the evidence from this study and others clearly suggests that women are vulnerable to expectations regarding their future success, whether the expectations come from societal stereotypes or from information about the prior performance of women on similar tasks. More encouraging, the evidence suggests that if women can be convinced that others have been successful in given domains, they may overcome even long-standing societal stereotypes.

We should also keep in mind that women are not the only group susceptible to society's stereotyping. Members of minority groups, such as African-Americans and Hispanic-Americans, are also vulnerable to stereotypes about academic success. In fact, Steele suggests that African-Americans may "disidentify" with academic success by putting forth less effort on academic tasks and generally downgrading the importance of academic achievement. Ultimately, such disidentification may act as a self-fulfilling prophecy, increasing the chances of academic failure (Steele & Aronson, 1995).

In sum, until society's stereotypes change, women and members of minority groups run the risk of academic failure because of their vulnerability to those stereotypes.

THE CHANGING COLLEGE STUDENT: NEVER TOO LATE TO GO TO COLLEGE?

If the words "average college student" bring to mind an image of a 19-year-old, you should begin to rethink your view. Increasingly, students are older. In fact, some 40 percent of students taking college courses for credit in the United States are 25 years or older. The average age of community college students is 31 (U.S. Bureau of the Census, 1990b).

Why are so many older, nontraditional students taking college courses? One reason is economic. As a college degree becomes increasingly important in obtaining a job, some workers feel compelled to get the credential. Furthermore, some employers encourage or require workers to undergo training to learn or update their skills. Finally, older students sometimes enroll in college classes simply for the joy of learning; they appreciate the opportunity for intellectual stimulation.

Some 40 percent of students taking college courses for credit in the United States are 25 years of age or older, and the average age of community college students is 31.

According to developmental psychologist Sherry Willis (1985), several broad goals underlie adults' participation in learning experiences. First, adults may be seeking to understand their own aging. As they get older, they try to figure out what is happening to them and what to expect in the future. Second, adults seek education to understand more fully the rapid technological and cultural changes that characterize modern life.

Furthermore, adult learners may be seeking a practical edge in combating obsolescence on the job. Some individuals also may be attempting to acquire new vocational skills. Finally, adult educational experiences might be seen as helpful in preparing for future retirement. As adults get older, they become increasingly concerned with shifting from a work orientation to a leisure orientation, and they may see education as a means of broadening their possibilities.

DROPPING OUT OF COLLEGE

Not everyone who enters colleges completes it. In fact, roughly half of all students who start college never receive a degree.

Why is the college dropout rate so high? There are several reasons. One has to do with finances: Given the high cost of college, many students are unable to afford the continued expense. Other people leave college because of changes in their life situations, such as marriage, the birth of a child, or the death of a parent.

Academic difficulties also may play a role. Some students simply find that they are not successful in their studies, and they are either forced by academic authorities to drop out or they leave on their own. However, in most cases students who drop out are not in academic jeopardy (Rotenberg & Morrison, 1993).

Dropping out is not always a step backward on a person's life path. In some cases it gives people breathing room to reassess their goals. For instance, students who view the college experience as simply marking time until they can get on with their "real" lives by earning a living can sometimes benefit from a period of full-time work. During the hiatus from college, they often get a different perspective on the realities of both work and school. Other individuals simply benefit by having some time off from school in which to mature psychologically.

TABLE 13-4

COLLEGE STUDENTS' PROBLEMS

Among the most prevalent problems of college students are the following:

For male students:	For female students:
Grades	What to do with their lives
Social life	Developing sexual and emotional relationships
Vocational decisions	Strain from too much work
The future	Grades
Sexual relationships	Adjustment
Peer pressures	Gaining independence
Adjusting to a new environment	Identity
Leaving family for the first time	Pressure from parents
Competition	Peer pressures
Depression	Morals

Source: Wechsler, Rohman, & Solomon (1981).

On the other hand, college students who drop out—intending to return one day, but never making it back because they become enmeshed in the nitty-gritty of everyday life—can experience real difficulties. They may become riveted as young adults to undesirable, low-paying jobs for which they are intellectually overqualified. A college education becomes a lost opportunity.

COLLEGE ADJUSTMENT: REACTING TO THE DEMANDS OF COLLEGE LIFE

When you began college, did you feel depressed, lonely, anxious, and withdrawn from others?

If you did, you weren't alone. Many students, particularly those who are recent high school graduates and who are living away from home for the first time, experience difficulties in adjustment during their first year in college. The **first-year adjustment reaction** is a group of psychological symptoms relating to the college experience. Although any first-year student might suffer from one or more of the symptoms of first-year adjustment reaction, it is particularly likely to occur among students who have been unusually successful, either academically or socially, in high school. When they begin college, their sudden change in status may cause them distress.

Most often, first-year adjustment reaction passes, as students make friends, experience academic success, and integrate themselves into campus life. In other cases, though, the problems remain and may fester, leading to more serious psychological difficulties.

Several other problems are common to college students (Duke & Nowicki, 1979). As Table 13-4 shows, male students are most likely to be concerned with their grades, social lives, and vocational decisions. In contrast, female students are concerned most with what to do with their lives, relationships, and the strain of too much work.

How prevalent are these concerns? Surveys find that almost half of all college students report having at least one significant psychological issue, and certain groups of students show particular problems. For example, overweight students report more psychological concerns, and minority women report having a higher frequency of problems relating to motivation than do white women (Wechsler, Rohman, Solomon, 1981; American Council on Education, 1995).

first-year adjustment reaction *a group of psychological symptoms relating to the college experience suffered by first-year college students*

The Informed Consumer of Development

When Do College Students Need Professional Help with Their Problems?

A college friend comes to you and says that she has been feeling depressed and unhappy and cannot seem to shake the feeling. She doesn't know what to do and thinks that she may need professional help. How do you answer her?

Although there are no hard-and-fast rules, several signals can be interpreted to determine if professional help is warranted. Among them (Engler & Goleman, 1992):

- psychological distress that lingers and interferes with a person's sense of well-being and ability to function;

- feelings that one is unable to cope effectively with the stress;

- hopeless or depressed feelings, with no apparent reason;

- the inability to build close relationships with others; and

- physical symptoms that have no apparent underlying cause.

If some of these signals are present, discussions with some kind of help-provider—such as a counseling psychologist, clinical psychologist, or other mental health worker—are warranted. (College students can find an appropriate provider by starting with their campus medical center; others can turn to their personal physicians or to local boards of health for referrals.)

Review and Rethink

REVIEW

- College enrollment differs across racial and ethnic lines, with a larger proportion of white high school graduates attending college than African-American or Hispanic-American graduates.

- In college, students learn not only a body of knowledge, but also a way of understanding the world that generally accepts more viewpoints and sees values in relativistic terms.

- Gender differences in treatment and expectations cause men and women to make different choices and engage in different behaviors in college. A similar situation often confronts minority students and presents barriers to their achievement.

- The average age of college students is steadily increasing as more adults return to college after spending time in the workforce. Temporarily dropping out of college is an increasingly widespread occurrence.

- New students, particularly those who enjoyed high status in high school, often find the transition to college difficult and experience first-year adjustment reaction.

RETHINK

◆ What are some advantages and disadvantages of multiple thinking and a relativistic view of values?

◆ Some African-American students are said to "disidentify" with academic success by downgrading its importance. Can you think of other situations in which people manifest this behavior?

◆ Why do college instructors behave differently toward male and female students? What factors contribute to this phenomenon? Can this situation be changed?

◆ How are older students likely to affect the college classroom, given what you know about human development?

◆ Are same-sex colleges the best way to address the problem of stereotyping and low expectations for women students? Why or why not?

LOOKING BACK

How does the body develop during early adulthood, and to what risks are young adults exposed?

1. The body and the senses generally reach their peak in early adulthood, with only moderate physical growth—if any—taking place. To reach their physical potential, people must exercise regularly and maintain proper diets, habits that bring many benefits to the heart, the muscles, and even the immune system.

2. Health risks during early adulthood are minimal, with accidents presenting the greatest risk of death, followed by AIDS, cancer, heart disease, and suicide. In the United States, violence is a significant cause of death among early adults, particularly among nonwhite segments of the population.

3. Eating the right quantity and types of food becomes even more important in early adulthood than it was in adolescence. Many young adults begin to put on weight because they fail to change poor eating habits developed earlier, and the percentage of adults classified as obese increases with every year of aging.

4. Obesity may be caused partly by biological factors, but environmental factors are also at work. Obese people appear to be overly sensitive to external eating cues and relatively insensitive to internal hunger cues that should regulate the desire for food. Additionally, obese people may have higher weight set points than others; consequently, they may find it especially difficult to lose weight and keep it off.

5. People with physical disabilities face many difficulties, many of them physical and material, but others are more subtle and psychological in nature, including prejudice and stereotyping.

What are the effects of stress, and what can be done about it?

6. Moderate, occasional stress is biologically healthy, producing physical reactions that facilitate the body's defense against threats, but long exposure to stressors produces damaging physical and psychosomatic effects. People pass through two stages in reacting to potentially stressful situations: primary appraisal of the situation itself, and secondary appraisal of their own coping abilities.

7. People cope with stress in a number of ways, including problem-focused coping, emotion-focused coping, and reliance on social support from others.

Does cognitive development continue in young adulthood?

8. According to Piaget, people's cognitive development reaches its peak by the end of adolescence with the formal operations stage, and their thinking remains qualitatively unchanged throughout adulthood.

9. More recent views of cognitive development find increasing evidence of postformal thought, which goes beyond formal logic to produce more flexible and subjective thinking that takes account of real-world complexity and yields subtler answers than those found during adolescence.

10. Psychologist K. Warner Schaie suggests that the development of thinking follows a set pattern of stages: the acquisitive stage, the achieving stage, the responsible stage, the executive stage, and the reintegrative stage.

How is intelligence defined today, and what causes cognitive growth in young adults?

11. Traditional views that equated IQ with intelligence are being questioned. According to Sternberg's triarchic theory, intelligence is made up of componential, experiential, and contextual components. Practical intelligence, generally similar to the contextual component in its reliance on observation of others to extract principles, seems to be related most closely with career success and to underlie social competence and physical and emotional health.

12. Creativity, which often seems to be a phenomenon of young adulthood, may in fact be unrelated to age and attributable instead to the fact that young people view problems in novel ways rather than in the familiar ways of their older peers.

13. Important life events, such as births and deaths, seem to contribute to cognitive growth by generating new insights into the self and revised views of the world.

Who attends college today, and how is the college population changing?

14. College attendance is growing more prevalent among minorities in the United States, although, compared to white high school graduates, a smaller percentage of African-American and Hispanic-American high school graduates enters college.

15. The profile of the typical college student in the United States has been changing steadily, with many current and future students being older than the 19-to-22-year-old image of the past. Many older students attend college for personal understanding and improvement, career advancement, and other reasons.

What do students learn in college, and what difficulties do they face?

16. What students learn in college goes beyond a body of knowledge. It includes a different way of understanding the world, manifested in the shift from dualistic (right-wrong; good-bad) thinking to multiple thinking, and even to a more relativistic view of values.

17. Significant differences in gender distribution among fields of study exist in college, with fewer women than men pursuing courses in engineering, the physical sciences, and math. This pattern seems to be due to societal stereotypes regarding women's supposed lack of competence in those areas.

18. There are gender differences in entering college students' expectations regarding their future careers and earnings, with women having lower expectations. The differences eventually become real as women's earnings and careers reflect their own, and society's, expectations.

19. College instructors treat women differently from men, in ways that reinforce societal stereotypes. This fact has led some to conclude that single-sex colleges may provide a better education and increased opportunities for women than coed institutions.

20. Many college students, particularly those who are experiencing a decline in status from their high school days, fall victim to the first-year adjustment reaction—feelings of depression, anxiety, and withdrawal that typically pass quickly as the students integrate themselves into their new surroundings.

KEY TERMS AND CONCEPTS

weight set point (p. 448)

stress (p. 450)

primary appraisal (p. 450)

secondary appraisal (p. 450)

psychosomatic disorders (p. 451)

coping (p. 452)

postformal thought (p. 457)

acquisitive stage (p. 457)

achieving stage (p. 457)

responsible stage (p. 458)

executive stage (p. 458)

reintegrative stage (p. 458)

triarchic theory of intelligence (p. 459)

practical intelligence (p. 459)

creativity (p. 462)

first-year adjustment reaction (p. 471)

Social and Personality Development

CHAPTER OUTLINE

PROLOGUE: SUDDENLY AN ADULT

Several years ago, my family gathered on Cape Cod for a weekend. My parents were there, my sister and her daughter, too, two cousins, and, of course, my wife, my son and me. We ate at one of those restaurants where the menu is scrawled on a blackboard held by a chummy waiter and had a wonderful time. With dinner concluded, the waiter set the check down in the middle of the table. That's when it happened. My father did not reach for the check.

In fact, my father did nothing. Conversation continued. Finally, it dawned on me. Me! I was supposed to pick up the check. After all these years, after hundreds of restaurant meals with my parents, after a lifetime of thinking of my father as the one with the bucks, it had all changed. I reached for the check and whipped out my American Express card. My view of myself was suddenly altered. With a stroke of the pen, I was suddenly an adult.

Some people mark off their life in years, others in events. I am one of the latter, and I think of some events as rites of passage. I did not become a young man at a particular year, like 13, but when a kid strolled into the store where I worked and called me "mister." I turned around to see whom he was calling. He repeated it several times—"Mister, mister"—looking straight at me. The realization hit like a punch. Me! He was talking to me. I was suddenly a mister.... (Cohen, 1987, p. 70)

LOOKING AHEAD

The notion that they are grown up dawns on most people during early adulthood. Until that time, people may think of themselves as children—or, if not children, at least not adultlike: full members of society with significant responsibilities. But it is during early adulthood that most people come to grips with the notion that they are no longer other people's children, but are viewed by others as nothing less than adults.

Early adulthood is a period during which a variety of developmental tasks must be faced (see Table 14-1). This chapter examines these challenges, concentrating on the development and course of relationships with others. We'll consider first how we establish and maintain love for others, distinguishing between liking and loving, and among different types of love. The chapter will look at how people choose partners, and how their choices are influenced by societal and cultural factors.

Next, the chapter turns to relationships during early adulthood. We will examine the choice of whether to marry, and the factors that influence the course and success of marriage. We also consider how the arrival of a child influences a couple's happiness and the kinds of roles children play within a marriage.

Finally, the chapter considers careers. We see how identity during early adulthood is often tied to one's job, and how people decide on the kind of work they wish to do. The chapter ends with a discussion of the reasons people work—it's not only to earn money, as we'll see—and techniques for choosing a career.

In short, after reading this chapter, you'll be able to answer the following questions:

- What are the types and causes of love, and how does love change over time?
- How do people choose spouses, and what do they look for in a marriage relationship?
- Why do people marry, and why do they divorce?
- How does the arrival of children affect a relationship?

TABLE 14-1

THE DEVELOPMENT TASKS OF ADULTHOOD

Adulthood (Ages 20–40)	Middle Adulthood (Ages 40–60)	Late Adulthood (Ages 60+)
1. Psychological separation from parents.	1. Dealing with body changes or illness and altered body image.	1. Maintaining physical health.
2. Accepting responsibility for one's own body.	2. Adjusting to middle-life changes in sexuality.	2. Adapting to physical infirmities or permanent impairment.
3. Becoming aware of one's personal history and time limitation.	3. Accepting the passage of time.	3. Using time in gratifying ways.
4. Integrating sexual experience (homosexual or heterosexual).	4. Adjusting to aging.	4. Adapting to losses of partner and friends.
5. Developing a capacity for intimacy with a partner.	5. Living through illness and death of parents, and contemporaries.	5. Remaining oriented to present and future, not preoccupied with the past.
6. Deciding whether to have children.	6. Dealing with realities of death.	6. Forming new emotional ties.
7. Having and relating to children.	7. Redefining relationship to spouse or partner.	7. Reversing roles of children and grandchildren (as caretakers).
8. Establishing adult relationships with parents.	8. Deepening relations with grown children or grandchildren.	8. Seeking and maintaining social contacts: companionship vs. isolation and loneliness.
9. Acquiring marketable skills.	9. Maintaining long-standing friendships and creating new ones.	9. Attending to sexual needs and (changing) expressions.
10. Choosing a career.	10. Consolidating work identity.	10. Continuing meaningful work and play (satisfying use of time).
11. Using money to further development.	11. Transmitting skills and values to the young.	11. Using financial resources wisely, for self and others.
12. Assuming a social role.	12. Allocating financial resources effectively.	12. Integrating retirement into new lifestyle.
13. Adapting ethical and spiritual values.	13. Accepting social responsibility.	
	14. Accepting social change.	

Source: Colarusso & Nemiroff (1981).

◆   Why is choosing a career such an important issue for young adults, and what factors influence the choice of a career?

◆   Why do people work, and what elements of a job bring satisfaction?

FORGING RELATIONSHIPS: LIKING AND LOVING

Asia Kaia Linn, whose parents chose her name while looking through a world atlas, met Chris Applebaum 6 years ago at Hampshire College in Massachusetts and fell in love with him one Saturday night while they were dancing.

Although many women might swoon over a guy with perfect hair and fluid dance steps, it was his silly haircut and overall lack of coordination that delighted her. "He's definitely a funny dancer, and he spun me around and we were just being goofy," Ms. Linn recalled. "I realized how much fun we were having, and I thought this is ridiculous and fabulous and I love him" (Brady, 1995, p. 47).

Asia followed her first instincts: Ultimately, she and Chris were married in an unconventional wedding ceremony at an art gallery, with guests wearing a psychedelic melange of clothes, and a ring-bearer delivering the wedding ring by steering a remote-control truck down the aisle of the gallery.

Not everyone falls in love quite as easily as Asia. For some, the road to love is tortuous, meandering through soured relationships and fallen dreams; for others, it is a road never taken. For some, love leads to marriage and a life befitting society's storybook view of home,

Chris Applebaum and Asia Linn.

children, and long years together as a couple. For many, it leads to a less happy ending, prematurely concluding in divorce and custody battles.

FALLING IN LOVE: WHEN LIKING TURNS TO LOVING

After a few chance encounters at the laundromat where they wash their clothes each week, Shoshana and Jerry begin to talk with one another. They find out they have a lot in common, and they begin to look forward to what are now semiplanned meetings. After several weeks, they go out on their first official date, and they discover they are well suited to each other.

If such a pattern seems predictable, it is: Most relationships develop in a fairly similar way, following a surprisingly regular progression (Burgess & Huston, 1979; Berscheid, 1985):

◆ Two people interact with each other more often and for longer periods of time. Furthermore, the range of settings increases.

◆ The two people increasingly seek out each other's company.

◆ They open up to each other more and more, disclosing more intimate information about themselves. They begin to share physical intimacies.

◆ The couple are more willing to share both positive and negative feelings, and they may offer criticism in addition to praise.

◆ They begin to agree on the goals they hold for the relationship.

◆ Their reactions to situations become more similar.

◆ They begin to feel that their own psychological well-being is tied to the success of the relationship, viewing it as unique, irreplaceable, and cherished.

◆ Finally, their definition of themselves and their behavior changes: They begin to see themselves and act as a couple, rather than as two separate individuals.

The evolution of a relationship can be seen in terms of what psychologist Bernard Murstein (1976, 1986, 1987) calls **stimulus-value-role (SVR) theory**, i.e., relationships proceed in a fixed order of three stages.

stimulus-value-role (SVR) theory   *the theory that relationships proceed in a fixed order of three stages: stimulus, value, and role*

passionate (or romantic) love *a state of powerful absorption in someone*

companionate love *the strong affection that we have for those with whom our lives are deeply involved*

In the first stage, the *stimulus stage*, relationships are built on surface, physical characteristics such as the way a person looks. Usually, this represents just the initial encounter. The second stage, the *value stage*, usually occurs between the second and the seventh encounter. In the value stage, the relationship is characterized by increasing similarity of values and beliefs. Finally, in the third stage, the *role stage*, the relationship is built on specific roles played by the participants. For instance, the couple may define themselves as boyfriend–girlfriend or husband–wife.

Although stimulus, value, and role factors dominate at particular stages, they are also influential at other junctures in the developing relationship. For instance, consider Figure 14-1, which illustrates the course of a typical relationship.

Of course, not every relationship follows a similar pattern, and this has led to criticism of SVR theory (Gupta & Singh, 1982; Sternberg, 1986). For instance, there seems to be no logical reason why value factors could not predominate early in a relationship, rather than stimulus factors. Consequently, additional approaches have been devised to explain the course of relationship development.

PASSIONATE AND COMPANIONATE LOVE: THE TWO FACES OF LOVE

Is "love" just a lot of "liking"? Most psychologists would answer negatively; love not only differs quantitatively from liking, but it represents a qualitatively different state. For example, love, at least in its early stages, involves relatively intense physiological arousal, an all-encompassing interest in another person, recurrent fantasies about the other individual, and rapid swings of emotion. As distinct from liking, love includes elements of closeness, passion, and exclusivity (Walster & Walster, 1978; Hendrick & Hendrick, 1989).

Not all love is the same, however. We don't love our mothers the same way we love girlfriends or boyfriends, brothers or sisters, or lifelong friends. What distinguishes these different types of love?

Passionate (or romantic) love is a state of powerful absorption in someone. It includes intense physiological interest and arousal, and caring for another's needs. In comparison, **companionate love** is the strong affection that we have for those with whom our lives are deeply involved (Hatfield, 1988; Hecht, Marston, & Larkey, 1994).

Distinguishing Between Passionate and Companionate Love.   Although it is clear that a difference exists between passionate and companionate love, drawing the distinction in practice is not always easy. One approach to determining when we love someone, as

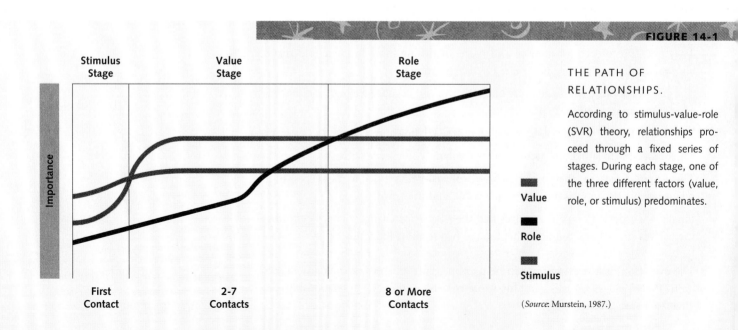

FIGURE 14-1

THE PATH OF RELATIONSHIPS.

According to stimulus-value-role (SVR) theory, relationships proceed through a fixed series of stages. During each stage, one of the three different factors (value, role, or stimulus) predominates.

Value

Role

Stimulus

(*Source*: Murstein, 1987.)

opposed to merely liking her or him, is through the use of questionnaires. For instance, psychologist Zick Rubin devised a series of questions to measure whether someone is liked or loved (Rubin, 1973). The love questionnaire consists of items like these:

♦ I feel that I can confide in _____ about virtually everything.

♦ I would do almost anything for _____.

♦ I feel responsible for _____'s well-being.

On the other hand, the questions designed to measure liking include these:

♦ I think that _____ is unusually well adjusted.

♦ I think that _____ is one of those people who quickly wins respect.

♦ _____ is one of the most likable people I know.

Couples who score high on the measures of "love" behave quite differently from those who score high on the "liking" scale (Rubin, 1973). They gaze more at each other, and their relationships are more apt to be intact six months after they fill out the questionnaire.

Understanding Passionate Love.   What is it that fuels the fires of passionate love? According to one theory, anything that produces strong emotions—even negative ones such as jealousy, anger, or fear of rejection—may be the source of deepening passionate love.

In psychologists Elaine Hatfield and Ellen Berscheid's **labeling theory of passionate love**, individuals experience romantic love when two events occur together: intense physiological arousal and situational cues that indicated that "love" is the appropriate label for the feelings they are experiencing (Berscheid & Walster, 1974). The physiological arousal can be produced by sexual arousal, excitement, or even negative emotions such as jealousy. However, if that arousal is subsequently labeled as "I must be falling in love" or "She makes my heart flutter" or "He really turns me on," then the experience is seen as due to passionate love.

The theory is particularly useful in explaining why people may feel deepened love even when they experience continual rejection or hurt from their assumed lover. It suggests that such negative emotions can produce strong physiological arousal. If this arousal is interpreted as being caused by "love," then people may decide that they are even more in love than they were before they experienced such negative emotions.

But why should people label an emotional experience as "love" when there are so many possible alternatives? One answer is that in Western cultures, passionate love is seen as possible, acceptable, desirable—an experience to be sought. The virtues of passion are extolled in love ballads, commercials, TV shows, and film. Consequently, young adults are primed and ready to see love in their lives (Dion & Dion, 1988; Hatfield & Rapson, 1993).

It is interesting to note that this is not the way it is in every culture. For instance, in many cultures passionate, romantic love is a foreign concept. Marriages are arranged in some societies, based upon economic and status considerations. Even in Western cultures, the concept of love is of relatively recent origin. For instance, the notion that couples need to be in love was not "invented" until the Middle Ages, when social philosophers first suggested that love ought to be a requirement for marriage. Their goal in making such a proposal: to provide an alternative to the raw sexual desire that had served as the primary basis for marriage (Lewis, 1958; Xiaohe & Whyte, 1990).

STERNBERG'S TRIANGULAR THEORY: THE THREE FACES OF LOVE

To psychologist Robert Sternberg, love is more complex than a simple division into passionate and companionate types. He suggests instead that love is made up of three components: intimacy, passion, and decision/commitment. The **intimacy component** encompasses feelings of closeness, affection, and connectedness. The **passion component**

labeling theory of passionate love   the theory that individuals experience romantic love when two events occur together: intense physiological arousal and situational cues suggesting arousal is due to love

intimacy component   the component of love that encompasses feelings of closeness, affection, and connectedness

passion component   the component of love that comprises the motivational drives relating to sex, physical closeness, and romance

In part, love involves companionship and mutual enjoyment of various activities.

comprises the motivational drives relating to sex, physical closeness, and romance. This component is exemplified by intense, physiologically arousing feelings of attraction. Finally, the third aspect of love, the **decision/commitment component**, embodies both the initial cognition that one loves another person and the longer-term determination to maintain that love (Sternberg, 1986, 1988).

By jointly considering whether each of the three components is either present or missing from a relationship, eight unique combinations of love can be formed (see Table 14-2). For instance, *nonlove* occurs for those with whom people have only the most casual of relationships; it consists of the absence of the three components of intimacy, passion, and decision/commitment. *Liking* develops for those for whom only intimacy is present; *infatuated love* exists for those about whom only passion is felt; and *empty love* exists in those cases where only decision/commitment is present.

Other types of love are more complex. For instance, *romantic love* occurs when intimacy and passion are present, and *companionate love* when intimacy and decision/commit-

decision/commitment component   *the third aspect of love that embodies both the initial cognition that one loves another person and the longer-term determination to maintain that love*

TABLE 14-2

THE COMBINATIONS OF LOVE

	COMPONENT*		
	Intimacy	Passion	Decision/Commitment
Nonlove	-	-	-
Liking	+	-	-
Infatuated love	-	+	-
Empty love	-	-	+
Romantic love	+	+	-
Companionate love	+	-	+
Fatuous love	-	+	+
Consummate love	+	+	+

*+ = component present; - = component absent.
Source: Sternberg (1986).

ment occur jointly. When a couple experience romantic love, they are drawn together physically and emotionally, but they do not necessarily view the relationship as lasting. Companionate love, on the other hand, may occur in long-lasting relationships in which physical passion has taken a backseat.

Fatuous love exists when passion and decision/commitment, without intimacy, are present. Fatuous love is a kind of mindless loving, in which there is no emotional bond between the partners.

Finally, the eighth kind of love is *consummate love*. In consummate love, all three components of love are present. Although we might assume that consummate love represents the "ideal" love, such a view may well be mistaken. Many long-lasting and entirely satisfactory relationships are based on types of love other than consummate love. Furthermore, the type of love that predominates in a relationship varies over time. As can be seen in Figure 14-2, in strong, loving relationships the level of decision/commitment peaks and remains fairly stable. By contrast, passion tends to peak early in a relationship, but then declines and levels off. Intimacy also increases fairly rapidly, but can continue to grow over time.

Sternberg's triangular theory of love emphasizes both the complexity of love and its dynamic, evolving quality. As people and relationships develop and change over time, so does their love.

CHOOSING A PARTNER: RECOGNIZING MR. OR MS. RIGHT

For many young adults, the search for a partner is a major pursuit during early adulthood. Certainly society offers a great deal of advice on how to succeed in this endeavor, as a glance at the array of magazines at any supermarket checkout counter confirms. Despite all the counsel, however, the road to identifying an individual to share one's life is not always easy.

Seeking a Partner: Is Love the Only Thing That Matters?   Most people have no hesitation in articulating that the major factor in choosing a spouse is love. Most people in the United States, that is: If we ask people in some other societies, love becomes a secondary consideration. For instance, consider the results of a survey, presented in Figure 14-3, in which college students were asked if they would marry someone they did not love. Hardly anyone in the United States, Japan, or Brazil would consider it. On the other hand, a goodly propor-

FIGURE 14-2

THE SHAPE OF LOVE.

Over the course of a relationship, the three aspects of love—intimacy, passion, and decision/commitment—vary in their strength.

(*Source:* Sternberg, 1986.)

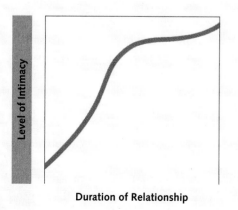

Duration of Relationship

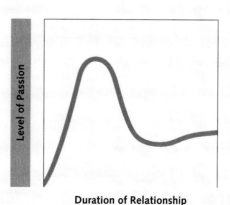

Duration of Relationship

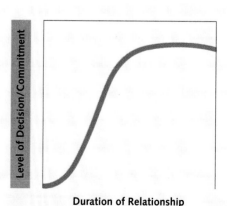

Duration of Relationship

FIGURE 14-3

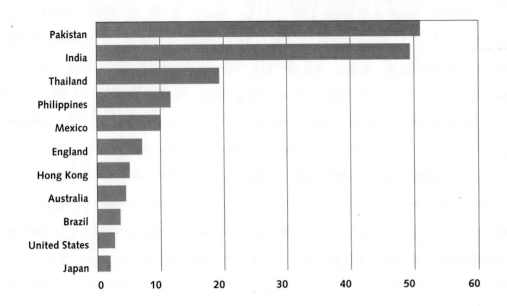

MARRY WITHOUT LOVE?

Shown are the percentages of people in various countries saying that they would marry someone even if they did not love that person.

(Adapted Levine, 1993.)

tion of college students in Pakistan and India would find it acceptable to marry without love (Levine, 1993).

If love is not the only important factor, what else matters? The characteristics differ considerably from one culture to another (see Table 14-3). For instance, a survey of nearly 10,000 respondents from around the world found that, while people in the United States believed that love and mutual attraction were the primary characteristics, in China men ranked good health most important and women rated emotional stability and maturity most critical. In contrast, in South Africa men from a Zulu background rated emotional stability first, and women rated dependable character of greatest concern (Buss et al., 1990).

On the other hand, commonalities exist across cultures. For instance, love and mutual attraction, even if not at the top of a specific culture's list, were relatively highly desired across all cultures. Furthermore, traits such as dependability, emotional stability, pleasing disposition, and intelligence were highly valued almost universally.

Certain gender differences in the preferred characteristics of a mate were similar across cultures—findings that have been confirmed by other surveys (e.g., Sprecher, Sullivan, & Hatfield, 1994). Men, more than women, prefer a potential marriage partner who is physically attractive. In contrast, women, more than men, prefer a potential spouse who is ambitious and industrious.

One explanation for cross-cultural similarities in gender differences rests on evolutionary factors. According to psychologist David Buss and colleagues (Buss et al., 1990), it is advantageous for human beings, as a species, to seek out certain characteristics in order to maximize the availability of beneficial genes. He argues that males in particular are genetically programmed to seek out mates with traits indicative of high reproductive capacity. Consequently, physically attractive, younger women might be more desirable as they are more capable of having children over a longer time period.

In contrast, women are genetically programmed to seek out men who have the potential to provide scarce resources so as to increase the likelihood that their offspring will survive. Consequently, they are attracted to mates who offer the highest potential of providing economic well-being (Feingold, 1992).

Although the evolutionary explanation makes logical sense, not everyone agrees. For instance, critics suggest that the similarities we find across cultures relating to different gen-

TABLE 14-3

MOST DESIRED CHARACTERISTICS IN A MARRIAGE PARTNER

	CHINA		SOUTH AFRICAN (ZULU)		UNITED STATES	
	Males	Females	Males	Females	Males	Females
Mutual Attraction–Love	4	8	10	5	1	1
Emotional Stability and Maturity	5	1	1	2	2	2
Dependable Character	6	7	3	1	3	3
Pleasing Disposition	13	16	4	3	4	4
Education and Intelligence	8	4	6	6	5	5
Good Health	1	3	5	4	6	9
Sociability	12	9	11	8	2	8
Desire for Home and Children	2	2	9	9	3	6
Refinement, Neatness	7	10	7	10	10	11
Ambition and Industriousness	10	5	8	7	11	7
Good Looks	11	15	14	16	7	14
Similar Education	15	12	12	12	12	12
Good Financial Prospects	16	14	18	13	16	10
Good Cook and Housekeeper	9	11	2	15	13	15
Favorable Social Status or Rating	14	13	17	14	14	13
Similar Religious Background	18	18	16	11	15	16
Chastity (no prior sexual intercourse)	3	6	13	18	17	18
Similar Political Background	17	17	15	17	18	17

Note: Numbers indicate rank ordering of characteristics.
Source: Buss et al., (1990).

der preferences may simply reflect similar patterns of gender stereotyping that have nothing to do with evolution. Such critics point out that, although some differences in what men and women prefer are consistent across cultures, there are also significant inconsistencies.

Filtering Models: Sifting Out a Spouse.   Although surveys assist in identifying the characteristics that are highly valued in a potential spouse, they are less helpful in determining how a specific individual is chosen as a partner. One approach that helps explain this is the filtering model developed by psychologists Louis Janda and Karen Klenke-Hamel (1980). They suggest that people seeking a mate screen potential candidates through successively finer-grained filters, just as we sift flour in order to remove undesirable material (see Figure 14-4).

The model assumes that people first filter for factors relating to broad determinants of attractiveness. Once these early screens have done their work, more sophisticated types of screening are used. The end result is a choice based on compatibility between the two individuals.

What determines compatibility? It is not only a matter of pleasing personality characteristics; several cultural factors also play an important role. For instance, people often marry according to the principle of **homogamy**, or the tendency to marry someone who is similar in age, race, education, religion, and other basic demographic characteristics. Homogamy is a dominant standard in most marriages in the United States (Surra, 1991; Kalmijn, 1991).

The marriage gradient represents another societal standard that determines who marries whom. The **marriage gradient** is the tendency for men to marry women who are

homogamy   the tendency to marry someone who is similar in age, race, education, religion, and other basic demographic characteristics

marriage gradient   the tendency for men to marry women who are slightly younger, smaller, and lower in status, and women to marry men who are slightly older, larger, and higher in status

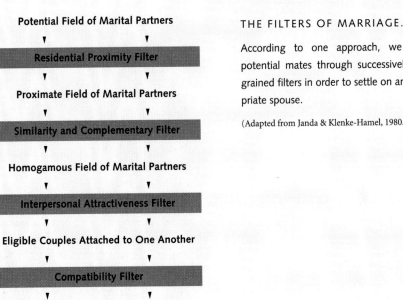

FIGURE 14-4

Potential Field of Marital Partners

Residential Proximity Filter

Proximate Field of Marital Partners

Similarity and Complementary Filter

Homogamous Field of Marital Partners

Interpersonal Attractiveness Filter

Eligible Couples Attached to One Another

Compatibility Filter

Eligible Couples With Role Fit

Married Couples

THE FILTERS OF MARRIAGE.

According to one approach, we screen potential mates through successively finer-grained filters in order to settle on an appropriate spouse.

(Adapted from Janda & Klenke-Hamel, 1980.)

slightly younger, smaller, and lower in status, and women to marry men who are slightly older, larger, and higher in status (Bernard, 1982).

The marriage gradient, which has a powerful influence on marriage in the United States, has important, and insidious, effects on partner choice. For one thing, it limits the number of potential mates for women, especially as they age, and allows men a wider choice. Furthermore, some men do not marry because they cannot find women of low enough status to meet the demands of the gradient, or cannot find women of the same or higher status who are willing to accept them as mates. Consequently, they are, in the words of sociologist Jessie Bernard (1982), "bottom of the barrel" men. On the other hand, some women will be unable to marry because they are higher in status than anyone in the available pool of men—"cream of the crop" women, in Bernard's words.

The marriage gradient makes finding a spouse particularly difficult for well-educated African-American women. Fewer African-American men attend college than do African-American women, making the potential pool of men who are suitable—as defined by society—relatively small. Consequently, relative to women of other races, African-American women are more apt to marry men who are less educated than they are (Taylor, Chatters, Tucker, & Lewis, 1991; Tucker & Mitchell-Kernan, 1995).

In addition to the principle of homogamy and the marriage gradient, other factors also influence the choices people make. In fact, some recent research suggests that the nature of the relationships we form as adults may be influenced by the style of parenting we experienced as infants—as considered in the Directions in Development section.

GAY AND LESBIAN RELATIONSHIPS: MEN WITH MEN AND WOMEN WITH WOMEN

Although most research conducted by psychologists has examined heterosexual relationships, an increasing number of studies have looked at relationships involving gay men and

Directions in Development

Attachment Styles and Romantic Relationships: Do Adult Loving Styles Reflect Attachment in Infancy?

Is the nature of attachment that people display during infancy reflected in their adult romantic relationships?

Increasing evidence suggests that it very well may be. As you may recall, attachment refers to the positive emotional bond that develops between a child and a particular individual (see Chapter 6). Infants generally are seen as falling into three attachment categories: *securely attached* (children with a healthy, positive, trusting relationship); *avoidant* (infants who are relatively indifferent to caregivers and who avoid interactions with them); and *anxious-ambivalent* (infants who show great distress when separated from a caregiver, but who appear angry upon the caregiver's return).

According to psychologist Phillip Shaver and colleagues, the influence of infants' attachment styles continues into adulthood and affects the nature of their romantic relationships (Hazan & Shaver, 1987; Shaver et al., 1988; Shaver, 1994). For instance, consider the following statements:

> *(1) I find it relatively easy to get close to others and am comfortable depending on them and having them depend on me. I don't often worry about being abandoned or about someone getting too close to me.*
> *(2) I am somewhat uncomfortable being close to others; I find it difficult to trust them completely, difficult to allow myself to depend on them. I am nervous when anyone gets too close, and often love partners want me to be more intimate than I feel comfortable being.*
> *(3) I find that others are reluctant to get as close as I would like. I often worry that my partner doesn't really love me or won't want to stay with me. I want to merge completely with another person, and this desire sometimes scares people away. (Shaver et al., 1988)*

According to Shaver's research, agreement with the first statement reflects a secure attachment style. Adults who agree with this statement readily enter into relationships and feel happy and confident about the future success of their relationships. Most young adults—just over half—display the secure style of attachment (Hazan & Shaver, 1987).

In contrast, adults who agree with the second statement typically display the avoidant attachment style. These individuals, who make up about a quarter of the population, tend to be less invested in relationships, have higher break-up rates, and often feel lonely.

Finally, agreement with the third category is reflective of an anxious-ambivalent style. Adults with an anxious-ambivalent style have a tendency to become overly invested in relationships, have repeated break-ups with the same partner, and have relatively low self-esteem. Around 20 percent of adults fall into this category (Simpson, 1987).

Recent research indicates that attachment style is also related to the nature of caregiving that adults give to their romantic partners. For instance, secure adults tend to provide sensitive caregiving, whereas anxious adults are more likely to provide compulsive, intrusive caregiving to partners who require assistance (Shaver, 1994).

It seems clear that there are continuities between infants' attachment styles and their behavior as adults. People who are having difficulty in relationships might well look back to their infancy to identify the root of their problem (Brennan & Shaver, 1995).

Homosexuals value similar attributes in their partners as do heterosexuals, and most seek to form loving, long-term, and meaningful relationships.

those involving lesbian women. The findings suggest that, compared to relationships between heterosexual couples, there are both similarities and differences.

For example, gay men describe successful relationships in ways that are similar to heterosexual couples' descriptions: Successful relationships involve greater appreciation for the partner and the couple as a whole, less conflict, and more positive feelings toward the partner. Similarly, lesbian women in a relationship show high levels of attachment, caring, intimacy, affection, and respect.

Despite the stereotype that gay males, in particular, find it difficult to form relationships and are interested in only sexual alliances, the reality is different. Most gays and lesbians seek loving, long-term, and meaningful relationships that differ little qualitatively from those desired by heterosexuals (Caldwell & Peplau, 1984; Peplau & Cochran, 1990; Kurdek, 1991, 1992).

Review and Rethink

REVIEW

- The course of relationships typically follows a pattern of increasing interaction, intimacy, and redefinition. SVR theory regards relationships as passing successively though *s*timulus, *v*alue, and *r*ole stages.

- According to the labeling theory of passionate love, people experience love when intense physiological arousal is accompanied by situational cues that the experience should be labeled "love."

- Types of love include passionate and companionate love. Sternberg's triangular theory identifies three basic components (intimacy, passion, and decision/commitment), which in combination can form eight types of love.

- In many Western cultures, love is the most important factor in selecting a partner. According to filtering models, people apply increasingly fine filters to potential partners, eventually choosing a mate according to the principles of homogamy and the marriage gradient.

◆ Attachment styles in infants appear to be linked to the ability to form romantic relationships in adulthood.

RETHINK

◆ How might a relationship that focuses first on values differ from one that focuses initially on external stimuli? Do any relationships focus first on roles?

◆ What has to change for a relationship to move from passionate to companionate love? From companionate to passionate love? In which direction is it more difficult for a relationship to move? Why?

◆ Through which of Sternberg's eight types of love do relationships tend to pass if they proceed from first acquaintance to a lifelong marriage?

◆ Do you accept the evolutionary explanation of gender differences in mate preferences proposed by Buss and colleagues? Why or why not? How would you test this theory?

◆ How do the principles of homogamy and the marriage gradient work to limit options for high-status women? How do they affect men's options?

THE COURSE OF RELATIONSHIPS

He wasn't being a chauvinist or anything, expecting me to do everything and him nothing. He just didn't *volunteer* to do things that obviously needed doing, so I had to put down some ground rules. Like if I'm in a bad mood, I may just yell: "I work eight hours just like you. This is half your house and half your child, too. You've got to do your share!" Jackson never changed the kitty litter box once in four years, but he changes it now, so we've made great progress. I just didn't expect it to take so much work. We planned this child together and we went through Lamaze together, and Jackson stayed home for the first two weeks. But then—wham—the partnership was over. (Cowan & Cowan, 1992, p. 63)

Relationships, like the individuals who comprise them, face a variety of challenges. As men and women move through early adulthood, they encounter significant changes in their lives as they work at starting and building their careers, having children, and establishing, maintaining, and sometimes ending relationships with others. One of the primary questions young adults face is whether and when they should marry.

MARRIAGE, POSSLQ, AND OTHER RELATIONSHIP CHOICES: SORTING OUT THE OPTIONS OF EARLY ADULTHOOD

For some people, the primary issue is not identifying a potential spouse, but whether to marry at all. Although surveys show that most heterosexuals say they want to get married, a significant number choose some other route. For instance, the past three decades have seen a dramatic rise in couples living together without being married, a status known as **cohabitation** (see Figure 14-5). These people, whom the U.S. Census Bureau calls *POSSLQs*, or *persons of the opposite sex sharing living quarters*, now make up about 4 percent of all couples in the United States. They tend to be young: Almost 40 percent are under 25. Although most are white, African-Americans are more likely to cohabit than whites. Furthermore, other countries have even higher cohabitation rates. In Sweden, for instance, about a quarter of all couples cohabit (Spanier, 1983; Bianchi & Spain, 1986; Popenoe, 1987).

Why do some couples choose to cohabit rather than to marry? Some feel they are not ready to make a lifelong commitment. Others feel the need to "practice" for marriage. Some reject the institution of marriage altogether, maintaining that marriage is outmoded and

cohabitation   *couples living together without being married*

FIGURE 14-5

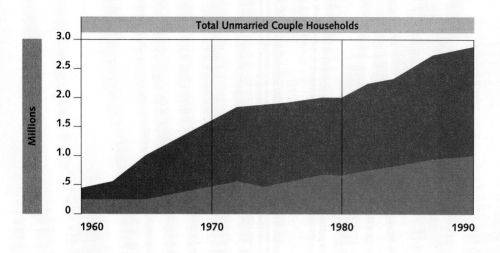

POSSLQS

The number of POSSLQs, or *persons of the opposite sex sharing living quarters,* has risen considerably in the last three decades.

(*Source*: U.S. Bureau of the Census, 1993.)

■ **Without Children**

■ **With Children**

that it is unrealistic to expect a couple to spend a lifetime together (Sarantakos, 1991; Hobart & Grigel, 1992; Cunningham & Antill, 1994).

On the other hand, marriage remains the preferred alternative for most people during early adulthood. Many see it as the appropriate culmination of a loving relationship; others feel it is the "right" thing to do after reaching a particular age in early adulthood. Others seek marriage because of the various roles that a spouse can fill (Nass, 1978). For instance, a spouse can play an economic role, providing security and financial well-being. Spouses also fill a sexual role, offering a means of sexual gratification and fulfillment that is fully accepted by society. Another role is therapeutic and recreational: Spouses provide a sounding-board to discuss one another's problems and act as partners for activities. Marriage also offers the only means of having children that is fully accepted by all segments of society. Finally, survey data suggest being married provides significant emotional, financial, and even health benefits, compared with remaining single or cohabiting (Waite, 1995).

Although it takes many forms, marriage is a central societal institution. In (a), we see a traditional wedding, while (b) shows 20,000 grooms and brides at a mass wedding ceremony conducted by the Unification Church.

(a)   (b)

"Your clock may be telling you to get married, but mine's telling me to have lunch."

Drawing by Cline; © 1995 The New Yorker Magazine, Inc.

Although marriage remains important, it is not a static institution. For example, fewer U.S. citizens are now married (62 percent) than at any time since the late 1890s. Part of this decline in marriage statistics is attributable to higher divorce rates (which we'll be discussing in Chapter 16), but the decision of people to marry later in life is also a contributing factor. The median age of first marriage in the United States is now 26 for men and 24 for women—the oldest age for women since national statistics were first collected in the 1880s (see Figure 14-6; Landers, 1990; Usdansky, 1992).

Does this mean that marriage is losing its viability as a social institution? Probably not. Most people—some 90 percent—eventually do wed, and national polls find that almost everyone endorses the notion that a good family life is important. Instead, the delay in marriage in part reflects economic concerns and the commitment to establishing a career. Choosing and starting a career presents an increasingly difficult series of choices, and some young adults feel that until they get a foothold on a career path and begin to earn an adequate salary, marriage plans should be put on hold.

FIGURE 14-6

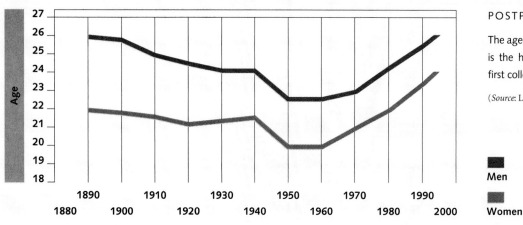

POSTPONING MARRIAGE.

The age at which women and men first marry is the highest since national statistics were first collected in the late 1800s.

(*Source*: Landers, 1990.)

Men

Women

WHAT MAKES MARRIAGE WORK? LOVE IS NOT ENOUGH

The statistics by now are so well known that they cause little surprise: Only about half of all marriages in the United States remain intact. Over a million marriages end in divorce each year, and there are 4.7 divorces for every 1,000 individuals. This figure actually represents a decline from the peak in the mid-1970s of 5.3 divorces per 1,000 people, and most experts think that the rate is leveling off (Edwards, 1995).

Furthermore, divorce is not just a problem in the United States. Countries around the world, both rich and poor, have shown increases in divorce during the last several decades (see Figure 14-7).

Although we'll discuss the consequences of divorce in greater detail in Chapter 16 when we consider middle age, divorce is a problem that has its roots in early adulthood and the early years of marriage. In fact, most divorces occur during the first 10 years of marriage.

Early Marital Conflict. According to some statistics, nearly half of newly married couples experience a significant degree of conflict. One of the major reasons is that partners may initially idealize one another, perceiving each other through the proverbial "starry eyes." However, as the realities of day-to-day living together and interacting begin to sink in, they become more aware of flaws (Pauker & Arond, 1989).

For instance, before marriage a man may take pride in his partner's frequent business trips to exotic locations. After their marriage, however, he may view the trips as a way for his wife to avoid responsibility at home, and he may become resentful of the time that she is absent (Bird & Melville, 1994).

Other factors may lead to marital conflict. For example, husbands and wives may have difficulty making the status transition from children of their parents to autonomous adults. Others have difficulty in developing an identity apart from their spouses, while some struggle to find a satisfactory allocation of time to share with the spouse, compared with time spent with friends and other family members (Tucker & Aron, 1993).

On the other hand, most married couples view the early years of marriage as deeply satisfying. For them, marriage can be a kind of extension of courtship. As they negotiate changes in their relationship and learn more about each other, many couples find themselves more deeply in love than before marriage. In fact, the newlywed period is for many couples one of the happiest of their entire married lives (Melville & Bird, 1994).

Can Divorce Be Predicted?   Researchers are obtaining increasing evidence that certain factors very accurately predict a later divorce. For instance, according to psychologist John Gottman, the accuracy of predicting divorce using certain variables can be higher than 90 percent (Gottman, Buehlman, & Katz, 1992; Gottman, 1993, 1995).

According to Gottman, the crucial factors, some of which are positive and some negative, include the following:

◆   affection displayed toward the spouse

◆   amount of negativity communicated to the spouse

◆   expansiveness or expressivity in communicating information about the relationship

◆   a sense of "we-ness," or perceiving oneself as part of an interdependent couple, rather than as one of two separate, independent individuals

◆   traditionality in gender roles

◆   volatility regarding the intensity of feelings in conflict situations

◆   a sense of control over one's life, as opposed to feelings of chaos

◆   pride in successfully getting through previous difficulties in the relationship

◆   disappointment and disenchantment with the marriage.

FIGURE 14-7

BREAKING FAMILY TIES AROUND THE WORLD.

Increases in divorce rates are not just a U.S. phenomena: Data from other countries also show significant increases.

(*Source*: Population Council, 1995.)

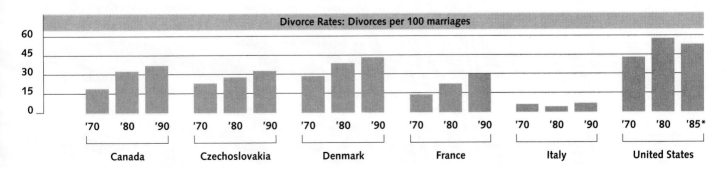

THE FAR SIDE   BY GARY LARSON

"Look, marriage is OK — but I also want
my own identity. ...I mean, how would *you* like it
if everyone referred to *you* as 'Chocolate Bar
and Chocolate Bar'?"

The Far Side © Far Works, Inc. Distributed by Universal Press
Syndicate. Reprinted with permission. All rights reserved.

The greatest likelihood of subsequent divorce occurred in cases in which husbands were low in affection, "we-ness," and expansiveness, but high in negativity and disappointment. Wives, on the other hand, displayed a different pattern. For them, the best predictors of divorce were low "we-ness" and high disappointment scores. The best single predictor of divorce was the degree of disappointment the husband felt about the marriage.

Other factors enter into the equation. For instance, divorce is more likely if spouses habitually attribute negative events to their partners. In this situation, when unpleasant things happen—even those that are not necessarily the spouse's fault—they are seen as connected to negative, unchangeable qualities of the spouse.

For example, consider the case of a husband who forgets to pick up a prescription for his wife at the drugstore. Wives who view such a mistake as an example of habitual forgetfulness, thoughtlessness, and irresponsibility are more prone to divorce than those who see the error as a one-time mistake, unrelated to enduring personality flaws. Generally, in solid marriages attributions about negative events tend to minimize the spouses' responsibility (Fincham & Bradbury, 1992; Bradbury & Fincham, 1992; Honeycutt, 1993).

Although it is clear that the nature of attributions differs in marriages that are at risk and those that are not, it is not clear whether the different attributional styles found in distressed marriages are the cause or the effect of the distress. Specifically, it may be that more dysfunctional attributions occur as a result of marital distress. Conversely, it is also plausible that negative attributional styles produce marital distress. If a man or woman continually misinterprets the causes of a spouse's behavior, seeing it in the worse possible light, it is not unlikely that the result will be an increase in marital discord.

PARENTHOOD: THE ARRIVAL OF CHILDREN

We had no idea what we were getting into when our first child was born. We certainly prepared for the event, reading magazine articles and books and even attending a class on child care. But when Sheanna was actually born, the sheer enormity of the task of taking care of her, her presence at every moment of the day, and the awesome responsibility of raising another human being weighed on us like nothing else we'd ever faced. Not that it was a burden. But it did make us look at the world with an entirely different perspective.

Like many parents, this couple was unable, before the fact, to grasp fully the tremendous, and sometimes overwhelming, nature of childrearing. The arrival of a child alters virtually every aspect of family life, in positive and, sometimes, negative ways.

Deciding To Have Children.   What makes a couple decide to have children in the first place? Childrearing certainly isn't economically advantageous: According to one estimate, a middle-class family with two children spends about $100,000 for each child by the time the child reaches the age of 18. Add in the costs of college and the figure comes to over $200,000 per child (Belkin, 1985; Cutler, 1990).

Instead, young adults typically cite psychological reasons for having children. They expect to derive pleasure from watching their children grow, fulfillment from their children's accomplishments, satisfaction from seeing them become successful, and enjoyment from forging a close bond with their youngsters. But there also may be a self-serving element in the decision to have children. For example, parents-to-be may hope that their children will provide for them in their old age, maintain a family business or farm, or simply offer companionship. Others have children because to do so is such a strong societal norm: More than 90 percent of all married couples have at least one child (Mackey, White, & Day, 1992).

For some couples, the decision to have children is inadvertent. Owing to the failure of birth control methods, some children are born without the benefit of being planned. In some cases, the family had been planning to have children at some point in the future, and so the pregnancy is not regarded as particularly undesirable and may even be welcomed. But in families that had actively *not* wanted to have children, or already had what they considered "enough" children, the pregnancy can be viewed as problematic (Clinton & Kelber, 1993).

The couples who are most likely to have unwanted pregnancies are often the most vulnerable in society. Unplanned pregnancies occur most frequently in younger, poorer, and less educated couples. On the other hand, there has been a dramatic rise in the use and effectiveness of contraceptives, and the incidence of undesired pregnancies has declined in the last several decades (Pratt, Mosher, Bachrach, & Horn, 1984).

The availability and use of effective contraceptives has also dramatically decreased the number of children in the average American family. As can be seen in Figure 14-8, over 40 percent of Americans polled in the 1970s desired families with three or more children, but by 1990 only 29 percent preferred three or more children. Today, most families seek to have no more than two children (Gallup & Newport, 1990).

These preferences have been translated into changes in the actual birth rate. In 1957, the *fertility rate* reached a post-World War II peak in the United States of 3.7 children per woman and then began to decline. Today, the rate remains below 2.0 children per woman, which is less than the *replacement level*, the number of children that one generation must produce to be able to replenish its numbers. Furthermore, by the year 2000 the number of couples who have no children is expected to rise by 12 percent from current levels (Exter, 1990).

What has produced this decline in the fertility rate? In addition to the availability of more reliable birth control methods, one reason is that increasing numbers of women have joined the workforce. The pressures of simultaneously holding a job and raising a child have convinced many women to have fewer children. Furthermore, many women who work outside the home are choosing to have children later in their childbearing years in order to

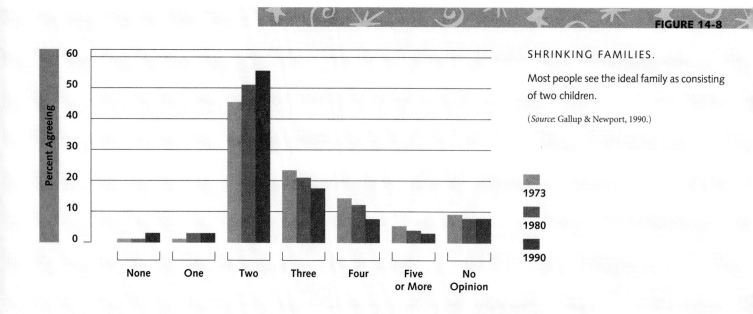

FIGURE 14-8

SHRINKING FAMILIES.

Most people see the ideal family as consisting of two children.

(*Source:* Gallup & Newport, 1990.)

1973

1980

1990

develop their careers. In fact, women between the ages of 30 and 34 are the only ones whose rate of births has actually increased over earlier decades. Still, because women who have their first children in their 30s have fewer years in which to have offspring, they ultimately cannot have as many children as women who begin childbearing in their 20s.

Finally, some of the traditional incentives for having children—such as their potential for providing economic support in old age—may no longer be as attractive. Potential parents may view Social Security and other pensions as a more predictable means of support when they are elderly. Furthermore, the sheer costs of raising a child, particularly the well-publicized increase in the cost of college, may act as a disincentive for bearing larger numbers of children (Bird & Melville, 1994).

The Impact of Children on Parents: Two's a Couple, Three's a Crowd?   How do couples react to the birth of a child? One fact is well established: For many couples, marital satisfaction takes a dive (Figley, 1973; Tucker & Aron, 1993). Before the birth of children, spouses are able to focus their attention on each other. They are able to respond to one another's needs, and they see their partners, as well as themselves, as autonomous individuals.

The birth of a child triggers a dramatic shift in the roles spouses must play. They are suddenly placed in new roles—"mother" and "father"—and these new positions may overwhelm their ability to respond in their older, although continuing, roles of "wife" and "husband" (Clulow, 1991). As one new father expressed his frustration with what he saw as his wife's willingness to allow their child to take precedence over him, "I keep asking her to get a sitter so we can go out for a quiet dinner, but she always finds a reason not to. It's like being turned down for a date week after week" (Cowan & Cowan, 1992, p. 61).

For many couples, the strains accompanying the birth of a child produce the lowest level of marital satisfaction of any point in their marriage. This is particularly true for women, who tend to be more dissatisfied than men with their marriages after the arrival of children. The most likely reason for this gender difference is that wives typically experience a greater increase in their responsibilities than do husbands (Glenn, 1990).

Wives' perception that men expend less effort in childrearing than they do is an accurate reading of reality. Even when both spouses hold jobs outside the home and work similar hours, the wife generally spends more time taking care of the children than the husband does (Biernat & Wortman, 1991; Kurdek, 1993; see Figure 14-9).

Parenthood expands the roles of both husbands and wives into that of fathers and mothers, a process that can have profound effects on couples' relationships.

FIGURE 14-9

WHO'S DOING THE WORK?

Although men and women work at their jobs a similar number of hours, women are apt to spend more time than their husbands in home chores and child-care activities.

(*Source*: Googans & Burden, 1987.)

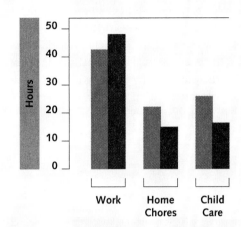

Married Females

Married Males

On the other hand, not all couples experience a decrease in marital satisfaction upon the birth of a child. Some, in fact, feel greater satisfaction during the years when they are most involved in childrearing. This is true primarily for couples who harbor realistic expectations regarding the extent of childrearing and other household responsibilities they face when children are born (Cowan & Cowan, 1988; Belsky et al., 1989; Hackel & Ruble, 1992).

Developmental Diversity

Gay and Lesbian Parents

In increasing numbers, children are being raised in families in which there are two Moms or two Dads. Rough estimates suggest that some 20 percent of gay men and lesbian women are parents (Falk, 1989; Turner, Scadden, & Harris, 1990).

How do lesbian and gay households compare to heterosexual households? To answer the question, we first need to consider some characteristics of gay and lesbian couples without children. According to studies comparing gay, lesbian, and heterosexual couples, labor tends to be divided more evenly in homosexual than in heterosexual households. Each partner in a homosexual relationship is more likely to carry out approximately the same number of different chores, compared with heterosexual partners. Furthermore, gay and lesbian couples cling more strongly to the ideal of an egalitarian allocation of household chores than do heterosexual couples (Deutsch, Lussier, & Servis, 1993; Kurdek, 1993; C.J. Patterson, 1992, 1994).

However, as with heterosexual couples, the arrival of a child (through adoption or artificial insemination) changes the dynamics of household life considerably in homosexual couples. Like heterosexual unions, a specialization of roles develops. According to recent research on lesbian mothers, for instance, childrearing tends to fall more to one member of the couple, while the other spends more time in paid employment. Although both partners usually say they share household tasks and decision making equally, biological mothers are more involved in child care. Conversely, the nonbiological mother in the couple is more likely to report spending greater time in paid employment (Patterson, 1995).

In short, research appears to indicate that the evolution of homosexual couples when children arrive is more similar to that of heterosexual couples than dissimilar, particularly in the increased role specialization occasioned by the requirements of child care. Of course, such research does not answer the question of what the consequences are for children being raised by homosexual parents. However, most research suggests that children raised in homosexual households show no differences in terms of eventual adjustment from those raised in heterosexual households. Although they may face greater challenges from a society in which the roots of prejudice against homosexuality are deep, children who have two Moms or two Dads ultimately seem to fare well (C.J. Patterson, 1992; Flaks et al., 1995).

Review and Rethink

REVIEW

◆ Cohabitation is an increasingly popular option for young adults, but most still choose marriage. The median age at which both men and women marry for the first time is rising, however.

◆ Divorce is prevalent in the United States, particularly within the first 10 years of marriage. The shift from an idealized view of married life to the reality can cause early discord.

◆ Factors that predict divorce include the levels of affection, negativity, and expressivity in the marriage. The attribution of negative events to a spouse's personality traits is also a significant predictor of divorce.

◆ Couples overwhelmingly desire to produce children, although both the availability of contraception and changes in women's roles in the workplace have combined to decrease average family size.

◆ Children bring pressures to both heterosexual and homosexual relationships, causing changes in focus, roles, and responsibilities.

RETHINK

◆ In what ways do you think cognitive changes in early adulthood (e.g., the emergence of postformal thought and practical intelligence) affect how young adults deal with questions of marriage, divorce, and childrearing?

◆ Why do you think society has established such a powerful norm in favor of marriage? What effects might such a norm have on a person who prefers to remain single?

◆ Why might spouses view each other's behaviors differently before and after marriage?

◆ Can people's attribution patterns regarding negative events in marriage be changed? Is this a basis for marriage counseling?

◆ Do the changes that children bring to a relationship affect husbands and wives equally? Do they affect each partner in a gay or lesbian relationship equally? Why or why not?

WORK: CHOOSING AND EMBARKING ON A CAREER

Why did I decide that I wanted to be a lawyer? The answer is a bit embarrassing. When I got to my senior year of college, I began to worry about what I was going to do when I graduated. My parents were asking, with increasing frequency, what kind of work I was thinking about, and I felt the pressure rising with each phone call from home. So I began to think seriously about the problem. At the time, the O.J. Simpson trial was in the news all the time, and it got me to thinking about what it might be like to be an attorney. I had always been fascinated by *L.A. Law* when it had been on television, and I could envision myself in one of those big corner offices with a view of the city. For these reasons, and just about none other, I decided to take the law boards and apply to law school.

For almost all of us, early adulthood is a period of decisions with lifelong implications. One of the most critical is choosing a career path. The choice we make goes well beyond determining how much money we will earn; it also relates to our status, our sense of self-worth, and the contribution that we will make in life. In sum, decisions about work go to the very core of a young adult's identity.

IDENTITY DURING YOUNG ADULTHOOD: THE ROLE OF WORK

According to psychiatrist George Vaillant, young adulthood is marked by a stage of development called **career consolidation**, a stage that is entered between the ages of 20 and 40, when young adults become centered on their careers. Based on a comprehensive longitudinal study of a large group of male graduates of Harvard begun when they were freshmen in the 1930s, Vaillant found a general pattern of psychological development (Vaillant, 1977; Vaillant & Vaillant, 1990).

In their early 20s, the men tended to be influenced by their parents' authority. But in their late 20s and early 30s, they started to act with greater autonomy. They married and began to have and raise children. At the same time, they started and began to focus on their careers—the period of career consolidation.

Based on his data, Vaillant drew a relatively uninspiring portrait of people in the career consolidation stage. The participants in his study tended to be rule-followers, worked very hard, were working their way up the corporate ladder, and sought to conform to the norms of their professions. Rather than showing the independence and questioning that they had displayed earlier while still in college, they threw themselves unquestioningly into their work.

Vaillant argues that work played such an important role in the lives of the men he studied that the career consolidation stage should be seen as an addition to Erik Erikson's stages of psychosocial identity. If you turn back to Table 12-1 in Chapter 12, you'll see that Erikson regards young adulthood as the time of the **intimacy-versus-isolation stage**. People in this stage, which spans the period of postadolescence into the early 30s, focus on developing close relationships with others. Those who experience difficulties during this stage are lonely and have a fear of relationships. On the other hand, people who successfully resolve the crisis of the stage are able to form intimate relationships on a physical, intellectual, and emotional level.

In the view of Vaillant, career concerns come to supplant the focus on intimacy, and the career consolidation stage marks a bridge between Erikson's intimacy-versus-isolation stage and Erikson's next period, that of generativity versus stagnation. (Generativity refers to an individual's contribution to society, as we'll discuss in Chapter 16.) However, there is little agreement on the accuracy of this contention. Critics point out, for instance, that Vaillant's sample, although relatively large, comprised a highly restricted, unusually bright group of people, all of them men. It is hard to know how generalizable the results are. Furthermore, societal norms have changed considerably since the time the study was begun in the late 1930s, and people's views of the importance of work may have shifted. Finally, the lack of women in the sample, and that fact that there have been major changes in the role of work in *women's* lives, make Vaillant's conclusions even less generalizable.

Still, it is hard to argue about the importance of work in most people's lives, and current research suggests that it makes up a significant part of both men's and women's iden-

career consolidation *a stage that is entered between the ages of 20 and 40 when young adults become centered on their careers*

intimacy-versus-isolation stage *according to Erik Erikson, the period of postadolescence into the early 30s that focuses on developing close relationships with others*

People enter the period of career choice in early adulthood, and seek information about specific career choices, as at this job fair.

fantasy period   *according to Eli Ginzberg, the period when career choices are made, and discarded, without regard to skills, abilities, or available job opportunities*

tentative period   *the second stage of Ginzberg's theory, which spans adolescence, and people begin to think in pragmatic terms about the requirements of various jobs and how their own abilities might fit with them*

tity—if for no other reason than many people spend more time working than they do on any other activity (Deaux, Reind, Mizrahi, & Ethier, 1995). We turn now to how people decide what careers to follow—and the implications of that decision.

PICKING AN OCCUPATION: CHOOSING LIFE'S WORK

Some people know from childhood that they want to be physicians or firefighters or go into business, and they follow invariant paths toward that goal. For others, the choice of a career is much a matter of chance, of turning to the want ads and seeing what's available.

Ginzberg's Career-choice Theory.   According to Eli Ginzberg (1972), people typically move through a series of stages in choosing a career. The first stage is the **fantasy period**, which lasts until a person is about 11. During the fantasy period, career choices are made, and discarded, without regard to skills, abilities, or available job opportunities. Instead, choices are made solely on the basis of what sounds appealing. Thus, a child may decide she wants to be a veterinarian—despite the fact that she is allergic to dogs and cats.

People begin to take practical considerations into account during the **tentative period**, which spans adolescence. People begin to think in pragmatic terms about the requirements of various jobs and how their own abilities might fit with them. They also consider their personal values and goals, exploring how well a particular occupation might satisfy them.

Speaking of Development

Henry Klein

Born: ···································· 1918

Education: ························· University of Pennsylvania, B.A. in English; University of Pennsylvania, M.A. in sociology; Temple University, Ph.D. in psychoeducational processes

Position: ························· Founder and director, American College and Career Counseling Center

Home: ························· Philadelphia, Pennsylvania

At one time or another everyone has pondered the question of which career to pursue, or whether to change a current job. For those facing that decision there are people like Henry Klein.

In 1962 Klein founded the American College and Career Counseling Center in Philadelphia. Its purpose is to help people find professions that are right for them.

A former columnist who wrote for 20 years on careers and education for several Philadelphia newspapers, Klein has also published a book that answers questions about getting into, and staying in, college.

Career counseling at Klein's center, which lasts about five sessions, begins with a basic interview and proceeds to the point where the counselor and the client have identified specific companies to pursue and outlined concrete strategies for approaching them.

"Before people come to me for career counseling I ask them to send me their résumés, and if they're close to graduation, copies of their transcripts," Klein explains. "I look through the transcript to find the strongest subject areas and try to get a baseline from that. I then look over the résumé to get a sense of the progression of jobs the person has passed through, as well as the functions and skills that the person has practiced.

Finally, in early adulthood, people enter the **realistic period**. Here young adults explore specific career options either through actual experience on the job or through training for a profession. After initially exploring what they might do, people begin to narrow their choices to a few alternative careers and eventually make a commitment to a particular one.

Although Ginzberg's theory makes sense, critics have charged that it oversimplifies the process of choosing a career. Because Ginzberg's research was based on subjects from middle socioeconomic levels, it may overstate the choices and options available to those in lower socioeconomic levels. Furthermore, the ages associated with the various stages might be too rigid. For instance, someone who does not attend college but begins to work immediately after high school graduation is likely to be making serious career decisions at a much earlier point than someone who attends college.

Holland's personality-type theory. Other theories of career choice emphasize how an individual's personality affects decisions about a career. According to John Holland, for instance, certain personality types match particularly well with certain careers. If the correspondence between personality and career is good, people will enjoy their careers more and be more likely to stay in them; but if the match is poor, they will be unhappy and more likely to shift into other careers (Holland, 1973, 1987; Gottfreedson & Holland, 1990).

According to Holland, six personality types are important in career choice:

realistic period *the stage of Ginzberg's theory that spans young adulthood during which people explore specific career options*

"We will try to find out if there's any common thread, no matter how small, that runs through each of the jobs—and there is usually something there that I can grab onto."

"You can't talk in terms of just one occupation; you have to think in terms of a career."

"I look for a particular trend in a field, and if there are no negatives, we go in that direction," he adds.

Although a fairly clear trend line is easier to work with, the person with a scattered, inconsistent history is more of a challenge, according to Klein.

"If the person's experience is scattered and there's no particular trend, we almost have to start from zero. In that case we have to ask a lot of basic questions, such as "What kind of person are you?' and "Where are you in your development?'

"We won't throw away all the things a person has been doing. We will try to find out if there's any common thread, no matter how small, that runs through each of the jobs—and there is usually *something* there that I can grab onto," he notes. "There might be a clue inside each job. It could be only a part of each of the jobs people have had, but they couldn't see it because they were always looking at the job as a whole."

While it is important to look at academic and work background, Klein points out that a person's character and development are equally important, if not more so.

"A person with a fairly stable life, who hasn't moved around a lot or job-hopped, produces a trend in careers and vocations that we can use," he says. "You have to work on personal development before you can commit to something in the longer term.

"Even if you fell into the perfect job, your personal development might push you out sooner or later if you were not up to a long-term career commitment. You can't talk in terms of just one occupation; you have to think in terms of a career."

♦ *Realistic.* These people are down-to-earth, practical problem-solvers, and physically strong, but their social skills are mediocre. They make good farmers, laborers, and truck drivers.

♦ *Intellectual.* Intellectual types are oriented toward the theoretical and abstract. Although not particularly good with people, they are well suited to careers in math and science.

♦ *Social.* The traits associated with the social personality type are related to verbal skills and interpersonal relations. Social types are good at working with people, and consequently make good salespersons, teachers, and counselors.

♦ *Conventional.* Conventional individuals prefer highly structured tasks. They make good clerks, secretaries, and bank tellers.

♦ *Enterprising.* These individuals are risk-takers and take-charge types. They are good leaders and may be particularly effective as managers or politicians.

♦ *Artistic.* Artistic types use art to express themselves, and they often prefer the world of art to interactions with people. They are best suited to occupations involving art.

Although Holland's enumeration of personality types is sensible, it suffers from a central flaw: Not everyone fits neatly into particular personality types. Furthermore, there are certainly exceptions to the typology, with jobs being held by people who do not have the particular personality that Holland would predict. Still, the basic notions of the theory have been validated, and they form the foundation of several measures designed to assess the occupational options for which a given person is particularly suited (Randahl, 1991).

Gender and Career Choices: Women's Work

WANTED: Full-time employee for small family firm. DUTIES: Including but not limited to general cleaning, cooking, gardening, laundry, ironing and mending, purchasing, bookkeeping and money management. Child care may also be required. HOURS: Avg. 55/wk but standby duty required 24 hours/day, 7 days/wk. Extra workload on holidays. SALARY AND BENEFITS: No salary, but food, clothing, and shelter provided at employer's discretion; job security and benefits depend on continued good will of employer. No vacation. No retirement plan. No opportunities for advancement. REQUIREMENTS: No previous experience necessary, can learn on the job. Only women need apply. (Unger & Crawford, 1992, p. 446)

Just two decades ago, many women entering early adulthood assumed that this admittedly exaggerated job description matched the work for which they were best suited and to which they aspired: housewife. Even those women who sought work outside the home were relegated to certain professions. For instance, until the 1960s employment ads in newspapers throughout the United States were almost always divided into two sections: "Help Wanted: Male" and "Help Wanted: Female." The men's job listings encompassed such professions as police officer, construction worker, and legal counsel; the women's listings were for secretaries, teachers, cashiers, and librarians.

The breakdown of jobs deemed appropriate for men and women reflected society's traditional view of what the two genders were best suited for. Traditionally, women were considered most appropriate for **communal professions**, occupations associated with relationships. In contrast, men were perceived as best suited for **agentic professions**, occupations associated with getting things accomplished. It is probably no coincidence that communal professions typically have lower status and pay less than do agentic professions (Eagly & Steffen, 1984, 1986).

communal professions *occupations associated with relationships*

agentic professions *occupations associated with getting things accomplished*

Although discrimination based on gender is far less blatant today than it was several decades ago—it is now illegal, for instance, to advertise a position specifically for a man or a woman—remnants of traditional gender-role prejudice persist. As we discussed in Chapter 13, women are less likely to be found in traditionally male-dominated professions such as engineering and computer programming. As shown in Figure 14-10, women in many professions earn less than do men in identical jobs. Although the discrepancy has been reduced in the last decade, this change has more to do with men's wages falling because of the disappearance of highly paid manufacturing jobs than with rises in women's wages (CIRE, 1990; U.S. Bureau of Labor Statistics, 1993).

Despite status and pay that are often lower than men's, more women are working outside the home than ever before. Between 1950 and 1990, the percentage of the female population (aged 16 and over) in the U.S. labor force increased from 35 percent to nearly 60 percent, and women today make up about 46 percent of the labor force. Almost all women expect to earn a living, and almost all do at some point in their lives. Furthermore, in about one-half of U.S. households, women earn about as much as their husbands (Lewin, 1995).

Furthermore, opportunities for women are in many ways considerably greater than they were in earlier years. Women are more likely to be physicians, lawyers, insurance agents, and bus drivers than they were in the past. However, within specific job categories, sex discrimination still occurs. For example, female bus drivers are more apt to have part-time school bus routes, while men hold better-paying full-time routes in cities. Similarly, female pharmacists are more likely to work in hospitals, while men work in higher-paying jobs in retail stores (Unger & Crawford, 1992).

In the same way, women (and also minorities) in high-status, visible professional roles may hit what has come to be called the *glass ceiling*, an invisible barrier within an organization that, because of discrimination, prevents individuals from being promoted beyond a

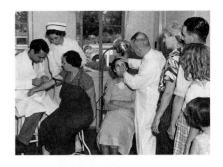

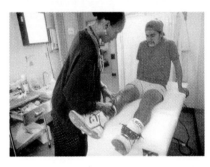

In the 1930s, it was the rare woman who would even consider becoming a doctor. Today, however, the story is different, and women make up an increasing proportion of physicians. Even so, women often earn less than men, even in identical professions.

FIGURE 14-10

THE PERSISTENT GENDER GAP.

The median wages of women in a given profession are shown as a proportion of the wages that men receive.

(*Source*: U.S. Bureau of Labor Statistics, 1992.)

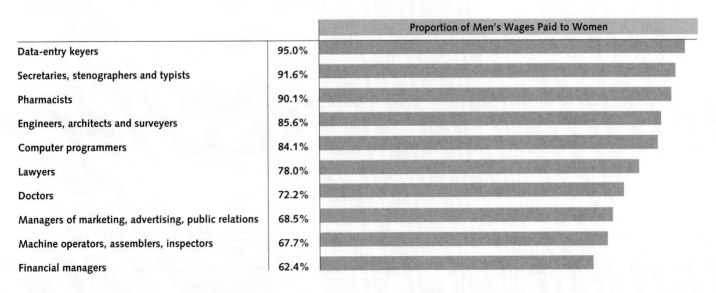

		Proportion of Men's Wages Paid to Women
Data-entry keyers	95.0%	
Secretaries, stenographers and typists	91.6%	
Pharmacists	90.1%	
Engineers, architects and surveyers	85.6%	
Computer programmers	84.1%	
Lawyers	78.0%	
Doctors	72.2%	
Managers of marketing, advertising, public relations	68.5%	
Machine operators, assemblers, inspectors	67.7%	
Financial managers	62.4%	

certain level. It operates subtly, and often the people responsible for keeping the glass ceiling in place are unaware of how their actions perpetuate discrimination against women and minorities (Larwood, Szwajkowski, & Rose, 1988; Morrison & von Gilnow, 1990; Snyder, Verderber, Langmeyer, & Myers, 1992).

WHY DO PEOPLE WORK?: MORE THAN EARNING A LIVING

The question of why people work would seem an easy one to answer: People work to earn a living. Yet the reality is different, for young adults express many reasons for seeking a job.

Intrinsic and Extrinsic Motivation. Certainly, people work to obtain various concrete rewards, or out of extrinsic motivation. **Extrinsic motivation** drives people to obtain tangible rewards, such as money and prestige (Singer, Stacey, & Lange, 1993).

On the other hand, people also work for factors relating to intrinsic motivation. **Intrinsic motivation** causes people to work for their own enjoyment, not for the rewards work may bring. For instance, people in many Western societies tend to subscribe to the *Puritan work ethic*, the notion that work is important in and of itself. According to this view, working is a meaningful act that brings psychological and (at least in the traditional view) even spiritual well-being and satisfaction (Stohs, 1992).

Work also brings a sense of personal identity. Consider, for instance, what people say about themselves when they first meet someone. After mentioning their names and where they live, they very typically tell what they do for a living. What people do is a large part of who they are (Repetti, & Cosmas, 1991).

Work also may be a central element in people's social lives. Because so much time is spent in work settings, work can be a source of young adults' friends and social activities. Social relationships forged at work may spill over into other parts of people's lives. In addition, there are often social obligations—dinner with the boss, or the annual seasonal party in December—that are related to work.

Finally, the kind of work that people do is a factor in determining **status**, which is the evaluation by society of the role a person plays. Various jobs are associated with a certain status, as indicated in Table 14-4. For instance, physicians and college teachers are near the top of the status hierarchy, while ushers and shoe shiners fall to the bottom.

extrinsic motivation *motivation that drives people to obtain tangible rewards, such as money and prestige*

intrinsic motivation *motivation that causes people to work for their own enjoyment, not for the rewards work may bring*

status *the evaluation of a role or person by other relevant members of a group or society*

Lawyers are high on the status hierarchy of professions, and some lawyers—such as Marcia Clark, prosecutor at the O.J. Simpson murder trial—achieve even greater status as a result of media exposure

TABLE 14-4

STATUS HIERARCHY OF VARIOUS PROFESSIONS

Occupation	Score	Occupation	Score
Physician	82	Bank teller	50
College teacher	78	Electrician	49
Lawyer	76	Police officer	48
Dentist	74	Insurance agent	47
Bank officer	72	Secretary	46
Airline pilot	70	Air traffic controller	43
Clergy	69	Mail carrier	42
Sociologist	66	Owner of a farm	41
Secondary school teacher	63	Restaurant manager	39
Registered nurse	62	Automobile mechanic	37
Pharmicist	61	Baker	34
Elementary school teacher	60	Salesclerk	29
Accountant	56	Gas station attendant	22
Painter	56	Waiter and waitress	20
Librarian	55	Laundry operator	18
Actor	55	Garbage collector	17
Funeral director	52	Janitor	16
Athlete	51	Usher	15
Reporter	51	Shoeshiner	12

Source: NORC (1990).

Satisfaction On the Job. The status associated with particular jobs affects people's satisfaction with their work. As might be expected, the higher the status of the job, the more satisfied people tend to be (Yankelovich, 1974). Furthermore, the status of the job of the major wage-earner can affect the status of other members of the family.

Of course, status isn't everything: Worker satisfaction depends on a number of factors, not the least of which is the nature of the job itself. For example, consider the plight of Patricia Alford, who worked at the Equitable Life Assurance Company. Her job consisted of entering data into a computer 9 hours each day except for two 15-minute breaks and an hour off for lunch. She never knew how much she was earning, because her salary depended on how many insurance claims she entered into the computer each day. The pay standards were so complicated that her salary varied from $217 to $400 a week, providing her with a weekly surprise at paycheck time (Booth, 1987).

Other people who work at computers are monitored on a minute-by-minute basis; supervisors can consistently see how many keystrokes they are entering. In some firms in which workers use the telephone for sales or to take customer orders, their conversations are monitored by supervisors. Not surprisingly, such forms of management produce worker dissatisfaction.

On the other hand, job satisfaction increases when workers have input into the nature of their jobs. Furthermore, variety is the spice of job life: People enjoy jobs that require several different types of skills more than those that require only a minimal number. Finally, the more influence employees have over others, either directly as supervisors or more informally, the greater their job satisfaction (Katzell & Guzzo, 1983; Steers & Porter, 1991).

The Informed Consumer of Development

Choosing a Career

One of the greatest challenges people face in early adulthood is making a decision that will have lifelong implications: the choice of a career. Although there is no single correct choice—most people can be happy in any of several different jobs—the options can be daunting. Here are some guidelines for at least starting to come to grips with the question of what occupational path to follow.

- Systematically evaluate a variety of choices. Libraries contain a wealth of information about potential career paths, and most colleges and universities have career centers that can provide occupational data and guidance.

- Know yourself. Evaluate your strengths and weaknesses, perhaps by completing a questionnaire at a college career center that can provide insight into your interests, skills, and values.

- Create a "balance sheet," listing the potential gains and losses that you will incur from a particular profession. First list the gains and losses that you will experience directly, and then list gains and losses for others. Next, write down your projected self-approval or self-disapproval from the potential career. Finally, list the projected social approval or disapproval you are likely to receive from others. By systematically evaluating a set of potential careers according to each of these criteria, you will be in a better position to compare different possibilities.

- "Try out" different careers through paid or unpaid internships. By seeing a job first-hand, interns are able to get a better sense of what an occupation is truly like.

- Remember that if you make a mistake, it is possible to change careers. In fact, people today increasingly change careers in early adulthood and even beyond. No one should feel locked into a decision made earlier in life. As we've seen throughout this book, people develop substantially over the course of their lives.

- It is reasonable to expect that shifting values, interests, abilities, and life circumstances might make a different career more appropriate later in life than the one chosen during early adulthood.

Review and Rethink

REVIEW

- Choosing a career is an important step in early adulthood, so important that George Vaillant considers career consolidation a developmental stage on a par with Erikson's intimacy-versus-isolation stage.

- According to Eli Ginzberg, people pass through three stages in considering careers: the fantasy period, the tentative period, and the realistic period.

◆ Other theories of career choice, such as John Holland's, attempt to match personality types to suitable careers.

◆ Gender stereotypes and traditional societal views regarding women's and men's work are changing, but women still experience subtle prejudice in career choices, roles, and wages.

◆ People work because of both extrinsic and intrinsic motivation factors. Job satisfaction results from characteristics such as status, control, job variety, and influence over others.

RETHINK

◆ If George Vaillant's study were performed today on women, in what ways do you think the results would be similar to or different from those of the original study?

◆ How good do you think the match is between personality characteristics and career choices? What issues relating to gender, ethnic, or cultural bias would be of concern to you in designing a career-oriented personality inventory?

◆ What sorts of unconscious behaviors and attitudes on the part of supervisors and co-workers contribute to the glass ceiling that affects women and minorities in the work-place?

◆ How does the division of jobs into communal and agentic relate to traditional views of male–female differences?

◆ How does the issue of motivation apply to workers of low socioeconomic status performing low-status jobs? How might opportunities for promotion and advancement be affected by low motivation?

LOOKING BACK

What are the types and causes of love, and how does love change over time?

1. The course of a relationship tends to proceed, according to stimulus-value-role theory, from a stage based on surface characteristics, through a stage based on values, to a final stage built on roles played by the participants.

2. Two main kinds of love are passionate, characterized by intense physiological arousal, intimacy, and caring, and companionate, characterized by respect, admiration, and affection.

3. According to the labeling theory of passionate love, feelings of love are brought about by a combination of intense physiological arousal (whether positive or negative) and situational and cultural cues that associate the label "love" with the experience.

4. Psychologist Robert Sternberg suggests that three components of love (intimacy, passion, and decision/commitment), combine to form eight types of love, through which a relationship can evolve.

How do people choose spouses, and what do they look for in a marriage relationship?

5. Although in Western cultures love tends to be the most important factor in selecting a partner, other cultures emphasize other factors. There are also gender differences in the characteristics that are sought in a partner.

6. According to filtering models, people filter potential partners initially for broad attractiveness factors, and then for compatibility factors, generally conforming to the princi-

ple of homogamy (relating to similarity) and to the marriage gradient (relating to status, size, and age).

7. Research suggests that people's attachment styles as infants tend to translate into their relative ease with romantic relationships as adults.

8. Gay men and lesbian women generally tend to seek the same qualities in relationships as do heterosexual men and women: attachment, caring, intimacy, affection, and respect.

Why do people marry, and why do they divorce?

9. In young adulthood, the question of marriage becomes urgent. Although cohabitation is increasingly popular, marriage remains the most attractive option for most young adults, although the median age of first marriage is rising for both men and women.

10. Divorce is prevalent in the United States, affecting nearly half of all marriages. Although the early years of a marriage are generally happy, discord can arise because of a shift from an ideal to a real view of the partner and the transition from being children to being adults.

11. Factors that predict divorce include the degree of affection or negativity expressed, expansiveness about the relationship, the sense of "we-ness" in the marriage, and feelings of disappointment with the marriage. Attribution also plays a role: Spouses who attribute negative events to unchanging personal characteristics in the spouse are more likely to divorce than are those who do not make such attributions.

How does the arrival of children affect a relationship?

12. The desire of couples to have children is very strong: More than 90 percent of married couples have at least one child. However, the size of the average family has decreased, and the U.S. fertility rate is now lower than the replacement level. This is due partly to birth control and partly to the changing roles of women in the workforce.

13. Children bring pressures to any marriage, including a shift in focus of the marriage partners, a change in their roles, and an increase in their responsibilities, especially the wife's.

14. Gay and lesbian couples with children experience similar changes in their relationships. Although the roles of the partners before children were more equal than in the typical heterosexual relationship, after children the roles tend to become just as divided, with one partner usually assuming the primary caregiver role.

Why is choosing a career such an important issue for young adults, and what factors influence the choice of a career?

15. According to George Vaillant, career consolidation is a developmental stage every bit as important as Erikson's intimacy-versus-isolation stage, and it should be separately considered. In his view, young adults are simultaneously involved in the critical task of defining both their careers and themselves. His views have been questioned because of the nonrepresentativeness of his research sample.

16. A model developed by Eli Ginzberg suggests that people typically move through three stages in choosing a career: the fantasy period of youth, the tentative period of adolescence, and the realistic period of young adulthood. This model has been criticized as overly simple, especially with regard to people of lower socioeconomic status.

17. Other theories attempt to match people's personality types with the kinds of careers that would suit them. This sort of research underlies most career-related inventories and measures used in career counseling.

18. Although traditional views of men's and women's occupations are yielding to more egalitarian attitudes, gender-role prejudice and stereotyping remain a problem in the workplace and in preparing for and selecting careers. Women tend to be pressured into certain occupations and out of others, and even when men and women perform the same work, women tend to earn less money.

Why do people work, and what elements of a job bring satisfaction?

19. People are motivated to work by both extrinsic factors, such as the need for money and prestige, and intrinsic factors, such as the enjoyment of work and its personal importance. Work helps determine a person's identity, social life, and status.

20. Job satisfaction is the result of many factors, including the nature and status of one's job, the amount of input one has into its nature, the variety of one's responsibilities, and the influence one has over others.

KEY TERMS AND CONCEPTS

stimulus-value-role (SVR) theory (p. 479)

passionate (or romantic) love (p. 480)

companionate love (p. 480)

labeling theory of passionate love (p. 481)

intimacy component (p. 481)

passion component (p. 481)

decision/commitment component (p. 482)

homogamy (p. 485)

marriage gradient (p. 485)

cohabitation (p. 489)

career consolidation (p. 499)

intimacy-versus-isolation stage (p. 499)

fantasy period (p. 500)

tentative period (p. 500)

realistic period (p. 501)

communal professions (p. 502)

agentic professions (p. 502)

extrinsic motivation (p. 504)

intrinsic motivation (p. 504)

status (p. 504)

PART

7

Middle Adulthood

Physical and Cognitive Development

CHAPTER OUTLINE

PROLOGUE: BRIAN SIPES

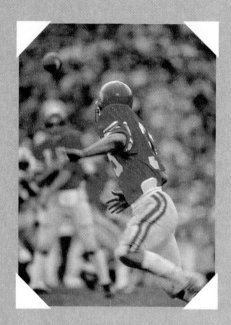

I thought I got better as I got older. I found out that wasn't the case in a real hurry last year. After going 12 years in professional football and 12 years before that in amateur football without ever having surgery performed on me, the last two seasons of my career I went under the knife three times. It happened very quickly and without warning, and I began to ask myself, "Is this age? Is this what's happening?" Because up until that moment, I'd never realized that I was getting older. . . .

When I got into professional football, it was always 1 year at a time, 1 day at a time. I thought that if football didn't work out, I was just gonna be a student of the world. So here I am, really just a kid again, starting a course of study and hoping I'll be better the second time around. . . .

For so long, my time was measured by my career. By football, by what was important to football. I'm anxious to put it behind me, to no longer be known as a football player. I will always be proud of what I did, but don't judge me by what I've done in the past.

In professional football I was constantly asked, "What are you gonna do when it's over? What are you gonna do when it's over?" And I used to manufacture answers, because I thought that these people need to know that the quarterback of their football team has something else going. He's not just a dumb jock. In reality, I've always wanted to walk out of football and have the curtain come down and say, "Okay, here's life. Here's life without football. It's been sports all my life, and here's a new life." What a great opportunity! How many people have a chance to do that? (Kotre & Hall, 1990, pp. 257, 259–260)

LOOKING AHEAD

For former professional football player Brian Sipes, entry into middle age occurred with unusual clarity. The closest witness to his body's gradual inability to keep up with the rigors of professional athletics, Sipes faced the challenge of transition that all of us, at some point during middle adulthood, encounter.

In this chapter we consider both physical and cognitive development during middle adulthood, roughly defined as the period from 40 to 60 years of age. For many people, it is a period when the passage of time becomes increasingly conspicuous as their bodies and their cognitive abilities begin, perhaps for the first time in their lives, to change in unwelcome ways. Yet at the same time, as we'll see in this and the following chapter, it is a period when many individuals are at the height of their success, when they are engaged in the process of shaping their lives as never before.

We begin the chapter by considering physical development. We consider changes in height, weight, and strength, and discuss the subtle decline in acuity of the senses. We also look at the role of sexuality in middle adulthood.

Next, we consider health. We examine both wellness and illness during middle age, and we pay particular attention to two of the major health problems of the period, heart disease and cancer.

Finally, the chapter focuses on cognitive development in middle age. We ask whether intelligence declines during the period, and we consider the difficulty of answering the question fully. We also look at memory, examining the ways in which memory capabilities change during middle adulthood.

In sum, after reading this chapter, you will be able to answer these questions:

◆   What sorts of physical changes affect people in middle adulthood?

◆   What changes in sexuality do middle-aged men and women experience?

◆   Is the middle age a time of health or disease for men and women?

◆   What sorts of people are likely to get coronary heart disease?

◆   What causes cancer and what tools are available to diagnose and treat it?

◆   What happens to a person's intelligence in middle adulthood?

◆   How does aging affect memory, and how can memory be improved?

PHYSICAL DEVELOPMENT

It crept up gradually on Sharon Boker-Tov. Soon after reaching the age of 40, she noticed that it took her a bit longer to bounce back from minor illnesses such as colds and the flu. Then she became conscious of changes in her eyesight: She needed more light to read fine print, and she had to adjust how far she held newspapers from her face in order to read them easily. Finally, she couldn't help but notice that the strands of gray hair on her head, which had begun to appear gradually in her late 20s, were becoming a virtual forest.

PHYSICAL TRANSITIONS: THE GRADUAL CHANGE IN THE BODY'S CAPABILITIES

Middle adulthood is the time when most people first become aware of the gradual changes in their bodies that mark the aging process. Of course, physical changes occur throughout the entire life span. Yet these changes take on new significance during middle adulthood, particularly in Western cultures that place a high value on youthful appearance. For many people, the psychological significance of such changes far exceeds the relatively minor and gradual changes that they are experiencing.

People's reactions to the physical changes of middle adulthood depend, in part, on their self-concepts. For those whose self-image is tied closely to their physical attributes—such as highly athletic men and women or those who are physically quite attractive—middle adulthood can be particularly difficult. On the other hand, because most people's views of themselves are not so closely tied to physical attributes, middle-aged adults generally report no less satisfaction than do younger adults with their body images (Berscheid, Walster, & Bohrnstedt, 1973).

Still, physical appearance plays an important role in determining how people view themselves, as well as how they are viewed by others. This is particularly the case for women, for whom societal pressures to retain a youthful appearance are especially strong in Western cultures. In fact, society applies a double standard to men and women in terms of appearance: Whereas older women tend to be viewed in unflattering terms, aging men are more frequently perceived as displaying a maturity that enhances their stature (Nowak, 1977; Katchadourian, 1987; M.B. Harris, 1994).

HEIGHT, WEIGHT, AND STRENGTH: THE BENCHMARKS OF CHANGE

For most people, height reaches a maximum during their 20s and remains relatively stable until about age 55. At that point, people begin a "settling" process in which the bones attached to the spinal column become less dense. Although the loss of height is very slow, ultimately women average a 2-inch decline and men a 1-inch decline over the rest of the life span (Rossman, 1977).

Women are more prone to a decline in height because of their greater risk of **osteoporosis**, a condition in which the bones become brittle, fragile, and thin, and which is often brought about by a lack of calcium in the diet. As we'll discuss further in Chapter 17, women can reduce the risk of osteoporosis by maintaining a diet high in calcium (which is found in milk, yogurt, cheese, and other dairy products) and by exercising regularly (Prince et al., 1991).

Both men and women continue to gain weight during middle adulthood, and the amount of body fat likewise tends to grow in the average person. Because height is not increasing, and actually may be declining, these weight and body fat gains lead to an increase in obesity. "Middle-age spread" is a visible symptom of this problem, as even those who have been relatively slim all their lives may begin to put on weight (Rodin, 1992).

The typical gains in weight that occur during middle adulthood are hardly preordained by genetic factors. In fact, people who maintain an exercise program during middle age tend to avoid obesity, as do individuals living in cultures where the typical life is more active and less sedentary than that of many Western cultures.

Changes in height and weight are also accompanied by declines in strength. Throughout middle adulthood, strength gradually decreases, particularly in the back and leg muscles. By the time they are 60, people have lost, on average, about 10 percent of their maximum strength. Still, such a loss in strength is relatively minor, and most people are easily able to compensate for it (Troll, 1985).

THE SENSES: THE SIGHTS AND SOUNDS OF MIDDLE AGE

One of the signs of middle age that most people find unmistakable is a change in the sensitivity of the sense organs. Although all the organs seem to shift at roughly the same rate, the changes are particularly noticeable in vision and hearing.

Vision.   Starting at about age 40, *visual acuity*—the ability to discern fine spatial detail in both close and distant objects—begins to decline (see Figure 15-1). One major reason is a change in the shape and elasticity of the eye's lens, which makes it harder to focus images sharply onto the retina. Furthermore, the lens becomes less transparent, which reduces the amount of light that passes through the eye (Pitts, 1982; DiGiovanna, 1994).

Beginning at around the age of 40, visual acuity, the ability to discern fine spatial detail, begins to drop. Most people begin to suffer from presbyopia, a decline in near vision.

FIGURE 15-1

THE DECLINE OF VISUAL ACUITY

Beginning about the age of 40, the ability to discern fine detail begins to drop.

(Adapted from Pitts, 1982.)

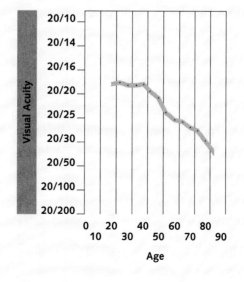

osteoporosis   *a condition in which the bones become brittle, fragile, and thin, often brought about by a lack of calcium in the diet*

presbyopia   *a nearly universal change in eyesight during middle adulthood that results in some loss of near vision*

glaucoma   *a condition where pressure in the fluid of the eye increases, either because the fluid cannot drain properly or because too much fluid is produced*

presbycusis   *the loss of the ability to hear sounds of high frequency*

A nearly universal change in eyesight during middle adulthood is the loss of near vision, called **presbyopia**. Even people who have never needed glasses or contact lenses find themselves holding reading matter at an increasing distance from their eyes in order to bring it into focus. Eventually, they need reading glasses. For those who were previously nearsighted, presbyopia may require bifocals or two sets of glasses (Kline & Schieber, 1985).

Other changes in vision also begin in middle adulthood. For instance, declines occur in depth perception, distance perception, and the ability to view the world in three dimensions. Furthermore, adaptation to darkness, which allows people to see in dimly lit environments, also declines. Such visual reductions may make it more difficult to climb stairs or to navigate around a dark room (Artal, Ferro, Miranda, & Navarro, 1993; Spear, 1993).

Although changes in vision are most often triggered by gradual aging processes, in some cases disease is involved. One of the most frequent causes of eye problems—which may, if left untreated, ultimately produce blindness—is **glaucoma**. This occurs when pressure in the fluid of the eye increases, either because the fluid cannot drain properly or because too much is produced. Approximately 1 to 2 percent of those over the age of 40 are afflicted by the disorder, and African-Americans are particularly susceptible (Wilson, 1989).

Initially, the increased pressure in the eye may constrict the neurons involved in peripheral vision and lead to tunnel vision. Ultimately, the pressure can become so high that all nerve cells are constricted, which causes complete blindness. Fortunately, glaucoma can be treated if it is detected early enough. Medication can reduce the pressure in the eye, as can surgery to restore normal drainage of eye fluid.

Hearing.   Like vision, hearing undergoes a gradual decline in acuity starting in middle adulthood. For the most part, however, the changes are less evident than those involving eyesight.

The primary sort of loss is for sounds of high frequency, a problem called **presbycusis**. About 12 percent of people between 45 and 65 suffer from presbycusis. There is also a gender difference: Men are more prone to hearing loss than are women, starting at about age 55. Finally, because the two ears are not equally affected by hearing difficulties, *sound localization*, the process by which the origin of a sound is identified, is diminished. This is true because sound localization depends on comparing the discrepancy in sound perceived by the two ears (DiGiovanni, 1994).

Some of the hearing losses of middle adulthood result from environmental factors. For instance, people whose professions keep them near loud noises—such as jet airplane mechanics and construction workers—are more apt to suffer debilitating and permanent hearing loss.

However, many changes are simply related to aging. For example, age brings a loss of *hair cells* in the inner ear, which transmit neural messages to the brain when vibrations bend them. Furthermore, the eardrum becomes less elastic with age, further reducing sound sensitivity (Olsho, Harkins, & Lenhardt, 1985).

Despite these physiological changes, declines in sensitivity to sounds do not markedly affect most people in middle adulthood. Most are able to compensate for the losses that do occur relatively easily—by asking others to speak up, raising the volume of a TV set, or paying greater attention to what others are saying.

REACTION TIME: NOT-SO-SLOWING DOWN

One common concern about aging is the notion that people begin to slow down once they reach middle adulthood. How valid is such a worry?

In most cases, not very. Although there is an increase in reaction time (meaning that it takes longer to react to a stimulus), usually the increase is fairly mild and hardly noticeable.

For instance, reaction time on simple tasks increases by around 20 percent from age 20 to 60. More complex tasks, which require the coordination of various skills—such as driving a car—show less of an increase. Still, it takes a bit more time for drivers to move the foot from the gas pedal to the brake when they are faced with an emergency situation. Increases in reaction time are largely produced by changes in the speed with which the nervous system processes nerve impulses (DiGiovanna, 1994).

On the other hand, because complex skills are often heavily practiced, or rehearsed, major declines in actual performance are generally avoided. In fact, middle-aged drivers tend to have fewer accidents than do younger ones. Although part of the reason for their better performance is that older drivers tend to be more careful and to take fewer risks than younger drivers, much of the cause is older drivers' greater amount of practice in the skill. In the case of reaction time, then, practice may indeed make perfect (Birren, Woods, & Williams, 1980; Siegler & Costa, 1985).

Can increases in reaction time, as well as other physical consequences of aging related to the muscle systems of the body, be slowed down? In many cases, the answer is yes. Specifically, involvement in an active exercise program retards the effects of aging, producing several important outcomes (see Figure 15-2). "Use it or lose it" is an aphorism with which developmentalists would agree.

SEX IN MIDDLE ADULTHOOD: THE ONGOING SEXUALITY OF MIDDLE AGE

Common wisdom, particularly among those under 40, suggests that sex is an activity of youth and early adulthood that generally fades away with age.

Most middle-aged people would tell a different story. Although it is true that the frequency of sexual intercourse declines with age (see Figure 15-3), sexual activities of various sorts remain a vital part of most middle-aged adults' lives (Whitbourne, 1990; T.W. Smith, 1991; Michael et al., 1994; Shaw, 1994).

FIGURE 15-2

USE IT OR LOSE IT

Many benefits accrue from maintaining a high level of physical activity throughout life.

(*Source*: DiGiovanni, 1994.)

The advantages of exercise include

Muscle System

Slower decline in energy molecules, muscle cell thickness, number of muscle cells, muscle thickness, muscle mass, muscle strength, blood supply, speed of movement, stamina

Slower increase in fat and fibers, reaction time, recovery time, development of muscle soreness

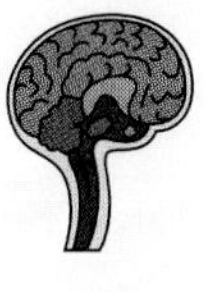

Nervous System

Slower decline in processing impulses by the central nervous system

Slower increase in variations in speed of motor neuron impulses

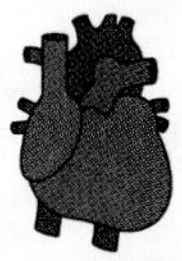

Circulatory System

Maintenance of lower levels of LDLs and higher HDL/cholesterol and HDL/LDL ratios

Decreased risk of high blood pressure, atherosclerosis, heart attack, stroke

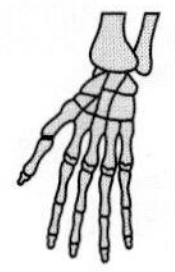

Skeletal System

Slower decline in bone minerals

Decreased risk of fractures and osteoporosis

FIGURE 15-3

FREQUENCY OF SEXUAL INTERCOURSE

As people age, the frequency of sexual intercourse declines.

(Adapted from Michael et al., 1994.)

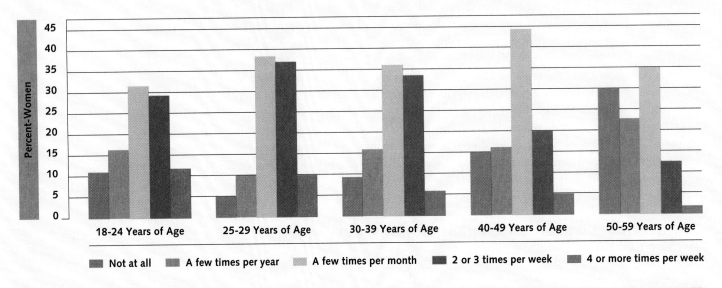

■ Not at all   ■ A few times per year   ■ A few times per month   ■ 2 or 3 times per week   ■ 4 or more times per week

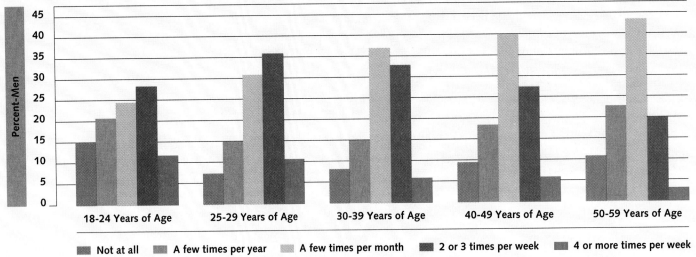

■ Not at all   ■ A few times per year   ■ A few times per month   ■ 2 or 3 times per week   ■ 4 or more times per week

In fact, many people experience a kind of sexual enjoyment and freedom that they lacked during their earlier lives. With their children grown and away from home, middle-aged couples may have more time to engage in uninterrupted sexual activities. Furthermore, if the female partner has passed through menopause, they may be liberated from the fear of pregnancy and may no longer need to employ birth control techniques (Sherwin, 1991).

Certainly, differences occur in the sexual experiences of women and men during middle adulthood. For instance, a man typically needs more time to achieve an erection, and it takes longer after an orgasm to have another. The volume of fluid that is ejaculated declines.

Contrary to popular opinion, sexuality continues to be a vital part of most couples' lives in middle adulthood.

Finally, the production of *testosterone*, the male sex hormone, declines with age (Hyde, 1994).

For women, the walls of the vagina become thinner and less elastic. The vagina shrinks and its entrance becomes compressed, potentially making intercourse painful.

The Female Climacteric and Menopause. Starting at about age 45, women enter a period known as the climacteric that lasts for some 15 to 20 years. The **female climacteric** marks the transition from being able to bear children to being unable to do so.

The most notable sign of the female climacteric is **menopause,** or the cessation of menstruation. For most women, menstrual periods begin to occur irregularly and less frequently during a 2-year period starting at about age 47 or 48, although it may begin as early as age 40 or as late as age 60. After a year goes by without a menstrual period, menopause is said to have occurred.

Menopause is important for several reasons. For one thing, it marks the point at which pregnancy is no longer possible. In addition, the production of estrogen and progesterone, the female sex hormones, begins to drop, producing a variety of hormone-related age changes (Hyde, 1994; DiGiovanna, 1994).

The changes in hormone production may produce a variety of symptoms, although the degree to which a woman experiences them varies significantly. One of the best known and most prevalent symptoms is "hot flashes," in which a woman senses an unexpected feeling of heat from the waist up. A woman may get red and begin to sweat when a hot flash occurs. Afterwards, she may feel chilled. Some women experience hot flashes several times a day; others, not at all.

Other symptoms may mark menopause. For instance, headaches, feelings of dizziness, heart palpitations, and aching joints are relatively common during the period. However, such complaints are far from universal. In one survey, for instance, only half of the women reported experiencing hot flashes. In general, only about one-tenth of all women have severe distress during menopause. And many—perhaps as many as half—have no significant symptoms at all (Hyde, 1994).

female climacteric   the period that marks the transition from being able to bear children to being unable to do so

menopause   the cessation of menstruation

male climacteric *the period of physical and psychological change relating to the male reproductive system that occurs during late middle age*

For women who do experience significant distress, one treatment is to take substitute hormones. In *estrogen-replacement therapy* (ERT), estrogen and progesterone are administered to alleviate the worst of the symptoms experienced by menopausal women. Using ERT reduces a variety of problems, such as hot flashes, loss of skin elasticity, and may help prevent osteoporosis, heart disease, colon cancer, and stroke (Schover & Jensen, 1988; Elias, 1990; Wallis, 1995).

Unfortunately, ERT is not without risk. Some research suggests that ERT is associated with later breast cancer, abnormal blood clots, and cancer of the uterine lining. These uncertainties make the routine use of ERT controversial, and many women face difficult choices in deciding whether the risks of the treatment outweigh the potential dangers (Steinberg et al., 1991; Wallis, 1995).

Does menopause produce psychological problems? Traditionally, experts, as well as the general population, believed that menopause was linked directly to depression, anxiety, crying spells, lack of concentration, and irritability. In fact, estimates of the incidence of severe depression ran as high as 10 percent of menopausal women. It was assumed that physiological changes in menopausal women's bodies brought about such disagreeable outcomes (Schmidt & Rubinow, 1991).

Today, however, most researchers view menopause from a different perspective. It now seems more reasonable to regard menopause as a normal part of aging that does not, by itself, produce psychological symptoms. Certainly some women experience psychological difficulties, but they do at other points in life as well.

Furthermore, research indicates that the expectations women have about menopause make a significant difference in their experience of it. Women who expect to have difficulties during menopause are more likely to attribute every physical symptom and emotional swing to it. On the other hand, those with more positive attitudes toward menopause may be less apt to attribute physical sensations to menopausal physiological changes. A woman's attribution of physical symptoms, then, affects her perception of the rigors of menopause—and ultimately her actual experience of the period (Leiblum, 1990).

Supporting such a view is the fact that women in non-Western cultures often have vastly different menopausal experiences. For instance, women of high castes in India report few symptoms of menopause. In fact, they look forward to menopause because being postmenopausal produces several social advantages, such as an end to taboos associated with menstruation and a perception of increased wisdom due to age. Similarly, Mayan women have no notion of hot flashes, and they generally look forward to the end of their childbearing years (Flint, 1982, 1989; Beck, 1992; Koster & Davidson, 1993).

The Male Climacteric. Do men experience the equivalent of menopause? Not really: Because they have never weathered anything akin to menstruation, they would have difficulty experiencing its discontinuation. Conversely, men experience some changes during middle age that are collectively referred to as the **male climacteric**, the period of physical and psychological change in the reproductive system that occurs during late middle age.

Because the changes happen gradually, it is hard to pinpoint the exact period of the male climacteric. For instance, despite progressive declines in the production of testosterone and sperm, men continue to be able to father children throughout middle age. Furthermore, it is no easier in men than in women to attribute psychological symptoms to subtle physiological changes.

One physical change that does occur quite frequently is enlargement of the *prostate gland*. By the age of 40, roughly 10 percent of men have enlarged prostates, and the percentage increases to half of all men by the age of 80. Enlargement of the prostate produces problems with urination, including difficulty starting urination or a need to urinate frequently at night.

Although the physical changes associated with middle age are unequivocal, whether they are the direct cause of any particular psychological symptoms or changes is unclear. Men, like women, clearly undergo psychological development during middle adulthood, but the extent to which psychological changes—which we'll discuss more in the next chapter—are associated with changes in reproductive capabilities remains an open question.

Exercise provides both physical and psychological benefits during the middle adulthood period.

The Informed Consumer of Development

It's Never Too Late to Start Exercising

Why bother?

That's a typical attitude of people in middle adulthood who never before have engaged seriously in exercise. They may assume that it is too late in life for exercise to have the beneficial effects touted by health providers.

Their reasoning is wrong. According to accumulating evidence, it is never too late to begin exercising. In fact, a regular exercise program may be as conducive to good health and to feeling good as quitting smoking or eating a low-fat diet, even if a person doesn't begin it until middle age (Baar, 1995).

According to recent guidelines suggested by the American College of Sports Medicine and the Centers for Disease Control and Prevention, every adult should get at least 30 minutes of moderate-intensity physical activity on most, and preferably all, days of the week. Not all of it need be traditional exercise: Such activities as walking a dog, gardening, or climbing up and down the stairs of a house during the course of the day count as exercise.

The benefits of exercise, as we have discussed in several places, are abundant. Not only does exercise help control weight gain, but it also can reduce the risk of heart disease, osteoporosis, and hypertension. Moreover, it may even prevent such ailments as the common cold (Nieman, 1990).

But exercise has benefits that extend beyond the physical. According to research conducted by John Foreyt of the Baylor College of Medicine, increasing evidence suggests that exercise also produces psychological benefits. In one study, for instance, Foreyt compared three groups of individuals who sought to lose weight. One group was put on a diet, a second group was given the diet plus an exercise regimen, and the third group just exercised, without dieting.

Although those who dieted and those who dieted and exercised lost weight initially, 2 years later both of those groups had regained their early weight loss. But those individuals who were in the exercise-only group had the greatest success. Although they showed less weight loss initially, 2 years later they were the only ones who had maintained their loss (Baar, 1995).

Foreyt attributes these results to the psychological benefits of exercise. He suggests that exercise increased the participants' sense of control and well-being, allowing them to develop better eating habits.

In short, regular exercise produces a variety of rewards. And anything is better than nothing: Even if a person doesn't exercise vigorously, keeping active in everyday activities is beneficial.

Review and Rethink

REVIEW

♦ People in middle adulthood experience changes in physical characteristics and appearance. Although most changes are gradual and minor, they can trouble people whose self-images are closely tied to physical attributes.

♦ The acuity of the senses, particularly vision and hearing, and speed of reaction also decline during middle age, but the losses are usually slight and produce few real problems.

♦ Sexuality in middle adulthood changes slightly, but not as dramatically as common wisdom supposes. Middle-aged couples, freed from concerns about children, can often progress to a new level of intimacy and enjoyment.

♦ Physiological changes relating to sexuality occur in both men and women. Both the female climacteric, which includes menopause, and the male climacteric seem to have physical and psychological symptoms.

♦ No matter how late it is begun, a regular program of exercise can have positive effects on overall wellness, susceptibility to illness and disease, weight and strength, and psychological well-being.

RETHINK

♦ Do you think a woman of 45 who works hard "not to look her age" combats or contributes to a cultural bias against middle-aged women? Why?

♦ What might be some effects on parents and children of the combination of later parenting and the physical changes of middle adulthood?

♦ What cultural factors in the United States might contribute to a woman's negative experience of menopause? How?

♦ Would you rather fly on an airplane with a middle-aged pilot or a young one? Why?

♦ Why do you think consistent exercise has positive effects not only on strength and agility but also on general health and psychological state?

HEALTH

It was an average exercise session for Jerome El-Neel. After the alarm went off at 5:30 A.M., he climbed onto his exercise bike and began vigorously peddling, trying to maintain, and exceed, his average speed of 14 miles per hour. Stationed in front of the television set, he used the remote control to tune to the morning business news. Occasionally glancing up at the TV, he began reading a report he had not finished the night before, swearing under his breath at some of the poor sales figures he was finding in the report. By the time he had completed exercising a half-hour later, he had gotten through the report, had managed to sign a few letters his secretary had typed for him, and had even left two voice-mail messages for some colleagues.

Most of us would be ready to head back to bed after such a packed half-hour. For Jerome El-Neel, however, it was routine: He consistently tried to accomplish several activities at the same time. Jerome thought of such behavior as efficient. Health care specialists might view it in another light, however: as symptomatic of a style of behavior that makes Jerome a likely candidate for coronary heart disease.

Although most people are relatively healthy in middle adulthood, they also become increasingly susceptible to a variety of health-related concerns. We will consider some of the typical health problems of middle age, focusing in particular on the relationship between health and stress.

WELLNESS AND ILLNESS: THE UPS AND DOWNS OF MIDDLE ADULTHOOD

For most people, middle age is a period of health. According to census figures, the vast majority of middle-aged adults report no chronic health difficulties and face no limitations on their activities (U.S. Bureau of the Census, 1990b).

In fact, in some ways people are better off, health-wise, in middle adulthood than in earlier periods of life. For instance, they are less apt to be involved in accidents, and people between the ages of 45 and 65 are less likely than are younger adults to experience infections, allergies, respiratory diseases, and digestive problems. In part, their relative protection from such diseases is due to the fact that they may have already experienced them and built up immunities during younger adulthood (Siegler & Costa, 1985; Sterns, Barrett, & Alexander, 1985).

On the other hand, it is during middle adulthood that people become particularly susceptible to chronic diseases. Arthritis typically begins after the age of 40, and diabetes is most likely to occur in people between the ages of 50 and 60. Hypertension (high blood pressure) is one of the most frequent chronic disorders found in middle age. Sometimes called the "silent killer" because it is symptomless, hypertension, if left untreated, greatly increases the risk of strokes and heart disease.

As a result of this greater susceptibility to disease, the death rate among middle-aged individuals is higher than it is in earlier periods of life. Still, the figures are not particularly grim: Statistically, only 3 out of every hundred 40-year-olds would be expected to die before the age of 50, and 8 out of every hundred 50-year olds would be expected to die before the age of 60. Furthermore, the death rate for people between 40 and 60 has declined dramatically over the past 50 years. For instance, the death rate now stands at just half of what it was in the 1940s (U.S. Census Bureau, 1991c).

Developmental Diversity

Individual Variation in Health: Ethnic and Gender Differences

Masked by the overall figures describing the health of middle-aged adults are vast individual differences. Although most people are relatively healthy, some are beset by a variety of ailments. Part of the cause is genetic. For instance, hypertension often runs in families.

Some of the causes of poor health are more insidious, however; they are related to social and environmental factors. For instance, the death rate for middle-aged African-Americans in the United States is twice the rate for Caucasians. Why should this be true?

The answer seems to lie not in race per se, but in socioeconomic status (SES) differences between majority and minority groups. For instance, when whites and African-Americans of the same SES level are compared, the death rate for African-Americans actually falls below that of whites. Furthermore, the lower a family's income, the more likely it is that a member will experience a disabling illness. Similarly, people living in lower SES households are more apt to labor in occupations that are dangerous, such as mining or construction

work. Ultimately, then, higher incidences of accidents and poor health, and ultimately a higher death rate, are linked to lower levels of income (U.S. Bureau of the Census, 1990b; Fingerhut & Makuc, 1992; see Figure 15-4).

Gender, like ethnicity and race, also makes a difference in health. Even though women's overall mortality rate is lower than men's—a trend that holds true from the time of infancy—the incidence of illness among middle-aged women is higher than among men.

Why are women more apt to be sick, but at the same time less likely to die? The answer is that women are more likely to experience minor, short-term, and non-life-threatening diseases, and men are more apt to experience more serious illnesses. Furthermore, the rate of cigarette smoking is lower among women than among men, which reduces their susceptibility to cancer and heart disease; women drink less alcohol than do men, which diminishes the risk of cirrhosis of the liver and auto accidents; and they work at less dangerous jobs (Verbrugge, 1985; Schaefer & Lamm, 1992).

One might reason that the higher incidence of illness in women would be accompanied by greater medical research targeted toward the types of disorders from which they suffer. However, this is not the case. In fact, the vast majority of medical research money is aimed at preventing life-threatening diseases faced mostly by men, rather than at chronic conditions that may cause disability and suffering, but not necessarily death. Even when research is carried out on diseases that strike both men and women, much of it has focused on men as subjects, rather than women. Although this bias is specifically being addressed in new initiatives announced in the mid-1990s by the U.S. National Institutes of Health, the historical pattern has been one of commiting less resources to research on women (Thorosen & Low, 1990).

The discrepancies in the lives of people of higher and lower socioeconomic status is associated with differences in death rates between the two groups.

FIGURE 15-4

DISABILITY AND INCOME LEVEL

Workers living in poverty are more likely to become disabled than are those with higher income levels.

(*Source*: U.S. Bureau of the Census, 1990a.)

Under $10,000 $20,000-$34,999

$10,000-$19,999 $35,000 and over

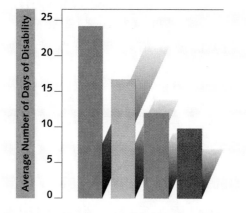

THE A'S AND B'S OF CORONARY HEART DISEASE: LINKING HEALTH AND PERSONALITY

More men die in middle age from diseases relating to the heart and circulatory system than from any other cause. Each year such diseases kill some 200,000 people under the age of 65, and they are responsible for more loss of work and disability days due to hospitalization than any other cause (American Heart Association, 1988).

Risk Factors for Heart Disease.   Although heart and circulatory diseases are a major problem, they are not equally deadly to all people. In fact, some individuals have a much lower risk than others. For instance, the death rate from these diseases in some countries, such as Japan, is only a quarter the rate in the United States (see Figure 15-5). Why should this be true?

The answer is that both genetic and experiential characteristics are involved. Some people seem genetically predisposed to develop heart disease. If a person's parents suffered from it, the likelihood is greater that she or he will, too. Similarly, sex and age are risk factors: Men are more likely to suffer from heart disease than are women, and the risk rises as people age.

However, several risk factors are a function of environmental and behavioral factors. For instance, cigarette smoking, a diet high in fats and cholesterol, and a relative lack of physical exercise all increase the likelihood of heart disease. Such factors may explain country-to-country variations in incidence. For example, the relatively low death rate attributable to heart disease in Japan may be due to differences in diet: The typical diet in Japan is much lower in fat than is the typical diet in the United States.

FIGURE 15-5

DEATH FROM HEART DISEASE

The risk of dying from cardiovascular disease differs significantly depending on the country in which one lives.

(*Source*: Working group on arteriosclerosis of the National Heart, Lung and Blood Institute, 1981, p. 514.)

* 1977

** 1976

*** 1975

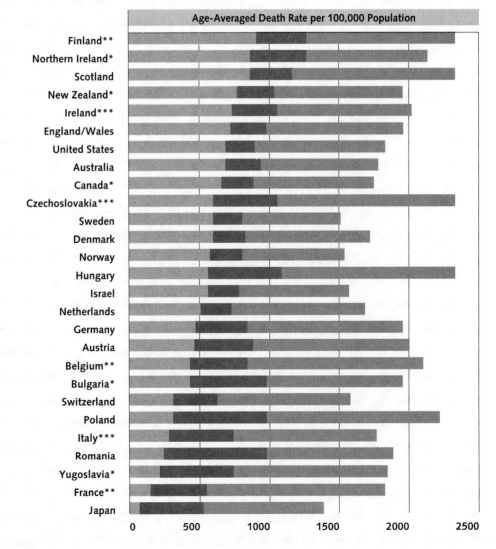

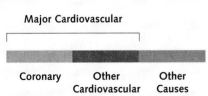

People who exhibit the Type A behavior pattern are competitive, impatient, and sometimes hostile. They also are more susceptible to coronary heart disease.

In addition, increasing evidence suggests that psychological factors might be associated with heart disease. In particular, certain personality characteristics appear to be related to the development of coronary heart disease—the Type A behavior pattern.

Type A and Type B.   For a certain proportion of adults, waiting patiently in a lengthy line at the grocery store is a near impossibility. Sitting in their cars at a long red light makes them seethe. And an encounter with a slow, inept clerk at a retail store turns them furious.

Such individuals—and those similar to Jerome El-Neel, who uses his exercise program as an opportunity to accomplish more work—have a set of personality characteristics known as **Type A behavior pattern**, which is characterized by competitiveness, impatience, and a tendency toward frustration and hostility. Type A people are driven to accomplish more than others, and they engage in *polyphasic activities*—multiple activities carried out simultaneously. They are easily angered and become both verbally and nonverbally hostile if they are prevented from reaching a goal they seek to accomplish.

In contrast to the Type A behavior pattern, many people have virtually the opposite characteristics in a pattern known as **Type B behavior pattern**, which is characterized by noncompetitiveness, patience, and a lack of aggression. In contrast to Type A, the Type B personality experiences little sense of time urgency and is rarely hostile.

Although most adults are not purely Type A or Type B, they do tend to fall predominantly into one of the two categories. Which category they fall into is of some importance, because a great deal of research suggests that the distinction is related to the incidence of coronary heart disease. Specifically, Type A men have twice the rate of coronary heart disease, a greater number of fatal heart attacks, and five times as many heart problems overall as do Type B men (Rosenman, Brand, Sholtz, & Friedman, 1976; Rosenman 1990; Strube, 1990).

Although it is not certain why Type A behavior increases the risk of heart problems, the most likely explanation is that when Type A people are in stressful situations, they become excessively aroused physiologically. Heart rate and blood pressure rise, and production of the hormones epinephrine and norepinephrine increases. Undue wear-and-tear on the body's circulatory system ultimately produces coronary heart disease (Matthews, 1982).

On the other hand, the links between Type A behavior and coronary heart disease are correlational, and no definitive evidence has been found that Type A behavior *causes* coronary heart disease. In fact, some evidence suggests that only certain components of Type A behavior are most involved in producing disease, and not the entire constellation of behaviors associated with the pattern. For instance, recent research suggests that the hostility and negative emotion components of the Type A pattern may be the central link to coronary heart disease (Wright, 1988; Evans, 1990; T.W. Smith, 1992; Suarez & Williams, 1992; Spicer, Jackson, & Spragg, 1993; Williams, 1993).

Although the relationship between at least some Type A behaviors and heart disease is clear, this does not mean that all middle-aged adults who can be characterized as Type A are destined to suffer form coronary heart disease. For one thing, it is possible to retrain individuals. For example, several programs have taught Type A people to behave differently—to slow their pace, to be less competitive, and in general to be more patient and less hostile with others. Such training is linked to declines in the risk of coronary heart disease (Williams, 1993; Cottreaux, 1993).

In addition, almost all the research conducted to date has focused on men, primarily because the incidence of coronary heart disease is much higher for males than for females. Consequently, until more research involving women is done, the findings that link the Type A behavior pattern to coronary heart disease apply primarily to males.

THE THREAT OF CANCER

Few diseases are as frightening as cancer, and many middle-aged individuals view a cancer diagnosis as a death sentence. Although the reality is different—many forms of cancer

type A behavior pattern   *behavior characterized by competitiveness, impatience, and a tendency toward frustration and hostility*

type B behavior pattern   *behavior characterized by noncompetitiveness, patience, and a lack of aggression*

respond quite well to medical treatment, and 40 percent of those diagnosed with the disease are still alive 5 years later—the disease raises many fears. And there is no denying the fact that cancer is the second-leading cause of death in the United States (American Cancer Society, 1992).

The precise trigger for cancer is still not known, but the process by which cancer spreads is straightforward. For some reason, particular cells in the body begin to multiply uncontrollably and rapidly. As they increase in number, these cells form tumors. If left unimpeded, they draw nutrients from healthy cells and body tissue. Eventually, they destroy the body's ability to function properly.

Like heart disease, cancer is associated with a variety of risk factors, some genetic and others environmental. Some kinds of cancer have clear genetic components. For example, a family history of breast cancer—which is the most common cause of cancer death among women—raises the risk for a woman.

However, several environmental and behavioral factors are also related to the risk of cancer. For instance, poor nutrition, smoking, alcohol use, exposure to sunlight, exposure to radiation, and particular occupational hazards (such as exposure to certain chemicals or asbestos) are all known to increase the chances of developing cancer.

Treating Cancer.   Treatment for cancer takes a variety of forms, depending on the type of cancer. One treatment is *radiation therapy*, in which the tumor is the target of radiation designed to destroy it. *Chemotherapy* involves the controlled ingestion of toxic substances meant, in essence, to poison the tumor. Finally, surgery may be used to remove the tumor (and often the surrounding tissue). The exact form of treatment is a function of how far the cancer has spread throughout a patient's body when it is first identified.

Because early cancer detection improves a patient's chances, diagnostic techniques that help identify the first signs of cancer are of great importance. This is particularly true during middle adulthood, when the risk of contracting certain types of cancer increases. Consequently, physicians urge that women routinely examine their breasts, and men routinely examine their testicles, for signs of cancer (Springer, 1991).

Sharon Driedger survived a bout of breast cancer following aggressive treatment with radiation therapy.

Directions in Development

Routine Mammograms: At What Age Should Women Begin Them?

> I found the lump in February 1990. Buried deep in my left breast, it was rock-hard, the size of a BB and it hurt. I wondered if it might be cancer. Like blue eyes and a sense of humor, the disease runs in my family. But not breast cancer. And not me. I was too young. OK. I had recently turned 40, but I was healthy. I worked out three times a week and I was *almost* a vegetarian. My next physical was only a month away. I'd have it checked then. (Driedger, 1994, p. 46)

For Sharon Driedger, feeling healthy, exercising, and eating a good diet was not enough: She did have cancer. But she was also lucky. After aggressive treatment with radiation therapy, she stands a good chance of a full recovery.

In part, her good luck is a result of the early identification of her cancer. Statistically, the earlier breast cancer is diagnosed, the better a woman's chances of survival. But just how to accomplish early identification has become a major source of contention in the medical

FIGURE 15-6

AGE AND THE RISK OF BREAST CANCER

Starting about the age of 30, the risk of breast cancer becomes increasingly likely, as these annual incidence figures show.

(Cited in Kaplan, Sallis, & Patterson, 1993.)

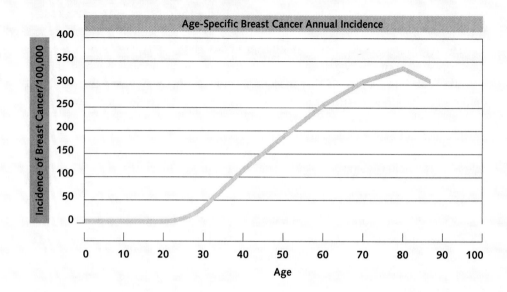

field, pitting one medical expert against another, and sometimes patients against physicians. Specifically, the controversy surrounds the use of mammograms, pictures produced by a process called *mammography*, and among the best means of detecting breast cancer in its earliest stages.

In mammography, a weak X-ray is used to examine breast tissue. The technique allows for the early identification of tumors while they are still very small, which permits treatment before the tumor has had time to grow and spread to other parts of the body. In short, mammograms have the potential for saving many lives, and both the National Cancer Institute and the American Cancer Society suggest that women over the age of 50 routinely obtain them.

But what about younger women? As can be seen in Figure 15-6, the risk of breast cancer does not suddenly rise at the age of 50. Instead, it begins to grow at about the age of 30 and then becomes increasingly more likely. For instance, the incidence of breast cancer in women between the ages of 40 and 44 is 112 out of 100,000, whereas the number almost doubles between the ages of 50 and 54 (Sondic, 1988). What, then, is so special about the age of 50?

To many observers, nothing much. According to them, women should have routine mammograms beginning at age 40, and some advocate the routine use of mammography even earlier. However, others dispute this advice because of two considerations. First, there is the problem of *false positives*, instances in which the test suggests something is wrong when in fact there is no problem. Because the breast tissue of younger women is denser than that of older women, younger women are more likely to have false positives. In fact, some estimates suggest that as many as a third of all younger women who have repeated mammograms are likely to have a false positive that necessitates further testing or a biopsy (A.B. Miller, 1991).

A second problem with routine mammograms for women under 50 is price. The average mammogram costs $100. If the incidence of breast cancer at age 40 is 112 cases out of 100,000, this means that it will cost $10 million to detect just 112 cases. Although one can argue that even one life saved is worth any financial expenditure, the medical establishment, plagued with increasing costs, is unlikely to find such reasoning compelling (Kaplan, Sallis, & Patterson, 1993).

In sum, the use of mammograms raises some difficult issues that involve medical, developmental, and societal considerations. Whether the current recommendation that only those over 50 undergo routine mammograms will evolve remains to be seen.

Psychological Factors Relating to Cancer: Mind Over Tumor?   Increasing evidence suggests that cancer is related not only to physiological causes but also to psychological factors. In particular, some research indicates that the emotional responses of people with cancer can influence their recovery. In one study, for instance, women who recently had had a breast removed as part of their treatment for breast cancer were categorized according to their attitudes. Some felt their situation was hopeless, while others stoically accepted their cancer, voicing no complaints. Other women expressed a "fighting spirit," contending that they would lick the disease. Finally, some simply denied that they had cancer, refusing to accept the diagnosis.

Ten years later, the researchers looked again at this group of women. They found clear-cut evidence that initial attitude was related to survival. A larger percentage of the women who had stoically accepted their cancer or had felt hopeless had died. The death rate was much lower for those who had a "fighting spirit" or who had denied that they had the disease (Pettingale, Morris, Greer, & Haybittle, 1985; see Figure 15-7).

Other studies suggest that the degree of social support people experience may be related to the onset and course of cancer. For example, some research finds that people with close family ties are less likely to develop cancer than those without them (C.B. Thomas, Duszynski, & Schaffer, 1979). Other studies show links between personality and cancer. For instance, cancer patients who are habitually optimistic report less physical and psychological distress than do those who are less optimistic (Baltrusch, Stangel, & Tirze, 1991; Carver, 1990; Carver & Scheier, 1993).

FIGURE 15-7

FIGHTING SPIRIT PAYS OFF

A woman's psychological reaction 3 months after her cancer operation was clearly associated with whether she was alive 10 years later.

(*Source:* Pettingale et al., 1985).

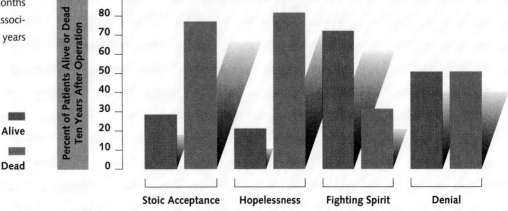

Finally, recent evidence suggests that participation in psychological therapy may give cancer patients an edge in treatment success. According to the preliminary results of a study done by psychiatrist David Spiegel, women in the advanced stages of breast cancer who participated in group therapy lived at least 18 months longer than did those who did not participate in therapy. Furthermore, the women who participated also experienced less anxiety and pain.

Such evidence, assuming it is valid, raises the question of the nature of the link between psychological state and cancer. One possibility is that patients who have the most positive attitudes and are involved in therapy might be more likely to adhere to intricate, complex, and often unpleasant medical treatments for cancer. Consequently, such patients are more likely to experience treatment success (Holland & Lewis, 1993).

However, there is another possibility. It may be that a positive psychological outlook benefits the body's *immune system*, the natural line of defense against disease. According to

Speaking of Development

Allen Levine

Born: ····························· 1949

Education: ························ Long Island University, B.A. in sociology; New York University, M.A. in social work; Long Island Institute for Mental Health, degree in psychoanalytic psychotherapy

Position: ························· Assistant director of social work at Cancer Care, Inc.

Home: ····························· New York City, New York

As a child of the 1960s, Allen Levine had a desire to help people in whatever profession he chose. This desire led him not only to academic degrees in social work, but also to his life's vocation at Cancer Care, Inc., in New York City.

Levine has worked at the care facility for 17 years, counseling people who have cancer. He has served as assistant director of social work for the past 2 years.

"In treatment it is important to get a good assessment of how a person has coped with serious issues in his or her life prior to the disease," he says. "By the time people have reached middle age, they have had to deal with a lot of life issues. You want to know how they coped before, and then find out how they are coping now.

this perspective, a positive emotional outlook bolsters the immune system, energizing the production of "killer" cells that fight the cancerous cells. In contrast, negative emotions and attitudes may impair the ability of the body's natural killer cells to fight off the cancer (Glaser et al., 1986; Kiecolt-Glaser & Glaser, 1991, 1993).

It is important to keep in mind that the link between attitudes and emotions, on the one hand, and cancer, on the other, is far from proven. Furthermore, we need to avoid blaming cancer patients for their illness. It is unjustified and unfair to assume that a cancer patient would be doing better if only he or she had a more positive attitude. On the other hand, it is reasonable to suggest that psychological therapy might be warranted as a routine component of cancer treatment, even if it does nothing more than improve the patient's psychological state and raise his or her morale (Zevon & Corn, 1990; Holland & Lewis, 1993).

"Serious illness puts a lot of pressure on the social system of the family."

"The crisis points of cancer are when most people need the most support. It is most important for the clinician at all stages to seek and understand the meaning of the disease."

"A person may have personal factors or a personal history that would make moving on with treatment difficult," Levine added. "You don't want to treat a person for cancer-related depression and then find out he or she has been depressed since adolescence. It's a different diagnosis in that case."

Levine notes that facing an illness such as cancer in middle age can affect a person's functioning at four basic levels.

"The first is the physical," he explains. "You have to look at the physical experiences the person has had with the disease. Is there disfigurement, weight loss or weight gain? Has there been surgery, chemotherapy? How is the cancer—and its treatment—affecting daily living, working, intimacy, playing with the kids? All of these factors need to be looked at.

"Second are the financial aspects of the disease. In middle age, many people are saving for retirement or college for their children. A chronic illness can be very expensive, and insurance doesn't cover everything. Financially, a major disease can really upset the apple cart.

"The third level is social. How deep is the family in terms of providing support for a person with a chronic illness? There's also the issue of parents having to deal with chronically ill children who may not survive them. Serious illness puts a lot of pressure on the social system of the family.

"The psychological aspect of cancer as a possibly life-threatening disease is the final level," Levine notes. "For instance, what does the disease mean to one's womanhood or manhood?

"The crisis points of cancer are when most people need the most support. It is most important for the clinician at all stages to seek and understand the *meaning* of the disease."

Review and Rethink

REVIEW

◆ In general, middle adulthood is a period of good health for most people, although susceptibility to chronic diseases, such as arthritis, diabetes, and hypertension, increases.

◆ Heart disease is a risk for middle-aged adults. Both genetic and environmental factors contribute to heart disease, including a set of high-pressure behaviors referred to as the Type A behavior pattern.

◆ The incidence of cancer begins to be significant in middle adulthood, owing both to genetic risk factors and experiential factors such as smoking, nutrition, and exposure to chemicals and radiation.

◆ Therapies such as radiation therapy, chemotherapy, and surgery can successfully treat cancer, and psychological factors, such as a fighting attitude and a refusal to accept the finality of cancer, can influence survival rates.

◆ The issue of the age at which women should begin to have regular mammograms is controversial, but there is substantial sentiment for lowering the generally accepted age from about 50 to about 40.

RETHINK

◆ Why is the incidence of disabling illness higher in lower socioeconomic status groups? Are there social-policy implications to this fact?

◆ Why do you think women's mortality rate in middle adulthood is lower than men's? Will this situation change as women's societal roles change?

◆ Are the Type A and Type B patterns primarily environmental or genetic? What evidence for your view do you find in this chapter?

◆ Does the effect of psychological attitude on cancer survival suggest that nontraditional healing techniques might have a place in cancer treatment? Why or why not?

◆ How do you view the issue of routine mammograms before age 50? Is the issue primarily one of health, economics, practicality, or ethics?

COGNITIVE DEVELOPMENT

It began innocently enough. Forty-five-year-old Bina Clingman couldn't remember whether she had mailed the letter that her husband had given her, and she wondered, in passing, whether this was a sign of aging. The very next day, her feelings were reinforced when she had to spend 20 minutes looking for a phone number that she knew she had written down on a piece of paper—somewhere. By the time she had found it, she was surprised and even a little anxious. "Am I losing my memory?" she asked herself, with both annoyance and some degree of concern.

Many people in their 40s will tell you that they feel more absentminded than they did 20 years earlier and that they harbor at least some concern about becoming less mentally able than when they were younger. Certainly, common wisdom suggests that people lose some cognitive nimbleness as they age. But how accurate is common wisdom? To answer the question, we need to consider a long tradition of research on intelligence and memory that began at the turn of the twentieth century.

DOES INTELLIGENCE DECLINE IN ADULTHOOD?

For years, researchers provided a clear, unwavering response when asked whether intelligence declined during adulthood. It was a response that most adults were not happy to hear: Intelligence peaked at the age of 18, stayed fairly steady until the mid-20s, and then began a gradual decline that continued until the end of life (Yerkes, 1923).

The Difficulties in Answering the Question.   The conclusion that intelligence starts to diminish when people are in their mid-20s was based on extensive research. In particular, *cross-sectional studies*—which test people of different ages at the same point in time—clearly showed that older subjects were more likely to score less well than were younger subjects on traditional intelligence tests, of the sort we first discussed in Chapter 9.

But consider the drawbacks of cross-sectional research—in particular the possibility that it may suffer from *cohort effects*. As you may recall from Chapter 1, cohort effects are influences associated with growing up at a particular historical time that affect people of a particular age.

For instance, suppose that, compared to the younger people, the older people in a cross-sectional study had had less adequate educations, were exposed to less stimulation in their jobs, or were relatively less healthy. In that case, the lower IQ scores of the older group could hardly be attributed solely, or perhaps even partially, to differences in intelligence between younger and older individuals. In sum, because they do not control for cohort effects, cross-sectional studies may well *underestimate* intelligence in older subjects.

In an effort to overcome the cohort problems of cross-sectional studies, researchers began to turn to *longitudinal studies*, in which the same people are studied periodically over a span of time. These studies began to reveal a different developmental pattern for intelligence: Adults tended to show fairly stable and even increasing intelligence test scores until they reached their mid-30s, and in some cases up to their 50s. At that point, though, scores began to decline (Bayley & Oden, 1955).

But let's step back a moment and consider the drawbacks of longitudinal studies. For instance, people who take the same intelligence test repeatedly may perform better simply because they become more familiar—and comfortable—with the testing situation. Similarly, because they have been exposed to the same test regularly over the years, they may even begin to remember some of the test items. Consequently, *practice effects* may account for the relatively superior performance of people on longitudinal measures of intelligence as opposed to cross-sectional measures.

Furthermore, it is difficult for researchers using longitudinal studies to keep their samples intact. Participants in a study may move away, decide they no longer want to participate, or become ill and die. In fact, as time goes on, participants who remain in the study may represent a healthier, more stable, and more psychologically positive group of people than those who are no longer part of the sample. If this is the case, then longitudinal studies may mistakenly *overestimate* intelligence in older subjects.

Crystallized and Fluid Intelligence.   The ability of developmental researchers to draw conclusions about age-related changes in intelligence faces still more hurdles, some of which are common to both cross-sectional and longitudinal studies. For instance, many IQ tests include sections based on physical performance, such as arranging a group of blocks, or contain timed sections that are scored on the basis of how quickly a question is completed. If older people take longer on physical tasks—and remember that reaction time slows with age, as we discussed earlier in the chapter—then their poorer performance on IQ tests may be a result of physical, rather than cognitive, changes (Schaie, 1991; Nettlebeck & Rabbitt, 1992).

To complicate the picture even further, many researchers believe that there are two kinds of intelligence: fluid intelligence and crystallized intelligence (Cattell, 1967, 1987). As we first noted in Chapter 9, **fluid intelligence** is the ability to deal with new problems and

fluid intelligence   *the ability to deal with new problems and situations*

crystallized intelligence   *the store of information, skills, and strategies that people have acquired through education and prior experiences, and through their previous use of fluid intelligence*

situations. For instance, a person who is asked to arrange a series of letters according to some rule or to memorize a set of numbers uses fluid intelligence. In contrast, **crystallized intelligence** is the store of information, skills, and strategies that people have acquired through education and prior experiences, and through their previous use of fluid intelligence. Someone who is solving a crossword puzzle or attempting to identify the murderer in a mystery story is using crystallized intelligence, relying on his or her past experience as a resource.

Initially, researchers believed that fluid intelligence was largely determined by genetic factors, and crystallized intelligence primarily by experiential, environmental factors. However, they later abandoned this distinction, largely because they found that crystallized intelligence is determined in part by fluid intelligence. For instance, a person's ability to solve a crossword puzzle (which involves crystallized intelligence) is a result of that person's proficiency with letters and patterns (a manifestation of fluid intelligence).

When developmental researchers looked at the two kinds of intelligence separately, they arrived at a new answer to the question of whether intelligence declines with age. Actually, they arrived at two answers: yes and no. Yes, because in general, fluid intelligence does show declines with age; no, because crystallized intelligence holds steady and in some cases actually improves (Baltes & Schaie, 1974; Schaie, 1993; Anstey, Stankov, & Lord, 1993; Wang & Kaufman, 1993; Heidrich & Denney, 1994, see Figure 15-8).

In fact, according to developmental psychologist K. Warner Schaie (1994), who has conducted extensive longitudinal research on the course of adult intellectual development, the broad division of intelligence into the fluid and crystallized categories masks true age-related differences and developments in intelligence. He argues that researchers should instead consider many particular types of ability, such as spatial orientation, numeric ability, verbal ability, and so on.

When looked at in this way, the question of how intelligence changes in adulthood yields yet another answer, but a more specific one. Schaie finds that certain abilities, such as inductive reasoning, spatial orientation, perceptual speed, and verbal memory, start a gradual decline at about age 25 and continue to decline through old age. On the other hand, numeric and verbal abilities show a quite different pattern. For instance, numeric ability tends to increase until the mid-40s, is lower at age 60, and then stays steady throughout the rest of life. Verbal ability rises until about the start of middle adulthood, around age 40, and stays fairly steady throughout the rest of the life span (Schaie, 1994).

Reframing the Issue: What Is the Source of Competence During Middle Adulthood?   It is clear that there is no simple answer to the question of whether intelligence declines during middle and later adulthood. The issue remains controversial; we will return to it when we consider older people in Chapter 17.

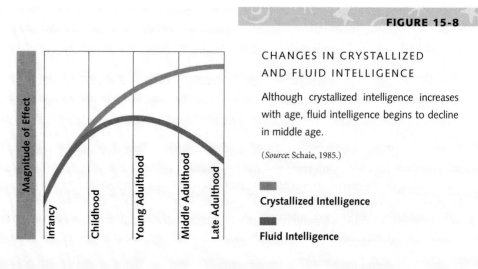

FIGURE 15-8

CHANGES IN CRYSTALLIZED AND FLUID INTELLIGENCE

Although crystallized intelligence increases with age, fluid intelligence begins to decline in middle age.

(*Source*: Schaie, 1985.)

■ **Crystallized Intelligence**

■ **Fluid Intelligence**

What is apparent is that even though overall IQ, as measured by traditional intelligence tests, drops in middle adulthood, almost all people in middle age show no apparent decline in general cognitive competence (Cunningham & Hamen, 1992). In fact, it is during the middle part of the life span that people come to hold some of the most important and powerful positions in society. How can we explain such continuing, and even growing, intellectual competence in the face of apparently ongoing declines in certain cognitive skills?

One answer comes from psychologist Timothy Salthouse (1989, 1994a), who suggests that there are four reasons why this discrepancy exists. For one thing, it is possible that typical measures of cognitive skills tap a different type of cognition from what is required to be successful in particular occupations. Recall the discussion of practical intelligence in Chapter 13, in which we considered the position that traditional IQ tests fail to measure cognitive abilities that are related to occupational success. Perhaps we would find no discrepancy between intelligence and cognitive abilities in middle adulthood if we used measures of practical intelligence rather than traditional IQ tests to assess intelligence.

A second factor also relates to the measurement of IQ and occupational success. It is possible that the most successful middle-aged adults are not representative of middle-aged adults in general. It may be that only a small proportion of people are highly successful, and the rest, who experience only moderate or little success, may have changed occupations, retired, or become sick and died. If we look at highly successful people, then, we are examining an unrepresentative sample of individuals.

It is also conceivable that the degree of cognitive ability required for professional success is simply not that high. According to this argument, people can be quite successful professionally and still be on the decline in certain kinds of cognitive abilities. In other words, their cognitive declines just don't matter all that much.

Finally, it may be that older people are successful because they have developed specific kinds of expertise and particular competencies. Whereas IQ tests measure reactions to novel situations, occupational success may be influenced by very specific sorts of well-practiced abilities. Consequently, although their overall intellectual skills may show a decline, middle-aged individuals might maintain and even expand the distinctive talents they need for professional accomplishment.

In fact, this last explanation is supported by what developmentalists Paul Baltes and Margaret Baltes term **selective optimization**, or the process by which people concentrate on particular skill areas to compensate for losses in other areas. Baltes suggests that cognitive development during middle and later adulthood is a mixture of growth and decline. As people begin to lose certain abilities owing to biological deterioration, they also advance in other areas by strengthening their skills. Ultimately, they are able to compensate for their losses, and they avoid showing any practical deterioration (Baltes & Baltes, 1990; P.B. Baltes, 1993; Staudinger, Marsiske, & Baltes, 1993; M.M. Baltes, 1995).

For instance, you'll recall from earlier in the chapter that reaction time lengthens as people get older. Because reaction time is a component of typing skill, we would expect that older typists would be slower than younger ones. However, this is not the case. Why? The answer is that, while their reaction time is increasing, older typists look further ahead in the material they are to type. This allows them to compensate for their lengthier reaction time (Salthouse, 1984).

In short, even minor declines in particular intellectual abilities are compensated for during middle adulthood. Overall cognitive competence, then, remains quite intact.

MEMORY: YOU MUST REMEMBER THIS

Whenever Mary Donovan cannot find her car keys, she mutters to herself that she is "losing her memory."

However, if she fits the pattern of most people in middle adulthood, her assessment is not necessarily accurate. According to research on memory changes in adulthood, most

selective optimization   *the process by which people concentrate on particular skill areas to compensate for losses in other areas*

people show only minimal memory losses, and many exhibit none at all during middle adulthood.

schemas   *organized bodies of information stored in memory*

Types of Memory.   To understand the nature of memory changes, it is necessary to consider the different types of memory. Memory is traditionally viewed in terms of three sequential components: sensory memory, short-term memory, and long-term memory. *Sensory memory* is an initial, momentary storage of information that lasts only an instant. Information is recorded by an individual's sensory system as a raw, meaningless stimulus. Next, information moves into *short-term memory*, which holds it for 15 to 25 seconds. Finally, if the information is rehearsed, it is moved into *long-term memory*, where it is stored on a relatively permanent basis.

The different types of memory storage vary with age in different ways. Both sensory memory and short-term memory show virtually no weakening during middle adulthood. The story is a bit different for long-term memory, which, for some people, shows some decline with age. However, the reason for the decline does not appear to be a fading or a complete loss of memory, but rather that the initial registering of the information and its storage become less efficient with age. Furthermore, memory declines may also be related to a reduction in the efficiency of information retrieval from memory. In other words, even if the information was stored efficiently in long-term memory, it may become more difficult to locate or isolate it (Hultsch, Masson, & Small, 1991; Salthouse, 1994b).

It is important to keep in mind that memory declines in middle age are relatively minor, and most can be compensated for by various cognitive strategies. For instance, paying greater attention to material when it is first encountered can aid in its later recall. Losing one's keys, for instance, may have relatively little to do with memory declines; instead, it may be the result of inattentiveness at an earlier moment. Furthermore, because of societal stereotypes about aging, people in middle adulthood may be prone to attribute their absentmindedness to aging, even though they have been absentminded throughout their lives. Consequently, it is the *meaning* they give to their forgetfulness that changes, rather than their actual ability to remember (Erber, Rothberg, & Szuchman, 1991).

Memory Schemas.   During adulthood, we recall material through the use of **schemas**, organized bodies of information stored in memory. Schemas not only help people represent the way the world is organized but they also allow them to categorize and interpret new information (Rumelhart, 1984; Fiske & Taylor, 1991).

People hold schemas for particular individuals (such as a mother, a wife, or a child) and for categories of people (mail carriers, lawyers, or professors). People's schemas serve to organize their behavior into coherent wholes, and they help them to interpret social events. For instance, psychologists Susan Fiske and Shelley Taylor (1991) give an example of an old Native American folktale in which the hero participates with several companions in a battle and is shot by an arrow. However, he feels no pain from the arrow. When he returns to his home and tells the story, something black emerges from his mouth, and he dies the next morning.

This tale is puzzling to many people because they are unschooled in the particular Native American culture to which the story belongs. People from Western societies tend to add, change, and omit details to fit their own existing schemas. However, to someone familiar with the Native American culture, the story makes perfect sense. The hero feels no pain because his companions are ghosts, and the "black thing" coming from his mouth is his departing soul.

In short, people's previous experiences within the context of a particular culture allow them to construct schemas in memory. In turn, their schemas allow them to comprehend and interpret new encounters. Furthermore, memory schemas influence people's recall of new information to which they are exposed. Material that is consistent with existing schemas is more likely to be recalled than is material that is inconsistent (Laszlo, 1986; Hansen, 1989; Van Manen & Pietromonaco, 1993).

Understanding a tale told by Native American story-tellers requires familiarity with the culture, due to the existence of particular schemas.

The Informed Consumer of Development

Effective Strategies for Remembering

mnemonics *formal strategies for organizing material in ways that make it more likely to be remembered*

All of us, at one time or another, are forgetful. However, certain techniques can enhance our memories and make it less likely that we will forget things that we wish to remember. **Mnemonics** (pronounced "nee-MON-iks") are formal strategies for organizing material in ways that make it more likely to be remembered. Among the mnemonics that work not only in middle adulthood but at other points of the life span are the following (Higbee & Kunihira, 1985; Mastropieri & Scruggs, 1991; Bellezza, Six, & Phillips, 1992).

♦ *Method of loci.* Developed by ancient Greek orators, the method of loci helps organize material. For instance, each part of a speech is mentally associated with a particular location in a well-known building. The first part might be thought of as located in the front entryway of one's own home, and the next part in the living room. Later portions of the talk might be pictured in the dining room, the kitchen, and so on, until the end of the speech is imagined to be in the basement of the house.

♦ *Encoding specificity phenomenon.* According to the encoding specificity phenomenon, people are most likely to recall information in environments that are similar to those in which they initially learned ("encoded") it (Tulving & Thompson, 1973). For instance, people are best able to recall information on a test if the test is held in the room in which they studied.

♦ *The keyword technique.* Anyone who has attempted to learn a foreign language knows that one of the greatest challenges is remembering vocabulary. To overcome the difficulty posed by long lists of unfamiliar words, memory experts have developed the keyword technique (first described in Chapter 9), in which a foreign word is paired with a common word in the learner's native language that has a similar *sound* to the foreign word. The native-language word is known as the *keyword.* For example, the keyword for the Spanish word for horse (*caballo*, pronounced *cob-eye-yo*) might be "eye." Once a keyword has been identified, the procedure is simple: The learner forms a mental picture in which the keyword is envisioned as "interacting" with the foreign word's translation (such as a horse with big eyes). Psychologists who study memory have found the keyword procedure to be effective, producing better recall than traditional techniques for memorizing lists of vocabulary words (Pressley & Levin, 1983; Pressley, 1987; Pressley & Van Meter, 1993).

♦ *Rehearsal.* In the realm of memory, practice makes perfect, or if not perfect, at least better. Adults of all ages can improve their memories if they expend more effort in rehearsing what they want to remember. By initially paying attention when they are exposed to new information, by purposefully thinking that they wish to recall it in the future, and by practicing what they wish to recall, people can substantially improve their recall of the material.

Review and Rethink

REVIEW

◆ The question of whether intelligence declines in middle adulthood is complicated by limitations in the two main methods of answering it: cross-sectional studies and longitudinal studies.

◆ Another complication in answering this question is the fact that intelligence appears to be divided into components, some of which decline while others hold steady or even improve.

◆ In general, cognitive competence in middle adulthood holds fairly steady despite declines in some areas of intellectual functioning, probably because of people's selective optimization of cognitive strategies that work well in their major areas of need.

◆ Memory may appear to decline in middle age, but in fact sensory and short-term memory are unaffected, and long-term memory deficits are probably due to ineffective strategies of memory storage and retrieval, which can be consciously improved.

◆ Mnemonics help people enhance their recall of information from memory, generally by forcing greater attention during memory storage.

RETHINK

◆ What are some advantages and disadvantages of cross-sectional and longitudinal research designs? Are there questions that can be answered best by each type of study?

◆ How might crystallized and fluid intelligence work together to help middle-aged people deal with novel situations and problems?

◆ How do you explain the apparent discrepancy between declining IQ scores and continuing cognitive competence in middle adulthood?

◆ How do memory schemas help people interpret social situations and novel events? How do you think people deal with elements of such situations that do not fit into existing schemas?

◆ How would you advise someone who complains of being unable to remember people's names? What strategies might be helpful?

LOOKING BACK

What sorts of physical changes affect people in middle adulthood?

1. During middle adulthood, roughly the period from 40 to 60, people typically decline slowly in height and strength and gain in weight. Height loss, especially in women, may be associated with osteoporosis, a thinning of the bones brought about by a lack of calcium in the diet. The best antidote for physical and psychological deterioration appears to be a healthful lifestyle, including regular exercise.

2. Visual acuity declines during this period as the eye's lens changes. People in middle adulthood tend to experience declines in near vision, depth and distance perception,

adaptation to darkness, and the ability to perceive in three dimensions. In addition, the incidence of glaucoma, a disease that can cause blindness, increases in middle adulthood.

3. Hearing acuity also declines slightly in this period, typically involving some loss of the ability to hear high-frequency sounds and a deterioration of sound localization.

4. Reaction time of middle-aged people begins to increase gradually, but slower reactions are largely offset in complex tasks by increased skill due to years of task rehearsal.

What changes in sexuality do middle-aged men and women experience?

5. Adults in middle age experience changes in sexuality, but these are less dramatic than commonly supposed, and many middle-aged couples experience new sexual freedom and enjoyment.

6. Women in middle age undergo the female climacteric, the change from being able to bear children to no longer being able to do so. The most notable sign is menopause, which is often accompanied by physical and emotional discomfort. Therapies and changing attitudes toward menopause appear to be lessening women's fears and experience of difficulty regarding menopause.

7. Men also undergo changes in their reproductive systems, sometimes referred to as the male climacteric. Generally, the production of sperm and testosterone declines and the prostate gland enlarges, causing difficulties with urination.

Is middle age a time of health or disease for men and women?

8. Middle adulthood is generally a healthy period, but people become more susceptible to chronic diseases, including arthritis, diabetes, and hypertension, and they have a higher death rate than before. However, the death rate among people in middle adulthood in the United States has been steadily declining.

9. Overall health in middle adulthood varies according to socioeconomic status (SES) and gender. People of higher SES are healthier and have lower death rates than do people of lower SES. Women have a lower mortality rate than men, but a higher incidence of illness. Researchers have generally paid more attention to the life-threatening diseases experienced by men than to the less fatal diseases typical of women.

What sorts of people are likely to get coronary heart disease?

10. Heart disease begins to be a significant factor in middle adulthood. Genetic characteristics, such as age, gender, and a family history of heart disease, are associated with the risk of heart disease, as are environmental and behavioral factors, including smoking, a diet high in fats and cholesterol, and a lack of exercise.

11. Psychological factors also play a role in heart disease. Behaviors associated with competitiveness, impatience, frustration, and hostility—called the Type A behavior pattern—are linked with a high risk of heart problems.

What causes cancer and what tools are available to diagnose and treat it?

12. Like heart disease, cancer becomes a threat in middle adulthood and is related to genetic and environmental factors. Treatments include radiation therapy, chemotherapy, and surgery.

13. Psychological factors appear to play a role in the treatment of cancer and even in the chances of developing cancer. Cancer patients who refuse to accept that they have the

disease or who fight back against it seem to have a higher survival rate than do patients who stoically accept their diagnosis or fall into hopelessness. Furthermore, individuals with strong family and social ties appear to be less likely to develop cancer than do those who lack such ties.

14. Breast cancer is a significant risk for women in middle adulthood. Mammography can help identify cancerous tumors early enough for successful treatment, but the age at which women should begin to have routine mammograms is a matter of controversy. For reasons of diagnostic accuracy and cost, standard practice today is about age 50, but many people believe that women should start earlier, at about age 40.

What happens to a person's intelligence in middle adulthood?

15. The question of whether intelligence declines in middle adulthood is challenging to answer because the two basic methods of addressing it have significant limitations. Cross-sectional methods, which study many subjects of different ages at one point in time, suffer from cohort effects. Longitudinal studies, which focus on the same subjects at several different points in time, are plagued by the difficulty of keeping a sample of subjects intact over many years.

16. Because intelligence appears to have several components, the question of intellectual decline is complex. Those who divide intelligence into two main types—fluid and crystallized—generally find that fluid intelligence slowly declines through middle adulthood, while crystallized intelligence holds steady or even improves. Those who divide intelligence into greater numbers of components find an even more complicated pattern.

17. People in middle adulthood generally display a high degree of overall cognitive competence despite demonstrated declines in particular areas of intellectual functioning. People tend to focus on and exercise specific areas of competence that generally compensate for areas of loss, a strategy known as selective optimization.

How does aging affect memory, and how can memory be improved?

18. Memory in middle adulthood may seem to be on the decline, but the problem is not with either sensory memory or short-term memory. Even apparent problems with long-term memory appear to relate to people's storage and retrieval strategies rather than to overall memory deterioration, and the problems are minor and relatively easy to overcome.

19. People interpret, store, and recall information in the form of memory schemas, which organize related bits of information to set up expectations and add meaning to phenomena. Prior experience contributes to memory schemas and facilitates interpretation of new situations and recall of information that fits the schema.

20. Mnemonic devices can help people improve their ability to recall information by forcing them to pay attention to information as they store it (the method of loci and the keyword technique), to use cues to enable retrieval (the encoding specificity phenomenon), or to practice information retrieval (rehearsal).

KEY TERMS AND CONCEPTS

osteoporosis (p. 514)   presbycusis (p. 516)
presbyopia (p. 516)   female climacteric (p. 519)
glaucoma (p. 516)   menopause (p. 519)

Social and Personality Development

CHAPTER OUTLINE

PROLOGUE: LINDA SMITH'S JOURNEY FROM VOLUNTEER TO BREADWINNER

For Linda Smith, as for many women [in their fifties], the experience she had accumulated as a volunteer and part-time entrepreneur during years of marriage and child-rearing is paying off in a late-in-life career. She is not the lawyer she once thought of becoming. But her job as director of development for Historic Deerfield in Deerfield, Massachusetts, helps keep alive a prominent museum of New England art and history. She raises millions of dollars each year.

Not that Mrs. Smith planned it this way. When her oldest child was born in 1968, "I did not have a career path," she said, although she had worked in advertising and in public relations for more than 5 years. "We as a couple decided that not only did we want to have children, but I wanted to be home with them."

But in the case of Mrs. Smith, motherhood included writing newsletters for free for the Board of Education in Pleasantville, N.Y., in Westchester County. She was also president of the P.T.A., president of the Junior League and president of the board of deacons at her church. "Some people seem to feel 'volunteer' has a negative connotation; it is very positive job experience," Mrs. Smith said. . . .

And then Mrs. Smith made the transition into a full-time career. . . . [After moving to New England], Mrs. Smith soon found herself on the payroll at Smith College, her alma mater (class of 1960), helping to raise funds. A friend put her in touch with Historic Deerfield, and she took her present job. . . .

"I want to see if I can do this job successfully," she said, dismissing retirement as way off in the future. "I am drawing on all my accumulated experience and schooling, and I am challenged. I have a lot on my plate, and I find it exciting." (Uchitelle, 1994, p. B8)

LOOKING AHEAD

Linda Smith's career path is not unusual: Many women who take time off to raise children return to the job market when their children have grown up and left a so-called empty nest. But Linda's path is also different from those taken by many other women and men as they reach middle age. In fact, one of the remarkable characteristics of middle age is its diversity, as the paths that different people travel continue to diverge.

This chapter focuses on the personality and social development that occurs in midlife. We begin by considering personality development. We examine the changes that occur during this period, according to various stage theorists, and the ways that people's "social clocks" continue their countdown through life's milestones. We also explore some of the controversies underlying developmentalists' understandings of midlife, including whether the midlife crisis, a phenomenon popularized in modern society, is fact or fiction.

We then turn to the relationships that evolve during middle adulthood. We consider the various familial ties that bind people together (or come unglued) during this period, including marriage, divorce, the empty nest, and grandparenting. We also look at a bleaker side of family relations: family violence, which is surprisingly prevalent.

Finally, the chapter considers the role of work and leisure during middle adulthood. We'll examine the changing role of work in people's lives and some of the difficulties associated with work, such as burnout and unemployment. The chapter concludes with a discussion of leisure time, which gains increasing importance during middle age.

In short, after reading this chapter, you'll be able to answer the following questions:

♦ In what ways does personality develop during middle adulthood?

- What are some current controversies in personality development?

- What are typical patterns of marriage and divorce in middle adulthood?

- What changing family situations do middle-aged adults face?

- What are the causes and characteristics of family violence in the United States?

- What are the characteristics of work and career in middle adulthood?

- How do people in midlife deal with career change, unemployment, and leisure time?

PERSONALITY DEVELOPMENT

In Western society, turning 40 represents an important milestone.

My 40th birthday was not an easy one. It's not that I woke up one morning and felt different—that's never been the case. But what did happen during my 40th year was that I came to the realization of the finiteness of life, and that the die was cast. I began to understand that I probably wasn't going to be president of the United States—a secret ambition—or even a captain of industry. Time was no longer on my side, but something of an adversary. But it was curious: Rather than following my traditional pattern of focusing on the future, planning to do this or do that, I began to appreciate what I had. I looked around at my life, was pretty well satisfied with some of my accomplishments, and began to focus on the things that were going right, not the things that I was lacking. But this state-of-mind didn't happen in a day; it took several years after turning 40 before I felt this way. Even now, it is hard to fully accept that I am middle-aged.

As this 47-year-old man suggests, the realization that one has entered middle adulthood does not always come easily. In many Western societies, the age of 40 has special meaning, bringing with it the inescapable fact that one is now middle-aged—at least in the view of others—and the suggestion, embodied in everyday common wisdom, that one is about to experience the throes of a "midlife crisis" (Gergen, 1990).

However, as we will see, the midlife crisis is far from inevitable, and many—perhaps most—people sail through middle age with little or no crisis or psychological turmoil. On the other hand, midlife does bring with it new psychological concerns, and those concerns do influence the nature and course of personality development.

ERIKSON'S STAGE OF GENERATIVITY VERSUS STAGNATION

As we first discussed in Chapter 12, psychoanalyst Erik Erikson suggests that middle adulthood encompasses the period of **generativity versus stagnation**. Generativity refers to an individual's contribution to family, community, work, and society as a whole. Generative people strive to play a role in guiding and encouraging future generations. They may work directly with younger individuals, acting as mentors, or they may satisfy their need for generativity through creative and artistic output, seeking to leave a lasting contribution. The focus of those who experience generativity, then, is beyond themselves, as they look toward the continuation of their own lives through others (McAdams, de St. Aubin, & Logan, 1993).

On the other hand, a lack of psychological success in this period means that people become stagnant. Focusing on the triviality of their own activity, people may come to feel that they have made only limited contributions to the world, that their presence has counted for little. In fact, some individuals find themselves floundering, still seeking new, and potentially more fulfilling, careers. Others become frustrated and bored.

Although Erikson provides a broad overview of personality development, some researchers have suggested that we need a more precise look at changes in personality during middle adulthood. For example, psychologist George Vaillant (1977) has suggested that an important period during middle adulthood is "keeping the meaning versus rigidity." *Keeping the meaning versus rigidity* occurs between about ages 45 and 55. During that

generativity versus stagnation *according to Erik Erikson the stage during middle adulthood in which people consider their contributions to family and society*

period, adults seek to extract the meaning from their lives, and they seek to "keep the meaning" by developing an acceptance of the strengths and weaknesses of others. Although they recognize the shortcomings of the world, they strive to preserve their world, and they are relatively content. On the other hand, those who are rigid become increasingly isolated from others.

LEVINSON'S SEASONS OF LIFE

According to psychologist Daniel Levinson (1986, 1990), the early 40s are a period of transition and crisis. Levinson based his contention on a comprehensive study of 40 men. Despite the relatively small sample size, and the fact that the study included no women, Levinson's view has been influential. It provided one of the first, and most far-reaching, descriptions of the stages through which people pass during adulthood.

Levinson suggests that adult men pass through a series of stages beginning with their entry into early adulthood at about age 20 and continuing into middle adulthood (see Figure 16-1). The beginning stages have to do with leaving one's family and entering the adult world. During this time of early adulthood, people construct what Levinson calls "The Dream," a broad, comprehensive vision of the future. The dream encompasses an individual's goals and aspirations, whether they entail becoming a captain of industry, a parent, or an elementary school teacher.

In early adulthood, people make, and sometimes discard, career choices as they come to grips with their capabilities and ultimately commit to long-term decisions. This leads to a period—the late 30s—of settling down. They establish themselves, throwing themselves into their chosen roles and moving toward the vision they created earlier in "The Dream."

However, between age 40 and 45, people move into a period that Levinson calls the *midlife transition*, or a time of questioning. People begin to focus on the finite nature of life, realizing and even growing obsessed with the fact that they will not live forever. They concentrate on the present rather than looking toward the future, and they begin to question some of their everyday, fundamental assumptions. They experience the first signs of aging, and they may begin to doubt the value of their accomplishments, finding them lacking in real meaning. More importantly, they confront the knowledge that they will be unable to accomplish all their aims before they die.

FIGURE 16-1

MEN'S STAGES OF ADULTHOOD

According to Daniel Levinson, men pass through a series of stages and crises. However, not everyone agrees with the universality of these stages, as well as their applicability to women.

(Adapted from Levinson, 1986.)

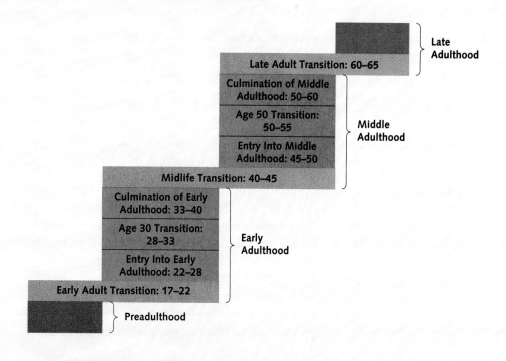

midlife crisis   *a stage of uncertainty and indecision brought about by the realization that life is finite*

social clock   *the psychological timepiece that records the major milestones in people's lives*

In Levinson's view, this period of assessment may lead to a **midlife crisis**, a stage of uncertainty and indecision brought about by the realization that life is finite. Facing signs of physical aging, people may also discover that even the accomplishments of which they are proudest have brought them less satisfaction than they expected. Looking toward the past, they may seek to define what went wrong and look for ways to correct their past mistakes. The midlife crisis, then, is a painful and tumultuous period of questioning.

What happens next depends on how successfully people deal with the midlife crisis. In Levinson's study, those men who came to grips with their aging found the remainder of their 40s productive and satisfying. Some took on new roles, such as mentors to younger people, and some even changed careers. On the other hand, those who were less successful in dealing with the midlife crisis entered a period of stagnation or even decline for the rest of their 40s. Such individuals were still struggling to find their places in the world well into their 50s.

For most people, though, the turmoil of the midlife crisis was resolved by the mid-40s. As they moved into their 50s, they felt secure in their worlds, comfortably looking forward to the future with a sense of fulfillment.

Levinson's view of middle adulthood clearly suggests that most people are susceptible to a fairly profound midlife crisis. But before accepting his view, we need to go back to some critical drawbacks to his research. First, his theorizing was based on a group of only 40 men. Although he interviewed them extensively, findings based on such a small sample of only one gender are difficult to generalize, particularly to women. Furthermore, the results of Levinson's interviews are not consistent. Some subjects had quite smooth midlife transitions, with little apparent turmoil, while others experienced psychological crises at ages when, according to the theory, crises should be relatively unlikely (McCrae & Costa, 1990).

In short, Levinson may have overstated the consistency and generality of the patterns he found in the sample of men he used to derive his theory. On the other hand, Levinson (1992), on the basis of more recent research, has argued that women generally go through the same stages as men, although with certain differences. For example, he suggests that women have greater difficulty in "The Dream" stage, experiencing trouble clearly articulating what their futures will encompass. The reason, he argues, is that women are more subject than men to conflict between the goals of having a career and raising a family.

Directions in Development

Charting the Social Clocks of Women's Lives: Marking Time

Having children. Receiving a promotion. Getting divorced. Changing jobs. Becoming a grandparent.

Each of these events marks a moment on what has been called the social clock of life. The **social clock** is the psychological timepiece that records the major milestones in people's lives. Each of us has such a social clock; it provides us with a sense of whether we have reached the major benchmarks of life early, late, or right on time in comparison to our peers.

Developmental psychologist Ravenna Helson and colleagues suggest that people have several social clocks from which to choose, and the selection they make has substantial implications for personality development during middle adulthood. Focusing on a sample of women who graduated from college during the early 1960s, Helson's longitudinal research has examined women whose social clocks were focused either on their families, on careers, or on a more individualistic target (Helson & Moane, 1987).

Helson found several broad patterns. Over the course of the study, which assessed participants at the ages of 21, 27, and 43, the subjects generally became more self-disciplined and committed to their duties. They also felt greater independence and confidence, and they were able to cope with stress and adversity more effectively.

Measures of traditional femininity changed over time. Although femininity measures increased from age 21 to age 27, they showed a decrease between the ages of 27 and 43. Helson speculates that the increase was related to a rise in sex-role specialization as the women became more involved in mothering. In contrast, the subsequent decline was likely a result of a decrease in child-care responsibilities as the women's children became older.

Helson's work also identified some intriguing similarities in personality development between women who chose to focus on family and those who focused on career. Both groups tended to show generally positive changes. In contrast, the women who had no strong focus on either family or career tended to show either little change or more negative shifts in personality development.

Helson's conclusion is that the particular social clock that a woman chooses may not be the critical factor in determining the course of personality development. Instead, involvement in some socially acceptable and justifiable social-clock pattern may be the key (Helson, Stewart, & Ostrove, 1995).

CONTROVERSIES IN PERSONALITY DEVELOPMENT DURING MIDDLE ADULTHOOD

Although they are also of concern at other stages of life, several controversies regarding the nature of personality development are particularly pronounced during middle adulthood. One issue is the reality of the midlife crisis. Another controversy is whether personality development proceeds through a series of age-related stages with associated crises or is instead tied to particular life events. Finally, a third basic issue relates to the degree of stability and change found in personality during adulthood.

The Midlife Crisis: Reality or Myth?   Central to Levinson's model of the seasons of life is the concept of "midlife crisis," a period of intense psychological turmoil that permeates the early 40s. The notion has taken on a life of its own: There is a general expectation in U.S. society that the age of 40 represents an important psychological juncture (Sheehy, 1976).

There's a problem, though, with such a view: The evidence for a widespread midlife crisis is simply lacking. In fact, most research suggests that for most people, the passage into middle age is relatively tranquil (Whitbourne, 1986). The majority of people regard midlife as a particularly rewarding time (Julian, McKenny, & McKelvey, 1992). Their children often have passed the period when childrearing is physically demanding, and in some cases children have left the home altogether, allowing parents the opportunity to rekindle an intimacy that they may have lost.

Furthermore, many middle-aged people find that their careers have blossomed—as we discuss later in this chapter—and far from being in crisis, they may feel quite content with

normative-crisis models *the approach that views personality development in terms of fairly universal stages, tied to a sequence of age-related crises*

life events models *the approach suggesting that the timing of particular events in an adult's life, rather than age per se, determines the course of personality development*

their lot in life. Rather than looking toward the future, they focus on the present, seeking to maximize their ongoing involvement with family, friends, and other social groups.

In sum, the evidence for a midlife crisis experienced by most people is no more compelling than the evidence for a stormy adolescence that we discussed in Chapter 12. Yet, like that notion, the idea that midlife crisis is nearly universal seems unusually well entrenched in "common wisdom." Why is this the case? One reason may be that people who do experience turmoil during middle age tend to be perceptually obvious and easily remembered by observers. For instance, a 40-year-old man who divorces his wife, replaces his sedate Ford Taurus station wagon with a red Saab convertible, and marries a much younger woman is likely to be more conspicuous than a happily married man who remains with his spouse (and Taurus) throughout middle adulthood. As a consequence, we attend to, and recall, marital difficulties more readily than the lack of them. In such ways is the myth of a blustery, and universal, midlife crisis perpetuated. The reality, though, is quite different: For most people, a midlife crisis is more the stuff of fiction than of reality.

Normative-crisis Versus Life Events: Two Broad Models of Adult Personality Development.   Traditional views of personality development during adulthood have suggested that people move through a fixed series of stages, each tied fairly closely to age. Furthermore, these stages are related to specific crises, in which an individual goes through an intense period of questioning and even psychological turmoil. This traditional perspective, exemplified by the approaches of Erikson and Levinson, is a feature of normative-crisis models of personality development. **Normative-crisis models** see personality development in terms of fairly universal stages that are tied to a sequence of age-related crises.

However, some critics suggest that normative-crisis models may be outmoded. They arose at a time when society had fairly rigid and uniform roles for people. Traditionally, men were expected to work and support a family; women were expected to stay at home, be housewives, and take care of the children. And the roles of men and women played out at relatively uniform ages.

Today, however, there is considerably more flexibility in people's roles, not only occupationally but also in the timing of major life events. For example, although some women follow the traditional model of bearing children in their early 20s and then staying home to raise them, many others are continuing their jobs and having children later. In sum, changes in society have called into question normative-crisis models that are tied closely to age.

Consequently, theorists such as Ravenna Helson focus on what might be called **life events models**, which suggest that the timing of particular events in an adult's life, rather than age per se, determines the course of personality development. For instance, a woman who has her first child at age 21 may experience psychological forces similar to those experienced by a woman who has her first child at age 39. The result is that the two women, despite their very different ages, share certain commonalities in terms of personality development (Neugarten, 1979; Hagestad & Neugarten, 1985; Helson & Wink, 1992).

We do not know for sure whether the normative-crisis view or the life events perspective will ultimately paint the more accurate picture of personality development and change during the course of adulthood. What is clear is that the various theorists we've discussed would all agree that middle adulthood is a time not of passivity and stagnation but of continued psychological growth (Helson & Roberts, 1994).

But how much psychological growth? The answer to that question raises a second major issue in the study of personality: the degree of stability versus change in personality.

Stability Versus Change in Personality.   Harry Hennesey, age 53 and a vice president of an investment banking firm, says that inside, he still feels like a kid.

Many middle-aged adults would agree with such a sentiment. Although most people tend to say that they have changed a good deal since they reached adolescence—and mostly for the better—many also contend that in terms of basic personality traits, they perceive important similarities between their present selves and their younger selves.

The degree to which personality is stable across the life span or changes as we age is one of the major issues of personality development during middle adulthood. Theorists such as Erikson and Levinson clearly suggest that there is substantial change over time. Erikson's stages and Levinson's seasons describe set patterns of change. The change may be predictable and age-related, but it is substantial.

On the other hand, an impressive body of research suggests that at least in terms of individual traits, personality is quite stable and continuous over the life span. Developmental psychologists Paul Costa and Robert McCrae find remarkable stability in particular traits. Even-tempered 20-year-olds are even-tempered at age 75; affectionate 25-year-olds become affectionate 50-year-olds; and disorganized 26-year-olds are still disorganized at age 60. Similarly, self-concept at age 30 is a good indication of self-concept at age 80 (Costa & McCrae, 1988, 1989; McCrae & Costa, 1990: also see Figure 16-2).

Furthermore, there is evidence that people's traits actually become more ingrained as they age. For instance, some research suggests that confident adolescents become more confident in their mid-50s, while diffident people become more diffident over the same time frame (Haan, Millsap, & Hartka, 1986).

Does such evidence for the stability of personality traits contradict the perspective of personality change championed by theorists such as Erikson and Levinson, or, for that matter, the social-clock approach of Helson? Not necessarily, for on closer inspection the contradictions of the two approaches may be more apparent than real.

It is likely that general personality is, in fact, relatively stable over time. People's basic traits do appear to show great continuity, particularly over the course of their adult lives. On the other hand, people are also susceptible to changes in their lives, and adulthood is jam-packed with major events, such as changes in family status, career, and even the economy. Furthermore, physical changes due to aging can provide the impetus for changes in the ways that people view themselves and the world at large (Krueger & Heckhausen, 1993).

In sum, personality development is marked by both stability and change. The challenge for developmentalists is to determine under what conditions and for which traits stability and change prevail. (The three major controversies involving personality development during middle adulthood are summarized in Table 16-1.)

FIGURE 16-2

THE STABILITY OF PERSONALITY

According to Paul Costa and Robert McCrae, basic personality traits such as openness, extroversion, and neuroticism are stable and consistent throughout adulthood.

(Adapted from Costa et al., 1986.)

Females

Males

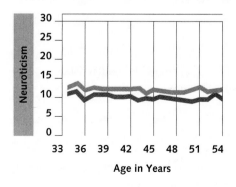

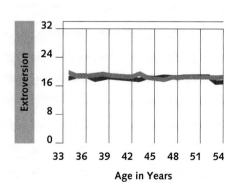

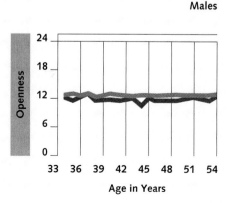

TABLE 16-1

THREE MAJOR CONTROVERSIES INVOLVING PERSONALITY DEVELOPMENT IN MIDDLE AGE

MIDLIFE CRISIS	According to Levinson, the early 40s are a period of intense psychological turmoil. There is now a general expectation in U.S. society that the age of 40 represents an important psychological juncture.
	However, most research suggests that for most people, the passage into middle age is relatively tranquil. The majority of people regard midlife as a particularly rewarding time, finding that their careers have blossomed; they focus on the present, seeking to maximize their ongoing involvement with family, friends, and other social groups.
NORMATIVE-CRISIS VERSUS LIFE EVENTS	Exemplified by the approaches of Erikson and Levinson, normative-crisis models suggest that people move through a fixed series of stages, each tied fairly closely to age.
	Helson, using a life events model, suggests that the timing of particular events in an adult's life, rather than age, determines the course of personality development.
STABILITY VERSUS CHANGE IN PERSONALITY	Most middle-aged adults tend to feel they have changed a good deal since adolescence, mostly for the better. Both Erikson and Levinson clearly suggest that there is substantial change in personality over time.
	Developmental psychologists Paul Costa and Robert McCrae, however, have found remarkable stability in particular traits, such as being even-tempered, affectionate, or disorganized. In addition, evidence shows that people's traits actually become more ingrained as they age.

Review and Rethink

REVIEW

- According to Erik Erikson, personality development in middle adulthood entails the "generativity versus stagnation" stage, while George Vaillant focuses more narrowly on a "keeping the meaning versus rigidity" period.

- Daniel Levinson calls the period the midlife transition, a confrontation with mortality that can lead to a midlife crisis. Levinson's research has been faulted for its small sample size and exclusive focus on men, shortcomings that he has attempted to remedy in follow-up work.

- Evidence for a midlife crisis in the majority of middle-aged people is lacking. Instead, midlife is generally a relatively tranquil and satisfying period for most adults.

- A major controversy among developmentalists is whether normative-crisis models, which portray people as passing through regular, age-related stages of development, or life events models, which view personality development in terms of specific changes in response to varying life events, are more accurate.

- A further controversy concerns the degree to which personality is changeable or stable over time. The resolution appears to be that broad personality characteristics are relatively stable, but more specific aspects of personality change in response to life events.

RETHINK

- How do you think the midlife transition is different for a middle-aged person whose child has just entered adolescence versus a middle-aged person who has just become a parent for the first time?

◆ What factors (in women, society, or the study) might account for Levinson's finding that women had more difficulty than men in articulating "The Dream"?

◆ In what ways might normative-crisis models of personality development be culture-specific?

◆ What are the implications of Ravenna Helson's social-clock theory for women who choose nontraditional social roles and career paths?

◆ How do you resolve the conflict between stability and change in personality? What sorts of personality characteristics might be more (or less) changeable in the face of events?

RELATIONSHIPS: FAMILY AND FRIENDS IN MIDDLE AGE

For Kathy and Bob, accompanying their son Jon to freshman orientation was like nothing they had ever experienced—or wished to experience again. When Jon had been accepted at a college on the other side of the country—his first choice—the reality that he would be leaving home in the fall was still fairly abstract. But the months flew by rapidly, and when the time came to leave him on his new campus, it was a wrenching experience. Not only did Kathy and Bob worry about their son in the way that parents always worry about their children, but they felt a sense of profound loss—a sense that their family would be changing in ways they could barely fathom, and that, to a large extent, their job of raising their son was over. Now he was largely on his own; their part was mostly done. It was a thought that filled them with pride and anticipation for his future, but with great sadness as well. They would miss him.

It is in middle age that most parents experience major changes in their relationships with their children. Although the number of exceptions to the pattern is increasing—some people do not even begin to have children until they are in their 40s—it is during their parents' middle adulthood that most children enter adolescence and ultimately move out of the household. Such shifts bring changes not only to parent–child relationships but also to parents' relationships with one another.

MARRIAGE AND DIVORCE

Fifty years ago, midlife was similar for most people. Men and women, who had married during early adulthood, were still married to one another. One hundred years ago, when life expectancy was much shorter than it is today, people in their 40s were most likely married—but not to the same person they had first married. Because the death of a spouse was a not infrequent occurrence, many people were often well into their second marriage by the time of middle age.

Today, however, the story is different, and quite mixed. During middle adulthood, many people's marriages end in divorce, and many families are in "blended" households, containing children and stepchildren from previous marriages. On the other hand, many couples still spend between 40 and 50 years together, the bulk of those years during middle adulthood. Furthermore, many people experience the peak of marital satisfaction during middle age.

The Ups and Downs of Marriage.   Even for happily married couples, marriage has its ups and downs, with satisfaction rising and falling over the course of the marriage. The most frequent pattern of satisfaction is the U-shaped configuration shown in Figure 16-3 (Figley, 1973). Marital satisfaction begins to decline just after the marriage, and it continues to fall until it reaches its lowest point following the births of the couple's children. However, at that

"Blended" families occur when previously-married husbands and wives remarry.

point, satisfaction begins to grow, eventually returning to the same level that it held before the marriage.

Middle-aged couples cite several sources of particular satisfaction (Levenson, Carstensen, & Gottman, 1993). For instance, in response to one survey, both men and women stated that their spouse was "their best friend" and that they liked their spouses as people. They also tended to view marriage as a long-term commitment, and to agree on their aims and goals. Finally, most also felt that their spouses had grown more interesting over the course of the marriage (Lauer & Lauer, 1985).

Although sexual satisfaction is related to general marital satisfaction, what matters is not how often married people have sex. (If the amount of sex were critical, most couples would be dissatisfied: Frequency of intercourse tends to decline with age.) Instead, for both men and women, being in agreement about their sex lives leads to satisfaction (Tavris & Sadd, 1977; Lauer & Lauer, 1985; Goleman, 1985).

For some couples, however, marital satisfaction, instead of rising again after the initial decline, continues to fall. For some, their dissatisfaction leads to divorce. Just as with younger couples, today's divorce rate for middle-aged couples is higher than in earlier

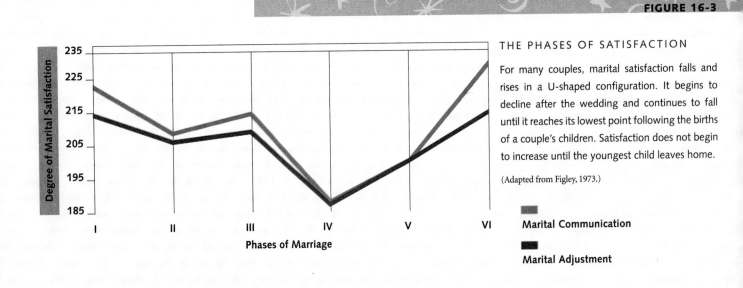

FIGURE 16-3

THE PHASES OF SATISFACTION

For many couples, marital satisfaction falls and rises in a U-shaped configuration. It begins to decline after the wedding and continues to fall until it reaches its lowest point following the births of a couple's children. Satisfaction does not begin to increase until the youngest child leaves home.

(Adapted from Figley, 1973.)

▬ **Marital Communication**

▬ **Marital Adjustment**

decades. For instance, about one woman in eight who is in her first marriage will get divorced after the age of 40 (Uhlenberg, Cooney, & Boyd, 1990).

Divorce can be especially difficult for women in midlife, particularly if they have followed the traditional female role of staying with their children and never performing substantial work outside the home. In such cases, divorced women, lacking recognized job skills, may be virtually unemployable. They also may face prejudice against older workers, finding that they are less likely to be hired than younger people, even in jobs with minimal requirements (Clarke-Stewart & Bailey, 1990; Morgan, 1991).

Remarriage.   On the other hand, many people who divorce—some 75 to 80 percent—end up marrying again, usually within 2 to 5 years. They are most likely to marry people who have also been divorced, partly because divorced people tend to be the ones in the available pool, but also because those who have gone through divorce share similar experiences (DeWitt, 1992).

Although the overall rate of remarriage is high, it is far higher in some groups than in others. For instance, although 75 percent of white women remarry, less than half of African-American women eventually get married again (Bumpass, Sweet, & Martin, 1990).

Similarly, it is harder for women to remarry than for men, particularly older women. Whereas 90 percent of women under the age of 25 remarry after divorce, less than one-third of women over the age of 40 remarry. The reason stems from the *marriage gradient* that we first discussed in Chapter 14: Societal norms push men to marry women who are younger, smaller, and lower in status than themselves (Bernard, 1982). As a consequence, the older a woman is, the fewer the socially acceptable men she has available to her. In addition, women have the disadvantage of harsh societal standards regarding physical attractiveness. Older women tend to be perceived as unattractive, whereas older men tend to be seen as "distinguished" and "mature" (Hatfield & Sprecher, 1986).

Still, remarriage is common. It is seen by most divorced people as more appealing than remaining single, for several reasons. One motivation to remarry is to avoid the social consequences of divorce. Even in the 1990s, where the breakup of marriages is common, divorce carries with it a certain stigma that people may attempt to overcome by remarrying.

Furthermore, divorced people miss the companionship that marriage provides. Divorced men, in particular, report feeling lonely and experience an increase in physical and mental health problems following divorce. Finally, marriage provides clear economic benefits (Ross, Mirowsky, & Goldsteen, 1991; Hallberg, 1992).

Second marriages are not the same as first marriages. Older couples tend to be more mature and realistic. They tend to look at marriage in less romantic terms than do younger couples, and they are more cautious. Furthermore, they show greater flexibility in terms of roles and duties; they share household chores more equitably and make decisions in a more participatory manner (Furstenberg & Spanier, 1984; Guisinger, Cowan, & Schuldberg, 1989).

Unfortunately, this doesn't make second marriages more durable than first ones. In fact, the divorce rate for second marriages is slightly higher than for first marriages. Several factors explain this phenomenon. One is that second marriages may be subject to stresses not present in first marriages, such as the strain of blending different families. For another, having experienced and survived divorce before, partners in second marriages may be more ready to walk away from unsatisfactory relationships (Cherlin, 1993).

Despite the high divorce rate for second marriages, many people settle into remarriage quite successfully. In such cases, people report as great a degree of satisfaction as do those who are in successful first marriages (Glenn & Weaver, 1977; Bird & Melville, 1994).

FAMILY EVOLUTIONS: FROM FULL HOUSE TO EMPTY NEST

For many couples, a major transition that typically occurs during middle adulthood is the departure of children, who may be either going to college, getting married, joining the mil-

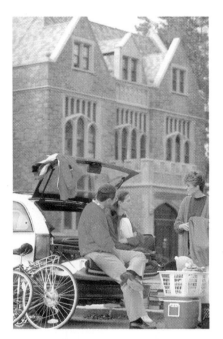

Leaving a daughter or son at college for the first time represents a significant transition for parents, producing an "empty nest."

itary, or taking a job far from home. Whatever the reason, their departure can be a wrenching experience—so wrenching, in fact, that it has been labeled the "empty nest syndrome." The **empty nest syndrome** refers to instances in which parents experience unhappiness, worry, loneliness, and depression from their children's departure from home.

Many parents report that major adjustments are required. Particularly for women who have followed the traditional societal model and stayed home to rear their children, the loss can be difficult. Certainly, if traditional homemakers have little or nothing else in their lives except their children, they do face a challenging period.

On the other hand, even mothers who have not worked outside the home have many other outlets for their physical and psychological energies, such as community or recreational activities. When the children leave, they may have more time for such activities. Moreover, they may feel that they now have the opportunity to get a job or to go back to school.

Consequently, for most people the empty nest syndrome is more myth than reality. There is little, if any, evidence to suggest that the departure of children produces anything more than temporary feelings of sadness and distress. This is especially true for women who have been working outside the home (Raup & Myers, 1989).

In fact, there are some discernible benefits when children leave home. Spouses have more time for one another. They can throw themselves into their own work, without having to worry about helping the youngsters with homework, carpools, and the like. The house stays neater, and the telephone rings less often.

It is important to keep in mind that most research examining the so-called empty nest syndrome has focused on women. Because men traditionally are not as involved as women in childrearing, it was assumed that the transition when children left home would be relatively smooth for men. However, at least some research suggests that men experience some degree of loss when their children depart. Although the nature of that loss may be different from that experienced by women.

empty nest syndrome   *the experience that relates to parents' feelings of unhappiness, worry, loneliness, and depression resulting from their children's departure from home*

"Your mother and I think it's time you got a place of your own. We'd like a little time alone before we die."

Drawing by Karen; © 1995 The New Yorker Magazine, Inc.

For example, one survey found that although most fathers expressed either happy or neutral feelings about the departure of their children, almost a quarter felt unhappy (R. Lewis, Freneau, & Roberts, 1979). Primarily they bemoaned lost opportunities, regretting things that they had not been able to do with their youngsters. For instance, some felt that they had been too busy for their children or had not been sufficiently nurturing or caring.

The concept of the empty nest syndrome first arose at a time when children, after growing up, tended to leave home for good. However, times change, and the empty nest often is not so empty after all, as we discuss in the Directions in Development section.

Directions in Development

Boomerang Children: Refilling the Empty Nest

Carole Olis doesn't know what to make of her 23-year-old son, Rob. He has been living at home since his graduation from college more than 2 years ago. Her six older children returned to the nest for just a few months and then bolted.

"I ask him, 'Why don't you move out with your friends?'" says Mrs. Olis, shaking her head. Rob has a ready answer: "They all live at home, too."

Carole Olis is not alone in being surprised and somewhat perplexed by the return of her son. There has been a significant increase in the United States in the number of young adults who come back to live in the homes of their middle-aged parents (see Figure 16-4).

Known as **boomerang children**, these returning offspring typically cite economic issues as the main reason for returning. Because of a difficult economy, many younger individuals are unable to find jobs after college, or the positions they do find pay so little that they have difficulty making ends meet.

Although the proportion of both men and women between the ages of 25 and 34 who return home is higher than at any time in the last 30 years, the increase is especially pronounced for men. The reasons for this are not entirely clear. One argument suggests that men are somehow lazier than women and seek the care and pampering that their parents, who are often economically well-off, are prepared to provide. However, parents often ask

boomerang children   *young adults who return, after leaving home for some period, to live in the homes of their middle-aged parents*

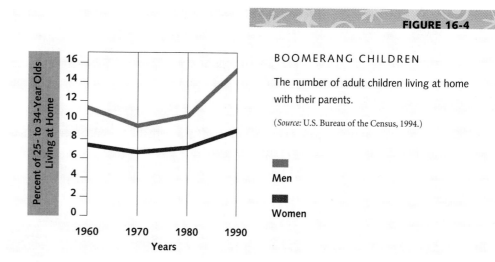

FIGURE 16-4

BOOMERANG CHILDREN

The number of adult children living at home with their parents.

(*Source:* U.S. Bureau of the Census, 1994.)

■ Men

■ Women

Boomerang children, adult offspring who have previously left home, but return to live with their parents, often experience conflicts over the degree of freedom they should have.

their children to pay rent and to participate in household chores, and the laziness explanation does not hold up very well.

A more likely explanation for the higher proportion of young men returning to their parents' homes probably relates to financial concerns. When young adults are unable to earn as much as they think they ought to, they are less eager to enter into marriage. Instead, they are more inclined to move back in with their middle-aged parents, where, even if they do pay rent, living is usually less expensive than it would be in an apartment of their own. Because men tend to marry at a later age than do women, it is men who are more apt to be single—and consequently more likely to be living at home.

But there is another reason that more men than women might prefer to move back home. It has to do with the freedom that parents provide their children. Whereas sons tend to get as much freedom as they want and can come and go at will, daughters are treated differently. Parents are apt to be stricter with their daughters, setting ground rules that they do not apply to their sons. In short, male children may see home as more inviting than female children (Duff, 1994).

Parents' reactions to the return of their children vary, largely according to the reasons for it. If their children are unemployed, their return to the previously empty nest may be a major irritant. Fathers in particular might not grasp the realities of the difficult job market that college graduates encounter, and might be decidedly unsympathetic to their children's return. Moreover, there may be some subtle parent–child rivalry for the attention of the spouse (J. Gross, 1991; Wilcox, 1992).

In contrast, mothers tend to be more sympathetic to children who are unemployed. Single mothers in particular may welcome the help and security provided by returning children. Furthermore, both mothers and fathers feel fairly positive about returning sons and daughters who work and contribute to the functioning of the household (Quinn, 1993).

In short, parents' reactions to boomerang children are both positive and negative. However, most middle-aged parents would probably agree with the sentiments expressed by comedian Bill Cosby: "Your parents want you out of the house. They really want you out of the house. They are worried about you. They love you but, God, they want you out of the house" (Wilcox, 1992, p. 83).

THE SANDWICH GENERATION: BETWEEN CHILDREN AND PARENTS

At the same time children are leaving the nest, or perhaps even returning as boomerang children, couples face another challenge during middle adulthood: growing responsibility for the care of their aging parents. Many couples feel squeezed between two generations, a fact that causes them to be called the sandwich generation. The **sandwich generation** refers to couples who in middle adulthood must fulfill the needs of both their children and their aging parents.

Being part of the sandwich generation is a relatively new phenomenon, produced by several converging trends. First, couples are marrying later and having children at an older age. At the same time, people are living longer. Consequently, the likelihood of simultaneously having children who still require a significant amount of nurturance, and parents who are still alive and in need of care, is growing.

The care of aging parents can be psychologically tricky. For one thing, there is a significant degree of role reversal. As we'll discuss further in Chapter 18, elderly people who were previously independent may resent and resist their children's efforts to help. They certainly do not want to be burdens on their offspring. For instance, almost all elderly people who live alone report that they do not wish to live with their children (CFCEPLA, 1986).

People in middle adulthood provide a range of care for their parents. In some cases, the care is merely financial, such as helping them make ends meet on meager pensions. In other situations, it takes the form of help in managing a household, such as taking down storm windows in the spring or shoveling snow in the winter.

In more extreme cases, parents may be invited to live in the home of a son or daughter. Such a situation can present the greatest difficulties, as roles are renegotiated. Suddenly, the children—who are no longer children—are in charge of the situation, and both they and their parents must find some common ground in determining how decisions are made. The loss of independence on the part of an elderly parent can be particularly difficult (Walker, Thompson, & Morgan, 1987; Mancini & Blieszner, 1991).

In many cases, the burden of caring for aging parents is not shared equally, with the larger share most often taken on by the wife. Even when both husband and wife are in the labor force, middle-aged women tend to be more involved in the day-to-day care of aging parents (Dean, Kolody, Wood, & Ensel, 1989; Green, 1991; Spitze & Logan, 1991; Walker & Pratt, 1991).

sandwich generation   couples who in middle adulthood must fulfill the needs of both their children and their aging parents

Couples in the "sandwich" generation must fulfill the needs of both their children and their aging parents.

Involved grandparents are actively engaged in grandparenting, and they influence their grandchildren's lives. By comparison, companionate and remote grandparents are less involved.

Despite the burden of being sandwiched in the middle of two generations, which can stretch the resources of the couple, there are also significant rewards. The psychological attachment between middle-aged children and their elderly parents can continue to grow. Both partners in the relationship can view each other more realistically. They can become closer, more accepting of each other's weaknesses and more appreciative of each other's strengths (Troll, 1986, 1989; Mancini & Blieszner, 1991).

BECOMING A GRANDPARENT: WHO, ME?

When her eldest son and daughter-in-law had their first child, Leah couldn't believe it. At age 54, she had become a grandmother! She kept telling herself that she felt far too young to be considered anybody's grandparent.

Middle adulthood often brings one of the unmistakable symbols of aging: becoming a grandparent. Grandparenting tends to fall into different styles (Cherlin & Furstenberg, 1986). *Involved* grandparents are actively engaged in grandparenting and have influence over their grandchildren's lives. They hold clear expectations about the ways in which their grandchildren should behave.

In contrast, *companionate* grandparents are more relaxed. Rather than taking responsibility for their grandchildren, companionate grandparents act as supporters and buddies to them. Finally, the most aloof type of grandparents are *remote*. Remote grandparents are detached and distant, and they show little interest in their grandchildren.

Marked gender differences characterize the extent to which grandparenthood is enjoyed. Generally, grandmothers are more interested, and experience greater satisfaction, than are grandfathers, particularly when grandmothers have a high level of interaction with younger grandchildren (J. Thomas, 1986; P.K. Smith, 1995).

Furthermore, African-American grandparents are more apt to be involved with their grandchildren than are white grandparents. The most likely explanation for this phenomenon is that the prevalence of three-generation families who live together is greater among African-Americans than among Caucasians. In addition, African-American families, which are more likely than white families to be headed by single parents, often rely substantially on the help of grandparents in everyday child care, and cultural norms tend to be highly supportive of grandparents taking an active role (Beck & Beck, 1989; Taylor et al., 1991).

FAMILY VIOLENCE: THE HIDDEN EPIDEMIC

> After finding an unidentified earring, the wife accused her husband of being unfaithful. His reaction was to throw her against the wall of their apartment, and then to toss her clothes out the window. In another incident, the husband became angry. Screaming at his wife, he threw her against a wall, and then picked her up and literally tossed her out of the house. Another time, the wife called 911, begging for the police to protect her. When the police came, the woman, with a black eye, a cut lip, and swollen cheeks, hysterically screamed, "He's going to kill me!"

If nothing else was clear about what was called the "murder trial of the century," there is ample evidence that the spousal abuse described above was an ingredient in the lives of O.J. Simpson and Nicole Brown Simpson. Allegations of abuse that came out during the trial were both chilling and, in another sense, all too familiar.

The Prevalence of Spousal Abuse.   Domestic violence is one of the ugly truths about marriage in the United States, occurring at epidemic levels. Some form of violence happens in one-fourth of all marriages, and more than half the women who were murdered in one recent 10-year period were killed by a partner. Between 21 and 34 percent of women will be slapped, kicked, beaten, choked, or threatened or attacked with a weapon at least once by an intimate partner. In fact, close to 15 percent of all marriages in the United States are characterized by continuing, severe violence (Straus, Gelles, & Steinmetz, 1980; Straus & Gelles, 1990; Browne, 1993; Browne & Williams, 1993; Holtzworth-Munroe, 1995).

No segment of society is immune from spousal abuse. Violence occurs across social strata, races, ethnic groups, and religions. It also occurs across genders: Although in the vast majority of cases of abuse a husband batters a wife, in about 8 percent of the cases wives physically abuse their husbands (Steinmetz & Lucca, 1988).

Certain factors increase the likelihood of abuse. For instance, families of lower socio-economic status (SES)—characterized by continuing economic concern, a high level of verbal aggression, and large size—are more likely to be involved in spousal abuse than are families in which such factors are not present. Furthermore, husbands and wives who grew up in families where violence was present are more likely to be violent themselves (Straus & Gelles, 1990).

The factors that put a family at risk are similar to those associated with child abuse, another form of family violence. Child abuse occurs most frequently in stressful environments, in lower socioeconomic strata, in single-parent families, and in situations with high levels of marital conflict (Dodge et al., 1990).

The Cycle of Violence. In many cases, violence breeds violence. Individuals who abuse their spouses and children were often as children the victims of abuse themselves. According to the **cycle-of-violence hypothesis**, abuse and neglect of children leads them to be predisposed to abusiveness as adults (Widom, 1989; Dodge et al., 1990).

Marital aggression by a husband typically occurs in three stages (L. Walker, 1984, 1989; see Figure 16-5). The first is the *tension-building* stage, in which a batterer becomes upset and shows dissatisfaction initially through verbal abuse. He may also show some preliminary physical aggression, in the form of shoving or grabbing. The wife may be desperately trying to avoid the impending violence, attempting to placate her spouse or withdraw from the situation. Such behavior may only serve to enrage the husband, who senses his wife's vulnerability.

The next stage consists of an *acute battering incident*, when the physical abuse actually occurs. It may last from several minutes to hours. Wives may be shoved against walls, choked, slapped, punched, kicked, and stepped on. Their arms may be twisted or broken, they may be shaken severely, thrown down a flight of stairs, or burned with cigarettes or scalding liquids. About a quarter of wives are forced to engage in sexual activities during this period, which takes the form of aggressive sexual acts and rape.

Finally, in some—but not all—cases, the episode moves into the *loving contrition* stage. At this point, the husband feels remorse and apologizes for his actions. He may minister to

cycle-of-violence hypothesis the theory that abuse and neglect of children leads them to be predisposed to abusiveness as adults

Parents who abuse their own spouses and children were often victims of abuse themselves as children, reflecting a cycle of violence.

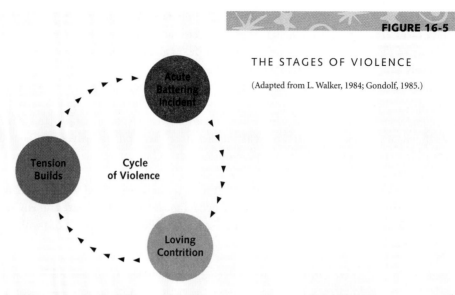

FIGURE 16-5

THE STAGES OF VIOLENCE

(Adapted from L. Walker, 1984; Gondolf, 1985.)

his wife, providing first aid and sympathy, and assuring her that he will never act violently again. Because wives may feel that in some way they were partly at fault in triggering the aggression, they may be motivated to accept the apology and forgive their husbands. They want to believe that the aggression will never occur again.

The "loving contrition" stage helps explain why many wives remain with abusive husbands and are the continuing victims of abuse. Wishing desperately to keep their marriages intact, and believing that they have no good alternatives, some wives remain out of a vague sense that they are responsible for the abuse. Others remain out of fear: They are afraid their husbands may come after them if they leave.

Still other wives stay with batterers because they, like their husbands, have learned a seemingly unforgettable lesson from childhood: that violence is an acceptable means of settling disputes. In line with social learning theory, the cycle-of-violence hypothesis suggests that family aggression is perpetuated from one generation to another as family members follow the lead of the previous generation. It is a fact that individuals who abuse their wives often have been raised in households in which they have witnessed spousal abuse, just as parents who abuse their children frequently have been the victims of abuse themselves as children (Feshbach, 1980; Straus et al., 1980).

However, growing up in a home where abuse occurs does not invariably lead to abusiveness as an adult. For instance, only about a third of people who were abused or neglected as children abuse their own children as adults, and fully two-thirds of abusers were not themselves abused as children. The cycle of violence, then, does not tell the full story of abuse (Kaufman & Zigler, 1987).

Spousal Abuse and Society: The Cultural Roots of Violence.   Consider these scenarios:

> After Dong Lu Chen beat his wife to death, he was sentenced to five years probation. He had confessed to the act but claimed that his wife had been unfaithful to him. His lawyer (and an anthropologist) had argued in court that traditional Chinese values might have led to his violent reaction to his wife's purported infidelity.
>
> After Lee Fong, a Laotian immigrant, had abducted a 16-year-old girl, he was acquitted of kidnapping, sexual assault, and menacing. During his trial, his lawyer argued that "bride stealing" is a traditional custom among the Hmong people of Laos.

Both cases were decided in courts in the United States. In both cases, lawyers based their arguments on the claim that in the Asian countries from which the defendants had emigrated, the use of violence against women was common and may even have received social approval. The juries obviously agreed with this "cultural defense" justification. (Findlen, 1990)

Although the tendency often is to see marital violence and aggression as a particularly North American phenomenon, in fact other cultures have traditions that establish an atmosphere in which violence is regarded as acceptable. For instance, wife battering is particularly prevalent in cultures in which women are viewed as inferior to men.

In fact, legal traditions in Western societies once suggested that wife beating was acceptable. According to English common law, which formed the foundation of the legal system in the United States, husbands were allowed to beat their wives. In the 1800s this law was modified to permit only certain kinds of beating. Specifically, a husband could not beat his wife with a stick or rod that was thicker than his thumb—the origin of the phrase "rule of thumb." It was not until the late nineteenth century that this law was removed from the books in the United States (T. Davidson, 1977).

Some experts on abuse suggest that the traditional power structure under which women and men function is a root cause of abuse. They argue that the more a society differentiates between men and women in terms of status, the more likely it is that abuse will occur (Pence & Shepard, 1988).

As evidence, they point to research examining the legal, political, educational, and economic roles of women and men. For example, some research has compared battering statistics across the various states in the United States. The findings are that states in which women's status is either relatively low or relatively high compared with women's status in other states show the highest levels of spousal abuse. Apparently, relatively low status makes women easy targets of violence. Conversely, unusually high status may make husbands feel threatened and consequently more likely to behave abusively (Yllo, 1983; Yllo & Bograd, 1988; Dutton, 1994).

The Informed Consumer of Development

Dealing With Spousal Assault

Despite the fact that spousal abuse occurs in some 25 percent of all marriages, efforts to deal with victims of abuse are underfunded and inadequate to meet current needs. In fact, some psychologists argue that the same factors that led society to underestimate the magnitude of the problem for many years now hinder the development of effective interventions. Still, there are several things that can be done to help the victims of spousal abuse (Dutton, 1988, 1992; Browne, 1993; Koss et al., 1993).

- ♦ Teach both wives and husbands a basic premise: Physical violence is *never*, under *any* circumstances, an acceptable means of resolving disagreements.

- ♦ Call the police. It is against the law to assault another person, including a spouse. Although it may be difficult to involve law enforcement officers, this is a realistic way of dealing with domestic abuse. Judges can also issue restraining orders requiring abusive husbands to stay away from their wives.

- ♦ If you are the victim of abuse, seek a safe haven. Many communities have shelters for the victims of domestic violence that can house women and their children. Because addresses of shelters are kept confidential, an abusive spouse will not be able to find you. Telephone numbers are listed in the yellow or blue pages of phone books, and local police should also have the numbers.

- Call the National Council on Child Abuse and Family Violence Helpline at 1-800-222-2000 for immediate advice.

- If you feel in danger from an abusive partner, go to court and seek a restraining order from a judge. Under a restraining order a spouse is forbidden to come near you, under penalty of law.

- Understand that the remorse shown by a spouse, no matter how heartfelt, may have no bearing on the possibility of future violence. Even if a husband shows loving contrition after a battering session and vows that he will never be violent again, such a promise is no guarantee against future abuse.

- Ultimately, men who batter must be taught more egalitarian views of male–female roles, and they must be led to deal with stress more effectively. Of course, for such strategies to be effective, men must be motivated to participate in programs that teach them new skills.

Review and Rethink

REVIEW

- For most couples, marital satisfaction rises during middle adulthood, but for some it falls steadily, leading to divorce and (usually) remarriage.

- Family changes faced by many people in middle adulthood include the departure of children for lives of their own and the appearance of grandchildren. Both changes can evoke complex emotional reactions.

- In addition to responsbilities for their children, middle-aged adults often have increasing responsibilities for their aging parents—an experience that can be both challenging and rewarding.

- Family violence is reaching epidemic proportions in the United States. Although violence occurs in every type of family, its incidence is higher in families of lower socioeconomic status. A "cycle of violence" from one generation to the next affords a partial explanation for the phenomenon.

- Marital violence tends to pass through three stages: the tension-building stage, an acute battering incident, and the loving contrition stage. Family violence has cultural roots, and complex interventions are needed to help its victims.

RETHINK

- What accounts for the typical U-shaped curve of satisfaction in most marriages?

- How does the experience of divorce differ for women with outside careers versus women who have stayed home to rear children? How does the marriage gradient affect women with outside careers?

- Are the phenomena of the empty nest, boomerang children, the sandwich generation, and grandparenting culturally dependent? Why might such phenomena be different in societies where multigenerational families are the norm?

- How do male–female status and power issues affect each of the three stages of marital violence?

- Should background culture be considered in U.S. courts as a mitigating factor in family violence cases? In other violent crimes?

WORK AND LEISURE

Enjoying a weekly game of golf . . . starting a neighborhood watch program . . . coaching a Little League baseball team . . . joining an investment club . . . traveling . . . taking a cooking class . . . attending a theater series . . . running for the local town council . . . going to the movies with friends . . . hearing lectures on New Age mysticism . . . fixing up a porch in the back of the house . . . chaperoning a high school class on an out-of-state trip . . . lying on a beach in Duck, North Carolina, reading a book during an annual vacation . . .

When we look at what people in the middle years of adulthood actually do, we find activities as varied as the individuals themselves. Although for most people middle adulthood represents the peak of on-the-job success and earning power, it is also a time when people throw themselves into leisure and recreational activities. In fact, middle age may be the period when work and leisure activities are balanced most easily. No longer feeling that they must prove themselves on the job, and increasingly valuing the contributions they are able to make to family, community, and—more broadly—society, middle-aged adults may find that work and leisure complement one another in ways that enhance overall happiness.

WORK AND CAREERS: JOBS AT MIDLIFE

For many, middle age is the time of greatest productivity, success, and earning power. It is also a time when occupational success may become considerably less alluring than it once was. This is particularly the case for those who may not have reached their goals, achieving less occupational success than they anticipated when they began their careers. In such cases, work becomes less valued, while family and other off-the-job interests become more important (Howard, 1992).

The factors that make a job satisfying often undergo a transformation during middle age. Whereas younger adults are more interested in abstract and future-oriented concerns, such as the opportunity for advancement or the possibility of recognition and approval, middle-aged employees care more about the here-and-now qualities of work. For instance, they are more concerned with pay, working conditions, and specific policies, such as the way vacation time is calculated. Furthermore, as at earlier stages of life, changes in overall job quality are associated with changes in distress for both men and women (Rosenfeld & Owens, 1965; Barnett et al., 1995).

In general, though, the relationship between age and work seems to be positive: The older workers are, the more overall job satisfaction they experience. This pattern is not altogether surprising, for younger adults who are dissatisfied with their positions will quit them and find new ones that they like better. Furthermore, older workers have fewer opportunities to change positions. Consequently, they may learn to live with what they have, and accept that the job they have is the best they are likely to get. Such acceptance may ultimately be translated into satisfaction (Doering, Rhodes, & Schuster, 1983; Schulz & Ewen, 1988).

Developmental Diversity

Immigrants on the Job: Making It in America

Seventeen years ago, Mankekolo Mahlangu-Ngcobo was placed in solitary confinement for 21 days in South Africa's Moletsane police station, falsely accused of terrorism. In 1980, once again in danger of imprisonment for her anti-apartheid protests, she fled to Botswana, leaving her 12-year-old son Ratijawe with her mother. She came to the U.S. in 1981, won political asylum in 1984 and now lives with her 13-year-old daughter Ntokozo in a $60,000 Baltimore row house. Her experiences left her with a deep appreciation of her adopted land. "If you have never lived somewhere else," she says, "you cannot know how much freedom you have here."

Ngcobo also found prosperity here. As with many of her fellow immigrants, the key was education. Since her arrival, she has earned a bachelor's degree, two master's and a doctorate in theology—which she paid for largely with scholarships or with her own money. Her academic credentials and dedication to helping others have won her two soul-satisfying careers, as a lecturer in public health at Baltimore's Morgan State University and as assistant minister at the Metropolitan African Methodist Episcopal Church in Washington, D.C. (J. Kim, 1995, p. 133)

Mankekolo Mahlangu-Ngcobo

If we were to rely solely on public opinion, we would probably view immigrants to the United States as straining the educational, health care, welfare, and prison systems while contributing little to U.S. society. But—as the story of Mankekolo Mahlangu-Ngcobo exemplifies—the assumptions that underlie anti-immigrant sentiment are, in fact, quite wrong.

With the number of immigrants entering the United States hovering around a million each year, residents born outside the country now represent close to 10 percent of the population, a percentage nearly twice what it was in 1980. In some states, almost a quarter of the population is foreign-born. (The proportion of foreign-born residents is still smaller than during the immigration wave in the early part of the century, when it reached 15 percent of the U.S. population.)

Critics of immigration contend that today's immigrants are somehow "different" from the earlier wave. In some ways, they are right. Only 38 percent are white, compared with 88 percent of immigrants who arrived before 1960. Critics also argue that new immigrants lack the skills that will allow them to make a contribution to the high-tech economy of the twenty-first century.

However, the critics are wrong in many fundamental respects. For instance, consider the following data (Topolnicki, 1995):

◆   Most legal *and* illegal immigrants are doing quite well financially. For example, U.S. Census Bureau figures show that immigrants who arrived in the United States prior to 1980 and have had a chance to establish themselves actually have a higher average family income than native-born Americans.

◆   Only a few immigrants come to the United States to get on welfare. Instead, most say they come because of opportunities to work and prosper in the United States. Nonrefugee immigrants who are old enough to work are less likely to be on welfare than are native-born U.S. citizens.

◆   Given time, immigrants contribute more to the economy than they take away. Although initially costly to the government, often because they hold low-paying jobs and therefore do not pay income taxes, immigrants become more productive as they get older. Ultimately, immigrants pay $25 billion to $30 billion a year more in taxes than they use in government services.

In short, the reality is that the vast majority of immigrants ultimately become contributing members of U.S. society. Furthermore, their contributions serve to invigorate not only the economy but the broader society as well.

CHALLENGES OF WORK: ON-THE-JOB DISSATISFACTION

Job satisfaction is not universal in middle adulthood. For some people, in fact, work becomes increasingly stressful as dissatisfaction with working conditions or with the nature of the job mounts. In some cases, conditions become so bad that the result is burnout or a decision to change jobs (Remondet & Hansson, 1991; Buunk & Janssen, 1992).

Burnout.   For 44-year-old Peggy Augarten, early-morning shifts in the intensive care unit of the suburban hospital where she worked were becoming increasingly difficult. Although it had always been hard to lose a patient, recently she found herself breaking into tears over her patients at the strangest moments: while she was doing the laundry, washing the dishes, or watching TV. When she began to dread going to work in the morning, she knew that her feelings about her job were undergoing a fundamental change.

Augarten's response can probably be traced to the phenomenon of **burnout**, which occurs when highly trained professionals experience dissatisfaction, disillusionment, frustration, and weariness from their jobs. It occurs most often in jobs that involve helping others, and it often strikes those who initially were the most idealistic and driven. In some ways, in fact, such workers may be overcommitted to their jobs, and the realization that they can make only minor dents in huge societal problems such as poverty and medical care is disappointing and demoralizing (Freudenberger & Richelson, 1980; Maslach, 1982; Hales, 1992).

burnout   *a situation that occurs when highly trained professionals experience dissatisfaction, disillusionment, frustration, and weariness from their jobs*

Burnout occurs when a professional experiences dissatisfaction, disillusionment, frustration, or weariness from his or her job. Those who experience it grow increasingly cynical or indifferent to their work.

One of the consequences of burnout is a growing cynicism about one's work, as well as indifference and lack of concern about how well one does it. The idealism with which a worker may have entered a profession is replaced by pessimism and the attitude that it is impossible to provide any kind of meaningful solution to a problem (Lock, 1992).

Burnout is not inevitable, even in professions with high demands and seemingly insurmountable burdens. Workers who are provided with realistic expectations about what can and cannot be accomplished are able to focus on what is practical and doable. Furthermore, jobs can be structured so that, although the "big picture" of disease, poverty, racism, and an inadequate educational system may look gloomy, workers experience small victories in their daily work.

Unemployment: The Dashing of the Dream.   Consider this observation of one particular worker:

> The dream is gone—probably forever. And it seems like it tears you apart. It's just disintegrating away. You look alongside the river banks . . . there's all flat ground. There used to be a big scrap pile there where steel and iron used to be melted and used over again, processed. That's all leveled off. Many a time I pass through and just happen to see it. It's hard to visualize it's not there anymore. (Kotre & Hall, 1990, p. 290)

It is hard not to view 52-year-old Matt Nort's description of an obsolete Pittsburgh steel mill as symbolic of his own life. Because he has been unemployed for several years, Matt's dreams for occupational success in his own life have died as much as the mill in which he once worked.

For many workers, unemployment is a hard reality of life, and the implications of not being able to find work are as much psychological as they are economic. For those who have been fired, laid-off by corporate downsizing, or forced out of jobs by technological advances, being out of work can be psychologically and even physically devastating (Sharf, 1992).

Because work plays a central role is so many people's lives, unemployment produces a void that is not just financial. Middle-aged adults who lose their jobs tend to stay unemployed longer than do younger workers, and people have fewer opportunities for gratifying work as they age.

Furthermore, employers may discriminate against older job applicants and make it more difficult to obtain new employment (Allan, 1990). Ironically, such discrimination is not only illegal but also based on misguided assumptions: Research finds that older workers have less absenteeism than do younger ones, hold their jobs longer, are more reliable, and are more willing to learn new skills (Birsner, 1991; Connor, 1992; Turner & Helms, 1993).

People who are unemployed frequently suffer from insomnia and feel anxious, depressed, and irritable. Their self-confidence may plummet, and they may be unable to concentrate. In fact, according to one analysis, every time the unemployment rate goes up 1 percent, there is a 4 percent rise in suicide, and admissions to psychiatric facilities go up by some 4 percent for men and 2 percent for women (I. Walker & Mann, 1987; Kates, Grieff, & Hagen, 1990; Connor, 1992).

Even aspects of unemployment that might at first seem positive, such as having more time to spend with one's family, often produce disagreeable consequences. For instance, the unemployed are less apt than employed people to participate in community activities, to use libraries, and to read. Furthermore, they are more likely to be late for appointments and even for meals (M. Jahoda, 1982; Fryer & Payne, 1986).

In sum, midlife unemployment is a wrenching experience. And for some people, especially those who never find meaningful work again, it taints their entire view of the world. For people forced into such involuntary—and premature—retirement, the loss of a job can lead to pessimism, cynicism, and despondency. Overcoming such feelings requires a major investment of psychological resources on the part of both the unemployed individuals and their families (Trippet, 1991).

SWITCHING—AND STARTING—CAREERS AT MIDLIFE

For some people, middle adulthood brings with it a hunger for change. For such individuals, who may be experiencing dissatisfaction with their jobs or simply returning to a job market they left years before, their developmental paths lead to new careers.

People who change careers in middle adulthood do so for several reasons. It may be that their jobs offer little challenge; they have achieved mastery, and what was once difficult is now routine. Other people change because their jobs have changed in ways they do not like. They may be asked to accomplish more with fewer resources, or technological advances may have made such drastic alterations in their day-to-day activities that they no longer enjoy what they do.

Still others are unhappy with the status they have achieved and wish to make a fresh start. Some are burned out, or feel that they are on a treadmill. In addition, some people simply do not like to think of themselves doing the same thing for the rest of their lives. For them, middle age is seen as the last point at which they can make a meaningful occupational change (Steers & Porter, 1991).

Finally, a significant number of people, almost all of them women, return to the job market after having taken time off to raise children. Since the mid-1980s, the number of women in the workforce who are in their 50s has grown significantly, as the story of Linda Smith at the beginning of the chapter exemplifies. Approximately 65 percent of women between the ages of 50 and 60—and 80 percent of those who graduated from college—are now in the workforce, with three-quarters in full-time jobs (see Figure 16-6).

For those who switch or start new careers, the outcome can be quite positive. They may feel invigorated by their work, and because of their prior work experience and their high level of motivation and enthusiasm, they may be especially valued employees (Adelmann, Antonucci, & Crohan, 1990; Connor, 1992; Bromberger & Matthews, 1994).

In other cases, the outcome is not so positive. People may enter new professions with unrealistically high expectations and be disappointed by the realities of the situation. Furthermore, middle-aged people who start new careers may find themselves in entry-level positions. As a consequence, their peers on the job may be considerably younger than they are (Sharf, 1992).

Still, for those people who change careers in middle adulthood, the potential rewards are great. In fact, some visionaries suggest that career changes might become the rule rather than the exception. According to this point of view, technological advances will occur so rapidly that people will be forced periodically to change dramatically what they do to earn a living. In such a scenario, people will have not one, but several, careers during their lifetimes.

Some people change careers in middle adulthood because they are not challenged in their current jobs, while others may simply wish to make a fresh start.

FIGURE 16-6

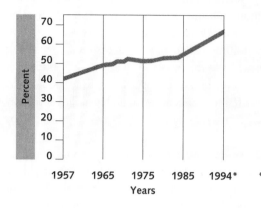

WOMEN AT WORK

The percentage of females, age 50 to 60, who are in the labor force has steadily increased over the last 40 years.

(*Source*: U.S. Bureau of Labor Statistics, 1995.)

*Through October

Speaking of Development

Cindy Marano

Born: ·············· 1947

Education: ············ B.A. in English, Northwestern University and George Mason University

Position: ············· Executive Director, Wider Opportunities for Women

Home: ·············· Washington, D.C.

Pursuing a career in today's highly competitive workforce can be a demanding and intimidating process, but few groups find the going as rough as the woman who, in middle age, must return to work.

Over the years Cindy Marano, Executive Director of Wider Opportunities for Women, has refined a process that she feels has been successful in helping women reenter the workforce in viable and well-paying jobs.

Wider Opportunities for Women (WOW) serves about 150 women a year in the local, Washington, D.C., area, but also works with about 600 programs across the country that, collectively, help a million girls and women.

According to Marano, the first step in working with women in trying to make the transition is evaluating labor market information. "Many women have a limited notion as to what the job market is, especially the current job market. Because women have been allowed so few job options, their perspective is narrowed. Consequently, you have to find out what the woman's interests are, given the current job market.

"The next step is a personal assessment where you look at her paid work experience, volunteer experiences, and hobbies. You have to find out the kind of transferable experiences in her life that can be translated into work," Marano added.

Marano noted that there are number of barriers that also need to be overcome, such as personal fears, family responsibilities, educational and literacy skills, and the lack of transportation.

Leisure Time: Life Beyond Work

With the typical work week hovering between 35 and 40 hours, most middle-aged adults have some 70 waking hours per week at their disposal. What do they do with their leisure time?

For one thing, they watch an awful lot of television. On average, middle-aged people view about 30 hours of TV each week. There are many reasons why this is less than ideal, not the least of which is that television is a sedentary activity that contributes to the lack of exercise common during middle adulthood.

But middle-aged adults do much more with their leisure time than watch television. In fact, for many people middle adulthood represents a renewed opportunity to become involved in activities outside the home. As children leave home, parents have substantial time freed up to participate more extensively in leisure activities.

In addition, people may come to the realization that their opportunity to make a lasting contribution to society may come less from their work achievements than from involvement in community activities. Consequently, some individuals turn to charitable projects or become involved in community boards and organizations.

"Because women have been allowed so few job options, their perspective is narrowed."

"Does she have four little children under 5, and what are the child-care implications?" Marano added. "It is almost like taking a photograph of this entire person and then digging beneath the surface. It is common to find a person with low self-esteem because of a lack of well-paid work experience. She may have had enormous personal leadership experience as a volunteer, or high skills in arts and crafts, but feels it is worthless in terms of the labor market."

In the third step of the process, WOW tries to look at the mesh between the labor market and the financial needs of the individual, according to Marano. Each woman participates in a 13-week prevocational program where basic skills are built and a variety of high-wage, nontraditional careers are explored. Many of the jobs have been predominantly filled by men in such fields as cable installation, repair maintenance, and the construction trades.

"We do have problems finding good skills training or getting financial assistance for education, and we struggle with sending women into a hostile work environment, but we do projects with unions and management to make the environment more hospitable," she added.

The two final steps are to identify the training needs of the individual and to help her market herself with practice interviewing and developing résumés.

"I have found that women tend to do this process best in groups. In fact, the development of a support system during the process of transition is the best thing the program can offer," Marano says.

" . . . The development of a support system during the process of transition is the best thing the program can offer."

Middle adulthood provides increasing opportunities to become involved in community activities, such as for this man who acts a "Big Brother" to a school-age child.

Furthermore, an increasing number of middle-aged people have turned to the information superhighway, via Internet and on-line computer services, for enjoyment. It is likely that the use of computers will grow as computer access improves, which will allow people to "surf the net"—to explore interactive, on-line computer capabilities at will.

Some of the motivation for developing leisure activities during middle adulthood comes from the desire to prepare for retirement. In fact, a significant number of people find the allure of leisure so great that they take early retirement. An increasing percentage of people in their 50s have voluntarily retired from their jobs. For those who make such a choice, and who have adequate financial resources to last the dozens of years that likely remain to them, life can be quite gratifying (J. Bond & Coleman, 1990; Cliff, 1991; Ransom, Sutch, & Williamson, 1991).

Review and Rethink

REVIEW

- People in middle age look at their jobs differently from before, placing more emphasis on short-term factors and less on career striving and ambition.

- Although job satisfaction tends to be high for most middle-aged people, some are dissatisfied because of disappointment with their accomplishments and for other reasons. Burnout is a factor, especially for people in the helping professions.

- Unemployment in midlife can have negative economic, psychological, and physical effects. Unemployed people have difficulty finding new jobs and must work hard to cope with feelings of despondency.

- Midlife career changes are becoming more prevalent, motivated usually by dissatisfaction, the need for more challenge or status, or the desire to return to the workforce after childrearing.

- People in middle adulthood usually have more leisure time than previously. Often they use it to become more involved outside the home in recreational and community activities.

RETHINK

- Why might striving for occupational success be less appealing in middle age than before? What cognitive and personality changes might contribute to this phenomenon?

- Why do you think immigrants' ambition and achievements are widely underestimated? Does the occurrence of conspicuous negative examples play a role (as it does in perceptions of the midlife crisis and stormy adolescence)?

- What practical, societal, and psychological factors contribute to the difficulty of midlife unemployment?

- What sorts of societal and attitudinal changes will have to occur to make frequent midlife career changes routine?

- What developmental changes help bring about increased involvement in charitable and community activities among middle-aged people?

LOOKING BACK

In what ways does personality develop during middle adulthood?

1. Considerable personality development occurs during middle adulthood. Erik Erikson suggests that the developmental conflict of the age is "generativity versus stagnation," ideally involving a shift in focus from oneself to the world beyond. George Vaillant views the main developmental issue similarly, but more narrowly, as "keeping the meaning versus rigidity," in which people seek to extract meaning from their lives and accept the strengths and weaknesses of others.

2. Daniel Levinson devised an influential theory of the seasons of life that focuses on the creation of "The Dream"—a global vision of one's future—in early adulthood, followed by the midlife transition of the early 40s, during which people confront their mortality and question their accomplishments, especially in terms of "The Dream." According to Levinson, the transition often entails a midlife crisis, as a result of which people either come to grips with their aging and their limitations or stagnate.

3. Levinson's theory has been criticized because it is based on a study involving a sample of only 40 men, from which it is difficult to generalize confidently. Later replications of his research involving women as well as men have produced generally similar results, although the nature of the stages of adulthood is somewhat different for women than for men.

What are some current controversies in personality development?

4. The notion of the midlife crisis has been particularly scrutinized and criticized. There is no evidence that most people go through such a crisis in the middle age, which is usually a time of relative satisfaction and tranquillity.

5. An important controversy concerns whether people tend to pass through a series of age-related developmental stages in a more or less uniform progression, as normative-crisis models indicate, or respond to a varying series of major life events at different times and in different orders, as life events models suggest.

6. Another controversy relates to the stability of personality. Theories such as Erikson's and Levinson's seem to imply a great deal of personality change over time, whereas those of other developmentalists emphasize the stability of major personality charac-

teristics from youth through old age. In fact, the general personality may be relatively stable over time, with particular aspects changing in response to life changes.

What are typical patterns of marriage and divorce in middle adulthood?

7. Middle adulthood is for most married couples a time of satisfaction, characterized by an upswing in feelings of friendship, commitment, mutual interest, and sexual harmony. However, for many couples marital satisfaction declines steadily and divorce results. Divorce can be especially difficult for women in midlife, particularly for those who have followed the traditional homemaker role.

8. Most people who divorce remarry, usually to another divorced person. Because of the marriage gradient, which dictates that men marry younger women, women over 40 find it harder to remarry than do men. People tend to remarry for a number of reasons, including removal of the social stigma of divorce, the desire for companionship, and the realization of economic benefits. Those who marry for a second time tend to be more realistic and mature than do people in first marriages, and to share roles and responsibilities more equitably. However, second marriages end in divorce even more often than do first marriages.

What changing family situations do middle-aged adults face?

9. The empty nest syndrome, a supposed psychological upheaval that many middle-aged people confront after their children have grown and left the home, is probably exaggerated. Although the departure of children is a major life transition and can produce powerful emotions, the reaction is generally of short duration. Furthermore, the permanent departure of children is occurring later and later as "boomerang" children increasingly return home for a number of years after having confronted the harsh realities of economic life.

10. Adults in the middle years often face responsibilities in two directions: In addition to caring for their children, they often must assume the care of their aging parents. Such adults have been called the "sandwich generation," and the experience can present difficulties. However, most people who care for their parents (and it is more often women than men who do so) find that the experience offers both rewards and challenges.

11. Another new experience for many middle-aged adults is becoming grandparents. Researchers have identified three distinct styles of grandparenting: involved, companionate, and remote. Styles tend to differ by gender and race, with women and African-Americans tending toward greater involvement with their grandchildren.

What are the causes and characteristics of family violence in the United States?

12. Family violence in the United States has reached epidemic proportions, with some form of violence occurring in a quarter of all marriages. Violence crosses lines of socioeconomic status, race, ethnicity, and religion, although the likelihood of violence is higher in families that are subject to economic or emotional stresses. In addition, people who were abused as children have a higher likelihood of becoming abusers as adults—a phenomenon termed the "cycle of violence."

13. Marital aggression typically proceeds through three stages: a tension-building stage, an acute battering incident, and a loving contrition stage. Despite contrition, abusers tend to remain abusers unless they get effective help. Wives may stay with battering husbands because they want desperately to preserve their marriages, assume part of the blame for the abuse, or come from family backgrounds in which violence was modeled as an acceptable way to settle disputes.

14. Spousal abuse in the United States often has cultural connections. Furthermore, researchers suggest that the power imbalance between women and men in many societies leads to an environment in which wife abuse is condoned.

What are the characteristics of work and career in middle adulthood?

15. For most people, midlife is a time of job satisfaction. Middle-aged workers tend to find career ambition less of a force in their lives than previously, and they begin to focus on the short-term features of work. In addition, family life and outside interests begin to be more valued.

16. The impression that many people in the United States have of immigrants is erroneous. Although many believe immigrants are not industrious and strain social support systems, immigrants as a group ultimately tend to be better off financially and less dependent on welfare than nonimmigrants. Furthermore, immigrants contribute far more to the economy in taxes than they receive in government services.

17. Job dissatisfaction is a factor for some people in middle age. Some are disappointed with their achievements and position in life, whereas others—especially those in the helping professions—may burn out because of their perceived failure to have made a difference in the insurmountable problems they have been working to address. Realistic expectations and a focus on small victories are the best antidotes to burnout for such individuals.

How do people in midlife deal with career change, unemployment, and leisure time?

18. Some people in middle adulthood must face unexpected unemployment, a condition with not only economic effects but also psychological and physical consequences. Middle-aged individuals who lose their jobs have an especially hard time because finding new ones is often made difficult by age discrimination and feelings of hopelessness.

19. A growing number of people change careers in midlife, some to increase job challenge, satisfaction, and status, others to return to a workforce they left years earlier to raise children. The result for many is a sense of invigoration and renewal. However, for people who hold unrealistic expectations about their new positions, the reality can bring disappointment.

20. Middle-aged people have substantial leisure time at their disposal. Though sedentary pursuits, such as television viewing, are a popular way to use leisure time, many people in midlife engage in social, recreational, and community activities. Leisure use in midlife serves as a good preparation for retirement.

KEY TERMS AND CONCEPTS

generativity versus stagnation (p. 544)
midlife crisis (p. 546)
social clock (p. 546)
normative-crisis models (p. 548)
life events models (p. 548)

empty nest syndrome (p. 554)
boomerang children (p. 555)
sandwich generation (p. 557)
cycle-of-violence hypothesis (p. 559)
burnout (p. 565)

Late Adulthood

Physical and Cognitive Development

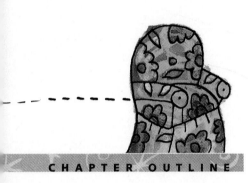

CHAPTER OUTLINE

The University of Arkansas campus is buzzing with talk of midterms and football. In a cafeteria, students are grousing about the food.

"Where are the dinner rolls?" says one. "I'm a vegetarian, and all they have is meat," complains another. Soon, though, everyone has moved on to complaining about classes.

A typical college scene—except for all the canes, hearing aids and white hair in evidence. This is Elderhostel, a program for people 60 and older run by a Boston nonprofit organization, formed in 1975, that recruits colleges to conduct weeklong educational sessions in everything from genealogy to the archaeology of ancient Egypt. . . .

Dorothy McAlpin, 63, is one of the program's most devoted students. A little more than a year ago, as she prepared to retire from a job as a correctional officer in a medium-security men's prison in Clarinda, Iowa, her biggest fear was "waking up in the morning alone and with nothing to do."

Rather than "play bridge and put on church bake sales," as older folks do in Clarinda, the grandmother, who wears her long silver hair tied back in a pink bow, decided to spend her retirement attending Elderhostel programs.

She studied the thick course directory and mapped out a route that allowed her to attend a different one in a different place just about every week. . . . Then, Mrs. McAlpin, who was divorced three years ago, became a vagabond. She gave up her apartment, bought a second-hand Winnebago and traveled around the country, from campus to campus.

In 52 weeks, Mrs. McAlpin, a community-college graduate, attended 45 Elderhostel programs, from Boston to Florida, Texas to Minnesota. (Stern, 1994, p. A1)

LOOKING AHEAD

Dorothy McAlpin is just one of the more than 300,000 people who enroll annually in thousands of classes organized by the Elderhostel program, the largest educational program for people in late adulthood. Represented on college campuses across the world, the Elderhostel movement is among the increasing evidence of the important intellectual growth and change that continue throughout people's lives, including late adulthood.

Old age used to be equated with loss: loss of brain cells, loss of intellectual capabilities, loss of energy, loss of sex drive. Increasingly, however, that view is being displaced as **gerontologists**, specialists who study aging, paint a very different picture of late adulthood. Rather than being viewed through the single lens of decline, late adulthood is now seen as a period of considerable diversity in which people continue to change—to grow in some areas, and, yes, to decline in others.

Even the definition of "old" is changing, for many people in the period of late adulthood, which begins at about age 60 and continues to death, are as vigorous and involved with life as people several decades younger. The reality, then, is that we cannot define old age by chronological years alone; we also must take into account people's physical and psychological well-being.

In this chapter, we'll consider both physical and cognitive development during late adulthood. We begin with a discussion of the myths and realities behind aging, examining some of the stereotypes that color our understanding of late adulthood. We look at the outward and inward signs of aging, and the ways in which the nervous system and senses change with age.

Next, we consider health and well-being in late adulthood. After examining some of the major disorders that affect older people, we consider what factors determine wellness and the relationship between aging and disease. We also focus on various theories that seek to explain the aging process, as well as gender, race, and ethnic differences in life expectancy.

gerontologists *specialists who study aging*

577

Finally, the chapter discusses intellectual development during late adulthood. We look at the nature of intelligence in older people, and the various ways in which cognitive abilities change. We also assess how different types of memory fare during late adulthood, and we consider ways to reverse intellectual declines in older people.

In sum, after reading this chapter, you'll be able to answer the following questions:

◆ What is it like to grow old in the United States today?

◆ What sorts of physical changes occur in old age?

◆ How are the senses affected by aging?

◆ What is the general state of health of older people, and to what disorders are they susceptible?

◆ Can wellness and sexuality be maintained in old age?

◆ How long can people expect to live, and why do they die?

◆ How well do older people function intellectually?

◆ Do people lose their memories in old age?

PHYSICAL DEVELOPMENT IN LATE ADULTHOOD

In 1875, the year Jeanne Louise Calment was born in Arles, in southern France, Victoria was Queen, Ulysses S. Grant was in the White House and horse-drawn carriages were the way to go.

Most remnants of that era are long gone, but not Jeanne Calment. Last month this daughter of a well-to-do boatbuilder and his wife turned 120. Still fond of a glass of port and always on the lookout for a box of good chocolates, she celebrated her birthday in a nursing home on the outskirts of the town where she was born. She is, according to the *Guinness Book of Records*, the oldest human being on earth whose age can be authenticated. (Art of Living, 1995, p. 69)

Jeanne Calment, whose major concession to age seems to have been giving up smoking at the age of 118, is a unique case. With the mean life expectancy of people in Western countries in the 70s—and even lower for people in less industrialized parts of the world—only a handful of people live beyond 100 years, let alone two decades more.

Why should this be the case? Is there some genetically determined limitation that prevents humans from staying alive beyond a certain age, or can they theoretically continue living for years and years? We'll consider these questions as we discuss the physical changes that occur in late adulthood and consider several theories about why people age.

AGING: MYTH AND REALITY

Late adulthood holds a unique distinction among the periods of human life: Because people are living longer, late adulthood is actually increasing in length. Whether we peg the start of the period at age 60, 65, or 70, there is a greater proportion of people alive in late adulthood than at any time in world history.

The Demographics of Late Adulthood.   At the start of this century, approximately 6 percent of the United States population was age 60 or older. By 1990, the comparable figure was more than 17 percent. And projections suggest that by the year 2050, nearly one-quarter of the population will be age 65 and above (see Figure 17-1).

Furthermore, the fastest-growing segment of the population is what has been termed the *oldest old*—people who are 85 or older. In the last two decades, the size of this group has nearly doubled.

Jeanne Calment at age 120.

FIGURE 17-1

THE FLOURISHING ELDERLY

The percentage of people over the age of 65 is projected to rise to almost 25 percent of the population by year 2050.

(Adapted from U.S. Bureau of the Census, 1990b.)

*Projected

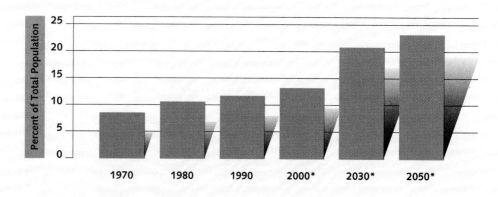

The population explosion among older people is not limited to the United States. In fact, the rate of increase is much higher in developing countries. For instance, by the year 2000, developing countries will show a 130 percent increase in the number of people over the age of 60, as compared with an increase of just over 50 percent in previously developed nations. Similarly, by the year 2025 the number of people age 80 and older will increase by 415 percent in developing countries and 132 percent in already developed countries. As can be seen in Figure 17-2, the sheer numbers of elderly are increasing substantially in countries around the globe (Grisby, 1991; Turner & Helms, 1993).

Ageism: Confronting the Stereotypes of Late Adulthood. Crotchety. Old codger. Old coot. Senile. Old geezer. Old hag.

Such are the labels of late adulthood. If you find that they do not draw a pretty picture, you are right: Such words are demeaning and biased, representing both overt and subtle **ageism**, prejudice and discrimination directed at older people.

Ageism is manifested in several ways. It is found in negative attitudes toward older people and the aging process that suggest that older people are in less than full command of

ageism   *prejudice and discrimination directed at older people*

The stereotyping of ageism, in which elderly people are viewed negatively, has a long history in western society, as evidenced in the character of Scrooge from Dickens' nineteenth century novel, *A Christmas Carol.*

FIGURE 17-2

THE ELDERLY POPULATION, WORLDWIDE

Some 23 nations already have more than 2 million elderly, and an additional 27 countries are projected to have elderly populations above 2 million by the year 2025.

(*Source:* Turner & Helms, 1994.)

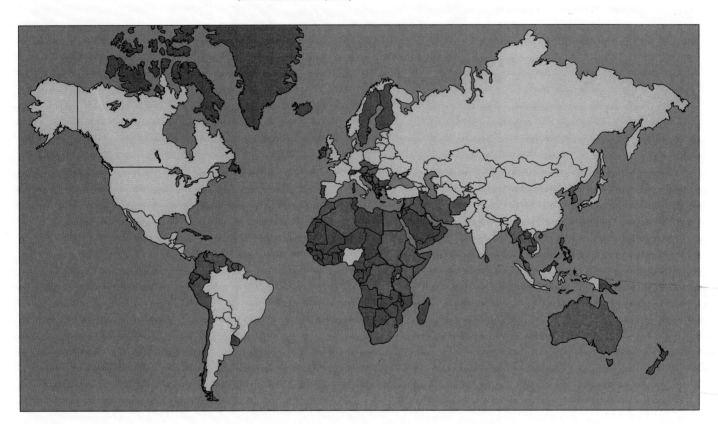

▨ **Nations currently having an elderly population of 2 million and above**

▨ **Additional nations expected to have an elderly population above 2 million by 2025**

their mental faculties (Secouler, 1992). In fact, meta-analyses of a large cross section of attitude studies have found that older adults are viewed more negatively than are younger ones on a variety of traits, particularly those having to do with general competence and attractiveness (Kite & Johnson, 1988).

Not only are older people held in lower esteem than are younger people, but they are also the objects of overt discrimination. For instance, elderly individuals seeking jobs may face open prejudice, being told in job interviews that the job would be better filled by people who are "less set in their ways" or "better equipped to compete in today's fast-paced world." Similarly, older applicants have been told that they have no business seeking positions that should be filled by younger persons with families to support. Such job discrimination persists even though it is illegal.

Furthermore, identical behavior carried out by an older and a younger person often is interpreted quite differently. For example, older adults who show memory lapses are viewed as chronically forgetful and likely to be suffering from some mental disorder. Similar behavior on the part of young adults is judged more charitably, merely as evidence of temporary forgetfulness produced by having too much on their minds (Erber, Szuchman, & Rothberg, 1990).

The ageism that produces such negative views of older people is reflected in their treatment. For instance, older adults in nursing homes are often the recipients of "baby-talk," the language and tone of voice that adults use to speak to infants (the type we discussed in Chapter 5). An 84-year-old woman might be addressed as "honey" or "baby," for example, and told that she has to go "night-night" (Whitbourne & Wills, 1993).

The ageism directed toward people in late adulthood is, in some ways, a peculiarly twentieth-century—and Western—cultural phenomenon. In the Colonial period of U.S. history, a long life was an indication that a person had led a particularly virtuous existence, and older people were held in high esteem. Similarly, people in most Asian societies venerate those who have reached old age because elders have attained special wisdom as a consequence of living so long. Likewise, many Native American societies traditionally have viewed older people as storehouses of information about the past.

In contrast, negative views of older people prevail in U.S. society, and they are based on widespread misinformation. For instance, to test you knowledge about aging, try answering the questions posed in Table 17-1. Most people score no higher than chance on the items, averaging about 50 percent correct (Palmore, 1988, 1992). In addition, a negative view of older people is supported by the reverence of youth and youthful appearance that characterizes many Western societies. It is the rare advertisement that includes an elderly person, unless it is for a product specifically designed for older adults. And when older people are portrayed in television programming, they are often presented as someone's mother, father, grandmother, or grandfather, rather than as individuals in their own right (Vernon, 1990).

Given the prevalence of ageist stereotypes in Western societies today, it is reasonable to ask how accurate these views are. Is there a kernel of truth in them?

The answer is largely no. As we will see in the remainder of this and the next chapter, aging produces consequences that vary greatly from one person to the next. Although some

TABLE 17-1

THE MYTHS OF AGING

1. The majority of old people (age 65 and older) are senile (have defective memory, are disoriented, or demented). **T or F?**
2. The five senses (sight, hearing, taste, touch, and smell) all tend to weaken in old age. **T or F?**
3. The majority of old people have no interest in, nor capacity for, sexual relations. **T or F?**
4. Lung vital capacity tends to decline in old age. **T or F?**
5. The majority of old people feel miserable most of the time. **T or F?**
6. Physical strength tends to decline in old age. **T or F?**
7. At least one-tenth of the aged are living in long-stay institutions (such as nursing homes, mental hospitals, and homes for the aged.) **T or F?**
8. Aged drivers have fewer accidents per driver than those under age 65. **T or F?**
9. Older workers usually cannot work as effectively as younger workers. **T or F?**
10. Over three-fourths of the aged are healthy enough to carry out their normal activities. **T or F?**
11. The majority of old people are unable to adapt to change. **T or F?**
12. Old people usually take longer to learn something new. **T or F?**
13. It is almost impossible for the average old person to learn something new. **T or F?**
14. Older people tend to react slower than do younger people. **T or F?**
15. In general, old people tend to be pretty much alike. **T or F?**
16. The majority of old people say they are seldom bored. **T or F?**
17. The majority old people are socially isolated. **T or F?**
18. Older workers have fewer accidents than do younger workers. **T or F?**

Scoring
All odd-numbered statements are false; all even-numbered statements are true. Most college students miss about six, and high school students miss about nine. Even college instructors miss an average of about three.

Source: Palmore, 1982.

elderly people are in fact physically frail, have cognitive difficulties, and require constant care, others are vigorous and independent—and sharp, brilliant, and shrewd thinkers. Furthermore, some problems that seem at first glance attributable to old age are actually a result of illness, improper diet, or insufficient nutrition. As we shall see, the autumn and winter of life can bring change and growth on a par with—and sometimes even better than—earlier periods of the life span.

PHYSICAL TRANSITIONS IN OLDER PEOPLE

"Feel the burn." That's what the Jane Fonda exercise tape says, and many of the 14 women in the group are doing just that. As the exercise tape continues through a variety of drills, the women participate to varying degrees. Some stretch and reach vigorously, while others mostly appear to be just swaying in time to the pounding beat of the music. It's not much different from thousands of exercise classes all over the United States. Yet to a youthful observer, there is one surprise: The youngest woman in this exercise group is 66 years old, and the oldest, dressed in sleek Spandex leotards, is 81.

The surprise registered by this observer reflects a popular stereotype of the elderly. Many people view those over 60 as sedentary and sedate, an image that certainly does not incorporate involvement in vigorous exercise.

The reality, however, is different. Although the physical capabilities of elderly people are not the same as they were in earlier stages of life, many older people remain remarkably agile and physically fit in later life (Paffenbarger et al., 1994).

Still, the changes in the body that began subtly during middle adulthood become unmistakable during old age. Both the outward indications of aging, and those related to internal functioning, become incontestable.

Outward Signs of Aging.   One of the most obvious signs of aging is the hair. Most people's hair becomes distinctly gray and eventually white, and it may thin out. The face and other parts of the body become wrinkled as the skin loses elasticity and *collagen*, the protein that forms the basic fibers of body tissue (Matteson, 1988; Bowers & Thomas, 1995).

People may become noticeably shorter, with some shrinking as much as 4 inches. Although this shortening is partially due to changes in posture, the primary cause is that the

Even in late adulthood, exercise is possible—and beneficial.

Although gray hair is often characterized as "distinguished" in men, the same trait in women is viewed more often as a sign of being "over the hill"—a clear double standard.

cartilage in the disks of the backbone has become thinner. This is particularly true for women, who are more susceptible than men to **osteoporosis**, or thinning of the bones.

Osteoporosis, which affects 25 percent of women over the age of 60, is a primary cause of broken bones among elderly people. It is also largely preventable, if people's calcium and protein intake are sufficient in earlier parts of life, and if they have engaged in sufficient exercise (Perlmutter & Hall, 1992; Guralnik et al., 1995).

Although negative stereotypes against appearing old operate for both men and women, they are particularly potent for women. In fact, in Western cultures there is a *double standard* for appearance, by which women who show signs of aging are judged more harshly than are men. For instance, gray hair in men is often viewed as "distinguished," a sign of character; the same characteristic in women is a signal that they are "over the hill" (Sontag, 1979; I.P. Bell, 1989).

As a consequence of the double standard, women are considerably more likely than men to feel compelled to hide the signs of aging. For instance, older women are much more likely than men to dye their hair and to have cosmetic surgery, and women's use of cosmetics is designed to make them look younger than their years (Unger & Crawford, 1992).

Internal Aging.   As the outward physical signs of aging become increasingly apparent, significant changes occur in the internal functioning of the organ systems. The capacities of many functions of the average 75-year-old pale in comparison to those of the average 30-year-old (see Figure 17-3; Shock, 1962; Turner & Helms, 1994).

The brain becomes smaller and lighter with age. As it shrinks, it pulls away from the skull, and the amount of space between brain and skull doubles from age 20 to age 70. Furthermore, there is a reduction in the flow of blood within the brain, which also uses less oxygen and glucose. The number of neurons, or brain cells, substantially declines in some parts of the brain (Scheibel, 1992; DiGiovanna, 1994).

The reduced flow of blood in the brain reflects in part reductions in the capacity of the heart to pump blood throughout the circulatory system. Because of hardening and shrinking of blood vessels throughout the body, the heart is forced to work harder, and it is typically unable to compensate fully. Consequently, 75-year-old men are able to pump less than three-quarters of the blood that they were able to pump during early adulthood (Shock, 1962; Kart, 1990).

osteoporosis a condition in which the bones become brittle, fragile, and thin, often brought about by a lack of calcium in the diet

FIGURE 17-3

1   Brain weight (56%)
2   Memory loss*
3   Slower speed of response*
4   Blood flow to brain (80%)
5   Speed of return to equilibrium of blood acidity (17%)
6   Cardiac output at rest (70%)
7   Number of glomeruli in kidney (56%)
8   Glomerular filtration rate (69%)
9   Kidney plasma flow (50%)
10 Number of nerve trunk fibers (63%)
11 Nerve conduction velocity (90%)
12 Number of taste buds (36%)
13 Maximum oxygen uptake during exercise (40%)
14 Maximum ventilation volume during exercise (53%)
15 Maximum voluntary breathing volume (43%)
16 Vital capacity (56%)
17 Less adrenal activity*
18 Less sexual activity*
19 Hand grip (55%)
20 Maximum work rate (70%)
21 Maximum work rate for short burst (40%)
22 Basal metabolic rate (84%)
23 Body water content (82%)
24 Body weight for males (88%)

*Percentages unavailable, although there is some
memory loss, slower speed or response and less
adrenal and sexual activity

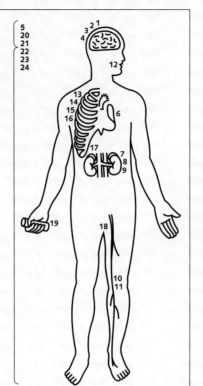

DECLINING PHYSICAL CAPACITIES

The percentages indicate the proportion of
capacity existing at age 75 relative to capacity
at age 30.

(*Source*: N.W. Shock, 1962.)

Other bodily systems work at lower capacity than they did earlier in life. For instance, the efficiency of the respiratory system declines with age, and the digestive system produces less digestive juice and is less efficient in pushing food through the system—which causes a higher incidence of constipation.

SLOWING REACTION TIME

As people get older, they take longer: longer to put on a tie, longer to reach a ringing phone, longer to open an envelope. One reason for this slowness is a lengthening of reaction time. As we discussed first in Chapter 15, reaction time begins to increase in middle age, and by late adulthood the rise can be significant (Fozard et al., 1994; Sliwinski et al., 1994).

It is not clear why people slow down. One explanation, known as the **peripheral slowing hypothesis**, suggests that overall processing speed declines in the peripheral nervous system. According to this notion, the peripheral nervous system, which encompasses the nerves that branch out from the spinal cord and brain and reach the extremities of the body, becomes less efficient with age. Because of this decrease in efficiency, it takes longer for information from the environment to reach the brain, and longer for commands from the brain to be transmitted to the body's muscles (Salthouse, 1989).

Other researchers have proposed an alternative explanation. According to the **generalized slowing hypothesis**, processing in all parts of the nervous system, including the brain, is less efficient. As a consequence, slowing occurs throughout the body, including the processing of both simple and complex stimuli and the transmission of commands to the muscles of the body (Cerella, 1990).

Although we do not know which explanation provides the more accurate account, it is clear that the slowing of reaction time and general processing results in a higher incidence

peripheral slowing hypothesis   the theory
that suggests that overall processing speed
declines in the peripheral nervous system

generalized slowing hypothesis   the the-
ory that processing in all parts of the nervous
system, including the brain, is less efficient

of accidents for elderly people. Because their reaction and processing time is slowed, they are unable to receive information efficiently from the environment that may indicate a dangerous situation, their decision-making processes may be slower, and ultimately their ability to remove themselves from harm's way is impaired (Whitbourne, Jacobo, & Munoz-Ruiz, 1995).

THE SENSES: SIGHT, SOUND, TASTE, AND SMELL

Old age brings with it distinct declines in the sense organs of the body, although in this area there is a great deal of variation. Sensory declines are of major psychological consequence because the senses serve as a person's link with the world outside the mind.

Vision.   Age-related changes in the physical apparatus of the eye—the cornea, lens, retina, and optic nerve—lead to a decrease in visual abilities. For instance, the lens becomes less transparent and the pupil shrinks. Even the optic nerve becomes less efficient in transmitting nerve impulses (Schieber, 1992).

As a result, vision declines along several dimensions. Vision of distant objects becomes less acute, more light is needed to see clearly, and it takes longer to adjust from dark to light places and vice versa.

The changes in vision produce everyday difficulties. For instance, driving, particularly at night, becomes more challenging (Ball & Rebok, 1994). Similarly, reading requires more lighting, and eye strain occurs more easily. On the other hand, eyeglasses and contact lenses can correct many of these problems, and the majority of older people can see reasonably well (Akutsu, 1991; Horowitz, 1994; Orr, 1991).

Several vision problems become more common during late adulthood. For instance, **cataracts**—cloudy or opaque areas on the lens of the eye that interfere with passing light—frequently develop. People with cataracts have blurred vision and tend to experience glare in bright light. If cataracts are left untreated, the lens becomes milky white and blindness is the eventual result. However, cataracts can be surgically removed, and eyesight can be restored through the use of eyeglasses, contact lenses, or *intraocular lens implants*, in which a plastic lens is permanently placed in the eye.

A second serious problem that afflicts many elderly individuals is glaucoma. As we noted first in Chapter 15, **glaucoma** occurs when pressure in the fluid of the eye increases, either because the fluid cannot drain properly or because too much fluid is produced. Glaucoma can also be treated by drugs or surgery if it is detected early enough.

Hearing.   Hearing loss is fairly common among elderly people. Roughly 30 percent of adults between the ages of 65 and 74 have some degree of hearing loss, and the figure rises to 50 percent among those aged 75 through 79. Overall, more than 10 million elderly people in the United States have hearing impairments of one kind or another (Hudson, 1990).

The ability to hear higher frequencies is particularly affected during old age. Loss of these frequencies makes it hard to hear conversations when there is considerable background noise or when several people are speaking simultaneously. Furthermore, some elderly people actually find loud noises painful.

Although hearing aids can help compensate and would probably be helpful in some 75 percent of the cases of permanent hearing loss, only 20 percent of elderly people wear them. One reason is that hearing aids are far from perfect. They amplify background noises as much as they amplify conversations, making it difficult for wearers to separate what they want to hear from other sounds. Moreover, a stigma is attached to wearing a hearing aid; many elderly people feel that the use of hearing aids makes them appear even older than they really are and causes them to be treated as though their minds were disabled (Hudson, 1990; Patterson, Dancer, & Clark, 1990).

Hearing loss can also harm the social lives of older people. Unable to hear conversations fully, some elderly people with hearing problems withdraw from others, avoiding situations

cataracts   cloudy or opaque areas on the lens of the eye that interfere with passing light

glaucoma   a condition where pressure in the fluid of the eye increases, either because the fluid cannot drain properly or because too much fluid is produced

in which many people are present. They may also be unwilling to respond to others, as they are unsure of what was said to them. In addition, such hearing losses can lead to feelings of isolation; able to catch only fragments of conversations, a hearing-impaired older adult can easily feel left out and lonely (Knutson & Lansing, 1990).

Taste and Smell.   Elderly people who have enjoyed food throughout their lives may experience a real decline in the quality of life because of changes in sensitivity to taste and smell. Both senses become less discriminating in old age, causing food to taste and smell less appetizing than it did earlier (Matteson, 1988; Myslinski, 1990; Scheiber, 1992; de Graaf, Polet, & van Staveren, 1994).

The reason for the decrease in taste and smell sensitivity can be traced to a decline in the number of taste buds in the tongue. Furthermore, the olfactory bulbs in the brain begin to shrivel, which reduces the ability to smell. Because smell is responsible in part for taste, the shrinkage of the olfactory bulbs makes food taste even more bland.

The loss of taste and smell sensitivity has an unfortunate side effect: Because food doesn't taste as good, people eat less and open the door to malnutrition. Furthermore, to compensate for the loss of taste buds, older people may oversalt their food, thereby increasing their chances of developing *hypertension*, or high blood pressure, one of the most common health problems of old age (Murphy, 1989; Stevens, Cain, Demarque, & Ruthruff, 1991).

The Informed Consumer of Development

Dealing with Sensory Impairments

There are several ways for younger people to help older people deal with declines that may occur in their sensory capabilities. Among them are the following:

- For people with vision problems, provide plenty of lighting, especially in critical areas like stairways. Keep rooms free of clutter, and do not rearrange furniture. Provide large-type reading materials. Many books and magazines are now printed in large-type editions, which people with visual problems find much easier to read. For those with severe vision problems, provide books on tape as an alternative to reading.

- When speaking to people with hearing impairments, speak at a distance of 3 to 6 feet, positioning yourself so that your face can be seen. Speak slightly louder than normal, but avoid screaming, which may do nothing but distort your words. Turn down radios and TVs when you are talking.

- Although using shorter, simpler sentences can be helpful, do not use baby talk or other linguistic devices that imply that those with hearing problems are mentally impaired.

- If an older person complains that food no longer tastes good, try cooking with more spices and stronger-tasting foods, such as tomato sauce or lamb. Do not go overboard on the salt, though; too much salt can lead to high blood pressure. Help ensure there is plenty of variety in the older person's diet.

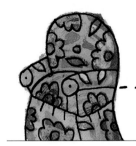

Review and Rethink

REVIEW

◆ Older people, who now represent a greater percentage of the population than ever before, are often the victims of ageism—prejudice and discrimination against old people.

◆ Physically, old age brings external changes—thinning and graying hair, wrinkles, and shorter stature—and internal changes—decreased brain size, fewer neurons, and diminished efficiency in circulation, respiration, and digestion.

◆ The two main hypotheses that seek to explain the increase in reaction time in old age are the peripheral slowing hypothesis and the generalized slowing hypothesis.

◆ The senses are susceptible to declines in old age. Vision may become more difficult at distances, in dim light, and when moving from darkness to light and vice versa.

◆ Hearing, especially of high frequencies, may diminish, causing social and psychological difficulties, and taste and smell may become less discriminating, leading to nutritional problems.

RETHINK

◆ What are some social implications of an increasing number and proportion of older people in the population?

◆ When jobs for all workers are scarce, is it right for elderly people to hold onto their current jobs or even seek new ones?

◆ When older people win praise and attention for being "vigorous," "active," and "youthful," is this a message that combats or supports ageism?

◆ What are some of the ways that ageism and other cultural attitudes toward aging affect those who are experiencing hearing loss?

◆ Should strict examinations for renewal of driver's licenses be imposed on older people? What issues should be taken into consideration?

HEALTH AND WELLNESS IN LATE ADULTHOOD

Like an actor settled into a long-running show, he continues to play the familiar role almost by rote: chopping wood, riding horses, visiting his office where, these days, the only business that awaits are letters from well-wishers and a jar of jelly beans. But nearly 4 months after his poignant handwritten note informing the world that he was suffering from Alzheimer's disease, former President Ronald Reagan, 84, is increasingly forgetting his lines and missing his cues. "About 6 months ago, he stopped recognizing me," Reagan's biographer, Edmund Morris, wrote recently. "Now I no longer recognize him." (Lambert, Armstrong, & Wagner, 1995, p. 32)

President Reagan became one of the 4 million Americans who suffer from Alzheimer's disease, a debilitating condition that saps both the physical and mental powers of its victims. In some ways, his disease symbolizes our view of elderly people, who, according to popular stereotypes, are more apt to be ill than healthy.

However, the reality is different: Most elderly people are in relatively good health for most of old age. According to surveys conducted in the United States, almost three-quarters of people 65 years old and above rate their health as good, very good, or excellent (USDHHS, 1990).

On the other hand, to be old is to be susceptible to a host of diseases. We now consider some of the major physical and psychological problems that beset older people.

RONALD REAGAN

Nov. 5, 1994

My Fellow Americans,

I have recently been told that I am one of the millions of Americans who will be afflicted with Alzheimer's Disease.

Upon learning this news, Nancy & I had to decide whether as private citizens we would keep this a private matter or whether we would make this news known in a public way.

In the past Nancy suffered from breast cancer and I had my cancer surgeries. We found through our open disclosures we were able to raise public awareness. We were happy that as a result many more people underwent testing. They were treated in early stages and able to return to normal, healthy lives.

So now, we feel it is important to share it with you. In opening our hearts, we hope this might promote greater awareness of this condition. Perhaps it will encourage a clearer understanding of the individuals and families who are affected by it.

In closing, let me thank you, the American people for giving me the great honor of allowing me to serve as your President. When the Lord calls me home, whenever that may be, I will leave with the greatest love for this country of ours and eternal optimism for its future.

I now begin the journey that will lead me into the sunset of my life. I know that for America there will always be a bright dawn ahead.

Thank you my friends. May God always bless you.

Sincerely,
Ronald Reagan

Portions of a letter, written by former president Ronald Reagan, poignantly discloses that he has Alzheimer's disease.

HEALTH PROBLEMS IN OLDER PEOPLE: PHYSICAL AND PSYCHOLOGICAL DISORDERS

Most of the illnesses and diseases found in late adulthood are not peculiar to old age; people of all ages suffer from cancer and heart disease, for instance. However, the incidence of these and many other diseases rises with age, raising the odds that an elderly person will be ill during this period. Moreover, while younger people can readily rebound from a variety of health problems, older people bounce back more slowly from illnesses. And ultimately, the illness may get the best of an older person, preventing a full recovery.

Common Physical Disorders.   Most older people have at least one chronic, long-term condition (AARP, 1990). For instance, *arthritis*, an inflammation of one or more joints, is common, striking around half of older people. Arthritis can cause painful swelling in various parts of the body, and it can be disabling. Sufferers can find themselves unable to carry out the simplest of everyday activities, such as unscrewing the cap of a jar of food or turning a key in a lock. Although aspirin and other drugs can relieve some of the swelling and reduce the pain, the condition cannot be cured (Burt & Harris, 1994).

Arthritis can produce swelling land inflammation in the joints of the hand.

Approximately one-third of older people have *hypertension*, or high blood pressure. Although it is symptomless, higher tension within the circulatory system can result in deterioration of the blood vessels and heart, and can raise the risk of cerebrovascular disease, or stroke, if it is not treated.

The leading causes of death in elderly people are heart disease, cancer, and stroke. Close to three-quarters of people in late adulthood die from these problems.

Psychological and Mental Disorders.   Like people in other age groups, older adults are susceptible to a variety of psychological disorders. Some 15 to 25 percent of those over age 65 are thought to show some symptoms of psychological malady (Haight, 1991).

One of the more prevalent problems is major depression, which is characterized by intense sadness, pessimism, and hopelessness. One obvious reason for its increased incidence in older people is the cumulative losses they experience as spouses and friends—often of the same age and sometimes even younger—die. Furthermore, declining health and physical capabilities, which may rob older people of a sense of control, can contribute to the prevalence of depression (Blazer, 1989; George, 1992; Bruce & Hoff, 1994; Smith, Christensen, Peck, & Ward, 1994).

Some psychological disorders are produced by combinations of drugs that elderly people may be taking for various medical conditions. Because of changes in metabolism, a dose of a particular drug that would be appropriate for a 25-year-old might be much too large for a person of 75. The effects of drug interactions can be subtle, and they can manifest themselves in a variety of psychological symptoms, such as drug intoxication or anxiety. Because of these possibilities, older people who take medications must be on guard, informing their physicians and pharmacists of every drug they take. They should also avoid medicating themselves with over-the-counter drugs, because a combination of nonprescription and prescription medications may be dangerous, or even deadly (Small, 1991; Perodeau, Poirier, Foisy, & Ostoj, 1994; Pollow, Stoller, Forster, & Duniho, 1994).

The most common mental disorder of elderly people is **dementia**, a broad category covering several diseases, each of which includes serious memory loss accompanied by declines in other mental functioning. Although dementia has many causes, the symptoms are similar: declining memory, lessened intellectual abilities, and impaired judgment. The chances of experiencing dementia increase with age. For example, although less than 2 percent of people between 60 and 65 years are diagnosed with dementia, the percentages double for every 5-year period past 65. Consequently, almost one-third of people over the age of 85 suffer from sort of dementia. On the other hand, dementia is hardly inevitable; most people do not suffer declines in their mental functioning.

Alzheimer's Disease.   The most common form of dementia is **Alzheimer's disease**, which represents one of the largest mental health problems faced by the aging population. Alzheimer's disease is a progressive brain disorder that produces loss of memory and confusion and kills 100,000 people in the United States each year. Furthermore, the number is sure to rise as the size of the elderly population grows. In fact, by the year 2040, if current trends continue, almost 7 million Americans over 85 will be victims of Alzheimer's disease (HMHL, 1995).

The symptoms of Alzheimer's disease develop gradually. Generally the first sign is unusual forgetfulness. A person may stop at a grocery store several times during the week, forgetting that he or she has already done the shopping. People may also have trouble recalling particular words during conversations. At first, recent memories are affected, and then older memories fade. Eventually, people with the disease are totally confused, unable to speak intelligibly or to recognize even their closest family and friends. In the final stages of the disease, they lose voluntary control of their muscles and are bedridden.

Because there is no cure for Alzheimer's disease at the present time, treatment deals only with the symptoms. Because victims of the disorder are initially aware that their mem-

dementia   the most common mental disorder of the elderly, it covers several diseases, each of which includes serious memory loss accompanied by declines in other mental functioning

Alzheimer's disease   a progressive brain disorder that produces loss of memory and confusion

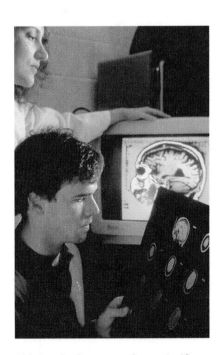

Alzheimer's disease produces significant changes to the brain, including shrinking and deterioration of several major structures. However, the cause of these changes remains unknown.

ories are failing and often understand quite well the future course of the disease, they may suffer from anxiety, fear, and depression—emotions not difficult to understand, given the grim prognosis.

Biologically, several changes are responsible for the disease. The brain shrinks, and several areas of the hippocampus and frontal and temporal lobes show deterioration. Furthermore, certain neurons die, which leads to a shortage of various neurotransmitters, such as acetylcholine.

Although the physical changes in the brain that produce the symptoms of Alzheimer's are clear, what is not known is what triggers the problem in the first place. Several explanations have been advanced. For instance, genetics clearly plays a role, with some families showing a much higher incidence of Alzheimer's than others. In fact, in certain families half the children appear to inherit the disease from their parents. On the other hand, in other families there is no discernible genetic pattern, so heredity is not the full story (M. Davidson, 1991; Barinaga, 1995a, 1995b; HMHL, 1995; Levy-Lahad et al., 1995).

Other explanations for the disease have also been investigated. For example, scientists are studying certain kinds of viruses, dysfunctions of the immune system, and hormone imbalances that may produce the disease. The research is far from definitive, however. In fact, some researchers now suggest that Alzheimer's disease is actually a family of disorders, with symptoms caused by a number of separate, distinct factors (R.D. Terry, 1994; Small et al., 1995).

Several drug treatments for Alzheimer's appear promising, although none are effective in the long term. The most promising drugs are related to the loss of the neurotransmitter acetylcholine (Ach) that occurs in some forms of Alzheimer's disease. Tacrine, or Cognex, has been shown in some studies to inhibit an enzyme that breaks down Ach, and it seems to alleviate some of the symptoms of the disease. Still, it is effective in only about 20 percent of Alzheimer's patients.

Other drugs being studied include anti-inflammatory drugs, which may reduce the brain inflammation that occurs in Alzheimer's. In addition, the chemicals in vitamins C and E are being tested; some evidence suggests that people who take such vitamins are at lower risk for developing the disorder. Still, at this point, it is clear that no drug treatment is truly effective (HMHL, 1995).

Ultimately, caregivers must provide total care for victims of Alzheimer's. As victims lose the ability to feed and clothe themselves, or even to control bladder and bowel functions, they must be cared for 24 hours a day. Because such care is typically impossible for even the most dedicated families, most Alzheimer's victims end their lives in nursing homes. Patients with Alzheimer's make up some two-thirds of those in nursing homes (Gray, Farish, & Dorevitch, 1992; Rovner & Katz, 1993).

People who care for the victims of Alzheimer's often become secondary victims of the disease. It is easy to become frustrated, angry, and exhausted by the demands of Alzheimer's patients, whose needs can be overpowering. In addition to the physical chore of providing total care, caregivers face the loss of a loved one, who may be visibly deteriorating. The burdens of caring for a person with Alzheimer's can be overwhelming (Talkington-Boyer & Snyder, 1994; Williamson & Schulz, 1993).

WELLNESS IN LATE ADULTHOOD: THE RELATIONSHIP BETWEEN AGING AND ILLNESS

Is getting sick an inevitable part of old age? Not necessarily. Whether an older person is ill or well depends less on age than on a variety of concerns, including past and present environmental factors, genetic predisposition, and psychological factors.

For instance, certain diseases, such as cancer and heart disease, have a clear genetic component. Some families have a higher incidence of breast cancer, for instance, than do others. At the same time, though, a genetic predisposition does not automatically mean that

Although these panels from the satirical "Senior Citizen Cookbook" imply that people should enjoy eating whatever they please in late adulthood, the reality is that adhering to nutritional guidelines remains important.
Drawing by R. Chast; © 1995 The New Yorker Magazine, Inc.

a person will get a particular illness. People's lifestyles—whether or not they smoke, the nature of their diets, their exposure to cancer-causing agents such as asbestos—can raise or lower their chances of coming down with such a disease. Furthermore, economic well-being also plays a role. For instance, as at all stages of life, living in poverty may restrict access to medical care.

Finally, psychological factors play an important role in determining people's susceptibility to illness—and ultimately the likelihood of death. For example, having a sense of control over one's environment, even in terms of making choices involving everyday matters, leads to a better psychological state and superior health outcomes (Taylor, 1991).

People can do specific things to enhance their physical well-being—as well as their longevity—during old age. It is probably no surprise that the right things to do are no different from what people should do during the rest of the life span: Eat a proper diet, exercise, and avoid obvious threats to health, such as smoking (Cesario & Hollander, 1991; Hickey & Stillwell, 1991; Ludwig, 1991; Hill, Storandt, & Malley, 1993).

Sometimes, however, older people experience difficulties that prevent them from following even these simple guidelines. For instance, varying estimates suggest that be-tween 16 and 50 percent of elderly people do not have adequate nutrition, and several million experience hunger every day (Manson & Shea, 1991; Burt & Harns, 1994; McCarthy, 1994).

The reasons for such malnutrition and hunger are varied. Some elderly people are too poor to purchase adequate food, and some are too infirm to shop or cook for themselves. Others feel little motivation to prepare and eat proper meals, particularly if they live alone. For those who have experienced significant declines in taste and smell sensitivity, eating well-prepared food may no longer be enjoyable. And some older people may never have eaten well-balanced meals in earlier periods of their lives (Ponza & Wray, 1990; Horwath, 1991).

Obtaining sufficient exercise might also prove problematic for older people. Although physical activity increases muscle strength and flexibility, reduces blood pressure and the risk of heart attack, and produces several other benefits, many older people do not get sufficient exercise to experience any of these benefits.

For instance, illness may prevent older adults from exercising, and even inclement weather during the winter might restrict a person's ability to get out of the house. Furthermore, problems can combine: A poor person with insufficient money to eat properly may as a consequence have little energy to put into physical activity.

Programs that offer food to poor, elderly adults provide a vital service, given the importance of good nutrition.

SEXUALITY IN OLD AGE: USE IT OR LOSE IT

Do your grandparents have sex? Quite possibly, yes. Although the answer may surprise you, increasing evidence suggests that people are sexually active well into their 80s and 90s. This happens despite societal stereotypes suggesting that it is somehow improper for two 75-year-olds to have sexual intercourse, and even worse for a 75-year-old to masturbate. Such negative attitudes are a function of societal expectations in the United States. In many other cultures, elderly people are expected to remain sexually active, and in some societies, people are expected to become less inhibited as they age (Winn & Newton, 1982; Hyde, 1994).

Two major factors determine whether an elderly person will engage in sexual activity (Masters, Johnson, & Kolodny, 1982). One is good physical and mental health. People need to be physically healthy, and to hold generally positive attitudes about sexual activity, in order for sex to take place. The other determinant of sexual activity during old age is previous, regular sexual activity. The longer elderly men and women have gone without sexual activity, the less likely is future sexual activity. "Use it or lose it" seems an accurate description of sexual functioning in older people.

And they do use it. For instance, one survey found that 43 percent of men and 33 percent of women over the age of 70 masturbated. The average frequency for those who masturbated was once a week. Furthermore, some two-thirds of men and women had sex with their spouses, again averaging about once per week (Brecher et al., 1984).

Of course, some changes in sexual functioning are related to age. It takes a longer time, and more stimulation, for men to get a full erection. The refractory period—the time following an orgasm during which men are unable to become aroused again—may last as long as a day or even several days. Women's vaginas become thin and inelastic, and they produce less natural lubrication, making intercourse more difficult.

Despite these changes in sexual functioning, sexual expression remains a full possibility (Schiavi, 1990; Crose & Drake, 1993; Kellett, 1993). In fact, most experts put no upward time limit on sexuality: Sex can last throughout the life span (Hyde, 1994).

APPROACHES TO AGING: WHY IS DEATH INEVITABLE?

Hovering over our discussion of health in late adulthood is the specter of death. At some point, no matter how healthy we have been throughout life, we know that we will experience physical declines and that life will end. But why?

Theories of Aging.   There are two major approaches to explaining why we undergo physical deterioration and death: genetic preprogramming theories and wear-and-tear theories (Bergener, Ermini, & Stahelin, 1985; Whitbourne, 1986). **Genetic preprogramming theories of aging** suggest that our body's DNA genetic code contains a built-in time limit for the reproduction of human cells. After a certain amount of time has gone by—determined genetically—the cells are no longer able to divide, and the individual begins to deteriorate.

There are actually several variations of the genetic preprogramming approach. One is that the genetic material contains a "death gene" that is programmed to direct the body to deteriorate and die. Another is that the genetic instructions for running the body can be read only a certain number of times before they become illegible. (Think of a computer disk containing a program that is used over and over and eventually just gives out.) As these instructions become incomprehensible, they produce bodily deterioration and ultimately death (Hayflick, 1974; Pereira-Smith et al., 1988; Finch, 1990).

The second explanation for physical decline consists of **wear-and-tear theories** of aging, which argue that the mechanical functions of the body simply wear out—the way cars and washing machines do. In addition, some wear-and-tear theorists suggest that the

genetic preprogramming theories of aging   *the theory that suggests that our body's DNA genetic code contains a built-in time limit for the reproduction of human cells*

wear-and-tear theories   *the theory that the mechanical functions of the body simply wear out with age*

According to genetic preprogramming theories of aging, people's DNA genetic code contains a built-in time limit on the length of life. Scientists are seeking to crack the code.

body's constant manufacture of energy to fuel its activities creates by-products. These by-products, combined with the toxins and threats of everyday life (such as radiation, chemical exposure, accidents, and disease), eventually reach such high levels that they impair the body's normal functioning. The ultimate result is deterioration and death.

Genetic preprogramming theories and wear-and-tear theories make different suggestions about the inevitability of death. Genetic preprogramming theories suggest that there is a built-in time limit to life—it is programmed in the genes, after all. On the other hand, wear-and-tear theories, particularly those that focus on the toxins that are built up during the course of life, paint a somewhat more optimistic view. They suggest that if a means can be found to eliminate the toxins produced by the body and by exposure to the environment, aging might well be prevented.

We do not know which class of theories provides the more accurate account of the reasons for aging. Each is supported by some research, and each seems to explain certain aspects of aging. Ultimately, then, just why the body begins to deteriorate and die remains something of a mystery (DiGiovanna, 1994).

Life Expectancy: How Long Have I Got?   Although the reasons for deterioration and death are not fully apparent, conclusions about average life expectancy can be stated quite clearly: Most of us can expect to live into old age. **Life expectancy**—the average age of death for members of a population—of a person born in 1980, for instance, is 74 years of age.

Average life expectancy has been steadily increasing. In 1776, average life expectancy in the United States was just 35. By the early 1900s, it had risen to 47. And in only four decades, between 1950 to 1990, it increased from 68 to over 75 years. Predictions are that it will continue to rise steadily, possibly reaching age 80 by the year 2050 (DiGiovanna, 1994).

Several reasons explain the steady increase in mean life expectancy over the past 200 years. Health conditions are generally better, with many diseases either wiped out entirely (e.g., smallpox) or better controlled through vaccines and preventive measures (e.g., measles and mumps). People's working conditions are generally better, and many products are safer than they once were. As environmental factors continue to improve, we can predict that life expectancy will continue to increase.

life expectancy   *the average age of death for members of a population*

One major question for gerontologists is just how far the life span can be increased. The most common answer is that the upper limit of life hovers around 120 years, the age of Jeanne Calment (described earlier in the chapter), the oldest person in the world whose age can be documented. Living beyond this age would probably require some major genetic alterations in humans, and that seems both technically and ethically improbable. Furthermore, experts suggest that life expectancy at birth is unlikely to go much beyond 85 years, unless a means is devised to control the rate at which the average body ages (Olshansky, Carnes, & Cassel, 1990).

It is also important to keep in mind that the figures for average life expectancy that we have been considering mask considerable gender, race, and ethnic disparities. These differences have important implications for society at large, as we discuss next.

Developmental Diversity

Gender, Race, and Ethnic Differences in Average Life Expectancy: Separate Lives, Separate Deaths

- The average Caucasian child born in the United States is likely to live 76 years. The average African-American child is likely to live 71 years.

- A child born in Japan has a life expectancy of 79 years; for a child born in Gambia, life expectancy is less than 45 years.

- A male born in the United States today is most likely to live to the age of 73; a female will probably live some 7 years longer.

Several reasons account for these discrepancies. Consider, for example, the gender gap in life expectancy, which is particularly pronounced. Across the industrialized world, women live longer than men by some 4 to 10 years (Holden, 1987). This female advantage begins just after conception: Although slightly more males are conceived, males are more likely to die during the prenatal period, infancy, and childhood. Consequently, by the age of 30 there are roughly equal numbers of men and women. But by the age of 65, 84 percent of females and 70 percent of males are still alive. For those over 85, the gender gap is even wider: For every male, 2.57 women are still alive (AARP, 1990).

There are several explanations for the gender gap. One is that the naturally higher levels of hormones such as estrogen and progesterone in women provide some protection from diseases such as heart attacks. Another possibility is that because women have been relegated to certain traditional professional roles, they experience less stress than do men. It is also possible that women engage in healthier behavior during their lives, such as eating well. However, no conclusive evidence supports either explanation fully (DiGiovanna, 1994).

Whatever its cause, the gender gap has continued to increase during much of the twentieth century. In the early part of the century, there was only a 2-year difference in favor of women. In contrast, the gap grew to 7 years in the 1980s. On the other hand, the size of the gap seems to have leveled off, owing largely to the fact that men are more likely than previously to engage in positive health behaviors (such as smoking less, eating better, and exercising more).

The racial and ethnic differences are troubling. They point out the disparities in socio-economic well-being of various groups in the United States. For example, life expectancy is almost 10 percent greater for whites than for African-Americans (see Figure 17-4). Furthermore, in contrast to whites, whose life expectancy keeps edging up, African-Americans have actually experienced slight declines in life expectancy in recent years.

FIGURE 17-4

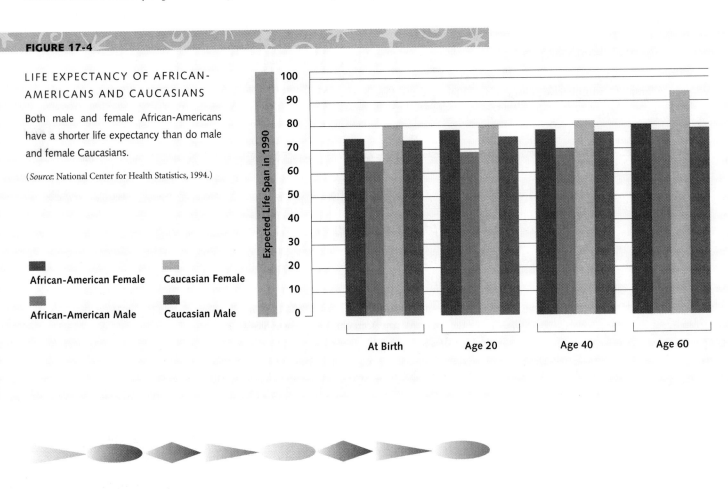

LIFE EXPECTANCY OF AFRICAN-AMERICANS AND CAUCASIANS

Both male and female African-Americans have a shorter life expectancy than do male and female Caucasians.

(*Source*: National Center for Health Statistics, 1994.)

African-American Female

Caucasian Female

African-American Male

Caucasian Male

The Informed Consumer of Development

Caring for People with Alzheimer's Disease

Alzheimer's disease is one of the most difficult illnesses to deal with, as a friend or loved one inexorably deteriorates mentally and physically. However, several things can be done to help deal with the situation.

- ◆ Make those with Alzheimer's disease feel secure in their home environments by keeping them occupied in everyday tasks of living as long as possible.
- ◆ Provide labels for everyday objects, furnish calendars and detailed but simple lists, and give oral reminders of time and place.
- ◆ Keep clothing simple: Provide clothes with few zippers and buttons, and lay them out in the order in which they should be put on.

◆ Put bathing on a schedule. People with Alzheimer's may be afraid of falling and of hot water, and may therefore avoid needed bathing.

◆ Prevent people with the disease from driving. Although patients often want to continue driving, and some 50 percent of those with the disease are still driving 2 years after diagnosis, their accident rate is high—some 20 times higher than average. Some families actually hide car keys or disable cars to prevent family members from driving.

◆ Monitor the use of the telephone. Some Alzheimer patients who answer the phone have been victimized by agreeing to requests of telephone salespeople and investment counselors.

◆ Provide opportunities for exercise, such as a daily walk. This prevents muscle deterioration and stiffness.

◆ Caregivers should remember to take time off. Although caring for an Alzheimer patient can be a full-time chore, caregivers need to lead their own lives. Seek out support from community service organizations. Keep in mind that ultimately it is likely to be impossible to keep a patient at home; most Americans with the disease end up in nursing homes.

◆ Call or write the Alzheimer's Association, which can provide support and information. The Association can be reached at 919 North Michigan Ave., Suite 1000, Chicago, IL 60611-1676; Tel. 1-800-272-3900.

Review and Rethink

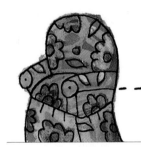

REVIEW

◆ Although most older people are healthy, the incidence of some serious diseases rises in old age and most people have at least one chronic ailment before they die. The leading causes of death among older people are heart disease, cancer, and stroke.

◆ Older people are susceptible to psychological disorders such as depression, which may be caused by the loss of loved ones, a sense of diminished control over the environment, or the side effects of prescription drugs.

◆ The most prevalent and damaging brain disorder among older people is Alzheimer's disease, which is caused by biological changes in the brain brought on by unknown factors.

◆ Proper diet, exercise, and avoidance of health risks can lead to prolonged wellness during old age, and sexuality can continue throughout the life span in healthy adults.

◆ Whether death is caused by genetic preprogramming or by general physical wear-and-tear is an unresolved question. Life expectancy has risen steadily for centuries, although expectancy is subject to gender, race, and ethnicity.

RETHINK

◆ In what ways might being the object of ageism contribute to depression in old age?

◆ What factors should a family take into account in deciding whether to care for a person with Alzheimer's at home or in a nursing facility?

◆ In what ways is socioeconomic status related to wellness in old age and to life expectancy?

◆ How might studies be designed to test whether the genetic preprogramming or wear-and-tear theory is more accurate?

◆ Are the reasons for the gender gap in life expectancy primarily genetic or cultural? Why?

COGNITIVE DEVELOPMENT IN LATE ADULTHOOD

Three women were talking about the inconveniences of growing old.

"Sometimes," one of them confessed, "when I go to my refrigerator, I can't remember if I'm putting something in or taking something out."

"Oh, that's nothing," said the second woman. "There are times when I find myself at the foot of the stairs wondering if I'm going up or if I've just come down."

"Well, my goodness!" exclaimed the third woman. "I'm certainly glad I don't have any problems like that"—and she knocked on wood. "Oh," she said, starting up out of her chair, "there's someone at the door." (Dent, 1984, p. 38)

It's an old joke, one that summons up the stereotypic view of aging. In fact, not too long ago many gerontologists would have subscribed to the view that older people are befuddled and forgetful.

Today, however, the view has changed dramatically. In terms of both overall intellectual ability and specific cognitive skills, such as memory and problem-solving abilities, the cognitive powers of older people are no longer seen as inevitably declining. In fact, with the appropriate practice and exposure to certain kinds of environmental stimuli, cognitive skills can actually improve.

INTELLIGENCE IN OLDER PEOPLE

The notion that older people become less cognitively adept initially arose from misinterpretations of research evidence. As we first noted in Chapter 15, early research on how intelligence changed as a result of aging typically drew a simple comparison between younger and older people's performance on the same IQ test, using traditional cross-sectional experimental methods. For example, a group of 30-year-olds and a group of 70-year-olds might have been given the same test and had their performance compared.

However, there are several drawbacks to such a procedure. One is that cross-sectional methods do not take into account *cohort effects*—influences attributable to growing up in a particular era. For example, if the mean educational attainment of the younger group—because of when they grew up—is greater than that of the older group, we might expect the younger group to do better on the test for that reason alone. Furthermore, because some traditional intelligence tests include timed portions or reaction-time components, the slower reaction time of older people might account for their inferior performance.

To try to overcome such problems, researchers turned to longitudinal studies, which followed the same individuals for many years. But these studies, too, raise some fundamental interpretive difficulties. Because of repeated exposure to the same test, subjects may, over time, become familiar with the test items, a fact that calls later results into question. Furthermore, it is quite difficult to keep a longitudinal sample intact, as subjects move away, quit participating, become ill, or die. In short, longitudinal studies have their drawbacks, and their use initially led to some erroneous conclusions about older people.

RECENT CONCLUSIONS ABOUT THE NATURE OF INTELLIGENCE IN OLDER PEOPLE

More recent research has attempted to overcome the drawbacks of both cross-sectional and longitudinal methods. In what is probably the most ambitious—and still ongoing—study of intelligence in older people, developmentalist K. Warner Schaie has employed cross-

Although some aspects of intelligence decline during late adulthood—as well as throughout earlier adulthood—crystallized intelligence (the store of information, skills, and strategies that people have acquired) remains steady and actually may improve.

sequential methods. As we discussed in Chapter 1, *cross-sequential studies* combine cross-sectional and longitudinal methods by examining several different age groups at a number of points in time.

In Schaie's massive study, carried out in Seattle, Washington, a battery of tests of cognitive ability was given to a group of 500 randomly chosen individuals. Participants belonged to different age groups, starting at age 20 and extending at 5-year intervals to age 70. Subjects were tested, and continue to be tested, every 7 years, and more subjects are added annually. At this point, more than 5,000 participants have been tested (Schaie, 1994).

The study, along with other research, supports several generalizations about the nature of intellectual change during old age. Among the major ones (Schaie, 1994):

♦ There is no uniform pattern in adulthood of age-related changes across all intellectual abilities. Some abilities gradually decline throughout adulthood, starting at about age 25, while others stay relatively steady (see Figure 17-5). In addition, as we discussed in Chapter 15, fluid intelligence (the ability to deal with new problems and situations)

FIGURE 17-5

CHANGES IN INTELLECTUAL FUNCTIONING

Although some intellectual abilities decline across adulthood, others stay relatively steady.

(*Source*: Schaie, 1994.)

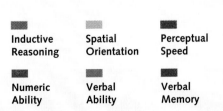

Inductive Reasoning   Spatial Orientation   Perceptual Speed

Numeric Ability   Verbal Ability   Verbal Memory

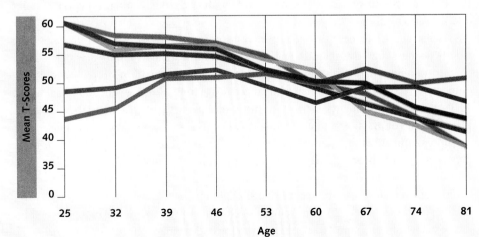

declines with age, whereas crystallized intelligence (the store of information, skills, and strategies that people have acquired) remains steady and in some cases actually improves (Baltes & Schaie, 1974; Schaie, 1993).

♦ For the average person, some cognitive declines are found in all abilities by age 67. However, these declines are minimal until the 80s. But even at age 81, less than half of the people tested showed consistent declines over the previous 7 years.

♦ Significant individual differences are found in the patterns of change in intelligence. For some, intellectual declines begin in their 30s, while for others no declines are experienced until they are in their 70s. In fact, roughly a third of those in their 70s score higher than the average young adult.

♦ Certain environmental and cultural factors are related to greater or lesser degrees of intellectual decline. For instance, characteristics associated with a lower probability of cognitive decline include the absence of chronic diseases, higher socioeconomic status (SES), involvement in an intellectually stimulating environment, a flexible personality style, being married to a bright spouse, maintenance of good perceptual processing speed, and feelings of self-satisfaction with one's accomplishment's in midlife or early old age.

The fact that environmental factors are related to intellectual declines—or, perhaps more importantly, to the lack of decline—suggests that it might be possible to develop procedures for maintaining intellectual skills. We discuss this possibility in the Directions in Development section.

Directions in Development

Reversing Intellectual Declines: Practice Makes Smarter

George Washington Carver was still a practicing scientist and educator at age 78. Oliver Wendell Holmes served as a Supreme Court justice at age 90. James Michener at age 82 wrote *Caribbean*. Simone de Beauvoir penned *Adieux: A farewell to Sartre* at age 73. I.M. Pei designed the Morton Meyerson Symphony Center at age 72.

Each of these individuals continued to make major intellectual contributions well into late adulthood. On the other hand, for some people old age marks a descent into a period of intellectual confusion, in which cognitive capabilities decline significantly.

Is there a way to prevent mental deterioration—and even allow people to *improve* their capabilities? The answer, according to research conducted by psychologists Sherry L. Willis and K. Warner Schaie, is a clear yes.

Willis and Schaie have carried out several studies examining methods for enhancing elderly people's cognitive skills. In one experiment, for instance, subjects participated in a 5-hour training program on reasoning and spatial skills (Schaie & Willis & Schaie, 1986). Subjects were 229 men and women who ranged in age from 64 to 95, with an average age of 73. Participants were taught general strategies for dealing with problems, and they also completed a series of practice test items similar to those used to measure cognitive skills.

After completing the training, participants were tested on a variety of skills. Of those people who had shown earlier declines in reasoning and spatial skills, most began to improve. Furthermore, the training boosted the performance of those elderly people whose abilities had remained relatively stable. Specifically, more than half of the subjects with prior declines in intellectual functioning showed significant improvement, and more than a third of the stable subjects improved significantly following training.

Subsequent research shows that cognitive training can have lasting effects. For example, one group of subjects received training three times over a 7-year period. By the end of the seven years, many of the subjects performed at a significantly higher level than they did at the start of the study. Furthermore, the study found that even adults in their late 70s showed significant improvement due to training (Willis & Nesselroade, 1990).

Perhaps of greatest importance is the fact that the success of training in bringing about growth in cognitive abilities was related to improvements in practical intelligence and on tasks associated with daily living (Willis, Jay, Diehl, & Marsiske, 1992). Such **plasticity**, or modifiability of behavior, suggests that there is nothing fixed about the changes that may occur in intellectual abilities during late adulthood. With the proper stimulation, practice, and motivation, older people can maintain their mental abilities. In mental life, then, as in so many other areas of human development, the motto "use it or lose it" is quite fitting (Shimamura et al., 1995).

MEMORY: REMEMBRANCE OF THINGS PAST—AND PRESENT

Composer Aaron Copland summed up what had happened to his memory in old age by remarking, "I have no trouble remembering everything that had happened 40 or 50 years ago—dates, places, faces, music. But I'm going to be 90 my next birthday, November 14th, and I find I can't remember what happened yesterday" (*Time*, 1980, p. 57). Our confidence in the accuracy of Copland's analysis is strengthened by an error in his statement: On his next birthday, he would be only 80 years old!

Is memory loss an inevitable part of aging? Not necessarily. For instance, cross-cultural research reveals that in societies where older people are held in relatively high esteem, such as in China, people are less likely to show memory losses than in societies where they are held in less regard (Levy & Langer, 1994).

Furthermore, even when memory declines that can be directly traced to aging do occur, they are limited primarily to *episodic memories*, which relate to specific life experiences. In contrast, other types of memory, such as *semantic memories* (general knowledge and facts) and *implicit memories* (memories about which people are not consciously aware) are largely unaffected by age (Graf, 1990; Russo & Parkin, 1993).

Still, it is clear that memory capacities change during old age. For instance, *short-term memory* slips gradually during adulthood until age 70, when the decline becomes more pronounced. The largest drop is for information that is presented quickly and verbally. In addition, information about things that are completely unfamiliar is more difficult to recall. For example, declines occur in memory for prose passages, names and faces of people, and even such critical information as the directions on a medicine label, possibly because new information is not registered and processed effectively when it is initially encountered. Although these age-related changes are generally minor, and their impact on everyday life negligible (because most elderly people automatically learn to compensate for them), memory losses are real (Light, 1991; Cherry & Park, 1993; Kausler, 1994; Grady et al., 1995).

Autobiographical Memory: Recalling the Days of Our Lives.   When it comes to **autobiographical memory**, memories of information about one's own life, older people are subject to some of the same principles of recall as are younger individuals. For instance, memory recall frequently follows the *Pollyanna principle*, in which pleasant memories are more likely to be recalled than are unpleasant memories. Similarly, people tend to forget information about their past that is not congruent with the way they currently see themselves, and they are more likely to make the material that they do recall "fit" their current conception of themselves (Bradburn, Rips, & Shevell, 1987; Conway & Rubin, 1993; Friedman, 1993).

Furthermore, particular periods of life are remembered better than others. As can be seen in Figure 17-6, 70-year-olds tend to recall autobiographical details from their 20s and

plasticity   *the degree to which a developing structure or behavior is susceptible to modification*

autobiographical memory   *memories of information about one's own life*

FIGURE 17-6

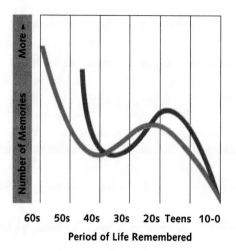

REMEMBRANCES OF THINGS PAST

Recall of autobiographical memories varies with age, with 70-year-olds recalling details from their 20s and 30s best, and 50-year-olds recalling memories from their teenage years and 20s. People of both ages also recall more recent memories best of all.

(*Source:* Rubin, 1986.)

■ **Recollection at Age 70**

■ **Recollection at Age 50**

Speaking of Development

Steven Weisler

Born: ···································· 1954

Education: ·························· Stanford University, Ph.d. in linguistics; Case Western University, B.A., M.A. in linguistics

Position: ··························· Elderhostel Instructor and Professor of Psychology, Hampshire College

Home: ································ Amherst, Massachusetts

For Steven Weisler, the stereotype of the elderly as doddering, confused, and befuddled is a complete myth. A teacher in the international Elderhostel program, Weisler has found that elders taking his courses are, in fact, generally more attentive and involved in the learning process than are younger college students.

"Some of the people are very smart but there is a range of intelligence levels," said Weisler, following the teaching of a 1-week linguistics course to a group of 40 elders. "The more ambitious the subject matter, the higher the education level of the students. We cover a huge amount of material in a 1-week period—the equivalent of half a semester's work with college students. An interesting question, of course, is if the courses lasted more than a week whether the tremendous high interest level of the elders, which far outstrips that of undergraduates, could be maintained."

Although the intensity and level of the subject matter may be the same as that experienced by the college student, the differences end there, according to Weisler.

"Everything is different about the program. First of all, the circumstances under which I teach elders are quite different in that the classes are shorter, lasting just a week, the elders are paying for it directly, and they choose to do it.

30s best. In contrast, 50-year-olds are likely to have more memories of their teenage years and their 20s. In both cases, recall of earlier years is better than recall of more recent events (Rubin, 1985; Fromholdt & Larsen, 1991; see Figure 17-6).

Explaining Memory Changes in Old Age.   Explanations for apparent changes in memory among older people tend to focus on three main categories: environmental factors, information-processing deficits, and biological factors.

- *Environmental factors.* Certain transitory factors that cause declines in memory may be found more frequently in older people. For example, older people are more apt than are younger ones to take the kinds of prescription drugs that hinder memory. The lower performance of older people on memory tasks may be related to drug taking and not to age per se. Similarly, declines in memory can sometimes be traced to life changes in late adulthood. For instance, retirees, no longer facing intellectual challenges from their jobs, may become less practiced in using memory. Also, their motivation to recall information may be lower than previously, accounting for lower performance on tasks involving memory.

- *Information-processing deficits.* Other explanations assume that memory declines not because of environmental factors, such as changes in lifestyle or motivation, but because of changes in information-processing capabilities. For example, one approach

"We cover a huge amount of material in a 1-week period—the equivalent of half a semester's work with college students."

"Probably the main difference is the elders' level of interest and attention tends to be much higher than that of undergraduates I've taught. In any given class about a third of the students are completely engaged with the material and another third are quite attentive, but quiet. I have found that in undergraduate courses it is rare for so many people to be excited and actively participating in the course. The elders listen very carefully, and if I say something they don't agree with, they're quick to let me know. And if I say something that excites them, it spurs them on, and they begin to ask questions and relate it to their own lives."

While Weisler doesn't formally test any of his elder students, he does feel that they have some intellectual advantages over their younger counterparts.

"It seems the elders are better at getting the 'big picture' than are undergraduates, and at figuring out the main outlines of the material and what the opposing points of view are," he explained. "They are absorbed in the material and have a seriousness of purpose and commitment of purpose that undergraduates sometimes don't have."

"The elders listen very carefully, and if I say something they don't agree with, they're quick to let me know."

suggests that as we reach later adulthood, our ability to inhibit irrelevant information and thoughts decreases, and that the presence of irrelevant thoughts interferes with successful problem solving. Similarly, some research suggests that the speed of information processing declines, which leads to the memory impairments observed in old age (Salthouse, 1991; Hartman & Hasher, 1991).

The information-processing-deficit approach that has received the most research support suggests that memory declines are due to changes in the ability to pay attention to and organize tasks involving memory skills. In this view, older adults concentrate less effectively than do younger individuals, and they have greater difficulty paying attention to appropriate stimuli and organizing material in memory. Furthermore, older people use less efficient processes to retrieve information from memory. These information-processing deficits subsequently lead to declines in recall abilities (Craik, 1984, 1994; Poon, 1985; Guttentag, 1985; Light, 1991).

♦ *Biological factors.* The last of the major approaches to explaining changes in memory during late adulthood concentrates on biological factors. According to these approaches, memory changes are a result of brain and body deterioration. For instance, some research finds that declines in episodic memory may be related to the deterioration of the frontal lobes of the brain (Albert & Kaplan, 1980; Poon, 1985). However, specific sorts of memory deficits occur in many older people without any evidence of underlying biological deterioration. In short, biological factors alone probably do not hold the key to understanding the memory impairments that occur in older people who are in good health.

LEARNING IN LATER LIFE: NEVER TOO LATE TO LEARN

The popularity of programs such as Elderhostel, which was discussed in the Speaking of Development section, attests to a growing trend among older people: the continuation of their education throughout late adulthood. Because the majority of older people have retired, they have time to delve into subjects in which they have always been interested, but which they have not previously been able to pursue.

Although sometimes classes are specially designed for older adults (as with Elderhostel), in other cases older people enroll in regular courses. For instance, many colleges encourage senior citizens to enroll in classes by providing them with free tuition.

Not everyone in late adulthood is able to take advantage of such educational opportunities. Because Elderhostels charge tuition, students who enroll in them tend to be of higher socioeconomic status, and the majority have postcollege graduate training of some sort (M. Beck, 1991).

In addition, some elderly people are doubtful about their intellectual capabilities and consequently avoid regular college classes in which they might have to compete with younger students. Their concern is largely misplaced, however: Older adults often have no trouble maintaining their standing in rigorous college courses. Furthermore, instructors and fellow students generally find the presence of older people, with their varied and substantial life experiences, a real educational benefit (Shevron & Lumsden, 1985).

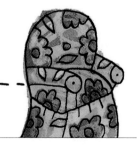

Review and Rethink

REVIEW

♦ Early studies of intellectual functioning among elderly people have been called into question because of concerns about the cross-sectional and longitudinal methods the studies employed.

◆ Schaie's more recent cross-sequential studies indicate that different aspects of intellectual functioning change in different ways in different people and under the influence of environmental and cultural factors.

◆ Schaie's studies also reveal that the human intellect retains considerable plasticity in old age and that older people can maintain their mental abilities with proper stimulation, practice, and motivation.

◆ Declines in memory affect mainly episodic memories, leaving semantic and implicit memories largely intact. Short-term memory declines gradually until age 70, when the decline grows steeper.

◆ Explanations of memory changes in old age have focused on environmental factors, information-processing declines, and biological factors.

RETHINK

◆ How does cross-sequential research attempt to overcome the shortcomings of longitudinal and cross-sectional methods?

◆ Do you think steady or increasing crystallized intelligence can partially or fully compensate for declines in fluid intelligence? Why or why not?

◆ How might cultural factors, such as the esteem in which a society holds its older members, work to affect an older person's memory performance?

◆ Do you believe short-term memory declines in old age relate more to information storage or information retrieval? Why? Can older people be trained to improve short-term memory?

◆ Why should older people's memories about "the good old days" and stories about their past lives be regarded with a bit of skepticism?

LOOKING
BACK

What is it like to grow old in the United States today?

1. Both the number and proportion of older people in the United States and in many other countries are larger than ever before, and elderly people are the fastest growing segment of the U.S. population.

2. Older people as a group are subjected to stereotyping and actual discrimination because of their age, a phenomenon referred to as "ageism." Many prevalent opinions and attitudes about older people are based on misinformation and are sustained by the bias toward youth that typifies many Western societies.

What sorts of physical changes occur in old age?

3. Old age is a period in which outward physical changes, such as graying and thinning hair, wrinkles, and bodily shrinkage, unmistakably indicate aging. However, many older people remain fit, active, and agile well into this period.

4. Inwardly, older people experience a decrease in brain size and in the number of neurons in the brain, and a reduction of blood flow (and oxygen) to all parts of the body including the brain. The circulatory, respiratory, and digestive systems all work with less efficiency.

5. Old age brings a slowing of reaction time, explanations of which include the peripheral slowing hypothesis (processing speed in the peripheral nervous system slows down)

and the generalized slowing hypothesis (processing in all parts of the nervous system slows down).

How are the senses affected by aging?

6. Physical changes in the eye bring declines in vision, particularly in the ability to discern distant and dimly lit objects and the ability to adjust from light to dark places and vice versa. Moreover, several eye conditions become more prevalent in old age, including cataracts and glaucoma.

7. Hearing also declines, particularly the ability to hear higher frequencies. Hearing loss has both psychological and social consequences, for it discourages older people from engaging in conversations and other social interactions, and thereby promotes isolation. Declines in the senses of taste and smell can have health consequences if they lead to oversalting of food or inadequate nutrition.

What is the general state of health of older people, and to what disorders are they susceptible?

8. Although most older people are healthy, the incidence of certain serious diseases rises in old age, and the ability of older people to bounce back from serious illness declines.

9. Most older people suffer from at least one chronic, long-term ailment, such as arthritis or hypertension. The leading causes of death in old age are heart disease, cancer, and stroke.

10. Older people are also susceptible to psychological disorders, such as depression, which can be brought about by the loss of family and friends that marks the period; by the loss of a sense of control over mind and body; and by the use of drugs, singly or in combination.

11. Brain disorders may also mark the period, especially Alzheimer's disease, a progressive, irreversible mental disorder caused by biological changes in the brain that are triggered by as yet unknown factors.

Can wellness and sexuality be maintained in old age?

12. Psychological and lifestyle factors can influence wellness in old age. A sense of control over one's life and environment can have positive effects, as can a proper diet, exercise, and the avoidance of risk factors, such as smoking.

13. Sexuality, despite some changes in sexual functioning, continues throughout old age, provided people are in good physical and mental health, have positive attitudes toward sex, and have maintained regular sexual activity previously.

How long can people expect to live, and why do they die?

14. Although death is inevitable, the reason why is still unknown. Two main theoretical approaches seek to explain death. Genetic preprogramming theories of aging claim that the body's DNA sets a built-in time limit on life, whereas wear-and-tear theories of aging maintain that the body simply wears out the way any machine does.

15. Life expectancy (now more than 75 years for those born in the United States today) has been rising steadily for centuries and continues to do so, although the expected life span of a person varies by gender, race, and ethnicity. Increases are due mainly to improvements in health and working conditions, and in general safety.

How well do older people function intellectually?

16. Negative views of intellectual functioning in old age, generally based on cross-sectional or longitudinal methods of research, have been discredited because of shortcomings in those methods.

17. Cross-sequential studies conducted by developmental psychologist K. Warner Schaie and his colleagues conclude that intellectual abilities tend to decline slowly throughout old age. However, the Schaie studies also demonstrate that different abilities change in different ways, that there are significant individual differences, and that environmental and cultural factors are related to intellectual changes.

18. Further studies indicate that training can affect cognitive abilities positively, and that with the proper stimulation, practice, and motivation, older people can maintain their mental abilities.

Do people lose their memories in old age?

19. Loss of memory in old age is not general or universal, but specific. Episodic memories are typically most affected, whereas semantic and implicit memories are largely unaffected. Short-term memory declines gradually until age 70, at which point the deterioration quickens, and autobiographical memory is affected by the same principles of recall—such as the Pollyanna principle and the need to "fit" past memory to present self-concept—to which it has always been subject.

20. Explanations of memory changes may focus on environmental factors (such as the effects of prescription drugs or age-related changes in circumstances), information-processing declines (such as a lessened ability to inhibit irrelevant thoughts, pay attention to appropriate stimuli, or organize information in memory), and biological factors (such as brain deterioration). Which approach is most accurate is not entirely settled.

KEY TERMS AND CONCEPTS

gerontologists (p. 577)

ageism (p. 579)

osteoporosis (p. 583)

peripheral slowing hypothesis (p. 584)

generalized slowing hypothesis (p. 584)

cataracts (p. 585)

glaucoma (p. 585)

dementia (p. 589)

Alzheimer's disease (p. 589)

genetic preprogramming theories of aging (p. 593)

wear-and-tear theories (p. 593)

life expectancy (p. 594)

plasticity (p. 601)

autobiograhical memory (p. 601)

Social and Personality Development

CHAPTER OUTLINE

"Well, I tell you," says Eva Solymosi, and so she does, starting at the beginning when she first met Joseph. The youngest of 13, she was a poor cook in Hungary, befriended by an old woman who shared this advice: "When a kind face comes by, keep him."

Eva saw Joseph, an 18-year-old chimney sweep, getting a drink of cold water by the public well. "He had a kind face. So that's it," she says and shrugs. They married the next year, moved to the U.S., and have been together since. She is 97 and he is 93....

The couple offers no great secrets to longevity and love. They married for better or worse. They were immigrants with little schooling, who worked hard and lived simply by her father's golden rules: "Always give people a day's work for their dollar. Be honest. Be good and people will love you for it...."

Joseph says it was Eva who married him. Eva laughs, "Yes, I was the wrecker. I wrecked your life." They tease each other gently. When she moves ahead of him in a story, he scolds her, "Keep your shirt on, Charlie." He sometimes calls her "my friend" or "boss," although, he adds, neither one of them is the boss.

They are partners. When one is telling a story, the other quietly gets up and fetches a pertinent picture or letter. They share the chores and praise the other's efforts....

They have been blessed, they say, not only with each other but with good friends. Look, they say. There's the dining room table from Hazel's grandmother, and the perfume from a lawyer and his wife who, before they died years ago, drove 70 miles to visit them every Sunday....

When Joseph is shopping or watching the news, Eva will spend hours going through her dozen photo albums. There is Joseph as a young man reading the newspaper, Eva eating an ear of corn in the 1920s, their first Christmas tree. Each album is like an old friend, inviting her back to her rose garden or to visit her mother's gravesite in Cleveland.

"I open it up and it gives me joy. To me it's something. To anyone else it means nothing," says Eva, almost apologetically. Joseph reassures her. "Oh Eva, it's wonderful. It's beautiful to look back."

She comes across a picture of him when he was 18. "Ah ha, that is the kind face I fell in love with. In my eyes he is still as handsome." He says nothing, but gently taps her cane with his (Ansberry, 1995, p. A1, a17).

LOOKING AHEAD

The warmth and affection between Joseph and Eva are unmistakable. Their relationship, spanning almost eight decades, continues to bring them quiet joy, and their mutual love and admiration reach the heights of human interconnectedness.

We turn in this chapter to the social and emotional aspects of late adulthood. We begin by considering how personality continues to develop in elderly individuals, and we then turn to an examination of various ways people can age successfully.

Next, we consider how various societal factors affect the day-to-day living conditions of older adults. We discuss options in living arrangements, as well as the ways in which economic and financial issues influence people's lives. We also look at how culture governs the way we treat older people, and we examine the influence of work and retirement on elderly individuals, considering the ways in which retirement can be optimized.

Finally, we consider relationships in late adulthood, not only among married couples but also among other relatives and friends. We'll see how the social networks of late adulthood continue to play an important—and sustaining—role in people's lives. We end with a discussion of how events such as the divorce of a parent, decades earlier, can still have a critical impact on the course of people's lives.

In sum, after reading this chapter, you'll be able to answer the following questions:

- In what ways does personality develop during late adulthood?
- How do people deal with aging?
- In what circumstances do older people live, and what difficulties do they face?
- Is retirement generally a period of enjoyment or difficulty?
- What is the state of marriage in late adulthood, and what changes typically occur in the marital relationship?
- What do older people go through when a spouse dies?
- What sorts of relationships are important in late adulthood?

PERSONALITY DEVELOPMENT AND SUCCESSFUL AGING

Greta Roach has a puckish manner, a habit of nudging you when she is about to say something funny. This happens often, because that is how she views the world. Even last year's knee injury, which forced her to drop out of her bowling league and halted the march of blue-and-chrome trophies across her living-room table, is not—in her mind—a frailty of age. Roach, who is 93, compares her plight to that of Olympic skater Nancy Kerrigan. "Same thing happened to my knee," she says, leaning over the arm of the sofa. Nudge. . . .

Roach takes the same spirited approach to life in her 90s as she did in her 20s, something not all elders can do. . . . "I enjoy life. I belong to all the clubs. I love to talk on the telephone. I write to my old friends." She pauses. "Those that are still alive." (Pappano, 1994, pp. 19, 30)

In many ways, Greta Roach, with her wit, high spirits, and enormous activity level, is much the same person she was in earlier years. Yet for other older adults, time and circumstances seem to bring changes in their outlook on life, in their views of themselves, and perhaps even in their basic personalities. In fact, one of the fundamental questions asked by psychologists concerns the degree to which personality remains stable, or changes, in later adulthood.

CONTINUITY AND CHANGE IN PERSONALITY DURING LATE ADULTHOOD

Is personality relatively stable throughout adulthood, or does it vary in significant ways? The answer, it turns out, depends on which facets of personality we wish to consider. According to developmental psychologists Paul Costa and Robert McCrae, whose work we first discussed in Chapter 16, basic personality traits are remarkably stable across adulthood. For instance, even-tempered people at age 20 are still even-tempered at age 75, and people who hold positive self-concepts early in adulthood still view themselves positively in late adulthood (Costa & McCrae, 1988, 1989; McCrae & Costa, 1990). Similarly, other longitudinal investigations have found that five basic personality traits remain quite stable (agreeableness, satisfaction, intellect, extroversion, and energy). Such research suggests that there is a fundamental continuity to personality (Field & Millsap, 1991).

On the other hand, the existence of stable basic personality traits does not preclude the possibility of change over time. As we noted in Chapter 16, the profound changes that occur throughout adulthood in people's social environments may produce fluctuations and changes in personality. What is important to a person at age 80 is not necessarily the same as what was important at age 40.

Some aspects of personality remain quite stable throughout the life span, consistent with the premise of this cartoon.
Drawing by R. Chast; © 1995 Worth Magazine.

ego-integrity-versus-despair stage *Erikson's final stage, characterized by a process of looking back over one's life, evaluating it, and coming to terms with it*

redefinition of self versus preoccupation with work-role *the theory that those in old age must redefine themselves in ways that do not relate to their work-roles or occupations*

body transcendence versus body preoccupation *a period in which people must learn to cope with and move beyond changes in physical capabilities as a result of aging*

ego transcendence versus ego preoccupation *the period in which elderly people must come to grips with their coming death*

Consequently, some theorists have focused their attention on the discontinuities of development. As we'll see next, the work of Erik Erikson, Robert Peck, and Daniel Levinson has focused on the changes in personality that occur as a result of new challenges that appear in later adulthood.

Ego-integrity-versus-despair: Erikson's Final Stage.   Psychoanalyst Erik Erikson's final word on personality concerns late adulthood, the time when elderly people move into the last of life's eight stages of psychosocial development. Labeled the **ego-integrity-versus-despair stage**, this last period is characterized by a process of looking back over one's life, evaluating it, and coming to terms with it.

Success in the ego-integrity-versus-despair stage is exemplified by a sense of satisfaction and accomplishment, which Erikson terms "integrity." When people achieve integrity, they feel that they have realized and fulfilled the possibilities that have come their way in life, and they have few regrets. On the other hand, some people look back on their lives with dissatisfaction. Feeling that they have missed important opportunities and have not accomplished what they wished, they experience gloom and despair, and their lives may lack integration. Such individuals may be unhappy, depressed, angry, or despondent over what they have done, or failed to do, with their lives.

Peck's Developmental Tasks.   Although Erikson's approach provides a picture of the broad possibilities of later adulthood, other theorists offer a more differentiated view of what occurs in the final stage of life. For instance, Robert Peck (1968) suggests that personality development in elderly people is occupied by three major developmental tasks or challenges.

In Peck's view, the first task is a **redefinition of self versus preoccupation with work-role**, in which those in old age must redefine themselves in ways that do not relate to their work-roles or occupations. As we'll see when we discuss retirement, the changes occurring when people stop working can trigger a difficult adjustment that has a major impact on the way individuals view themselves. Peck suggests that people must adjust their value systems to achieve a self-concept and a sense of self-esteem in which work is not involved.

The second major developmental task in late adulthood is **body transcendence versus body preoccupation**. As we saw in Chapter 17, elderly individuals can undergo significant changes in their physical capabilities as a result of aging. In the body transcendence versus body preoccupation stage, people must learn to cope with and move beyond those physical changes (transcendence). If they do not, they become preoccupied with their physical deterioration, to the detriment of their personality development.

Finally, the third developmental task faced by those in old age is **ego transcendence versus ego preoccupation**, in which elderly people must come to grips with their coming death. They need to understand that although death is inevitable, and probably not too far off, they have made contributions to society. If people in late adulthood see these contributions, which can take the form of children or work- and civic-related activities, as lasting beyond their own lives, they will experience ego transcendence. If not, they may become preoccupied with the question of whether their lives had value and worth to society.

Levinson's Final Season: The Winter of Life.   According to Daniel Levinson, people enter late adulthood by passing through a transition stage that typically occurs about age 60 to 65 (Levinson, 1986, 1990). During this transition period, people come to view themselves as entering late adulthood—or, ultimately, as being "old." Knowing full well what society's stereotypes about elderly individuals are, and how negative they can be, people struggle with the notion that they are now in this category.

For those who found it hard to accept being "middle aged," passing into the category of "old" can be even more difficult. People ultimately make this transition, however, and then enter a period characterized by definite physical changes and the increasing occurrence of serious illness and death among loved ones and friends. Such changes produce both a heightened recognition that one is aging and a sense of one's own mortality.

The other realization that comes with age is that one is no longer on the center stage of life, but is increasingly playing bit parts. This loss of power, respect, and authority can be difficult for individuals accustomed to having control in their lives.

On the other hand, people in late adulthood can serve as resources to younger individuals, and they may find themselves regarded as "venerated elders" whose advice is sought and relied upon. Furthermore, old age can bring with it a new freedom to do things for the simple sake of the enjoyment and pleasure they bring, rather than because they are obligations.

life review   *the point in life in which people examine and evaluate their lives*

Life Review and Reminiscence: The Common Theme of Personality Development.
Erikson, Peck, and Levinson all suggest that a major characteristic of personality development in old age is looking backward. In fact, **life review**, in which people examine and evaluate their lives, is a common theme for most personality theorists who focus on late adulthood.

According to gerontologist Robert Butler, life review is triggered by the increasingly obvious prospect of one's death (Butler, 1968, 1990; Butler & Lewis, 1981). As people age, they look back on their lives, remembering and reconsidering what has happened to them.

We might at first suspect that such reminiscence may be harmful, as people relive the past, wallow in past problems, and revive old wounds, but this is not the case at all. By reviewing the events of the past, elderly people often come to a better understanding of their past. They may be able to resolve lingering problems and conflicts, and they may feel they can face their current lives with greater wisdom and serenity (Fishman, 1992; Sherman, 1994).

There are other benefits from the process of life review. For example, reminiscence may lead to a sense of sharing and mutuality, a feeling of interconnectedness with others. Moreover, it can be a source of social interaction, as older adults seek to share their prior experiences with others (Unruh, 1989; Sherman, 1991).

Reminiscence might even have cognitive benefits, serving to improve memory in older people. By reflecting on the past, individuals activate a variety of memories about people and events in their lives. In turn, these memories may trigger other, related memories, and

Older adults may become "venerated elders," whose advice is sought and relied upon.

may bring back sights, sounds, and even smells of the past (Thorsheim & Roberts, 1990; Kartman, 1991).

On the other hand, the outcomes of life review and reminiscence are not always positive. People who become obsessive about the past, reliving old insults and mistakes that cannot be rectified, may end up feeling guilt, depression, and anger against those from the past who may not even still be alive. In such cases, reminiscence produces declines in psychological functioning (DeGenova, 1993).

Overall, though, the process of life review and reminiscence can play an important role in the ongoing lives of elderly individuals. It provides continuity between past and present, and may increase awareness of the contemporary world. It also can provide new insights into the past and into others, allowing people to continue personality growth and to function more effectively in the present (Stevens-Ratchford, 1993; Turner & Helms, 1994).

SUCCESSFUL AGING: WHAT IS THE SECRET?

At age 77, Elinor Reynolds spends most of her time at home, leading a quiet, routine existence. Never married, Elinor receives visits from her two sisters every few weeks, and some of her nieces and nephews stop by on occasion. But for the most part, she keeps to herself. When asked, she says she is quite happy.

In contrast, Carrie Masterson, also 77, is involved in something different almost every day. If she is not visiting the Senior Center, participating in some kind of activity, she is out shopping. Her daughter complains that Carrie is "never home" when she tries to reach her by phone, and Carrie replies that she has never been busier—or happier.

Clearly, there is no single way to age successfully (Bond, Cutler, & Grams, 1995). How people age depends on personality factors and the circumstances in which they find themselves. Two major approaches provide alternative explanations: disengagement theory and activity theory.

Disengagement Theory: Gradual Retreat.   According to **disengagement theory**, late adulthood marks a gradual withdrawal from the world on physical, psychological, and social levels (Cummings & Henry, 1961). On a physical level, elderly people have lower energy levels and tend to slow down progressively. Psychologically, they begin to withdraw from others, showing less interest in the world around them and spending more time looking inward. Finally, on a social level, they engage in fewer interactions with others, in terms of both day-to-day, face-to-face encounters and participation in society as a whole. Older adults also become less involved and invested in the lives of others.

Disengagement theory suggests that withdrawal is a mutual process. Because of norms and expectations about aging, society in general begins to disengage from those in late adulthood. For example, mandatory retirement ages compel elderly people to withdraw from work-related roles, thereby accelerating the process of disengagement.

Contrary to what we might expect, such withdrawal is not necessarily a negative experience for those in old age. In fact, most theorists who subscribe to disengagement theory argue that the outcomes of disengagement are largely positive. According to this view, the gradual withdrawal of people in late adulthood permits them to become more reflective about their own lives and to become less constrained by social roles. Furthermore, people can become more discerning in their social relationships, focusing on those who best meet their needs. In a sense, then, disengagement can be liberating (C.L. Johnson & Barer, 1992; Carstensen, 1995).

Similarly, decreased emotional investment in others can be viewed as beneficial. By investing less emotional energy in their social relationships with others, people in late adulthood are better able to adjust to the increasing frequency of serious illness and death among their peers.

Does disengagement theory provide an accurate account of late adulthood? An initial study, examining close to 300 people aged 50 to 90, discovered clear evidence for disen-

disengagement theory   *the period in late adulthood that marks a gradual withdrawal from the world on physical, psychological, and social levels*

gagement (Cummings & Henry, 1961). For instance, the researchers found that specific events, such as retirement or the death of a spouse, were accompanied by a gradual disengagement in which the level of social interaction with others plummeted.

However, later research has not been so supportive of disengagement theory. For example, a follow-up study involving about half the subjects in the original study found contradictory results (Havighurst, Neugarten, & Tobin, 1968; Havighurst, 1973). In this second look at the subjects, researchers found that although some of the subjects were happily disengaged, others, who had remained quite involved and active, were as happy as those who showed signs of disengagement, and sometimes even happier.

Other evidence argues against disengagement theory. In many non-Western cultures, for instance, people remain engaged, active, and busy throughout old age. In such cultures, where late adulthood is viewed as little different from earlier periods of life, the expectation is that people will remain actively involved in everyday life (Palmore, 1975). Clearly, then, disengagement is not an automatic, universal process for all people in late adulthood.

Given the limitations of disengagement theory, gerontologists have developed an alternative approach: activity theory.

Activity Theory: Continued Involvement.   According to **activity theory**, the people who are most likely to be happy in late adulthood are those who are fully involved and engaged with the world. This theory suggests that successful aging occurs when people maintain the interests and activities they pursued during middle age, and they resist any decrease in the amount and type of social interaction they have with others (Blau, 1973; Palmore, 1979).

In the view of activity theorists, elderly people are happiest when their behavior shows continuity with earlier periods of life. Happiness and satisfaction with life are assumed to spring from a high level of involvement with the world. Moreover, successful aging occurs when older adults adapt to inevitable changes in their environments not by withdrawing, but by resisting reductions in their social involvement (J.Z. Bell, 1978).

Activity theory suggests, then, that late adulthood should reflect a continuation of activities in which elderly people participated earlier. Furthermore, in cases in which it is no longer possible to participate in certain activities—such as work, following retirement—activity theory argues that successful aging occurs when replacement activities are found.

activity theory   the theory suggesting that successful aging occurs when people maintain the interests, activities, and social interactions with which they were involved during middle age

While disengagement theory suggests that people in late adulthood begin to gradually withdraw from the world, activity theory argues that successful aging occurs when people maintain their involvement with others.

Like disengagement theory, activity theory has drawn critics. For one thing, activity theory makes little distinction between various types of activities. Surely not every activity will have an equal impact on a person's happiness and satisfaction with life, and being involved in various activities just for the sake of remaining engaged is unlikely to be satisfying. In sum, the specific nature and quality of the activities in which people engage are likely to be more critical than the mere quantity or frequency of their activities (J.G. Gubrium, 1973; Burrus-Bammel & Bammel, 1985).

A more significant criticism is that for some people in late adulthood, the principle of "less is more" clearly holds. For such individuals, less activity brings greater enjoyment of life. They are able to slow down and do only the things that bring them the greatest satisfaction (Ward, 1984). In fact, some people view the ability to moderate their pace as one of the bounties of late adulthood. For them, a relatively inactive, and perhaps even solitary, existence is welcomed (Hansson & Carpenter, 1994).

In short, neither disengagement theory nor activity theory provides a complete picture of successful aging. For some people, a gradual disengagement occurs, and this leads to relatively high levels of happiness and satisfaction. For others, preserving a significant level of

Speaking of Development

Gloria Stielow

Born: ·································· 1954

Education: ························· Attended Laramie County Community College, Cheyenne, Wyoming: Certified Human Services Provider.

Position: ··························· Project coordinator, Senior Services Department, Laramie County, Wyoming

Home: ······························ Pine Bluff, Wyoming

Just outside Cheyenne, Wyoming, is a triangle of three small towns. Pine Bluff is the largest with a population of about 1,100, followed by Burns with just under 300 inhabitants, and Albin with about 200.

For Gloria Stielow, who wears many hats as the Laramie County project coordinator for the Senior Services Department, these three small towns are her "office."

In addition to serving as supervisor for 20 housing units for the elderly, overseer of three senior centers, office clerk, and bus driver, Stielow is also the activities director, a position she finds quite rewarding.

"We're like a big family out here," she says of the 75 active senior citizens she serves. "I'm not just an employee, and they're not just clients. Instead, they're like grandparents, aunts, and uncles."

To meet the social needs of the seniors, Stielow makes sure that any activities she plans are what the majority of her clients want.

activity and involvement leads to greater satisfaction (C.L. Johnson & Barer, 1992; Rapkin & Fischer, 1992).

Ultimately, the best predictor of whether disengagement or activity will lead to successful aging may be one's behavior prior to late adulthood (Maddox & Campbell, 1985). Highly socially-involved younger adults may be the ones for whom activity leads to the greatest satisfaction. In contrast, for those people who were relatively socially independent, uninvolved, or withdrawn as young adults, disengagement during late adulthood may be perfectly satisfying.

Selective Optimization with Compensation: A General Model of Successful Aging. It seems clear that no single pattern of aging is linked to success in late adulthood. For some, an active, involved life may lead to happiness, while for others, a relatively disengaged style may be best.

Furthermore, factors other than the relative degree of engagement and activity are associated with satisfaction in late adulthood. For instance, good physical and mental health are clearly important in determining an elderly person's overall sense of well-being.

"I'm not just an employee, and they're not just clients. Instead, they're like grandparents, aunts, and uncles."

"You can set up as many different programs and activities as you want, but if they're not what the seniors are interested in, they won't show."

"If I notice that several of the seniors have the same type of need, I go out into the community and contact agencies that meet that sort of need. I try to get a feel for the seniors' needs and preferences," she explains. "You can set up as many different programs and activities as you want, but if they're not what the seniors are interested in, they won't show."

The top two favorites, according to Stielow, are dances and the theater.

"They basically enjoy anything that permits them to get out and shine," she says. "We have two gentlemen who are in their 90s. Now, they have a little trouble walking, but you get them out there on the dance floor and they have pretty good rhythm. They just love it.

"Most of the people we take are single men and women. We used to go straight home after the dances ended—around 6 in the evening," Stielow says. "One day someone mentioned that they didn't really want to go home and cook for themselves, and suggested we stop for dinner. I took a poll and—guess what?—now we stop off and have dinner in Cheyenne."

Every other month from fall through spring the seniors attend the Cheyenne Little Theater, where they enjoy primarily comedies and romances. But the big event is the Senior Citizen Prom.

"For the past three years we have put on an April prom in conjunction with the local junior high school, and coordinated through the outreach program at Laramie County Community College," says Stielow. "We get between 100 and 120 people every year. They have to register a month in advance.

"All the participants are given programs and dance cards, and we have a local country-western band for music. In addition we provide a complete dinner menu. It's an event where they can all get dressed up and earn some extra attention. Fellowship is extremely important for these folks. The purpose of our events is to get them out of their quiet homes so they can socialize with others."

selective optimization   the process by
which people concentrate on particular skill
areas to compensate for losses in other areas

Similarly, having enough financial security to provide for basic needs, including food, shelter, and medical care, is critical. In addition, a sense of autonomy, independence, and personal control over one's life is a significant advantage (Abeles, Gift, & Ory, 1994).

Finally, the way in which elderly people perceive old age can influence their happiness and satisfaction. Those who view late adulthood in terms of positive attributes—such as the possibility of gaining knowledge and wisdom—are apt to perceive themselves in a more positive light than those who view old age in a more pessimistic and unfavorable way (Heckhausen, Dixon, & Baltes, 1989; Thompson, 1993).

In considering the factors that lead to successful aging, developmentalists Paul Baltes and Margret Baltes focus on the "selective optimization with compensation" model. As we first noted in Chapter 15, the assumption underlying the model is that late adulthood brings with it changes and losses in underlying capabilities, which vary from one person to another. However, it is possible to overcome such shifts in capabilities through **selective optimization**, or the process by which people concentrate on particular skill areas to compensate for losses in other areas. They do this by seeking to fortify their general motivational, cognitive, and physical resources, while also, through a process of selection, focusing on particular areas of special interest (Baltes & Baltes, 1990; Staudinger et al., 1993; P.B. Baltes, 1993; M.M. Baltes, 1995).

At the same time, the model suggests that elderly individuals engage in compensation for the losses that they have sustained due to aging. Compensation may take the form, for instance, of employing a hearing aid to offset losses in hearing. Similarly, a person who has run marathons all her life may have to cut back or give up entirely other activities in order to increase her training. By forgoing other activities, she may be able to maintain her running skills through concentration on them.

Piano virtuoso Arthur Rubinstein provides another example of selective optimization with compensation. In his later years, he maintained his concert career and was acclaimed for his playing. To manage this, he used several strategies that illustrate the model of selective optimization with compensation.

First, Rubinstein reduced the number of pieces he played at concerts—an example of being selective in what he sought to accomplish. Second, he practiced those pieces more often, thus using optimization. Finally, in an example of compensation, he slowed

Piano virtuoso Artur Rubinstein provided an example of selective optimization, the process by which people concentrate on a particular skill to compensate for losses in other areas. To accomplish this, he reduced the number of pieces he played at concerts and practiced them more often.

down the tempo of musical passages immediately preceding faster passages, thereby fostering the illusion that he was playing just as fast as he had ever played (Baltes & Baltes, 1990).

In short, the model of selective optimization with compensation (summarized in Figure 18-1) illustrates the fundamentals of successful aging. Although late adulthood may bring about various changes in underlying capabilities, people who focus on optimizing their achievements in particular areas may well be able to compensate for any limitations and losses that do occur. The outcome is a life that is reduced in some areas, but is also transformed and modified and, ultimately, is effective and successful.

FIGURE 18-1

SELECTIVE OPTIMIZATION WITH COMPENSATION

According to the model proposed by Paul Baltes and Margret Baltes, successful aging occurs when an older adult focuses on his or her most important areas of functioning and compensates for loses in other areas.

(Adapted from Baltes & Baltes, 1990.)

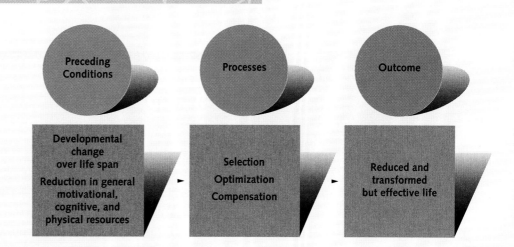

The Informed Consumer of Development

The Keys to Successful Aging

The research on successful aging suggests several strategies for dealing with the changes in capabilities that may occur during late adulthood. Among the general principles suggested by Baltes and Baltes (1990) are the following:

- Engaging in healthy lifestyles can reduce the probability of physical declines.

- People should strengthen their underlying resources through educational, motivational, and health-related activities. In so doing, they can draw upon these resources to compensate for specific losses as they age.

- Because there are limitations on the extent to which underlying resources can be drawn upon, society should provide compensatory supports. For instance, home environments should be designed to support mobility limitations that might occur, and effective home health care systems should be developed.

♦ People in late adulthood need to understand that although they will inevitably experience losses in various capabilities, they can often compensate for those losses. Not every
activity can be maintained throughout life, but it is possible to offset losses with new
gains.

♦ Because people vary significantly in the way they age and how their capabilities change
over the life span, individuals must follow their own paths, seeking to understand
which particular skills to optimize. In sum, there is no single path to successful aging,
and each person must find his or her own way.

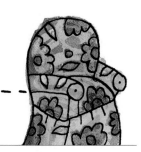

Review and Rethink

REVIEW

♦ Although some basic aspects of personality remain stable throughout life, others develop
to reflect changes in the social environments through which people pass as they age.

♦ Erik Erikson calls older adulthood the ego-integrity-versus-despair stage, whereas
Robert Peck focuses on three tasks that define the period: redefinition of self versus preoccupation with work-role, body transcendence versus body preoccupation, and ego
transcendence versus ego preoccupation.

♦ According to Daniel Levinson, people pass through a struggle with the notion of being
old, which, once resolved, can bring a sense of liberation and self-regard.

♦ Disengagement theory suggests that older people gradually withdraw from the world,
which can lead to reflection and satisfaction. In contrast, activity theory suggests that
the happiest people continue to be engaged with the world. The two theories seem to
represent a choice people make on the basis of personality factors.

♦ The most successful model for aging may be selective optimization with compensation,
through which people focus on a few important aspects of life and work to compensate
for failing abilities.

RETHINK

♦ Why might one set of personality traits be relatively stable over the life span while others change? Does this have to do with the heredity versus environment distinction?

♦ How might personality traits account for success or failure in achieving satisfaction
through the life review process?

♦ Do societal attitudes affect older people's ability to resolve their final developmental
conflicts successfully? How?

♦ How might cultural factors affect an older person's likelihood of pursuing either the
disengagement strategy or the activity strategy?

♦ Do only older people engage in selective optimization with compensation? Might such
a strategy be usefully employed by younger people?

THE DAILY LIFE OF LATE ADULTHOOD

I hear all these retired folks complaining that they don't have this and they don't have that.... I'm not pinched.... My house is paid for. My car is paid for. Both my sons are grown up. I don't need many new clothes. Every time I go out and eat somewhere, I get a senior citizen's discount. This is the happiest period of my life. These are my golden years. (Gottschalk, 1983, p. 1)

This positive view of life in late adulthood was expressed by a 74-year-old retired shipping clerk. Although the story is certainly not the same for all retirees, many, if not most, find their postwork lives happy and involving. We'll consider some of the ways in which people lead their lives in late adulthood, beginning with where they live.

LIVING ARRANGEMENTS: THE PLACES AND SPACES OF THEIR LIVES

Think "old age," and, if you are like most people, your thoughts soon turn to nursing homes. Popular stereotypes place most elderly people in lonely, unpleasant, institutional surroundings, under the care of strangers.

The reality, however, is quite different. Although it is true that some people finish their lives in nursing homes, they are a tiny minority—only 5 percent. Most people live out their entire lives in home environments, typically in the company of at least one other family member. Let us consider the various living arrangements of late adulthood.

Living with Family Members.   Roughly two-thirds of people over the age of 65 live with other members of the family. In most cases they live with spouses, in other cases with siblings, and in still others they live in multigenerational settings with their children, grandchildren, and even occasionally great-grandchildren.

The consequences of living with a family member are quite varied, depending on the nature of the setting. For married couples, living with a spouse represents continuity with earlier life. On the other hand, for people who move in with their children, the adjustment to life in a multigenerational setting can be jarring. Not only is there a potential loss of independence and privacy, but older adults may feel uncomfortable with the way in which their children are raising their grandchildren. Unless there are some ground rules about the specific roles that people are to play in the household, friction can ensue (Sussman & Sussman, 1991).

For some groups, living in extended families is more typical than for other groups. For instance, African-Americans are more likely to live in multigenerational families than are whites. Furthermore, the amount of influence that family members have over one another and the interdependence of extended families are generally greater in both African-American and Hispanic families than in Caucasian families (Mutran, 1985; Gibson, 1986; McAdoo, 1988).

Specialized Living Environments.   For some 10 percent of those in late adulthood, home is an institution. Specialized environments in which elderly people live run the gamut from life-care communities—made up of a group of older individuals who initially live in separate houses or apartments—to the traditional nursing homes of popular stereotypes (Moos & Lemke, 1985).

One of the most recent innovations in living arrangements is the **life-care community**, which typically offers an environment in which all the residents are of retirement age or older and need various levels of care. Residents sign contracts under which the community makes a commitment to provide care at whatever level is needed, starting with occasional home care and extending all the way to full-time nursing care, which is often provided at an on-site nursing home.

Life-care communities tend to be fairly homogeneous in terms of religious, racial, and ethnic backgrounds, and they are often organized by private or religious organizations.

life-care community   *a community that offers an environment in which all the residents are of retirement age or older and need various levels of care*

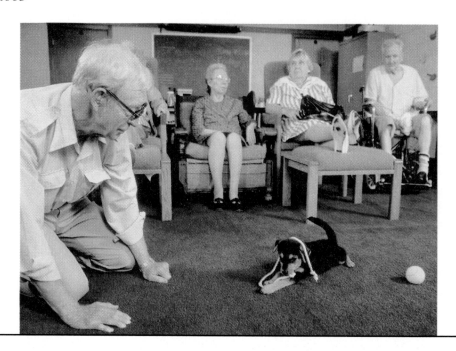

Adult life-care communities provide care at several different levels, according to the particular needs of residents.

Because joining may involve a substantial initial payment, members of such communities tend to be relatively well-off financially (Forrest & Forrest, 1991).

Several types of nursing institutions exist, ranging from those that provide part-time day care to homes that offer 24-hour-a-day, live-in care. In **adult day-care facilities**, elderly individuals receive care only during the day, but spend nights and weekends in their own homes. During the time that they are at the facility, people receive nursing care, take their meals, and participate in scheduled activities. Sometimes adult facilities are combined with infant and child day-care programs, an arrangement that allows for interaction between the old and the young (Kocarnik & Ponzetti, 1991; Quade, 1994).

Other institutional settings provide more extensive care. The most intensive institutions are **skilled-nursing facilities**, which provide full-time nursing care for people who have chronic illnesses or who are recovering from a temporary medical condition. Although skilled-nursing facilities, which are traditional nursing homes, house only 5 percent of the population over 65, the percentage increases with age. For instance, just over 1 percent of people between the ages of 64 and 74 are in nursing homes, whereas for those 85 and older, the proportion climbs to 25 percent (USDHHS, 1990).

The greater the extent of nursing home care, the greater the adjustment that is required of residents. Although some newcomers adjust relatively rapidly, the loss of independence brought about by institutional life can lead to difficulties. In addition, elderly people are as susceptible to society's stereotypes about nursing homes as are other members of society, and their expectations may be particularly negative. They may see themselves as just marking time until they eventually die, forgotten and discarded by a society that venerates youth (Biedenharn & Normoyle, 1991).

Although such fears may be exaggerated, they can lead to **institutionalism**, a psychological state in which people develop apathy, indifference, and a lack of caring about themselves (Butler & Lewis, 1981). Institutionalism is brought about, in part, by a sense of *learned helplessness*, a belief that one has no control over one's environment.

The sense of helplessness brought about by institutionalism can literally have deadly consequences. Consider, for instance, what happens when people enter nursing homes in late adulthood. One of the most conspicuous changes from their independent past is that they no longer have control over their most basic activities. They may be told when and what to eat; their sleeping schedules may be arranged by others; and even their visits to the bathroom may be regulated.

adult day-care facilities   *a facility in which elderly individuals receive care only during the day, but spend nights and weekends in their own homes*

skilled-nursing facilities   *a facility that provides full-time nursing care for people who have chronic illnesses or are recovering from a temporary medical condition*

institutionalism   *a psychological state in which people develop apathy, indifference, and a lack of caring about themselves*

A classic experiment showed the consequences of such a loss of control. In the study, psychologists Ellen Langer and Irving Janis (1979) divided elderly residents of a nursing home into two groups. In one group, the residents were encouraged to make a variety of choices about their day-to-day activities; in the other group, residents were given no choices and were encouraged to let the nursing home staff care for them. The results were clear. Not only were the participants who had choices happier, but their health was also better. In fact, 18 months after the experiment began, only 15 percent of the choice group had died—compared to 30 percent of the comparison group.

In short, the loss of control experienced by residents of nursing homes and other institutions can have a profound effect on their sense of well-being. At the same time, however, some nursing homes are considerably better than others. The best go out of their way to permit residents to make basic life decisions, and they attempt to give people in late adulthood a sense of control over their lives.

FINANCIAL ISSUES: THE ECONOMICS OF LATE ADULTHOOD

People in late adulthood range from one end of the socioeconomic spectrum to the other. In many ways, in fact—including financial condition—they are not much different from younger populations. Those who were relatively affluent during their working years tend to remain relatively affluent, while those who were poor at earlier stages of life tend to remain poor when they reach late adulthood.

At the same time, people who reach late adulthood today may experience growing economic pressure as a result of increasing human longevity. Furthermore, the social inequities that various groups experience during their earlier lives become magnified with increasing age (Duncan & Smith, 1989; Ben-Porath, 1991).

Some 12 percent of people age 65 and older live below the poverty line, a proportion that is quite close to that for people under age 65. However, significant differences exist in gender and racial groups. For instance, women are almost twice as likely as men to be living in poverty. Of those elderly women living alone, about one-fourth live on incomes below the poverty line. A married woman may also slip into poverty if she becomes widowed, for she may have used up savings to pay for her husband's final illness, and the husband's pension may cease with his death (Burkhauser, Holden, & Feaster, 1988; Grambs, 1989).

During late adulthood, the range of socioeconomic well-being mirrors that of earlier years.

Furthermore, although only 7 percent of whites in late adulthood live below the poverty level, 18 percent of Hispanic men and a quarter of African-American men live in poverty. Minority women fare the worst of any category. For example, some 82 percent of African-American elderly women are either "poor" or "near-poor," according to U.S. Census Bureau statistics (Bahr & Peterson, 1989; U.S. Bureau of the Census, 1991b).

One source of financial vulnerability for people in late adulthood is the reliance on a fixed income for support. Unlike that of a younger person, the income of an elderly person, which typically comes from a combination of Social Security benefits, pensions, and savings, rarely keeps up with inflation.

Consequently, as inflation drives the price of goods such as food and clothing even higher, income does not rise as quickly. What may have been a reasonable income at age 65 is worth much less 20 years later, as the elderly person gradually slips into poverty (Brock, 1991).

Another important source of financial vulnerability in older adults is rising health care costs. During one of the great national debates in the United States during the mid-1990s, efforts were made to curb the growing cost to the U.S. treasury of entitlements such as Medicare, which provides health care insurance to elderly people.

Even before any Medicare cuts, people in late adulthood were hardly protected: By the late 1980s, the average older person was spending close to 20 percent of his or her income for health care costs. Moreover, for those elderly individuals who require care in nursing home facilities, the financial costs can be staggering, running an average of $30,000 to $40,000 annually (Hess, 1990).

To complicate the problem even further, unless major changes are made in the way that Social Security and Medicare are financed, the costs borne by younger U.S. citizens in the workforce must rise significantly. Increasing expenditures mean that a larger proportion of younger people's pay must be taxed to fund benefits for the elderly. Such a situation is apt to lead to increasing friction and segregation between younger and older generations. And as we discuss next, cultural values relating to elderly people in the United States (and other Western societies) already may result in major conflicts between young and old.

Developmental Diversity

How Culture Shapes the Way We Treat People in Late Adulthood

> The elderly Eskimo grandmother is bundled up in a parka, placed in a boat, and rowed to a large ice floe floating in the sea. She leaves the boat, walks out onto the ice. The boat pulls away, leaving her to die a certain and lonely death.

The situation described above has reached the level of folklore, with some people assuming that the Arctic Ocean is full of aged Eskimos waiting to die on ice floes. But this view is just plain wrong: Although isolated cases of abandonment are reported, the truth is that it rarely happens (Fry, 1985).

Now consider another scene relating to the treatment of elderly individuals, drawn from a different society:

Older people are held in considerably higher regard in many non-western cultures than in western ones, although there is great individual variability.

> The elderly grandmother is seated at the head of the table, in a place of honor, as the Chinese family sits down to dinner. She is given the first choice of food, and is fussed over throughout the meal. At the end of the meal, she rises and leaves, making no effort to help clean up. No one expects her to—she is held in such high regard by her family and Chinese society that she never has to lift a finger.

Such veneration of aging people in Asian families seems hardly surprising to most people in Western cultures. Most of us have been taught that citizens of many non-Western cultures hold older individuals in far greater esteem than do citizens of Western cultures, treating them at all times with the utmost respect and consideration.

Yet in some ways, this view of the treatment of elderly individuals is as overdrawn as the folklore about elderly Eskimos. In neither society is the treatment of older adults invariably bad, nor invariably good.

Even those societies that articulate strong ideals regarding the treatment of older people do not always live up to those standards. For instance, careful research on the Chinese people, whose admiration, respect, and even worship for individuals in late adulthood are strong, shows that actual behavior is not so positive in almost every segment of the society except for the most elite. Furthermore, it is typically sons and their wives who are expected to care for elderly parents; parents with just daughters may find themselves with no one to care for them in late adulthood. In short, conduct toward elderly people in particular cultures is quite variable, and we must be careful not to make broad, global statements about how older adults are treated in a given society (Sankar, 1981; Harrell, 1981; Fry, 1985).

On the other hand, some generalizations can be supported. For example, Asian societies, in general, do hold elderly people, particularly members of their own families, in higher esteem than Western cultures tend to. Although the strength of this standard has been declining in areas of Asia in which industrialization has been increasing rapidly, such as Japan, the view of aging and the treatment of people in late adulthood still tend to be more positive than in Western cultures (Fry, 1985; Ikels, 1989).

What is it about Asian cultures that leads to higher levels of esteem for old age? In general, cultures that hold the elderly in high regard are relatively homogeneous in socioeconomic terms. In addition, the roles that people play in those societies entail greater responsibility with increasing age, and elderly people control resources to a relatively large extent.

Moreover, roles display continuity throughout the life span, and older adults continue to engage in activities that are valued by society. Finally, cultures in which older adults are held in higher regard tend to be organized around extended families, in which the older generations are well integrated into the family structure (Press & McKool, 1972; Fry, 1985; Sangree, 1989).

WORK AND RETIREMENT IN LATE ADULTHOOD

When to retire is a major decision faced by the majority of individuals in late adulthood. Although for some the decision is easy, many people experience a fair amount of difficulty in making the identity shift from "worker" to "retiree." For others, though, retirement represents a major opportunity, offering the chance to lead, perhaps for the first time in adulthood, a life of leisure.

Retirement occupies a growing proportion of people's lives. Because the typical retirement age is moving downward, toward age 60, and because people's life spans are expanding, people today spend far more time in retirement than did those from previous generations. Moreover, because the number of people in late adulthood continues to increase, retirees are an increasingly significant and influential segment of the U.S. population.

Older Workers: Combating Age Discrimination.   Although the number of retirees is on the rise, many people continue to work, either full-time or part-time, for some part of late adulthood. They can do so largely because of legislation that was passed in the late 1970s, in which mandatory retirement ages were made illegal in almost every profession. Part of broader legislation that makes age discrimination illegal, these laws gave most workers the opportunity either to remain in jobs they held previously or to begin working in entirely different fields (Borgatta, 1991).

Despite laws making age discrimination illegal, it remains a reality. Some employers encourage older workers to leave their jobs in order to replace them with younger employees whose salaries will be considerably lower. Furthermore, some employers believe that older workers are not up to the demands of the job or are less willing to adapt to a changing workplace—stereotypes about the elderly that are enduring, despite legislative changes.

The reality is that there is little evidence to support supposed declines in older workers' ability to perform their jobs. Even in those few professions that were specifically exempted from laws prohibiting mandatory retirement ages—those involving public safety—the evidence does not support the notion that workers should be retired at an arbitrary age. For instance, one large-scale, careful study of older police officers, firefighters, and prison guards concluded that age did not predict accurately whether a worker was likely to be incapacitated on the job, or the level of his or her general work performance. Instead, a case-by-case analysis of individual workers' performance was a more reasonable approach (Landy, 1994).

Ongoing age discrimination and several other factors have led to a marked decline over the last three decades in the number of people who continue working in late adulthood. Part of the reason for the decline is that Social Security and other pensions provide workers with enough income to live sufficiently well to make retirement an appealing option. Another reason is that a disincentive for working is built into the Social Security laws: Workers who are collecting Social Security are taxed at higher rates both on their earnings *and* on their Social Security pensions, meaning that their net earnings can be minimal. Such factors increase the probability that the later years of life will be spent in retirement rather than work.

Retirement: Filling a Life of Leisure.   Why do people retire? Although the basic reason seems apparent—to stop working—the retirement decision is actually based on a variety of factors. For instance, sometimes workers are burned out after a lifetime of work; they seek a respite from the tension and frustration of their jobs, and from the sense that they are not accomplishing as much as they once wished they could. Others retire because their health has declined, and still others because they are offered incentives by their employers in the form of bonuses or increased pensions if they retire by a certain age. Finally, some people have planned for years to retire and intend to use their increased leisure to travel, study, or spend more time with their children and grandchildren.

Whatever the reason they retire, people often pass through a series of retirement stages, summarized in Table 18-1 (Atchley, 1982, 1985). Retirement may begin with a *honeymoon* period, in which former workers engage in a variety of activities, such as travel, that were previously hindered by full-time work. The next phase may be *disenchantment*, in which retirees conclude that retirement is not all they thought it would be. They may miss the stimulation of their previous jobs, or they may find it hard to keep busy.

The next phase is *reorientation*, in which retirees reconsider their options and become engaged in new, more fulfilling activities. If successful, this leads to the *retirement routine* stage, in which they come to grips with the realities of retirement and feel fulfilled in this new phase of life. Not all people reach this stage; some may feel disenchanted with retirement for years.

Finally, the last phase of the retirement process is *termination*. Although some people terminate retirement by going back to work, termination for most people results from major physical deterioration. In this case, health becomes so bad that the person can no longer function independently.

TABLE 18-1

STAGES OF RETIREMENT

Stage	Characteristic
Honeymoon	In this period, former workers engage in a variety of activities, such as travel, that were previously hindered by working full-time.
Disenchantment	In this stage, retirees feel that retirement is not all that they thought it would be. They may miss the stimulation of a job or may find it difficult to keep busy.
Reorientation	At this point, retirees reconsider their options and become engaged in new, more fulfilling activities. If successful, it leads them to the next stage.
Retirement Routine	Here the retiree comes to grips with the realities of retirement and feels fulfilled with this new phase of life. Not all reach this stage; some may feel disenchanted with retirement for years.
Termination	Although some people terminate retirement by going back to work, termination occurs for most people because of major physical deterioration where their health becomes so bad they can no longer function independently.

Source: Atchley, 1982.

Obviously, not everyone passes through all these stages, and the sequence is not universal. In large measure, a person's reactions to retirement stem from the reasons he or she retired in the first place. For example, a person forced into retirement for health reasons will have a very different experience from someone who eagerly chose to retire at a particular age. Similarly, the retirement of people who loved their jobs might be a quite different experience from that of people who despised their work.

In short, the psychological consequences of retirement vary a great deal from one individual to the next. For many people, though, retirement is a continuation of a life well-lived, and they use it to the fullest.

The Informed Consumer of Development

Planning for—and Living—a Good Retirement

What makes for a good retirement? Gerontologists suggest that several factors are related to success (Herzog, House, & Morgan, 1991; Kelly & Wescott, 1991).

- *Plan ahead financially.* Because most financial experts suggest that Social Security pensions will be inadequate in the future, personal savings are critical. Similarly, having adequate health-care insurance is essential.

- *Consider tapering off from work gradually.* Sometimes it is possible to enter into retirement by shifting from full-time to part-time work. Such a transition may be helpful in preparing for eventual full-time retirement.

- *Explore your interests before you retire.* Assess what you like about your current job and think how that might be translated into leisure activities.

◆   *Plan to volunteer your time.* People who retire have an enormous wealth of skills, and these are often need by nonprofit organizations and small businesses. Organizations such as the Retired Senior Volunteer Program or the Foster Grandparent Program can help match your skills with people who need them.

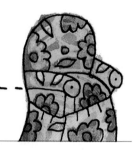

Review and Rethink

REVIEW

◆   Elderly people live in a variety of settings: their own homes, the homes of their families, life-care facilities, skilled-nursing facilities, and other settings.

◆   Financial issues can trouble older people, largely because their incomes are fixed, health-care costs are increasing, and the life span is lengthening.

◆   Societies in which elderly people are respected are generally characterized by social homogeneity, extended families, responsible roles for older people, and control of significant resources by older people.

◆   Older people are often under considerable pressure to retire from their jobs, and the success with which they deal with retirement depends on a number of factors, including personality characteristics and the circumstances surrounding the retirement decision.

◆   Retired people may pass through stages, including a honeymoon period, disenchantment, reorientation, retirement routine, and termination.

RETHINK

◆   What are some advantages and disadvantages of an elderly person's living with the family of a son or daughter? What cultural conditions might affect the balance?

◆   What policies might a nursing home institute to minimize the chances that its residents will develop "institutionalism"? Why are such policies relatively uncommon?

◆   How does the marriage gradient contribute to the likelihood that a woman will fall into poverty when she reaches old age?

◆   Why might the level of industrialization that a society has reached affect the way it regards older people?

◆   How might a person avoid becoming stuck in the disenchantment stage following retirement?

RELATIONSHIPS: OLD AND NEW

Philip Cassidy, 88, and Viola Cassidy, 85, live in the 1-½-story Needham Cape that Philip's uncle built in 1930, when the couple were first married. They have no health problems and take no daily medications. Together they do arts-and-crafts projects and make Christmas ornaments for their grandchildren. In June, they traveled to Alaska for two weeks. They socialize at the Needham Council on Aging and are regulars at Thursday cribbage games. Viola volunteers at her church and takes ceramics classes. Philip is a member of the hospitality committee of the Retired Men's Club and plays golf.

"This is an easy time," says Viola. "You don't have to do all the things you do when you are younger. You don't have to get up early. It's a different life altogether." (Pappano, 1994, p. 28)

The life the Cassidys lead is the sort that many couples envision for themselves: time for family, friends, travel, and doing the things that they couldn't do before they retired. Yet it is also something of a rarity for those in the last stage of life. For every older person who is part of a couple, many more are alone.

What is the nature of the social world of people in late adulthood? To answer the question, let us first consider the nature of marriage in that period.

MARRIAGE IN THE LATER YEARS: TOGETHER, THEN ALONE

It's a man's world—at least when it comes to marriage after the age of 65. The proportion of men over the age of 65 who are married is far greater than that of women (see Figure 18-2). One reason for this disparity is that 70 percent of women outlive their husbands by at least a few years. Because there are fewer men available (they've died), these women are unlikely to remarry (Barer, 1994).

Furthermore, the marriage gradient that we first discussed in Chapter 14 is still a powerful influence. Reflecting societal norms that suggest that women should marry men older than themselves, the marriage gradient works to keep women single even in the later years of life. At the same time, it makes remarriage for men much easier, for the available pool of eligible partners is much larger (Treas & Bengtson, 1987; AARP, 1990).

The vast majority of people who are still married in later life report that they are satisfied with their marriages. They indicate that their partners provide substantial companionship and emotional support. Because at this period in life they have typically been together for a long time, they have great insight into their partners (Brubaker, 1991; Levenson, Carstensen, & Gottman, 1993).

At the same time, not every aspect of marriage is equally satisfying, and marriages may undergo severe stress as spouses experience changes in their lives. For instance, the retirement of one or both spouses can alter the nature of a couple's relationship (Askham, 1994).

For some couples, the stress is so great that one spouse or the other seeks a divorce. Although the exact numbers are hard to come by, at least 2 percent of divorces in the United States involve women over the age of 60 (Uhlenberg et al., 1990).

The reasons for divorce at such a late stage of life are varied. Women who divorce often do so because their husbands are abusive or alcoholic. But in the more frequent case of a husband seeking a divorce from his wife, the reason is often that he has found a younger woman. Often the divorce occurs soon after retirement, when men who have been highly involved in their careers are in psychological turmoil (Cain, 1982).

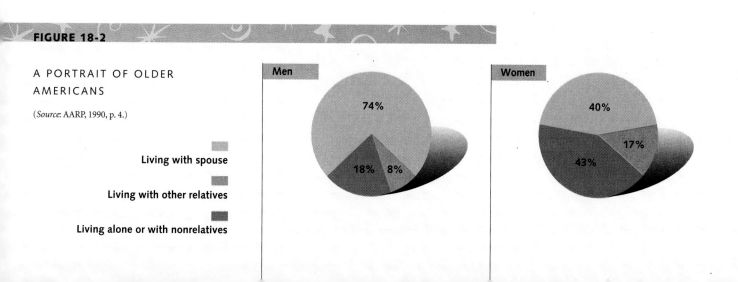

FIGURE 18-2

A PORTRAIT OF OLDER AMERICANS

(*Source*: AARP, 1990, p. 4.)

Living with spouse

Living with other relatives

Living alone or with nonrelatives

Men

74%

18%   8%

Women

40%

17%

43%

Divorce so late in life is particularly difficult for women. Because of the marriage gradient and the limited size of the potential pool of eligible men, it is unlikely that a late-divorced woman will remarry. Furthermore, for many women, marriage has been their primary role and the center of their identities, and they may view divorce as a major failure. As a consequence, happiness and the quality of life for divorced women often plummet (Chiriboga, 1982; Burrus-Bammel & Bammel, 1985; Goldscheider, 1994). (Another aspect of divorce—the surprisingly lingering impact on older people of their *parents'* divorce, years earlier—is discussed in the Directions in Development section).

It is important to keep in mind that some people enter late adulthood having never married. For those who have remained single throughout their lives—about 5 percent of the population—late adulthood may bring fewer transitions, since the status of living alone does not change. In fact, never-married individuals report feeling less lonely than do most people their age, and they have a greater sense of independence (F.F. Gubrium, 1975; Essex & Nam, 1987).

Directions in Development

The Lasting Influence of Childhood: Evidence from the Terman Study

It was more than three-quarters of a century ago that psychologist Lewis M. Terman searched California's schools for children who tested in the genius range on his then newly devised intelligence test. The 1,500 children that he found are still being studied in what is probably the longest-running longitudinal study in the field of psychology.

The people in the study—who began to refer to themselves as "Termites" as the study wore on—are still being tested every 5 years or so. Now in their 80s, they continue to provide a wealth of new information, and previous data continue to be mined for nuggets of understanding about the course of human development.

The latest analyses have examined the impact that several types of psychological stresses experienced by the participants during childhood have had on their current lives—and deaths. One of the most unexpected findings from a recent analysis of the data reveals that participants whose parents divorced faced a one-third greater risk of an earlier death than did participants whose parents remained married at least until the participants reached age 21 (H.S. Friedman et al., 1995a, 1995b).

Lewis Terman

Specifically, the average age of death for men whose parents divorced during their childhoods was 76, whereas the average age of death was 80 for men whose parents did not divorce. For women, those whose parents divorced, on average died at age 82; those whose parents did not divorce lived to an average age of 86 (Schwartz et al., in press).

To gather the data, psychologist Howard Friedman tracked down the death certificates of the participants in the study who had died and examined their backgrounds. He suggests that the surprising findings are due to the greater stigma attached to divorce during the childhoods of the study participants, who were born about 1910.

In addition, further analyses revealed that the children of divorce also tended to have greater marital instability themselves during their adult years. Such marital instability was also linked to an increased risk of premature death (Winger, 1993).

Finally, the study examined the links between several types of personality factors and longevity. The results suggest that childhood social dependability, or "conscientiousness," is related to length of life. Participants in the study, particularly males, who were rated during childhood as prudent, conscientious, truthful, and free from vanity had a 30 percent lower chance of dying in a particular year. It is plausible that such a cluster of factors produces greater adherence to healthful behaviors and more careful living in general, thereby accounting for the longer lives of those with such traits. Figure 18-3 illustrates the joint effects of conscientiousness and parental divorce for the males in the study.

On the other hand, and somewhat to the surprise of the researchers, childhood cheerfulness was related to a *shorter* life. Perhaps a cheery disposition leads to a carelessness or carefreeness that in turn produces poor health habits, thereby shortening a person's life.

Although the full explanation for these findings is not apparent, it is clear that parental divorce, marital instability, and childhood personality traits are all related to longevity. Without doubt, the Terman longitudinal study continues to yield important and interesting findings, even as the study itself moves through a healthy old age.

FIGURE 18-3

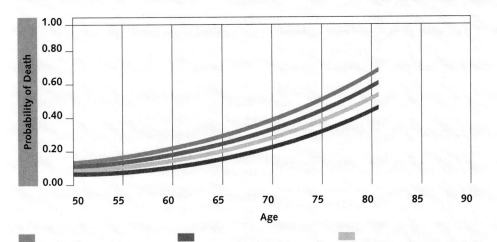

Conscientiousness—and the consequences of divorce—last a lifetime. Individuals who were high in conscientiousness early in life had a lower probability of dying throughout adulthood. Similarly, parental divorce was associated with a higher probability of death.

(*Source:* Friedman et al., 1995b.)

Males whose parents divorced– Low conscientiousness

Males whose parents divorced– High conscientiousness

Males whose parents did not divorce– Low conscientiousness

Males whose parents did not divorce– High conscientiousness

Dealing with Retirement: Too Much Togetherness? When Morris Abercrombie finally stopped working full-time, his wife, Roxanne, found some aspects of his increased presence at home troubling. Although their marriage was strong, his intrusion into her daily routine, and his constant questioning about whom she was on the phone with and where she was going when she went out, were irksome. Finally, she began to wish he would spend less time around the house. It was an ironic thought: She had passed much of Morris's preretirement years wishing that he would spend more time at home.

The situation that Morris and Roxanne found themselves in is not unique. For many couples, retirement means that relationships need to be refashioned. In some cases, retirement results in a couple spending more time together than at any other point in their marriage. In others, retirement provides an opportunity to alter the long-standing distribution of household chores, with men taking on more responsibility than before for the everyday functioning of the household.

In fact, research suggests that it is not unusual for gender-stereotyped roles to become reversed in late adulthood. In contrast to the early years of marriage, when wives, more than husbands, typically desire greater companionship with their spouses, in late adulthood husbands' companionship needs tend to be greater than their wives'. The power structure of marriage also changes: Men become more affiliative and less competitive following retirement. At the same time, women become more assertive and autonomous (Blumstein & Schwartz, 1989; Bird & Melville, 1994).

Caring for an Aging Spouse.   The shifts in health that accompany late adulthood sometimes require women and men to care for their spouses in ways that they never envisioned. Consider, for example, one woman's comments of frustration:

> I cry a lot because I never thought it would be this way. I didn't expect to be mopping up the bathroom, changing him, doing laundry all the time. I was taking care of babies at twenty; now I'm taking care of my husband. (Doress et al., 1987, pp. 199–200)

At the same time, some people view caring for an ailing and dying spouse in a more positive light, regarding it in part as a final opportunity to demonstrate love and devotion. In fact, some caregivers report feeling quite satisfied as a result of fulfilling what they see as their responsibility to their spouse. And some of those who experience emotional distress initially find that the distress declines as they successfully adapt to the stress of caregiving (Lawton et al., 1989; Townsend, Noelker, Deimling, & Bass, 1989; Zarit & Reid, 1994).

Yet even if giving care is viewed in such a light, there is no getting around the fact that it is an arduous chore, made more difficult by the fact that the spouses providing the care are probably not in the peak of physical health themselves. In fact, caregiving may be detrimental to the provider's own physical and psychological well-being. For instance, caregivers report lower levels of satisfaction with life than do noncaregivers (Vitaliano, Dougherty, & Siegler, 1994).

In most cases, it should be noted, the spouse who provides the care is the wife. Just under three-quarters of people who provide care to a spouse are women. Part of the reason is demographic: Men tend to die earlier than women, and consequently they contract the diseases leading to death earlier than women. A second reason, though, relates to society's traditional gender roles, which view women as "natural" caregivers. As a consequence, health care providers may be more likely to suggest that a wife care for her husband than that a husband care for his wife (Polansky, 1976; Unger & Crawford, 1992).

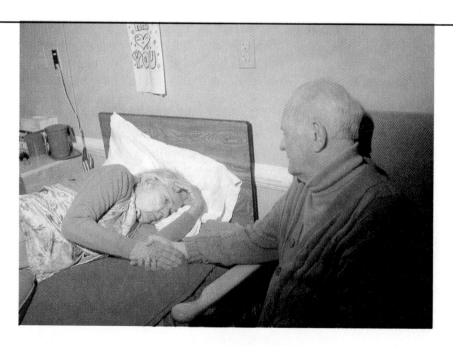

One of the most difficult responsibilities of later adulthood is caring for one's ill spouse.

The Death of a Spouse: Becoming Widowed.   Hardly any event is more painful and stressful than the loss of one's spouse. Especially for those who married young, the death of a spouse leads to profound feelings of loss, and often brings about drastic changes in economic and social circumstances. If the marriage has been a good one, the death of the partner means the loss of a companion, a lover, a confidante, a helper.

Upon a partner's death, spouses suddenly assume a new and unfamiliar societal role: widowhood. At the same time, they lose the role with which they were most familiar: spouse. Suddenly, widowed people are no longer part of a couple; instead, they are viewed by society, and themselves, solely as individuals. All this occurs as they are dealing with profound and sometimes overwhelming grief (which we'll discuss more in Chapter 19).

Widowhood brings a variety of new demands and concerns. There is no longer a companion with whom to share the day's events. If the deceased spouse primarily carried out household chores, the surviving spouse must learn how to do these tasks and must perform them every day. Although initially family and friends provide a great deal of support, this assistance quickly fades into the background, and newly widowed people are left to make the adjustment to being single on their own (Wortman & Silver, 1990).

Following the death of a spouse, people's social lives often change drastically. Typically, married couples tend to socialize with other married couples; the widowed may feel like "fifth wheels" as they seek to maintain the friendships they enjoyed as couples. Eventually, such friendships may cease, although they may be replaced by friendships with other single people (van den Hoonaard, 1994).

Economic issues are of major concern to many widowed people. Although many have insurance, savings, and pensions to provide economic security, some individuals, most often women, experience a decline in their economic well-being as the result of a spouse's death. In such cases, the change in financial status can force wrenching decisions, such as selling the house in which the couple spent their entire married lives (O'Bryant & Morgan, 1989; Hoskins, 1992).

According to sociologists Gloria Heinemann and Patricia Evans (1990), the process of adjusting to widowhood encompasses three stages (see Figure 18-4). In the first stage, *preparation*, spouses prepare, in some cases years and even decades ahead of time, for the eventual death of the partner. Consider, for instance, the purchase of life insurance, the preparation of a will, and the decision to have children who may eventually provide care in one's old age. Each of these actions helps prepare for the eventuality that one will be widowed and will require some degree of assistance (Heinemann & Evans, 1990).

The second stage of adjustment to widowhood, *grief and mourning*, is an immediate reaction to the death of a spouse. It starts with the shock and pain of loss, and continues as the survivor works through the period of grief and mourning. The length of time a person spends in this period depends both on the degree of support received from others and on personality factors. In some cases, the grief and mourning period may extend for years; in others it lasts a few months.

The last stage of adjustment is *adaptation*. In adaptation, the widowed individual starts a new life. The period begins with the acceptance of one's loss, and it continues with the reorganization of roles and the formation of new friendships. The adaptation stage also encompasses a period of reintegration, in which a new identity—as an unmarried person—is developed.

For most people, life returns to normal and becomes enjoyable once again. For others, life is viewed as all right, but just barely: The life they had before their spouse's death is seen as qualitatively better than their current existence. And for a minority of those who are widowed, there is no recovery; they constantly experience a strong sense of loss that overwhelms their current efforts at achieving happiness.

It is important to keep in mind that the model of loss and change proposed by Heinemann and Evans (1990) may not apply to everyone. Certainly, vast individual differences exist in the ways people react to the death of a spouse. Furthermore, the timing of the various stages in the model differs substantially from one person to the next.

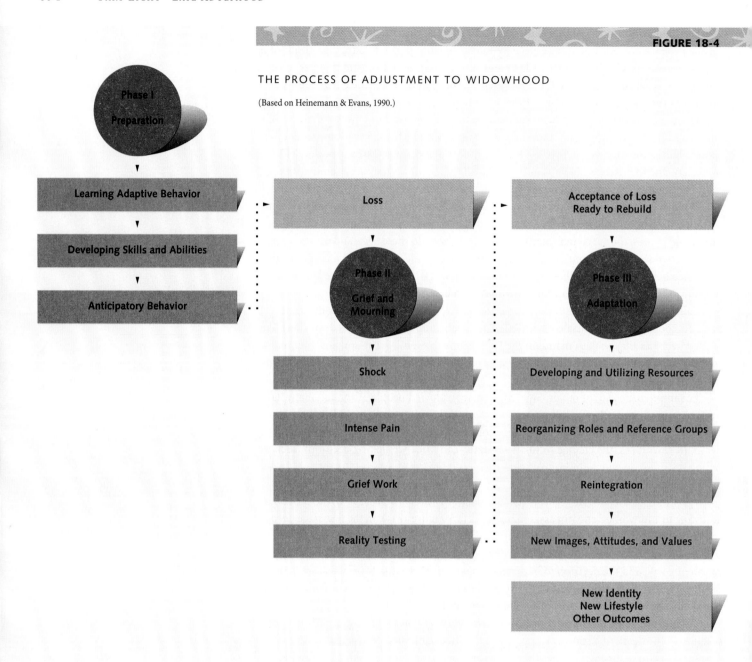

FIGURE 18-4

THE PROCESS OF ADJUSTMENT TO WIDOWHOOD

(Based on Heinemann & Evans, 1990.)

Phase I

Preparation

Learning Adaptive Behavior

Developing Skills and Abilities

Anticipatory Behavior

Loss

Phase II

Grief and Mourning

Shock

Intense Pain

Grief Work

Reality Testing

Acceptance of Loss
Ready to Rebuild

Phase III

Adaptation

Developing and Utilizing Resources

Reorganizing Roles and Reference Groups

Reintegration

New Images, Attitudes, and Values

New Identity
New Lifestyle
Other Outcomes

Without fail, however, the death of a spouse is a profound event in any period of life. During late adulthood its implications are particularly powerful, because it can be seen as a forewarning of one's own mortality (Howie, 1993).

THE SOCIAL NETWORKS OF LATE ADULTHOOD

Elderly people enjoy friends as much as younger people do, and friendships play an important role in the lives of those in late adulthood. In fact, time spent with friends is often valued more highly during late adulthood than time spent with the family, and friends are often seen as more important providers of support than are family members. Furthermore, a third of older persons report that they made a new friend within the past year (Armstrong, 1991; Hartshorne, 1994; Hansson & Carpenter, 1994).

Friendship: Why Friends Matter in Late Adulthood.   One reason for the importance of friendship relates to the element of control. In friendship relationships, unlike family relationships, we choose whom we like and whom we dislike, meaning that we have considerable control. Because late adulthood may bring with it a gradual loss of control in other areas, such as in one's health, the ability to maintain friendships may take on more importance than in other stages of life (Marshall, 1986; Chappell, 1991: Krause & Borawski-Clark, 1994).

In addition, friendships—especially ones that have developed recently—may be more flexible than family ties, given that recent friendships are not likely to have a history of obligations and past conflicts. In contrast, family ties may have a long and sometimes stormy record that can reduce the emotional sustenance they provide (Hartshorne, 1994).

Another reason for the importance of friendships in late adulthood relates to the increasing likelihood, over time, that one will be without a marital partner. When a spouse dies, people typically seek out the companionship of friends to help deal with their loss and also to replace some of the social functions that were provided by the deceased spouse.

Of course, it is not only spouses who die during old age; friends also die. The way in which adults view friendship in late adulthood determines how vulnerable they are to the death of a friend. If the friendship has been defined as irreplaceable, then the loss of the friend may be quite difficult. On the other hand, if the friendship is defined as a role relationship that fulfills companionship needs, then the death of a friend might be less traumatic. In such cases, older adults are more likely to become involved subsequently with new friends (Hartshorne, 1994).

Social Support: The Significance of Others.   Friendships also provide one of the basic social needs: social support. **Social support** is assistance and comfort supplied by a network of caring, interested people. Such support plays a critical role in successful aging (Antonucci, 1990; Antonucci & Akiyama, 1991).

The benefits of social support are considerable. For instance, people can provide emotional support by lending a sympathetic ear and providing a sounding board for one's concerns. Furthermore, social support from people who are experiencing similar problems—such as the loss of a spouse—can provide an unmatched degree of understanding and a pool of helpful suggestions for coping strategies that would be less credible coming from others.

In addition, people can furnish material support, such as helping with rides or picking up groceries. They can provide help in solving problems, such as dealing with a difficult landlord or fixing a broken appliance.

The benefits of social support do not come only from other humans. One researcher found that owners of pets were less apt to need medical care following exposure to high levels of stress than were those without pets. Dogs were especially good in providing social support, although other animals were adequate as well (Siegel, 1990; Hoffman, 1991).

What kinds of social support are most effective and appropriate? It depends on the situation, but one factor is that a mechanism should exist whereby those who receive support can reciprocate in some fashion. In Western societies, older adults—like younger people—value relationships in which reciprocity is possible. *Reciprocity* is the expectation that if someone provides something positive to another person, a return benefit ought to be received. Conversely, someone who receives something of benefit from another individual expects to provide something in return (M.S. Clark, Mills, & Corcoran, 1989; M. Clark & Mills, 1993).

On the other hand, with increasing age, it may be progressively more difficult to reciprocate the social support that one receives. As a consequence, relationships can become more asymmetrical, placing the recipient in a difficult psychological position (Roberto, 1987; Selig, Tomlinson, & Hickey, 1991).

FAMILY RELATIONSHIPS: THE TIES THAT BIND

Even after the death of a spouse, most older adults are part of a larger family unit. Connections with siblings, children, grandchildren, and even great-grandchildren continue, and they may provide an important source of comfort to adults in the last years of their lives.

social support   *assistance and comfort supplied by another person or a network of caring, interested people*

Siblings can provide unusually strong emotional support during late adulthood. Because they often share old, pleasant memories of childhood, and because they usually represent the oldest existing relationships a person has, siblings provide important support. Although not every memory of childhood may be pleasant, continuing interaction with brothers and sisters still provides substantial emotional support during late adulthood (Bengston, Rosenthal, & Burton, 1990; Moyer, 1992).

Children.   Even more important than siblings, however, are children and grandchildren. Societal obligations are strong for parent–child relationships, even in an age in which geographic mobility is high. Moreover, parents and children tend to share similar views of how adult children should behave toward their parents (see Table 18-2). In particular, they expect that children should help their parents understand their resources, provide emotional support, and talk over matters of importance (Hamon & Blieszner, 1990).

Because the great majority of older adults have at least one child who lives fairly close, family members still provide significant aid to one another. Furthermore, it is most often children who end up caring for their aging parents when they require assistance (Stone, Cafferata, & Sangl, 1987; Eggebeen & Hogan, 1990; Wolfson et al., 1993).

Conversely, the bonds between parents and children are sometimes asymmetrical, with parents seeking a closer relationship and children a more distant one. Parents have a greater *developmental stake* in close ties because they see their children as perpetuating their beliefs, values, and standards. On the other hand, children are motivated to maintain their autonomy and live independently from their parents. These divergent perspectives make parents more likely to minimize conflicts they experience with their children, and children more likely to maximize them (Bengston et al., 1985; O'Connor, 1994).

Still, most parents and children remain fairly close, both geographically and psychologically. Some 75 percent of children live within a 30-minute drive of their parents, and parents and children visit and talk with one another frequently. However, daughters tend to

TABLE 18-2

PARENTS AND CHILDREN SHARE SIMILAR VIEWS OF HOW ADULT CHILDREN SHOULD BEHAVE TOWARD THEIR PARENTS

Item	Children's Rank	Parents' Rank
Help understand resources	1	2
Give emotional support	2	3
Discuss matters of importance	3	1
Make room in home in emergency	4	7
Sacrifice personal freedom	5	6
Care when sick	6	9
Be together on special occasions	7	5
Provide financial help	8	13
Give parents advice	9	4
Adjust family schedule to help	10	10
Feel responsible for parent	11	8
Adjust work schedule to help	12	12
Believe that parent should live with child	13	15
Visit once a week	14	11
Live close to parent	15	16
Write once a week	16	14

(Adapted from Hamon & Blieszner, 1990.)

be in more frequent contact with their parents than sons are. Furthermore, mothers tend to be the recipients of communication more frequently than fathers (Hoffman, McManus, & Brackbill, 1987; Field & Minkler, 1988; Krout, 1988).

For parents, their children remain a source of great interest and concern. Some surveys show, for instance, that even in late adulthood parents talk about their children nearly every day, particularly if the children are having some sort of problem. At the same time, children may turn to their elderly parents for advice, information, and sometimes tangible help, such as money (Greenberg & Becker, 1988).

Grandchildren and Great-grandchildren.   As we discussed first in Chapter 16, not all grandparents are equally involved with their grandchildren. Even those grandparents who take great pride in their grandchildren may be relatively detached from them, avoiding any direct care role (Cherlin & Furstenberg, 1986).

As we saw in Chapter 16, grandmothers tend to be more involved with their grandchildren than are grandfathers; similarly, there are gender differences in the feelings grandchildren have toward their grandparents. Specifically, most young adult grandchildren feel closer to their grandmothers than to their grandfathers. In addition, most express a preference for their maternal grandmothers over their paternal grandmothers (Kennedy, 1990; Kalliopuska, 1994).

Furthermore, African-American grandparents tend to be more involved with their grandchildren than are white grandparents, and African-American grandchildren often feel closer to their grandparents. Moreover, grandfathers seem to play a more central role in the lives of African-American children than in the lives of white children. The reason for these racial differences probably stems in large measure from the higher proportion of multigenerational families among African-Americans than among whites. In such families, grandparents usually play a central role in childrearing (Beck & Beck, 1989; Kivett, 1991; Taylor et al., 1991).

Great-grandchildren play less of a role in the lives of both Caucasian and African-American great-grandparents. Most great-grandparents do not have close relationships with their great-grandchildren. Close relationships tend to occur only when the great-grandparents and great-grandchildren live relatively near one another (Doka & Mertz, 1988).

In four-generation families, the relationship between great-grandparent and great-grandchild is often remote.

There are several explanations for the relative lack of involvement of great-grandparents with great-grandchildren. One is that by the time they reach great-grandparenthood, elderly adults are so old that they do not have much physical or psychological energy to expend on forming relationships with their great-grandchildren. Another is that there may be so many great-grandchildren that great-grandparents do not feel strong emotional ties to them. In fact, it is not uncommon for a great-grandparent who has had a large number of children to have so many great-grandchildren that they are difficult to keep track of. For example, when President John Kennedy's mother, Rose Kennedy (who had given birth to a total of nine children), died at the age of 104 in 1995, she had 30 grandchildren and 41 great-grandchildren!

Still, even though most great-grandparents may not have close relationships with their great-grandchildren, they still profit emotionally from the mere fact that they have great-grandchildren. For instance, great-grandparents may see their great-grandchildren as representing both their own and their family's continuation, as well as providing a concrete sign of their longevity (Doka & Mertz, 1988).

ELDER ABUSE: RELATIONSHIPS GONE WRONG

> With good health and a sizable pension, 76-year-old Mary T. should have been enjoying a comfortable retirement. But in fact, her life was made miserable by a seemingly endless barrage of threats, insults, and indignities from her live-in adult son.
>
> A habitual gambler and drug user, the son was merciless: he spat at Mary, brandished a knife in her face, stole her money, and sold her possessions. After several emergency room trips and two hospitalizations, social workers convinced Mary to move out and join a support group of other elderly people abused by their loved ones. With a new apartment and understanding friends, Mary finally had some peace. But her son found her, and feeling a mother's guilt and shame, Mary took him back—and opened another round of heartache. (Minaker & Frishman, 1995, p. 9)

It would be easy to assume that such cases are rare. The truth of the matter, however, is that they are considerably more common than we would like to believe. According to some estimates, the incidence of **elder abuse**, the physical or psychological mistreatment or neglect of elderly individuals, may affect as many as 2 million people above the age of 60 each year. Even these estimates might be too low, for people who are abused are often too embarrassed or humiliated to report their plight. And as the number of elderly people increases, experts believe that the number of cases of elder abuse will also rise (Brubaker, 1991).

Elder abuse is most frequently directed at family members and particularly toward elderly parents. Those most at risk are likely to be less healthy and more isolated than the average person in late adulthood, and they are more likely to be living within a caregiver's home. Although there is no single cause for elder abuse, it often is the result of a combination of economic, psychological, and social pressures on caregivers who must provide high levels of care, 24 hours a day. Thus, people with Alzheimer's disease or other sorts of dementia are particularly likely to be targets of abuse (Pillemer & Suitor, 1988; Williams & Griffen, 1991).

The best way to deal with elder abuse is to prevent it from occurring in the first place. Family members caring for an older adult should take occasional breaks. Social support agencies can be contacted; they can provide advice and concrete support. For instance, the National Family Caregivers Association (800-896-3650) maintains a caregivers' network and publishes a newsletter. Furthermore, anyone suspecting that an elderly person is being abused should contact authorities in the local or state adult protective services.

---

elder abuse   *the physical or psychological mistreatment or neglect of elderly individuals*

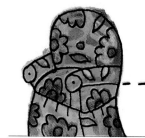

Review and Rethink

REVIEW

- Although marriages in older adulthood are generally happy, stresses due to aging can bring divorce. Women may divorce an alcoholic or abusive husband, whereas men often divorce to pursue a younger woman. Divorce is usually harder on women than on men because of the marriage gradient and societal attitudes.

- Life events can trigger a redefinition of the marital relationship. Retirement often causes a reworking of power relationships within the marriage, while the need to care for an ailing spouse can be a test of love and devotion.

- The death of a spouse brings highly significant psychological, social, and material changes to the life of the survivor. People may pass through the stages of preparation, grief and mourning, and adaptation in dealing with such a death.

- Friendships are very important in later life, especially for the social support they bring from people who may be going through some of the same life changes and experiences. The notion of reciprocity in such relationships is crucial.

- Family relationships are a continuing part of most older people's lives, especially relationships with siblings and children. Relationships with extended family members, including grandchildren and great-grandchildren, are also important but to a lesser extent, and they are often influenced by culture.

RETHINK

- What are some factors that can combine to make older adulthood a more difficult time for women than for men?

- Why might people who experienced as children the divorce of their parents be likely to die younger than those who had no such experience?

- What are some ways in which the retirement of a spouse can bring stress to a marriage? Is retirement less stressful in households where both spouses work, or twice as stressful?

- Do you think there are cultural differences in the experience of widowhood? If so, what sorts of differences?

- Why are their children so important to older people, and why is the relationship between older parents and children asymmetrical?

LOOKING BACK

In what ways does personality develop during late adulthood?

1. Some fundamental aspects of personality remain relatively stable throughout the life span, but others change in response to changes in people's social environments as they age.

2. Erik Erikson calls the last stage of psychosocial development the ego-integrity-versus-despair stage. As people reflect on their lives, they can either feel satisfaction, which leads to integration, or dissatisfaction, which can lead to despair and a lack of integration.

3. Robert Peck divides the period of late adulthood into three main tasks: redefinition of self versus preoccupation with work-role, body transcendence versus body preoccupation, and ego transcendence versus ego preoccupation.

4. Daniel Levinson regards people as passing through a transitional stage on the way to late adulthood, during which they struggle with the notion of being "old" and with societal stereotypes about aging. If they make the transition successfully, they can achieve liberation and self-respect.

5. Life review is a common theme of developmental theories of late adulthood. Life review can help people resolve past conflicts and problems and enjoy a sense of wisdom and serenity. On the other hand, some people become obsessive about past errors and slights that cannot be undone, and their obsession can lead to difficulties.

How do people deal with aging?

6. Two contrasting theories—disengagement theory and activity theory—present opposite ends of a spectrum of methods to deal successfully with aging. The way people deal with aging depends partly on their prior habits and personalities.

7. The model of selective optimization with compensation can be most effective for dealing with aging. It involves focusing on a limited number of personally important areas of functioning, and actively compensating for ability losses induced by aging.

In what circumstances do older people live, and what difficulties do they face?

8. Many living arrangements are available for elderly people, depending on their preferences and physical abilities. Arrangements include staying at home, living with family members, participating in adult day-care, residing in life-care communities, and living in skilled-nursing facilities.

9. Although most elderly people continue the general financial condition they experienced earlier in life, certain factors in old age make them financially vulnerable. These factors include a generally longer life span, a fixed income, and rising health care costs. The financial condition of an elderly person is also related to gender and race.

10. In general, Western societies do not hold elderly people in as high esteem as do many Asian societies. Societies with a high regard for older people tend to be those with a high degree of social homogeneity, extended families, responsible roles for older people, and control of resources by older people.

Is retirement generally a period of enjoyment or difficulty?

11. The circumstances of retirement—whether it was somewhat forced or entirely voluntary; whether it was from a job one loved or hated—partly determine the satisfaction a retired person will experience. People who retire must fill an increasingly longer span of leisure time. Those who are most successful plan ahead and have varied interests, often including worthwhile volunteer work.

12. People who retire often pass through stages, including a honeymoon period, disenchantment, reorientation, a retirement routine stage, and termination. Although the psychological effects of retirement differ from one person to the next, many retirees experience deep satisfaction.

What is the state of marriage in late adulthood, and what changes typically occur in the marital relationship?

13. Marriages in later life generally remain happy, although stresses brought about by major life changes that accompany aging can cause rifts and lead to divorce.

14. Divorce in later life is usually harder on the woman than on the man, partly because of the continuing influence of the marriage gradient. Women who leave their husbands often do so because the husband is abusive or alcoholic. In the far more common case of a man leaving his wife, the reason is often the pursuit of a younger woman.

15. The retirement of a spouse can lead to significant changes in the marital relationship, including a decrease in gender stereotyping of home roles and chores, and a redefinition of power structures within the relationship. The result can be stressful or beneficial.

16. Deterioration in the health of a spouse can lead an older person to assume the role of caregiver. Although the experience can be disturbing and difficult, many people report feelings of satisfaction with their new role. Because of demographic factors and societal attitudes and expectations, more women than men find themselves caring for aging spouses.

What do older people go through when a spouse dies?

17. The death of a spouse forces several difficult changes on the widowed partner, including assumption of a new societal role, accommodation to the absence of a companion and chore-sharer, creation of a new social life, and resolution of financial problems. Again, it is women more than men who must face these changes.

18. Sociologists Gloria Heinemann and Patricia Evans have identified three stages in the process of adjusting to widowhood: preparation, grief and mourning, and adaptation. Some people never reach the adaptation stage.

What sorts of relationships are important in late adulthood?

19. Friendships continue to be important in later life because they represent an area of control and flexibility, offer companionship, and provide an important means of social support from peers who may have similar problems and experiences. Reciprocity is often an important element of satisfying friendships.

20. Family relationships provide a great deal of emotional support for people in later life. Siblings, with whom the older person has a long history, and children are particularly important. Grandchildren may also be important, but this is less typical, and relations with great-grandchildren are even less likely to be close.

KEY TERMS AND CONCEPTS

ego-integrity-versus-despair stage (p. 612)
redefinition of self versus preoccupation with work-role (p. 612)
body transcendence versus body preoccupation (p. 612)
ego transcendence versus ego preoccupation (p. 612)
life review (p. 613)
disengagement theory (p. 614)

activity theory (p. 615)
selective optimization (p. 618)
life-care community (p. 621)
adult day-care facilities (p. 622)
skilled-nursing facilities (p. 622)
institutionalism (p. 622)
social support (p. 635)
elder abuse (p. 638)

Endings

CHAPTER 19

ENDINGS

Death and Dying

CHAPTER OUTLINE

PROLOGUE: CHOOSING DEATH

Domenic Ponzo's wife was able to say good-bye to her husband just moments before he died.

Domenic Ponzo's final journey began at 3 A.M. one day last May, when he awakened at his East Boston home with a sharp pain in his side. His visit to the local health clinic turned up a serious gallbladder problem, and soon after Ponzo found himself in one of the 12 private rooms at the Medical Intensive Care Unit (MICU) at Boston's Beth Israel Hospital. His gangrenous gallbladder had been removed, his kidneys had completely collapsed, his lungs were laboring to inflate on their own, his heart was weakened by a coronary during or soon after the gallbladder surgery.

It all happened with such numbing swiftness. Just 2 weeks after his predawn agony, Ponzo's medical options were dwindling. As his hope for life faded, replacing it was not the peaceful certainty of death but the terrifying unknown of dying. His body could not tolerate more surgery. Although poisonous wastes were building up in his system, dialysis had to be halted because it triggered his angina. He was slipping in and out of consciousness; soon his lungs would be no more able to gather in oxygen than a punctured balloon. . . .

The doctors explained that there were no reasonable medical options. A ventilator to breathe for him, drugs to support his blood pressure, electric shocks to jump-start his sputtering heart might keep him alive for another week or so. But to what end? The best course, they said, was to keep him comfortable and permit him a peaceful, dignified death. . . .

Early the next morning, the cloud seemed to lift from Ponzo's mind, and for a brief few moments he saw his wife, and perhaps his end, with a calm lucidity. They exchanged a final "I love you." "I just held him in my arms," Mrs. Ponzo said. "I took off his [oxygen] mask—he didn't need it any more—and held him and held him until his final breath." (Begley, 1991, p. 43)

LOOKING AHEAD

If ever death can be said to be good, this was a good death. After 69 years, Domenic Ponzo slipped away in the arms of someone he loved.

Death is an experience that will befall all of us at some time, as universal to the human condition as birth. As such, it represents a milestone of life that is central to an understanding of the life span. In fact, death is omnipresent throughout every period of life, a possibility from the moment following conception, in infancy and childhood, and throughout adulthood, increasingly likely the longer we live.

Despite the ubiquity of death and dying, however, the study of the topic is a relative newcomer to the domain of developmentalists. Only in the past several decades has serious study been given to the developmental implications of dying.

In this chapter we discuss death and dying from several perspectives. We begin by considering how we define death—an exercise that is trickier than it seems. We then examine how people view and react to death at different points in the life span, beginning in infancy and continuing through late adulthood. And we consider the very different views of death held by various societies.

Next, we look at how people confront their own death. We discuss the stages people seem to move through as they come to grips with their approaching demise. We also look at how people seek to control their own death through the use of living wills and assisted suicide.

Finally, we consider reactions to bereavement (the fact that one has experienced a loss) and grief (the emotional response to a death). We examine the difficulties in distinguishing normal from unhealthy grief, and we discuss the consequences of a loss. The chapter also looks at mourning and funerals, discussing how people can prepare themselves for the inevitability of death.

In short, after reading this chapter, you'll be able to answer the following questions:

- What is death, and how does its meaning change throughout the life span and across cultures?

- In what ways do people face the prospect of their own imminent death?

- How can people exert some measure of control over their own process of dying?

- What are grief and bereavement, and how do people work through them?

- How can individuals be helped to prepare for and cope with death?

DYING AND DEATH ACROSS THE LIFE SPAN

Karen Ann Quinlan's parents faced significant ethical issues in their determination to remove her from a respirator after she was in a coma.

It took them close to a year to do it, but eventually Karen Ann Quinlan's parents won the right to remove her from a respirator. Lying in a hospital bed in New Jersey in what physicians call a "persistent vegetative state," Quinlan was never expected to regain consciousness following an automobile accident. After the state Supreme Court allowed her parents to have the respirator removed, Quinlan lived on in a coma for close to a decade until she died.

Were Quinlan's parents right in asking for the removal of her respirator? Was she already dead when it was turned off? Were her constitutional rights unfairly ignored by her parents' action?

The difficulty of answering such questions illustrates the complexity of what are, literally, matters of life and death. Death is not only a biological event; it also involves psychological aspects. We need to consider not only issues relating to the definition of death, but also the ways in which our conception of death changes across various points in the life span.

DEFINING DEATH: DETERMINING THE POINT AT WHICH LIFE ENDS

What is death? Although the question seems straightforward, defining the point at which life ceases and death occurs is surprisingly complex. In fact, medicine over the last few decades has advanced to the point where some people who would have been considered dead in the past would now be considered alive.

Functional death is defined by an absence of heartbeat and breathing. Although this definition seems unambiguous, it is not completely straightforward. For example, a person whose heart has stopped beating and whose breathing has ceased for as long as 5 minutes may be resuscitated and suffer little damage as a consequence of the experience. Does this mean that the person who is now alive was dead, as the functional definition would have it?

Because of the ambiguities involved in using heartbeat and respiration to determine the moment of death, medical experts have turned to a measure of brain functioning. In **brain death**, all signs of brain activity, as measured by electrical brain waves, have ceased. When brain death occurs, there is no possibility of restoring brain functioning.

On the other hand, some medical experts suggest that a definition of death that relies solely on a lack of brain waves is inappropriate. Instead, they argue that a lack of the qualities that make people human—the ability to think, reason, feel, and experience the world—may be sufficient to declare a person dead. In this view, which takes psychological considerations into account, a person who suffers irreversible brain damage, who is in a coma, and who will never experience anything approaching a human life can be considered dead. In such a case, the argument goes, death can be judged to have arrived, even if some sort of primitive brain activity is still occurring (Veatch, 1984).

functional death   the absence of a heartbeat and breathing

brain death   a diagnosis of death based on the cessation of all signs of brain activity, as measured by electrical brain waves

Not surprisingly, such an argument, which moves us from strictly medical criteria to moral and philosophical considerations, is controversial. As a result, the legal definition of death in most localities in the United States relies on the absence of brain functioning. However, some localities still employ a definition relating to the absence of respiration and heartbeat, and the reality is that, no matter where a death occurs, in most cases people do not bother to measure brain waves. Usually, the brain waves are closely monitored only in certain circumstances—when the time of death is significant, when organs may potentially be transplanted, or when criminal or legal issues might be involved.

DEATH ACROSS THE LIFE SPAN: CAUSES AND REACTIONS

Death is something we associate with old age. However, for many individuals, death comes earlier. In such cases, in part because it seems "unnatural" for a younger person to die, the reactions are particularly extreme. Let us consider several age groups.

Death in Infancy and Childhood.   Despite its economic wealth, the United States has a relatively high infant mortality rate, as we first discussed in Chapter 3. Although the rate has declined since the mid-1960s, the United States ranks behind 22 other industrialized countries in the proportion of infants who die during the first year of life (Wegman, 1993; National Center for Health Statistics, 1993b).

As these statistics indicate, the number of parents who experience the death of an infant is substantial, and their reactions may be profound. They typically experience the same reactions they would following the death of an older person, and sometimes even more severe effects as they struggle to deal with a death at such an early age. One of the most common reactions is extreme depression (DeFrain et al., 1991; Brockington, 1992).

Another kind of death that is exceptionally difficult to deal with is prenatal death, or *miscarriage*. Parents typically form psychological bonds with their unborn child, and consequently they often feel profound grief if it dies before it is born. Moreover, many times friends and relatives do not attribute as much meaning to miscarriage as do the parents, isolating the parents and making them feel their loss all the more more keenly.

Another form of death that produces extreme stress, in part because it is so unanticipated, is sudden infant death syndrome. In **sudden infant death syndrome**, or **SIDS**, a seemingly healthy baby stops breathing and dies of unexplained causes. Usually occurring between the ages of 2 and 4 months, SIDS strikes unexpectedly; a robust, hardy baby is placed into a crib at nap time or at night and never wakes up.

Afterwards, parents often feel intense guilt, and acquaintances may be suspicious of the "true" cause of death. There is no known cause for SIDS, which seems to strike randomly (Downey, Silver, & Wortman, 1990).

During childhood, the most frequent cause of death is accidents, most of them due to motor vehicle crashes, fires, and drowning. However, a substantial number of children in the United States are victims of homicides, which have nearly tripled in number since 1960. By the early 1990s, death by homicide had become the fourth leading cause of death for children between the ages of 1 and 9 (National Center for Health Statistics, 1994).

About the age of 5, children begin to develop a concept of death. Although they are well aware of death before that time, it usually is thought of as a temporary state involving a *reduction* in living, rather than a *cessation*. For instance, a preschool-age child might say, "Dead people don't get hungry—well, maybe a little" (Kastenbaum, 1985, p. 629).

Some preschoolers think of death in terms of sleep—with the consequent possibility of waking up, just as Sleeping Beauty was awakened in the fairy tale. For children who believe this, death is not particularly fearsome; rather, it is something of a curiosity. If people merely tried hard enough—by administering medicine, providing food, or using magic—dead people might "return" (Bluebond-Langner, 1977; Lonetto, 1980).

In some cases, children's misunderstanding of death can produce devastating emotional consequences. Children sometimes leap to the erroneous conclusion that they are

sudden infant death syndrome (SIDS) *the unexplained death of a seemingly healthy baby*

Adolescents' views of death may be highly romantic and dramatic.

somehow responsible for a person's death. In some cases, for instance, they assume they could have prevented the death by being better behaved. In the same way, they may believe that if the person who died really wanted to, he or she could return.

Past the age of 5, the finality and irreversibility of death become better understood. In some cases, children personify death as some kind of ghostlike or devilish figure. At first, though, they do not think of death as universal, but rather as something that happens only to certain people. By about age 9, however, they come to accept the universality of death and its finality (Nagy, 1948). By middle childhood, children also learn about some of the customs involved with death, such as funerals, cremation, and cemeteries.

For parents, the death of a child produces the most profound sense of loss and grief. In fact, there is no worse death in the eyes of most parents, including the loss of a spouse or of parents. Parents' extreme reaction is partly based on the sense that the natural order of the world, in which children "should" outlive their parents, has somehow collapsed. Furthermore, parents feel that it is their primary responsibility to protect their children from any harm, and they may feel that they have failed in this task when a child dies.

Parents are almost never well equipped to deal with the death of a child, and they may obsessively ask themselves afterward, over and over, why the death occurred. Because the bond between children and parents is so strong, parents sometimes feel that a part of themselves has died as well (Sanders, 1988; Stroebe, Stroebe, & Hansson, 1993).

Death in Adolescence.   We might expect the significant advances in cognitive development that occur during adolescence to bring about a sophisticated, thoughtful, and reasoned view of death. However, in many ways, adolescents' views of death are as unrealistic as those of younger children, although along different lines.

Although adolescents clearly understand the finality and irreversibility of death, their view often tends to be highly romantic. As we discussed in Chapter 11, adolescents develop a *personal fable*, a set of beliefs that causes them to feel unique and special. Such thinking can lead to quite risky behavior, as personal fables induce a sense of invulnerability (Pattison, 1977; Elkind, 1985).

Many times, this risky behavior causes death in adolescence. For instance, the most frequent cause of death among adolescents is accidents, most often involving motor vehicles. Other frequent causes include homicide, suicide, cancer, and AIDS (National Center for Health Statistics, 1994).

When adolescent feelings of invulnerability confront the likelihood of death due to an illness, the results can be shattering. Adolescents who learn that they have a terminal illness often feel angry and cheated—that life has been unjust to them. Because they feel—and act—so negatively, it may be difficult for medical personnel to treat them effectively.

In contrast, some adolescents diagnosed with a terminal illness react with total denial. Feeling indestructible, they may find it impossible to accept the seriousness of their illness. If it does not interfere with their acceptance of medical treatment, some degree of denial may actually be useful, as it allows an adolescent to continue with his or her normal life as long as possible (Blumberg, Lewis, & Susman, 1984).

Death in Young Adulthood.   Young adulthood is the time when most people feel primed to begin their lives. Past the preparatory time of childhood and adolescence, they are on the threshold of making their mark on the world. Because death at such a point in life seems close to unthinkable, its occurrence is particularly difficult. Because they are actively pursuing their goals for life, they are angry and impatient with any illness that threatens their future.

In early adulthood, the leading cause of death continues to be accidents, followed by suicide, homicide, AIDS, and cancer. By the end of early adulthood, however, disease becomes a more prevalent cause of death.

For those people facing death in early adulthood, several concerns are of particular importance (A.S. Cook & Oltjenbruns, 1989). One is the desire to develop intimate relationships and express sexuality, each of which is inhibited, if not completely prevented, by a terminal illness. For instance, people who test positive for the AIDS virus may find it quite difficult to start new relationships. The role of sexual activities within evolving relationships presents even more challenging issues (Rabkin, Remien, & Wilson, 1994).

Another particular concern during young adulthood involves future planning. At a time when most people are mapping out their careers and deciding at what point to start a family, young adults who have a terminal illness face additional burdens. Should they marry, even though it is likely that the partner will soon end up widowed? Should a couple seek to conceive a child if it is clear that the child is likely to be raised by only one parent? How soon should one's employer be told about a terminal illness, when it is clear that employers sometimes discriminate against unhealthy workers? None of these questions are easily answered.

Like adolescents, young adults sometimes make poor patients. They are outraged at their plight and feel the world is unfair, and they may direct their anger at care providers and loved ones. In addition, they may make the medical staff who provide direct care—nurses and orderlies—feel particularly vulnerable, since the staff themselves are often young (Kastenbaum, 1977; A.S. Cook & Oltjenbruns, 1989).

Death in Middle Adulthood.   For people in middle adulthood, the shock of a life-threatening disease—which is the most common cause of death in this period—is not so great. In fact, by this point, people are well aware of the fact that they are going to die sometime, and they may be able to consider the possibility of death in a fairly realistic manner.

On the other hand, their sense of realism does not make the possibility of dying any easier. In fact, fears about death are often greater in middle adulthood than at any time previously—or even in later life. These fears may lead people to look at life in terms of the number of years they have remaining, as opposed to their earlier orientation toward the number of years they have already lived (Kalish & Reynolds, 1976; Neugarten, 1967; Levinson, 1990).

The most frequent cause of death in middle adulthood is heart attack or stroke. Although the unexpectedness of such a death does not allow for preparation, in some ways it is easier than a slow, protracted, and painful death from a disease such as cancer. It is certainly the kind of death that most people prefer: When asked, they say they would like an instant and painless death that does not involve loss of any body part (Taylor, 1991).

Death in Late Adulthood.   By the time they reach late adulthood, people know with some certainty that their time is coming to an end. They think about death, they typically begin to make preparations for their demise, and they may have already begun to pull away from the world owing to diminishing physical and psychological energy (Cummings & Henry, 1961). Furthermore, they face an increasing number of losses in their environment. Spouses, siblings, and friends may have already died, a constant reminder of their own mortality.

The prevalence of death in the lives of elderly people makes them less anxious about dying than they were at earlier stages of life. This does not mean that people in late adulthood welcome death. Rather, it implies that they are more realistic and reflective about it (Gesser, Wong, & Reker, 1988; Turner & Helms, 1994).

Some elderly individuals actively seek out death, turning to suicide. In fact, the suicide rate for men climbs steadily during the course of late adulthood, and no age group has a higher rate of suicide than Caucasian men over the age of 85. (Adolescents and young adults commit suicide in greater numbers, but their *rate* of suicide is actually lower.) Suicide is often a consequence of severe depression or some form of dementia or can be due to the loss of a spouse. And, as we'll discuss later in the chapter, some individuals, struck down with a terminal illness, seek the assistance of others in committing suicide (Blazer, 1991).

One particularly salient issue for older adults suffering from a terminal illness is whether their lives still have value. More than younger individuals suffering from terminal illnesses, elderly people who are dying harbor concerns that they are burdens to their family or to society. Furthermore, they may be given the message, sometimes inadvertently, that their value to society has ended and that they have attained the status of "dying" as opposed to being "very sick" (Kastenbaum, 1985).

Do older people wish to know if death is impending? The answer, in most cases, is yes. Like younger patients, who usually state that they wish to know the true nature of an ailment, older people want the details of their illnesses (Blumenfield, Levy, & Kaplan, 1979; S.M. Miller & Mangan, 1983). Ironically, candor is not something caregivers wish to provide: Physicians usually prefer to avoid telling dying patients that their illnesses are terminal (Feifel, 1963).

Conversely, not all people wish to learn the truth about their condition or to know that they are dying. In fact, it is important to keep in mind that individuals react to death in substantially different ways. In part, their reaction is produced by personality factors. For example, a person's general level of anxiety and sense of how quickly time passes have been linked to concerns about death (Kastenbaum, 1985). In addition, there are significant cultural differences in how people view, and react to, death, as we consider next.

Developmental Diversity

Differing Conceptions of Death

In the midst of a tribal celebration, an older man waits for his oldest son to place a cord around his neck and lift him to his death. The son complies with the request.

In India, Hindus do not see death as an ending, but rather as part of a continual cycle. Because they believe in reincarnation, death is thought to be followed by rebirth into a new life. Death, then, is seen as a companion to life.

People's responses to death take many forms, particularly in different cultures. But even within Western societies, reactions to death and dying are quite diverse. For instance, consider which is better: for a man to die after a full life, in which he has raised a family and been successful in his job, or for a courageous and valiant young soldier to die defending his country in wartime. Has one person died a better death than the other?

The answer depends on one's values, which are largely attributable to cultural and subcultural teachings. For instance, some societies view death as a punishment or as a judgment about one's contributions to the world. Others see death as redemption from an earthly life of travail. Still others view death as the start of an eternal life, while others believe that there is no heaven or hell and that an earthly life is all there is.

Given that religious teachings regarding the meaning of life and death are quite diverse, it is not surprising that views of death and dying vary substantially. For instance, one study found that Christian and Jewish 10-year-olds tended to view death from a more "scientific" vantage point than did Sunni Moslem and Druze children of the same age. We cannot be sure whether such differences are due to the different religious and cultural backgrounds of the children, or if differences in exposure to dying people influence the rate at which the understanding of death develops. However, it is clear that members of the

Differing conceptions of death lead to different rituals, as this ceremony on the Ganges River in India illustrates.

various groups had very different conceptions of death (Florian & Kravetz, 1985; Segall et al., 1990).

In addition, members of some cultures seem to learn about death at an earlier age than others. For instance, exposure to high levels of violence and death may lead to an awareness of death earlier in some cultures than in those in which violence is less a part of everyday life. Research shows that children in Northern Ireland and Israel understood the finality, irreversibility, and inevitability of death at an earlier age than do children in the United States and Britain (Smilansky, 1980; McWhirter, Young, & Majury, 1983).

Review and Rethink

REVIEW

◆ Definitions of the point at which death occurs have included the cessation of heartbeat and respiration (functional death), the absence of electrical brain waves (brain death), and the loss of qualities that make a person human.

◆ Death may happen at any point in the life span, with varying effects. The death of an infant or young child can be particularly difficult for parents, and for an adolescent death appears to be unthinkable.

◆ Death in young adulthood can appear unfair, and the issues faced by a terminally ill young adult are considerable. In middle adulthood, people have begun to appreciate the reality of death, a realization that can actually increase the fear of death.

◆ By the time they reach late adulthood, people know they will die and begin to make preparations. The key issue for older people who face death is whether their lives still have value.

◆ Cultural differences in attitudes and beliefs about death strongly influence people's reactions to it. It is possible that exposure to death can affect the age at which the reality of death is understood.

RETHINK

◆ What decision-making process regarding life support would you recommend to a parent faced with a child in a "persistent vegetative state"?

◆ Given their developmental level and understanding of death, how do you think preschool children react to the death of a parent?

◆ What aspects of their development make terminally ill young adults become concerned about marriage, childbearing, and work?

◆ Do you believe people who are going to die should be told? Does your response differ depending on age?

◆ In what ways do you think older people's sense of worth can be affected, negatively and positively, by family attitudes, caregiver actions, and other environmental influences?

> Helen Reynolds, 63, had undergone operations in January and April to repair and then replace a heart valve that was not permitting a smooth flow of blood. But by May her feet had turned the color of overripe eggplants, their mottled purple black an unmistakable sign of gangrene. . . . In June she chose to have first her right leg, and then her left, amputated in hopes of stabilizing her condition. The doctors were skeptical about the surgery, but deferred to her wishes. . . .
>
> Even when the April heart operation at Beth Israel forced her onto a ventilator, she never withdrew from what her life had become. She delighted in the MICU [intensive care] nurses doing her hair and makeup. When doctors turned down her television so they could talk during their morning rounds to her room, she gestured for it to be turned back up immediately after they left. In May she and her family celebrated her 63rd birthday, with balloons, flowers and a 2-foot-tall Happy Birthday From All of Us card, there on the ninth-floor MICU with its picture-window view of Boston's western suburbs. . . .
>
> But then Reynolds uncharacteristically began talking about her pain. On that Sunday afternoon in June, a nurse beckoned intern Dr. Randall Evans. Evans, a graduate of the University of New Mexico Medical School who planned a career in the critical-care field, was immensely popular with the nursing staff for his cordial and sympathetic manner. But, unlike the MICU nurses, he had difficulty reading Reynolds's lips (the ventilator made it impossible for her to speak aloud), and asked her to write down her request. Laboriously, she scrawled 16 words on the note pad: "I have decided to end my life as I do not want to live like this." (Begley, 1991, pp. 44–45)

Less than a week later, after the ventilator that helped her to breathe had been removed at her request, Helen Reynolds died.

Like other deaths, Reynolds's raises a myriad of difficult questions. Was her request to remove the respirator equivalent to suicide? Should the medical staff have complied with the request? Was she coping with her impending death effectively? How do people come to terms with death, and how do they react and adapt to it? Psychologists and other specialists in death and dying have struggled, with great difficulty, to find answers to such questions.

THE STAGES OF DEATH: UNDERSTANDING THE PROCESS OF DYING

No individual has had a greater influence on our understanding of the way in which people confront death than Elisabeth Kübler-Ross. A psychiatrist, Kübler-Ross developed a stage theory of death and dying, built on extensive interviews with people who were dying and with those who cared for them (Kübler-Ross, 1969, 1982).

Based on her observations, Kübler-Ross suggests that people pass through five basic stages (summarized in Figure 19-1):

Denial.   "No, I can't be dying! There must be some mistake."

It is typical for people to protest in such a manner on learning that they have a terminal disease. Such objections represent the first stage of dying, *denial*. In denial, people resist the idea that they are going to die. They may argue that their test results have been mixed up, that an X-ray has been read incorrectly, or that their physician doesn't know what he or she is talking about.

Denial comes in several forms. A patient may flatly reject the diagnosis, simply refusing to believe the news. In extreme cases, memories of weeks in the hospital are forgotten. In other forms of denial, patients fluctuate between refusing to accept the news and, at other times, confiding that they know they are going to die (Carroll, 1985).

FIGURE 19-1

THE STAGES OF DEATH

(*Source*: Kübler-Ross, 1975.)

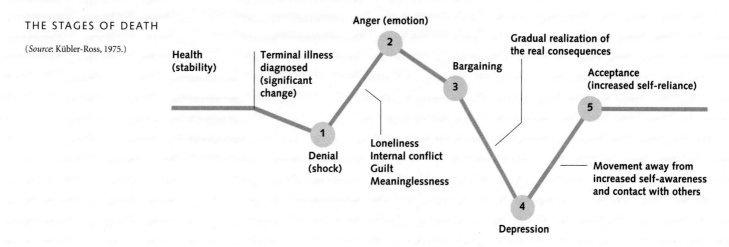

Although we might view the loss of reality implied by denial as a sign of deteriorating mental health, in fact many experts view denial in positive terms. Denial is a defense mechanism that can permit people to absorb the unwelcome news on their own terms, according to their own timetables. Only when they are able to recognize the news can they move on and eventually come to grips with the reality that they are truly going to die.

Anger.   After they move beyond denial, people typically pass into the next stage, *anger*. A dying person may be angry at everyone: people who are in good health, their spouses and other family members, their children, those who are caring for them. They may lash out at others, and wonder—sometimes aloud—why *they* are dying and not someone else. They may be furious at God, reasoning that they have led good lives and that there are far worse people in the world who should be dying.

It may not be easy to be around people in the anger stage. As they focus their anger on others, they may say and do things that are painful and sometimes unfathomable. Eventually, though, most patients move beyond the anger phase into the next stage—bargaining.

Bargaining.   "If you're good, you'll be rewarded." Most people learn this equation in their childhoods, and they typically revert to it after passing through the anger stage. In this case, "good" means promising to be a better person, and the "reward" is staying alive.

In the *bargaining* stage, dying people try to negotiate their way out of death. They may declare that they will dedicate their lives to the poor if God saves them. They may promise that if they can just live long enough to see a son married, they will willingly accept death later. They may say that if just one request is granted to them, they won't ask for a postponement of death any longer.

However, the promises that are part of the bargaining process are rarely kept. If one request appears to be granted, people typically seek another, and yet another. Furthermore, they may be unable to fulfill their promises because their illnesses keep progressing and prevent them from achieving what they said they would do.

In some ways, bargaining seems to have positive consequences. Although death cannot be postponed indefinitely, having a goal of attending a particular event or living until a certain time may in fact delay death until then. For instance, death rates of Jewish people decline just before the holiday of Passover, and rise just after it. Similarly, the death rate among older Chinese women falls before and during important holidays, and rises after. It is as if the people involved have negotiated to stay alive until after the holidays have passed (D. Phillips & Smith, 1990; D. Philips, 1992).

In the end, of course, all the bargaining in the world is unable to overcome the inevitability of death. When people realize that death is unavoidable, they move into the next stage, depression.

Depression.   Eventually, people proceed to the *depression* stage. Realizing that the issue is settled and they cannot bargain their way out of death, people are overwhelmed with a deep sense of loss. They know that they are losing their loved ones and that their lives really are coming to end.

The depression they experience may be of two types. In *reactive depression*, the feelings of sadness are based on events that have already occurred: the loss of dignity that may accompany medical procedures, the end of a job, or the knowledge that one will never return from the hospital to one's home.

On the other hand, dying people also experience preparatory depression. In *preparatory depression*, individuals feel sadness over future losses. They know that death will bring an end to their relationships with others, and that they will never see future generations. The reality of death is inescapable in this stage, and it brings about profound sadness over the unalterable conclusion of one's life.

Acceptance.   The final stage of dying is *acceptance*. In this last stage, people are fully aware that death is impending. Unemotional and uncommunicative, they have virtually no feelings—positive or negative—about the present or future. They have made peace with themselves, and they may wish to be left alone. For them, death holds no sting.

Evaluating Kübler-Ross's Stage Theory.   Kübler-Ross has had an enormous impact on the way we look at death. As one of the first people to observe systematically how people approach their own deaths, she is recognized as a pioneer.

On the other hand, her work has drawn criticism. For one thing, there are some obvious limitations to her conception of dying. It is largely limited to those who are aware that they are dying and who die in a relatively leisurely fashion. For people who suffer from diseases in which the prognosis is ambiguous as to when or even if they will die, her theory is not applicable.

More important, Kübler-Ross's stage theory must be evaluated against the standards of the other stage theories that we have discussed throughout this book. In particular, we must ask whether the stages are universal and occur in the same sequence for all individuals. The answer is no on both counts. Not every person passes through every stage on the way to death, and some people move through the stages in a different sequence. Some even go through the same stage several times (Schulz & Aderman, 1974). Depressed patients may show bursts of anger, and an angry patient may bargain for more time.

Furthermore, Kübler-Ross's enumeration of stages may be too restrictive. For example, other researchers suggest that anxiety plays an important role throughout the process of dying. The anxiety may be about one's upcoming demise, or it may relate to fear of the symptoms of the disease. A person with cancer, then, may fear death less than the uncontrollable pain that may be a future possibility (Hinton, 1967; Schulz & Aderman, 1974; Taylor, 1991).

Finally, there are substantial differences in people's reactions to impending death. The specific cause of dying, how long the process of dying lasts, a person's age, sex, and personality, and the social support available from family and friends all influence the course of dying and one's responses to it (Zautra, Reich, & Guarnaccia, 1990; Stroebe, Stroebe et al., 1993).

In short, there are significant concerns about the accuracy of Kübler-Ross's account of how people react to impending death. On the other hand, her contributions have been influential, particularly among those who provide direct care to the dying. Furthermore, Kübler-Ross was almost single-handedly responsible for bringing into public awareness the phenomenon of death, which previously had languished out of sight in Western societies. Consequently, she remains an important figure.

CHOOSING THE NATURE OF DEATH: IS DNR THE WAY TO GO?

The letters "DNR" written on a patient's medical chart have a simple and clear meaning. Standing for "Do not resuscitate," DNR signifies that, rather than administering any and every procedure that might possibly keep a patient alive, no extraordinary means are to be taken. For terminally ill patients, DNR may mean the difference between dying immediately or living additional days, months, or even years, kept alive only by the most extreme, invasive, and even painful medical procedures.

The decision to use or not to use extreme medical interventions entails several issues. One is the differentiation of "extreme" and "extraordinary" measures from those that are simply routine. There are no hard-and-fast rules, since in part the determination of what is "extreme" is dependent on the specific patient, his or her prior medical history, and factors such as age and even religion. For instance, different definitions might apply to a 12-year-old patient and an 85-year-old patient with the same medical condition.

Other questions concern quality of life. How can we determine an individual's current quality of life and whether it will be improved or diminished by a particular medical intervention? Who makes such decisions—the patient, a family member, or medical personnel?

One thing is clear: Medical personnel are reluctant to carry out the wishes of the terminally ill and their families to suspend aggressive treatment. Even when it is certain that a patient is going to die, and patients determine that they do not wish further treatment, physicians often claim to be unaware of their patients' wishes. Furthermore, even when they are told, physicians frequently do not enter a "Do not resuscitate" order on a patient's medical chart. For instance, one survey of dying patients found that although a third of the patients asked not to be resuscitated, only 47 percent of their physicians stated that they knew of their patients' preference (see Table 19-1). In addition, only 49 percent of patients had their wishes entered on their medical charts (Knaus et al., 1995).

Living Wills.   To gain more control over decisions regarding the nature of their death, people are increasingly signing **living wills**, i.e., legal documents that designate the medical treatments they want or do not want if they cannot express their wishes (see Figure 19-2).

living wills *legal documents designating what medical treatments people want or do not want if they cannot express their wishes*

TABLE 19-1

DYING HARD: EXPERIENCES OF 4,301 PATIENTS WITH END-OF-LIFE CARE

Percentage of terminal patients who did not want resuscitation	31%
Of those patients who did not want resuscitation, percentage whose physicians were aware of their preference	47%
Of those patients who did not want resuscitation, percentage whose preferences were entered on their charts	49%

(*Source:* Knaus et al., 1995.)

euthanasia   *the practice of assisting people who are terminally ill to die more quickly*

Some living wills designate a specific person, called a *health-care proxy*, to act as an individual's representative in making health-care decisions. Wills might cover all medical care problems or only terminal illnesses. In such cases, nonterminal problems, such as coma, would not be addressed.

Assisted Suicide.   Dr. Jack Kevorkian became well known—and well prosecuted—in the early 1990s for his invention and promotion of a "suicide machine," in which a terminal patient can push a button that releases anesthesia and a drug that stops the heart. Because Kevorkian did not administer the drug himself, the process is known as *assisted suicide*, a death in which a person provides the means for a terminally ill individual to commit suicide.

Although Kevorkian was first charged with murder, the initial cases were dismissed. However, the State of Michigan, where the assisted suicides took place, passed a law prohibiting the practice, and new charges were lodged against Kevorkian when he continued to aid people in their deaths.

In other countries, assisted suicide is an accepted practice. For instance, although The Netherlands has laws that prohibit any person from assisting in the suicide of another, it is an acceptable practice for medical personnel to help end their dying patients' lives. However, several conditions must be met to make the practice permissible: At least two physicians must determine that the patient is terminally ill, there must be unbearable physical or mental suffering, the patient must give informed consent in writing, and relatives must be informed beforehand (Gomez, 1991; Simons, 1995).

Assisted suicide is one form of **euthanasia**, the practice of assisting terminally ill people to die more quickly. Popularly known as "mercy killing," euthanasia involves either actively hastening death or withholding treatment that might be expected to postpone death.

Euthanasia is a highly controversial practice, in part because it centers on decisions about who should control life. Does the right belong solely to an individual, a person's physicians, his or her dependents, the government, or some deity? Because, at least in the United States, we assume that everyone has the absolute right to create lives by bringing children into the world, some people argue that we should also have the absolute right to end our own lives. Such arguments make discussions of euthanasia highly emotional (Solomon, 1995).

Dr. Jack Kevorkian assisted in the suicides of more than a dozen individuals.

FIGURE 19-2

A LIVING WILL

MY LIVING WILL

TO MY FAMILY, MY PHYSICIAN, MY LAWYER AND ALL OTHERS WHOM IT MAY CONCERN

Death is as much a reality as birth, growth, maturity and old age–it is the one certainty of life. If the time comes when I can no longer take part in decisions for my own future, let this statement stand as an expression of my wishes and directions, while I am still of sound mind.

If at such a time the situation should arise in which there is no reasonable expectation of my recovery from extreme physical or mental disability, I direct that I be allowed to die and not be kept alive by medications, artificial means or "heroic measures". I do, however, ask that medication be mercifully administered to me to alleviate suffering even though this may shorten my remaining life.

This statement is made after careful consideration and is in accordance with my strong convictions and beliefs. I want the wishes and directions here expressed carried out to the extent permitted by law. Insofar as they are not legally enforceable, I hope that those to whom this Will is addressed will regard themselves as morally bound by these provisions.

Optional specific provisions to be made in this space.

DURABLE POWER OF ATTORNEY (optional)

I hereby designate _____ to serve as my attorney-in-fact for the purpose of making medical treatment decisions. This power of attorney shall remain effective in the event that I become incompetent or otherwise unable to make such decisions for myself. Optional Notarization:

"Sworn and subscribed to before me this
_____ day of _____ , 19 ___ ."

_____
Notary Public
(seal)

Signed _____
Date _____
Witness _____
Address _____
Witness _____
Address _____

Copies of this request have been given to _____
_____

(Optional)   My Living Will is registered with Concern for Dying (No. _____)

home care   *an alternative to hospitalization in which dying people stay in their homes and receive treatment from their families and visiting medical staff*

CARING FOR THE TERMINALLY ILL: THE PLACE OF DEATH

Although most people in the United States die in hospitals, it does not have to be that way. In fact, there are several reasons why hospitals are among the least desirable locales in which to face death. Hospitals are typically impersonal, with staff rotating throughout the day. Because visiting hours are limited, people frequently die alone, without the comfort of loved ones at the bedside. Furthermore, hospitals are designed to make people better, not to deal with the dying, and it is extraordinarily expensive to provide custodial care for dying people. In addition, and perhaps more importantly, hospitals typically do not have the resources required to deal adequately with the emotional requirements of terminal cases.

As a consequence, several alternatives to hospitalization have become increasingly popular in the last few decades. In **home care**, dying people stay in their homes and receive treatment from their families and visiting medical staff. Many dying patients prefer home care,

Speaking of Development

Robert P. Picard, R.N.

Born: ·································· 1942

Education: ····················· Community College of Rhode Island, Warwick, A.S. in science and nursing

Position: ······················· Director of nurses and hospice services, Visiting Nurse Service of Greater Woonsocket

Home: ·························· Woonsocket, Rhode Island

From the age of 17, when he became a hospital corpsman in the U.S. Navy, Robert P. Picard has been involved in the more intense side of medicine. He worked in emergency medicine, in life-support systems, and as a surgical technician before moving into home care in 1988.

Even now his focus is on what many would consider an intense side of life: its end. Picard has spent a number of years with the Visiting Nurse Service of Greater Woonsocket, first as manager of its hospice program, and now as director of nurses and hospice services.

"Hospice deals not only with patients who are dying, but with their families as well," he says. "Before gaining admission to hospice, the patient and the family members have made a decision that the patient will be the recipient of no extraordinary act that is curative in nature. They arrive at this decision after two physicians have given a terminal diagnosis and have confirmed that the patient understands that the disease is terminal."

Once admitted to the hospice, the patient is assigned a team that includes a nurse, a social worker, a psychiatric nurse, a member of the clergy, a physician, and volunteers.

"The approach we take is different for each individual, due to the culture of the patient, the family dynamics surrounding the patient, and the patient's understanding of or need for relief of symptoms, as opposed to measures designed to seek a cure.

"When it comes to the family, every case has to be different," he adds. "Some families are disorganized, and some are very close. The nature of the family affects the patient significantly."

Ever since AIDS emerged as a major terminal illness, Picard has noticed great differences in the ways AIDS patients deal with death, as compared with patients who have cancer.

because they can spend their final days in a familiar environment, with people they love and a lifetime accumulation of treasures around them (Brescia, Sadof, & Barstow, 1984).

Although the dying may prefer home care, it can be quite difficult for family members. Untrained in nursing, they may provide less than optimal medical care. Furthermore, it is extraordinarily draining, both physically and emotionally, to be on call 24 hours a day. On the other hand, furnishing final care can offer family members a good deal of emotional solace because they are giving something precious to people they love.

Another alternative to hospitalization that is becoming increasingly prevalent is **hospice care**, or care for the dying provided in institutions devoted to the dying. In the Middle Ages, hospices were facilities that provided comfort and hospitality to travelers. Drawing on that concept, today's hospices are designed to provide a warm, supportive environment for the dying. They do not focus on extending people's lives, but rather on

hospice care   *care provided for the dying in institutions devoted to those who are terminally ill*

"Hospice deals not only with patients who are dying, but with their families as well."

"Patients who are told, as cancer patients are, that based on the best medical knowledge, they will die in 6 to 9 months, regardless of medical intervention, seem to accept the fact more readily," Picard says. "What you hear from the cancer patients is how long it's going to be before they die. We want them to have hope, but we also know that there are some cancers that, no matter how aggressively we treat them, will not be cured.

"It is different with AIDS patients, who are generally between the ages of 20 and 45. With AIDS, we don't have any firm figures on when our patients are going to die, and there is no drug to cure them. Understandably, AIDS patients—mostly younger than cancer patients and hopeful that a cure may be found at any moment—want every medical intervention up to the last minute.

"AIDS patients tend to be more informed than other patients. They do research, they read, they study experimental drugs, and they insist on treatment after treatment," he adds.

One dominating factor that determines how a patient is attended in the hospice is the individual life development of each patient, according to Picard. "You have to respect where the person is coming from, the personal background. You let your patients be themselves.

"Some people are raised to expect that they will have suffering and pain, while others focus on pain avoidance to the extent of overcompensation. But we're not judgmental. We feel that the patient is the only one who knows what the pain level is. My subjective pain, my pain threshold, is different from yours.

"Ultimately the hospice provides a place to die with dignity. The only person who can define that dignity is the patient," Picard says.

"Ultimately the hospice provides a place to die with dignity. The only person who can define that dignity is the patient."

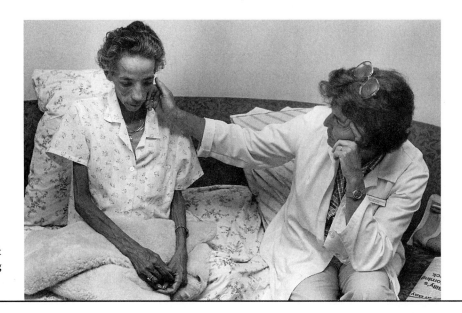

This 39-year-old cancer patient is dying at home, cared for by her family and visiting medical staff.

making their final days pleasant and meaningful. Typically, people who go to hospices are removed from treatments that are painful, and no extraordinary or invasive means are employed to make their lives longer. The emphasis is on making patients' lives as full as possible, not on squeezing out every possible moment of life at any cost (McCracken & Gerdsen, 1991).

Although the research is far from conclusive, hospice patients appear to be more satisfied with the care they receive than are those who receive treatment in more traditional settings (Kane et al., 1984). Hospice care provides a clear alternative to traditional hospitalization for the terminally ill. (For more on hospice care, see the accompanying Speaking of Development feature.)

Review and Rethink

REVIEW

- Elisabeth Kübler-Ross has identified five stages of dying: denial, anger, bargaining, depression, and acceptance.

- Although Kübler-Ross's theory has been criticized as lacking universal applicability, she is respected for having brought the process of dying into the daylight and she remains very influential.

- Issues surrounding dying are highly controversial, including the measures that physicians should apply to keep dying patients alive and who should make the decision. Living wills are a way for people to take some control over the decision.

- Assisted suicide and, more generally, euthanasia are not permitted in the United States, although many people believe they should be, with appropriate safeguards and sign-offs.

- Although most people in the United States die in hospitals, increasing numbers are choosing home care or hospice care for their final days.

RETHINK

♦ Do you think Kübler-Ross's five stages of dying might be subject to cultural influences? Age differences? Why or why not?

♦ Should quality-of-life issues play a part in resuscitation decisions? If so, who should make such a determination?

♦ Do you think assisted suicide should be permissible? What about other forms of euthanasia? Why or why not?

♦ What advice would you give someone who is considering offering home care to a terminally ill relative?

♦ Do you believe the stresses associated with attending dying patients are greater for hospice workers or for traditional hospital workers? Why?

GRIEF AND BEREAVEMENT

No one ever told me that grief felt so like fear. I am not afraid, but the sensation is like being afraid. The same fluttering in the stomach, the same restlessness, the yawning. I keep on swallowing.

    At other times it feels like being mildly drunk, or concussed. There is a sort of invisible blanket between the world and me. I find it hard to take in what anyone says. Or perhaps, hard to want to take it in. It is so uninteresting. (C.S. Lewis, 1985, p. 394)

For something that is a universal experience, most of us are surprisingly ill-prepared for the grief that follows the death of a loved one. Particularly in Western societies, where life expectancy is long and mortality rates lower than at any time in history, people are apt to view death as an atypical event rather than an expected part of life. This attitude makes grief all the more difficult to bear, particularly when we compare the present day with historical eras in which people lived shorter lives and the death rate was considerably higher (Gluhoski, Leader, & Wortman, 1994).

BEREAVEMENT AND GRIEF: ADJUSTING TO THE DEATH OF A LOVED ONE

After the death of a loved one, a painful period of adjustment follows, involving bereavement and grief. **Bereavement** is acknowledgment of the objective fact that one has experienced a death, whereas **grief** is the emotional response to one's loss. Although grief and other reactions to bereavement are quite individualistic, there are certain similarities in the ways people in Western societies adjust to the loss (Malinak, Hoyt, & Patterson, 1979; Silverman, 1986; Sanders, 1989; Rando, 1993).

The first stage typically entails shock, numbness, disbelief, or outright denial. People may avoid the reality of the situation, although the pain may break through, causing anguish, fear, and deep sorrow and distress. If the pain is too severe, however, the person may cycle back to numbness. In some ways, such a psychological state might be beneficial, for it permits the survivor to make funeral arrangements and carry out other psychologically difficult tasks. Typically, people pass through this stage in a few days or weeks, although in some cases it lasts longer.

In the next phase, people begin to confront the death and realize the extent of their loss. They fully experience their grief, and they react to the reality that the separation from the dead person will be permanent. In so doing, mourners may experience depression, yearn for the dead individual, be impatient or lethargic, and suffer deep unhappiness. However, they also begin to view their past relationship realistically, warts and

bereavement *acknowledgment of the objective fact that one has experienced a death*

grief *the emotional response to one's loss*

After a death, people move through a painful period of bereavement and grief. These adolescents in Bosnia mourn the loss of a friend who was killed by an enemy bombardment.

all. As a result, they begin to free themselves from some of the bonds that tied them to their loved ones.

Finally, people who have lost a loved one reach the accommodation stage. They begin to pick up the pieces of their lives, and to construct new identities. For instance, rather than seeing herself as someone's widowed spouse, a woman whose husband has died may come to regard herself as a single person.

Ultimately, most people are able to live new lives, independent from the person who has died. They form new relationships, and some even find that coping with the death has helped them to grow as individuals. They become more self-reliant and more appreciative of life.

It is important to keep in mind that not everyone passes through the stages of grief in the same manner and in the same order. People display vast individual differences, partly dependent on personality, the nature of the relationship with the deceased, and the post-death opportunities that are available to them for continuing their lives. As with Kübler-Ross's stages of dying, then, the stages of grieving do not unfold in the same way for all people.

Differentiating Unhealthy Grief from Normal Grief.   Although ideas abound about what separates normal grief from unhealthy grief, careful research has shown that many of the assumptions that both laypersons and clinicians hold are wrong. For instance, there is no evidence that a particular timetable for grieving exists, especially the common notion that that grieving should be complete a year after a spouse has died. Increasing evidence suggests that for some people (but not all) grieving may take considerably longer than a year. Research also contradicts the common assumption that depression is widespread: In fact, just 15 to 30 percent of people show relatively deep depression following the loss of a loved one (Wortman & Silver, 1989; Prigerson et al., 1995).

Similarly, it is often assumed that people who show little initial distress over a death are simply not facing up to reality, and that as a consequence they are likely to have problems later. This is not the case: There is little evidence that slight initial grief leads to later consequences. In fact, those who show the most intense distress immediately after a death are the most apt to have adjustment difficulties and health problems later on (Wortman & Silver, 1989; Gluhoski et al., 1994).

The Consequences of Grief and Bereavement.   In a sense, death is catching, at least in terms of survivors' mortality. A good deal of evidence suggests that widowed people are particularly at risk of dying. Some studies find that the risk of death is as much as 7 times higher than normal in the first year following the loss of a spouse. At particular risk are men and younger women who have been widowed (Gluhoski et al., 1994).

On the other hand, remarriage seems to lower the risk of death for survivors. This is particularly true for widowers, although the reasons are not clear.

Several factors increase the likelihood that bereavement will produce negative consequences. For instance, people who are already insecure, anxious, or fearful are less able to cope effectively. Furthermore, people whose relationships were marked by ambivalence before death are more apt to suffer poor post-death outcomes than are those who were secure in their relationships. Similarly, those who were dependent on their partners, and who therefore feel more vulnerable without them, are apt to suffer more after the death (Sanders, 1988).

Finally, the suddenness of a loved one's death appears to affect the course of grieving. People who unexpectedly lose partners are less able to cope than are those who were able to anticipate the death. For instance, in one study, people who experienced a sudden death still had not fully recovered 4 years later. In part, this may be due to the fact that sudden, unanticipated deaths are often the result of violence, which occurs more frequently among younger individuals (Sanders, 1988; Rando, 1993).

Although there is no way to erase the pain associated with the loss of a loved one, there are ways to prepare for it. As we consider in the Directions in Development section, **thanatologists**, people who study death and dying, suggest that death education should be an important component of everyone's schooling.

thanatologists   *people who study death and dying*

Directions in Development

Death Education: Preparing for the Inevitable

"When will Mom come back from being dead?" "Why did Barry have to die?" "Did Grampa die because I was bad?"

Children's questions illustrate why many psychologists suggest that learning about death is a necessary adjunct to both children's and adult's educational experiences. One result is a relatively new area of instruction, termed *death education*, encompassing programs that teach about death, dying, and grief. Death education is designed to help people of all ages deal better with death and dying—both the deaths of others and their own personal mortality.

Why is death education necessary? Probably the most important reason relates to the way in which we hide death, at least in most Western societies. We typically give hospitals the task of dealing with dying people, and we do not talk to children about death or allow them to go to funerals for fear of disturbing them. Even those most familiar with death, such as emergency workers and medical specialists, are uncomfortable talking about the subject. Because it is discussed so little, and is so removed from everyday life, people of all ages may have little opportunity to confront their feelings about death. As a result, death provokes even more anxiety (Bertman, 1991).

Several types of death education programs have been developed. Among the major kinds are the following:

♦   *Crisis intervention education.* When the Oklahoma City federal building was bombed, killing scores of people, children in the area were the subjects of several kinds of crisis intervention designed to deal with their anxieties. Because the victims included youngsters in a day-care center in the building, younger children were especially susceptible to feelings that they, too, might die in a blast. These younger children, whose conceptions of death were shaky at best, needed explanations geared to their levels of cognitive development. In this situation, psychologists provided counseling intervention on an emergency basis.

◆ *Routine death education.* Although there is relatively little curricular material on death available at the elementary school level, course work in high schools is becoming increasingly common. For instance, some high schools have specific courses on death and dying, and one survey found that the majority of teachers discuss death as part of other lessons (Cappiello & Troyer, 1979). Furthermore, colleges and universities increasingly include courses relating to death in such departments as psychology, human development, sociology, and education.

◆ *Death education for members of the helping professions.* Professionals who will deal with death, dying, and grief as part of their careers have a special need for death education. Almost all medical and nursing schools now offer some form of death education to help their students. The most successful programs not only provide intellectual content regarding death, but also allow students to explore their feelings about the topic (Kastenbaum, 1977; Dickinson, Summer, & Durand, 1987).

Although no single form of death education will be sufficient to demystify death, the types of programs described above may help people to come to grips more effectively with what is, along with birth, the most universal—and certain—of all human experiences.

MOURNING AND FUNERALS: FINAL RITES

Death is a big business in the United States. The average funeral costs $4,000. The buying of an ornate, polished coffin, preparation of the deceased for preservation and viewing, and transportation to and from the cemetery in a limousine are among the services that people typically purchase in planning a funeral (Lynwander, 1995).

In part, the relatively grandiose nature of funerals is due to the vulnerability of those planning the funeral, who are typically close survivors of the deceased. Wishing to demonstrate love and affection, the survivors are susceptible to suggestions to "provide the best" for the deceased.

But it is not only the pressure of enterprising salespersons that leads many people to spend thousands of dollars on a funeral. In large measure, the nature of funerals is also determined by social norms and customs. Because an individual's death represents an important transition, not only for loved ones but for an entire community, the rites associated with death take on an added importance. In a sense, then, a funeral is not only a public acknowledgment that an individual has died, but a recognition of everyone's ultimate mortality and an acceptance of the cycle of life (DeSpelder & Strickland, 1992).

In Western societies, funeral rituals follow a typical pattern, despite some surface variations. Prior to the funeral, the body is prepared in some way and is dressed in special clothing. Funerals usually include the celebration of a religious rite, the delivery of a eulogy, a procession of some sort, and some formal time period, such as the wake for Irish Catholics and shivah for Jews, in which relatives and friends visit the mourning family and pay their respects. Military funerals typically include the firing of weapons and a flag draped over the coffin.

At the time of a loved one's death, relatives are easy targets for unscrupulous funeral home operators, who may convince the family to purchase a costly, elaborate funeral package.

Other cultures include funeral rituals of quite different sorts. For instance, in some societies mourners shave their heads as a sign of grief; in others they allow the hair to grow and men stop shaving for a period of time. In other cultures, mourners may be hired to wail and grieve. Sometimes noisy celebrations take place at funerals; in other cultures silence is the norm. Even the nature of emotional displays, such as the amount and timing of crying, are determined culturally (Rosenblatt, 1988).

Historically, some cultures have developed funeral rites that strike us as extreme. For example, in *suttee*, a traditional Hindu practice in India that is now illegal, a widow was expected to throw herself into the fire that consumed her husband's body. In ancient China, servants were sometimes buried (alive) with their masters' bodies.

Ultimately, no matter what the particular ritual, all funerals basically serve the same underlying function: They mark the endpoint for the life of the person who has died—and the starting point for the survivors, from which they can resume their lives.

In the Cajun tradition of New Orleans, jazz bands are included to provide the appropriate spirit following a funeral.

The Informed Consumer of Development

Helping a Child Cope With Grief

Because of their limited understanding of death, younger children need special help in coping with grief. Among the strategies that can help are the following.

- Be honest. Don't say that a dead person is "sleeping" or "on a long trip." Tell children the truth—that the person is no longer alive and will never be alive again.

- Encourage expressions of grief. Do not tell children not to cry or to show their feelings. Instead, tell them that it is understandable to feel terrible, and that they may always miss the deceased. At the same time, assure them that they will always have good memories of the person who has died.

- Reassure children that they are not to blame for the death. Children sometimes attribute a loved one's death to their own behavior—if they hadn't misbehaved, they mistakenly reason, the person would not have died. Help them understand the error of such logic.

- Understand that children's grief may surface in unanticipated ways. Children may show little or no grief at the time of the death, but later they may become upset for no apparent reason. Keep in mind that death can be overwhelming for a child, and try to be consistently loving and supportive.

Review and Rethink

REVIEW

- Bereavement refers to the objective fact of the loss of a loved one; grief refers to the emotional response to that loss. For many people, grief passes through several stages, from denial, through sorrow, to accommodation.

- There are many common misconceptions about how people deal with a death, but in fact the expression of grief is highly individual. Depression is far from universal, and reactions to death are partly determined by its suddenness and other factors.

- Thanatologists recommend that death education become a part of people's normal course of learning, to replace the nearly total lack of attention most people now give death and dying.

- Funeral rites, though trying and expensive, play a significant role in helping people acknowledge the death of a loved one, recognize their own mortality, and proceed with their lives.

♦ Children need special help coping with grief. Psychologists advise honesty, encouraging the child to express grief, allaying thoughts of guilt and responsibility, and preparing for delayed and indirect expressions of grief.

RETHINK

♦ What cultural beliefs in U.S. society do you believe contribute to people's reluctance to think about death?

♦ How might coping with the death of a loved one strengthen a person?

♦ Why do you think the risk of death is so high for people who have recently lost a spouse? Why might remarriage lower the risk?

♦ Would you recommend death education for children in elementary school? At what age would you start to deal with the subject of death? Why?

♦ In some societies, eating, drinking, socializing, and even merrymaking are normal parts of the funeral ritual. What function might such displays serve?

LOOKING BACK

What is death, and how does its meaning change throughout the life span and across cultures?

1. The precise point at which death occurs is difficult to determine. *Functional death* refers to the absence of heartbeat and respiration, although people in this state can sometimes be resuscitated. *Brain death* refers to the absence of electrical activity in the brain, which is irreversible. Some people argue that death occurs when people can no longer use characteristically human faculties, such as feeling and reasoning.

2. Preschool youngsters begin to develop a concept of death at around age 5, although its finality is not grasped until about age 9. The death of an infant or a young child is among the most devastating experiences for parents, largely because it seems unnatural and entirely incomprehensible.

3. Adolescents have an unrealistic sense of invulnerability that makes them susceptible to hazardous situations and accidental death. Denial often makes it impossible for terminally ill adolescents to accept the seriousness of their condition.

4. For young adults, death is virtually unthinkable. If they must face death, young adults are confronted with serious issues relating to marriage, childbearing, and work. Young adults who are terminally ill can be difficult patients because of a strong sense of the injustice of their fate.

5. In middle adulthood, disease becomes the leading cause of death. For the first time, fear of death may become substantial because middle-aged adults are fully aware of its reality.

6. People in late adulthood begin to prepare for death, partly because they sense its arrival in their own bodies, and partly because their close environment provides so many examples of death. Older people generally prefer to know if death is near, and the main issue they have to deal with is whether their lives continue to have value.

7. Responses to death are in part determined by culture. Death in some cultures is viewed as a release from the pains of the world or the beginning of a pleasurable afterlife. In other cultures, it is regarded as a punishment or judgment, and in still others as a sim-

ple and complete end to life. There is some evidence that differences in exposure to death can cause differences in conceptions of and attitudes toward it.

In what ways do people face the prospect of their own imminent death?

8. The presence of death raises many difficult issues for the person who is dying and for caregivers who must deal with the patient's reactions and coping strategies.

9. Elisabeth Kübler-Ross suggests that people pass through five basic stages on their way to death. At first they deny that they will die, then they become angry, and then they attempt to bargain for more time. Next they become depressed, and finally they accept the fact of their impending demise.

10. Kübler-Ross's theory has been criticized because its applicability is limited to those who have time to go through five stages of dying and because of its lack of universality and invariability. On the other hand, no one has done more to raise awareness of the dying process than she, and her work remains influential.

How can people exert some measure of control over their own process of dying?

11. Although many people prefer not to have "extraordinary measures" applied to save them from dying, the distinction between extraordinary and normal measures is ambiguous and the question of who makes the decision is controversial.

12. A living will is a means of asserting control over decisions surrounding one's death. Such wills specify the medical treatments that people want and do not want in life-threatening situations, and they often designate health-care proxies to represent them in case they cannot express their wishes themselves.

13. Assisted suicide is a form of euthanasia, a controversial practice that is illegal in the United States. The main controversy involves who should have control over life-and-death decisions.

14. Although most deaths in the United States occur in hospitals, an increasing number of terminal patients are opting for either home care, where they may conclude their lives among familiar surroundings and people, or hospices, where they will receive professional care designed to help them reach the end of their lives in comfort and dignity.

What are grief and bereavement, and how do people work through them?

15. The death of a loved one brings a period of adjustment involving bereavement and grief. Bereavement refers to the objective fact of the loss, whereas grief refers to the emotional response to it.

16. Grief often, but by no means always, proceeds through recognizable stages reminiscent of Kübler-Ross's stages of dying. The first stage typically involves shock or even denial. In the second stage, people begin to confront their loss, to experience grief, and to accept the permanence of their separation from the loved one. Finally, people reach the accommodation stage, in which they begin to construct identities apart from the person who has died.

17. Individuals vary considerably in their expressions of grief, and only a minority of people experience depression. Furthermore, common assumptions about the need to express one's distress in order to avoid problems later are misguided. However, a genuine consequence of bereavement is an increase in the risk of death for the survivor, which can be lessened by remarriage.

How can people be helped to prepare for and cope with death?

18. Because death is virtually a forbidden topic in many Western societies, death education has been devised to help people learn about death and consider their own mortality

realistically. Death education might involve routine instruction of schoolchildren, crisis intervention, and special training for those in the helping professions.

19. Funeral rituals in many Western societies follow a similar pattern, including preparation of the body, a religious rite, a eulogy, a procession, and an established time period for visitation of the bereaved family. Funerals serve a dual function: acknowledging the death of a loved one and recognizing and anticipating the mortality of all who participate.

20. Children in particular need help in dealing with the death of someone close. Psychologists counsel honesty, encouragement of expressions of grief, reassurance that the death was in no way due to the child's behavior, and understanding that the child's grief may be delayed and indirect.

KEY TERMS AND CONCEPTS

functional death (p. 646)

brain death (p. 646)

sudden infant death syndrome (SIDS) (p. 647)

living wills (p. 655)

euthanasia (p. 656)

home care (p. 658)

hospice care (p. 659)

bereavement (p. 661)

grief (p. 661)

thanatologists (p. 663)

Glossary

Abstract modeling   The process by which modeling paves the way for the development of more general rules and principles (Ch. 8)

Acceleration   Special programs that allow gifted students to move ahead at their own pace, even if this means skipping to higher grade levels (Ch. 9)

Accommodation   Changes in existing ways of thinking that occur in response to encounters with new stimuli or events (Ch. 1, 5)

Achieving stage   The point reached by young adults in which intelligence is applied to specific situations involving the attainment of long-term goals regarding careers, family, and societal contributions (Ch. 13)

Acquired immunodeficiency syndrome (AIDS)   A sexually transmitted disease, produced by the HIV virus, that has no cure and ultimately causes death (Ch. 11)

Acquisitive stage   According to Schaie, the first stage of cognitive development, encompassing all of childhood and adolescence, in which the main developmental task is to acquire information (Ch. 13)

Activity theory   The theory suggesting that successful aging occurs when people maintain the interests, activities, and social interactions with which they were involved during middle age (Ch. 18)

Addictive drugs   Drugs that produce a biological or psychological dependence in users, leading to increasingly powerful cravings for them (Ch. 11)

Adolescence   The developmental stage that lies between childhood and adulthood (Ch. 11)

Adolescent egocentrism   A state of self-absorption in which the world is viewed from one's own point-of-view (Ch. 11)

Adult day-care facilities   A facility in which elderly individuals receive care only during the day, but spend nights and weekends in their own homes (Ch. 18)

Age of viability   The point at which an infant can survive a premature birth (Ch. 3)

Ageism   Prejudice and discrimination directed at older people (Ch. 17)

Agentic professions   Occupations associated with getting things accomplished (Ch. 14)

Aggression   Intentional injury or harm to another person (Ch. 8)

Ainsworth strange situation   A sequence of staged episodes that illustrate the strength of attachment between a child and (typically) his or her mother (Ch. 6)

Alzheimer's disease   A progressive brain disorder that produces loss of memory and confusion (Ch. 17)

Amniocentesis   The process of identifying genetic defects by examining a small sample of fetal cells drawn by a needle inserted into the amniotic fluid surrounding the unborn fetus (Ch. 2)

Androgynous   A state in which gender roles encompass characteristics thought typical of both sexes (Ch. 8)

Anorexia nervosa   A severe eating disorder in which individuals refuse to eat, while denying that their behavior and appearance, which may become skeleton-like, are out of the ordinary (Ch. 11)

Apgar scale   A standard measurement system that looks for a variety of indications of good health in newborns (Ch. 3)

Artificial insemination   A process of fertilization in which a man's sperm is placed directly into a woman's vagina by a physician (Ch. 2)

Assimilation   The process in which people understand an experience in terms of their current stage of cognitive development and way of thinking (Ch. 1, 5)

Associative play   When two or more children actually interact with one another by sharing or borrowing toys or materials, although they do not do the same thing (Ch. 8)

Attachment   The positive emotional bond that develops between a child and a particular individual (Ch. 6)

Attention-deficit hyperactivity disorder (ADHD)   A learning disability marked by inattention, impulsiveness, a low tolerance for frustration, and generally a great deal of inappropriate activity (Ch. 9)

Attributions   People's understanding of the reasons behind their behavior (Ch. 10)

Auditory impairment   A special need that involves the loss of hearing or some aspect of hearing (Ch. 9)

Authoritarian parents   Parents who are controlling, punitive, rigid, cold (Ch. 8)

Authoritative parents   Parents who are firm, setting clear and consistent limits (Ch. 8)

Autobiographical memory   Memories of information about one's own life (Ch. 7, 17)

Autonomy   Having independence and a sense of control over one's life (Ch. 12)

Autonomy-versus-shame-and-doubt-stage   The period during which children develop independence and autonomy if parents encourage exploration and freedom (Ch. 8)

Babbling   Making speechlike but meaningless sounds (Ch. 5)

Bayley Scales of Infant Development   A measure that evaluates an infant's development from 2 to 30 months (Ch. 5)

Behavior modification   A formal technique for promoting the frequency of desirable behaviors and decreasing the incidence of unwanted ones (Ch. 1)

Behavioral genetics   The study of the effects of heredity on behavior (Ch. 2)

Behavioral perspective   The approach that suggests that the keys to understanding development are observable behavior and outside stimuli in the environment (Ch. 1)

Bereavement   Acknowledgment of the objective fact that one has experienced a death (Ch. 19)

Bicultural identity   The maintaining of one's original cultural identity while integrating into the dominant culture (Ch. 9)

Bilingualism   The use of more than one language (Ch. 9)

Blended families   A remarried couple that has at least one stepchild living with them (Ch. 10)

Body transcendence versus body preoccupation   A period in which people must learn to cope with and move beyond changes in physical capabilities as a result of aging (Ch. 18)

Bonding   Close physical and emotional contact between parent and child during the period immediately following birth, argued by some to affect later relationship strength (Ch. 3)

Boomerang children   Young adults who return, after leaving home for some period, to live in the homes of their middle-aged parents (Ch. 16)

Brain death   A diagnosis of death based on the cessation of all signs of brain activity, as measured by electrical brain waves (Ch. 19)

Brazelton Neonatal Behavioral Assessment Scale (NBAS)   A measure designed to determine infants' neurological and behavioral responses to their environment (Ch. 4)

Bulimia   An eating disorder characterized by binges on large quantities of food, followed by purges of the food through vomiting or the use of laxatives (Ch. 11)

Burnout   A situation that occurs when highly trained professionals experience dissatisfaction, disillusionment, frustration, and weariness from their jobs (Ch. 16)

Career consolidation   A stage entered between the ages of 20 and 40 when young adults become centered on their careers (Ch. 14)

Cataracts   Cloudy or opaque areas on the lens of the eye that interfere with passing light (Ch. 17)

Centration   The process of concentrating on one limited aspect of a stimulus and ignoring other aspects (Ch. 7)

Cephalocaudal principle   The principle that growth follows a pattern that begins with head and upper body parts (Ch. 4)

Cesarean delivery   A birth in which the baby is surgically removed from the uterus, rather than traveling through the birth canal (Ch. 3)

Chlamydia   The most common sexually transmitted disease, caused by a parasite (Ch. 11)

Chorionic villus sampling (CVS)   A test used to find genetic defects that involves taking samples of hairlike material that surrounds the embryo (Ch. 2)

Chromosomes   Rod-shaped portions of DNA that are organized in 23 pairs (Ch. 2)

Chronological (or physical) age   The actual age of the child taking the intelligence test (Ch. 9)

Classical conditioning   A type of learning in which an organism responds in a particular way to a neutral stimulus that normally does not bring about that type of response (Ch. 1, 5)

Cliques   Groups of from two to twelve people whose members have frequent social interactions with one another (Ch. 12)

Cluster suicide   A situation in which one suicide leads to attempts by others to kill themselves (Ch. 12)

Cognitive development   Development involving the ways that growth and change in intellectual capabilities influence a person's behavior. (Ch. 1)

Cognitive perspective   The approach that focuses on the processes that allow people to know, understand, and think about the world (Ch. 1)

Cohabitation   Couples living together without being married (Ch. 14)

Cohort   A group of people born at around the same time in the same place (Ch. 1)

Collectivistic orientation   The orientation promoting the notion of interdependence in which people tend to regard themselves as parts of a larger social network (Ch. 8)

Communal professions   Occupations associated with relationships (Ch. 14)

Companionate love   The strong affection that we have for those with whom our lives are deeply involved (Ch. 14)

Concrete operational stage   The period of cognitive development between 7 and 12 years of age, which is characterized by the active, and appropriate, use of logic (Ch. 9)

Conservation   The knowledge that quantity is unrelated to the arrangement and physical appearance of objects (Ch. 7)

Constructive play   Play in which children manipulate objects to produce or build something (Ch. 8)

Continuous change   Gradual development in which achievements at one level build on those of previous levels (Ch. 1)

Control group   The group that receives either no treatment or alternative treatment (Ch. 1)

Cooperative play   Activity in which children genuinely play with one another, taking turns, playing games, or devising contests (Ch. 8)

Coping   The effort to control, reduce, or tolerate the threats that lead to stress (Ch. 13)

Correlational research   Research that seeks to identify whether an association or relationship exists between two factors (Ch. 1)

Critical period   A specific, but limited, time span, usually early in an organism's life, during which the organism is particularly susceptible to environmental influences relating to some particular facet of development (Ch. 4)

Cross-sectional research   Research in which people of different ages are compared at the same point in time (Ch. 1)

Cross-sequential studies The process by which researchers examine a number of different age groups over several points in time (Ch. 1)

Crowds A larger group than a clique, comprised of individuals who share particular characteristics but who may not interact with one another (Ch. 12)

Crystallized intelligence The store of information, skills, and strategies that people have acquired through education and experiences, and through their previous use of fluid intelligence (Ch. 9, 15)

Cultural assimilation model The model that fostered the view of American society as the proverbial melting pot (Ch. 9)

Cycle of violence hypothesis The theory that abuse and neglect that children suffer predispose them as adults to abuse and neglect their own children (Ch. 8, 16)

Day care centers Places that typically provide care for children all day, while their parents are at work (Ch. 7)

Decentering The ability to take multiple aspects of a situation into account (Ch. 9)

Decision/commitment component The third aspect of love that embodies both the initial cognition that one loves another person and the longer-term determination to maintain that love (Ch. 14)

Deferred imitation An act in which a person who is no longer present is imitated later by children after they have witnessed such scenes (Ch. 5)

Dementia The most common mental disorder of the elderly, it covers several diseases, each of which includes serious memory loss accompanied by declines in other mental functioning (Ch. 17)

Developmental quotient An overall developmental score that relates to performance in four domains: motor skills, language use, adaptive behavior, and personal-social skills (Ch. 5)

Differential emotions theory Emotional expressions that not only reflect emotional experiences, but also help in the regulation of emotion itself (Ch. 6)

Discontinuous change Development that occurs in distinct steps or stages, with each stage bringing about behavior that is assumed to be qualitatively different from behavior at earlier stages (Ch. 1)

Disengagement theory The period in late adulthood that marks a gradual withdrawal from the world on physical, psychological, and social levels (Ch. 18)

Dizygotic twins Twins who are produced when two separate ova are fertilized by two separate sperm at roughly the same time (Ch. 2)

Dominance hierarchy Rankings that represent the relative social power of those in a group hierarchy (Ch. 10)

Down syndrome A disorder produced by the presence of an extra chromosome on the 21st chromosome pair; once referred to as mongolism (Ch. 2)

Ecological approach The concept that different levels of the environment simultaneously influence individuals (Ch. 1)

Ego transcendence versus ego preoccupation The period in which elderly people must come to grips with their coming death (Ch. 18)

Ego-integrity-versus-despair stage Erikson's final life stage, characterized by a process of looking back over one's life, evaluating it, and coming to terms with it (Ch. 18)

Ego According to Freud, the part of personality that is rational and reasonable (Ch. 1)

Egocentric thought Thinking that does not take into account the viewpoints of others (Ch. 7)

Elder abuse The physical or psychological mistreatment or neglect of elderly individuals (Ch. 18)

Embryonic stage The period from 2 to 8 weeks following fertilization during which significant growth occurs in the major organs and body systems (Ch. 2)

Empathy An emotional response that corresponds to the feelings of another person (Ch. 6, 8)

Empty nest syndrome The experience that relates to parents' feelings of unhappiness, worry, loneliness, and depression resulting from their children's departure from home (Ch. 16)

Enrichment An approach through which students are kept at grade level but are enrolled in special programs and given individual activities to allow greater depth of study on a given topic (Ch. 9)

Erikson's theory of psycholosocial development The theory that considers how individuals come to understand themselves and the meaning of others'—and their own—behavior (Ch. 6)

Euthanasia The practice of assisting people who are terminally ill to die more quickly (Ch. 19)

Executive stage The period in middle adulthood when people take a broader perspective than earlier, including concerns about the world (Ch. 13)

Experiment A process in which an investigator, called an experimenter, devises two different experiences for subjects or participants (Ch. 1)

Experimental research Research designed to discover causal relationships between various factors (Ch. 1)

Extrinsic motivation Motivation that drives people to obtain tangible rewards, such as money and prestige (Ch. 14)

Fantasy period According to Eli Ginzberg, the period when career choices are made, and discarded, without regard to skills, abilities, or available job opportunities (Ch. 14)

Female climacteric The period that marks the transition from being able to bear children to being unable to do so (Ch. 15)

Fertilization The process by which a sperm and an ovum—the male and female gametes, respectively—join to form a single new cell (Ch. 2)

Fetal alcohol syndrome (FAS) A disorder caused by the pregnant mother consuming substantial quantities of alcohol during pregnancy, potentially resulting in mental retardation and delayed growth in the child (Ch. 2)

Fetal stage The stage that begins at about 8 weeks after conception and continues until birth (Ch. 2)

Field study   A research investigation carried out in a naturally occurring setting (Ch. 1)

First-year adjustment reaction   A group of psychological symptoms relating to the college experience suffered by first-year college students (Ch. 13)

Fixation   Behavior reflecting an earlier stage of development (Ch. 1)

Fluid intelligence   The ability to deal with new problems and situations (Ch. 9, 15)

Formal operations period   The stage at which people develop the ability to think abstractly (Ch. 11)

Functional death   The absence of a heartbeat and breathing (Ch. 19)

Functional play   Simple, repetitive activities typical of 3-year-olds (Ch. 8)

Gametes   The sex cells from the mother and father that form a new cell at conception (Ch. 2)

Gender schema   A cognitive framework that organizes information relevant to gender (Ch. 8)

Gender   The sense of being male or female (Ch. 6)

Generalized slowing hypothesis   The theory that processing in all parts of the nervous system, including the brain, is less efficient (Ch. 17)

Generation gap   A divide between parents and children in attitudes, values, aspirations, and worldviews (Ch. 12)

Generativity versus stagnation   According to Erik Erikson the stage during middle adulthood in which people consider their contributions to family and society (Ch. 16)

Genes   The basic unit of genetic information (Ch. 2)

Genetic counseling   The discipline that focuses on helping people deal with issues relating to inherited disorders (Ch. 2)

Genetic preprogramming theories of aging   The theory that suggests that our body's DNA genetic code contains a built-in time limit for the reproduction of human cells (Ch. 17)

Genital herpes   A common sexually transmitted disease that is a virus and is not unlike cold sores that sometimes appear around the mouth (Ch. 11)

Genotype   The underlying combination of genetic material present (but not outwardly visible) in an organism (Ch. 2)

Germinal stage   The first—and shortest—stage of the prenatal period, which takes place during the first 2 weeks following conception (Ch. 2)

Gerontologists   Specialists who study aging (Ch. 17)

Gifted and talented   Children who show evidence of high performance capability in areas such as intellectual, creative, artistic, leadership, or specific academic fields (Ch. 9)

Glaucoma   A condition where pressure in the fluid of the eye increases, either because the fluid cannot drain properly or because too much fluid is produced (Ch. 15, 17)

Grammar   The system of rules that determines how our thoughts can be expressed (Ch. 7)

Grief   The emotional response to one's loss (Ch. 19)

Habituation   The decrease in the response to a stimulus that occurs after repeated presentations of the same stimulus (Ch. 5)

Handedness   The preference of using one hand over another (Ch. 7)

Heteronomous morality   The initial stage of moral development, in which rules are seen as invariant, unchangeable, and beyond people's influence and control (Ch. 8)

Holophrases   One-word utterances that depend on the particular context in which they are used to determine meaning (Ch. 5)

Home care   An alternative to hospitalization in which dying people stay in their homes and receive treatment from their families and visiting medical staff (Ch. 19)

Homogamy   The tendency to marry someone who is similar in age, race, education, religion, and other basic demographic characteristics (Ch. 14)

Hospice care   Care provided for the dying at home or in institutions devoted to those who are terminally ill (Ch. 19)

Id   According to Freud, the raw, unorganized, inborn part of personality that is present at birth (Ch. 1)

Identification   The process in which children attempt to be similar to their same-sex parent, incorporating the parent's attitudes and values (Ch. 8)

Identity achievement   The particular identity to which teenagers commit following a period of crisis during which they consider various alternatives (Ch. 12)

Identity diffusion   The category in which adolescents consider various identity alternatives, but never commit to one, or never even consider identity options in any conscious way (Ch. 12)

Identity foreclosure   The state of adolescents who prematurely commit to an identity without adequately exploring alternatives (Ch. 12)

Identity-versus-role-diffusion stage   The period during which teenagers seek to determine what is unique and distinctive about themselves (Ch. 12)

Imaginary audience   Fictitious observers who pay as much attention to the adolescents' behavior as the adolescents do themselves (Ch. 11)

Immanent justice   The notion that rules that are broken earn immediate punishment (Ch. 8)

In vitro fertilization (IVF)   A procedure in which a woman's ova are removed from her ovaries, and a man's sperm are used to fertilize the ova in a laboratory (Ch. 2)

Individualistic orientation   The orientation that emphasizes personal identity and uniqueness of the individual (Ch. 8)

Industry-versus-inferiority stage   The period from age 6 to 12 characterized by a focus on efforts to attain competence in meeting the challenges presented by parents, peers, school, and the other complexities of the modern world (Ch. 10)

Infant mortality   Death within the first year of life (Ch. 3)

Infantile amnesia   The lack of memory for experiences that occurred prior to 3 years of age (Ch. 5)

Infertility The inability to conceive after 12 to 18 months of trying to become pregnant (Ch. 2)

Information-processing approaches The model that seeks to identify the way that individuals take in, use, and store information (Ch. 5, 11)

Initiative-versus-guilt-stage The period when preschoolers come to realize that they are people in their own right, and they begin to make decisions and to shape the kind of people that they will become (Ch. 8)

Institutionalism A psychological state in which people develop apathy, indifference, and a lack of caring about themselves (Ch. 18)

Intelligence quotient (IQ score) A measure of intelligence that takes into account a student's mental *and* chronological age (Ch. 9)

Intelligence The capacity to understand the world, think with rationality, and use resources effectively when faced with challenges (Ch. 9)

Intimacy component The component of love that encompasses feelings of closeness, affection, and connectedness (Ch. 14)

Intimacy-versus-isolation stage According to Erik Erikson, the period of postadolescence into the early 30s that focuses on developing close relationships with others (Ch. 14)

Intrinsic motivation Motivation that causes people to work for their own enjoyment, not for the rewards work may bring (Ch. 14)

Intuitive thought Thinking that reflects preschoolers' use of primitive reasoning and their avid acquisition of knowledge about the world (Ch. 7)

Klinefelter's syndrome A disorder resulting from the presence of an extra *X* chromosome that produces underdeveloped genitals, extreme height, and enlarged breasts (Ch. 2)

Kwashiorkor A disease in which a child's stomach, limbs, and face swell with water (Ch. 4)

Labeling theory of passionate love The theory that individuals experience romantic love when two events occur together: intense physiological arousal and situational cues suggesting arousal is due to love (Ch. 14)

Laboratory study A research investigation conducted in a controlled setting explicitly designed to hold events constant (Ch. 1)

Language-acquisition device (LAD) A neural system that both permits the understanding of language structure and provides a set of strategies and techniques for learning the particular characteristics of the language to which a child is exposed (Ch. 7)

Language The systematic, meaningful arrangement of symbols that provides the basis for communication (Ch. 5)

Latchkey children Children who let themselves into their homes after school and wait alone until their caretakers return from work (Ch. 10)

Laterlization The process in which certain functions are located more in one hemisphere than the other (Ch. 7)

Learning disabilities Difficulties in the acquisition and use of listening, speaking, reading, writing, reasoning, or mathematical abilities (Ch. 9)

Learning theory approach The theory that language acquisition follows the basic laws of reinforcement and conditioning (Ch. 7)

Least restrictive environment The setting that is most similar to that of children without special needs (Ch. 9)

Life events models The approach suggesting that the timing of particular events in an adult's life, rather than age per se, determines the course of personality development (Ch. 16)

Life expectancy The average age of death for members of a population (Ch. 17)

Life review The point in life in which people examine and evaluate their lives (Ch. 18)

Life-care community A community that offers an environment in which all the residents are of retirement age or older and need various levels of care (Ch. 18)

Life span developmental psychology The branch of psychology that studies patterns of growth, change, and stability in behavior occurring throughout the entire life span (Ch. 1)

Living wills Legal documents designating what medical treatments people want or do not want if they cannot express their wishes (Ch. 19)

Longitudinal research Research in which the behavior of one or more individuals is measured as the subjects age (Ch. 1)

Low-birthweight infants Infants that weight less than 2,500 grams (about $5\frac{1}{2}$ pounds) at birth (Ch. 3)

Mainstreaming An educational approach in which exceptional children are integrated to the extent possible into the traditional educational system and are provided with a broad range of educational alternatives (Ch. 9)

Male climacteric The period of physical and psychological change relating to the male reproductive system that occurs during late middle age (Ch. 15)

Marasmus A disease characterized by the cessation of growth (Ch. 4)

Marriage gradient The tendency for men to marry women who are slightly younger, smaller, and lower in status, and women to marry men who are slightly older, larger, and higher in status (Ch. 14)

Masturbation Sexual self-stimulation (Ch. 12)

Memory The process by which information is initially recorded, stored, and retrieved (Ch. 5, 8)

Menarche The onset of menstruation (Ch. 11)

Menopause The cessation of menstruation (Ch. 15)

Mental age The typical intelligence level found for people at a given chronological age (Ch. 9)

Mental retardation A significantly subaverage level of intellectual functioning that occurs with related limitations in two or more skill areas (Ch. 9)

Meta-memory An understanding about the processes that underlie memory, which emerges and improves during middle childhood (Ch. 9)

676

Metacognition The knowledge that people have about their own thinking processes, and their ability to monitor their cognition (Ch. 11)

Metalinguistic awareness An understanding of one's own use of language (Ch. 9)

Midlife crisis A stage of uncertainty and indecision brought about by the realization that life is finite (Ch. 16)

Mild retardation Retardation in which IQ scores are in the range of 50 or 55 to 70 (Ch. 9)

Mnemonics Formal strategies for organizing material in ways that make it more likely to be remembered (Ch. 15)

Moderate retardation Retardation in which IQ scores are from about 35 or 40 to 50 or 55 (Ch. 9)

Monozygotic twins Twins who are genetically identical (Ch. 2)

Moral development The changes in people's sense of justice and of what is right and wrong, and in their behavior related to moral issues (Ch. 8)

Moratorium The category in which adolescents may have explored various identity alternatives to some degree, but have not yet committed themselves (Ch. 12)

Motherese A type of speech directed toward infants that is characterized by short, simple sentences (Ch. 5)

Multicultural education A form of education in which the goal is to help minority students develop competence in the culture of the majority group while maintaining positive group identities that build on their original cultures (Ch. 9)

Multifactorial transmission Traits that are determined by a combination of both genetic and environmental factors in which a genotype provides a range within which a phenotype may be expressed (Ch. 2)

Multimodal approach to perception The approach that considers how information that is collected by various individual sensory systems is integrated and coordinated (Ch. 4)

Mutual regulation model The model in which infants and parents learn to communicate emotional states to one another and to respond appropriately (Ch. 6)

Neglected children Children who receive relatively little attention from their peers in the form of either positive or negative interactions (Ch. 10)

Neonate The term used for newborns (Ch. 3)

Nonnormative life events Specific, atypical events that occur in a particular person's life at a time when they do not happen to most people (Ch. 1)

Normative age-graded influences Biological and environmental influences that are similar for individuals in a particular age group, regardless of when or where they are raised (Ch. 1)

Normative history-graded influences Biological and environmental influences associated with a particular historical moment (Ch. 1)

Normative-crisis models The approach that views personality development in terms of fairly universal stages, tied to a sequence of age-related crises (Ch. 16)

Norms The average performance of a large sample of children of a given age (Ch. 4)

Obesity Body weight more than 20 percent higher than the average weight for a person of a given age and height (Ch. 7)

Object permanence The realization that people and objects exist even when they cannot be seen (Ch. 5)

Onlooker play Play in which children simply watch others at play but do not actually participate themselves (Ch. 8)

Operant conditioning A form of learning in which a voluntary response is strengthened or weakened, depending on its association with positive or negative consequences (Ch. 1, 5)

Operations Organized, formal, and logical mental processes (Ch. 7)

Osteoporosis A condition in which the bones become brittle, fragile, and thin, often brought about by a lack of calcium in the diet (Ch. 15, 17)

Overextension Words used too broadly, overgeneralizing their meaning (Ch. 5)

Parallel play Play in which children play with similar toys, in a similar manner, but do not interact with each other (Ch. 8)

Passion component The component of love that comprises the motivational drives relating to sex, physical closeness, and romance (Ch. 14)

Passionate (or romantic) love A state of powerful absorption in someone (Ch. 14)

Peer pressure The influence of one's peers to conform to their behavior and attitudes (Ch. 12)

Perception The sorting out, interpretation, analysis, and integration of stimuli involving the sense organs and brain (Ch. 4)

Peripheral slowing hypothesis The theory suggesting that overall processing speed declines in the peripheral nervous system (Ch. 17)

Permissive parents Parents who provide lax and inconsistent feedback (Ch. 8)

Personal fables The view held by some adolescents that what happens to them is unique, exceptional, and shared by no one else (Ch. 11)

Personality development Development involving the ways in which the enduring characteristics that differentiate one person from another change over the life span (Ch. 1)

Personality The sum total of the enduring characteristics that begin during infancy and that differentiate one individual from another (Ch. 6)

Phenotype The observable trait; the trait that actually is seen (Ch. 2)

Physical development Development involving the body's physical makeup, including the brain, nervous system, muscles, and senses, and the need for food, drink, and sleep (Ch. 1)

Plasticity The degree to which a developing structure or behavior is susceptible to experience (Ch. 4, 17)

Pluralistic society model The concept that American society is made up of diverse, coequal cultural groups that should preserve their individual cultural features (Ch. 9)

Polygenic inheritance Inheritance in which a combination of multiple gene pairs is responsible for the production of a particular trait (Ch. 2)

Postformal thought Thinking that acknowledges that adult predicaments must sometimes be solved in relativistic terms (Ch. 13)

Postmature infants Infants still unborn 2 weeks after the mother's due date (Ch. 3)

Practical intelligence Intelligence that is learned primarily by observing others and modeling their behavior (Ch. 13)

Prelinguistic communication Communication through sounds, facial expressions, gestures, imitation, and other non-linguistic means (Ch. 5)

Preoperational stage The stage where children's use of symbolic thinking grows, mental reasoning emerges, and the use of concepts increases, according to Jean Piaget (Ch. 7)

Presbycusis The loss of the ability to hear sounds of high frequency (Ch. 15)

Presbyopia A nearly universal change in eyesight during middle adulthood that results in some loss of near vision (Ch. 15)

Preschools (or nursery schools) A child-care facility designed to provide intellectual and social experiences for children (Ch. 7)

Preterm infants Infants who are born prior to 38 weeks after conception (also known as premature infants) (Ch. 3)

Primary appraisal The assessment of an event to determine whether its implications are positive, negative, or neutral (Ch. 13)

Primary sex characteristics Characteristics associated with the development of the organs and structures of the body that directly relate to reproduction (Ch. 11)

Principle of hierarchical integration The principle stating that simple skills typically develop separately and independently but are later integrated into more complex skills (Ch. 4)

Principle of the independence of systems The principle of growth suggesting that different body systems grow at different rates (Ch. 4)

Private speech Spoken language that is not intended for others (Ch. 7)

Profound retardation Retardation in which IQ scores are below 20 or 25 (Ch. 9)

Proximodistal principle The principle that development proceeds from the center of the body outward (Ch. 4)

Psychoanalytic theory The theory proposed by Freud that suggests that unconscious forces act to determine personality and behavior (Ch. 1)

Psychodynamic perspective The approach that states behavior is motivated by inner forces, memories, and conflicts of which a person has little awareness or control (Ch. 1)

Psychological maltreatment Abuse that occurs when parents or other caregivers harm children's behavioral, cognitive, emotional, or physical functioning (Ch. 8)

Psychosexual development According to Freud, a series of stages that children pass through in which pleasure, or gratification, is focused on a particular biological function and body part (Ch. 1)

Psychosocial development The approach that encompasses changes both in the understanding individuals have of their interactions with others, others' behavior, and of themselves as members of society (Ch. 1, 8)

Psychosomatic disorders Medical problems caused by the interaction of psychological, emotional, and physical difficulties (Ch. 13)

Puberty The period during which the sexual organs mature, beginning earlier for girls than for boys (Ch. 11)

Race dissonance The phenomenon in which minority children indicate preferences for majority values or people (Ch. 8)

Rapid eye movement (REM) sleep The period of sleep that is found in older children and adults and is associated with dreaming (Ch. 4)

Realistic period The stage that spans adolescence during which people begin to think in pragmatic terms about the requirements of various jobs and how their own abilities might fit with them (Ch. 14)

Reciprocal socialization A process in which infants' behaviors invite further responses from parents and other caregivers (Ch. 6)

Redefinition of self versus preoccupation with work-role The theory that those in old age must redefine themselves in ways that do not relate to their work-roles or occupations (Ch. 18)

Reference group Groups of people with whom one compares oneself (Ch. 12)

Reflexes Unlearned, organized involuntary responses that occur automatically in the presence of certain stimuli (Ch. 3, 4)

Reintegrative stage The period of late adulthood during which the focus is on tasks that have personal meaning (Ch. 13)

Rejected children Children who are actively disliked, and whose peers may react to them in an obviously negative manner (Ch. 10)

Resilience The ability to overcome circumstances that place a child at high risk for psychological or physical damage (Ch. 8)

Responsible stage The stage where the major concerns of middle-aged adults relate to their personal situations, including protecting and nourishing their spouses, families, and careers (Ch. 13)

Rhythms Repetitive, cyclical patterns of behavior (Ch. 4)

Sandwich generation People who in middle adulthood must fulfill the needs of both their children and their aging parents (Ch. 16)

Schemas Organized bodies of information stored in memory (Ch. 15)

Scheme An organized pattern of sensorimotor functioning (Ch. 5)

School day care Child-care facility provided by some local school systems in the United States (Ch. 7)

Secondary appraisal The assessment of whether one's coping abilities and resources are adequate to overcome the harm, threat, or challenge posed by the potential stressor (Ch. 13)

Secondary sex characteristics The visible signs of sexual maturity that do not involve the sex organs directly (Ch. 11)

Selective optimization The process by which people concentrate on particular skill areas to compensate for losses in other areas (Ch. 15, 18)

Self-concept Peoples' beliefs about what they are like as individuals (Ch. 8)

Self-efficacy Learned expectations that one is capable of carrying out a behavior or producing a desired outcome in a particular situation (Ch. 10)

Self-esteem An individual's overall and specific positive and negative self-evaluation (Ch. 10)

Sensation The stimulation of the sense organs (Ch. 4)

Sensorimotor stage According to Piaget the initial stage of cognitive development, spanning from birth to about 2 years of age, during which knowledge develops from physically acting on objects. (Ch. 5)

Severe retardation Retardation in which IQ scores range from about 20 or 25 to 35 or 40 (Ch. 9)

Sex cleavage Sex segregation in which boys interact primarily with boys, and girls primarily with girls (Ch. 12)

Sexually transmitted disease (STD) A disease that is spread through sexual contact (Ch. 11)

Sickle-cell anemia A blood disorder that gets its name from the shape of the red blood cells in those who have it (Ch. 2)

Skilled-nursing facilities A facility that provides full-time nursing care for people who have chronic illnesses or who are recovering from a temporary medical condition (Ch. 18)

Small-for-gestational-age infants Infants who, because of delayed fetal growth, weigh 90 percent or less than the average weight of infants of the same gestational age (Ch. 3)

Social clock The psychological timepiece that records the major milestones in people's lives (Ch. 16)

Social comparison The desire to evaluate one's own behavior, abilities, expertise, and opinions by comparing them to those of others (Ch. 10)

Social competence The collection of individual social skills that permits people to perform successfully in social settings (Ch. 10)

Social development The way in which individuals' interactions with others and their social relationships grow, change, and remain stable over the course of life (Ch. 1)

Social learning Learning by observing the behavior of another person, called a model (Ch. 1)

Social problem-solving The use of strategies for solving social conflicts in ways that are satisfactory both to oneself and to others (Ch. 10)

Social referencing The intentional search for information to help explain the meaning of uncertain circumstances and events (Ch. 6)

Social smile Smiling in response to other individuals (Ch. 6)

Social speech Speech directed toward another person and meant to be understood by that person (Ch. 7)

Social support Assistance and comfort supplied by another person or a network of caring, interested people (Ch. 18)

Socialized delinquents Adolescents who know and subscribe to the norms of society; they are fairly normal psychologically (Ch. 12)

Sociobiologists Scientists who consider the biological roots of social behavior (Ch. 8)

Speech impairment Speech that is impaired when it deviates so much from the speech of others that it calls attention to itself, interferes with communication, or produces maladjustment in the speaker (Ch. 9)

Stanford-Binet Intelligence Scale A test consisting of a series of items that vary according to the age of the person being tested (Ch. 9)

State The degree of awareness displayed to both internal and external stimulation (Ch. 4)

Status The evaluation of a role or person by other relevant members of a group or society (Ch. 10, 14)

Stillbirth The delivery of a child who is not alive, occurring in less than one delivery in 100 (Ch. 3)

Stimulus-value-role (SVR) theory The theory that relationships proceed in a fixed order of three stages: stimulus, value, and role (Ch. 14)

Stress The response to events that threaten or challenge people (Ch. 13)

Stuttering Substantial disruption in the rhythm and fluency of speech; the most common speech impairment (Ch. 9)

Sudden infant death syndrome (SIDS) The unexplained death of a seemingly healthy baby (Ch. 4, 19)

Superego According to Freud, the aspect of personality that represents a person's conscience, incorporating distinctions between right and wrong (Ch. 1)

Syntax The way in which an individual combines words and phrases to form sentences (Ch. 7)

Tay-Sachs disease A disorder for which there is no treatment and that produces blindness and muscle degeneration prior to death (Ch. 2)

Teacher expectancy effect The cycle of behavior in which a teacher transmits an expectation about a child and thereby actually brings about the expected behavior (Ch. 10)

Telegraphic speech Speech in which words not central or critical to the message are left out (Ch. 5)

Temperament Patterns of arousal and emotionality that are consistent and enduring characteristics of an individual (Ch. 6)

Tentative period The second stage of Eli Ginzberg's theory that spans adolescence, when people begin to think in pragmatic terms about the requirements of various occupations and how their own abilities might fit with them (Ch. 14)

Teratogen A factor that produces a birth defect (Ch. 2)

Thanatologists   People who study death and dying (Ch. 19)

Theories   Explanations and predictions concerning phenomena of interest, providing a framework for understanding the relationships among an organized set of facts or principles (Ch. 1)

Theory of mind   Knowledge and beliefs about a child's mental world (Ch. 6)

Transformation   The process in which one state or condition is changed into another (Ch. 7)

Treatment   A procedure applied by an investigator based on two different experiences devised for subjects and participants (see **Experiment**) (Ch. 1)

Treatment group   The group receiving the treatment in an experiment (Ch. 1)

Triarchic theory of intelligence   The model that states that intelligence consists of three aspects of information processing: the componential element, the experiential element, and the contextual element (Ch. 9, 13)

Trust-versus-mistrust stage   The period during which infants develop a sense of trust or mistrust, largely depending on how well their needs are met by their caretakers (Ch. 6)

Type A behavior pattern   Behavior characterized by competitiveness, impatience, and a tendency toward frustration and hostility (Ch. 15)

Type B behavior pattern   Behavior characterized by non-competitiveness, patience, and a lack of aggression (Ch. 15)

Ultrasound sonography   A process in which high-frequency sound waves scan the mother's womb to produce an image of the unborn baby whose size and shape can then be assessed (Ch. 2)

Underextension   The act of using words too restrictively, common among children just mastering spoken language (Ch. 5)

Undersocialized delinquents   Adolescents who are raised with little discipline, or with harsh, uncaring parental supervision (Ch. 12)

Universal grammar   Norm Chomsky's theory that all the world's languages share a similar underlying structure (Ch. 7)

Very-low-birthweight infants   Infants who weigh less than 1250 grams (about 2¼ pounds) or, regardless of weight, have been in the womb under 30 weeks (Ch. 3)

Visual impairment   Difficulties in seeing that may include blindness or partial sightedness (Ch. 9)

Visual-recognition memory   The memory of and recognition of a stimulus that has been previously seen; related to IQ (Ch. 5)

Wear-and-tear theories   The theory that the mechanical functions of the body simply wear out with age (Ch. 17)

Wechsler Adult Intelligence Scale–Revised (WAIS–R)   A test for adults that provides separate measures of verbal and performance (or nonverbal) skills, as well as a total score (Ch. 9)

Wechsler Intelligence Scale for Children–Revised (WISC–R)   A test for children that provides separate measures of verbal and performance (or nonverbal) skills, as well as a total score (Ch. 9)

Weight set point   The particular level of weight that the body strives to maintain (Ch. 13)

Zone of proximal development (ZPD)   The level at which a child can *almost,* but not fully, comprehend or perform a task on her or his own, according to Lev Vygotsky (Ch. 7)

Zygote   The new cell formed by the process of fertilization (Ch. 2)

References

AAMR (American Association on Mental Retardation). (1992). *Mental retardation: Definition, classification, and systems of support.* Washington, DC: Author.

AAP/ACOG (American Academy of Pediatrics /American College of Obstetricians and Gynecologists). (1992). *Guidelines for perinatal care.* Elk Grove, IN: Author.

AARP (American Association of Retired Persons). (1990). *A profile of older Americans.* Washington, DC: Author.

Abeles, R.P., Gift, H.C., & Ory, M.G. (Eds.). (1994). *Aging and quality of life.* New York: Springer.

Able, E.L., & Sokol, R.J. (1987). Incidence of fetal alcohol syndrome and economic impact of FAS-related anomalies. *Drug and Alcohol Dependence, 19,* 51–70.

Aboud, F.E., & Skerry, S.A. (1983). Self and ethnic concepts in relation to ethnic constancy. *Canadian Journal of Behavioral Science, 15,* 14–26.

Achenbach, T.A. (1992). Developmental psycholopathology. In M.H. Bornstein & M.E. Lamb (Eds.), *Developmental psychology: An advanced textbook.* Hillsdale, NJ: Erlbaum.

ACOG (American College of Obstetricians and Gynecologists). (1994, February). *Guidelines for exercise during pregnancy and the postpartum period.* Washington, DC: Author.

Adams, R.J., Mauer, D., & Davis, M. (1986). Newborns' discrimination of chromatic from achromatic stimuli. *Journal of Experimental Child Psychology, 41,* 267–281.

Adelmann, P.K., Antonucci, T.C., & Crohan, S.E. (1990). A causal analysis of employment and health in midlife women. *Women and Health, 16,* 5–20.

Adler, P.A., Kless, S.J., & Adler, P. (1992). Socialization to gender roles: Popularity among elementary school boys and girls. *Sociology of Education, 65,* 169–187.

Ainsworth, M.D. (1989). Attachments beyond infancy. *American Psychologist, 44,* 709–716.

Ainsworth, M.D.S., Blehar, M.C., Waters, E., & Wall, S. (1978). *Patterns of attachment: A psychological study of the strange situation.* Hillsdale, NJ: Erlbaum.

Ainsworth, M.D.S., & Bowlby, J. (1991). An ethological approach to personality development. *American Psychologist, 46,* 333–341.

Ainsworth, M.S. (1993). Attachment as related to mother–infant interaction. *Advances in Infancy Research, 8,* 1–50.

Aitken, R.J. (1995, July 7). The complexities of conception. *Science, 269,* 39–40.

Akutsu, H. (1991). Psychophysics of reading—X. Effects of age-related changes in vision. *Journal of Gerontology: Psychological Sciences, 46,* 325–331.

Alan Guttmacher Institute (1988). *Pregnancy rates around the world.* New York: Author.

Alan Guttmacher Institute. (1993a). *Report on viral sexual diseases.* Chicago: Author.

Alan Guttmacher Institute. (1993b). *Survey of male sexuality.* Chicago: Author.

Alan Guttmacher Institute (1994). *National teenage pregnancy rate.* New York: Author.

Albers, L.L., & Krulewitch, C.J. (1993). Electronic fetal monitoring in the United States in the 1980s. *Obstetrics & Gynecology, 82,* 8–10.

Albert, M.S., & Kaplan, E. (1980). Organic implications of neuropsychological deficits in the elderly. In L.W. Poon, J.L. Fozard, L.S. Cermak, D. Arenberg, & L.W. Thompson (Eds.), *New directions in memory and aging: Proceedings of the George A. Talland memorial conference.* Hillsdale, NJ: Erlbaum.

Alessandri, S.M., Sullivan, M.W., Imaizumi, S., & Lewis, M. (1993). Learning and emotional responsivity in cocaine-exposed infants. *Developmental Psychology, 29,* 989–997.

Alexander, G.M., & Hines, M. (1994). Gender labels and play styles: Their relative contributions to children's selection of playmate. *Child Development, 65,* 869–879.

Allan, P. (1990). Looking for work after forty: Job search experiences of older unemployed managers and professionals. *Journal of Employment Counseling, 27,* 113–121.

Allen, L.S., Hines, M., Shryne, J.E., & Gorski, R.A. (1989). Two sexually dimorphic cell groups in the human brain. *Journal of Neuroscience, 9,* 497–506.

Als, H. (1992). Individualized, family-focused developmental care for the very low-birthweight preterm infant in the NICU. In S.L. Friedman & M.D. Sigman (Eds.), *The psychological development of low birthweight children.* Norwood, NJ: Ablex.

Ambuel, B. (1995). Adolescents, unintended pregnancy, and abortion: The struggle for a compassionate social policy. *Current Directions in Psychological Science, 4,* 1–5.

American Academy of Pediatrics. (1989b) *The facts on breastfeeding.* Elk Grove Village, IL: Author.

American Academy of Pediatrics. (1992). The use of whole cow's milk in infancy. *Pediatrics, 89,* 1105–1109.

American Academy of Pediatrics Committee on Drugs. (1978). Effects of medication during labor and delivery on infant outcome. *Pediatrics, 62* (3), 402–403.

American Academy of Pediatrics Committee on Sports Medicine and Committee on School Health. (1989a). Organized athletics for pre-adolescent children. *Pediatrics, 84* (3), 583–584.

American Academy of Pediatrics. (1982). The promotion of breast feeding. *Pediatrics, 72* (6), 891–894.

American Academy of Pediatrics. (1988). Committee on sports medicine: Infant exercise programs. *Pediatrics, 82,* 800–825.

American Cancer Society. (1992). *Cancer facts and figures.* New York: Author.

American Council on Education. (1995). *The American freshman: National norms for fall 1994.* Los Angeles: University of California Los Angeles Higher Education Research Institute.

American Heart Association. (1988). *Heart facts.* Dallas, TX: Author.

American Humane Association. (1991). Annual cases reported. Englewood, CO: Author.

American Psychological Association. (1992). Ethical principles of psychologists and code of conduct. *American Psychological Association.* Washington, DC: Author.

Amsel, A. (1988). *Behaviorism, neobehaviorism, and cognitivism in learning theory.* Hillsdale, NJ: Erlbaum.

Anand, K.J.S., & Hickey, P.R. (1987). Pain and its effect in the human neonate and fetus. *New England Journal of Medicine, 317* (21), 1321–1329.

Anand, K.J.S., & Hickey, P.R. (1992). Halothane-morphine compared with high-dose sufentanil for anesthesia and post-operative analgesia in neonatal cardiac surgery. *New England Journal of Medicine, 326* (1), 1–9.

Anders, T.F., & Taylor, T. (1994). Babies and their sleep environment. *Children's Environments, 11* 123–134.

Anderson, D.A. (1994). Lesbian and gay adolescents: Social and developmental considerations. *High School Journal, 77,* 13–19.

Andersson, T., & Magnusson, D. (1990). Biological maturation in adolescence and the development of drinking habits and alcohol abuse among young males: A prospective longitudinal study. *Journal of Youth and Adolescence, 19,* 33–42.

Ansberry, C. (1995, February 14). After seven decades, couple still finds romance in the 90s. *The Wall Street Journal,* pp. A1, A17.

Anstey, K., Stankov, L., & Lord, S. (1993). Primary aging, secondary aging, and intelligence. *Psychology and Aging, 8,* 562–570.

Antonucci, T.C. (1990). Social supports and social relationships. In R.H. Binstock & L.K. George (Eds.), *Handbook of aging and the social sciences.* San Diego, CA: Academic Press.

Antonucci, T.C., & Akiyama, H. (1991). Social relationships and aging well. *Generations, 15,* 39–44.

APA (American Psychological Association). A public interest directorate. (1993, August 10). *Violence and youth: Psychology's response.* Washington, DC: Author.

Apgar, V. (1953). A proposal for a new method of evaluation in the newborn infant. *Current Research in Anesthesia and Analgesia, 32,* 260.

Appelbaum, M. (1995, March). Paper presented at the biennial meeting of the Society for Research in child Development. Indianapolis, IN.

Apter, A., Galatzer, A., Beth-Halachmi, N., & Laron, Z. (1981). Self-image in adolescents with delayed puberty and growth retardation. *Journal of Youth and Adolescence, 10,* 501–505.

Archer, S.L., & Waterman, A.S. (1994). Adolescent identity development: Contextual perspectives. In C.B. Fisher & R.M. Lerner (Eds.), *Applied developmental psychology.* New York: McGraw-Hill.

Archibald, W.P. (1974). Alternative explanations for the self-fulfilling prophecy. *Psychological Bulletin, 81,* 74–84.

Ardila, A., & Rosselli, M. (1994). Development of language, memory, and visuospatial ability in 5- to 12-year-old children using a neuropsychological battery. *Developmental Neuropsychology, 10,* 97–120.

Ards, S., & Harrell, A. (1993). Reporting of child maltreatment: A secondary analysis of the national incidence surveys. *Child Abuse & Neglect, 17,* 337–344.

Arias, R. (1995, January 23). *People Weekly,* pp. 34–39.

Aries, P. (1962). *Centuries of childhood.* New York: Knopf.

Armstrong, M.J. (1991). Friends as a source of informal support for older women with physical disabilities. *Journal of Women and Aging, 3,* 63–83.

Arnett, J. (1995). The young and reckless: Adolescent reckless behavior. *Current Directions in Psychological Science, 4,* 67–71.

Art of Living. (1995, March 20). *People Weekly,* p. 69.

Artal, P., Ferro, M., Miranda, I., & Navarro, R. (1993). Effects of aging in retinal image quality. *Journal of the Optical Society of America, 10,* 1656–1662.

Aseltine, R.H., Gore, S., & Colten, M.E. (1994). Depression and the social developmental context of adolescence. *Journal of Personality and Social Psychology, 67,* 252–263.

Asendorpf, J.B., & Baudonniere, P.M. (1993). Self-awareness and other-awareness: Mirror self-recognition and synchronic imitation among unfamiliar peers. *Developmental Psychology, 29,* 88–95.

Asher, S.R. (1983). Social competence and peer status: Recent advances and future directions. *Child Development, 54,* 1427–1434.

Asher, S.R., Hymel, S., & Renshaw, P.D. (1984). Loneliness in children. *Child Development, 55,* 1456–1464.

Asher, S.R., & Parker, J.G. (1991). The significance of peer relationship problems in childhood. In B.H. Schneider, G. Attili, J. Nadel, & R.P. Weisberg (Eds.), *Social competence in developmental perspective.* Amsterdam, The Netherlands: Kluwer.

Asher, S.R., Singleton, L.C., & Taylor, A.R. (1982). *Acceptance vs friendship.* Paper presented at the meeting of the American Research Association, New York.

Askham, J. (1994). Marriage relationships of older people. *Reviews in Clinical Gerontology, 4,* 261–268.

Aslin, R.N. (1987). Visual and auditory development in infancy. In J.D. Osofsky (Ed.), *Handbook of infant development* (2nd ed.). New York: Wiley.

Atchley, R.C. (1982). Retirement: Leaving the world of work. *Annals of the American Academy of Political and Social Science, 464,* 120–131.

Atchley, R.C. (1985). *Social forces and aging: An introduction to social gerontology.* Belmont, CA: Wadsworth.

Atkins, C.J., Senn, K., Rupp, J., & Kaplan, R.M. (1990). Attendance at health promotion programs: Baseline predictors and program outcomes. *Health Education Quarterly, 17,* 417–428.

Atwater, L.E. (1992). Beyond cognitive ability: Improving the prediction of performance. *Journal of Business and Psychology, 7,* 27–44.

Aved, B.M., Irwin, M.M., Cummings, L.S., & Findeisen, N. (1993). Barriers to prenatal care for low-income women. *Western Journal of Medicine, 158,* 493–498.

Aviezer, O., Van Ijzendoorn, M.H., Sagi, A., & Schuengel, C. (1994). "Children of the dream" revisited: 70 Years of collective early child care in Israeli kibbutzim. *Psychological Bulletin, 116,* 99–116.

Azar, B. (1995, January). "Gifted" label stretches, it's more than high IQ. *APA Monitor,* p. 25.

Azar, B., & McCarthy, K. (1994, October). Psychologists recommend vigilance against aggression. *APA Monitor,* p. 45.

Azuma, S., & Chasnoff, I. (1993). Outcome of children prenatally exposed to cocaine and other drugs: An analysis of three-year data. *Pediatrics, 92,* 396–402.

Baar, K. (1995, March 29). Time for a fitness pyramid? *The New York Times,* pp. C1, C6.

Babad, E. (1992). Pygmalion—25 years after interpersonal expectations in the classroom. In P.D. Blanck (Ed.), *Interpersonal expectations: Theory, research and application.* Cambridge: Cambridge University Press.

Backer, P. (1993, February 28). On turning 13: Reports from the front lines. *The New York Times,* sec. 4, p. 2.

Bahr, S.J., & Peterson, E.T. (Eds.). (1989). *Aging and the family.* Lexington, MA: Lexington Books.

Bahrick, L.E. (1989). Intermodal learning in infancy: Learning on the basis of two kinds of invariant relations in audible and visible events. *Child Development, 50,* 197–209.

Bahrick, L.E., & Pickens, J.N. (1988). Classification of bimodal English and Spanish language passages by infants. *Infant Behavior and Development, 11,* 277–296.

Baillargeon, R. (1987). Object permanence in $3\frac{1}{2}$-and $4\frac{1}{2}$-month-old infants. *Developmental Psychology, 23* (5), 655–670.

Baillargeon, R., & DeVos, J. (1991). Object permanence in young infants: Further evidence. *Child Development, 62,* 1227–1246.

Baker, D.B. (1994). Parenting stress and ADHD: A comparison of mothers and fathers. *Journal of Emotional and Behavioral Disorders, 2,* 46–50.

Baldwin, W. (1993). The consequences of early childbearing: A perspective. *Journal of Research on Adolescence, 3,* 349–352.

Ball, J.A. (1987). *Reactions to motherhood.* New York: Cambridge University Press.

Ball, K., & Rebok, G.W. (1994). Evaluating the driving ability of older adults. Special Issue: Research translation in gerontology: A behavioral and social perspective. *Journal of Applied Gerontology, 13,* 20–38.

Baltes, M.M. (1995). Dependency in old age: Gains and losses. *Current Directions in Psychological Science, 4,* 14–19.

Baltes, P.B. (1987). Theoretical propositions of life-span developmental psychology: On the dynamics between growth and decline. *Developmental Psychology, 23,* 611–626.

Baltes, P.B. (1993). The aging mind: Potential and limits. *Gerontologist, 33,* 580–594.

Baltes, P.B., & Schaie, K.W. (1974, March). The myth of the twilight years. *Psychology Today,* pp. 35–38.

Baltes, P.B., Reese, H.W., & Lipsitt, L. (1980). Life-span developmental psychology. *Annual Review of Psychology, 31,* 65–110.

Baltes, P.B., & Baltes, M.M. (1990). Psychological perspectives on successful aging: the model of selective optimization with compensation. In P.B. Baltes & M.M. Baltes (Eds.), *Successful aging: Perspectives from the behavioral sciences.* Cambridge: Cambridge University Press.

Baltrusch, H.J., Stangel, W., & Tirze, I. (1991). Stress, cancer and immunity: New developments in biopsychosocial and psychoneuroimmunologic research. *Acta Neurologica, 13,* 315–327.

Bandura, A. (1977). *Social learning theory.* Englewood Cliffs, NJ: Prentice-Hall.

Bandura, A. (1978). Social learning theory of aggression. *Journal of Communication, 28,* 12–29.

Bandura, A. (1986). *Social foundations of thought and action.* Englewood Cliffs, NJ: Prentice-Hall.

Bandura, A. (1988). Perceived self-efficacy: Exercise of control through self-belief. In J.P. Dauwalder, M. Perrez, & V. Hobbi (Eds.), *Annual series of Euopean research in behavior therapy* (Vol. 2). Lisse, The Netherlands: Swets & Zeilinger.

Bandura, A. (1991). Social cognitive theory of moral thought and action. In W.M. Kurtines & J.L. Gewirtz (Eds.), *Handbook of moral behavior and development.* Hillsdale, NJ: Erlbaum.

Bandura, A. (1993). Perceived self-efficacy in cognitive development and functioning. *Educational Psychologist, 28,* 117–148.

Bandura, A., Grusec, J.E., & Menlove, F.L. (1967). Vicarious extinction of avoidance behavior. *Journal of Personality and Social Psychology, 5,* 16–23.

Bandura, A., & Schunk, D.H. (1981). Cultivating competence, self-efficacy, and intrinsic interest through proximal self-motivation. *Journal of Personality and Social Psychology, 67,* 601–607.

Bandura, A., Ross, D., & Ross, S. (1963). Vicarious extinction of avoidance behavior. *Journal of Personality and Social Psychology, 67,* 601–607.

Barer, B.M. (1994). Men and women aging differently. *International Journal of Aging and Human Development, 38,* 29–40.

Barinaga, M. (1995, June 30). New Alzheimer's gene found. *Science, 268,* 1845–1846.

Barinaga, M. (1995, August 18). Missing Alzheimer's gene found. *Science, 269,* 917–918.

Barkley, R.A. (1995). *Taking charge of ADHD: The complete, authoritative guide for parents.* New York: Guilford Press.

Barnett, R.C., & Rivers, C. (1992). The myth of the miserable working woman. *Working Woman, 2,* 62–65, 83–85.

Barnett, R.C., Raudenbush, S.W., Brennan, R.T., Pleck, J.H., & Marshall, N.L. (1995). Change in job and marital experiences and change in psychological distress: A longitudinal study of dual-earner couples. *Journal of Personality and Social Psychology, 69,* 839–850.

Barr, H.M., Streissguth, A.P., Darby, B.L., & Sampson, P.D. (1990). Prenatal exposure to alcohol, caffeine, tobacco, and aspirin: Effects on fine and gross motor performance in 4-year-old children. *Developmental Psychology, 26* (3), 339–348.

Barr, R.G., Konner, M., Bakeman, R., & Adamson, L. (1991). Crying in ~KungSan infants: A test of the cultural specificity hypothesis. *Developmental Medicine and Child Neurology, 33,* 601–610.

Barrett, D.E., & Frank, D.A. (1987). *The effects of undernutrition on children's behavior.* New York: Gordon & Breach.

Barrett, D.E., & Radke-Yarrow, M.R. (1985). Effects of nutritional supplementation on children's responses to novel, frustrating, and competitive situations. *American Journal of Clinical Nutrition, 42,* 102–120.

Bartecchi, C.E., MacKenzie, T.D., & Schrier, R.W. (1995, May). The global tobacco epidemic. *Scientific American,* pp. 44–51.

Bates, E., Bretherton, I., & Snyder, L. (1988). *From first words to grammar: Individual differences and dissociable mechanisms.* New York: Cambridge University Press.

Bates, J.E., Marvinney, D., Bennett, D.S., Dodge, K.A., Kelly, T., & Pettit, G.S. (1991). *Children's daycare history and kindergarten adjustment.* Paper presented at the biennial meeting of the Society for Research in Child Development, Seattle, WA.

Bates, J.E., Marvinney, D., Kelly, T., Dodge, K.A., Bennett, D.S., & Pettit, G.S. (1994). Child-care history and kindergarten adjustment. *Developmental Psychology, 30,* 690–700.

Baumeister, R.F. (Ed.). (1993). *Self-esteem: The puzzle of low self-regard.* New York: Plenum Press.

Baumrind, D. (1971). Current patterns of parental authority. *Developmental Psychology Monographs, 4* (1, Pt. 2).

Baumrind, D. (1980). New directions in socialization research. *Psychological Bulletin, 35,* 639–652.

Bayer, C.L., & Cegala, D.J. (1992). Trait verbal aggressiveness and argumentativeness: Relations with parenting style. *Western Journal of Communication, 56,* 301–310.

Bayley, N. (1949). Consistency and variability in the growth of intelligence from birth to eighteen years. *Journal of Genetic Psychology, 75,* 165–196.

Bayley, N. (1969). *Manual for the Bayley scales of infant development.* New York: The Psychological Corporation.

Bayley, N., & Oden, M. (1955). The maintenance of intellectual ability in gifted adults. *Journal of Gerontology, 10,* 91–107.

Beal, C.R. (1994). *Boys and girls: The development of gender roles.* New York: McGraw-Hill.

Beal, C.R., & Belgrad, S.L. (1990). The development of message evaluation skills in young children. *Child Development, 61,* 705–712.

Bear, G.G., & Rys, G.S. (1994). Moral reasoning, classroom behavior, and sociometric status among elementary school children. *Developmental Psychology, 30,* 633–638.

Becahy, R. (1992, August 3). AIDS epidemic. *Newsweek,* p. 49.

Beck, M. (1991, November 11). School days for seniors. *Newsweek,* pp. 60–65.

Beck, M. (1992, May 25). Menopause. *Newsweek,* pp. 71–79.

Beck, R.W., & Beck, S.W. (1989). The incidence of extended households among middle-aged black and white women. *Journal of Family Issues, 10,* 147–168.

Beckwirth, L., & Rodning, C. (1991). Intellectual functioning in children born preterm: Recent research. In L. Okagaki & R.J. Sternberg (Eds.), *Directors of development: Influences on the development of children's thinking.* Hillsdale, NJ: Erlbaum.

Begley, S. (1991, August 26). Choosing death. *Newsweek,* pp. 43–46.

Behrend, D.A. (1988). Overextensions in early language comprehension: Evidence from a signal detection approach. *Journal of Child Language, 15,* 63–75.

Beilin, H., & Pufall, P. (Eds.). (1992). *Piaget's theory: Prospects and possibilities.* Hillsdale, NJ: Erlbaum.

Belkin, L. (1985, May 23). Parents weigh costs of children. *The New York Times,* p. A14.

Bell, A., & Weinberg, M.S. (1978). *Homosexuality: A study of diversities among men and women.* New York: Simon & Schuster.

Bell, I.P. (1989). The double standard: Age. In J. Freeman (Ed.), *Women: A feminist perspective* (4th ed.). Mountain View, CA: Mayfield.

Bell, J.Z. (1978). Disengagement versus engagement—a need for greater expectation. *Journal of the American Geriatrics Society, 26,* 89–95.

Bell, S.M., & Ainsworth, M.D.S. (1972). Infant crying and maternal responsiveness. *Child Development, 43,* 1171–1190.

Bellack, A.S., Hersen, M., & Kazdin, A.E. (1990). *International handbook of behavior modification and therapy*. New York: Plenum Press.

Bellezza, F.S., Six, L.S., & Phillips, D.S. (1992). A mnemonic for remembering long strings of digits. *Bulletin of the Psychonomic Society, 30,* 271–274.

Belluck, P. (1995, January 25). At 15, Westinghouse finalist grasps Holy Grail of math. The *The New York Times,* p. A1.

Belmont, J.M. (1994). Discussion: A view from the empiricist's window. *Educational Psychologists, 30,* 99–102.

Belsky, J., & Rovine, M. (1987). Temperament and attachment in the strange situation: An empirical rapprochement. *Child Development, 58,* 787–795.

Belsky, J., & Rovine, M. (1988). Nonmaternal care in the first year of life and infant–parent attachment security. *Child Development, 59,* 157–167.

Belsky, J., Fish, M., & Isabella, R. (1991). Continuity and discontinuity in infant negative and positive emotionality: Family antecedents and attachment consequences. *Developmental Psychology, 27,* 421–431.

Belsky, J., Rovine, M., & Fish M. (1989). The developing family system. In M. Gunnar (Ed.), *Systems and development: Minnesota symposium on child psychology* (Vol. 22). Hillsdale, NJ: Erlbaum.

Belsky, J., Rovine, M., & Taylor, D.G. (1984). The Pennsylvania infant and family development project: III. The origins of individual differences in infant–mother attachment: Maternal and infant contributions. *Child Development, 55,* 718–728.

Belsky, J., Steinberg, L., & Walker, A. (1982). The ecology of day care: A critical review. *Child Development, 49,* 929–949.

Bem, S. (1987). Gender schema theory and its implications for child development: Raising gender-aschematic children in a gender-schematic society. In M.R. Walsh (Ed.), *The psychology of women: Ongoing debates.* New Haven, CT: Yale University Press.

Ben-Porath, Y. (1991). Economic implications of human life span extension. In F.C. Ludwig (Ed.), *Life span extension: Consequences and open questions.* New York: Springer.

Benedict, H. (1979). Early lexical development: Comprehension and production. *Journal of Child Language, 6,* 183–200.

Benenson, J.F., & Apostoleris, N.H. (1993, March). *Gender differences in group interaction in early childhood.* Paper presented at the biennial meeting of the Society for Research in Child Development, New Orleans.

Benenson, J.F. (1994). Ages four to six years: Changes in the structures of play networks of boys and girls. *Merrill-Palmer Quarterly, 40,* 478–487.

Bengston, V.L., Cutler, N.E., Mangen, D.J., & Marshall, V.W. (1985). Generations, cohorts, and relations between age groups. In R.H. Binstock & E. Shanas (Eds.), *Handbook of aging and the social sciences* (2nd ed.). New York: Van Nostrand Reinhold.

Bengston, V.L., Rosenthal, C., & Burton, L. (1990). Families and aging: Diversity and heterogeneity. In R.H. Binstock & L.K. George (Eds.), *Handbook of aging and the social sciences* (3rd ed.). San Diego, CA: Academic Press.

Bennet, A. (1992, October 14). Lori Schiller emerges from the torments of schizophrenia. *The Wall Street Journal,* pp. A1, A10.

Benoit, D., & Parker, K.C.H. (1994). Stability and transmission of attachment across three generations. *Child Development, 65,* 1444–1456.

Benson, H. (1993). The relaxation response. In D. Goleman & J. Guerin (Eds.), *Mind-body medicine: How to use your mind for better health.* Yonkers, NY: Consumer Reports Publications.

Berenbaum, S.A., & Hines, M. (1992). Early androgens are related to sex-typed toy preferences. *Psychological Science, 3,* 202–206.

Berenbaum, S.A., & Snyder, E. (1995). Early hormonal influences on childhood sex-typed activity and playmate preferences: Implications for the development of sexual orientation. Special Issue: Sexual orientation and human development. *Developmental Psychology, 31,* 31–42.

Bergeman, C., Chipuer, H., Plomin, R., Pedersen, N., McClearn, G., Nesselroade, J., Costa, P., & McCrae, R. (1993). Genetic and environmental effects on openness to experience, agreeableness, and conscientiousness: An adoption/twin study. *Journal of Personality, 61,* 159–179.

Bergener, M., Ermini, M., & Stahelin, H.B. (Eds.). (1985, February). *Thresholds in aging.* The 1984 Sandoz Lectures in Gerontology, Basel, Switzerland.

Berk, L.E. (1992). Children's private speech: An overview of the theory and the status of research. In R.M. Diaz & L.E. Berk (Eds.), *Private speech: From social interaction to self-regulation.* Hillsdale, NJ: Erlbaum.

Berk, L.E., & Landau, S. (1993). Private speech of learning disabled and normally achieving children in classroom academic and laboratory contexts. *Child Development, 64,* 556–571.

Berko, J. (1958). The child's learning of English morphology. *Word, 14,* 150–177.

Berkowitz, G.S., Skovron, M.L., Lapinski, R.H., & Berkowitz, R.L. (1990). Delayed childbearing and the outcome of pregnancy. *New England Journal of Medicine, 322,* 659–664.

Berkowitz, L. (1993). *Aggression: Its causes, consequences, and control.* New York: McGraw-Hill.

Berman, A.L., & Jobes, D.A. (1991). *Adolescent suicide: Assessment and intervention.* Washington, DC: American Psychological Association.

Bernal, M.E. (1994, August). *Ethnic identity of Mexican-American children.* Address at the annual meeting of the American Psychological Association, Los Angeles.

Bernard, J. (1982). *The future of marriage.* New Haven, CT: Yale University Press.

Berscheid, E. (1985). Interpersonal attraction. In G. Lindzey & E. Aronson (Eds.), *Handbook of social psychology* (3rd ed.). New York: Random House.

Berscheid, E., & Walster, E. (1974a). Physical attractiveness. In G. Lindzey & E. Aronson (Eds.), *Handbook of social psychology* (3rd ed.). New York: Random House.

Berscheid, E., & Walster, E. (1974b). Physical attractiveness. In L. Berkowitz, (Ed.), *Advances in experimental social psychology* (Vol. 7, pp. 157–215). New York: Academic Press.

Berscheid, E., Walster, E., & Bohrnstedt, G. (1973, June). The happy American body: A survey report. *Psychology Today,* pp. 119–131.

Bersoff, D.M.N., & Ogned, D.W. (1991). APA amicus curiae briefs: Furthering lesbian and gay male civil rights. *American Psychologist, 46,* 950–956.

Bertman, S.L. (1991). *Facing death: Images, insights, and interventions.* Bristol, PA: Hemisphere.

Bianchi, S.M., & Spain, D. (1986). *American women in transition.* New York: Russell Sage Foundation.

Biedenharn, B.J., & Normoyle, J.B. (1991). Elderly community residents' reactions to the nursing home: An analysis of nursing home-related beliefs. *Gerontologist, 31,* 107–115.

Bierman, K.L., & Furman, W. (1984). The effects of social skills training and peer involvement on the social adjustment of preadolescents. *Child Development, 55,* 151–162.

Bierman, K.L., Miller, C.L., & Stabb, S.D. (1987). Improving the social behavior and peer acceptance of rejected boys: Effects of social skill training with instructions and prohibitions. *Journal of Consulting and Clinical Psychology, 55,* 194–200.

Biernat, M., & Wortman, C.B. (1991). Sharing of home responsibilities between professionally employed women and their husbands. *Journal of Personality and Social Psychology, 60,* 844–860.

Bijeljac-Babic, R., Bertoncini, J., & Mehler, J. (1993). How do 4-day-old infants categorize multisyllabic utterances? *Developmental Psychology, 29,* 711–721.

Bing, E.D. (1983). *Dear Elizabeth Bing: We've had our baby.* New York: Pocket Books.

Bird, G., & Melville, K. (1994). *Families and intimate relationships.* New York: McGraw-Hill.

Biron, O., Mongeau, J.G., & Bertrand, D. (1977). Familial resemblance of bodyweight and weight/height in 374 homes with adopted children. *Journal of Pediatrics, 91,* 555–558.

Birren, J.E., Woods, A.M., & Williams, M.V. (1980). Behavioral slowing with age: Causes, organization and consequences. In L.W. Poon (Ed.), *Aging in the 1980s.* Washington, DC: American Psychological Association.

Birsner, P. (1991). *Mid-career job hunting.* New York: Simon & Schuster.

Bisanz, J., Morrison, F.J., & Dunn, M. (1995). Effects of age and schooling on the acquisition of elementary quantitative skills. *Developmental Psychology, 31,* 221–236.

Bjorklund, D.F., Schneier, W., Cassel, W.S., & Ashley, E. (1994). Training and extension of a memory strategy: Evidence of utilization deficiencies in the acquisition of an organizational strategy in high- and low-IQ children. *Child Development, 65,* 951–965.

Black, J.E., & Greenough, W.T. (1986). Induction of pattern in neural structure by experience: Implication for cognitive development. In M.E. Lamb, A.L. Brown, & B. Rogoff (Eds.), *Advances in developmental psychology* (Vol. 4). Hillsdale, NJ: Erlbaum.

Blair, S.N., Kohl, H.W., Paffenberger, R.S., Clark, D.G., Cooper, K.H., & Gibbons, L.W. (1989). Physical fitness and all-cause mortality: A prospective study of healthy men and women. *Journal of the American Medical Association, 262,* 2395–2401.

Blake, J., & de Boysson-Bardies, B. (1992). Patterns in babbling: A cross-linguistic study. *Journal of Child Language, 19,* 51–74.

Blass, E.M., Ganchrow, J.R., & Steiner, J.E. (1984). Classical conditioning in newborn humans 2–48 hours of age. *Infant Behavior and Development, 7,* 223–235.

Blau, Z.S. (1973). *Old age in a changing society.* New York: New Viewpoints.

Blazer, D. (1989). Depression in the elderly. *The New England Journal of Medicine, 320* (3), 164–166.

Blazer, D. (1991). Suicide risk factors in the elderly: An epidemiological study. *Journal of Geriatric Psychiatry, 24,* 175–190.

Bloch, H. (1989). On early coordinations and their future. In A. de Ribaupierre (Ed.), *Transition mechanisms in child development: The longitudinal perspective* (pp. 259–282). New York: Cambridge University Press.

Bloom, L. (1993). *The transition from infancy to language: Acquiring the power of expression.* New York: Cambridge University Press.

Blount, B.G. (1982). Culture and the language of socialization: Parental speech. In D.A. Wagner & H.W. Stevenson (Eds.), *Cultural perspectives on child development.* San Francisco: Freeman.

Bluebond-Langner, M. (1977). Meanings of death to children. In H. Feifel (Ed.), *New meanings of death.* New York: McGraw-Hill.

Blumberg, B.D., Lewis, M.J., & Susman, E.J. (1984). Adolescence: A time of transition. In M.G. Eisenberg, L.C. Sutkin, & M.A. Jansen (Eds.), *Chronic illness and disability through the life span: Effects on self and family.* New York: Springer.

Blumenfield, M., Levy, N.B., & Kaplan, D. (1979). The wish to be informed of a fatal illness. *Omega, 9,* 323–326.

Blumstein, P., & Schwartz, P. (1989). *American couples: Money, work, sex.* New York: Morrow.

Blustein, D.L., & Palladino, D.E. (1991). Self and identity in late adolescence: A theoretical and empirical integration. *Journal of Adolescent Research, 6,* 437–453.

Bogatz, G.A., & Ball, S. (1972). *The second year of Sesame Street: A continuing evaluation.* Princeton, NJ: Educational Testing Service.

Boismier, J.D. (1977). Visual stimulation and wake-sleep behavior in human neonates. *Developmental Psychology, 10,* 219–227.

Boivin, M., Dodge, K.A., & Coie, J.D. (1995). Individual-group behavioral similarity and peer status in experimental play groups of boys: The social misfit revisited. *Journal of Personality and Social Psychology, 69,* 269–279.

Bolger, K.E., Patterson, C.J., Thompson, W.W., & Kupersmidt, J.B. (1995). Psychosocial adjustment among children experiencing persistent and intermittent family economic hardship. *Child Development, 66,* 1107–1129.

Bond, J., & Coleman, P. (1990). Aging into the twenty-first century. In J. Bond & P. Coleman (Eds.), *Aging in society: An introduction to social gerontology.* Newbury Park, CA: Sage.

Bond, L.A., Cutler, S.J., & Grams, A.E. (1995). *Promoting successful and productive aging.* Newbury Park, CA: Sage.

Booth, A., & Edwards, J.N. (1989). Transmission of marital and family quality over the generations: The effect of parental divorce and unhappiness. *Journal of Divorce, 13,* 41–58.

Booth, W. (1987, October 2). Big Brother is counting your keystrokes. *Science, 238,* 17.

Borgatta, E.F. (1991). Age discrimination issues. *Research on Aging, 13,* 476–484.

Bornstein, M.H. (1989a). Sensitive periods in development: Structural characteristics and causal interpretations. *Psychological Bulletin, 105,* 179–197.

Bornstein, M.H. (1989b). Stability in early mental development: From attention and information processing in infancy to language and cognition in childhood. In M.H. Bornstein & N.A. Krasnegor (Eds.), *Stability and continuity in mental development: Behavioral and biological perspectives* (pp. 147–170). Hillsdale, NJ: Erlbaum.

Bornstein, M.H., & Lamb, M.E. (1992). *Development in infancy: An introduction.* New York: McGraw-Hill.

Bornstein, M.H., & Lamb, M.E. (Eds.). (1992). *Developmental psychology: An advanced textbook* (p. 135). Hillsdale, NJ: Erlbaum.

Bornstein, M.H., & Ruddy, M.G. (1984). Infant attention and maternal stimulation. In H. Bouma & D.G. Bouwhuis (Eds.), *Attention and performance* (Vol. 10). London: Erlbaum.

Bornstein, M.H., & Sigman, M.D. (1986). Continuity in mental development from infancy. *Child Development, 57,* 251–274.

Bornstein, M.H., & Tamis-LeMonda, C.S. (1989). Maternal responsiveness and cognitive development in children. In M.H. Bornstein (Ed.), *Maternal responsiveness: Characteristics and consequences* (pp. 49–61). San Francisco: Jossey-Bass.

Botvin, G.J., Epstein, J.A., Schinke, S.P., & Diaz, T. (1994). Predictors of cigarette smoking among inner-city minority youth. *Journal of Developmental and Behavioral Pediatrics, 15,* 67–73.

Bouchard, C., Tremblay, A., Despres, J.P., Nadeau, A., et al. (1990a). The response to long-term overfeeding in identical twins. *New England Journal of Medicine, 322,* 1477–1482.

Bouchard, T.J., Jr. (1994, June 17). Genes, environment, and personality. *Science, 264,* 1700–1701.

Bouchard, T.J., Jr., Lykken, D.T., McGue, M., Segal, N.L., et al. (1990b, October 12). Sources of human psychological differences: The Minnesota study of twins reared apart. *Science, 250,* 223–228.

Bouchard, T.J., & McGue, M. (1981). Familial studies of intelligence: A review. *Science, 212,* 1055–1059.

Boulton, M.J., & Smith, P.K. (1990). Affective bias in children's perceptions of dominance relationships. *Child Development, 61,* 221–229.

Bowen, D.J., Kahl, K., Mann, S.L., & Peterson, A.V. (1991). Descriptions of early triers. *Addictive Behaviors, 16,* 95–101.

Bower, B. (1985). The left hand of math and verbal talent. *Science News, 127,* 263.

Bower, T.G.R. (1974). *Development in infancy.* San Francisco: Freeman.

Bower, T.G.R. (1977). *A primer of infant development.* San Francisco: Freeman.

Bowers, K.E., & Thomas, P. (1995, August). Handle with care. *Harvard Health Letter,* pp. 6–7.

Bowlby, J. (1951). Maternal care and mental health. *Bulletin of the World Health Organization, 3,* 355–534.

Boyd, G.M., Howard, J., & Zucker, R.A. (Eds.). (1995). *Alcohol problems among adolescents: Current directions in prevention research.* Hillsdale, NJ: Erlbaum.

Boylan, P. (1990). Induction of labor, complications of labor, and postmaturity. *Current Opinion in Obstetrics & Gynecology, 2,* 31–35.

Boysson-Bardies, B. de, Sagart, L., & Durand, C. (1984). Discernible differences in the babbling of infants according to target language. *Journal of Child Language, 11,* 1–15.

Boysson-Bardies, B., de & Vihman, M.M. (1991). Adaptation to language: Evidence from babbling and first words in four languages. *Language, 67,* 297–307.

Brackbill, Y. (1979). Obstetrical medication and infant behavior. In J.D. Osofsky (Ed.), *Handbook of infant development.* New York: Wiley.

Brackbill, Y., & Broman, S.H. (1979). *Obstetrical medication and development in the first year of life.* Unpublished manuscript.

Bradburn, N.M., Rips, L.J., & Shevell, S.K. (1987). Answering autobiographical questions: The impact of memory and inference on surveys. *Science, 236,* 157–161.

Bradbury, T.N., & Fincham, F.D. (1992). Attributions and behavior in marital interaction. *Journal of Personality and Social Psychology, 63,* 613–628.

Braddick, O. (1993). Orientation- and motion-selective mechanisms in infants. In K. Simons (Ed.), *Early visual development: Normal and abnormal* (pp. 163–177). New York: Oxford University Press.

Bradley, R.H., Whiteside, L., Mundfrom, D.J., Casey, P.H., Kelleher, K.J., & Pope, S.K. (1994). Early indications of resilience and their relation to experiences in the home environments of low birthweight, premature children living in poverty. *Child Development, 65,* 346–360.

Brady, L.S. (1995, January 29). Asia Linn and Chris Applebaum. *The New York Times,* p. 47.

Bray, G.A. (1983). Obesity. In N.M. Kaplan & J. Stamler (Eds.), *Prevention of coronary heart disease.* Philadelphia: Saunders.

Bray, G.A. (1990). Exercise and obesity. In C. Bouchard, R.J. Shephard, T. Stephens, J.R. Sutton, & B.D. McPherson (Eds.), *Exercise, fitness, and health: A consensus of current knowledge.* Champaign, IL: Human Kinetics.

Brazelton, T.B. (1973). *The neonatal behavioral assessment scale.* Philadelphia: Lippincott.

Brazelton, T.B. (1983). *Infants and mothers: Differences in development* (rev. ed.). New York: Delta.

Brazelton, T.B. (1990). Saving the bathwater. *Child Development, 61,* 1661–1671.

Brazelton, T.B. (1991). Discussion: Cultural attitudes and actions. In M.H. Bornstein (Ed.), *Cultural approaches to parenting.* Hillsdale, NJ: Erlbaum.

Brazelton, T.B., Nugent, J.K., & Lester, B.M. (1987) Neonatal Behavioral Assessment Scale. In J.D. Osofsky (Ed.), *Handbook of infant development* (2nd ed.). New York: Wiley.

Breakwell, G.M. (1992). *Social psychology of identity and the self-concept.* New York: Academic Press.

Brecher, E.M., and the Editors of Consumer Reports Books. (1984). *Love, sex, and aging.* Mount Vernon, NY: Consumers Union.

Bredekamp, S. (Ed.). (1989). *Developmentally appropriate practice in early childhood programs serving children from birth through age 8.* Washington, DC: National Association for the Education of Young Children.

Bregman, J., & Kimberlin, L.V. (1993). Developmental outcome in extremely premature infants: Impact of surfactant. *Pediatric Clinics of North America, 40,* 937–953.

Brennan, K.A., & Shaver, P.R. (1995). Dimensions of adult attachment, affect regulation, and romantic relationship functioning. *Personality and Social Psychology Bulletin, 21,* 267–283.

Brent, D.A., Perper, J.A., Moritz, G., & Liotus, L. (1994). Familial risk factors for adolescent suicide: A case-control study. *Acta Psychiatrica Scandinavica, 89,* 52–58.

Brescia, F.J., Sadof, M., & Barstow, J. (1984). Retrospective analysis of a home care hospice program. *Omega, 15,* 37–44.

Bridges, J.S. (1993). Pink or blue: Gender-stereotypic perceptions of infants as conveyed by birth congratulations cards. *Psychology of Women Quarterly, 17,* 193–205.

Brislin, R. (1993). *Understanding culture's influence on behavior.* Fort Worth, TX: Harcourt Brace Jovanovich.

Brock, A.M. (1991). Economics of aging. In E.M. Baines (Ed.), *Perspectives on gerontological nursing.* Newbury Park, CA: Sage.

Brockington, I.F. (1992). Disorders specific to the puerperium. *International Journal of Mental Health, 21,* 41–52.

Brody, J. (1994a, February 2). Fitness and the fetus: A turnabout in advice. *The New York Times,* p. C13.

Brody, J.E. (1994b, April 6). The value of breast milk. *The New York Times,* p. C11.

Brody, L.E., & Benbow, C.P. (1987). Accelerative strategies: How effective are they for the gifted? *Gifted Child Quarterly, 3,* 105–110.

Brody, N. (1993). Intelligence and the behavioral genetics of personality. In R. Plomin & G.E. McClearn (Eds.), *Nature, nurture and psychology.* Washington, DC: American Psychological Association.

Bromberger, J.T., & Matthews, K.A. (1994). Employment status and depressive symptoms in middle-aged women: A longitudinal investigation. *American Journal of Public Health, 84,* 202–206.

Bronfenbrenner, U. (1979). *The ecology of human development.* Cambridge, MA: Harvard University Press.

Bronfenbrenner, U. (1989). Ecological systems theory. In R. Vasta (Ed.), *Six theories of child development.* Greenwich, CT: JAI Press.

Brooks-Gunn, J., & Matthews, W.S. (1979). *He and she: How children develop their sex role identity.* Englewood Cliffs, NJ: Prentice-Hall.

Brooks-Gunn, J., & Reiter, E. (1990). The role of pubertal processes. In S. Feldman & G. Elliott (Eds.), *At the threshold: The developing adolescent.* Cambridge, MA: Harvard University Press.

Brooks-Gunn, J., & Ruble, D. (1982). The development of menstrual-related beliefs and behaviors during early adolescence. *Child Development, 53,* 1567–1577.

Brooks-Gunn, J., Petersen, A.C., & Compas, B.E. (1994). What role does biology play in childhood and adolescent depression? In I.M. Goodyer (Ed.), *Mood disorders in childhood and adolescence.* New York: Cambridge University Press.

Brouwers, P., Moss, H., Wolters, P., Eddy, J., Balis, F., Poplack, D.G., & Pizzo, P.A. (1990). Effect of continuous-infusion zidovudine therapy on neuropsychologic functioning in children with symptomatic human immunodeficiency virus. *The Journal of Pediatrics, 117,* 980–985.

Brown, B. (1990). Peer groups. In S. Feldman & G. Elliott (Eds.), *At the threshold: The developing adolescent.* Cambridge, MA: Harvard University Press.

Brown, B., Lohr, M., & Trujillo, C. (1983). *Adolescent peer group stereotypes, member conformity, and identity development.* Paper presented at the meeting of the Society for Research in Child Development, Detroit, MI.

Brown, J.D. (1991). Staying fit and staying well: Physical fitness as a moderator of life stress. *Journal of Personality and Social Psychology, 60,* 368–375.

Brown, J.D., & McGill, K.L. (1989). The cost of good fortune: When positive life events produce negative health consequences. *Journal of Personality and Social Psychology, 57,* 1103–1110.

Brown, J.L. (1987, February). Hunger in the U.S. *Scientific American, 256,* pp. 37–41.

Brown, R. (1973). *A first language.* Cambridge, MA: Harvard University Press.

Brown, R., & Fraser, C. (1963). The acquisition of syntax. In C.N. Cofer & B. Musgrave (Eds.), *Verbal behavior and learning: Problems and processes.* New York: McGraw-Hill.

Browne, A. (1993). Violence against women by male partners: Prevalence, outcomes, and policy implications. *American Psychologist, 48,* 1077–1087.

Browne, A., & Williams, K.R. (1993). Gender, intimacy, and lethal violence: Trends from 1976–1987. *Gender & Society, 7,* 78–98.

Brownell, C. (1986). Convergent developments: Cognitive-developmental correlates of growth in infant/toddler peer skills. *Child Development, 57,* 275–286.

Brownell, K.D., & Rodin, J. (1994). The dieting maelstrom: Is it possible and advisable to lose weight? *American Psychologist, 49,* 781–791.

Brubaker, T. (1991). Families in later life: A burgeoning research area. In A. Booth (Ed.), *Contemporary families.* Minneapolis, MN: National Council on Family Relations.

Brubaker, T. (Ed.). (1990). *Family relationships in later life.* Beverly Hills, CA: Sage.

Bruce, M.L., & Hoff, R.A. Social and physical health risk factors for first-onset major depressive disorder in a community sample. *Social Psychiatry and Psychiatric Epidemiology, 29,* 165–171.

Buchanan, M., & Robbins, C. (1990). Early adult psychological consequences for males of adolescent pregnancy and its resolution. *Journal of Youth and Adolescence, 19,* 413–424.

Buchholz, E., & Korn-Bursztyn, C. (1993). Children of adolescent mothers: Are they at risk for abuse? *Adolescence, 28,* 361–382.

Bullock, J. (1988). Altering aggression in young children. *Early Childhood Education, 15,* 24–27.

Bullock, M. (1995, July/August). What's so special about a longitudinal study? *Psychological Science Agenda,* pp. 9–10.

Bullough, V.L. (1981). Age at menarche. *Science, 213,* 365–366.

Bumpass, L., Sweet, J., & Martin, T. (1990). Changing patterns of remarriage. *Journal of Marriage and the Family, 52,* 747–756.

Burbules, N.C., & Linn, M.C. (1988). Response to contradiction: Scientific reasoning during adolescence. *Journal of Educational Psychology, 80,* 67–75.

Burgess, R.L., & Huston, T.L. (Eds.). (1979). *Social exchanges in developing relationships.* New York: Academic Press.

Buriel, R. (1993). Acculturation, respect for cultural differences, and biculturalism among three generations of Mexican American and Euro-American school children. *Journal of Genetic Psychology, 154,* 531–543.

Burkhauser, R.V., Holden, K.C., & Feaster, D. (1988). Incidence, timing, and events associated with poverty: A dynamic view of poverty in retirement. *Journal of Gerontology, 43* (2), S46–S52.

Burnham, D.K., & Harris, M.B. (1992). Effects of real gender and labeled gender on adults' perceptions of infants. *Journal of Genetic Psychology, 153,* 165–183.

Burns, B., & Lipsett, L.P. (1991). Behavioral factors in crib death: Toward an understanding of the sudden infant death syndrome. *Journal of Applied Developmental Psychology, 12,* 159–184.

Burrus-Bammel, L.L., & Bammel, G. (1985). Leisure and recreation. In J.E. Birren & K.W. Schaie (Eds.), *Handbook of the psychology of aging.* New York: Van Nostrand Reinhold.

Burt, V.L., & Harris, T. (1994). The third National Health and Nutrition Examination Survey: Contributing data on aging and health. *Gerontologist, 34,* 486–490.

Bushman, B.J. (1993). Human aggression while under the influence of alcohol and other drugs: An integrative research review. *Current Directions in Psychological Science, 2,* 148–152.

Bushman, B.J., & Geen, R.G. (1990). Role of cognitive-emotional mediators and individual differences in the effects of media violence on aggression. *Journal of Personality and Social Psychology, 58,* 156–163.

Buss, D.M., et al. (1990). International preferences in selecting mates: A study of 37 cultures. *Journal of Cross-Cultural Psychology, 21,* 5–47.

Bussey, K. (1992). Lying and truthfulness: Children's definition, standards, and evaluative reactions. *Child Development, 63,* 1236–1250.

Butler, R.N. (1968). The life review: An interpretation of reminiscence in the aged. In B. Neugarten (Ed.), *Middle age and aging.* Chicago: University of Chicago Press.

Butler, R.N. (1990). The contributions of late-life creativity to society. *Gerontology and Geriatrics Education, 11,* 45–51.

Butler, R.N., & Lewis, M.I. (1981). *Aging and mental health.* St. Louis, MO: C.V. Mosby.

Butterfield, E., & Siperstein, G. (1972). Influence of contingent auditory stimulation upon nonnutritional suckle. In J. Bosma (Ed.), *Oral sensation and perception: The mouth of the infant.* Springfield, IL: Chas. C Thomas.

Butterworth, G. (1994). Infant intelligence. In J. Khalfa (Ed.), *What is intelligence? The Darwin College lecture series* (pp. 49–71). Cambridge: Cambridge University Press.

Button, E. (1993). *Eating disorders: Personal construct theory and change.* New York: Wiley.

Buunk, B.P., & Janssen, P.P. (1992). Relative deprivation, career issues, and mental health among men in midlife. *Journal of Vocational Behavior, 40,* 338–350.

Byne, W., & Parsons, B. (1994, February). Biology and human sexual orientation. *Harvard Mental Health Letter,* pp. 5–7.

Cain, B.S. (1982, December 19). Plight of the gray divorcee. *The New York Times Magazine,* pp. 89–93.

Cairns, E., McWhirter, L., Duffy, U., & Barry, R. (1990). The stability of self-concept in late adolescence: Gender and situational effects. *Personality and Individual Differences, 11,* 937–944.

Caldwell, M.A., & Peplau, L.A. (1984). The balance of power in lesbian relationships. *Sex Roles, 23,* 713–725.

Calkins, S.D., & Fox, N.A. (1992). The relations among infant temperament, security of attachment, and behavioral inhibition at twenty-four months. *Child Development, 63,* 1456–1472.

Caminiti, S. (1992, August 10). Who's minding America's kids? *Fortune,* pp. 50–53.

Campbell, F.A., & Ramey, C.T. (1994). Effects of early intervention on intellectual and academic achievement: A follow-up study of children from low-income families. *Child Development, 65,* 684–698.

Campbell, J., Poland, M., Waller, J., & Ager, J. (1992). Correlates of battering during pregnancy. *Research in Nursing and Health, 15,* 219–226.

Campos, J.J., & Stenberg, C. (1981). Perception, appraisal, and emotions: The onset of social referencing. In M.E. Lamb & L.R. Sherrod (Eds.), *Infant social cognition: Empirical and theoretical considerations.* Hillsdale, NJ: Erlbaum.

Campos, J.J., Langer, A., & Krowitz, A. (1970). Cardiac responses on the visual cliff in prelocomotor human infants. *Science, 170,* 196–197.

Camras, L.A., Malatesta, C., & Izard, C.E. (1991). The development of facial expressions in infancy. In R.S. Feldman & B. Rimé (Eds.), *Fundamentals of nonverbal behavior.* Cambridge: Cambridge University Press.

Camras, L.A., & Sachs, V.B. (1991). Social referencing and caretaker expressive behavior in a day care setting. *Infant Behavior and Development, 14,* 27–36.

Caplan, L.J., & Barr, R.A. (1989). On the relationship between category intensions and extensions in children. *Journal of Experimental Child Psychology, 47,* 413–429.

Cappiello, L.A., & Troyer, R.E. (1979). A study of the role of health educators in teaching about death and dying. *Journal of School Health, 49,* 397–399.

Cardon, L.R., DiLalla, L.F., Plomin, R., DeFries, J.C., et al. (1990). Genetic correlations between reading performance and IQ in the Colorado Adoption Project. *Intelligence, 14,* 245–257.

Cardon, L.R., Fulker, D.W., DeFries, J.C., & Plomin, R. (1992). Continuity and change in general cognitive ability from 1 to 7 years of age. *Developmental Psychology, 28,* 64–73.

Cardon, R., & Fulker, D. (1993). Genetics of specific cognitive abilities. In R. Plomin & G. McClearn (Eds.), *Nature, nurture and psychology* (pp. 99–120). Washington, DC: American Psychological Association.

Carlsson-Paige, N., & Levin, D.E. (1994). *Power rangers and aggression.* Unpublished study, Lesley College, Massachusetts.

Carmody, D. (1990, March 7). College drinking: Changes in attitude and habit. *The New York Times,* p. A1.

Carnegie Task Force on Meeting the Needs of Young Children. (1994). *Starting points: Meeting the needs of our youngest children*. New York: Carnegie Corporation.

Carroll, D. (1985). *Living with dying*. New York: McGraw-Hill.

Carson, R.C., Butcher, J.N., & Coleman, J.C. (1988). *Abnormal psychology and modern life* (9th ed.). Glenview, IL: Scott, Foresman.

Carstensen, L.L. (1995). Evidence for a life-span theory of socioemotional selectivity. *Current directions in Psychological Science, 4,* 151–156.

Carver, C. (1990). *Optimism and coping with cancer.* Paper presented at the conference on "Hostility, coping and health." Lake Arrowhead, CA.

Carver, C.S., & Scheier, M.F. (1993). On the power of positive thinking: The benefits of being optimistic. *Current Directions in Psychological Science, 2,* 26–30.

Case, R. (1991). Stages in the development of the young child's first sense of self. *Developmental Review, 11,* 210–230.

Caspi, A., & Moffitt, T.E. (1991). Individual differences are accentuated during periods of social change: The sample case of girls at puberty. *Journal of Personality and Social Psychology, 61,* 157–168.

Caspi, A., & Moffitt, T.E. (1993). *Continuity amidst change: A paradoxical theory of personality coherence.* Manuscript submitted for publication.

Caspi, A., Henry, B., McGee, R.O., Moffitt, T.E., et al. (1995). Temperamental origins of child and adolescent behavior problems: From age three to age fifteen. *Child Development, 66,* 55–68.

Cassidy, J., & Berlin, L.J. (1994). The insecure/ambivalent pattern of attachment: Theory and research. *Child Development, 65,* 971–991.

Catania, J.A., Coates, T.J., Stall, R., Turner, H., Peterson, J., Hearst, N., Dolcini, M.M., Hudes, E., Gagnon, J., Wiley, J., & Groves, R. (1992). Prevalence of AIDS-related risk factors and condom use in the United States. *Science, 258,* 1101–1106.

Catell, R.B. (1967). *The scientific analysis of personality.* Chicago: Aldine.

Catell, R.B. (1987). *Intelligence: Its structure, growth, and action.* Amsterdam, The Netherlands: North-Holland.

Caughy, M.O., DiPietro, J.A., & Strobino, D.M. (1994). Day-care participation as a protective factor in the cognitive development of low-income children. *Child Development, 65,* 457–471.

CDC (Center for Disease Control). (1991, January 9). *Morbidity and Mortality Report,* pp. 183–184.

Ceci, S.J., & Bruck, M. (1993). The suggestibility of the child witness: A historical review and synthesis. *Psychological Bulletin, 113,* 403–439.

Ceci, S.J., & DeSimone, M. (1992). *Group distortion effects in preschoolers' reports.* Paper presented at the Biennial Meeting of the American Psychology & Law Society, San Diego, CA.

Ceci, S.J., & Hembrooke, H. (1993). The contextual nature of earliest memories. In J.M. Puckett & H.W. Reese (Eds.), *Mechanisms of everyday cognition* (pp. 117–136). Hillsdale, NJ: Erlbaum.

Center on Addiction and Substance Abuse. (1994). *Report on college drinking.* New York: Columbia University Press.

Cerella, J. (1990). Aging and information-processing rate. In J.E. Birren & K.W. Schaie (Eds.), *Handbook of the psychology of aging* (3rd ed.). San Diego, CA: Academic Press.

Cernoch, J.M., & Porter, R.H. (1985). Recognition of maternal axillary odors by infants. *Child Development, 56,* 1593–1598.

Cesario, T.C., & Hollander, D. (1991). Life span extension by means other than control of disease. In F.C. Ludwig (Ed.), *Life span extension: Consequences and open questions.* New York: Springer.

CFCEPLA (Commonwealth Fund Commission on Elderly People Living Alone). (1986). *Problems facing elderly Americans living alone.* New York: Louis Harris & Associates.

Chalmers, I., Enkin, M., & Keirse, M.J. (Eds.). (1989). *Effective care in pregnancy and childbirth.* New York: Oxford University Press.

Chao, R.K. (1994). Beyond parental control and authoritarian parenting style: Understanding Chinese parenting through the cultural notion of training. *Child Development, 65,* 1111–1119.

Chappell, N.L. (1991). In-group differences among elders living with friends and family other than spouses. *Journal of Aging Studies, 5,* 61–76.

Chase-Lansdale, P. & Owen, M. (1987). Maternal employment in a family context: Effect on infant–mother and infant–father attachment. *Child Development, 58,* 1505–1512.

Chasnoff, I.J., Hunt, C.E., & Kaplan, D. (1989). Prenatal cocaine exposure as associated with respiratory pattern abnormalities. *American Journal of Diseases of Childhood, 143,* 583–587.

Chen, C., & Stevenson, H.W. (1995). Motivation and mathematics achievement: A comparative study of Asian-American, Caucasian-American, and East Asian high school students. *Child Development, 66,* 1215–1234.

Cherlin, A. (1993). *Marriage, divorce, remarriage.* Cambridge, MA: Harvard University Press.

Cherlin, A., & Furstenberg, F. (1986). *The New American grandparent.* New York: Basic Books.

Cherry, K.E., & Park, D.C. (1993). Individual difference and contextual variables influence spatial memory in younger and older adults. *Psychology and Aging, 8,* 517–526.

Child Health USA '93. (1993). *Recommended child vaccination schedule* (p. 43). Washington, DC: U.S. Department of Health & Human Services.

Chira, S. (1994, July 10.) Teen-agers, in a poll, report worry and distrust of adults. *The New York Times,* pp. 1, 16.

Chiriboga, D.A. (1982). Adaptation to marital separation in later and earlier life. *Journal of Gerontology, 37,* 109–114.

Chollat-Traquet, C. (1992). *Women and tobacco.* Geneva: World Health Organization.

Chomsky, N. (1968). *Language and mind.* New York: Harcourt Brace Jovanovich.

Chomsky, N. (1978). On the biological basis of language capacities. In G.A. Miller & E. Lennenberg (Eds.), *Psychology and biology of language and thought* (pp. 199–220). New York: Academic Press.

Chomsky, N. (1991). Linguistics and cognitive science: Problems and mysteries. In A. Kasher (Ed.), *The Chomskyan turn.* Cambridge, MA: Blackwell.

Chomsky, N. (1993). On the nature, use, and acquisition of language. In A.I. Goldman (Ed.), *Readings in philosophy and cognitive science* (pp. 511–534). Cambridge, MA: MIT Press.

Cicchetti, D., & Beeghly, M. (Eds.). (1990). *Children with Down syndrome.* Cambridge: Cambridge University Press.

CIRE (Cooperative Institutional Research Program of the American Council on Education). (1990). *The American freshman: National norms for fall 1990.* Los Angeles: American Council on Education.

Clark, E. (1983). Meanings and concepts. In J. Flavell & E. Markham (Eds.), *Handbook of child psychology: Cognitive development* (Vol. 3). New York: Wiley.

Clark, J.E., & Humphrey, J.H. (Eds.). (1985). *Motor development: Current selected research.* Princeton, NJ: Princeton Book Company.

Clark, K.B., & Clark, M.P. (1947). Racial identification and preference in Negro children. In T.M. Newcomb & E.L. Hartley (Eds.), *Readings in social psychology.* New York: Holt, Rinehart & Winston.

Clark, M., & Mills, J. (1993). The difference between communal and exchange relationships: What it is and is not. *Personality and Social Psychology Bulletin, 19,* 684–691.

Clark, M.S., Mills, J.R., & Corcoran, D.M. (1989). Keeping track of needs and inputs of friends and strangers. *Personality and Social Psychology Bulletin, 15,* 533–542.

Clarke-Stewart, A. (1993). *Daycare.* Cambridge, MA: Harvard University Press.

Clarke-Stewart, A., & Friedman, S. (1987). *Child development: Infancy through adolescence.* New York: Wiley.

Clarke-Stewart, K.A. (1989). Infant day care: Maligned or malignant? Special Issue: Children and their development: Knowledge base, research agenda, and social policy application. *American Psychologist, 44,* 266–273.

Clarke-Stewart, K.A., & Bailey, B. (1990). Adjusting to divorce: Why do men have it easier? *Journal of Divorce, 13,* 75–94.

Clarke-Stewart, K.A., Gruber, C.P., & Fitzgerald, L.M. (1994). *Children at home and in day care.* Hillsdale, NJ: Erlbaum.

Cliff, D. (1991). Negotiating a livable retirement: Further paid work and the quality of life in early retirement. *Aging and Society, 11,* 319–340.

Clifton, R. (1992). The development of spatial hearing in human infants. In L.A. Werner, & E.W. Rubel (Eds.), *Developmental psychoacoustics* (pp. 135–157). Washington, DC: American Psychological Association.

Clinton, J.F., & Kelber, S.T. (1993). Stress and coping in fathers of newborns: Comparisons of planned versus unplanned pregnancy. *International Journal of Nursing Studies, 30,* 437–443.

Clulow, C. (1991). Partners becoming parents: A question of difference. *Infant Mental Health Journal, 12,* 256–266.

Cnattingius, S., Berendes, H., & Forman, M. (1993). Do delayed childbearers face increased risks of adverse pregnancy outcomes after the first birth? *Obstetrics & Gynecology, 81,* 512–516.

Coats, E., & Feldman, R.S. (1995). The role of television in the socialization of nonverbal behavioral skills. *Basic and Applied Social Psychology, 17,* 327–341.

Coccaro, E., Bergeman, C., & McClearn, G. (1993). Heritability of irritable impulsiveness: A study of twins reared together and apart. *Psychiatry Research, 48,* 229–242.

Cohen, R. (1987, May). Suddenly I'm the adult? *Psychology Today, 21,* pp. 65–72.

Cohen, S., Tyrell, D.A., & Smith, A.P. (1993). Negative life events, perceived stress, negative affect, and susceptibility of the common cold. *Journal of Personality and Social Psychology, 64,* 131–140.

Cohen, S.E. (1995). Biosocial factors in early infancy as predictors of competence in adolescents who were born prematurely. *Journal of Developmental & Behavioral Pediatrics, 16,* 36–41.

Cohn, J.F., & Tronick, E.Z. (1983). Three-month-old infants' reaction to simulated maternal depression. *Child Development, 54,* 185–193.

Cohn, J.F., & Tronick, E.Z. (1989). Mother–infant face-to-face interaction: Influence is bidirectional and unrelated to periodic cycles in either partner's behavior. *Developmental Psychology, 24,* 386–392.

Colarusso, C.A., & Nemiroff, R.A. (1981). *Adult development: A new dimension in psychodynamic theory and practice.* New York: Plenum Press.

Colby, A., & Damon, W. (1987). Listening to a different voice: A review of Gilligan's *In a different voice.* In M.R. Walsh (Ed.), *The psychology of women.* New Haven, CT: Yale University Press.

Colby, A., & Kohlberg, L. (1987). *The measurement of moral adjudgment* (Vols. 1–2). New York: Cambridge University Press.

Cole, M. (1992). Culture in development. In M.H. Bornstein, & M.E. Lamb (Eds.), *Developmental psychology: An advanced textbook* (3rd ed.). Hillsdale, NJ: Erlbaum.

Coleman, J. (1961). *The adolescent society.* Glencoe, IL: Free Press.

Coleman, J.C. (1980). Friendship and the peer group in adolescence. In J. Adelson (Ed.), *Handbook of adolescent psychology.* New York: Wiley.

Coles, R., & Stokes, G. (1985). *Sex and the American teenager.* New York: Harper & Row.

Collins, W.A. (1983). Interpretation and inference in children's television. In J. Bryant & D.R. Anderson (Eds.), *Children's understanding of television.* New York: Academic Press.

Committee for Rights and Legal Matters. (1989). Corporal punishment in schools. *American Journal of Psychiatry, 146,* 1524.

Committee on Children, Youth and Families. (1994). *When you need child day care.* Washington, DC: American Psychological Association.

Committee to Study the Prevention of Low Birthweight (1985). *Preventing low birthweight.* Washington, DC: National Academy Press.

Compas, B.E., Hinden, B.R., & Gerhardt, C.A. (1995). Adolescent development: Pathways and processes of risk and reliance. *Annual Review of Psychology, 46,* 265–293.

Comstock, G., & Strasburger, V.C. (1990). Deceptive appearances: Television violence and aggressive behavior. Conference: Teens and television (1988, Los Angeles, California). *Journal of Adolescent Health Care, 11,* 31–44.

Condit, V. (1990). Anorexia nervosa: Levels of causation. *Human Nature, 1,* 391–413.

Condry, J. (1989). *The psychology of television.* Hillsdale, NJ: Erlbaum.

Condry, J., & Condry, S. (1976). Sex differences: A study of the eye of the beholder. *Child Development, 47,* 812–819.

Conel, J.L. (1930–1963), *Postnatal development of the human cerebral cortex* (Vols. 1–6). Cambridge, MA: Harvard University Press.

Conger, J. (1977). *Adolescence and youth* (2nd ed.). New York: Harper & Row.

Connor, R. (1992). *Cracking the over-50 job market.* New York: Penguin Books.

Conway, M., & Rubin, D. (1993). The structure of autobiographical memory. In A.F. Collins, S.E. Gathercole, M.A. Conway, & P.E. Morris (Eds.), *Theories of memory.* Hillsdale, NJ: Erlbaum.

Cook, A.S., & Oltjenbruns, K.A. (1989). *Dying and grieving: Lifespan and family perspectives.* New York: Holt, Rinehart & Winston.

Cook, S.W. (1984). Cooperative interaction in multiethnic contexts. In N. Miller & M. Brewer (Eds.), *Groups in contact: The psychology of desegregation.* New York: Academic Press.

Cook, W.J., & Wollersheim, J.P. (1976). The effect of labeling of special education students and the perception of contact versus noncontant peers. *Journal of Special Education, 10,* 187–198.

Cook-Deegan, R. (1994). *The gene wars: Science, politics, and the human genome.* New York: W.W. Norton & Co., Inc.

Coons, S., & Guilleminault, C. (1982). Developments of sleep-wake patterns and non-rapid eye movement sleep stages during the first six months of life in normal infants. *Pediatrics, 69* (6), 793–798.

Cooper, R.P., & Aslin, R.N. (1990). Preference for infant-directed speech in the first month after birth. *Child Development, 61,* 1584–1595.

Cooper, R.P., & Aslin, R.N. (1994). Developmental differences in infant attention to the spectral properties of infant-directed speech. *Child Development, 65,* 1663–1677.

Corbin, C. (1973). *A textbook of motor development.* Dubuque, IA: Wm.C. Brown.

Coren, S. (1989). Left-handedness and accident-related injury risk. *American Journal of Public Health, 79,* 1–2.

Coren, S., & Halpern, D.F. (1991). Left-handedness: A marker for decreased survival fitness. *Psychological Bulletin, 109* (1), 90–106.

Costa, P.T., Busch, C.M., Zonderman, A.B., & McCrae, R.R. (1993). Correlations of MMPI factor scales with measures of the five-factor model of personality. *Journal of Personality Assessment, 50,* 640–650.

Costa, P.T., Jr., & McCrae, R.R. (1988). Personality in adulthood: A six-year longitudinal study of self-report and spouse ratings on the NEO Personality Inventory. *Journal of Personality and Social Psychology, 54,* 853–863.

Costa, P.T., Jr., & McCrae, R.R. (1989). Personality continuity and the changes of adult life. In M. Storandt & G.R. VandenBos (Eds.), *The adult years: Continuity and change.* Washington, DC: American Psychological Association.

Cottreaux, J. (1993). Behavioral psychotherapy applications in the medically ill. *Psychotherapy and Psychosomatics, 60,* 116–128.

Cowan, C.P., & Cowan, P.A. (1992). *When partners become parents.* New York: Wiley.

Cowan, N. (1992). Verbal memory span and the timing of spoken recall. *Journal of Memory and Language, 31,* 668–684.

Cowan, P.A., & Cowan, C.P. (1988). Changes in marriage during the transition to parenthood: Must we blame the baby? In G.Y. Michaels & W.A. Goldberg (Eds.), *The transition to parenthood: Current theory and research.* Cambridge: Cambridge University Press.

Cox, M.J., Owen, M.T., Henderson, V.K., & Margand, N.A. (1992). Prediction of infant–father and infant–mother attachment. *Developmental Psychology, 28,* 474–483.

Cox, M.J., & Cox, R.D. (1985). (Eds.). *Foster care: Current issues, policies, and practices.* Norwood, NJ: Ablex.

Craik, F.I.M. (1984). Age differences in remembering. In L.R. Squire & N. Butters (Eds.), *Neuropsychologoy of memory.* New York: Guilford Press.

Craik, F.I.M. (1994). Memory changes in normal aging. *Current Directions in Psychological Science, 3,* 155–158.

Crandall, C., & Biernat, M. (1990). The ideology of anti-fat attitudes. *Journal of Applied Social Psychology, 20,* 227–243.

Cratty, B. (1979). *Perceptual and motor development in infants and children* (2nd ed.). Englewood Cliffs, NJ: Prentice-Hall.

Cratty, B. (1986). *Perceptual and motor development in infants and children* (3rd ed.). Englewood Cliffs, NJ: Prentice-Hall.

Crews, D. (1993). The organizational concept and vertebrates without sex chromosomes. *Brain, Behavior, and Evolution, 42,* 202–214.

Crockenberg, S.B. (1986). Are temperamental differences in babies associated with predictable differences in care-giving? In J.V. Lerner & A.C. Peterson (Eds.), *Temperament and social interaction in infants and children (New Dimensions in Child Development)* (Vol. 30, pp. 75–88). San Francisco: Jossey-Bass.

Crockett, L.J., & Crouter, A.C. (Eds.). (1995). *Pathways through adolescence: Individual development in relation to social contexts.* Hillsdale, NJ: Erlbaum.

Cromwell, E.S. (1994). *Quality child care: A comprehensive guide for administrators and teachers.* Boston: Allyn & Bacon.

Crook, C.K. (1978). Taste perception in the newborn infant. *Infant Behavior and Development, 1,* 52–69.

Crook, C.K. (1987). Taste and olfaction. In P. Salapatek & L.B. Cohen (Eds.), *Handbook of infant perception* (Vol. 1). New York: Academic Press.

Crosby, W. (1991). Studies in fetal malnutrition. *American Journal of Diseases of Children, 145,* 871–876.

Crose, R., & Drake, L.K. (1993). Older women's sexuality. *Clinical Gerontologist, 12,* 51–56.

Croyle, R.T., & Hunt, J.R. (1991). Coping with health threat: Social influence processes in reactions to medical test results. *Journal of Personality and Social Psychology, 60,* 382–389.

Crystal, D.S., Chen, C., Fuligni, A.J., Stevenson, H.W., et al. (1994). Psychological maladjustment and academic achievement: A cross-cultural study of Japanese, Chinese, and American high school students. *Child Development, 65,* 738–753.

Csikszentmihalyi, M., & Larson, R. (1984). *Being adolescent: Conflict and growth in the teenage years.* New York: Basic Books.

Culbertson, J.L., & Gyurke, J. (1990). Assessment of cognitive and motor development in infancy and childhood. In J.H. Johnson & J. Goldman (Eds.), *Developmental assessment in clinical child psychology: A handbook* (pp. 100–131). New York: Pergamon Press.

Cummings, E., & Henry, W.E. (1961). *Growing old.* New York: Basic Books.

Cummings, E.M., Iannotti, R.J., & Zahn-Waxler, C. (1989). Aggression between peers in early childhood: Individual continuity and developmental change. *Child Development, 60,* 887–895.

Cunningham, J.D., & Antill, J.K. (1994). Cohabitation and marriage: Retrospective and predictive comparisons. *Journal of Social and Personal Relationships, 11,* 77–93.

Cunningham, W.R., & Hamen, K. (1992). Intellectual functioning in relation to mental health. In J.E. Birren, R.B., Sloane, & G.D. Cohen (Eds.), *Handbook of mental health and aging.* San Diego, CA: Harcourt Brace.

Cutler, B. (1990). Rock-a-buy baby. *American Demographics, 12*(1), 35–39.

Dainton, M. (1993). The myths and misconceptions of the step-mother identity. *Family Relations, 42,* 93–98.

Daly, T., & Feldman, R.S. (1994). *Benefits of social integration for typical preschool children.* Unpublished manuscript.

Damon, W. (1977). *The social world of the child.* San Francisco: Jossey-Bass.

Damon, W. (1983). *Social and personality development.* New York: W.W. Norton & Co., Inc.

Damon, W. (1988). *The moral child.* New York: The Free Press.

Damon, W., & Hart, D. (1988). *Self-understanding in childhood and adolescence.* New York: Cambridge University Press.

Damon, W., & Hart, D. (1992). Self-understanding and its role in social and moral development. In M.H. Bornstein & M.E. Lamb (Eds.), *Developmental psychology: An advanced textbook* (3rd ed.). Hillsdale, NJ: Erlbaum.

Darling, N., & Steinberg, L. (1993). Parenting style as context: An integrative model. *Psychological Bulletin, 113,* 487–496.

Dasen, P.R. (1977). Are cognitive processes universal? A contribution to cross-cultural Piagetian psychology. In N. Warren (Ed.), *Studies in cross-cultural psychology* (Vol. 1). London: Academic Press.

Dasen, P., Inhelder, B., Lavallee, M., & Retschitzki, J. (1978). *Naissance de l'intelligence chez l'enfant Baoule de Cote d'Ivorie.* Berne, Switzerland: Hans Huber.

Dasen, P., Ngini, L., & Lavallee, M. (1979). Cross-cultural training studies of concrete operations. In L.H. Eckenberger, W.J. Lonner, & Y.H. Poortinga (Eds.), *Cross-cultural contributions to psychology.* Amsterdam, The Netherlands: Swets & Zeilinger.

Davidson, M. (Ed.). (1991). Alzheimer's disease. *Psychiatric Clinics of North America, 14,* 112–120.

Davidson, T. (1977). Wifebeating: A recurring phenomenon throughout history. In M. Roy (Ed.), *Battered women: A psychosociological study of domestic violence.* New York: Van Nostrand Reinhold.

Davies, P.T., & Cummings, E.M. (1994). Marital conflict and child adjustment: An emotional security hypothesis. *Psychological Bulletin, 116,* 387–411.

Davis-Floyd, R.E. (1994). The technocratic body: American childbirth as cultural expression. *Social Science & Medicine, 38,* 1125–1140.

Davydov, V.V. (1995). The influence of L.S. Vygotsky on education theory, research, and practice. *Educational Researcher, 24,* 12–21.

de Graaf, C., Polet, P., & van Staveren, W.A. (1994). Sensory perception and pleasantness of food flavors in elderly subjects. *Journal of Gerontology, 49,* P93–P99.

Dean, A., Kolody, B., Wood, P., & Ensel, W. (1989). Measuring the communication of social support from adult children. *Journal of Marriage and the Family, 44,* 71–79.

DeAngelis, T. (1994, December). What makes kids ready, set for school? *APA Monitor,* pp. 36–37.

Deaux, K., Reind, A., Mizrahi, K., & Ethier, K.A. (1995). Parameters of social identity. *Journal of Personality and Social Psychology, 68,* 280–291.

Decarrie, T.G. (1969). A study of the mental and emotional development of the thalidomide child. In B.M. Foss (Ed.), *Determinants of infant behavior* (Vol. 4). London: Methuen.

DeCasper, A.J., & Fifer, W.P. (1980). Of human bonding: Newborns prefer their mothers' voices. *Science, 208,* 1174–1176.

DeCasper, A.J., & Prescott, P. (1984). Human newborns' perception of male voices: Preference, discrimination, and reinforcing value. *Developmental Psychobiology, 17,* 481–491.

DeCasper, A.J., & Spence, M.J. (1986). Prenatal material speech influences newborns' perception of speech sounds. *Infant Behavior and Development, 9,* 133–150.

deChateau, P. (1980). Parent–neonate interaction and its long-term effects. In E.G. Simmel (Ed.), *Early experiences and early behavior.* New York: Academic Press.

DeClercq, E.R. (1992). The transformation of American midwifery: 1975 to 1988. *American Journal of Public Health, 82,* 680–684.

DeFrain, J., Martens, L., Stork, J., & Stork, W. (1991). The psychological effects of a stillbirth on surviving family members. *Omega: Journal of Death and Dying, 22,* 81–108.

DeGenova, M.K. (1993). Reflections of the past: New variables affecting life satisfaction in later life. *Educational Gerontology, 19,* 191–201.

Delemarre-van de Wall, H. (1993). Environmental factors influencing growth and pubertal development. *Environmental Health Perspectives, 101* (Suppl. 2), 39–44.

Demetriou, A., Shayer, M., & Efklides, A. (Eds.). (1993). *Neo-Piagetian theories of cognitive development: Implications and applications for education.* London: Routledge.

Demo, D.H., & Acock, A. (1991). The impact of divorce on children. In A. Booth (Ed.), *Contemporary families.* Minneapolis, MN: National Council on Family Relations.

Dennis, W. (1966). Age and creative productivity. *Journal of Gerontology, 21,* 1–8.

Dennis, W. (1966). Creative productivity between the ages of 20 and 80 years. *Journal of Gerontology, 11,* 331–337.

Dent, J. (1984, March). Laughter is the best medicine. *Reader's Digest,* p. 38.

DeRosier, M.E., Kupersmidt, J.B., & Patterson, C.J. (1994). Children's academic and behavioral adjustment as a function of the chronicity and proximity of peer rejection. *Child Development, 65,* 1799–1813.

Desforges, D.M., Lord, C.G., Ramsey, S.L., Mason, J.A., VanLeeuwen, M.D., West, S.C., & Lepper, M.R. (1991). Effects of structured cooperative contact on changing negative attitudes toward stigmatized social groups. *Journal of Personality and Social Psychology, 60,* 531–544.

DeSpelder, L., & Strickland, A.L. (1992). *The last dance: Encountering death and dying* (3rd ed.). Palo Alto, CA: Mayfield.

Deutsch, F.M., Lussier, J.B., & Servis, L.J. (1993). Husbands at home: Predictors of paternal participation in childcare and housework. *Journal of Personality and Social Psychology, 65,* 1154–1166.

Deveny, K. (1994, December 5). Chart of kindergarten awards. *The Wall Street Journal,* p. B1.

deVilliers, P.A., & deVilliers, J.G. (1992). Language development. In M.H. Bornstein & M.E. Lamb (Eds.), *Developmental psychology: An advanced textbook.* Hillsdale, NJ: Erlbaum.

deVries, M.W. (1984). Temperament and infant mortality among the Masai of East Africa. *American Journal of Psychiatry, 141,* 1189–1194.

deVries, R. (1969). Constancy of generic identity in the years 3 to 6. *Monographs of the Society for Research in Child Development, 34,* (3, Serial No. 127).

DeWitt, P.M. (1992). The second time around. *American Demographics, 14,* 60–63.

Diamond, A. (Ed.). (1991). Frontal lobe involvement in cognitive changes during the first year of life. In K. Gibwon, M. Konner, & A. Patterson (Eds.), *Brain and behavioral development.* Hillsdale, NJ: Erlbaum.

Dickenson, G. (1975). Dating behavior of black and white adolescents before and after desegregation. *Journal of Marriage and the Family, 37,* 602–608.

Dickinson, G.E. (1981). Death education in U.S. medical schools: 1975–1980. *Journal of Medical Education, 56,* 111–114.

Dickinson, G.E., Summer, E.D., & Durand, R.P. (1987). Death education in the U.S. professional colleges: Medical, nursing, and pharmacy. *Death Studies, 11,* 57–61.

Dietz, W.H. (1987). Childhood obesity. *Annals of the New York Academy of Sciences, 499,* 47–54.

DiFranza, J.R., & Lew, R.A. (1995). Effect of maternal cigarette smoking on pregnancy complications and sudden infant death syndrome. *The Journal of Family Practice, 40,* 385–394.

DiGiovanna, A.G. (1994). *Human aging: Biological perspectives* (p. 159). New York: McGraw-Hill.

DiLalla, L.F., Thompson, L.A., Plomin, R., Phillips, K., et al. (1990). Infant predictors of preschool and adult IQ: A study of infant twins and their parents. *Developmental Psychology, 26,* 433–440.

Dinges, M.M., & Oetting, E.R. (1993). Similarity in drug use patterns between adolescents and their friends. *Adolescence, 28,* 253–266.

Dion, K.K. (1972). Physical attractiveness and evaluations of children's transgressions. *Journal of Personality and Social Psychology, 24,* 207–213.

Dion, K.L., & Dion, K.K. (1988). Romantic love: Individual and cultural perspectives. In R.J. Sternberg & M.L. Barnes (Eds.), *The psychology of love.* New Haven, CT: Yale University Press.

Dodge, K.A. (1985a). A social information processing model of social competence in children. In M. Perlmutter (Ed.), *Minnesota symposia on child psychology* (Vol. 18, pp. 77–126). Hillside, NJ: Erlbaum.

Dodge, K.A. (1985b). Facets of social interaction and the assessment of social competence in children. In B.H. Schneider, K.H. Rubin, & J.E. Ledingham (Eds.), *Children's peer relations: Issues in assessment and intervention.* New York: Springer-Verlag.

Dodge, K.A., Bates, J.E., & Petit, G.S. (1990, December 20). Mechanisms in the cycle of violence. *Science, 250,* 1678–1683.

Dodge, K.A., & Coie, J.D. (1987). Social information-processing factors in reactive and proactive aggression in children's peer groups. *Journal of Personality and Social Psychology, 53,* 1146–1158.

Dodge, K.A., & Crick, N.R. (1990). Social information-processing bases of aggressive behavior in children. *Personality and Social Psychology Bulletin, 16,* 8–22.

Dodge, K.A., & Price, J.M. (1994). On the relation between social information processing and socially competent behavior in early school-aged children. *Child Development, 65,* 1385–1397.

Dodge, K.A., Pettit, G.S., McClasky, C.L., & Brown, M.M. (1986). Social competence in children. *Monographs of the Society for Research in Child Development, 51,* (2, Serial No. 213).

Doering, M., Rhodes, S.R., & Schuster, M. (1983). *The aging worker: Research and recommendations.* Beverly Hills, CA: Sage.

Doka, K.J., & Mertz, M.E. (1988). The meaning and significance of great-grandparenthood. *Gerontologist, 28,* 192–197.

Dolcini, M.M., Coh, L.D., Adler, N.E., Millstein, S.G., et al. (1989). Adolescent egocentrism and feelings of invulnerability: Are they related? *Journal of Early Adolescence, 9,* 409–418.

Doress, P.B., Siegal, D.L., & the Midlife and Old Women Book Project. (1987). *Ourselves, growing older.* New York: Simon & Schuster.

Dornbusch, S., Carlsmith, J., Bushwall, S., Ritter, P., Leiderman, P., Hastorf, A., & Gross, R. (1985). Single parents, extended households, and the control of adolescents. *Child Development, 56,* 326–341.

Dornbusch, S.M., Ritter, P.L., & Steinberg, L. (1991). Differences between African Americans and non-Hispanic Whites in the relation of family statuses to adolescent school performance. *American Journal of Education, 99,* 543–567.

Douglas, M.J. (1991). Potential complications of spinal and epidural anesthesia for obstetrics. *Seminars in Perinatology, 15,* 368–374.

Douvan, E., & Adelson, J. (1966). *The adolescent experience.* New York: Wiley.

Dove, A. (1968, July 15). Taking the chitling test. *Newsweek.*

Downey, G., Silver, R.C., & Wortman, C.B. (1990). Reconsidering the attribution-adjustment relation following a major negative event: Coping with the loss of a child. *Journal of Personality and Social Psychology, 59,* 227–236.

Dreyer, P.H. (1982). Sexuality during adolescence. In B.B. Woman (Ed.), *Handbook of developmental psychology.* Englewood Cliffs, NJ: Prentice-Hall.

Driedger, S.D. (1994, July 11). "Cancer made me stronger." *McCleans,* p. 46.

Dromi, E. (1987). *Early lexical development.* Cambridge: Cambridge University Press.

Dromi, E. (1993). The development of prelinguistic communication: Implications for language evaluation. In N.J. Anastasiow & S. Harel (Eds.), *At-risk infants: Interventions, families, and research* (pp. 19–26). Baltimore: Paul Brookes.

Dryfoos, J.G. (1990). *Adolescents at risk: Prevalence and prevention.* New York: Oxford University Press.

DuBois, D.L., & Hirsch, B.J. (1990). School and neighborhood friendship patterns of blacks and whites in early adolescence. *Child Development, 61,* 524–536.

Duckitt, J. (1994). Conformity to social pressure and racial prejudice among White South Africans. *Genetic, Social, and General Psychology Monographs, 120,* 121–143.

Duff, C. (1994, September 12). Cool pad, fab food, one catch: Mom lives there, too. *The Wall Street Journal,* pp. A1, A8.

Duke, M., & Nowicki, S., Jr. (1979). *Abnormal psychology: Perspectives on being different.* Monterey, CA: Brooks/Cole.

Duke, M.P., & Nowicki, S., Jr. (1986). *Abnormal psychology: A new look.* New York: Holt, Reinhart & Winston.

Duke, R., & Martinez, R. (1994). The impact of gender on self-esteem among adolescents. *Adolescence, 29,* 105–115.

Duncan, G.J., & Smith, K.R. (1989). The rising affluence of the elderly: How far, how fair, and how frail. *Annual review of sociology.* Palo Alto, CA: Annual Reviews.

Duncan, G.J., Brooks-Gunn, J., & Klebanov, P.K. (1994). Economic deprivation and early childhood development. *Child Development, 65,* 296–318.

Duncan, P., Ritter, P., Dornbusch, S., Gross, R., et al. 1985). The effects of pubertal timing on body image, school behavior, and deviance. *Journal of Youth and Adolescence, 14,* 227–236.

Dunham, R.M., Kidwell, J.S., & Wilson, S.M. (1986). Rites of passage at adolescence: A ritual process paradigm. *Journal of Adolescent Research, 1,* 139–153.

Dunn, A. (1995, January 28). Cram schools: Immigrants' tools for success. *The New York Times,* pp. 1, 24.

Dunn, J. (1991). Understanding others: Evidence from naturalistic studies of children. In W. Whiten (Ed.), *Natural theories of mind: Evolution, development and stimulation of everyday mindreading.* Oxford: Blackwell.

Dunn, L.M. (1968). Special education for the mildly retarded—Is much of it justifiable? *Exceptional Child, 35,* 5–22.

Dunphy, D.C. (1963). The social structure of urban adolescent peer groups. *Society, 26,* 230–246.

Dutton, D.G. (1988). *The domestic assault of women: Psychological and criminal justice perspectives.* Boston: Allyn & Bacon.

Dutton, D.G. (1994). *The domestic assault of women: Psychological and criminal justice perspectives* (2nd ed.). Vancouver: University of British Columbia Press.

Dutton, M.A. (1992) *Empowering and healing the battered woman: A model of assessment and intervention.* New York: Springer.

Dweck, C.S., & Bush, E.S. (1976). Sex differences in learned helplessness: I. Differential debilitation with peer and adult evaluators. *Developmental Psychology, 12,* 147–156.

Dweck, C.S. (1991). Self-theories and goals: Their role in motivation, personality and development. In R. Dienstbier (Ed.), *Nebraska symposium on motivation* (Vol. 36). Lincoln: University of Nebraska Press.

Eagly, A.H., & Steffen, V.J. (1984). Gender stereotypes stem from the distribution of women and men into social roles. *Journal of Personality and Social Psychology, 46,* 735–754.

Eagly, A.H., & Steffen, V.J. (1986). Gender and aggressive behavior: A meta-analytic review of the social psychological literature. *Psychological Bulletin, 100,* 309–330.

Eakins, P.S. (Ed.). (1986). *The American way of birth.* Philadelphia: Temple University Press.

Eaton, W.O., & Enns, L.R. (1986). Sex differences in human motor activity level. *Psychological Bulletin, 100,* 19–28.

Eaton, W.O., & Yu, A.P. (1989). Are sex differences in child motor activity level a function of sex differences in maturational status? *Child Development, 60,* 1005–1011.

Eaves, L., Silberg, J., Hewitt, J.K., Meyer, J., et al. (1993). Genes, personality, and psychopathology: A latent class analysis of liability to symptoms of attention-deficit hyperactivity disorder in twins. In R. Plomin, & G.E. McClearn (Eds.), *Nature, nurture, and psychology.* Washington, DC: American Psychological Association.

Eberstadt, N. (1994, Spring). Why babies die in D.C. *The Public Interest, 115,* pp. 3–16.

Eccles, J.S., Amberton, A., Buchanan, C.M., Jacobs, J., Flanagan, C., Harold, R., MacIver, D., Midgley, C., Reuman, D., & Wigfield, A. (1993). School and family effects on the ontogeny of children's interests, self-perceptions, and activity choice. In J. Jacobs (Ed.), *Nebraska symposium on motivation, 1992.* Lincoln: University of Nebraska Press.

Eccles, J.S., Wigfield, A., Flanagan, C., Miller, C., et al. (1989). Self-concepts, domain values, and self-esteem: Relations and changes at early adolescence. *Journal of Personality and Social Psychology, 57,* 283–310.

Ecenbarger, W. (1993, April 1). America's new merchants of death. *Reader's Digest,* p. 50.

Eckerman, C.O., & Oehler, J.M. (1992). Very low birthweight newborns and parents as early social partners. In S.L. Friedman & M.D. Sigman (Eds.), *The psychological development of low-birthweight children.* Norwood, NJ: Ablex.

Eden, D. (1990). Pygmalion without interpersonal contrast effects: Whole groups gain from raising manager expectations. *Journal of Applied Psychology, 75,* 394–398.

Eder, R.A. (1990). Uncovering young children's psychological selves: Individual and developmental differences. *Child Development, 61,* 849–863.

Edwards, R. (1995, February). New tools help gauge marital success. *APA Monitor,* p. 6.

Egan, M.C. (1994). Public health nutrition: A historical perspective. *Journal of the American Dietetic Association, 94,* 298–304.

Egeland, B., & Farber, E.A. (1984). Infant–mother attachment: Factors related to its development and changes over time. *Child Development, 55,* 753–771.

Egeland, B., & Hiester, M. (1995). The long-term consequences of infant day-care and mother–infant attachment. *Child Development, 66,* 474–485.

Egeland, B., Pianta, R., & O'Brien, M.A. (1993). Maternal intrusiveness in infancy and child maladaptation in early school years. *Development and Psychopathology, 5,* 359–370.

Eggebeen, D.J., & Hogan, D.P. (1990). Giving between generations in American families. *Human Nature, 1,* 211–232.

Ehlers, C.L., Frank, E., & Kupfer, D.J. (1988). Social zeitgebers and biological rhythms: A unified approach to understanding the etiology of depression. *Archives of General Psychiatry, 45,* 948–952.

Eiger, M.S. (1987). The feeding of infants and children. In R.A. Hoekelman, S. Blatman, S.B. Friedman, N.M. Nelson, & H.M. Seidel (Eds.), *Primary pediatric care.* St. Louis, MO: C.V. Mosby.

Eiger, M.S., & Olds, S.W. (1987). *The complete book of breastfeeding.* New York: Workman, Bantam.

Eimas, P.D., Sigueland, E.R., Jusczyk, P., & Vigorito, J. (1971). Speech perception in infants. *Science, 171,* 303–306.

Einbinder, S.D. (1992). *A statistical profile of children living in poverty: Children under three and children under six, 1990.* Unpublished document from the National Center for Children in Poverty. New York: Columbia University, School of Public Health.

Eisenberg, N., & Fabes, R. (1991). Prosocial behavior and empathy: A multimethod, developmental perspective. In.M.S. Clark (Ed.), *Review of personality and social psychology* (Vol. 12). Newbury Park, CA: Sage.

Eisenberg, N., Wolchik, S.A., Hernandez, R., & Pasternack, J.F. (1985). Parental socialization of young children's play: A short-term longitudinal study. *Child Development, 56,* 1506–1513.

Ekman, P., & O'Sullivan, M. (1991). Facial expression: Methods, means, and moues. In R.S. Feldman & B. Rime (Eds.), *Fundamentals of nonverbal behavior.* Cambridge: Cambridge University Press.

Elias, M. (1990, March 12). Women weighing the benefits and risks of estrogen therapy. *Norwich Bulletin,* p. C5.

Elkind, D. (1967). Egocentrism in adolescence. *Child Development, 38,* 1025–1034.

Elkind, D. (1984). *All grown up and no place to go.* Reading, MA: Addison-Wesley.

Elkind, D. (1985). Egocentrism redux. *Developmental Review, 5,* 218–226.

Elkind, D. (1988). *Miseducation.* New York: Knopf.

Ellsberg, P. (1994, May 6). What's New Orleans? *Commonweal,* p. 31.

Endo, S. (1992). Infant–infant play from 7 to 12 months of age: An analysis of games in infant–peer triads. *Japanese Journal of Child and Adolescent Psychiatry, 33,* 145–162.

Engler, J., & Goleman, D. (1992). *The consumer's guide to psychotherapy.* New York: Simon & Schuster.

Ennett, S.T., Tobler, N.S., Ringwalt, C.L., & Flewelling, R.L. (1994, September). How effective is drug abuse resistance education? A meta-analysis of Project DARE outcome evaluations. *American Journal of Public Health, 84,* 1394–1401.

Enright, M.K., Rovee-Collier, C.K., Fagen, J.W., & Caniglia, K. (1983). The effects of distributed training on retention of operant conditioning in human infants. *Journal of Experimental Child Psychology, 36,* 209–225.

Epstein, J.A., Botvin, G.J., Diaz, T., Toth, V., et al. (1995). Social and personal factors in marijuana use and intentions to use drugs among inner-city minority youth. *Journal of Development & Behavioral Pediatrics, 16,* 14–20.

Epstein, K. (1993). The interactions between breast-feeding mothers and their babies during the breastfeeding session. *Early Child Development and Care, 87,* 93–104.

Epstein, L.H. (1992). Exercise and obesity in children. *Journal of Applied Sport Psychology, 4,* 120–133.

Epstein, S. (1994). An integration of the cognitive and the psychodynamic unconscious. *American Psychologist, 49,* 709–724.

Epstein, S., & Meier, P. (1989). Constructive thinking: A broad coping variable with specific components. *Journal of Personality and Social Psychology, 57,* 332–350.

Erber, J.T., Rothberg, S.T., & Szuchman, L.T. (1991). Appraisal of everyday memory failures by middle-aged adults. *Educational Gerontology, 17,* 63–72.

Erber, J.T., Szuchman, L.T., & Rothberg, S.T. (1990). Everyday memory failure: Age differences in appraisal and attribution. *Psychology and Aging, 5,* 236–241.

Erikson, E.H. (1963). *Childhood and society.* New York: W.W. Norton & Co., Inc.

Eron, L.D., & Huesmann, L.R. (1985). The control of aggressive behavior by changes in attitude, values, and the conditions of learning. In R.J. Blanchard & C. Blanchard (Eds.), *Advances in the study of aggression.* New York: Academic Press.

Eron, L.D., Gentry, J., & Schlegel, P. (1994). *Reason to hope: A psychosocial perspective on violence and youth.* Washington, DC: American Psychological Association.

Erwin, P. (1993). *Friendship and peer relations in children.* Chichester, UK: Wiley.

Espenschade, A. (1960). Motor development. In W.R. Johnson (Ed.), *Science and medicine of exercise and sports.* New York: Harper & Row.

Essex, M.J., & Nam, S. (1987). Marital status and loneliness among older women: The differential importance of close family and friends. *Journal of Marriage and the Family, 49,* 92–106.

Evans, P.D. (1990). Type A behavior and coronary heart disease: When will the jury return? *British Journal of Psychology, 81,* 147–157.

Eveleth, P., & Tanner, J. (1976). *Worldwide variation in human growth.* New York: Cambridge University Press.

Eyer, D. (1992). The bonding hype. In M.E. Lamb & J.B. Lancaster (Eds.), *Birth management: Biosocial perspectives.* Hawthorne, NY: Aldine de Gruyter.

Eyer, D.E. (1994). Mother–infant bonding: A scientific fiction. *Human Nature, 5,* 69–94.

Eysenck, H.J. (1976). Structure of social attitudes. *Psychological reports, 39,* 463–466.

Fabsitz, R.R., Carmelli, D., & Hewitt, J.K. (1992). Evidence for independent genetic influences on obesity in middle age. *International Journal of Obesity and Related Metabolic Disorders, 16,* 657–666.

Fagot, B.I. (1978). The influence of sex of child on parental reactions to toddler children. *Child Development, 49,* 459–465.

Fagot, B.I. (1979). Sex differences in toddlers' behavior and parental reaction. *Developmental Psychology, 10,* 554–558.

Fagot, B.I. (1991, March). *Peer relations in boys and girls from two to seven.* Paper presented at the biennial meeting of the Society for Research in Child Development, Seattle, WA.

Fagot, B.I., & Hagan, R. (1991). Observation of parent reaction to sex-stereotyped behaviors: Age and sex effects. *Child Development, 62,* 617–628.

Fagot, B.I., & Leinbach, M.D. (1993). Gender-role development in young children: From discrimination to labeling. *Developmental Review, 13,* 205–224.

Fairburn, C.C., Jones, R., Peveler, R.C., et al. (1993). Psychotherapy and bulimia nervosa. *Archives of General Psychiatry, 50,* 419–428.

Falk, P.J. (1989). Lesbian mothers: Psychosocial assumptions in family law. *American Psychologist, 44,* 941–947.

Fangman, J.J., Mark, P.M., Pratt, L., Conway, K.K., et al. (1994). *American Journal of Obstetrical Gynecology, 170,* 744–750.

Fanshel, D., Finch, S.J., & Grundy, J.F. (1990). *Foster children in a life course perspective.* New York: Columbia University Press.

Fanshel, D., Finch, S.J., & Grundy, J.F. (1992). *Serving the urban poor.* Westport, CT: Praeger.

Fantz, R. (1963). Pattern vision in newborn infants. *Science, 140,* 296–297.

Fantz, R.L. (1961). The origin of form perception. *Scientific American,* p. 72.

Farley, C.F. (1993, April 19). CNN/Time national poll. *Time,* p. 15.

Farrington, D. (1991). Childhood aggression and adult violence: Early precursors and later-life outcomes. In D. Pepler & K. Rubin (Eds.), *The development and treatment of childhood aggression.* Hillsdale, NJ: Erlbaum.

Farver, J.M., & Branstetter, W.H. (1994). Preschoolers' prosocial responses to their peers' distress. *Developmental Psychology, 30,* 334–341.

Farver, J.M., Kim, Y.K., & Lee, Y. (1995). Cultural differences in Korean- and Anglo-American preschoolers' social interaction and play behaviors. *Child Development, 66,* 1088–1099.

Feather, N.T. (1980). Values in adolescence. In Joseph Adelson (Ed.), *Handbook of adolescent psychology.* New York: Wiley.

Feifel, H. (1963). Relationship of physician to terminally ill patient. In N.L. Farberow (Ed.), *Taboo topics* (pp. 8–12). New York: Atherton.

Fein, G.G., Gariboldi, A., & Boni, R. (1993). The adjustment of infants and toddlers to group care: The first 6 months. *Early Childhood Research Quarterly, 8,* 1–14.

Feingold, A. (1992). Matching for attractiveness in romantic partners and same-sex friends: A meta-analysis and theoretical critique. *Psychological Bulletin, 111,* 304–341.

Feldman, R.S. (1982). *Development of nonverbal behavior in children.* New York: Springer-Verlag.

Feldman, R.S. (Ed.). 1990. *The social psychology of education.* Cambridge: Cambridge University Press.

Feldman, R.S., & Rimé, B. (Eds.). (1991). *Fundamentals of nonverbal behavior.* Cambridge: Cambridge University Press.

Feldman, R.S. (Ed.). (1992). *Applications of nonverbal behavioral theories and research.* Hillsdale, NJ: Erlbaum.

Feldman, R.S., & Prohaska, T. (1979). The student as Pygmalion: Effect of student expectation on the teacher. *Journal of Educational Psychology, 4,* 485–493.

Feldman, R.S., & Theiss, A.J. (1982). The teacher and student as Pygmalions: The joint effects of teacher and student expectation. *Journal of Educational Psychology, 74,* 217–223.

Feldman, R.S., Philippot, P., & Custrini, R.J. (1991). Social competence and nonverbal behavior. In R.S. Feldman & B. Rimé (Eds.), *Fundamentals of nonverbal behavior.* Cambridge: Cambridge University Press.

Feldman, S.S., Biringen, Z.C., & Nash, S.C. (1981). Fluctuations of sex-related self-attributions as a function of stage of family life cycle. *Developmental Psychology, 17,* 24–35.

Feldman, S.S., & Rosenthal, D.A. (1990). The acculturation of autonomy expectations in Chinese high schoolers residing in two Western nations. *International Journal of Psychology, 25,* 259–281.

Feldman, W., Feldman, E., & Goodman, J.T. (1988). Culture versus biology: Children's attitudes toward thinness and fatness. *Pediatrics, 81,* 190–194.

Feng, T. (1993). Substance abuse in pregnancy. *Current Opinion in Obstetrics & Gynecology, 5,* 16–23.

Fenwick, K., & Morrongiello, B. (1991). Development of frequency perception in infants and children. *Journal of Speech, Language Pathology, and Audiology, 15,* 7–22.

Fernald, A. (1984). The perceptual and affective salience of mothers' speech to infants. In L. Feagans, C. Garvey, & R. Golinkoff (Eds.), *The origins and growth of communication.* Norwood, NJ: Ablex.

Fernald, A. (1989). Intonation and communicative intent in mothers' speech to infants: Is the melody the message? *Child Development, 60,* 1497–1510.

Fernald, A. (1991). Prosody in speech to children: Prelinguistic and linguistic functions. In R. Vasta (Ed.), *Annals of child development* (Vol. 8, pp. 43–80). London: Jessica Kingsley.

Fernald, A., & Kuhl, P. (1987). Acoustic determinants of infant preference for motherese speech. *Infant Behavior and Development, 10,* 279–293.

Fernald, A., Taeschner, T., Dunn, J., Papousek, M., et al. (1989). A cross-language study of prosodic modifications in mothers' and fathers' speech to preverbal infants. *Journal of Child Language, 16,* 477–501.

Ferrarri, F., Kelsall, A.W., Rennie, J.M., & Evans, D.H. (1994). The relationship between cerebral blood flow velocity fluctuations and sleep state in normal newborns. *Pediatric Research, 35,* 50–54.

Feshbach, S. (1980). Child abuse and the dynamics of human aggression and violence. In J. Gerbner, C.J. Ross, & E. Zigler (Eds.), *Child abuse: An agenda for action.* New York: Oxford University Press.

Festinger, L. (1954). A theory of social comparison processes. *Human Relations, 7,* 117–140.

Field, D. (1987). A review of preschool conservation training: An analysis of analyses. *Developmental Review, 7,* 210–251.

Field, D., & Minkler, M. (1988). Continuity and change in social support between young-old and old-old or very-old age. *Journal of Gerontology, 43*(4), 100–106.

Field, T. (1990). *Infancy.* Cambridge, MA: Harvard University Press.

Field, T., Cohen, D., Garcia, R., & Greenberg, R. (1984). Mother–stranger face discrimination by the newborn. *Infant Behavior and Development, 7,* 19–27.

Field, T., Dempsey, J., & Shuman, H.H. (1983). Five-year follow-up of preterm respiratory distress syndrome and post-term postmaturity syndrome infants. In T. Field & A. Sostek (Eds.), *Infants born at risk: Physiological, perceptual and cognitive processes.* New York: Grune & Stratton.

Field, T., Greenberg, R., Woodson, R., Cohen, D., et al. (1984). Facial expression during Brazelton neonatal assessments. *Infant Mental Health Journal, 5,* 61–71.

Field, T., Masi, W., Goldstein, S., Perry, S., et al. (1988). Infant daycare facilitates preschool social behavior. *Early Childhood Research Quarterly, 3,* 341–359.

Field, T., & Roopnarine, J.L. (1982). Infant–peer interactions. In T. Field, A. Huston, H. Quay, & G. Finley (Eds.), *Review of human development.* New York: Wiley.

Field, T., & Walden, T. (1982). Perception and production of facial expression in infancy and early childhood. In H. Reese & L. Lipsitt (Eds.), *Advances in child development and behavior* (Vol. 16). New York: Academic Press.

Field, T.M. (1978). Interaction of primary versus secondary caretaker fathers. *Developmental Psychology, 14,* 183–184.

Field, T.M. (1979). Games parents play with normal and high-risk infants. *Child Psychiatry and Human Development, 10,* 41–48.

Field, T.M. (1981). Infant gaze aversion and heart rate during face-to-face interactions. *Infant Behavior and Development, 4,* 307–313.

Field, T.M. (1982). Individual differences in the expressivity of neonates and young infants. In R.S. Feldman (Ed.), *Development of nonverbal behavior in children.* New York: Springer-Verlag.

Field, T.M. (1987). Interaction and attachment in normal and atypical infants. *Journal of Consulting and Clinical Psychology, 14,* 183–184.

Field, T.M. (Ed.). (1988). *Stress and coping across development.* Hillsdale, NJ: Erlbaum.

Field, T.M. (1990). Alleviating stress in newborn infants in the intensive care unit. In B.M. Lester & E.Z. Tronick (Eds.), *Stimulation and the preterm infant: The limits of plasticity.* Philadelphia: Saunders.

Field, T.M. (1991). Reducing stress in child and psychiatric patients by massage and relaxation therapy. In T.M. Field, P.M. McCabe, & D. Schneiderman (Eds.), *Stress and coping in infancy and childhood* (Vol. 4). Hillsdale, NJ: Erlbaum.

Field, T.M. (1995). Infant massage therapy. In T.M. Field (Ed.), *Touch in early development.* Hillsdale, NJ: Erlbaum.

Field, T.M., & Millsap, R.E. (1991). Personality in advanced old age: Continuity or change? *Journal of Gerontology: Psychological Sciences, 46,* P299–P308.

Field, T.M., Woodson, R., Greenberg, R., & Cohen, D. (1982). Discrimination and imitation of facial expressions by neonates. *Science, 218,* 179–181.

Fifer, W. (1987). Neonatal preference for mother's voice. In N.A. Kasnegor, E.M. Blass, & M.A. Hofer, (Eds.), *Perinatal development: A psychobiological perspective. Behavioral biology* (pp. 111–124). Orlando, FL: Academic Press.

Figley, C.R. (1973). Child density and the marital relationship. *Journal of Marriage and the Family, 35,* 272–282.

Finch, C.E. (1990). *Longevity, senescence, and the genome.* Chicago: University of Chicago Press.

Fincham, F.D., & Bradbury, T.N. (1992). Assessing attributions in marriage: The relationship attribution measure. *Journal of Personality and Social Psychology, 62,* 457–468.

Findlen, B. (1990, Sept.-Oct.). Culture: A refuge for murder. *Ms.,* pp. 1, 47.

Fingerhut, L.A., & Kleinman, J.C. (1990). International and interstate comparisons of homicide among young males. *Journal of the American Medical Association, 263,* 3292–3295.

Fingerhut, L.A., & MaKuc, D.M. 1992). Mortality among minority populations in the United States. *American Journal of Public Health, 82,* 1168–1170.

Fishbein, H.D., & Imai, S. (1993). Preschoolers select playmates on the basis of gender and race. *Journal of Applied Developmental Psychology, 14,* 303–316.

Fishel, E. (1993, September). Starting kindergarten. *Parents,* pp. 165–169.

Fisher, C.B., & Fryrberg, D. (1994). Participant partners: College students weigh the costs and benefits of deceptive research. *American Psychologist, 49,* 417–427.

Fisher, C.B., & Lerner, R.M. (1994). *Applied developmental psychology.* New York: McGraw-Hill.

Fishman, S. (1992). Relationships among an older adult's life review, ego integrity, and death anxiety. *International Psychogeriatrics, 4,* (Suppl. 2), 267–277.

Fiske, S.T., & Taylor, S.E. (1991). *Social cognition* (2nd ed.). New York: McGraw-Hill.

Fivush, R. (Ed.). (1995). *Long-term retention of infant memories.* Hillsdale, NJ: Erlbaum.

Flaks, D.K., Ficher, I., Masterpasqua, F., & Joseph, G. (1995). Lesbians choosing motherhood: A comparative study of lesbian and heterosexual parents and their children. Special Issue: Sexual-orientation and human development. *Developmental Psychology, 31*, 105–114.

Flavell, J.H. (1979). Metacognitive aspects of problem solving. In L. Resnick (Ed.), *The nature of intelligence.* Hillsdale, NJ: Erlbaum.

Flavell, J.H. (1985). *Cognitive development* (2nd ed.). Englewood Cliffs, NJ: Prentice-Hall.

Flavell, J.H. (1993). Young children's understanding of thinking and consciousness. *Current Directions in Psychological Science, 2*, 40–43.

Flavell, J.H. (1994). Cognitive development: Past, present, and future. In R.D. Parke, P.A. Ornstein, J.J. Rieser, & C. Zahn-Waxler (Eds.), *A century of developmental psychology.* Washington, DC: American Psychological Association.

Flavell, J.H., Green, F.L., & Flavell, E.R. (1995). The development of children's knowledge about attentional focus. *Developmental Psychology, 31*, 706–712.

Fleming, J.E., & Offord, D.R. (1990). Epidemiology of childhood depressive disorders: A critical review. *Journal of the American Academy of Child and Adolescent Psychiatry, 29*, 571–580.

Fletcher, A.C., Darling, N.E., Steinberg, L., & Dornbusch, S.M. (1995). The company they keep: Relation of adolescents' adjustment and behavior to their friends' perceptions of authoritative parenting in the social network. *Developmental Psychology, 31*, 300–310.

Flint, M. (1982). Male and female menopause: A cultural put on. In A. Voda, M. Dinnerstein, & S. O'Donnell (Eds.), *Changing perspectives on menopause.* Austin: University of Texas Press.

Flint, M. (1989). Cultural and subcultural meanings to the menopause. *Menopause Management, 2*(3), 11.

Florian, V., & Kravetz, S. (1985). Children's concepts of death: A cross-cultural comparison among Muslims, Druze, Christians, and Jews in Israel. *Journal of Cross-cultural psychology, 16*, 174–189.

Flum, H. (1994). The evolutive style of identity formation. *Journal of Youth and Adolescence, 23*, 489–498.

Fogel, A. (1980). Peer vs. mother-directed behavior in one- to three-month-old infants. *Infant Behavior and Development, 2*, 215–226.

Folkman, S., & Lazarus, R.S. (1980). An analysis of coping in a middle-aged community sample. *Journal of Health and Social Behavior, 21*, 219–239.

Folkman, S., & Lazarus, R.S. (1988). Coping as a mediator of emotion. *Journal of Personality and Social Psychology, 54*, 466–475.

Forrest, R., & Forrest, M.B. (1991). *Retirement living: A guide to housing alternatives.* New York: Facts on File.

Forslund, M. (1992). Growth and motor performance in preterm children at 8 years of age. *Acta Paediatrica, 81*, 840–842.

Fowler, W. (1990). *Talking from infancy: How to nurture and cultivate early language development.* Cambridge, MA: Brookline Books.

Fowles, D.C. (1992). Schizophrenia: Diathesis-stress revisited. *Annual Review of Psychology, 43*, 303–336.

Fox, J.L. (1984). International group suspends Nestlè boycott. *Science, 223*, 569.

Fox, N., Kimmerly, N.L., & Schafer, W.D. (1991). Attachment to mother/attachment to father: A meta-analysis. *Child Development, 62*, 210–225.

Fox, N.F. (Ed.). (1994). *The development of emotion regulation: Biological and behavioral considerations. Monographs of the Society for Research in Child Development.* (2–3, Serial No. 240).

Fozard, J.L., Vercruyssen, M., Reynolds, S.L., Hancock, P.A., et al. (1994). Age differences and changes in reaction time: The Baltimore Longitudinal Study of Aging. *Journal of Gerontology, 49*, 179–189.

Franck, I., & Brownstone, D. (1991). *The parent's desk reference.* New York: Prentice-Hall.

Frankenburg, W.K., Dodds, J., Archer, P., Shapiro, H., et al. (1992). The Denver II: A major revision and restandardization of the Denver Developmental Screening Test. *Pediatrics, 89*, 91–97.

Franzoi, S.L., Davis, M.H., & Vasquez-Suson, K.A. (1994). Two social worlds: Social correlates and stability of adolescent status groups. *Journal of Personality and Social Psychology, 67*, 462–473.

Freedman, D.G. (1979, January). Ethnic differences in babies. *Human nature,* pp. 15–20.

Frenkel, L.D., & Gaur, S. (1994). Perinatal HIV infection and AIDS. *Clinics in Perinatology, 21*, 95–107.

Freud, S. (1920). *A general introduction to psychoanalysis.* New York: Boni & Liveright.

Freud, S. (1959). *Group psychology and the analysis of the ego.* London: Hogarth Press. (Original work published 1922)

Freudenberger, H.J., & Richelson, G. (1980). *Burnout: The high cost of high achievement.* New York: Bantam.

Fried, P.A., & Watkinson, B. (1990). 36- and 48-Month neurobehavioral follow-up of children prenatally exposed to marijuana, cigarettes, and alcohol. *Developmental and Behavioral Pediatrics, 11*, 49–58.

Friedman, D., Berman, S., & Hamberger, M. (1993). Recognition memory and ERPs: Age-related changes in young, middle-aged, and elderly adults. *Journal of Psychophysiology, 7*, 181–201.

Friedman, H.S., Tucker, J.S., Schwartz, J.E., Martin, L.R., et al. (1995a). Childhood conscientiousness and longevity: Health behaviors and cause of death. *Journal of Personality and Social Psychology, 68*, 696–703.

Friedman, H.S., Tucker, J.S., Schwartz, J.E., Tomlinson-Keasey, C., et al. (1995b). Psychosocial and behavioral predictors of longevity: The aging and death of the "Termites." *American Psychologist, 50*, 69–78.

Friedman, S.L., & Sigman, M.D. (1992). *The psychological development of low birthweight children.* Norwood, NJ: Ablex.

Friedman, W.J. (1993). Memory for the time of past events. *Psychological Bulletin, 113*, 44–66.

Fromholt, P., & Larsen, S.F. (1991). Autobiographical memory in normal, aging and primary degenerative dementia (dementia of the Alzheimer type). *Journal of Gerontology, 46*, 85–91.

Fromme, K., & Rivet, K. (1994). Young adults' coping style as a predictor of their alcohol use and response to daily events. *Journal of Youth and Adolescence, 23*, 85–97.

Fry, C.L. (1985). Culture, behavior, and aging in the comparative perspective. In J.E. Birren & K.W. Schaie (Eds.), *Handbook of the psychology of aging.* New York: Van Nostrand Reinhold.

Fryer, D., & Payne, R. (1986). Being unemployed: A review of the literature on the psychological experience of unemployment. In C.L. Cooper & I.T. Robertson (Eds.), *International review of industrial and organizational psychology.* Chichester, UK: Wiley.

Fuchs, D., & Fuchs, L.S. (1994). Inclusive schools movement and the radicalization of special education reform. *Exceptional Children, 60*, 294–309.

Furman, W., & Bierman, K.L. (1983). Developmental changes in young children's conceptions of friendship. *Child Development, 54*, 549–556.

Furstenberg, F., & Spanier, G. (1984). *Recycling the family: Remarriage after divorce.* Beverly Hills, CA: Sage.

Furstenberg, F.F., Jr., Brooks-Gunn, J., & Morgan, S.P. (1987). *Adolescent mothers in later life.* New York: Cambridge University Press.

Gaddis, A., & Brooks-Gunn, J. (1985). The male experience of pubertal change. *Journal of Youth and Adolescence, 14*, 61–70.

Gaertner, S.L., Mann, J.A., Dovidio, J.F., Murrell, A.J., & Pomare, M. (1990). How does cooperation reduce intergroup bias? *Journal of Personality and Social Psychology, 59*, 692–704.

Gagne, F. (1985). Giftedness and talent: Re-examining a reexamination of the definitions. *Gifted Child Quarterly, 29*, 103–112.

Galambos, N.L., & Dixon, R.A. (1984). Toward understanding and caring for latchkey children. *Child Care Quarterly, 13*, 116–125.

Gallagher, J.J. (1994). Teaching and learning: New models. *Annual Review of Psychology, 45,* 171–195.

Gallant, J.L., Braun, J., & VanEssen, D.C. (1993, January 1). Selectivity for polar, hyperbolic, and Cartesian gratings in macaque visual cortex. *Science, 259,* 100–103.

Gallup, G.G., Jr. (1977). Self-recognition in primates: A comparative approach to the bidirectional properties of consciousness. *American Psychologist, 32,* 329–337.

Gallup, G.H., & Newport, F. (1990). Virtually all adults want children, but many of the reasons are intangible. *The Gallup Poll Monthly, 297.*

Gangon, L., & Coleman, M. (1989). Preparing for remarriage: Anticipating the issues, seeking solutions. *Family Relations, 38,* 28–33.

Gans, J.E., Blyth, D.A., Elsby, A.B., & Gaveras, C.C. (1990). America's adolescents: How healthy are they? *AMA profiles of adolescent health series.* (Vol.1). Chicago: American Medical Association.

Garbaciak, J.A. (1990). Labor and delivery: Anesthesia, induction of labor, malpresentation, and operative delivery. *Current Opinion in Obstetrics and Gynecology, 2,* 773–779.

Garbarino, J. (1985). *Adolescent development: An ecological perspective.* Columbus, OH: Chas.E. Merrill.

Garbarino, J., & Asp, C. (1981). *Successful schools and competent students.* Lexington, MA: Lexington Books.

Garbarino, J., Dubrow, N., Kostelny, K., & Pardo, C. (1992). *Children in danger: Coping with the consequences of community violence.* San Francisco: Jossey-Bass.

Garber, M. (1981). Malnutrition during pregnancy and lactation. In G.H. Bourne (Ed.), *World review of nutrition and dietetics* (Vol. 36). Basel, Switzerland: Karger.

Gardner, H., & Hatch, T. (1989). Multiple intelligences go to school. *Educational Researcher, 18*(8), 4–10.

Garland, A.F., & Zigler, E. (1993). Adolescent suicide prevention: Current research and social policy implications. *American Psychologist, 48,* 169–182.

Garner, P.W., Jones, D.C., & Miner, J.L. (1994). Social competence among low-income preschoolers: Emotion socialization practices and social cognitive correlates. *Child Development, 65,* 622–637.

Garner, R., & Alexander, P.A. (1989). Metacognition: Answered and unanswered questions. *Educational Psychologist, 24,* 143–158.

Gaulden, M.E. (1992). Maternal age effect: The enigma of Down syndrome and other trisomic conditions. *Mutation Research, 296,* 69–88.

Gazzaniga, M.S. (1983). Right-hemisphere language following brain bisection: A twenty-year perspective. *American Psychologist, 38,* 525–537.

Geary, D.C., Fan, L., & Bow-Thomas, C.C. (1992). Even before formal instruction, Chinese children out-perform American children in mental addition. *Cognitive Development, 8,* 517–529.

Gelles, R.J. (1994). *Contemporary families.* Newbury Park, CA: Sage.

Gelles, R.J., & Cornell, C. (1990). *Intimate violence in families.* Beverly Hills, CA: Sage.

Gelman, D. (1994, April 18). The mystery of suicide. *Newsweek,* pp. 44–49.

Gelman, R. (1972). Logical capacity of very young children: Number invariance rules. *Child Development, 43,* 75–90.

Gelman, R., & Baillargeon, R. (1983). A review of some Piagetian concepts. In P.H. Mussen (Ed.), *Handbook of child psychology: Vol. 3. Cognitive Development* (4th ed., pp 167–230). New York: Wiley.

Gelman, S.A., & Kalish, C.W. (1993). Categories and causality. In R. Pasnak & M.L. Howe (Eds.), *Emerging themes in cognitive development. Vol. II: Competencies.* New York: Springer-Verlag.

Genesee, F. (1994). Bilingualism. In V.S. Ramachandran (Ed.), *Encyclopedia of human behavior.* San Diego, CA: Academic Press.

George, L.K. (1992). Social factors and the onset and outcome of depression. In K.W. Schaie, D. Blazer, & J.S. House (Eds), *Aging, health behaviors, and health outcomes: Social structure and aging.* Hillsdale, NJ: Erlbaum.

Gerard, H.B. (1988). School desegregation: The social science role. In P.A. Katz & K.A. Taylor (Eds.), *Eliminating racism: Profiles in controversy.* New York: Plenum Press.

Gergen, M.M. (1990). Finished at 40: Women's development within the patriarchy. *Psychology of Women Quarterly, 14,* 471–493.

Gesell, A.L. (1946). The ontogenesis of infant behavior. In L. Carmichael (Ed.), *Manual of child psychology.* New York: Harper.

Gesser, G., Wong, P.T., & Reker, G.T. (1988). Death attitudes across the lifespan: The development and validation of the Death Attitude Profile (DAP). *Omega: Journal of Death and Dying, 18,* 113–128.

Gibbins, A. (1994, September 2). Children's vaccine initiative stumbles. *Science, 265,* 1376–1377.

Gibson, E.J., & Walk, R.D. (1960). The "visual cliff." *Scientific American,* 64–71.

Gibson, R.C. (1986). Older black Americans. *Generations, 10*(4), 35–39.

Gil, D.G. (1970). *Violence against children: Physical abuse in the United States.* Cambridge, MA: Harvard University Press.

Gilbert, L.A. (1994). Current perspectives on dual-career families. *Current Directions in Psychological Science, 3,* 101–105.

Gilligan, C. (1982). *In a different voice: Psychological theory and women's development.* Cambridge, MA: Harvard University Press.

Gilligan, C. (1987). Adolescent development reconsidered. In C.E. Irwin (Ed.), *Adolescent social behavior and health.* San Francisco: Jossey-Bass.

Gilligan, C., Lyons, N.P., & Hammer, T.J. (Eds.). (1990). *Making connections.* Cambridge, MA: Harvard University Press.

Gilligan, C., Ward, J.V., & Taylor, J.M. (Eds.). (1988). *Mapping the moral domain: A contribution of women's thinking to psychological theory and education.* Cambridge, MA: Harvard University Press.

Ginzberg, E. (1972). Toward a theory of occupational choice: A restatement. *Vocational Guidance Quarterly, 12,* 10–14.

Gjerde, P., Block, J., & Block, J. (1988). Depressive symptoms and personality during late adolescence: Gender differences in the externalization–internalization of symptom expression. *Journal of Abnormal Psychology, 97,* 475–486.

Gladue, B. (1984). Hormone markers for homosexuality. *Science, 225,* 198.

Gladue, B.A. (1994). The biopsychology of sexual orientation. *Current Directions in Psychological Science, 3,* 150–154.

Glaser, R., Rice, J., Speicher, C.E., Stout, J.C., et al. (1986). Stress depresses interferon production by leukocytes concomitant with a decrease in natural killer cell activity. *Behavioral Neuroscience, 100,* 675–678.

Gleason, J.B. (1987). Sex differences in parent–child interaction. In S.U. Philips, S. Steele, & C. Tanz (Eds.), *Language, gender, and sex in comparative perspective.* New York: Cambridge University Press.

Gleason, J.B., Perlmann, R.Y., Ely, R., & Evans, D.W. (1991). The babytalk register: Parents' use of diminutives. In J.L. Sokolov & C.E. Snow (Eds.), *Handbook of research in language development using CHILDES.* Hillsdale, NJ: Erlbaum.

Gleick, E., Reed, S., & Schindehette, S. (1994, October 24). The baby trap. *People Weekly,* pp. 38–56.

Glenn, N.D., & Weaver, C.N. (1977). The marital happiness of remarried divorced persons. *Journal of Marriage and the Family, 39,* 331–337.

Glenn, N.D., & Weaver, C.N. (1990). Quantitative research on marital quality in the 1980s: A critical review. *Journal of Marriage and the Family, 52,* 818–831.

Glick, P. (1989). Remarried families, stepfamilies, and stepchildren: A brief demographic analysis. *Family Relations, 38,* 24–27.

Glick, P., Zion, C., & Nelson, C. (1988). What mediates sex discrimination in hiring decisions? *Journal of Personality and Social Psychology, 55,* 178–186.

Glover, J.A., Ronning, R.R., & Reynolds, C.R. (Eds.). (1992). *Handbook of creativity.* New York: Plenum Press.

Gluhoski, V., Leader, J., & Wortman, C.B. (1994). Grief and bereavement. In V.S. Ramachandran (Ed.), *Encyclopedia of human behavior.* San Diego, CA: Academic Press.

Gold, P.W., Gwirtsman, H., Avgerinos, P.C., Nieman, L.K., et al. (1986). Abnormal hypothalmic-pituitary-adrenal function in anorexia nervosa. *New England Journal of Medicine, 314,* 1335–1342.

Goldberg, S. (1983). Parent–infant bonding: Another look. *Child Development, 54,* 1355–1382.

Goldberg, S., & DiVitto, B. (1983). *Born too soon.* San Francisco: Freeman.

Goldscheider, F.K. (1994). Divorce and remarriage: Effects on the elderly population. *Reviews in Clinical Gerontology, 4,* 253–259.

Goldsmith, H.H., & Harman, C. (1994). Temperament and attachment: Individuals and relationships. *Current Directions in Psychological Science, 3,* 53–57.

Goldstein, A. (1994, August). School violence. Paper presented at the annual meeting of the American Psychological Association, Los Angeles.

Goleman, D. (1985, February 5). Mourning: New studies affirm its benefits. *The New York Times,* pp. C1, C6.

Golinkoff, R.M. (1993). When is communication a "meeting of minds"? *Journal of Child Language, 20,* 199–207.

Golombok, S., & Fivush, R. (1994). *Gender development.* Cambridge: Cambridge University Press.

Golombok, S., Cook, R., Bish, A., & Murray, C. (1995). Families created by the new reproductive technologies: Quality of parenting and social and emotional development of the children. *Child Development, 66,* 285–298.

Gomez, C.F. (1991). *Regulating death: Euthanasia and the case of the Netherlands.* New York: The Free Press.

Gondolf, E.W. (1985). Fighting for control: A clinical assessment of men who batter. *Social Casework, 66,* 48–54.

Gongla, P., & Thompson, E.H. (1987). Single-parent families. In M.B. Sussman & S.K. Steinmetz (Eds.), *Handbook of marriage and the family.* New York: Plenum Press.

Goodman, G.S., & Reed, R.S. (1986). Age differences in eyewitness testimony. *Law and Human Behavior, 10,* 317–332.

Goodwin, M.H. (1980). Directive-response speech sequences in girls' and boys' task activities. In S. McConnell-Ginet, R. Borker, & N. Furman (Eds.), *Women and language in literature and society* (pp. 157–173). New York: Praeger.

Goodwin, M.H. (1990). Tactical uses of stories: Participation frameworks within girls' and boys' disputes. *Discourse Processes, 13,* 33–71.

Googans, B., & Burden, D. (1987). Vulnerability of working parents: Balancing work and home roles. *Social Work, 32,* 295–300.

Goossens, F.A., & Van-Ijzendoorn, M.H. (1990). Quality of infants' attachments to professional caregivers: Relation to infant–parent attachment and day-care characteristics. *Child Development, 61,* 832–837.

Goren, G.C., Sarty, M., & Wu, P.Y.K. (1975). Visual following and pattern discrimination of facelike stimuli by newborn infants. *Pediatrics, 56,* 544–549.

Gorman, K.S., & Pollitt, E. (1992). Relationship between weight and body proportionality at birth, growth during the first year of life, and cognitive development at 36, 48, and 60 months. *Infant Behavior and Development, 15,* 279–296.

Gortmaker, S.L., Dietz, W.H., Sobol, A.M., & Welher, C.A. (1987). Increasing pediatric obesity in the United States. *American Journal of the Diseases of Children, 141,* 535–540.

Gottesman, I.I. (1991). *Schizophrenia genesis: The origins of madness.* New York: W.H. Freeman.

Gottesman, I.I. (1993). Origins of schizophrenia: Past as prologue. In R. Plomin, & G.E. McClearn (Eds.), *Nature, nurture, and psychology.* Washington, DC: American Psychological Association.

Gottfredson, G.D., & Holland, J.L. (1990). A longitudinal test of the influence of congruence: Job satisfaction, competency utilization, and counterproductive behavior. *Journal of Counseling Psychology, 37,* 389–398.

Gottfried, A.E., & Gottfried, A.W. (Eds.). (1994). *Redefining families.* New York: Plenum Press.

Gottlieb, G. (1991). Experimental canalization of behavioral development: Theory. *Developmental Psychology, 27,* 373–381.

Gottman, J., & Parkhurst, J. (1980). A developmental theory of friendship and acquaintance processes. In W.A. Collins (Ed.), *Development of cognition, affect, and social relations.* Hillsdale, NJ: Erlbaum.

Gottman, J.M. (1986). The world of coordinated play: Same- and cross-sex friendship in young children. In J.M. Gottman & J.G. Parker (Eds.), *Conversations of friends: Speculations on affective development* (pp. 139–191). Cambridge: Cambridge University Press.

Gottman, J.M. (1993). *What predicts divorce? The relationship between marital processes and marital outcomes.* Hillsdale, NJ: Erlbaum.

Gottman, J.M. (Ed.). (1995). *What predicts divorce? The measures.* Hillsdale, NJ: Erlbaum.

Gottman, J.M., Buehlman, K.T., & Katz, L.F. (1992). Factors determining divorce. *Journal of Family Psychology, 1,* 37–43.

Gottman, J.M., & Katz, L.F. (1989). Effects of marital discord on young children's peer interaction and health. *Developmental Psychology, 25,* 373–381.

Gottschalk, E.C., Jr. (1983, February 21). Older Americans: The aging made gains in the 1970s, outpacing rest of the population. *The Wall Street Journal,* pp. 1, 20.

Gottwald, S.R., & Thurman, S.K. (1994). The effects of prenatal cocaine exposure on mother–infant interaction and infant arousal in the newborn period. *Topics in Early Childhood Special Education, 14,* 217–231.

Gould, S.J. (1977). *Ontogeny and phylogeny.* Cambridge, MA: Harvard University Press.

Gouvier, W.D., Steiner, D.D., Jackson, W.T., & Schlater, D. (1991). Employment discrimination against handicapped job candidates: An analog study of the effects of neurological causation, visibility of handicap, and public contact. *Rehabilitation Psychology, 36,* 121–129.

Graber, J.A., Brooks-Gunn, J., Paikoff, R.L., & Warren, M.P. (1994). Prediction of eating problems: An 8-year study of adolescent girls. *Developmental Psychology, 30,* 823–834.

Graber, J.A., Brooks-Gunn, J., & Warren, M.P. (1995). The antecedents of menarcheal age: Heredity, family environment, and stressful life events. *Child Development, 66,* 346–359.

Grady, C.L., McIntosh, A.R., Horwitz, B., Maison, J.M., et al. (1995, July 14). Age-related reductions in human recognition memory due to impaired encoding. *Science, 269,* 218–221.

Graf, P. (1990). Life span changes in implicit and explicit memory. Bulletin of the *Psychonomic Society, 28,* 353–358.

Graham, E. (1995, February 9). Leah: Life is all sweetness and insecurity. *The Wall Street Journal,* p. B1.

Graham, J.R. (1990). *MMPI-2: Assessing personality and psychopathology.* New York: Oxford University Press.

Graham, J.W., Marks, G., & Hansen, W.B. (1991). Social influence processes affecting adolescent substance use. *Journal of Applied Psychology, 76,* 291–298.

Graham, S. (1992). "Most of the subjects were white and middle class": Trends in published research on African Americans in selected APA journals. *American Psychologist, 47,* 629–639.

Graham, S. (1994). Motivation in African Americans. *Review of Educational Research, 64,* 55–117.

Grambs, J.D. (1989). *Women over forty: Visions and realities.* New York: Springer.

Grant, V.J. (1994). Sex of infant differences in mother–infant interaction: A reinterpretation of past findings. *Developmental Review, 14,* 1–26.

Grantham-McGregor, S., Powell, C., Walker, S., Chang, S., et al. (1994). The long-term follow-up of severely malnourished children who participated in an intervention program. *Child Development, 65,* 428–439.

Gratch, G., & Schatz, J.A. (1987). Cognitive development: The relevance of Piaget's infancy books. In J.D. Osofsky (Ed.), *Handbook of infant development* (2nd ed.). New York: Wiley.

Grattan, M.P., DeVos, E.S., Levy, J., & McClintock, M.K. (1992). Asymmetric action in the human newborn: Sex differences in patterns of organization. *Child Development, 63,* 273–289.

Gray, L.C., Farish, S.J., & Dorevitch, M. (1992). A population-based study of assessed applicants to long-term nursing home care. *Journal of the American Geriatric Society, 40,* 596–600.

Green, C.P. (1991). Clinical considerations: Midlife daughters and their aging parents. *Journal of Gerontological Nursing, 17,* 6–12.

Greenberg, J., & Becker, M. (1988). Aging parents as family resources. *Gerontologist, 28,* 786–790.

Greenberg, M.T., Cicchetti, D., & Cummings, E.M. (Eds.). (1990). *Attachment in the preschool years: Theory, research, and intervention.* Chicago: University of Chicago Press.

Greenfield, P. (1995, Winter). Culture, ethnicity, race, and development: Implications for teaching theory and research. *SRCD Newsletter.* Chicago: Society for Research in Child Development.

Greenfield, P.M. (1966). On culture and conservation. In J.S. Bruner, R.R. Olver, & P.M. Greenfield (Eds.), *Studies in cognitive growth.* New York: Wiley.

Greenfield, P.M. (1976). Cross-cultural research and Piagetian theory: Paradox and progress. In K.F. Riegel & J.A. Meacham (Eds.), *The developing individual in a changing world: Vol. 1.* The Hague, The Netherlands: Mouton.

Greenglass, E.R., & Burke, R.J. (1991). The relationship between stress and coping among Type A's. *Journal of Social Behavior and Personality, 6,* 361–373.

Gregory, S. (1856). *Facts for young women.* Boston.

Greven, P. (1990). *Spare the child: The religious roots of punishment and the psychological impact of physical abuse.* New York: Knopf.

Grieser, T., & Kuhl, P. (1988). Maternal speech to infants in atonal language: Support for universal prosodic features in motherese. *Developmental Psychology, 24,* 14–20.

Grisby, J.S. (1991). Paths for future population aging. *Gerontologist, 31,* 195–203.

Grolnick, W.S., & Slowiaczek, M.L. (1994). Parents' involvement in children's schooling: A multidimensional conceptualization and motivation model. *Child Development, 65,* 237–252.

Gross, J. (1991, June 16). More young single men hang on to apron strings. *The New York Times,* pp. A1, A18.

Gross, P.A. (1991). *Managing your health: Strategies for lifelong good health.* Yonkers, NY: Consumer Reports Publications.

Gross, R.T., McCormick, M.C., Brooks-Gunn, J., Shapiro, S., Benasich, A.A. & Black, G. (1990). Health care use among young children in day care. Results in a randomized trial of early intervention. *Journal of the American Medical Association, 265,* 2212–2217.

Gross, R.T., Brooks-Gunn, J., & Spiker, D. (1992). Efficacy of comprehensive early intervention for low-birthweight premature infants and their families: The infant health and development program. In S.L. Friedman & M.D. Sigman (Eds.), *The psychological development of low-birthweight children.* Norwood, NJ: Ablex.

Grossmann, K.E., Grossman, K., Huber, F., & Wartner, U. (1982). German children's behavior towards their mothers at 12 months and their fathers at 18 months in Ainsworth's strange situation. *International Journal of Behavioral Development, 4,* 157–181.

Grusec, J.E. (1982). Socialization processes and the development of altruism. In J.P. Rushton & R.M. Sorrentino (Eds.), *Altruism and helping behavior.* Hillsdale, NJ: Erlbaum.

Grusec, J.E. (1991). The socialization of altruism. In M.S. Clark (Ed.), *Prosocial behavior.* Newbury Park, CA: Sage.

Grusec, J.E., & Goodnow, J.J. (1994a). Summing up and looking to the future. *Developmental Psychology, 30,* 29–31.

Grusec, J.E., & Goodnow, J.J. (1994b). Impact of parental discipline methods on the child's internalization of values: A reconceptualization of current points of view. *Developmental Psychology, 30,* 4–19.

Gubrium, F.F. (1975). Being single in old age. *International Journal of Aging and Human Development, 6,* 29–41.

Gubrium, J.G. (1973). *The myth of the golden years: A socio-environmental theory of aging.* Springfield, IL: Chas. C Thomas.

Guerin, D.W., & Gottfried, A.W. (1994). Developmental stability and change in parent reports of temperament: A ten-year longitudinal investigation from infancy through preadolescence. *Merrill-Palmer Quarterly, 40,* 334–355.

Guisinger, S., Cowan, P., & Schuldberg, D. (1989). Changing parent and spouse relations in the first year of remarriage of divorced fathers. *Journal of Marriage and the Family, 51,* 445–456.

Gullotta, T.P., Adams, G.R., & Montemayor, R. (Eds.). (1995). *Substance misuse in adolescence.* Thousand Oaks, CA: Sage.

Gupta, U., & Singh, P. (1982). An exploratory study of love and liking and type of marriages. *Indian Journal of Applied Psychology, 19,* 92–97.

Gur, R.C., Gur, R.E., Obrist, W.D., Hungerbuhler, J.P., Younkin, D., Rosen, A.D., Skilnick, B.E., & Reivich, M. (1982). Sex and handedness differences in cerebral blood flow during rest and cognitive activity. *Science, 217,* 659–661.

Guralnik, M.D., Ferrucci, L., Simonsick, E.M., Salive, M.E., et al. (1995). Lower-extremity function in persons over the age of 70 years as a predictor of subsequent disability. *New England Journal of Medicine, 332,* 556–561.

Gurman, E.B. (1994). Debriefing for all concerned: Ethical treatment of human subjects. *Psychological Science, 5,* 139.

Guthrie, G., & Lonner, W. (1986). Assessment of personality and psychopathology. In W. Lonner & J. Berry (Eds.), *Field methods in cross-cultural research.* Newbury Park, CA: Sage.

Guttentag, R.E. (1985). Memory and aging: Implications for theories of memory development during childhood. *Developmental Review, 5,* 56–82.

Guttman, J. (1993). *Divorce in psychosocial perspective: Theory and research.* Hillsdale, NJ: Erlbaum.

Haan, N. (1985). Processes of moral development: Cognitive or social disequilibrium? *Developmental Psychology, 21,* 996–1006.

Haan, N., Millsap, R., & Hartka, E. (1986). As time goes by: Change and stability in personality over fifty years. *Psychology and Aging, 1,* 220–232.

Hack, M., Klein, N.K., & Taylor, H.G. (1995). Long-term developmental outcomes of low birth weight infants. *The Future of Children, 5,* 176–197.

Hackel, L.S., & Ruble, D.N. (1992). Changes in the marital relationship after the first baby is born: Predicting the impact of expectancy disconfirmation. *Journal of Personality and Social Psychology, 62,* 944–957.

Hagestad, G.O., & Neugarten, B.L. (1985). Age and the life course. In R.H. Binstock & E. Shanas (Eds.), *Handbook of aging and the social sciences.* (2nd ed.). New York: Van Nostrand Reinhold.

Haggerty, R., Garmezy, N., Rutter, M., & Sherrod, L. (Eds.). (1994). *Stress, risk, and resilience in childhood and adolescence.* New York: Cambridge University Press.

Haight, B.K. (1991). Psychological illness in aging. In E.M. Baines (Ed.), *Perspectives on gerontological nursing.* Newbury Park, CA: Sage.

Haith, M.H. (1991, April). *Setting a path for the 90s: Some goals and challenges in infant sensory and perceptual development.* Paper presented at the biennial meeting of the Society for Research in Child Development. Seattle, WA.

Haith, M.M. (1980). *Rules that babies look by.* Hillsdale, NJ: Erlbaum.

Haith, M.M. (1986). Sensory and perceptual processes in early infancy. *Journal of Pediatrics, 109* (1), 158–171.

Haith, M.M. (1991). Gratuity, perception-action integration and future orientation in infant vision. In F. Kessel, M. Bornstein, & A. Sameroff (Eds.), *Contemporary constructions of the child.* Hillsdale, NJ: Erlbaum.

Hakuta, K.U., & Garcia, E.E. (1989). Bilingualism and education. *American Psychologist, 44,* 374–379.

Hales, D. (1992). *An invitation to health: Taking charge of your life.* Menlo Park, CA: Benjamin/Cummings.

Hales, K.A., Morgan, M.A., & Thurnau, G.R. (1993). Influence of labor and route of delivery on the frequency of respiratory morbidity in term neonates. *International Journal of Gynecology & Obstetrics, 43,* 35–40.

Halford, G.S., Maybery, M.T., O'Hare, A.W., & Grant, P. (1994). The development of memory and processing capacity. *Child Development, 65,* 1338–1356.

Hall, E.G., & Lee, A.M. (1984). Sex differences in motor performance of young children: Fact or fiction? *Sex Roles, 10,* 217–230.

Hallberg, H. (1992). Life after divorce: A five-year follow-up study of divorced middle-aged men in Sweden. *Family Practice, 9,* 49–56.

Halliday, M.A.K. (1975). *Learning how to mean—Explorations in the development of language.* London: Edward Arnold.

Hallinan, M.T., & Williams, R.A. (1989). Interracial friendship choices in secondary schools. *American Sociological Review, 54,* 67–78.

Halverson, C.F., Jr., Kohnstamm, G.A., & Martin, R.P. (Eds.). (1994). *The developing structure of temperament and personality from infancy to adulthood.* Hillsdale, NJ: Erlbaum.

Hammen, C. (1991). *Depression runs in families.* New York: Springer-Verlag.

Hammer, R.P. (1984). The sexually dimorphic region of the preoptic area in rats contains denser opiate receptor binding sites in females. *Brain Researcher, 308,* 172–176.

Hamon, R.R., & Blieszner, R. (1990). Filial responsibility expectations among adult child–older parent pairs. *Journal of Gerontology, 45,* 110–112.

Hampson, J., & Nelson, K. (1993). The relation of maternal language to variation in rate and style of language acquisition. *Journal of Child Language, 20,* 313–342.

Hanna, E., & Meltzoff, A.N. (1993). Peer imitation by toddlers in laboratory, home, and day-care contexts: Implications for social learning and memory. *Developmental Psychology, 29,* 701–710.

Hansen, C.H. (1989). Priming sex-role stereotypic schemas with rock music videos: Effects on impression favorability, trait inferences, and recall of subsequent male–female interaction. *Basic and Applied Social Psychology, 10,* 371–391.

Hansson, R.O., & Carpenter, B.N. (1994). *Relationships in old age: Coping with the challenge of transition.* New York: Guilford Press.

Harkness, S., & Super, C.M. (1985). The cultural context of gender segregationing children's peer groups. *Child Development, 56,* 219–224.

Harlow, H.F., & Zimmerman, R.R. (1959). Affectional responses in the infant monkey. *Science, 130,* 421–432.

Harrell, S. (1981). Growing old in rural Taiwan. In P.T. Amoss & S. Harrell (Eds.), *Other ways of growing old.* Stanford, CA: Stanford University Press.

Harris, M.B. (1994). Growing old gracefully: Age concealment and gender. *Journal of Gerontology, 49,* 149–158.

Harris, M.J., Milich, R., Corbitt, E.M., Hoover, D.W., et al. (1992). Self-fulfilling effects of stigmatizing information on children's social interactions. *Journal of Personality and Social Psychology, 63,* 41–50.

Harris, M.J., & Rosenthal, R. (1986). Four factors in the mediation of teacher expectancy effects. In R.S. Feldman (Ed.), *The social psychology of education.* Cambridge: Cambridge University Press.

Harris, P.L. (1983). Infant cognition. In M. Haith & J.J. Campos (Eds.), *Infancy and developmental psychobiology* (Vol. 2). In P.H. Mussen (Gen. Ed.), *Handbook of child psychology.* New York: Wiley.

Harris, P.L. (1987). The development of search. In P. Sallapatek & L. Cohen (Eds.), *Handbook of infant perception: From perception to cognition* (Vol. 2, pp. 155–207). Orlando, FL: Academic Press.

Hart, B., & Risley, T.R. (1995). *Meaningful differences in the everyday experience of young American children.* Baltimore: Paul Brookes.

Hart, S.N., & Brassard, M.R. (1987). A major threat to children's mental health. *American Psychologist, 42,* 160–165.

Harter, S. (1983). Developmental perspectives on the self-system. In Paul H. Mussen (Ed.), *Handbook of child psychology: Vol. 4. Socialization, personality and social development.* New York: Wiley.

Harter, S. (1990a). Identity and self-development. In S. Feldman & G. Elliott (Eds.), *At the threshold: The developing adolescent.* Cambridge, MA: Harvard University Press.

Harter, S. (1990b). Issues in the assessment of self-concept of children and adolescents. In A. LaGreca (Ed.), *Through the eyes of a child.* Boston: Allyn & Bacon.

Hartman, M., & Hasher, L. (1991). Aging and suppression: Memory for previously relevant information. *Psychology and aging, 6,* 587–594.

Hartshorne, T.S. (1994). Friendship. In V.S. Ramachandran (Ed.), *Encyclopedia of human behavior.* San Diego, CA: Academic Press.

Hartup, W.W. (1970). Peer relations. In T.D. Spencer & N. Kass (Eds.), *Perspectives in child psychology: Research and review.* New York: McGraw-Hill.

Hartup, W.W. (1983). Peer relations. In P.H. Mussen (Ed.), *Handbook of child psychology* (4th ed., Vol. 4). New York: Wiley.

Hartup, W.W. (1989). Social relationships and their developmental significance. *American Psychologist, 44,* 120–126.

Hartup, W.W. (1992). Friendships and their developmental significance. In H. McGurk (Ed.), *Childhood social development: Contemporary perspectives.* London: Erlbaum.

Haskins, R. (1985). Public school aggression among children with varying day-care experience. *Child Development, 56,* 689–703.

Haskins, R. (1989). Beyond metaphor: The efficacy of early childhood education. *American Psychologist, 44,* 274–282.

Hatfield, E. (1988). Passionate and companionate love. In R.J. Sternberg & M.L. Barnes (Eds.), *The psychology of love* (pp. 191–217). New Haven, CT: Yale University Press.

Hatfield, E., & Rapson, R.L. (1993). Historical and cross-cultural perspectives on passionate love and sexual desire. *Annual Review of Sex Research, 4,* 67–97.

Hatfield, E., & Sprecher, S. (1986). *Mirror, mirror . . . The importance of looks in everyday life.* Albany: State University of New York Press.

Hattie, J. (1992). *Self-concept.* Hillsdale, NJ: Erlbaum.

Haug, H. (1991). Aging of the brain. In F.C. Ludwig (Ed.), *Life span extension: Consequences, intimacy, and close relationships.* New York: Springer.

Havighurst, R.J. (1973). Social roles, work, leisure, and education. In C. Eisdorfer & M.P. Lawton (Eds.), *The psychology of adult development and aging.* Washington, DC: American Psychological Association.

Havighurst, R.J., Neugarten, B.L., & Tobin, S.S. (1968). Disengagement and patterns of aging. In B.L. Neugarten (Ed.), *Middle age and aging.* Chicago: University of Chicago Press.

Hawton, K. (1986). *Suicide and attempted suicide among children and adolescents.* Newbury Park, CA: Sage.

Hay, D.F. (1984). Social conflict in early childhood. In G. Whitehurst (Ed.), *Annals of child development* (Vol. 1). Greenwich, CT: JAI Press.

Hayflick, L. (1974). The strategy of senescence. *The Journal of Gerontology, 14,* 37–45.

Hayne, H., & Rovee-Collier, C. (1995). The organization of reactivated memory in infancy. *Child Development, 66,* 893–906.

Hazell, P. (1993). Adolescent suicide clusters: Evidence, mechanisms and prevention. *Australian and New Zealand Journal of Psychiatry, 27,* 653–665.

Hazen, C., & Shaver, P. (1987). Romantic love conceptualized as an attachment process. *Journal of Personality and Social Psychology, 52,* 511–524.

Heatherton, T.F., Polivy, J., & Herman, C.P. (1991). Restraint, weight loss, and variability of body weight. *Journal of Abnormal Psychology, 100,* 78–83.

Hebbeler, K. (1985). An old and a new question on the effects of early education for children from low income families. *Educational Evaluation and Policy Analysis, 7,* 207–216.

Hecht, M.L., Marston, P.J., & Larkey, L.K. (1994). Love ways and relationship quality in heterosexual relationships. *Journal of Social and Personal Relationships, 11,* 25–43.

Heckhausen, J., Dixon, R.A., & Baltes, P.B. (1989). Gains and losses in development throughout adulthood as perceived by different adult age groups. *Developmental Psychology, 25,* 109–121.

Heidrich, S.M., & Denney, N.W. (1994). Does social problem solving differ from other types of problem solving during the adult years? *Experimental Aging Research, 20,* 105–126.

Heinemann, G.D., & Evans, P.L. (1990). Widowhood: Loss, change, and adaptation. In T.H. Brubaker (Ed.), *Family relationships in later life.* Newbury Park, CA: Sage.

Hellige, J.B. (1994). *Hemispheric asymmetry: What's right and what's left.* Cambridge, MA: Harvard University Press.

Hellman, P. (1987, November 23). Sesame Street smart. *New York,* pp. 49–53.

Helson R., & Moane, G. (1987). Personality change in women from college to midlife. *Journal of Personality and Social Psychology, 53,* 176–186.

Helson, R., & Roberts, B.W. (1994). Ego development and personality change in adulthood. *Journal of Personality and Social Psychology, 66,* 911–920.

Helson, R., Stewart, A.J., & Ostrove, J. (1995). Identity in three cohorts of midlife women. *Journal of Personality and Social Psychology, 69,* 544–557.

Helson, R., & Wink, P. (1992). Personality change in women from the early 40s to the early 50s. *Psychology and Aging, 7,* 46–55.

Hendrick, C., & Hendrick S. (1989). Research on love: Does it measure up? *Journal of Personality and Social Psychology, 56,* 784–794.

Henry, C.S., Stephenson, A.L., Hanson, M.F., & Hargett, W. (1993). Adolescent suicide and families: An ecological approach. *Adolescence, 28,* 291–308.

Hepper, P.G., Scott, D., & Shahidullah, S. (1993). Response to maternal voice. *Journal of Reproductive and Infant Psychology, 11,* 147–153.

Herbst, A.L. (1981). Diethylstilbestrol and other sex hormones during pregnancy. *Obstetrics & Gynecology, 58,* 355–405.

Herbst, A.L. (1994). The epidemiology of ovarian carcinoma and the current status of tumor markers to detect disease. *American Journal of Obstetrics and Gynecology, 170,* 1099–1105.

Herek, G.M. (1993). Sexual orientation and military service: A social science perspective. *American Psychologist, 48,* 538–549.

Herrgard, E., Luoma, L., Tuppurainen, K., Karjalainen, S., & Martikainen, A. (1993). Neurodevelopmental profile at five years of children born at < or = 32 weeks gestation. *Developmental Medicine and Child Neurology, 35,* 1083–1096.

Herrnstein, R.J., & Murray, C. (1994). *The bell curve: Intelligence and class structure in American life.* New York: The Free Press.

Herzog, A.R., House, J.S., & Morgan, J.N. (1991). Relation of work and retirement to health and well-being in older age. *Psychology and Aging, 6,* 202–211.

Hess, J.L. (1990). The catastrophic health care fiasco. *The Nation, 250,* 193–203.

Hetherington, E.M., & Blechman, E.A. (Eds.). (1996). *Stress, coping, and resiliency in children and families.* Hillsdale, NJ: Erlbaum.

Hetherington, E.M., & Clingempeel, W. (1992). Coping with marital transitions: A family systems perspective. *Monographs of the Society for Research in Child Development, 57* (2–3, Serial No. 227).

Hetherington, E.M., Stanley-Hagan, M., & Anderson, E. (1989). Marital transitions: A child's perspective. *American Psychologist, 44,* 303–312.

Hetherington, T.F., & Weinberger, J. (Eds.). (1993). *Can personality change?* Washington, DC: American Psychological Association.

Heward, W.L., & Orlansky, M.D. (1988, October). The epidemiology of AIDS in the U.S. *Scientific American,* pp. 72–81.

Hewett, F.M., & Forness, S.R. (1974). *Education of exceptional learners.* Boston: Allyn & Bacon.

Hickey, T., & Stillwell, D.L. (1991). Health promotion for older people: All is not well. *Gerontologist, 31,* 822–829.

Higbee, K.L., & Kunihira, S. (1985). Cross-cultural applications of Yodai mnemonics. *Educational Psychologist, 20,* 57–64.

Higher Education Research Institute, UCLA (1991). *The American freshman: National norms for fall 1990.* Los Angeles: Author.

Hill, R.D., Storandt, M., & Malley, M. (1993). The impact of long-term exercise training on psychological function in older adults. *Journal of Gerontology, 48,* P12–P17.

Hinde, R.A., Tamplin, A., & Barrett, J. (1993). Social isolation in 4-year-olds. *British Journal of Developmental Psychology, 11,* 211–236.

Hines, M., & Kaufman, F.R. (1994). Androgen and the development of human sex-typical behavior: Rough-and-tumble play and sex of preferred playmates in children with congenital adrenal hyperplasia (CAH). *Child Development, 65,* 1042–1053.

Hinton, J.M. (1967). *Dying.* Baltimore: Penguin Books.

Hirsch, H.V., & Spinelli, D.N. (1970). Visual experience modifies distribution of horizontally and vertically oriented receptive fields in cats. *Science, 168,* 869–871.

Hirshberg, L. (1990). When infants look to their parents: II. Twelve-month-olds' response to conflicting parental emotional signals. *Child Development, 61,* 1187–1191.

Hirshberg, L., & Svejda, M. (1990). When infants look to their parents: I. Infants' social referencing of mothers compared to fathers. *Child Development, 61,* 1175–1186.

HMHL (Harvard Mental Health Letter). (1994, February). AIDS and Mental health—Part II. *Harvard Mental Health Letter,* pp. 1–4.

HMHL (Harvard Mental Health Letter). (1995, February). *Update on Alzheimer's disease—Part I.* Cambridge, MA: Harvard Medical School.

Hobart, C., & Grigel, F. (1992). Cohabitation among Canadian students at the end of the eighties. *Journal of Comparative Family Studies, 23,* 311–337.

Hoff-Ginsberg, E. (1986). Function and structure in maternal speech. *Child Development, 22,* 155–163.

Hoffman, L.W. (1989). Effects of maternal employment in the two-parent family. *American Psychologist, 44,* 283–292.

Hoffman, L.W., McManus, K.A., & Brackbill, Y. (1987). The value of children to young and elderly parents. *International Journal of Aging and Human Development, 25,* 309–312.

Hoffman, R.G. (1991). Companion animals: A therapeutic measure for elderly patients. *Journal of Gerontological Social Work, 18,* 195–205.

Holahan, C.J., & Moos, R.H. (1987). Personal and contextual determinants of coping strategies. *Journal of Personality and Social Psychology, 52,* 946–955.

Holahan, C.J., & Moos, R.H. (1990). Life stressors, resistance factors, and improved psychological functioning: An extension of the stress resistance paradigm. *Journal of Personality and Social Psychology, 58,* 909–917.

Holden, C. (1987, October 9). Why do women live longer than men? *Science, 233,* 158–160.

Holland, A., Sicotte, N., & Treasure, L. (1988). Anorexia nervosa: Evidence for a genetic basis. *Journal of Psychosomatic Research, 32,* 561–571.

Holland, J.C., & Lewis, S. (1993). Emotions and cancer: What do we really know? In D. Goleman & J. Gurin (Eds.), *Mind-body medicine.* Yonkers, NY: Consumer Reports Books.

Holland, J.L. (1973). *Making vocational choices: A theory of careers.* Englewood Cliffs, NJ: Prentice-Hall.

Holland, J.L. (1987). Current status of Holland's theory of careers: Another perspective. *Career Development Quarterly, 36,* 24–30.

Holland, N. (1994, August). *Race dissonance—implications for African-American children.* Paper presented at the annual meeting of the American Psychological Association, Los Angeles.

Hollenbeck, A.R., Gewirtz, J.L., Sebris, S.L., & Scanlon, J.W. (1984). Labor and delivery medication influences parent–infant interaction in the first post-partum month. *Infant Behavior and Development, 7,* 201–209.

Holman, R.L. (1991, December 21). Exam hell linked to depression. *The Wall Street Journal,* p. 4.

Holmbeck, G.N., Crossman, R.E., Wandrei, M.L., & Gasiewski, E. (1994). Cognitive development, egocentrism, self-esteem, and adolescent contraceptive knowledge, attitudes, and behavior. *Journal of Youth and Adolescence, 23,* 169–193.

Holmes, D.L., Reich, J.N., & Gyurke, J.S. (1989). The development of high-risk infants in low-risk families. In F.J. Morrison, C. Lord, & D. Keating (Eds.), *Psychological development in infancy.* San Diego, CA: Academic Press.

Holmes, J. (1994). *John Bowlby and attachment theory.* New York: Routledge.

Holmes, T.H., & Rahe, R.H. (1967). The Social Readjustment Scale. *Journal of Psychosomatic Research, 11,* 257–261.

Holtzworth-Munroe, A. (1995, August). Marital violence. *The Harvard Mental Health Letter,* pp. 4–6.

Honeycutt, J.M. (1993). Marital happiness, divorce status and partner differences in attributions about communication behaviors. *Journal of Divorce and Remarriage, 21,* 177–205.

Hopkins, B., & Westra, T. (1988). Maternal handling and motor development: An intracultural study. *Genetic Psychology Monographs, 114,* 377–420.

Hopkins, B., & Westra, T. (1989). Maternal expectations of their infants' development: Some cultural differences. *Developmental Medicine and Child Neurology, 31,* 384–390.

Hopkins, B., & Westra, T. (1990). Motor development, maternal expectation, and the role of handling. *Infant Behavior and Development, 13,* 117–122.

Horgan, J. (1993, February). Genes and crime (controversial National Institutes of Health initiative). *Scientific American, 268,* p. 24.

Horn, D.L., & Donaldson, G. (1980). Cognitive development: II. Adulthood development of human abilities. In O.G. Brim & J. Kagan (Eds.), *Constancy and change in human development.* Cambridge, MA: Harvard University Press.

Hornik, R., & Gunnar, M.R. (1988). A descriptive analysis of infant social referencing. *Child Development, 59,* 626–634.

Hornik, R., Risenhoover, N., & Gunner, M. (1987). The effects of maternal positive, neutral, and negative affective communications on infant response to new toys. *Child Development, 58,* 937–944.

Horowitz, A. (1994). Vision impairment and functional disability among nursing home residents. *Gerontologist, 34,* 316–323.

Horwath, C.C. (1991). Nutrition goals for older adults: A review. *Gerontologist, 31,* 811–821.

Hoskins, I. (1992). Social security protection of women: Prospects for the 1990s. *Aging International, 19,* 27–32.

Houle, R., & Feldman, R.S. (1991). Emotional displays in children's television programming. *Journal of Nonverbal Behavior, 15,* 261–271.

Howard, A. (1992). Work and family crossroads spanning the career. In S. Zedeck (Ed.), *Work, families and organizations.* San Francisco: Jossey-Bass.

Howe, M.L., & O'Sullivan, J.T. (1990). The development of strategic memory: Coordinating knowledge, metamemory, and resources. In D.F. Bjorklund (Ed.), *Children's strategies: Contemporary view of cognitive development.* Hillsdale, NJ: Erlbaum.

Howes, C. (1987). Social competence with peers in young children: Developmental sequences. *Developmental Review, 7,* 252–272.

Howes, C., Phillips, D.A., & Whitebook, M. (1992). Thresholds of quality: Implications for the social development of children in center-based child care. *Child Development, 63,* 449–460.

Howes, C., Unger, O., & Seidner, L.B. (1989). Social pretend play in toddlers: Parallels with social play and with solitary pretend. *Child Development, 60,* 77–84.

Howes, C., & Wu, F. (1990). Peer interactions and friendships in an ethnically diverse school setting. *Child Development, 61,* 537–541.

Howie, L. (1993). Old women and widowhood: A dying status passage. *Omega, 26,* 223–233.

Howie, P.W., et. al. (1990). Protective effect of breast feeding against infection. *British Journal of Medicine, 300,* 11.

Hsu, L.K.G. (1990). *Eating disorders.* New York: Guilford Press.

Hubbard, J., & Coie, J.D. (1994). Emotional correlates of social competence in children's peer relationships. *Merrill-Palmer Quarterly, 40,* 1–20.

Hubel, D.H., & Wiesel, T.N. (1979, September). Brain mechanisms of vision. *Scientific American, 241,* pp. 150–162.

Hudson, M.J. (1990). Hearing and vision loss in an aging population: Myths and realities. *Educational Gerontology, 16,* 87–96.

Huesmann, L.R. (1986). Psychological processes promoting the relations between exposure to media violence and aggressive behavior by the viewer. *Journal of Social Issues, 42,* 125–139.

Huesmann, L.R., & Eron, L.D. (Eds.). (1986). *Television and the aggressive child: A cross-national comparison.* Hillsdale, NJ: Erlbaum.

Huesmann, L.R., Eron, L.D., Klein, R., Brice, P., et al. (1983). Mitigating the imitation of aggressive behaviors by changing children's attitudes about media violence. *Journal of Personality and Social Psychology, 5,* 899–910.

Hultsch, D.F., Masson, M.E., & Small, B.J. (1991). Adult age difference in direct and indirect tests of memory. *Journal of Gerontology: Psychological Sciences, 46,* 22–30.

Humphreys, L.G. (1992). Commentary: What both critics and users of ability tests need to know. *Psychological Science, 3,* 271–274.

Hunt, J., & Hunt, L. (1975). Racial inequality and self-image: Identity maintenance as identity diffusion. *Sociology and Social Research, 61,* 539–559.

Hunt, M. (1974). *Sexual behaviors in the 1970s.* New York: Dell.

Hunt, M. (1993). *The story of psychology.* New York: Doubleday.

Huston, A. (Ed.). (1991). *Children in poverty: Child development and public policy.* Cambridge: Cambridge University Press.

Huston, A.C., & Wright, J.C. (1995, May). *The effects of educational television viewing of lower income preschoolers on academic skills, school readiness, and school adjustment 1 to 3 years later: Report to Children's Television Workshop.* Lawrence, KS: Center for Research on the Influences of Television on Children, Department of Human Development, University of Kansas.

Hyde, J.S. (1994). *Understanding human sexuality* (5th ed.). New York: McGraw-Hill.

Iacono, W.G., & Grove, W.M. (1993). Schizophrenia reviewed: Toward an integrative genetic model. *Psychological Science, 4,* 273–276.

Ijzendoorn, M.H. van, & Kroonenberg P.M. (1988). Cross-cultural patterns of attachment: A meta-analysis of the strange situation. *Child Development, 59,* 147–156.

Ijzendoorn, M.H. van, & Tavecchio, L.W.C. (1987). The development of attachment theory as a Lakatosian research program: Philosophical and methodological aspects. In L.W.C. Travecchio & M.H. van Ijzendoorn (Eds.), *Attachment in social networks: Contributions to the Bowlby-Ainsworth attachment theory* (pp. 3–31). Amsterdam, The Netherlands: North-Holland.

Ikels, C. (1989). Becoming a human being in theory and practice: Chinese views of human development. In D.I. Kertzer & K.W. Schaie (Eds.), *Age structuring in comparative perspective.* Hillsdale, NJ: Erlbaum.

Illingworth, R.S. (1973). *Basic developmental screening: 0–2 years.* Oxford: Blackwell Scientific.

Infant Health and Development Program. (1990). *Journal of the American Medical Association, 263,* 3035–3042.

Insel, P.M., & Roth, W.T. (1991). *Core concepts in health* (6th ed.). Mountain View, CA: Mayfield.

Irwin, E.G. (1993). A focused overview of anorexia nervosa and bulimia: I. Etiological issues. *Archives of Psychiatric Nursing, 7*, 342–346.

Isabella, R.A. (1993). Origins of attachment: Maternal interactive behavior across the first year. *Child Development, 64*, 605–621.

Isaksen, S.G., & Murdock, M.C. (1993). The emergence of a discipline: Issues and approaches to the study of creativity. In S.G. Isaksen, M.C. Murdock, R.L. Firestein, & D.J. Treffinger (Eds.), *The emergence of a discipline* (Vol. 1). Norwood, NJ: Ablex.

Isay, R.A. (1990). *Being homosexual: Gay men and their development*. New York: Avon Books.

Israeloff, R. (1991, July). First steps. *Parents*, pp. 53–59.

Izard, C., & Malatesta, C. (1987). Perspectives on emotional development: I. Differential emotions theory of early emotional development. In J.D. Osofsky (Ed.), *Handbook of infant development*. New York: Wiley.

Izard, C.E. (1977). *Human emotions*. New York: Plenum Press.

Jacklin, C.N., Snow, M.E., & Maccoby, E.E. (1981). Tactile sensitivity and muscle strength in newborn boys and girls. *Infant Behavior and Development, 4*, 261–268.

Jackson, L.A., Gardner, P.D., & Sullivan, L.A. (1992). Explaining gender differences in self-pay expectations: Social comparison standards and perceptions of fair pay. *Journal of Applied Psychology, 77*, 651–663.

Jacobsen, L., & Edmondson, B. (1993, August). *American Demographics*, pp. 22–27.

Jacobson, N.S. (1987). Family type, visiting patterns, and children's behavior in the stepfamily: A linked family system. In K. Pasley & M. Ihinger-Tallman (Eds.), *Remarriage and stepparenting*. New York: Guilford Press.

Jacobson, S.W., Fein, G.G., Jacobson, J.L., Schwartz, P.M., et al. (1985). The effect of intrauterine PCB exposure on visual recognition memory. *Child Development, 56*, 853–860.

Jacoby, L.L., & Kelley, C.M. (1992). A process-dissociation framework for investigating unconscious influences: Freudian slips, projective tests, subliminal perception, and signal detection theory. *Current Directions in Psychological Science, 1*, 174–179.

Jacoby, R., & Glauberman, N. (Eds.). (1995). *The bell curve debate*. New York: Times Books/Random House.

Jadack, R.A., Hyde, J.S., Moore, C.F., & Keller, M.L. (1995). Moral reasoning about sexually transmitted diseases. *Child Development, 66*, 167–177.

Jahoda, G. (1980). Theoretical and systematic approaches in mass-cultural psychology. In H.C. Triandis & W.W. Lambert (Eds.), *Handbook of cross-cultural psychology* (Vol. 1). Boston: Allyn & Bacon.

Jahoda, G., & Lewis, I.M. (1988). *Acquiring culture: Cross-cultural studies in child development*. London: Croom Helm.

Jahoda, M. (1982). *Employment and unemployment*. Cambridge: Cambridge University Press.

Jakobson, R. (1971). Why "Mama" and "Papa"? In A. Bar-Adon & W.F. Leopold (Eds.), *Child language*. Englewood Cliffs, NJ: Prentice-Hall.

James, W. (1950). *The principles of psychology*. New York: Holt. (original work published 1890).

Jamieson, D.W., Lydon, J.E., Stewart, G., & Zanna, M.P. (1987). Pygmalion revisited: New evidence for student expectancy effects in the classroom. *Journal of Educational Psychology, 79*, 461–466.

Janda, L.H., & Klenke-Hamel, K.E. (1980). *Human sexuality*. New York: Van Nostrand.

Jarvik, M.E. (1990, October 19). The drug dilemma: Manipulating the demand. *Science, 250*, 387–392.

Jensen, A. (1969). How much can we boost IQ and scholastic achievement? *Harvard Educational Review, 39*, 10123.

Jepson, H.A., Talashek, M.L., & Tichy, A.M. (1991). The Apgar score: Evolution, limitations, and scoring guidelines. *Birth, 18*, 83–92.

Johnson, A.M., Wadsworth, J., Wellings, K., & Bradshaw, S. (1992). Sexual lifestyles and HIV risk. *Nature, 360*, 410–412.

Johnson, C.L., & Barer, B.M. (1992). Patterns of engagement and disengagement among the oldest old. *Journal of Aging Studies, 6*, 351–364.

Johnson, J.L., Primas, P.J., & Coe, M.K. (1994). Factors that prevent women of low socioeconomic status from seeking prenatal care. *Journal of the American Academy of Nurse Practitioners, 6*, 105–111.

Johnson, S.L., & Birch, L.L. (1994). Parents' and children's adiposity and eating style. *Pediatrics, 94*, 653–661.

Johnson, W., Emde, R.N., Pannabecker, B., Stenberg, C., & Davis, M. (1982). Maternal perception of infant emotion from birth through 18 months. *Infant Behavior and Development, 5*, 313–322.

Johnston, C.C. (1989). Pain assessment and management in infants. *Pediatrician, 16*, 16–23.

Jones, S.S., & Raag, T. (1989). Smile production in older infants: The importance of a social recipient for the facial signal. *Child Development, 60*, 811–818.

Jones, S.S., Collins, K., & Hong, H. (1991). An audience effect on smile production in 10-month-old infants. *Psychological Science, 2*, 45–49.

Jost, H., & Songtag, L. (1944). The genetic factor in autonomic nervous system function. *Psychosomatic Medicine, 6*, 308–310.

Julian, T., McKenny, P.C., & McKelvey, M.W. (1992). Components of men's well-being at mid-life. *Issues in Mental Health Nursing, 13*, 285–299.

Julien, R.M. (1995). *A primer of drug action* (6th ed.). New York: W.H. Freeman.

Juvenile Justice Clearinghouse. (1995). Current statistics on World Wide Web page. Washington, DC: Author.

Juvenile offenders and victims: A focus on violence. Rockville, MD: Juvenile Justice Clearinghouse.

Kagan, J. (1981). Universals in human development. In R.H. Munroe, R.L. Munroe, & B.B. Whiting (Eds.), *Handbook of crosscultural human development* (pp. 53–62). New York: Garland.

Kagan, J. (1994). Yesterday's premises, tomorrow's promises. In R.D. Parke, P.A. Ornstein, J.J. Rieser, & C. Zahn-Waxler (Eds.), *A century of developmental psychology*. Washington, DC: American Psychological Association.

Kagan, J., & Snidman, N. (1991). Infant predictors of inhibited and uninhibited profiles. *Psychological Science, 2*, 40–44.

Kagan, J., Arcus, D., & Snidman, N. (1993). The idea of temperament: Where do we go from here? In R. Plomin, & G.E. McClearn (Eds.), *Nature, nurture, and psychology*. Washington, DC: American Psychological Association.

Kagan, J., Arcus, D., Snidman, N., Feng, W.Y., et al. (1994). Reactivity in infants: A cross-national comparison. *Developmental Psychology, 30*, 342–345.

Kagan, J., Reznick, S., & Gibbons, I. (1989). Inhibited and uninhibited life of children. *Child Development, 60*, 838–845.

Kahn, S., Zimmerman, G., Csikszentmihalyi, M., & Getzels, J.W. (1985). Relations between identity in young adulthood and intimacy at midlife. *Journal of Personality and Social Psychology, 49*, 1316–1322.

Kaitz, M., Meschulach-Sarfaty, O., Auerbach, J., & Eidelman, A. (1988). A re-examination of newborns' ability to imitate facial expressions. *Developmental Psychology, 24*, 3–7.

Kalish, R.A., & Reynolds, D.K. (1976). *An overview of death and ethnicity*. Farmingdale, NY: Baywood.

Kalliopuska, M. (1994). Relations of retired people and their grandchildren. *Psychological Reports, 75*, 1083–1088.

Kalmijn, M. (1991). Status homogamy in the United States. *American Journal of Sociology, 97*, 496–523.

Kamerman, S., & Hayes, C. (1982). *Families that work: Children in a changing world*. Washington, DC: National Academy Press.

Kamhi, A. (1986). The elusive first word: The importance of the naming insight for the development of referential speech. *Journal of Child Language, 13*, 155–161.

Kane, R.I., Wales, J., Bernstein, L., Leibowitz, A., & Kaplan, S. (1984). A randomized controlled trial of hospice care. *The Lancet, 302,* 890–894.

Kaplan, H., & Dove, H. (1987). Infant development among the Ache of eastern Paraguay. *Developmental Psychology, 23,* 190–198.

Kaplan, R.M., Sallis, J.F., Jr., & Patterson, T.L. (1993). *Health and human behavior.* New York: McGraw-Hill.

Karmel, B.Z., Gardner, J.M., & Magnano, C.L. (1991). Attention and arousal in early infancy. In M.J.S. Weiss, & P.R. Zelazo (Eds.), *Newborn attention: Biological constraints and the influence of experience* (pp. 339–376). Norwood, NJ: Ablex.

Kart, C.S. (1990). *The realities of aging* (3rd ed.). Boston: Allyn & Bacon.

Kartman, L.L. (1991). Life review: One aspect of making meaningful music for the elderly. *Activities, Adaptations, and Aging, 15,* 42–45.

Kastenbaum, R. (1985). Dying and death: A life-span approach. In J.E. Birren & K.W. Schaie (Eds.), *Handbook of the psychology of aging.* New York: Van Nostrand Reinhold.

Kastenbaum, R.J. (1977). *Death, society and human experience.* St. Louis, MO: C.V. Mosby.

Katchadourian, H.A. (1987). *Biological aspects of human sexuality* (3rd ed.). New York: Holt, Rinehart & Winston.

Kates, E. (1995). Escaping poverty: The promise of higher education. *Social Policy Report: Society for Research in Child Development, 9,* 1–21.

Kates, N., Grieff, B., & Hagen, D. (1990). *The psychosocial impact of job loss.* Washington, DC: American Psychiatric Press.

Katrowitz, B. (1988, May 16). Preemies. *Newsweek,* pp. 62–67.

Katrowitz, B., & Wingert, P. (1990, Winter/Spring). Step by step. *Newsweek Special Edition,* pp. 24–34.

Katz, L.G. (1989, December). Beginners' ethics. *Parents,* p. 213.

Katz, P.A. (Ed.). (1976). *Towards the elimination of racism.* New York: Pergamon Press.

Katzell, R.A., & Guzzo, R.A. (1983). Psychological approaches to productivity improvement. *American Psychologist, 38,* 468–472.

Kauffman, J.M. (1993). How we might achieve the radical reform of special education. *Exceptional Children, 60,* 6–16.

Kaufman, J., & Zigler, E. (1987). Do abused children become abused parents? *American Journal of Orthopsychiatry, 57,* 186–192.

Kausler, D.H. (1994). *Learning and memory in normal aging.* San Diego, CA: Academic Press.

Keating, D. (1980). Thinking processes in adolescence. In J. Adelson (Ed.), *Handbook of adolescent psychology.* New York: Wiley.

Keating, D. (1990). Adolescent thinking. In S. Feldman & G. Elliott (Eds.), *At the threshold: The developing adolescent.* Cambridge, MA: Harvard University Press.

Keating, D.P., & Clark, L.V. (1980). Development of physical and social reasoning in adolescence. *Developmental Psychology, 16,* 23–30.

Kellett, J.M. (1993). Sexuality in later life. *Reviews in Clinical Gerontology, 3,* 309–314.

Kelly, J.A. (1995). *Changing HIV risk behavior: Practical strategies.* New York: Guilford Press.

Kelly, J.R., & Wescott, G. (1991). Ordinary retirement: Commonalities and continuity. *International Journal of Aging and Human Development, 32,* 81–89.

Kemper, R.L., & Vernooy, A.R. (1994). Metalinguistic awareness in first graders: A qualitative perspective. *Journal of Psycholinguistic Research, 22,* 41–57.

Kennedy, G.E. (1990). College students' expectations of grandparent and grandchild role behavior. *Gerontologist, 30,* 43–48.

Kessen, W. (1979). The American child and other cultural inventions. *American Psychologist, 34,* 815–820.

Kiecolt-Glaser, J.K., & Glaser, R. (1986). Behavioral influences on immune function: Evidence for the interplay between stress and health. In T. Field, P. McCabe, & N. Schneiderman (Eds.), *Stress and coping* (Vol. 2). Hillsdale, NJ: Erlbaum.

Kiecolt-Glaser, J.K., & Kiecolt-Glaser, R. (1991). Psychosocial factors, stress, disease, and immunity. In R. Ader, D.L. Felten, & N. Cohen (Eds.), *Psychoneuroimmunology.* San Diego, CA: Academic Press.

Kiecolt-Glaser, R., & Kiecolt-Glaser, J.K. (1993). Mind and immunity. In D. Goleman, & J. Gurin, (Eds.), *Mind-body medicine.* Yonkers, NY: Consumer Reports Books.

Kihlstrom, J.F. (1987, September 18). The cognitive unconscious. *Science, 237,* 1445–1452.

Killen, M., & Hart, D. (Eds.). (1995). *Morality in everyday life: Developmental perspectives.* New York: Cambridge University Press.

Kim, B., Triandis, H.C., Kagiteibais, C., Choi, S., et al. (Eds.). (1994). *Individualism and collectivism: Theory, method, and applications.* Thousand Oaks, CA: Sage.

Kim, J. (1995, January). "You cannot know how much freedom you have here." *Money,* p. 133.

Kim, U., Triandis, H.C., Kagitebasi, C., & Yoon, G. (1994). *Individualism and collectivism: Theory, method, and applications.* Newbury Park, CA: Sage.

Kim, Y., & Stevens, J.H. (1987). The socialization of prosocial behavior in children. *Childhood Education, 63,* 200–206.

Kimball, J.W. (1983). *Biology* (5th ed.). Reading, MA: Addison-Wesley.

Kimble, G.A. (1993). Evolution of the nature-nurture issue in the history of psychology. In R. Plomin, & G.E. McClearn (Eds.), *Nature, nurture, and psychology.* Washington, DC: American Psychological Association.

Kinsey, A.C., Pomeroy, W.B., & Martin, C.E. (1948). *Sexual behavior in the human male.* Philadelphia: Saunders.

Kite, M.E., & Johnson, B.T. (1988). Attitudes toward older and younger adults: A meta-analysis. *Psychology and Aging, 3(3),* 232–244.

Kitterle, F.L. (1991). (Ed.). *Cerebral laterality: Theory and research.* Hillsdale, NJ: Erlbaum.

Kivett, V.R. (1991). Centrality of the grandfather role among older rural black and white men. *Journal of Gerontology: Social Sciences, 46,* S250–S258.

Klaus, H.M., & Kennell, J.H. (1976). *Maternal–infant bonding.* St. Louis, MO: C.V. Mosby.

Klein, L., German, P., McPhee, S., Smith, C., & Levine, D. (1982). Aging and its relationship to health knowledge and medication compliance. *Gerontologist, 22,* 384–387.

Klein, M.C., Gauthier, R.J., Robbins, J.M., Kaczorowski, J., et al. (1994). Relationship of episiotomy to perineal trauma and morbidity, sexual dysfunction, and pelvic floor relaxation. *American Journal of Obstetrics and Gynecology, 171,* 591–598.

Kleinman, A. (1991, July). The psychiatry of culture and culture of psychiatry. *Havard Mental Health Letter,* p. 8.

Kleinman, J.C. (1992). The epidemiology of low birthweight. In S.L. Friedman & M.D. Sigman (Eds.), *The psychological development of low birthweight children.* Norwood, NJ: Ablex.

Kline, D.W., & Schieber, F. (1985). Vision and aging. In J.E. Birren & K.W. Schaie (Eds.), *Handbook of the psychology of aging* (2nd ed.). New York: Van Nostrand Reinhold.

Klinnert, M. (1984). The regulation of infant behavior by maternal facial expression. *Infant Behavior and Development, 7,* 447–465.

Klinnert, M., Campos, J.J., Sorce, J., Emde, R.N., et al. (1983). Emotions as behavioral regulators: Social referencing in infancy. In R. Plutchik & H. Kerrman (Eds.), *Emotions in early development: Vol. 2. The emotions.* New York: Academic Press.

Knaus, W.A., Conners, A.F., Dawson, N.V., Desbiens, N.A., et al. (1995). A controlled trial to improve care for seriously ill hospitalized patients. The study to understand prognoses and preferences for outcomes and risks of treatments (SUPPORT). *Journal of the American Medical Association, 273,* 1591–1598.

Knight, K. (1994, March). Back to basics. *Essence,* pp. 122–138.

Knittle, J.L. (1975). Early influences on development of adipose tissue. In G.A. Bray (Ed.), *Obesity in perspective.* Washington, DC: U.S. Government Printing Office.

Knutson, J.F., & Lansing, C.R. (1990). The relationship between communication problems and psychological difficulties in persons with profound acquired hearing loss. *Journal of Speech and Hearing Disorders, 55,* 656–664.

Kocarnik, R.A., & Ponzetti, J.J., Jr. (1991). The advantages and challenges of intergenerational programs in long-term care facilities. *Journal of Gerontological Social Work, 16,* 97–107.

Kochanska, G. (1995). Children's temperament, mothers' discipline, and security of attachment: Multiple pathways to emerging internalization. *Child Development, 66,* 597–615.

Kohlberg, L. (1969). Stage and sequence: The cognitive-developmental approach to socialization. In D. Goslin (Ed.), *Handbook of socialization theory and research.* Chicago: Rand McNally.

Kohlberg, L. (1975). Counseling and counselor education: A developmental approach. *Counselor Education and Supervision, 14,* 250–256.

Kohlberg, L. (1984). *The psychology of moral development: Essays on moral development* (Vol. 2). San Francisco: Harper & Row.

Kolata, G. (1991, May 15). Drop in casual sex tied to AIDS peril. *The New York Times,* pp. A1, A9.

Kolata, G. (1994, August). Selling growth drug for children: The legal and ethical questions. *The New York Times,* pp. A1, A11.

Kolb, B. (1989). Brain development, plasticity, and behavior. *American Psychologist, 44*(9), 1203–1212.

Kopp, C.B., & Kaler, S.R. (1989). Risk in infancy: Origins and implications. *American Psychologist, 44,* 224–230.

Kornhaber, M., Krechevsky, M., & Gardner, H. (1991). Engaging intelligence. *Emotional Psychologist, 25,* 177–199.

Koss, M.P., Goodman, L.A., Browne, A., Fitzgerald, L.F., et al. (1993). *No safe haven: Violence against women, at home, at work, and in the community.* Final report of the American Psychological Association Women's Programs Office Task Force on Violence Against Women. Washington, DC: American Psychological Association.

Koster, A., & Davidsen, M. (1993). Climacteric complaints and their relation to menopausal development: A retrospective analysis. *Maturitas, 17,* 155–166.

Kotre, J., & Hall, E. (1990). *Seasons of life.* Boston: Little, Brown.

Kraemer, H.C., Korner, A., Anders, T., Jacklin, C.N., & Dimiceli, S. (1985). Obstetric drugs and infant behavior: A re-evaluation. *Journal of Pediatric Psychology, 10,* 345–353.

Krause, N., & Borawski-Clark, E. (1994). Clarifying the functions of social support in later life. *Research on Aging, 16,* 251–279.

Krout, J.A. (1988). Rural versus urban differences in elderly parents' contact with their children. *Gerontologist, 28,* 198–203.

Krueger, J., & Heckhausen, J. (1993). Personality development across the adult life span: Subjective conceptions vs cross-sectional contrasts. *Journal of Gerontology, 48,* 100–108.

Kryter, K.D. (1983). Presbycusis, sociocusis, and nosocusis. *Journal of the Acoustical Society of America, 73,* 1897–1917.

Kübler-Ross, E. (1969). *On death and dying.* New York: Macmillan.

Kübler-Ross, E. (1982). *Working it through.* New York: Macmillan.

Kübler-Ross, E. (Ed.). (1975). *Death: The final stage of growth.* Englewood Cliffs, NJ: Prentice-Hall.

Kuchuk, A., Vibbert, M., & Bornstein, M.H. (1986). The perception of smiling and its experimental correlates in three-month-old infants. *Child Development, 57,* 1054–1061.

Kuczynski, L. (1984). Socialization goals and mother–child interaction: Strategies for long-term and short-term compliance. *Developmental Psychology, 20,* 1061–1073.

Kuczynski, L., & Kochanska, G. (1990). Development of children's noncompliance strategies from toddlerhood to age 5. *Developmental Psychology, 26,* 398–408.

Kupfermann, I. (1991). Hypothalamus and limbic system: Petidergic neurons, homeostatis, and emotional behavior. In E.R. Kandel, J.H. Schwartz, & T.M. Jessell (Eds.), *Principles of neural science* (3rd ed.). New York: Elsevier.

Kupfersmid, J., & Wonderly, D. (1980). Moral maturity and behavior: Failure to find a link. *Journal of Youth and Adolescence, 9,* 249–261.

Kurdek, L.A. (1991). Correlates of relationship satisfaction in cohabiting gay and lesbian couples: Integration of contextual, investment, and problem-solving models. *Journal of Personality and Social Psychology, 61,* 910–922.

Kurdek, L.A. (1992). Relationship stability and relationship satisfaction in cohabiting gay and lesbian couples: A prospective longitudinal test of the contextual and interdependence models. *Journal of Social and Personal Relationships, 9,* 125–142.

Kurdek, L.A. (1993). The allocation of household labor in gay, lesbian, and heterosexual married children. *Journal of Social Issues, 49,* 127–139.

Kurtines, W.M., & Gewirtz, J.L. (1987). *Moral development through social interaction.* New York: Wiley.

Labouvie-Vief, G. (1980). Beyond formal operations: Uses and limits of pure logic in life-span development. *Human Development, 23,* 141–161.

Labouvie-Vief, G. (1986). Modes of knowledge and the organization of development. In M.L. Commons, L. Kohlberg, F. Richards, & J. Sinnott (Eds.), *Beyond formal operations 3: Models and methods in the study of adult and adolescent thought.* New York: Praeger.

Labouvie-Vief, G. (1990). Modes of knowledge and the organization of development. In M.L. Commons, C. Armon, L. Kohlberg, F.A. Richards, et al. (Eds.), *Adult development: Vol. 2. Models and methods in the study of adolescent thought.* New York: Praeger.

LaBuda, M., Gottesman, I., & Pauls, D. (1993). Usefulness of twin studies for exploring the etiology of childhood and adolescent psychiatric disorders. *American Journal of Medical Genetics, 48,* 47–59.

Ladd, G.W. (1983). Social networks of popular, average and rejected children in social settings. *Merrill-Palmer Quarterly, 29,* 282–307.

LaFromboise, T., Coleman, H.L., & Gerton, J. (1993). Psychological impact of biculturalism: Evidence and theory. *Psychological Bulletin, 114,* 395–412.

Lagercrantz, H., & Slotkin, T.A. (1986). The "stress" of being born. *Scientific American, 254* (4), pp. 100–107.

Lamaze, F. (1970). *Painless childbirth: The Lamaze method.* Chicago: Regnery.

Lamb, D.R. (1984). *Physiology of exercise: Response and adaptation* (2nd ed.). New York: Macmillan.

Lamb, M. (1982). The bonding phenomenon: Misinterpretations and their implications. *Journal of Pediatrics, 101,* 555–557.

Lamb, M. (1994). Infant-care practices and the application of knowledge. In C.B. Fisher & R.M. Lerner (Eds.), *Applied developmental psychology.* New York: McGraw-Hill.

Lamb, M.E. (1977). The development of mother–infant and father–infant attachments in the second year of life. *Developmental Psychology, 13,* 637–648.

Lamb, M.E. (1982). Paternal influences on early socio-emotional development. *Journal of Child Psychology and Psychiatry and Allied Disciplines, 23,* 185–190.

Lamb, M.E. (Ed.). (1986). *The father's role: Applied perspectives.* New York: Wiley.

Lamb, M.E. (1987). Predictive implications of individual differences in attachment. *Journal of Consulting and Clinical Psychology, 55,* 817–824.

Lamb, M.E., Ketterlinus, R.D., & Fracasso, M.P. (1992). Parent–child relationships. In M.H. Bornstein & M.E. Lamb (Eds.), *Developmental psychology: An advanced textbook* (3rd ed.). Hillsdale, NJ: Erlbaum.

Lamb, M.E., Morrison, D.C., & Malkin, C.M. (1987). The development of infant social expectations in face-to-face interaction. *Merrill-Palmer Quarterly, 33,* 241–254.

Lamb, M.E., Sternberg, K.J., Hwang, C.P., & Broberg, A.G. (Eds.). *Child care in context: Cross-cultural perspectives.* Hillsdale, NJ: Erlbaum.

Lamb, M.E., Thompson, R.A., Gardner, W.P., Charnov, E., & Estes, D. (1984). Security of infantile attachment as assessed in the strange situation: Its study and biological interpretation. *Behavioral and Brain Sciences, 7,* 127–147.

Lambert, P., Armstrong, L., & Wagner, J. (1995, February 27). The vanishing. *People Weekly,* pp. 32–42.

Lambert, W.E., & Peal, E. (1972). The relation of bilingualism to intelligence. In A.S. Dil (Ed.), *Language, psychology, and culture* (3rd ed.). New York: Wiley.

Lampl, M., Cameron, N., Veldhuis, J.D., & Johnson, M.L. (1995, April 21). Patterns of human growth. *Science, 268,* 442–447.

Lander, E.S., & Schork, N.J. (1994, September 30). Genetic dissection of complex traits. *Science, 265,* 2037–2048.

Landers, R.K. (1990, July 6). Are Americans still in love with marriage? *Editorial Research Reports,* pp. 382–394.

Landy, F.J. (1994, July/August). Mandatory retirement age: Serving the public welfare? *Psychological Science Agenda,* pp. 10–13.

Lang, J.S. (1987, April 13). Happiness is a reunited set of twins. *U.S. News & World Report,* pp. 63–66.

Langer, E., & Janis, I. (1979). *The psychology of control.* Beverly Hills, CA: Sage.

Langford, P.E. (1995). *Approaches to the development of moral reasoning.* Hillsdale, NJ: Erlbaum.

Langlois, J.H., Ritter, J.M., Roggman, L.A., & Vaughn, L.S. (1991). Facial diversity and infant preferences for attractive faces. *Developmental Psychology, 27,* 79–84.

Larsen-Freeman, D., & Long, M.H. (1991). *An introduction to second language acquisition research.* London: Longman.

Larwood, L., Szwajkowski, E., & Rose, S. (1988). Sex and race discrimination resulting from manager–client relationships: Applying the rational bias theory of managerial discrimination. *Sex Roles, 18,* 9–29.

Lask, B., & Bryant-Waugh, R. (Eds.). (1993). *Childhood onset of anorexia nervosa and related eating disorders.* Hillsdale, NJ: Erlbaum.

Laszlo, J. (1986). Scripts for interpersonal situations. *Studia Psychologia, 28,* 125–135.

Lauer, J., & Lauer, R. (1985, June). Marriages made to last. *Psychology Today, 31,* pp. 22–26.

Laursen, B., & Collins, W.A. (1994). Interpersonal conflict during adolescence. *Psychological Bulletin, 115,* 197–209.

Lawton, M.P., Kleban, M.H., Moss, M., Rovine, M., et al. (1989). Measuring caregiving appraisal. *Journal of Gerontology: Psychological Sciences, 44,* 61–71.

Lazarus, R.S. (1968). Emotions and adaptations: Conceptual and empirical relations. In W. Arnold (Ed.), *Nebraska symposium on motivation.* Lincoln: University of Nebraska Press.

Lazarus, R.S. (1991). *Emotion and adaptation.* New York: Oxford University Press.

Lazarus, R.S., & Folkman, S. (1984). *Stress, appraisal, and coping.* New York: Springer.

Leboyer, F. (1975). *Birth without violence.* New York: Knopf.

Lecanuet, J.-P., Fifer, W.P., Krasnegor, N.A., & Smotherman, W.P. (Eds.). (1995a). *Fetal development: A psychobiological perspective.* Hillsdale, NJ: Erlbaum.

Lecanuet, J.-P., Granier-Deferre, C., & Busnel, M.-C. (1995b). Human fetal auditory perception. In J.-P. Lecanuet, W.P. Fifer, N.A. Krasnegor, & W.P. Smotherman (Eds.), *Fetal development: A psychobiological perspective.* Hillsdale, NJ: Erlbaum.

Lecours, A.R. (1982). Correlates of developmental behavior in brain maturation. In T. Bever (Ed.), *Regressions in mental development.* Hillsdale, NJ: Erlbaum.

Lee, H., & Barratt, M.S. (1993). Cognitive development of preterm low birthweight children at 5 to 8 years old. *Developmental and Behavioral Pediatrics, 14,* 242–249.

Lee, V.E., Brooks-Gunn, J., Schnur, E., & Liau, F. (1990). Are Head Start effects sustained? A longitudinal follow-up comparison of disadvantaged children attending Head Start, no preschool, and other preschool programs. *Child Development, 61,* 495–507.

Lefkowitz, M.M. (1981). Smoking during pregnancy: Long-term effects on offspring. *Developmental Psychology, 17,* 192–194.

Legerstee, M. (1990). Infants use multimodal information to imitate speech sounds. *Infant Behavior and Development, 13,* 343–354.

Leiblum, S.R. (1990). Sexuality and the midlife woman. Special Issue: Women at midlife and beyond. *Psychology of Women Quarterly, 14,* 495–508.

Leigh, B.C., Morrison, D.M., Trocki, K., & Temple, M. (1994). Sexual behavior of American adolescents: Results from a U.S. national survey. *Journal of Adolescent Health, 15,* 117–125.

Leitenberg, H., Detzer, M.J., & Srebnik, D. (1993). Gender differences in masturbation and the relation of masturbation experience in preadolescence and/or early adolescence to sexual behavior and sexual adjustment in young adulthood. *Archives of Sexual Behavior, 22,* 87–98.

Leiter, J., & Johnsen, M.C. (1994). Child maltreatment and school performance. *American Journal of Education, 102,* 154–189.

Lelwica, M., & Haviland, J. (1983). *Ten-week-old infants' reactions to mothers' emotional expressions.* Paper presented at the biennial meeting of the Society for Research in Child Development.

Lepore, S.J., Evans, G.W., & Schneider, M.L. (1991). Dynamic role of social support in the link between chronic stress and psychological distress. *Journal of Personality and Social Psychology, 61,* 889–909.

Lepore, S.J., Palsane, M.N., & Evans, G.W. (1991). Daily hassles and chronic strains: A hierarchy of stressors? *Social Science and Medicine, 33,* 1029–1036.

Leslie, A.M. (1987). Pretense and representation: The origins of "theory of mind." *Psychological Review, 94,* 412–426.

Lester, B.M., & Brazelton, T.B. (Eds.). (1989). The cultural context of infancy. *Vol. 2. Multicultural and interdisciplinary approaches to parent–infant relations* (pp. 39–61). Norwood, NJ: Ablex.

Lester, B.M., & Tronick, E.Z. (1990). Introduction. In B.M. Lester & E.Z. Tronick (Eds.), *Stimulation and the preterm infant: The limits of plasticity.* Philadelphia: Saunders.

Lester, R., & Van Theil, D.H. (1977). Gonadal function in chronic alcoholic men. *Advances in Experimental Medicine and Biology, 85A,* 339–414.

Levano, K.J., Cunningham, F.G., Nelson, S., Roark, M., et al. (1986). A prospective comparison of selective and universal electronic fetal monitoring in 34,995 pregnancies. *New England Journal of Medicine, 315,* 615–619.

LeVay, S. (1993). *The sexual brain.* Cambridge, MA: MIT Press.

Levenson, R.W., Carstensen, L.L., & Gottman, J.M. (1993). Long-term marriage: Age, gender, and satisfaction. *Psychology and Aging, 8,* 301–313.

Levine, R.V. (1993, February). Is love a luxury? *American Demographics,* pp. 37–39.

Levinson, D. (1992). *The seasons of a woman's life.* New York: Knopf.

Levinson, D.J. (1986). A conception of adult development. *American Psychologist, 41,* 3–13.

Levinson, D.J. (1990, August). *The seasons of a woman's life: Implications for women and men.* Paper presented at the meeting of the American Psychological Association, Boston.

Levy, B.L., & Langer, E. (1994). Aging free from negative stereotypes: Successful memory in China and among the American deaf. *Journal of Personality and Social Psychology, 66,* 989–997.

Levy-Lahad, E., Wijsman, E.M., Nemens, E., Anderson, L., et al. (1995, August 18). A familial Alzheimer's disease locus on Chromosome 1. *Science, 269,* 970–976.

Lewin, T. (1995, May 11). Women are becoming equal providers: Half of working women bring home half the household income. *The New York Times,* p. A14.

Lewinsohn, P.M., Roberts, R.E., Seeley, J.R., & Rohde, P. (1994). Adolescent psychopathology: II. Psychosocial risk factors for depression. *Journal of Abnormal Psychology, 103,* 302–315.

Lewinsohn, P.M., Rohde, P., & Seeley J.R. (1994). Psychosocial risk factors for future adolescent suicide attempts. *Journal of Consulting and Clinical Psychology, 62,* 297–305.

Lewis, C., & Mitchell, P. (Eds.). (1994). *Children's early understanding of mind: Origins and development.* Hillsdale, NJ: Erlbaum.

Lewis, C.S. (1958). *The allegory of love: A study in medieval traditions.* New York: Oxford University Press.

Lewis, C.S. (1985). A grief observed. In E.S. Shneidman (Ed.), *Death: Current perspectives* (3rd ed.). Palo Alto, CA: Mayfield.

Lewis, D.O., Yeager, C.A., Loveley, R., et al. (1994). A clinical follow-up of delinquent males: Ignored vulnerabilities, unmet needs, and the perpetuation of violence. *Journal of the American Academy of Child and Adolescent Psychiatry, 33,* 518–528.

Lewis, M., & Brooks-Gunn, J. (1979). *Social cognition and the acquisition of self.* New York: Plenum Press.

Lewis, M., & Bendersky, M. (Eds.). (1995). *Mothers, babies, and cocaine: The role of toxins in development.* Hillsdale, NJ: Erlbaum.

Lewis, M., Feiring, C., McGuffog, C., & Jaskir, J. (1984). Predicting psychopathology in six-year-olds from early social relations. *Child Development, 55,* 123–136.

Lewis, R., Freneau, P., & Roberts, C. (1979). Fathers and the postparental transition. *Family Coordinator, 28,* 514–520.

Lewit, E.M., Baker, L.S., Corman, H., & Shiono, P.H. (1995). *The Future of Children, 5,* 35–56.

Leyens, J.P., Camino, L., Parke, R.D., & Berkowitz, L. (1975). Effects of movie violence on aggression in a field setting as a function of group dominance and cohesion. *Journal of Personality and Social Psychology, 32,* 346–360.

Liaw, E.-R., & Brooks-Gunn, J. (1993). Patterns of low-birthweight children's cognitive development. *Developmental Psychology, 29,* 1024–1035.

Lieberman, M.A. (1992). Adult life crises. In J.E. Birren, R.B. Sloane, & G.D. Cohen (Eds.), *Handbook of mental health and aging* (2nd ed.). San Diego, CA: Harcourt Brace.

Liebert, R.M., & Sprafkin, J. (1988). *The early window: Effects of television on children and youth* (3rd ed.). New York: Pergamon Press.

Light, L.L. (1991). Memory and aging: Four hypotheses in search of data. *Annual Review of Psychology, 42,* 333–376.

Lindholm, K.J. (1991). Two-way bilingual/immersion education: Theory, conceptual issues, and pedagogical implications. In R.V. Padilla & A. Benavides (Eds.), *Critical perspectives on bilingual education research.* Tempe, AZ: Bilingual Review Press.

Lindhout, D., Frets, P.G., & Niermeijer, M.F. (1991). Approaches to genetic counseling. *Annals of the New York Academy of Sciences, 630,* 223–229.

Linz, D.G., Donnerstein, E., & Penrod, S. (1988). Effects of long-term exposure to violent and sexually degrading depictions of women. *Journal of Personality and Social Psychology, 55,* 758–768.

Lipka, R.P., & Brinthaupt, T.M. (Eds.). (1992). *Self-perspectives across the life span.* Albany: State University of New York Press.

Lipman, J. (1992, March 10). Surgeon General says it's high time Joe Camel quit. *The Wall Street Journal,* pp. B1, B7.

Lipsitt, L.P. (1986). Learning in infancy: Cognitive development in babies. *Journal of Pediatrics, 109*(1), 172–182.

Lipsitt, L.P. (1986). Toward understanding the hedonic nature of infancy. In L.P. Lipsitt & J.H. Cantor (Eds.), *Experimental child psychologist: Essays and experiments in honor of Charles C. Spiker* (pp. 97–109). Hillsdale, NJ: Erlbaum.

Liskin, L. (1985, Nov./Dec.) Youth in the 1980s: Social and health concerns: 4. *Population Reports, 8,* (5).

Livingston, R., Adam, B.S., & Bracha, H.S. (1993). Season of birth and neurodevelopmental disorders: Summer birth is associated with dyslexia. *Journal of the American Academy of Child and Adolescent Psychiatry, 32,* 612–616.

Livson, N., & Peskin, H. (1980). Perspectives on adolescence from longitudinal research. In J. Adelson (Ed.), *Handbook of adolescent psychology.* New York: Wiley.

Lloyd, B., & Duveen, G. (1991). Expressing social gender identities in the first year of school. *European Journal of Psychology of Education, 6,* 437–447.

Lock, R.D. (1992). *Taking charge of your career direction* (2nd ed.). Pacific Grove, CA: Brooks/Cole.

Locke, J.L. (1983). *Phonological acquisition and change.* New York: Academic Press.

Loehlin, J.C. (1992). *Genes and environment in personality development.* Newbury Park, CA: Sage.

Logue, A.W. (1991). *The psychology of eating and drinking* (2nd ed.). New York: W.H. Freeman.

Lonetto, R. (1980). *Children's conception of death.* New York: Springer.

Long, T., & Long, L. (1983). *Latchkey children.* New York: Penguin Books.

Lorenz, K. (1957). Companionship in bird life. In C. Scholler (Ed.), *Instinctive behavior.* New York: International Universities Press.

Lorenz, K. (1966). *On aggression.* New York: Harcourt Brace Jovanovich.

Lorenz, K. (1974). *Civilized man's eight deadly sins.* New York: Harcourt Brace Jovanovich.

Lorenz, K.Z. (1965). *Evolution and the modification of behavior.* Chicago: University of Chicago Press.

Lowe, M.R. (1993). The effects of dieting on eating behavior: A three-factor model. *Psychological Bulletin, 114,* 100–121.

Lowrey, G.H. (1986). *Growth and development of children* (8th ed.). Chicago: Year Book Medical Publishers.

Lucas, A., Morley, R., Cole, T.J., Lister, G., et al. (1992). Breast milk and subsequent intelligence quotient in children born preterm. *Lancet, 339,* 261–264.

Ludwig, F.C. (Ed.). (1991). *Life span extension: Consequences and open questions.* New York: Springer.

Lust, B., Hermon, G., & Kornfilt, J. (Eds.). (1994). *Syntactic theory and first language acquisition: Binding, dependencies, and learnability.* Hillsdale, NJ: Erlbaum.

Lust, B., Suner, M., & Whitman, J. (Eds.). (1995). *Syntactic theory and first language acquisition.* Hillsdale, NJ: Erlbaum.

Luster, T., & McAdoo, H.P. (1994). Factors related to the achievement and adjustment of young African American children. *Child Development, 65,* 1080–1094.

Lykken, D., Bouchard, T., McGue, M., & Tellegen, A. (1993a). Heritability of interests: A twin study. *Journal of Applied Psychology, 78,* 649–661.

Lykken, D.T., McGue, M., Tellegen, A., & Bouchard, T.J., Jr. (1993b). Emergenesis: Genetic traits that may not run in families. *American Psychologist, 47,* 1565–1577.

Lynwander, L. (1995, February 5). Burying the poor. *The New York Times,* Section 13NJ, p. 1.

Maccoby, E.E. (1980). *Social development: Psychological growth and the parent–child relationship.* New York: Harcourt Brace Jovanovich.

MacCoun, R.J. (1993). Drugs and the law: A psychological analysis of drug prohibition. *Psychological Bulletin, 113,* 497–512.

Mackey, M.C. (1990). Women's preparation for the childbirth experience. *Maternal-Child Nursing Journal, 19,* 143–173.

Mackey, W.C., White, U., & Day, R. (1992). Reasons American men become fathers: Men's divulgences, women's perceptions. *Journal of Genetic Psychology, 153,* 435–445.

Mackey, W.E., & Hess, D.J. (1982). Attention structure and stereotype of gender on television: An empirical analysis. *Genetic Psychology Monographs, 106,* 199–215.

MacPhee, D., Kreutzer, J.C., & Fritz, J.J. (1994). Infusing a diversity perspective into human development courses. *Child Development, 65,* 699–715.

MacWhinney, B. (1991). Connectionism as a framework for language acquisition. In J. Miller (Ed.), *Research on child language disorders.* Austin, TX: Pro-ed.

Maddox, G.L., & Campbell, R.T. (1985). Scope, concepts, and methods in the study of aging. In R.H. Binstock & E. Shanas (Eds.), *Handbook of aging and the social sciences* (2nd ed.). New York: Van Nostrand Reinhold.

Major, B., & Konar, E. (1984). An investigation of sex differences in pay expectations and their possible causes. *Academy of Management Journal, 27,* 777–792.

Malina, R.M. (1979). Secular changes in size and maturity. *Monographs of the Society for Research in Child Development, 54* (1–2, Serial No. 219).

Malinak, D.P., Hoyt, M.F., & Patterson, V. (1979). Adults' reactions to the death of a parent: A preliminary study. *American Journal of Psychiatry, 136,* 1152–1156.

Malinosky-Rummell, R., & Hansen, D.J. (1993). Long-term consequences of childhood physical abuse. *Psychological Bulletin, 114,* 68–79.

Malinowski, C.I., & Smith, C.P. (1985). Moral reasoning and moral conduct: An investigation prompted by Kohlberg's theory. *Journal of Personality and Social Psychology, 49,* 1016–1027.

Malott, R.W., Whaley, D.L., & Malott, M.E. (1993). *Elementary principles of behavior* (2nd ed.). Englewood Cliffs, NJ: Prentice-Hall.

Mancini, J.A., & Blieszner, R. (1991). Aging parents and adult children. In A. Booth (Ed.), *Contemporary families.* Minneapolis, MN: National Council on Family Relations.

Mandich, M., Simons, C.J., Ritchie, S., Schmidt, D., et al. (1994). Motor development, infantile reactions and postural responses of preterm, at-risk infants. *Developmental Medicine and Child Neurology, 36,* 397–405.

Mandler, J.M. (1990). A new perspective on cognitive development in infancy. *American Scientist, 78,* 236–243.

Mangelsdorf, S., Gunnar, M., Kestenbaum, R., Lang, S., et al. (1990). Infant proneness-to-distress temperament, maternal personality, and mother–infant attachment: Association and goodness of fit. *Child Development, 61,* 820–831.

Manson, A., & Shea, S. (1991). Malnutrition in elderly ambulatory medical patients. *American Journal of Public Health, 81,* 1195–1197.

Maratsos, M.P. (1983). Some current issues in the study of the acquisition of grammar. In P.H. Mussen (Ed.), *Handbook of child psychology* (Vol. 3, 4th ed.). New York: Wiley.

Marche, T.A., & Howe, M.L. (1995). Preschoolers report misinformation despite accurate memory. *Developmental Psychology, 31,* 554–567.

Marcia, J.E. (1966). Development and validation of ego identity status. *Journal of Personality and Social Psychology, 3*(5), 551–558.

Marcia, J.E. (1980). Identity in adolescence. In J. Adelson (Ed.), *Handbook of adolescent psychology.* New York: Wiley.

Margolin, G. (1995, January). Paper presented at the conference titled "Violence against children in the family and the community: A conference on causes, developmental consequences, interventions and prevention." Los Angeles: University of Southern California.

Marjoribanks, K. (1994). Cross-cultural comparisons of family environments of Anglo-, Greek-, and Italian-Australians. *Psychological Reports, 74,* 49–50.

Markus, H.R., & Kitayama, S. (1991). Culture and the self: Implications for cognition, emotion, and motivation. *Psychological Review, 98,* 224–253.

Marsh, H.W. (1990). Influences of internal and external frames of reference on the formation of math and English self-concepts. *Journal of Educational Psychology, 82,* 107–116.

Marsh, H.W., & Holmes, I.W.M. (1990). Multidimensional self-concepts: Construct validation of responses by children. *American Educational Research Journal, 27,* 89–118.

Marsh, H.W., & Parker, J.W. (1984). Determinants of student self-concept: Is it better to be a relatively large fish in a small pond even if you don't learn to swim as well? *Journal of Personality and Social Psychology, 47,* 213–231.

Marsh, H.W., & Shavelson, R. (1985). Self-concept: Its multifaceted, hierarchical structure. *Educational Psychologist, 20,* 107–123.

Marshall, V.W. (Ed.). (1986). *Later life: The social psychology of aging.* Beverly Hills, CA: Sage.

Martin, B.A. (1989). Gender differences in salary expectations. *Psychology of Women Quarterly, 13,* 87–96.

Martin, C.L. (1993). New directions for investigating children's gender knowledge. *Developmental Review, 13,* 184–204.

Martin, G.B., & Clark, R.D. (1982). Distress crying in neonates: Species and peer specificity. *Developmental Psychology, 18,* 3–9.

Martinez, R., & Dukes, R.L. (1991). Ethnic and gender differences in self-esteem. *Youth and Society, 22,* 318–338.

Marx, M.B., Garrity, T.F., & Bowers, F.R. (1975). The influence of recent life experience on the health of college freshman. *Journal of Psychosomatic Research, 19,* 87–98.

Maslach, C. (1982). *Burnout—the cost of caring.* Englewood Cliffs, NJ: Prentice-Hall.

Masters, W.H., Johnson, V., & Kolodny, R.C. (1982). *Human sexuality.* Boston: Little, Brown.

Mastropieri, M.A., & Scruggs, T.E. (1991). *Teaching students ways to remember: Strategies for learning mnemonically.* Cambridge, MA: Brookline Books.

Mathew, A., & Cook, M.L. (1990). The control of reaching movements by young infants. *Child Development, 61,* 1238–1257.

Mathews, J.J., & Zadak, K. (1991). The alternative birth movement in the United States: History and current status. *Women and Health, 17,* 39–56.

Matlin, M.M. (1987). *The psychology of women.* New York: Holt.

Matlock, J.R., & Green, V.P. (1990). The effects of day care on the social and emotional development of infants, toddlers and preschoolers. *Early Child Development and Care, 64,* 55–59.

Matson, J.L., & Mulick, J.A. (Eds.). (1991). *Handbook of mental retardation* (2nd ed.). New York: Pergamon Press.

Matteson, M.A. (1988). Age-related changes in the integument. In M.A. Matteson & E.S. McConnell (Eds.), *Gerontological nursing: Concepts and practice.* Philadelphia: Saunders.

Matthews, K.A. (1982). Psychological perspectives on the Type A behavior pattern. *Psychological Bulletin, 91,* 293–323.

McAdams, D.P., de St. Aubin, E., & Logan, R.L. (1993). Generativity among young, midlife, and older adults. *Psychology and Aging, 8,* 221–230.

McAdoo, H.P. (1988). *Black families.* Newbury Park, CA: Sage.

McCabe, M. (1984). Toward a theory of adolescent dating. *Adolescence, 19,* 159–169.

McCall, R.B. (1979). *Infants.* Cambridge, MA: Harvard University Press.

McCarthy, M.J. (1994, November 8). Hunger among elderly surges: Meal programs just can't keep up. *The Wall Street Journal,* pp. A1, A11.

McCartney, K. (1984). Effect of quality of day care environment on children's language development. *Developmental Psychology, 20,* 244–260.

McClearn, G.E. (1993). Behavioral genetics: The last century and the next. In R. Plomin & G.E. McClearn (Eds.), *Nature, nurture, and psychology.* Washington, DC: American Psychological Association.

McClelland, D.C. (1993). Intelligence is not the best predictor of job performance. *Current Directions in Psychological Research, 2,* 5–8.

McCormick, M.C. (1992). Advances in neonatal intensive care technology and their possible impact on the development of low-birthweight infants. In S.L. Friedman & M.D. Sigman (Eds.), *The psychological development of low-birthweight children.* Norwood, NJ: Ablex.

McCracken, A.L., & Gerdsen, L. (1991). Sharing the legacy: Hospice care principles for the terminally ill elders. *Journal of Gerontological Nursing, 17,* 4–8.

McCrae, R.R., & Costa, P.T., Jr. (1990). *Personality in adulthood.* New York: Guilford Press.

McDaniel, K.D. (1986). Pharmacologic treatment of psychiatric and neurodevelopmental disorders in children and adolescents: III. *Clinical Pediatrics, 25,* 198–204.

McDonald, R.M., & Towberman, D.B. (1993). Psychosocial correlates of adolescent drug involvement. *Adolescence, 28,* 925–936.

McGraw, K.M., & Bloomfield, J. (1987). Social influence on group moral decisions: The interactive effects of moral reasoning and sex-role orientation. *Journal of Personality and Social Psychology, 53,* 1080–1087.

McGue, M. (1993). From proteins to cognitions: The behavioral genetics of alcoholism. In R. Plomin & G.E. McClearn (Eds.), *Nature, nurture, and psychology.* Washington, DC: American Psychological Association.

McGue, M., Bouchard, T., Iacono, W., & Lykken, D. (1993). Behavioral genetics of cognitive ability: A life-span perspective. In R. Plomin & G. McClearn (Eds.), *Nature, nurture and psychology* (pp. 59–76). Washington, DC: American Psychological Association.

McGuinness, D. (1972). Hearing: Individual differences in perceiving. *Perception, 1,* 465–473.

McKenna, J.J. (1983). Primate aggression and evolution: An overview of sociobiological and anthropological perspectives. *Bulletin of the American Academy of Psychiatry and the Law, 11,* 105–130.

McKey, R.H., Condelli, L., Ganson, H., Barrett, B.J., McConkey, C., & Plantz, M.C. (1985). *The impact of Head Start on children, families, and communities.* Washington, DC: CSR, Inc.

McWhirter, D.P., Sanders, S., & Reinisch, J.M. (1990). *Homosexuality, heterosexuality: Concepts of sexual orientation.* New York: Oxford University Press.

McWhirter, L., Young, V., & Majury, Y. (1983). Belfast children's awareness of violent death. *British Journal of Psychology, 22,* 81–92.

Mead, M. (1942). *Environment and education, a symposium held in connection with the fiftieth anniversary celebration of the University of Chicago.* Chicago: University of Chicago.

Mednick, S.A. (1962). The associative basis of the creative process. *Psychological Review, 69,* 220–232.

Mednick, S.A. (1963). Research creativity in psychology graduate students *Journal of Consulting Psychology, 27,* 265–266.

Mehler, J., & Dupoux, E. (1994). *What infants know: The new cognitive science of early development.* Cambridge, MA: Blackwell.

Meisels, S.J., & Plunket, J.W. (1988). Developmental consequences of preterm birth: Are there long-term deficits? In P.B. Baltes, D.L. Featherman, & R.M. Lerner (Eds.), *Lifespan development and behavior* (Vol. 9). Hillsdale, NJ: Erlbaum.

Meltzoff, A.N. (1981). Imitation, intermodal coordination and representation in early infancy. In G. Butterworth (Ed.), *Infancy and epistemology.* Brighton, UK: Harvester Press.

Meltzoff, A.N., & Moore M.K., (1977). Imitation of facial and manual gestures by human neonates. *Science, 198,* 75–78.

Meltzoff, A.N., & Moore, M.K. (1989). Imitation in newborn infants: Exploring the range of gestures imitated and the underlying mechanisms. *Developmental Psychology, 25* (6), 954–962.

Meltzoff, A.N., & Moore, M.K. (1994). Imitation, memory, and the representation of persons. *Infant Behavior and Development, 17,* 83–99.

Mendelson, M.J., Aboud, F.E., & Lanthier, R.P. (1994). Personality predictors of friendship and popularity in kindergarten. *Journal of Applied Developmental Psycholology, 15,* 413–435.

Menyuk, P. (1995). *Early language development in full term and premature infants.* Hillsdale, NJ: Erlbaum.

Mercer, C. (1992). *Students with learning disabilities* (4th ed.). Columbus, OH: Chas.E. Merrill.

Mercer, J.R. (1973). *Labeling the mentally retarded.* Berkeley: University of California Press.

Meyer-Bahlburg, H.F.L., Ehrhardt, A.A., Rosen, L.R., Gruen, R.S., et al. (1995). Prenatal estrogens and the development of homosexual orientation. *Developmental Psychology, 31,* 12–21.

Meyerhoff, M.K., & White, B.L. (1986, September). Making the grade as parents. *Psychology Today,* pp. 38–45.

Michael, R.T., Gagnon, J.H., Laumann, E.O., & Kolata, G. (1994). *Sex in America: A definitive survey.* Boston: Little, Brown.

Michel, G.L. (1981). Right-handedness: A consequence of infant supine head-orientation preference? *Science, 212,* 685–687.

Midlarsky, E., & Bryan, J.H. (1972). Affect expressions and children's imitative altruism. *Journal of Experimental Research in Personality, 6,* 195–203.

Miller, A.B. (1991). Is routine mammography screening appropriate for women 40–49 years of age? *American Journal of Preventive Medicine, 7,* 55–62.

Miller, B.C. (1992). Adolescent parenthood, economic issues, and social policies. *Journal of Family and Economic Issues, 13,* 467–475.

Miller, C.A. (1987). A review of maternity care programs in western Europe. *Family Planning Perspectives, 19* (5), 207–211.

Miller, D.A., McCluskey-Fawcett, K., & Irving, L. (1993). Correlates of bulimia nervosa: Early family mealtime experiences. *Adolescence, 28,* 621–635.

Miller, N., & Brewer, M. (1984). *Groups in contact: The psychology of desegregation.* New York: Academic Press.

Miller, N., & Brewer, M.B. (1990). Social categorization theory and team learning procedures. In R.S. Feldman (Ed.), *The social psychology of education: Current research and theory.* Cambridge: Cambridge University Press.

Miller, S.M., & Mangan, C.E. (1983). Interacting effects of information and coping style in adapting to gynecologic stress: Should the doctor tell all? *Journal of Personality and Social Psychology, 45,* 223–236.

Miller, W. (1958). Lower-class culture as a generation milieu of gang delinquency. *Journal of Social Issues, 14,* 5–19.

Miller-Bernal, L. (1993). Single-sex versus coeducational environments: A comparison of women students' experiences at four colleges. *American Journal of Education, 102,* 23–54.

Miller-Jones, D. (1989). Culture and testing. *American Psychologist, 44,* 360–366.

Milner, J. (1995, January). Paper presented at a conference titled "Violence against children in the family and the community: A conference on causes, developmental consequences, interventions and prevention." Los Angeles: University of Southern California.

Minaker, K.I., & Frishman, R. (1995, October). Love gone wrong. *Harvard Health Letter,* pp. 9–12.

Minde, K. (1992). Aggression in preschoolers: Its relation to socialization. *Journal of the American Academy of Child and Adolescent Psychiatry, 31,* 853–862.

Miner, D. (1983). *Children and race.* Beverly Hills, CA: Sage.

Minkowski, A. (1967). *Regional development of the brain in early life.* Oxford: Blackwell.

Minorities in Higher Education. (1995). Annual status report on minorities in higher education. Washington, DC: American Council on Education.

Mistretta, C.M. (1990). Taste development. In J.R. Coleman (Ed.), *Development of sensory systems in mammals* (pp. 567–613). New York: Wiley.

Mittendorf, R., Williams, M.A., Berkey, C.S., & Cotter, R.F. (1990). The length of uncomplicated human gestation. *Obstetrics & Gynecology, 75,* 73–78.

MMWR (Morbidity & Mortality Weekly Report). (1989). Progress toward achieving the 1990 national objectives for physical fitness and exercise. *MMWR, 38,* 449–453.

Mones, P. (1995, July 28). Life and death and Susan Smith. *The New York Times,* p. A27.

Money, J., & Ehrhardt, A.A. (1972). *Man and woman, boy and girl: The differentiation and dimorphism of gender identity from conception to maturity.* Baltimore: Johns Hopkins University Press.

Montemayor, R., Adams, G.R., & Gulotta, T.P. (Eds). (1994). *Personal relationships during adolescence.* Newbury Park, CA: Sage.

Moon, C., Cooper, R.P., & Fifer, W. (1993). Two-day-olds prefer their native language. *Infant Behavior and Development, 16,* 495–500.

Moore, K.L. (1974). *Before we are born: Basic embryology and birth defects.* Philadelphia: Saunders.

Moore, S.M., & Rosenthal, D.A. (1991). Condoms and coitus: Adolescents' attitudes to AIDS and safe sex behavior. *Journal of Adolescence, 14,* 211–227.

Moos, R.H., & Lemke, S. (1985). Specialized living environments for older people. In J.E. Birren & K.W. Schaie (Eds.), *Handbook of the psychology of aging.* New York: Van Nostrand Reinhold.

Morelli, G.A., Rogoff, B., Oppenheim, D., & Goldsmith, D. (1992). Cultural variation in infants' sleeping arrangements: Questions of independence. Special section: Cross-cultural studies of development. *Developmental Psychology, 28,* 604–613.

Morgan, L. (1991). *After marriage ends.* Newbury Park, CA: Sage.

Morgane, P., Austin-LaFrance, R., Bronzino, J., Tonkiss, J., Diaz-Cintra, S., Cintra, L., Kemper, T., & Galler, J. (1993). Prenatal malnutrition and development of the brain. *Neuroscience and Biobehavioral Reviews, 17,* 91–128.

Morrison, A.M., & von Glinow, M.A. (1990). Women and minorities in management. *American Psychologist, 45,* 200–208.

Morse, R.M., & Flavin, D.K. (1992). The definition of alcoholism. *Journal of the American Medical Association, 268,* 1012–1014.

Moses, L.J., & Chandler, M.J. (1992). Traveler's guide to children's theories of mind. *Psychological Inquiry, 3,* 286–301.

Moshman, D., Glover, J.A., & Bruning, R.H. (1987). *Developmental psychology.* Boston: Little, Brown.

Moss, H.A. (1974). Early sex differences and mother–infant interaction. In R.C. Friedman, R.N. Richart, & R.L. Verde Wicle (Eds.), *Sex differences in behavior.* New York: Wiley.

Moyer, M.S. (1992). Sibling relationships among older adults. *Generations, 16,* 55–58.

Mueller, E., & Vandell, D. (1979). Infant–infant interactions. In J. Osofsky (Ed.), *Handbook of infant development.* New York: Wiley.

Murphy, C. (1989). Aging and chemosensory perception of and preference for nutritionally significant stimuli. Conference on Nutrition and the Chemical Senses in Aging: Recent advances and current research needs, Sarasota, Florida. *Annals of the New York Academy of Sciences, 561,* 251–266.

Murray, A.D., Dolby, R.M., Nation, R.L., & Thomas, D.B. (1981). Effects of epidural anesthesia on newborns and their mothers. *Child Development, 52,* 71–82.

Murray, M. (1995, February 9). Alex: Fun, games, and harsh truths at the age of 10. *The Wall Street Journal,* pp. B1–B2.

Murstein, B.I. (1976). *Whom will marry whom? Theories and research in marital choice.* New York: Springer.

Murstein, B.I. (1986). *Paths to marriage.* Beverly Hills, CA: Sage.

Murstein, B.I. (1987). A clarification and extension of the SVR theory of dyadic pairing. *Journal of Marriage and the Family, 49,* 929–933.

Musick, J. (1993). *Young, poor, and pregnant: The psychology of teenage motherhood.* New Haven, CT: Yale University Press.

Mussen, P.H. (1969). Early sex-role development. In D.A. Goslin (Ed.), *Handbook of socialization theory and research,* (pp. 707–732). Chicago: Rand McNally.

Mussen, P.H., & Jones, M.C. (1957). Self-conceptions, motivations, and interpersonal attitudes of late- and early-maturing boys. *Child Development, 28,* 243–256.

Mutran, E. (1985). Intergenerational family support among blacks and whites. *Journal of Gerontology, 40,* 382–389.

Mutryn, C.S. (1993). Psychosocial impact of cesarean section on the family: A literature review. *Social Science and Medicine, 37,* 1271–1281.

Myerhoff, B. (1982). Rites of passage: Process and paradox. In V. Turner (Ed.), *Celebration: Studies in festivity and ritual.* Washington, DC: Smithsonian Press.

Myers, B.J. (1987). Mother–infant bonding: The status of this critical-period hypothesis. In M.H. Bornstein (Ed.), *Sensitive periods in development: Interdisciplinary perspectives.* Hillsdale, NJ: Erlbaum.

Myers, B.J., Britt, G.C., Lodder, D.E., Kendall, K.A., et al. (1992). Effects of cocaine exposure on infant development: A review. *Journal of Child and Family Studies, 1,* 393–415.

Myers, N.A., Clifton, R.K., & Clarkson, M.G. (1987). When they were very young: Almost-threes remember two years ago. *Infant Behavior and Development, 10,* 123–132.

Myklebust, B.M., & Gottlieb, G.L. (1993). Development of the stretch reflex in the newborn: Reciprocal excitation and reflex irradation. *Child Development, 64,* 1036–1045.

Myslinski, N.R. (1990). The effects of aging on the sensory systems of the nose and mouth. *Topics in Geriatric Rehabilitation, 5,* 21–30.

Nagel, K.L., & Jones, K.H. (1992). Predisposition factors in anorexia nervosa. *Adolescence, 27,* 381–386.

Nagy, M. (1948). The child's theories concerning death. *Journal of Genetic Psychology, 73,* 3–27.

Nakagawa, M., Lamb, M.E., & Miyaki, K. (1992). Antecedents and correlates of the Strange Situation behavior of Japanese infants. *Journal of Cross-Cultural Psychology, 23,* 300–310.

Nass, G.G. (1978). *Marriage and the family.* Reading, MA: Addison-Wesley.

National Center for Education Statistics (1991). *Digest of education statistics 1990.* Washington DC: Author.U.S. Department of Education, pp. 113, 116, 118, 120, 121.

National Center for Health Statistics. (1993a). *Health United States, 1992.* (DHHS Publication No. PHS 92–1232). Hyattsville, MD: Public Health Service.

National Center for Health Statistics. (1993b). *Vital Statistics of the United States. Forthcoming, 1990. Vol. II: Mortality, Part A.* Washington, DC: Public Health Service.

National Center for Health Statistics. (1993c). Advance Report of Final Natality Statistics, 1991. *Monthly Vital Statistics Report: Vol. 42.* Washington, DC: Public Health Service.

National Center for Health Statistics. (1994). Division of Vital Statistics. Washington, DC: Public Health Service.

National Center for Health Statistics (1995). Advance Report of Final Natality Statistics, 1993. *Monthly Vital Statistics Report: Vol. 44.* Washington, DC: Public Health Service.

National Joint Committee on Learning Disabilities. (1989). *Letter from NJCLD to member organizations. Topic: Modifications to the NJCLD definition of learning disabilities.* Washington, DC.

National Research Council. (1991). *Caring for America's children.* Washington, DC: National Academy Press.

Nelson, C.A. (1987). The recognition of facial expressions in the first two years of life: Mechanisms of development. *Child Development, 58,* 889–909.

Nelson, C.A. (1995). The ontogeny of human memory: A cognitive neuroscience perspective. *Developmental Psychology, 31,* 723–738.

Nelson, K. (1981). Individual differences in language development: Implications for development and language. *Developmental Psychology, 17* (2), 170–187.

Nelson, K. (1986). *Event knowledge: Structure and function in development.* Hillsdale, NJ: Erlbaum.

Nelson, K. (1989). Remembering: A functional developmental perspective. In P.R. Solomon, G.R. Goethels, C.M. Kelley, & B.R. Stephens (Eds.), *Memory: An interdisciplinary approach.* New York: Springer-Verlag.

Nelson, K. (1992). Emergence of autobiographical memory at age 4. *Human Development, 35,* 172–177.

Nelson, T.O. (1990). Metamemory: A theoretical framework and new findings. In G.H. Bower (Ed.), *The psychology of learning and motivation.* San Diego, CA: Academic Press.

Nelson, T.O. (1994). Metacognition. In V.S. Ramachandran (Ed.), *Encyclopedia of human behavior* (Vol. 3). San Diego, CA: Academic Press.

Nettelbeck, T., & Rabbitt, P.M. (1992). Aging, cognitive performance, and mental speed. *Intelligence, 16,* 189–205.

Nettles, S.M., & Pleck, J.H. (1990). Risk, resilience, and development: The multiple ecologies of black adolescents. In R.J. Haggerty, N. Garmezy, M. Rutter, & L. Sherrod (Eds.), *Risk and resilience in children: Developmental approaches.* New York: Cambridge University Press.

Neugarten, B. (1967). The awareness of middle age. In R. Owen (Ed.), *Middle Age*. London: BBC.

Neugarten, B.L. (1979). Time, age, and the life cycle. *American Journal of Psychiatry, 136*, 887–893.

Neuringer, M. (1993). Cerebral cortex docosahexaenoic acid is lower in formula-fed than in breast-fed infants. *Nutrition Review, 51*, 228–241.

Newcomb, A.F., & Bagwell, C.L. (1995). Children's friendship relations: A meta-analytic review. *Psychological Bulletin, 117*, 306–347.

Newcomb, A.F., Bukowski, W.M., & Pattee, L. (1993). Children's peer relations: A meta-analytic review of popular, rejected, neglected, controversial, and average sociometric status. *Psychological Bulletin, 113*, 99–128.

Newcombe, N., & Fox, N.A. (1994). Infantile amnesia: Through a glass darkly. *Child Development, 65*, 31–40.

Ney, P.G., Fung, T., & Wickett, A.R. (1993). Child neglect: The precursor to child abuse. *Pre- and Peri-Natal Psychology Journal, 8*, 95–112.

NIAAA (National Institute on Alcohol Abuse and Alcoholism). (1990). *Alcohol and Health*. Washington, DC: U.S. Government Printing Office.

Nihart, M.A. (1993). Growth and development of the brain. *Journal of Child and Adolescent Psychiatric and Mental Health Nursing, 6*, 39–40.

Nisbett, R. (1994, October 31). Blue genes. *New Republic*, p. 15.

Nisbett, R.E. (1972). Hunger, obesity and the ventromedial hypothalamus. *Psychological Review, 79*, 433–453.

Noble, G. (1983). Social learning from everyday television. In M. Howe (Ed.), *Learning from television: Psychological and educational research*. New York: Academic Press.

Nolen-Hoeksema, S., & Girgus, J.S. (1994). The emergence of gender differences in depression during adolescence. *Psychological Bulletin, 115*, 424–443.

NORC (National Opinion Research Center). (1990). *General social surveys 1972–1990: Cumulative codebook*. Chicago: National Opinion Research Center.

Notzon, F.C. (1990). International differences in the use of obstetric interventions. *Journal of the American Medical Association, 263* (24), 3286–3291.

Nowak, C.A. (1977). Does youthfulness equal attractiveness? In L.E. Troll, J. Israel, & K. Israel (Eds.), *Looking ahead*. Englewood, Cliffs, NJ: Prentice-Hall.

Nowak, R. (1994a, March 18). Nicotine scrutinized as FDA seeks to regulate cigarettes. *Science, 263*, 1555–1556.

Nowak, R. (1994b, July 22). Genetic testing set for takeoff. *Science, 265*, 464–467.

Nowicki, S., & Duke, M.P. (1994). Individual differences in the nonverbal communication of affect: The Diagnostic Analysis of Nonverbal Accuracy Scale. Special Issue: Development of nonverbal behavior: II. Social development and nonverbal behavior. *Journal of Nonverbal Behavior, 18*, 9–35.

NSFH (National Survey of Families and Households). (1993, August). Married fathers with preschoolers. *American Demographics*, p. 25.

Nugent, J.K., Lester, B.M., & Brazelton, T.B. (Eds.). (1989). *The cultural context of infancy: Vol. 1. Biology, culture, and infant development*. Norwood, NJ: Ablex.

Nwokah, E., & Fogel, A. (1993). Laughter in mother–infant emotional communication. *Humor: International Journal of Humor Research, 6*, 137–161.

Nyhan, W.L. (1990). Structural abnormalities. *Clinical Symposia, 42*, 2.

O'Leary, S.G. (1995). Parental discipline mistakes. *Current Directions in Psychological Science, 4*, 11–13.

O'Malley, P.M., Johnston, L.D., & Bachman, J.G. (1995). Adolescent substance abuse: Epidemiology and implications for public policy. *Pediatric Clinics of North America, 42*, 241–260.

O'Neill, C. (1994, May 17). Exercise just for the fun of it. *Washington Post*, p. WH18.

O'Bryant, S.L., & Morgan, L.A. (1989). Financial experience and well-being among mature widowed women. *Gerontologist, 29*, 245–251.

O'Connor, M.J., Sigman, M., & Brill, N. (1987). Disorganization of attachment in relation to maternal alcohol consumption. *Journal of Consulting and Clinical Psychology, 55* (6), 831–836.

O'Connor, P. (1994). Very close parent/child relationships: The perspective of the elderly person. *Journal of Cross-Cultural Gerontology, 9*, 53–76.

O'Sullivan, J.T. (1993). Applying cognitive developmental principles in classrooms. In R. Pasnak & M.L. Howe (Eds.), *Emerging themes in cognitive development* (Vol. 2). New York: Springer-Verlag.

Ogbu, J. (1992). Understanding cultural diversity and learning. *Educational Researcher, 21*, 5–14.

Ogbu, J.U. (1988). Black education: A cultural-ecological perspective. In H.P. McAdoo (Ed.), *Black families*. Beverly Hills, CA: Sage.

Ogilvy, C.M. (1994). Social skills training with children and adolescents: A review of the evidence on effectiveness. *Educational Psychology, 14*, 73–83.

Olewus, D. (1982). Development of stable aggressive reaction patterns in males. In R. Blanchard & C. Blanchard (Eds.), *Advances in the study of aggression* (Vol. 1). New York: Academic Press.

Oliver, M.B., & Hyde, J.S. (1993). Gender differences in sexuality: A meta-analysis. *Psychological Bulletin, 114*, 29–51.

Olshansky, S.J., Carnes, B.A., & Cassel, C. (1990). In search of Methuselah. Estimating the upper limits to human longevity. *Science, 250*, 634–640.

Olsho, L.W., Harkins, S.W., & Lenhardt, M.L. (1985). Aging and the auditory system. In J.E. Birren & K.W. Schaie (Eds.), *Handbook of the psychology of aging* (2nd ed.). New York: Van Nostrand Reinhold.

Ono, Y. (1995, October 15). Ads do push kids to smoke, study suggests. *The Wall Street Journal*, pp. B1–B2.

Onslow, M. (1992). Choosing a treatment program for early stuttering: Issues and future directions. *Journal of Speech and Hearing Research, 35*, 983–993.

Orr, A.L. (1991). The psychosocial aspects of aging and vision loss. *Journal of Gerontological Social Work, 17*, 1–14.

Ozecki, M. (1993, February 28). On turning 13: Reports from the front lines. *The New York Times*, sec. 4, p. 2.

Paffenbarger, R.S., Kampert, J.B., Lee, I.M., Hyde, R.T., et al. (1994). Changes in physical activity and other lifeway patterns influencing longevity. *Medicine and Science in Sports and Exercise, 26*, 857–865.

Paikoff, R.L., & Brooks-Gunn, J. (1990). Physiological processes: What role do they play during the transition to adolescence? In R. Montemayor, G.R. Adams, & T.P. Gulotta (Eds.), *From childhood to adolescence: A transitional period?* Newbury Park, CA: Sage.

Palmore, E. (1975). *The honorable elders: A cross-cultural analysis of aging in Japan*. Durham, NC: Duke University Press.

Palmore, E. (1979). Predictors of successful aging. *Gerontologist, 19*, 427–431.

Palmore, E.B. (1988). *The facts on aging quiz*. New York: Springer.

Palmore, E.B. (1992). Knowledge about aging: What we know and need to know. *Gerontologist, 32*, 149–150.

Paneth, N.S. (1995). The problem of low birth weight. *The Future of Children, 5*, 19–34.

Panneton, R.K. (1985). *Prenatal auditory experience with melodies: Effects on postnatal auditory preferences in human newborns*. Unpublished doctoral dissertation, University of North Carolina at Greensboro.

Papousek, H., & Bernstein, P. (1969). The functions of conditioning stimulation in human neonates and infants. In A. Ambrose (Ed.), *Stimulation in early infancy*. New York: Academic Press.

Papousek, H., & Papousek, M. (1991). Innate and cultural guidance of infants' integrative competencies: China, the United States, and Germany. In M.H. Borstein (Ed.), *Cultural approaches to parenting*. Hillsdale, NJ: Erlbaum.

Pappano, L. (1994, November 27). The new old generation. *Boston Glove Magazine*, pp. 18–38.

Papps, F., Walker, M., Trimboli, A., & Trimboli, C. (1995). Parental discipline in Anglo, Greek, Lebanese, and Vietnamese cultures. *Journal of Cross-Cultural Psychology, 26,* 49–64.

Park, K.A., Lay, K., & Ramsay, L. (1993). Individual differences and developmental changes in preschoolers' friendships. *Developmental Psychology, 29,* 264–270.

Parke, R., Ornstein, P.A., Rieser, J.J., & Zahn-Waxler, C. (1994). The past as prologue: An overview of a century of developmental psychology. In R.D. Parke, P.A. Ornstein, J.J. Rieser, & C. Zahn-Waxler (Eds.), *A century of developmental psychology.* Washington, DC: American Psychological Association.

Parke, R., & Slaby, R. (1983). The development of aggression. In E.M. Hetherington (Ed.), *Handbook of child psychology: Vol. 4. Socialization, personality, and social development* (pp. 547–642). New York: Wiley

Parke, R.D. (1981). *Fathers.* Cambridge, MA: Harvard University Press.

Parke, R.D. (1989). Social development in infancy: A twenty-five-year perspective. In D. Palermo (Ed.), *Advances in child development and behaviors.* New York: Academic Press.

Parke, R.D. (1990). In search of fathers: A narrative of an empirical journey. In I. Sigel & G. Brody (Eds.), *Methods of family research.* (Vol. 1). Hillsdale, NJ: Erlbaum.

Parke, R.D., & Sawin, D.B. (1980). The family in early infancy: Social interactional and attitudinal analyses. In F.A. Pedersen (Ed.), *The father–infant relationship: Observational studies in the family setting.* New York: Praeger Special Studies.

Parke, R.D., & Tinsley, B.J. (1987). Family interaction in infancy. In J. Osofsky (Ed.), *Handbook of infant development* (2nd ed.). New York: Wiley.

Parmalee, A.H., Jr., & Sigman, M.D. (1983). Prenatal brain development and behavior. In P.H. Mussen (Ed.), *Handbook of child psychology* (Vol. 2, 4th ed.). New York: Wiley.

Parmalee, A.H., Wenner, W., & Schulz, H. (1964). Infant sleep patterns from birth to 16 weeks of age. *Journal of Pediatrics, 65,* 572–576.

Parritz, R.H., Mangelsdorf, S., & Gunnar, M.R. (1992). Control, social referencing, and the infants' appraisal of threat. In S. Feinman (Ed.), *Social referencing and the social construction of reality in infancy.* New York: Plenum Press.

Parten, M.B. (1932). Social participation among preschool children. *Journal of Abnormal and Social Psychology, 27,* 243–269.

Pascoe, J.M. (1993). Social support during labor and duration of labor: A community-based study. *Public Health Nursing, 10,* 97–99.

Patterson, C.J. (1992). Children of lesbian and gay parents. *Child Development, 63,* 1025–1042.

Patterson, C.J. (1994). Lesbians and gay families. *Current Directions in Psychological Science, 3,* 62–64.

Patterson, C.J. (1995). Families of the baby boom: Parents' division of labor and children's adjustment. Special Issue: Sexual orientation and human development. *Developmental Psychology, 31,* 115–123.

Patterson, G.R., DeBaryshe, B.D., & Ramsey, E. (1989). A developmental perspective on antisocial behavior. *American Psychologist, 44,* 330–335.

Patterson, K., Dancer, J., & Clark, D. (1990). Myth perceptions of hearing loss, hearing aids, and aging. *Educational Gerontology, 16,* 289–296.

Pattison, E.M. (1977). The experience of dying. In E.M. Pattison (Ed.), *The experience of dying.* Englewood Cliffs, NJ: Prentice-Hall.

Pauker, S., & Arond, M. (1989). *The first year of marriage: What to expect, what to accept and what you can change.* New York: Warner Books.

Pavlov, I.P. (1927). *Conditioned reflexes.* London: Oxford University Press.

Payne, J.S., Kauffman, J.M., Brown, G.B., & DeMott, R.M. (1974). *Exceptional children in focus.* Columbus, OH: Chas.E. Merrill.

Peck, R.C. (1968). Psychological developments in the second half of life. In B.L. Neugarten (Ed.), *Middle age and aging.* Chicago: University of Chicago Press.

Pedersen, N.L., Plomin, R., Nesselroade, J.R., & McClearn, G.E. (1992). A quantitative genetic analysis of cognitive abilities during the second half of the life span. *Psychological Science, 3,* 346–353.

Pederson, D.R., Moran, G., Sitko, C., Campbell, K., Ghesquire, K., & Acton, H. (1990). Maternal sensitivity and the security of infant–mother attachment: A q-sort study. *Child Development, 61,* 1974–1983.

Pedlow, R., Sanson, A., Prior, M., & Oberklaid, F. (1993). Stability of maternally reported temperament from infancy to 8 years. *Developmental Psychology, 29,* 998–1007.

Pence, E., & Shepard, M. (1988). Integrating feminist theory and practice: The challenge of the battered women's movement. In K. Yllo & M. Bograd (Eds.), *Feminist perspectives on wife abuse.* Berkely, CA: Sage.

Peplau, L.A., & Cochran, S.D. (1990). A relationship perspective on homosexuality. In D.P. McWhirter, S.A. Sanders, & J.M. Reinisch (Eds.), *Homosexuality/heterosexuality: The Kinsey scale and current research.* New York: Oxford University Press.

Pereira, J. (1994, December 7). Caution: "Morphing" may be hazardous to your teacher. *The Wall Street Journal,* pp. A1, A8.

Pereira-Smith, O., Smith, J., et al. (1988, August). Paper presented at the annual meeting of the International Genetics Congress, Toronto.

Perez, C.M., & Midom, C.S. (1994). Childhood victimization and long-term intellectual and academic outcomes. *Child Abuse & Neglect, 18,* 617–633.

Perleth, C., Lehwald, G., & Browder, C.S. (1993). Indicators of high ability in young children. In K. Heller, F.J. Monks, & A.H. Passow (Eds.), *International handbook of research and development of giftedness and talent* (pp. 283–310). Oxford: Pergamon Press.

Perlmann, R.Y., & Gleason, J.B. (1990, July). *Patterns of prohibition in mothers' speech to children.* Paper presented at the Fifth International Congress for the Study of Child Language, Budapest, Hungary.

Perlmutter, M., & Hall, E. (1992). *Adult development and aging* (2nd ed.). New York: Wiley.

Perodeau, G.M., Poirier, S., Foisy, P., & Ostoj, M. (1992). Potential drug interactions among the elderly in a home care program. *Journal of Geriatric Drug Therapy, 6,* 41–60.

Perozzi, J.A., & Sanchez, M.C. (1992). The effect of instruction in L1 on receptive acquisition of L2 for bilingual children with language delay. *Language, Speech, and Hearing Services in Schools, 23,* 348–352.

Perris, E.E., Myers, N.A., & Clifton, R.K. (1990). Long-term memory for a single infancy experience. *Child Development, 61,* 1796–1807.

Perry, W.G. (1970). *Forms of intellectual and ethical development in the college years.* New York: Holt.

Petersen, A. (1985). Adolescent development. *Annual Review of Psychology, 39,* 583–607.

Petersen, A. (in press). A longitudinal investigation of adolescents' changing perceptions of pubertal timing. *Developmental Psychology.*

Petersen, A.C., & Crockett, L. (1985). Pubertal timing and grade effects on adjustment. *Journal of Youth and Adolescence, 14,* 191–206.

Petersen, A.C., Compas, B., & Brooks-Gunn, J. (1991). *Depression in adolescence: Implications of current research for programs and policy.* Report prepared for the Carnegie Council on Adolescent Development, Washington, DC.

Petersen, A.C., Compas, B.E., Brooks-Gunn, J., Stemmler, M., Ey, S., & Grant, K.E. (1993). Depression in adolescence. *American Psychologist, 48,* 155–168.

Petersen, A.C., Sarigiani, P.A., & Kennedy, R.E. (1991). Adolescent depression: Why more girls? *Journal of Youth and Adolescence, 20,* 247–271.

Peterson, A.C. (1988, September). Those gangly years. *Psychology Today,* pp. 28–34.

Peterson, B.E., & Stewart, A.J. (1993). Generativity and social motives in young adults. *Journal of Personality and Social Psychology, 65,* 186–198.

Peterson, L. (1994). Child injury and abuse-neglect: Common etiologies, challenges, and courses toward prevention. *Current Directions in Psychological Science, 3,* 116–120.

Petitto, L.A., & Marentette, P.F. (1991, March 22). Babbling in the manual mode: Evidence for the ontogeny of language. *Science, 251,* 1493–1496.

Petraitis, J., Flay, B.R., & Miller, T.Q. (1995). Reviewing theories of adolescent substance use: Organizing pieces in the puzzle. *Psychological Bulletin, 117,* 67–86.

Pettingale, K.W., Morris, T., Greer, S., & Haybittle, J.L. (1985). Mental attitudes to cancer: An additional prognostic factor. *The Lancet, 310,* 750.

Phelan, P., Yu, H.C., & Davidson, A.L. (1994). Navigating the psychosocial pressures of adolescence: The voices and experiences of high school youth. *American Educational Research Journal, 31,* 415–447.

Philippot, P., & Feldman, R.S. (1990). Age and social competence in preschoolers' decoding of facial expression. *British Journal of Social Psychology, 29,* 43–54.

Phillips, D. (1992). Death postponement and birthday celebrations. *Psychosomatic Medicine, 26,* 12–18.

Phillips, D., & Smith, D. (1990). Postponement of death until symbolically meaningful occasions. *Journal of the American Medical Association, 269,* 27–38.

Phillips, D.A., & Zimmerman, M. (1990). The developmental course of perceived competence and incompetence among competent children. In R. Sternberg & J. Kolligian (Eds.), *Competence considered.* New Haven, CT: Yale University Press.

Phillips, D.A., Voran, M., Kisker, E., Howes, C., & Whitebook, M. (1994). Child care for children in poverty: Opportunity or inequity? *Child Development, 65,* 472–492.

Phillips, R.D., Wagner, S.H., Fells, C.A., & Lynch, M. (1990). Do infants recognize emotion in facial expressions? Categorical and "metaphorical" evidence. *Infant Behavior and Development, 13,* 71–84.

Phillips, S., King, S., & DuBois, L. (1978). Spontaneous activities of female versus male newborns. *Child Development, 49,* 590–597.

Phinney, J., Lochner, B., & Murphy, R. (1990). Ethnic identity development and psychological adjustment in adolescence. In A. Stiffman & L. Davis (Eds.), *Advances in adolescent mental health: Vol. 5. Ethnic issues.* Greenwich, CT: JAI Press.

Phinney, J.S., & Alipuria, L.L. (1990). Ethnic identity in college students from four ethnic groups. *Journal of Adolescence, 13,* 171–183.

Piaget, J. (1932). *The moral judgment of the child.* New York: Harcourt, Brace & World.

Piaget, J. (1952). *The origins of intelligence in children.* New York: International Universities Press.

Piaget, J. (1954). *The construction of reality in the child* (M. Cook, Trans.). New York: Basic Books.

Piaget, J. (1962). *Play, dreams and imitation in childhood.* New York: W.W. Norton & Co., Inc.

Piaget, J. (1983). Piaget's theory. In W. Kessen (Ed.) & P.H. Mussen (Series Ed.), *Handbook of child psychology: Vol 1. History, theory, and methods* (pp. 103–128). New York: Wiley.

Piaget, J., & Inhelder, B. (1958). *The growth of logical thinking from childhood to adolescence* (A Parsons & S. Seagrin, Trans.). New York: Basic Books.

Piaget, J., & Inhelder, B. (1969). *The psychology of the child* (H. Weaver, Trans.). New York: Basic Books.

Piaget, J., Inhelder, B., & Szenubsjam A. (1960). *The child's conception of geometry.* New York: Basic Books. (Original work published 1948).

Pillemer, K., & Suitor, J. (1988). Elder abuse. In V. VanHasselt, R. Morrison, A. Bellack, & M. Hersen (Eds.), *Handbook of family violence.* New York: Plenum Press.

Pinker, S. (1989). Resolving a learnability paradox in the acquisition of the verb lexicon. In M. Rice & R. Schiefelbusch (Eds.), *The teachability of language.* Baltimore: Paul Brookes.

Pinker, S. (1994). *The language instinct.* New York: Morrow.

Pipp, S., Easterbrooks, M., & Brown, S.R. (1993). Attachment status and complexity of infants' self- and other-knowledge when tested with mother and father. *Social Development, 2,* 1–14.

Pitts, D.G. (1982). The effects of aging upon selected visual functions. In R. Sekuler, D. Kline, & K. Dismukes (Eds.), *Aging and human visual function.* New York: Alan R. Liss.

Plomin, R. (1990). The role of inheritance in behavior. *Science, 248,* 183–188.

Plomin, R. (1994a). *Genetics and experience: The interplay between nature and nurture.* Newbury Park, CA: Sage.

Plomin, R. (1994b). Nature, nurture, and social development. *Social Development, 3,* 37–53.

Plomin, R. (1994c). The genetic basis of complex human behaviors. *Science, 264,* 1733–1739.

Plomin, R., & McClearn, G.E. (Eds.). (1993). *Nature, nurture, and psychology.* Washington, DC: American Psychological Association.

Plomin, R., Corley, R., DeFries, J.C., & Fulker, D.W. (1990). Individual differences in television viewing in early childhood: Nature as well as nurture. *Psychological Science, 1,* 371–377.

Plomin, R., DeFries, J.C., & McClearn, G.E. (1990). *Behavioral genetics: A primer.* New York: W.H. Freeman.

Poest, C.A., Williams, J.R., Witt, D.D., & Atwood, M.E. (1990). Challenge me to move: Large muscle development in young children. *Young Children, 45,* 4–10.

Polansky, E. (1976). Take him home, Mrs. Smith. *Healthright, 2* (2).

Polivy, J., & Herman, C.P. (1985). Dieting and binging: A casual analysis. *American Psychologist, 40,* 193–201.

Polivy, J., & Herman, C.P. (1991). Good and bad dieters: Self-perception and reaction to a dietary challenge. *International Journal of Eating Disorders, 10,* 91–99.

Pollitt, E. (1994). Poverty and child development: Relevance of research in developing countries to the United States. *Child Development, 65,* 283–295.

Pollitt, E., Gorman, K.S., Engle, P.L., Martorell, R., & Rivera, J. (1993). Early supplementary feeding and cognition: Effects over two decades. *Monographs of the Society for Research in Child Development, 58,* v–99.

Pollow, R.L., Stoller, E.P., & Forster, L.E. (1994). Drug combinations and potential for risk of adverse drug reaction among community-dwelling elderly. *Nursing Research, 43,* 44–49.

Pomerleau, A., Bolduc, D., Malcuit, G., & Cossette, L. (1990). Pink or blue: Environmental gender stereotypes in the first two years of life. *Sex Roles, 22,* 359–367.

Pomerleau, O.F., & Pomerleau, C.S. (1989). A bio-behavioral perspective on smoking. In T. Ney & A. Gale (Eds.), *Smoking and human behavior.* New York: Wiley.

Ponomarev, D. (1993, February 28). On turning 13: Reports from the front lines. *The New York Times,* sec. 4, p. 2.

Ponza, M., & Wray, L. (1990). *Evaluation of the food assistance needs of the low-income elderly and their participation in USDA Programs: Final results of the elderly programs study.* Princeton, NJ: Mathematical Policy Research.

Poon, L.W. (1985). Differences in human memory with aging: Nature, causes, and clinical implications. In J.E. Birren & K.W. Schaie (Eds.), *Handbook of the psychology of aging* (2nd ed.). New York: Van Nostrand Reinhold.

Popenoe, D. (1987). Beyond the nuclear family: A statistical portrait of the changing family in Sweden. *Journal of Marriage and the Family, 49,* 173–183.

Population Council Report. (1995, May 30). The decay of families is global, studies say. *The New York Times,* p. A5.

Porges, S.W., & Lipsitt, L. (1993). Neonatal responsivity to gustatory stimulation: The gustatory-vagal hypothesis. *Infant Behavior & Development, 16,* 487–494.

Porter, F.L., Porges, S.W., & Marshall, R.E. (1988). Newborn pain cries and vagal tone: Parallel changes in response to circumcision. *Child Development, 59,* 495–515.

Porter, R.H., Balogh, R.D., & Makin, J.W. (1988). Olfactory influences on mother–infant interactions. In C. Rovee-Collier & L. Lipsitt (Eds.), *Advances in infancy research* (Vol. 5). Norwood, NJ: Ablex.

Potter, M.C. (1990). Remembering. In D.N. Osherson & E.E. Smith (Eds.), *Thinking.* Cambridge, MA: MIT Press.

Poulin-Dubois, D., Serbin, L.A., Kenyon, B., & Derbyshire, A. (1994). Infants' intermodal knowledge about gender. *Developmental Psychology, 30,* 436–442.

Power, T.G., & Parke, R.D. (1982). Play as a context for early learning: Lab and home analyses. In L.M. Laosa & I.E. Sigal (Eds.), *The family as a learning environment.* New York: Plenum Press.

Pratt, W.F., Mosher, W.D., Bachrach, C., & Horn, M. (1984). *Understanding U.S. fertility: Findings from the National Survey of Family Growth.* Washington, DC: Population Reference Bureau.

Prechtl, H.F.R. (1982). Regressions and transformations during neurological development. In T.G. Bever (Ed.), *Regressions in mental development.* Hillsdale, NJ: Erlbaum.

Prentice, A. (1991). Can maternal dietary supplements help in preventing infant malnutrition? *Acta Paediatrica Scandinaica* (Supplement 374), 67–77.

Prescott, C., & Gottesman, I. (1993). Genetically mediated vulnerability to schizophrenia. *Psychiatric Clinics of North America, 16,* 245–267.

Press, I., & McKool, M., Jr. (1972). Social structure and status of the aged: Toward some valid cross-cultural generalizations. *Aging and Human Development, 3,* 297–306.

Pressley, M. (1987). Are keyword method effects limited to slow presentation rates? An empirically based reply to Hall and Fuson (1986). *Journal of Educational Psychology, 79,* 333–335.

Pressley, M., & Levin, J.R. (1983). *Cognitive strategy research: Psychological foundations.* New York: Springer-Verlag.

Pressley, M., & Van Meter, P. (1993). Memory strategies: Natural development and use following instruction. In R. Pasnak & M.L. Howe (Eds.), *Emerging themes in cognitive development* (Vol. 2). New York: Springer-Verlag.

Pressley, M., Cariglia-Bull, T., Deane, S., & Schneider, W. (1987). Short-term memory, verbal competence, and age as predictors of imagery instructional effectiveness. *Journal of Experimental Child Psychology, 43,* 194–211.

Price, D.W., & Goodman, G.S. (1990). Visiting the wizard: Children's memory for a recurring event. *Child Development, 61,* 664–680.

Price, R., & Gottesman, I. (1991). Body fat in identical twins reared apart: Roles for genes and environment. *Behavior Genetics, 21,* 1–7.

Prigerson, H.G., Frank, E., Kasl, S.V., et al. (1995). Complicated grief and bereavement-related depression as distinct disorders: Preliminary empirical validation in elderly bereaved spouses. *American Journal of Psychiatry, 152,* 22–30.

Prince, R.L., Smith, M., Dick, I.M., Price, R.I., et al. (1991). Prevention of postmenopausal osteoporosis. A comparative study of exercise, calcium supplementation, and hormone replacement therapy. *New England Journal of Medicine, 325,* 1189–1195.

Prodromidis, M., Brams, S., Field, T., Scafidi, F., et al. (1994). Psychosocial stressors among depressed adolescent mothers. *Adolescence, 29,* 331–343.

Purdy, M. (1995, November 6). A kind of sexual revolution. *The New York Times,* pp. B1, B6.

Putallaz, M. (1983). Predicting children's sociometric status from their behavior. *Child Development, 54,* 1417–1426.

Putnam, F. (1995, January). Paper presented at a conference titled "Violence against children in the family and the community: A conference on causes, developmental consequences, interventions and prevention." Los Angeles: University of Southern California.

Pyryt, M.C., & Mendaglio., S. (1994). The multidimensional self-concept: A comparison of gifted and average-ability adolescents. *Journal for the Education of the Gifted, 17,* 299–305.

Pyszczynski, T., Greenberg, J., & LaPrelle, J. (1985). Social comparison after success and failure: Biased search for information consistent with a self-servicing conclusion. *Journal of Experimental Social Psychology, 21,* 195–211.

Quade, R. (1994, July 10). Day care brightens young and old. *The New York Times,* p. B8.

Quay, L.C., & Blaney, R.L. (1992). Verbal communication, nonverbal communication, and private speech in lower and middle socioeconomic status preschool children. *Journal of Genetic Psychology, 153,* 129–138.

Quinn, J.B. (1993, April 5). What's for dinner, Mom? *Newsweek,* p. 68.

Quinn, M. (1990, January 29). Don't aim that pack at us. *Time,* p. 60.

Rabkin, J., Remien, R., & Wilson, C. (1994). *Good doctors, good patients: Partners in HIV treatment.* New York: NCM Publishers.

Radetsky, P. (1994, December 2). Stopping premature births before it's too late. *Science, 266,* 1486–1488.

Radke-Yarrow, M., Zahn-Waxler, C., & Chapman, M. (1983). Children's prosocial dispositions and behavior. In E.M. Hetherington, (Ed.), *Handbook of child psychology: Vol. 4. Socialization, personality, and social development* (pp. 469–545). New York: Wiley.

Rahe, R.H., & Arthur, R.J. (1978). Life change and illness studies: Past history and future directions. *Human Stress, 4,* 3–15.

Ramsay, D.S. (1980). Onset of unimanual handedness in infants. *Infant Behavior and Development, 3,* 377–385.

Ramsey, P.G. (1995). Changing social dynamics in early childhood classrooms. *Child Development, 66,* 764–773.

Ranade, V. (1993). Nutritional recommendations for children and adolescents. *International Journal of Clinical Pharmacology, Therapy, and Toxicology, 31,* 285–290.

Randahl, G.J. (1991). A typological analysis of the relations between measured vocational interests and abilities. *Journal of Vocational Behavior, 38,* 333–350.

Rando, T.A. (1993). *Treatment of complicated mourning.* Champaign, IL: Research Press.

Ransom, R.L., Sutch, R., & Williamson, S.H. (1991). Retirement: Past and present. In A.H. Munnell (Ed.), *Retirement and public policy: Proceedings of the Second Conference of the National Academy of Social Insurance. Washington, DC.* Dubuque, IA: Kendall/Hunt.

Rapkin, B.D., & Fischer, K. (1992). Personal goals of older adults: Issues in assessment and prediction. *Psychology and Aging, 7,* 127–137.

Rauch-Elnekave, H. (1994). Teenage motherhood: Its relationship to undetected learning problems. *Adolescence, 29,* 91–103.

Raup, J., & Myers, J. (1989). The empty nest syndrome: Myth or reality? *Journal of Counseling and Development, 68,* 180–183.

Rauscher, F.H., Shaw, G.L., Levine, L.J., Ky, K.N., & Wright, E.L. (1994, August). *Music and spatial task performance—A causal relationship.* Paper presented at the annual meeting of the American Psychological Association, Los Angeles.

Ravitch, D. (1985). *The troubled crusade: American education 1945–1980.* New York: Basic Books.

Reinis, S., & Goldman, J.M. (1980). *The development of the brain: Biological and functional perspectives.* Springfield, IL: Chas. C Thomas.

Reiss, I.L. (1960). *Premaraital sexual standards in America.* New York: The Free Press.

Reiss, M.J. (1984). Human sociobiology. *Zygon Journal of Religion and Science, 19,* 117–140.

Reissland, N. (1988). Neonatal imitation in the first hour of life: Observations in rural Nepal. *Developmental Psychology, 24,* 450–469.

Reitman, V. (1994, February 15). Tots do swimmingly in language-immersion programs. *The Wall Street Journal,* p. B1.

Remondet, J.H., & Hansson, R.O. (1991). Job-related threats to control among older employees. *Journal of Social Issues, 47,* 129–141.

Repetti, R.L., & Cosmas, K.A. (1991). The quality of the social environment at work and job satisfaction. *Journal of Applied Social Psychology, 21,* 840–854.

Reynolds, A.J. (1994). Effects of a preschool plus follow-on intervention for children at risk. *Developmental Psychology, 30,* 787–804.

Ricciardelli, L.A. (1992). Bilingualism and cognitive development in relation to threshold theory. *Journal of Psycholinguistic Research, 21,* 301–316.

Ricciuti, H.N. (1993). Nutrition and mental development. *Current Directions in Psychological Science, 2,* 43–46.

Rice, M.L., Huston, A.C., Truglio, R., & Wright, J. (1990). Words from "Sesame Street": Learning vocabulary while viewing. *Developmental Psychology, 26* (3), 421–428.

Richards, H.D., Bear, G.G., Stewart, A.L., & Norman, A.D. (1992). Moral reasoning and classroom conduct: Evidence of a curvilinear relationship. *Merrill-Palmer Quarterly, 38*, 176–190.

Richards, M.H., & Duckett, E. (1991). Maternal employment and adolescents. In J.V. Lerner & N. Galambos (Eds.), *Employed mothers and their children.* New York: Garland.

Richards, M.H., & Duckett, E. (1994). The relationship of maternal employment to early adolescent daily experience with and without parents. *Child Development, 65*, 225–236.

Richards, R., Kinney, D.K., Benet, M., & Merzel, A.P.C. (1990). Assessing everyday creativity: Characteristics of the lifetime creativity scales and validation with three large samples. *Journal of Personality and Social Psychology, 54*, 476–485.

Richardson, G.A., & Day, N.L. (1994). Detrimental effects of prenatal cocaine exposure: Illusion or reality? *Journal of the American Academy of Child & Adolescent Psychiatry, 33*, 28–34.

Richardson, V., & Champion, V. (1992). The relationship of attitudes, knowledge, and social support to breast-feeding. *Issues in Comprehensive Pediatric Nursing, 15*, 183–197.

Rief, S.F. (1995). *How to reach and teach ADD/ADHD children.* West Nyack, NY: Center for Applied Research in Education.

Riese, M.L. (1987). Temperamental stability between the neonatal period and 24 months. *Developmental Psychology, 23*, 216–222.

Riese, M.L. (1990). Neonatal temperament in monozygotic and dizygotic twin pairs. *Child Development, 61*, 1230–1237.

Rimm, S.B., & Lovance, K.J. (1992). The use of subject and grade skipping for the prevention and reversal of underachievement. Special Issue: Challenging the gifted: Grouping and acceleration. *Gifted Child Quarterly, 36*, 100–105.

Rist, M.C. (1990, January). The shadow children. *The American School Board Journal*, pp. 19–24.

Robbins, M.W. (1990, December 10). Sparing the child: How to intervene when you suspect abuse. *New York*, pp. 42–53.

Robbins, W.J. (1929). *Growth.* New Haven, CT: Yale University Press.

Roberto, K.A. (1987). Exchange and equity in friendships. In R.G. Adams & R. Blieszner (Eds.), *Older adult friendships: Structure and process.* Newbury Park, CA: Sage.

Robertson, S.S. (1982). Intrinsic temporal patterning in the spontaneous movement of awake neonates. *Child Development, 53*, 1016–1021.

Rochat, P., & Goubet, N. (1995). Development of sitting and reaching in 5- and 6-month old infants. *Infant Behavior & Development, 18*, 53–68.

Rodin, J. (1986, September 19). Aging and health: Effects of the sense of control. *Science, 233*, 1271–1276.

Rodin, J. (1992). Determinants of body fat localization and its implications for health. *Annals of Behavioral Medicine, 14*, 275–281.

Rodin, J., & Hall, E. (1987). A sense of control. In E. Hall, *Growing and changing.* New York: Random House.

Roffwarg, H.P., Muzio, J.N., & Dement, W.C. (1966). Ontogenic development of the human sleep-dream cycle. *Science, 152*, 604–619.

Rogan, W.J., & Gladen, B.C. (1993). Breast-feeding and cognitive development. *Early Human Development, 31*, 181–193.

Rolfe, S.A. (1994). Does assessment of cognitive functioning in infancy hold the key to early detection of developmental disabilities? A review of research. *Australia and New Zealand Journal of Developmental Disabilities, 19*, 61–72.

Romaine, S. (1994). *Bilingualism* (2nd ed.). London: Blackwell.

Rönkä, A., & Pulkkinen, L. (1995). Accumulation of problems in social functioning in young adulthood: A developmental approach. *Journal of Personality and Social Psychology, 69*, 381–391.

Roodenrys, S., Hulme, C., & Brown, G. (1993). The development of short-term memory span: Separable effects of speech rate and long-term memory. *Journal of Experimental Child Psychology, 56*, 431–442.

Roopnarine, J. (1992). Father–child play in India. In K. MacDonald (Ed.), *Parent–child play.* Albany: State University of New York Press.

Roopnarine, J., & Honig, A.S. (1985, September). The unpopular child. *Young Children*, pp. 59–64.

Roopnarine, J.L., Johnson, J.E., & Hooper, F.H. (Eds.). *Children's play in diverse cultures.* Albany: State University of New York Press.

Rose, S.A., & Feldman, J.F. (1995). Prediction of IQ and specific cognitive abilities at 11 years from infancy measures. *Developmental Psychology, 31*, 685–696.

Rose, S.A., Feldman, J.F., & Wallace, I.F. (1992). Infant information processing in relation to six-year cognitive outcomes. *Child Development, 63*, 1126–1141.

Rose, S.A., Feldman, J.F., Wallace, I.F., & McCarton, C. (1991). Information processing at 1 year: Relation to birth status and developmental outcome during the first 5 years. *Developmental Psychology, 27*, 723–737.

Rose, S.A., & Ruff, H.A. (1987). Cross-modal abilities in infants. In J.D. Osofsky (Ed.), *Handbook of infant development* (2nd ed.). New York: Wiley.

Rosemond, J. (1988, September). Taming the TV monster and why that's so important. *Better Homes and Gardens*, pp. 26–27.

Rosen, W.D., Adamson, L.B., & Bakeman, R. (1992). An experimental investigation of infant social referencing: Mothers' messages and gender differences. *Developmental Psychology, 28*, 1172–1178.

Rosenblatt, P.C. (1988). Grief: The social context of private feelings. *Journal of Social Issues, 44*, 67–78.

Rosenfeld, M., & Owens, W.A., Jr. (1965, April). *The intrinsic-extrinsic aspects of work and their demographic correlates.* Paper presented at the Midwestern Psychological Association, Chicago.

Rosenman, R.H. (1990). Type A behavior pattern: A personal overview. *Journal of Social Behavior and Personality, 5*, 1–24.

Rosenman, R.H., Brand, R.J., Sholtz, R.I., & Friedman, M. (1976). Multivariate prediction of coronary heart disease during 8.5-year follow-up in the Western Collaborative Group Study. *American Journal of Cardiology, 37*, 903–910.

Rosenstein, D., & Oster, H. (1988). Differential facial responses to four basic tastes in newborns. *Child Development, 59*, 1555–1568.

Rosenthal, D.A., & Shepherd, H. (1993). A six-month follow-up of adolescents' sexual risk-taking, HIV/AIDS knowledge, and attitudes to condoms. *Journal of Community and Applied Social Psychology, 3*, 53–65.

Rosenthal, R. (1987). Pygmalion effects: Existence, magnitude, and social importance. *Educational Researcher, 16*, 37–40.

Rosenthal, R. (1994). Interpersonal expectancy effects: A 30-year perspective. *Current Directions in Psychological Science, 3*, 176–179.

Rosenthal, R., & Jacobson, L. (1968). *Pygmalion in the classroom: Teacher expectation and pupils' intellectual development.* New York: Holt, Rinehart & Winston.

Rosenzweig, M.R., & Bennett, E.L. (1976). Enriched environments: Facts, factors, and fantasies. In L. Petrinovich & J.L. McGaugh (Eds.), *Knowing, thinking, and believing.* New York: Plenum Press.

Rosnow, R.L., Rotheram-Borus, M.J., Ceci, S.J., Blanck, P.D., et al. (1993). The institutional review board as a mirror of scientific and ethical standards. *American Psychologist, 48*, 821–826.

Ross Laboratories. (1993). *Ross Laboratories mothers' survey, 1992.* Division of Abbott Laboratories, USA, Columbus, OH. Unpublished data.

Ross, C.E., Mirowsky, J., & Goldsteen, K. (1991). The impact of the family on health. In A. Booth (Ed.), *Contemporary families.* Minneapolis, MN: National Council on Family Relations.

Ross, R.K., & Yu, M.C. (1994). Breast feeding and breast cancer. *New England Journal of Medicine, 330*, 1683–1684.

Rosser, P.L., & Randolph, S.M. (1989). Black American infants: The Howard University normative study. In J.K. Neugent, B.M. Lester, & T.B. Brazelton (Eds.), *The cultural context of infancy: Vol. 1. Biology, culture, and infant development.* Norwood, NJ: Ablex.

Rossman, I. (1977). Anatomic and body composition changes with aging. In C.E. Finch & L. Hayflick (Eds.), *Handbook of the biology of aging.* New York: Van Nostrand Reinhold.

Rotenberg, K.J., & Morrison, J. (1993). Loneliness and college achievement: Do loneliness scale scores predict college drop-out? *Psychological Reports, 73,* 1283–1288.

Rothbart, M.K., Ahadi, S.A., & Hershey, K.L. (1994). Temperament and social behavior in childhood. *Merrill-Palmer Quarterly, 40,* 21–39.

Rothblum, E.D. (1990). Women and weight: Fad and fiction. *Journal of Psychology, 124,* 5–24.

Roush, W. (1995, March 31). Arguing over why Johnny can't read. *Science, 267,* 1896–1998.

Rovee-Collier, C. (1993). The capacity for long-term memory in infancy. *Current Directions in Psychological Science, 2,* 130–135.

Rovee-Collier, C.K. (1984). The ontogeny of learning and memory in human infancy. In R.V. Kail, Jr., & N.E. Spear (Eds.), *Comparative perspectives on the development of memory.* Hillsdale, NJ: Erlbaum.

Rovee-Collier, C.K. (1987). Learning and memory in infancy. In J.D. Osofsky (Ed.), *Handbook of infant development* (2nd ed.). New York: Wiley.

Rovee-Collier, C., Borza, M.A., Adler, S.A., & Boller, K. (1993). Infants' eyewitness testimony: Effects of postevent information on a prior memory representation. *Memory & Cognition, 21,* 267–279.

Rovee-Collier, C.K., & Hayne, H. (1987). Reactivation and infant long-term memory. In H.W. Reese (Ed.), *Advances in child development and behavior* (Vol. 20). New York: Academic Press.

Rovner, B.W., & Katz, I.R. (1993). Psychiatric disorders in the nursing home: A selective review of studies related to clinical care. *International Journal of Geriataric Psychiatry, 8* (Special Issue), 75–87.

Rowe, D.C. (1993). Genetic perspectives on personality. In R. Plomin & G.E. McClearn (Eds.), *Nature, nurture, and psychology.* Washington, DC: American Psychological Association.

Rubenstein, J., Howes, C., & Boyule, P. (1981). A two-year follow-up of infants in community-based day care. *Journal of Child Psychology and Psychiatry, 22,* 209–218.

Rubin, D.C. (1985, September). The subtle deceiver: Recalling our past. *Psychology Today,* pp. 39–46.

Rubin, D.C. (1986). *Autobiographical memory.* Cambridge: Cambridge University Press.

Rubin, D.H., Krasilnikoff, P.A., Leventhal, J.M., Weile, B., & Berget, A. (1986). Effects of passive smoking on birthweight. *The Lancet, 315,* 415–417.

Rubin, K.H., Daniels-Beirness, T., & Hayvren, M. (1982). Social and social-cognitive correlates of sociometric status in preschool and kindergarten children. *Canadian Journal of Behavioral Science, 14,* 338–349.

Rubin, K.H., Fein, G., & Vandenberg, B. (1983). In E.M. Hetherington (Ed.), *Handbook of child psychology: Vol. 4. Socialization, personality and social development* (pp. 693–774). New York: Wiley.

Rubin, Z. (1973). *Liking and loving.* New York: Holt.

Ruble, D. (1983). The development of social comparison processes and their role in achievement-related self-actualization. In E.T. Higgins, D.N. Ruble, and W.W. Hartup (Eds.), *Social cognition and social development.* New York: Cambridge University Press.

Ruble, D., & Brooks-Gunn, J. (1982). The experience of menarche. *Child Development, 53,* 1557–1566.

Ruble, D.N., Boggiano, A.K., Feldman, N.S., & Loebl, J.H. (1989). Developmental analysis of the role of social comparison in self-evaluation. *Developmental Psychology, 16,* 105–115.

Ruff, H.A. (1989). The infant's use of visual and haptic information in the perception and recognition of objects. *Canadian Journal of Psychology, 43,* 302–319.

Rule, B.G., & Ferguson, T.J. (1986). The effects of media violence on attitudes, emotions and cognitions. *Journal of Social Issues, 42,* 29–50.

Rumelhart, D.E. (1984). Schemata and the cognitive system. In R.S. Wyer, Jr., & T.K. Siull (Eds.), *Handbook of social cognition.* Hillsdale, NJ: Erlbaum.

Russell, G., & Radojevic, M. (1992). The changing role of fathers: Current understandings and future directions for research and practice. Special Section: Australian Regional Meeting: Attachment and the relationship of the infant and caregivers. *Infant Mental Health Journal, 13,* 296–311.

Russo, R., & Parkin, A.J. (1993). Age differences in implicit memory: More apparent than real. *Memory & Cognition, 21,* 73–80.

Russon, A.E., & Waite, B.E. (1991). Patterns of dominance and imitation in an infant peer group. *Ethology and Sociobiology, 12,* 55–73.

Rusting, R. (1990, March). Safe passage? *Scientific American,* p. 36.

Rutter, M., & Garmezy, N. (1983). Developmental psychopathology. In E.M. Hetherington (Ed.), *Handbook of child psychology: Vol. 4. Socialization, personality, and social development.* New York: Wiley.

Rutter, M. (1987). Continuities and discontinuities from infancy. In J.D. Osofsky (Ed.), *Handbook of infant development* (2nd ed.). New York: Wiley.

Saarni, C., & Borg, V. (in press). Television's influence on children's understanding of emotions and social control. In A. Dorr (Ed.), *Television and affect.* Hillsdale, NJ: Erlbaum.

Sacks, M.H. (1993). Exercise for stress control. In D. Goleman & J. Gurin (Eds.), *Mind-body medicine.* Yonkers, NY: Consumer Reports Books.

Sadker, M., & Sadker, D. (1994). *Failing at fairness: How America's schools cheat girls* (pp. 168–170) New York: Scribner's.

Sagi, A. (1990). Attachment theory and research from a cross-cultural perspective. *Human Development 1990, 33,* 10–22.

Sagi, A., Donnell, F., van Ijzendoorn, M.H., Mayseless, O., & Aviezer, O. (1994). Sleeping out of home in a kibbutz communal arrangement: It makes a difference for infant–mother attachment. *Child Development, 65,* 992–1004.

Sagi, A., Ijzendoorn, M.H., & Koren-Karie, N. (1991). Primary appraisal of the Strange Situation: A cross-cultural analysis of preseparation episodes. *Developmental Psychology, 27,* 587–596.

Sagi, A., Lewkowicz, K.S., Shoham, R., Dvir, R., & Estes, D. (1985). Security of infant–mother, father, multiple attachments among kibbutz-reared Israeli children. In I. Bretherton & E. Waters (Eds.), *Growing points of attachment theory and research. Monographs of the Society for Research in Child Development, 50 (1–2,* Serial No. 209), 257–275.

Sagi, A., Van-Ijzendoorn, M.H., & Koren-Karie, N. (1991). Primary appraisal of the Strange Situation: A cross-cultural analysis of preseparation episodes. *Developmental Psychology, 27,* 587–596.

Salber, E.J., Freeman, H.E., & Abelin, T. (1968). Needed research on smoking: Lessons from the Newton study. In E.F. Borgatta & R.R. Evans (Eds.), *Smoking, health, and behavior.* Chicago: Aldine.

Salmon, D.K. (1993, September). Getting through labor. *Parents,* pp. 62–66.

Salthouse, T.A. (1984). Effects of age and skill in typing. *Journal of Experimental Psychology: General, 113,* 345–371.

Salthouse, T.A. (1989). Age-related changes in basic cognitive processes. In APA Master Lectures, *The adult years: Continuity and change.* Washington, DC: American Psychological Association.

Salthouse, T.A. (1991). Mediation of adult age differences in cognition by reductions in working memory and speed of processing. *Psychological Science, 2,* 179–183.

Salthouse, T.A. (1993). Speed mediation of adult age differences in cognition. *Developmental Psychology, 29,* 722–738.

Salthouse, T.A. (1994a). Aging associations: Influence of speed on adult age differences in associative learning. *Journal of Experimental Psychology: Learning, Memory, and Cognition, 20,* 1486–1503.

Salthouse, T.A. (1994b). The aging of working memory. *Neuropsychology, 8,* 535–543.

Samaritans. (1989). *Annual report, 1989.* Boston: Author.

Sanders, C.M. (1988). Risk factors in bereavement outcome. *Journal of Social Issues, 44,* 97–111.

Sanders, C.M. (1989). *Grief: The mourning after.* New York: Wiley.

Sanderson, C.A., & Cantor, N. (1995). Social dating goals in late adolescence: Implications for safer sexual activity. *Journal of Personality and Social Psychology, 68,* 1121–1134.

Sandler, B. (1994, January 31). First denial, then a near-suicidal plea: "Mom, I need your help." *People Weekly,* pp. 56–58.

Sandyk, R. (1992). Melatonin and maturation of REM sleep. *International Journal of Neuroscience, 63,* 105–114.

Sangree, W.H. (1989). Age and power: Life-course trajectories and age structuring of power relations in East and West Africa. In D.I. Kertzer & K.W. Schaie (Eds.), *Age structuring in comparative perspective.* Hillsdale, NJ: Erlbaum.

Sankar, A. (1981). The conquest of solitude: Singlehood and old age in traditional Chinese society. In C.L. Fry (Ed.), *Dimensions: Aging, culture and health.* New York: Praeger.

Sanoff, A.P., & Minerbrook, S. (1993, April 19). Race on campus. *U.S. News & World Report,* pp. 52–64.

Sanson, A., & diMuccio, C. (1993). The influence of aggressive and neutral cartoons and toys on the behavior of preschool children. *Australian Psychologist, 28,* 93–99.

Sanson, A.V., Smart, D.F., Prior, M., Oberklaid, F., & Pedlow, R. (1994). The structure of temperament from age 3 to 7 years: Age, sex, and sociodemographic influences. *Merrill-Palmer Quarterly, 40,* 233–252.

Sarantakos, S. (1991). Cohabitation revisited: Paths of change among cohabiting and non-cohabiting couples. *Australian Journal of Marriage and the Family, 12,* 144–155.

Sarason, I.G., Sarason, B.R., & Pierce, G.R. (1991). Anxiety, cognitive interference, and performance. *Journal of Social Behavior and Personality, 5,* 1–18.

Sarason, S., Johnson, J.H., & Siegel, J.M. (1978). Assessing the impact of life changes: Development of the Life Experiences Survey. *Journal of Consulting and Clinical Psychology, 46,* 932–946.

Sarnat, H.B. (1978). Olfactory reflexes in the newborn infant. *Journal of Pediatrics, 92,* 624–626.

Sasser-Coen, J.R. (1993). Qualitative changes in creativity in the second half of life: A life-span developmental perspective. *Journal of Creative Behavior, 27,* 18–27.

Savage-Rumbaugh, E.S., Murphy, J., Sevcik, R.A., Brakke, K.E., et al. (1993). Language and comprehension in ape and child. *Monographs of the Society for Research in Child Development, 58* (3–4, Serial No. 233).

Savin-Williams, R., & Demo, D. (1983). Situational and transituational determinants of adolescent self-feelings. *Journal of Personality and Social Psychology, 44,* 824–833.

Savin-Williams, R.C., & Berndt, T.J. (1990). Friendship and peer relations. In S. Feldman & G. Elliott (Eds.), *At the threshold: The developing adolescent.* Cambridge, MA: Harvard University Press.

Scanlon, J.W., & Hollenbeck, A.R. (1983). Neonatal behavioral effects of anesthetic exposure during pregnancy. In A.E. Friedman, A. Milusky, & A. Gluck (Eds.), *Advances in perinatal medicine.* New York: Plenum Press.

Scarr, S. (1992). Developmental theories for the 1990s: Development and individual differences. *Child Development, 63,* 1–19.

Scarr, S. (1993). Biological and cultural diversity: The legacy of Darwin for development. *Child Development, 64,* 1333–1353.

Scarr, S., & Carter-Saltzman, L. (1982). Genetics and intelligence. In R.J. Sternberg (Ed.), *Handbook of human intelligence* (pp. 792–896). Cambridge: Cambridge University Press.

Scarr, S., Phillips, D., & McCartney, K. (1989). Working mothers and their families. *American Psychologist, 44,* 1402–1409.

Schachter, S., Goldman, R., & Gordon, A. (1968). Effects of fear, food deprivation, and obesity on eating. *Journal of Personality and Social Psychology, 10,* 91–97.

Schaefer, R.T., & Lamm, R.P. (1992). *Sociology* (4th ed.). New York: McGraw-Hill.

Schaffer, H.R. (1971). *The growth of sociability.* Hammondsworth, UK: Penguin Books.

Schaffer, H.R., & Emerson, P.E. (1964). The development of social attachments in infancy. *Monographs of the Society for Research in Child Development, 29* (No. 94).

Schaie, K.W. (1977–1978). Toward a stage theory of adult cognitive development. *Journal of Aging and Human Development, 8,* 129–138.

Schaie, K.W. (1991). Developmental designs revisited. In S.H. Cohen & H.W. Reese (Eds.), *Life-span developmental psychology: Methodological innovations.* Hillsdale, NJ: Erlbaum.

Schaie, K.W. (1993). The Seattle longitudinal studies of adult intelligence. *Current Directions in Psychological Science, 2,* 171–175.

Schaie, K.W. (1994). The course of adult intellectual development. *American Psychologist, 49,* 304–313.

Schaie, K.W., & Willis, S.L. (1993). Age difference patterns of psychometric intelligence in adulthood: Generalizability within and across ability domains. *Psychology and Aging, 8,* 44–55.

Schaie, K.W., Willis, S.L., Jay, G., & Chipuer, H. (1989). Structural invariance of cognitive abilities across the adult life span: A cross-sectional study. *Developmental Psychology, 25,* 652–662.

Schaie, W. (1985). *Longitudinal studies of psychological development.* New York: Guilford Press.

Schanberg, S., & Field, T.M. (1987). Sensory deprivation stress and supplemental stimulation in the rat pup and preterm human neonate. *Child Development, 58,* 1431–1447.

Schanberg, S., Field, T., Kuhn, C., & Bartolome, J. (1993). Touch: A biological regulator of growth and development in the neonate. *Verhaltenstherapie, 3* (Suppl. 1), 15.

Schatz, M. (1994). *A toddler's life.* New York: Oxford University Press.

Schechtman, V.L., & Harper, R.M. (1991). Time of night effects on heart rate variation in normal neonates. *Journal of Developmental Physiology, 16,* 349–353.

Scheibel, A.B. (1992). Structural changes in the aging brain. In J.E. Birren, R.B. Sloane, & G.D. Cohen (Eds.), *Handbook of mental health and aging* (2nd ed.). San Diego, CA: Harcourt Brace.

Scheiber, F. (1992). Aging and the senses. In J.E. Birren, R.B. Sloane, & G.D. Cohen (Eds.), *Handbook of mental health and aging* (2nd ed.). San Diego, CA: Harcourt Brace.

Scheier, M.F., & Carver, C.S. (1992). Effects of optimism on psychological and physical well-being: Theoretical overview and empirical update. *Cognitive Therapy and Research, 16,* 201–228.

Schiavi, R.C. (1990). Sexuality and aging in men. *Annual Review of Sex Research, 1,* 227–249.

Schlicker, S.A., Borra, S.T., & Regan, C. (1994). The weight and fitness status of United States children. *Nutrition Reviews, 52,* 11–17.

Schmidt, P.J., & Rubinow, D.R. (1991). Menopause-related affective disorders: A justification for further study. *American Journal of Psychiatry, 148,* 844–852.

Schmidt, U., & Treasure, J. (1993). *Getting better bit(e) by bit(e): A survival kit for sufferers of bulimia nervosa and binge eating disorders.* Hillsdale, NJ: Erlbaum.

Schneider, B.A., Bull, D., & Trehub, S.E. (1988). Binaural unmasking in infants. *Journal of the Acoustical Society of America, 83,* 1124–1132.

Schneider, B.A., Trehub, S.E., & Bull, D. (1980). High-frequency sensitivity in infants. *Science, 207,* 1003–1004.

Schneider, W., & Pressley, M. (1989). *Memory between two and twenty.* New York: Springer-Verlag.

Schneiderman, N. (1983). Animal behavior models of coronary heart disease. In D.S. Kranz, A. Baum, & J.E. Singer (Eds.), *Handbook of psychology and health* (Vol. 3). Hillsdale, NJ: Erlbaum.

Schofield, J.W., & Francis, W.D. (1982). An observational study of peer interaction in racially mixed "accelerated" classrooms. *Journal of Educational Psychology, 74*, 722–732.

Schorr, L. (1988). *Without our reach: Breaking the cycle of disadvantage.* New York: Anchor Press.

Schover, L.R., & Jensen, S.B. (1988). *Sexuality and chronic illness.* New York: Guilford Press.

Schulenberg, J.E., Asp, C.E., & Peterson, A.C. (1984). School from the young adolescent's perspective. *Journal of Early Adolescence, 4*, 107–130.

Schulman, M. (1991). *The passionate mind: Bringing up an intelligent and creative child.* New York: The Free Press.

Schulman, P., Keith, D., & Seligman, M. (1993). Is optimism heritable? A study of twins. *Behavior Research and Therapy, 31*, 569–574.

Schultz, A.H. (1969). *The life of primates.* New York: Universe Books.

Schultz, R., & Curnow, C. (1988). Peak performance and age among superathletes: Track and field, swimming, baseball, tennis, and golf. *Journal of Gerontology, 43*, P113–P120.

Schulz, R., & Aderman, D. (1974). Clinical research and the stages of dying. *Omega, 6*, 137–143.

Schulz, R., & Aderman, D. (1976). How medical staff copes with dying patients. *Omega, 7*, 11–21.

Schulz, R., & Ewen, R.B. (1988). *Adult development and aging: Myths and emerging realities.* New York: Macmillan.

Schunk, D.H. (1991). Self-efficacy and academic motivation. Special Issue: Current issues and new directions in motivational theory and research. *Educational Psychologist, 26*, 207–231.

Schuster, C.S., & Ashburn, S.S. (1986). *The process of human development* (2nd ed.). Boston: Little, Brown.

Schwartz, J.E., Friedman, H.S., Tucker, J.S., Tomlinson-Keasey, C., et al. (in press). Childhood sociodemographic and psychosocial factors as predictors of longevity across the life-span. *American Journal of Public Health.*

Schwebel, M., Maher, C.A., & Fagley, N.S. (Eds.). (1990). *Promoting cognitive growth over the life span.* Hillsdale, NJ: Erlbaum.

Schweinhart, L.J., Barnes, H.V., & Weikart, D.P. (1993). *Significant benefits: The High/Scope Perry Preschool Study through age 27* (Monographs of the High/Scope Educational Research Foundation, No. 10). Ypsilanti, MI: High/Scope Press.

Scruggs, T.E., & Mastropieri, M.A. (1994). Successful mainstreaming in elementary science classes: A qualitative study of three reputational cases. *American Educational Research Journal, 31*, 785–811.

Secouler, L.M. (1992). Our elders: At high risk for humiliation. Special Issue: The humiliation dynamic: Viewing the task of prevention from a new perspective: II. *Journal of Primary Prevention, 12*, 195–208.

Segal, J., & Segal, & Z. (1992, September). No more couch potatoes. *Parents*, p. 235.

Segal, N.L. (1993). Twin, sibling, and adoption methods: Tests of evolutionary hypotheses. *American Psychologist, 48*, 943–956.

Segall, M.H., Dasen, P.R., Berry, J.W., & Poortinga, Y.H. (1990). *Human behavior in global perspective.* Boston: Allyn & Bacon.

Seibel, M., & McCarthy, J.A. (1993). Infertility, pregnancy, and the emotions. In D. Goleman & J. Gurin (Eds.), *Mind-body medicine.* Yonkers, NY: Consumer Reports Books.

Seidman, S.N., & Rieder, R.O. (1994). A review of sexual behavior in the United States. *American Journal of Psychiatry, 151*, 330–341.

Selig, S., Tomlinson, T., & Hickey, T. (1991). Ethical dimensions of intergenerational reciprocity: Implications for practice. *Gerontologist, 31*, 624–630.

Serbin, L.A., Moller, L., Powlishta, K., & Gulko, J. (1991, April). *The emergence of gender segregation and behavioral compatibility in toddlers' peer preferences.* Paper presented at the biennial meeting of the Society for Research in Child Development. Baltimore.

Serow, R.C. (1994). Called to teach: A study of highly motivated preservice teachers. *Journal of Research and Development in Education, 27*, 65–72.

Sesser, S. (1993, September 13). Opium war redux. *New Yorker*, pp. 78–89.

Shafer, R.G. (1990, March 12). An anguished father recounts the battle he lost trying to rescue a teenage son from drugs. *People Weekly*, pp. 81–83.

Shankaran, S., Cohen, S.N., Linver, M., & Zonia, S. (1988). Medical care costs of high-risk infants after neonatal intensive care: A controlled study. *Pediatrics, 81*, 372–378.

Sharf, R.S. (1992). *Applying career development theory to counseling.* Pacific Grove, CA: Brooks/Cole.

Sharpe, R. (1994, July 18). Better babies: School gets kids to do feats at a tender age, but it's controversial. *The Wall Street Journal*, pp. A1, A6.

Shavelson, R., Hubner, J.J., & Stanton, J.C. (1976). Self-concept: Validation of construct interpretations. *Review of Educational Research, 46*, 407–441.

Shaver, P. (1994, August). *Attachment and care giving in adult romantic relationships.* Invited address presented at the annual meeting of the American Psychological Association, Los Angeles.

Shaver, P.R., Hazan, C., & Bradshaw, D. (1988). Love as attachment: The integration of three behavioral systems. In R.J. Sternberg & M.L. Barnes (Eds.), *The psychology of love* (pp. 68–99). New Haven, CT: Yale University Press.

Shaw, J. (1994). Aging and sexual potential. *Journal of Sex Education and Therapy, 20*, 134–139.

Shea, J.D. (1985). Studies of cognitive development in Papua New Guinea. *International Journal of Psychology, 20*, 33–61.

Shealy, C.N. (1995). From *Boys Town* to *Oliver Twist*: Separating fact from fiction in welfare reform and out-of-home placement of children and youth. *American Psychologist, 50*, 565–580.

Shearer, E.L. (1993). Cesarean section: Medical benefits and costs. *Social Science and Medicine, 37*, 122–1231.

Sheehy, G. (1976). *Passages.* New York: Dutton.

Sheingold, K., & Tenney, Y.J. (1982). Memory for a salient childhood event. In U. Neisser (Ed.), *Memory observed.* New York: W.H. Freeman.

Shepard, G.B. (1991). A glimpse of kindergarten—Chinese style. *Young Children, 47*, 11–15.

Sherman, E. (1991). *Reminiscence and the self in old age.* New York: Springer.

Sherman, E. (1993). Mental health and successful adaptation in later life. *Generations, 17*, 43–46.

Sherman, E. (1994). The structure of well-being in the life narratives of the elderly. *Journal of Aging Studies, 8*, 149–158.

Sherry, B., Springer, D.A., Connell, F.A., & Garrett, S.M. (1992). Short, thin, or obese? Comparing growth indexes of children from high- and low-poverty areas. *Journal of the American Dietetic Association, 92*, 1092–1095.

Sherwin, B.B. (1991). The psychoendocrinology of aging and female sexuality. *Annual Review of Sex Research, 2*, 181–198.

Shevron, R.H., & Lumsden, D.B. (1985). *Introduction to educational gerontology* (2nd ed.). New York: Hemisphere.

Shields, J. (1973). Heredity and psychological abnormality. In H. Eysenck (Ed.), *Handbook of abnormal psychology* (pp. 540–603). San Diego, CA: Edits Publishers.

Shimamura, A.O., Berry, J.M., Mangels, J.A., Rusting, C.L., & Jurica, P.J. (1995). Memory and cognitive abilities in university professors: Evidence for successful aging. *Psychological Science, 6*, 271–277.

Shiono, P.H., & Behrman, R.E. (1995). Low birth weight: Analysis and recommendations. *The Future of Children, 5*, 4–18.

Shirley, M.M. (1933). *The first two years: A study of twenty-five babies* (Vol. 2). Minneapolis: University of Minnesota Press.

Shock, N.W. (1962). *The physiology of aging.* San Francisco: Freeman.

Shore, C.M. (1994). *Individual differences in language development.* Newbury Park, CA: Sage.

Shostak, M. (1981). *Nissa: The life and words of a !Kung woman.* Cambridge, MA: Harvard University Press.

Shriver, M.D., & Piersel, W. (1994). The long-term effects of intrauterine drug exposure: Review of recent research and implications for early childhood special education. *Topics in Early Childhood Special Education, 14,* 161–183.

Shrum, W., Cheek, N., Jr., & Hunter, S.M. (1988). Friendship in school: Gender and racial homophily. *Sociology of Education, 61,* 227–239.

Shucard, J., Shucard, D., Cummins, K., & Campso, J. (1981). Auditory-evoked potentials and sex-related differences in brain development. *Brain and Language, 13,* 91–102.

Shurkin, J.N. (1992). *Terman's kids: The groundbreaking study of how the gifted grow up.* Boston: Little, Brown.

Siegel, J.M. (1990). Stressful life events and use of physician services among the elderly: The moderating role of pet ownership. *Journal of Personality and Social Psychology, 58,* 1081–1086.

Siegel, L.A. (1983). The prediction of possible learning disabilities in preterm and full-term children. In T. Field & A. Sostek (Eds.), *Infants born at risk: Physiological, perceptual and cognitive processes.* New York: Grune & Stratton.

Siegel, L.S. (1989). A reconceptualization of prediction from infant test scores. In M.H. Bornstein & N.A. Krasnegor (Eds.), *Stability and continuity in mental development: Behavioral and biological perspectives.* Hillsdale, NJ: Erlbaum.

Siegler, I.C., & Costa, P.T. (1985). Health behavior relationships. In J.E. Birren & K.W. Schaie (Eds.), *Handbook of the psychology of aging* (2nd ed.). New York: Van Nostrand Reinhold.

Siegler, R.S. (1991). *Children's thinking* (2nd ed.). Englewood Cliffs, NJ: Prentice-Hall.

Siegler, R.S. (1994). Cognitive variability: A key to understanding cognitive development. *Current Directions in Psychological Science, 3,* 1–5.

Siegler, R.S., & Richards, D. (1982). The development of intelligence. In R. Sternberg (Ed.), *Handbook of human intelligence.* London: Cambridge University Press.

Sigman, M. (1995). Nutrition and child development: More food for thought. *Current Directions in Psychological Science, 4,* 52–55.

Sigman, M., Cohen, S.E., Beckwith, L., Asarnow, R., et al. (in press). Continuity in cognitive abilities from infancy to 12 years of age. *Cognitive Development.*

Sigman, M., Neumann, C., Jansen, A.A.J., & Bwibo, N. (1989). Cognitive abilities of Kenyan children in relation to nutrition, family characteristics, and education. *Child Development, 60,* 1463–1474.

Sigman, M.D., Cohen, S.E.K., Beckwith, L., Asarnow, R., et al. (1992). The prediction of cognitive abilities at 8 and 12 years of age from neonatal assessments of preterm infants. In S.L. Friedman & M.D. Sigman (Eds.), *The psychological development of low birthweight children.* Norwood, NJ: Ablex.

Signorella, M.L., Bigler, R.S., & Liben, L. (1993). Development differences in children's gender schemata about others: A meta-analytic review. *Developmental Review, 13,* 106–126.

Signorelli, N. (1987). Children and adolescents on television: A consistent pattern of devaluation. *Journal of Early Adolescence, 7,* 255–268.

Signorielli, N. (1990). Children, television, and gender roles: Messages and impact. *Journal of Adolescent Health Care, 11,* 50–58.

Silbereisen, R., Peterson, A., Albrecht, H., & Krache, B. (1989). Maturational timing and the development of problem behavior: Longitudinal studies in adolescence. *Journal of Early Adolescence, 9,* 247.

Silverman, P.R. (1986). *Widow to widow.* New York: Springer.

Simmons, R., & Blyth, D. (1987). *Moving into adolescence.* New York: Aldine de Gruyter.

Simmons, R., Brown, L., Bush, D., & Blyth, D. (1978). Self-esteem and achievement of black and white adolescents. *Social Problems, 26,* 86–96.

Simmons, R., & Rosenberg, F. (1975). Sex, sex roles, and self-image. *Journal of Youth and Adolescence, 4,* 229–258.

Simons, M. (1995, September 11). Dutch doctors to tighten rules on mercy killings. *The New York Times,* p. A7.

Simonton, D.K. (1989). The swan-song phenomenon: Last-works effects for 172 classical composers. *Psychology and Aging, 4,* 42–47.

Simpson, J.A. (1987). The dissolution of romantic relationships: Factors involved in relationship stability and emotional distress. *Journal of Personality and Social Psychology, 53,* 683–692.

Singer, J.L., & Singer, D.G. (1983). Psychologists look at television. *American Psychologist, 38,* 826–834.

Singer, M.S., Stacey, B.G., & Lange, C. (1993). The relative utility of expectancy-value theory and social cognitive theory in predicting psychology student course goals and career aspirations. *Journal of Social Behavior and Personality, 8,* 703–714.

Singh, G.K., & Yu, S.M. (1995). Infant mortality in the United States: Trends, differentials, and projections 1950 through 2010. *The American Journal of Public Health, 85,* 957–964.

Singleton, L.C., & Asher, S.R. (1979). Racial integration and children's peer preferences. *Child Development, 50,* 936–941.

Skinner, B.F. (1957). *Verbal behavior.* New York: Appleton-Century-Crofts.

Skinner, B.F. (1975). The steep and thorny road to a science of behavior. *American Psychologist, 30,* 42–49.

Skipper, J.K., & Nass, G. (1966). Dating behavior: A framework of analysis and an illustration. *Journal of Marriage and the Family, 28,* 412–420.

Slater, A. (1995). Individual differences in infancy and later IQ. *Journal of Child Psychology and Psychiatry and Allied Disciplines, 36,* 69–112.

Slater, A., Mattock, A., & Brown, E. (1990). Size constancy at birth: Newborn infants' responses to retinal and real size. *Journal of Experimental Child Psychology, 49,* 314–322.

Sliwinski, M., Buschke, H., Kuslansky, G., & Senior, G. (1994). Proportional slowing and addition speed in old and young adults. *Psychology and Aging, 9,* 72–80.

Slobin, D. (1970). Universals of grammatical development in children. In G. Flores D'Arcais & W. Levelt (Eds.), *Advances in psycholinguistics.* New York: American Elsevier.

Small, G.W. (1991). Recognition and treatment of depression in the elderly. The clinician's challenge: Strategies for treatment of depression in the 1990s, Phoenix, Arizona. *Journal of Clinical Psychiatary, 52* (Suppl.) 11–22.

Small, G.W., Mazziotta, J.C., Collins, M.T., et al. (1995). Apolipoprotein E, type 4 allele and cerebral glucose metabolism in relatives at risk for familial Alzheimer's disease. *Journal of the American Medical Association, 273,* 942–947.

Smetana, J. (1988). Concepts of self and social convention: Adolescents' and parents' reasoning about hypothetical and actual family conflicts. In M. Gunnar (Ed.), *21st Minnesota symposium on child psychology.* Hillsdale, NJ: Erlbaum.

Smetana, J. (1989). Adolescents' and parents' reasoning about actual family conflict. *Child Development, 60,* 1052–1067.

Smetana, J.G. (1995). Parenting styles and conceptions of parental authority during adolescence. *Child Development, 66,* 299–316.

Smetana, J., Yau, J., & Hanson, S. (1991). Conflict resolution in families with adolescents. *Journal of Research on Adolescence, 1,* 189–206.

Smilansky, S.N. (1980). The concept of death among Israeli children. In A. Raviv, A. Klingman, & M. Horowitz (Eds.), *Children in situations of death and crisis.* Tel-Aviv: Atzer Hamoreh.

Smith, D. (1993). Brain, environment, and personality. *Psychological Reports, 72,* 3–13.

Smith, M. (1990). Alternative techniques. *Nursing Times, 86,* 43–45.

Smith, P.K. (1978). A longitudinal study of social participation in preschool children: Solitary and parallel play reexamined. *Developmental Psychology, 12,* 517–523.

Smith, P.K. (1995). Grandparenthood. In M.H. Bornstein (Ed.), *Handbook of parenting.* Hillsdale, NJ: Erlbaum.

Smith, T.W. (1991). Adult sexual behavior in 1989: Number of partners, frequency of intercourse, and risk of AIDS. *Family Planning, Perspectives, 23*, 102–107.

Smith, T.W. (1992). Hostility and health: Current status of a psychosomatic hypothesis. *Health Psychology, 11*, 139–150.

Smith, T.W., Christensen, A.J., Peck, J.R., & Ward, J.R. (1994). Cognitive distortion, helplessness, and depressed mood rheumatoid arthritis: A four-year longitudinal analysis. *Health Psychology, 13*, 213–217.

Smuts, A.B., & Hagen, J.W. (1985). History of the family and of child development: Introduction to Part 1. *Monographs of the Society for Research in Child Development, 50* (4–5, Serial No. 211).

Snarey, J.R. (1985). Cross-cultural universality of social-moral development. A critical review of Kohlbergian research. *Psychological Bulletin, 97*, 202–232.

Snow, C.E. (1977a). Mother's speech research: From input to interaction. In C.E. Snow & C.A. Ferguson (Eds.), *Talking to children: Language input and acquisition.* London: Cambridge University Press.

Snow, C.E. (1977b). The development of conversation between mothers and babies. *Journal of Child Language, 4*, 1–22.

Snow, R. (1969). Unfinished Pygmalion. *Contemporary Psychology, 14*, 197–199.

Snyder, M. (1974). The self-monitoring of expressive behavior. *Journal of Personality and Social Psychology, 30*, 526–537.

Snyder, M. (1987). *Public appearances/private realities: The psychology of self-monitoring.* New York: W.H. Freeman.

Snyder, R.A., Verderber, K.S., Langmeyer, L., & Myers, M. (1992). A reconsideration of self- and organization-referent attitudes as "causes" of the glass ceiling effect. *Group and Organization Management, 17*, 260–278.

Socolar, R.R.S., & Stein, R.E.K. (1995). Spanking infants and toddlers: Maternal belief and practice. *Pediatrics, 95*, 105–111.

Sohlberg, S., & Strober, M. (1994). Personality in anorexia nervosa: An update and a theoretical integration. *Acta Psychiatrica Scandinavica, 89* (Suppl. 378), 1–16.

Solomon, A. (1995, May 22). A death of one's own. *New Yorker*, pp. 54–69.

Sontag, S. (1979). The double standard of aging. In J.H. Williams (Ed.), *Psychology of women: Selected readings.* New York: W.W. Norton & Co., Inc.

Soper, D.E. (1993). Infections following cesarean section. *Current Opinion in Obstetrics and Gynecology, 5*, 517–520.

Sorensen, K. (1992). Physical and mental development of adolescent males with Klinefelter syndrome. *Hormone Research, 37* (Suppl. 3), 55–61.

Sorensen, T., Nielsen, G., Andersen, P., & Teasdale, T. (1988). Genetic and environmental influences on premature death in adult adoptees. *New England Journal of Medicine, 318*, 727–732.

Spanier, G.B., (1983). Married and unmarried cohabitation in the United States: 1980. *Journal of Marriage and the Family, 45*, 277–288.

Spear, P.D. (1993). Neural bases of visual deficits during aging. *Vision Research, 33*, 2589–2609.

Spearman, C. (1927). *The abilities of man.* London: Macmillan.

Spelke, E. (1987). The development of intermodal perception. In P. Salapatek & L. Cohen (Eds.), *Handbook of infant perception* (Vol. 2). Orlando, FL: Academic Press.

Spelke, E.S. (1991). Physical knowledge in infancy: Reflections on Piaget's theory. In S. Carey & R. Gelman (Eds.), *The epigenesis of mind.* Hillsdale, NJ: Erlbaum.

Spencer, M.B. (1991). Minority development of identity. In R.M. Lerner, A.C. Petersen, & J. Brooks-Gunn (Eds), *Encyclopedia of adolescence* (Vol. 1). New York: Garland.

Spencer, M.B., & Dornbusch, S.M. (1990). Challenges in studying minority youth. In S. Feldman & G. Elliott (Eds.), *At the threshold: The developing adolescent.* Cambridge, MA: Harvard University Press.

Spicer, J., Jackson, R., & Spragg, R. (1993). The effects of anger management and social contact on risk of myocardial infarction in Type As and Type Bs. *Psychology and Health, 8*, 243–255.

Spiegel, D. (1993). Social support: How friends, family, and groups can help. In D. Goleman & J. Gurin (Eds.), *Mind-body medicine.* Yonkers, NY: Consumer Reports Books.

Spira, A., Bajos, N., Bejin, A., & Beltzer, N. (1992). AIDS and sexual behavior in France. *Nature, 360*, 407–409.

Spitze, G., & Logan, J. (1990). More evidence on women (and men) in the middle. *Research on Aging, 12*, 182–198.

Sprecher, S., Sullivan, Q., & Hatfield, E. (1994). Mate selection preferences: Gender differences examined in a national sample. *Journal of Personality and Social Psychology, 66*, 1074–1080.

Springer, I. (1991, April 28). Afraid to feel. *Boston Globe Health*, pp. 14, 30.

Springer, S.P., & Deutsch, G. (1989). *Left brain, right brain* (3rd ed.). New York: W.H. Freeman.

Squires, S. (1991, September 17). Lifelong fitness depends on teaching children to love exercise. *Washington Post*, p. WH16.

Sroufe, L.A. (1994). Pathways to adaptation and maladaptation: Psychopathology as developmental deviation. In D. Cicchetti (Ed.), *Developmental psychopathology: Past, present, and future.* Hillsdale, NJ: Erlbaum.

Stabler, B., Clopper, R.R., Siegel, P.T., Stoppani, C., et al. (1994). Academic achievement and psychological adjustment in short children. *Developmental and Behavioral Pediatrics, 14*, 1–6.

Stack, D., & Muir, D. (1992). Adult tactile stimulation during face-to-face interactions modulates five-month-olds' affect and attention. *Child Development, 63*, 1509–1525.

Stacy, A.W., Sussman, S., Dent, C.W., Burton, D., et al. (1992). *Personality and Social Psychology Bulletin, 18*, 163–172.

Stallone, D.D., & Stunkard, A.J. (1991). The regulation of body weight: Evidence and clinical implications. *Annals of Behavioral Medicine, 13*, 220–230.

Stangor, C., Lynch, L., Changming, D., & Glass, B. (1992). Categorization of individuals on the basis of multiple social features. *Journal of Personality and Social Psychology, 62*, 207–218.

Stanjek, K. (1978). Das Uberreichen von Gaben: Funktion und Entwicklung in den ersten Lebensjahren. *Zeitschrif· fur Entwicklungspsychologie und Pedagogische Psychologie, 10*, 103–113.

Stanley, J.C. (1980). On educating the gifted. *Educational Researcher, 9*, 8–12.

Stanley, J.C., & Benbow, C.P. (1983). SMPY's first decade: Ten years of posing problems and solving them. *Journal of Special Education, 17*, 11–25.

Staub, E. (1977). A child in distress: The influence of nurturance and modeling on children's attempts to help. *Developmental Psychology, 5*, 124–133.

Staudinger, U.M., Marsiske, M., & Baltes, P.B. (1993). Resilience and levels of reserve capacity in later adulthood: Perspectives from lite-span theory. *Development and Psychopathology, 5*, 541–566.

Steele, C.M. (1992, April). Race and the schooling of Black America. *Atlantic Monthly*, pp. 68–80.

Steele, C.M., & Aronson, J. (1995). Stereotype threat and the intellectual test performance of African Americans. *Journal of Personality and Social Psychology, 69*, 797–811.

Steers, R.M., & Porter, L.W. (1991). *Motivation and work behavior* (5th ed.). New York: McGraw-Hill.

Stein, J.H., & Reiser, L.W. (1994). A study of white middle-class adolescent boys' responses to "semenarche" (the first ejaculation). *Journal of Youth and Adolescence, 23*, 373–384.

Stein, Z., Susser, M., Saenger, G., & Marolla, F. (1975). *Famine and human development: The Dutch hunger winter of 1944–1945.* New York: Oxford University Press.

Steinberg, K.K., Thacker, S.B., Smith, S.J., Stroup, D.F., et al. (1991). A meta-analysis of the effect of estrogen replacement therapy on the risk of breast cancer. *Journal of the American Medical Association, 265*, 1985–1990.

Steinberg, L. (1986). Latchkey children and the susceptibility of adolescents to antisocial peer pressure. *Child Development, 58,* 269–275.

Steinberg, L. (1990). Autonomy, conflict, and harmony in the family relationship. In S. Feldman & G. Elliott (Eds.), *At the threshold: The developing adolescent.* Cambridge, MA: Harvard University Press.

Steinberg, L. (1993). *Adolescence.* New York: McGraw-Hill.

Steinberg, L., Dornbusch, S., & Brown, B.B. (1992). Ethnic differences in adolescent achievement: An ecological perspective. *American Psychologist, 47,* 723–729.

Steinberg, L., Lamborn, S.D., Darling, N., Mounts, N., et al. (1994). Over-time changes in adjustment and competence among adolescents from authoritative, authoritarian, indulgent, and neglectful families. *Child Development, 65,* 754–770.

Steinberg L., & Silverberg, S. (1986). The vicissitudes of autonomy in early adolescence. *Child Development, 57,* 841–851.

Steiner, J.E. (1977). Facial expressions of the neonate infant indicating the hedonics of food-related chemical stimuli. In J.M. Weiffenbach (Ed.), *Taste and development.* Bethesda, MD: Department of Health, Education, and Welfare.

Steiner, J.E. (1979). Human facial expressions in response to taste and smell stimulation. *Advances in Child Development and Behavior, 13,* 257.

Steinhauer, J. (1995, April 10). Big benefits in marriage, studies say. *The New York Times,* p. A8.

Steinmetz, S.K. (1987). Family violence. In S.K. Steinmetz & M. Sussman (Eds.), *Handbook of marriage and the family.* New York: Plenum Press.

Steinmetz, S.K., & Lucca, J. (1988). Husband battering. In V. Van Hasselt, R. Morrison, A. Bellack, & M. Hersen (Eds.), *Handbook of family violence.* New York: Plenum Press.

Stephan, W.G. (1985). Intergroup relations. In G. Lindzey & E. Aronson (Eds.), *Handbook of social psychology* (Vol. 3, pp. 181–206). Hillsdale, NJ: Erlbaum.

Stephan, W.G. (1986). The effects of school desegregation: An evaluation 30 years after *Brown.* In M.J. Saks & L. Saxe (Eds.), *Advances in applied social psychology* Hillsdale, NJ: Erlbaum.

Steri, A.O., & Spelke, E.S. (1988). Haptic perception of objects in infancy. *Cognitive Psychology 20,* 1–23.

Stern, G. (1994, November, 30). Going back to college has special meaning for Mrs. McAlpin. *The Wall Street Journal,* p. A1.

Stern, M., & Karraker, K.H. (1989). Sex stereotyping of infants: A review of gender labeling studies. *Sex Roles, 20,* 501–522.

Sternberg, J., & Wagner, R.K. (1993). The g-ocentric view of intelligence and job performance is wrong. *Current Directions in Psychological Science, 2,* 1–5.

Sternberg, R.J. (1982). Reasoning, problems solving, and intelligence. In R.J. Sternberg (Ed.), *Handbook of human intelligence* (pp. 225–307). Cambridge: Cambridge University Press.

Sternberg, R.J. (1985a). *Beyond IQ: A triarchic theory of human intelligence.* New York: Cambridge University Press.

Sternberg, R.J. (1985b). Implicit theories of intelligence, creativity, and wisdom. *Journal of Personality and Social Psychology, 49,* 607–627.

Sternberg, R.J. (1986). Triangular theory of love. *Psychological Review, 93,* 119–135.

Sternberg, R.J. (1987). Liking versus loving: A comparative evaluation of theories. *Psychological Bulletin, 102,* 331–345.

Sternberg, R.J. (1988). Triangulating love. In R.J. Sternberg & M.J. Barnes (Eds.), *The psychology of love.* New Haven, CT: Yale University Press.

Sternberg, R.J. (1990). *Metaphors of mind: Conceptions of the nature of intelligence.* Cambridge: Cambridge University Press.

Sternberg, R.J. (1991). Theory-based testing of intellectual abilities: Rationale for the Sternberg triarchic abilities test. In H.A.H. Rowe (Ed.), *Intelligence: Reconceptualization and measurement.* Hillsdale, NJ: Erlbaum.

Sternberg, R.J., Conway, B.E., Ketron, J.L., & Bernstein, M. (1981). Peoples' conceptions of intelligence. *Journal of Personality and Social Psychology, 41,* 37–55.

Sternberg, R.J., & Lubart, T.I. (1992). Buy low and sell high: An investment approach to creativity. *Current Directions in Psychological Science, 1,* 1–5.

Sterns, H.L., Barrett, G.V., & Alexander, R.A. (1985). Accidents and the aging individual. In J.E. Birren & K.W. Schaie (Eds.), *Handbook of the psychology of aging* (2nd ed.). New York: Van Nostrand Reinhold.

Stevens, J.C., Cain, W.S., Demarque, A., & Ruthruff, A. (1991). On the discrimination of missing ingredients: Aging and salt flavor. *Appetite, 16,* 129–140.

Stevens-Ratchford, R.G. (1993). The effect of life review reminiscence activities on depression and self-esteem in older adults. *American Journal of Occupational Therapy, 47,* 413–420.

Stevens-Simon, C., & White, M.M. (1991). Adolescent pregnancy. *Pediatric Annals, 20,* 322–331.

Stevenson, H.W. (1992, December). Learning from Asian schools. *Scientific American,* pp. 70–75.

Stevenson, H.W., & Lee, S. (1990). Contexts of achievement: A study of American, Chinese, and Japanese children. *Research in Child Development, 55,* Nos. 1–2.

Stevenson, H.W., & Stigler, J.W. (1992). *The learning gap: Why our schools are failing and what we can learn from Japanese and Chinese education.* New York: Summit Books.

Stevenson, H.W., Chen, C., & Lee, S.Y. (1992). A comparison of the parent–child relationship in Japan and the United States. In L.L. Roopnarine & D.B. Carter (Eds.), *Parent–child socialization in diverse cultures.* Norwood, NJ: Ablex.

Steward, E.P. (1995). *Beginning writers in the zone of proximal development.* Hillsdale, NJ: Erlbaum.

Stipek, D.J., & Hoffman, J. (1980). Development of children's performance-related judgments. *Child Development, 51,* 912–914.

Stohs, J.H. (1992). Intrinsic motivation and sustained art activity among male fine and applied artists. *Creativity Research Journal, 5,* 245–252.

Stone, R., Cafferata, G.L., & Sangl, J. (1987). Caregivers of the frail elderly: A national profile. *Gerontologist, 27,* 616–626.

Storfer, M. (1990). *Intelligence and giftedness: The contributions of heredity and early environment.* San Francisco: Jossey-Bass.

Strassberg, Z., Dodge, K.A., Pettit, G.S., & Bates, J.E. (1994). Spanking in the home and children's subsequent aggression toward kindergarten peers. *Development and Psychopathology, 6,* 445–461.

Straus, M., Gelles, R., & Steinmetz, S.K. (1980). *Behind closed doors: Violence in the American family.* Garden City, NY: Anchor Press.

Straus, M.A., & Gelles, R.J. (1990). *Physical violence in American families.* New Brunswick, NJ: Transaction Books.

Streissguth, A.P., Barr, H.M., & Sampson, P.D. (1990). Moderate prenatal alcohol exposure: Effects on child IQ and learning problems at age 7-[1/2] years. *Alcohol Clinical and Experimental Research, 54,* 662–669.

Stroebe, M.S., Stroebe, W., & Hansson, R.O. (Eds.). (1993). *Handbook of bereavement: Theory, research, and intervention.* Cambridge: Cambridge University Press.

Strube, M. (Ed.). (1990). Type A behavior [Special Issue]. *Journal of Social Behavior and Personality, 5.*

Sturner, W., Sweeney, K., Callery, R., & Haley, N. (1991). Cocaine babies: The scourge of the '90s. *Journal of Forensic Sciences, 36,* 34–39.

Suarez, E.C., & Williams, R.B., Jr. (1992). Interactive models of reactivity: The relationship between hostility and potentially pathogenic physiological responses to social stressors. In N. Schneiderman, P. McCabe, & A. Baum (Eds.), *Stress and disease processes.* Hillsdale, NJ: Erlbaum.

Sugarman, S. (1988). *Piaget's construction of the child's reality.* Cambridge: Cambridge University Press.

Sugden, J. (1995, January 23). Sanctuaries for broken children. *People Weekly,* p. 39.

Sullivan, M.W., Rovee-Collier, C.K., & Tynes, D.M. (1979). A conditioning analysis of infant long-term memory. *Child Development, 50,* 152–162.

Suls, J., & Wills, T.A. (Eds.). (1991). *Social comparison: Contemporary theory and research.* Hillsdale, NJ: Erlbaum.

Sulzer-Azaroff, B., & Mayer, R. (1991). *Behavior analysis and lasting change.* New York: Holt.

Sung, B.L. (1985). Bicultural conflicts in Chinese immigrant children. *Journal of Comparative Family Studies, 16,* 255–270.

Sung, I.K., Borh, B., & Oh, W. (1993). Growth and neurodevelopmental outcome of very low birth weight infants with intrauterine growth retardation: Comparison with control subjects matched by birth weight and gestational age. *Journal of Pediatrics, 123,* 618–624.

Super, C.M. (1976). Environmental effects on motor development: A case of African infant precocity. *Developmental Medicine and Child Neurology, 18,* 561–576.

Super, C.M., & Harkness, S. (1982). The infant's niche in rural Kenya and metropolitan America. In L. Adler (Ed.), *Issues in cross-cultural research.* New York: Academic Press.

Suro, R. (1992, May 26). For women, varied reasons for single motherhood. *The New York Times,* p. A12.

Surra, C.A. (1991). Mate selection and premarital relationships. In A. Booth (Ed.), *Contemporary families* (pp. 54–57). Minneapolis, MN: National Council on Family Relations.

Suskind, R. (1994, September 24). Class struggle: Poor, black, and smart. *The New York Times,* p. A1.

Sussman, S.K., & Sussman, M.B. (Eds.). (1991). *Families: Intergenerational and generational connections.* Binghamton, NY: Haworth.

Swanson, L.A., Leonard, L.B., & Gandour, J. (1992). Vowel duration in mothers' speech to young children. *Journal of Speech and Hearing Research, 35,* 617–625.

Tajfel, H. (1982). *Social identity and intergroup relations.* London: Cambridge University Press.

Takahashi, K. (1986). Examining the strange situation procedure with Japanese mothers and 12-month-old infants. *Developmental Psychology, 22,* 265–270.

Takahashi, K. (1990). Are the key assumptions of the "strange situation" procedure universal? A view from Japanese research. *Human Development, 33,* 23–30.

Talkington-Boyer, S., & Snyder, D.K. (1994). Assessing impact on family caregivers to Alzheimer's disease patients. *American Journal of Family Therapy, 22,* 57–66.

Tamis-LeMonda, C.S., & Bornstein, M.H. (1993). Antecedents of exploratory competence at one year. *Infant Behavior and Development, 16,* 423–439.

Tannen, D. (1991). *You just don't understand.* New York: Ballantine.

Tanner, J. (1972). Sequence, tempo, and individual variation in growth and development of boys and girls aged twelve to sixteen. In J. Kagan & R. Coles (Eds.), *Twelve to sixteen: Early adolescence.* New York: W.W. Norton & Co., Inc.

Tanner, J.M. (1978). *Education and physical growth* (2nd ed.). New York: International Universities Press.

Tate, D.C., Reppucci, N.D., & Mulvey, E.P. (1995). Violent juvenile delinquents: Treatment effectiveness and implications for future action. *American Psychologist, 50,* 777–781.

Tavris, C., & Sadd, S. (1977). *The Redbook report on female sexuality.* New York: Delacorte.

Taylor, M.S., Locke, E.A., Lee, C., & Gist, M.E., (1984). Type A behavior and faculty research productivity: What are the mechanisms? *Organizational Behavior and Human Performance, 34,* 402–418.

Taylor, R.J., Chatters, L.M., Tucker, M.B., & Lewis, E. (1991). Developments in research on black families. In A. Booth (Ed.), *Contemporary families.* Minneapolis, MN: National Council on Family Relations.

Taylor, S.E. (1991). *Health psychology* (2nd ed.). New York: McGraw-Hill.

Tegano, D.W., Lookabaugh, S., May, G.E., & Burdette, M.P. (1991). Constructive play and problem solving: The role of structure and time in the classroom. *Early Child Development and Care, 68,* 27–35.

Tellegen, A., Lykken, D.T., Bouchard, T.J., Jr., Wilcox, K.J., Segal, N.L., & Rich, S. (1988). Personality similarity in twins reared apart and together. *Journal of Personality and Social Psychology, 54,* 1031–1039.

Terman, L.M., & Oden, M.H. (1959). *The gifted group at mid-life: Thirty-five years' follow-up of the superior child.* Stanford, CA: Stanford University Press.

Termine, N.T., & Izard, C.E. (1988). Infants' responses to their mothers' expressions of joy and sadness. *Developmental Psychology, 24,* 223–229.

Terry, D. (1994, December 12). When the family heirloom is homicide. *The New York Times,* pp. A1, B7.

Terry, R.D. (Ed.). (1994). *Alzheimer's disease.* New York: Raven Press.

Tharp, R.G. (1989). Psychocultural variables and constants: Effects on teaching and learning in schools: Special Issue: Children and their development: Knowledge base, research agenda, and social policy application. *American Psychologist, 44,* 349–359.

The world factbook. (1994). The Central Intelligence Agency: Washington, DC.

Thelen, E. (1979). Rhythmical stereotypes in normal human infants. *Animal Behavior, 27,* 699–715.

Thelen, E. (1994). Three-month-old infants can learn task-specific patterns of interlimb coordination. *Psychological Science, 5,* 280–285.

Thelen, E. (1995). Motor development: A new synthesis. *American Psychologist, 50,* 79–95.

Thoman, E.B. (1990). Sleeping and waking states in infants: A functional perspective. *Neuroscience and Biobehavioral Review, 14,* 93–107.

Thoman, E.B., & Whitney, M.P. (1989). Sleep states of infants monitored in the home: Individual differences, developmental trends, and origins of diurnal cyclicity. *Infant Behavior and Development, 12,* 59–75.

Thoman, E.B., & Whitney, M.P. (1990). Behavioral states in infants: Individual differences and individual analyses. In J. Colombo & J. Fagen (Eds.), *Individual differences in infancy: Reliability, stability, prediction* (pp. 113–136). Hillsdale, NJ: Erlbaum.

Thomas, A., & Chess, S. (1977). *Temperament and development.* New York: Brunner/Mazel.

Thomas, A., & Chess, S. (1980). *The dynamics of psychological development.* New York: Brunner/Mazel.

Thomas, A., & Chess, S. (1984). Genesis and evolution of behavioral disorders: From infancy to early adult life. *American Journal of Orthopsychiatry, 141*(1), 1–9.

Thomas, A., Chess, S., & Birch, H.G. (1968). *Temperament and behavior disorders in children.* New York: New York University Press.

Thomas, C.B., Duszynski, K.R., & Schaffer, J.W. (1979). Family attitudes reported in youth as potential predictors of cancer. *Psychosomatic Medicine, 4,* 287–302.

Thomas, J. (1986). Gender differences in satisfaction with grandparenting. *Psychology and Aging, 1,* 215–219.

Thomas, P. (1994, September 6). Washington's infant mortality rate, more than twice the U.S. average, reflects urban woes. *The Wall Street Journal,* p. A14.

Thompson, L.A., Fagen, J.F., & Fulker, D.W. (1991). Longitudinal prediction of specific cognitive abilities from infant novelty preference. *Child Development, 62,* 530–538.

Thompson, P. (1993). "I don't feel old": The significance of the search for meaning in later life. *International Journal of Geriatric Psychiatry, 8,* 685–692.

Thoreson, C.E., & Low, K.G. (1990). Women and the Type A behavior pattern: Review and commentary. *Journal of Social Behavior and Personality, 5,* 117–133.

Thornburg, K.R., Pearl, P., Crompton, D., & Ispa, J.M. (1990). Development of kindergarten children based on child care arrangements. *Early Childhood Research Quarterly, 5,* 27–42.

Thorne, B. (1986). Girls and boys together, but mostly apart. In W.W. Hartup & Z. Rubin (Eds.), *Relationships and development* (pp. 167–184). Hillsdale, NJ: Erlbaum.

Thorpe, J.A., Hu, D.H., Albin, R.M., McNitt, J., et al. (1993). The effect of intrapartum epidural analgesia on nulliparous labor: A randomized, controlled prospective trial. *American Journal of Obstetrics & Gynecology, 169,* 851–858.

Thorsheim, H.I., & Roberts, B.B. (1990). *Reminiscing together: Ways to help us keep mentally fit as we grow older.* Minneapolis: CompCare Publishers.

Time (1980, September 8). People section.

Tobin, J.J., Wu, D.Y.H., & Davidson, D.H. (1989). *Preschool in three cultures: Japan, China, and the United States.* New Haven, CT: Yale University Press.

Toch, T. (1995, January 2). Kids and marijuana: The glamour is back. *U.S. News & World Report,* p. 12.

Toda, S., & Fogel, A. (1993). Infant response to the still-face situation at 3 and 6 months. *Developmental Psychology, 29,* 532–538.

Tomlinson-Keasey, C. (1985). *Child development: Psychological, sociological, and biological factors.* Homewood, IL: Dorsey.

Topolnicki, D.M. (1995, January). The real immigrant story: Making it big in America. *Money,* pp. 129–138.

Touwen, B.C.L. (1984). Primitive reflexes—conceptual or semantic problem? In H.F.R. Prechtl (Ed.), *Continuity of neural functions from prenatal to postnatal life* (pp. 115–125). Philadelphia: Lippincott.

Townsend, A., Noelker, L., Deimling, G., & Bass, D. (1989). Longitudinal impact of interhousehold caregiving on adult children's mental health. *Psychology and Aging, 4,* 393–401.

Treas, J., & Bengtson, V.L. (1987). The family in later years. In M.B. Sussman & S.K. Steinmetz (Eds.), *Handbook of marriage and the family.* New York: Plenum Press.

Treasure, J., & Tiller, J. (1993). The aetiology of eating disorders: Its biological basis. *International Review of Psychiatry, 5,* 23–31.

Treffers, P.E., Eskes, M., Kleiverda, G., & van Alten, D. (1990). Home births and minimal medical interventions. *Journal of the American Medical Association, 262* (7), 2203, 2207–2208.

Trehub, S.E., Schneider, B.A., Morrongiello, B.A., & Thorpe, L.A. (1988). Auditory sensitivity in school-age children. *Journal of Experimental Child Psychology, 46,* 272–285.

Trehub, S.E., Schneider, B.A., Morrongiello, B.A., & Thorpe, L.A. (1989). Developmental changes in high-frequency sensitivity. *Audiology, 28,* 241–249.

Trehub, S.E., Thorpe, L.A., & Morrongiello, B.A. (1985). Infants' perception of melodies: Changes in a single tone. *Infant Behavior & Development, 8,* 213–223.

Triandis, H.C. (1994). *Culture and social behavior.* New York: McGraw-Hill.

Triandis, H.C. (1995). *Individualism and collectivism.* Boulder, CO: Westview Press.

Trippet, S.E. (1991). Being aware: The relationship between health and social support among older women. *Journal of Women and Aging, 3,* 69–80.

Troiano, R.P., Flegal, K.M., Kuczmarski, R.J., Campbell, S.M., et al. (1995). Overweight prevalence and trends for children and adolescents: The National Health and Nutrition Examination Surveys, 1963–1992. *Archives of Pediatric and Adolescent Medicine, 10,* 1085–1091.

Troll, L.E. (1985). *Early and middle adulthood* (2nd ed.). Monterey, CA: Brooks/Cole.

Troll, L.E. (1986). Parents and children in later life. *Generations, 10,* 23–25.

Troll, L.E. (1989). Myths of midlife intergenerational relationships. In S. Hunter & M. Sundel (Eds.), *Midlife myths.* Newbury Park, CA: Sage.

Tronick, E.Z. (1995). Touch in mother–infant interactions. In T.M. Field (Ed.), *Touch in early development.* Hillsdale, NJ: Erlbaum.

Tronick, E.Z., & Gianino, A.F. (1986). The transmission of maternal depression to the infant. In E.Z. Tronick & T. Field (Eds.), *Maternal depression and infant disturbance.* San Francisco: Jossey Bass.

Tronick, E.Z., Thomas, R.B., & Daltabuit, M. (1994). The Quechua manta pouch: A caretaking practice for buffering the Peruvian infant against the multiple stressors of high altitude. *Child Development, 65,* 1005–1013.

Tucker, J.S. (1993). *The association of marital status with mortality across the life span for females and males.* Unpublished doctoral dissertation, University of California, Riverside.

Tucker, M.B., & Mitchell-Kernan, C. (1995). *The decline in marriage among African Americans.* New York: Russell Sage Foundation.

Tucker, P., & Aron, A. (1993). Passionate love and marital satisfaction at key transition points in the family life cycle. *Journal of Social and Clinical Psychology, 12,* 135–147.

Tulving, E., & Thompson, D.M. (1973). Encoding specificity and retrieval processes in episodic memory. *Psychological Review, 80,* 352–373.

Turner, J.S., & Helms, D.B. (1994). *Contemporary adulthood* (5th ed.). Fort Worth, TX: Harcourt Brace.

Turner, J.S., & Helms, D.B. (1995). *Lifespan development* (5th ed.). Fort Worth, TX: Harcourt Brace College Publishers.

Turner, P.H., Scadden, L., & Harris, M.B. (1990). Parenting in gay and lesbian families. *Journal of Gay and Lesbian Psychotherapy, 1,* 55–66.

Turner, P.J., Gervai, J., & Hinde, R.A. (1993). Gender-typing in young children: Preferences, behavior and cultural differences. *British Journal of Developmental Psychology, 11,* 323–342.

Turner, P.J., & Gervai, J. (1995). A multidimensional study of gender typing in preschool children and their parents: Personality, attitudes, preferences, behavior, and cultural differences. *Developmental Psychology, 31,* 759–772.

U.S. Advisory Board on Child Abuse and Neglect. (1995). *A nation's shame: Fatal child abuse and neglect in the United States.* Washington, DC: Superintendent of Documents.

U.S. Bureau of Labor Statistics. (1993). *Average wages earned by women compared to men.* Washington, DC: U.S. Department of Labor.

U.S. Bureau of Labor Statistics. (1995). *Workforce demographics and makeup.* Washington, DC: U.S. Department of Labor.

U.S. Bureau of the Census. (1990a). *Statistical Abstract of the United States: 1990* (110th ed.). Washington, DC: U.S. Government Printing Office.

U.S. Bureau of the Census. (1990b). *Studies in marriage and the family: Single parents and their children* (Current Population Reports, Series P-23, No. 167). Washington, DC: U.S. Government Printing Office.

U.S. Bureau of the Census. (1990c). *Current population reports* (pp. 25–917, 25–1095). Washington, DC: U.S. Government Printing Office.

U.S. Bureau of the Census. (1990d). *Statistical abstract of the United States* (110th ed.). Washington, DC: U.S. Government Printing Office.

U.S. Bureau of the Census. (1991a). *Statistical abstract of the United States: 1991* (111th ed.) Washington, DC: U.S. Government Printing Office.

U.S. Bureau of the Census. (1991b). *Population profile of the United States: 1991* (Current Population Reports, Series P-23, No. 173). Washington, DC: U.S. Government Printing Office.

U.S. Bureau of the Census. (1991c). *Studies in household formation: Remarriage among women in the United States* (Current Population Reports, Series P-23, No. 169). Washington, DC: U.S. Government Printing Office.

U.S. Bureau of the Census. (1991d). Population profile of the United States: 1991. *Current population reports* (Series P-23, No. 173). Washington, DC: U.S. Government Printing Office.

U.S. Bureau of the Census. (1992). Poverty in the United States: 1991. *Current population reports* (Series P-60, No. 181). Washington, DC: U.S. Government Printing Office.

U.S. Bureau of the Census. (1993). *Child health USA.* Washington, DC: U.S. Government Printing Office.

U.S. Bureau of the Census. (1994). Household statistics, 1993. *Current population reports.* Washington, DC: Author.

U.S. Commission on Civil Rights. (1983). *Statistics of minority groups.* Washington, DC: Author.

U.S. Department of Agriculture. (1992). *Dietary guidelines.* Washington, DC: Author.

U.S. Department of Education. (1988). *James Madison Elementary School: A curriculum for American students.* Washington, DC: U.S. Government Printing Office

U.S. Department of Education. (1992, April). *Experiences in child care and early childhood programs of first and second graders.* Washington, DC: National Center for Education Statistics.

U.S. Department of Education, Office of Special Education and Rehabilitative Services. (1987). *Eighth Annual Report to Congress on the Implementation of the Education of the Handicapped Act, 1986.* Washington, DC: U.S. Government Printing Office.

U.S. Department of Labor. (1992). *Occupational outlook handbook.* Washington, DC: U.S. Government Printing Office.

U.S. National Center for Health Statistics. (1994). *Vital statistics of the United States. Annual.* Washington, DC: U.S. Government Printing Office.

U.S. Surgeon General. (1988). *Report on nutrition and health.* Washington, DC: U.S. Government Printing Office.

Ubell, E. (1995, February 12). Sex-education programs that work—and some that don't. *Parade Magazine,* pp. 18–20.

Uchitelle, L. (1994, November 28). Women in their 50's follow man paths into workplace. *The New York Times,* pp. A1, B8.

Uhlenberg, P., Cooney, T., & Boyd, R. (1990). Divorce for women after midlife. *Journal of Gerontology, 45* (1), S3–S11.

UNESCO (1990). *Compendium of statistics on illiteracy,* No. 31. Paris: Author.

Unger, R., Kreeger, L., & Christoffel, K.K. (1990). Childhood obesity. Medical and familial correlates and age of onset. *Clinical Pediatrics, 29,* 368–373.

Unger, R., & Crawford, M. (1992). *Women and gender.* New York: McGraw-Hill.

Ungrady, D. (1992, October 19). Getting physical: Fitness experts are helping shape up young America. *Washington Post,* p. B5.

United Nations. (1990). *Declaration of the world summit for children.* New York: Author.

United Nations. (1994). *World social situation in the 1990s.* New York: United Nations Publications.

University of Michigan. (1994). *Monitoring the future study.* Ann Arbor: University of Michigan Press.

Unruh, D. (1989). Toward a social psychology of reminiscence. In D. Unruh & G.S. Livings (Eds.), *Personal history through the life course.* Greenwich, CT: JAI Press.

Urberg, K.A. (1982). The development of the concepts of masculinity and femininity in young children. *Sex Roles, 8,* 659–668.

Usdansky, M.L. (1992, July 17). Wedded to the single life: Attitudes, economy delaying marriages. *USA Today,* p. A8.

USDHHS (U.S. Department of Health and Human Services). (1990). *Health United States (1989)* (DHHS Publication No. PHS 90–1232). Washington, DC: U.S. Government Printing Office.

Vaillant, G.E. (1977). *Adaptation to life.* Boston: Little, Brown.

Vaillant, G.E., & Vaillant, C.O. (1981). Natural history of male psychological health: X. Work as a predictor of positive mental health. *The American Journal of Psychiatry, 138,* 1433–1440.

Vaillant, P.E., & Vaillant, C.O. (1990). Natural history of male psychological health: XII. A 45-year study of predictors of successful aging. *American Journal of Psychiatry, 147* (1), 31–37.

van den Hoonaard, D.K. (1994). Paradise lost: Widowhood in a Florida retirement community. *Journal of Aging Studies, 8,* 121–132.

Van Manen, S., & Pietromonaco, P. (1993). *Acquaintance and consistency influence memory from interpersonal information.* Unpublished manuscript. University of Massachusetts at Amherst.

Van Riper, C. (1972). *Speech correction: Principles and methods.* Englewood Cliffs, NJ: Prentice-Hall.

Vandell, D.L., & Hembree, S.E. (1994). Peer social status and friendship: Independent contributors to children's social and academic adjustment. *Merrill-Palmer Quarterly, 40,* 461–477.

Van Evra, J. (1990). *Television and child development.* Hillsdale, NJ: Erlbaum.

Van Tassel-Baska, J., Olszewski-Kubilius, P., & Kulieke, M. (1994). A study of self-concept and social support in advantaged and disadvantaged seventh and eighth grade gifted students. *Roeper Review, 16,* 186–191.

Vaughn, B.E., Lefever, G.B., Seifer, R., & Barglow, P. (1989). Attachment behavior, attachment security, and temperament during infancy. *Child Development, 60,* 728–737.

Vaughn, B.E., Stevenson-Hinde, J., Waters, E., Kotsaftis, A., et al. (1992). Attachment security and temperament in infancy and early childhood: Some conceptual clarifications. *Developmental Psychology, 28,* 463–473.

Vaughn, V., McKay, R.J., & Behrman, R. (1979). *Nelson textbook of pediatrics* (11th ed.). Philadelphia: Saunders.

Veatch, R.M. (1984). Brain death. In E.S. Shneidman (Ed.), *Death: Current perspectives* (3rd ed.) Palo Alto, CA: Mayfield.

Verbrugge, L.M. (1985). Gender and health: An update on hypotheses and evidence. *Journal of Health and Social Behavior, 26,* 156–182.

Vercellini, P., Zuliani, G., Rognoni, M., Trespidi, L., et al. (1993). Pregnancy at forty and over: A case-control study. *European Journal of Obstetrics, Gynecology, & Reproductive Biology, 48,* 191–195.

Vernberg, E.M. (1990). Psychological adjustment and experiences with peers during early adolescence: Reciprocal, incidental, or unidirectional relationships? *Journal of Abnormal Child Psychology, 18,* 187–198.

Vernon, J.A. (1990). Media stereotyping: A comparison of the way elderly women and men are portrayed on prime-time television. *Journal of Women and Aging, 2,* 55–68.

Vihman, M.M. (1991). Early syllables and the construction of phonology. In C.A. Ferguson, L. Menn, & C. Stoel-Gammon (Eds.), *Phonological development: Models, research, implications* (pp. 69–84). Hillsdale, NJ: Erlbaum.

Vincze, M. (1971). Examinations on the social contacts between infants and young children reared together. *Magyar Pszichologiai Szemle, 28,* 58–61.

Vitaliano, P.P., Dougherty, C.M., & Siegler, I.C. (1994). Biopsychosocial risks for cardiovascular disease in spouse caregivers of persons with Alzheimer's disease. In R.P. Abeles, H.C. Gift, & M.G. Ory (Eds.), *Aging and quality of life.* New York: Springer.

Vitaro, F., & Pelletier, D. (1991). Assessment of children's social problem-solving skills in hypothetical and actual conflict situations. *Journal of Abnormal Child Psychology, 19,* 505–518.

Volling, B.L., & Belsky, J. (1992). The contribution of mother–child and father–child relationships to the quality of sibling interaction: A longitudinal study. *Child Development, 63,* 1209–1222.

Volling, B.L., Mackinnon-Lewis, C., Rabiner, D., & Baradaran, L.P. (1993). Children's social competence and sociometric status: Further exploration of aggression, social withdrawal, and peer rejection. *Development and Psychopathology, 5,* 459–483.

Vondra, J.I., Barnett, D., & Cicchetti, D. (1990). Self-concept, motivation, and competence among preschoolers from maltreating and comparison families. *Child Abuse and Neglect, 14,* 525–540.

Vygotsky, L.S. (1962). *Selected psychological investigations.* Moscow: Izdstel'sto Akademii Pedagogicheskikh Nauk SSSR.

Vygotsky, L.S. (1979). *Mind in society: The development of higher mental processes.* Cambridge, MA: Harvard University Press. (Original works published 1930, 1933, and 1935)

Vygotsky, L.S. (1986). *Thought and language* (A. Kozulin, Trans.). Cambridge, MA: MIT Press. (Original work published 1934).

Wachs, T.D. (1992). *The nature of nurture.* Newbury Park, CA: Sage.

Wachs, T.D. (1993). The nature–nurture gap: What we have here is a failure to collaborate. In R. Plomin & G.E. McClearn (Eds.), *Nature, nurture, and psychology.* Washington, DC: American Psychological Association.

Wadsworth, B.J. (1971). *Piaget's theory of cognitive development.* New York: Longman.

Wagner, R.K., & Sternberg, R.J. (1985). Alternate conceptions of intelligence and their implications for education. *Review of Educational Research, 54,* 179–223.

Wagner, R.K., & Sternberg, R.J. (1986). Tacit knowledge and intelligence in the everyday world. In R.J. Sternberg & R.K. Wagner (Eds.), *Practical intelligence: Nature and orgins of competence in the everyday world.* Cambridge: Cambridge University Press.

Wagner, R.K., & Sternberg, R.J. (1991). *Tacit knowledge inventory.* San Antonio, TX: The Psychological Corporation.

Walden, T.A., & Baxter, A. (1989). The effect of context and age on social referencing. *Child Development, 60,* 1230–1240.

Walden, T.A., & Ogan, T.A. (1988). The development of social referencing. *Child Development, 59,* 1230–1240.

Walker, A.J., & Pratt, C.C. (1991). Daughters' help to mothers: Intergenerational aid versus caregiving. *Journal of Marriage and the Family, 53,* 3–12.

Walker, A.J., Thompson, L., & Morgan, C.S. (1987). Two generations of mothers and daughters: Role position and interdependence. *Psychology of Women Quarterly, 11,* 195–208.

Walker, I., & Mann, L. (1987). Unemployment, relative deprivation, and social protest. *Personality and Social Psychology Bulletin, 13,* 275–283.

Walker, L. (1984). *The battered woman syndrome.* New York: Springer.

Walker, L.E. (1989). Psychology and violence against women. *American Psychologist, 44,* 695–702.

Walker-Andrews, A.S., & Grolnick, W. (1983). Infants' discrimination of vocal expressions. *Infant Behavior and Development, 6,* 491–498.

Walker-Andrews, A.S., & Lennon, E. (1991). Infants' discrimination of vocal expressions: Contributions of auditory and visual information. *Infant Behavior and Development, 14,* 131–142.

Waller, N.G., Kojetin, B.A., Bouchard, T.J., Jr., Lykken, D.T., et al. (1990). Genetic and environmental influences on religious interests, attitudes, and values: A study of twins reared apart and together. *Psychological Science, 1,* 138–142.

Wallerstein, J.S., & Kelly, J.B. (1989). *Second chances: Men, women, and children a decade after divorce.* New York: Ticknor & Fields.

Wallis, C. (1995, June 26.) The estrogen dilemma. *Time,* pp. 46–53.

Wallis, C. (1994, July 18). Life in overdrive. *Time,* pp. 42–50.

Walster, H.E., & Walster, G.W. (1978). *Love.* Reading, MA: Addison-Wesley.

Walters, E., & Gardner, H. (1986). The theory of multiple intelligences: Some issues and answers. In R.J. Sternberg & R.K. Wagner (Eds.), *Practical intelligence.* Cambridge: Cambridge University Press.

Wang, J., & Kaufman, A.S. (1993). Changes in fluid and crystallized intelligence across the 20- to 90-year age range on the K-BIT. *Journal of Psychoeducational Assessment, 11,* 29–37.

Wang, M.C., Peverly, S.T., & Catalano, R. (1987). Integrating special needs students in regular classes: Programming, implementation, and policy issues. *Advances in Special Education, 6,* 119–149.

Wang, Z.W., Black, D., Andreasen, N.C., & Crowe, R.R. (1993). A linkage study of chromosome 11q in schizophrenia. *Archives of General Psychiatry, 50,* 212–216.

Ward, R.A. (1984). *The aging experience: An introduction to social gerontology* (2nd ed.). New York: Harper & Row.

Warrick, P. (1991, October 30). What the doctors have to say. *Los Angeles Times,* p. E4.

Wasserman, A.L., Thompson, E.I., Wilimas, J.A., & Fairclough, D. (1967). *Middle age.* London: BBC.

Watanabe, T. (1992, September 14). A lesson for Japan's kids: Play! *Los Angeles Times,* p. 111.

Waterman, A. (1982). Identity development from adolescence to adulthood: An extension of theory and a review of research. *Developmental Psychology, 18,* 341–358.

Waterman, A., & Waterman, M. (1981). A longitudinal study of changes in ego identity status during the freshman year at college. *Developmental Psychology, 5,* 167–173.

Watson, J.B., & Rayner, R. (1920). Conditioned emotional reactions. *Journal of Experimental Psychology, 3,* 1–14.

Weber, K.S., Frankenberger, W., & Heilman, K. (1992). The effects of Ritalin on the academic achievement of children diagnosed with attention-deficit hyperactivity disorder. *Developmental Disabilities Bulletin, 20,* 49–68.

Webster, R.A., Hunter, M., & Keats, J.A. (1994). Peer and parental influences on adolescents' substance use: A path analysis. *International Journal of the Addictions, 29,* 647–657.

Wechsler, D. (1975). Intelligence defined and undefined. *American Psychologist, 30,* 135–139.

Wechsler, H., Davenport, A., Dowdall, G., Moeykens, B., et al. (1994). Health and behavioral consequences of binge drinking in college: A national survey of students at 140 campuses. *Journal of the American Medical Association, 272,* 1672–1677.

Wechsler, H., Isaac, N.E., Grodstein, F., & Sellers, D.E. (1994). Continuation and initiation of alcohol use from the first to the second year of college. *Journal of the Study of Alcohol, 55,* 41–45.

Wechsler, H., Rohman, M., & Solomon, R. (1981). Emotional problems and concerns of New England college students. *American Journal of Orthopsychiatry, 51,* 719.

Weed, K., Ryan, E.B., & Day, J. (1990). Metamemory and attributions as mediators of strategy use and recall. *Journal of Educational Psychology, 82,* 849–855.

Wegman, M.E. (1993). Annual summary of vital statistics—1992. *Pediatrics, 92,* 743–754.

Weinberg, R.A. (1989). Intelligence and IQ: Landmark issues and great debates. *American Psychologist, 44* (2), 98–104.

Weiner, B. (1985). *Human motivation.* New York: Springer-Verlag.

Weiner, B. (1994). Integrating social and personal theories of achievement striving. *Review of Educational Research, 64,* 557–573.

Welker, W.J. (1991). Is sparing the rod a wise, or ill-advised strategy? *Pediatric News, 25,* 5.

Wellman, H.M. (1990). *The child's theory of mind.* Cambridge, MA: MIT Press.

Wellman, H.M., & Gelman, S.A. (1992). Cognitive development: Foundational theories of core domains. *Annual Review of Psychology, 43,* 337–375.

Wells, A.S., & Crain, R.L. (1994). Perpetuation theory and the long-term effects of school desegregation. *Review of Educational Research, 64,* 531–555.

Werner, E.E. (1972). Infants around the world: Cross-cultural studies of psychomotor development from birth to two years. *Journal of Cross-Cultural Psychology, 3,* 111–134.

Werner, E.E. (1993). Risk resilience and recovery: Perspectives from the Kauai Longitudinal Study. *Development and Psychopathology, 5,* 503–515.

Werner, E.E. (1995). Resilience in development. *Current Directions in Psychological Science, 4,* 81–85.

Werner, E.E., & Smith, R.S. (1992). *Overcoming the odds: High-risk children from birth to adulthood.* Ithaca, NY: Cornell University Press.

Wertsch, J.V., & Tulviste, P. (1992). L.S. Vygotsky and contemporary developmental psychology. *Developmental Psychology, 28,* 548–557.

Westen, D. (1990). Psychoanalytic approaches to personality. In L.A. Previn (Ed.), *Handbook of personality: Theory and research.* New York: Guilford Press.

Wheeden, A., Scafidi, F.A., Field, T., & Ironson, G., (1993). Massage effects on cocaine-exposed preterm neonates. *Journal of Developmental and Behavioral Pediatrics, 14,* 318–322.

Whitbourne, S., Jacobo, M., & Munoz-Ruiz, M. (1996). Adversity in the elderly. In R.S. Feldman (Ed.), *The psychology of adversity.* Amherst: University of Massachusetts Press.

Whitbourne, S.K. (1986). *Adult development* (2nd ed). New York: Praeger.

Whitbourne, S.K. (1990). Sexuality in the aging male. *Generations, 14,* 28–30.

Whitbourne, S.K., Zuschlag, M.K., Elliot, L.B., & Waterman, A.S. (1992). Psychosocial development in adulthood: A 22-year sequential study. *Journal of Personality and Social Psychology, 63,* 260–271.

Whitbourne, S.K., & Wills, K. (1993). Psychological issues in institutional care of the aged. In S.B. Goldsmith (Ed.), *Long-term care.* Gaithersburg, MD: Aspen.

Whiting, B.B., & Edwards, C.P. (1988). *Children of different worlds: The formation of social behavior.* Cambridge, MA: Harvard University Press.

Wideman, M.V., & Singer, J.F. (1984). The role of psychological mechanisms in preparation for childbirth. *American Psychologist, 34,* 1357–1371.

Widom, C.S. (1989). Does violence beget violence? A critical examination of the literature. *Psychological Bulletin, 106,* 3–28.

Wierson, M., & Forehand, R. (1994). Parent behavioral training for child noncompliance: Rationale, concepts, and effectiveness. *Current Directions in Psychological Science, 3,* 146–150.

Wierson, M., Long, P.J., & Forehand, R.L. (1993). Toward a new understanding of early menarche: The role of environmental stress in pubertal timing. *Adolescence, 28,* 913–924.

Wilcox, A., Skjaerven, R., Buekens, P., & Kiely, J. (1995). Birth weight and perinatal mortality: A comparison of the United States and Norway. *Journal of the American Medical Association, 273,* 709–711.

Wilcox, M.D. (1992). Boomerang kids. *Kiplinger's Personal Finance Magazine, 46,* 83–86.

Williams, B.C. (1990). Immunization coverage among preschool children: The United States and selected European countries. *Pediatrics, 86,* 1052–1056.

Williams, B.C., & Miller, C.A. (1992). Preventive health care for young children: Findings from a 10-country study and directions for United States policy. *Pediatrics, 89* (Suppl.).

Williams, D., & Griffen, L. (1991). Elder abuse in the black family. In R. Hampton (Ed.), *Black family violence: Current research and theory.* Lexington, MA: Lexington Books.

Williams, R.B., Jr. (1993). Hostility and the heart. In D. Goleman & J. Gurin (Eds.), *Mind-body medicine.* Yonkers, NY: Consumer Reports Books.

Williamson, G.M., & Schulz, R. (1993). Coping with specific stressors in Alzheimer's disease caregiving. *Gerontologist, 33,* 747–755.

Willis, S.L. (1985). Educational psychology of the older adult learner. In J.E. Birren & K.W. Schaie (Eds.), *Handbook of the psychology of aging* (2nd ed.). New York: Van Nostrand Reinhold.

Willis, S.L., Jay, G.M., Diehl, M., & Marsiske, M. (1992). Longitudinal change and prediction of everyday task competence in the elderly. *Research on Aging, 14,* 68–91.

Willis, S.L., & Nesselroade, C.S. (1990). Long-term effects of fluid ability training in old-old age. *Developmental Psychology, 26,* 905–910.

Willis, S.L., & Schaie, K.W. (1986). Training the elderly on the ability factors of spatial orientation and inductive reasoning. *Psychology and Aging, 1,* 239–247.

Wilson, M.N. (1989). Child development in the context of the black extended family. *American Psychologist, 44,* 380–385.

Wilson, R.S. (1983). The Louisville Twin Study: Developmental synchronies in behavior. *Child Development, 54,* 298–316.

Windle, M. (1994). A study of friendship characteristics and problem behaviors among middle adolescents. *Child Development, 65,* 1764–1777.

Wineburg, S.S. (1987). The self-fulfillment of the self-fulfilling prophecy. *Educational Researcher, 16,* 28–37.

Winn, R.L., & Newton, N. (1982). Sexuality in aging: A study of 106 cultures. *Archives of Sexual Behavior, 11,* 283–298.

Wisnia, S. (1994, June 27). On the right track. *Washington Post,* p. D5.

Witelson, S. (1989, March). *Sex differences.* Paper presented at the annual meeting of the New York Academy of Science, New York.

Wolf, A.M., Gortmaker, S.L., Cheung, L., & Gray, H.M. (1993). Activity, inactivity, and obesity: Racial, ethnic, and age differences among schoolgirls. *American Journal of Public Health, 83,* 1625–1627.

Wolff, P.H. (1963). Observations of the early development of smiling. In B.M. Foss (Ed.), *Determinants of infant behaviour* (Vol 4). London: Methuen.

Wolfson, C., Handfield-Jones, R., Glass, K.C., McClaran, J., et al. (1993). Adult children's perceptions of their responsibility to provide care for dependent elderly parents. *Gerontologist, 33,* 315–323.

Wood, J. (1989). Theory and research concerning social comparisons of personal attributes. *Psychological Bulletin, 106,* 231–248.

Wood, W., Wong, F.Y., & Chachere, J.G. (1991). Effects of media violence on viewers' aggression in unconstrained social interaction. *Psychological Bulletin, 109,* 371–383.

Woolfolk, A.E. (1993). *Educational psychology* (5th ed.). Boston: Allyn & Bacon.

World Conference on Education for All. (1990, April). *World Declaration on Education for All and Framework for Action to Meet Basic Learning Needs:* Preamble (p. 1). New York: Author.

World Food Council. (1992). *The global state of hunger and malnutrition: 1992 Report.* Table 2 (p. 8). New York: Author.

Worobey, J., & Bajda, V.M. (1989). Temperament ratings at 2 weeks, 2 months, and 1 year: Differential stability of activity and emotionality. *Developmental Psychology, 25,* 257–263.

Wortman, C., & Silver, R.C. (1989). The myths of coping with loss. *Journal of Consulting and Clinical Psychology, 57,* 349–357.

Wortman, C.B., & Silver, R.C. (1990). Successful mastery of bereavement and widowhood: A life-course perspective. In P.B. Baltes & M.M. Baltes (Eds.), *Successful aging: Perspectives from the behavioral sciences.* Cambridge: Cambridge University Press.

Wright, J.C., Huston, A.C., Reitz, A.L., & Piemyat, S. (1994). Young children's perceptions of television reality: Determinants and developmental differences. *Developmental Psychology, 30,* 229–239.

Wright, L. (1988). The Type A behavior pattern on coronary artery disease. *American Psychologist, 43,* 2–14.

Wynn, K. (1992). Addition and subtraction by human infants. *Nature, 358,* 749–750.

Xiohe, X., & Whyte, M.K. (1990). Love matches and arranged marriages: A Chinese replication. *Journal of Marriage and the Family, 52,* 709–722.

Yankelovich, D. (1974, December). Turbulence in the working world: Angry workers, happy grads. *Psychology Today,* pp. 80–87.

Yarrow, L. (1990, September). Does my child have a problem? *Parents,* p. 72.

Yarrow, L. (1992, November). Giving birth: 72,000 moms tell all. *Parents,* pp. 148–159.

Yarrow, M.R., Scott, P.M., & Waxler, C.Z. (1973). Learning concern for others. *Developmental Psychology, 8,* 240–260.

Yee, M., & Brown, R. (1994). The development of gender differentiation in young children. *British Journal of Social Psychology, 33,* 183–196.

Yelland, G.W., Pollard, J., & Mercuri, A. (1993). The metalinguistic benefits of limited contact with a second language. *Applied Psycholinguistics, 14,* 423–444.

Yerkes, R.M. (1923). *A point scale for measuring mental ability: A 1923 revision.* Baltimore: Warwick & York.

Yllo, K. (1983). Using a feminist approach in quantitative research: A case study. In D. Finkelhor, R.J. Gelles, G. Hotaling, & M.A. Straus (Eds.), *The dark side of families.* Beverly Hills, CA: Sage.

Yllo, K., & Bograd, M. (Eds.). (1988). *Feminist perspectives on wife abuse.* Berekely, CA: Sage.

Young, H., & Ferguson, L. (1979). Developmental changes through adolescence in the spontaneous nomination of reference groups as a function of decision context. *Journal of Youth and Adolescence, 8,* 239–252.

Youniss, J. (1989). Parent–adolescent relationships. In William Damon (Ed.), *Child development today and tomorrow.* San Francisco: Jossey-Bass.

Youniss, J., & Haynie, D.L. (1992). Friendship in adolescence. *Journal of Developmental and Behavioral Pediatrics, 13,* 59–66.

Yuill, N., & Perner, J. (1988). Intentionality and knowledge in children's judgments of actor's responsibility and recipient's emotional reaction. *Developmental Psychology, 24,* 358–365.

Zahn-Waxler, C., & Radke-Yarrow, M. (1990). The origins of empathic concern. *Motivation and Emotion, 14,* 107–130.

Zahn-Waxler, C., Robinson, J.L., & Emde, R.N. (1992). The development of empathy in twins. *Developmental Psychology, 28,* 1038–1047.

Zaidel, D.W. (1994). Worlds apart: Pictorial semantics in the left and right cerebral hemispheres. *Current Directions in Psychological Science, 3,* 5–8.

Zarbatany, L., Hartmann, D.P., & Rankin, D.B. (1990). The psychological functions of preadolescent peer activities. *Child Development, 61,* 1067–1080.

Zarit, S.H., & Reid, J.D. (1994). Family caregiving and the older family. In C.B. Fisher & R.M. Lerner (Eds)., *Applied developmental psychology.* New York: McGraw-Hill.

Zautra, A.J., Reich, J.W., & Guarnaccia, C.A. (1990). Some everyday life consequences of disability and bereavement for older adults. *Journal of Personality and Social Psychology, 59,* 550–561.

Zelazo, N., Zelazo, P.R., Cohen, K., & Zelazo, P.D. (1993). Specificity of practice effects on elementary neuromotor patterns. *Developmental Psychology, 29,* 686–691.

Zelazo, P.R. (1983). The development of walking: New findings on old assumptions. *Journal of Motor Behavior, 2,* 99–137.

Zelazo, P.R., Zelazo, N.A., & Kolb, S. (1972). "Walking" in the newborn. *Science, 176,* 314–315.

Zeskind, P.S., & Ramey, D.T. (1981). Preventing intellectual and interactional sequels of fetal malnutrition: A longitudinal, transactional, and synergistic approach to development. *Child Development, 52,* 213–218.

Zevon, M., & Corn, B. (1990). Paper presented at the annual meeting of the American Psychological Association, Boston.

Zhang, J., Dawson, V.L., Dawson, T.M., & Snyder, S.H. (1994a, February 4). Nitric oxide activation of poly (ADP-ribose) synthetase in neurotoxicity. *Science, 263,* 687–689.

Zhang, Y., Proenca, R., Maffel, M., Barone, M., et al. (1994b). Positional cloning of the mouse *obese* gene and its human homologue. *Nature, 372,* 425–432.

Zigler, E. (1994). Early intervention to prevent juvenile delinquency. *Harvard Mental Health Newsletter,* pp. 5–7.

Zigler, E., & Styfco, S.J. (1994). Head Start: Criticism in a constructive context. *American Psychologist, 49,* 127–132.

Zigler, E., Styfco, S.J., & Gilman, E. (1993). The national Head Start program for disadvantaged preschoolers. In E. Zigler & S.J. Styfco (Eds.), *Head Start and beyond: A national plan for extended childhood intervention* (pp. 1–41). New Haven, CT: Yale University Press.

Zill, N. (1983). *Marital disruption and the child's need for psychological help.* Washington, DC: National Institute for Mental Health.

Zillman, D. (1993). Mental control of angry aggression. In D.M. Wegner & J.W. Pennebaker (Eds.), *Handbook of mental control.* Englewood Cliffs, NJ: Prentice-Hall.

Acknowledgments

Photographs

About the Author: P. xx, Robert Feldman

Chapter 1 Page 4 Howard Schatz, Graphostock; p. 5 J. Pat Carter, Gamma-Liaison, Inc.; p. 6 David Young-Wolff, PhotoEdit; p. 7 H. Dratch, The Image Works; p. 14 Todd Buchanan, New York Times Pictures; p. 17 Lewis Hime, Bettman; p. 17 Bettman; p. 18 Jon Erikson, Simon & Shcuster/PH College; p.21 Ken Heyman, Black Star; p. 25 Keren Su, Stock Boston; p. 29 (top left) Alexander Tsiaras, Stock Boston; (bottom left) Mary Kate Denny, PhotoEdit; (right) LeDuc, Monkmeyer Press; p. 32 Donald J. Hernandez, Ph.D.

Chapter 2 Page 40 Niki Mareschal, Image Bank; p. 41 Bob Scaha; p. 42 D.W.Fawcett, Photo Researchers, Inc.; p. 44 L. Willatt, E. Anglan Regional Genetics Service/Science Photo Library, Photo Researchers, Inc.; p. 45 Aaron Haupt, Stock Boston; p. 47 Murray Alcosser, The Image Bank; p. 52 SIU Biomed Comm, Custom Medical Stock Photo; p. 56 Lopa Malkan Wani; p. 59 Peter Glass, Monkmeyer Press; p. 65 Sandra Scarr; p. 68 Jason Burns/ACE Phototake NYC; p. 68 Steve Allen, The Image Bank; p. 73 American Cancer Society

Chapter 3 Page 78 Barbara Campbell, Gamma-Liaison, Inc.; p. 79 Comstock; p. 80 (left) Comstock; (right) M. Greenlar, The Image Works; p. 82 Henry Schleichkorn, Custom Medical Stock Photo; p. 85 Byron, Monkmeyer Press; p. 87 Lawrence Migdale, Stock Boston; p. 88 Kathy McKain; p. 92 Ansell Horn, Phototake NYC; p. 104 Jose L. Pelaez, The Stock Market; pp. 104 & 105 Tiffany M. Field, Ph.D.

Chapter 4 Page 112 Comstock; p. 113 Lawrence Migdale; p. 118 (left & right) Comstock; p. 120 Ed Bock The Stock Market; p. 123 (left) Laura Elliot, Comstock; (center) L.J.Weinstein, Woodfin Camp & Associates; (right) Laura Dwight Photography; p. 131 (top) Jose L. Pelaez, The Stock Market; (bottom) Comstock; p. 132 J. Kenneth Whitt; p. 135 Bob Daemmrich, The Image Works; p. 137 Mark Richards, PhotoEdit; p. 139 Dion Ogust, The Image Works; p. 141 Laura Dwight Photography

Chapter 5 Page 146 Comstock; p. 147 Lawrence Migdale; p. 148 Bettman; p. 154 Owen Franken, Stock Boston; p. 155 David Sanders, The Arizona Star ; p. 157 The Granger Collection; p. 160 Rovee Collier; p. 161 Laura Dwight; p. 163 Robert Brenner, PhotoEdit; p. 164 Bill Mitchell Photography, Ellen Sackoff; p. 169 B. Dauleaux/Explorer, Photo Researchers, Inc.; p. 170 Dr. Laura Ann Petitto, McGill University; p. 173 Laura Dwight

Chapter 6 Page 180 Tom McCarthy, Stock Market; p. 181 David J. Sama, Stock Boston; p. 182 (top right, left; bottom right) Dr. Carroll Izard; (bottom left) Dr. Murray L. Barr; p. 184 Comstock; p. 185 M.K.Denny, PhotoEdit; p. 186 Laura Dwight; p. 187 Fredrik D. Bodin, Stock Boston; p. 188 Laura Dwight; p. 189 Primate Laboratory, University of Wisconsin; p. 190 Daniel Grogan Photography; p. 191 William Hamilton, Johns Hopkins University; p. 193 Collins, Monkmeyer Press; p. 194 Stacy Pick, Stock Boston; p. 195 Laura Dwight; p. 197 Elizabeth Hathon, Stock Market; p. 203 Goodwin, Monkmeyer Press; p. 204 (left) Bettman; (right) Photofest; p. 205 Lawrence Migdale; p. 206 Melinda Rauch

Chapter 7 Page 214 Joseph Schuyler, Stock Boston; p. 215 Michael Newman, PhotoEdit; p. 218 Laura Dwight; p. 220 Dr. M.E. Raichle; p. 222 (left) Bob Daemmrich, The Image Works; (right) Charles Gupton, Stock Boston; p. 229 (left & right) Laura Dwight; p. 232 Al Cook; p. 233 Catjerine Karnow, Woodfin Camp & Associates; p. 234 Bob Daemmrich, The Image Works; p. 244 Collins, The Image Works; p. 246 Yolanda Garcia

Chapter 8 Page 254 Gabe Palmer, The Stock Market; p. 255 (T/K); p. 257 Rick Browne, Stock Boston; p. 258 (left) Ursula Markus, Photo Researchers, Inc.; (right) Laura Dwight; p. 260 (left)Spencer Grant, Stock Boston; (right) (T/K); p. 265 Collins, Monkmeyer Press; p. 267 Brady, Monkmeyer Press; p. 271 Stephen Ferry, Gamma-Liaison, Inc.; p. 274 David Kurtz, Ph.D.; p. 280 Catherine Ursillo, Photo Researchers, Inc.; p. 281 Kopstein, Monkmeyer Press; p. 282 Albert Bandura

Chapter 9 Page 292 Comstock; p. 293 Frank Steiman, Stock Boston; p. 295 Jose Azel, Aurora; p. 296 Alexandra Avakian, Stock Market; p. 304 Lawrence Migdale; p. 306 Penny Tweedie, Woodfin Camp & Associates; p. 310 Bonnie Kamin, PhotoEdit; p. 312 Lauro Cavazos; p. 320 Bettman; p. 328 Richard Hutchings, Photo Researchers, Inc.

Chapter 10 Page 336 Rocher/Jerrican, Photo Researchers, Inc.; p. 337 Lori Grinker, Contact Press Images; p. 340 Robert Hopuser Comstock; p. 342 Merrim, Monkmeyer Press; p. 352 Bob Daemmrich, Stock Boston; p. 354 Jonathan Nourak PhotoEdit; p. 359 Comstock; p. 360(left) Bettman; (right) Melchoir DiGiacomo, Boys Town; p. 362 Sam Schmidt; p. 364 J. Wishnetsky, Comstock

Chapter 11 Page 374 Russell D. Cutris, Photo Researchers, Inc.; p. 375 Marty Katz; p. 378 (top) C/B Productions, Stock Market; (bottom) Dana White, PhotoEdit; p. 381 Archive Photos; p. 396 Doreen Branch; p. p. 383 Adam Fernandez; p. 390 Tony Freeman, PhotoEdit; p. 395 (T/K); p. 398 Collins, Monkmeyer Press; p. 400 Jacques Chenet, Woodfin Camp & Associates; p. 408 Michael A. Keller Studios, Ltd., Stock Market

Chapter 12 Page 406 Werner Bokelberg, The Image Bank; p. 407 Torleif Svensson, Stock Market; p. 408 Paul Howell, Gamma-Liaison, Inc.; p. 413 G&M David de Lossy, Image Bank; p. 415 UPI, Bettmann; p. 421 David Young-Wolff, PhotoEdit; pp. 423 & 424 Bob Daemmrich, Stock Boston; p. 426 Ron Chapple, FPG International; p. 440 Paula Lerner, Woodfin Camp & Associates; p. 433 Bob Daemmrich, The Image Works; p. 436 Patricia Canessa

Chapter 13 Page 442 Rob Gage, FPC International; p. 443 Bob Daemmrich, The Image Works; p. 445 Adam Butler/Topham-PA, The Image Works; p. 446 Jeff Widener, Sygma; p. 449 David Pollack, The Stock Market; p. 450 (left) Bob Daemmrich, The Image Works; (right) Eastcott/Momatiuk, Woodfin Camp & Associates; p. 452 Dr. Patricia Norris; p. 457 Joseph Nettis, Stock Boston; p. 462 Gary Hershorn/Reuters, Bettmann; p. 468 Kopstein, Monkmeyer Press; p. 470 Bernard Wolf, Monkmeyer Press

Chapter 14 Page 476 Comstock; p. 477 Campolungo, The Image Bank; p. 479 Edward Keating, New York Times Pictures; p. 482 Comstock; p. 488 Bob Daemmrich, Stock Boston; p. 490 (left) Gabe Palmer, The Stock Market; (right) Yun Sukbong/Reuters, Bettmann; p. 496 Mark Richards, PhotoEdit; p. 499 Bob Daemmrich, Stock Boston; p. 500 Dr. Henry Klein; p. 503 (top) UPI, Bettmann; (bottom) Andy Levin, Photo Researchers, Inc.; p. 504 Reuters, Bettmann

Chapter 15 Page 512 Lori Adamski Peek, Tony Stone Images; p. 513 John Kelly, Image Bank; p. 515 Conklin Monkmeyer Press; p. 519 C/B Productions, Stock Market; p. 521 Jerry Wachter, Photo Researchers, Inc.; p. 524 (top) Paul Barton, Stock Market; (bottom) Goodwin, Monkmeyer Press; p. 526 Marc Romanelli, Image Bank; p. 527 Peter Bregg, MacLean's; p. 530 Allen Levine; p. 536 Lawrence Migdale

Chapter 16 Page 542 Dreyfuss, Monkmeyer Press; p. 543 Jon Crispin, New York Times Pictures; p. 544 D. Van Kirk, Image Bank; p. 552 Phil Borden, PhotoEdit; p. 554 Flip Chalfant, Image Bank; p. 556 Addison Geary, Stock Boston; p. 557 M. Siluk, The Image Works; p. 558 Stock Market; p. 559 Richard Abamo, Stock Market; p. 564 Penny Wolin; p. 565 L.D. Grodon, The Image Bank; p. 567 Cindy Marano; p. 568 Goldberg, Monkmeyer Press; p. 570 John Moore, The Image Works

Chapter 17 Page 576 S. Gazin, The Image Works; p. 577 Lawrence Migdale; p. 578 Florian Launette, AP/Wide World Photos; p. 579 UPI, Bettman; p. 582 Joe Sohm, The Stock Market; p. 583 (left) Comstock;(right) Benn Mitchell, The Image Bank; p. 588 API/Wide World Photos; p. 588 Comstock; p. 589 Will & Deni McIntyre, Photo Researchers, Inc.; p. 592 Bob Daemmrich, Stock Boston; p. 594 Peter Menzel, Stock Boston; p. 599 David Woods, The Stock Market; p. 602 Steven Weisler

Chapter 18 Page 608 Bruce Ayres, Tony Stone Images; p. 609 Hazel Hankin, Impact Visuals Photos & Graphics, Inc.; p. 613 Cont/Reininger, Woodfin Camp & Associates; p. 615 (left) Nathan Benn, Woodfin Camp & Associates; (right) Lawrence Migdale; p. 616 Gloria Stielow; p. 618 Bettmann; p. 622 Bob Daemmrich, Stock Boston; p. 623 (left, right) Comstock; p. 624 Keren Su, Stock Boston; p. 630 Stock Montage, Inc.; p. 632 Sidney, Monkmeyer Press; p. 637 M. Antman, The Image Works

Chapter 19 Page 644 Rob Boudreau, Tony Stone Images; p. 645 Ira Wyman, Sygma; p. 646 UPI, Bettman; p. 648 Paul Rezendes, Positive Images; p. 650 Arvind Garg, Photo Researchers, Inc.; p. 656 Detroit News/Gary Porter, Gamma-Liaison, Inc.; p. 658 Robert Picard; p. 660 Carl Glassman, The Image Works; p. 662 Azerud, Sygma; p. 665 Comstock; p. 665 Janeart, Image Bank

Figures and Tables

Chapter 2   Figure 2-2 - Copyright 1995, USA Weekend. Reprinted with permission.; Figure 2-5 - From John W. Kimball, *Biology*, 5th ed. Copyright © 1983 Addison Wesley Publishing Company, Reading, MA. Reprinted by permission of Times Mirror Higher Education Group, Inc., Dubuque, Iowa. All Rights reserved.; Figure 2-8 - Tellegen, A. et al. (1988). Personality similarity in twins reared apart and together. *Journal of Personality and Social Psychology*, 54, 10311-1039. Copyright © 1988 by the American Psychological Association. Adapted with permission.; Figure 2-9 - From: *Schizophrenia Genesis* by Gottesman. Copyright © 1991 by Irving I. Gottesman. Used with Permission of W.H. Freeman and Company.; Figures 2-10 Bornstein, M.H., & Lamb, M.E. (eds.). (1992). *Development in Infancy: An introduction* (3rd ed.). New York:

McGraw-Hill. Reproduced with permission of the McGraw-Hill Companies.; Table 2-2 - Kagan, J., Arcus, D., & Snidman, N. (1993). The idea of temperament. Where do we go from here? In Plomin, R., & McCleary G. E. (eds.), *Nature, nurture, and psychology*. Washington, DC: American Psychological Association. Copyright © 1993 by the American Psychological Association. Adapted with permission.

Chapter 3   Figure 3-2 - Reprinted with permission of the publishers from Infancy by Tiffany Field, Cambridge, Mass: Harvard University Press, Copyright © by the President and Fellows of Harvard College.; Table 3-2 - Reprinted with permission from *Preventing low birthweight*. Copyright 1985 by the National Academy of Sciences. Courtesy of the National Academy Press, Washington, DC.; Table 3-3 - From Fortune Magazine, August 10, 1992. © 1992 Time Inc. All rights reserved.

Chapter 4   Figures 4-1 - From Cratty, B.J. (1979). *Perceptual and motor development in infants and children*. All rights reserved. Reprinted by permission of Allyn & Bacon.; Figure 4-3 - Bornstein, M.H., & Lamb, M.E. (eds.). (1992). *Development psychology: An advanced textbook*. p. 135. Hillsdale, NJ: Erlbaum.; Figure 4-5 - Reprinted from Roffwarg, H.P., Muzio, J.N., & Dement, W.C. (1966). Ontogenic development of the human sleep-dream cycle. *Science, 152*, 604-619. Copyright 1966 American Association for the Advancement of Science.; Figure 4-9 - Used with permission of Ross Products Division, Abbott Laboratories, Columbus, OH 43216. From Mother's Survey © 1993 Ross Products Division, Abbott Laboratories.; Figure 4-11 - Adapted from *The origin of form perception*, by R. L. Fantz. Copyright © 1961 by Scientific American. All rights reserved.; Table 4-2 - Adapted from: Thoman, E.B., & Whitney, M.P. (1990). Behavioral states in infants: *Individual differences and individual analyses*. In J. Columbo, & J. Fagen (Eds), *Individual differences in infancy: Reliability, stability, prediction*. Hillsdale, NJ: Erlbaum.

Chapter 5   Figure 5-6 Bornstein, M.H. & Lamb, M.E. (Eds). (1992). *Development in Infancy: An Introduction* (3rd ed.) New York: McGraw-Hill. Reproduced with permission of the McGraw-Hill Companies.; Figure 5-7 - Gleason, J.B., Perlmann, R.Y., Ely, R., & Evans, D.W. (1991). The babytalk registry: Parents' use of diminutive. In J.L. Sokolov, & CE. Snow (Eds), *Handbook of Research in Language Development using CHILDES*. Hillsdale, NJ: Erlbaum.; Figure 5-8 - Fernald, A., Taeschner, T., Dunn, J., Papousek, M., Boysson-Bardies, B., & Fukui, I. (1989). A cross-language study of prosodic modifications in mothers' and fathers' speech to preverbal infants. *Journal of Child Language, 16*, 477-501. Reprinted with the permission of Cambridge University Press.; Table 5-4 - Bayley Scales of Infant Development. Copyright © by The Psychological Corporation. Reproduced by permission. All rights reserved.; Table 5-5 - Adapted from Benedict, H. (1979). Early lexical development: Comprehension and production. *Journal of Child Language, 6*, 183-200. Copyright 1979. Reprinted by permission of Cambridge University Press.; Table 5-7 - From: *Cultural Perspectives on Child Development* by Wager and Stevenson. Copyright © 1982 by W.H. Freeman and Company. Used with permission.

Chapter 6   Figure 6-3 - American Demographics magazine © 1993. Reprinted with permission; Figure 6-4 - Adapted from Bell, S. M., & Ainsworth, M. D. (1972). Infant crying and maternal responsiveness. *Child Development, 43*, 1171-1190. © The Society for Research in Child Development, Inc.; Figure 6-4 - From Tomlinson-Keasey, C. (1985). *Child development: Psychological, sociological and biological factors*. Homewood, IL: Dorsey Press. Reprinted with the permission of Dr. Carol Tomlinson-Keasey.; Table 6-1 - Adapted from Waters, (1978). © The Society for Research in Child Development, Inc.

Chapter 7 Figure 7-8 - Hart, B., Risley, R. T, (1995). *Meaningful differences in the everyday experience of young American children.* Paul H. Brookes Publishing, P.O. Box 10624, Baltimore, MD 21285-0624.; Figure 7-9 - From Wright, J.C., & Huston, A.C. (1995). *Effects of educational TV viewing of lower income preschoolers on academic skills, school readiness, and school adjustment one to three years later.* Lawrence, KS: Center for Research on the Influences of Television on Children, University of Kansas.; Table 7-1 - Adapted with permission from Charles C. Corbin, *A textbook of motor development.* Copyright © 1973 Times Mirror Higher Education Group, Inc., Dubuque, Iowa. All rights reserved.

Chapter 8 Figure 8-1 - Adapted from: Farver, J.M., Kim, Y.K., & Lee, Y. (1995). Cultural differences in Korean- and Anglo-American preschooler's interaction and play behaviors. *Child Development, 66,* 1088-1099. © The Society for Research in Child Development, Inc.

Chapter 9 Figure 9-1 - Barrett, D. E., & Radke-Yarrow, M. (1985). Effects of nutritional supplementation on children's responses to novel, frustrating, and competitive situations. *American Journal of Clinical Nutrition, 42,* 102-120. © American Journal of Clinical Nutrition. American Society for Clinical Nutrition.; Figure 9-2 - From Cratty, B.J. (1979). *Perceptual and motor development in infants and children.* All rights reserved. Reprinted by permission of Allyn & Bacon.; Figure 9-6 - © UNESCO 1990. Reproduced by permission of UNESCO.; Table 9-2 - Walters, E., & Gardner, H. (1986). The theory of multiple intelligences: Some issues and answers. In R.J. Sternberg & R.K. Wagner (eds.), *Practical Intelligence.* Cambridge University Press. Copyright 1986. Reprinted with the permission of Cambridge University Press.

Chapter 10 Figure 10-1 - Shavelson, R., Hubner, J.J., & Stanton, J.C. 1976). Self-concept: Validation of construct interpretations. *Review of Educational Research, 46,* 407-441. Reprinted with the permission of the American Educational Research Association.; Figure 10-3 - Adapted from Dodge, K.A. (1985). A social information processing model of social competence in children. In M. Perlmutter (Ed.), *Minnesota Symposia on Child Psychology* (Vol 18), 77-126. Hillsdale, NJ: Erlbaum.; Figure 10-4 - Suro, R. (1992, May 26). For women, varied reasons for single motherhood. The New York Times, A12. Copyright © 1992 by The New York Times Company. Reprinted by permission.; Figure 10-5 - Adapted from Stevenson, H.W., & Lee, S. (1990). Contexts of achievement: A study of American, Chinese, and Japanese children. Research in Child Development. Monographs. No. 221, 55, Nos. 1-2. © The Society for Research in Child Development, Inc; Table 10-3 - Adapted from Zarbatany, L., Hartmann, D.P., & Rankin, B.D. (1990). The psychological functions of preadolescent peer activities. *Child Development, 61,* 1067-1080. © The Society for Research in Child Development, Inc.; Table 10-4 - Shealy, C. N. (1995). From Boys Town to Oliver Twist: Separating fact from fiction in welfare reform and out-of-home placement of children and youth. *American Psychologist, 50,* 565-580. Copyright © 1995 by the American Psychological Association. Adapted with permission.

Chapter 11 Figure 11-1 - From Cratty, B.J. (1979). *Perceptual and motor development in infants and children.* All rights reserved. Reprinted by permission of Allyn & Bacon.; Figure 11-2 - Adapted from Eveleth, P., & Tanner, J. (1976). *Worldwide variation in human growth.* New York: Cambridge University Press. Copyright 1976. Reprinted with the permission of Cambridge University Press.; Figure 11-4 - *Journal of Genetic Psychology, 75,* 165-196. 1949. Reprinted with permission of the Helen Dwight Reid Educational Foundation. Published by Heldref

Publications, 1319 Eighteenth St., N.W., Washington, DC 20036-1802. Copyright © 1949.; Figure 11-6 - Adapted from Crystal, D.S., Chen, C., Fuligni, A.J., et al (1994). Psychological maladjustment and academic achievement: A cross cultural study of Japanese, Chinese, and American high school students. *Child Development, 65,* 738-753. © The Society for Research in Child Development, Inc.; Figure 11-9 - Adapted from Alan Guttmacher Institute (1993). *Sexually transmitted diseases (STDs) in the United States.* New York: Alan Guttmacher Institute.

Chapter 12 Figure 12-1 - AMA Profiles of Adolescent Health: *America's adolescents: How healthy are they?* American Medical Association, copyright 1990.; Figure 12-3 - Steinberg, L., & Silverberg, S. B. (1986). Influences on marital satisfaction during middle stages of the family life cycle. *Journal of Marriage and the Family, 49,* 751-760. Copyrighted 1986 by the National Council on Family Relations, 3989 Central Ave. NE, Suite 550, Minneapolis, MN 55421. Reprinted by permission.; Figure 12-4 - Adapted from Brown, B., Loher, M., & Trujillo, C. (1983). Adolescent peer group stereotypes, member conformity, and identity development. Paper presented at the meeting of the Society for Research in Child Development. © The Society for Research in Child Development, Inc.; Figure 12-6 - Adapted from Alan Guttmacher Institute (1988). *Pregnancy rates around the world.* New York: Alan Guttmacher Institute.; Table 12-1 - From Childhood and Society by Erik H. Erikson. copyright 1950. © 1963 by W. W. Norton & Company, Inc., renewed © 1978, 1991 by Erik H. Erikson. Reprinted by permission of W.W. Norton & Company, Inc.; Table 12-2 - Adapted from Marcia, J.E. (1990). Identity in adolescence. In J. Adelson (Ed.), *Handbook of adolescent psychology.* New York: Wiley. Copyright © 1990. Reprinted by permission of John Wiley & Sons, Inc.

Chapter 13 Figure 13-1 - Blair, S.N., Kohl, H. W., Paggenberger, R.S., et al. (1989). Physical fitness and all-cause mortality: A prospective study of healthy men and women. *Journal of the American Medical Assn., 262,* 2395-2401. Copyright 1989, American Medical Association.; Figure 13-4 - Lazarus, R.S., & Folkman, S. *Stress, appraisal and coping.* © 1984 by Springer Publishing Company, Inc., New York 10012. Used by permission.; Figure 13-5 - Adapted from Schaie, K.W. (1977-1978). Toward a stage of adult theory of adult cognitive development. *International Journal of Aging and Human Development, 8,* 129-138. Copyright © 1978 Baywood Publishing Co., Inc.; Figure 13-6 - Adapted from Sternberg, R.J. (1985). *Beyond IQ: A triarchic theory of human intelligence.* New York: Cambridge University Press. Copyright 1985. Reprinted with the permission of Cambridge University Press.; Figure 13-7 - Sternberg, R.J., & Wagner, R.K. (1993). The g-ocentric view of intelligence and job performance is wrong. *Current Directions in Psychological Science, 2,* 1-5.; Figure 13-10 - From Astin, A. W., Korn, W. S., & Berz, E. R. (1990). *The American freshman: National norms for Fall, 1990.* Los Angeles: Higher Education Research Institute, Graduate School of Education, UCLA.; Table 13-1 - Rahe, K.H., & Arthur, R.J. (1978). Life change and illness studies: Past history and future directions. *Human Stress, 4,* 3-15. Reprinted with permission of the Helen Dwight Reid Educational Foundation. Published by Heldref Publications, 1319 Eighteenth St., N.W., Washington, D.C. 20036-1802.; Table 13-4 - From Wechsler, H., Rohman, M., & Solomon, R. (1981). Emotional problems and concerns of New England College Students. *American Journal of Orthopsychiatry, 51,* 719. Reprinted with permission, from the American Journal of Orthopsychiatry. Copyright 1981 by the American Orthopsychiatric Association, Inc.

Chapter 14 Figure 14-1 - Murstein, B.I. (1987). FEEDBACK: A clarification and extension of the SVR Theory of dyadic pairing. *Journal of Marriage and the Family, 49,* 929-933. Copyrighted 1986 by the

National Council on Family Relations, 3989 Central Ave. NE, Suite 550, Minneapolis, MN 55421. Reprinted by permission.; Figure 14-2 - Sternberg, R.J. (1986). Triangular theory of love. *Psychological Review, 93,* 119-135. Copyright © 1986 by the American Psychological Association. Adapted with permission.; Figure 14-3 - American Demographics magazine, © 1993. Reprinted with permission.; Table 14-2 - Sternberg, R.J. (1986). Triangular theory of love. *Psychological Review, 93,* 119-135. Copyright © 1986 by the American Psychological Association. Adapted with permission.; Table 14-3 - Buss, D. M. et al. (1990). International preferences in selecting mates: A study of 37 cultures. *Journal of Cross-Cultural Psychology, 21,* 5-47. Copyright © 1990 by Sage Publications. Reprinted by permission of Sage Publications.; Figure 14-7 - Adapted from Judith Bruce, Cynthia B. Lloyd, and Ann Leonard, *Families in Focus: New Perspectives on Mothers, Fathers and Children.* (New York: The Population Council 1995) p. 20 and p. 73.; Figure 14-8 - Gallup, G.H., & Newport, F. (1990). Virtually all adults want children, but many of the reasons are intangible. *The Gallup Poll Monthly, Vol 297.* Information collected by the Gallup Organization and published by The Gallup Poll.; Figure 14-9 - Googans, B., & Burden, D. (1987).Vulnerability of working parents: Balancing work and home roles. *Social Work, 32,* 295-300. Copyright 1987, National Association of Social Workers, Inc.

Chapter 15   Figure 15-2 - DiGiovanna, A. G. (1994). *Human aging: Biological perspectives.* p. 159. New York: McGraw-Hill. Reproduced with permission of the McGraw-Hill Companies.; Figure 15-6 - Kaplan, R.M., Sallis, J.F., Jr., Patterson, T.L. (1993). *Health and human behavior.* p. 254. "Age specific breast cancer annual incidence". New York: McGraw-Hill. Reproduced with permission of the McGraw-Hill Companies.; Figure 15-7 - Pettingale, K. W., Morris, T., Greer, S., & Haybittle, J. L. (1985). *Mental attitudes to cancer: An additional prognostic factor.* Lancet, 310, p. 750. © by The Lancet Ltd. 1985.

Chapter 16   Figure 16-1 - From *The seasons of a man's life* by Daniel J. Levinson et al. Copyright © 1978 by Daniel J. Levinson. Reprinted by permission of Alfred A. Knopf, Inc.; Figure 16-2 - Adaptations from Costa, P.T., et al. (1993). Correlations of MMPI factor scales with measures of the five factor model of personality. *Journal of Personality Assessment, 50,* 640-650.; Figure 16-3 - Figley, C.R. (1973). Child density

and the marital relationship. *Journal of Marriage and the Family, 35,* 272-282. Copyrighted 1973 by the National Council on Family Relations, 3989 Central Ave. NE, Suite 550, Minneapolis, MN 55421. Reprinted by permission.

Chapter 17   Figure 17-2 - Figure from *Contemporary adulthood,* 5th Edition by Jeffrey S. Turner and Donald B. Helms, Copyright © 1994 by Holt, Rinehart and Winston, Inc., reproduced by permission of the publisher.; Figure 17-3 - From: *The Physiology of Aging* by Shock. Copyright © 1962 by W.H. Freeman and Company. Used with permission.; Figure 17-5 - Schaie, K.W. (1994). The course of adult intellectual development. *American Psychologist, 49,* 304-313, pg. 307. Copyright © 1994 by the American Psychological Association. Reprinted with permission.; Figure 17-6 - Rubin, D.C., Wetzler, S.E., & Nebes, R.D. (1986). Autobiographical memory across the life span. In D.C. Rubin (Ed.), *Autobiographical memory.* Cambridge, England, Cambridge University Press. Copyright 1986. Reprinted with the permission of Cambridge University Press.; Table 17-1 - Palmore, E.B. *The facts on aging quiz.* © 1982 by Springer Publishing Company, Inc., New York 10012. Used by permission.

Chapter 18   Figure 18-2 - Reprinted with the permission of the American Association of Retired Persons.; Figure 18-3 - Friedman, N.S., et al. (1995). Childhood conscientiousness and longevity: Health behaviors and cause of death. *Journal of Personality and Social Psychology, 68,* 696-703. Copyright © 1995 by the American Psychological Association. Adapted with permission.; Figure 18-4 - Heinemann, G.D., Evans, P.L. (1990). Widowhood: Loss, change, and adaptation. In T.H. Brubaker (ed.), *Family relationships in later life.* Newbury Park, CA: Sage. Copyright © 1990 by Sage Publications. Reprinted by permission of Sage Publications.; Table 18-1 - Atchley, R.C. (1982). Retirement: Leaving the world of work. *Annals of the American Academy of Political and Social Science, 464,* 120-131. Copyright © 1982 by Sage Publications. Reprinted by permission of Sage Publications.

Chapter 19   Figure 19-1 - Reprinted with permission of Simon & Schuster from *Death: The final stage of growth* by Elisabeth Kübler-Ross. Copyright © 1975 by Elisabeth Kübler-Ross.

Name Index

Subject Index

Ageism, 579-80

Agentic professions, 502

Age of mothers, affects on prenatal development, 71, 94

Age of viability, 93

Age ranges, defined, 7-9

Aging

See also Adulthood (late)

demographics of, 578-79, 580

internal, 583-84

keys to successful, 614-20

myths of, 581

outward signs of, 582-83

theories of, 593-94

Aggression

See also Violence

cognitive perspective of, 284

defined, 281

guidelines for reducing, 285

how to deal effectively with, 15

minor forms of, 15

preschool period and, 280-85

roots of, 281-82

social learning perspective of, 282-83

television viewing and, 282-83

AIDS (acquired immune deficiency syndrome)

adolescence and, 399-400

prenatal development and, 71-72

prevention methods, 401

Ainsworth strange situation, 190-91, 192

Aka Pygmy, 195

Alcohol

abuse in adolescence, 395-97

prenatal development affected by, 73

signs of abuse, 402

Alzheimer's disease, 589-90, 596-97

American Academy of Neurology, 163

American Academy of Pediatrics, 35, 86, 124, 135, 140, 163, 275, 299

American Association on Mental Retardation (AAMR), 328-29

American Cancer Society, 528

American College of Obstetricians and Gynecologists, 74, 86

American College of Sports Medicine, 521

American Medical Association, 35

American Psychological Association, 34, 35, 208

America's Children: Resources from Family, Government and the Economy (Hernandez), 32

Americans with Disabilities Act (ADA) (1990), 449

Amniocentesis, 53

Androgynous, 261

Animal research, use of, 57-58, 189

Anorexia nervosa, 381-82

Anoxia, 83

Apgar scale, 83

Arthritis, 588

Artificial insemination, 55

Asian cultures

See also under name of country

adolescence and autonomy in, 420

attributional patterns and academic success, 364-65

collectivistism in, 10, 25

dating in, 430

educational performance and, 388-92

illiteracy rates, 315

marriage without love in, 484

middle school years and physical development of children, 296

parenting styles in, 269-70

play in, 266

self-concept in, 256

spousal abuse in, 560-61

temperament of children in, 63

treatment of elderly, 624-25

Assimilation, 23, 148

Associative play, 265-66

Attachment

Ainsworth strange situation, 190-91, 192

Behavioral System, 196

Bowlby and, 189-90, 191, 193-94

classifications of, 190-91

cultural differences, 191-92

defined, 189

fathers, role of, 193-95

impact of, in infancy on adult relationships, 487

in infancy, 189-95

infant behavior and, 193

mothers, role of, 192-93

reciprocal socialization, 196

research on, 189-90

Attention-deficit hyperactivity disorder (ADHD), 294-95, 301-2

Attention spans, preschool period and, 233

Attributions

cultural differences, 364-68

defined, 362-63

Auditory impairment, 300

Australia

concrete operational thought in Aborigine children, 306, 305

death from heart disease in, 525

father-child relationships in, 195

marriage without love in, 484

mortality rates for, 447

Austria

death from heart disease in, 525

smoking in, 398

Authoritarian parents, 267

Authoritative parents, 268

Autobiographical memory, 232, 601, 603

Autonomy, adolescence and, 419-20

Autonomy-versus-shame-and-doubt stage, 257

Awa tribe, 376

Babbling, 169-70

Baghdad, menarche/menstruation in, 378

Bantu, menarche/menstruation in, 378

Bayley, Nancy, 162, 164

Bayley Scales of Infant Development, 162, 164

Behavioral genetics, 49-50

Behavioral perspective, 20-22, 24

Behavioral states, primary, 119

Behavior modification, 21

Belgium

death from heart disease in, 525

mortality rates for, 447

preschools in, 245

Bell Curve controversy, 13-14, 324-26

Bell Curve, The (Herrnstein and Murray), 13, 325-26, 388

Bereavement

See also Grief and bereavement

defined, 661

Bicultural identity, 319

Bilingualism

benefits of, 311-13

defined, 310

statistics on, 311

Binet, Alfred, 320-21

Biological perspectives on gender differences, 259-60

Birth(s)

See also Childbirth; Childbirth complications

multiple, 44

out-of-wedlock, cultural differences, 493

weights for, 92-94

Birthing centers, 88-90

Birthing chair, 84

Blended families, 358

Body transcendence versus body preoccupation, 612

Bonding, 84

Boomerang children, 555-56

Bottle-feeding, breast-feeding versus, 131-35

Bowlby, John, 189-90, 191, 193-94

Brain death, 646

Brain development

in infancy, 116-17

in preschool period, 220-21

Braxton-Hicks contractions, 81

Brazelton Neonatal Behavioral Assessment Scale (NBAS), 126-27

Brazil

concrete operational thought in children, 306

marriage without love in, 483, 484

Breast cancer, 527-29

Breast-feeding versus bottle-feeding, 131-35

Bulimia, 382

Burnout, 565-66

Canada

adolescent pregnancy in, 434

bilingualism in, 310

death from heart disease in, 525

divorce rates in, 493

mortality rates in, 447

Cancer, 526-31